Compensation

Fourteenth Editic

Barry Gerhart

University of Wisconsin-Madison

COMPENSATION, FOURTEENTH EDITION

Published by McGraw Hill LLC, 1325 Avenue of the Americas, New York, NY 10019.

This book is printed on acid-free paper.

1 2 3 4 5 6 7 8 9 LCR 27 26 25 24 23 22

ISBN 978-1-264-08090-8 (bound edition)
MHID 1-264-08090-5 (bound edition)
ISBN 978-1-264-41524-3 (loose-leaf edition)
MHID 1-264-41524-9 (loose-leaf edition)

Portfolio Director: *Michael Ablassmeir*
Lead Product Developer: *Michele Janicek*
Marketing Manager: *Debbie Clare*
Content Project Managers: *Melissa M. Leick; Katie Reuter*
Buyer: *Rachel Hirschfield*
Content Licensing Specialist: *Gina Oberbroeckling*
Cover Image: *De Space Studios/Shutterstock*
Compositor: *Straive*

Library of Congress Cataloging-in-Publication Data

Name: Gerhart, Barry A., author.
Title: Compensation / Barry Gerhart, University of Wisconsin–Madison. Description: Fourteenth edition. | New York, NY : McGrawHill Education, [2023] | Includes bibliographical references and index.
Identifiers: LCCN 2021045979 |
ISBN 9781264080908 (hardcover ; alk. paper)
Subjects: LCSH: Compensation management.
Classification: LCC HF5549.5.C67 M54 2023 | DDC 658.3/2–dc22
LC record available at https://lccn.loc.gov/2021045979

mheducation.com/highered

Table of Contents

About the Author

BARRY GERHART

Barry Gerhart is the Bruce R. Ellig Distinguished Chair in Pay and Organizational Effectiveness, School of Business, University of Wisconsin–Madison. Professor Gerhart received his B.S. in Psychology from Bowling Green State University and his Ph.D. in Industrial Relations from the University of Wisconsin–Madison. Professor Gerhart is a recipient of the Scholarly Achievement Award, the International Human Resource Management Scholarly Achievement Award (twice), the Herbert Heneman Jr. Career Achievement Award, and the Mahoney Mentoring Award, all from the Human Resources Division, Academy of Management. He has also received the Michael R. Losey Excellence in Human Resource Research Award, the career achievement award of the Society for Human Resource Management. Professor Gerhart is a Fellow of the Academy of Management and of the American Psychological Association. He has served as a department chair and/or area coordinator at Cornell, Vanderbilt, and Wisconsin, as well as senior associate dean and interim dean at Wisconsin. He has held visiting appointments at Bayreuth University, King's College London, and Copenhagen Business School.

Preface

Compensation is uniquely important in organizations because it typically represents the single largest operating cost, especially where employee skills or human capital are the source of competitive advantage (e.g., Google/Alphabet, Facebook; investment banking, law, accounting, and consulting firms; professional sports teams; universities). Compensation is also important because employees regularly report it as the most important factor that goes into their decision of whether to take a job or stay in a job. Compensation also plays a major role in what employees choose to do on the job: their effort level, where they direct their effort/what goals they pursue, how cooperative they are, how flexible they are, how ethical they are, and so forth. These all add up to determine how efficient, innovative, customer-oriented and (in the case of for-profit) how profitable an organization is over time. Profits, in turn, create jobs. In the absence of profits, jobs disappear. An organization that pays too much, pays too little, ties too much compensation up as fixed costs, and/or pays for the wrong things puts the company, its investors, and its employees at risk. On the other hand, designing and executing an effective compensation strategy can play a key role in great shared success.

Compensation challenges ebb and flow with changes in the economy. The Financial Crisis of 2008 and the related Great Recession brought job cuts (with the national unemployment rate rising to 10 percent, the highest since 1983), reduced hours, reduced employer contributions to 401(k) retirement plans, reduced bonus/profit-sharing payments, and some wage cuts. With revenue and profits down and with labor costs often the single largest operating cost, employers cut labor costs in these ways. Eventually, as company revenues picked up again, we gradually saw employers put less emphasis on cutting labor costs and more emphasis on hiring. However, job growth was initially quite modest. At the beginning of 2013, the unemployment rate was still at 8 percent. Why? Employers have become increasingly careful about adding new workers because they want to keep costs under control and they don't want to have to reduce the workforce if they guess wrong about increasing revenue growth/product demand (and the need for more workers). As economic growth continued, however, competition for employees increased and employers began to hire. The U.S. unemployment rate declined every year until it was below 4 percent in 2018 and 2019, the lowest it has been since 1969. However, wage gains remain modest. That is because employers are careful not only about hiring, as we have noted. They are also careful about giving wage/salary increases because once those are added to base pay, "they are there forever." Increasingly, employers seek to make labor costs variable, which means greater reliance on bonuses and/or profit-sharing, where payments to employees go up during good times, but automatically go down during bad times when profits and revenues go down. Nevertheless, the low unemployment rates and the scarcity of workers it signaled resulted in a number of employers raising base wages.

Then, of course, the pandemic hit. The unemployment rate went from 3.5 percent in February 2020 to 14.8 percent by April 2020. Employers followed all of the same actions to cut labor costs in 2020 they had followed in response to the Great Recession that began in 2008. Suddenly, many employers went from having to raise wages to be able to hire and retain enough employees to run their businesses to instead having too many employees costing too much to survive without dramatic action. Business strategy became "cut costs enough to survive, while being ready to go when business picks back up." A Conference Board survey reported that one quarter of employers laid off or furloughed employees and 34 percent reduced working hours. Some companies announced salary cuts (temporary) of 30 percent to 50 percent. Contributions to 401k plans were stopped at about 1 in 10 employers. The millions of workers who lost their jobs or who took pay cuts still had bills to pay. Government aid helped some business owners and employees, but not everyone and not always enough.

For some, there was opportunity. Amazon's business strategy continued to be growth, and it added 427,300 employees (a more than 50 percent increase) between January and October of 2020. That this was necessary can be seen from the fact it grew its revenue from $87.4 billion in the quarter ending December 31, 2019 to $125.6 billion in the quarter ended December 31, 2020. Amazon paid many workers bonuses to work through the pandemic and remain with Amazon. There were some retailers who went beyond bonuses and raised wages to make sure they would have the workforce to respond to growth in business. In June 2020, Target announced it would increase its hourly minimum to $15, following increases to $11 in 2017 and $13 in 2019. The new hourly minimum allows Target to compete better for workers with Amazon and Costco, which had a $15 minimum hourly wage (Costco subsequently raised it to $16/hour in February 2021) and with Walmart, which also raised wages. By August 2020, many companies that had made temporary salary or benefits (usually 401k) cuts began to rescind them. Economic forecasts suddenly began to turn positive with the deployment of effective vaccines. In early 2021, The Congressional Budget Office (CBO) projected a rapid economic recovery to pre-pandemic levels by 2022, including a strong drop in the unemployment rate and thus a return to wide competition for employees. (Further, that projection did not consider the impact on economic growth of the $1.9 trillion American Rescue Plan Act of 2021 enacted in March 2021.) Things were about to go full circle, from economic boom until early 2020, to economic hard times (for most, not all) starting March 2020, and looking in the crystal ball (or using forecasts like that of CBO just above), employers need to shift back to recruiting (and retention) mode (and quickly) to be able to take advantage of the strong business recovery unfolding in 2021. (The unemployment rate was down to 6.0 % by April 2021.) Success in recruiting and retention will depend on competitive compensation. Not acting quickly enough or not setting compensation at a sufficiently competitive level means losing out on employees who choose to work elsewhere and thus losing out on sales and profits.

We will also talk about the use of pay as an incentive to influence choices of effort and behavior. Let's just take a trip part-way around the globe here. To take a not so down to earth example, if you were a Russian cosmonaut, you could earn a bonus of $1,000 for every space walk you took (technically known as "extravehicular activity"), up to three per space trip. A contract listing specific tasks to be done on a space mission permits you to earn up to $30,000 above the $20,000 you earn while you are on the ground. Conclusion: *Pay matters.*

(As a small aside, in contrast to the Russian cosmonauts, private citizens have the opportunity to visit the International Space Station, without having to meet the troublesome requirements and preparation to become a cosmonaut or an astronaut. But, it will cost them. Axiom Space, based in Houston, using a SpaceX rocket, will give a ride to three customers in 2022, each of whom will pay around $55 million for the trip and an 8-day stay.)

After you have read this book, you will also better understand that *what you pay for matters.* Many years ago, when Green Giant discovered too many insect parts in the pea packs from one of its plants, it designed a bonus plan that paid people for finding insect parts. Green Giant got what it paid for: insect parts. Innovative Green Giant employees brought insect parts from home to add to the peas just before they removed them and collected the bonus.

The Houston public school district also got what it paid for when it promised teachers bonuses of up to $6,000 if their students' test scores exceeded targets. Unfortunately, several teachers were later fired when it was discovered that they had leaked answers to their students and adjusted test scores. Teachers were motivated to raise test scores, just not to raise them in the way desired (improved student learning). Wells Fargo wanted customers to sign up for more of its products to increase its potential for revenue and profit growth. To achieve this goal, Wells Fargo incentivized its employees so they would be rewarded for achieving this goal (and/or penalized if they did not achieve it). This incentive certainly "worked," if you think this includes employees setting up fake accounts, which the customers did not sign up for, in order to achieve their targets for performance (new account sign-ups). Again, employees were motivated to achieve the outcome, but not necessarily in the appropriate way.

Such problems are global. A British telephone company paid a cash bonus to operators based on how quickly they completed requests for information. Some operators discovered that the fastest way to complete a request was to give out a wrong number or–even faster–just hang up on the caller. "We're actually looking at a new bonus scheme," says an insightful company spokesperson. Conclusion: *What you pay for matters.*

After you have read this book, you will also have learned that *how you pay matters.* Motorola ended its old-fashioned pay system that employees said guaranteed a raise every six months if you were still breathing. The new system paid for learning new skills and working in teams. Sound good? It wasn't. Employees resented those team members who went off for six weeks of training at full pay while remaining team members picked up their work. Motorola was forced to get rid of its new-fashioned system, too.

Wells Fargo also, not surprisingly, had to change *how* it pays and *what* it pays for.[2] Specific changes made include:

- No product sales goals.
- Performance evaluation based on customer service, usage and growth, not simply on new accounts opened.
- Incentives associated with direct customer feedback and product usage.
- A higher percentage of employee compensation comprised of base salary, rather than variable incentives.
- More employee performance metrics focused on the goals of a given bank branch, instead of on an individual worker.

To summarize, compensation is a powerful tool that has major consequences for the success or failure of an organization. Our aim is to put you in a better position to design and/or execute compensation strategies to make success more likely. That will be helpful whatever the scale and scope of your responsibility, from a unit of a few employees to an entire organization. Our book will also help you better understand how your own compensation is managed and how that can help you achieve your own career goals.

ABOUT THIS BOOK

This book focuses on the strategic choices in managing compensation. We introduce these choices, real-world issues that managers confront from New York to New Zealand and all points between, in the total compensation model in Chapter 1. This model provides an integrating framework that is used throughout the book. Major compensation issues are discussed in the context of current theory, research, and practice. The practices illustrate new developments as well as established approaches to compensation decisions.

We live in interesting times. Anywhere you look on the globe today, economic and social pressures are forcing managers to rethink how people get paid and what difference it makes. Traditional approaches to compensation are being questioned. But what is being achieved by all this experimentation and change? What is merely fad and fashion, and what, instead, is supported by the evidence? In this book, we strive to separate beliefs from facts, wishful thinking from demonstrable results, and opinions from research. Yet when all is said and done, managing compensation is part science, but also part art.

Each chapter contains at least one *e-Compensation box* to point you to some of the vast compensation information on the Internet. Real-life *Your Turn* cases ask you to apply the concepts and techniques discussed in each chapter. For example, the Your Turn in Chapter 9 draws on Jerry Newman's experience when he worked undercover for 14 months in seven fast-food restaurants. The case takes you into the gritty details of the employees' behaviors (including Professor Newman's) during rush hour, as they desperately worked to fill customers' orders and meet their own performance targets set by their manager. You get to recommend which rewards will improve employees' performance (including Professor Newman's) and customers' satisfaction. We tackle major compensation issues from three sides: theory, research, and practice–no problem can survive that onslaught!

The author, together with George Milkovich, also publishes *Cases in Compensation,* an integrated casebook designed to provide additional practical skills that apply the material in this book. The casebook is available directly from the authors (e-mail: cases.in.compensation@gmail.com). Completing the integrated cases will help you develop skills readily transferable to future jobs and assignments. Instructors are invited to e-mail for more information on how *Cases in Compensation* can help translate compensation research and theory into practice and build competencies for on-the-job decisions.

But *caveat emptor!* "Congress raises the executive minimum wage to $565.15 an hour," reads the headline in the satirical newspaper *The Onion* (**www.onion.com**, "America's Finest News Source"). The article says that the increase will help executives meet the federal standard-of-easy-living. "Our lifestyles are expensive to maintain," complains one manager. Although the story in *The Onion* may clearly be fiction, sometimes it is more difficult to tell. One manager told us that when she searched for this textbook in her local bookstore, store personnel found the listing in their information system–under fiction!

WHAT'S NEW

All chapters have been revised, in recognition of ongoing changes at organizations and in their competitive environments around the world. Many examples are provided of the current pay strategies or practices used in specific, named companies. Some of these are well established and successful (Apple, IBM, Lincoln Electric, Microsoft, Merrill Lynch, Nucor, SAS Institute, Tesla, Toyota, Walmart), some face real problems (airlines, domestic car companies), and others are using unique practices (Google, Whole Foods). Whenever possible, we observe how the challenges faced by these companies have evolved over time. We have created six brand new end- of-chapter *Your Turn* cases, which include an examination of the role of compensation at companies such as Amazon, Walmart, Apple, and Starbucks. This includes a focus on environmental, social, and governance (ESG) issues. Other new Your Turns have to do with new benefits, including those important during the pandemic. We have also introduced a dozen new exhibits, many of which document the causes and consequences of compensation (e.g., how much does pay increase when someone voluntarily changes jobs?). This edition continues to emphasize the importance of total compensation and its relevance for achieving sustainable competitive advantage. It reinforces our conviction that beyond *how much* people are paid, *how* they are paid really matters. Managing pay means ensuring that the right people get the right pay for achieving objectives in the right way. Greater emphasis is given to theoretical advances and evidence from research. Throughout the book,+ we translate this evidence into guidance for improving the management of pay.

ACKNOWLEDGMENTS

A very special thanks goes to **George T. Milkovich**, who was the lead author on the first 11 editions of *Compensation*. George has long been my mentor, colleague, and friend since our days together at Cornell. His influence on me and on *Compensation* continues. Sincere thanks also goes to **Jerry M. Newman**, who co-authored the first 13 editions of *Compensation*. With Jerry, like George, his influence on *Compensation* will also be long-lasting. Jerry and I did not have as much of a chance to work together, but I enjoyed working with him very much as well. An interesting note on Jerry is that he decided he wanted to learn more about work and compensation from a different perspective. To do this, he did something unusual: he stepped away (temporarily!) from being a distinguished professor and actually went to work as a crew member (he knows his way around a deep fryer) at several well-known quick service restaurants. (Think Undercover Boss.) You might enjoy reading about it in his interesting and fun book, *My Secret Life on the McJob.*

All to say, I am grateful to have had the honor (and good fortune) to work with two people like George and Jerry and to carry on their work in *Compensation* going forward. Indeed, you will often find the use of "we" instead of "I" in the book, indicating that what you read reflects the influence of all three of us.

Many other people have contributed to our understanding of compensation and to the preparation of this textbook over the years and editions. We owe a special, continuing debt of gratitude to our students. In the classroom, they motivate and challenge us, and as returning seasoned managers they try mightily to keep our work relevant:

Kenneth Abosch
Aon
Stephanie Argentine
Rich Products
Patrick Beall
Lockheed Martin
Joseph Bruno
Kodak
Karee Buerger
Greater Chicago Area
Federico Castellanos
IBM EMEA
Cindy Cohen
Impac
Andrew Doyle
Oppenheimer Fund
Brian Dunn
Maclagan
Bruce Ellig
Author and Pfizer (emeritus)
Thomas Fentner
Health Now
Rich Floersch
McDonald's USA
Beth Florin
Pearl Meyer & Partners
Richard Frings
Johnson & Johnson
Takashi Fujiwara
Mitsubishi
Yuichi Funada
Toshiba
Ted Grasela
Cognigen
Thomas Gresch
General Motors
Peter Hearl
YUM Brands (emeritus)
Lada Hruba
Bristol Meyers Squibb
Richard Ivey
KFC
Tae-Jin Kim
SK Group
Jed Kortens
Cisco
Joe Kreuz
Advantage Professionals
Hiroshi Kurihara
Fuji Xerox
Christian LeBreton
IBM EMEA
Mitch Linnick
IBM
Tony Marchak
IBM EMEA

Masaki Matsuhashi
Toshiba
Randy McDonald
IBM
Nancy McGough
Room & Board
Matt Milkovich
Registry Nursing
Michael Milkovich
brightpeak financial
Sarah Milkovich
Jet Propulsion Laboratory
Sonja Milkovich
Sled Dog Software
Pat Murtha
Pizza Hut
David Ness
Medtronic
Erinn Newman
American Express
Kelly Newman
Presbyterian Residence
Terrie Newman
HR Foundations
Stephen O'Byrne
Shareholder Value Advisors
Tony Ragusa
Stereo Advantage
Jaime Richardson
Align Technology
Lindsay Scott
Lindsay Scott & Associates
Jason Sekanina
Linear Technology
Rich Severa
Accretive Partners & Strategies LLC
Diana Southall
HR Foundations
Cassandra Steffan
Frito-Lay
Masanori Suzuki
Google Japan
Ichiro Takemura
Toshiba
Richard Their
Xerox
Jan Tichy
Merck
Andrew Thompson
Link Group Consultants
Jose Tomas
Burger King
Karen Velkey
Northrop Grumman
Ian Ziskin
Northrop Grumman

Our universities, past and present, Cornell, SUNY-Buffalo and the University of Wisconsin-Madison, and Vanderbilt have provided forums for the interchange of ideas among students, experienced managers, and academic colleagues. We value this interchange. Other academic colleagues have also played a role in our research and thinking and/or provided helpful comments on this and previous editions of the book. We particularly thank:

Martha Andrews
University of North Carolina, Wilmington
Tom Arnold
Westmoreland Community College
Lubica Bajzikova
Comenius University, Bratislava
David Balkin
University of Colorado
Stuart Basefsky
Cornell University
Glenda Barrett
University of Maryland University College

Melissa Barringer
University of Massachusetts

Rebecca Bennett
Louisiana Tech University

Matt Bloom
University of Notre Dame

James T. Brakefield
Western Illinois University

Timothy Brown
San Jose State University

Lisa Burke
University of Tennessee-Chattanooga

Wayne Cascio
University of Colorado-Denver

Michael Chase
Indiana Wesleyan University

Dennis Cockrell
Washington State University-Pullman

H. Kristi Davison
University of Mississippi

Rebecca Decardenas
Barry University

Lee Dyer
Cornell University

Allen D. Engle Sr.
Eastern Kentucky University

Meiyu Fang
National Central University

Jie (Jasmine) Feng
Rutgers University

Dwight D. Frink
University of Mississippi

Ingrid Fulmer
Rutgers University

Marilyn Gagné
Curtin University

Kubilay Gok
Winona State University

Mary Graham
Syracuse University

Luis Gomez-Mejia
Arizona State University

Nina Gupta
University of Arkansas

Thomas Hall
Penn State University

Kevin Hallock
Cornell University

Robert Heneman
Ohio State University

Vandra Huber
University of Washington

Greg Hundley
Purdue

Debra D. Kuhl
Pensacola State College

Frank Krzystofiak
SUNY-Buffalo

David I. Levine
University of California-Berkeley

Frank B. Markham
The University of Mississippi

Janet Marler
SUNY-Albany

Patrenia McAbee
Delaware County Community College

Atul Mitra
Northern Iowa University

Michael Moore
Michigan State University

Bahaudin Mujtaba
Nova Southeastern University

Brian Murray
University of Dallas

Teresa S. Nelson
Butler County Community College

Anthony J. Nyberg
University of South Carolina

Rick Opland
California State University, Long Beach

Sanghee Park
Rutgers University

Bryan J. Pesta
Cleveland State University

Richard Posthuma
University of Texas at El Paso

Janez Prasnikar
University of Ljubljana

Vlado Pucik
IMD

Hesan Ahmed Quazi
Nanyang Business School

Greg Reilly
University of Connecticut

Sara Rynes
University of Iowa

Donald P. Schwab
University of Wisconsin-Madison

Dow Scott
Loyola University Chicago

James Sesil
University of Wisconsin-Madison

Jason Shaw
Nanyang Technical University

Thomas Stone
Oklahoma State University

Warren Scott Stone
University of Arkansas at Little Rock

Michael Sturman
Rutgers University

Ningyu Tang
Shanghai Jiao Tong University

Thomas Li-Ping Tang
Middle Tennessee State University

Tom Timmerman
Tennessee Tech University

Charlie Trevor
University of Wisconsin-Madison

Lee Tyner
University of Central Oklahoma

Yingchun Wang
University of Houston Downtown

Zhong-Ming Wang
Zhejiang University

Yoshio Yanadori
University of South Australia

Tae Seok Yang
Western Illinois University

Nada Zupan
University of Ljubljana

Part I
Introducing The Pay Model And Pay Strategy

Why do we work? If we are fortunate, our work brings meaning to our lives, challenges us in new and exciting ways, brings us recognition, and gives us the opportunity to interact with interesting people and create friendships. Oh yes—we also get a paycheck. Here in Part 1 of the book, we begin by talking about what we mean by "pay" and how paying people in different ways can influence them and, in turn, influence organization success. Wages and salaries, of course, are part of compensation, but so too, for some employees, are bonuses, health care benefits, stock options, and/or work/life balance programs.

Compensation is one of the most powerful tools organizations have to influence their employees. Managed well, it can play a major role in organizations successfully executing their strategies through their employees. We will see how companies like Costco, Whole Foods, Nucor, the SAS Institute, Microsoft, Alphabet/Google, and others use compensation to attract, motivate, and retain the right employees to execute their strategies. We will also see how companies like Apple sell premium products at attractive price points, to an important degree by using suppliers that have low labor costs. When they are managed less well—as bankruptcies at General Motors, Chrysler (now part of Stellantis), Lehman Brothers, and American Airlines (which stated at the time that it needed to reduce labor costs by $1.25 billion per year to be competitive), for example, might indicate—compensation decisions can also come back to haunt you. In Part 1, we describe the compensation policies and techniques that organizations use and the multiple objectives they hope to achieve by effectively managing these compensation decisions.

Although compensation has its guiding principles, we will see that "the devil is in the details"—how a compensation program is specifically designed and implemented will help determine its success. We want you to bring a healthy skepticism when you encounter simplistic or sweeping claims about whether a particular way of managing compensation does or does not work. For example, organizations, in general, benefit from pay for performance, but there are many types of pay-for-performance programs, and it is not always easy to design and implement a program that has the intended consequences and avoids *unintended* consequences. (As examples of what can go wrong, search the Web for Wells Fargo or Novartis and the term, scandal.) So, general principles are helpful, but only to a point.

Thus, in Part 1, our aim is to also help you understand how compensation strategy decisions interact with the specific context of an organization (e.g., its business and human resource strategies) to influence organization success. We emphasize that good theory and research are fundamental, not only to understanding compensation's likely effects, but also to developing that healthy skepticism we want you to have toward simplistic claims about what works and what does not.

Chapter **One**
The Pay Model

Chapter Outline

COMPENSATION: DOES IT MATTER? (OR, "SO WHAT?")

Why should you care about compensation? Do you find that life goes more smoothly when there is at least as much money coming in as going out? (Refer, e.g., to the lyrics for the Beatles' song "Money."[1] To exaggerate a bit, they say something like: Money doesn't buy everything, but if money can't buy it, I can't use it.) In the movie, It's a Wonderful Life, George Bailey is in a difficult spot. An (inexperienced) guardian angel by the name of Clarence has been sent to help George. When Clarence implores George to let him help, George asks if he has $8,000 on him. Clarence replies "No, we don't use money in Heaven" to which George responds: "Well, it comes in real handy down here, bud!"

Of course, it is the same for companies. It really does help to have as much money coming in (actually, more is better) as going out. Until recently, production workers at Chrysler received total compensation (i.e., wages plus benefits) of about $76 per hour. U.S. workers doing the same jobs at Toyota received $48 per hour, and the average total compensation per hour in U.S. manufacturing was $25 (and $3 in Mexico–not surprisingly, many new automobile supply and assembly plants have gone to Mexico in recent years). It is one thing to pay more than your competitors if you get something more (e.g., higher productivity and/or quality) in return. But Chrysler was not. So its "strategy" was not sustainable. Chrysler ended up going through bankruptcy, being bought out by Fiat, and then reducing worker compensation costs as part of its strategy for a return to competitiveness. Specifically, Chrysler took steps (as part of its bankruptcy plan) to bring its hourly labor costs down to about $49.[2] (Fiat Chrysler is now part of Stellantis.)

General Motors (GM), like Chrysler, has for decades paid its workers well–too well, perhaps, for what it received in return. So what? Well, in 1970, GM had 150 U.S. plants and 395,000 hourly workers. In sharp contrast, GM now has 32 U.S. manufacturing plants (including 11 vehicle assembly plants) and 87,000 U.S. workers (up from 57,000 U.S. hourly workers a few years ago).[3] In June 2009, GM, like Chrysler, had to file for bankruptcy (avoiding it for a while thanks to loans from the U.S. government–i.e., you, the taxpayer). Not all of GM's problems were compensation related. Building too many vehicles that consumers did not want was also a problem. But having labor costs higher than the competition's, without corresponding advantages in efficiency, quality, and customer service, does not seem to have served GM or its stakeholders well. Its stock price peaked at $93.62/share in April 2000. Its market value was about $60 billion in 2000. That shareholder wealth was wiped out in bankruptcy. Think also of the billions of dollars the U.S. taxpayer had to put into GM. Think of all the jobs that have been lost over the years and the effects on communities that have lost those jobs. (The good news is that as of 2021, GM's market value was over $80 billion. However, that is a ways behind what is now the most valuable U.S. carmaker, Tesla, at $635 billion, depending on the day, or about 8x greater than GM.)

On the other hand, Nucor Steel pays its workers very well, relative to what other companies inside and outside of the steel industry pay. But Nucor also has much higher productivity than is typical in the steel industry. The result: Both the company and its workers do well. Apple Computer is able to charge lower prices for its iPads and iPhones by outsourcing manufacturing to China in facilities owned by the Hon Hai Precision Industry Co., Ltd. (Foxconn), a Taiwanese company. (See **Chapter 7**.) As we will see later, doing so generates billions (yes, billions with a "b") of dollars in cost savings per year. Google and Facebook are companies that are known for paying very well. So far that seems to have worked, in that their high pay allows them to be very selective in who they hire and who they keep, and they would say that their talent-rich strategy has helped them to foster growth and innovation.

Wall Street financial services firms and banks used **incentive** plans that rewarded people for developing "innovative" new financial investment vehicles and for taking risks to earn a lot of money for themselves and their firms.[4] But several years ago, during the Great Financial Crisis of 2008, the markets discovered that many such risks had gone bad. Blue chip firms such as Lehman Brothers slid quickly into bankruptcy, whereas others, like Bear Stearns and Merrill Lynch, survived to varying degrees by finding other firms (J.P. Morgan and Bank of America, respectively) to buy them. The issue has not gone away. U.S. Federal Reserve officials have "made it clear that they believe bad behavior at banks goes deeper than a few bad apples and are advising firms to track warning signs of excessive risk taking and other cultural breakdowns." In the words of one Fed official, "Risk takers are drawn to finance like they are to Formula One racing." An important driver of risk taking among traders and others is the incentive system that encourages them to be "confident and aggressive" and that often results in those who thrive under this incentive rising to top leadership positions at the banks.[5]

Novartis is a health care solutions company based in Switzerland that includes medicines, pharmaceuticals, and eye care. The U.S. Justice Department announced a $678 million settlement with Novartis over improper inducements to persuade doctors to prescribe Novartis drugs, including Lotrel for hypertension. It is the largest whistleblower settlement under federal law. The key whistleblower was Ozzie Bilotta. According to NBC News, when he began working at Novartis, it was his dream job. But, "he never thought he'd be bribing doctors and wearing a wire for the feds." He ended up taking this sort of "drastic action" because he felt it was necessary to change how the pharmaceutical industry operated. Novartis subsequently changed its sales compensation such that pay no longer depends only on sales. It also now depends on an evaluation of whether sales were achieved in a way that is consistent with the Novartis Code of Ethics. There is also an Anti-Bribery Policy document that includes directing employees to "Always ask yourself before offering, giving, or promising anything of value to any person if what you are considering could be viewed as having an illegitimate purpose. If the answer is yes, you must not proceed."[6] Novartis has also increased its investment in data collection and analytics to monitor compliance with its Code of Ethics.

How people are paid affects their behaviors at work (as we have seen, for good or bad), which affect an organization's success.[7] For most employers, compensation is a major part of total cost, and often it is the single largest part of operating cost. These two facts together mean that well-designed compensation systems can help an organization achieve and sustain competitive advantage. On the other hand, as we have recently seen, poorly designed compensation systems can likewise play a major role in undermining organization success.

Our book, we hope, can play a role in helping to better educate you, the reader, about the design of compensation systems, both for managers and for workers. That includes not only how compensation can make things work better, but just as importantly, how compensation can make things go wrong, sometimes very wrong, as in our above examples.

COMPENSATION: DEFINITION, PLEASE (STAKEHOLDERS)

How people view compensation affects how they behave. It does not mean the same thing to everyone. Your view will probably differ depending on whether you look at compensation from the perspective of a member of society, a stockholder, a manager, or an employee. Thus, we begin by recognizing different perspectives.

EXHIBIT 1.1 **Indicators of Economic Standard of Living, United States (all dollar amounts in constant $), by Year**

	1990	2000	2010	2020	Growth 1990-2020
Panel A. Gross Domestic Product (GDP) per Employed Person[a]					
	84,062	100,468	118,578	127,378	52%

	1990	2000	2010	2020	Growth 1990-2020
Panel B. Average Annual Earnings[b]					
	42,518	44,711	45,758	52,156	23%

	1990	2000	2010	2017	Growth 1990-2017
Panel C. Household Income, by Income Level[c]					
Before Transfers and Taxes					
All	76,500	100,100	98,000	110,700	45%
Top 1 Percent	886,000	1,722,800	1,561,800	1,961,500	121%
Top 1 Percent Share (of Income)	13%	21%	19%	22%	64%
Highest Quintile	182,500	264,500	260,600	309,400	70%
Middle Quintile	60,100	68,600	68,800	49,700	−17%
Lowest Quintile	15,700	19,600	20,100	21,300	36%
After Transfers and Taxes					
All	61,900	79,700	84,200	93,300	51%
Top 1 Percent	640,300	1,167,100	1,105,800	1,343,000	110%
Top 1 Percent Share (of Income)	12%	17%	15%	17%	46%
Highest Quintile	137,200	191,400	198,800	229,700	67%
Middle Quintile	49,700	57,900	62,900	68,000	37%
Lowest Quintile	21,400	26,900	32,800	35,900	68%

Panel D. Net Household Wealth and Population					
	1990	2000	2010	2020	Growth 1990-2020
Net Household Wealth (millions)[d]	44,832,962	66,745,710	78,832,798	130,154,587	190%
Population[e]	250,181,000	282,398,000	309,774,000	330,152,000	32%
Panel E. Net Individual Wealth Share[f]					
	1990	2000	2010	2018	Growth 1990-2018
Top 1% Wealth Share	30%	33%	37%	38%	27%
Top 10% Wealth Share	68%	73%	77%	77%	13%

[a]Adjusted for Purchasing Power, 2017 Dollars. Source: WorldBank.
https://data.worldbank.org/indicator/SL.GDP.PCAP.EM.KD

[b]U.S. Bureau of Labor Statistics. Usual Weekly Earnings. Multiplied by 52 and converted to 2020 dollars.

[c]2017 Dollars. Source: Congressional Budget Office (2020). The Distribution of Household Income, 2017. October 2020. Transfers are means-tested (i.e., depend on income) and include, for example, Medicaid. Taxes are federal and include income tax, payroll tax, corporate, and excise tax.
https://www.cbo.gov/system/files/2020-10/56575-Household-Income.pdf

[d]2020 Dollars. Source: Board of Governors of the Federal Reserve (U.S.). Households and Nonprofit Organizations; New Worth, Level.
https://fred.stlouisfed.org/series/HNONWRA027N

[e]https://fred.stlouisfed.org/series/POPTOTUSA647NWDB

[f]Emmanuel Saez and Gabriel Zucman. The Rise of Income and Wealth Inequality in America: Evidence from Distributional Macroeconomic Accounts. Journal of Economic Perspectives, 2020, 34, 3–26. Uses "tax units" (individuals) rather than households.

Society

Exhibit 1.1 summarizes information on indicators of economic standard of living. All dollar amounts are in constant (also called real) dollars (i.e., adjusted for price changes/inflation). At the top, we start with Panel A, economic output (GDP) per Employed Person, a measure of national productivity. We see that productivity has increased by 52 percent since 1990. As a general rule, increases in productivity are necessary to generate increases in income and wealth for most of the population. We also note that the level of productivity in the United States in 2020, $127,378, is the highest among the 30 largest economies in the world. Panel B shows that (real) average annual earnings have increased 23 percent since 1990. Panel C moves from individual earnings from work to household income from all sources, including earnings, but other sources also (e.g., employer contributions for health care premiums, unemployment compensation, business income, capital income/gains, among others). We provide two sets of household income, before and after taxes (generally higher at higher income levels) and (means-test, meaning based on income) transfers (e.g., Medicaid; Children's Health Insurance Program; these transfers are generally higher at lower income levels). We see that income overall (All) has grown by 45 percent since 1990, before transfers and taxes and 51 percent after adjusting for taxes and transfers. Growth in economic output is the basis for growth in overall income (and wealth). However, the way income and wealth is distributed is also important. We show the income shares for the top 1 percent of income group and for selected quintiles (each one-fifth of the distribution). We see that income of the top 1 percent in 2020, after transfers and taxes, was $1,343,000 and it has grown by 110 percent since 1990. In contrast, the other quintiles have income that is considerably lower in 2020 (e.g., 68,000 in the middle quintile) and, although their growth rates are positive and significant, ranging from 37 percent to 68 percent, their growth has been considerably lower than for the top 1 percent group. Finally, Panels D and E show household wealth and individual wealth, including shares at the top. Again, there is good news in that household wealth has grown substantially over time, nearly tripling from 1990 to 2020. In this case, we need to account for the fact that the population also grew. Clearly, however, population growth was much smaller, indicating that the wealth of Americans really has increased substantially over time. However, wealth is very concentrated. We see that the top 10 percent hold 77 percent of the country's wealth and the top 1 percent hold 38 percent of its wealth. We also see that the concentration of wealth has increased since 1990.

The focus on the distribution of income and its implications for justice or equity is also seen in the attention paid to earnings differences by demographic groups.[8] For example, a comparison of earnings between men and women highlights what many consider inequities in pay decisions. Among full-time, year-round workers in the United States, women earn 82 percent of what men earn (up from 60 percent in 1980).[9] If women had the same characteristics as men, especially years and continuity of work experience and worked in the same occupations and industries, the gap narrows by one-half or more (see **Chapter 17**).[10] However, even with that, women would earn 93 percent of what comparable men earn, thus still leaving a sizable gap. Society has taken an interest in such earnings differentials. One indicator of this interest is the introduction of laws and regulations aimed at eliminating the discrimination that causes them.[11] (See **Chapter 17**.)

Based on the discussion above, it seems clear that people care greatly about their income. However, one well-known study on this issue by Kahneman and Deaton has sometimes been incorrectly (and/or incompletely interpreted) to mean that money only matters up to a point.[12] For example, based on the study, $75,000 (let's call it more like $95,000 adjusted for inflation) has been identified as the magic amount of annual income that makes people happy and paying them more had severely diminishing returns such that annual income beyond $75,000 did not increase their happiness any further. However, that result is based on asking people about the emotional well-being ("happiness) they experienced yesterday. Perhaps not surprisingly, having had a "headache" yesterday or reporting "zero social time with friends or family yesterday, including telephone and email-contact" had much larger effects on the emotional well-being/affect they felt yesterday than did whether their annual income was above $75,000. In contrast, when asked about life evaluation on a scale ranging from 0 ("worst possible life for you") to 10 ("the best possible life for you"), there was almost no diminishing return to higher income (measured on a log scale, equivalent to using percentage increases in income). As Kahneman and Deaton put it, there is "a fairly steady rise in life evaluation" in proportion to increases in income "over the entire range." Even returning to "happiness," Deaton and Kahneman caution: "Our data speak only to differences; they do not imply that people will not be happy with a raise from $100,000 to $150,000, or that they will be indifferent to an equivalent drop in income." In summary, the Deaton and Kahneman findings can be interpreted to mean, first, that increases in income that help people avoid poverty or the threat of poverty (or what is called financial precarity) have a major positive impact on both happiness and life evaluation. Second, these increases in income have diminishing returns for increasing happiness (as measured by emotional well-being the day before) beyond $95,000 in today's dollars. Third, it would be a mistake to think that reducing anyone's pay to $95,000 would do anything but make them unhappy. Fourth, higher pay is associated with higher life satisfaction and that association continues beyond $95,000.

Benefits given as part of a total compensation package, like wages/salaries, may also be seen as a reflection of equity or justice in society. As we will see, private sector employers spend about 42 cents for benefits on top of every dollar paid for **wages** and **salaries.** (State and local government employers pay even more: 62 cents in benefits on top of every wage dollar.)[13] Individuals and businesses in the United States spend $3.6 trillion per year, or about 17 percent of U.S. economic output (gross domestic product) on health care.[14] Nevertheless, as we will see, many (over 30 million) of people in the United States (over 8 percent of the population) have no health insurance.[15] (Prior to implementation of The Affordable Care Act of 2010, over 48 million were uninsured.)[16] A major reason is that the great majority of people who are under the age of 65 and not below the poverty line obtain health insurance through their employers, but small employers, which account for a substantial share of employment, are much less likely than larger employers to offer health insurance to their employees. As a result, the great majority of uninsured in the United States are from working families. (Of the uninsured, 85 percent have a full-time worker in the family and another 11 percent have a part-time worker in the family.)[17] Given that those who do have insurance typically have it through an employer, it also follows that whenever the unemployment rate increases, health care coverage declines further. (Some users of online dating services provide information on their employer-provided health care insurance. Dating service "shoppers" say they view health insurance coverage as a sign of how well a prospect is doing in a career.)

Job losses (or gains) within a country over time are partly a function of relative labor costs (and productivity) across countries. People in the United States worry about losing manufacturing jobs to Mexico, China, and other nations. (Increasingly, white-collar work in areas like finance, computer programming, and legal services is also being sent overseas.) **Exhibit 1.2** reveals that annual salary cost per employee (these numbers do not include benefits) in Mexico is $17,594, or about one-quarter of the $65,836 average salary in the United States. China's estimated annual salary of $12,430 is less than one-fifth of the U.S. rate. However, the value of what is produced also needs to be considered. Productivity in China is also roughly one-fifth that of U.S. workers, whereas Mexican worker productivity is about one-third of the U.S. level. Finally, if low wages are the goal, there always seems to be somewhere that pays less. Some companies (e.g., Coach) are now moving work out of China because its hourly wage, especially after recent increases, is not nearly as low as in countries like Vietnam, India, and the Philippines.[18] However, for other companies–such as Foxconn, which builds iPhones and iPads for Apple–even with increases in wages in China, labor costs remain very low in China compared to those in the United States and other advanced economies. Foxconn appears to be poised to continue having a large presence in China, a part of the world where most of its supply chain is. However, recent events are leading it, like others, to work to diversify its production and supply chain to be less dependent on any one country. We return to the topic of international comparisons in **Chapter 7** and **Chapter 16**.)

Some consumers know that pay increases often lead to price increases. They do not believe that higher labor costs benefit them. But other consumers lobby for higher wages. While partying revelers were collecting plastic beads at New Orleans' Mardi Gras, filmmakers were showing video clips of the Chinese factory that makes

EXHIBIT 1.2 Annual Salary and Economy-Wide Productivity (Gross Domestic Product [GDP] per Employed Person), in U.S. Dollars

	Annual Salary (excludes benefits)	Productivity (GDP per employee)
United States	65,836	127,378
Mexico	17,594	45,172
Japan	38,617	78,297
China	12,430	30,074
Germany	53,638	105,234
Czechia	29,281	81,079

Source: Annual salary (not including benefits) is from the Organization for Economic Cooperation and Development (OECD.org). https://data.oecd.org/earnwage/average-wages.htm, Salary data for China are from: Table 4-12, China Statistical Yearbook 2019. National Bureau of Statistics of China. http://www.stats.gov.cn/tjsj/ndsj/2019/indexeh.htm. Converted from yuan to USD using average exchange rate for 2019. Productivity is gross domestic product (GDP), in constant 2017 PPP $, divided by total employment in the economy. Purchasing power parity (PPP) adjustments are made to adjust for what can be purchased in different countries with the equivalent of a U.S. dollar. Source: The World Bank. https://data.worldbank.org/indicator/SL.GDP.PCAP.EM.KD.

the beads. In the video, the plant manager describes the punishment (5 percent reduction in already low pay) that he metes out to the young workers for workplace infractions. After viewing the video, one reveler complained, "It kinda takes the fun out of it."[19]

Stockholders

Stockholders are also interested in how employees are paid. Some believe that using stock to pay employees creates a sense of ownership that will improve performance, which in turn will increase stockholder wealth. But others argue that granting employees too much ownership dilutes stockholder wealth. Google's stock plan cost the company $600 million in its first year of operation. So people who buy Google stock (stockholders) are betting that this $600 million will motivate employees to generate more than $600 million in extra stockholder wealth.

Stockholders (also called shareholders) have a particular interest in executive pay.[20] (Executive pay will be discussed further in **Chapter 14**.)[21] To the degree that the interests of executives are aligned with those of shareholders (e.g., by paying executives on the basis of company performance measures such as shareholder return), the hope is that company performance will be higher. There is debate, however, about whether executive pay and company performance are strongly linked in the typical U.S. company.[22] In the absence of such a linkage, concerns arise that executives can somehow use their influence to obtain high pay without necessarily performing well. **Exhibit 1.3** provides descriptive data on chief executive officer (CEO) compensation. Note the large numbers (total annual compensation of $12.3 million) and also that the bulk of compensation (stock-related) is connected to shareholder return or other (primarily short-term, or one year or less) performance measures (bonus). As such, one would expect changes in CEO wealth and shareholder wealth to generally be aligned. We will return to this topic in more depth in **Chapter 14**.

In **Chapter 14** we will suggest that, on average, CEO interests and shareholder interests appear to be significantly aligned, but there are important exceptions and it is certainly an ongoing challenge to ensure that executives act in the best interest of shareholders. For example, during the meltdown in the financial services industry, top executives at Bear Stearns and Lehman Brothers regularly exercised stock options and sold stock during the period 2000–2008 prior to the meltdown. One estimate is that these stock-related gains plus bonus payments generated $1.4 billion for the top five executives at Bear Stearns and $1 billion for those at Lehman Brothers during the 2000–2008 period. "Thus, while the long-term shareholders in their firms were largely decimated, the executives' performance-based compensation kept them in positive territory." The problem here is that shareholders paid a huge penalty for what appears to have been overly aggressive risk-taking by

EXHIBIT 1.3 **Annual Compensation of Chief Executive Officers, U.S. (S&P 500) Public Companies**

Compensation Component	Median
Salary	$ 1,200,000
Bonus	$ 2,000,000
Stock Grants	$ 6,500,000
Stock Option Awards	$ 0[a]
Total Annual Compensation	$ 12,300,000

[a]The mean was $2.0 million.

Source: Equilar, CEO Pay Trends. Equilar.com. Because medians are used, compensation components do not add up to equal total annual compensation.

executives, but the executives, in contrast, did quite well because of "their ability to claim large amounts of compensation based on short-term results."[23]

Shareholders can influence executive compensation decisions in a variety of ways (e.g., through shareholder proposals and election of directors in proxy votes). In addition, the Dodd-Frank Wall Street Reform and Consumer Protection Act (see **Chapter 14**) was signed into law in 2010. Among its provisions is "say on pay," which requires public companies to submit their executive compensation plan to a vote by shareholders. The vote is not binding. However, companies seem to be intent on designing compensation plans that do not result in negative votes. In addition, clawback provisions (designed to allow companies to reclaim compensation from executives in some situations) are available under Dodd-Frank and have also been adopted in stronger form by some companies.[24]

Customers

Employment costs in the form of compensation are often the largest single operating cost for an organization. Thus, for companies whose business strategy depends on low product/service cost to compete for customers, they also may focus on keeping compensation costs low. As we will see shortly, that is certainly true of Walmart. It certainly seems to have worked in the eyes of customers as it is year after year the largest company in the world in terms of revenues. As a different example, we will see that Costco's business strategy is less exclusively cost-based. They are concerned about employment costs, but their business strategy depends on paying higher wages to attract and retain employees more successfully than Walmart does, as well as employees who can provide a higher level customer experience. Compensation also increasingly comes into play for customers who want to purchase from a company that acts with responsibility with respect to environmental, social, and governance (ESG) issues. This can take a variety of forms in the employment and compensation area. For example, customers may base their buying decisions on how they believe the company's employees are treated and/or how workers employed by other companies, but part of the company's supply chain, are treated. For example, Apple has supplier responsibility standards and an extensive system to monitor supplier adherence to these standards, including in the area of employment.[25]

Managers

For managers, compensation influences their success in two ways. First, it is a major expense that must be managed. Second, it is a major determinant of employee attitudes and behaviors (and thus, organization performance). We begin with the cost issue. Competitive pressures, both global and local, force managers to consider the affordability of their compensation decisions. Labor costs can account for more than 50 percent of total costs. In some industries, such as financial or professional services and in education and government, this figure is even higher. However, even within an industry, labor costs as a percentage of total costs vary among individual firms. For example, small neighborhood grocery stores, with labor costs between 15 percent and 18 percent, have been driven out of business by supermarkets that delivered the same products at a lower cost of labor (9 to 12 percent). Supermarkets today are losing market share to the warehouse club stores such as Sam's Club and Costco, which enjoy an even lower cost of labor (4 to 6 percent), even though Costco pays wages that are above average for the industry. And, now Amazon has entered the grocery business by purchasing Whole Foods, which is expected to cause further cost reductions and disruption.

Exhibit 1.4 compares the hourly pay rate for retail workers at Costco to that at Walmart and Sam's Club (which is owned by Walmart). Wages for the three jobs in **Exhibit 1.4** are higher at Costco. The Costco wages are increasing further because as of 2021, its minimum wage will go to $16/hour. Walmart's minimum wage remains at $11/hour. Each retailer tries to provide a unique shopping experience. Walmart and Sam's Club compete on low prices, with Sam's Club being a "warehouse store" with especially low prices on a narrower range of products, often times sold in bulk. Costco also competes on the basis of low prices, but with a mix that includes more high-end products aimed at a higher customer income segment. To compete in this segment, Costco appears to have chosen to pay higher wages, perhaps as a way to attract and retain a higher quality workforce.[26] A Costco's annual report states, "With respect to expenses relating to the compensation of our employees, our philosophy is not to seek to minimize the wages and benefits that they earn. Rather, we believe that achieving our longer-term objectives of reducing employee turnover and enhancing employee satisfaction requires maintaining compensation levels that are better than the industry average for much of our workforce." By comparison, Walmart simply states in a previous annual report that they "experience significant turnover in associates [i.e., employees] each year."[27] Based on **Exhibit 1.4**, Costco is quite successful, relative to its competitors, in terms of employee retention, customer satisfaction, and the efficiency with which it generates sales (see revenue per square foot and revenue per employee). So, although Costco's labor costs are higher than those of Sam's Club and Walmart, it appears that this model works for Costco because it helps it gain an advantage over its competitors.

Thus, rather than treating pay only as an expense to be minimized, a manager can also use it to influence employee behaviors and to improve the organization's performance. High pay, as long as it can be documented to bring high returns through its influences on employees, can be a successful strategy. As our Costco (versus Sam's Club and Walmart) example seems to suggest, the way people are paid affects the quality of their work and their attitude toward customers.[28] It may also affect their willingness to be flexible, learn new skills, or suggest innovations. On the other hand, people may become interested in unions or legal action against their employer based on how they are paid (e.g., if they perceive their pay to be unfairly low). This potential to influence employees' behaviors, and subsequently the productivity and effectiveness of the organization, means that the study of compensation is well worth your time, don't you think?[29]

Employees

The pay individuals receive in return for the work they perform and the value they create is usually the major source of their financial security. Hence, pay plays a vital role in a person's economic and social well-being. Employees may see compensation as a *return in an exchange* between their employer and themselves, as an **entitlement** for being an employee of the company, as an incentive to decide to take/stay in a job and invest in performing well in that job, or as a reward for having done so. Compensation can be all of these things.[30]

The importance of pay is apparent in many ways. Employees are less likely to quit current jobs that pay more and are likely to increase their pay when they quit voluntarily to take another job. (See **Chapter 7**.) Wages and benefits are a major focus of labor unions' efforts to serve their members' interests. (See **Chapter 14**.) The extensive legal framework governing pay–including minimum wage, living wage, overtime, and nondiscrimination regulations–also points to the central importance of pay to employees in the employment relationship. (See **Chapter 17**.) Next, we turn to how pay influences employee behaviors.

HOW PAY INFLUENCES BEHAVIORS: INCENTIVE AND SORTING EFFECTS

Pay can influence employee **motivation** and behavior in two ways. First, and perhaps most obviously, pay can affect the motivational intensity, direction, and persistence of current employees. Motivation, together with employee **ability** and work/organizational design (which can help or hinder employee performance), determines employee behaviors such as performance. We will refer to this effect of pay as an **incentive effect,** the degree to which pay influences individual and aggregate motivation among the employees we have at any point in time.

EXHIBIT 1.4 Pay Rates at Retail Stores, Customer Satisfaction, Employee Turnover, and Sales/Square Ft.

	Average Pharmacy Tech Annual Wage	Average Stocker Hourly Wage	Average Cashier Hourly Wage	Customer Satisfaction (100 = highest)	Employee Annual Turnover	On Best Employer List?	Stores	Revenues	Store Size Average (Sq. ft.)	Number of Employees	Revenue per Sq. ft.	Revenue per Employee
Costco	$17 to $24	$14 to $15	$15 to $16	81	lower	Yes[a]	795	$163 billion	146,038	273,000	$1,406	$597,875
Sam's Club	$14 to $16	$11 to $12	$11 to $12	79			599	$64 billion	133,995	—	$ 796	—
Walmart	$13 to $17	$11 to $12	$11 to $12	71	higher	No	4,473	$370 billion	148,225	—	$ 526	—
Walmart + Sam's Club							5,342	$434 billion	146,624	1,600,000	$ 554	$271,171

Sources: Customer Satisfaction data from American Customer Satisfaction Index TM, http://www.theacsi.org/, retrieved April 4, 2021; Number of Stores, Revenues, Store Size, Number of Employees from Wal-Mart 10-K (Annual Report) and Costco 10-K (Annual Report). For Walmart, used only U.S. data; Average Wage from www.glassdoor.com, retrieved April 4, 2021. Note: There are wage and compensation data in Costco's Annual Report (Form 10-K) and in Walmart's Annual Report (Form 10-K) and more in Walmart's Environmental, Social, and Governance Report. However, the data reported by Costco is total compensation, primarily for full-time U.S. employees, whereas Walmart includes many non-U.S. employees and reports wage or salary (rather than total compensation). Note: Revenue per sq. ft. equals Revenues/(Stores × Store Size Average)

[a] #4 on Forbes 2021 list. Top 50 in Glassdoor 2021 list.

However, pay can also have an indirect, but important, influence via a **sorting effect** on the composition of the workforce.[31] That is, different types of pay strategies may cause different types of people to apply to and stay with (i.e., self-select into) an organization. In the case of pay structure/level, it may be that higher pay levels help organizations attract more high-quality applicants, allowing them to be more selective in their hiring. Similarly, higher pay levels may improve employee retention. (In **Chapter 7**, we will talk about when paying more is most likely to be worth the higher costs.)

In other words, although perhaps less obvious, it is not only how much but *how* an organization pays that can result in sorting effects.[32] Ask yourself: Would people who are highly capable and have a strong work ethic and an interest in earning a lot of money prefer to work in an organization that pays about the same amount to all employees doing the same job, regardless of their performance? Or would they prefer to work in an organization where their pay can be much higher (or lower) depending on how they perform? If you chose the latter answer, then you believe that sorting effects matter. People differ regarding which type of pay arrangement they prefer. The question for organizations is simply this: Are you using the pay policy that will attract and retain the types of employees you want? Keep in mind that high performers have more alternative job opportunities and that more opportunities, all else being equal (e.g., if they are not paid more for their higher performance), translate into higher turnover–which is likely to be a significant problem if it is the high performers who are leaving, especially if high performers in particular roles create a disproportionately high amount of value for organizations. This would be the case, for example, if performance, instead of following a normal distribution, follows a power law distribution, which allows more extreme values (e.g., in the form of very high and valuable performance).[33]

This also raises the issue of dealing with outside offers that employees receive. We know that a substantial share of employee turnover results from receiving unsolicited outside offers. In other words, turnover is not always in response to dissatisfaction. Sometimes it is driven by opportunity. These are likely to be some of the most valuable employees, and thus policies and practices for dealing with outside offers (hopefully informed by research) are important.[34]

Let's take a look at one especially informative study conducted by Edward Lazear regarding incentive and sorting effects.[35] Individual worker productivity was measured before and after a glass installation company switched one of its plants from a salary-only (no pay for performance) system to an individual incentive plan under which each employee's pay depended on his/her own performance. An overall increase in plant productivity of 44 percent was observed comparing before and after. Roughly one-half of this increase was due to individual employees becoming more productive. However, the remaining one-half of the productivity gain was not explained by this fact. So, where did the other one-half of the gain come from? The answer: Less-productive workers were less likely to stay in their jobs under the new individual incentive system because it was less favorable to them. When they left, they tended to be replaced by more-productive workers (who were happy to have the chance to make more money under a system that rewards performance than they might make elsewhere). Thus, focusing only on the incentive effects of pay (on current workers) can miss the other major mechanism (sorting) by which pay decisions influence employee behaviors.

Some research looks at "stars." For example, one study used data on individual security analysts in investment banks and found that newly hired "stars" from other firms generally did less well in their new firms, but their performance decline was less when moving with other members of their team, rather than alone.[36] Thus, there are implications. First, star performance may be somewhat firm-specific. Second, a firm cannot necessarily "buy talent" and be sure that talent will perform at the same level as at its previous firm. Third, to the degree that is the case, the firm-specificity may stem at least partly from the additional value created by being part of a well-functioning team. Other research on stars, this time in the hedge fund industry, finds that, compared to other members of their team, stars get more credit when things go well and more blame when things go poorly. Thus, working "in someone's shadow" can be a plus when things don't go well, but can lead to less credit when things go well.[37]

The pay model that comes later in this chapter includes compensation policies and the **objectives** (efficiency, fairness, compliance) these are meant to influence. Our point here is that compensation policies work through employee incentive and sorting effects to either achieve or not achieve those objectives.

Global Views—*Vive la Différence*

In English, *compensation* means something that counterbalances, offsets, or makes up for something else. However, if we look at the origin of the word in different languages, we get a sense of the richness of the meaning, which combines entitlement, return, and reward.[38]

In China, the traditional characters for the word "compensation" are based on the symbols for logs and water, suggesting that compensation provides the necessities in life. In the recent past the state owned all Chinese enterprises, and compensation was treated as an entitlement. In today's China, compensation takes on a more subtle meaning. A new word, *dai yu,* is used. It refers to how you are being treated–your wages, benefits, training opportunities, and so on. When people talk about compensation, they ask each other about the *dai yu* in their companies. Rather than assuming that everyone is entitled to the same treatment, the meaning of compensation now includes a broader sense of returns as well as entitlement.[39]

"Compensation" in Japanese is *kyuyo,* which is made up of two separate characters (*kyu* and *yo*), both meaning "giving something." *Kyu* is an honorific used to indicate that the person doing the giving is someone of high rank, such as a feudal lord, an emperor, or a samurai leader. Traditionally, compensation is thought of as something given by one's superior. Today, business consultants in Japan try to substitute the word *housyu,* which means "reward" and has no associations with notions of superiors. The many allowances that are part of Japanese compensation systems translate as *teate,* which means "taking care of something." *Teate* is regarded as compensation that takes care of employees' financial needs. This concept is consistent with the family, housing, and commuting allowances that are still used in many Japanese companies.[40]

These contrasting ideas about compensation–multiple views (societal, stockholder, managerial, employee, and even global) and multiple meanings (returns, rewards, entitlement)–add richness to the topic. But they can also cause confusion unless everyone is talking about the same thing. So let's define what we mean by "compensation" or "pay" (the words are used interchangeably in this book):

> **Compensation** refers to all forms of financial returns and tangible services and benefits employees receive as part of an employment relationship.

FORMS OF PAY

Exhibit 1.5 shows the variety of returns people receive from work. Total returns are categorized as **total compensation** and **relational returns.** The relational returns (learning opportunities, status, challenging work, and so on) are psychological.[41] Total compensation returns are more transactional. They include pay received directly as cash (e.g., base, merit, incentives, cost-of-living adjustments) and indirectly as benefits (e.g., pensions, medical insurance, programs to help balance work and life demands, brightly colored uniforms).[42] So pay comes in different forms, and programs to pay people can be designed in a wide variety of ways. WorldatWork has a Total Rewards Model that is similar and includes compensation, benefits, work-life, performance/recognition, and development/career opportunities.[43] The importance of monetary rewards as a motivator relative to other rewards (e.g., intrinsic rewards such as how interesting the work is) has long been a topic of interest, as have the conditions under which money is more or less important to people (and even whether money is sometimes too important to people).[44] Although scholars and pundits have sometimes debated which is more important (and have sometimes argued that money does not motivate or even that it demotivates), our reading of the research indicates that both types of rewards are important and that it is usually not terribly productive to debate which is more important.[45] It will no doubt come as little surprise that we will focus on monetary rewards (total compensation) in a book called *Compensation.* Whatever other rewards employees value, it is our experience that they expect to be paid for their work, that how and how much they are paid affects their attitudes, performance, and job choice, as well as their standard of living. These effects of compensation on employees (as well as the cost of employee compensation) have major implications for how successfully organizations can execute their strategies and achieve their goals, as we will see.

Cash Compensation: Base

Base wage is the cash compensation that an employer pays for the work performed. Base wage tends to reflect the value of the work or skills and generally ignores differences attributable to individual employees. For example, the base wage for machine operators may be $20 an hour. However, some individual operators may receive more because of their experience and/or performance. Some pay systems set base wage as a function of the skill or education an employee possesses; this is common for engineers and schoolteachers.[46]

A distinction is often made in the United States between wage and salary, with **salary** referring to pay for employees who are **exempt** from regulations of the Fair Labor Standards Act (FLSA) and hence do not receive overtime pay.[47] Managers and professionals usually fit this category. Their pay is calculated at an annual or monthly rate rather than hourly, because hours worked do not need to be recorded. In contrast, workers who are covered by overtime and reporting provisions of the Fair Labor Standards Act–*nonexempts*–have their pay calculated as an hourly wage. Some organizations, such as IBM, Eaton, and Walmart, label all base pay as "salary." Rather than dividing employees into separate categories of salaried and wage earners, they believe that an "all-salaried" workforce reinforces an organizational **culture** in which all employees are part of the same team. However, merely changing the terminology does not negate the need to comply with the FLSA.

EXHIBIT 1.5 Total Returns for Work

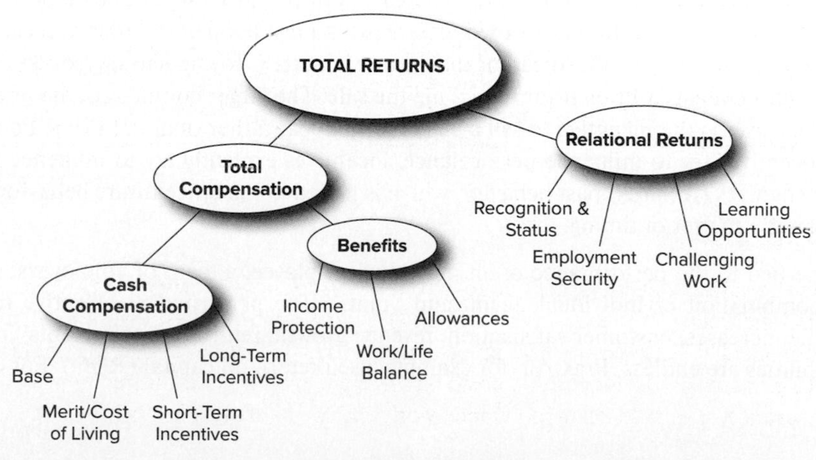

Cash Compensation: Merit Increases/Short-Term Incentives (Merit Bonuses)/COLAs

A cost of living adjustment (COLA) to base wages may be made on the basis of changes in what other employers are paying for the same work, changes in living costs, or changes in experience or skill. Such provisions are less common than in the past as employers continually try to control fixed costs and link pay increases to individual and/or company performance.

Merit increases are given as increments to base pay and are based on performance.[48] According to a WorldatWork survey, 94 percent of U.S. firms use merit pay increases.[49] Given that 22 percent of respondents to the survey were in the nonprofit, not-for-profit, or public sectors where we know that the use of merit pay is less,[50] it may be that nearly 100 percent of U.S. private sector organizations use merit pay. Merit payments are based on an assessment (or rating) of recent past performance made (with or without a formal performance evaluation). In recent years, merit increase budgets (or average merit increases) have been around 3 percent.[51] Survey data indicate that, on average, an outstanding performer receives a 4.8 percent increase, an average performer a 2.9 percent increase, and a poor performer a 0.2 percent increase.[52] Finally, companies increasingly use merit bonuses.[53] As with merit increases, *merit bonuses* are based on a performance rating but, unlike merit increases, are paid in the form of a lump sum rather than becoming (a permanent) part of the base salary.[54] Merit bonuses (also referred to as short-term incentives) may now be more important than traditional merit increases. "Indeed, merit bonuses now appear to account for more of the pay-performance relationship than do the traditional and most often discussed form of pay for individual performance, merit pay."[55] In companies that use merit bonuses and among those workers who receive them, the average annual merit bonus in recent years has been about 6 percent for hourly employees, 7 percent for lower level salaried employees, and 11 percent for higher level (but below officers/executives) salaried employees, all much larger than the more often discussed recent merit increase pools of around 3 percent.[56] We return to this issue in **Chapter 18**.

Cash Compensation: Incentives

Incentives also tie pay increases to performance.[57] However, incentives differ from merit adjustments. First, incentives are tied to objective performance measures (e.g., sales) usually in a formula-based way, whereas a merit increase program typically relies on a subjective performance rating. There is also some subjectivity in the size of the pay increase awarded for a particular rating. Second, incentives do not increase the base wage and so must be re-earned each pay period. Third, the potential size of the incentive payment will generally be known (given the use of a formula) beforehand. Whereas merit pay programs evaluate past performance of an individual and then decide on the size of the increase, what must happen in order to receive the incentive payment is called out very specifically ahead of time. For example, a Toyota salesperson knows the **commission** on a Land Cruiser versus a Prius prior to making the sale. The larger commission he or she will earn by selling the Land Cruiser is the incentive to sell a customer that car rather than the Prius. Fourth, while both merit pay and incentives try to influence performance, incentives explicitly try to influence future behavior whereas merit recognizes (rewards) past behavior, which is hoped to influence future behavior. The incentive-reward distinction is a matter of timing.

Incentives can be tied to the performance of an individual employee, a team of employees, a total business unit, or some combination of individual, team, and unit.[58] The performance objective may be expense reduction, volume increases, customer satisfaction, revenue growth, return on investments, increase in stock value–the possibilities are endless. Prax Air, for example, used return on capital (ROC). For every quarter in which a 6 percent ROC target is met or exceeded, Prax Air awarded bonus days of pay. An 8.6 percent ROC means two extra days of pay for that quarter for every employee covered by the program. An ROC of 15 percent means 8.5 extra days of pay.

Because incentives are one-time payments, they do not permanently increase labor costs. When performance declines, incentive pay automatically declines, too. Consequently, incentives (and sometimes merit bonuses also) are frequently referred to as **variable pay.**

Incentives can have powerful effects, both good and bad, on performance. On average, these effects are positive and substantial.[59] However, incentives are risky, and they can go wrong in spectacular fashion.[60] One example is the Great Financial Crisis, which apparently stemmed in large part from improper and aggressive incentives paid to encourage loan officers to give home loans (mortgages) to people who were unlikely to be able to pay them back. (Recent events at Wells Fargo provide further examples.) We will talk about more examples in later chapters.

Long-Term Incentives

Incentives may be short- or long-term. Long-term incentives are intended to focus employee efforts on multiyear results. Typically they are in the form of stock ownership or else options to buy stock at a fixed price (thus leading to a monetary gain to the degree the stock price later goes up). The belief underlying stock ownership is that employees with a financial stake in the organization will focus on long-term financial objectives: return on investment, market share, return on net assets, and the like. Bristol-Myers Squibb grants stock to selected "Key Contributors" who make outstanding contributions to the firm's success. Stock options are often the largest component in an executive pay package. Some companies extend stock ownership beyond the ranks of executives and/or other high salary employees. Examples of companies that provide both broad-based equity awards and employee stock purchase plans include Cisco, Intuit, Adobe Systems, and Goldman Sachs.[61]

Benefits: Income Protection

Exhibit 1.5 showed that benefits, including income protection, work/life services, and allowances, are also part of total compensation. Indeed,benefits add an average of $0.46 in cost for every $1.00 in wages and salaries. (See **Chapter 12**.) Some income protection programs are legally required in the United States; employers must pay into a fund that provides income replacement for workers who become disabled or unemployed. Employers are also required to pay one-half the payroll tax for each employee to fund Social Security coverage. (Employees pay the other half.) Different countries have different lists of mandatory benefits.

Medical insurance, retirement programs, life insurance, and savings plans are common benefits. They help protect employees from the financial risks inherent in daily life. Often companies can provide these protections to employees more cheaply than employees can obtain them for themselves. In the United States, employers spend roughly $725 billion per year just on health care costs, or 19 percent of all U.S. health care expenditures.[62] Among employers that provide health insurance, the cost to provide family coverage is $21,342 per year per employee. The average employer pays $15,574 (74 percent) of that and the average employee pays the remaining $5,588 (26 percent).[63] Given the magnitude of such costs, it is no surprise that employers have sought to rein in or reduce benefits costs. One approach has been to shift costs to employees (e.g., having employees pay a larger share of health insurance premiums).[64] Some companies have allowed their benefits costs to get so far out of control that more drastic action has been taken. For example, as noted, companies like Chrysler, GM, and American Airlines have recently gone through bankruptcy, which has been used to reduce benefits costs and labor costs more generally. GM benefits costs had gotten so high that GM was sometimes described as a pension and health care provider that also makes cars.

Benefits: Work/Life Balance

Programs that help employees better integrate their work and life responsibilities include time away from work (vacations, jury duty), access to services to meet specific needs (drug counseling, financial planning, referrals for child and elder care), and flexible work arrangements (e.g., remote work, nontraditional schedules, nonpaid time off). Responding to the changing demographics of the workforce (two-income families or single parents who need work-schedule flexibility to meet their family obligations), many U.S. employers are giving a higher priority to these benefit forms. (This trend was reinforced by the pandemic.) Medtronic, for example, touts its Total Well-Being Program that seeks to provide "resources for growth–mind, body, heart, and spirit" for each employee. Health and wellness, financial rewards and security, individual and family well-being, and a fulfilling work environment are part of this "total well-being."[65] Medtronic believes that this program permits employees to be "fully present" at work and less distracted by conflicts between their work and nonwork responsibilities.

Benefits: Allowances

Allowances often grow out of whatever is in short supply. In Vietnam and China, housing (dormitories and apartments) and transportation allowances are frequently part of the pay package. Many decades after the end of World War II–induced food shortages, some Japanese companies still continue to offer a "rice allowance" based on the number of an employee's dependents. Almost all foreign companies in China discover that housing, transportation, and other allowances are expected.[66] Companies that resist these allowances must come up with other ways to attract and retain employees. In many European countries, managers assume that a car will be provided–only the make and model are negotiable.[67]

Total Earnings Opportunities: Present Value of a Stream of Earnings

Up to this point we have treated compensation as something received at a moment in time. But a firm's compensation decisions have a temporal effect. Say you have a job offer at $50,000 a year. If you stay with the firm for five years and receive an annual increase of 4 percent, in five years you will be earning $60,833 a year. For your employer, the five-year cost commitment of the decision to hire you turns out to be $331,649 in cash. If you add in an additional 30 percent for benefits, the decision to hire you implies a commitment of over $430,000 from your employer. Will you be worth it? You will be, after this course.

A present-value perspective shifts the comparison of today's initial offers to consideration of future bonuses, merit increases, and promotions. Sometimes a company will tell applicants that its relatively low starting offers will be overcome by larger future pay increases. In effect, the company is selling the present value of the future stream of earnings. But few candidates apply that same analysis to calculate the future increases required to offset the lower initial offers. Hopefully, everyone who reads **Chapter 1** will now do so.

Relational Returns from Work

Why do Google millionaires continue to show up for work every morning? Why does Andy Borowitz write the funniest satirical news site on the web (***www.borowitzreport.com***) for free? There is no doubt that nonfinancial returns from work have a substantial effect on employees' behavior.[68] **Exhibit 1.5** includes such relational returns from work as recognition and status, employment security, challenging work, and opportunities to learn. Other forms of relational return might include personal satisfaction from successfully facing new challenges, teaming with great co-workers, receiving new uniforms, and the like.[69] Such factors are part of the total return, which is a broader umbrella than total compensation. Interestingly, as you may have noticed, the types of rewards just listed, other than money, are sometimes viewed as being, for lack of a better word, more noble (or higher order as Maslow and Herzberg might say) than money. In fact, at least one study reports that candidates for a job who come across as more motivated by money are sometimes inferred to have lower levels of higher order motivations, resulting in them being evaluated lower. The researchers refer to this as "motivation purity bias."[70] So, as always, think about how you want to present yourself (including in terms of your motivation purity) and come across when you interview!

The Organization as a Network of Returns

Sometimes it is useful to think of an organization as a network of returns created by all these different forms of pay, including total compensation and relational returns. The challenge is to design this network so that it helps the organization to succeed.[71] As in the case of crew rowers pulling on their oars, success is more likely if all are pulling in unison rather than working against one another. In the same way, the network of returns is more likely to be useful if bonuses, development opportunities, and promotions all work together.

So the next time you walk through an employer's door, look beyond the cash and health care offered to search for all the returns that create the network. Even though this book focuses on compensation, let's not forget that compensation is only one of many factors affecting people's decisions about work. (You might enjoy listening to Roger Miller's song "Kansas City Star," or Chely Wright's "It's the Song" for some other reasons people choose their work.)

A PAY MODEL

The pay model shown in **Exhibit 1.6** serves as both a framework for examining current pay systems and a guide for most of this book. It contains three basic building blocks: (1) the compensation objectives, (2) the policies that form the foundation of the compensation system, and (3) the techniques that make up the compensation system. Because objectives drive the system, we will discuss them first.

Compensation Objectives

Pay systems are designed to achieve certain objectives. The basic objectives, shown at the right side of the model, include efficiency, fairness, ethics, and compliance with laws and regulations. *Efficiency* can be stated more specifically: (1) improving performance, increasing quality, delighting customers and stockholders, and (2) controlling labor costs.

Compensation objectives at Medtronic and Whole Foods are contrasted in **Exhibit 1.7**. Medtronic is a medical technology company that pioneered cardiac pacemakers. Its compensation objectives emphasize performance, business success, minimizing fixed costs, and attracting and energizing top talent.

EXHIBIT 1.6 The Pay Model

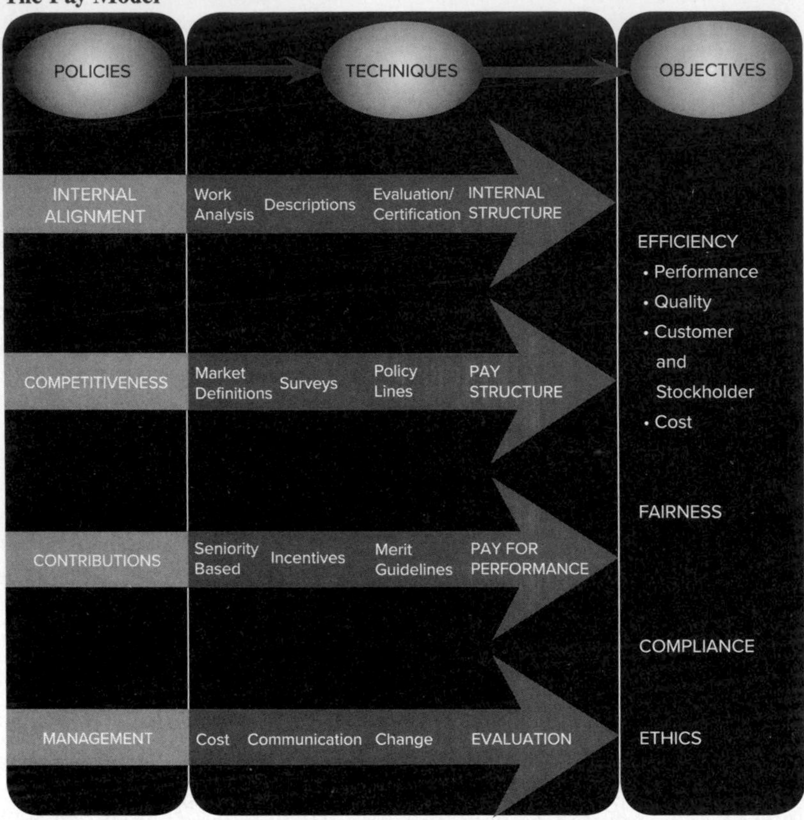

EXHIBIT 1.7 Pay Objectives at Medtronic and Whole Foods

Medtronic	Whole Foods
Support Medtronic mission and increased complexity of business	Increase long-term shareholder value
Minimize increases in fixed costs	Earn profits daily through voluntary exchange with our customers
Attract and engage top talent	Through profits, create capital for growth, prosperity, opportunity, job satisfaction, and job security
Emphasize personal, team, and Medtronic performance	Support team member happiness and excellence
Recognize personal and family total well being	Acknowledge that team outcomes are collective
Ensure Fair Treatment: and Acknowledge that team outcomes are collective should be on their own line.	

Whole Foods is the nation's largest organic- and natural-foods grocer. Its markets are a "celebration of food": bright, well stocked, and well staffed.[72] The company describes its commitment to offering the highest quality and least processed foods as a shared responsibility. Its first compensation objective is "Increase long-term shareholder value."

Fairness (sometimes called equity) is a fundamental objective of pay systems.[73] In Medtronic's objectives, fairness means to "ensure fair treatment" and "recognize personal and family well-being." Whole Foods's pay objectives discuss a "shared fate." In their egalitarian work culture, pay beyond base wages is linked to team performance, and employees have some say about who is on their team.

The fairness objective calls for fair treatment for all employees by recognizing both employee contributions (e.g., higher pay for greater performance, experience, or training) and employee needs (e.g., a fair wage as well as fair procedures). *Procedural fairness* refers to the process used to make pay decisions.[74] It suggests that the way a pay decision is made may be equally as important to employees as the results of the decision *(distributive fairness).*

Compliance as a pay objective means conforming to federal and state compensation laws and regulations. If laws change, pay systems may need to change, too, to ensure continued compliance. As companies go global, they must comply with the laws of all the countries in which they operate.

Ethics

Asian philosophy gives us the concept of yin and yang—complementary opposites rather than substitutes or trade-offs. It is not yin *or* yang; part of yin is in yang, and part of yang is in yin. So it is with objectives in the pay model. It is not efficiency versus fairness versus compliance. Rather, the aim is to achieve all three simultaneously. The tension of working toward all objectives at once creates fertile grounds for ethical dilemmas.

Ethics means the organization cares about how its results are achieved.[75] Scan the websites or lobby walls of corporate headquarters and you will inevitably find statements of "Key Behaviors," "Our Values," and "Codes of Conduct." One company's code of conduct is shown in **Exhibit 1.8**. The challenge is to put these statements into daily practice. The company in the exhibit is the formerly admired, now reviled, Enron, whose employees lost not only their Enron jobs, but also the money they invested in Enron stock (in some cases, their entire retirement nest egg).

Because it is so important, it is inevitable that managing pay sometimes creates ethical dilemmas. Manipulating results to ensure executive bonus payouts, misusing (or failing to understand) statistics used to measure competitors' pay rates, repricing or backdating stock options to manipulate (increase) their value, encouraging employees to invest a portion of their wages in company stock while executives are bailing out, offering just enough pay to get a new hire in the door while ignoring the relationship to co-workers' pay, and shaving the hours recorded in employees' time card—these are all-too-common examples of ethical lapses.

Some, but not all, compensation professionals and consultants remain silent during ethical misconduct and outright malfeasance. Absent a professional code, compensation managers must look to their own ethics—and the pay model, which calls for combining the objectives of efficiency and fair treatment of employees as well as compliance.[76]

There are probably as many statements of pay objectives as there are employers. In fact, highly diversified firms such as General Electric and Eaton, which operate in multiple lines of businesses, may have different **pay objectives** for different business units. At General Electric, each unit's objectives must meet GE overall objectives.

Objectives serve several purposes. First, they guide the design of the pay system. If an objective is to increase customer satisfaction, then incentive programs and merit pay might be used to pay for performance. Another employer's objective may be to develop innovative new products. Job design, training, and team building may be used to reach this objective. The pay system aligned with this objective may include salaries that are at least equal to those of competitors (external competitiveness) and that go up with increased skills or knowledge (internal alignment). This pay system could be very different from our first example, where the focus is on increasing customer satisfaction. Notice that policies and techniques are the means to reach the objectives.

In summary, objectives guide the design of pay systems. They also serve as the standards for judging the success of the pay system. If the objective is to attract and retain the best and the brightest skilled employees, but they are leaving for higher-paying jobs elsewhere, the system may not be performing effectively. Although there may be many nonpay reasons for such turnover, objectives provide standards for evaluating the effectiveness of a pay system.[77]

Four Policy Choices

Every employer must address the policy decisions shown on the left side of the pay model: (1) internal alignment, (2) external competitiveness, (3) employee contributions, and (4) management of the pay system. These policies are the foundation on which pay systems are built. They also serve as guidelines for managing pay in ways that accomplish the system's objectives.

EXHIBIT 1.8 Enron's Ethics Statement

Foreword

"As officers and employees of Enron Corp., its subsidiaries, and its affiliated companies, we are responsible for conducting the business affairs of the companies in accordance with all applicable laws and in a moral and honest manner. . . . We want to be proud of Enron and to know that it enjoys a reputation for fairness and honesty and that it is respected. . . . Enron's reputation finally depends on its people, on you and me. Let's keep that reputation high."

July 1, 2000
Kenneth L. Lay
Chairman and Chief Executive Officer

Values

Respect	We treat others as we would like to be treated ourselves. We do not tolerate abusive or disrespectful treatment. Ruthlessness, callousness, and arrogance don't belong here.
Integrity	We work with customers and prospects openly, honestly, and sincerely. When we say we will do something, we will do it; when we say we cannot or will not do something, then we won't do it.
Communication	We have an obligation to communicate. Here, we take the time to talk with one another . . . and to listen.
Excellence	We are satisfied with nothing less than the very best in everything we do. . . . The great fun here will be for all of us to discover just how good we can really be.

Source: Enron's Code of Ethics, *The Smoking Gun*, July 2000.

Internal Alignment

Internal alignment refers to comparisons among jobs or skill levels inside a single organization. Jobs and people's skills are compared in terms of their relative contributions to the organization's business objectives. How, for example, does the work of the programmer compare with the work of the systems analyst, the software engineer, and the software architect? Does one contribute to solutions for customers and satisfied stockholders more than another? What about two marketing managers working in different business units of the same organization? Internal alignment pertains to the pay rates both for employees doing equal work and for those doing dissimilar work. In fact, determining what is an appropriate difference in pay for people performing different work is one of the key challenges facing managers. Whole Foods tries to manage differences with a salary cap that limits the **total cash** compensation (wages plus bonuses) of any executive to 19 times the average cash compensation of all full-time employees. The cap originally started at eight times the average. However, attraction and retention problems were cited as a need for raising the cap several times since. (Note that the cap does not include stock options.)

Pay relationships within the organization affect all three compensation objectives. They affect employee decisions to stay with the organization, to become more flexible by investing in additional training, or to seek greater responsibility. By motivating employees to choose increased training and greater responsibility in dealing with customers, internal pay relationships indirectly affect the capabilities of the workforce and hence the efficiency of the entire organization. Fairness is affected through employees' comparisons of their pay to the pay of others in the organization. Compliance is affected by the basis used to make internal comparisons. Paying on the basis of race, gender, age, or national origin is illegal in the United States.

External Competitiveness

External competitiveness refers to pay comparisons with competitors. *How much* do we wish to pay in comparison to what other employers pay?

Many organizations claim their pay systems are market-driven–that is, based almost exclusively on what competitors pay. "Market-driven" gets translated into practice in different ways.[78] Some employers may set their pay levels higher than their competition, hoping to attract the best applicants. Of course, this assumes that someone is able to identify and hire the "best" from the pool of applicants. And what is the appropriate market? When, for example, should international pay rates be considered? Should the pay of software engineers in New Delhi or Minsk influence pay for engineers in Silicon Valley or Boston?

External competitiveness decisions–both how much and what forms–have a twofold effect on objectives: (1) to ensure that the pay is sufficient to attract and retain employees–if employees do not perceive their pay as competitive in comparison to what other organizations are offering for similar work, they may be more likely to leave–and (2) to control labor costs so that the organization's prices of products or services can remain competitive in a global economy.

Employee Contributions

How much emphasis should there be on paying for performance? Should one programmer be paid differently from another if one has better performance and/or greater seniority? Or should there be a **flat rate** for programmers? Should the company share any profits with employees? Should it share with all employees, part-time as well as full-time?

The emphasis to place on **employee contributions** (or nature of **pay mix**) is an important policy decision because it directly affects employees' attitudes and work behaviors. Eaton and Motorola use pay to support other "high-performance" practices in their workplaces.[79] Both use team-based pay and corporate profit-sharing plans.

Starbucks emphasizes stock options and sharing the success of corporate performance with the employees. General Electric uses different performance-based pay programs at the individual, division, and company-wide levels. Performance-based pay affects fairness, in that employees need to understand the basis for judging performance in order to believe that their pay is fair.

What mix of pay forms–base, incentives, stock, benefits–do our competitors use in comparison to the pay mix we use? Whole Foods combines base pay and **team incentives** to offer higher pay if warranted by team performance. Nucor targets base pay below market, but targets total cash compensation (including profit sharing and gain-sharing/plant production bonuses) at well above the market median. Medtronic sets its base pay to match its competitors but ties bonuses to performance. It offers stock to all its employees, based on overall company performance.[80] Further, Medtronic believes that its benefits, particularly its emphasis on programs that balance work and life, make it a highly attractive place to work. It believes that *how* its pay is positioned and *what forms* it uses create an advantage over competitors.

The external competitiveness and employee contribution decisions should be made jointly. Clearly, an above-market compensation level is most effective and sustainable when it exists together with above-market employee contributions to productivity, quality, customer service, or other important strategic objectives.

Management

A policy regarding management of the pay system is the last building block in our model. Management means ensuring that the *right people* get the *right pay* for *achieving the right objectives in the right way*. The greatest system design in the world is useless without competent management.

Managing compensation means answering the "So What?" question. So what is the impact of this policy, this technique, this decision? Although it is possible to design a system that is based on internal alignment, external competitiveness, and employee contributions, what difference does it make? Does the decision help the organization achieve its objectives?[81]

The ground under compensation management has shifted. The traditional focus on how to administer various techniques is long gone, replaced by more strategic thinking–managing pay as part of the business. It goes beyond simply managing pay as an expense to better understanding and analyzing the impact of pay decisions on people's behaviors and organizations' success. The impact of pay decisions on expenses is one result that is easily measured and well understood. But other measures–such as pay's impact on attracting and retaining the right people, and engaging these people productively–are not yet widely used in the management of compensation. Efforts to do so are increasing, and the perspective is shifting from "How to" toward trying to answer the "So What?" question.[82] Ease of measurement is not the same as importance; costs are easy to measure (and, of course, important), so there is a tendency to focus there. Yet the consequences of pay, although often less amenable to measurement, are nonetheless just as important.

Pay Techniques

The remaining portion of the pay model in **Exhibit 1.6** shows the techniques that make up the pay system. The exhibit provides only an overview since techniques are discussed throughout the rest of the book. Techniques tie the four basic policies to the pay objectives.

Uncounted variations in **pay techniques** exist; many are examined in this book. Most consultant firms tout their surveys and techniques on their web pages. You can obtain updated information on various practices by simply surfing the web.

e-Compensation

WorldatWork (***www.worldatwork.org***) provides information on its compensation-related journals and special publications, as well as short courses aimed at practitioners. The Society of Human Resource Management (***www.shrm.org***) also offers compensation-related information as well as more general human resource management (HRM) information. The society's student services section offers guidance on finding jobs in the field of human resources. Both sites are good sources of information for people interested in careers in HRM. Information on pay trends in Europe is available from the European Industrial Relations Observatory (***http://www.eurofound.europa.eu/observatories/eurwork***). The International Labour Organization (***www.ilo.org***) maintains a database that can be browsed either by subject (conditions of employment) or country. Cornell University's Industrial and Labor Relations School offers a "research portal" for articles of interest in human resource management (***http://guides.library.cornell.edu/hrm***). The Employee Benefits Research Institute (EBRI) includes links to other benefits sources on its website (***www.ebri.org***). Every chapter in this book also mentions interesting websites. Use them as a starting point to search out others.

BOOK PLAN

Compensation is such a broad and compelling topic that there are several books devoted to it. This book focuses on the design and management of compensation systems. To aid in understanding how and why pay systems work, our pay model provides the structure for much of the book. **Chapter 2** discusses how to formulate and execute a compensation strategy. We analyze what it means to be strategic about how people are paid and how compensation can help achieve and sustain an organization's competitive advantage.[83]

The pay model plays a central role in formulating and implementing an organization's pay strategy. The model identifies four basic policy choices that are the core of the pay strategy. After we discuss strategy, the next sections of the book examine each of these policies in detail. **Part 2** on *internal alignment* (**Chapters 3**, **4**, **5**, and **6**) examines pay relationships within a single organization. **Part 3** (**Chapters 7** and **8**) examines *external competitiveness*–the pay relationships among competing organizations–and analyzes the influence of market-driven forces.

Once the compensation rates and structures are established, other issues emerge. How much should we pay each individual employee? How much and how often should a person's pay be increased, and on what basis–experience, seniority, or performance? Should pay increases be contingent on the organization's and/or the employee's performance? How should the organization share its success (or failure) with employees? These are questions of *employee contributions,* the third building block in the model, covered in **Part 4** (**Chapters 9**, **10**, and **11**).

In **Part 5**, we cover employee services and benefits (**Chapters 12** and **13**). How do benefits fit in the company's overall compensation package? What choices should employees have in their benefits? In **Part 6**, we cover systems tailored for special groups–sales representatives, executives, contract workers, unions (**Chapters 14** and **15**)–and we provide more detail on global compensation systems (**Chapter 16**). **Part 7** concludes with information essential for *managing the compensation system*. The government's role in compensation is examined in **Chapter 17**. **Chapter 18** includes understanding, communicating, budgeting, and evaluating results.

Even though the book is divided into sections that reflect the pay model, pay decisions are not discrete. All of them are interrelated. Together, they influence employee behaviors and organization performance and can create a pay system that can be a source of competitive advantage.

Throughout this book our intention is to examine alternative approaches. We believe that there rarely is a single correct approach; rather, alternative approaches exist or can be designed. The one most likely to be effective depends on the circumstances. We hope that this book will help you become better informed about these options, how to evaluate and select the most effective ones, and how to design new ones. Whether as an employee, a manager, or an interested member of society, you should be able to assess the effectiveness and fairness of pay systems.

CAVEAT EMPTOR—BE AN INFORMED CONSUMER

Most managers do not read research. They do not subscribe to research journals; they find them too full of jargon and esoterica, and they see them as impractical and irrelevant.[84] However, a study of 5,000 HR managers compared their beliefs to the research evidence in several areas and identified seven common and important misconceptions held by managers.[85] The study authors concluded that being unaware of key research findings may prove costly to organizations. For example, when it comes to motivating workers, organization efforts may be somewhat misguided if they do not know that "money is the crucial incentive . . . no other incentive or motivational technique comes even close to money with respect to its instrumental value."[86]

So it pays to read the research. There is no question that some studies are irrelevant and poorly performed. But if you are not a reader of research literature, you become prey for the latest business self-help fad. Belief, even enthusiasm, is a poor substitute for informed judgment. Therefore, we end this chapter with a consumer's guide to research that includes three questions to help make you a critical reader–and a better-informed decision maker.

1. Is the Research Useful?

How useful are the variables in the study? How well are they measured? For example, many studies purport to measure organization performance. However, performance may be accounting measures such as return on assets or cash flow, financial measures such as earnings per share, operational measures such as scrap rates or defect indicators, or qualitative measures such as customer satisfaction. It may even be the opinions of compensation managers, as in, "How effective is your gain-sharing plan?" (Answer choices are "highly effective," "effective," "somewhat," "disappointing," "not very effective." "Disastrous" is not usually one of the choices.) The informed consumer must ask, Does this research measure anything useful?

2. Does the Study Separate Correlation from Causation?

Once we are confident that the variables are useful and accurately measured, we must be sure that they are actually related. Most often this is addressed through the use of statistical analysis. The **correlation coefficient** is a common measure of association and indicates how changes in one variable are related to changes in another. Many research studies use a statistical analysis known as *regression analysis.* One output from a regression analysis is the R^2. The R^2 is a squared correlation and tells us what percentage of the variation in the outcome variable is accounted for by the variables we are using to predict or explain.

But even if there is a relationship, correlation does not ensure causation. For example, just because a manufacturing plant initiates a new incentive plan and the facility's performance improves, we cannot conclude that the incentive plan caused the improved performance. Perhaps new technology, **reengineering,** improved marketing, or the general expansion of the local economy underlies the results. The two changes are associated or related, but causation is a tough link to make.

Too often, case studies, benchmarking studies of best practices, or consultant surveys are presented as studies that reveal cause and effect. They do not. Case studies are descriptive accounts whose value and limitations must be recognized. Just because the best-performing companies are using a practice does not mean the practice is causing the performance. IBM provides an example of the difficulty of deciding whether a change is a cause or an effect. Years ago, IBM pursued a no-layoff policy. While IBM was doing well, the no-layoff policy was cited as part of the reason. Later, when performance declined, IBM eventually ended the no-layoff policy as a partial response. Did the policy contribute to company success at one time, but not later due to changing circumstances? Did it always act as a drag on company success? Or was it a mistake to get rid of it? Causality is difficult to infer as we do not know what would have happened had IBM never had the policy and/or if they had it and kept it (versus ending it). Perhaps because of such challenges in inference, compensation research often does attempt to answer questions of causality. Yet good policy decisions rest on making good causal inferences.[87] Thus, we need to strive to overcome the challenges to answer key questions such as: How does the use of performance-based pay influence employee ability and motivation, customer satisfaction, product quality, and company performance?

3. Are There Alternative Explanations?

Consider a hypothetical study that attempts to assess the impact of a performance-based pay program. The researchers measure performance by assessing quality, productivity, customer satisfaction, employee satisfaction, and the facility's performance. The final step is to see whether future periods' performance improves compared to this period's. If it does, can we safely assume that it was the incentive pay that caused performance? Or is it equally likely that the improved performance has alternative explanations, such as the fluctuation in the value of currency, changes in competition, or perhaps a change in leadership or other human resource practices in the facility?

In this case, causality evidence seems weak. Alternative explanations exist. If the researchers had measured the performance indicators several years prior to and after installing the plan, then the evidence of causality is perhaps a bit stronger. The evidence would be stronger if an equivalent group (a control group) had no pay program change and experienced no increase in performance. Further, if the researchers repeated this experiment in other facilities and the results were similar, then the preponderance of evidence is stronger yet. It could then be concluded that clearly the organization is doing something right, and incentive pay is part of it.

The best way to establish causation is to account for competing explanations, either statistically or through control groups. The point is that alternative explanations often exist. And if they do, they need to be accounted for to establish causality. It is very difficult to disentangle the effects of pay plans to clearly establish causality. However, it is possible to look at the overall pattern of evidence to make judgments about the effects of pay.

So we encourage you to become a critical reader of all management literature, including this book. As Hogwarts' famous Professor Alastor Moody cautions, have "constant vigilance for sloppy analysis masquerading as research."[88]

Your Turn
Compensation at the World's Largest Company

Walmart is the largest company in the world in terms of revenue and employees. It is also a company that gets talked about a lot. Take this opportunity to do a bit of research on how compensation works there. Do a search for Walmart's Environmental, Social & Governance Report. It should be readily available. (You can also check whether the following links are still active: https://corporate.walmart.com/esgreport2019/ and https://corporate.walmart.com/esgreport/.) Download the most recent report and, if available, download the two most recent full reports. Go to the Social section of both reports and examine the information related to pay (including benefits), promotion, and opportunity for Walmart employees.

QUESTIONS:

1. What is the minimum pay at Walmart? What is the average pay at Walmart? To what degree has each changed year to year?
2. Promotion to higher job levels is the main way that pay increases over the course of one's career. What are the promotion opportunities like at Walmart? How much is opportunity is there for career and pay growth?
3. To what degree has Walmart achieved desirable levels of diversity and inclusion? What steps is the company taking to improve in this area?
4. How does Walmart describe its approach to safeguarding the treatment of workers (including fair pay) in its supply chain?
5. We know that Walmart keeps a careful eye on compensation cost of its employees, as part of its strategy of keeping its product prices low. What about workers it does not employ, but that are in its supply chain? Of what relevance is Walmart's supply chain (and the workers in it) to Walmart keeping its prices low?
6. Walmart recently announced a commitment to sourcing $10 billion in India-made goods by 2027. (https://corporate.walmart.com/newsroom/2020/12/10/walmart-commits-to-sourcing-10-billion-of-india-made-goods-each-year-by-2027). Search the web for data on wage levels (minimum wage or actual wages) in India. How do wages in India compare to those in the United States? How will sourcing more goods from India help Walmart with its low price strategy? Where else does Walmart source from and how do wages in those countries compare to those in the United States?

Still Your Turn
Who Are Amazon's Peer Companies for Comparing Compensation?

A *Wall Street Journal* article on April 4, 2021, "Amazon's Labor Unrest May Show at the Margins," described Amazon as having "thin margins by tech standards," noting that Amazon's revenue/employee was only about one-fifth as large as "peers" such as Alphabet (Google), Apple, Facebook, and Microsoft. The *Journal* seemed to be suggesting that if unionization is successful at Amazon (on a significant scale, i.e., beyond the one current location where a union organizing drive is taking place), that Amazon's labor costs will increase and it cannot afford that if its margins are already thin. Why would the *Journal* use these tech companies as peers? Isn't Walmart a better peer comparison?

To get better insight, go to the most recent annual reports (form 10-k), readily available on the web, and compute revenue per employee for Walmart and Amazon. (At Amazon, use net sales as revenue.) Also, compute the ratio of operating income to revenue by business segment for Walmart and Amazon. (Revenue per employee is not possible to compute based on the Amazon annual report.) Each company has three business segments.

QUESTIONS:

1. How do the revenue/employee numbers compare across companies?
2. How does the ratio of operating income to revenue compare across segments within and across the companies? Focusing on Amazon, how do these operating income/revenue ratios differ across its segments?
3. We will see that choosing peer companies to compare compensation includes those that are product market competitors, as well as labor market competitors. Based on the ratios you have computed and examined, who are Amazon's product market competitors?

Summary

The model presented in this chapter provides a structure for understanding compensation systems. The three main components of the model are the compensation objectives, the policy decisions that guide how the objectives are going to be achieved, and the techniques that make up the pay system and link the policies to the objectives. The following sections of the book examine each of the four policy decisions–internal alignment, external competitiveness, employee performance, and management–as well as the techniques, new directions, and related research.

Two questions should constantly be in the minds of managers and readers of this text. First, Why do it this way? There is rarely one correct way to design a system or pay an individual. Organizations, people, and circumstances are too varied. But a well-trained manager can select or design a suitable approach. Second, So what? What does this technique do for us? How does it help achieve our goals? If good answers to the "So What?" question are not apparent, there is no point to the technique. Adapting the pay system to meet the needs of the employees and helping to achieve the goals of the organization is what this book is all about.

The basic premise of this book is that compensation systems do have a profound impact. Yet, too often traditional pay systems seem to have been designed in response to some historical but long-forgotten problem. The practices continue, but the logic underlying them is not always clear or even relevant. Hopefully, the next generation of pay systems will be more flexible–designed to achieve specific objectives under changing conditions.

Review Questions

1. How do differing perspectives affect our views of compensation?
2. What is your definition of compensation? Which meaning of compensation seems most appropriate from an employee's view: return, reward, or entitlement? Compare your ideas with someone with more experience, someone from another country, someone from another field of study.
3. What is the "network of returns" that your college offers your instructor? What returns do you believe make a difference in teaching effectiveness? What "returns" would you change or add, to increase the teaching effectiveness?

4. What are the four policy issues in the pay model? What purposes do the objectives in the pay model serve?
5. List all the forms of pay you receive from work. Compare your list to someone else's list. Explain any differences.
6. Answer the three questions in the section ***Caveat Emptor*–Be an Informed Consumer** for any study or business article that tells you how to pay people.

Endnotes

1. Written by Jenny Bradford and Berry Gordy Jr. Performed by The Beatles on *The Beatles' Second Album* (1964).
2. Brent Snavely, "Labor Costs to Be Sticking Point of UAW Talks with Automakers," *Los Angeles Times,* July 8, 2011; Chris Woodyard, "VW Exec Knows of No Talks to Unionize Tennessee Plant," *USA Today,* August 1, 2011; Jerry Hirsch, "Automakers Plan to Hire Thousands of Workers This Year," *Los Angeles Times,* January 12, 2012.
3. General Motors 2021 Annual Report (10-K); General Motors 2018 Annual Report (10-K), https:/./investor.gm; https://media.gm.com/media/us/en/gm/plants-facilities.html.
4. W. G. Sanders and D. C. Hambrick, "Swinging for the Fences: The Effects of CEO Stock Options on Company Risk Taking and Performance," *Academy of Management Journal* 50 (2007), pp. 1055–1078; Cynthia E. Devers, Gerry McNamara, Robert M. Wiseman, and Mathias Arrfelt, "Moving Closer to the Action: Examining Compensation Design Effects on Firm Risk," *Organization Science* 19 (July–August 2008), pp. 548–566.
5. Emily Glazer and Christina Rexrode, "As Regulators Focus on Culture, Wall Street Struggles to Define It," *The Wall Street Journal*, February 2, 2015. p. A1.
6. https://www.novartis.com/our-company/corporate-responsibility/ethics-risk-compliance/anti-bribery-anti-corruption. Accessed April 3, 2021; A. Kanski, "Novartis Revises Bonus Structure to Promote Ethical Behavior," *MM&M*, September 21, 2018; J. Miller, "Novartis Links Bonuses to Ethics in Bid to Rebuild Reputation," *Reuters*, September 17, 2018.
7. B. Gerhart and M. Fang, "Pay, Intrinsic Motivation, Extrinsic Motivation, Performance, and Creativity in the Workplace: Revisiting Long-Held Beliefs," *Annual Review of Organizational Psychology and Organizational Behavior* 2 (2015), pp. 489–521; B. Gerhart and M. Fang, "Pay for (Individual) Performance: Issues, Claims, Evidence and the Role of Sorting Effects," *Human Resource Management Review* 24 (2014), pp. 41–52; K. F. Hallock, *Pay: Why People Earn What They Earn and What You Can Do Now to Make More* (Cambridge: Cambridge University Press, 2012); N. Gupta and J. D. Shaw, "Employee Compensation: The Neglected Area of HRM Research," *Human Resource Management Review* 24, no. 1 (2014), pp. 1–4; G. E. Ledford, "The Changing Landscape of Employee Rewards: Observations and Prescriptions," *Organizational Dynamics* 43, no. 3 (2014), pp. 168–179; B. Gerhart, S. L. Rynes, and I. S. Fulmer, "Pay and Performance: Individuals, Groups, and Executives," *Academy of Management Annals* 3 (2009), pp. 251–315; B. Gerhart and S. L. Rynes, *Compensation: Theory, Evidence, and Strategic Implications* (Thousand Oaks, CA: Sage, 2003); James H. Dulebohn and Stephen E. Werling, "Compensation Research: Past, Present, and Future," *Human Resource Management Review* 17 (2007), pp. 191–207; Steve Werner and Stephanie Ward, "Recent Compensation Research: An Eclectic Review," *Human Resource Management Review* 14 (2004), pp. 201–227; S. L. Rynes, B. Gerhart, and K. A. Minette, "The Importance of Pay in Employee Motivation: Discrepancies between What People Say and What They Do," *Human Resource Management* 43 (2004), pp. 381–394.

8. B. Gerhart, "Gender Differences in Current and Starting Salaries: The Role of Performance, College Major, and Job Title," *Industrial and Labor Relations Review* 43 (1990), pp. 418–433; G. G. Cain, "The Economic Analysis of Labor-Market Discrimination: A Survey," in *Handbook of Labor Economics*, ed. O. Ashenfelter and R. Layard (New York: North-Holland, 1986), pp. 694–785; F. D. Blau and L. M. Kahn, "The Gender Pay Gap: Have Women Gone as Far as They Can?" *Academy of Management Perspectives*, February 2007, pp. 7–23.
9. U.S. Bureau of the Census. Historical Income Tables, Table P-40.
10. Blau, F. D., & Kahn, L. M. (2017). The gender wage gap: Extent, trends, and explanations. *Journal of economic literature*, 55(3), 789–865.
11. U.S. Department of Labor, Bureau of Labor Statistics, "Highlights of Women's Earnings in 2010," *Report 1031,* July 2011; Francine D. Blau and Lawrence M. Kahn, "The Gender Pay Gap: Have Women Gone as Far as They Can?" *Academy of Management Perspectives* 21 (February 2007), pp. 7–23.
12. Daniel Kahneman and Angus Deaton. (September 21, 2010). High income improves evaluation of life but not emotional well-being. *Proceedings of the National Academy of Sciences* 107, 16489–16493.
13. "Employer Costs for Employer Compensation—December 2020," March 18, 2021, USDL-21-0437, *www.bls.gov.*
14. Organization for Economic Cooperation and Development. OECD Health Statistics 2020 and Health Expenditures Funding. www.OECD.org. Accessed March 8, 2021.
15. The Henry J. Kaiser Foundation, Julia Foutz, Anthony Damico, Ellen Squires, and Rachel Garfield, "The Uninsured: A Primer—Key Facts about Health Insurance and the Uninsured under the Affordable Care Act," https://www.kff.org/uninsured/report/the-uninsured-a-primer-key-facts-about-health-insurance-and-the-uninsured-under-the-affordable-care-act/.
16. National Center for Health Statistics. Fact Sheet, November 2020 (and previous years). www.cdc.gov; R.A. Cohen et al. Health Insurance Coverage: Early Release of Estimates from the National Health Interview Survey. January – June 2020. Released February 2021.
17. Henry J. Kaiser Foundation, Key Facts about the Uninsured Population, September 19, 2017, updated November 29, 2017, https://www.kff.org/uninsured/fact-sheet/key-facts-about-the-uninsured-population/.
18. John Gapper and Barney Jopson, "Coach to Cut Output in China," *Financial Times,* May 13, 2011; Ben Blanchard, "Foxconn to Raise Wages Again at China Plant," www.reuters.com, retrieved October 19, 2010; Joe Manget and Pierre Mercier, "As Wages Rise, Time to Leave China?" *Bloomberg Businessweek,* December 1, 2010; Shai Oster, "China's Rising Wages Propel U.S. Prices," *The Wall Street Journal,* May 9, 2011; Tim Worstall, "Apple's Foxconn to Double Wages Again," *Forbes,* May 28, 2012.
19. David Redmon, director, *Mardi Gras: Made in China, www.mardigrasmadeinchina.com/news.html;* B. Powell and D. Skarbek, "Sweatshops and Third World Living Standards: Are the Jobs Worth the Sweat?" *Journal of Labor Research,* Spring 2006, pp. 263–290.
20. L. Bebchuk and J. M. Fried, *Pay without Performance* (Cambridge, MA: Harvard University Press, 2004); M. J. Conyon, "Executive Compensation and Incentives," *Academy of Management Perspectives* 21 (February 2006), pp. 25–44; S. N. Kaplan, "Are CEOs Overpaid?" *Academy of Management Perspectives* 22, no. 2 (2008), pp. 5–20; J. P. Walsh, "CEO Compensation: The Responsibilities of the Business Scholar to Society," *Academy of Management Perspectives* 22, no. 2 (2008), pp. 26–33; A. J. Nyberg, I. S. Fulmer, B. Gerhart, and M. A. Carpenter, "Agency Theory Revisited: CEO Returns and Shareholder Interest Alignment," *Academy of Management Journal* 53 (2010), pp. 1029–1049.
21. Information on executive pay can be found in the following sources: Bruce R. Ellig, *The Complete Guide to Executive Compensation*, 3rd ed. (New York: McGraw-Hill, 2014); I. S. Fulmer, "Labor Market

Influences on CEO Compensation," *Personnel Psychology* 62 (2009), pp. 659–696; B. Gerhart, S. L. Rynes, and I. S. Fulmer, "Pay and Performance: Individuals, Groups, and Executives," *Academy of Management Annals* 3 (2009), pp. 251–315; C. Frydman and D. Jenter, "CEO Compensation," *Annual Review of Financial Economics* 2 (2010), pp. 75–102; K. J. Murphy, "Executive Compensation," in *Handbook of Labor Economics,* vol. 3B, ed. O. C. Ashenfelter and David Card (Amsterdam: Elsevier/North Holland, 2009).

22. C. E. Devers, A. A. Cannella, G. P. Reilly, and M. E. Yoder, "Executive Compensation: A Multidisciplinary Review of Recent Developments," *Journal of Management* 33 (2007), pp. 1016–1072; I. S. Fulmer, "The Elephant in the Room: Labor Market Influences on CEO Compensation," *Personnel Psychology,* in press; A. Nyberg, I. S. Fulmer, B. Gerhart, and M. A. Carpenter, "Agency Theory Revisited: CEO Returns and Shareholder Interest Alignment," *Academy of Management Journal* 53 (2010), pp. 1029–1049.

23. Lucian Bebchuk, Alma Cohen, and Holger Spamann, "Paid to Fail," Project Syndicate, March 2010. www.project-syndicate.com, retrieved May 18, 2012; Lucian Bebchuk et al., "The Wages of Failure: Executive Compensation at Bear Stearns and Lehman 2000–2008," *Yale Journal on Regulation* 27 (2010), pp. 257–282.

24. Joann S. Lublin, "Firms Feel 'Say on Pay' Effect: Companies Work Harder to Win Shareholder Votes on Executive Compensation," *The Wall Street Journal,* May 2, 2011; Gretchen Morgenson, "When Shareholders Make Their Voices Heard," *The New York Times,* April 7, 2012; Steven M. Davidoff, "After $2 Billion Loss, Will JPMorgan Move to Claw Back Pay?" *The New York Times,* May 14, 2012, https://dealbook.nytimes.com/2012/05/14/after-2-billion-trading-loss-will-jpmorgan-claw-back-pay

25. Apple 2020 Progress Report. Supplier Responsibility. https://www.apple.com/supplier-responsibility/pdf/Apple_SR_2020_Progress_Report.pdf.

26. Wayne F. Cascio, "The High Cost of Low Wages," *Harvard Business Review* 84 (December 2006), p. 23; Liza Featherstone, "Wage against the Machine," *Slate,* June 27, 2008.

27. Costco 10-K (annual report), filed October 14, 2011; Walmart 10-K (annual report), filed March 27, 2012.

28. Jerry Newman, *My Secret Life on the McJob* (New York: McGraw-Hill, 2007); Edward Lawler III, *Treat People Right! How Organizations and Individuals Can Propel Each Other into a Virtuous Spiral of Success* (San Francisco: Jossey-Bass, 2003).

29. K. Bartol and E. Locke, "Incentives and Motivation," chap. 4 in *Compensation in Organizations, ed.* S. Rynes and B. Gerhart (San Francisco: Jossey-Bass, 2000), pp. 104–150; B. Gerhart, S. L. Rynes, and I. S. Fulmer, "Pay and Performance: Individuals, Groups, and Executives," *Academy of Management Annals* 3 (2009), pp. 251–315.

30. Edward E. Lawler III, *Pay and Organizational Effectiveness: A Psychological View* (New York: McGraw-Hill, 1971); T. L. P. Tang, "The Meaning of Money Revisited," *Journal of Organizational Behavior* 13, no. 2 (1992), pp. 197–202.

31. E. P. Lazear, "Salaries and Piece Rates," *Journal of Business* 59 (1986), pp. 405–431; B. Gerhart and G. T. Milkovich, "Employee Compensation: Research and Practice," in *Handbook of Industrial & Organizational Psychology,* 2nd ed., ed. M. D. Dunnette and L. M. Hough (Palo Alto, CA: Consulting Psychologists Press, 1992); B. Gerhart and S. L. Rynes, *Compensation: Theory, Evidence, and Strategic Implications* (Thousand Oaks, CA: Sage, 2003).

32. D. M. Cable and T. A. Judge, "Pay Preferences and Job Search Decisions: A Person-Organization Fit Perspective," *Personnel Psychology* 47 (1994), pp. 317–348; C. B. Cadsby, F. Song, and F. Tapon, "Sorting and Incentive Effects of Pay-for-Performance: An Experimental Investigation," *Academy of Management Journal* 50 (2007), pp. 387–405; C. Q. Trank, S. L. Rynes, and R. D. Bretz, Jr., "Attracting

Applicants in the War for Talent: Differences in Work Preferences among High Achievers," *Journal of Business and Psychology* 16 (2001), pp. 331–345; C. O. Trevor, B. Gerhart, and J. W. Boudreau, "Voluntary Turnover and Job Performance: Curvilinearity and the Moderating Influences of Salary Growth and Promotions," *Journal of Applied Psychology* 82 (1997), pp. 44–61; A. Salamin and P. W. Hom, "In Search of the Elusive U-Shaped Performance-Turnover Relationship: Are High Performing Swiss Bankers More Liable to Quit?" *Journal of Applied Psychology* 90 (2005), pp. 1204–1216; J. D. Shaw and N. Gupta, "Pay System Characteristics and Quit Patterns of Good, Average, and Poor Performers," *Personnel Psychology* 60 (2007), pp. 903-928; B. Schneider, "The People Make the Place," *Personnel Psychology* 40 (1987), pp. 437–453; A. Nyberg, "Retaining Your High Performers: Moderators of the Performance-Job Satisfaction-Voluntary Turnover Relationship," *Journal of Applied Psychology* 95 (2010), pp. 440–453; J. D. Shaw, B. Dineen, R. Fang, and R. F. Vellella, "Employee-Organization Exchange Relationships, HRM Practices, and Quit Rates of Good and Poor Performers," *Academy of Management Journal* 52 (2009), pp. 1016–1033; M. Lynn, R. J. Kwortnik, and M. C. Sturman, "Voluntary Tipping and the Selective Attraction and Retention of Service Workers in the USA: An Application of the ASA Model," *International Journal of Human Resource Management* 22 (2011), pp. 1887–1901; T. Dohmen and A. Falk, "Performance Pay and Multidimensional Sorting: Productivity, Preferences, and Gender," *The American Economic Review* 2011, pp. 556–590; B. Gerhart and M. Fang, "Pay for (Individual) Performance: Issues, Claims, Evidence and the Role of Sorting Effects," *Human Resource Management Review* 24 (2014), pp. 41–52; B. D. Blume, R. S. Rubin, and T. T. Baldwin, "Who Is Attracted to an Organisation Using a Forced Distribution Performance Management System?" *Human Resource Management Journal* 23, no. 4 (2013), pp. 360–378; W. J. Becker and R. Cropanzano, "Dynamic Aspects of Voluntary Turnover: An Integrated Approach to Curvilinearity in the Performance-Turnover Relationship," *Journal of Applied Psychology* 96 (2011), pp. 233–246; B. W. Swider, W. R. Boswell, and R. D. Zimmerman, "Examining the Job Search-Turnover Relationship: The Role of Embeddedness, Job Satisfaction, and Available Alternatives," *Journal of Applied Psychology* 96 (2011), pp. 432–441.

33. E. H. O'Boyle and H. Aguinis, "The Best and the Rest: Revisiting the Norm of Normality of Individual Performance," *Personnel Psychology* 65 (2012), pp. 79–119; J. W. Beck, A. S. Beatty, and P. R. Sackett, "On the Distribution of Job Performance: The Role of Measurement Characteristics in Observed Departures from Normality," *Personnel Psychology* 67 (2014), pp. 531–566; H. Aguinis and E. O'Boyle, "Star Performers in Twenty-First Century Organizations," *Personnel Psychology* 67, no. 2 (2014), pp. 313–350; H. Aguinis, E. O'Boyle, E. Gonzalez-Mulé, and H. Joo, H., "Cumulative Advantage: Conductors and Insulators of Heavy-Tailed Productivity Distributions and Productivity Stars," *Personnel Psychology* 69 (2014).

34. T. H. Lee, B. Gerhart, I. Weller, and C. O. Trevor, "Understanding Voluntary Turnover: Path-Specific Job Satisfaction Effects and the Importance of Unsolicited Job Offers," *Academy of Management Journal* 51 (2008), pp. 651–671; W. I. MacKenzie Jr, B. S. Klaas, and J. A. McClendon, "Information Use in Counter-Offer Decisions: An Examination of Factors That Influence Management Counter-Offer Decisions," *Journal of Labor Research* 33, no. 3 (2012), 370–387.

35. E. Lazear, "Performance Pay and Productivity," *American Economic Review* 90 (2000), pp. 1346–1361.

36. Groysberg, B., & Lee, L. E. (2009). Hiring stars and their colleagues: Exploration and exploitation in professional service firms. *Organization Science*, *20*(4), 740–758. See p. 752.

37. Rebecca R. Kehoe, F. Scott Bentley. Shadows and shields: Stars limit their collaborators' exposure to attributions of both credit and blame *Personnel Psychology*, 2020.

38. Atul Mitra, Matt Bloom, and George Milkovich, "Crossing a Raging River: Seeking Far-Reaching Solutions to Global Pay Challenges," *WorldatWork Journal* 22, no. 2 (Second Quarter 2002); Mark Fenton-O'Creevy, "HR Practice: Vive la Différence," *Financial Times,* October 2002, pp. 6–8; Mansour

Javidan, Peter Dorman, Mary Sully DeLuque, and Robert House, "In the Eye of the Beholder: Cross Cultural Lessons in Leadership from Project GLOBE," *Academy of Management Perspectives,* February 2006, pp. 67–90.

39. Anne Tsui and Chung-Ming Lau, *The Management of Enterprises in the People's Republic of China* (Boston: Kluwer Academic, 2002).
40. Sanford Jacoby, *The Embedded Corporation: Corporate Governance and Employment Relations in Japan and the United States* (Princeton, NJ: Princeton University Press, 2004); Yoshio Yanadori, "Minimizing Competition? Entry-Level Compensation in Japanese Firms," *Asia Pacific Journal of Management* 21 (December 2004), pp. 445–467.
41. Chun Hui, Cynthia Lee, and Denise M. Rousseau, "Psychological Contract and Organizational Citizenship Behavior in China: Investigating Generalizability and Instrumentality," *Journal of Applied Psychology* 89 (2004), pp. 311–321; N. Conway and R. Briner, *Understanding Psychological Contracts at Work: A Critical Evaluation of Theory and Research* (Oxford: Oxford University Press, 2005); WorldatWork has developed a total rewards model, described in Jean Christofferson and Bob King, "The 'It' Factor: A New Total Rewards Model Leads the Way," *Workspan,* April 2006.
42. "Brightly Colored Uniforms Boost Employee Morale," *The Onion* 36(43), November 30, 2000.
43. Jean Christofferson and Bob King, "New Total Rewards Model," *Workspan,* April 2006, pp. 1–8.
44. F. Herzberg, "One More Time: How Do You Motivate Employees?" *Harvard Business Review,* September–October 1987, pp. 5–16; E. L. Deci, R. Koestner, and R. M. Ryan, "A Meta-Analytic Review of Experiments Examining the Effects of Extrinsic Rewards on Intrinsic Motivation," *Psychological Bulletin* 25 (1999), pp. 627–668. R. Eisenberger and J. Cameron, "Detrimental Effects of Reward: Reality or Myth?" *American Psychologist* 51 (1996), pp. 1153–1166. D. Pink, *Drive: The Surprising Truth about What Motivates Us* (New York: Penguin Group, 2009); S. E. DeVoe, J. Pfeffer, and B. Y. Lee, "When Does Money Make Money More Important? Survey and Experimental Evidence," *Industrial & Labor Relations Review* 66, no. 5 (2013), pp. 1078–1096; T. L. P. Tang, R. Luna-Arocas, I. Q. Pardo, and T. L. N. Tang, "Materialism and the Bright and Dark Sides of the Financial Dream in Spain: The Positive Role of Money Attitudes' The Matthew Effect," *Applied Psychology* 63, no. 3 (2014), pp. 480–508; J. Chen, T. L. P. Tang, and N. Tang, "Temptation, Monetary Intelligence (Love of Money), and Environmental Context on Unethical Intentions and Cheating," *Journal of Business Ethics* 123, no. 3 (2014), pp. 197–219; B. Gerhart and S. L. Rynes, *Compensation: Theory, Evidence, and Strategic Implications* (Thousand Oaks, CA: Sage, 2003), chap. 3; Edward E. Lawler III, *Pay and Organizational Effectiveness: A Psychological View* (New York: McGraw-Hill, 1971).
45. B. Gerhart and M. Fang, "Intrinsic Motivation, Pay for Performance, and Effectiveness (in the Workplace): Theories and Evidence," *Annual Review of Organizational Psychology and Organizational Behavior* (2015); P. C. Cerasoli, J. M. Nicklin, and M. T. Ford, "Intrinsic Motivation and Extrinsic Incentives Jointly Predict Performance: A 40-Year Meta-Analysis," *Psychological Bulletin* 140 (2014), pp. 980–1008; G. E. Ledford Jr., M. Fang, and B. Gerhart, "Negative Effects of Extrinsic Rewards on Intrinsic Motivation: More Smoke than Fire," *World at Work Journal* 22, no. 2 (2013), pp. 17–29; A. A. Grandey, N. W. Chi, and J. A. Diamond, "Show Me the Money! Do Financial Rewards for Performance Enhance or Undermine the Satisfaction from Emotional Labor?" *Personnel Psychology* 66, no. 3 (2013), pp. 569–612; R. Hewett and N. Conway, "The Undermining Effect Revisited: The Salience of Everyday Verbal Rewards and Self-Determined Motivation," *Journal of Organizational Behavior* 37, no. 3 (2016), pp. 436–455; M. Fang and B. Gerhart, "Does Pay for Performance Diminish Intrinsic Interest? A Workplace Test Using Cognitive Evaluation Theory and the Attraction-Selection-Attrition Model," *International Journal of Human Resource Management* (2012); M. Gagné and E. L. Deci, "Self-Determination Theory and Work Motivation," *Journal of Organizational*

Behavior 26 (2005), pp. 331–362; E. L. Deci, A. H. Olafsen, and R. M. Ryan, "Self-Determination Theory in Work Organizations: The State of a Science," *Annual Review of Organizational Psychology and Organizational Behavior* 4 (2017), pp. 19–43; [Note: Our view is that Deci et al. 2017 is generally wrong in its characterization of previous work (e.g., Gerhart and Fang 2015, in the same publication). But we include it here to provide a full range of views.] B. Gerhart and M. Fang, "Competence and Pay for Performance," In *Handbook of Competence and Motivation: Theory and Application,* 2nd ed., ed. A. J. Elliot, C. S. Dweck, and D. S. Yeager (New York: Guilford Press, 2017).

46. Allan Odden and Carolyn Kelley, *Paying Teachers for What They Know and Do: New and Smarter Compensation Strategies to Improve Schools,* 2nd ed. (Thousand Oaks, CA: Corwin Press, 2002); Ralph Blumenthal, "Houston Ties Teachers' Pay to Test Scores," *The New York Times,* January 13, 2006, p. A12.
47. U.S. Department of Labor, Fair Labor Standards Act, *http://www.dol.gov/compliance/laws/comp-flsa.htm*.
48. B. Gerhart and M. Fang, "Pay for (Individual) Performance: Issues, Claims, Evidence and the Role of Sorting Effects," *Human Resource Management Review* 24 (2014), pp. 41–52; S. L. Rynes, B. Gerhart, and L. Parks, "Personnel Psychology: Performance Evaluation and Pay for Performance," *Annual Review of Psychology* 56 (2005), pp. 571–600; R. L. Heneman, *Merit Pay: Linking Pay Increases to Performance Ratings* (New York: Addison-Wesley, 1992); G. Milkovich and A. Wigdor, *Pay for Performance: Evaluating Performance Appraisal and Merit Pay* (Washington, DC: National Academy Press, 1991); M. C. Sturman, C. O. Trevor, J. W. Boudreau, and B. Gerhart, "Is It Worth It to Win the Talent War? Evaluating the Utility of Performance-Based Pay," *Personnel Psychology* 56 (2003), pp. 997–1035; Michael Sturman, "How versus How Much You Pay: The Effects of Various Pay Components on Future Performance," working paper, Hotel School, Ithaca, NY (2006); John J. Schaubroeck, Jason D. Shaw, and Michelle K. Duffy, "An Under-Met and Over-Met Expectations Model of Employee Reactions to Merit Raises," *Journal of Applied Psychology* 93 (2008), pp. 424–434; S. E. Scullen, P. K. Bergey, and L. Aiman-Smith, "Forced Distribution Rating Systems and the Improvement of Workforce Potential: A Baseline Simulation," *Personnel Psychology* 58 (2005), pp. 1–32.
49. WorldatWork. (2016). Compensation programs and practices. Scottsdale, AZ: WorldatWork.
50. WorldatWork, *Compensation Programs and Practices* (Scottsdale, AZ: Author, 2012).
51. One issue is to determine how large a pay increase must be to be meaningful. A. Mitra, A. Tenhiälä, and J. D. Shaw, "Smallest Meaningful Pay Increases: Field Test, Constructive Replication, and Extension," *Human Resource Management* 55, no. 1 (2016), pp. 69–81.
52. Mercer, *2019/2020 US Compensation Planning Survey,* www.mercer.com.
53. Willis Towers Watson. "Most U.S. Employers Planning Raises, Bonuses for 2021." www.willistowerswatson.com.Carol Patton. Here are the latest trends in employee bonuses: More companies are basing bonuses on multiple factors of performance. Human Resource Executive, December 31, 2019. https://hrexecutive.com/
54. A. J. Nyberg, J. R. Pieper, and C. O. Trevor, "Pay-for-Performance's Effect on Future Employee Performance Integrating Psychological and Economic Principles toward a Contingency Perspective," *Journal of Management,* 42 (2016): 1753–1783; B. Gerhart and M. Fang, "Pay for (Individual) Performance: Issues, Claims, Evidence and the Role of Sorting Effects," *Human Resource Management Review* 24 (2014), pp. 41–52; AON Hewitt Survey, U.S. Salary Increases 1991/1992 and 2011/2012.
55. B. Gerhart and M Fang, "Pay for (Individual) Performance: Issues, Claims, Evidence and the Role of Sorting Effects," *Human Resource Management Review* 24 (2014), pp. 41–52.

56. *Ibid.* WorldatWork, *Compensation Programs and Practices 2012* (Scottsdale, AZ: Author, 2012); see also K. Abosch, "Why Can't (Won't) We Differentiate?" presentation at Wisconsin School of Business, University of Wisconsin–Madison, May 2012.

57. B. Gerhart, "Incentives and Pay for Performance in the Workplace," *Advances in Motivation Science* 4 (2017), pp. 91–140; J. D. Shaw and N. Gupta, "Let the Evidence Speak Again! Financial Incentives Are More Effective than We Thought," *Human Resource Management Journal* 25, no. 3 (2015), pp. 281–293; D. G. Jenkins Jr., A. Mitra, N. Gupta, and J. D. Shaw, "Are Financial Incentives Related to Performance? A Meta-analytic Review of Empirical Research," *Journal of Applied Psychology* 83 (1998), pp. 777–787; Steve Kerr, "The Best Laid Incentive Plans," *Harvard Business Review,* January 2003; Michael C. Sturman and J. C. Short, "Lump Sum Bonus Satisfaction: Testing the Construct Validity of a New Pay Satisfaction Dimension," *Personnel Psychology* 53 (2000), pp. 673–700; A. D. Stajkovic and F. Luthans, "A Meta-Analysis of the Effects of Organizational Behavior Modification on Task Performance, 1975–1995," *Academy of Management Journal* 40 (1997), pp. 1122–1149; T. M. Nisar, "Bonuses and Investment in Intangibles," *Journal of Labor Research* (Summer 2006), pp. 381–396; W. F. Whyte, *Money and Motivation: An Analysis of Incentives in Industry* (New York: Harper Brothers, 1955); E. E. Lawler III, *Pay and Organizational Effectiveness: A Psychological View* (New York: McGraw-Hill, 1971); D. Roy, "Quota Restriction and Gold Bricking in a Machine Shop," *American Journal of Sociology* 57 (1952), pp. 427–442; B. Gerhart and S. L. Rynes, *Compensation: Theory, Evidence, and Strategic Implications* (Thousand Oaks, CA: Sage, 2003).

58. Anthony J. Nyberg, Mark A. Maltarich, Dhuha "Dee" Abdulsalam, Spenser M. Essman, and Ormonde Cragun, "Collective Pay for Performance: A Cross-Disciplinary Review and Meta-Analysis," *Journal of Management,* April 20, 2018, https://doi.org/10.1177/0149206318770732; S. De Spiegelaere, G. Van Gyes, and G. Van Hootegem, "Innovative Work Behaviour and Performance-Related Pay: Rewarding the Individual or the Collective?" *International Journal of Human Resource Management* 29, no. 12 (2018), pp. 1900–19. M. A. Maltarich, A. J. Nyberg, G. Reilly, D. D. Abdulsalam, and M. Martin, "Pay-for-Performance, Sometimes: An Interdisciplinary Approach to Integrating Economic Rationality with Psychological Emotion to Predict Individual Performance," *Academy of Management Journal* 60 (2017), pp. 2155–2174; L. Bareket-Bojmel, G. Hochman, and D. Ariely, "It's (Not) All About the Jacksons: Testing Different Types of Short-Term Bonuses in the Field," *Journal of Management* 43, no. 2 (2017), pp. 534–554; S. Conroy and N. Gupta, "Team Pay-for-Performance: The Devil Is in the Details," *Group & Organization Management* 41, no. 1 (2016), pp. 32–65.

59. Kim, J. H., Gerhart, B., & Fang, M. (2021). "Do Financial Incentives Help or Harm Performance in Interesting Tasks?"*Journal of Applied Psychology*.

60. B. Gerhart, "Incentives and Pay for Performance in the Workplace," *Advances in Motivation Science* 4 (2017), pp. 91–140; M. S. Giarratana, M. Mariani, and I. Weller, "Rewards for Patents and Inventor Behaviors in Industrial Research and Development," *Academy of Management Journal* 61, no. 1 (2018), pp. 264–292; B. Gerhart, C. Trevor, and M. Graham, "New Directions in Employee Compensation Research," in *Research in Personnel and Human Resources Management,* ed. G. R. Ferris (1996), pp. 143–203; J. M. Beus and D. S. Whitman, "Almighty Dollar or Root of All Evil? Testing the Effects of Money on Workplace Behavior," *Journal of Management* 43, no. 7 (2017), pp. 2147–2167.

61. Corey Rosen. "Broad-Based Stock Plans Remain Prevalent in Fortune Best 100 Companies to Work For." National Center for Employee Ownership. nceo.org, February 21, 2020.

62. Centers for Medicare and Medicaid Services, National Health Expenditures Data, NHE Fact Sheet, Table 5. www.cms.gov.

63. Henry J. Kaiser Family Foundation, *2020 Employer Health Benefits Survey (Report), www.kff.org.*

64. Barbara Mannino, "Employees Get Pinched: Health Insurance Costs More," May 9, 2012, http://www.foxbusiness.com/personal-finance/2012/03/09/employees-get-pinched-health-insurance-costs-more/, retrieved May 17, 2012.

65. *www.medtronic.com*

66. Mei Fong, "A Chinese Puzzle," *The Wall Street Journal,* August 16, 2004, p. B1.

67. The websites for the International Labour Organization (*www.ilo.org*) and the European Industrial Relations Observatory On-Line (*www.eiro.eurofound.ie*) publish news of developments in HR in Europe. Also see Paul Boselie and Jaap Paauwe, *HR Function Competencies in European Companies* (Ithaca, NY: CAHRS Working Paper, 2005).

68. Gary P. Latham, *Work Motivation: History, Theory, Research, and Practice* (Thousand Oaks, CA: Sage, 2007); A. H. Maslow, "A Theory of Human Motivation," *Psychological Review* 50 (1943), pp. 370–396; F. Herzberg, B. Mausner, R. O. Peterson, and D. F. Capwell, *Job Attitudes: Review of Research and Opinion* (Pittsburgh: Psychological Service of Pittsburgh, 1957); B. Gerhart and S. L. Rynes, *Compensation: Theory, Evidence, and Strategic Implications* (Thousand Oaks, CA: Sage, 2003): R. Sage, G. Kanfer, G. Chen, and R. D. Pritchard, eds., *Motivation: Past, Present, and Future* (New York: Taylor and Francis, 2008).

69. Austin Collins, "Pay in Theoretical Physics," *California Institute of Technology Newspaper,* May 23, 1997, p. 3; Richard P. Feynman, *The Pleasure of Finding Things Out* (Cambridge, MA: Helix Books, 1999); "Brightly Colored Uniforms Boost Employee Morale," *The Onion* 36 (43), November 30, 2000; Just Racz, *50 Jobs Worse Than Yours* (New York: Bloomsbury, 2004).

70. Derfler-Rozin, R., & Pitesa, M. (2020). Motivation purity bias: Expression of extrinsic motivation undermines perceived intrinsic motivation and engenders bias in selection decisions. *Academy of Management Journal*, 63(6), 1840–1864.

71. Park, S., & Sturman, M. C. (2016). "Evaluating Form and Functionality of Pay-for-Performance Plans: The Relative Incentive and Sorting Effects of Merit Pay, Bonuses, and Long-Term Incentives." *Human Resource Management,* 55(4), 697–719.

72. Charles Fishman, "The Anarchist's Cookbook," *Fast Company,* July 2004, *http://www.fastcompany.com/magazine/84/wholefoods.html.* Further information on each company's philosophy and way of doing business can be deduced from their websites: *www.medtronic.com* and *www.wholefoods.com.*

73. Readers of earlier editions of this book will note that we now at times substitute "fairness" for "equity." The word "equity" has taken on several meanings in compensation, such as stock ownership and pay discrimination. In some cases, "fairness" better conveys our meaning in this book.

74. Charlie O. Trevor and David L. Wazeter, "A Contingent View of Reactions to Objective Pay Conditions: Interdependence among Pay Structure Characteristics and Pay Relative to Internal and External Referents," *Journal of Applied Psychology* 91 (2006), pp. 1260–1275; Quinetta M. Roberson and Jason A. Colquitt, "Shared and Configural Justice: A Social Network Model of Justice in Teams," *Academy of Management Review* 30, no. 3 (2005), pp. 595–607; Don A. Moore, Philip E. Tetlock, Lloyd Tanlu, and Max H. Bazerman, "Conflicts of Interest and the Case of Auditor Independence: Moral Seduction and Strategic Issue Cycling," *Academy of Management Review* 31, no. 1 (2006), pp. 10–29; Maurice E. Schweitzer, Lisa Ordonez, and Bambi Douma, "Goal Setting as a Motivator of Unethical Behavior," *Academy of Management Journal* 47, no. 3 (2004), pp. 422–432; Vikas Anand, Blake E. Ashforth, and Mahendra Joshi, "Business as Usual: The Acceptance and Perpetuation of Corruption in Organizations," *Academy of Management Executive* 19, no. 4 (2005), pp. 9–22.

75. John W. Budd and James G. Scoville, eds., *The Ethics of Human Resources and Industrial Relations* (Ithaca, NY: Cornell University Press, 2004); Richard M Locke, Fei Qin, and Alberto Brause, "Does Monitoring Improve Labor Standards? Lessons from Nike," *Industrial & Labor Relations Review* 61 (2007), p. 3.

76. "Academy of Management Code of Ethical Conduct," *Academy of Management Journal* 48, no. 6 (2005), pp. 1188–1192; Barrie E. Litzky, Kimberly A. Eddleston, and Deborah L. Kidder, "The Good, the Bad, and the Misguided: How Managers Inadvertently Encourage Deviant Behaviors," *Academy of Management Perspectives* 20, no. 1 (February 2006), pp. 91–103; Frederic W. Cook, "Compensation Ethics: An Oxymoron or Valid Area for Debate?" featured speech at ACA International Conference Workshop, 1999; Stuart P. Green, *Lying, Cheating, and Stealing: A Moral Theory of White-Collar Crime* (Boston: Oxford University Press, 2006); Tom Stone, "Ethics in HRM," Oklahoma State HR Conference, May 2005, see *www.shrm.org/ethics/code-of-ethics/asp*. Stone identifies an integrity test at *www.hoganassessments.com* and *www.epredix.com*. The site for the Ethics Resource Center is *www.ethics.org*. The Josephson Institute of Ethics publishes online their pamphlet *Making Ethical Decisions*, *www.josephsoninstitute.org*.

77. Michael Gibbs and Wallace Hendricks, "Do Formal Pay Systems Really Matter?" *Industrial & Labor Relations Review* (October 2004), pp. 71–93; John Boudreau and Pete Ramstad, *Beyond Cost-Per-Hire and Time to Fill: Supply-Chain Measurement for Staffing* (Los Angeles: Center for Effective Organizations, 2006); Christopher Collins, Jeff Ericksen, and Matthew Allen, *HRM Practices, Workforce Alignment, and Firm Performance* (Ithaca, NY: CAHRS Working Paper, 2005).

78. *Market Pricing: Methods to the Madness* (Scottsdale, AZ: WorldatWork, 2002).

79. Rosemary Batt, "Managing Customer Services: Human Resource Practices, Quit Rates, and Sales Growth," *Academy of Management Journal* 45, no. 3 (2002), pp. 587–597; Paul Osterman, "The Wage Effects of High Performance Work Organization in Manufacturing," *Industrial and Labor Relations Review* (January 2006), pp. 187–204; Patrick Wright, Timothy Gardner, Lisa Moynihan, and Mathew Allen, "The Relationship between HR Practices and Firm Performance: Examining Causal Order," *Personal Psychology* (Summer 2005), pp. 409–446; Robert D. Mohr and Cindy Zoghi, "High-Involvement Work Design and Job Satisfaction," *Industrial & Labor Relations Review* 61 (2008), p. 275; Eileen Appelbaum, Thomas Bailey, Peter Berg, and Arne Kalleberg, *Manufacturing Advantage: Why High Performance Work Systems Pay Off* (Ithaca, NY: Cornell University Press, 2000).

80. Mary Graham, Rick Welsh, and George Mueller, "In the Land of Milk and Money: One Dairy Farm's Strategic Compensation System," *Journal of Agribusiness* 15, no. 2 (1997), pp. 171–188.

81. J. Paauwe, *HRM and Performance: Unique Approaches in Order to Achieve Long-term Viability* (Oxford: Oxford University Press, 2004).

82. John Boudreau and Pete Ramstad, *Beyond Cost-Per-Hire and Time to Fill: Supply-Chain Measurement for Staffing* (Los Angeles: Center for Effective Organizations, 2006); Ed Lawler, Dave Ulrich, Jac Fitz-Enz, and James Madden, *HR Business Process Outsourcing* (San Francisco: Jossey-Bass, 2004); D. Scott, D. Morajda, T. McMullen, and R. Sperling, "Evaluating Pay Program Effectiveness," *WorldatWork Journal* 15, no. 2 (Second Quarter 2006), pp. 50–59; S. Raza, *Optimizing Human Capital Investments for Superior Shareholder Returns* (New York: Hewitt Associates, 2006); M. Huselid and B. Becker, "Improving HR Analytical Literacy: Lessons from Moneyball," chap. 32 in M. Losey, S. Meisinger, and D. Ulrich, eds., *The Future of Human Resource Management* (Hoboken, NJ: Wiley, 2005).

83. Y. Yanadori and J. H. Marler, "Compensation Strategy: Does Business Strategy Influence Compensation in High-Technology Firms?" *Strategic Management Journal* 27 (2006), pp. 559–570.

84. Jeffrey Pfeffer and Robert Sutton, "Management Half-Truth and Nonsense: How to Practice Evidence-Based Management," *California Management Review* (Spring 2006); Denise Rousseau, "Is There Such a Thing as 'Evidence-Based Management'?" *Academy of Management Review* 31, no. 2 (2006), pp. 258–269; Sara L. Rynes, Amy E. Colbert, and Kenneth G. Brown, "HR Professionals' Beliefs about Effective Human Resource Practices: Correspondence between Research and Practice," *Human Resource Management* 41, no. 2 (Summer 2002), pp. 149–174; Sara L. Rynes, Amy E. Colbert, and Kenneth G. Brown, "Seven Common Misconceptions about Human Resource Practices: Research Findings versus Practitioner Beliefs," *Academy of Management Executive* 16, no. 3 (2002), pp. 92–102.

85. Sara L. Rynes, Amy E. Colbert, and Kenneth G. Brown, "Seven Common Misconceptions about Human Resource Practices: Research Findings versus Practitioner Beliefs," *Academy of Management Executive* 16, no. 3 (2002), pp. 92–102.

86. E. A. Locke, D. B. Feren, V. M. McCaleb, et al., "The Relative Effectiveness of Four Ways of Motivating Employee Performance," in *Changes in Working Life,* ed. K. D. Duncan, M. M. Gruenberg, and D. Wallis (New York: Wiley, 1980), pp. 363–388. See also S. L. Rynes, B. Gerhart, and L. Parks, "Personnel Psychology: Performance Evaluation and Pay-for-Performance," *Annual Review of Psychology* 56 (2005), pp. 571–600.

87. B. Gerhart, "Modeling Human Resource Management—Performance Linkages," in *The Oxford Handbook of Human Resource Management,* ed. P. Boxall, J. Purcell, and P. Wright (Oxford: Oxford University Press, 2007); P. M. Wright, T. M. Gardner, L. M. Moynihan, and M. R. Allen, "The Relationship between HR Practices and Firm Performance: Examining the Causal Order," *Personnel Psychology* 52 (2005), pp. 409–446.

88. J. K. Rowling, *Harry Potter and the Goblet of Fire* (London: Scholastic, 2000).

Chapter Two

Strategy: The Totality Of Decisions

Chapter Outline

You probably think you can skip this chapter. After all, what can be so challenging about a compensation strategy? How about this for a strategy: We'll let the market decide what we need to pay people! Unfortunately, a dose of reality quickly reveals that employers do not behave so simply. Even if they did, deciphering what "the market" has "decided" requires an investment in information search and cognitive processing. Information has a cost, and in processing information, people are only "boundedly rational" (to use a term coined by Nobel Laureate Herbert Simon).

SIMILARITIES AND DIFFERENCES IN STRATEGIES

In **Exhibit 2.1** we compare compensation strategies at Google, Nucor, and Merrill Lynch. Google is a popular Internet search engine company. Nucor is a pioneer in recycling steel scrap and other metallics into steel products, including rebar, angles, rounds, channels, flats, sheet, beams, plate, and other products. Merrill Lynch, now part of Bank of America, is a financial services organization that had an eventful several years (following the 2008 Great Financial Crisis) and advises companies and clients worldwide. We will focus primarily on financial advisors ("brokers") at Merrill Lynch. All three have been innovators in their industries. Their decisions on the five dimensions of compensation strategy are both similar and different. All three formulate their pay strategies to support their business strategies. All three emphasize outstanding employee performance and commitment. However, there are major differences.

Google (now called Alphabet), while in fact one of the largest companies in the world with a market value of over $1.8 trillion, positions itself as still being, at heart, the feisty start-up populated by nerds and math whizzes. It offers employees such generous stock programs that many of them have become millionaires. Its benefits are "way beyond the basics" compared to its competitors. (Yes, there is a free lunch, a gym, a grand piano, bocce courts, a bowling alley, and roller hockey in the parking lot. There is also food: 25 cafés in the

EXHIBIT 2.1 Three Compensation Strategies

	Google (Alphabet)	Nucor	Merrill Lynch
Objectives	Emphasis on innovation Commitment to cost containment	Focus on customer Most productive Highest quality	Focus on customer Attract, motivate, and retain the best talent Fair, understandable policies and practices
Internal Alignment	Minimize hierarchy Everyone wears several hats Emphasize collaboration	Succeed by working together No defined career paths, but many opportunities	Pay fairly internally Job sized on four factors: knowledge/skill, complexity, business impact, strategic value
Externally Competitive	Market leader in pay and benefits Unique benefits	Below market for base Market leader for total cash compensation	Market competitive in base and benefits Market competitive in incentive/bonus and stock
Employee Contributions	Recognize individual contributions Significant stock programs	Bonuses based on plant production and company profits	Financial advisors work under a strong incentive system based on client wealth management fees/commissions and total wealth of their client base
Management	Love employees, want them to know it	Not for everyone No layoff practice, but income fluctuates	Understandable, consistent message

company, all free.) Not surprisingly, Google was named the best company to work for by *Fortune* six years in a row, and #1 on the 2020 Forbes World's Best Employers list. Google has traditionally not emphasized cash compensation (base plus bonus) in its communications, but the reality is different. For example, Google was ranked #1 on Glassdoor's list of Top Companies for Compensation & Benefits.[1] According to Glassdoor, the mean salary for a senior software engineer at Google is $183,413 plus an average $33,000 in additional variable pay (e.g., bonuses) for a total of $209,838, compared to the national average of $124,784 plus $11,000, a total of $134,784. A few years ago, Google implemented an across-the-board 10 percent increase in base pay, reportedly based on employee survey results indicating that Google employees "consider salary more important than bonuses or equity."[2] Google also believes strongly in pay for performance. Laszlo Bock, its former Head of People Operations, in his book, *Work Rules!*, recommends that organizations "Pay unfairly (it's more fair!)." Bock explains that a small percentage of employees create a large percentage of the value and that their pay must recognize their disproportionate contributions.

At Nucor Steel, the emphasis is on high productivity, high quality, and low-cost products. Nucor provides an opportunity for those who are willing to work hard to make a lot of money by helping the company be productive and profitable. Consider that in a good year, an hourly worker can make $75,000 or more per year in wages and bonuses combined. That compares to a median annual earning for the occupation, production workers, in the United States of roughly $45,000 (as well as typically less job security).[3] In addition, Nucor has had no layoffs, even when sales dropped from $23.7 billion in 2008 to $11.2 billion in 2009. Thus, when Nucor says in its corporate mission statement that it succeeds by "working together" and that all of its customers are important (including employees), its actions show it takes these words seriously. However, some workers at Nucor did experience substantial reductions in pay (primarily in bonus payouts) a few years ago when competition in the steel industry, including from imports, drove steel prices and profits lower.[4] Thus, Nucor's labor costs are flexible downward when necessary, but that flexibility is not achieved through the use of layoffs. (Indeed, designing the system to build in this labor cost flexibility without having to resort to layoffs helps avoid layoffs.) One plant manager observes that "We will use the folks to do things like maintenance, housekeeping, training and cross training, but we keep them working."[5] This plant manager also describes how hiring at the plant works at Nucor. "When we hire someone for the shop floor, that decision is made by a team from the shop floor. I don't make the decision who we hire. It's made by the folks who will depend on this person for their workplace safety and their pay." (We will see this is similar to the way Whole Foods hires.)[6]

Merrill Lynch pay objectives are straightforward: to attract, motivate, and retain the best talent. Merrill Lynch relies heavily on the human capital of its employees to compete. One of its segments is Global Markets and Investment Banking, an area where a lot of money can be made, but also where a lot of money can be lost, as we saw during the financial crisis late in the last decade. Our focus here is on the Global Wealth Management segment and its key group, financial advisors (brokers). There are over 17,000 advisors at Merrill Lynch and average annual fees and commission per broker is just over $1.1 million.[7] For every $100 million in client assets under management, about $1 million in fees and commissions (referred to as "production") is generated.[8] A financial advisor at Merrill Lynch generating $5 million or more of production (i.e., someone with $500 million in client assets) would receive a bonus equal to 50 percent of this amount, or $2,500,000. Advisors with smaller production would receive a smaller percentage. For example, a financial associate with production of $500,000 would receive 40 percent, or $200,000. Over time, depending on the year (and strategic focus), there have also been separate incentives for team production, adding new clients, and growth in production.[9] One recent change has been to gradually reduce bonus payouts for client accounts having assets under management of less than $250,000, culminating most recently in no bonus payouts to advisors for such accounts.[10] (Another part of Bank America, Merrill Edge, serves these smaller accounts.)

Merrill Lynch went through a turbulent period, having been acquired by Bank of America in a deal brokered by the U.S. Treasury Department. However, unlike its former key competitors like Lehman Brothers, which entered bankruptcy, and Bear Stearns, which appears to have lost its identity within J.P. Morgan after being acquired, Merrill Lynch has retained its separate identity and is structured as a wholly owned subsidiary of Bank of America. Its compensation approach for brokers, its key employee group, remains essentially unchanged.[11]

The aggressive pay-for-performance approach at Merrill Lynch was traditionally seen as a key factor in generating substantial wealth both for shareholders and for many of its employees over the years. However, that same aggressive pay-for-performance approach at Merrill Lynch (and at its competitors), most notably in the Global Markets and Investment Banking segment, is now seen as having been a key factor in the "meltdown" in the financial industry. A widely held view is that this aggressive approach led to too much risk-taking (e.g., in areas of the business like subprime lending and currency trading) and consequently the downfall of firms in the financial industry. So, the same aggressive approach that was seen as the core of a culture that generated substantial wealth for Merrill Lynch shareholders, and many employees, subsequently was identified as the culprit in the downfall of Merrill Lynch and its peers. What about going forward? Merrill, like the rest of the industry, has adjusted and to date, has not had similar problems. Further, it has in a number of years produced a disproportionately high (for its size) share of Bank of America overall net income.[12]

These three companies are in very different businesses, facing different conditions, serving different customers, and employing different talent. So the differences in their pay strategies may not surprise you. Pay strategies can also differ among companies competing for the same talent and similar customers.[13]

Different Strategies within the Same Industry

Google, Microsoft, and SAS all compete for software engineers and marketing skills. In its earlier years Microsoft adopted a strategy very similar to Google's, except its employees "put some skin in the game"; that is, they accepted less base pay to join a company whose stock value was increasing exponentially.[14] But when its stock quit performing so spectacularly, Microsoft shifted its strategy to increase base and bonus from the 45th percentile of competitors' pay to the 65th percentile. It still retained its strong emphasis on (still nonperforming) stock-related compensation, but eliminated its long-standing, broad-based stock option plan in favor of stock grants. Its benefits continue to lead the market. More recently, Microsoft, as CNET put it, "took another step toward middle age" by "significantly scaling back its stock awards for employees, replacing that with cash." CNET describes this shift as "implicitly acknowledging that its stock performance isn't enough [any more] to retain top talent." Microsoft has gone from being #8 on the first (1998) list of 100 Best Companies to Work For to being #86 on the 2014 list. More recently, it was #4 on the 2020 Forbes World's Best Employers List and #15 on the Forbes Best Large Employers 2021 List.

SAS Institute, the world's largest privately owned software company, takes a very different approach. It emphasizes its work/life programs over cash compensation and gives only limited bonuses and no stock awards. Like Google, SAS is regularly one of the top companies on the 100 Best Companies to Work For list (e.g., #1 in 2011, #3 in 2012, #2 in 2013, #2 in 2014, #4 in 2015, #8 in 2016, #37 in 2017, #61 in 2020). SAS, headquartered in Cary, North Carolina, includes free onsite child care centers, subsidized private schools for children of employees, doctors on site for free medical care, plus recreation facilities.[15] Working more than 35 hours per week is discouraged. By removing as many of the frustrations and distractions of day-to-day life as possible, SAS believes people will focus on work when they are at work and won't burn out. SAS feels, for example, that programming code written by someone working a 35-hour week will be better than that written by tired employees. Google so far retains the excitement of a start-up, Microsoft has morphed into "the new Boeing–a solid place to work for a great salary."[16] SAS emphasizes its work/family programs and work/nonwork balance.

So, all these examples illustrate the variance in strategic perspectives among companies in different industries (Google, Nucor, Merrill Lynch) and even among companies in the same industry (Google, Microsoft, SAS).

Different Strategies within the Same Company (between business units/markets)

Sometimes different business units within the same corporation will have very different competitive conditions, adopt different business strategies, and thus fit different compensation strategies. The business units at United Technologies include Otis Elevator, Pratt & Whitney aircraft engines, Sikorsky Aircraft, Climate Controls/Security, Aerospace, and Building/Industrial Systems. These businesses face very different competitive conditions. The Korean company SK Holdings has even more variety in its business units. They include a gasoline retailer, a cellular phone manufacturer, and SK Construction. SK has different compensation strategies aligned to each of its very different businesses.[17]

A simple "let the market decide our compensation" approach doesn't work internationally either. In many nations, markets do not operate as in the United States or may not even exist. People either do not–or in some cases, cannot–easily change employers. In China, central Asia, and some eastern European countries, markets for labor have emerged only relatively recently. Even in some countries with highly developed economies, such as Germany and France, the labor market is highly regulated. Consequently, there is less movement of people among companies than is common in the United States, Canada, or even Korea and Singapore.[18]

The point is that a strategic perspective on compensation is more complex than it first appears. So we suggest that you continue to read this chapter.

Different Strategies within the Same Company (Evolution over Time)

It also follows that when business strategies change, pay systems should change, too. A classic example is IBM's strategic and cultural transformation. For years IBM placed a strong emphasis on internal alignment. Its well-developed job evaluation plan, clear hierarchy for decision making, work/life balance benefits, and policy of no layoffs served well when the company dominated the market for high-profit mainframe computers. But it did not provide flexibility to adapt to competitive changes and changes in what their customers wanted and who their customers were. Thus, IBM "exited commoditizing businesses like personal computers and hard disk drives."[19] Instead, it shifted to a focus on "high-growth, high value segments of the [information technology] industry." In its most recent annual report, IBM now describes its business as "We create value for clients by providing integrated solutions and products that leverage: data, information technology, deep expertise in industries and business processes, with trust and security and a broad ecosystem of partners and alliances."

It goes on to say that "As technology has increasingly become a key engine of business success, enterprises around the world are prioritizing digital transformation. The pressing need to adapt to evolving market requirements and adopt new business models that improve customer experience and streamline business performance has accelerated the urgency of this transformation." Along the way, the move to a new business strategy meant a new compensation strategy. This included streamlining the organization by cutting layers of management, redesigning jobs to build in more flexibility, increasing incentive pay to more strongly differentiate on performance, and keeping a constant eye on costs. So far, the strategy has not worked, at least in terms of how IBM's stock price has performed relative to the broader market. However, IBM is a Fortune 40 company (which is based on revenue) and, according to Fortune, it is the largest U.S. company in the information technology services industry. For an example of a company that has had made more gradual changes in its business strategy and how it changed is compensation strategy to support those changes, see our discussion of Microsoft just above. In Microsoft's case, its stock price performance has far exceeded that of the broader market and is currently a Fortune 25 company, but more notably, the second or third largest (depending on the day) company in the world by market value. Indeed, the substantial growth in market value at Microsoft in recent years might raise some questions about whether its compensation strategy needs to evolve somewhat again.

STRATEGIC CHOICES

Strategy refers to the fundamental directions that an organization chooses.[20] An organization defines its strategy through the trade-offs it makes in choosing what (and what not) to do. **Exhibit 2.2** ties these strategic choices to the quest for competitive advantage. At the corporate level, the fundamental strategic choice is: *What business should we be in?* At the business unit level, the choice shifts to: *How do we gain and sustain competitive advantage in this business?* At the functional level the strategic choice is: *How should total compensation help this business gain and sustain competitive advantage?* The ultimate purpose–the "So What?"–is to gain and sustain competitive advantage.

A **strategic perspective** focuses on those compensation choices that help the organization gain and sustain competitive advantage.

EXHIBIT 2.2 Strategic Choices

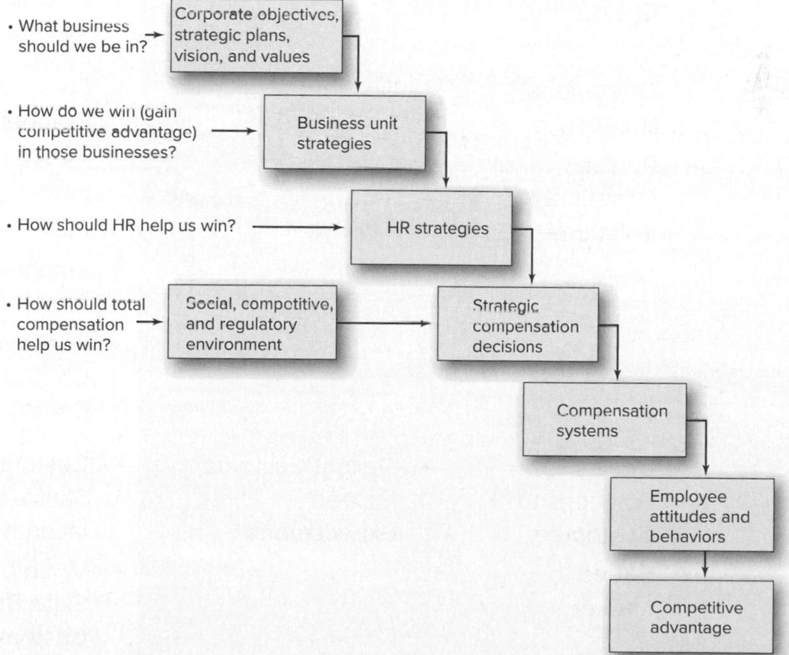

SUPPORT BUSINESS STRATEGY

A currently popular theory found in almost every business book and consultant's report tells managers to tailor their pay systems to align with the organization's business strategy. The rationale is based on contingency notions. That is, differences in a firm's business strategy should be supported by corresponding differences in its human resource strategy, including compensation. The underlying premise is that the greater the alignment, or fit, between the organization and the compensation system, the more effective the organization.[21]

Exhibit 2.3 gives an example of how compensation systems might be tailored to three general business strategies. The **innovator** stresses new products and short response time to market trends. A supporting compensation approach places less emphasis on evaluating skills and jobs and more emphasis on incentives designed to encourage innovations. The **cost cutter's** efficiency-focused strategy stresses doing more with less by minimizing costs, encouraging productivity increases, and specifying in greater detail exactly how jobs should be performed. The **customer-focused** business strategy stresses delighting customers and bases employee pay on how well they do this.

Other business strategy frameworks rely on similar ideas. In Michael Porter's strategy work, firms that cut costs would be said to follow a *cost leadership* strategy, whereas those that seek to provide a unique and/or innovative product or service at a premium price are said to follow a *differentiation* strategy. Likewise, Miles

EXHIBIT 2.3 **Tailor the Compensation System to the Strategy**

Strategy	Business Response	HR Program Alignment	Compensation Systems
Innovator: Increase Product Complexity and Shorten Product Life Cycle	• Product Leadership • Shift to Mass Customization • Cycle Time	• Committed to Agile, Risk-Taking, Innovative People	• Reward Innovation in Products and Processes • Market-Based Pay • Flexible—Generic Job Descriptions
Cost Cutter: Focus on Efficiency	• Operational Excellence • Pursue Cost-Effective Solutions	• Do More with Less	• Focus on Competitors' Labor Costs • Increase Variable Pay • Emphasize Productivity • Focus on System Control and Work Specifications
Customer Focused: Increase Customer Expectations	• Deliver Solutions to Customers • Speed to Market	• Delight Customer, Exceed Expectations	• Customer Satisfaction Incentives • Value of Job and Skills Based on Customer Contact

and Snow refer to *defenders* as those that operate in stable markets and compete on cost, whereas *prospectors* are more focused on innovation, new markets, and so forth.[22] These are known as generic strategy frameworks. Conventional wisdom would be that competing on cost requires lower compensation, whereas competing through innovation is likely to be more successful with high-powered incentives/pay for performance.[23]

Most firms, however, do not have generic strategies. Instead, as our discussion below suggests, they tend to have aspects of cost and innovation. Likewise, compensation strategies do not necessarily line up neatly with generic business strategies.[24] Although Lincoln Electric, Nucor Steel, and Southwest Airlines rely heavily on cost leadership in their strategies, they pay their employees well above market (e.g., using stock and profit-sharing plans) when (and, importantly, only when) firm performance is strong. SAS follows a customer and innovation strategy, but uses little in the way of pay for performance. If you think about it, if a particular business strategy automatically meant that a particular pay strategy would work best, there would not be much need for managers. These generic business strategy and pay strategy ideas are a good starting point.[25] But to do better than its competitors, a firm must consider how to fashion its own unique way of adding value through matching its business strategy and pay strategy.[26]

How do Google, Nucor, and Merrill Lynch fit into these generic business strategies? Look again at **Exhibit 2.3**. At first pass, Google might be an innovator and Merrill Lynch customer focused. Nucor is an innovator in its capability to recycle scrap steel while also being a dedicated cost cutter and productivity-focused. Yet managers in these companies would probably say that their company is a combination of all three descriptors. Merrill Lynch is also an innovator in financial investment derivatives and seeks to control costs. So like our discussion of yin and yang in **Chapter 1**, the reality for each company is a unique blending of all three strategies.

SUPPORT HR STRATEGY

Although a compensation strategy that supports the business strategy implies alignment between compensation and overall HR strategies, this topic is important enough that we want to explicitly deal with it. In the literature on so-called high-performance work systems (HPWS) and HR strategy, Boxall and Purcell describe a "very basic theory of performance," which they refer to as "AMO theory":

$$P = f(\mathrm{A,M,O})$$

P is performance, which is specified to be a function (*f*) of three factors: *A* is **ability,** *M* is **motivation,** and *O* is **opportunity.**[27] In other words, the *AMO* logic is that HR systems will be most effective when employee ability is developed through selective hiring and training and development, when the compensation system motivates employees to act on their abilities, and when roles are designed to allow employees to be involved in decisions and have an impact. (It is also common to refer to the O part as E, for environment.) Compensation (through incentive and sorting effects) is the key to attracting, retaining, and motivating employees with the abilities necessary to execute the business strategy and handle greater decision-making responsibilities. Compensation is also the key to motivating them to fully utilize those abilities. As such, higher pay levels and pay for performance are often part of such an HPWS.

Consider alignment between compensation and other aspects of HR at SAS. Rather than being sold in a one-time transaction, SAS's software is licensed. This is part of a business strategy by which SAS gets ongoing and substantial feedback from customers regarding how products can be continually improved and also regarding what new products customers would like. To support this long-term customer relationship, SAS seeks to have low employee turnover. Its heavy emphasis on benefits in compensation seems to be helpful in retaining employees. SAS also gets many job applications, which allows it to be very selective in its hiring. That no doubt helps build a highly able workforce and allows selection of those who fit SAS's emphasis on teamwork and idea sharing. The deemphasis on pay for individual performance probably reduces the risk that competition among employees will undermine this objective. As we discuss in the next section, Whole Foods also is team-based. Unlike SAS, however, it relies heavily on pay for performance. But it is team performance that matters. (Contrast the deemphasis on differences in individual performance at SAS and Whole Foods with the very different approach–strong emphasis on individual pay for performance–that seems to fit the business and HR strategies of companies such as General Electric, Nucor Steel, Lincoln Electric, and Merrill Lynch.) How effective can a compensation strategy be in supporting business strategy if it is at cross-purposes with the overall HR strategy? While reading about Whole Foods below, ask yourself how well its reliance on teams and giving workers wide decision latitude would work with a different compensation strategy. Such a mismatch happens surprisingly often.[28]

Compensation strategy and HR strategy are central to successful business strategy execution. **Exhibit 2.4** seeks to capture that idea, the importance of AMO and fit. It also makes the very simple, but very important, observation that all of this comes down to effects on either revenues or costs. Compensation strategy, HR strategy, and business strategy ultimately seek to decrease costs or increase revenues, relative to competitors.[29] At the same time, key stakeholders (e.g., employees, customers, shareholders) must be happy with their "deal" or relationship with the company. To the extent all of this happens, effectiveness is more likely to follow.

THE PAY MODEL GUIDES STRATEGIC PAY DECISIONS

Let us continue our discussion of Whole Foods. The competitive advantage of Whole Foods is apparent with the first visit to one of its grocery stores, described as "a mouth-watering festival of colors, smells, and textures; an homage to the appetite."[30] What started out in 1978 as a small health food store in Austin, Texas, has, through strategic decisions, grown to become the world's leading natural and organic foods supermarket, whose objective is to change the way Americans eat. Along the way, Whole Foods' managers have designed a total compensation system to support the company's phenomenal growth from 10,000 "team members" and $900 million in sales in 1996 to 87,000 "team members" and sales of $16 billion as of 2017. (Whole Foods was acquired in 2017 for $13.7 billion by Amazon. Whole Foods data are not reported separately by Amazon.) Whole Foods was on the Fortune list of Best Companies to Work for 20 consecutive years and is on the 2021 Forbes list of America's Best Large Employers. John Mackey has so far continued as CEO of Whole Foods, which would suggest planned continuity.)[31] Mackey, when asked what it's like to "finally have a boss" says the question "completely misunderstands the way most corporations operate," explaining "I've always had a boss. I always reported to the board of directors at Whole Foods."[32]

Using our pay model, let us consider the five strategic compensation choices facing Whole Foods managers:

EXHIBIT 2.4 Fit between HR Strategy and Compensation Strategy and Effectiveness

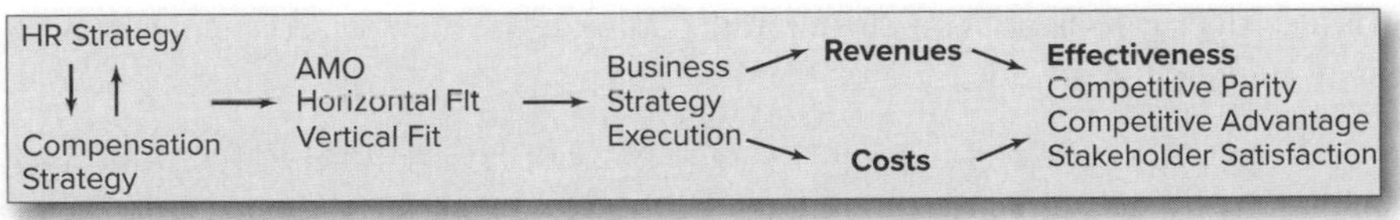

Horizontal Fit: Fit of Compensation Strategy with overall HR Strategy
Vertical Fit: Fit of Compensation Strategy and HR Strategy with the Business Strategy
AMO = Ability, Motivation, Opportunity

1. ***Objectives:*** How should compensation support the business strategy and be adaptive to the cultural and regulatory pressures in a global environment? (Whole Foods objectives: Increase shareholder value through profits and growth; go to extraordinary lengths to satisfy and delight customers; seek and engage employees who are going to help the company make money—every new hire must win a two-thirds vote from team members before being given a permanent position.)

2. ***Internal Alignment:*** How differently should the different types and levels of skills and work be paid within the organization? (Whole Foods: Store operations are organized around eight to ten self-managed teams; these teams make the types of decisions [e.g., what products to order and stock] that are often reserved for managers. Egalitarian, shared-fate philosophy means that executive salaries do not exceed 19 times the average pay of full-time employees [the ratio used to be 8 times; note that for top executives, salary typically accounts for well under one-half of total compensation]; all full-time employees qualify for stock.)

3. ***External Competitiveness:*** How should total compensation be positioned against competitors? (Whole Foods: Offer a unique deal compared to competitors.) What **forms of compensation** should be used? (Whole Foods: Provide health insurance for all employees working at least 20 hours/week and 20 hours of paid time a year to do volunteer work.) At Whole Foods, a store team leader (store manager) can earn over $100,000 per year based on salary, bonus, and restricted stock units.[33] No college degree is necessary. Median earnings for someone 25 and over with a high school degree in the United States is under $40,000.

4. ***Employee Contributions:*** Should pay increases be based on individual and/or team performance, on experience and/or continuous learning, on improved skills, on changes in cost of living, on personal needs (housing, transportation, health services), and/or on each business unit's performance? (Whole Foods: A shared fate—every four weeks the performance of each team is measured in terms of revenue per hour worked, which directly affects what they get paid. [This is one reason staffers are given some say in who gets hired—co-workers want someone who will help them make money!])

5. ***Management:*** How open and transparent should the pay decisions be to all employees? Who should be involved in designing and managing the system? ("You Decide"—employees recently voted to pick their health insurance rather than having one imposed by leadership.) In the area of pay transparency, Whole Foods practices "No-secrets" management: Every store has a book listing the previous year's pay for every employee, including executives. Mackey says that pay transparency is an important source of motivation in that "It gives people something to strive for." The idea is that employees think "Wow, I had no idea" I could make that much in that job. I want that job." For example, "I really want to be a store team leader because I had no idea" they can make over $100,000. [34]

These decisions, taken together, form a pattern that becomes an organization's compensation strategy.

Stated versus Unstated Strategies

All organizations that pay people have a compensation strategy. Some may have written compensation strategies for all to see and understand. Others may not even realize they have a compensation strategy. Ask a manager at one of these latter organizations about its compensation strategy and you may get a pragmatic response: "We do whatever it takes." Its compensation strategy is inferred from the pay decisions it has made.[35] Managers in all organizations make the five strategic decisions discussed earlier. Some do it in a rational, deliberate way, while others do it more chaotically–as ad hoc responses to pressures from the economic, sociopolitical, and regulatory context in which the organization operates. But in any organization that pays people, there is a compensation strategy at work.

DEVELOPING A TOTAL COMPENSATION STRATEGY: FOUR STEPS

Developing a compensation strategy involves four simple steps, shown in **Exhibit 2.5**. While the steps are simple, executing them is complex. Trial and error, experience, and insight play major roles. Research evidence can also help.[36]

Step 1: Assess Total Compensation Implications

Think about any organization's past, present, and–most vitally–future. What factors in its business environment have contributed to the company's success? Which of these factors are likely to become more (or less) important as the company looks ahead? **Exhibit 2.5** classifies the factors as competitive dynamics, culture/values, social and political context, employee/union needs, and other HR systems.

EXHIBIT 2.5 **Key Steps in Formulating a Total Compensation Strategy**

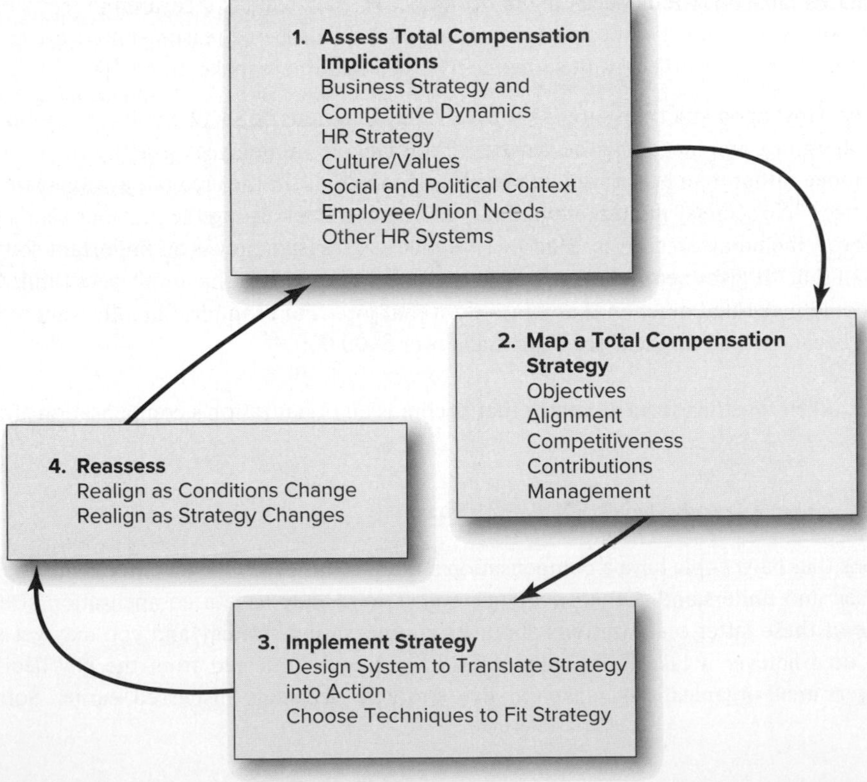

Business Strategy and Competitive Dynamics—Understand the Business

This first step includes an understanding of the specific industry in which the organization operates and how the organization plans to compete in that industry. This corresponds with the first two decisions in **Exhibit 2.2**: What business should we be in, and how do we win in that business?[37] To cope with the turbulent competitive dynamics, focus on what factors in the business environment (i.e., changing customer needs, competitors' actions, changing labor market conditions, changing laws, globalization) are important today. What will be important in the future?

What is your company's strategy? How do you compete to win? How should the compensation system support that strategy? Learn to gauge the underlying dynamics in your business (or build relationships with those who can). We have already discussed aligning different compensation strategies with different business strategies using the examples of cost cutter, customer centered, and innovator (**Exhibit 2.3**). But be cautious: As we have already pointed out, reality is more complex and chaotic. Organizations are innovators *and* cost cutters *and* customer centered. All three, and more. The orderly image conveyed in the exhibits does not adequately capture the turbulent competitive dynamics underlying this process.[38]

Competitive dynamics can be assessed globally.[39] However, comparing pay among countries is complex. In **Chapter 1**, we noted differences in hourly labor costs and productivity (output per dollar of wages) among countries. But as we shall see in **Chapter 16** on global pay, countries also differ on the average length of the workweek, the average number of paid holidays, the kinds of national health care and retirement programs, and even how pay is determined. Nevertheless, managers must become knowledgeable about competitive conditions both globally and locally.

HR Strategy: Pay as a Supporting Player or a Catalyst for Change?

As noted earlier, the pay strategy is also influenced by how it fits with other HR systems in the organization.[40] Whatever the overall HR strategy, a decision about the prominence of pay in that HR strategy is required. Pay can be a supporting player, as in the high-performance approach, or it can take the lead and be a catalyst for change. Whatever the role, compensation is embedded in the total HR approach.[41]

So, the compensation implications of all the above factors–the organization's business strategy, global competitive dynamics, culture and values, the sociopolitical context, employee preferences, and how pay fits with other HR systems–all are necessary to formulate a compensation strategy.

Culture/Values

A pay system reflects the values that guide an employer's behavior and underlie its treatment of employees. The pay system mirrors the company's image and reputation. As we noted in **Chapter 1**, most companies publish a values statement on their websites. Medtronic publishes theirs in 24 languages. Part of it is in **Exhibit 2.6**. Medtronic's value #5 recognizes employees' worth by fostering "personal satisfaction in work accomplished, security, advancement opportunity, and means to share in the company's success." Its compensation strategy reflects this value by including work/life balance programs for security, incentives, and stock ownership to share the company's success.

But there are some skeptics out there. Mission statements have been described as "an assemblage of trite phrases" that impress no one.[42] In contrast, Johnson and Johnson, like Medtronic, considers its statement its "moral compass" and "recipe for business success."[43]

Social and Political Context

Context refers to a wide range of factors, including legal and regulatory requirements, cultural differences, changing workforce demographics, expectations, and the like. These also affect compensation choices. In the case of Whole Foods, its business is very people intensive. Consequently, Whole Foods managers may find that an increasingly diverse workforce and increasingly diverse forms of pay (child care, chemical dependency counseling, educational reimbursements, employee assistance programs) may add value and be difficult for competitors (other supermarkets) to imitate.

Because governments are major stakeholders in determining compensation, lobbying to influence laws and regulations can also be part of a compensation strategy. In the United States, employers will not sit by while Congress considers taxing employee benefits. Similarly, the European Union's "social contract" is a matter of interest.[44] And in China, every foreign company has undoubtedly discovered that building relationships with government officials is essential. So, from a strategic perspective, managers of compensation may try to shape the sociopolitical environment as well as be shaped by it.

Employee Preferences

The simple fact that employees differ is too easily overlooked in formulating a compensation strategy. Individual employees join the organization, make investment decisions, interact with customers, design new products, assemble components, and so on. Individual employees receive the pay. A major challenge in the

EXHIBIT 2.6 **Medtronic Values (Medtronic Mission Statement)**

Written in 1960, our Mission dictates that our first and foremost priority is to contribute to human welfare. Over a half-century later, the Mission continues to serve as our ethical framework and inspirational goal for our employees around the world.

1. To contribute to human welfare by application of biomedical engineering in the research, design, manufacture, and sale of instruments or appliances that **alleviate pain, restore health, and extend life**.
2. **To direct our growth in the areas of biomedical engineering** where we display maximum strength and ability; to gather people and facilities that tend to augment these areas; to continuously build on these areas through education and knowledge assimilation; to avoid participation in areas where we cannot make unique and worthy contributions.
3. **To strive without reserve for the greatest possible reliability and quality** in our products; to be the unsurpassed standard of comparison and to be recognized as a company of dedication, honesty, integrity, and service.
4. **To make a fair profit** on current operations to meet our obligations, sustain our growth, and reach our goals.
5. **To recognize the personal worth of employees** by providing an employment framework that allows personal satisfaction in work accomplished, security, advancement opportunity, and means to share in the company's success.
6. **To maintain good citizenship** as a company.

Source: https://www.medtronic.com/us-en/about/mission.html. Accessed April 8, 2021.

design of next-generation pay systems is how to better satisfy individual needs and preferences. Offering more choice is one approach. Older, highly paid workers may wish to defer taxes by putting their pay into retirement funds, while younger employees may have high cash needs to buy a house, support a family, or finance an education. Dual-career couples who have double family coverage may prefer to use more of their combined pay for child care, automobile insurance, financial counseling, or other benefits such as flexible schedules. Employees who have young children or dependent parents may desire dependent care coverage.[45] Whole Foods, in fact, as described in its annual report each year, holds an employee vote every three years to determine the nature of their benefits program.

As an example of employee preference data that can be collected, based on the opinions of 10,000 U.S. workers, Hudson found that:

- Nearly three out of four U.S. workers claim to be satisfied with their compensation, yet a large portion of the same sample (44 percent) say they would change their mix of cash and benefits if given the chance.
- When given their choice of unconventional benefits, most employees would select a more flexible work schedule (33 percent) or additional family benefits (22 percent), including parental leaves and personal days, over job training (13 percent) or supplemental insurance (16 percent).
- One in five workers say better health care benefits would make them happier with their compensation package. On the other hand, 41 percent said that the single thing that would make them happier is more money.[46]

Choice Is Good. Yes, No, Maybe?[47]

Contemporary pay systems in the United States do offer some choices. Flexible benefits and choices among health care plans and investment funds for retirement are examples. As noted above, Whole Foods employees vote on the benefits they want. Netflix employees can choose the mix of stock options and salary. General Mills similarly allows many employees to swap several weeks' salary for stock awards. The company believes that allowing employees their choice adds value and is difficult for other companies to imitate–it is a source of competitive advantage for General Mills. Whether or not this belief is correct remains to be studied.

Some studies have found that people do not always choose well. They do not always understand the alternatives, and too many choices simply confuse them. Thus, the value added by offering choices and satisfying preferences may be offset by the expense of communicating and simply confusing people.[48]

In addition to possibly confusing employees, unlimited choice would be a challenge to design and manage. Plus, it would meet with disapproval from the U.S. Internal Revenue Service (health benefits are not viewed by the IRS as income). Offering greater choice to employees in different nations would require meeting a bewildering maze of codes and regulations. On the other hand, the U.S. federal government, including the IRS, already offers its employees a bit of choice in their work schedules. Forty-three percent avail themselves of the option to take compensatory time off for extra hours worked. In contrast, U.S. private sector workers covered by the Fair Labor Standards Act (i.e., **nonexempt** employees) must be paid time-and-a-half overtime if they work over 40 hours in a week. A compensatory time option is not permitted.[49]

Union Preferences

Pay strategies need to take into account the nature of the union–management relationship.[50] Even though less than 7 percent of U.S. private sector workers are now in labor unions, union influence on pay decisions remains significant in key sectors (e.g., manufacturing, health care, education). Union preferences for different forms of pay (e.g., protecting retirement and health care plans) and their concern with job security affect pay strategy.

Unions' interests can differ. In Denver, Colorado, a merit pay plan was developed collaboratively by the Denver Public Schools and the Denver Classroom Teachers Association, the local union affiliate. Teachers approved the agreement by a 59 percent to 41 percent vote, and Denver voters approved a $25 million property tax increase to pay for it. Conversely, many teachers in Springfield, Massachusetts, left for neighboring, higher-paying school districts in part because the district wanted to impose a merit pay plan.[51]

Compensation deals with unions can be costly to change. The U.S. auto companies negotiated "The Jobs Bank" program that began in 1984 with the United Auto Workers. Employees who were no longer needed to make cars continued to get paid until they were needed again. Some received up to $100,000 a year, including benefits. Their job: Do nothing but wait for a job to open up. But for a number of people, those jobs never materialized. In various cities around the United States, about 15,000 employees showed up at designated locations (to be paid not to work) at 6 a.m. each day and stayed until 2:30 p.m., with 45 minutes off for lunch. Some volunteered for approved community projects or took classes. Jerry Mellon claims, "They paid me like $400,000 over 6 years to learn how to deal blackjack."[52] Readers may wonder if the Jobs Bank was a compensation strategy that trumped the business strategy. No wonder GM eventually bought its way out of the Bank. No wonder GM recently found it necessary to go through bankruptcy.

Step 2: Map a Total Compensation Strategy

The compensation strategy is made up of the elements in the pay model: objectives, and the four policy choices of alignment, competitiveness, contributions, and management. Mapping these decisions is Step 2 in developing a compensation strategy.

Mapping is often used in marketing to clarify and communicate a product's identity. A strategic map offers a picture of a company's compensation strategy. It can also clarify the message that the company is trying to deliver with its compensation system.

Exhibit 2.7 maps the compensation strategies of Microsoft and SAS. The five dimensions are subdivided into a number of descriptors rated on importance. These ratings are from your fearless (read "tenured") authors. They are not ratings assigned by managers in the companies. The descriptors used under each of the strategy dimensions can be modified as a company sees fit.

Objectives: Prominence is the measure of how important total compensation is in the overall HR strategy. Is it a catalyst, playing a lead role? Or is it less important, playing a more supporting character to other HR programs? At Microsoft, compensation is rated highly prominent, whereas at SAS it is more supportive.

Internal Alignment: This is described as the degree of internal hierarchy. For example, how much does pay differ among job levels and how well does compensation support career growth? Both SAS and Microsoft use pay to support flexible work design and promotions. But pay differences at SAS, whose philosophy is "Everyone is part of the SAS family," are smaller than at Microsoft, where differences in pay are seen as returns for superior performance.

External Competitiveness: This includes comparisons on two issues. How much are our competitors paying, and what forms of pay are they using? The importance of work/life balance achieved via benefits and services is also part of external competitiveness. According to the strategy map, Microsoft's **competitive position** is critical to its pay strategy, whereas SAS competes on work/family balance in family-oriented benefits such as private schools and doctors on the company's campus.

Employee Contributions: These two companies take a very different approach to performance-based pay. SAS uses only limited individual-based performance pay. This is consistent with its overall egalitarian approach. Microsoft makes greater use of pay based on individual and company performance.

Management: Ownership refers to the role non-HR managers play in making pay decisions. *Transparency* refers to openness and communication about pay. As one might expect, both Microsoft and SAS rate high on the use of technology to manage the pay system, and Microsoft offers greater choices in their health care and retirement investment plans.

Each company's profile on the strategy map reflects its main message or "pay brand."

Microsoft: Total compensation is prominent, with a strong emphasis on market competitiveness, individual accomplishments, and performance-based returns.

SAS: Total compensation supports its work/life balance. Competitive market position, company-wide success sharing, and egalitarianism are the hallmarks.

In contrast to the verbal description earlier in this chapter, strategic maps provide a visual reference. They are useful in analyzing a compensation strategy that can be more clearly understood by employees and

EXHIBIT 2.7 Contrasting Maps of Microsoft and SAS

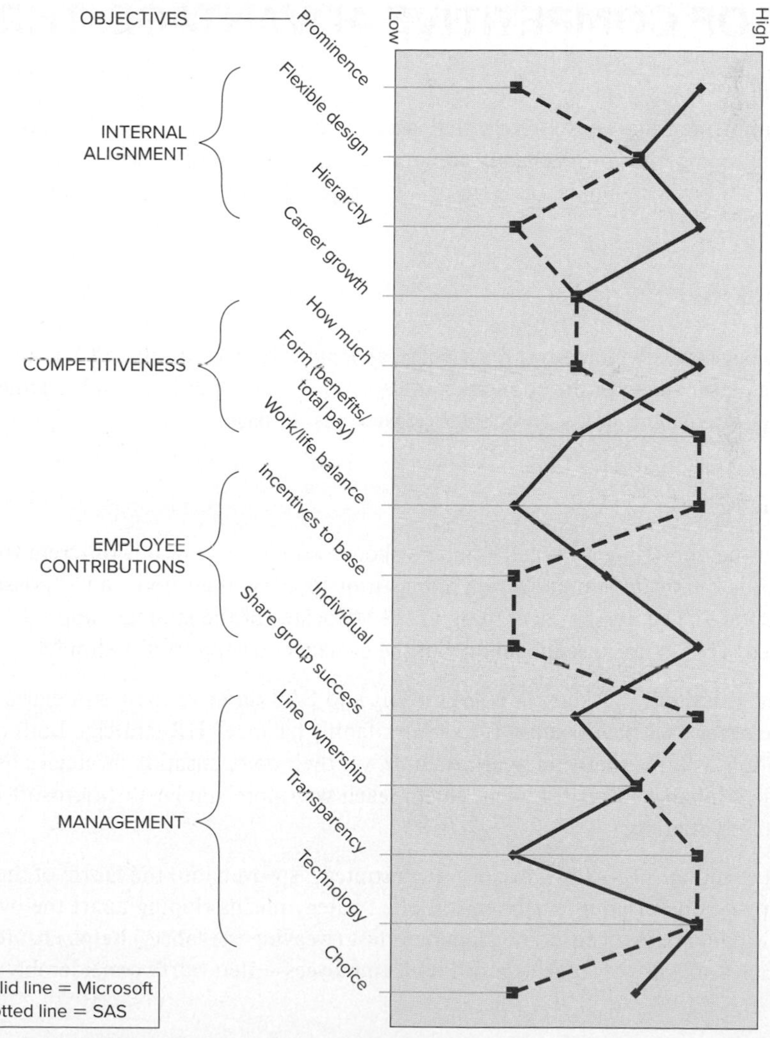

managers.[53] Maps *do not* tell which strategy is "best." Rather, they provide a framework and guidance. Just like a road map, they can show where you are and where you are going.[54]

The rest of this book discusses compensation decisions in detail. It is important to realize, however, that the decisions in the pay model work in concert. It is the totality of these decisions that forms the compensation strategy.

Steps 3 and 4: Implement and Reassess

Step 3 in **Exhibit 2.5** is to implement the strategy through the design and execution of the compensation system. The compensation system translates strategy into practice–and into people's bank accounts.

Step 4, Reassess and Realign, closes the loop. This step recognizes that the compensation strategy must change to fit changing conditions. Thus, periodic reassessment is needed to continuously learn, adapt, and improve. The results from using the pay system need to be assessed against the objectives we are trying to achieve.

SOURCE OF COMPETITIVE ADVANTAGE: THREE TESTS

Developing and implementing a pay strategy that is a source of sustained competitive advantage is easier said than done. Not all compensation decisions are strategic or a source of competitive advantage. Three tests determine whether a pay strategy is a source of advantage: (1) Is it aligned? (2) Does it differentiate? (3) Does it add value?

Align

Alignment of the pay strategy includes three aspects, as we have already discussed: (1) align with the business strategy, (2) align externally with the economic and sociopolitical conditions, and (3) align internally within the overall HR system. Alignment is probably the easiest test to pass.

Differentiate

Some believe that the only thing that really matters about a strategy is how it is different from everyone else's. If the pay system is relatively simple for any competitor to copy, then how can it possibly be a source of competitive advantage? The answer, according to the advocates of the strategic approach, is in how the pay system is managed. This rhetoric is appealing, but the evidence to support it is slim.[55]

The map profiles in **Exhibit 2.7** show how Microsoft and SAS differ in their strategies. One uses pay as a strong signal; the other uses pay to support its "work/family balance" HR strategy. Both organizations claim to have organization cultures that value performance, yet their compensation strategies differ. (In our earlier examples, Google/Alphabet, Merrill Lynch, Nucor, each was more similar to Microsoft in the emphasis on pay and strong differentiation.)

Are they difficult to imitate? Probably, because each strategy is woven into the fabric of the company's overall HR strategy. Copying one or another dimension of a strategy means ripping apart the overall approach and patching in a new one. So, in a sense, the alignment test (weaving the fabric) helps ensure passing the differentiation test. Microsoft's use of stock awards for all employees–often worth considerably more than people's base pay–is difficult for its competitors to copy. SAS's work-family-balance (like Medtronic's total-presence-at-the-workplace strategy) is difficult to copy. It may be relatively easy to copy any individual action a competitor takes (i.e., grant stock options to more employees or offer more choice in their health insurance). But the strategic perspective implies that it is the *way* programs fit together and fit the overall organization that is hard to copy. Simply copying others by blindly benchmarking best practices amounts to trying to get in and/or stay in the race, not win it.[56] (Of course, being in the race, or achieving competitive parity, may be a major improvement for some organizations.)

It is also important to note that in any specific organization, the term "simply copying" is simply too simple. It is often not easy to copy under conditions of imperfect information on how well management practices work, what it will cost to implement, and uncertainty about how well it will work for you.[57] Jeffrey Pfeffer captures this with his "one-eighth rule": (1) only one-half of company leaders believe a practice will work, (2) only one-half of those decide to try it, and (3) only one-half of that group are able to successfully implement it.[58] Thus, only 1/8 (1/2 x 1/2 x 1/2 = 1/8) are able to successfully pull of "simply copying" a best practice used by another company. Further, as suggested above, in cases where "copying" actually takes place, the practice is not likely to be a copy, even if it has the same label. "Pay for performance" can take many forms and different levels of coverage/intensity of implementation.[59] During implementation, there is likely to be at least some effort to align its particular form with other parts of the compensation and HR strategy, resulting in some uniqueness.

e-Compensation: Compensation Consultants

Compensation consultants are major players, and practically every organization uses at least one for data and advice. So learning more about the services these consultants offer is useful. Go to the websites of at least two of them. You can choose from the consulting firms listed below or find others.

FW Cook **https://www.fwcook.com/**
Korn Ferry Haygroup ***www.kornferry.com/haygroup.com***
Mercer ***www.mercer.com***
Aon Hewitt ***www.aon.com***
Willis Towers Watson ***www.towerswatson.com***
Newport Group ***www.newportgroup.com***

1. Compare consultants. From their websites, construct a chart comparing their stated values and culture and their business strategies, and highlight the services offered.
2. Critically assess whether their strategies and services are unique and/or difficult to imitate. Which one would you select (based on the web information) to help you formulate a company's total compensation strategy?
3. Based on the web information, which one would you prefer to work for? Why?
4. Be prepared to share this information with others in class.

Return on the Investment: If everyone does a great job on this e-compensation, you will all have useful information on consultants.

For more background, see Lewis Pinault, *Consulting Demons: Inside the Unscrupulous World of Global Corporate Consulting* (New York: Harpers Business, 2000), and Fred Cook, "A Personal Perspective of the Consulting Profession," *ACA News*, October 1999, pp. 35–43.

Add Value

Organizations continue to look for the return they are getting from their incentives, benefits, and even base pay. Compensation is often a company's largest controllable expense. Because consultants and a few researchers treat different forms of pay as investments, the task is to come up with ways to calculate the return on investments (ROI). But this is a difficult proposition. As one writer put it, "It is easier to count the bottles than describe the wine."[60] Costs are easy to fit into a spreadsheet, but any value created as a result of those costs is difficult to specify, much less measure.[61] Current attempts to do so are described in **Chapter 18**, Management.

Trying to measure an ROI for any compensation strategy implies that people are "human capital," similar to other factors of production. Many people find this view dehumanizing. They argue that viewing pay as an investment with measurable returns diminishes the importance of treating employees fairly.[62] In **Chapter 1** we discussed the need to keep all objectives, including efficiency and fairness, in mind at the same time. No doubt about it, of the three tests of strategy–align, differentiate, add value–the last is the most difficult.

Are there advantages to an innovative compensation strategy? We do know that in products and services, first movers (innovators) have well-recognized advantages that can offset the risks involved–high margins, market share, and mind share (brand recognition).[63] But we do not know whether such advantages accrue to innovators in total compensation. What, if any, benefits accrued to Microsoft, one of the first to offer very large stock options to all employees, once its competitors did the same thing? What about General Mills, who was among the first to offer some managers a choice of more stock options for smaller base pay? Does a compensation innovator attract more and better people? Induce people to stay and contribute? Are there cost advantages? Studies are needed to find the answers.

"BEST PRACTICES" VERSUS "BEST FIT"?

The premise of any strategic perspective is that if managers align pay decisions with the organization's strategy and values, are responsive to employees and union relations, and are globally competitive, then the organization is more likely to achieve competitive advantage.[64] The challenge is to design the "fit" with the environment, business strategy, and pay plan. The better the fit, the greater the competitive advantage.

But not everyone agrees. In contrast to the notion of strategic fit, some believe that (1) a set of **best-pay practices** exists and (2) these practices can be applied universally across situations. Rather than having a better fit between business strategy and compensation plans that yields better performance, they say that best practices result in better performance with almost any business strategy.[65]

These writers believe that adopting best-pay practices allows the employer to gain preferential access to superior employees. These superior employees will in turn be the organization's source of competitive advantage. The challenge here is to select from various recommended lists which are "the" best practices.[66] Which practices truly are the best? We believe that research over the past few years is beginning to point the way to improve our choices.[67]

GUIDANCE FROM THE EVIDENCE

There is consistent research evidence that the following practices do matter to the organization's objectives.

- *Internal alignment:* Both smaller and larger pay differences among jobs inside an organization can affect results. Smaller internal pay differences and larger internal pay differences can both be a "best" practice. Which one depends on the context; that is, the fit with business strategy, other HR practices, the organization culture, and so on.[68]

- *External competitiveness:* Paying higher than the average paid by competitors can affect results. Is higher competitive pay a "best" practice? Again, it depends on the context.
- *Employee contributions:* Performance-based pay can affect results. Is pay-for-performance a "best" practice? Although the most effective form/design likely depends on the context, the evidence is strong that pay-for-performance of some form, due to positive incentive and sorting effects (see **Chapter 1**) is likely to be more effective than a system where people's pay is independent of their performance.[69]
- *Managing compensation:* Rather than focusing on only one dimension of the pay strategy (e.g., pay for performance or internal pay differences), all dimensions need to be considered together.[70]
- *Compensation strategy:* Finally, embedding compensation strategy within the broader HR strategy affects results. Compensation does not operate alone; it is part of the overall HR perspective.[71]

So, specific pay practices appear to be more beneficial in some contexts than in others.[72] Thus, best practice versus best fit does not appear to be a useful way to frame the question. A more useful question is, *What practices pay off best under what conditions?* Much of the rest of this book is devoted to exploring this question.

VIRTUOUS AND VICIOUS CIRCLES

A group of studies suggests specific conditions to look at when making strategic pay decisions. One study examined eight years of data from 180 U.S. companies.[73] The authors reported that while *pay levels* (external competitiveness) differed among these companies, they were not related to the companies' subsequent financial performance. However, when combined with differences in the size of bonuses and the number of people eligible for stock options, the pay levels were related to future financial success of the organizations. This study concluded that it is not only *how much* you pay but also *how* you pay that matters.[74]

Think of pay as part of a circle. **Exhibit 2.8** suggests that performance-based pay works best when there is success to share. An organization whose profits or market share is increasing is able to pay larger bonuses and stock awards. And paying these bonuses fairly improves employee attitudes and work behaviors, which in turn improves their performance.[75] The circle gains upward momentum.[76] Employees receive returns that compensate for the risks they take. And they behave like owners, since they are sharing in the organization's success.

Additionally, there are several studies that analyzed pay strategies as part of the "high-performance workplace" approaches discussed earlier. This research focused on specific jobs and workplaces, such as sales

EXHIBIT 2.8 **Virtuous and Vicious Circles**

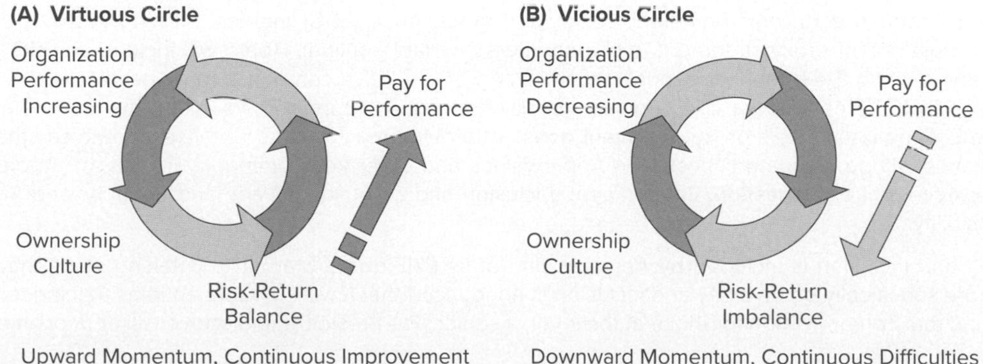

and service representatives in call service centers and jobs in factories.[77] They indicate that performance-based pay that shares success with employees does improve employee attitudes, behaviors, and performance—especially when coupled with the other "high-performance" practices. One study even reported that the effects of the compensation strategy equaled the impact of all the other practices (high involvement, teams, selective hiring, and training programs) combined.[78] These findings are near and dear to our hearts. So other "high-performance" HR practices also become factors that support improved performance and the virtuous circle.

It cannot have escaped your attention that circles can also gain momentum going downward to become a vicious circle. As shown in **Exhibit 2.8**, when organization performance declines, performance-based pay plans do not pay off; there are no bonuses, and the value of stock declines—with potentially negative effects on organization performance. Declining organization performance increases the risks facing employees—risks of still smaller bonuses, demotions, wage cuts, and even layoffs. Unless the increased risks are offset by larger returns, the risk-return imbalance will reinforce declining employee attitudes and speed the downward spiral. Unfortunately, we do not yet know what compensation practices can be used to shift an organization caught in a downward spiral into an upward one.

Perhaps we believe so strongly that pay matters and that studying it in the workplace is beneficial, that this is what we see—believing is seeing. So, caution and more evidence are required. Nevertheless, these studies do seem to indicate that performance-based pay may be a best practice, under the right circumstances. (Could performance-based pay sometimes be a "worst practice"? Yes, when incentive systems don't pay off and they alienate employees or lead to government investigation of possible stock option manipulation.) Additionally, we do not have much information about how people perceive various pay strategies. Do all managers "see" the total compensation strategy at Merrill Lynch or Google the same way? Some evidence suggests that if you ask ten managers about their company's HR strategy, you get ten different answers. If the link between the strategy and people's perceptions is not clear, then maybe we are using evidence to build on unstable ground.

Your Turn

Using Compensation to Improve Environmental, Social, and Governance (including Diversity & Inclusion) Performance: Apple and Starbucks[79]

As with most companies, Apple measures and compensates senior executive performance primarily on the basis of meeting key financial goals. Now, for the first time, Apple will also compensate its executives based on their performance on environmental, social, and governance (ESG) metrics. Starting in 2021, according to is most recent proxy statement to shareholders (available online), Apple will include an ESG "modifier" in determining the bonus (or annual incentive) part of executive compensation. Specifically, the bonus can be up to 10 percent larger if ESG goals are fully met versus 10 percent lower for low performance in meeting ESG goals. Apple's proxy statement does not provide much further detail, except to say that ESG performance will be evaluated "based on Apple values and other key community initiatives." Apple's values are: Accessibility, Education, Environment, Inclusion and Diversity, Privacy and Security, and Supplier Responsibility.

Diversity and Inclusion is included by Apple as part of its ESG goals. Starbucks is taking steps that focus even more specifically on diversity and inclusion. It announced that it will mandate antibias training for executives and that compensation for those at the level of senior vice president and above will depend in part on their success in increasing minority representation in the Starbucks workforce. Starbucks said its goal is to have at least 30 percent of corporate employees and at least 40 percent of its U.S. retail and manufacturing employees be people of color by 2025. It says that it currently does not meet those goals in nine of the fourteen job levels that it tracks. In 2018, two black men sitting at a table in a Philadelphia Starbucks were arrested. The company subsequently apologized and closed its U.S. corporate stores for one day to conduct antibias training. The Starbucks proxy statement provides some detail on how diversity and inclusion will play a larger role in executive compensation. In contrast to Apple, there will be a modifier not only in the bonus (annual incentive) plan, but also in the long-term incentive plan. One specific target is to increase Black, Indigenous, and LatinX representation by 5 percent or more over a three-year period.

QUESTIONS:

1. In **Chapter 1**, we saw the major components of chief executive officer compensation. Apple's ESG incentive focuses primarily on the bonus. In thinking about the (a) typical size of the bonus relative to total chief executive compensation and (b) taking into account the size of the ESQ "modifier" Apple will use (based on ESG performance), do you consider the incentive to achieve ESG goals to be too small, too large, or just about right? Explain.
2. In looking at the ESG incentive at Starbucks, is it about the same, stronger, or weaker than what Apple will use? Explain. Given Starbuck's business strategy and its stakeholders, would it make sense for Starbucks to use the same, stronger, or weaker ESG incentives, especially in the diversity and inclusion area, compared to Apple?
3. Do you have any suggestions for either or both companies that might make their ESG incentives more effective?

Still Your Turn Mapping Compensation Strategies

Take any organization that you know—current employer, business school, the place you interned, or a friend's employer. Look at **Exhibit 2.7**, "Contrasting Maps of Microsoft and SAS." Map your organization's compensation strategy then compare it to that of Microsoft and SAS.

1. Summarize the key points of your company's strategy.
2. What are the key differences compared to the strategies of Microsoft and SAS?

Or ask several managers in the *same* organization to map that organization's compensation strategy. You may need to assist them. Then compare the managers' maps.

3. Summarize the key similarities and differences.
4. Why do these similarities and differences occur?
5. How can maps be used to clarify and communicate compensation strategies to leaders? To employees?

Summary

Managing total compensation strategically means fitting the compensation system to the business and environmental conditions. We believe the best way to proceed is to start with the pay model–the objectives and four policy choices–and take the steps discussed in this chapter: (1) assess implications for the total compensation of your organization's situation; (2) map out the compensation objectives and four policy choices to achieve them (internal alignment, external competitiveness, employee contributions, and management); (3) translate these policies into the workplace via the compensation system and implement it; and (4) reassess by comparing your results against the pay objectives. And continue to learn, adapt, and improve. Sounds simple? It isn't. The major challenge in managing total compensation is to understand how your pay system can add value and make the organization more successful. We believe that research is beginning to offer useful evidence-based guidance, with the promise of more to come.

Review Questions

1. Select a familiar company or analyze the approach your college uses to pay teaching assistants or faculty. Infer its compensation strategy using the five dimensions (objectives, alignment, competitiveness, employee considerations, and management). How does your company or school compare to Microsoft and Merrill Lynch? What business strategy does it seem to "fit" (i.e., cost cutter, customer centered, innovator, or something else)?
2. Contrast the essential differences between the best-fit and best-practices perspectives.
3. Reread **Exhibit 2.6**. Discuss how those values might be reflected in a compensation system. Are these values consistent with "Let the market decide"?
4. Three tests for any source of competitive advantage are align, differentiate, and add value. Discuss whether these tests are difficult to pass. Can compensation really be a source of competitive advantage?
5. Set up a debate over the following proposition: Nonfinancial returns (great place to work, opportunities to learn, job security, and flexible work schedules) are more important (i.e., best practice) than pay.

Endnotes

1. Top Companies for Compensation & Benefits. glassdoor.com. Retrieved February 5, 2015.
2. Martin Peers, "Searching Google for Pay," *The Wall Street Journal,* November 11, 2010; Laszlo Bock. *Work Rules!* (New York: Grand Central, 2015); Laszlo Bock "Google's 10 Things to Transform Your Team and Your Workplace," *Fortune*, March 5, 2015.
3. U.S. Bureau of Labor Statistics. Occupational Employment and Wages, May 2020. https://www.bls.gov/oes/current/oes510000.htm.
4. Joseph S. Pete, "Sobering: Steelmakers Warn More Layoffs Could Occur," Nwitimes.com, March 26, 2015.
5. Rick Barrett. Steelmaker Nucor says it doesn't do layoffs. That's helped make it a Top Workplace for 10 years. Milwaukee Journal Sentinel, April 12, 2019. www.jsonline.com.
6. Rick Barrett. Steelmaker Nucor says it doesn't do layoffs. That's helped make it a Top Workplace for 10 years. Milwaukee Journal Sentinel, April 12, 2019. www.jsonline.com.
7. Janet Levaux. Merrill Lowers Key Comp Target, Again. www.thinkadvisor.com, June 9, 2020.
8. Jed Horowitz, "Analysis: Broker Bonus Bidding War Comes at a Cost," *NewsDaily,* April 10, 2012, www.newsdaily.com.
9. Payout Grids 2012, www.onwallstreet.com/global/payout_grids.html, retrieved April 17, 2012; Lisa Beilfuss, "Merrill Lynch Revamps Broker Pay to Reward Referrals, Stronger Growth," *Wall Street Journal*, November 8, 2017; Jed Horowitz and Mason Braswell, "2018 Comp: Merrill Lynch Adds Penalties/Rewards to Spur Asset Growth," Advisorhub.com, November 8, 2017.

10. Jed Horowitz. "2021 Comp: Merrill Keeps Grids Intact, Eliminates Pay on Small Accounts. www.advisorhub.com, December 3, 2020.
11. David Mildenbers, "Bank of America's Merrill Adds $5 Billion to Deposits in Month," *www.Bloomberg.com,* June 5, 2009; "Merrill Tweaks Advisor Pay for 2015," http://wealthmanagement.com; Michael Wursthorn. "Brokerages to Advisers: Follow the Carrot in 2015," *The Wall Street Journal,* December 19, 2014, www.wsj.com.
12. Lisa Beilfuss, "Merrill Lynch Boosts Profit, Fee-Based Assets Clients of Bank of America's Global Wealth Unit Moved $27.5 Billion into Fee-Based Accounts during the Latest Quarter," *The Wall Street Journal,* July 18, 2017; Michael Wursthorn, "Merrill Contributes More to Bank of America's Bottom Line," *The Wall Street Journal,* January 15, 2015. Halah Touryalai, "Here's Why Bank of America Loves Merrill Lynch," *Forbes,* April 19, 2012, www.forbes.com.
13. Timothy M. Gardner, "Interfirm Competition for Human Resources: Evidence from the Software Industry," *Academy of Management Journal* 48(2), 2005, pp. 237–256; Yoshio Yanadori and Janet Marler, "Compensation Strategy: Does Business Strategy Influence Compensation in High Technology Firms?" *Strategic Management Journal* (June 2006), pp. 559–570.
14. An *option* is the opportunity to buy stock at a set price. If the value of shares increases, then the option has value (market price minus the set option price). Awards grant employees stock whose value is its market price. Later chapters discuss stock options and awards in detail. See Kevin F. Hallock and Craig A. Olson, "The Value of Stock Options to Non-Executive Employees," Working paper, Institute of Labor and Industrial Relations, University of Illinois Urbana/Champaign, January 2006.
15. "SAS Institute," Stanford Business School case; also, "SAS: The Royal Treatment," *60 Minutes,* October 13, 2002.
16. Rich Karlgaard, "Microsoft's IQ Dividend," *The Wall Street Journal,* July 28, 2004, p. A13; Holman W. Jenkins Jr., "Stock Options Are Dead, Long Live Stock Options," *The Wall Street Journal,* July 16, 2003.
17. M. Treacy and F. Wiersma, *The Discipline of Market Leaders* (Reading, MA: Addison-Wesley, 1997).
18. Daniel Vaughan-Whitehead, "Wage Reform in Central and Eastern Europe," in *Paying the Price,* ed. Daniel Vaughn-Whitehead (New York: St. Martin's Press, 2000); Marshall Meyer, Yuan Lu, Hailin Lan, and Xiaohui Lu, "Decentralized Enterprise Reform: Notes on the Transformation of State-Owned Enterprises," in *The Management of Enterprises in the People's Republic of China,* ed. Anne S. Tsui and Chung-Ming Lau (Boston: Kluwer Academic, 2002), pp. 241–274; Mei Fong, "A Chinese Puzzle," *The Wall Street Journal,* August 16, 2004, p. B1.
19. IBM, "Our Strategy," *www.ibm.com/investor/strategy/,* retrieved May 22, 2009.
20. Michael Porter, "What Is Strategy?" *Harvard Business Review,* November–December 1996, pp. 61–78. Deepak K. Datta, James P. Guthrie, and Patrick M. Wright, "Human Resource Management and Labor Productivity: Does Industry Matter?" *Academy of Management Journal* 48(5), 2005, pp. 135–145; Yoshio Yanadori and Janet Marler, "Compensation Strategy: Does Business Strategy Influence Compensation in High Technology Firms?" *Strategic Management Journal* (June 2006), pp. 559–570; Henry Mintzberg, "Five Tips for Strategy," in *The Strategy Process: Concepts and Contexts,* Henry Mintzberg and James Brian Quinn, eds. (Englewood Cliffs, NJ: Prentice-Hall, 1992); J. E. Delery and D. H. Doty, "Models of Theorizing in Strategic Human Resource Management," *Academy of Management Journal* 39(4), 1996, pp. 802–835; Edilberto F. Montemayor, "Congruence between Pay Policy and Competitive Strategy in High-Performing Firms," *Journal of Management* 22(6), 1996, pp. 889–908; B. Gerhart, "Pay Strategy and Firm Performance," in *Compensation in Organizations:*

Current Research and Practice, S. L. Rynes and B. Gerhart, eds. (San Francisco, CA: Jossey-Bass, 2000); Barry Gerhart and Sara Rynes, *Compensation: Theory, Evidence, and Strategic Implications* (Thousand Oaks, CA: Sage, 2003).

21. For comprehensive reviews of theory and research on this topic, see Luis R. Gomez-Mejia, Pascual Berrone, and Monica Franco-Santos, *Compensation and Organizational Performance* (Armonk, NY: M. E. Sharpe, 2010); and Luis R. Gomez-Mejia and David B. Balkin, *Compensation, Organizational Strategy, and Firm Performance* (Cincinnati: South-Western, 1992).
22. Michael E. Porter, *Competitive Strategy* (New York: Free Press, 1980); R. E. Miles and C. C. Snow, *Organizational Strategy, Structure, and Process* (New York: McGraw-Hill, 1978).
23. A. Tenhiala and T. Laamanen, "Right on the Money? The Contingent Effects of Strategic Orientation and Pay System Design on Firm Performance," *Strategic Management Journal* 39 (2018), pp. 3408–33; M. S. Giarratana, M. Mariani, and I. Weller, "Rewards for Patents and Inventor Behaviors in Industrial Research and Development," *Academy of Management Journal* 61, no. 1 (2018), pp. 264–92. B. R. Ellig, "Compensation Elements: Market Phase Determines the Mix," *Compensation and Benefits Review* 13, no. 3 (1981), pp. 30–38; Gomez-Mejia and Balkin, *Compensation, Organizational Strategy, and Firm Performance*; Y. Yanadori and J. H. Marler, "Compensation Strategy: Does Business Strategy Influence Compensation in High-Technology Firms?" *Strategic Management Journal* 27 (2006), pp. 559–70; B. Gerhart, "Compensation Strategy and Organizational Performance" in *Compensation in Organizations*, ed. S. L. Rynes and B. Gerhart (San Francisco: Jossey-Bass, 2000);
24. George T. Milkovich, "A Strategic Perspective on Compensation," *Research in Personnel and Human Resources Management* 6 (1988), pp. 263–268; B. Gerhart and S. L. Rynes, *Compensation: Theory, Evidence, and Strategic Implications* (Thousand Oaks, CA: Sage, 2003).
25. Y. Yanadori and J. H. Marler, "Compensation Strategy: Does Business Strategy Influence Compensation in High-Technology Firms?" *Strategic Management Journal* 27 (2006), pp. 559–570; N. Rajagopalan, "Strategic Orientations, Incentive Plan Adoptions, and Firm Performance: Evidence From Electrical Utility Firms," *Strategic Management Journal* 18 (1996), pp. 761–785; Luis R. Gomez-Mejia and David B. Balkin, *Compensation, Organization Strategy, and Firm Performance* (Cincinnati: South-Western, 1992); B. Gerhart, "Compensation Strategy and Organizational Performance," in *Compensation in Organizations,* ed. S. L. Rynes and B. Gerhart, Frontiers of Industrial and Organizational Psychology series (San Francisco: Jossey-Bass, 2000).
26. B. Gerhart, C. Trevor, and M. Graham, "New Directions in Employee Compensation Research," in *Research in Personnel and Human Resources Management,* ed. G. R. Ferris (Amsterdam: Elsevier, 1999), pp. 143–203.
27. Peter Boxall and John Purcell, *Strategy and Human Resource Management,* 2nd ed. (Basingstoke, UK: Palgrave MacMillan, 2007); Rosemary Batt, "Managing Customer Services: Human Resource Practices, Quit Rates, and Sales Growth," *Academy of Management Journal* 45 (2002), pp. 587–597; Eileen Appelbaum, Thomas Bailey, Peter Berg, and Arne Kalleberg, *Manufacturing Advantage: Why High Performance Work Systems Pay Off* (Ithaca, NY: Cornell University Press, 2000); I. S. Fulmer, B. Gerhart, and K. S. Scott, "Are the 100 Best Better? An Empirical Investigation of the Relationship between Being a 'Great Place to Work' and Firm Performance," *Personnel Psychology* 56 (2003), pp. 965–993; H. C. Katz, T. A. Kochan, and M. R. Weber, "Assessing the Effects of Industrial Relations Systems and Efforts to Improve the Quality of Working Life on Organizational Effectiveness," *Academy of Management Journal* 28 (1985), pp. 509–526; Mark A. Huselid, "The Impact of Human Resource Management Practices on Turnover, Productivity, and Corporate Financial Performance," *Academy of Management Journal* 38 (1995), pp. 635–672; John Paul Macduffie, "Human Resource Bundles and Manufacturing Performance: Organizational Logic and Flexible Production

Systems in the World Auto Industry," *Industrial and Labor Relations Review* 48 (1995), pp. 197–221. For a review, see B. Gerhart, "Horizontal and Vertical Fit in Human Resource Systems," in *Perspectives on Organizational Fit,* ed. C. Ostroff and T. Judge, SIOP Organizational Frontiers series (New York: Erlbaum, 2007).

28. P. M. Wright, G. McMahan, S. Snell, and B. Gerhart, "Comparing Line and HR Executives' Perceptions of HR Effectiveness: Services, Roles, and Contributions," *Human Resource Management* 40 (2001), pp. 111–124.
29. B. Becker and B. Gerhart, "The Impact of Human Resource Management on Organizational Performance: Progress and Prospects," *Academy of Management Journal* 39 (1996), pp. 779–801.
30. Charles Fishman, "The Anarchist's Cookbook," *Fast Company,* July 2004, *http://www.fastcompany.com/magazine/84/wholefoods.html,* July 2004; Whole Foods Market, Inc. Annual Report (Form 10-K), November 26, 2008, *www.sec.gov.*
31. Ronald Orol, "Whole Foods CEO John Mackey: Meeting Amazon Was Like 'Falling in Love.'" TheStreet.com, March 5, 2018.
32. Catherine Clifford. Whole Foods founder John Mackey on having Jeff Bezos as a boss: 'People had this wrong stereotype that the CEO is like a god.' CNBC.com, January 3, 2021.
33. Catherine Clifford. Whole Foods CEO John Mackey: Store managers could be making 'well over $100,000,' without a college degree. CNBC.com, November 5, 2020.
34. Catherine Clifford. "Whole Foods CEO John Mackey: Store managers could be making 'well over $100,000,' without a college degree." November 5, 2020. CNBC.com.
35. H. Mintzberg, "Crafting Strategy," *Harvard Business Review* (July–August 1970), pp. 66–75.
36. M. Brown, M. C. Sturman, and M. Simmering, "Compensation Policy and Organizational Performance: The Efficiency, Operational, and Financial Implications of Pay Levels and Pay Structure," *Academy of Management Journal* 46 (2003), pp. 752–762; Yoshio Yanadori and Janet Marler, "Compensation Strategy: Does Business Strategy Influence Compensation in High Technology Firms?" *Strategic Management Journal,* June 2006, pp. 559–570.
37. Timothy M. Gardner, "Interfirm Competition for Human Resources: Evidence from the Software Industry," *Academy of Management Journal* 48(2), 2005, pp. 237–256; H. Mintzberg, "Crafting Strategy," *Harvard Business Review* (July–August 1970), pp. 66–75.
38. S. Chatterjee, "Core Objectives: Clarity in Designing Strategy," *California Management Review* 47(2), 2005, pp. 33–49.
39. M. Bloom and G. Milkovich, "Strategic Perspectives on International Compensation and Reward Systems," in *Research and Theory in Strategic HRM: An Agenda for the Twenty-First Century,* ed. Pat Wright, et al. (Greenwich, CT: JAI Press, 1999); M. Bloom, G. Milkovich, and A. Mitra, "International Compensation: Learning from How Managers Respond to Variations in Local Host Contexts," *International Journal of Human Resource Management* (Special Issue, 2003); Allen D. Engle Sr. and Mark Mendenhall, "Transnational Roles and Transnational Rewards: Global Integration in Executive Compensation," presentation at International HR conference, Limerick, Ireland, June 2003; Paul Evans, Vlado Pucik, and Jean-Louis Barsoux, *The Global Challenge* (New York: McGraw-Hill, 2002); *Global Rewards: A Collection of Articles from WorldatWork* (Scottsdale, AZ: WorldatWork, 2005).
40. George Milkovich and Thomas A. Mahoney, "Human Resource Planning Models: A Perspective," *Human Resource Planning* 1(1) (1978), pp. 1–18.
41. Rosemary Batt, Alexander J. S. Colvin, and Jeffrey Keefe, "Employee Voice, Human Resource Practices, and Quit Rates: Evidence from the Telecommunications Industry," *Industrial and Labor Relations Review* 55(4), July 2002, pp. 573–594; A. Colvin, R. Batt, and H. Katz, "How High

Performance HR Practices and Workforce Unionization Affect Managerial Pay," *Personnel Psychology* 54 (2001), pp. 903–934; Paul Osterman, "The Wage Effects of High Performance Work Organization in Manufacturing," *Industrial and Labor Relations Review* (January 2006), pp. 187–204.

42. Study by Christopher K. Bart cited in Steven Greenhouse, "The Nation: Mission Statements; Words that Can't Be Set to Music," *The New York Times,* February 13, 2000.
43. https://www.jnj.com/credo.
44. See the website for Federation of European Employers, at *www.fedee.com.* Also, Watson Wyatt Worldwide, "Strategic Rewards: Managing through Uncertain Times," survey report (2001–2002).
45. Jason Shaw, Michelle Duffy, Atul Mitra, Daniel Lockhart, and Matthew Bowler, "Reactions to Merit Pay Increases: A Longitudinal Test of a Signal Sensitivity Perspective," *Journal of Applied Psychology* 88 (2003), pp. 538–544; Loretta Chao, "For Gen Xers, It's Work to Live," *The Wall Street Journal,* November 29, 2005, p. B6; Eduardo Porter, "Choice Is Good. Yes, No or Maybe?" *The New York Times,* March 27, 2005, p. WK12; Melissa Barringer and George Milkovich, "Employee Health Insurance Decisions in a Flexible Benefit Environment," *Human Resource Management* 35 (1996), pp. 293–315; M. P. Patterson, "Health Benefit Evolutions for the 21st Century: Vouchers and Other Innovations?" *Compensation and Benefits Review* 32(4), July/August 2000, pp. 6–14.
46. Hudson, *Rising Above the Average: Hudson's 2007 Compensation and Benefits Report,* https://us.hudson.com/Portals/US/documents/White%20Papers/us-whitepapers-comp-ben-2007.pdf. See also "Employee Job Satisfaction and Engagement: Revitalizing a Changing Workforce," Society for Human Resource Management, https://www.shrm.org/hr-today/trends-and-forecasting/research-and-surveys/Documents/2016-Employee-Job-Satisfaction-and-Engagement-Report.pdf.
47. Eduardo Porter, "Choice Is Good. Yes, No or Maybe?" *The New York Times,* March 27, 2005, p. WK12.
48. S. S. Iyengar, R. E. Wells, and B. Schwartz, "Doing Better but Feeling Worse: Looking for the 'Best' Job Undermines Satisfaction," *Psychological Science* 17(2), 2003, pp. 143–150; R. Chua and S. S. Iyengar, "Empowerment through Choice? A Critical Analysis of the Effects of Choice in Organizations," in *Research on Organizational Behavior,* ed. B. Shaw and M. Kramer (Oxford: Elsevier, 2006).
49. Karen Strossel, "Make My (Mother's) Day . . . ," *The Wall Street Journal,* May 12, 2006, p. A13; John Deckop, Kimberly Merriman, and Gary Blau, "Impact of Variable Risk Preferences on the Effectiveness of Control by Pay," *Journal of Occupational and Organizational Psychology* 77 (2004), pp. 63–80.
50. Morris M. Kleiner, Jonathan S. Leonard, and Adam M. Pilarski, "How Industrial Relations Affects Plant Performance: The Case of Commercial Aircraft Manufacturing," *Industrial and Labor Relations Review* 55(2), January 2002, pp. 195–218; Sean Karimi and Gangaram Singh, "Strategic Compensation: An Opportunity for Union Activism," *Compensation and Benefits Review* (March/April 2004), pp. 62–67; Henry S. Faber, "Union Success in Representation Elections: Why Does Unit Size Matter?" *Industrial and Labor Relations Review* 54(2), 2001, pp. 329–348.
51. Maria Sacchetti, "Teachers Study Merit Proposal," *Boston Globe*, August 8, 2005; Karla Dial, "Denver Voters Approve Merit Pay for Teachers," *School Reform News,* December 1, 2005.
52. Jeffrey McCracken, "Detroit's Symbol of Dysfunction: Paying Employees Not to Work," *The Wall Street Journal,* March 1, 2006, pp. A1, A12; Lauren Etter, "Is General Motors Unraveling?" *The Wall Street Journal,* April 8, 2006, p. A7; "GM Offers Huge Employee Buyout," Associated Press, March 22, 2006.
53. George Milkovich and Carolyn Milkovich, *Cases in Compensation,* 9th ed. (Santa Monica, CA: Milkovich, 2004), p. 8; Aaron Chatterji and David Levine, "Breaking Down the Wall of Codes: Evaluating Non-Financial Performance Measurement," *California Management Review* 48(2), Winter 2006, pp. 29–51.

54. W. Chan Kim and Renee Mauborgne, "Pursuing the Holy Grail of Clear Vision," *Financial Times,* August 6, 2002, p. 8; Robert S. Kaplan and David P. Norton, "Having Trouble with Your Strategy? Then Map It," *Harvard Business Review,* September–October 2000, pp. 167–176; S. Chatterjee, "Core Objectives: Clarity in Designing Strategy," *California Management Review* 47(2), 2005.

55. L. Bossidy, R. Charman, and C. Burck, *Execution: The Discipline of Getting Things Done* (New York: Crown Business Publishers, 2002); R. Preston McAffee, *Competitive Solutions: The Strategist's Toolkit* (Princeton, NJ: Princeton University Press, 2005).

56. J. Pfeffer, "When It Comes to 'Best Practices,' Why Do Smart Organizations Occasionally Do Dumb Things?" *Organizational Dynamics* 25 (1997), pp. 33–44; J. Pfeffer, *The Human Equation: Building Profits by Putting People First* (Boston: Harvard Business School Press, 1998); Barry Gerhart, Charlie Trevor, and Mary Graham, "New Directions in Employee Compensation Research," in *Research in Personnel and Human Resources Management,* vol. 14, ed. G. R. Ferris (Greenwich, CT: JAI Press, 1996), pp. 143–203.

57. Gerhart, B. & Feng, J. (2021). The Resource-Based View of the Firm, Human Resources, and Human Capital: Progress and Prospects. Journal of Management; Gerhart, B., Trevor, C. O., & Graham, M. E. 1996. New directions in compensation research: Synergies, risk, and survival. Research in Personnel and Human Resources Management, 14: 143–204.

58. Pfeffer, J. 1994. Competitive advantage through people: Unleashing the power of the workforce. Boston, MA: Harvard Business School Press.; Jewell, D., Jewell, S., & Kaufman, B. 2020. Designing and implementing high-performance work systems: Insights from consulting practice for academic researchers. Human Resource Management Review, forthcoming.

59. Gerhart, B. & Feng, J. (2021). The Resource-Based View of the Firm, Human Resources, and Human Capital: Progress and Prospects. *Journal of Management;* Becker, B. E., & Gerhart, B. 1996. The impact of human resource management on organizational performance: Progress and prospects. Academy of Management Journal, 39: 779–801.

60. Samir Raza, "Optimizing Human Capital Investments for Superior Shareholder Returns," *Valuation Issues,* 2006, *www.valuationissues.com;* M. Huselid and B. Becker, "Improving HR Analytical Literacy: Lessons from Moneyball," chap. 32 in M. Losey, S. Meisinger, and D. Ulrich, *The Future of Human Resource Management* (Hoboken, NJ: Wiley, 2005); Lindsay Scott, "Managing Labor Costs Using Pay-for-Performance," Lindsay Scott & Associates, Inc., *www.npktools.com,* 2006; Thomas Stewart, *Intellectual Capital: The New Wealth of Organizations* (New York: Currency, 1997); D. Scott, D. Morajda, and T. McMullen, "Evaluating Pay Program Effectiveness," *WorldatWork Journal,* First Quarter 2006; D. Scott, T. McMullen, and R. Sperling, "Evaluating Pay Program Effectiveness: A National Survey of Compensation and Human Resource Professionals," *WorldatWork Journal* 15(2), Second Quarter 2006, pp. 50–59.

61. Richard Donkin, "Measuring the Worth of Human Capital," *Financial Times,* November 7, 2002; Peter F. Drucker, "They're Not Employees, They're People," *Harvard Business Review,* February 2002, pp. 70–77; Stephen Gates, *Value at Work: The Risks and Opportunities of Human Capital Measurement and Reporting* (New York: Conference Board, 2002).

62. John Boudreau and Pete Ramstad, "Beyond Cost-per-Hire and Time to Fill: Supply-Chain Measurement for Staffing," Working Paper T04-16 (468) (Los Angeles, CA: Center for Effective Organizations, 2006).

63. Connie Willis, *Bellwether* (London: Bantam Books 1996); M. Gladwell, *The Tipping Point: The Next Big Thing* (Boston: Little, Brown, 2000).

64. J. Purcell, "Best Practices and Best Fit: Chimera or Cul-de-Sac?" *Human Resources Management Journal* 9(3) (1999), pp. 26–41.

65. B. Gerhart, "Pay Strategy and Firm Performance," in *Compensation in Organizations: Current Research and Practice,* ed. S. Rynes and B. Gerhart (San Francisco: Jossey-Bass, 2000); B. Gerhart and G. Milkovich, "Employee Compensation," in *Handbook of Industrial and Organization Psychology,* 3rd ed., ed. M. Dunnette and L. Hough (Palo Alto, CA: Consulting Psychologists Press, 1992).

66. P. K. Zingheim and J. R. Schuster, *Pay People Right!* (San Francisco: Jossey-Bass, 2000); J. Pfeffer, "Seven Practices of Successful Organizations," *California Management Review* 49(2), 1998, pp. 96–124; E. Lawler, *Rewarding Excellence* (San Francisco: Jossey-Bass, 2000).

67. Gerhart, B. & Feng, J. (in press). The Resource-Based View of the Firm, Human Resources, and Human Capital: Progress and Prospects. Journal of Management

68. Jason Shaw, Michelle Duffy, Atul Mitra, Daniel Lockhart, and Matthew Bowler, "Reactions to Merit Pay Increases: A Longitudinal Test of a Signal Sensitivity Perspective," *Journal of Applied Psychology* 88 (2003), pp. 538–544; M. Bloom and G. Milkovich, "Relationships Among Risk, Incentive Pay, and Organization Performance," *Academy of Management Journal* 41(3), 1998, pp. 283–297; Charlie O. Trevor and David L. Wazeter, "A Contingent View of Reactions to Objective Pay Conditions: Interdependence Among Pay Structure Characteristics and Pay Relative to Internal and External Referents," *Journal of Applied Psychology,* in press; Charlie Trevor, Barry Gerhart, and Greg Reilly, "Decoupling Explained and Unexplained Pay Dispersion to Predict Organizational Performance," presentation at Academy of Management meeting Atlanta, Georgia, August 11–16, 2006; Matthew C. Bloom, "The Performance Effects of Pay Structures on Individuals and Organizations," *Academy of Management Journal* 42(1), 1999, pp. 25–40; Mark Brown, Michael C. Sturman, and Marcia Simmering, "Compensation Policy and Organizational Performance: The Efficiency, Operational, and Financial Implications of Pay Levels and Pay Structure," *Academy of Management Journal* 46 (2003), pp. 752–762; E. P. Lazear, *Personnel Economics* (Cambridge, MA: MIT Press, 1995).

69. Gerhart, B. (2017). Incentives and pay for performance in the workplace. In *Advances in motivation science* (Vol. 4, pp. 91-140). Elsevier; Gerhart, B., Rynes, S. L., & Rynes, S. (2003). *Compensation: Theory, evidence, and strategic implications*. Sage.

70. Edilberto F. Montemayor, "Congruence between Pay Policy and Competitive Strategy in High-Performing Firms," *Journal of Management* 22(6), 1996, pp. 889–908; L. R. Gomez-Mejia and D. B. Balkin, *Compensation, Organization Strategy, and Firm Performance* (Cincinnati: Southwestern, 1992); Trevor, C. O., Reilly, G., & Gerhart, B. (2012). Reconsidering pay dispersion's effect on the performance of interdependent work: Reconciling sorting and pay inequality. *Academy of Management Journal*, 55(3), 585–610.

71. Mark A. Huselid, Brian E. Becker, and Richard W. Beatty, *The Workforce Scorecard* (Boston: Harvard Business School Press, 2005); David Ulrich and Wayne Brockbank, *The HR Value Proposition* (Boston: Harvard Business School Press, 2005); Brian Becker, Mark Huselid, and Dave Ulrich, *The HR Scorecard: Linking People, Strategy, and Performance* (Boston: Harvard Business School Press, 2001); Rosemary Batt, Virginia Doellgast, and Hyunji Kwon, *The U.S. Call Center Industry 2004: National Benchmarking Report–Strategy, HR Practices, and Performance* (Ithaca, NY: Industrial and Labor Relations School, 2005); D. Scott, D. Morajda, and T. McMullen, "Evaluating Pay Program Effectiveness," *WorldatWork Journal,* First Quarter 2006; and D. Scott, T. McMullen, and R. Sperling, "Evaluating Pay Program Effectiveness: A National Survey of Compensation and Human Resource Professionals," *WorldatWork Journal* 15(2), Second Quarter 2006, pp. 50–59; B. Becker and M. Huselid, "High Performance Work Systems and Firm Performance: A Synthesis of Research and Managerial Implications," in *Research in Personnel and Human Resources*, ed. G. Ferris (Greenwich, CT: JAI Press, 1997); Paul Osterman, "The Wage Effects of High Performance Work Organization in Manufacturing," *Industrial and Labor Relations Review*, January 2006, pp. 187–204.

72. Deepak K. Datta, James P. Guthrie, and Patrick M. Wright, "Human Resource Management and Labor Productivity: Does Industry Matter?" *Academy of Management Journal* 48(5), pp. 135–145.

73. K. Murphy and M. Jensen, "It's Not How Much You Pay, But How," *Harvard Business Review,* May–June 1990, pp. 138–149.

74. B. Gerhart and G. Milkovich, "Organization Differences in Managerial Compensation and Financial Performance," *Academy of Management Journal* 90(33), pp. 663–691.

75. Barry Gerhart and Sara Rynes, *Compensation: Theory, Evidence, and Strategic Implications* (Thousand Oaks, CA: Sage, 2003).

76. Bartolome Deya-Tortella, Luis R. Gomez-Mejia, Julio O. DeCastro, and Robert M. Wiseman, "Incentive Alignment or Perverse Incentives?" *Management Research* 3(2), 2005; Stephane Renaud, Sylvie St-Onge, and Michel Magnan, "The Impact of Stock Purchase Plan Participation on Workers' Individual Cash Compensation," *Industrial Relations,* January 2004, pp. 120–147; Ingrid Smithey Fulmer, Barry Gerhart, and Kimberly Scott, "Are the 100 Best Better? An Empirical Investigation of the Relationship between Being a 'Great Place to Work' and Firm Performance," *Personnel Psychology* 56 (2003), pp. 965–993; S. Werner and H. Tosi, "Other People's Money: The Effects of Ownership on Compensation Strategy," *Academy of Management Journal* 38(6), pp. 1672–1691.

77. Rosemary Batt, Virginia Doellgast, and Hyunji Kwon, *The U.S. Call Center Industry 2004: National Benchmarking Report–Strategy, HR Practices, and Performance* (Ithaca, NY: Industrial and Labor Relations School, 2005); Rosemary Batt, Alexander J. S. Colvin, and Jeffrey Keefe, "Employee Voice, Human Resource Practices, and Quit Rates: Evidence from the Telecommunications Industry," *Industrial and Labor Relations Review* 55(4), July 2002, pp. 573–594; N. Bloom and J. Van Reenen, "Discussion Paper No. 716," London School of Economics, March 2006.

78. Brian Becker and Mark Huselid, "High Performance Work Systems and Firm Performance: A Synthesis of Research and Managerial Implications," in *Research in Personnel and Human Resource Management,* ed. G. R. Ferris (Greenwich, CT: JAI Press, 1997).

79. Eric Rosenbaum. "Apple's new executive bonus formula is designed for the fast-changing world we live in." CNBC.com, January 16, 2021. Apple Proxy Statement, January 5, 2021. www.sec.gov (Form DEF14a). Starbucks Proxy Statement, January 8, 2021. www.sec.gov (Form DEF14a). Heather Haddon. Starbucks Ties Executive Pay to 2025 Diversity Targets. Wall Street Journal, October 14, 2020. WSJ.com.

Part II
Internal Alignment: Determining The Structure

According to the U.S. Department of Labor's Bureau of Labor Statistics (BLS), Occupational Employment Statistics, there are large differences in pay as a function of position/job. The average annual pay for a licensed practical nurse working at a hospital is $47,310.[1] For a registered nurse working at a hospital, it is $81,680. For physicians and surgeons, median annual pay for those in primary care, specifically internal medicine, is $210,960, compared to $251,650 for a specialist, specifically a surgeon. Another physician compensation survey by Medscape reports that the average compensation is $243,000 in primary care and $346,000 for a specialist, including $357,000 in emergency medicine, and $511,000 in orthopedics.[2] Speaking of visits to the emergency room and orthopedics, let's look a bit at sports. In soccer (or what most countries outside of the United States call football), we see that position once again matters. When the Los Angeles Galaxy won the MLS Cup several years ago, their highest-paid forward, Robbie Keane, earned $4.5 million and their highest-paid midfielder, Landon Donovan, earned $4.5 million. What about the highest-paid defender on the Galaxy? That was Omar Gonzalez at $1,000,000 (a major increase from the $197,000 he earned a few years before that). A look at the 10 highest paid players in MLS that year found seven forwards, three midfielders, and no defenders. The Galaxy did not win the championship last year. The Columbus Crew did. Interestingly, the top-paid defender for the Crew, Jonathan Mensah, earned $800,000, more than the top-paid midfielder, Darlington Nagbe at $665,000 and more than all but two of the forwards.[3] Did the Columbus Crew just discover a new strategy on position differentials that is the path to success in soccer? (Or, will the L.A. Galaxy model prove superior? Or, maybe the L.A. Galaxy model fits the L.A. market and the Columbus Crew model fits the Columbus market?) Why does position matter so much when it comes to pay? Why don't hospitals and soccer teams just pay all types of "jobs" the same? In the examples above, can one get promoted to earn more money? For example, can a registered nurse become a physician? Can a defender move up to midfielder and then to forward? What about at law firms and consulting firms? Can an associate become a partner? If so, what is the payoff?

EXHIBIT II.1 The Pay Model

POLICIES	TECHNIQUES				OBJECTIVES
INTERNAL ALIGNMENT	Work Analysis	Descriptions	Evaluation/ Certification	INTERNAL STRUCTURE	EFFICIENCY • Performance • Quality • Customer and Stockholder • Cost
COMPETITIVENESS	Market Definitions	Surveys	Policy Lines	PAY STRUCTURE	FAIRNESS
CONTRIBUTIONS	Seniority Based	Incentives	Merit Guidelines	PAY FOR PERFORMANCE	COMPLIANCE
MANAGEMENT	Cost	Communication	Change	EVALUATION	ETHICS

Chapter **Three**
Defining Internal Alignment

Chapter Outline

> For the kingdom of heaven is like unto a man that is an householder, which went out early in the morning to hire labourers into his vineyard. And when he had agreed with the labourers for a penny a day, he sent them into his vineyard. And he went out about the third hour, and saw others standing idle in the marketplace, And said unto them; Go ye also into the vineyard, and whatsoever is right I will give you. And they went their way. Again he went out about the sixth and ninth hour, and did likewise. And about the eleventh hour he went out, and found others standing idle, and saith unto them, Why stand ye here all the day idle? They say unto him, Because no man hath hired us. He saith unto them, Go ye also into the vineyard; and whatsoever is right, that shall ye receive. So when even was come, the lord of the vineyard saith unto his steward, Call the labourers, and give them their hire, beginning from the last unto the first. And when they came that were hired about the eleventh hour, they received every man a penny. But when the first came, they supposed that they should have received more; and they likewise received every man a penny. And when they had received it, they murmured against the goodman of the house, Saying, These last have wrought but one hour, and thou hast made them equal unto us, which have borne the burden and heat of the day. But he answered one of them, and said, Friend, I do thee no wrong: didst not thou agree with me for a penny? Take that thine is, and go thy way: I will give unto this last, even as unto thee.[4]

Matthew's parable raises age-old questions about internal alignment and pay structures within a single organization.[5] The laborers felt that those who "have borne the burden and heat of the day" should be paid more than those who worked fewer hours. But apparently the householder was looking at an individual's needs. He ignored (1) the content of the work, (2) the skills and knowledge required to perform it, and (3) its relative value for achieving the organization's objectives. These three are common bases for today's pay structure. And if the procedures to determine the structure are not acceptable to the parties involved, today's employees murmur, too. That murmuring translates into turnover, an unwillingness to try new technologies, even indifference to the quality of the grapes or the customer's satisfaction with them. This chapter examines internal alignment and its consequences.

JOBS AND COMPENSATION

As we just saw in the **Part II** Introduction, pay varies significantly according to the job. We will see in this chapter that organizations design their pay structures around jobs and job levels and that, in many organizations, an employee's pay (and by implication, their pay growth over time) depends on both the nature of the job and the job level (and thus promotion rate).[6]

COMPENSATION STRATEGY: INTERNAL ALIGNMENT

Setting objectives is our first issue in a strategic approach to pay. Our second issue, **internal alignment,** addresses relationships *inside* the organization. Matthew doesn't tell us how the work in the vineyard was organized. Perhaps laborers worked in teams: some trimmed while others tied the vines. Does trimming require more judgment than tying? How do the responsibilities and pay of the trimmer relate to the responsibilities and pay of the tier, the householder's cook, or the steward? Internal alignment addresses the logic underlying these relationships. The relationships form a pay structure that should *support the organization strategy, support the work flow,* and *motivate behavior toward organization objectives.*

> **Internal alignment,** often called *internal equity,* refers to the pay relationships among different jobs/skills/competencies within a single organization.[7]

Exhibit 3.1 shows a structure for engineering work at a division of Lockheed Martin, the world's largest defense contractor. Lockheed also builds rockets, shuttles, and Mars rovers for NASA. Lockheed has the contract to build the next shuttle that will take crewed flights back to the moon and on to Mars. The six levels in Lockheed's structure range from entry to consultant. You can see the relationships in the descriptions of each level. Decisions on how to pay each level create a **pay structure.**

EXHIBIT 3.1 Engineering Structure at Lockheed Martin

Engineer
Limited use of basic principles and concepts. Develops solutions to limited problems. Closely supervised.

Senior Engineer
Full use of standard principles and concepts. Provides solutions to a variety of problems. Under general supervision.

Systems Engineer
Wide applications of principles and concepts, plus working knowledge of other related disciplines. Provides solutions to a wide variety of difficult problems. Solutions are imaginative, thorough, and practicable. Works under only very general direction.

Lead Engineer
Applies extensive expertise as a generalist or specialist. Develops solutions to complex problems that require the regular use of ingenuity and creativity. Work is performed without appreciable direction. Exercises considerable latitude in determining technical objectives of assignment.

Advisor Engineer
Applies advanced principles, theories, and concepts. Contributes to the development of new principles and concepts. Works on unusually complex problems and provides solutions that are highly innovative and ingenious. Works under consultative direction toward predetermined long-range goals. Assignments are often self-initiated.

Consultant Engineer
Exhibits an exceptional degree of ingenuity, creativity, and resourcefulness. Applies and/or develops highly advanced technologies, scientific principles, theories, and concepts. Develops information that extends the existing boundaries of knowledge in a given field. Often acts independently to uncover and resolve problems associated with the development and implementation of operational programs.

Pay structure refers to the array of pay rates for different work or skills within a single organization. The *number of levels*, the *differentials* in pay between the levels, and the *criteria* used to determine those differences describe the structure.

Supports Organization Strategy

Lockheed decided that six levels of engineering work would support the company's strategy of researching, designing, and developing advanced technology systems.

Supports Work Flow

Work flow refers to the process by which goods and services are delivered to the customer. The pay structure ought to support the efficient flow of that work and the design of the organization.[8] For example, financial service firms in the United States traditionally offer investment advice and products through client centers. At Merrill Lynch, customer associates used to take all calls from clients or new prospects and route them to financial advisors (FAs). If the caller wanted a specific transaction, such as purchasing a stock, mutual fund, or certificate of deposit, the customer associate passed the information on to an FA who was legally certified to make the purchase. No one at Merrill Lynch "owned" a client. Personal long-term relationships were not emphasized.

Nevertheless, Merrill Lynch recognized that its clients' investment needs varied, depending on their net worth, among other factors. Ultra-high-net-worth individuals with more than $25 million to invest were not interested in CDs or stock transactions. They wanted advice specific to their circumstances from someone they knew and trusted. And instead of waiting for calls from these customers, the FAs should initiate calls to them. That would help build the long-term relationship around adding value to clients' investments. Merrill Lynch also noticed that meeting the needs of these high-net-worth clients was very profitable (i.e., higher margins on the fees and the products).[9] So Merrill Lynch redesigned the flow of work to better reflect its clients' needs–and increase its profits.

Merrill Lynch divided its clients into five groups, based on net worth: investor, emerging affluent, affluent, high net worth, and ultra-high net worth (the "whales"). Then it revamped its job structure to match. The work of FA was divided into five job levels, ranging from assistant vice president, investments (AVPI), to senior vice president, investments (SVPI). These new job levels were defined by the amount of client assets the advisor manages and the expertise and knowledge the advisor possesses. Building those long-term relationships with the "whales" requires complex interactions. The smaller ("investor") clients are still buying stocks, bonds, and CDs through the FA centers. Newly trained and experienced FAs are now building relationships with individuals in the various client groups. In addition to the FA centers, Merrill Lynch also created private banking hubs to serve clients with very high net worth.

To support the new FA job structure, Merrill Lynch designed a new pay structure. The differential in base pay between the top-level (the SVPI) and the entry-level FA is about 8 to 1. Aggressive bonus and stock incentives are a substantial part of the new pay structure. The pay difference between entry-level FAs, AVPIs, and SVPIs was a major issue–just as it is for Lockheed engineers, health care workers, soccer players, and the laborers in the vineyard.

Motivates Behavior

Internal pay structures are part of the network of returns discussed in **Chapter 1:** pay increases for promotions, for more challenging work, and for greater responsibility as employees move up in the structure. The challenge is to design structures that will engage people to help achieve organization objectives. Merrill Lynch FAs work to meet the specific needs of their clients by building long-term relationships. Lockheed engineers work together to share knowledge with each other and with their customers. Is taking on a "bigger" job worth it? Does it pay off to take more training to get promoted? It will in a well-designed pay structure.

The structure ought to make clear the relationship between each job and the organization's objectives. This is an example of **"line-of-sight."** Employees should be able to "see" the links between their work, the work of others, and the organization's objectives. And the structure ought to be fair to employees. The vineyard owner's internal pay structure may have been aligned with his business strategy, but the employee dissatisfaction raises concerns about its fairness to employees.

STRUCTURES VARY AMONG ORGANIZATIONS

An internal pay structure can be defined by (1) the number of *levels* of work, (2) the pay *differentials* between the levels, and (3) the *criteria or bases* used to determine those levels and differentials.

Number of Levels

One feature of any pay structure is its hierarchical nature: the number of levels and reporting relationships. Some are more hierarchical, with multiple levels; others are compressed, with few levels.[10] The stated goal of GE Healthcare is to provide "transformational medical technologies and services that are shaping a new age of patient care." One of their many product lines is magnetic resonance imaging (MRI). In comparison to Lockheed's six levels for engineering alone (**Exhibit 3.1**), GE Healthcare uses five broad levels, described in **Exhibit 3.2**, to cover all professional and executive work, including engineering. GE Healthcare would probably fit the Lockheed Martin structure into two or three levels.

EXHIBIT 3.2 **Career Bands at GE Healthcare**

GE Band	Nature of Work
Associate	Front line, administrative, and secretarial
Professional	Developing professional
Lead Professional	Team leader, supervisor, or experienced individual contributor
Senior Professional	Manager or seasoned professional
Executive	Key member of management team and/or individual contributor with major impact on business
	Career band is determined by job scope, accountability, and skills

Source: GE Healthcare.

Differentials

The pay differences among levels are referred to as **differentials.** If we assume that an organization has a compensation budget of a set amount to distribute among its employees, there are a number of ways it can do so. It can divide the budget by the number of employees to give everyone the same amount. The Moosewood Restaurant in Ithaca, New York, adopts this approach. But few organizations in the world are that egalitarian. In most, pay varies among employees.[11] Work that requires more knowledge or skills, is performed under unpleasant working conditions, or adds more value is usually paid more.[12] **Exhibit 3.3** shows the percent differentials (on the right vertical axis) traditionally attached to Lockheed Martin's engineering structure. (Actual pay levels are now somewhat higher for the entire structure due to inflation.) Northrup Grumman uses a similar six-level engineering structure with similar differentials. One intention of these differentials is to motivate people to strive for promotion to a higher-paying level. As **Exhibit 3.3** shows, the same basic structure, in terms of percent differentials, can be paired with different pay-level policies. For example, although a lead engineer gets paid more in the structure on the right, the percent differential between the lead engineer and systems engineer is the same in both (28 percent).

Criteria: Content and Value

Work content and its value are the most common bases for determining internal structures. **Content** refers to the work performed in a job and how it gets done (tasks, behaviors, knowledge required, etc.). **Value** refers to the worth of the work: its relative contribution to the organization objectives. A structure based on content typically ranks jobs on skills required, complexity of tasks, problem solving, and/or responsibility. In contrast, a structure based on the value of the work focuses on the *relative contribution* of these skills, tasks, and responsibilities to the organization's goals. While the resulting structures may be the same, there are important differences. In addition to relative contribution, external market value (i.e., what competitors pay for this job) may also be included. Or it may include rates agreed upon through collective bargaining, or even legislated rates (minimum wage). In centrally planned economies such as Cuba, job values in all organizations are set by a government agency. Following the now-discarded approaches of the former Soviet Union and China, Cuba's government dictates a universal structure: 8 levels for industrial workers, 16 levels for technical and engineering work, and 26 levels for government employees.

Use Value and Exchange Value

Use value reflects the value of goods or services an employee produces in a job. **Exchange value** is whatever wage the employer and employee agree on for a job. Think about IBM software engineers living in Bangalore, Kiev, and Purchase, New York. Their work content is very similar in all three locations. Now think about them working together on the same project–same company, same job content, same internal job. They have the same use value. Wage rates in Bangalore and Kiev are a lot lower than in Purchase, New York. The jobs' exchange value varies.[13] For promotions, IBM treats these jobs as being at the same level in the structure. But the external markets in India, Ukraine, and the United States yield very different pay rates.

The difference between exchange value and use value also surfaces when one firm acquires another. IBM's acquisition of the consulting business of PricewaterhouseCoopers (PWC), where consultants were the lifeblood of the business, is a case in point. At the time, IBM was moving from being a computer company to becoming a provider of information technology solutions whose applications were broader than the IT department. PWC consultants could help IBM's marketing teams engage with clients at a higher organization level. The use value of the PWC consultants within IBM differed from their use value within PWC (how they contributed to IBM or PWC objectives). So, similar marketing jobs in two different companies may be valued differently based on how they contribute to organization objectives. Alternatively, the same work content in the same company (IBM's software engineers) may have different exchange value based on different geographies.

Job- and Person-Based Structures

A **job-based structure** relies on the work content–tasks, behaviors, responsibilities. A **person-based structure** shifts the focus to the employee: the *skills, knowledge,* or *competencies* the employee possesses, whether or not they are used in the employee's particular job. The engineering structure at Lockheed Martin (**Exhibit 3.1**) uses the work performed as the criterion. GE Healthcare (**Exhibit 3.2**) uses the individual employees' competencies/knowledge required at each level of work.

EXHIBIT 3.3 **Pay Structure (for Engineering) at Lockheed Martin, under Two Alternative Pay-Level Policies**

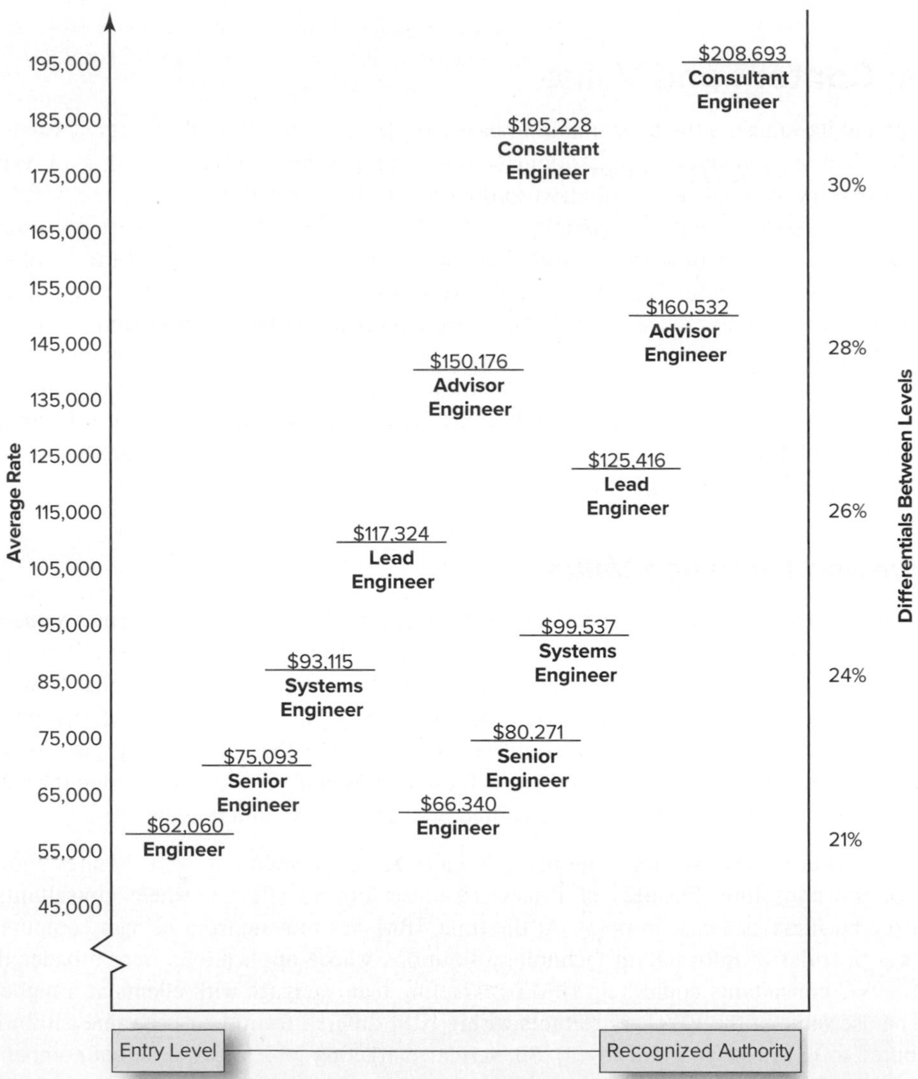

In the real workplace, it is often hard to describe a job without reference to the jobholder's knowledge and skills. Conversely, it is hard to define a person's job-related knowledge or competencies without referring to work content. So rather than a job- *or* person-based structure, reality includes both job *and* person.

WHAT SHAPES INTERNAL STRUCTURES?

The major factors that shape internal structures are shown in **Exhibit 3.4**. We categorize them as *external* and *organization* factors, even though they are connected and interact. Exactly how they interact is not always well understood. As we discuss the factors, we will also look at various theories.[14]

Economic Pressures

Adam Smith was an early advocate of letting economic market forces influence pay structures. He was the first to ascribe both an exchange value and a use value to human resources. Smith faulted the new technologies associated with the Industrial Revolution for increasing the use value of labor without a corresponding increase in exchange value (i.e., higher wages).

EXHIBIT 3.4 What Shapes Internal Structures?

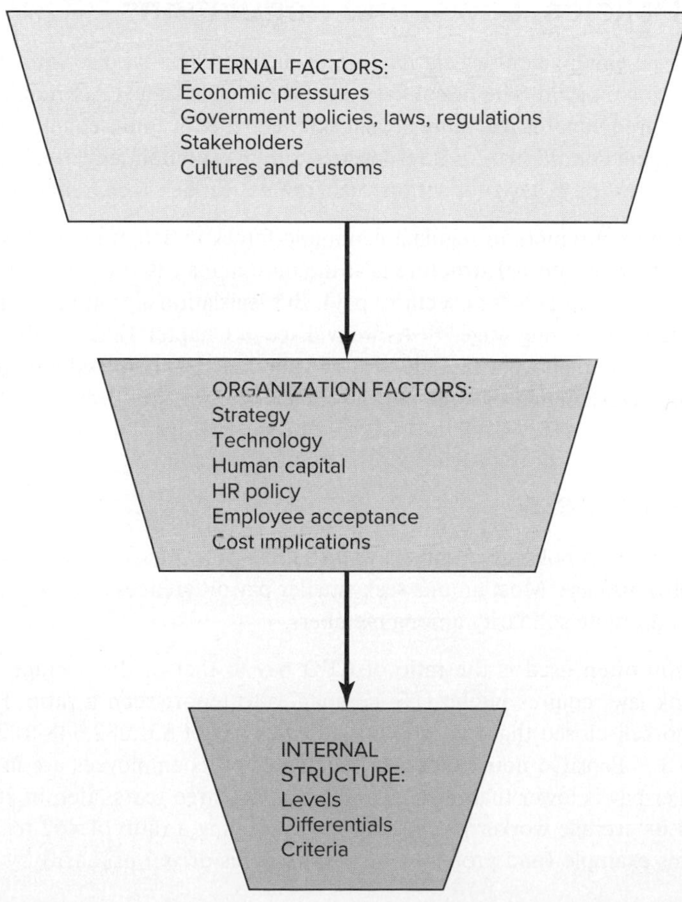

Karl Marx took this criticism even further.[15] He said that employers unfairly pocketed the **surplus value** created by the difference between use and exchange value. He urged workers to overthrow capitalistic systems to become owners themselves and reap the full use value of their labor.

A countering theory put forth in the last half of the 19th century, **marginal productivity,** says that employers do in fact pay use value.[16] Unless an employee can produce a value equal to the value received in wages, it will not be worthwhile to hire that worker. One job is paid more or less than another because of differences in relative productivity of the job and/or differences in how much a consumer values the output. In the short run especially, interesting things can happen. For example, some advanced practice nurses with extensive training (specifically, nurse anesthetists) now earn an average of $189,190 per year, which is more than some primary care doctors. These nurses earn less than physician anesthesiologists, $271,440 (an alternative survey estimate is $398,000), but can perform some of the same tasks.[17] Not surprisingly, they are in high demand. Surgeons may be fine with the situation because it removes a possible constraint on being able to do surgery. Hence, differences in skill and productivity provide a rationale for the internal pay structure.

In addition to supply and demand for labor, supply and demand for products and services also affect internal structures.[18] Turbulent changes, either in competitors' products/services (as in the rise of online shopping) or in customers' tastes (as in the popularity of electric vehicles), force organizations to redesign work flow and force employees to continuously learn new skills. Unpredictable external conditions require pay structures that support agile organizations and flexible people.[19]

Government Policies, Laws, and Regulations

In the United States, equal employment legislation forbids pay systems that discriminate on the basis of gender, race, religion, or national origin. The Equal Pay Act and the Civil Rights Act require "equal pay for equal work," with work considered equal if it requires equal skill, equal effort, and equal responsibility and is performed under equal working conditions. An internal structure may contain any number of levels, with differentials of any size, as long as the criteria for setting them are not gender, race, religion, or national origin.

Much pay-related legislation attempts to regulate economic forces to achieve social welfare objectives. The most obvious place to affect an internal structure is at the minimums (minimum-wage legislation) and maximums (special reporting requirements for executive pay). But legislation also aims at the differentials. A contemporary U.S. example is the "living wage."[20] As we will see in Chapter 17, a number of U.S. cities require minimum hourly wage rates well above what federal law requires. The anticipated outcome of such legislation is a flatter, more compressed structure of wage rates in society.

External Stakeholders

Unions, stockholders, and even political groups have a stake in how internal pay structures are determined. Unions are the most obvious case. Most unions seek smaller pay differences among jobs and seniority-based promotions as a way to promote solidarity among members.

One specific comparison often used is the ratio of CEO pay to that of the average or entry-level worker. Indeed, the Dodd-Frank law requires public U.S. companies to report such a ratio. For example, PepsiCo in its first required report disclosed that the ratio of its CEO's pay of $31,082,648 to its average worker pay of $47,801 was 650 to 1.[21] PepsiCo noted that more than half of its employees are in developing/emerging economies where worker pay is lower than in the United States. Three years later, in 2021, Pepsi's CEO was paid $21,486,692 and its average worker pay was $46,546, yielding a ratio of 462 to 1.[22] Thus, the change in the CEO ratio in this example (and probably in most cases) is driven primarily by changes in CEO pay.

Looking at averages across companies, estimates vary by what data are used, but they range from CEO pay that is 110 times to over 500 times the pay for manufacturing jobs.[23] The AFL-CIO website (**https://aflcio.org/paywatch**) has a tool called Executive Pay Watch. It reports an average CEO-to-worker pay ratio of 264 to 1 (down from 347 to 1, three years ago). The degree to which employees compare their pay to that of their CEO is not known, as no systematic data have been reported.

Cultures and Customs

One former radio show host defined culture by what songs we know in common–camp songs, religious hymns, the big hits of the year when we were 15. A General Mills executive says culture is the foods we eat. A more academic definition of culture is "the mental programming for processing information that people share in common."[24] People who share a mind-set might agree on what size pay differential is fair. In ancient Greece, Plato declared that societies are strongest when the richest earn a maximum of four times the lowest pay. Aristotle favored a five-times limit. In 1942, President Franklin Roosevelt proposed a maximum wage: a 100 percent tax on all income above 10 times the minimum wage.

Historians note that in 14th-century western Europe, the Christian church endorsed a **"just wage" doctrine,** which supported the existing class structure. The doctrine was an effort to end the economic and social chaos resulting from the death of one-third of the population from plague. The resulting shortage of workers gave ordinary people power to demand higher wages, much to the dismay of church and state. Market forces such as skills shortages (higher exchange value) were explicitly denied as appropriate determinants of pay structures. Today, advocates of the living wage are trying to change societal judgments about what wage is just.

Even today, cultural factors play a role in shaping pay structures. Many traditional Japanese employers place heavy emphasis on experience in their internal pay structures. But pressures from global competitors plus an aging workforce have made age-based pay structures very expensive. Consequently, some Japanese employers are shifting older employees to lower-paying business units, emphasizing performance and downplaying seniority.[25] (This change is particularly irksome; as the authors have grown older, the wisdom of basing pay on age has become more and more obvious to us!)

Organization Strategy

You have already read how organization strategies influence internal pay structures. The belief is that pay structures that are not aligned with the organization strategy may become obstacles to the organization's success. However, aligned structures today may become an obstacle tomorrow. So aligned, yet adaptable, may be required.

Organization Human Capital

Human capital–the education, experience, knowledge, abilities, and skills required to perform the work–is a major influence on internal structures.[26] The greater the value added by the skills and experience, the more pay those skills will command. Lockheed's structure pays consultant engineers more than lead or senior engineers because the human capital required in the consultant engineer job brings a greater return to Lockheed. It is more crucial to Lockheed's success.

Organization Work Design

Technology used in producing goods and services influences the *organizational design,* the *work* to be performed, and the *skills/knowledge* required to perform the work. The technology required to produce precision military hardware differs from that used to develop and manufacture plastics. These differences contribute to the different structures observed at Lockheed and GE Healthcare.

Multiple structures often exist within the same organization for different types of work. For example, Northrup Grumman has supervisory, engineering, technical, administrative, and nonexempt structures, each having five to six base-pay groupings/levels.

The design of organizations is undergoing profound changes. A lot of people who work in organizations are not employees of these organizations. (See the last part of Chapter 13 and the section, Employee or Independent Contractor?, in Chapter 17.) They may be employed by either a supplier (e.g., an IT services supplier such as IBM or Accenture) or perhaps a *temporary* work supplier (e.g., Allegis Group). Or they may be working under a temporary contract for a limited amount of time or on a limited project. The security guards, software engineers, or accountants may be supplied by **outsourcing** specialists. Pay for these employees is based on the internal structure of their home employer (e.g., IBM or Accenture) rather than that of the workplace at which they are currently located. Another major work design change is **delayering.**[27] Entire levels of work have disappeared. Just weeks after arriving at Hewlett Packard, its then new CEO Mark Hurd began hearing complaints about HP's sluggish response to customer needs. He discovered that internal organization layers were delaying responses. HP cut levels of management from 11 to 8 and customers immediately applauded the reduced response time.[28] Likewise, when Satya Nadella became CEO at Microsoft, he announced job cuts, but not just to cut costs, but also to change how decisions got made. In a memo to employees, he explained that "work simplification" was a driving force because of the need to "become more agile and move faster." As part of that, "we plan to have fewer layers of management, both top down and sideways, to accelerate the flow of information and decision making." That would happen by "flattening" the hierarchy and "increasing the span of control (i.e., increasing the number direct reports) of people managers."[29] Thus, delayering can cut unnecessary, noncontributing work, cutting costs and getting things done faster and better. It can also add work to other jobs, enlarging them. Through the use of self-managed work teams in production work, entire levels of supervisory jobs are removed and the responsibility for more decisions is delegated to the teams.[30] This will change a job's value and the job structure. Importantly, keep in mind that organizations often "iterate" back and forth, moving toward decentralization (as in the examples above), but then often moving back toward more centralization (and control) at other times. A term that is used to describe an especially strong philosophy of decentralization, lack of management hierarchy, and strong autonomy for employees is holocracy.[31] Again, the organization work design that is most effective will depend on the organization and its strategy.[32]

Overall HR Policies

The organization's other human resource policies also influence internal pay structures. Most organizations tie money to promotions in order to induce employees to apply for higher-level positions.[33] If an organization has more levels, it can offer more promotions, but there may be smaller pay differences between levels. The belief is that more frequent promotions (even without significant pay increases) offer a sense of "career progress" to employees.[34]

Internal Labor Markets: Combining External and Organization Factors

Internal labor markets combine both external and organizational factors. Internal labor markets consist of the rules and procedures that (1) determine the pay for the different jobs within a single organization and (2) allocate employees among those different jobs.[35] In the organization depicted in **Exhibit 3.5**, individuals are recruited only for entry-level jobs (an engineer would be hired right out of college; a senior engineer would have a few years' experience). They are later promoted or transferred to other jobs inside the organization. Because the employer competes in the external market for people to fill these **entry jobs,** their pay must be high enough to attract a pool of qualified applicants. In contrast, pay for jobs filled via transfer and promotions is connected to external market forces, but the connection is less direct. External markets are dominant influences on pay for entry jobs. However, the fact that external markets' influence on nonentry jobs is less direct does not mean it is not important.[36]

EXHIBIT 3.5 **Illustration of an Internal Labor Market**

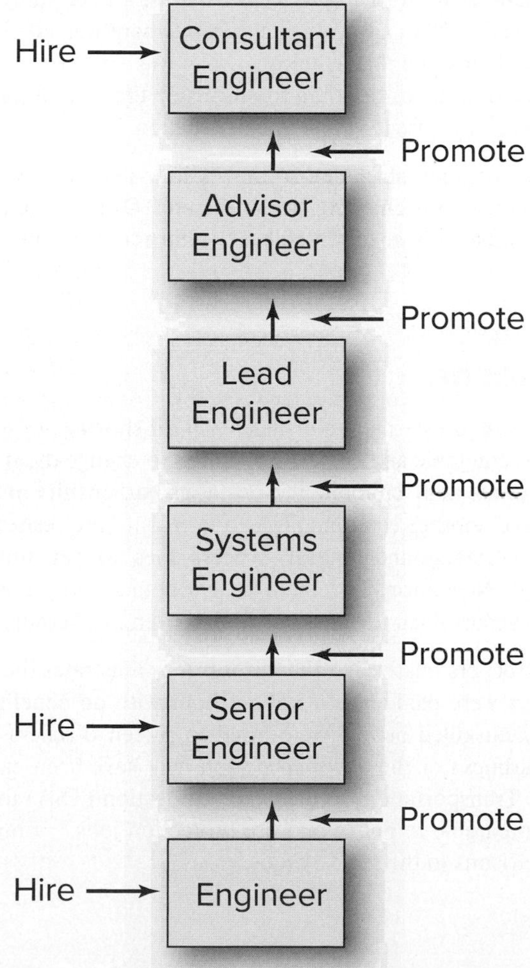

Employee Acceptance and Perceived Fairness

Employees judge the fairness of their pay through comparisons with the compensation paid to others for work related in some fashion to their own.[37] Accordingly, an important factor influencing the internal pay structure is its *acceptability to the employees involved.*[38] Employees make multiple pay comparisons to assess the fairness of an internal pay structure. They compare both with other jobs in the same internal structure and with the pay for their job in the external market (i.e., at competing employers).[39]

Two sources of fairness are important: the procedures for determining the pay structure, called **procedural justice;** and the results of those procedures–the pay structure itself–called **distributive justice.**

Suppose you are given a ticket for speeding. *Procedural justice* refers to the process by which a decision is reached: the right to an attorney, the right to an impartial judge, and the right to receive a copy of the arresting officer's statement. *Distributive justice* refers to the fairness of the decision: guilty. Researchers report that employees' perceptions of procedural fairness significantly influence their acceptance of the results; employees and managers are more willing to accept low pay if they believe that the way this result was obtained was fair. This research also suggests that pay procedures are more likely to be perceived as fair (1) if they are consistently applied to all employees, (2) if employees participated in the process, (3) if appeals procedures are included, and (4) if the data used are accurate. Nevertheless, a later study raises a question about the usefulness of employee participation.[40] In a low-wage company, there was no connection between employee participation and pay fairness. It may be that employees' pay was so low that no amount of participation could overcome their dissatisfaction. So rather than tossing aside the idea of participation, it may be that in extreme cases (very low wages) a pay raise may trump participation.

Applied to internal structures, procedural justice addresses how design and administration decisions are made and whether procedures are applied in a consistent manner. Distributive justice addresses whether the actual pay differences among employees are acceptable. We return to distributive justice later in this chapter when we discuss equity theory.

Pay Structures Change

Pay structures change in response to external factors such as skill shortages. Over time, distorted pay differences may become accepted as equitable and customary; efforts to change them are resisted. Thus, pay structures established for organizational and economic reasons at an earlier time may be maintained for cultural or political reasons. It may take another economic jolt to overcome the resistance. Then new norms form around the new structure. This "change-and-congeal" process does not yet support the continuous changes occurring in today's economy.[41] New norms for employee acceptance will probably need to include recognition that people must become accustomed to constant change, even in internal pay relationships.

The pay for airport security screeners relative to other airport jobs illustrates the change-and-congeal process. Prior to 9/11, airport screeners were paid about $5.50 an hour with no benefits. Recent immigrants, some undocumented, and relatively unskilled people were hired to screen travelers and their luggage. The people working at the airport Starbucks or the newspaper shop may have been earning more than the screeners. After the 9/11 attack, the Transportation Security Administration (TSA) took over airport security and screening. Wages are now comparable to police and fire protection jobs.[42] Employees in other airport jobs have had to revise their comparisons to the security jobs.[43]

STRATEGIC CHOICES IN DESIGNING INTERNAL STRUCTURES

Aligned pay structures support the way the work gets done, fit the organization's business strategy, and are fair to employees. Greater internal alignment–fit–is more likely to lead to success. Misaligned structures become obstacles. They may still motivate employee behavior, but it may be undesirable behavior. Wayne Knight's computer programmer character (Dennis Dedry) might never have stolen dinosaur embryos in the movie *Jurassic Park* if he had been given the pay raise he felt he deserved.

But what does it mean to fit or tailor the pay structure to be internally aligned? Two strategic choices are involved: (1) how specifically tailored to the organization's design and work flow to make the structure and (2) how to distribute pay throughout the levels in the structure.

Tailored versus Loosely Coupled

A low-cost, customer-focused business strategy such as that followed by McDonald's or Walmart may be supported by a closely tailored structure. Jobs are well defined with detailed tasks or steps to follow. You can go into a McDonald's in Cleveland, Prague, or Shanghai and find they all are similar in key ways. Their pay structures are, too. There are seven jobs in each McDonald's (under supervisors and managers). All are very well defined in order to eliminate variance in how they are performed. Cooking french fries takes nine steps. It seems hard to make a mistake in these jobs.[44] It is also hard to be the very best french fryer in the whole company. Differences in pay among jobs are very small.

In contrast to McDonald's, 3M's business strategy requires constant product innovation and short product-design-to-market cycle times. The 3M competitive environment is turbulent and unpredictable. No steps at all are laid out. 3M engineers might work on several teams developing several products at the same time. 3M's pay structures are more loosely linked to the organization in order to provide flexibility.

Hierarchical versus Egalitarian and Layered versus Delayered Structures

Pay structures can range from hierarchical to egalitarian. **Exhibit 3.6** clarifies the differences. Egalitarian structures have fewer levels and/or smaller differentials between adjacent levels and between the highest- and lowest-paid workers.

EXHIBIT 3.6 **Hierarchical versus Egalitarian Structures**

	Hierarchical ←——→	**Egalitarian**
Levels	Many	Fewer
Differentials	Depends	Depends
Criteria	Person or job	Person or job
Supports:	Close fit	Loose fit
Work Organization	Individual performers	Teams
Fairness	Performance	Equal treatment
Behaviors	Opportunities for promotion	Cooperation

Structures can also be said to vary from layered to delayered. In **Exhibit 3.7**, the layered structure has eight levels, with relatively small between-level differentials in comparison to the delayered structure, which has only three levels. The layered structure is more hierarchical than the delayered structure and less egalitarian in terms of number of levels; the multiple levels would include detailed descriptions of work done at each level and outline who is responsible for what. Hierar chies send the message that the organization values the differences in work content, individual skills, and contributions to the organization.[45]

In the delayered structure, several levels of job titles are removed so that all employees at all levels become responsible for a broader range of tasks but also have greater freedom (with less close supervision) to determine how best to accomplish what is expected of them. The delayered structure is more egalitarian in that it sends the message that all employees are valued equally. Employees are less closely supervised and they are given more autonomy (less close supervision), in hopes of allowing them to exercise independent thought, initiative, and action. The assumption is that more equal treatment will improve employee satisfaction, support cooperation, and therefore affect workers' performance. Of course, if there are fewer levels in a delayered structure and if the difference between the lowest and highest compensation in the organization is the same as in a layered structure (as implied in **Exhibit 3.7**), then the pay differentials between levels would actually be larger in the delayered structure, not smaller. To more completely fit the egalitarian criteria laid out in **Exhibit 3.6**, the delayered structure in **Exhibit 3.7** would need to raise the pay of the Associate Engineer and bring down the pay of the Chief Engineer, relative to the layered structure. That would decrease overall pay differentiation (variance/dispersion) between employees, making it more egalitarian. For example, Costco tries to maintain CEO cash compensation (base plus bonus) at 8 times the average of Costco unionized employees. Whole Foods aims for no more than 19 times. They believe the more delayered structure better fits their emphasis on cooperative employee teams. (CEOs at both companies nevertheless typically have higher total compensation that is more than 8 times or 19 times that of the average employee due to the value of their stock options.)

Yet egalitarian structures are not problem free. For example, Ben and Jerry's Homemade, purveyors of premium ice cream, tried to maintain a ratio of only 7 to 1. (When the company started, the spread was 5 to 1.) The relatively narrow differential reflected the company's philosophy that the prosperity of its production workers and its management should be closely linked. However, it eventually became a barrier to recruiting. Ben and Jerry's was forced to abandon this policy when it needed to hire an accounting manager and a new CEO. And only when the company was acquired by Unilever did the press report the value of Ben and Jerry's stock, which netted cofounders Ben Cohen $19 million and Jerry Greenfield $42 million–far beyond the 7-to-1 ratio.

Still, it is hard to be against anything called "egalitarian." If we instead use the word "averagism," as Chinese workers do when describing the pay system under socialism's state-owned enterprises, where maximum

EXHIBIT 3.7 Layered versus Delayered Structures

Layered	Delayered
Chief Engineer	Chief Engineer
Engineering Manager	
Consulting Engineer	
Senior Lead Engineer	
Lead Engineer	Consulting Engineer
Senior Engineer	
Engineer	
Engineer Trainee	Associate Engineer

differentials of 3 to 1 were mandated, some of the possible drawbacks of this approach become clear.[46] Equal treatment (i.e., a lack of pay for performance, either through within-grade or between-grade pay growth) can mean that the more knowledgeable and high-performing employees–the stars–feel underpaid. They may quit to go to an employer that better recognizes their contributions with higher pay (i.e., there is the risk of a negative sorting effect) or simply refuse to do anything (e.g., because of negative incentive effects and/or perceptions of inequity) that is not specifically required of them. Their change in behavior will lower overall performance. So a case can be made for both egalitarian and hierarchical structures.

Keep in mind, though, that the choice is rarely either/or. Instead, the differences are a matter of degree: Levels can range from many to few, differentials can be large or small, and the criteria can be based on the job, the person, or some combination of the two.

GUIDANCE FROM THE EVIDENCE

Before managers recommend a pay structure for their organizations, we hope they will not only look at organization strategy, work flow, fairness, and employee motivation, but also look at the research. Both economists and psychologists have something to tell us about the effects of various structures.

Equity Theory: Fairness

As we noted earlier, employees judge the equity (fairness) of their pay by making multiple comparisons.[47] Evidence based on a study of 2,000 school teachers suggests that teachers are more likely to feel their internal pay structures are fair when they are paid relatively highly within the structure. They will also feel pay structures are fair even when they are relatively low in the internal structure if they work in a high-paying school district. Applying these findings to Lockheed's engineers, advisors, and consultant engineers, we would assume they are more likely to say the internal structure is fair if they are in one of the higher pay levels. Engineers at lower levels will think Lockheed's structure is fair only if Lockheed pays more than its aerospace defense industry competitors. What we don't know is how the lead engineer with 10 years experience will judge the pay structure if Lockheed hires new people into lead engineer jobs with only five years of experience. This kind of situation is unlikely to occur with unionized teachers' pay structures, but it is very common in other organizations.

So the research suggests that employees judge the fairness of their organization's internal pay structure by making multiple comparisons:

- Comparing to jobs similar to their own (internal equity),
- Comparing their job to others at the same employer (internal equity), and
- Comparing their jobs' pay against external pay levels (external equity).

What evidence do we have on the degree to which employees make internal and external equity comparisons? **Exhibit 3.8** provides some data. Among the organizations surveyed, external and internal pay comparisons appear to be about equally common, at least in terms of which types of comparisons employees raise with managers.[48] Note that about one-quarter to one-third of the organizations report that employees raise these comparisons frequently or constantly. Thus, it appears that a job as a compensation professional requires not only designing a compensation system that supports the organization's objectives but also being able to explain to employees on a regular and ongoing basis the rationale for the compensation system choices.

The results from these comparisons depend in part on the *accuracy* of employee knowledge of other employees' jobs, internal structures, and external pay levels.[49] Teachers' pay schedules are generally public knowledge, but this is seldom the case in private sector organizations like Lockheed. Evidence from 30-year-old research shows employees often are misinformed about their relative standing in the pay structure.[50] Equity theory could support either egalitarian or hierarchical structures, depending on the comparisons and the accuracy of information about them.

It is important to be clear that the terms *equity* and *equal* are not interchangeable. Outcomes such as pay can be unequal across employees, but pay can nevertheless be perceived as equitable or fair, if those perceived as making larger performance contributions are the ones receiving higher pay. Equity theory says that people compare the ratio of their own outcomes (e.g., pay, status, enjoyment) to inputs (e.g., effort, ability, performance) with the outcome to input ratio as noted above, one or more comparison with others (internal, external, or themselves in a past or future situation). Perceived equity results if the ratios are very similar. The ratios can be similar despite differences in pay if performance differences are perceived to exist.[51]

A study of a wide range of organizations found that those having larger pay differentials among top executives experienced slightly higher executive turnover, perhaps because of perceptions on inequity. An increase of 1 standard deviation in the size of pay differentials was associated with 2% to 6% lower average tenure among executives. However, the study did not examine the degree to which pay differentials were based on performance and the performance levels of those leaving was also not examined. Thus, we cannot make an assessment of the perceived equity implications, and we also don't know what (if any) kind of sorting effect (whether it was high or low performers who were more likely to leave) large versus small pay differentials had. We only know that turnover was higher in organizations having larger pay differentials. Other studies have also reported that greater pay dispersion is related to higher turnover among executives, but again the performance of the leavers and stayers has not typically been compared.[52]

Tournament Theory (and Pay Dispersion): Motivation and Performance

Economists have focused more directly on the motivational effects of structures as opposed to people's perceptions of structures. Consider, for example, a golf tournament where the prizes total, say, $100,000. How that $100,000 is distributed affects the performance of all players in the tournament. Compare a 3-prize

EXHIBIT 3.8 How Often Do Employees Express Concerns about the Lack of Internal or External Equity/Fairness?

	Internal Equity/Fairness			External Equity/Fairness		
	Frequently or Constantly	**Occasionally**	**Seldom or Never**	**Frequently or Constantly**	**Occasionally**	**Seldom or Never**
Base Pay Amount	21%	45%	34%	28%	51%	22%
Base Pay Merit Increases	27%	45%	28%	24%	42%	34%

Source: Adapted from D. Scott, T. McMullen, and M. Royal. *WorldatWork Journal,* Fourth Quarter, 2011, 50–64. Survey of 568 compensation professionals (primarily mid-level to senior-level).

schedule of $60,000, $30,000, and $10,000 with a 10-prize schedule of $19,000, $17,000, $15,000, $13,000, and so on. According to **tournament theory,** *all* players will play better in the first tournament, where the prize differentials are larger.[53] There is some evidence to support this. Raising the total prize money by $100,000 in the Professional Golf Association tournament lowered each player's score, on average, by 1.1 strokes over 72 holes.[54] And the closer the players got to the top prize, the more their scores were lowered. (Note to non-golfers: A lower score is an improvement.)

Applying these results to organization structures, the greater the differential between your salary and your boss's salary, the harder you (and everyone else but the boss) will work. If Lockheed pays its advisor engineers $125,000 and its consultant engineers $162,000, the tournament model says that increasing the consultants' pay to $200,000 will cause everyone (except the consultants) to work harder. Rather than resenting the big bucks going to the consultants, engineers at all levels will work harder to be a "winner," that is, get promoted to the next level on the way to becoming consultants themselves.[55] Within limits, the bigger the prize for getting to the next level of the structure, the greater the motivational impact of the structure. Several studies support tournament theory. One reported that giving larger raises with a promotion increases effort and reduces absenteeism.[56] Others find that performance improves with larger differentials at the top levels of the structure. The "winner-take-all" idea springs from these studies.[57]

Differentiation and Dispersion in Teams

But what about team settings?[58] Virtually all the research that supports hierarchical structures and tournament theory was conducted in situations where individual performance matters most (auto racing, bowling, golf tournaments) or, at best, where the demand for cooperation among a small group of individuals is relatively low (professors, stockbrokers, truck drivers).[59]

In contrast to individual performers, team sports provide a setting where both an individual player's performance as well as the cooperative efforts of the entire team make a difference.[60] Using eight years of data on Major League Baseball, Matt Bloom found that teams with small differences in player salaries did better than those with large differentials. In addition to affecting team performance, egalitarian structures had a sizable effect on individual players' performance, too. A mediocre player improved more on a team with an egalitarian structure than on a team with a hierarchical structure. It may also be that the egalitarian pay structure reflects a more flexible, supportive organization culture in which a mediocre player is given the training and support needed to improve.

Although the baseball study was important in providing a paradigm for studying the effects of pay dispersion (egalitarian versus hierarchical pay), one potential issue is that baseball is not a sport characterized by a great deal of interdependence nor is it a sport where there is much in the way of (discretionary) cooperative effort. A later study was conducted using hockey teams, a setting where there is substantial task interdependence and a player does have discretion regarding cooperative behavior. The hockey study found that teams that differentiated salaries more greatly as a function of individual performance (as opposed to factors not related to performance) did better, in large part because such teams were more successful in attracting and retaining the most talented players. In other words, larger differentials based on performance generated positive sorting effects. Without differentials based on performance, the most talented players go elsewhere to play.[61] Also, it is important to remember that *equal* and *equitable* mean different things. Equal pay may actually be seen as inequitable (unfair), especially by stronger performers.[62] Other studies similarly suggest that the performance consequences of dispersion depend on contingency factors such as the basis (how justifiable) of dispersion and also the degree (too much or too little may be less effective).[63] However, there continues to be a debate about the effects of dispersion and the moderating role of contextual factors.[64]

e-Compensation

Salaries for players and teams in Major League Baseball and the National Hockey League are listed at ***http://www.usatoday.com/sports/mlb/salaries*** *and* ***http://www.usatoday.com/sports/nhl/salaries***. Pick some of your favorite teams and compare the highest- and lowest-paid players on the team. Based on the differentials, which teams do the models and research discussed in this chapter predict will have the better record?

Information on team standings is available at *USA Today* and other sources. Question: Would you bet your tuition on the relationship between player salary differentials on a team and the team's performance? (What about player salary levels and/or the relationship between player performance and pay as the basis for predicting team success?)

When you look at an association/correlation, it does not have to be perfect to be important. For example, smoking does not guarantee health problems, but ... So, when you look at major league team salaries, paying a lot does not guarantee a title, but does it make it more likely and, if so, how much more likely (and is it worth the cost?)

Institutional Theory: Copy Others and Conform

Sometimes internal pay structures are adopted because they have been called a "best practice."[65] Organizations simply copy or imitate others. Recent examples of such "benchmarking" behavior include the rush to outsource jobs, to emphasize teams, to deemphasize individual contributions, and to shift to a **competency-based pay system,** often with little regard to whether any of these practices fit the organization or its employees and add value.

Institutional theory sees firms as responding/conforming to normative pressures in their environments so as to gain legitimacy and to reduce risk. As such, institutional theory predicts that very few firms are "first movers"; instead, most firms copy innovative practices after innovators have learned how to make the practices work. The potential drawback of such mimetic behavior is that what aligns with the strategy of another organization may not align with the organization's own strategy. And according to the resource-based view of the firm, it is not possible to out perform one's competitors if you simply imitate their practices.[66] However, as noted earlier, for a firm that is performing worse than competitors, learning from other organizations, which may entail some imitation, may be quite useful in achieving competitive parity and may represent a significant improvement for the firm.[67]

(More) Guidance from the Evidence

Exhibit 3.9 summarizes the effects attributed to internally aligned structures. The impact of internal structures depends on the context in which they operate.

- More hierarchical structures are related to greater performance when the work flow depends on individual contributors (e.g., consulting and law practices, surgical units, stockbrokers, even university researchers).
- High performers quit less under more hierarchical systems when pay is based on performance rather than seniority and when people have knowledge of the structure.

- More egalitarian structures are related to greater performance when close collaboration and sharing of knowledge are required (e.g., firefighting and rescue squads, manufacturing teams, global software design teams). The competition fostered in the "winner-take-all" tournament hierarchies appears to have negative effects on performance when the work flow and organization design require teamwork.
- The impact of any internal structure on organization performance is affected by the other dimensions of the pay model; pay levels (competitiveness), employee performance (contributions), and employee knowledge of the pay structure (management).[68]

Beyond these points, much remains to be studied. There is practically no research on the optimal size of the promotional increase or its effects on behavior, satisfaction, or performance. Nor is much known about whether more frequent promotions with minimal change in the nature of the work are better (or worse) than less frequent promotions with major changes in work. Informal expectations often develop at each workplace. ("You can expect to get promoted here after about three years, and a 10 percent raise usually goes with it.") In universities, promotion from assistant to associate professor tends to occur after six years, although there is no norm on accompanying pay increases. In Japanese pay structures, promotion from associate to *kakari-cho* occurs after five years in a company. Similar norms exist in the military. Little is known about how these rules of thumb develop and what their original logic was. But they do matter. Promotions sooner (or later) than expected, accompanied by a larger (or smaller) pay increase, send a powerful message.

So what should be the size of the pay differentials among the engineering levels within Lockheed? To answer this question, we would need to understand how differentials within the **career path** support Lockheed's business strategy and work flow, whether the differentials motivate engineers to contribute to Lockheed's success, and whether they are considered fair by the engineers. The next several chapters discuss how to manage these internal structures.

CONSEQUENCES OF STRUCTURES

Let's turn again to that "So what?" question and the pay model. Why worry about internal alignment at all? Why not simply pay employees whatever it takes to get them to take a job and to show up for work every day? Why not let external market forces or what competitors are paying determine internal wage differentials? Or why not let a government agency decide?

EXHIBIT 3.9 Some Consequences of an Internally Aligned Structure

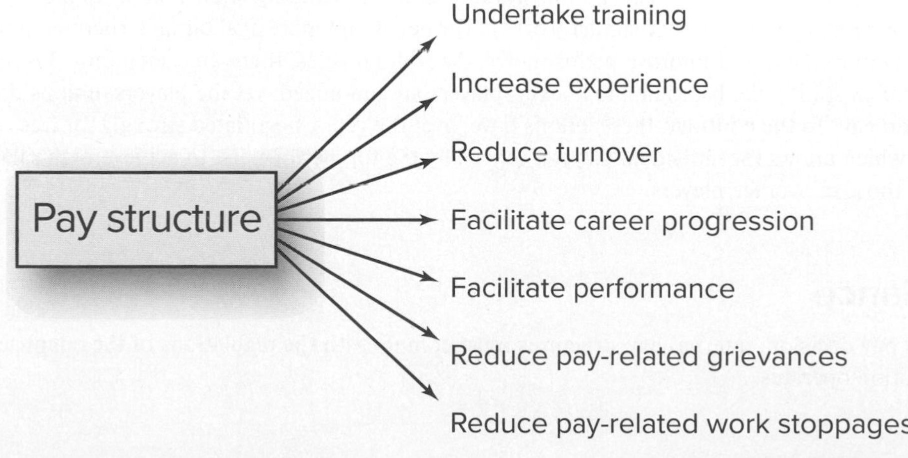

Efficiency (including Retention)

Research shows that an aligned structure can lead to better organization performance.[69] If the structure does not motivate employees to help achieve the organization's objectives, then it is a candidate for redesign.

Internal pay structures imply future returns. The size of the differentials between the entry level in the structure and the highest level can encourage employees to remain with the organization, increase their experience and training, cooperate with co-workers, and seek greater responsibility.[70]

In most organizations, "hiring from within" (i.e., promotion) continues to be used to fill a large share of jobs and these internal hires often outperform outside hires (and are also less costly on average).[71] Employers typically have more and better information available on current employees (inside applicants) versus outside applicants when estimating performance. Likewise, employees generally have better information on their fit to a job in their current organization than do outside applicants.[72]

The inside hiring works best when positions are publicly posted to generate the largest and strongest applicant pool, as opposed to reliance on using only one's personal/informal network to hire internal candidates.[73] Of course, to the degree an organization is growing and/or needs to grow certain skill areas not readily available or efficiently developed inside the organization, external hiring necessarily increases in importance.[74] Other research indicates that vertical wage dispersion reduces employee turnover, presumably because of the greater payoff to promotion on one's current organization. On the other hand, horizontal wage dispersion was found to increase turnover, in this case one presumes because of perceptions of pay inequity, at least where the performance/contribution basis is not clear and credible.[75]

Chapter 2 raised the strategy question, Do you want to be difficult to imitate? We already noted that the number of levels and titles in a career path may be rewarding beyond the pay attached to the titles. Microsoft added a "distinguished engineer" title to its structure. The consulting firm McKinsey and Company added an "associate partner." Their rationale was that employees are motivated by these more frequent steps in the career ladder. These are new titles and levels that are not yet reflected in the external market.

Fairness

Writers have long agreed that departures from an acceptable wage structure will occasion turnover, grievances, and diminished motivation.[76] But that is where the agreement ends. One group argues that if fair (i.e., sizable) differentials among jobs are not paid, individuals may harbor ill will toward the employer, resist change, change employment if possible, become depressed, and "lack that zest and enthusiasm which makes for high efficiency and personal satisfaction in work."[77] Others, including labor unions, argue for only small differentials within pay levels and for similar work, in the belief that more egalitarian structures support cooperation and commitment and improve performance. As with all rules, there are exceptions. For example, in U.S. professional sports like baseball and hockey, players are unionized, yet the players' unions do not strive for egalitarian pay. To the contrary, these unions have, over the years, negotiated strongly for free agent rights for players, which allows for individual players, especially the top performers, to achieve high salaries, much higher than those of average players.

Compliance

As with any pay decision, internal pay structures must comply with the regulations of the countries in which the organization operates.

While the research on internal alignment is very informative, there is still a lot we do not know. What about the appropriate number of levels, the size of the differentials, and the criteria for advancing employees through a structure? We believe the answers lie in understanding the factors discussed in this chapter: the organization's strategic intent, its design and work flow, human capital, and the external conditions, regulations, and customs it faces. We also believe that aligning the pay structure to fit the organization's conditions is more likely to lead to competitive advantage for the organization and a sense of fair treatment for employees. On the other hand, sometimes people take the notion of internal alignment too far. At a Houston oil company, official policy was that wall hangings were related to position in the structure. Top brass got original art, while employees at the bottom of the structure got photos of the company's oil refineries. One analyst commented, "It was so level specific that you could tell immediately upon entering an office the minimum salary level of that person."[78]

Your Turn So You Want to Lead an Orchestra!

Peter Drucker calls orchestras an example of an organization design that will become increasingly popular in the 21st century, in that they employ skilled and talented people, joined together as a team to create products and services. Drucker may hear what he wants to hear. Others say orchestras are autocratic. The conductor dictates what is played and how it is played. Rather than basking in the glow of orchestral teamwork, jokes like the following are common among orchestra members: *Q. Why do so many people take an instant dislike to the viola? A. It saves time.*

Job descriptions for orchestras look simple: Play the music. *(Q. How is lightning like a keyboardist's fingers? A. Neither strikes the same place twice.)* Violins play violin parts; trumpets play trumpet parts. Yet one study reported that job satisfaction for orchestra members ranks below that of prison guards. However, orchestra members were more satisfied than operating room nurses and hockey players.

Exhibit 3.10 shows the pay structure from several years ago for a regional chamber orchestra. *(Q. How can you make a clarinet sound like a French horn? A. Play all the wrong notes.)* The pay covers six full orchestra concerts, one Caroling by Candlelight event, three Sunday Chamber Series concerts, several Arts in Education elementary school concerts, two engagements for a flute quartet, and one Ring In the Holidays brass event as well as the regularly scheduled rehearsals. *(Q. How can you tell when a trombonist is playing out of tune? A. When the slide is moving.)*

1. Describe the orchestra's pay structure in terms of levels, differentials, and job- or person-based approach.
2. Discuss what factors may explain the structure. Why does violinist I receive more than the oboist and trombonist? Why does the principal trumpet player earn more than the principal cellist and principal clarinetist but less than the principal viola and principal flute players? What explains these differences? Does the relative supply versus the demand for violinists compare to the supply versus the demand for trombonists? Is it that violins play more notes?
3. What is the pay differential between the principal viola and next highest paid viola? What about between the principal trumpet and the next highest paid trumpet? Why these differentials between the principal and other? Why aren't they larger? Smaller? Why is the differential between trumpet players different than between the viola players?
4. How well do equity and tournament models apply? Do custom and tradition play any role? What about institutional theory?

EXHIBIT 3.10 **Orchestra Compensation Schedule**

Instrument	Fee	Instrument	Fee
Violin, Concertmaster	$6,970	Violin I	$2,483
Principal Bass and Conductor	5,070	Violin I	2,483
Principal Viola	5,036	Violin II	2,483
Principal Flute	4,337	Violin II	2,483
Principal Trumpet	4,233	Viola	2,483
Principal Cello	4,181	Violin II	1,975
Principal Clarinet	4,146	Viola	2,212
Trumpet	3,638	Oboe	2,206
Principal Oboe	3,615	Trombone	2,137
Principal Violin II	3,488	Viola	2,033
Principal Horn	3,390	Violin II/Viola	1,784
Keyboard I	3,361	Cello	1,634
Cello	3,228	Clarinet	1,548
Principal Percussion	3,049	Horn	1,548
Violin I	2,899	Flute	1,455
Cello	2,882	Keyboard II	1,392
Principal Bassoon	2,824	Bassoon	1,265
Violin I	2,685	Violin II	1,178

Still Your Turn (If You Don't Want to Lead the Orchestra...)

Use another example of how different jobs/skills get paid differently and how lines of career progression operate. You can use the health care or sports examples from the **Part II** Introduction earlier. Or, you can choose another example. You can use the pay structure in **Exhibit 3.11** at Pennsylvania Power & Light that was negotiated with the International Brotherhood of Electrical Workers (IBEW). Address the same general questions raised above in the orchestra example regarding the size of pay differentials and why they exist.

EXHIBIT 3.11 Pay Structure for Selected Job Families, Pennsylvania Power & Light

Annual Salary (Min)	Annual Salary (Max)	Pay Grade	Bookkeeping	Coal Equipment Operator	Nuclear Plant Operator	Electrical Equipment Repair	Technician Effluents	Technician Radiation Protection
36,660	43,992	1	Clerk Cash Receipts					
40,352	47,684	2					Handyman Effluents	
43,992	51,376	3						
47,684	55,016	4						
51,376	58,656	5		Coal Equipment Operator I			Helper Effluents	
55,016	62,348	6				Electrical Equipment Repair 3rd Class		
58,656	65,988	7					Effluents Technician I	
62,348	69,680	8		Coal Equipment Operator II				
65,988	73,320	9	Cash Receipts Leader	Coal Equipment Operator III		Electrical Equipment Repair 2nd Class		
69,680	77,012	10					Effluents Technician II	
73,320	80,652	11	Bookkeeper	Coal Equipment Operator IV				
77,012	84,344	12	Bookkeeper Senior					
80,652	87,984	13				Electrical Equipment Repair 1st Class		Radiation Protection Technician Junior
84,344	91,676	14						
87,984	95,368	15				Electrical Equipment		Radiation Protection

Annual Salary (Min)	Annual Salary (Max)	Pay Grade	Bookkeeping	Coal Equipment Operator	Nuclear Plant Operator	Electrical Equipment Repair	Technician Effluents	Technician Radiation Protection
						Repair Leader		Technician Senior
91,676	99,008	16						
95,368	102,700	17			Nuclear Plant Oper Trainee			
103,220	103,220	18						
113,568	113,568	19			Nuclear Plant Oper			

Source: Agreement between Local Union No. 1600 of the International Brotherhood of Electrical Workers, AFL-CIO, and Pennsylvania Power and Light Company. Pay rates shown are effective May 9, 2016. http://www.dol.gov/olms/regs/compliance/cba/pdf/2014/private/K9292.pdf. See also: https://ibew1600.org/wp-content/uploads/2020/01/2017-Labor-Agrmnt-Fullsize.pdf.

Still (yes, still) Your Turn NCAA

$8.5 billion. That is the estimated annual revenue received by NCAA Division 1 Schools from sports, with about 58 percent of that coming from men's football and basketball. College players do not get paid. Some receive scholarships. There is an ongoing legal challenge to the status quo of not paying the players. A few years ago, the five power conferences in the NCAA decided to increase the value of a scholarship by additionally providing a cost-of-living stipend of $200 to $400 per month to pay for expenses beyond tuition, books, and housing. Is that enough? Or should players be paid as employees and paid an amount that is more consistent with the revenue they generate for their universities? Note that the issue is currently before the Supreme Court. Thus, you will soon have a chance (or likely you already can) compare your opinion with that of the highest court in the land.

After considering that issue, consider next the question of how such a system should be designed. Develop a pay strategy to have at the ready (a contingency plan) in case players are to be paid like employees in the future. In evaluating design options, take into account the following issues raised early on in this issue's history by NCAA men's basketball tournament analysts (and former college and pro basketball stars) Kenny Smith, Charles Barkley, and Clark Kellogg. Kenny Smith believes players should get paid, but only if they graduate. Charles Barkley believes that it would be unfair, even discriminatory, to pay basketball players, but not fencers, gymnasts, softball players, and swimmers. Barkley also warns against letting college athletes sign sponsorship deals (e.g., with shoe or apparel companies). He says it would ruin team chemistry. He says that if he is an offensive lineman and the quarterback "is making money and I'm not, I'm not blocking for him." Clark Kellogg believes players should get paid, in part, because the time commitment has grown to be so large, in season and off-season. He notes that it is not possible to even have a summer job anymore. Another analyst, former college coach Bill Raftery, is concerned that paying players would make for even less parity in NCAA college sports because the small schools may not be able to afford to pay their players and/or to pay them as much as larger schools.

In summary, please address the following three questions:

1. Should NCAA athletes get paid as employees?
2. If NCAA athletes are paid as employees, either because of legal action or colleges/universities deciding on their own to change the system, how should the pay strategy be designed to "work" and avoid the potential pitfalls identified above?
3. What would your pay strategy design cost and how would it be funded? What impact would the required level of funding have on colleges and universities? How would athletes outside of sports such as basketball and football be affected?
4. If the U.S. Supreme Court has ruled on this issue by the time you read this, what did they decide, how will their decision be implemented, and how well do you think it will all work out? What challenges do you expect?

Sources: Tommy Beer. "Supreme Court Set to Hear Case That Could Shape the Future of College Athletics." Forbes.com, March 30, 2021; Brent Kendall and Louise Radnofsky. NCAA Pressed by Supreme Court Justices on Player Compensation. *The Wall Street Journal,* March 31, 2021. wsj.com; Matthew Futterman, "The Debate Continues: Should the Players Get Paid?" *The Wall Street Journal,* March 19, 2015, D8; Steve Berkowitz, "NCAA Increases Value of Scholarships in Historic Vote," *USA Today*, January 17, 2015; Joe Nocera, "It's Business, NCAA. Pay the Players: Only the Magic of the Market Can Cure What Ails College Sports," *Bloomberg View*, October 13, 2017, www.bloomberg.com.

Summary

This chapter discusses internal alignment and how it affects employees, managers, and employers. Internal alignment refers to the pay relationships among jobs/skills/competencies within a single organization. The potential consequences of internal pay structures are vital to organizations and individuals. Recent research plus experience offers guidance concerning the design and management of internal pay structures.

Pay structures–the array of pay rates for different jobs within an organization–are shaped by societal, economic, organizational, and other factors. Employees judge a structure to be fair by comparing to other jobs within the organization and to what competitors pay for jobs similar to theirs. Acceptance by employees of the pay differentials among jobs is a key test of an equitable pay structure. Such structures are part of the network of returns offered by organizations. They offer career paths to higher-paying jobs and a sense of achievement.

Keep the goals of the entire compensation system in mind when thinking about internal pay structures. There is widespread experience and increasing research to support the belief that differences in internal pay structures, coupled with the other dimensions of compensation systems, influence people's attitudes and work behaviors and therefore the success of organizations.

Review Questions

1. Why is internal alignment an important policy in a strategic perspective of compensation?
2. Discuss the factors that influence internal pay structures. Based on your own experience, which ones do you think are the most important? Why?
3. Internal structures are part of the incentives offered in organizations. Look into any organization: your college, workplace, or the grocery store where you shop. Describe the flow of work. How is the job structure aligned with the organization's business, the work flow, and its objectives? How do you believe it influences employee behaviors?
4. What is the "just-wage" doctrine? Can you think of any present-day applications?
5. A typical structure within colleges is instructor, assistant professor, associate professor, full professor. Is this egalitarian or hierarchical? What added information would you need to decide? What behaviors by the faculty do you believe the structure influences? Is it aligned? Difficult to copy? Does it add value?

Endnotes

1. U.S. Bureau of Labor Statistics. https://www.bls.gov/oes/current/oes_nat.htm#29-0000. March 31, 2021.
2. L. Kane, "Medscape Physician Compensation Report 2020." May 14, 2020. medscape.com. Exhibit 4.
3. C. Smith. SoccerPrime. https://soccerprime.com/columbus-crew-sc-player-salaries. Accessed April 7, 2021.
4. Matthew 20: 1-14. *The Holy Bible, King James Version*. Retrieved from https://www.biblegateway.com/passage/?search=matthew 20&version=KJV
5. For a history of the different standards for pay, see T. Mahoney, *Compensation and Reward Perspectives* (Burr Ridge, IL: Irwin, 1979); G. Milkovich and J. Stevens, "From Pay to Rewards: 100 Years of Change," *ACA Journal* 9(1) (2000), pp. 6-18; D. F. Schloss, *Methods in Industrial Remuneration* (New York: Putnam's, 1892).

6. P. Doeringer and M. Piore, *Internal Labor Markets and Manpower Analysis* (Armonk, NY: Sharpe, 1985). E. P. Lazear, *Personnel Economics* (Cambridge: MIT Press, 1995). One study, for example, found that education level and work experience explained about 30 percent of the variance in salaries in a large company. Job level explained an additional 50 percent of the variance in salaries. See B. Gerhart and G. T. Milkovich, "Salaries, Salary Growth, and Promotions of Men and Women in a Large Private Firm," in *Pay Equity: Empirical Inquiries,* eds. R. Michael and H. Hartmann (Washington, D.C.: National Academy Press, 1989).
7. "Equity" could refer to stock, to some perceived balance of effort and rewards, and/or pay discrimination (gender equity). We believe "internal alignment" better reflects the meaning and importance underlying pay structures.
8. H. K. Doerr, T. Freed, T. Mitchell, C. Schriesheim, and X. (Tracy) Zhou, "Work Flow Policy and Within-Worker and Between-Workers Variability in Performance," *Journal of Applied Psychology* 89(5), 2004, pp. 911–921.
9. K. McNamara, "Push Is on to Advise the Very Wealthy," *The Wall Street Journal,* May 27, 2006, p. B4.
10. J. B. Quinn, P. Anderson, and S. Finkelstein, "Leveraging Intellect," *Academy of Management Executive* 19(4), 2005, pp. 78–94.
11. Researchers use a statistic called the *gini coefficient* to describe the distribution of pay. A gini of zero means everyone is paid the identical wage. The higher the gini coefficient (maximum = 1), the greater the pay differentials among the levels.
12. D. T. Mortensen, *Wage Dispersion: Why Are Similar Workers Paid Differently?* (Cambridge, MA: MIT Press, 2005); B. Gerhart and S. Rynes, *Compensation: Theory, Evidence, and Strategic Implications* (Thousand Oaks, CA: Sage, 2003); R. Gibbons and M. Waldman, "A Theory of Wage and Promotion Dynamics Inside Firms," *Quarterly Journal of Economics,* November 1999, pp. 1321–1358; G. Baker, M. Gibbs, and B. Holmstrom, "The Internal Economics of the Firm: Evidence from Personnel Data," *Quarterly Journal of Economics* (November 1994), pp. 881–919; M. Bloom and G. Milkovich, "Money, Managers, and Metamorphosis," in *Trends in Organizational Behavior,* 3rd ed., ed. D. Rousseau and C. Cooper (New York: Wiley, 1996).
13. D. Kirkpatrick, "The Net Makes It All Easier–Including Exporting U.S. Jobs," *Fortune,* May 26, 2003, p. 146.
14. Y. Yanadori, "Cascading Model of Compensation Management: The Determinants of Compensation of Top Executives and Employees," Vancouver, BC: Sauder School of Business working paper, January 2006.
15. C. Tucker, ed., *The Marx-Engels Reader* (New York: Norton, 1978).
16. A. M. Carter, *Theory of Wages and Employment* (Burr Ridge, IL: Irwin, 1959); U.S. Bureau of Labor Statistics, Occupational Employment Statistics. May 2017, https://www.bls.gov/oes/current/oes291151.htm.
17. The nurse anesthetist salary and the lower anesthesiologist salary estimates are from the U.S. Bureau of Labor Statistics. https://www.bls.gov/oes/. The higher anesthesiologist salary estimate is from Medscape, Medscape Anesthesiologist Compensation Report 2020. medscape.com.
18. Dana Matlioli, "Help-Wanted: Senior-Level Job, Junior Title, Pay," *The Wall Street Journal,* April 12, 2008.
19. B. Gerhart and G. Milkovich, "Employee Compensation," in *Handbook of Industrial and Organization Psychology*, vol. 3, ed. M. Dunnette and L. Hough (Palo Alto, CA: Consulting Psychologists Press, 1992); S. Brown and K. Eisenhardt, *Competing on the Edge: Strategy and Structured Chaos* (Boston: Harvard Business Press, 1998); G. Baker, M. Gibbs, and B. Holmstrom, "The Internal Economics of

the Firm: Evidence from Personnel Data," *Quarterly Journal of Economics* (November 1994), pp. 881–919; M. Gibbs, "Incentive Compensation in a Corporate Hierarchy," *Journal of Accounting and Economics* 19 (1995), pp. 247–277.

20. S. Adams and D. Neumark, "The Effects of Living Wage Laws: Evidence from Failed and Derailed Living Wage Campaigns," NBER working paper 11342, May 2005.
21. B. Murray, "Revealed: You're Finally Learning a Lot More about the Chasm between CEO and Worker Pay," FastCompany, April 10, 2018, https://www.fastcompany.com/40557116/revealed-youre-finally-learning-a-lot-more-about-the-chasm-between-ceo-and-worker-pay.
22. Pepsico. Notice of 2021 Annual Meeting of Shareholders and Proxy Statement. pepsico.com, March 24, 2021.
23. J. Phan. CEO Pay Ratio: A Deep Data Dive. Harvard Law School Forum on Corporate Governance and Financial Regulation. May 31, 2018. https://corpgov.law.harvard.edu/2018/05/31/ceo-pay-ratio-a-deep-data-dive/
24. G. Hoefstede, *Culture's Consequences: International Differences in Work Relationships and Values* (Thousand Oaks, CA: Sage, 1980); R. Donkin, "The Pecking Order's Instinctive Appeal," *Financial Times,* August 23, 2002; A. Mitra, M. Bloom, and G. Milkovich, "Crossing a Raging River: Seeking Far-Reaching Solutions to Global Pay Challenges," *WorldatWork Journal* 11(2), Second Quarter 2002; F. Trompenaars, *Riding the Waves of Culture: Understanding Diversity in Global Business* (Burr Ridge, IL: Irwin, 1995); J. Brockner, Y. Chen, K. Leung, and D. Skarlick, "Culture and Procedural Fairness: When the Effects of What You Do Depend on How You Do It," *Administrative Science Quarterly* 45(2000), pp. 138–159; T. Li-Ping Tang, V. Wai-Mei Luk, and R. K. Chiu, "Pay Differentials in the People's Republic of China: An Examination of Internal Equity and External Competitiveness," *Compensation and Benefits Review* 32(3), May/June 2000, pp. 43–49.
25. Y. Yanadori, "Minimizing Competition? Entry-Level Compensation in Japanese Firms," *Asia Pacific Journal of Management* 21 (December 2004), pp. 445–467.
26. D. Levine, D. Belman, G. Charness, et al., *The New Employment Contract: How Little Wage Structures at U.S. Employers Have Changed* (Kalamazoo, MI: Upjohn, 2001).
27. R. G. Rajan and J. Wulf, "The Move from Tall to Flat: How Corporate Hierarchies Are Changing," working paper, Wharton School, August 2003.
28. P.-W. Tam, "Hurd's Big Challenge at H-P: Overhauling Corporate Sales," *The Wall Street Journal,* April 3, 2006, pp. A1, A13.
29. Text: Microsoft CEO Satya Nadella's Memo on Job Cuts. *Wall Street Journal*, July 17, 2014. wsj.com.
30. R. Batt, A. J. S. Colvin, and J. Keefe, "Employee Voice, Human Resource Practices, and Quit Rates: Evidence from the Telecommunications Industry," *Industrial and Labor Relations Review* 55(4), July 2002, pp. 573–594; W. F. Cascio, "Strategies for Responsible Restructuring," *Academy of Management Executive* 19(4), 2005, pp. 39–50.
31. https://www.holacracy.org.
32. Herman Vantrappen and Frederic Wirtz. When to Decentralize Decision Making, and When Not To. Harvard Business Review. hbr.org, December 26, 2017; Ethan Bernstein, John Bunch, Niko Canner, and Michael Lee. Beyond the holacracy hype. Harvard Business Review. hbr.org, July-August 2016; Aimee Groth. Zappos has quietly backed away from holacracy. Quartz. qz.com, January 29, 2020.
33. P. Schumann, D. Ahlburg, and C. B. Mahoney, "The Effects of Human Capital and Job Characteristics on Pay," *Journal of Human Resources* 29(2), 1994, pp. 481–503; A. Kohn, *Punished by Rewards: The Trouble with Gold Stars, Incentive Plans, A's, Praise and Other Bribes* (Boston: Houghton Mifflin, 1993);

J. Greenberg and S. Ornstein, "High Status Job Titles as Compensation for Underpayment: A Test of Equity Theory," *Journal of Applied Psychology* 68(2), 1983, pp. 285–297.

34. Specialized studies of competitors' pay structures are conducted by some consulting firms. These are discussed in Chapter 8.

35. Thomas A. Mahoney, "Organizational Hierarchy and Position Worth," *Academy of Management Journal,* December 1979, pp. 726–737; Barry Gerhart and Sara Rynes, *Compensation: Theory, Evidence, and Strategic Implications* (Thousand Oaks, CA: Sage, 2003).

36. Doeringer, P. B., & Piore, M. J. (1985). *Internal labor markets and manpower analysis*. Armonk, N.Y: M.E. Sharpe; E. R. Livernash, "The Internal Wage Structure," in *New Concepts in Wage Determination*, ed. G. W. Taylor and F. C. Pierson (New York: McGraw-Hill, 1957), pp. 140–172; Gerhart, B., & Feng, J. The Resource-Based View of the Firm, Human Resources, and Human Capital: Progress and Prospects. *Journal of Management*, 2021.

37. E. R. Livernash, "The Internal Wage Structure," in *New Concepts in Wage Determination,* eds. G. W. Taylor and F. C. Pierson (New York: McGraw-Hill, 1957), pp. 143–172.

38. T. Judge and H. G. Heneman III, "Pay Satisfaction," in *Compensation in Organizations: Current Research and Practice,* eds. S. Rynes and B. Gerhart (San Francisco: Jossey-Bass, 2000); R. Folger and M. Konovsky, "Effects of Procedural and Distributive Justice on Reactions to Pay Raise Decisions," *Academy of Management Journal* (March 1989), pp. 115–130; M. L. Williams, M. A. McDaniel, and N. Nguyen, "A Meta-Analysis of the Antecedents and Consequences of Pay Level Satisfaction," *Journal of Applied Psychology* 91 (2006), pp. 392–413.

39. C. O. Trevor and D. L. Wazeter, "A Contingent View of Reactions to Objective Pay Conditions: Interdependence among Pay Structure Characteristics and Pay Relative to Internal and External Referents," *Journal of Applied Psychology* 91 (2006), pp. 1260–1275; J. S. Adams, "Towards an Understanding of Inequity," *Journal of Abnormal and Social Psychology* 67 (1963), p. 422; Paul S. Goodman, "An Examination of Referents Used in the Evaluation of Pay," *Organizational Behavior and Human Performance* 12 (1974), pp. 170–195.

40. F. P. Morgeson, M. A. Campion, and C. P. Maertz, "Understanding Pay Satisfaction: The Limits of a Compensation System Implementation," *Journal of Business & Psychology* 16(1), Fall 2001, pp. 133–163.

41. P. England, P. Allison, Y. Wu, and M. Ross, "Does Bad Pay Cause Occupations to Feminize, Does Feminization Reduce Pay, and How Can We Tell with Longitudinal Data?" paper presented at annual meeting of the American Sociological Association, August 2004, San Francisco.

42. A. Smith, "TSA officers 'desperate' to unionize," CNN.com, November 24, 2010, http://money.cnn.com/2010/11/24/news/economy/tsa_screener_union/index.htm.

43. "Federal Uniformed Police: Selected Data on Pay, Recruitment, and Retention at 13 Police Forces in the Washington, D.C. Metropolitan Area," GAO-03-658, June 13, 2003.

44. This statement does not apply to professors who work in McDonald's while on sabbatical. See J. Newman, *My Secret Life on the McJob* (New York: McGraw-Hill, 2007).

45. E. Jaques, "In Praise of Hierarchies," *Harvard Business Review,* January–February 1990, pp. 32–40; Matthew C. Bloom, "The Performance Effects of Pay Structures on Individuals and Organizations," *Academy of Management Journal* 42(1), 1999, pp. 25–40.

46. Daniel Z. Ding, Keith Goodall, and Malcolm Warner, "The End of the 'Iron Rice-Bowl': Whither Chinese Human Resource Management?" *International Journal of Human Resource Management* 11(2), April 2000, pp. 217–236; Thomas Li-Ping Tang, Vivenne Wai-Mei Luk, and Randy K. Chiu, "Pay Differentials in the People's Republic of China: An Examination of Internal Equity and External

Competitiveness," *Compensation and Benefits Review* 32(3), May/June 2000, pp. 43–49; Li Hua Wang, "Pay Policies and Determination in China," working paper, Northwestern University, 2003.

47. E. E. Lawler, *Pay and Organizational Effectiveness: A Psychological View* (New York: McGraw-Hill, 1971); T. A. Mahoney, *Compensation and Reward Perspectives* (Homewood, IL: Irwin, 1979); Charlie O. Trevor and David L. Wazeter, "A Contingent View of Reactions to Objective Pay Conditions: Interdependence among Pay Structure Characteristics and Pay Relative to Internal and External Referents," *Journal of Applied Psychology* 91 (2006), pp. 1260–1275; E. Lawler III, *Treat People Right! How Organizations and Individuals Can Propel Each Other into a Virtuous Spiral of Success* (San Francisco: Jossey-Bass, 2003); Kim, T. Y., Wang, J., Chen, T., Zhu, Y., & Sun, R. (2019). Equal or equitable pay? Individual differences in pay fairness perceptions. *Human Resource Management*, 58(2), 169–186.
48. For more evidence on employee pay comparisons and their consequences, see the following sources: P. S. Goodman, "An Examination of Referents Used in the Evaluation of Pay," *Organizational Behavior and Human Performance* 12(1974), pp. 170–195; C. O. Trevor and D. L. Wazeter, "A Contingent View of Reactions to Objective Pay Conditions: Interdependence among Pay Structure Characteristics and Pay Relative to Internal and External Referents," *Journal of Applied Psychology* 91(2006), pp. 1260–1275; M. M. Harris, F. Anseel, and F. Lievens, "Keeping Up with the Joneses: A Field Study of the Relationships among Upward, Lateral, and Downward Comparisons and Pay Level Satisfaction," *Journal of Applied Psychology* 93, no. 3 (May 2008), pp. 665–673; Gordon D. A. Brown, Jonathan Gardner, Andrew J. Oswald, and Jing Qian, "Does Wage Rank Affect Employees' Well-Being? " *Industrial Relations* 47, no. 3 (July 2008), p. 355; D. Card, A. Mas, E. Moretti, and E. Saez, "Inequality at Work: The Effect of Peer Salaries on Job Satisfaction," Working Paper 16396, National Bureau of Economic Research, September 2010.
49. J. Shaw and N. Gupta, "Pay System Characteristics and Quit Rates of Good, Average, and Poor Performers," University of Kentucky working paper, May 2006.
50. G. Milkovich and P. H. Anderson, "Management Compensation and Secrecy Policies," *Personnel Psychology* 25 (1972), pp. 293–302.
51. J. S. Adams, "Toward an Understanding of Inequity," *Journal of Abnormal and Social Psychology* 67(5), 1963, pp. 422–436; C.O. Trevor, G. Reilly, and B. Gerhart, "Reconsidering Pay Dispersion's Effect on the Performance of Interdependent Work: Reconciling Sorting and Pay Inequality," *Academy of Management Journal* 55 (2012), pp. 585–610.
52. J. G. Messersmith, J. P. Guthrie, Y. Y. Ji, and J. Y. Lee, "Executive Turnover: The Influence of Dispersion and Other Pay Characteristics," *Journal of Applied Psychology* 96 (2011), pp. 457–469.
53. B. E. Becker and M. A. Huselid, "The Incentive Effects of Tournament Compensation Systems," *Administrative Science Quarterly* 37, 1992, pp. 336–350; E. Lazear and S. Rosen, "Rank-Order Tournaments as Optimum Labor Contracts," *Journal of Political Economy* 89, 1981, pp. 841–864; Matthew C. Bloom, "The Performance Effects of Pay Structures on Individuals and Organizations," *Academy of Management Journal* 42(1), 1999, pp. 25–40; Michael L. Bognanno, "Corporate Tournaments," *Journal of Labor Economics* 19(2), 2001, pp. 290–315; B. L. Connelly, L. Tihanyi, T. R. Crook, and K. A. Gangloff, "Tournament Theory: Thirty Years of Contests and Competitions," *Journal of Management*, 40(1), 2014, pp. 16–47.
54. R. G. Ehrenberg and M. L. Bognanno, "The Incentive Effects of Tournaments Revisited: Evidence from the European PGA Tour," *Industrial and Labor Relations Review* 43 (1990), pp. 74S–88S; Tor Eriksson, "Executive Compensation and Tournament Theory: Empirical Tests on Danish Data," *Journal of Labor Economics,* April 1999, pp. 262–280.

55. T. Y. Park, S. Kim, and L. K. Sung, "Fair Pay Dispersion: A Regulatory Focus Theory View," *Organizational Behavior and Human Decision Processes* 142, 2017, pp. 1-11.

56. E. P. Lazear, *Personnel Economics* (Cambridge, MA: MIT Press, 1995).

57. R. H. Frank and P. J. Cook, *The Winner-Take-All Society: Why the Few at the Top Get So Much More Than the Rest of Us* (New York: Penguin, 1996).

58. J. Pfeffer and N. Langton, "The Effect of Wage Dispersion on Satisfaction, Productivity, and Working Collaboratively: Evidence from College and University Faculty," *Administrative Science Quarterly* 38 (1993), pp. 382-407; Edward P. Lazear, "Pay Equality and Industrial Politics," *Journal of Political Economy* 97(3), 1989, pp. 561-580.

59. J. D. Shaw and N. Gupta, "Pay System Characteristics and Quit Patterns of Good, Average, and Poor Performers," *Personnel Psychology* 60 (2007), pp. 903-928.

60. M. C. Bloom, "The Performance Effects of Pay Structures on Individuals and Organizations," *Academy of Management Journal* 42(1), 1999, pp. 25-40; J. M. Beus and D. S. Whitman, "Almighty Dollar or Root of All Evil? Testing the Effects of Money on Workplace Behavior," *Journal of Management*, https://doi.org/10.1177%2F0149206314565241.

61. C. O. Trevor, G. Reilly, and B. Gerhart, "Reconsidering Pay Dispersion's Effect on the Performance of Interdependent Work: Reconciling Sorting and Pay Inequality," *Academy of Management Journal* 55 (2012), pp. 585-610.

62. C. O. Trevor, G. Reilly, and B. Gerhart, "Reconsidering Pay Dispersion's Effect on the Performance of Interdependent Work: Reconciling Sorting and Pay Inequality," *Academy of Management Journal* 55 (2012), pp. 585-610; Y. Garbers and U. Konradt, "The Effect of Financial Incentives on Performance: A Quantitative Review of Individual and Team-Based Financial Incentives," *Journal of Occupational and Organizational Psychology* 87(1), 2014, 102-137; E. E. Lawler, *Pay and Organizational Effectiveness: A Psychological View* (New York: McGraw-Hill, 1971).

63. I. Grabner and M. A. Martin, "The effect of horizontal pay dispersion on the effectiveness of performance-based incentives." *Accounting, Organizations and Society*, 88 (2021); S. A. Conroy and N. Gupta. "Disentangling horizontal pay dispersion: Experimental evidence." *Journal of Organizational Behavior,* 40(3), 2019, 248-263; H. Yang and B. S. Klaas, "Pay Dispersion and the Financial Performance of the Firm: Evidence from Korea," *International Journal of Human Resource Management* 22 (2011), pp. 2147-2166; J. W. Fredrickson, A. Davis-Blake, and W. M. G. Sanders, "Sharing the Wealth: Social Comparisons and Pay Dispersion in the CEO's Top Team," *Strategic Management Journal* 31 (2010), pp. 1031-1055; C. Anderson and C. E. Brown, "The Functions and Dysfunctions of Hierarchy," *Research in Organizational Behavior* 30 (2010), pp. 55-89; M. J. Pearsall, M. S. Christian, and A. P. J. Ellis, "Motivating Interdependent Teams: Individual Rewards, Shared Rewards, or Something in Between," *Journal of Applied Psychology* 95 (2010), pp. 183-191; S. Kepes, J. E. Delery, and N. Gupta, "Contingencies in the Effects of Pay Range on Organizational Effectiveness," *Personnel Psychology* 62(3), 2009, pp. 497-531.

64. J. D. Shaw, "Pay Dispersion," *Annual Review of Organizational Psychology and Organizational Behavior* 1(1), 2014, pp. 521-544; P. E. Downes and D. Choi, "Employee Reactions to Pay Dispersion: A Typology of Existing Research," *Human Resource Management Review* 24(1), 2014, pp. 53-66; A. Bucciol, N. J. Foss, and M. Piovesan, "Pay Dispersion and Performance in Teams," *PloS One* 9(11), 2014, p. e112631; Y. Yanadori and V. Cui, "Creating Incentives for Innovation? The Relationship between Pay Dispersion in R&D Groups and Firm Innovation Performance," *Strategic Management Journal* 34(12), 2013, pp. 1502-1511.

65. P. S. Tolbert and L. G. Zucker, "Institutionalization of Institution Theory," in *Handbook of Organization Studies,* ed. G. Glegg, C. Hardy, and W. Nord (London: Sage, 1996), pp. 175–199; M. Barringer and G. Milkovich, "A Theoretical Exploration of the Adoption and Design of Flexible Benefit Plans: A Case of HR Innovation," *Academy of Management Review* 23(2), 1998, pp. 305–324.
66. Jay B. Barney, "Firm Resources and Sustained Competitive Advantage," *Journal of Management* 17 (1991), pp. 99–120.
67. Gerhart, B., & Feng, J. The Resource-Based View of the Firm, Human Resources, and Human Capital: Progress and Prospects. *Journal of Management,* 2021.
68. M. Brown, M. C. Sturman, and M. Simmering, "Compensation Policy and Organizational Performance: The Efficiency, Operational, and Financial Implications of Pay Levels and Pay Structure," *Academy of Management Journal* 46 (2003), pp. 752–762; J. Shaw and N. Gupta, "Pay System Characteristics and Quit Rates of Good, Average, and Poor Performers," University of Kentucky working paper, May 2006.
69. M. Brown, M. C. Sturman, and M. Simmering, "Compensation Policy and Organizational Performance: The Efficiency, Operational, and Financial Implications of Pay Levels and Pay Structure," *Academy of Management Journal* 46 (2003), pp. 752–762.
70. E. Lazear, "Labor Economics and Psychology of Organization," *Journal of Economic Perspectives* 5 (1991), pp. 89–110; D. Wazeter, "Determinants and Consequences of Pay Structures," Ph.D. dissertation, Cornell University, 1991.
71. M. Bidwell, "Paying More to Get Less: The Effects of External Hiring versus Internal Mobility," *Administrative Science Quarterly*, 56 (2011), 369–407; P. S. DeOrtentiis, C. H. Van Iddekinge, R. E. Ployhart, and T. D. Heetderks, "Build or Buy? The Individual and Unit-Level Performance of Internally versus Externally Selected Managers Over Time. *Journal of Applied Psychology*, 103(8), 2018, 916. It also, of course, matters why someone is moving. To the degree it is not voluntary or to the degree their skills are not a better match with the new job, that helps explain the inside hire advantage. For more on attributes of inside hires (and transfers) and external hires, see: J. DeVaro, A. Kauhanen, and N. Valmari, "Internal and External Hiring," *ILR Review*, 72(4), 2019, 981–1008.
72. B. Gerhart and J. Feng, "The Resource-Based View of the Firm, Human Resources, and Human Capital: Progress and Prospects," *Journal of Management*, 2021; J. R. Keller, "Posting and Slotting: How Hiring Processes Shape the Quality of Hire and Compensation in Internal Labor Markets," *Administrative Science Quarterly*, *63*(4), 2018, 848–878; M. Bidwell, "Paying More to Get Less: The Effects of External Hiring versus Internal Mobility," *Administrative Science Quarterly*, *56*(3), 2018, 369–407; S. J. George, "Information in the Labor Market," *Journal of Political Economy,* 70(5), Part 2 (1962): 94–105.
73. J. R. Keller, "Posting and Slotting: How Hiring Processes Shape the Quality of Hire and Compensation in Internal Labor Markets," *Administrative Science Quarterly*, 63 (2018), pp. 848–878; P. S. DeOrtentiis, C. H. Van Iddekinge, R. E., Ployhart, and T. D. Heetderks, "Build or Buy? The Individual and Unit-Level Performance of Internally versus Externally Selected Managers Over Time," *Journal of Applied Psychology,* 103(8), 2018, p. 916.
74. B. Gerhart and J. Feng, "The Resource-Based View of the Firm, Human Resources, and Human Capital: Progress and Prospects,"' *Journal of Management*, 2021.
75. Kacperczyk and C. Balachandran, "Vertical and Horizontal Wage Dispersion and Mobility Outcomes: Evidence from the Swedish Microdata," *Organization Science,* 29, no. 1 (2018), pp. 17–38.
76. E. Robert Livernash, "The Internal Wage Structure," in *New Concepts in Wage Determination,* eds. G. W. Taylor and F. C. Pierson (New York: McGraw-Hill, 1957), pp. 143–172.

77. E. Jaques, "In Praise of Hierarchies," *Harvard Business Review* (January–February 1990), pp. 32–46.

78. J. Sandberg, "Apportioning Furniture by Rank Can Stir Up Anger, Envy, Rebellion," *The Wall Street Journal,* November 10, 2004, p. B1.

Chapter Four
Job Analysis

Chapter Outline

Three people sit in front of their keyboards scanning their monitors. One is a customer representative in Ohio, checking the progress of an order for four dozen web-enabled cell phones from a retailer in Texas, who just placed the four dozen into his shopping cart on the company's website. A second is an engineer logging in to the project design software for the next generation of these phones. Colleagues in China working on the same project last night (day, in China) sent some suggestions for changes in the new design; the team in the United States will work on the project today and have their work waiting for their Chinese colleagues when they come to work in the morning. A third employee, in Ireland, is using the business software recently installed worldwide to analyze the latest sales reports. In today's workplace, people working for the same company no longer need to be down the hallway from one another. They can be on-site and overseas. Networks and business software link them all. Yet all their jobs are part of the organization's internal structure.

If pay is to be based on work performed, some way is needed to discover and describe the differences and similarities among these jobs–observation alone is not enough. **Job analysis** is that systematic method. Two products result from a job analysis. A **job description** is the list of tasks, duties, and responsibilities that make up a job. These are observable actions. A **job specification** is the list of knowledge, skills, abilities, and other characteristics that are necessary for an individual to have to perform the job. Thus, the description focuses on the job and the specification focuses on the person.

STRUCTURES BASED ON JOBS, PEOPLE, OR BOTH

Exhibit 4.1 outlines the process for constructing a work-related internal structure. No matter what the approach, the process begins by looking at people at work. Job-based structures look at what people are doing and the expected outcomes; skill- and competency-based structures look at the person. However, the underlying purpose of each phase of the process, called out in the left-hand side of the exhibit, remains the same for both job- and person-based structures: (1) collect and summarize work content information that identifies similarities and differences, (2) determine what to value, (3) assess the relative value, and (4) translate the relative value into an internal structure. (The blank areas in the person-based structure will be filled in when we get to **Chapter 6**.) This chapter and **Chapter 5** focus on the job-based structure.[1]

Exhibit 4.2 is part of a job description for a registered nurse. The job summary section provides an overview of the job. The section on relationships to other jobs demonstrates where the job fits in the organization structure: which jobs are supervised by this jobholder, which job supervises this jobholder, and the nature of any internal and external relationships.

EXHIBIT 4.1 Many Ways to Create Internal Structure

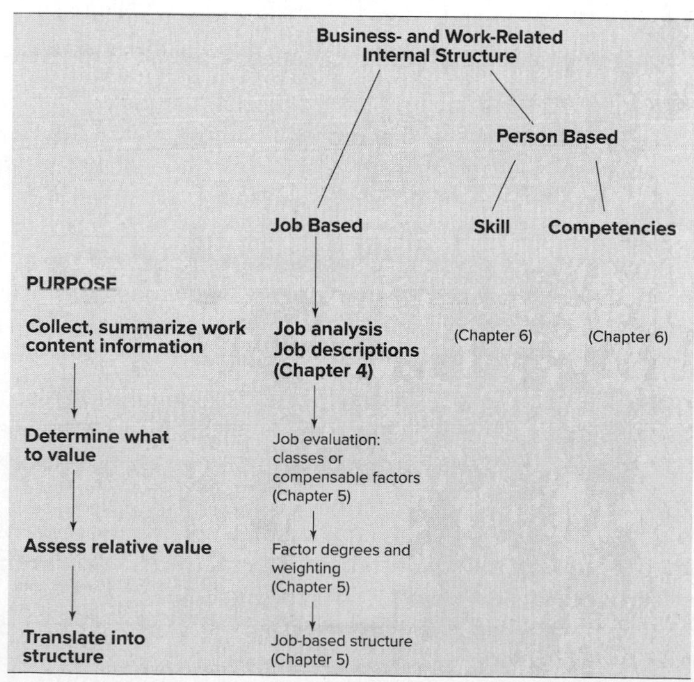

The section on essential responsibilities elaborates on the summary: "Provides a written assessment of patient within one hour of admission and at least once a shift." Collecting information on these essential responsibilities is the heart of job analysis.

EXHIBIT 4.2 Contemporary Job Description for Registered Nurse

Job Title: Registered Nurse

Job Summary

Accountable for the complete spectrum of patient care from admission through transfer or discharge through the nursing process of assessment, planning, implementation, and evaluation. Each R.N. has primary authority to fulfill responsibility of the nursing process on the assigned shift and for projecting future needs of the patient/family. Directs and guides patient teaching and activities for ancillary personnel while maintaining standard of professional nursing.

Relationships

Reports to: Head Nurse or Charge Nurse.

Supervises: Responsible for the care delivered by L.P.N.s, nursing assistants, and orderlies.

Works with: Ancillary Care Departments.

External relationships: Physicians, patients, patients' families.

Qualifications

Education: Graduate of an accredited school of nursing.

Work experience: Critical care requires one year of recent medical/surgical experience (special care nursing preferred), medical/surgical experience (new graduates may be considered for noncharge positions).

License or registration requirements: Current R.N. license or permit in the State of Minnesota.

Physical requirements:
A. Ability to bend, reach, or assist to transfer up to 50 pounds.
B. Ability to stand and/or walk 80 percent of 8-hour shift.
C. Visual and hearing acuity to perform job-related functions.

Essential Responsibilities

1. Assess physical, emotional, and psychosocial dimensions of patients.
   Standard: Provides a written assessment of patient within one hour of admission and at least once a shift. Communicates this assessment to other patient care providers in accordance with hospital policies.
2. Formulates a written plan of care for patients from admission through discharge.
   Standard: Develops short- and long-term goals within 24 hours of admission. Reviews and updates care plans each shift based on ongoing assessment.
3. Implements plan of care.
   Standard: Demonstrates skill in performing common nursing procedures in accordance with but not limited to the established written R.N. skills inventory specific to assigned area.

Note: Additional responsibilities omitted from exhibit.

JOB-BASED APPROACH: MOST COMMON

Exhibit 4.3 shows how job analysis and the resulting job description fit into the process of creating an internal structure. Job analysis provides the underlying information. It identifies the content of the job. This content serves as input for describing and valuing work.

> **Job analysis** is the systematic process of collecting information that identifies similarities and differences in the work.

Exhibit 4.3 also lists the major decisions in designing a job analysis: (1) Why are we performing job analysis? (2) What information do we need? (3) How should we collect it? (4) Who should be involved? (5) How useful are the results?

Why Perform Job Analysis?

Potential uses for job analysis have been suggested for every major human resource function. Often the type of job analysis data needed varies by function. For example, identifying the skills and experience required to perform the work clarifies hiring and promotion standards and identifies training needs. In performance evaluation, both employees and supervisors look to the required behaviors and results expected in a job to help assess performance. At one point, IBM identified every role (490 in all) performed by its 300,000-plus workers, managers, and executives. For example, IBM's vice president for learning had the roles of learning leader and manager. IBM also measured and monitored 4,000 skill sets.[2]

An internal structure based on job-related information provides both managers and employees a work-related rationale for pay differences. Employees who understand this rationale can see where their work fits into the bigger picture and can direct their behavior toward organization objectives. Job analysis data also help managers defend their decisions when challenged.

In compensation, job analysis has two critical uses: (1) It establishes similarities and differences in the work contents of the jobs and (2) it helps establish an internally fair and aligned job structure. If jobs have equal content, then in all likelihood the pay established for them will be equal (unless they are in different geographies). If, on the other hand, the job content differs, then the differences, along with the market rates paid by competitors, are part of the rationale for paying jobs differently.

EXHIBIT 4.3 Determining the Internal Job Structure

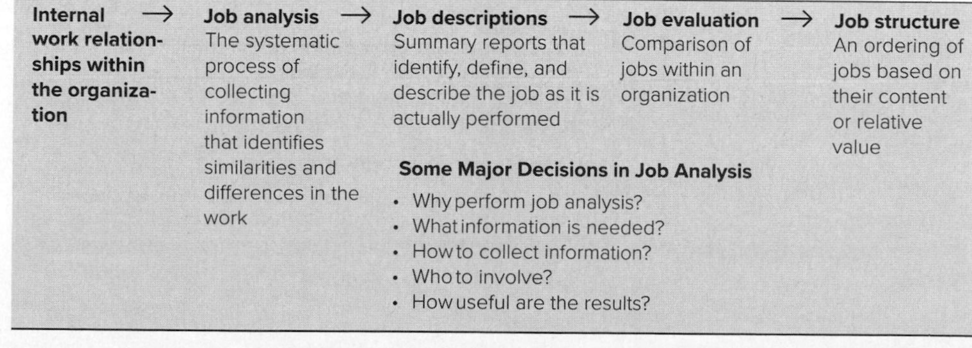

The key issue for compensation decision makers is still to ensure that the data collected are useful and acceptable to the employees and managers involved. As the arrows in **Exhibit 4.3** indicate, collecting job information is only an interim step, not an end in itself.

JOB ANALYSIS PROCEDURES

Exhibit 4.4 summarizes some job analysis terms and their relationship to each other. Job analysis usually collects information about specific tasks or behaviors.[3] A group of tasks performed by one person makes up a *position.* Identical positions make a *job,* and broadly similar jobs combine into a **job family.**[4]

The U.S. federal government, one of the biggest users of job analysis data, has developed a step-by-step approach to conducting **conventional job analysis.**[5] The government's procedures, shown in **Exhibit 4.5**, include developing preliminary information, interviewing jobholders and supervisors, and then using the information to create and verify job descriptions. The picture that emerges from reading the steps in the exhibit is of a very stable workplace where the division from one job to the next is clear, with little overlap.

In this workplace, jobs follow a steady progression in a hierarchy of increasing responsibility, and the relationship between jobs is clear. So is how to qualify for promotion into a higher-level job. While some argue that such a traditional, stable structure is a shrinking part of the workplace landscape, such structures nevertheless persist, in varying degrees, in many large organizations.[6] Thus, the federal Department of Labor's description of conventional job analysis provides a useful "how-to" guide.

EXHIBIT 4.4 **Job Analysis Terminology**

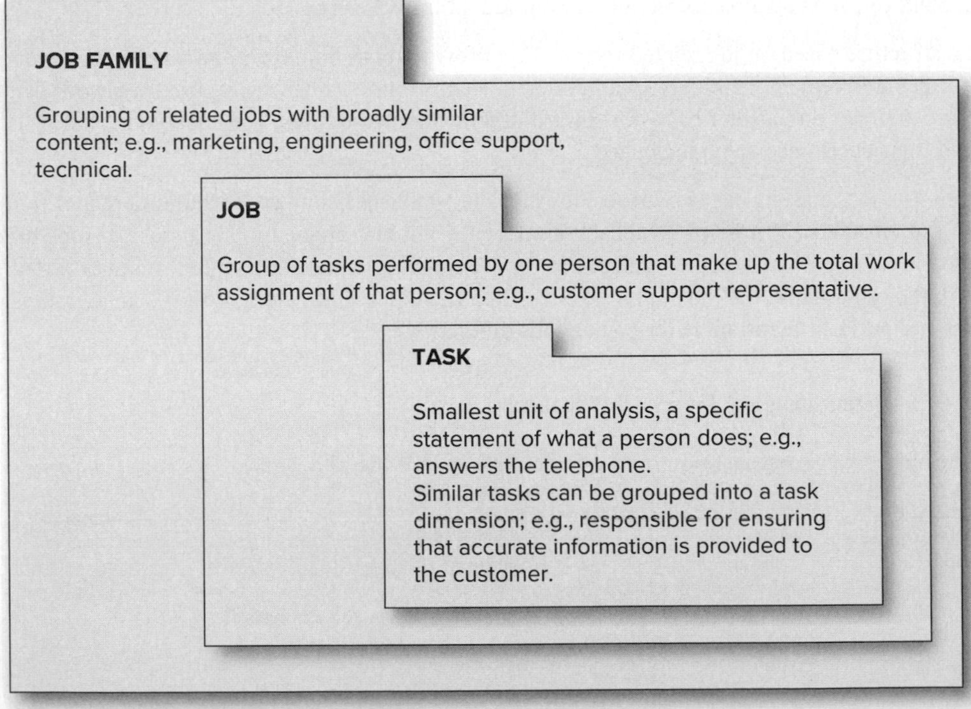

EXHIBIT 4.5 Conventional Job Analysis Procedures

Step	Things to Remember or Do
1. Develop preliminary job information	*a.* Review existing documents in order to develop an initial "big-picture" familiarity with the job: its main mission, its major duties or functions, work flow patterns. *b.* Prepare a preliminary list of duties that will serve as a framework for conducting the interviews. *c.* Make a note of major items that are unclear or ambiguous or that need to be clarified during the data-gathering process.
2. Conduct initial tour of work site	*a.* The initial tour is designed to familiarize the job analyst with the work layout, the tools and equipment that are used, the general conditions of the workplace, and the mechanics associated with the end-to-end performance of major duties. *b.* The initial tour is particularly helpful in those jobs where a firsthand view of a complicated or unfamiliar piece of equipment saves the interviewee the thousand words required to describe the unfamiliar or technical. *c.* For continuity, it is recommended that the first-level supervisor-interviewee be designated the guide for the job-site observations.
3. Conduct interviews	*a.* It is recommended that the first interview be conducted with the first-level supervisor, who is considered to be in a better position than the jobholders to provide an overview of the job and how the major duties fit together. *b.* For scheduling purposes, it is recommended that no more than two interviews be conducted per day, each interview lasting no more than three hours.
Notes on selection of interviewees	*a.* The interviewees are considered subject-matter experts by virtue of the fact that they perform the job (in the case of job incumbents) or are responsible for getting the job done (in the case of first-level supervisors). *b.* The job incumbent to be interviewed should represent the *typical*/employee who is knowledgeable about the job (*not* the trainee who is just learning the ropes *or* the outstanding member of the work unit). *c.* Whenever feasible, the interviewees should be selected with a view toward obtaining an appropriate race/sex mix.
4. Conduct second tour of work site	*a.* The second tour of the work site is designed to clarify, confirm, and otherwise refine the information developed in the interviews. *b.* As in the initial tour, it is recommended that the same first-level supervisor-interviewee conduct the second walk-through.

Step	Things to Remember or Do
5. Consolidate job information	*a.* The consolidation phase of the job study involves piecing together into one coherent and comprehensive job description the data obtained from several sources: supervisor, jobholders, on-site tours, and written materials about the job.
	b. Past experience indicates that one minute of consolidation is required for every minute of interviewing. For planning purposes, at least five hours should be set aside for the consolidation phase.
	c. A subject-matter expert should be accessible as a resource person to the job analyst during the consolidation phase. The supervisor-interviewee fills this role.
	d. The job analyst should check the initial preliminary list of duties and questions—all must be answered or confirmed.
6. Verify job description	*a.* The verification phase involves bringing all the interviewees together for the purpose of determining if the consolidated job description is accurate and complete.
	b. The verification process is conducted in a group setting. Typed or legibly written copies of the job description (narrative description of the work setting *and* list of task statements) are distributed to the first-level supervisor and the job incumbent interviewees.
	c. Line by line, the job analyst goes through the entire job description and makes notes of any omissions, ambiguities, or needed clarifications.
	d. The job analyst collects all materials at the end of the verification meeting.

WHAT INFORMATION SHOULD BE COLLECTED?

As **Exhibit 4.5** suggests, a typical analysis starts with a review of information already collected in order to develop a framework for further analysis. Job titles, major duties, task dimensions, and work flow information may already exist. However, it may no longer be accurate. So the analyst must clarify existing information, too.

Generally, a good job analysis collects sufficient information to adequately identify, define, and describe a job. **Exhibit 4.6** lists some of the information that is usually collected. The information is categorized as "related to the job" and "related to the employee."

Job Data: Identification

Job titles, departments, the number of people who hold the job, and whether it is exempt from the Fair Labor Standards Act are all examples of information that identifies a job.

While a job title may seem pretty straightforward, it may not be. An observer of the U.S. banking system commented that "every employee over 25 seems to be a vice president." A study accuses the U.S. government of creating more new job titles in a recent six-year period than in the preceding 30 years.[7] Some of the newer positions include deputy to the deputy secretary, principal assistant deputy undersecretary, and associate principal deputy assistant secretary. Most of these titles were created at the highest levels of government service, often to attract a specific person with unique skills. Our personal favorite is at the Jet Propulsion Laboratory in Pasadena, California, where the head of the Interplanetary Network Directorate is, naturally, the director of the Directorate.[8] On the other hand, your tax dollars were at one point paying the wages of 484 deputy assistant secretaries, 148 associate assistant secretaries, 220 assistant assistant secretaries, and 82 deputy assistant assistant secretaries.

Job Data: Content

This is the heart of job analysis. Job content data involve the elemental tasks or units of work, with emphasis on the purpose of each task. An excerpt from a job analysis questionnaire that collects task data is shown in **Exhibit 4.7**. The inventory describes the job aspect of communication in terms of actual tasks, such as "read technical publications" and "consult with co-workers." The inventory takes eight items to cover "obtain technical information" and another seven for "exchange technical information." In fact, the task inventory from which the exhibit is excerpted contains 250 items and covers only systems and analyst jobs. New task-based questions need to be designed for each new set of jobs.

In addition to the emphasis on the task, the other distinguishing characteristic of the inventory in the exhibit is the emphasis on the objective of the task, for example, "read technical publications to keep current on industry" and "consult with co-workers to exchange ideas and techniques." **Task data** reveal the actual work performed and its purpose or outcome.

EXHIBIT 4.6 **Typical Data Collected for Job Analysis**

Data Related to Job	
Job Identification	**Job Content**
Title	Tasks
Department in which job is located	Activities
Number of people who hold job	Constraints on actions
	Performance criteria
	Critical incidents
	Conflicting demands
	Working conditions
	Roles (e.g., negotiator, monitor, leader)

Data Related to Employee		
Employee Characteristics	**Internal Relationships**	**External Relationships**
Professional/technical knowledge	Boss and other superiors	Suppliers
Manual skills	Peers	Customers
Verbal skills	Subordinates	Regulatory
Written skills		Professional industry
Quantitative skills		Community
Mechanical skills		Union/employee groups
Conceptual skills		
Managerial skills		
Leadership skills		
Interpersonal skills		

Employee Data

We can look at the kinds of behaviors that will result in the outcomes. **Exhibit 4.6** categorizes employee data as employee characteristics, internal relationships, and external relationships. **Exhibit 4.8** shows how communication can be described with verbs (e.g., negotiating, persuading). The verbs chosen are related to the employee characteristic being identified (e.g., bargaining skills, interpersonal skills). The rest of the statement helps identify whether the behavior involves an internal or external relationship. So both **Exhibit 4.7** and **Exhibit 4.8** focus on communication, but they come at it with different approaches.

The excerpt in **Exhibit 4.8** is from the **Position Analysis Questionnaire (PAQ),** which groups work information into seven basic factors: information input, mental processes, work output, relationships with other persons, job context, other job characteristics, and general dimensions. Similarities and differences among jobs are described in terms of these seven factors, rather than in terms of specific aspects unique to each job.[9] The communication behavior in this exhibit is part of the relationships-with-other-persons factor.

EXHIBIT 4.7 Communication: Task-Based Data

1. Mark the circle in the "Do This" column for tasks that you currently perform.
2. At the end of the task list, write in any unlisted tasks that you currently perform.
3. Rate each task that you perform for relative time spent by marking the appropriate circle in the "Time Spent" column.

Please use a No. 2 pencil and fill all circles completely.

PERFORM COMMUNICATION ACTIVITIES	Do This	Time spent in current position: Very small amount / Much below average / Below average / Slightly below average / About average / Slightly above average / Above average / Much above average / Very large amount
Obtain technical information		
421. Read technical publications about competitive products.	○	①②③④⑤⑥⑦⑧⑨
422. Read technical publications to keep current on industry.	○	①②③④⑤⑥⑦⑧⑨
423. Attend required, recommended, or job-related courses and/or seminars.	○	①②③④⑤⑥⑦⑧⑨
424. Study existing operating systems/programs to gain/maintain familiarity with them.	○	①②③④⑤⑥⑦⑧⑨
425. Perform literature searches necessary to the development of products.	○	①②③④⑤⑥⑦⑧⑨
426. Communicate with system software group to see how their recent changes impact current projects.	○	①②③④⑤⑥⑦⑧⑨
427. Study and evaluate state-of-the-art techniques to remain competitive and/or lead the field.	○	①②③④⑤⑥⑦⑧⑨
428. Attend industry standards meetings.	○	①②③④⑤⑥⑦⑧⑨
Exchange technical information		
429. Interface with coders to verify that the software design is being implemented as specified.	○	①②③④⑤⑥⑦⑧⑨
430. Consult with co-workers to exchange ideas and techniques.	○	①②③④⑤⑥⑦⑧⑨
431. Consult with members of other technical groups within the company to exchange new ideas and techniques.	○	①②③④⑤⑥⑦⑧⑨
432. Interface with support consultants or organizations to clarify software design or courseware content.	○	①②③④⑤⑥⑦⑧⑨

Source: Excerpted from Control Data Corporation's Quantitative Job Analysis.

EXHIBIT 4.8 **Communication: Behavioral-Based Data**

Section 4 Relationships with Others	***Code Importance to This job (1)***
This section deals with different aspects of interaction between people involved in various kinds of work.	N Does not apply 1 Very minor 2 Low 3 Average 4 High 5 Extreme

4.1 Communication

Rate the following in terms of how important the activity is to the completion of the job. Some jobs may involve several or all of the items in this section.

4.1.1 Oral (communicating by speaking)

99 ______	Advising (dealing with individuals in order to counsel and/or guide them with regard to problems that may be resolved by legal, financial, scientific, technical, clinical, spiritual, and/or professional principles)
100 ______	Negotiating (dealing with others in order to reach an agreement on solution, for example, labor bargaining, diplomatic relations, etc.)
101 ______	Persuading (dealing with others in order to influence them toward some action or point of view, for example, selling, political campaigning, etc.)
102 ______	Instructing (the teaching of knowledge or skills, in either an informal or a formal manner, to others, for example, a public school teacher, a machinist teaching an apprentice, etc.)
103 ______	Interviewing (conducting interviews directed toward some specific objective, for example, interviewing job applicants, census taking, etc.)
104 ______	Routine information exchange job related (the giving and/or receiving of *job-related* information of a routine nature, for example, ticket agent, taxicab dispatcher, receptionist, etc.)
105 ______	Nonroutine information exchange (the giving and/or receiving of *job-related* information of a nonroutine or unusual nature, for example, professional committee meetings, engineers discussing new product design, etc.)
106 ______	Public speaking (making speeches or formal presentations before relatively large audiences, for example, political addresses, radio/TV broadcasting, delivering a sermon, etc.)

4.1.2 Written (communicating by written/printed material)

107 ______	Writing (for example, writing or dictating letters, reports, etc., writing copy for ads, writing newspaper articles, etc.; do *not* include transcribing activities described in item 4.3 but only activities in which the incumbent creates the written material)

Source: E. J. McConnick, P. R. Jeanneret, and R. C. Mecham, *Position Analysis Questionnaire,* copyright ©1969 Purdue Research Foundation. Licensed by ERI Economic Research Institute, Inc.

The entire PAQ consists of 194 items. Its developers claim that these items are sufficient to analyze any job. However, you can see from the exhibit that the reading level is quite high. A large proportion of employees need help to get through the whole thing.

Another, more nuanced view of "communication" focuses on the nature of the interactions required plus knowledge underlying them. Interactions are defined as the knowledge and behaviors involved in searching, monitoring, and coordinating required to do the work. Some interactions are transactional–routine, "do it by the book." The nine steps of a McFry job, shown in **Exhibit 4.9**, seem transactional to us. Other interactions are more tacit–complex and ambiguous. Work content that involves more tacit interactions is believed to add greater value than more transactional tasks.[10]

The content of communications that occurs between the Merrill Lynch financial advisor and a client to complete a stock transaction differs substantively from that between a Merrill Lynch senior vice president investor and client who aims to build a long-term relationship to manage a client's $10 million in assets. Communication in both settings includes interactions with clients, but "building long-term relationships" versus "complete transactions" reveals substantive differences in content.

However appealing it may be to rationalize job analysis as the foundation of all HR decisions, collecting all of this information for so many different purposes is very expensive. In addition, the resulting information may be too generalized for any single purpose, including compensation. If the information is to be used for multiple purposes, the analyst must be sure that the information collected is accurate and sufficient for each use. Trying to be all things to all people often results in being nothing to everyone.

"Essential Elements" and the Americans with Disabilities Act

In addition to the job description having sections that identify, describe, and define the job, the **Americans with Disabilities Act (ADA)** requires that **essential elements** of a job–those that cannot be reassigned to other

EXHIBIT 4.9 The McFry Nine-Step Program

1. Open a bag of fries.
2. Fill basket about half full (at McDonald's, a machine does this step because we humans might make a mistake. At most places, the task is manual.)
3. Place basket in deep fryer.
4. Push timer button to track cooking time.
5. Play Pavlov's dog—remove basket from fryer when buzzer rings and tip so fries go into holding tray. Be careful; this takes two hands, and hot grease can be flying about. Don't spill even a drop of grease on the floor or you will be skating—not walking—in it for the rest of the day.
6. Salt fries.
7. Push another button that signals when seven minutes are up, the "suggested holding time" for fries.
8. Check screen for size fries requested on next order.
9. Fill the corresponding fry container with fries and place in holding bin.

Source: Jerry Newman. *My Secret Life on the McJob* (New York: McGraw-Hill, 2007).

workers—must be specified for jobs covered by the legislation. If a job applicant can perform these essential elements, it is assumed that the applicant can perform the job. After that, reasonable accommodations must be made to enable an otherwise-qualified handicapped person to perform those elements.[11]

ADA regulations state that "essential functions refers to the fundamental job duties of the employment position the individual with a disability holds or desires." The difficulty of specifying essential elements varies with the discretion in the job and with the stability of the job. Technology changes tend to make some tasks easier for all people, including those with disabilities, by reducing the physical strength or mobility required to do them. Unfortunately, employment rates for people with disabilities are still low.

The law does not make any allowances for special pay rates or special benefits for people with disabilities. Say, for example, a company subsidizes paid parking for its employees. An employee who does not drive because of a disability requests that the employer provide the cash equivalent of the parking subsidy as a reasonable accommodation so that the money can be used to pay for alternative transportation.

While the law does not require any particular kind of analysis, many employers have modified the format of their job descriptions to specifically call out the essential elements. A lack of compliance places an organization at risk and ignores one of the objectives of the pay model.

Level of Analysis

The job analysis terms defined in **Exhibit 4.4** are arranged in a hierarchy. The level at which an analysis begins influences whether the work is similar or dissimilar. The three jobs described in the beginning of the chapter—customer representative, engineer, account analyst—all involve use of computers, but a closer look showed that the jobs are very different. At the job-family-level bookkeepers, tellers, and accounting clerks may be considered to be similar jobs, yet at the job level they are very different. An analogy might be looking at two grains of salt under a microscope versus looking at them as part of a serving of french fries. If job data suggest that jobs are similar, the jobs must be paid equally; if jobs are different, they can be paid differently.[12]

e-Compensation

Many companies post a sample of job openings on their websites. You can also check LinkedIn, Glassdoor, and a host of other websites. Compare the job postings from several companies. How complete are the job descriptions included with the postings? Are "essential elements" listed? Are job titles specific or generic? Can you get any sense of a company's culture from its job postings?

Does this mean that the microscopic approach is best? Not necessarily. Many employers find it difficult to justify the time and expense of collecting task-level information, particularly for flexible jobs with frequently changing tasks. They may collect just enough job-level data to make comparisons in the external market for setting wages. However, the ADA's essential-elements requirement for hiring and promotion decisions seems to require more detail than what is required for pay decisions. Designing career paths, staffing, and legal compliance may also require more detailed, finely grained information.

Using broad, generic descriptions that cover a large number of related tasks closer to the job-family level in **Exhibit 4.4** is one way to increase flexibility. Two employees working in the same broadly defined jobs may be doing entirely different sets of related tasks. But for pay purposes, they may be doing work of equal value. Employees in these broadly defined jobs can switch to other tasks that fall within the same broad range without the bureaucratic burden of making job transfer requests and wage adjustments. Thus, employees can more easily be matched to changes in the work flow. Recruiter, compensation analyst, and training specialist could each be analyzed as a separate, distinct job, or could all be combined more broadly in the category "HR associate."

Still, a countervailing view deserves consideration. A promotion to a new job title is part of the organization's network of returns. Reducing the number of titles may reduce the opportunities to reinforce positive employee behavior. E*Trade experienced an increase in turnover after it retitled jobs. It reduced its vice presidents and directors to 85, down from around 170 before the retitling.[13] Moving from the federal government job of assistant secretary to that of associate assistant secretary (or reverse) may be far more meaningful than people outside Washington, DC, imagine.

HOW CAN THE INFORMATION BE COLLECTED?

Conventional Methods

The most common way to collect job information is to ask the people who are doing a job to fill out a questionnaire. Sometimes an analyst will interview the jobholders and their supervisors to be sure they understand the questions and that the information is correct. Or the analyst may observe the person at work and take notes on what is being done.

Exhibit 4.10 shows part of a job analysis questionnaire. Questions range from "Give an example of a particularly difficult problem that you face in your work. Why does it occur? How often does it occur? What special skills and/or resources are needed to solve this difficult problem?" to "What is the nature of any contact you have with individuals or companies in countries other than the United States?" These examples are drawn from the Complexity of Duties section of a job analysis questionnaire used by 3M. Other sections of the questionnaire are Skills/Knowledge Applied (19 to choose from), Impact This Job Has on 3M's Business, and Working Conditions. It concludes by asking respondents how well they feel the questionnaire has captured their particular job.

The advantage of conventional questionnaires and interviews is that the involvement of employees increases their understanding of the process. However, the results are only as good as the people involved. If important aspects of a job are omitted, or if the jobholders themselves either do not realize or are unable to express the importance of certain aspects, the resulting job descriptions will be faulty. If you look at the number of jobs in an organization, you can see the difficulty in expecting a single analyst to understand all the different types of work and the importance of certain job aspects. Different people have different perceptions, which may result in differences in interpretation or emphasis. The whole process is open to bias and favoritism.[14] As a result of this potential subjectivity, as well as the huge amount of time the process takes, conventional methods have given way to more quantitative (and systematic) data collection.

Quantitative Methods

Increasingly, employees are directed to a website where they complete a questionnaire online.[15] Such an approach is characterized as **quantitative job analysis (QJA),** because statistical analysis of the results is possible. **Exhibits 4.7** and **4.8** are excerpts from quantitative questionnaires. In addition to facilitating statistical analysis of the results, quantitative data collection allows more data to be collected faster.

A questionnaire typically asks jobholders to assess each item in terms of whether or not that particular item is part of their job. If it is, they are asked to rate how important it is and the amount of job time spent on it. The responses can be machine-scored, similar to the process for a multiple-choice test (only there are no wrong answers), and the results can be used to develop a profile of the job. Questions are grouped around five compensable factors (discussed in **Chapter 5**): knowledge, accountability, reasoning, communication, and working conditions. Knowledge is further subcategorized as range of depth, qualifications, experience, occupational skills, management skills, and learning time. Assistance is given in the form of prompting questions and a list of jobs whose holders have answered each question in a similar way. Results can be used to prepare a job profile based on the compensable factors. If more than one person is doing a particular job, results of several people in the job can be compared or averaged to develop the profile. Profiles can be compared across jobholders in both the same and different jobs.

EXHIBIT 4.10 3M's Structured Interview Questionnaire

I. Job Overview

Job Summary	What is the main purpose of your job? (Why does it exist and what does the work contribute to 3M?) Examples: To provide secretarial support in our department by performing office and administrative duties. To purchase goods and services that meet specifications at the least cost. To perform systems analysis involved in the development, installation, and maintenance of computer applications. Hint: It may help to list the duties first before answering this question.
Duties and Respon-sibilities	What are your job's main duties and responsibilities? (These are the major work activities that usually take up a significant amount of your work time and occur regularly as you perform your work.) In the spaces below, list your job's five most important or most frequent duties. Then, in the boxes, estimate the percentage of the time you spend on each duty each day. — Percentage of Time Spent (Total may be less than but not more than 100%) 1.

II. Skills/Knowledge Applied

Formal Training or Education	What is the level of formal training/education that is needed to start doing your job? Example: High School, 2 Year Vo-Tech in Data Processing. Bachelor of Science in Chemistry. In some jobs, a combination of education and job-related experience can substitute for academic degrees. Example: Bachelor's Degree in Accounting or completion of 2 years of general business plus 3–4 years' work experience in an accounting field.
Experience	Months: Years: None
Skills/ Compet-	What important skills, competencies, or abilities are needed to do the work that you do? (Please give examples for each skill that you identify.) **A. Coordinating Skills** (such as scheduling activities, organizing/maintaining records) Are coordinating skills required? ☐ Yes ☐ No If yes, give examples of specific skills needed Example **B. Administrative Skills** (such as mo

III. Complexity of Duties

Structure and Variation of Work	How processes and tasks within your work are determined, and how you do them are important to understanding your work at 3M. Describe the work flow in your job. Think of the major focus of your job or think of the work activities on which you spend the most time. 1. From whom/where (title, not person) do you receive work? 2. What processes or tasks do you perform to comple
Problem Solving and Analysis	3. Give an example of a particularly difficult problem that you face in your work. Why does it occur? How often does it occur? What special skills and/or resources are needed to solve this difficult problem?

VI. General Comments

General Comments	What percentage of your job duties do you feel was captured in this questionnaire? ☐ 0–25% ☐ 26–50% ☐ 51–75% ☐ 76–100% What aspect of your job was not covered adequately by this questionnaire?

Quantitative inventories can be tailored to the needs of a specific organization or to a specific family of jobs, such as data/information-processing jobs.[16] Many organizations find it practical and cost-effective to modify these existing inventories rather than to develop their own analysis from ground zero. But, remember, as we have said, the results depend on the quality of the inputs. Here, the items on the questionnaire matter. If important aspects of a job are omitted or if the jobholders themselves do not realize the importance of certain aspects, the resulting job descriptions will be faulty. In one study, the responses of high-performing stockbrokers on amounts of time spent on some tasks differed from those of low performers. The implication is that any analysis needs to include good performers to ensure that the work is usefully analyzed.[17]

Who Collects the Information?

Collecting job analysis information through one-on-one interviews can be a thankless task. No matter how good a job you do, some people will not be happy with the resulting job descriptions. In the past, organizations often assigned the task to a new employee, saying it would help the new employee become familiar with the jobs of the company. Today, if job analysis is performed at all, human resource generalists and supervisors do it. The analysis is best done by someone thoroughly familiar with the organization and its jobs and trained in how to do the analysis properly.[18]

Who Provides the Information?

The decision on the source of the data (jobholders, supervisors, and/or analysts) hinges on how to ensure consistent, accurate, useful, and acceptable data. Expertise about the work resides with the jobholders and the supervisors; hence, they are the principal sources. For key managerial/professional jobs, supervisors "two levels above" have also been suggested as valuable sources since they may have a more strategic view of how jobs fit in the overall organization. In other instances, subordinates and employees in other jobs that interface with the job under study are also involved.

The number of incumbents per job from which to collect data probably varies with the stability of the job, as well as the ease of collecting the information. An ill-defined or changing job will require either the involvement of more respondents or a more careful selection of respondents. Obviously, the more people involved, the more time-consuming and expensive the process, although computerization helps mitigate these drawbacks.

Whether through a conventional analysis or a quantitative approach, completing a questionnaire requires considerable involvement by employees and supervisors. Involvement can increase their understanding of the process, thereby increasing the likelihood that the results of the analysis will be acceptable.[19] But it also is expensive.

What about Discrepancies?

What happens if the supervisor and the employees present different pictures of the jobs? While supervisors, in theory, ought to know the jobs well, they may not, particularly if jobs are changing. People actually working in a job may change it. They may find ways to do things more efficiently, or they may not have realized that certain tasks were supposed to be part of their jobs.

3M had an interesting problem when it collected job information from a group of engineers. The engineers listed a number of responsibilities that they viewed as part of their jobs; however, the manager realized that those responsibilities actually belonged to a higher level of work. The engineers had enlarged their jobs beyond what they were being paid to do. No one wanted to tell these highly productive employees to slack off. Instead, 3M looked for additional ways to reward these engineers rather than bureaucratize them.

What should the manager do if employees and their supervisors do not agree on what is part of the job? Differences in job data may arise among the jobholders as well. Some may see the job one way, some another. The best answer is to collect more data. Enough data are required to ensure consistent, accurate, useful, and acceptable results. Holding a meeting of multiple jobholders and supervisors in a focus group to discuss discrepancies and then asking both employees and supervisors to sign off on the revised results helps ensure agreement on, or at least understanding of, the results. Disagreements can be an opportunity to clarify expectations, learn about better ways to do the job, and document how the job is actually performed. Discrepancies among employees may even reveal that more than one job has been lumped under the same job title.

Top Management (and Union) Support Is Critical

In addition to involvement by analysts, jobholders, and their supervisors, support of top management is absolutely essential. Support of union officials in a unionized workforce is as well. They know (hopefully) what is strategically relevant. They must be alerted to the cost of a thorough job analysis, its time-consuming nature, and the fact that changes will be involved. For example, jobs may be combined; pay rates may be adjusted. If top managers (and unions) are not willing to seriously consider any changes suggested by job analysis, the process is probably not worth the bother and expense.

JOB DESCRIPTIONS SUMMARIZE THE DATA

So now the job information has been collected, maybe even organized. But it still must be summarized and documented in a way that will be useful for HR decisions, including job evaluation (**Chapter 5**). As noted previously, that summary of the job is the **job description.** The job description provides a "word picture" of the job. Let us return to **Exhibit 4.2**, our job description for a registered nurse. It contains information on the tasks, people, and things included. Trace the connection between different parts of the description and the job analysis data collected. The job is identified by its title and its relationships to other jobs in the structure. A job summary provides an overview of the job. The section on essential responsibilities elaborates on the summary. It includes the tasks. Related tasks may be grouped into task dimensions.

This particular job description also includes very specific standards for judging whether an essential responsibility has been met–for example, "Provides a written assessment of patient within one hour of admission and at least once a shift." A final section lists the qualifications necessary in order to be hired for the job. These are the **job specifications** that can be used as a basis for hiring–the knowledge, skills, and abilities required to adequately perform the tasks. But keep in mind that the summary needs to be relevant for pay decisions and thus must focus on similarities and differences in content.

Using Generic Job Descriptions

To avoid starting from scratch (if writing a job description for the first time) or as a way to cross-check externally, it can be useful to refer to generic job descriptions that have not yet been tailored to a specific organization. One readily accessible source is the Occupational Information Network, or O*NET (***www.onetcenter.org***). **Exhibit 4.11** shows the information O*NET provides using the job of computer programmer as an example.

EXHIBIT 4.11 O*NET Code Connector

Help **Search**

Software Developers, Applications - 15-1132.00

O*NET-SOC Description

Develop, create, and modify general computer applications software or specialized utility programs. Analyze user needs and develop software solutions. Design software or customize software for client use with the aim of optimizing operational efficiency. May analyze and design databases within an application area, working individually or coordinating database development as part of a team. May supervise computer programmers.

Sample of Reported Job Titles

- Application Developer
- Application Integration Engineer
- Applications Developer
- Computer Consultant
- Information Technology Analyst (IT Analyst)
- Software Architect
- Software Developer
- Software Development Engineer
- Software Engineer
- Technical Consultant

Tasks

 All 15 displayed

- Analyze information to determine, recommend, and plan computer specifications and layouts, and peripheral equipment modifications.
- Analyze user needs and software requirements to determine feasibility of design within time and cost constraints.
- Confer with systems analysts, engineers, programmers and others to design system and to obtain information on project limitations and capabilities, performance requirements and interfaces.
- Consult with customers about software system design and maintenance.
- Coordinate software system installation and monitor equipment functioning to ensure specifications are met.
- Design, develop and modify software systems, using scientific analysis and mathematical models to predict and measure outcome and consequences of design.
- Determine system performance standards.

- Develop and direct software system testing and validation procedures, programming, and documentation.
- Modify existing software to correct errors, allow it to adapt to new hardware, or to improve its performance.
- Obtain and evaluate information on factors such as reporting formats required, costs, and security needs to determine hardware configuration.
- Recommend purchase of equipment to control dust, temperature, and humidity in area of system installation.
- Specify power supply requirements and configuration.
- Store, retrieve, and manipulate data for analysis of system capabilities and requirements.
- Supervise the work of programmers, technologists and technicians and other engineering and scientific personnel.
- Train users to use new or modified equipment.

Detailed Work Activities

5 of 17 displayed

- Analyze project data to determine specifications or requirements.
- Apply mathematical principles or statistical approaches to solve problems in scientific or applied fields.
- Assess database performance.
- Collaborate with others to determine design specifications or details.
- Coordinate software or hardware installation.

Source: This page includes information from O*NET Code Connector by the U.S. Department of Labor, Employment and Training Administration (USDOL/ETA). Used under the CC BY 4.0 license. O*NET® is a trademark of USDOL/ETA. https://www.onetonline.org.

e-Compensation

Use O*NET to find the knowledge, skills, and other characteristics needed to be a computer programmer (or an occupation of your choice).

Go to *http://online.onetcenter.org/*

Choose: Find Occupations

Enter the occupation name into space under "Keyword or O*NET-SOC code"

Click on "go"

Then click on the name of the occupation to see the knowledge, skills, etc. required.

Would this information from O*NET be useful to you if you needed to write job descriptions in your organizations?

Describing Managerial/Professional Jobs

Descriptions of managerial/professional jobs often include more detailed information on the nature of the job, its scope, and accountability. One challenge is that an individual manager will influence the job content.[20] Professional/managerial job descriptions must capture the relationship between the job, the person performing it, and the organization objectives–how the job fits into the organization, the results expected, and what the person performing it brings to the job. Someone with strong information systems and finance expertise performing the compensation manager's job will probably shape it differently, based on this expertise, than someone with strong negotiation and/or counseling expertise.

Exhibit 4.12 excerpts this scope and accountability information for a nurse manager. Rather than emphasizing the tasks to be done, this description focuses on the accountabilities (e.g., "responsible for the coordination, direction, implementation, evaluation, and management of personnel and services; provides leadership; participates in strategic planning and defining future direction").

Verify the Description

The final step in the job analysis process is to verify the accuracy of the resulting job descriptions (step 6 in **Exhibit 4.5**). Verification often involves the jobholders as well as their supervisors to determine whether the proposed job description is accurate and complete. The description is discussed, line by line, with the analyst, who makes notes of any omissions, ambiguities, or needed clarifications (an often excruciating and thankless task). It would have been interesting to hear the discussion between our nurse from 100 years ago, whose job is described in **Exhibit 4.13**, and her supervisor. The job description paints a vivid picture of expectations at that time, although we suspect the nurse probably did not have much opportunity for input regarding the accuracy of the job description.

EXHIBIT 4.12 Job Description for a Manager

Title: Nurse Manager

Department: ICU

Position Description:

Under the direction of the Vice President of Patient Care Services and Directors of Patient Care Services, the Nurse Manager assumes 24-hour accountability and responsibility for the operations of defined patient specialty services. The Nurse Manager is administratively responsible for the coordination, direction, implementation, evaluation, and management of personnel and services. The Nurse Manager provides leadership in a manner consistent with the corporate mission, values, and philosophy and adheres to policies and procedures established by Saint Joseph's Hospital and the Division of Patient Care Services. The Nurse Manager participates in strategic planning and defining future direction for the assigned areas of responsibility and the organization.

Qualification:

Education: Graduate of accredited school of nursing. A bachelor's degree in nursing or related field required. Master's degree preferred. Current license in State of Wisconsin as a Registered Nurse, Experience: A minimum of three years' clinical nursing is required. Minimum of two years' management experience or equivalent preferred.

JOB ANALYSIS: BEDROCK OR BUREAUCRACY?

HRNet, an Internet discussion group related to HR issues, provoked one of its largest responses ever with the query, "What good is job analysis?" Some felt that managers have no basis for making defensible, work-related decisions without it. Others called the process a bureaucratic boondoggle. Yet job analysts are an endangered species. Many employers, as part of their drive to contain expenses, no longer have job analysts. The unknown costs involved are too difficult to justify.

One expert writes, "Whenever I visit a human resources department, I ask whether they have any [job analysis]. I have not had a positive answer in several years, except in government organizations."[21] Yet if job analysis is the cornerstone of human resource decisions, what are such decisions based on if work information is no longer rigorously collected?

This disagreement centers on the issue of flexibility. Many organizations today are using fewer employees to do a wider variety of tasks in order to increase productivity and reduce costs. Reducing the number of different jobs and cross-training employees can make work content more fluid and employees more flexible.[22]

Generic job descriptions that cover a larger number of related tasks (e.g., "associate") can provide flexibility in moving people among tasks without adjusting pay. Employees may be more easily matched to changes in the work flow; the importance of flexibility in behavior is made clear to employees.

Traditional job analysis that makes fine distinctions among levels of jobs has been accused of reinforcing rigidity in the organization. Employees may refuse to do certain tasks that are not specifically called out in

EXHIBIT 4.13 Job Description for Nurse 100 Years Ago

In addition to caring for your 50 patients each nurse will follow these regulations:

1. Daily sweep and mop the floors of your ward, dust the patient's furniture and window sills.
2. Maintain an even temperature in your ward by bringing in a scuttle of coal for the day's business.
3. Light is important to observe the patient's condition. Therefore, each day, fill kerosene lamps, clean chimneys, and trim wicks. Wash the windows once a week.
4. The nurse's notes are important in aiding the physician's work. Make your pens carefully, you may whittle nibs to your individual taste.
5. Each nurse on the day duty will report every day at 7 a.m. and leave at 8 p.m. except on the Sabbath on which day you will be off from 12:00 noon to 2:00 p.m.
6. Graduate nurses in good standing with the director of nurses will be given an evening off each week for courting purposes, or two evenings a week if you go regularly to church.
7. Each nurse should lay aside from each pay day a goodly sum of her earnings for her benefit during her declining years, so that she will not become a burden. For example, if you earn $30 a month you should set aside $15.
8. Any nurse who smokes, uses liquor in any form, gets her hair done at a beauty shop, or frequents dance halls will give the director good reason to suspect her worth, intentions, and integrity.
9. The nurse who performs her labors and serves her patients and doctors faithfully and without fault for a period of five years will be given an increase by the hospital administration of five cents a day, provided there are no hospital debts that are outstanding.

their job descriptions. It should be noted, however, that this problem mainly arises where employee relations are already poor. In unionized settings, union members may "work to the rules" (i.e., not do anything that is not specifically listed in their job descriptions) as a technique for putting pressure on management.

In some organizations, analyzing work content is now conducted as part of **work flow analysis.** This analysis looks at how an organization does its work: activities pursued to accomplish specific objectives for specific customers. A "customer" can be internal or external to the organization. So Starbucks, in its continuous quest for improved service, frets over "average wait time." If the time to put that Venti Double Chocolate Chip Frappuccino Blended Creme in your hand is increased because customers in front of you are musing over the new CD for sale at the register, you may decide that the Dunkin' Donuts across the street might be a better choice. Starbucks shaved 20 seconds off its wait time by redesigning the barista job to include "floating." Floaters walk the queue, take your order, mark the cup, and hand the cup to the barista who will actually fill your order–all before you get to the cash register. Floaters also "communicate" with the customers to make the experience enjoyable. Notice that as part of a work flow study, job analysis is conducted to understand the work and how it adds value. Is the barista job content now different with the floating tasks? Yes.[23]

JOB ANALYSIS AND CHANGE IN WORK: GLOBALIZATION AND AUTOMATION (INCLUDING AI)

Change in Work

Whether because of changes in technology, consumer preferences, or other factors, the content of work continually changes and evolves over time. As we will see later in this chapter (under "**Currency**"), it is thus important to use job analysis to keep job descriptions up to date. **Exhibit 4.14** helps us see how work changes over time. In the top (Part A), we can see that from 1940 until today, employment in farming and mining occupations declined from 18 percent of all employment to just 2 percent. Employment of production workers has likewise had a steep decline. On the other hand, employment in professional and managerial occupations has increased substantially. Also notable is the last column, which shows that, overall, 63% of detailed occupational titles (within the broad occupational categories in the left column) did not exist in 1940. This is most true of occupations within the Health Services and Professionals categories. Part B of **Exhibit 4.14** provides some examples of new occupational titles that have been added over the years.

As a more specific example of change in work, consider the job of landman, which entails tracking down (before competitors) the owners of land to get them to sign over drilling rights to valuable oil and natural gas deposits on their land. At one point, especially during the shale boom, drilling rights in East Texas could cost more than $15,000 per acre and landmen earned six-figure incomes. Now, however, demand for fossil fuels has weakened and interest in shale-based deposits has been especially hard hit. Thus, some landmen like Carter Collum and Tami Hughes decided they needed to adapt. Some now work at securing prime wind and solar fields as growth in renewable energy ramps up. It remains to be seen how things will play out. By its nature, renewable energy does not "run out." That would suggest there will be less need to find new land than is the case for fossil fuels. If so, a shift to renewables will mean less landmen. However, demand for other jobs (e.g., in construction of renewable energy generation) should grow. In the meantime, landmen's pitch to landowners is less money up front, but payments that last longer. For example, one Texas couple with 450 acres receive about $20,000 per year for two wind turbines on their property, which they plan to use to help their retirement. They also like that it is "low-impact income."[24]

Susceptibility to Offshoring

Offshoring refers to the movement of jobs to locations beyond a country's borders. Historically, manual, low-skill jobs were most susceptible to offshoring. As we saw in **Chapter 1**, there are substantial differences in hourly compensation costs across countries for manufacturing workers; this has played an important role in

EXHIBIT 4.14 **How Work Changes over Time**

Part A. Change in Employment Share and New Occupations Since 1940

Occupation (broad)	Employment Share		Share of Occupations (detailed) New Since 1940
	1940	2018	
Farming & Mining	18	2	51%
Production	27	7	48%
Professionals	13	23	75%
Health Services	1	4	82%
Managers	8	15	43%
Clerical & Administrative	8	14	67%
All Occupations	NA	NA	63%

Part B. Examples of New Occupational Titles Added to Census over Time

Year	
1940	Automatic welding operator
1950	Beautician
1960	Textile chemist
1970	Engineer computer application
1980	Controller, remotely piloted vehicle
1990	Certified medical technician
2000	Wind turbine specialist
2018	Drama therapist

Source: Autor, D., Mindell, D., & Reynolds, E. The Work of the Future: Building Better Jobs in an Age of Intelligent Machines. Cambridge: MIT. Figure 2. Original data from David Autor, Anna Salomons, and Bryan Seegmiller, "New Frontiers: The Origins and Content of New Work, 1940–2018." *MIT Mimeo*, 2020.

companies' decisions about where to locate production operations. Similar differences in cost in other low-skill occupations (e.g., in call centers) have had similar ramifications. (So, when you call for an airline reservation or help with your printer, you may well reach someone in another country.) Of course, as we also noted, labor cost is only part of the story. There are productivity differences across countries as well, meaning that lower labor costs may in some cases be offset by lower productivity. Availability of workers with needed education and skills is another potential constraint. Proximity to customers is yet another issue. Sometimes that argues for moving offshore, sometimes it does not.

Increasingly, susceptibility to offshoring is no longer limited to low-skill jobs. White-collar jobs are also increasingly at risk.[25] Is there a way to systematically measure which jobs are most susceptible to offshoring? The U.S. Bureau of Labor Statistics has attempted to do just this with respect to service-providing occupations. **Exhibit 4.15** shows the list of occupations it found to have the highest and lowest susceptibility to offshoring. The offshoring susceptibility scores are based on the sum of scores on the four items shown. So, jobs are most susceptible to outsourcing when inputs and outputs can easily be transmitted electronically, little interaction with other workers is required, little local knowledge is required, and the work can be routinized.

EXHIBIT 4.15 Susceptibility of Occupations to Offshoring and Projected Employment Growth

Susceptibility Score	Occupation	Projected 10-Year Employment Growth
	Highest Susceptibility to Offshoring	
16	Computer programmers	−4%
16	Pharmacy technicians	32%
16	Parts salespersons	−2%
16	Telephone operators	−4.9%
16	Billing and posting clerks and machine operators	−39%
16	Computer operators	4%
16	Data entry keyers	−25%
16	Word processors and typists	−5%
15	Tax preparers	−11%
15	Medical transcriptionists	−9%
15	Telemarketers	14%
15	Payroll and timekeeping clerks	−10%
15	Proofreaders and copy markers	6%
	Lowest Susceptibility to Offshoring	
6	Chief executives	2%
6	General and operations managers	1%
6	Administrative services managers	12%
6	Computer and information systems managers	16%

Susceptibility Score	Occupation	Projected 10-Year Employment Growth
6	Wholesale and retail buyers, except farm products	0%
6	Computer systems analysts	29%
6	Landscape architects	16%
6	Industrial engineers	21%
6	Animal scientists	9%
6	Advertising sales agents	21%
5	Advertising and promotions managers	6%
5	Marketing managers	15%
5	Sales managers	10%
5	Public relations managers	17%
5	Engineering managers	7%
5	Natural science managers	12%
5	Management analysts	22%
5	Civil engineers	18%
5	Art directors	9%
4	Environmental engineers	26%

Offshoring susceptibility questions (maximum score = 16, minimum score = 4)?

1. To what degree can the inputs and outputs of the occupation be transmitted electronically?

Very low degree (1 point)	Low degree (2 point)	High degree (3 point)	Very high degree (4 point)

2. To what degree do the duties of this occupation require interaction with other types of workers?

Very low degree (1 point)	Low degree (2 point)	High degree (3 point)	Very high degree (4 point)

3. To what degree is knowledge of social and cultural idiosyncrasies, or other local knowledge, needed to carry out the tasks of this occupation?

Very low degree (4 point)	Low degree (3 point)	High degree (2 point)	Very high degree (1 point)

4. To what degree can the work of the occupation be routinized or handled by following a script?

Very low degree (1 point)	Low degree (2 point)	High degree (3 point)	Very high degree (4 point)

Source: R. J. Moncarz, M. G. Wolf, and B Wright, "Service-Providing Occupations, Offshoring and The Labor Market." *Monthly Labor Review,* December 2008, 71–86.

Interestingly, highly susceptible jobs include not only those that require little education and training, such as data entry keyers and telemarketers, but also computer programmers and tax preparers. Turning to jobs with low susceptibility to outsourcing, we see various managerial positions and also positions where local knowledge is required (e.g., marketing managers presumably need to know consumer preferences in particular regions of the world) or where being "on the ground" (literally, in the case of landscape architects) is necessary.

To our knowledge, the system for assessing susceptibility to offshoring has not been rigorously validated to see how well it predicts actual offshoring of occupations. Nevertheless, as **Exhibit 4.15** indicates, growth rates (in the United States) for jobs on the highly susceptible list are generally small or negative, while jobs on the low susceptibility list have shown strong growth. Unless the two sets of jobs have different growth rates across countries, the differential growth rates seem consistent with the possibility that jobs on the highly susceptible list have lower growth rates, at least in part because they have experienced greater offshoring. Also, there are certainly numerous examples of jobs on the highly susceptible list (e.g., data entry keyers, telemarketers, and computer programmers) being offshored. In **Chapter 7**, we return to the topic of offshoring to discuss labor cost and effectiveness ramifications.

Susceptibility to Automation and AI

In **Exhibit 4.16**, we provide an example of applying automation to a production worker's job. In this example, there is no reduction in the number of workers (just one in this case), but there certainly could be in other situations. What is most notable about this example is that automation does not eliminate the job. Instead, it changes it. The job becomes less about manual labor and more about doing other types of tasks, including handling customer orders and interacting with customers.

In **Exhibit 4.17**, we also report the probability that various jobs can be automated (their susceptibility to automation). The estimates are based on (1) expert judgment of potential automation, based on answers to the question "Can the tasks of this job be sufficiently specified, conditional on the availability of big data, to be performed by state of the art computer-controlled equipment" and (2) an estimate of the "potential bottlenecks" to automation, as indicated by the following job attributes/requirements: finger dexterity, manual dexterity, cramped workspace/awkward position, originality, fine arts, social perceptiveness, negotiation, persuasion, and assisting/caring for others. For example, with respect to manual dexterity, a low level, which would increase probability of automation, would correspond to "Screw a light bulb into a light socket";

EXHIBIT 4.16 Example of Changes to a Worker's Tasks in a Firm Using a Collaborative Robot

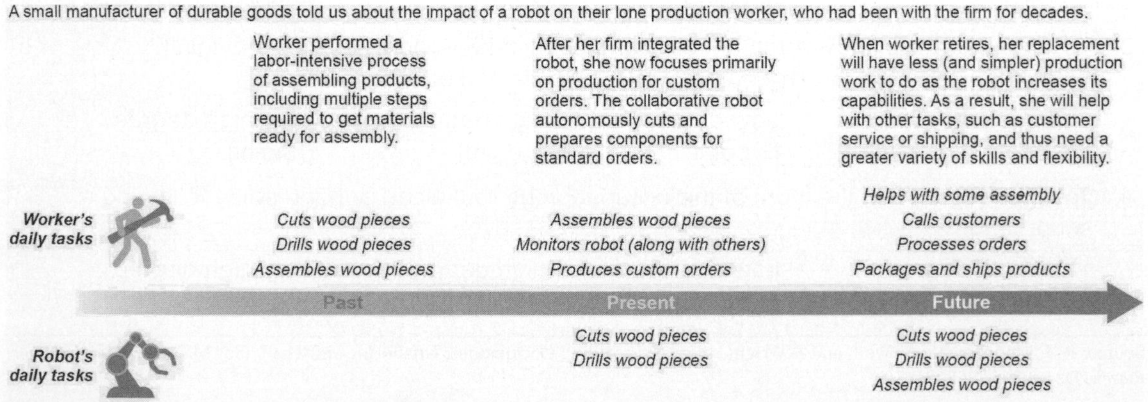

A small manufacturer of durable goods told us about the impact of a robot on their lone production worker, who had been with the firm for decades.

	Past	Present	Future
	Worker performed a labor-intensive process of assembling products, including multiple steps required to get materials ready for assembly.	After her firm integrated the robot, she now focuses primarily on production for custom orders. The collaborative robot autonomously cuts and prepares components for standard orders.	When worker retires, her replacement will have less (and simpler) production work to do as the robot increases its capabilities. As a result, she will help with other tasks, such as customer service or shipping, and thus need a greater variety of skills and flexibility.
Worker's daily tasks	*Cuts wood pieces* *Drills wood pieces* *Assembles wood pieces*	*Assembles wood pieces* *Monitors robot (along with others)* *Produces custom orders*	*Helps with some assembly* *Calls customers* *Processes orders* *Packages and ships products*
Robot's daily tasks		*Cuts wood pieces* *Drills wood pieces*	*Cuts wood pieces* *Drills wood pieces* *Assembles wood pieces*

Source: U.S. Government Accountability Office. Workforce Automation. March 2019. GAO-19-257.

medium (level) would be "Pack oranges in crates as quickly as possible"; and a high (level) would be "Perform open heart surgery with surgical instruments."[26] We thus see, for example, that there is a very low probability that the jobs of physicians and surgeons will be (completely) automated. In contrast, there is a high probability that the jobs of cashiers and tellers will become automated. Perhaps less expected, a number of white-collar jobs (e.g., real estate brokers, loan officers, tax preparers) have a high probability, as do models and umpires. An example of applying automation to a manual job and how that can change it to be a more cognitive job is shown in **Exhibit 4.16**.

One last observation on **Exhibit 4.17** is the high (98%) susceptibility to automation of Driver/sales workers. CBS's 60 Minutes has done an interesting story on driverless trucks, which is available online.[27] Of course, the ultimate goal of companies like Uber is to provide ride-sharing services without using drivers. Tesla is another company known for pursuing driverless technology. Indeed, its head, Elon Musk, has argued that it is worth it to Tesla owners and prospective owners to pay $10,000 for "full self-driving capability" in part because he claims owners will "soon" be able to make that money and more back by deploying their cars as driverless "robotaxis." This type of automation brings us to the topic of AI.

EXHIBIT 4.17 Susceptibility of Occupations to Automation

Probability of Automation	
Very Low	
0.30%	First-line supervisors of mechanics, installers, and repairers
0.30%	Audiologists
0.40%	Occupational therapists
0.40%	Healthcare social workers
0.40%	Dietitians and nutritionists
0.40%	Lodging managers
0.40%	Sales engineers
0.40%	Physicians and surgeons
0.44%	First-line supervisors of police and detectives
0.44%	Dentists, general
0.44%	Elementary school teachers
0.48%	Clinical, counseling, and school psychologists
0.60%	Human resources managers
Medium	
48%	Aerospace engineering and operations technicians
48%	Computer programmers
49%	Telecommunications line installers and repairers
49%	Police, fire, and ambulance dispatchers
50%	Installation, maintenance, and repair workers

Probability of Automation	
51%	Demonstrators and product promoters
51%	Dental assistants
51%	Architectural and civil drafters
Very High	
97%	Ophthalmic laboratory technicians
97%	Cashiers
97%	Real estate brokers
98%	Models
98%	Bookkeeping, accounting, and auditing clerks
98%	Driver/sales workers
98%	Credit analysts
98%	Packaging and filling machine operators and tenders
98%	Tellers
98%	Umpires, referees, and other sports officials
98%	Loan officers
99%	Tax preparers
99%	Insurance underwriters
99%	Title examiners, abstractors, and searchers
99%	Telemarketers

Source: C. B. Frey, & M. A. Osborne, "The Future of Employment: How Susceptible Are Jobs to Computerisation?," *Technological Forecasting and Social Change* 114 (2017), pp. 254–280.

"Artificial intelligence (AI), or machine learning, refers to algorithms that learn to complete tasks by identifying statistical patterns in data, rather than following instructions provided by humans." [28] AI can be applied to a job like driver (see above), but also to jobs that require higher education and have high earnings. an example of the latter is a radiologist. Computers are beginning to be used to read images such as X-rays to determine whether the image is consistent with a disease such as pneumonia. "The technology could free up medical personnel to spend more time with patients or examine less clear-cut cases–and it could reduce the overall need for radiologists." [29] **Exhibit 4.18** provides the results of an effort to identify which occupations are most "exposed" (susceptible) to AI. At the top are market research analysts and marketing specialists, sales managers, computer programmers, and personal financial advisors. These are occupations where an algorithm may be able to identify and use patterns of data to complete tasks. Least susceptible to automation seem to be positions where social interaction is important. Also, in contrast to the case with automation more broadly, some more manual occupations (e.g., cooks) are less, not more susceptible to AI. Consistent with this, we see in the middle and bottom parts of **Exhibit 4.18** that occupations with higher education and higher pay are more susceptible to the use of AI.

The wealth management industry provides another interesting example. The search for lower costs and new revenue sources continues in the wealth management industry and financial services more broadly. The growth of passive investing means that investors have low-cost alternatives to traditional (active) asset managers. Goldman Sachs is testing a new automated investment service it anticipates offering to customers soon. The idea is to capture (automate) expertise once available only to Goldman's richest clients in this digital service and offer it to a broader customer base. The new product will rely on the firm's smart-beta ETFs and asset allocation models designed by its private wealth management group. At UBS, Chris Purves, head of UBS Group AG's Strategic Development Lab, has worked on bringing algorithmic trading and machine learning to wealth management. He talks of the need to focus on what he calls human survivors of the tech revolution in wealth management. Likewise, another observer noted that "Good traders used to be easily identifiable" and extremely valuable. But, now, trading is very commoditized" and expert individual judgment is "being replaced by platforms and robots and people with different skillsets." Cornell professor Marcos Lopez de Prado, the former head of machine learning at the hedge fund AQR Capital Management LLC, says that many of the 6 million employed in finance and insurance will lose their jobs "because they are not trained to work alongside algorithms" (i.e., AI).[30]

EXHIBIT 4.18 Occupations Most Exposed (susceptible) to Artificial Intelligence (AI), Most to Least

	AI Exposure (100 % = most susceptible)
Occupation	
Market research analysts and marketing specialists	100%
Sales managers	100%
Computer programmers	98%
Personal financial advisors	91%
All occupations	50%
Human resources specialists	42%
Welders, cutters, solderers, and brazers	36%
Dental assistants	21%
Combined food preparation and serving workers	16%
Cooks, restaurant	9%
Education Level	
Graduate or Professional Degree	56%
Bachelor's Degree	58%
Some College	51%
High School	52%
Less than High School	50%

Occupational Wage Percentile	
100	66%
60	66%
40	58%
20	48%

Source: Mark Muro, Jacob Whiton, and Robert Maxim. November 2019. What Jobs Are Affected by AI? Better-paid, better-educated workers face the most exposure. Metropolitan Policy Program at Brookings. November 2019.

Note: Muro et al. use Michael Webb's method to measure AI exposure. Webb examines patent descriptions to identify predictions of the commercial relevance of AI technological applications. His method looks for verb-object pairs such as "diagnose-disease" to identify AI technological capabilities. He then uses machine learning to quantify the extent to which each occupation description (from O*NET) highlights similar capabilities. The higher the overlap between capabilities described in patents and occupations, the greater that occupation's exposure (susceptibility) to the application of AI.

Source: Michael Webb. The Impact of Artificial Intelligence on the Labor Market. January 2020. Stanford University.

Note: Percentiles computed based on standard normal (z) scores reported in original.

Job Analysis Information and Comparability across Borders

As firms spread work across multiple countries, there is an increasing need to analyze jobs to either maintain consistency in job content or else be able to measure the ways in which jobs are similar and different. For example, for a software development team to work equally effectively with programmers in the United States and India, the job descriptions and job specifications need to be measured and understood. One potential challenge is that norms or perceptions regarding what is and what is not part of a particular job may vary across countries. However, a study of three different jobs (first-line supervisor, general office clerk, and computer programmer) in the United States, China, Hong Kong, and New Zealand found that ratings of the importance and amount of work activities and job requirements were "quite similar" across countries, suggesting that job analysis information "is likely to transport quite well across countries."[31]

JUDGING JOB ANALYSIS

Beyond beliefs about its usefulness—or lack thereof—for satisfying both employees and employers, there are several ways to judge job analysis.

Reliability

If you measure something tomorrow and get the same results you got today, or if I measure and get the same result you did, the measurement is considered to be reliable. This doesn't mean it is right—only that repeated measures give the same result. **Reliability** is a measure of the consistency of results among various analysts, various methods, various sources of data, or over time. Reliability is a necessary, but not sufficient, condition for **validity.**

The mean correlation between work content ratings of jobs from two different raters, a typical way to estimate reliability, is .083.[32] So, using a single rater to conduct a job analysis typically results in very poor reliability. By using multiple raters and taking their average rating, the reliability increases. With 5 raters, it is .312. With 15 raters, it is .488. These are still not terribly high reliabilities and indicate that the outcome of a job analysis depends to an important degree on who conducts it. There is higher reliability between professional job analysts and also when more specific tasks are rated (as opposed to more general job requirements or knowledge and skill requirements).[33] Research on employee and supervisor agreement in job analysis information is mixed.[34] For instance, experience may change an employee's perceptions about a job since the employee may have found new ways to do it or added new tasks to the job. The supervisor may not realize the extent of change. In such cases, the job the employee is actually doing may not be the same as the job originally assigned by the supervisor. Differences in performance seem to influence reliability. Other research finds that reliability is lower for jobs that are more interdependent with other jobs, and have more autonomy/are less routine.[35] Research does not show that gender and race differences affect reliability.[36] Obviously, the way to increase reliability in a job analysis is to understand and reduce sources of difference. Quantitative job analysis helps do this. But we need to be sure that we do not eliminate the richness of responses while eliminating the differences. Sometimes there really may be more than one job. Training can also improve reliability.[37]

See the section "**Reliability of Job Evaluation Techniques**" in **Chapter 6** for further details on how reliability can affect pay outcomes.

Validity

Does the analysis create an accurate portrait of the work? There is almost no way of showing statistically the extent to which an analysis is accurate, particularly for complex jobs. No gold standard exists; how can we know? Consequently, *validity* examines the convergence of results among sources of data and methods. If several job incumbents, supervisors, and peers respond in similar ways to questionnaires, then it is more likely that the information is valid. However, a sign-off on the results does not guarantee the information's validity.[38] It may mean only that all involved were sick to death of the process and wanted to get rid of the analyst so they could get back to work.

Acceptability

If job holders and managers are dissatisfied with the initial data collected and the process, they are not likely to buy into the resulting job structure or the pay rates attached to that structure. An analyst collecting information through one-on-one interviews or observation is not always accepted because of the potential for subjectivity and favoritism. One writer says, "We all know the classic procedures. One [worker] watched and noted the actions of another . . . at work on [the] job. The actions of both are biased and the resulting information varied with the wind, especially the political wind."[39] However, quantitative computer-assisted approaches may also run into difficulty, especially if they give in to the temptation to collect too much information for too many purposes. After four years in development, one application ran into such severe problems due to its unwieldy size and incomprehensible questions that managers simply refused to use it.

Currency

To be valid, acceptable, and useful (see below), job information must be up to date. Some jobs stay relatively stable over time, while others may change in important ways, even over short time periods. As **Exhibit 4.19** shows, most organizations report that they have up-to-date job information, but a substantial portion report that job information is not up to date. That can hinder not only compensation practice and decision-making, but also employee selection, training, and development. Most organizations do not engage in any regular (e.g., annual or biannual) updating of job analysis information, instead being more likely to update job information when the significant changes are believed to have occurred or when the job is being reevaluated for compensation purposes.[40] It may be useful to develop a systematic protocol for evaluating when job information needs to be updated.[41]

Usefulness

Usefulness refers to the practicality of the information collected. For pay purposes, job analysis provides work-related information to help determine how much to pay for a job–it helps determine whether the job is similar to or different from other jobs. If job analysis does this in a reliable, valid, and acceptable way and can be used to make pay decisions, then it is useful.[42]

As we have noted, some see job analysis information as useful for multiple purposes, such as hiring and training. But multiple purposes may require more information than is required for pay decisions. The practicality of all-encompassing quantitative job analysis plans, with their relatively complex procedures and analysis, remains in doubt. Some advocates get so taken with their statistics and computers that they ignore the role that judgment must continue to play in job analysis. Dunnette's point, made more than 35 years ago, still holds true today: "I wish to emphasize the central role played in all these procedures by human judgment. I know of no methodology, statistical technique or objective measurements that can negate the importance of, nor supplement, rational judgment."[43]

A Judgment Call

In the face of all the difficulties, time, expense, and dissatisfaction, why on earth would you as a manager bother with job analysis? Because work-related information is needed to determine pay, and differences in

EXHIBIT 4.19 Updated Job Descriptions

How many jobs in your organization have up-to-date position, job, or role descriptions in place?

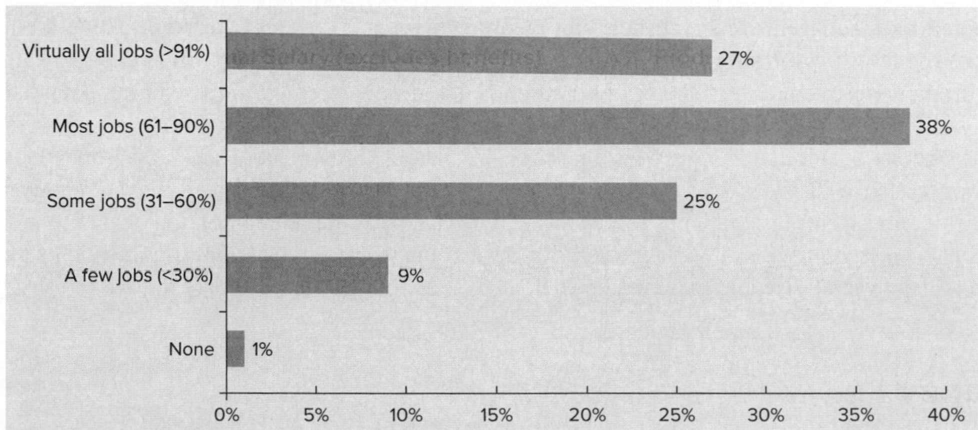

Source: "Job Evaluation and Market-Pricing Practices Survey," February 2020. WorldatWork. ©WorldatWork. Reprinted with permission from WorldatWork. Content is licensed for use by purchaser only. No part of this article may be reproduced, excerpted or redistributed in any form without express written permission from WorldatWork.

work determine pay differences. There is no satisfactory substitute that can ensure the resulting pay structure will be work-related or will provide reliable, accurate data for making and explaining pay decisions.

If work information is required, then the real issue should be, How much detail is needed to make these pay decisions? The answer is, Enough to help set individual employees' pay, encourage continuous learning, increase the experience and skill of the work force, and minimize the risk of pay-related grievances. Omitting this detail and contributing to an incorrect and costly decision by uninformed managers can lead to unhappy employees who drive away customers with their poor service, file lawsuits, or complain about management's inability to justify their decisions. The response to inadequate analysis ought not to be to dump the analysis; rather, the response should be to obtain a more useful analysis.

Your Turn — The Customer-Service Agent

Read the article on a day in the work life of Bill Ryan. Then write a job description for the job of customer-service agent. Use the exhibits in this chapter to guide you in deciding what information in the story is relevant for job analysis.

To work on this Your Turn, you will need to access the following article online: Alex Frangos, "The Customer-Service Agent," *Wall Street Journal,* July 16, 2001. If you have a subscription to the *Wall Street Journal,* you can access this article at **https://www.wsj.com/articles/SB995046210750147553**. If you do not have a subscription, you will may be able to access it through a simple web search. Otherwise, you need to access the article via one of your library databases (e.g., ABI/Inform, Proquest, or other databases that include *Wall Street Journal* articles). Alternatively, you can choose a different job that you and your teammate have observed and answer the following questions using that job.

1. Does the day diary include sufficient information?
2. Identify the specific information in the article that you found useful.
3. What additional information do you require? How would that information help you?

Pick a teammate (or the instructor will assign one) and exchange job descriptions with your teammate.

1. How similar/different are the two descriptions? You and your teammate started with exactly the same information. What might explain any differences?
2. What process would you go through to understand and minimize the differences?
3. What are some of the relational returns of the job?

Summary

Encouraging employee behaviors that help achieve an organization's objectives and fostering a sense of fairness among employees are two hallmarks of a useful internal pay structure. One of the first strategic pay decisions is how much to align a pay structure internally compared to aligning it to external market forces. Do not be misled. The issue is *not* achieving internal alignment versus alignment with external market forces. Rather, the strategic decision focuses on sustaining the optimal balance of internally aligned and externally responsive pay structures that helps the organization achieve its mission. *Both are required.* This part of the book focuses on one of the first decisions managers face in designing pay systems: how much to emphasize pay structures that are internally aligned with the work performed, the organization's structure, and its strategies. Whatever the choice, the decision needs to support (and be supported by) the organization's overall human resource strategy.

Next, managers must decide whether job and/or individual employee characteristics will be the basic unit of analysis supporting the pay structure. This is followed by deciding what data will be collected, what method(s) will be used to collect the information, and who should be involved in the process.

A key test of an effective and fair pay structure is acceptance of results by managers and employees. The best way to ensure acceptance of job analysis results is to involve employees as well as supervisors in the process. At the minimum, all employees should be informed of the purpose and progress of the activity.

If almost everyone agrees about the importance of job analysis, does that mean everyone does it? Of course not. Unfortunately, job analysis can be tedious and time-consuming. Often the job is given to newly hired compensation analysts, ostensibly to help them learn the organization, but perhaps there's also a hint of "rites of passage" in such assignments.

Alternatives to job-based structures such as *skill-based* or *competency-based systems* are being experimented with in many firms. The premise is that basing structures on these other criteria will encourage employees to become more flexible, and thus fewer workers will be required for the same level of output. This may be the argument, but as experience increases with the alternatives, managers are discovering that they can be as time consuming and bureaucratic as job analysis. Bear in mind, job content remains the conventional criterion for structures.

Review Questions

1. Job analysis has been considered the cornerstone of human resource management. Precisely how does it support managers making pay decisions?
2. What does job analysis have to do with internal alignment?
3. Describe the major decisions involved in job analysis.
4. Distinguish between task data and behavioral data.
5. What is the critical advantage of quantitative approaches over conventional approaches to job analysis?
6. How would you decide whether to use job-based or person-based structures?
7. Why do many managers say that job analysis is a colossal waste of their time and the time of their employees? Are they right?

Endnotes

1. S. Bing, *100 Bullshit Jobs . . . And How to Get Them* (New York: HarperColllins, 2006); J. Racz, *50 Jobs Worse Than Yours* (New York: Bloomsbury, 2004). Our personal favorite is the ride operator at the "It's a Small World" ride at Disney.
2. R. J. Grossman, "IBM's HR Takes a Risk," *HR Magazine*, April 2007.
3. M. T. Brannick, E. L. Levine, and F. P. Morgeson, *Job and Work Analysis: Methods, Research, and Applications for Human Resource Management*, 2nd ed. (Los Angeles: Sage, 2007).
4. E. J. McCormick, "Job and Task Analysis," in *Handbook of Industrial and Organizational Psychology*, ed. M. D. Dunnette (Chicago, IL: Rand McNally, 1976), pp. 651–696; R. J. Harvey, "Job Analysis," in *Handbook of Industrial and Organizational Psychology,* vol. 2, ed. M. D. Dunnette and L. Hough (Palo Alto, CA: Consulting Psychologists Press, 1991), pp. 72–157.
5. Particularly valuable sources of information on job analysis definitions and methods are U.S. Department of Labor, Manpower Administration, *Revised Handbook for Analyzing Jobs* (Washington,

DC: U.S. Government Printing Office, 1992); R. J. Harvey, "Job Analysis," in *Handbook of Industrial and Organizational Psychology,* vol. 2, eds. M. D. Dunnette and L. Hough (Palo Alto, CA: Consulting Psychologists Press, 1991), pp. 72–157; B. Lister, *Evaluating Job Content* (Scottsdale, AZ: WorldatWork, 2006).

6. W. Cascio, "Strategies for Responsible Restructuring," *Academy of Management Executive* 19(4), 2005, pp. 39–50; J. Marler, M. Barringer, and G. Milkovich, "Boundaryless and Traditional Contingent Employees: Worlds Apart," *Journal of Organizational Behavior* 23 (2002), pp. 425–453.
7. P. C. Light, *The True Size of Government* (Washington, DC: Brookings Institute, 1999); C. Prendergast, "The Role of Promotion in Inducing Specific Human Capital Acquisition," *Quarterly Journal of Economics,* May 1993, pp. 523–534.
8. D. Neil, "All Rays Lead to Pasadena," *Los Angeles Times,* February 5, 2006.
9. Much of the developmental work and early applications of the PAQ were done in the 1960s and 1970s. See, for example, E. J. McCormick, "Job and Task Analysis," in *Handbook of Industrial and Organizational Psychology,* ed. M. D. Dunnette (Chicago: Rand McNally, 1976), pp. 651–696; E. J. McCormick et al., "A Study of Job Characteristics and Job Dimensions as Based on the Position Analysis Questionnaire," Occupational Research Center, Purdue University, West Lafayette, IN, 1969. The PAQ is available from the Economic Research Institute. https://www.erieri.com/paq.
10. T. H. Davenport, "The Coming Commoditization of Processes," *Harvard Business Review,* June 2005, pp. 101–108.
11. *Benefits Compliance: An Overview for the HR Professional* (Scottsdale, AZ: WorldatWork, 2006). Society for Human Resource Management. ADA: Job Analysis/Job Description Physical Activities Checklist. February 5, 2018. https://www.shrm.org/resourcesandtools/tools-and-samples/hr-forms/pages/ada_jobanalysisjobdescriptionadalist.aspx.
12. V. L. Huber and S. R. Crandall, "Job Measurement: A Social-Cognitive Decision Perspective," in *Research in Personnel and Human Resources Management,* vol. 12, ed. Gerald R. Ferris (Greenwich, CT: JAI Press, 1994), pp. 223–269; Juan I. Sanchez, I. Prager, A. Wilson, and C. Viswesvaran, "Understanding within-Job Title Variance in Job-Analytic Ratings," *Journal of Business and Psychology* 12 (1998), pp. 407–419.
13. Susanne Craig, "E*Trade Lowers Corporate Titles," in "Move That Could Spur Departures," *The Wall Street Journal,* September 6, 2001, pp. C1, C14.
14. Theresa M. Glomb, John D. Kammeyer-Mueller, and Maria Rotundo, "Emotional Labor Demands and Compensating Wage Differentials," *Journal of Applied Psychology* 89(4), 2004, pp. 700–714; Juan I. Sanchez and Edward L. Levine, "Is Job Analysis Dead, Misunderstood, or Both? New Forms of Work Analysis and Design," in *Evolving Practices in Human Resource Management: Responses to a Changing World of Work,* ed. A. I. Kraut and A. K. Korman (San Francisco: Jossey-Bass, 1999), pp. 43–68.
15. Handel, M. J. (2016). The O* NET content model: strengths and limitations. *Journal for Labour Market Research*, *49*(2), 157–176. R. Reiter-Palmon, M. Brown, D. Sandall, C. Buboltz, and T. Nimps, "Development of an O*NET Web-Based Job Analysis and Its Implementation in the U.S. Navy: Lessons Learned," *Human Resources Management Review* 16 (2006), pp. 294–309.
16. Handel, Michael J. "What do people do at work?" *Journal for Labour Market Research* 49, 2 (2016): 177. Sanchez, J. I., & Levine, E. L. (2012). The rise and fall of job analysis and the future of work analysis. *Annual Review of Psychology*, 63, 397–425. Manson, T. M., Levine, E. L., & Brannick, M. T. (2000). The construct validity of task inventory ratings: A multitrait-multimethod analysis. *Human Performance*, 13(1), 1–22.

17. Juan I. Sanchez and Edward L. Levine, "Accuracy or Consequential Validity: Which Is the Better Standard for Job Analysis Data?" *Journal of Organizational Behavior* 21 (2000), pp. 809–818; W. C. Borman, D. Dorsey, and L. Ackerman, "Time-Spent Responses and Time Allocation Strategies: Relations with Sales Performance in a Stockbroker Sample," *Personnel Psychology* 45 (1992), pp. 763–777.

18. R. Arvey, E. M. Passino, and J. W. Lounsbury, "Job Analysis Results as Influenced by Sex of Incumbent and Sex of Analyst," *Journal of Applied Psychology* 62(4), 1977, pp. 411–416.

19. V. L. Huber and S. R. Crandall, "Job Measurement: A Social-Cognitive Decision Perspective," in *Research in Personnel and Human Resources Management,* vol. 12, ed. Gerald R. Ferris (Greenwich, CT: JAI Press, 1994), pp. 223–269.

20. David Levine, Dale Belman, Gary Charness, Erica Groshen, and K. C. O'Shaughnessy, *Changes in Careers and Wage Structures at Large American Employers* (Kalamazoo, MI: Upjohn Institute, 2003).

21. See commentary by Charlie Fay in "The Future of Salary Management," *Compensation and Benefits Review,* July/August 2001, p. 10.

22. A. I. Kraut, P. R. Pedigo, D. D. McKenna, and M. D. Dunnette, "The Role of the Manager: What's Really Important in Different Management Jobs," *Academy of Management Executive* 19(4), 2005, pp. 122–129; L. Dyer and R. A. Shafer, "From HR Strategy to Organizational Effectiveness," in *Strategic Human Resources Management in the Twenty-First Century,* Suppl. 4, eds. P. M. Wright, L. D. Dyer, J. W. Boudreau, and G. T. Milkovich (Stamford, CT: JAI Press, 1999).

23. M. Farnham and E. Hutchinson, "The Effect of Multiskilling on Labor Productivity, Product Quality, and Financial Performance,' in *Advances in the Economic Analysis of Participatory and Labor-Managed Firms* (pp. 35–62). Emerald Group Publishing Limited; S. Steven Gray, "Coffee on the Double," *The Wall Street Journal,* April 12, 2005, pp. B1–B7; K. H. Doerr, T. Freed, T. Mitchell, C. Schriesheim, and X. (Tracy) Zhou, "Work Flow Policy and Within-Worker and Between-Workers Variability in Performance," *Journal of Applied Psychology,* October 2004, pp. 911–921.

24. Rebecca Elliott. Oil-and-Gas Landmen Now Hunt for Wind and Sun: Job to secure drilling rights shifts to deals to place turbines, solar panels. Wall Street Journal, April 19, 2021, A1.

25. S. Kuruvilla and E. Noronha, "From Pyramids to Diamonds: Legal Process Offshoring, Employment Systems, and Labor Markets for Lawyers in the United States and India," *ILR Review* 69(2), 2016, pp. 354–377.

26. Frey, C. B., & Osborne, M. A. (2017). The future of employment: how susceptible are jobs to computerisation? Technological Forecasting and Social Change, 114, 254–280; quotation at p. 263.

27. Jon Wertheim. Automated trucking, a technical milestone that could disrupt hundreds of thousands of jobs, hits the road. Companies are already testing driverless trucks on America's roads. The technology will bring untold profits, but it may cost thousands of truckers their livelihoods. 60 Minutes, March 15, 2020. https://www.cbsnews.com/news/driverless-trucks-could-disrupt-the-trucking-industry-as-soon-as-2021-60-minutes-2020-03-15/.

28. M. Webb. *The Impact of Artificial Intelligence on the Labor Market*. January 2020. Stanford University. page 1.

29. E. Morath. AI Is the Next Workplace Disrupter—and It's Coming for High-Skilled Jobs. Wall Street Journal, February 23, 2020. www.wsj.com.

30. Hugh Son. Goldman Sachs, once reserved for the rich, is close to offering wealth management for the masses. CNBC.com. December 22, 2020; Katie Linsell and Lananh Nguyen. The End of the Bonus Culture Is Coming to Wall Street. www.bloomberg.com. January 13, 2020; H. Son, "Bank of America CEO Moynihan Says He Cut Jobs Equal to the Workforce of Delta Air Lines," *CNBC*, October 16,

2018. CNBC.com. S. Krouse, "BlackRock Shake-Up Favors Computers over Humans," *Wall Street Journal*, March 29, 2017.

31. P. Taylor, W.-D. Li, Kan Shi, and W. Borman, "The Transportability of Job Information across Countries," *Personnel Psychology* 61 (2008), pp. 69–111.
32. E. Dierdorff and M. Wilson, "A Meta-Analysis of Job Analysis Reliability," *Journal of Applied Psychology,* August 2003, pp. 635–646. Dierdorff and Wilson did not report the mean correlation between two raters. We used the Spearman–Brown Prophecy formula to compute it based on their other reported results. The formula is available in any psychometrics book, including J. C. Nunnally, *Psychometric Theory,* 2nd ed. (New York: McGraw-Hill, 1978).
33. Ibid.; Erich C. Dierdorff and Frederick P. Morgeson, "Effects of Descriptor Specificity and Observability on Incumbent Work Analysis Ratings," *Personnel Psychology* 62 (2009), pp. 601–628.
34. Juan I. Sanchez and E. L. Levine, "The Impact of Raters' Cognition on Judgment Accuracy: An Extension to the Job Analysis Domain," *Journal of Business and Psychology* 9 (1994), pp. 47–57; Juan I. Sanchez and Edward L. Levine, "Accuracy or Consequential Validity: Which Is the Better Standard for Job Analysis Data?" *Journal of Organizational Behavior* 21 (2000), pp. 809–818; Frederick P. Morgeson and Michael A. Campion, "Accuracy in Job Analysis: Toward an Inference-Based Model," *Journal of Organizational Behavior* 21 (2000), pp. 819–827; Erich Dierdorff and Mark Wilson, "A Meta-Analysis of Job Analysis Reliability," *Journal of Applied Psychology,* August 2003, pp. 635–646. DuVernet, A. M., Dierdorff, E. C., & Wilson, M. A. (2015). Exploring factors that influence work analysis data: A meta-analysis of design choices, purposes, and organizational context. *Journal of Applied Psychology,* 100(5), 1603.
35. Erich C. Dierdorff and Frederick Morgeson, "Consensus in Role Requirements: The Influence of Discrete Occupational Context on Role Expectations," *Journal of Applied Psychology* 92 (2007), pp. 1228–1241.
36. Richard Arvey, Emily M. Passino, and John W. Lounsbury, "Job Analysis Results as Influenced by Sex of Incumbent and Sex of Analyst," *Journal of Applied Psychology* 62(4), 1977, pp. 411–416; Sara L. Rynes, Caroline L. Weber, and George T. Milkovich, "Effects of Market Survey Rates, Job Evaluation, and Job Gender on Job Pay," *Journal of Applied Psychology* 74(1), 1989, pp. 114–123.
37. Filip Lievens and Juan I. Sanchez, "Can Training Improve the Quality of Inferences Made by Raters in Competency Modeling? A Quasi-Experiment," *Journal of Applied Psychology* 92 (2008), pp. 812–819.
38. Juan I. Sanchez and E. L. Levine, "The Impact of Raters' Cognition on Judgment Accuracy: An Extension to the Job Analysis Domain," *Journal of Business and Psychology* 9 (1994), pp. 47–57; Juan I. Sanchez and Edward L. Levine, "Accuracy or Consequential Validity: Which Is the Better Standard for Job Analysis Data?" *Journal of Organizational Behavior* 21 (2000), pp. 809–818; Frederick P. Morgeson and Michael A. Campion, "Accuracy in Job Analysis: Toward an Inference-Based Model," *Journal of Organizational Behavior* 21 (2000), pp. 819–827.
39. E. M. Ramras, "Discussion," in *Proceedings of Division of Military Psychology Symposium: Collecting, Analyzing, and Reporting Information Describing Jobs and Occupations,* 77th Annual Convention of the American Psychological Association, Lackland Air Force Base, TX, September 1969, pp. 75–76. Tony Simons and Quinetta Roberson, "Why Managers Should Care about Fairness: The Effects of Aggregate Justice Perceptions on Organizational Outcomes," *Journal of Applied Psychology,* June 2003, pp. 432–443.
40. WorldatWork, "Job Evaluation and Market-Pricing Practices," www.worldatwork.org/waw/adimLink?id=31378, 2009.

41. P. Bobko, P. L. Roth, and M. A. Buster, "A Systematic Approach for Assessing the Currency ('Up-to-Dateness') of Job-Analytic Information," *Public Personnel Management* 37 (2008), pp. 261–277.

42. Wyse, A. E., & Babcock, B. (2018). A Comparison of Subject Matter Experts' Perceptions and Job Analysis Surveys. *Practical Assessment, Research & Evaluation*, 23(10). Edward L. Levine, Ronald A. Ash, Hardy Hall, and Frank Sistrunk, "Evaluation of Job Analysis Methods by Experienced Job Analysts," *Academy of Management Journal* 26(2), 1983, pp. 339–348.

43. M. D. Dunnette, L. M. Hough, and R. L. Rosse, "Task and Job Taxonomies as a Basis for Identifying Labor Supply Sources and Evaluating Employment Qualifications," in *Affirmative Action Planning, ed.* George T. Milkovich and Lee Dyer (New York: Human Resource Planning Society, 1979), pp. 37–51.

Chapter **Five**
Job-Based Structures and Job Evaluation

Chapter Outline

How does any organization go about valuing work? The next time you go to the supermarket, check out the different types of work there: store manager, produce manager, front-end manager, deli workers, butchers, stock clerks, checkout people, bakers–the list is long, and the work surprisingly diverse. If you managed a supermarket, how would you value work? (Fortunately, you will have the opportunity to address this very question in the **Your Turn** at the end of this chapter!)

This chapter and **Chapter 6** discuss techniques used to value work. Both chapters focus on "how-to"–the specific steps involved. Job evaluation techniques are discussed in this chapter. Person-based techniques, both skill-based and competency-based, are discussed in **Chapter 6**. All of these techniques are used to design pay structures that will influence employee behavior and help the organization sustain its competitive advantage.

As you read this chapter, you will see that job evaluation serves three major purposes (which we will explain in more detail later):

1. To help set pay for jobs where market pay survey data are unavailable (non-key or non-benchmark jobs) by helping compare the internal value of these non-key jobs to jobs for which market pay data are available (key jobs or benchmark jobs).

2. To match a job in a particular company to a comparable job of similar value in a market pay survey, which is necessary to identify the market pay for the company job.
3. To pay jobs in a particular company in part based on which jobs are most important to the company's strategy, not just on the basis of what other companies pay those jobs, as indicated by market survey pay data.

JOB-BASED STRUCTURES: JOB EVALUATION

Exhibit 5.1 is a variation on **Exhibit 4.1** in the previous chapter. It orients us to the process used to build a job-based internal structure. Our job analysis and job descriptions (**Chapter 4**) collected and summarized work information. In this chapter, the focus is on what to value in the jobs, how to assess that value, and how to translate it into a **job-based structure.** Job evaluation is a process for determining the **relative value of jobs.**

> **Job evaluation** is the process of systematically determining the relative worth of jobs to create a job structure for the organization. The evaluation is based on a combination of job content, skills required, value to the organization, organizational culture, and the external market. This potential to blend organizational forces and external market forces is both a strength and a challenge of job evaluation.

EXHIBIT 5.1 **Many Ways to Create Internal Structure**

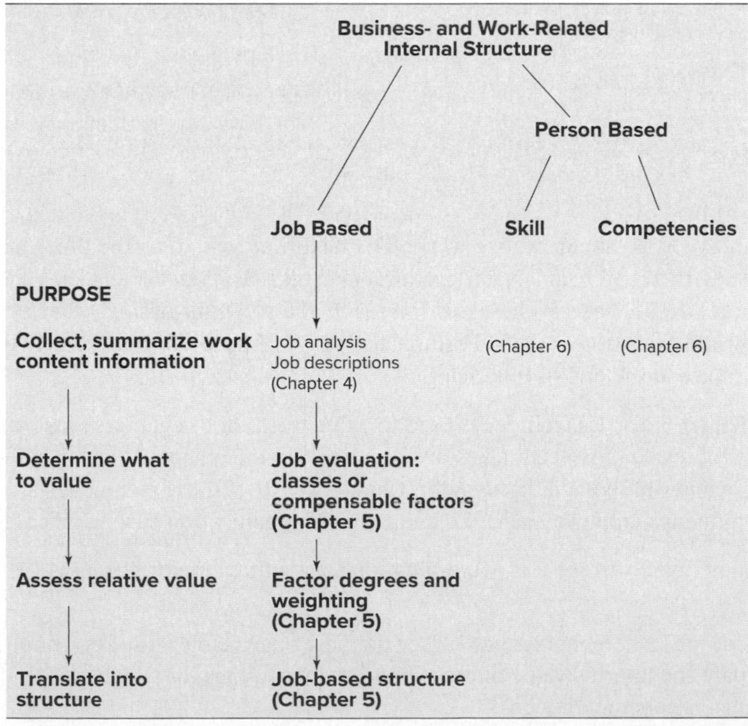

DEFINING JOB EVALUATION: CONTENT, VALUE, AND EXTERNAL MARKET LINKS

Content and Value

We noted in **Chapter 3** that **content** refers to what work is performed and how it gets done. Perspectives differ on whether job evaluation is based on **job content** or job value. Internal alignment based on content orders jobs on the basis of the skills required for the jobs and the duties and responsibilities associated with the jobs. A structure based on job value orders jobs on the basis of the relative contribution of the skills, duties, and responsibilities of each job to the organization's goals. But can this structure translate directly into pay rates, without regard to the external market, government regulations, or any individual negotiation process? Most people think not. Recall that internal alignment is just one of the building blocks of the pay model. Job content matters, but it is not the only basis for pay. Job value may also include the job's value in the external market (*exchange value*). Plus, pay rates may be influenced by collective bargaining or other negotiations.

In addition, the value added by the same work may be more (or less) in one organization than in another. We observed in **Chapter 3** that the value added by consultants in PricewaterhouseCoopers (PWC), where earnings were generated directly by consultants, may differ from the value added by the same consultants now that they are merged into IBM, where revenues come through a wide variety of services. At PWC, consultants were critical to organization objectives. At IBM, they are less so. As a result, those who remained with IBM may have had their base pay frozen but received larger bonuses until their base pay fit IBM's structure. So, while we talk about internal job value based on contributions to organization objectives, external market value may differ. There is not necessarily a one-to-one correspondence between internal job value and pay rates.

Linking Content with the External Market

Some see job evaluation as a process for linking job content and internal value with external market rates. Aspects of job content (e.g., skills required and customer contacts) take on value based on their relationship to market wages. Because higher skill levels or willingness to work more closely with customers usually commands higher wages in the labor market, then skill level and nature of customer contacts become useful criteria for establishing differences among jobs. If some aspect of job content, such as stressful working conditions, is not related to wages paid in the external labor market, then that aspect may be excluded in the job evaluation. In this perspective, the value of job content is based on what it can command in the external market; it has no intrinsic value.[1] But not everyone agrees. Job evaluation, as we will see, is an important tool for organizations that wish to differentiate themselves from competitors if, for example, their particular strategy relies more heavily on certain jobs or skills than is the case in other organizations (i.e., in the market).

Technical and Process Dimensions

Researchers, too, have their own perspective on job evaluation. Some say that if job evaluation can be made sufficiently rigorous and systematic (objective, numerical, generalizable, documented, and reliable), then it can be judged according to technical standards. Just as with employment tests, the reliability, validity, and usefulness of job evaluation plans can be compared. (We cover these issues in **Chapter 6**.)

Those using job evaluation to make pay decisions sometimes see things differently. They see job evaluation also as a process that helps gain acceptance of pay differences among jobs–an administrative procedure through which the parties become involved and committed. Its statistical validity is not the only issue. Its usefulness also comes from providing a framework for give-and-take–an exchange of views. Employees, union representatives, and managers haggle over "the rules of the game" for determining the relative value of work. If all participants agree that skills, effort, responsibilities, and working conditions are important, then work is evaluated based on these factors. As in sports and games, we are more willing to accept the results if we accept the rules and believe they are applied fairly.[2] This interpretation is consistent with the history of job evaluation, which began as a way to bring peace and order to an often-chaotic and dispute-riven wage-setting process between labor and management.[3]

Exhibit 5.2 summarizes the assumptions that underlie the perspectives on job evaluation. Some say the content of jobs has intrinsic value that the evaluation will uncover; others say the only fair measure of job value is found in the external market. Some say contemporary job evaluation practices are just and fair; others say they are just fair. "Beneath the superficial orderliness of job evaluation techniques and findings, there is much that smacks of chaos."[4] We try to capture all these perspectives in this chapter.

"HOW-TO": MAJOR DECISIONS

Exhibit 5.3 shows job evaluation's role in determining the internal structure. You already know that the process begins with job analysis, in which the information on jobs is collected, and that job descriptions summarize the information and serve as input for the evaluation. The exhibit calls out some of the major decisions in the job evaluation process. They are as follows: (1) establish the purpose(s), (2) decide on single versus multiple plans, (3) choose among alternative methods, (4) obtain involvement of relevant stakeholders, and (5) evaluate the usefulness of the results.

Establish the Purpose

Job evaluation is part of the process for establishing an internally aligned pay structure. Recall from **Chapter 2** that a structure is aligned if it supports the organization strategy, fits the work flow, is fair to employees, and motivates their behavior toward organization objectives.

EXHIBIT 5.2 Assumptions Underlying Different Views of Job Evaluation

Aspect of Job Evaluation	Assumption
Assessment of job content	Content has intrinsic value outside external market.
Assessment of relative value	Stakeholders can reach consensus on value.
External market link	Value cannot be determined without external market.
Measurement	Honing instruments will provide objective measures.
Negotiation	Negotiating brings rationality to a social/political process; establishes rules of the game and invites participation.

- *Supports organization strategy:* Job evaluation aligns with the organization's strategy by including what it is about work that adds value–that contributes to pursuing the organization's strategy and achieving its objectives. Job evaluation helps answer, How does this job add value?[5]
- *Supports work flow:* Job evaluation supports work flow in two ways. It integrates each job's pay with its relative contributions to the organization, and it helps set pay for new, unique, or changing jobs.
- *Is fair to employees:* Job evaluation can reduce disputes and grievances over pay differences among jobs by establishing a workable, agreed-upon structure that reduces the role of chance, favoritism, and bias in setting pay.
- *Motivates behavior toward organization objectives:* Job evaluation clarifies for employees what it is about their work that the organization values, how their jobs support the organization's strategy and its success. It can also help employees adapt to organization changes by improving their understanding of what is valued in their new assignments and why that value may have changed. Thus, job evaluation helps create the network of rewards (promotions, challenging work) that motivates employees.

If the purpose of the evaluation is not clearly stated, it becomes too easy to get lost in complex procedures, negotiations, and bureaucracy. The job evaluation process becomes the end in itself instead of a way to achieve an objective. Establishing its purpose can help ensure that the evaluation actually is a useful systematic process.

Single versus Multiple Plans

Rarely do employers evaluate all jobs in the organization at one time. More typically, a related group of jobs, for example, manufacturing, technical, or administrative, will be the focus. As we saw in **Chapter 3**, for example, Northrup Grumman has four different structures. Many employers design different evaluation plans for different types of work. They do so because they believe that the work content is too diverse to be usefully evaluated by one plan. For example, production jobs may vary in terms of manipulative skills, knowledge of statistical quality control, and working conditions. But these tasks and skills may not be relevant to engineering and finance jobs. Rather, the nature of the contacts with customers may be relevant. Consequently, a single, universal plan may not be acceptable to employees or useful to managers if the work covered is highly diverse. Even so, there are some plans that have been successfully applied across a wide breadth and depth of work. The most prominent examples include the Hay plan (more on this later) and the **Position Analysis Questionnaire** (discussed in **Chapter 4**).

EXHIBIT 5.3 **Determining an Internally Aligned Job Structure**

Internal Alignment: Work Relationships within the Organization → Job Analysis → Job Description → Job Evaluation → Job Structure

Some Major Decisions in Job Evaluation

- Establish purpose of evaluation.
- Decide whether to use single or multiple plans.
- Choose among alternative approaches.
- Obtain involvement of relevant stakeholders.
- Evaluate plan's usefulness.

Benchmark Jobs—A Sample

To be sure that all relevant aspects of work are included in the evaluation, an organization may start with a sample of **benchmark (key) jobs.** In **Exhibit 5.4**, benchmark jobs would be identified for as many of the levels in the structure and groups of related jobs (administrative, manufacturing, technical) as possible. The heavy shading in the exhibit marks the benchmark jobs.

A benchmark job has the following characteristics:

- Its contents are well known and relatively stable over time.
- The job is common across a number of different employers. It is not unique to a particular employer.
- A reasonable proportion of the workforce is employed in this job.

A representative sample of benchmark jobs will include the entire domain of work being evaluated–administrative, manufacturing, technical, and so on–and capture the diversity of the work within that domain.

Diversity in the work can be thought of in terms of depth (vertically) and breadth (horizontally). The *depth of work* in most organizations probably ranges from strategic leadership jobs (CEOs, general directors) to the filing and mail distribution tasks in entry-level office jobs. Horizontally, the *breadth of work* depends on the nature of business. Relatively similar work can be found in specialty consulting firms (e.g., compensation or executive search firms). The breadth of work performed in some multinational conglomerates such as General Electric mirrors the occupations in the entire nation. GE includes jobs in businesses spanning financial services, entertainment (NBC), aircraft engines, medical instruments, power systems, and home appliances.

Typically, a job evaluation plan is developed using benchmark jobs, and then the plan is applied to the remaining nonbenchmark jobs. Selecting benchmark jobs from each level ensures coverage of the entire work domain, thus helping to ensure the accuracy of the decisions based on the job evaluation.

The number of job evaluation plans used hinges on how detailed an evaluation is required to make pay decisions and how much it will cost. There is no ready answer to the question of "one plan versus many." Current practice (not always the best answer for the future, since practice is based on the past) is to use separate plans for major domains of work: top-executive/leadership jobs, managerial/professional jobs, operational/technical jobs, and office/administrative jobs. Open the door on some organizations and you will find additional plans for sales, legal, engineers/scientists, and skilled trades.

EXHIBIT 5.4 Benchmark Jobs

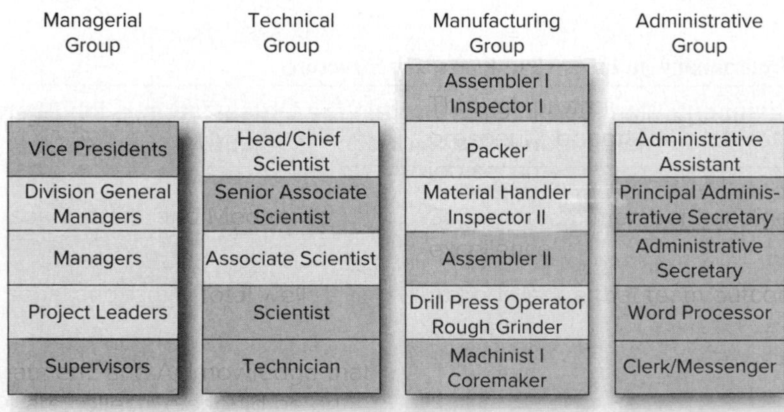

Note: More heavily shaded jobs have been selected as benchmarks.

The costs associated with all these plans (including time) give impetus to the push to simplify job structures (reduce titles and levels). Some employers, notably Hewlett-Packard, simplify by using a single plan with a core set of common factors for all jobs and additional factors specific to particular occupational or functional areas (finance, manufacturing, software and systems, sales).

Choose among Job Evaluation Methods

Ranking format, classification, and **point (factor) method** are the most common job evaluation methods, though uncounted variations exist. Research over 40 years consistently finds that different job evaluation plans generate different pay structures. So the method you choose matters.

Exhibit 5.5 compares the methods. They all begin by assuming that a useful job analysis has been translated into job description methods.

JOB EVALUATION METHODS

A survey of roughly 1,000 members of WorldatWork, the association for compensation professionals, asked which primary job evaluation method was used in their organizations. As **Exhibit 5.6** indicates, the most common response was "Well, not really any job evaluation method." Instead, **market pricing** was overwhelmingly chosen (68% to 74%, depending on the job level) as the primary method of job evaluation. What is market pricing? We will return to this topic in more detail later, especially in **Chapter 8**. For now, think of market pricing as directly matching as many of your own organization's jobs as possible to jobs described in the external pay surveys you use. To the extent that such matches can be made, the pay rate for your job will be based on the survey data. Internal equity is greatly de-emphasized (as is the organization's strategy–more on this in **Chapter 8**).

Note that **Exhibit 5.6** does indicate that somewhere between 1 in 3 and 1 in 4 organizations continue to use traditional job evaluation approaches as their *primary* methods. Further, it is likely that job evaluation is also used widely even in organizations that rely primarily on market pricing, because it is usually not possible to directly match all jobs to market survey jobs. Thus, job evaluation is still needed and we now discuss three job evaluation methods, with most of our attention given to point or point factor approaches.

EXHIBIT 5.5 Comparison of Job Evaluation Methods

	Advantage	Disadvantage
Ranking	Fast, simple, easy to explain.	Cumbersome as number of jobs increases. Basis for comparisons is not called out.
Classification	Can group a wide range of work together in one system.	Descriptions may leave too much room for manipulation.
Point	Compensable factors call out basis for comparisons. Compensable factors communicate what is valued.	Can become bureaucratic and rule-bound.

Ranking

Ranking simply orders the job descriptions from highest to lowest, based on a global definition of relative value or contribution to the organization's success. Ranking is simple, fast, and easy to understand and explain to employees; it is also the least expensive method, at least initially. However, it can create problems that require difficult and potentially expensive solutions because it doesn't tell employees and managers what it is about their jobs that is important.

Two ways of ranking are common: **alternation ranking** and **paired comparison.** *Alternation ranking* orders job descriptions alternately at each extreme. Evaluators reach agreement on which jobs are the most and least valuable (i.e., which is a 10, which is a 1), then the next most and least valued (i.e., which is a 9, which is a 2), and so on, until all the jobs have been ordered. The *paired-comparison* method uses a matrix to compare all possible pairs of jobs. **Exhibit 5.7** shows that the higher-ranked job is entered in the cell of the matrix. When all comparisons have been completed, the job most frequently judged "more valuable" becomes the highest-ranked job, and so on.

Alternation-ranking and paired-comparison methods may be more reliable (produce similar results consistently) than simple ranking. Nevertheless, ranking has drawbacks. The criteria on which the jobs are ranked are usually so poorly defined, if they are specified at all, that the evaluations become subjective opinions that are impossible to justify in strategic and work-related terms. Further, evaluators using this method must be knowledgeable about every single job under study. The numbers alone turn what should be a simple task into a formidable one—50 jobs require 1,225 comparisons—and as organizations change, it is difficult to remain knowledgeable about all jobs. Some organizations try to overcome this difficulty by ranking jobs within single departments and merging the results. However, even though the ranking appears simple, fast, and inexpensive, in the long run the results are difficult to defend and costly solutions may be required to overcome the problems created.

EXHIBIT 5.6 Primary Method of Job Evaluation

	What is the *primary* method of job evaluation used by your organization?		
	Market Pricing	**Point Factor**	**Other**
Executives	72%	16%	10%
Senior Management	69%	19%	11%
Middle Management	67%	21%	12%
Professional	66%	21%	12%
Sales	71%	18%	10%
Administrative	67%	19%	13%
Production	66%	17%	14%

Source: WorldatWork, "Job Evaluation and Market-Pricing Practices," February 2020. N = 472 organizations.

Classification

Picture a bookcase with many shelves. Each shelf is labeled with a paragraph describing the kinds of books on that shelf and, perhaps, one or two representative titles. This same approach describes the *classification* method of job evaluation. A series of classes covers the range of jobs. Class descriptions are the labels. A job description is compared to the class descriptions to decide which class is the best fit for that job. Each class is described in such a way that the "label" captures sufficient work detail yet is general enough to cause little difficulty in slotting a job description onto its appropriate "shelf" or class. The classes may be described further by including titles of benchmark jobs that fall into each class.

Determining the number of classes and writing class descriptions to define the boundaries between each class (e.g., how many bookshelves and what distinguishes each from the other–fiction, nonfiction, mysteries, biographies, etc.) are something of an art form. One way to begin is to find the natural breaks or changes in the work content. At Lockheed, the engineering work discussed in previous chapters has obvious natural breaks between engineers (individual contributors) and lead engineers (responsible for overall projects). But how many classes within each of these make sense? **Exhibit 5.8** shows classifications used by Clark Consulting to conduct salary surveys of engineering salaries at many different employers. Managerial work includes three classes, while there are five classes of individual contributors. Information to guide the writing of class descriptions can come from managers, job incumbents, job descriptions, and career progression considerations.

Writing class descriptions can be troublesome when jobs from several job families are covered by a single plan. Although greater specificity of the class definition improves the reliability of evaluation, it also limits the variety of jobs that can easily be classified. For example, class definitions written with sales jobs in mind may make it difficult to slot office or administrative jobs and vice versa. One issue with the job classification method is that trying to include a diverse set of jobs in one class can result in vagueness of job descriptions, leaving a lot of room for "judgment."[6] Including titles of benchmark jobs for each class can help make the descriptions more concrete.

In practice, with a classification method the job descriptions not only are compared to the class descriptions and benchmark jobs but also can be compared to each other to be sure that jobs within each class are more similar to each other than to jobs in adjacent classes.

EXHIBIT 5.7 Paired-Comparison Ranking

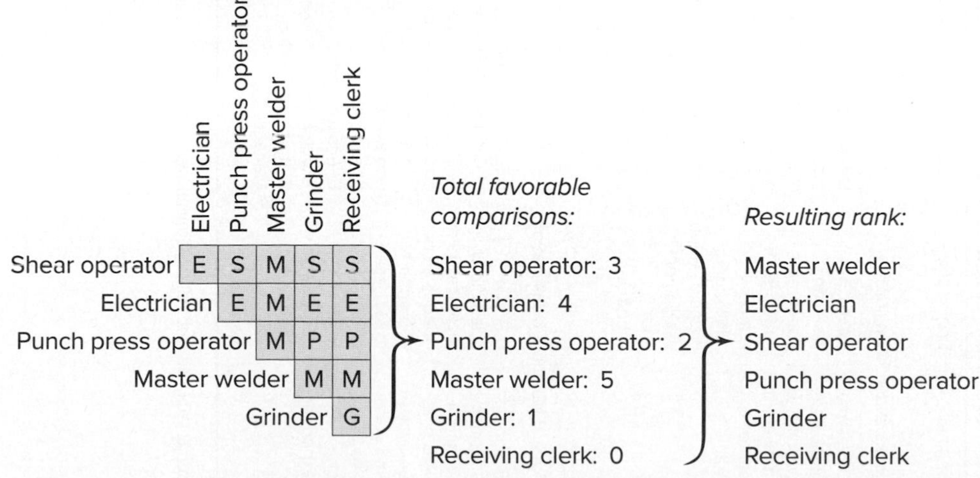

EXHIBIT 5.8 **Classifications for Engineering Work Used by Clark Consulting**

Engineer 1	Engineer 2	Engineer 3	Engineer 4	Engineer 5	Engineering Manager 1	Engineering Manager 2	Engineering Manager 3
Tasks and Responsibilities							
Develops, tests, and documents software as part of a team.	Develops, tests, and documents software that is more challenging. Helps develop assignment and schedules.	Develops project plans, including technical specifications and schedules. Designs and performs analysis on complex programs and systems. Provides input into product designs and updates.	Leads complex project design and development. Proposes new products and oversees their implementation.	Provides technical expertise and advice to management in strategic planning process. Provides technical expertise in research, design, and development for new technologies Provides guidance to support staff.	Manages design and development of new software and/or technologies while adhering to cost and schedule targets. Helps develop management policies. Manages up 10 employees.	Creates work environment for developing and implementing complete products/systems. Plays role in strategic planning. Manages 10 to 25 employees, including first-level managers.	Leads strategic planning for families of products, including their marketing and pricing. Manages engineering product group while adhering to quality and timeliness goals. Manages over 25 employees from multiple disciplines.
Typical Minimum Qualifications							
B.S. in a scientific or technical field or equivalent and up to two years of experience.	B.S. in a scientific or technical field or equivalent and up to two to four years of experience, or an M.S. degree and up to two years of experience.	B.S. in engineering, computer science, or related technical field and four to six years of experience or an M.S. and two to four years of experience. Education and experience at or above that of Engineering Manager 1	B.S. in engineering, computer science, or a related technical field and six or more years of experience or an M.S. and four to six years of experience	B.S. in engineering, computer science, or a related technical field and ten or more years of experience or an M.S. and six or more years of experience	Education and experience at or above that of Engineer 5	Education and experience at or above that of Engineering Manager 1	Education and experience at or above that of Engineering Manager 2

Source: Adapted from Clark Consulting.

The end result is a job structure made up of a series of classes with a number of jobs in each. All these comparisons are used to ensure that this structure is based on the organization strategy and work flow, is fair, and focuses behaviors on desired results. The jobs within each class are considered to be equal (similar) work and will be paid equally. Jobs in different classes should be dissimilar and may have different pay rates.

The Wall Street Journal once compiled a list of the 10 most unusual U.S. government jobs. It included Smokey Bear's manager, a Supreme Court seamstress (job responsibility: keeping the Supremes in stitches), a gold stacker, condom tester, currency reconstructor, and Air Force art curator. The Office of Personnel Management publishes The Classifiers Handbook (45 pages) and Introduction to the Position Classification Standards (73 pages), which together provide instructions on how to classify jobs into the General Schedule.[7] Visit the site to discover the level of detail in the government's approach. Contrast that with "Big Blue" (IBM), which puts its complete classification plan on a single page.

Point Method

Point methods have three common characteristics: (1) compensable factors, with (2) factor degrees numerically scaled, and (3) weights reflecting the relative importance of each factor.[8] Each job's relative value, and hence its location in the pay structure, is determined by the total points assigned to it.

Point plans are the most commonly used job evaluation approach in the United States and Europe. They represent a significant change from ranking and classification methods in that they make explicit the criteria for evaluating jobs: *compensable factors*.[9]

Compensable factors are based on the strategic direction of the business and how the work contributes to these objectives and strategy. The factors are scaled to reflect the degree to which they are present in each job and weighted to reflect their overall importance to the organization. Points are then attached to each **factor weight.** The total points for each job determine its position in the job structure.

There are eight steps in the design of a point plan.

1. Conduct job analysis.
2. Determine compensable factors.
3. Scale the factors.
4. Weight the factors according to importance.
5. Select criterion pay structure.
6. Communicate the plan and train users.
7. Apply to nonbenchmark jobs.
8. Develop online software support.

1. Conduct Job Analysis

Just as with ranking and classification, point plans begin with job analysis. Typically a representative sample of jobs, that is, benchmark jobs, is drawn for analysis. The content of these jobs is the basis for defining, **scaling,** and weighting the compensable factors.

2. Determine Compensable Factors

Compensable factors play a pivotal role in the point plan. These factors reflect how work adds value to the organization. They flow from the work itself and the strategic direction of the business.

> **Compensable factors** are those characteristics in the work that the organization values, that help it pursue its strategy and achieve its objectives.

To select compensable factors, an organization asks itself, What is it about the work that adds value? Organizations can often begin with existing compensable factor frameworks, which we discuss below. **Exhibit 5.9** provides an example of a compensable factor called job controls and complexity. Organizations can then adapt existing compensable factors and/or add new ones that are more specific to their strategies. For example, one company decided to include decision making, which is somewhat similar to job controls and complexity in **Exhibit 5.9**, as a compensable factor. The definition of *decision making* is three-dimensional: (1) the risk and complexity (hence the availability of guidelines to assist in making the decisions), (2) the impact of the decisions, and (3) the time that must pass before the impact is evident.

In effect, this firm determined that its competitive advantage depends on decisions employees make in their work. And the relative value of the decisions depends on their risk, their complexity, and their impact on the company. Hence, this firm is signaling to all employees that jobs will be valued based on the nature of the decisions required by employees in those jobs. Jobs that require riskier decisions with greater impact have a higher relative worth than jobs that require fewer decisions with less consequence.

To be useful, compensable factors should be

- Based on the strategy and values of the organization.
- Based on the work performed.
- Acceptable to the stakeholders affected by the resulting pay structure.

Based on the Strategy and Values of the Organization

The leadership of any organization is the best source of information on where the business should be going and how it is going to get there. Clearly, the leaders' input into factor selection is crucial. If the business strategy involves providing innovative, high-quality products and services designed in collaboration with customers and suppliers, then jobs with greater responsibilities for product innovation and customer contacts should be valued higher. Or if the business strategy is more Walmart-like, "providing goods and services to delight customers at the lowest cost and greatest convenience possible," then compensable factors might include impact on **cost containment,** customer relations, and so on.

Compensable factors reinforce the organization's culture and values as well as its business direction and the nature of the work. If the direction changes, then the compensable factors may also change. For example, strategic plans at many companies call for increased globalization. Procter & Gamble and 3M include a "multinational responsibilities" factor in their managerial job evaluation plan. Multinational responsibilities are defined in terms of the type of responsibility (in developing policies and strategies, whether the role is assisting, leading, or having full responsibility, including approval authority), the percent of time devoted to international issues, and the number of countries covered. (Do you suppose that managers at 3M or P&G got raises when Czechoslovakia, Yugoslavia, and the Soviet Union rearranged themselves into a greater number of smaller, independent countries?)

EXHIBIT 5.9 Compensable Factor Example: Job Controls and Complexity (3 of the 8 levels)

Factor Definition: The amount and type of direction received, the complexity of work, and the nature of the work within a job.

Level 1

- Employee does not deviate from detailed directions given by the supervisor and guides; e.g., standard operating procedures (SOPs), handbooks, and reference manuals.

AND

- Tasks are clear-cut and related. There is little choice in deciding what to do or how to do it. The level of complexity is low.

AND

- Work relieves others in the unit/office of simple, repetitive tasks. The work has minimal impact outside of the immediate organizational unit.

Level 4

- Employee either (a) carries out work with minimal supervision (i.e., the supervisor sets only goals, priorities, and deadlines; and the employee uses guidelines that cover most situations), **or** (b) the employee follows the supervisor's directions on methods and desired results but modifies methods to resolve unforeseen situations and problems.

AND

- Processes, procedures, or software vary from one assignment to the next, although assignments are related in function and objective. Based on the assignment, the employee must use diverse but conventional methods, techniques, or approaches.

AND

- Work product or service affects the accuracy, reliability, or acceptability of further processes or services.

Level 8

- Employee works (a) with only administrative and policy direction **and** (b) must make decisions based on broadly stated guidelines that lack specificity or proven validity, e.g., general policy statements, basic laws, or scientific theory. The employee defines objectives, plans work, and develops new methods or hypotheses that have led to recognition as a technical authority.

AND

- Work requires many different processes and methods applied to an established administrative or professional field. Problems are typically the result of unusual circumstances, variations in approach, and incomplete or conflicting data. The employee must interpret data and refine methods to complete assignments.

AND

- Work affects the work of other experts, influences important professional or administrative activities of the establishment, or impacts the well being of many groups of people.

Source: U.S. Bureau of Labor Statistics, *National Compensation Survey: Guide for Evaluating Your Firm's Jobs and Pay,* May 2013 (revised).

Factors may also be eliminated if they no longer support the business strategy. The railway company Burlington Northern revised its job evaluation plan to omit the factor "number of subordinates supervised." It decided that a factor that values increases to staff runs counter to the organization's objective of reducing bureaucracy and increasing efficiency. Major shifts in the business strategy are not daily occurrences, but when they do occur, compensable factors should be reexamined to ensure they are consistent with the new directions.[10]

Based on the Work Itself

Employees and supervisors are experts in the work actually done in any organization. Hence, it is important to seek their answers to what should be valued in the work itself. Some form of documentation (i.e., job descriptions, job analysis, employee and/or supervisory focus groups) must support the choice of factors. Work-related documentation helps gain acceptance by employees and managers, is easier to understand, and can withstand a variety of challenges to the pay structure. For example, managers may argue that the salaries of their employees are too low in comparison to those of other employees or that the salary offered a job candidate is too low. Union leaders may wonder why one job is paid differently from another. Allegations of **pay discrimination** may be raised. Employees, line managers, union leaders, and compensation managers must understand and be able to explain why work is paid differently or the same. Differences in factors that are obviously based on the work itself provide that rationale or even diminish the likelihood of the challenges arising.

Reliable and Valid

See the **Chapter 4** and **Chapter 6** discussions of reliability and validity.

Acceptable to the Stakeholders

Acceptance of the compensable factors used to slot jobs into the pay structure may depend, at least in part, on tradition. For example, people who work in hospitals, nursing homes, and child care centers make the point that responsibility for people is used less often as a compensable factor, and valued lower, than responsibility for property.[11] This omission may be a carryover from the days when nursing and child care service were provided by family members, usually women, without reimbursement. People now doing these jobs for pay say that properly valuing a factor for people responsibility would raise their wages. So the question is, acceptable to whom? The answer ought to be the stakeholders.

Using Existing Standardized Plans or Adapting Factors from Existing Plans

The use of existing, standardized plans (e.g., the Hay Group plan described below) offers the advantage of being able to compare the relative scope, content, and internal value of jobs in the organization to similar jobs in other organizations, which can be very helpful in deciding what to pay jobs relative to similar jobs in other organizations. However, as noted, to the degree that job value and pay are to be uniquely tailored to the organization's strategy and values, the job evaluation system will also need to be tailored. Although a wide variety of factors are used in standard existing plans, the factors tend to fall into four generic groups: skills required, effort required, responsibility, and working conditions. These four were used more than 60 years ago in the **National Electrical Manufacturers Association (NEMA) plan** and are also included in the Equal Pay Act (1963) to define equal work. Many of these early point plans, such as those of the **National Metal Trades Association (NMTA)** and NEMA, and the Steel Plan, were developed for manufacturing and/or office jobs.

Since then, point plans have also been applied to managerial and professional jobs. The *National Compensation Survey (NCS),* available from the U.S. Bureau of Labor Statistics (BLS), uses as compensable factors knowledge, job controls/complexity, contacts, and physical environment, and can be applied to a wide range of jobs. The NCS can be used by employers to match their jobs to jobs in the (free and publicly available) BLS pay surveys.[12]

The Korn Ferry[13] *Hay Group Guide Chart–Profile Method*[SM], used by more than 8,000 employers worldwide (including 150 of the 500 largest U.S. corporations), is perhaps the most widely used. This methodology considers work to be a process in which knowledge/skill/ability is applied to various issues and challenges in order to create an output that is of value to the organization (see **Exhibit 5.10**).

The three Hay factors–know-how, problem solving, and accountability–use Guide Charts to quantify the requirement for each factor in more detail. **Exhibit 5.11** summarizes the basic definitions of the three Hay factors. A fourth factor, working conditions, can be applied where appropriate or required by law.

In **Exhibit 5.12**, the Hay factor Know-How is considered in terms of the depth and breadth of specialized knowledge (A to H scale) required, the amount of "managerial" capability to plan/organize/coordinate/integrate resources to achieve results (T to V scale), and the degree of communicating and influencing skills required to achieve results through interacting with others (1 to 3 scale). The cell that corresponds to the right level of all three dimensions for the job being evaluated is located on the Guide Chart and this gives the points allocated for this factor. In the exhibit, the Factory Manager gets 400 points for Know-How. A similar process utilizes Guide Charts for Problem Solving and Accountability to determine the points for those factors, which leads to a total point score for the job.

How Many Factors?

A remaining issue to consider is how many factors should be included in the plan. Some factors may have overlapping definitions or may fail to account for anything unique in the criterion chosen. In fact, the NEMA plan explicitly states that the compensable factor experience should be correlated with education. One writer calls this the "illusion of validity"–we want to believe that the factors are capturing divergent aspects of the

EXHIBIT 5.10 **Hay Group, Role of Compensable Factors of Accountability, Problem Solving, and Know-How**

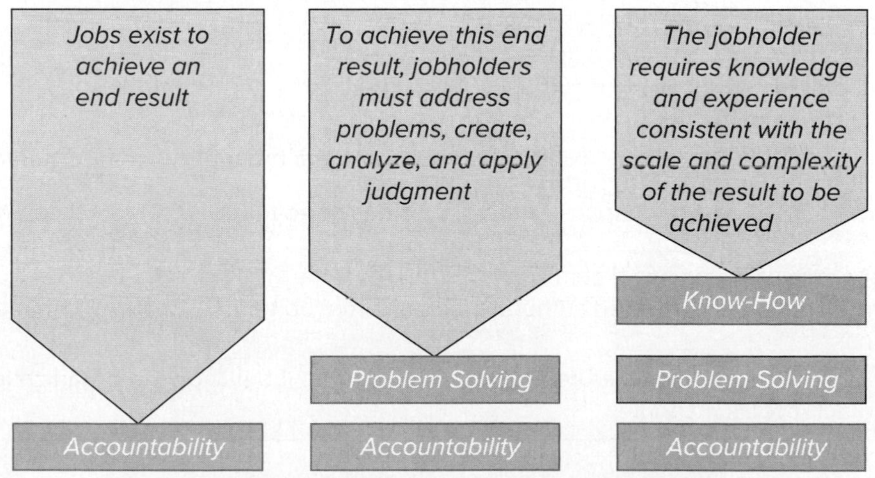

The Hay Group method uses three universal compensable elements to measure the relative size of jobs

job and that both are important.[14] It has long been recognized that factors overlap or are highly correlated, raising the concern about double counting the value of a factor. Indeed, in the Hay plan, problem solving is calculated as a percentage of Know-How. So, by definition, one builds on the foundation established by the other. It is a central principle of the Hay plan that the factors are not independent–the reason that know-how is required is because of the problems that have to be solved in order to achieve the results that are required (accountability)–and that the relative proportions of the factors that come together in a job provide important insights to the job. This notion of relative proportions is the *Profile* concept in the *Hay Group Guide Chart–Profile Method.*

Another challenge is called "small numbers." If even one job in our benchmark sample has a certain characteristic, we tend to use that factor for the entire work domain. Unpleasant working conditions are a common example. If even one job is performed in unpleasant working conditions, it is tempting to make those conditions a compensable factor and apply it to all jobs. Once a factor is part of the system, other workers are likely to say their jobs have it, too. For example, office staff may feel that ringing telephones or leaky toner cartridges constitute stressful or hazardous conditions.

In one plan, a senior manager refused to accept a job evaluation plan unless the factor working conditions was included. The plan's designer, a recent college graduate, showed through statistical analysis that working conditions did not vary enough among 90 percent of the jobs to have a meaningful effect on the resulting pay structure. Nevertheless, the manager pointed out that the recent grad had never worked in the plant's foundry, where working conditions were extremely meaningful. In order to get the plan accepted by the foundry workers, the working-conditions factor was included.

EXHIBIT 5.11 Hay Group, Compensable Factors Definitions

Know-how: the sum total of all knowledge and skill, however acquired, required to do the job competently.
Know-how typically has three dimensions:

- Practical, technical, and specialized knowledge and skill (includes depth and breadth)
- Planning, organizing, coordinating, and integrating knowledge
- Communicating and influencing skills

Problem solving: measuring the nature and complexity of the issues and challenges that the job has to face.
Problem solving typically has two dimensions:

- Environment—the availability of guidance for the thinking in terms of policies, procedures, guidelines, and instructions, along with the degree of definition around the problems
- Challenge—the inherent complexity of the issues and the thought process required

Accountability: the measured impact that the job is designed to have on the success of the enterprise.
Accountability typically has two dimensions:

- Freedom to act—the delegated authority vested in the job to act, approve, or make decisions
- Impact—the magnitude and nature of the impact that the job has on the organization's ability to achieve its mandate

This situation is not unusual. In one study, a 21-factor plan produced the same rank order of jobs that could be generated using only 7 of the factors. Further, the jobs could be correctly slotted into pay classes using only three factors. Yet the company decided to keep the 21-factor plan because it was "accepted and doing the job." Research as far back as the 1940s demonstrates that the skills dimension explains 90 percent or more of the variance in job evaluation results; three factors generally account for 98 to 99 percent of the variance.[15] Nevertheless, as we demonstrate in **Chapter 6**, even under such circumstances where reliability is high, the job evaluation points assigned to at least some jobs can vary depending on the choice of raters or factors.

3. Scale the Factors

Once the factors are determined, scales reflecting the different degrees (i.e., levels) within each factor are constructed. Each degree may also be anchored by the typical skills, tasks, and behaviors taken from the benchmark jobs that illustrate each factor degree. Returning to **Exhibit 5.9**, there are 8 levels or degrees of the Job Controls and Complexity compensable factor (of which 3 levels or degrees are shown).

Most **factor scales** consist of four to eight degrees. In practice, many evaluators use extra, undefined degrees such as plus and minus around a scale number. So what starts as a 5-degree scale–1, 2, 3, 4, 5–ends up as a 15-degree scale, with −1, 1, 1+, −2, 2, 2+, and so on. The reason for adding plus/minus is that users of the plan believe more degrees are required to adequately differentiate among jobs. If we are trying to design 15 levels into the job structure but the factors use only three or five degrees, such users may be right.[16] However, all too often inserting pluses and minuses gives the illusion of accuracy of measurement that is simply not the case.

EXHIBIT 5.12 **Hay Group, Compensable Factors Scoring**

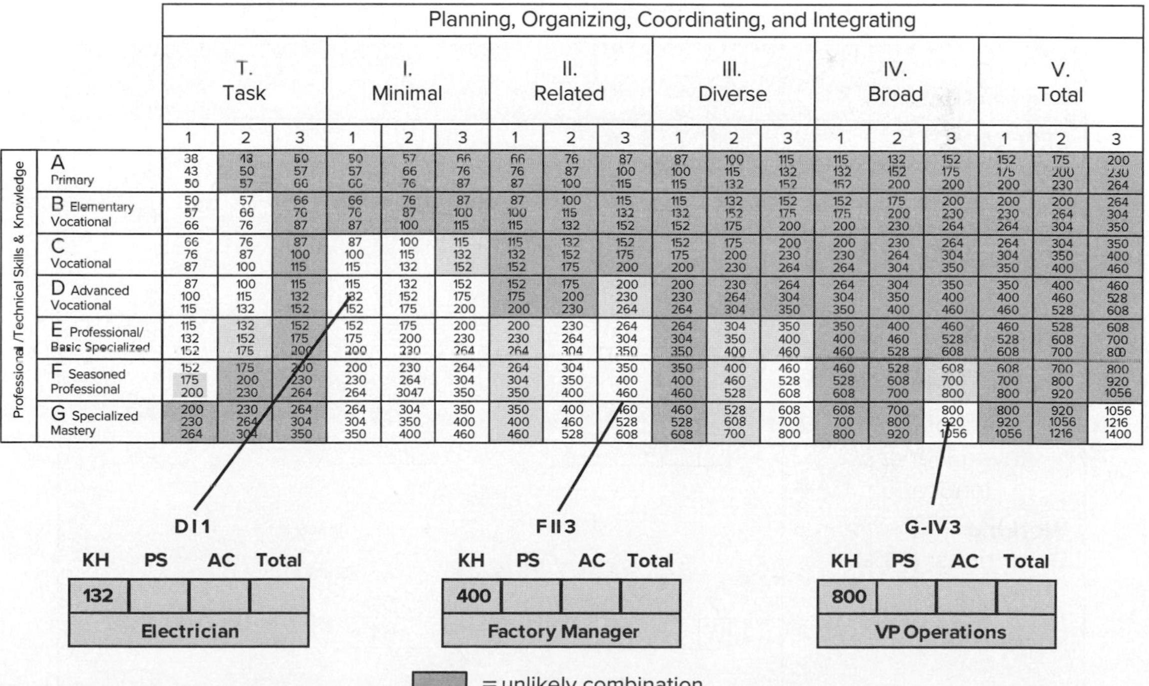

Professional/Technical Skills & Knowledge	Planning, Organizing, Coordinating, and Integrating																	
	T. Task			I. Minimal			II. Related			III. Diverse			IV. Broad			V. Total		
	1	2	3	1	2	3	1	2	3	1	2	3	1	2	3	1	2	3
A Primary	38 43 50	43 50 57	50 57 66	50 57 66	57 66 76	66 76 87	66 76 87	76 87 100	87 100 115	87 100 115	100 115 132	115 132 152	115 132 152	132 152 200	152 175 200	152 175 200	175 200 230	200 230 264
B Elementary Vocational	50 57 66	57 66 76	66 76 87	66 76 87	76 87 100	87 100 115	87 100 115	100 115 132	115 132 152	115 132 152	132 152 175	152 175 200	152 175 200	175 200 230	200 230 264	200 230 264	200 264 304	264 304 350
C Vocational	66 76 87	76 87 100	87 100 115	87 100 115	100 115 132	115 132 152	115 132 152	132 152 175	152 175 200	152 175 200	175 200 230	200 230 264	200 230 264	230 264 304	264 304 350	264 304 350	304 350 400	350 400 460
D Advanced Vocational	87 100 115	100 115 132	115 132 152	115 132 152	132 152 175	152 175 200	152 175 200	175 200 230	200 230 264	200 230 264	230 264 304	264 304 350	264 304 350	304 350 400	350 400 460	350 400 460	400 460 528	460 528 608
E Professional/ Basic Specialized	115 132 152	132 152 175	152 175 200	152 175 200	175 200 230	200 230 264	200 230 264	230 264 304	264 304 350	264 304 350	304 350 400	350 400 460	350 400 460	400 460 528	460 528 608	460 528 608	528 608 700	608 700 800
F Seasoned Professional	152 175 200	175 200 230	200 230 264	200 230 264	230 264 3047	264 304 350	264 304 350	304 350 400	350 400 460	350 400 460	400 460 528	460 528 608	460 528 608	528 608 700	608 700 800	608 700 800	700 800 920	800 920 1056
G Specialized Mastery	200 230 264	230 264 304	264 304 350	264 304 350	304 350 400	350 400 460	350 400 460	400 460 528	460 528 608	460 528 608	528 608 700	608 700 800	608 700 800	700 800 920	800 920 1056	800 920 1056	920 1056 1216	1056 1216 1400

Source: Hay Group, personal communication, August 10, 2012.

Another major issue in determining degrees is whether to make each degree equidistant from the adjacent degrees **(interval scaling).** For example, on a scale with 8 degrees, the interval scaling would aim for the difference between the first and second degrees to approximate the difference between the fourth and fifth degrees.

The following criteria for scaling factors have been suggested: (1) Ensure that the number of degrees is necessary to distinguish among jobs, (2) use understandable terminology, (3) anchor degree definitions with benchmark-job titles and/or work behaviors, and (4) make it apparent how the degree applies to the job.

4. Weight the Factors According to Importance

Once the degrees have been assigned, the factor weights can be determined. Factor weights reflect the relative importance of each factor to the overall value of the job. Different weights reflect differences in importance attached to each factor by the employer. For example, the National Electrical Manufacturers Association plan weights education at 17.5 percent; another employer's association weights it at 10.6 percent; a consultant's plan recommends 15.0 percent; and a trade association weights education at 10.1 percent.

Weights are often determined through an advisory committee that allocates 100 percent of the value among the factors.[17] In the illustration in **Exhibit 5.13**, a committee allocated 40 percent of the value to skill, 30 percent to effort, 20 percent to responsibility, and 10 percent to working conditions. Each factor has two subfactors, with five degrees each. In the example for the bookstore manager, the subfactor mental skill gets half the 40 percent given to skill and the subfactor experience gets the other half: 4 degrees of mental skill times 20 equals 80 points, and 3 degrees of experience times 20 equals another 60 points.[18]

EXHIBIT 5.13 Job Evaluation Form

Job *bookstore manager*

Check one: ☒ Administrative ☐ Technical

Compensable Factors	Degree (1 2 3 4 5)	×	Weight	=	Total
Skill: (40%)					
Mental	4 (X)		20%		80
Experience	3 (X)		20%		60
Effort: (30%)					
Physical	2 (X)		15%		30
Mental	4 (X)		15%		60
Responsibility: (20%)					
Effect of Error	4 (X)		10%		40
Inventiveness/ Innovation	3 (X)		10%		30
Working Conditions: (10%)					
Environment	1 (X)		5%		5
Hazards	1 (X)		5%		5
					310

5. Select Criterion Pay Structure

Job evaluation has traditionally supplemented committee judgment for determining weights with statistical analysis.[19] The committee members recommend the **criterion pay structure,** that is, a pay structure they wish to duplicate with the point plan. The criterion structure may be the current rates paid for benchmark jobs, market rates for benchmark jobs, rates for jobs held predominantly by males (in an attempt to eliminate gender bias), or union-negotiated rates.[20] Once a criterion structure is agreed on, statistical modeling techniques are used to determine the weight for each factor and the factor scales that will reproduce, as closely as possible, the chosen structure. The statistical approach is often labeled **policy capturing** to differentiate it from the **committee a priori judgment approach.** Not only do the weights reflect the relative importance of each factor, but research clearly demonstrates that the weights influence the resulting pay structure.[21] Thus, selecting the appropriate pay rates to use as the criteria is critical. The job evaluation and its results are based on it.[22]

Perhaps the clearest illustration can be found in municipalities. Rather than using market rates for firefighters, some unions have successfully negotiated a link between firefighters' pay and police rates. So the criterion structure for firefighters becomes some percentage of whatever wage structure is used for police. We describe this process in more detail in **Chapter 8**.

6. Communicate the Plan and Train Users

Once the job evaluation plan is designed, a manual is prepared so that other people can apply the plan. The manual describes the method, defines the compensable factors, and provides enough information to permit users to distinguish varying degrees of each factor. The point of the manual is to allow users who were not involved in the plan's development to apply the plan as its developers intended. One measure of success in this training would be high (inter)rater reliability. Users will also require training on how to apply the plan and background information on how the plan fits into the organization's total pay system. An **appeals process** may also be included so that employees who feel their jobs are unfairly evaluated have some recourse. Employee acceptance of the process is crucial if the organization is to have any hope that employees will accept the resulting pay as fair. In order to build this acceptance, communication to all employees whose jobs are part of the process used to build the structure is required. This communication may be done through informational meetings, websites, or other methods.

7. Apply to Nonbenchmark Jobs

Recall that the compensable factors and weights were derived using a sample of benchmark jobs. The final step is to apply the plan to the remaining jobs. If the policy-capturing approach described above (and in **Chapter 9**) is used, then an equation can be used to translate job evaluation points into salaries. This can be done by people who were not necessarily involved in the design process but have been given adequate training in applying the plan. Increasingly, once the plan is developed and accepted, it becomes a tool for managers and HR specialists. They evaluate new positions that may be created or reevaluate jobs whose work content has changed. They may also be part of panels that hear appeals from murmuring employees.

8. Develop Online Software Support

Online job evaluation is widely used in larger organizations. It becomes part of a Total Compensation Service Center for managers and HR generalists to use.[23]

WHO SHOULD BE INVOLVED?

If the internal structure's purpose is to aid managers–and if ensuring high involvement and commitment from employees is important–those managers and employees with a stake in the results should be involved in the process of designing it. A common approach is to use committees, task forces, or teams that include representatives from key operating functions, including nonmanagerial employees. In some cases, the group's role is only advisory; in others, the group designs the evaluation approach, chooses compensable factors, and approves all major changes. Organizations with unions often find that including union representatives helps gain acceptance of the results. Task forces involving both unions and management participated in the design of a new evaluation system for the federal government. However, other union leaders believe that philosophical differences prevent their active participation. They take the position that collective bargaining yields more equitable results. So the extent of union participation varies. No single perspective exists on the value of active participation in the process, just as no single management perspective exists.

Exhibit 5.14 shows further results from the survey of WorldatWork members discussed earlier. We see that compensation professionals (i.e., usually compensation analysts, sometimes also those at higher levels such as the compensation manager) are primarily responsible for most job evaluations for most jobs. Although that holds true for senior management jobs as well, we see that the higher level compensation manager is more likely to be charged with the job evaluation in this case and that consultants also play a much larger role here.

The Design Process Matters

Research suggests that attending to the fairness of the design process and the approach chosen (job evaluation, skill/competency-based plan, and market pricing), rather than focusing solely on the results (the internal pay structure), is likely to achieve employee and management commitment, trust, and acceptance of the results. The absence of participation may make it easier for employees and managers to imagine ways the structure might have been rearranged to their personal liking. Two researchers note, "If people do not participate in decisions, there is little to prevent them from assuming that things would have been better, 'if I'd been in charge.'"[24]

EXHIBIT 5.14 **Who Typically Conducts the Job Evaluation?**

	Compensation Staff	Employee Committee	Consultant	Senior Management or Manager
Executives	56%	4%	27%	14%
Senior Management	83%	4%	7%	6%
Middle Management	88%	5%	3%	4%
Professional	87%	5%	3%	5%
Sales	87%	6%	3%	5%
Administration	88%	5%	3%	4%
Production	86%	6%	3%	6%

Source: WorldatWork, "Job Evaluation and Market-Pricing Practices Survey," February 2020. N = 341 organizations.

e-Compensation

O*Net, the Occupational Information Network, is the U.S. Department of Labor's database that identifies and describes occupations; worker knowledge, skills, and abilities; and workplace requirements for jobs across the country in all sectors of the economy. For more information, visit O*Net's website: ***www.onetcenter.org***.

How can public sector agencies use this information? Go to an occupation that is of interest to you. Compare the information offered by the Department of Labor to the job-opening descriptions you looked at for specific companies (Chapter 4's **e-Compensation**).

Why are they different? What purpose does each serve?

Additional research is needed to ascertain whether the payoffs from increased participation offset potential costs (time involved to reach consensus, potential problems caused by disrupting current perceptions, etc.). We noted earlier that no amount of participation overcomes low wages. In multinational organizations the involvement of both corporate compensation and country managers raises the potential for conflict due to their differing perspectives. Country managers may wish to focus on the particular business needs in their markets, whereas corporate managers may want a system that operates equally well (or poorly) across all countries. The country manager has operating objectives, does not want to lose key individuals, and views compensation as a mechanism to help accomplish these goals; corporate adopts a worldwide perspective and focuses on ensuring that decisions are consistent with the overall global strategy.

Appeals/Review Procedures

No matter what the technique, no job evaluation plan anticipates all situations. It is inevitable that some jobs will be incorrectly evaluated—or at least employees and managers may suspect that they were. Consequently, review procedures for handling such cases and helping to ensure procedural fairness are required. In the past, the compensation manager handled reviews, but increasingly teams of managers and even peers are used. Sometimes these reviews take on the trappings of formal grievance procedures (e.g., documented complaints and responses and levels of approval). Problems may also be handled by managers and the employee relations generalists through informal discussions.[25]

When the evaluations are completed, approval by higher levels of management is usually required. An approval process helps ensure that any changes that result from evaluating work are consistent with the organization's operations and directions.

"I Know I Speak for All of Us When I Say I Speak for All of Us"

One study found that more powerful departments in a university were more successful in using the appeals process to change the pay or the classification of a job than were weaker departments.[26] This is consistent with other research that showed that a powerful member of a **job evaluation committee** could sway the results.[27] Consequently, procedures should be judged for their susceptibility to political influences. "It is the decision-making process, rather than the instrument itself, that seems to have the greatest influence on pay outcomes," writes one researcher.[28]

THE FINAL RESULT: STRUCTURE

The final result of the job analysis–job description–job evaluation process is a *structure,* a hierarchy of work. As shown in **Exhibit 5.3** at the beginning of this chapter, this hierarchy translates the employer's internal alignment policy into practice. **Exhibit 5.15** shows four hypothetical job structures within a single organization. These structures were obtained via different approaches to evaluating work. The jobs are arrayed within four basic functions: managerial, technical, manufacturing, and administrative. The managerial and administrative structures were obtained via a point job evaluation plan; the technical and manufacturing structures, via two different person-based plans (**Chapter 6**). The manufacturing plan was negotiated with the union. The exhibit illustrates the results of evaluating work: structures that support a policy of internal alignment.

Organizations commonly have multiple structures derived through multiple approaches that apply to different functional groups or units (see **Exhibit 5.16**). Although some employees in one structure may wish to compare the procedures used in another structure with their own, the underlying premise in practice is that internal alignment is most influenced by fair and equitable treatment of employees doing similar work in the same skill/knowledge group.

BALANCING CHAOS AND CONTROL

Looking back at the material we have covered in the past three chapters (determining internal alignment, job analysis, job evaluation), you may be thinking that we have spent a lot of time and a lot of our organization's money to develop techniques. But we have yet to pay a single employee a single dollar. Why bother with all this? Why not just pay whatever it takes and get on with it?

Prior to the widespread use of job evaluation, employers in the 1930s and 1940s did just that, and got irrational pay structures–the legacy of decentralized and uncoordinated wage-setting practices. Pay differences were a major source of unrest among workers. American Steel and Wire, for example, had more than 100,000 pay rates. Employment and wage records were rarely kept; only the foreman knew with any accuracy how

EXHIBIT 5.15 Resulting Internal Structures–Job, Skill, and Competency Based

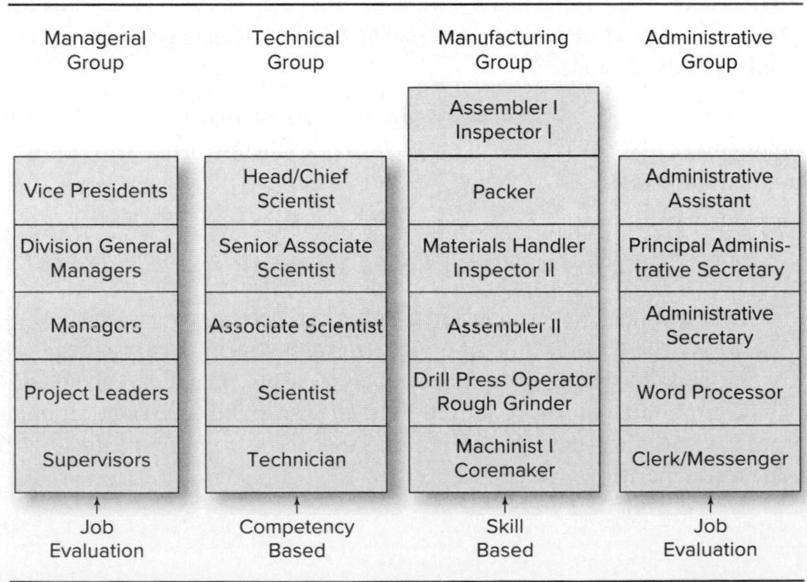

many workers were employed in his department and the rates they received. Foremen were thus "free to manage," but they used wage information to vary the day rate for favored workers or assign them to jobs where piece rates were loose.

Job evaluation, with its specified procedures and documented results, helped change that. The technique provided work-related and business-related order and logic. However, over time, complex procedures and creeping bureaucracy can cause users to lose sight of the objectives, focusing instead on "how-to" rather than "so what does this do to help accomplish our objectives." Too often we become so enamored with our techniques that we slip into knowing more and more about less and less.

At the same time, the world of work is changing. The work of many people now requires that they figure out what to do in a given situation (tacit knowledge) instead of simply invoking a canned routine (transactional work). They must identify problems and opportunities, make decisions, plan courses of action, marshal support, and, in general, design their own work methods, techniques, and tools. The challenge is to ensure that job evaluation plans afford flexibility to adapt to changing conditions.

Generic factors and vague descriptions such as "associates" or "technicians" may be very attractive to managers coping with increased competitive pressures and the need to restructure work and reduce costs. This flexibility avoids bureaucracy and leaves managers "free to manage"–just like the American Steel and Wire foremen. But it also reduces control and guidelines, and this in turn may make it harder to ensure that people are treated fairly. Some balance between chaos and control is required. History suggests that when flexibility without guidelines exists, chaotic and irrational pay rates too frequently result. Removing inefficient bureaucracy is important, but balanced guidelines are necessary to ensure that employees are treated fairly and that pay decisions help the organization achieve its objectives.

EXHIBIT 5.16 Number of Pay Structures in Organizations

Number of Pay Structures	Frequency
1	27%
2	13%
3	16%
4	9%
5 or more	62%

Source: WorldatWork. *Compensation Programs and Practices Survey*. 2019.

N = 322 organizations.

Job Evaluation at Whole Foods

Rather than wait until you are next in a supermarket to check out the different types of work, we brought some of the jobs at Whole Foods Market to you. Now that you have some background in job evaluation, it is time to try it out. As a first step, Whole Foods has done job analysis and prepared job descriptions. The results are shown below. Now a job structure is needed. The manager has assigned this job to you.

1. Divide into teams of four to six each. Each team should evaluate the jobs (i.e., assign job evaluation points to each job) and prepare a job structure based on its evaluation. Assign titles to each job, and show your structure by title and job letter. A broad hint: Recall from our discussions of Whole Foods' business and pay strategies in **Chapters 2** and **3** that teams play an important role.
2. Your team should describe the process it went through to arrive at that job structure. The job evaluation techniques and compensable factors used should be described, and the reasons for selecting them should be stated.
3. Each team should put its job structure (i.e., points assigned to each job) on the board. Comparisons can then be made among job structures of the various teams. What is the average correlation between columns of job evaluation points from different teams? Is this correlation high enough to obtain a sufficient level of reliability? (You may wish to skip ahead to the section "Reliability of Job Evaluation Techniques" in **Chapter 6** and pay special attention to the example of how even "high" reliability may not eliminate important salary differences that result from whose ratings are used.) Does the job evaluation method used appear to affect the results? Do the compensable factors chosen affect the results? Does the process affect the results?
4. Evaluate the job descriptions. What parts of them were most useful? How could they be improved?

JOB A (TEAM MEMBER, DELI)[29]

Kind of Work

Provide excellent customer service. Follow and comply with all applicable health and sanitation procedures. Prepare food items: sandwiches, slice deli meats and cheeses. Prepare items on station assignment list and as predetermined. Stock and rotate products, stock supplies and paper goods in a timely basis; keep all utensils stocked. Check dates on all products in stock to ensure freshness and rotate when necessary. Use waste sheets properly, as directed. Operate and sanitize all equipment in a safe and proper manner. Comply with and follow Whole Foods Market Safety Procedures. Follow established Weights and Measures procedures (tares). Answer the phone and pages to department quickly and with appropriate phone etiquette. Practice proper use of knives, slicer, trash compactor, baler (must be 18 years of age or older), and all other equipment used during food preparation and cleanup. Perform other duties as assigned, and follow through on supervisor requests in a timely manner.

Requirements

- Some deli experience preferred.
- Clear and effective communicator.
- Patient and enjoys working and mentoring people.
- Ability to perform physical requirements of position.
- Ability to learn proper use of knives, slicer, baler (must be 18 years of age or older) and all other equipment used during food preparation and cleanup.
- Ability to work well with others as a team.
- Knowledge of all relevant Whole Foods Market policies and standards.
- Understands and can communicate quality goals to customers.

JOB B (CASHIER)

Kind of Work

Assist and focus on customers during entire checkout process. Perform all cash register functions according to established procedures. Maintain a positive company image by providing courteous, friendly, and efficient customer service. Check out customer groceries efficiently and accurately. Pass entry-level PLU code test. Maintain a professional demeanor at all times. Stock registers with supplies as needed. Follow proper check-receiving procedure. Clean, stock, and detail front-end area with special attention to own register. Change journal tapes and ribbon as needed. Walk produce department at the beginning of every shift to identify and learn new produce codes. Comply with all posted state health and safety codes.

Requirements

- Excellent communication skills necessary for good customer and team relations.
- Ability to work well with others.
- Ability to learn proper use of baler (must be 18 or older).
- Desire to learn and grow.
- Ability to work in a fast-paced environment, with a sense of urgency.
- Understanding the importance of working as a team.
- Good math skills.
- Patience.

JOB C (TEAM LEADER, PREPARED FOODS)

Kind of Work

Reports to store team leader and to associate store team leader. Provides overall management and supervision of the Prepared Foods Department. Responsible for team member hiring, development, and terminations. Also responsible for profitability, expense control, buying/merchandising, regulatory compliance, and special projects as assigned. Complete accountability for all aspects of department operations. Consistently communicate and model Whole Foods vision and goal. Interview, select, train, develop, and counsel team members in a manner that builds and sustains a high-performing team and minimizes turnover. Make hiring and termination decisions with guidance of store team leader. Establish and maintain a positive work environment. Manage inventory to achieve targeted gross profit margin. Manage the ordering process to meet Whole Foods Market quality standards. Maintain competitive pricing and achieve targeted sales. Establish and maintain positive and productive vendor relationships. Develop and maintain creative store layout and product merchandising in support of regional and national vision. Establish and maintain collaborative and productive working relationships. Model and cultivate effective inter-department and inter-store communication. Provide accurate, complete information in daily, weekly, monthly, annual, and "ad hoc" management reports. Maintain comprehensive knowledge of, and ensure compliance with, relevant regulatory rules and standards.

Requirements

- Two years' relevant experience as a team leader, assistant team leader, supervisor, or buyer.
- Thorough knowledge of products, buying, pricing, merchandising, and inventory management.
- Excellent verbal and written communication skills.

- Strong organizational skills.
- Knowledge of all relevant Whole Foods Market policies and standards.
- Computer skills.

JOB D (TEAM MEMBER, PREPARED FOODS)

Kind of Work

Perform all duties and responsibilities of Prepared Foods Team Member. Provide excellent customer service. Assist team leader in nightly team operations. Report all actions of team members that violate policies or standards to the team leader or associate team leader. Mentor and train team members. Maintain quality standards in production and counter display. Comply with all applicable health and safety codes. Help implement and support all regional programs.

Requirements

- Minimum six months' retail food production experience, or equivalent.
- Overall knowledge of both front and back of the house operations.
- Comprehensive product knowledge.
- Comprehensive knowledge of quality standards.
- Excellent organizational skills.
- Excellent interpersonal skills, and ability to train others.
- Demonstrated decision-making ability, and leadership skills.
- Ability to perform physical requirements of position.
- Able to work a flexible schedule based on the needs of the store.

JOB E (TEAM MEMBER, KITCHEN)

Kind of Work

Performs all duties related to dishwashing: unloading kitchen deliveries and cleaning all dishes, utensils, pots, and pans. May be prep work. Maintain food quality and sanitation in kitchen. Maintain a positive company image by being courteous, friendly, and efficient. Wash and sanitize all dishes, utensils, and containers. Assist with proper storage of all deliveries. Rotate and organize products. Perform prep work as directed. Provide proper ongoing maintenance of equipment. Maintain health department standards when cleaning and handling food. Perform deep-cleaning tasks on a regular basis. Take out all of the garbage and recycling materials. Sweep and wash floors as needed.

Requirements

- Entry-level position.
- Able to perform physical requirements of job.
- Practices safe and proper knife skills.
- Ability to work box baler (must be 18 years of age or older).
- Works well with others and participates as part of a team.

JOB F (TEAM MEMBER II, STOCK AND DISPLAY)

Kind of Work

Performs all functions related to breaking down deliveries and moving back stock to floor. Assists in organizing and developing promotional displays; maintains back room, training entry-level grocery clerks. Trained and capable of operating any of the sub-departments as needed. Maintains and ensures retail standards during their shift. Responsible for implementing team's break schedule. Performs all duties and responsibilities of grocery team member. Builds displays and requests appropriate signage. Supervises shift to ensure standards are maintained. Implements break schedule for shift. Responsible for problem solving in team leader or associate team leader's absence. Fully responsible for completion of all opening or closing checklists. Responsible for checking in deliveries.

Requirements

- Minimum one year retail grocery experience, or equivalent.
- Proficient in math skills (addition, subtraction, multiplication, and division).
- Ability to perform physical requirements of position.
- Ability to properly use baler (must be 18 years of age or older).
- Able to direct team members and implement break schedule.
- Ability to work well with others.

JOB G (ASSOCIATE TEAM LEADER, PREPARED FOODS)

Kind of Work

Reports directly to Prepared Foods Team Leader. Assists in overall management and supervision of the Prepared Foods Department. Can be responsible for team member hiring, development, and terminations. Also responsible for profitability, expense control, buying/merchandising, regulatory compliance, and special projects as assigned. Complete accountability for all assigned aspects of department operations. Consistently communicate and model Whole Foods vision and goals. Assist in the interview, selection, training, development, and counseling of team members in a manner that builds and sustains a high-performing team and minimizes turnover. Discuss hiring and termination decisions with guidance of others. Establish and maintain a positive work environment. Manage inventory to achieve targeted gross profit margin. Manage the ordering process to meet Whole Foods Market quality standards, maintain competitive pricing, and achieve targeted sales. Develop and maintain creative store layout and product merchandising in support of regional and national vision. Establish and maintain collaborative and productive working relationships. Model and cultivate effective inter-department and inter-store communication. Provide accurate, complete information in daily, weekly, monthly, annual, and "ad hoc" management reports. Maintain comprehensive knowledge of, and ensure compliance with, relevant regulatory rules and standards.

Requirements

- One to two years of department experience, or industry equivalent.
- Analytical ability and proficiency in math needed to calculate margins, monitor profitability, and manage inventory.
- Clear and effective communicator.
- Patient and enjoys working and mentoring people.

- Strong organizational skills.
- Knowledge of all relevant Whole Foods Market policies and standards.
- Computer skills.

JOB H (REGIONAL TEAM LEADER)

Kind of Work

Rotate among stores. Assist and support the store team leader with all store functions. Interview, select, evaluate, counsel, and terminate team members. Coordinate and supervise all store products and personnel. Follow through on all customer and team member questions and requests. Evaluate customer service and resolve complaints. Operate the store in an efficient and profitable manner. Have a firm understanding of store financials and labor budgets. Establish and achieve sales, labor, and contribution goals. Review department schedules and research productivity improvements. Order store equipment and supplies in a timely manner. Enforce established food safety, cleaning, and maintenance procedures. Inspect store; ensure cleanliness; visit off-hours for consistency. Maintain accurate retail pricing and signage. Ensure that product is cross-merchandised in other departments. Coordinate, supervise, and report physical inventory. Analyze product transfers, waste, and spoilage. Manage expenses to maximize the bottom line. Provide, maintain, and safety-train team members on all equipment and tools. Resolve safety violations and hazards immediately. Maintain store security and ensure that opening and closing procedures are followed. Show EVA improvement over a designated period. Leverage sales growth to improve store profitability. Assist in handling liability claims and minimize their occurrence. Establish and maintain good community relations. Create a friendly, productive, and professional working environment. Communicate company goals and information to team members. Ensure and support team member development and training. Evaluate team member duties, dialogues, raises, and promotions. Keep regional leadership informed of all major events that affect the store. Ensure store policies and procedures are followed. Visit the competition on a regular basis and react to current industry trends.

Requirements

- A passion for retailing.
- Complete understanding of Whole Foods Market retail operations.
- Strong leadership and creative ability.
- Management and business skills with financial expertise.
- Well organized with excellent follow-through.
- Detail oriented with a vision and eye for the big picture.
- Self-motivated and solution oriented.
- Excellent merchandising skills and eye for detail.
- Ability to delegate effectively and use available talent to the best advantage.
- Strong communicator/motivator; able to work well with others and convey enthusiasm.
- Ability to maintain good relationships with vendors and the community.
- Can train and inspire team members to excellence in all aspects of the store.
- Ability to make tough decisions.
- Love and knowledge of natural foods.
- Strong computer skills.

JOB I (TEAM MEMBER, STOCK AND DISPLAY)

Kind of Work

Performs all functions related to breaking down deliveries and moving back stock to floor. May assist in organizing and developing promotional displays; maintains back room. Stock and clean grocery shelves, bulk bins, frozen and dairy case. Maintain back stock in good order. Sweep floors and face shelves throughout the store. Comply with all applicable health and safety codes. Provide excellent customer service. Log and expedite customers' special orders. Retrieve special orders for customers by request and offer service out to car. Respond to all grocery pages quickly and efficiently. Build displays and request appropriate signage.

Requirements

- Retail grocery or natural foods experience a plus.
- Proficient in math skills (addition, subtraction, multiplication, and division).
- Ability to learn basic knowledge of all products carried in department.
- Ability to perform physical requirements of position.
- Proper and safe use of box cutter, baler (must be 18 years of age or older), and all equipment.
- Ability to work well with others.

Summary

The differences in the rates paid for different jobs and skills affect the ability of managers to achieve their business objectives. Differences in pay matter. They matter to employees, because their willingness to take on more responsibility and training, to focus on adding value for customers and improving quality of products, and to be flexible enough to adapt to change all depend at least in part on how pay is structured for different levels of work. Differences in the rates paid for different jobs and skills also influence how fairly employees believe they are being treated. Unfair treatment is ultimately counterproductive.

So far, we have examined the most common approach to designing pay differences for different work: job evaluation. In **Chapter 6** we will examine several alternative approaches. However, any approach needs to be evaluated for how useful it is.

Job evaluation has evolved into many different forms and methods. Consequently, wide variations exist in its use and how it is perceived. This chapter discussed some of the many perceptions of the role of job evaluation and reviewed the criticisms leveled at it. No matter how job evaluation is designed, its ultimate use is to help design and manage a work-related, business-focused, and agreed-upon pay structure.

Review Questions

1. How does job evaluation translate internal alignment policies (loosely coupled versus tight fitting) into practice? What does (a) organization strategy and objectives, (b) flow of work, (c) fairness, and (d) motivating people's behaviors toward organization objectives have to do with job evaluation?
2. Why are there different approaches to job evaluation? Think of several employers in your area (the college, hospital, retailer, 7-Eleven, etc.). What approach would you expect them to use? Why?
3. What are the advantages and disadvantages of using more than one job evaluation plan in any single organization?

4. Why bother with job evaluation? Why not simply market price? How can job evaluation link internal alignment and external market pressures?
5. Consider your college or school. What are the compensable factors required for your college to evaluate jobs? How would you go about identifying these factors? Should the school's educational mission be reflected in your factors? Or are the more generic factors used in the Hay plan okay? Discuss.
6. You are the manager of ten people in a large organization. All of them become very suspicious and upset when they receive a memo from the HR department saying their jobs are going to be evaluated. How do you reassure them?

Endnotes

1. *Job Evaluation and Market Pricing Practices* (Scottsdale, AZ: WorldatWork, November 2015); Donald P. Schwab, "Job Evaluation and Pay Setting: Concepts and Practices," *in Comparable Worth: Issues and Alternatives, ed.* E. Robert Livernash (Washington, DC: Equal Employment Advisory Council, 1980), pp. 49–77.
2. Rupp, D. E., Shapiro, D. L., Folger, R., Skarlicki, D. P., & Shao, R. (2017). "A critical analysis of the conceptualization and measurement of organizational justice: Is it time for reassessment?" Academy of Management Annals, 11(2), 919–959. M. A. Konovsky, "Understanding Procedural Justice and Its Impact on Business Organizations," *Journal of Management* 26(3), 2000, pp. 489–511; Frederick P. Morgeson, Michael A. Campion, and Carl P. Maertz, "Understanding Pay Satisfaction: The Limits of a Compensation System Implementation," *Journal of Business and Psychology* 16(1), Fall 2001, pp. 133–149. Herbert Simon, "From Substantive to Procedural Rationality," in Spiro J. Latsis, ed. Methodological Appraisal in Economics, Cambridge 1976.
3. E. Robert Livernash, "Internal Wage Structure," in *New Concepts in Wage Determination,* ed. George W. Taylor and Frank C. Pierson (New York: McGraw-Hill, 1957).
4. M. S. Viteles, "A Psychologist Looks at Job Evaluation," *Personnel* 17 (1941), pp. 165–176.
5. Armstrong, Michael, and Duncan Brown, "Job Evaluation Versus Market Pricing: Competing or Combining Methods of Pay Determination?" Compensation & Benefits Review (2018). Robert L. Heneman and Peter V. LeBlanc, "Developing a More Relevant and Competitive Approach for Valuing Knowledge Work," *Compensation and Benefits Review,* July/August 2002, pp. 43–47; Robert L. Heneman and Peter V. LeBlanc, "Work Valuation Addresses Shortcomings of Both Job Evaluation and Market Pricing," *Compensation and Benefits Review,* January/February 2003, pp. 7–11.
6. Howard Risher and Charles Fay, *New Strategies for Public Pay* (Saratoga Springs, NY: AMACOM, 2000). The Office of Personnel Management (OPM) does special studies on the Federal Civil Service. They are on the OPM's website at www.opm.gov/studies/index.htm.
7. www.opm.gov/fedclass/clashnbk.pdf.www.opm.gov/fedclass/gsintro.pdf.
8. Factor comparison, another method of job evaluation, bears some similarities to the point method in that compensable factors are clearly defined and the external market is linked to the job evaluation results. However, factor comparison is used by less than 10 percent of employers that use job evaluation. The method's complexity makes it difficult to explain to employees and managers, thus limiting its usefulness.
9. Liccione, William J., "Linking the market and internal values of jobs: Rethinking the market line." Compensation & Benefits Review 46.2 (2014): 80–88. John Kilgour, "Job Evaluation Revisited: The Point Factor Method," *Compensations Benefits Review,* June/July 2008, pp. 37–46.

10. Robert L. Heneman, "Job and Work Evaluation: A Literature Review," *Public Personnel Management,* Spring 2003; C. Ellis, R. Laymon, and P. LeBlanc, "Improving Pay Productivity with Strategic Work Valuation," *WorldatWork,* Second Quarter 2004, pp. 56–65.

11. Hornsby, Jeffrey S., Brien N. Smith, and Jatinder ND Gupta, "The impact of decision-making methodology on job evaluation outcomes: A look at three consensus approaches," Group & Organization Management 19.1 (1994): 112–128. M. K. Mount and R. A. Ellis, "Investigation of Bias in Job Evaluation Ratings of Comparable Worth Study Participants," *Personnel Psychology* 40 (1987), pp. 85–96; Morley Gunderson, "The Evolution and Mechanics of Pay Equity in Ontario," *Canadian Public Policy,* vol. XXVIII, Suppl. 1 (2002), pp. S117–S131.

12. See http://www.bls.gov/ncs/ocs/sp/ncbr0004.pdf. May 2013.

13. Korn Ferry | HayGroup. Job Evaluation: Foundations and applications. https://www.kornferry.com/content/dam/kornferry/docs/pdfs/job-evaluation.pdf 2017.

14. D. F. Harding, J. M. Madden, and K. Colson, "Analysis of a Job Evaluation System," *Journal of Applied Psychology* 44 (1960), pp. 354–357.

15. See a series of studies conducted by C. H. Lawshe and his colleagues published in the *Journal of Applied Psychology* from 1944 to 1947. For example, C. H. Lawshe, "Studies in Job Evaluation: II. The Adequacy of Abbreviated Point Ratings for Hourly Paid Jobs in Three Industrial Plans," *Journal of Applied Psychology* 29 (1945), pp. 177–184. Also see Theresa M. Welbourne and Charlie O. Trevor, "The Roles of Departmental and Position Power in Job Evaluation," *Academy of Management Journal* 43 (2000), pp. 761–771.

16. Tjarda Van Sliedregt, Olga F. Voskuijl, and Henk Thierry, "Job Evaluation Systems and Pay Grade Structures: Do They Match?" *International Journal of Human Resource Management* 12(8), December 2001, pp. 1313–1324; R. M. Madigan and D. J. Hoover, "Effects of Alternative Job Evaluation Methods on Decisions Involving Pay Equity," *Academy of Management Journal,* March 1986, pp. 84–100.

17. Hornsby, Jeffrey S., Brien N. Smith, and Jatinder ND Gupta, "The impact of decision-making methodology on job evaluation outcomes: A look at three consensus approaches," Group & Organization Management 19.1 (1994): 112–128. John R. Doyle, Rodney H. Green, and Paul A. Bottomley, "Judging Relative Importance: Direct Rating and Point Allocation Are Not Equivalent," *Organizational Behavior and Human Decision Processes* 70(1), April 1997, pp. 65–72.

18. Some contemporary job evaluation plans include the factor weight directly in each factor scale. So rather than a 1-to-5 scale for each factor, each factor has a unique scale. An illustration: The weight or relative importance of skill/knowledge is 40 percent; each degree on a 1 to 5 scale is worth 40 points. The point range is 40 to 200. In practice, statistically modeling values for factor scales often yields more results.

19. Paul M. Edwards, "Statistical Methods in Job Evaluation," *Advanced Management,* December 1948, pp. 158–163.

20. Paula England, "The Case for Comparable Worth," *Quarterly Review of Economics and Finance* 39 (1999), pp. 743–755; N. Elizabeth Fried and John H. Davis, *Developing Statistical Job-Evaluation Models* (Scottsdale, AZ: WorldatWork, 2004); M. Gunderson, "The Evolution and Mechanics of Pay Equity in Ontario," *Canadian Public Policy,* vol. XXVIII, Suppl. 1 (2002), pp. S117–S131.

21. M. K. Mount and R. A. Ellis, "Investigation of Bias in Job Evaluation Ratings of Comparable Worth Study Participants," *Personnel Psychology* 40 (1987); Tjarda Van Sliedregt, Olga F. Voskuijl, and Henk Thierry, "Job Evaluation Systems and Pay Grade Structures: Do They Match?" *International Journal of Human Resource Management* 12(8), December 2001, pp. 1313–1324; Judith M. Collins and Paul M. Muchinsky, "An Assessment of the Construct Validity of Three Job Evaluation Methods: A Field Experiment," *Academy of Management Journal* 36(4), 1993, pp. 895–904; Robert M. Madigan and

David J. Hoover, "Effects of Alternative Job Evaluation Methods on Decisions Involving Pay Equity," *Academy of Management Journal* 29 (1986), pp. 84–100.

22. The importance of appropriate criterion pay structure is particularly relevant in "pay equity studies" to assess gender bias. See *Canadian Telephone Employees Association et al. v. Bell Canada*; Canada Equal Wages Guidelines, 1986.
23. See, for example, https://nl.hudson.com/nl-nl/talent-management/talent-management-door-hudson/talent-management-tools/persoonlijkheidsvragenlijst/compas-online.
24. Carl F. Frost, John W. Wakely, and Robert A. Ruh, *The Scanlon Plan for Organization Development: Identity, Participation, and Equity* (East Lansing: Michigan State Press, 1974); E. A. Locke and D. M. Schweiger, "Participation in Decision Making: One More Look," in *Research in Organization Behavior* (Greenwich, CT: JAI Press, 1979); G. J. Jenkins, Jr., and E. E. Lawler III, "Impact of Employee Participation in Pay Plan Development," *Organizational Behavior and Human Performance* 28 (1981), pp. 111–128.
25. B. Carver and A. A. Vondra, "Alternative Dispute Resolution: Why It Doesn't Work and Why It Does," *Harvard Business Review,* May–June 1994, pp. 120–129. Blood, Milton R., William K. Graham, and Sheldon Zedeck, "Resolving Compensation Disputes with Three-party Job Evaluation," Applied Psychology 36.1 (1987): 39–50.
26. T. M. Welbourne and C. O. Trevor, "The Roles of Departmental and Position Power in Job Evaluation," *Academy of Management Journal* 43 (2000), pp. 761–771.
27. N. Gupta and G. D. Jenkins, Jr., "The Politics of Pay," paper presented at the annual meeting of the Society for Industrial and Organizational Psychology, Montreal, 1992.
28. V. Huber and S. Crandall, "Job Measurement: A Social-Cognitive Decision Perspective," in *Research in Personnel and Human Resources Management,* vol. 12, Gerald R. Ferris, ed. (Greenwich, CT: JAI Press, 1994).
29. The job titles used here may differ from those used at Whole Foods.

Chapter Six
Person-Based Structures

Chapter Outline

History buffs tell us that some form of job evaluation was in use when the pharaohs built the pyramids. Chinese emperors managed the Great Wall construction with the assistance of job evaluation. In the United States, job evaluation in the public sector came into use in the 1880s, when Chicago reformers were trying to put an end to patronage in government hiring and pay practices. To set pay based not on your connections but instead on the work you did was a revolutionary old idea.

The logic underlying job-based pay structures flows from scientific management, championed by Frederick Taylor in the early 20th century. Work was broken into a series of steps and analyzed so that the "one best way," the most efficient way to perform every element of the job (right down to how to shovel coal), could be specified. Strategically, Taylor's approach fit with mass production technologies that were beginning to revolutionize the way work was done.

Taylorism still pervades our lives. Not only are jobs analyzed and evaluated in terms of the "best way" (i.e., McFry's nine steps, **Exhibit 4.9**), but cookbooks and software manuals specify the methods for baking a cake or using a program as a series of simple, basic steps. Golf is analyzed as a series of basic tasks that can be combined successfully to lower one's handicap. At work, at play, in all daily life, "Taylor's thinking so permeates the soil of modern life we no longer realize it is there."[1]

In today's organizations, work is also analyzed with an eye toward increasing competitiveness and success. Routine work **(transactional work)** is separated from more complex work **(tacit work)**. Investment bankers can isolate routine transactions–even routine analysis of financial statements–from more-complex analysis and problem solving required to make sound investment recommendations to clients. Legal work such as patent searches, entering documents into readable databases, and even vetting simple contracts can be broken out from more complex client relationships. The more routine work generates lower revenues and requires less knowledge. People doing this work are likely paid less than people doing the more complex work that yields greater profits.

Once fragmented, work processes can be rebundled into new, different jobs.[2] Pay structures based on each person's skills, knowledge, and experience offer flexibility to align talent with continuously redesigned workplaces. A few years ago, machine operators on Eaton's assembly line needed to know how to operate one machine; now, as part of a manufacturing cell, they are members of self-managing teams. Eaton assembly lines now require people to be multiskilled, continuously learning, and flexible, and to possess problem-solving and negotiating skills. The search is on for pay systems that support the fragmented and rebundled work flows. Routine work may even be outsourced, though outsourcing a McFryer is not on the horizon.

More complex work requires pay systems that support continuous learning, improvement, and flexibility. Person-based structures hold out that promise. Person-based approaches are the topic of this chapter. At the end of this chapter, we shall discuss the usefulness of the various job-based and person-based approaches for determining internal structures.

Exhibit 6.1 points out the similarities in the logic underlying job-based versus people-based approaches. No matter the basis for the structure, a way is needed to (1) collect and summarize information about the work, (2) determine what about the work is of value to the organization, (3) quantify that value, and (4) translate that value into an internal structure.

PERSON-BASED STRUCTURES: SKILL PLANS

The majority of applications of **skill-based pay** have been in manufacturing, where the work often involves teams, multiskills, and flexibility. An advantage of a skill-based plan is that people can be deployed in a way that better matches the flow of work, thus avoiding bottlenecks as well as idle hands.[3]

Types of Skill Plans

Skill plans can focus on *depth* (specialists in corporate law, finance, or welding and hydraulic maintenance) and/or *breadth* (generalists with knowledge in all phases of operations including marketing, manufacturing, finance, and human resources).

Specialist: Depth

The pay structures for your elementary or high school teachers were likely based on their knowledge as measured by education level. A typical teacher's contract specifies a series of steps, with each step corresponding to a level of education. A bachelor's degree in education is step 1 and is the minimum required for hiring. To advance a step to higher pay requires additional education. Each year of seniority also is associated with a pay increase. The result can be that two teachers may receive different pay rates for doing essentially the same job—teaching English to high school juniors. The pay is based on the knowledge of the individual doing the job (measured by number of college credits and years of teaching experience) rather than on job content or output (performance of students).[4] The presumption is that more knowledge will translate into higher teaching effectiveness.

EXHIBIT 6.1 **Many Ways to Create Internal Structure**

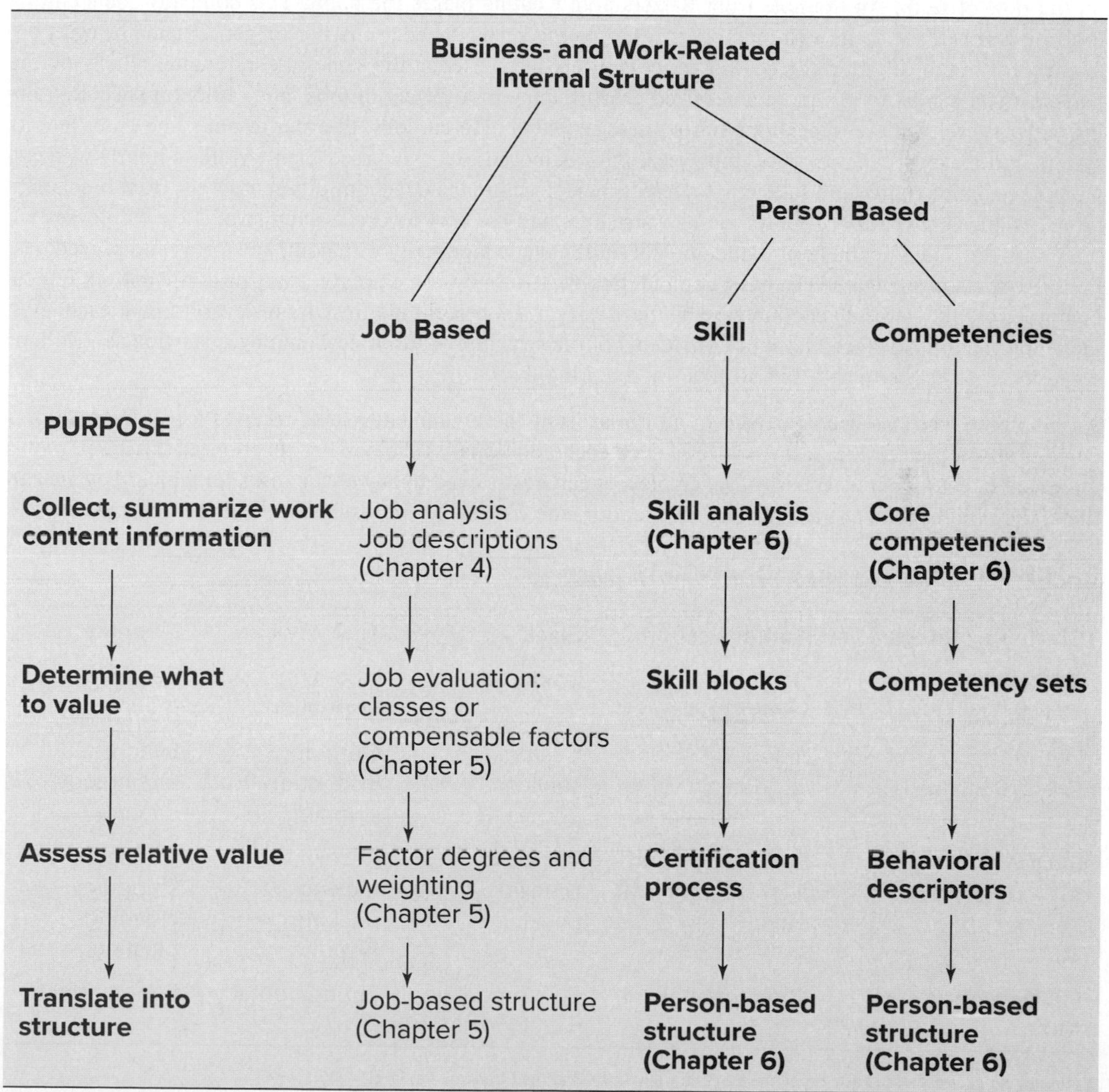

> **Skill-based structures** link pay to the depth or breadth of the skills, abilities, and knowledge a person acquires that are relevant to the work. In structures based on skill, individuals are paid for all the skills for which they have been certified, regardless of whether the work they are doing requires all or just a few of those particular skills. The wage attaches to the person. In contrast, a job-based plan pays employees for the job to which they are assigned, regardless of the skills they possess.

Generalist/Multiskill-Based: Breadth

As with teachers, employees in a **multiskill system** earn pay increases by acquiring new knowledge, where the knowledge is specific to a range of related jobs. Pay increases come with certification of new skills rather than with job assignments. Employees can then be assigned to any of the jobs for which they are certified, based on the flow of work. An example from Balzers Tool Coating makes the point. This company coats cutting tools by bombarding them with metal ions. The coating keeps the edge sharper longer. Originally, eight different jobs were involved in the coating process. Everyone started at the same rate, no matter which job the person was assigned to. Employees received cross-training in a variety of jobs, but without a specific training path or level. Different locations started new people in different jobs. In order to put some order into its system and make better use of its employees, Balzers moved to a skill-based plan for all its hourly workers, including administrative and sales employees. Its new structure included four different levels, from fundamental to advanced. **Exhibit 6.2** shows the new structure and the skill blocks in each level. New employees are hired into the fundamental level. Fundamental skills include familiarity with company forms and procedures, basic product knowledge, safety, basic computer usage, and so on. An employee starting at the bottom Fundamental level (100 percent) can increase his/her salary by 93 percent if s/he acquires every skill at each level, including the top Advanced level (193 percent) of the structure. Thus, a new employee starting at $10/hour could increase his/her pay to $19.30/hour by acquiring skills.

An employee who has been certified in all the skills at the fundamental level receives a pay increase of 7 percent and moves to the basic skill level. For each additional skill-block certification at this level, pay is increased by 5 to 6 percent. Basic-level employees can be assigned to any of the tasks for which they are certified; they will be paid at their highest certification rate. The same approach is used at the intermediate and

EXHIBIT 6.2 Skill Ladder at Balzers Tool Coating

Grade Pay Range	Administration	Sales	Tool	Machine
Advanced 150–193%	Office administration	Inside sales	Incoming inspection	Service Arc technology
Intermediate 136–179%	Blueprint expediting	Customer service pricing–B	Outgoing inspection shipping	Evaporation technology coating
Basic 107–164%	Software pricing file/route general office	Van driver licensing packing courier	Receiving racking packing fixturing	Degas stripping cleaning blasting
Fundamental 100%	Fundamental	Fundamental	Fundamental	Fundamental

Note: Pay range is expressed as a percentage of entry pay (100%) at the Fundamental level.

advanced levels. A person certified at the very top of the structure could be assigned to any of the tasks in the structure. The advantage to Balzers is workforce flexibility–staffing assignments can be better matched to the work flow.[5] The advantage to employees is that the more they learn, the more they earn.

The system at Balzers differs from the system for teachers in that the responsibilities assigned at Balzers can change drastically over a short period of time, whereas teachers' basic responsibilities do not vary on a day-to-day basis. Additionally, the Balzers system is designed to ensure that all the skills are clearly work-related. Training improves skills that the company values. In contrast, a school district has no guarantee that courses taken improve teaching skills (or students' knowledge and performance).

Purpose of the Skill-Based Structure

Skill-based structures can be evaluated using the objectives already specified for an internally aligned structure: supports the organization strategy, supports work flow, is fair to employees, and directs their behavior toward organization objectives.

Supports the Strategy and Objectives

The skills on which to base a structure need to be directly related to the organization's objectives and strategy. In practice, however, the "line of sight" between changes in the specific work skills (fundamental to advanced) required to operate the Balzers coaters and increased shareholder returns is difficult to make clear. In some cosmic sense, we know that these operating skills matter, but the link to the plant's performance is clearer than the link to corporate goals.

Supports Work Flow

The link here is clearer. One of the main advantages of a skill-based plan is that it facilitates matching people to a changing work flow.[6] For example, one national hotel chain moves many of its people to the hotel's front desk between 4 p.m. and 7 p.m., when the majority of guests check in. After 7 p.m., these same employees move to the food and beverage service area to match the demand for room service and dining room service. The hotel believes that by ensuring that guests will not have to wait long to check in or to eat, it can provide a high level of service with fewer staff.

Is Fair to Employees

Employees like the potential of higher pay that comes with learning. And by encouraging employees to take charge of their own development, skill-based plans may give them more control over their work lives.

However, favoritism and bias may play a role in determining who gets first crack at the training necessary to become certified at higher-paying skill levels. Employees complain that they are forced to pick up the slack for those who are out for training. Additionally, the courts have not yet been asked to rule on the legality of having two people do the same task but for different (skill-based) pay.

Motivates Behavior toward Organization Objectives

Person-based plans have the potential to clarify new standards and behavioral expectations. The fluid work assignments that skill-based plans permit encourage employees to take responsibility for the complete work process and its results, with less direction from supervisors.[7] If less direction from supervisors is needed, then fewer supervisors may be needed. Indeed, research at nine manufacturing plants concluded that the number of managers in plants under skill-based pay was as much as 50 percent lower compared to traditional plants.[8] Having fewer supervisors can result in substantial labor cost savings, but, of course, supervisors can see this potential consequence as well, which can certainly dampen their enthusiasm for skill-based pay and the often related practice of using teams and moving some decision responsibility from supervisors to workers.[9]

"HOW-TO": SKILL ANALYSIS

Exhibit 6.3 depicts the process for determining a skill-based structure. It begins with an analysis of skills, which is similar to the task statements in a job analysis. Related skills can be grouped into a **skill block;** skill blocks can be arranged by levels into a skill structure. To build the structure, a process is needed to describe, certify, and value the skills.

Exhibit 6.3 also identifies the major **skill analysis** decisions: (1) What is the objective of the plan? (2) What information should be collected? (3) What methods should be used? (4) Who should be involved? (5) How useful are the results for pay purposes? These are exactly the same decisions as in job analysis.

> **Skill analysis** is a systematic process of identifying and collecting information about skills required to perform work in an organization.

What Information to Collect?

There is far less uniformity in the use of terms in person-based plans than there is in job-based plans. Equipment manufacturer FMC assigns points and groups skills as foundation, core electives, and optional electives. Its plan for technicians is more fully developed in **Exhibit 6.4**.

- Foundation skills include a quality seminar, videos on materials handling and hazardous materials, a three-day safety workshop, and a half-day orientation. All foundation skills are mandatory and must be certified to reach the Technician I level.

EXHIBIT 6.3 Determining the Internal Skill-Based Structure

Internal Alignment: Work Relationships Within the Organization	→	Skill Analysis	→	Skill Blocks	→	Skill Certification	→	Skill-Based Structure

Basic Decisions

- What is the objective of the plan?
- What information should be collected?
- What methods should be used to determine and certify skills?
- Who should be involved?
- How useful are the results for pay purposes?

- Core electives having to do with the facility's operations (e.g., fabrication, welding, painting, finishing, assembly, inspection) are necessary. Each skill is assigned a point value.
- Optional electives are additional specialized competencies ranging from computer applications to team leadership and consensus building.

To reach Technician I (114 percent of entry level pay), 40 core elective points (of 370) must be certified, in addition to the foundation competencies. To reach Technician II, an additional 100 points of core electives must be certified, plus one optional elective.

A fully qualified Technician IV (certified in the foundations, 365 points of core electives, and 5 optional electives) is able to perform all work in any cell at the facility. Technician IV earns 162 percent of what an entry-level employee earns no matter what task they are doing. FMC's approach should look familiar to any college student: required courses, required credits chosen among specific categories, and optional electives. There is a minor difference, of course–FMC employees get paid for passing these courses, whereas college students pay to take courses!

The FMC plan illustrates the kind of information that underpins skill-based plans: very specific information on every aspect of the production process. This makes the plans particularly suited for continuous-flow technologies where employees work in teams.

EXHIBIT 6.4 **FMC's Technician Skill-Based Structure**

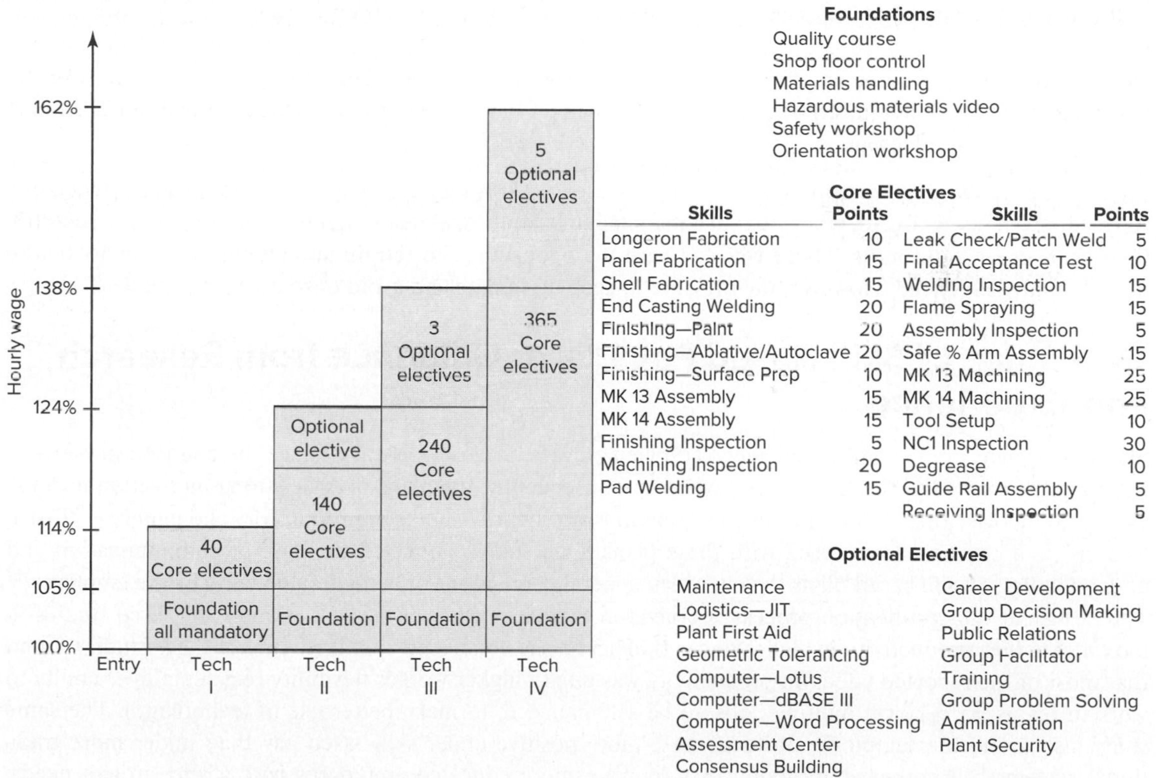

Foundations

Quality course
Shop floor control
Materials handling
Hazardous materials video
Safety workshop
Orientation workshop

Core Electives

Skills	Points	Skills	Points
Longeron Fabrication	10	Leak Check/Patch Weld	5
Panel Fabrication	15	Final Acceptance Test	10
Shell Fabrication	15	Welding Inspection	15
End Casting Welding	20	Flame Spraying	15
Finishing—Paint	20	Assembly Inspection	5
Finishing—Ablative/Autoclave	20	Safe % Arm Assembly	15
Finishing—Surface Prep	10	MK 13 Machining	25
MK 13 Assembly	15	MK 14 Machining	25
MK 14 Assembly	15	Tool Setup	10
Finishing Inspection	5	NC1 Inspection	30
Machining Inspection	20	Degrease	10
Pad Welding	15	Guide Rail Assembly	5
		Receiving Inspection	5

Optional Electives

Maintenance	Career Development
Logistics—JIT	Group Decision Making
Plant First Aid	Public Relations
Geometric Tolerancing	Group Facilitator
Computer—Lotus	Training
Computer—dBASE III	Group Problem Solving
Computer—Word Processing	Administration
Assessment Center	Plant Security
Consensus Building	

Note: Pay range is expressed as a percentage of entry pay (100%) at the Entry level.

Whom to Involve?

Employee involvement is almost built into skill-based plans. Employees and managers are the source of information on defining the skills, arranging them into a hierarchy, bundling them into skill blocks, and certifying whether a person actually possesses the skills. At Balzers and FMC, a committee consisting of managers from several sites developed the skill listing and certification process for each of the four skill ladders, with input from employees.

Establish Certification Methods

Organizations may use peer review, on-the-job demonstrations, or tests to certify that employees possess skills and are able to apply them. Honeywell evaluates employees during the six months after they have learned the skills. Leaders and peers are used in the certification process. Still other companies require successful completion of formal courses. However, we do not need to point out to students that sitting in the classroom doesn't guarantee that anything is learned. School districts address this issue in a variety of ways. Some will certify for any courses; others only for courses in the teacher's subject area. However, no districts require evidence that the course and certification improve teaching effectiveness.

Newer skill-based applications appear to be moving away from an on-demand review and toward scheduling fixed review points in the year. Scheduling makes it easier to budget and control payroll increases. Other changes include ongoing recertification, which replaces the traditional one-time certification process and helps ensure skills are kept fresh, and removal of certification (and accompanying pay) when a particular skill is deemed obsolete.[10] However, it can be difficult to change certification procedures once a system is in place. TRW Automotive faced this problem in regard to using formal classes for its Mesa, Arizona, airbag facility. TRW felt that some employees were only putting in "seat time." Yet no one was willing to take the responsibility for refusing to certify, since an extra sign-off beyond classroom attendance had not been part of the original system design.

Many plans require that employees be recertified, since the skills may get rusty if they are not used frequently. At its Ome facility in Tokyo, where Toshiba manufactures laptops, all team members are required to recertify their skills every 24 months. Those who fail have the opportunity to retrain and attempt to recertify before their pay rate is reduced. However, the pressure to keep up to date and avoid obsolescence is intense.

Outcomes of Skill-Based Pay Plans: Guidance from Research and Experience

Skill-based plans are generally well accepted by employees because it is easy to see the connection between the plan, the work, and the size of the paycheck. Consequently, the plans provide strong motivation for individuals to increase their skills and this can result in major improvements in productivity and quality.[11] "Learn to earn" is a popular slogan used with these plans. One study connected the ease of communication and understanding of skill-based plans to employees' general perceptions of being treated fairly by the employer.[12] The design of the certification process is crucial in this perception of fairness. Two of the three studies to look at whether productivity is higher under skill-based pay concluded that it is. One of these studies found that most of the reported effect on productivity was due to higher worker flexibility (e.g., employee ability to work in teams, to perform multiple jobs, to be self-managed, to make better use of technology). The same study also found that employee attitudes were more positive under skill-based pay than under more traditional systems.[13] Another study found that younger, more educated employees with strong growth needs, organizational commitment, and a positive attitude toward workplace innovations were more successful in acquiring new skills.[14] Nevertheless, for reasons not made clear, the study's authors recommend allocating training opportunities by seniority.

Skill-based plans become increasingly expensive as the majority of employees become certified at the highest pay levels. As a result, the employer may have an average wage higher than competitors who are not using skill-based plans. Unless the increased flexibility permits leaner staffing, the employer may experience higher labor costs. Some employers are combating this by requiring that employees stay at a rate a certain amount of time before they can take the training to move to a higher rate. Motorola abandoned its skill-based plan because at the end of three years, everyone had topped out (by accumulating the necessary skill blocks). TRW, too, found that after a few years, people at two airbag manufacturing plants on skill-based systems had all **topped out.** They were flexible and well trained. So now what? What happens in the next years? Does everybody automatically receive a pay increase? Do the work processes get redesigned? In a firm with labor-intensive products, the increased labor costs under skill-based plans may become a source of competitive disadvantage.

So what kind of workplace seems best suited for a skill-based plan? Early researchers on skill-based plans found that about 60 percent of the companies in their original sample were still using skill-based plans seven years later. One of the key factors that determined a plan's success was how well it was aligned with the organization's strategy. Plans were more viable in organizations that follow a cost-cutter strategy (see **Chapter 2**)–doing more with less. The reduced numbers of highly trained, flexible employees that skill-based pay promises fit this strategy very well.[15]

On the other hand, it has also been argued that the higher labor costs under skill-based pay (estimated as between 10 and 15 percent) mean that it may be a better fit to companies in industries where labor costs are a small share of total costs, such as paper and forest products, chemicals, and food processing. If labor costs are 15 percent of total costs and skill-based pay translates into labor costs higher by 10 percent, then total costs would be higher by 1.5 percent due to skill-based pay.[16] The question then is whether this increase in labor costs is more than offset by gains in productivity, quality, customer responsiveness, flexibility, or worker retention, for example.

A final question is whether a multiskilled "jack-of-all-trades" might really be the master of none. Some research suggests that the greatest impact on results occurs immediately after just a small amount of increased flexibility.[17] Greater increments in flexibility achieve fewer improvements. There may be an optimal number of skills for any individual to possess. Beyond that number, productivity returns are less than the pay increases. Additionally, some employees may not be interested in giving up the job they are doing. Such a "camper" creates a bottleneck for rotating other employees into that position to acquire those skills. Organizations should decide in advance whether they are willing to design a plan to work around campers or whether they will force campers into the system.

The bottom line is that skill-based approaches may be only short-term initiatives for specific settings. Unfortunately, the longitudinal study of survival rates discussed above does not address the 40 percent of cases where skill-based pay did not survive beyond six years.

PERSON-BASED STRUCTURES: COMPETENCIES

As with job evaluation, there are several perspectives on what **competencies** are and what they are supposed to accomplish. Are they a skill that can be learned and developed, or are they a trait that includes attitudes and motives? Do competencies focus on the minimum requirements that the organization needs to stay in business, or do they focus on outstanding performance? Are they characteristics of the organization or of the employee? Unfortunately, the answer to all of these questions is yes.[18] A lack of consensus means that competencies can be a number of things; consequently, they stand in danger of becoming nothing.

By now you should be able to draw the next exhibit (**Exhibit 6.5**) yourself. The top part shows the process of using competencies to address the need for internal alignment by creating a **competency-based structure.** All approaches to creating a structure begin by looking at the work performed in the organization. While *skill-based* and **job-based systems** hone in on information about specific tasks, competencies take the opposite approach. They try to abstract the underlying, broadly applicable knowledge, skills, and behaviors that form the foundation for success at any level or job in the organization. These are the *core* **competencies.** Core competencies are often linked to mission statements that express an organization's philosophy, values, business strategies, and plans.

Competency sets translate each core competency into action. For the core competency of *business awareness,* for example, competency sets might be related to organizational understanding, cost management, third-party relationships, and ability to identify business opportunities.

Competency indicators are the observable behaviors that indicate the level of competency within each set. These indicators may be used for staffing and evaluation as well as for pay purposes.

TRW's competency model for its human resource management department, shown in **Exhibit 6.6**, includes the four core competencies considered critical to the success of the business.[19] All HR employees are expected to demonstrate varying degrees of these competencies. However, not all individuals would be expected to reach the highest level in all competencies. Rather, the HR function should possess all levels of mastery of all the core competencies within the HRM group. Employees would use the model as a guide to what capacities the organization wants people to develop.

The *competency indicators* anchor the degree of a competency required at each level of complexity of the work. **Exhibit 6.7** shows five levels of competency indicators for the competency *impact and influence.* These behavioral anchors make the competency more concrete. The levels range from "uses direct persuasion" at level 1 to "uses experts or other third parties to influence" at level 5. Sometimes the behavioral anchors might include scales of the intensity of action, the degree of impact of the action, its complexity, and/or the amount of effort expended. Scaled competency indicators are similar to job analysis questionnaires and degrees of compensable factors, discussed in **Chapters 4** and **5**.

EXHIBIT 6.5 Determining the Internal Competency-Based Structure

Internal Alignment: Work Relationships Within the Organization ⟶ **Core Competencies** ⟶ **Competency Sets** ⟶ **Behavioral Descriptors** ⟶ **Competency-Based Structure**

Basic Decisions

- What is objective of plan?
- What information to collect?
- What methods are used to determine and certify competencies?
- Who is involved?
- How useful for pay purposes?

Defining Competencies

As supporters of planet Pluto have discovered, definitions matter. Because competencies are trying to get at what underlies work behaviors, there is a lot of fuzziness in defining them. Early conceptions of competencies focused on five areas:

1. Skills (demonstration of expertise)
2. Knowledge (accumulated information)
3. Self-concepts (attitudes, values, self-image)
4. Traits (general disposition to behave in a certain way)
5. Motives (recurrent thoughts that drive behaviors)[20]

EXHIBIT 6.6 **TRW Human Resources Competencies**

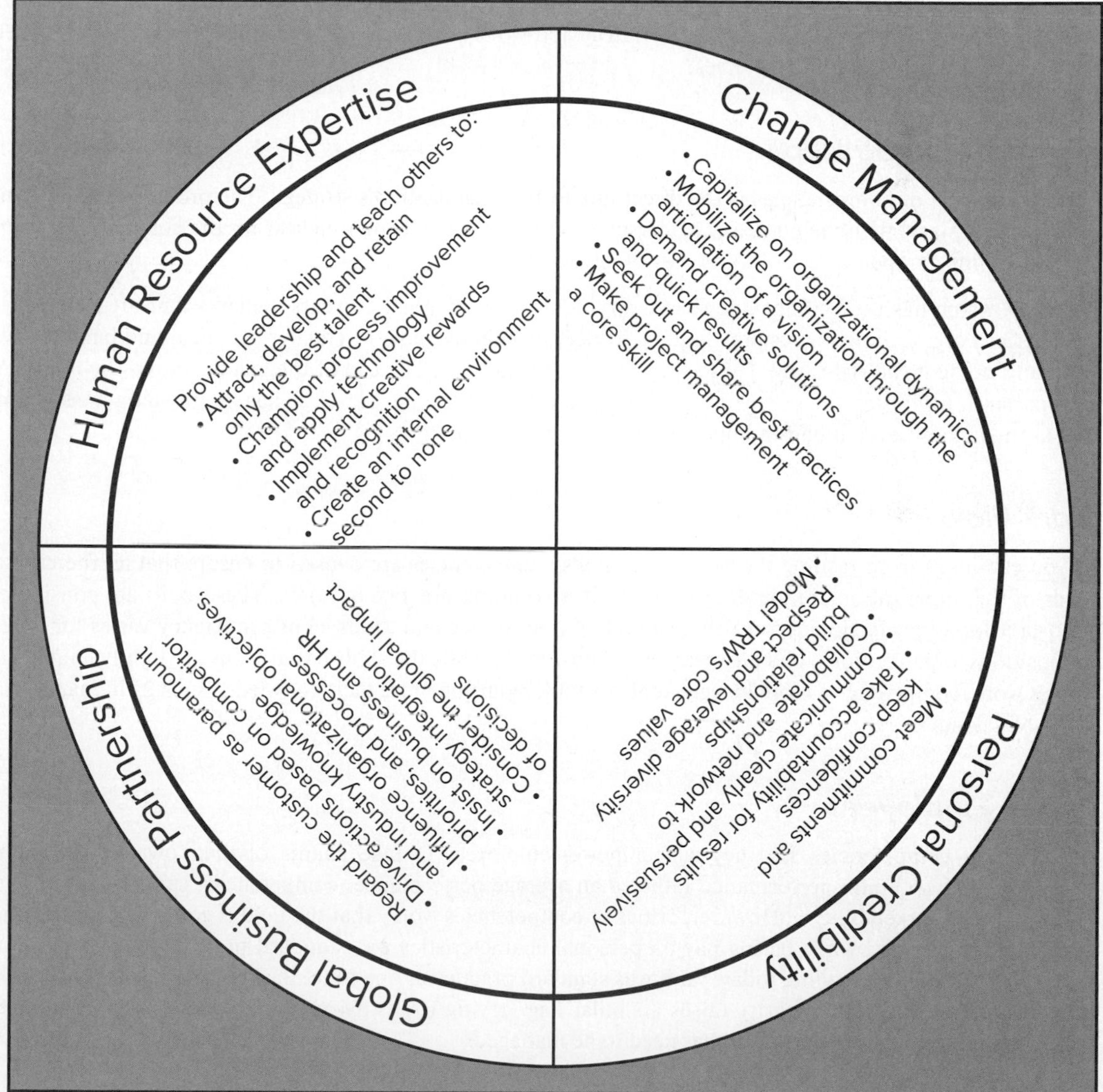

As experience with competencies has grown, organizations seem to be moving away from the vagueness of self-concepts, traits, and motives. Instead, they are placing greater emphasis on business-related descriptions of behaviors "that excellent performers exhibit much more consistently than average performers." Competencies are becoming "a collection of observable behaviors (not a single behavior) that require no inference, assumption or interpretation."[21] **Exhibit 6.7** shows behavioral anchors for the competency: Impact and Influence. Comparison with examples of compensable factors used in job evaluation from **Chapter** 5–Decision Making (**Exhibit 5.9**) and Multinational Responsibilities (**Exhibit 5.10**)–reveal the greater behavioral orientation of competencies. However, differences can be rather small. For example, "consult with technical experts" anchors level 6 of the job evaluation Decision Making compensable factor in **Exhibit 5.9** and "uses experts" anchors the Impact and Influence behavioral competency shown in **Exhibit 6.7**.

Purpose of the Competency-Based Structure

Do competencies help support an internally aligned structure? Using our by-now-familiar yardstick, how well do competencies support the organization strategy and work flow, treat employees fairly, and motivate their behavior toward organization objectives?

Organization Strategy

The main appeal of competencies is the direct link to the organization's strategy. The process of identifying competencies starts with the company leadership deciding what will spell success for the company. It resembles identifying compensable factors as part of job evaluation.

Frito-Lay, which has used competency-based structures for more than 10 years, believes four are required in managerial work: leading for results, building work-force effectiveness, leveraging technical and business systems, and doing it the right way. These are shown in **Exhibit 6.8**. The top of the exhibit shows the levels. At the first level, exhibiting the competency affects the team. At the next level, it has an impact across teams. And at the highest level, it has an impact on the entire location.

Work Flow

As you can judge from reading the previous exhibits, competencies are chosen to ensure that all the critical needs of the organization are met. For example, it is common practice to note: "These skills are considered important for all professionals but the weighting of importance and the level of proficiency varies for different positions, organizations, and business conditions."[22] So while the skills-based plans are tightly coupled to today's work, competencies more loosely apply to work requiring more tacit knowledge such as in managerial and professional work.

Fair to Employees

Advocates of competencies say they can empower employees to take charge of their own development. By focusing on optimum performance rather than average performance, competencies can help employees maintain their marketability.[23] However, critics of competencies worry that the field is going back to the middle of the last century, when basing pay on personal characteristics was standard practice.[24] Basing pay on race or gender seems appalling today, yet it was standard practice at one time. Basing pay on someone's judgment of another person's integrity raises a similar flag. Trying to justify pay differences based on inferred personal competencies creates risks that need to be managed.

EXHIBIT 6.7 **Sample Behavioral Competency Indicators**

Impact and Influence: The intention to persuade, convince, or influence to have a specific impact. It includes the ability to anticipate and respond to the needs and concerns of others. *"Impact and Influence" is one of the competencies considered "most critical."*

Level	Behaviors
0: Not shown	• Let things happen • Quotes policy and issues instruction
1: Direct persuasion	• Uses direct persuasion in a discussion or presentation • Appeals to reason; uses data or concrete examples • Does not adapt presentation to the interest and level of the audience • Reiterates the same points when confronted with opposition
2: Multiple attempts to persuade	• Tries different tactics when attempting to persuade without necessarily making an effort to adapt to the level or interest of an audience (e.g., making two or more different arguments or points in a discussion)
3: Builds trust and fosters win-win mentality (expected performance level)	• Tailors presentations or discussions to appeal to the interest and level of others • Looks for the "win-win" opportunities • Demonstrates sensitivity and understanding of others in detecting underlying concerns, interests, or emotions, and uses that understanding to develop effective responses to objections
4: Multiple actions to influence	• Takes more than one action to influence, with each action adapted to the specific audience (e.g., a group meeting to present the situation, followed by individual meetings) • May include taking a well-thought-out unusual action to have a specific impact
5: Influences through others	• Uses experts or other third parties to influence • Develops and maintains a planned network of relationships with customers, internal peers, and industry colleagues • When required, assembles "behind the scenes" support for ideas regarding opportunities and/or solving problems

Source: Reprinted from *Raising the Bar: Using Competencies to Enhance Employee Performance.* Contents ©WorldatWork. Reprinted with permission from WorldatWork. Content is licensed for use by purchaser only. No part of this article may be reproduced, excerpted or redistributed in any form without express written permission from WorldatWork.

e-Compensation

Look again at the Your Turn at the end of **Chapter 4**. How much do you think Bill Ryan, the customer service representative, is paid? Go to ***www.salary.com*** and search for some information. How does your job description for Mr. Ryan's job compare to those on salary.com? Does it matter?

Motivate Behavior toward Organization Objectives

Competencies in effect provide guidelines for behavior and keep people focused. They can also provide a common basis for communicating and working together. This latter possibility has become increasingly important as organizations go global, and as employees with widely differing viewpoints and experiences fill leadership positions in these global organizations.

e-Compensation

Go to **www.shrm.org/hrcompetencies**. Examine the competencies identified as important to be successful for human resource professionals and how they vary according to career stage. Consider how you would use this competency information in paying human resource professionals.

EXHIBIT 6.8 **Frito-Lay Managerial Competencies**

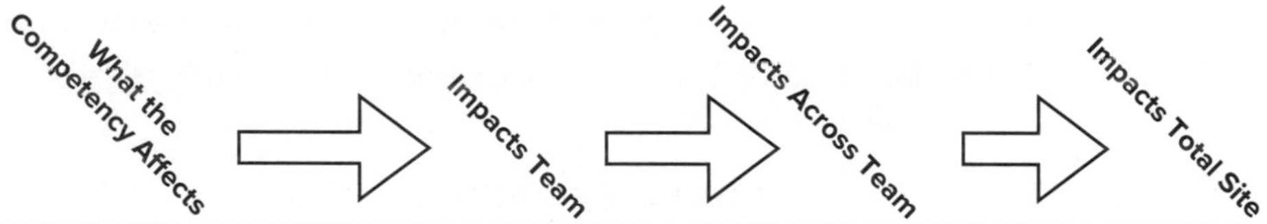

Competency Dimension	Behaviors
Leading for results	Using initiative and influence with others to drive results and promote continuous improvement.
Building workforce effectiveness	Coaching individual development and building capability of operational, project, or cross-functional teams to achieve business results.
Leveraging technical and business systems	Acquiring and applying a depth and/or breadth of knowledge, skills, and experience to achieve functional excellence.
Doing it the right way	Modeling, teaching, and coaching company values.

Source: Nancy Jagmin, "Assessing and Rewarding Competencies: The Ten-Year Tune-Up at Frito-Lay," presentation for the Center for Organization Effectiveness, April 2003, Marina del Rey, CA.

"HOW-TO": COMPETENCY ANALYSIS

The bottom part of **Exhibit 6.5** shows the basic decisions in creating a competency-based structure.[25] The first decision, and by far the most important, is to clarify the objective of the plan.

Objective

We have already pointed out that one of the pitfalls of competency systems is trying to do too many things with ill-suited systems. Competencies may have value for personal development and communicating organization direction. However, the vagueness and subjectivity (what exactly *are* this person's motives?) make competencies a "risky foundation for a pay system."[26] The competency structure may exist on paper by virtue of the competency sets and scaled behavioral indicators but bear little connection to the work employees do. In contrast, companies like Frito-Lay have been using theirs for 10 years. Perhaps paying for competencies is the only way to get people to pay attention to them.

What Information to Collect?

A number of schemes for classifying competencies have been proposed.[27] One of them uses three groups:

1. *Personal characteristics:* These have the aura of the Boy Scouts about them: trustworthy, loyal, courteous. In business settings, the relevant characteristics might be personal integrity, maturity of judgment, flexibility, and respect for others. Employees are expected to come in the door with these characteristics and then develop and demonstrate them in increasingly complex and ambiguous job situations.
2. *Visionary:* These are the highest-level competencies. They might be expressed as possessing a global perspective, taking the initiative in moving the organization in new directions, and able to articulate the implications for the organization of trends in the marketplace, in world events, in the local community.
3. *Organization specific:* Between the above two groups are the competencies that are tied specifically to the particular organization and to the particular function where they are being applied. They generally include leadership, customer orientation, functional expertise (e.g., able to leap tall buildings and explain the difference between competencies and compensable factors), and developing others–whatever reflects the company values, culture, and strategic intent.

At 3M, for example, competencies were developed internally for its global executives.[28] Behavioral anchors are used to rate an executive on each of these competencies. There are three competency areas: Fundamental (ethics and integrity, intellectual capability), Essential (customer orientation, developing people, inspiring others, business health and results), and Visionary (global perspective, vision and strategy, nurturing innovation, building alliances, organizational agility). Executives' ratings on these competencies are used to assess and develop executives worldwide. Because 3M relies heavily on promotion from within, competency ratings help develop executive talent for succession planning. Again, the link to development is clear; the link to pay is less clear.

Because they stem from each organization's mission statement or its strategy to achieve competitive advantage, you might conclude that the core competencies would be unique for each company. In fact, they are not. One analysis showed that most organizations appear to choose from the same list of 20 core competencies (**Exhibit 6.9**).[29] What does appear to differ among organizations is how they apply competencies. This parallels an issue in the strategy chapter (**Chapter 2**): There may be only slight differences in the words, but the actions differ. It is the actions that are the source of competitive advantage. 3M, for example, is known for innovation. Its competency, nurturing innovation, is defined as "Creates and sustains an environment that supports experimentation, rewards risk taking, reinforces curiosity, and challenges the status quo through freedom and openness without judgment. Influences the future to 3M's advantage." This competency, especially in terms of how 3M uniquely executes it, is thought to be a key to 3M's competitive advantage.

Whom to Involve?

Like compensable factors, competencies are derived from the executive leadership's beliefs about the organization and its strategic intent. However, anecdotal evidence indicates that not all employees understand that connection. Employees at one bank insisted that processing student tuition loans was a different competency from processing auto loans. The law department at Polaroid generated a list of over 1,000 competencies it felt were unique to the law department and that created value for the organization. (Is it possible that Polaroid, which has since gone bankrupt, would have been better served by devoting more time and energy to the effect of digital photography on film-based cameras?)

EXHIBIT 6.9 The Top 20 Competencies

Achievement orientation
Concern for quality
Initiative
Interpersonal understanding
Customer service orientation
Influence and impact
Organization awareness
Networking
Directiveness
Teamwork and cooperation
Developing others
Team leadership
Technical expertise
Information seeking
Analytical thinking
Conceptual thinking
Self-control
Self-confidence
Business orientation
Flexibility

Exhibit 6.10 shows part of the competencies used by a major toy company. This is one of eight competencies for the marketing department. Other departments have separate competencies. Notice the mind-numbing level of detail. While this approach may be useful for career development, it is doubtful that all this information is useful, much less necessary, for compensation purposes. The initial promise of simplicity and flexibility in person-based systems remains unfulfilled.

Establish Certification Methods

The heart of the person-based plan is that employees get paid for the relevant skills or competencies they possess, whether or not those skills are used. Skill-based plans assume that possessing these skills will make it easier to match work flow with staffing levels, so whether or not an individual is *using* a particular skill on a particular day is not an issue. Competency-based plans assume–what? That all competencies are used all the time? The assumptions are not clear. What is clear, however, is the requirement that if people are to be paid based on their competencies, then there must be some way to demonstrate or certify to all concerned that a person possesses that level of competency. Although consultants discuss competencies as compatible with 360-degree feedback and personal development, they are silent on objectively certifying whether a person possesses a competency.

Resulting Structure

Recall that internal structures are described in terms of number of levels, pay differentials, and criterion on which the job structure is based. In practice, competency-based structures generally are designed with relatively few levels–four to six–and relatively wide differentials for increased flexibility. **Exhibit 6.11** depicts the toy company's structures based on the four phases (levels) shown in **Exhibit 6.10**. Such a generic structure could be applied to almost any professional work, even the work of a university faculty.

Competencies and Employee Selection and Training/Development

In **Chapter 2**, we noted that human resource strategies can be thought of as influencing effectiveness through their impact on workforce ability, motivation, and ability to contribute (AMO). In the case of competencies, there is clear evidence that ability (broadly defined to include personality traits) is related to general competencies. Like **Exhibit 6.9**, **Exhibit 6.12** shows a set of generic competencies, called the Great Eight, that seem to capture in an efficient way the themes found in the array of competency frameworks available. What **Exhibit 6.12** adds are hypotheses regarding how these competencies relate to the individual characteristics of personality ("Big Five"), motivation, and ability. So, for example, based on **Exhibit 6.12**, if we wish to have managers who are competent in leading and deciding, we need to select or train and develop people high in need for power, need for control, and who have extroverted personalities. Failure to adequately screen employees on these individual characteristics would not only put more pressure on training and development, but also potentially demotivate employees who are seeking to acquire and demonstrate these competencies, but who may not be well suited to do so. Competency-based pay would be less likely to succeed in this situation.

EXHIBIT 6.10 Product Development Competency for Marketing Department at a Toy Company

Manages the product development process by:

- Analyzing and evaluating marketplace to identify niches/opportunities
- Evaluating product/concepts
- Developing marketing strategies
- Coordinating and evaluating research/testing
- Generating product recommendations and obtaining management support
- Driving product schedules/activities

Phase I: Baseline Expectation	Phase II: Competent/Proficient	Phase III: Advanced/Coach	Phase IV: Expert/Mentor
• Analyzes market/competitive data (e.g., TRST, NPD) and provides top-line trend analysis, with supervision • Evaluates products/concepts (see Toy Viability competency) • Contributes to product brainstorming sessions • Oversees market research activities and ensures timely completion • Obtains Account Management input to the product development effort • Develops and implements marketing strategy, with supervision: product, positioning, pricing/financial, promotion, packaging, merchandising, and advertising • Facilitates cost reductions to achieve price/profit goals; ensures execution of cost meeting next steps • Ensures adherence to product schedules • Coordinates licensor approval of product concept/models	• Monitors and analyzes market/competitive data (e.g., TRST, NPD) with minimal supervision, and provides recommendations for product development opportunities • Makes substantial contributions in product brainstorming sessions • Analyzes market research results and makes appropriate product recommendations • Partners with Account Management group to obtain their buy-in to the product development effort • Develops and implements marketing strategy, with minimal supervision • Drives cost reductions to achieve price/profit goals • Drives product schedules and resolves product scheduling issues (late delivery, late debug) • Negotiates with licensors to obtain product approvals	• Independently monitors and analyzes market/competitive data (e.g., TRST, NPD), provides recommendations for product development opportunities, and coaches others to do so • Leads and facilitates formal product brainstorming sessions • Coaches others in analyzing market research results and making product recommendations • Develops innovative marketing plans (e.g., new channels of distribution, niche markets) • Independently develops and implements marketing strategy, and coaches others to do so • Identifies/evaluates cost reduction opportunities, and coaches others to do so • Identifies and implements product schedule improvement tactics • Coaches others to manage product schedules • Shares product ideas/strategies with other teams/categories	• Reviews/approves recommendations for product development opportunities • Provides short- and long-term vision and goals for developing the corporate product portfolio across categories or brands • Reviews/approves marketing strategy, and proactively adjusts strategy in response to internal/external changes • Approves cost reduction recommendations • Anticipates critical issues that may impact product schedules and develops alternate plans • Ensures on-strategy delivery

Guidance (and Caution) from the Research on Competencies

While the notion of competencies may have value in identifying what distinguishes typical from truly outstanding performance, there is debate on whether competencies can be translated into a measurable, objective basis for pay. Competencies often morph into compensable factors. But, that can cause difficulties if they were not developed for that purpose.[30]

Thus far, research is limited. An area of research with potential application to competencies deals with human capital and knowledge management.[31] Viewing the competencies of employees as a portfolio similar to a diversified investment portfolio highlights the fact that some competencies deliver greater returns than others. The focus then changes to managing existing competencies and developing new ones in ways that maximize the overall returns to the organization.[32] In one study, managers' competencies were related to their performance ratings, but there was no relationship to unit-level performance.[33] (Perhaps future studies will report different results.) As organizations globalize, they may rebalance their values and perspectives to allow a global strategy to function.[34] They seek the right balance among the range and depth of cultural, functional, and product competencies in the global organization. But this is speculative and remains to be translated into pay practices.

The basic question remains: Is it appropriate to pay you for what I believe you are *capable of doing* versus what you are doing? Isn't it likely to be more effective, for pay purposes, to focus on what is easily measurable and directly related to organizational success (i.e., knowledge and skills that are job/performance related)? Also, a question raised earlier is whether competency-based systems are more susceptible to discrimination based on individual employee demographic characteristics.

ONE MORE TIME: INTERNAL ALIGNMENT REFLECTED IN STRUCTURES (PERSON-BASED OR JOB-BASED)

Now that we have spent three chapters examining all the trees, let's look again at the forest. The purpose of job- and person-based procedures is really very simple–to design and manage an internal pay structure that helps the organization succeed.

As with job-based evaluation, the final result of the person-based plan is an internal structure of work in the organization. This structure should reflect the organization's internal alignment policy (loosely versus tightly linked, egalitarian versus hierarchical) and support its business operations. Further, managers must ensure that the structure *remains* internally aligned by reassessing work/skills/competencies when necessary. Failure to do so risks pay structures that open the door to bias and potentially unethical and misdirected behavior.

EXHIBIT 6.11 Toy Company's Structure Based on Competencies

Level	Phase	Title
4	Expert	Visionary; Champion; Executive
3	Advanced	Coach; Leader
2	Resource	Contributor; Professional
1	Proficient	Associate

In practice, when evaluating higher-value, nonroutine work, the distinction between job- versus person-based approaches blurs. The focus is on what factors (*both* job and person) create value for the organization. The person influences the job content in managerial and professional work. Skill-based fits more easily with manufacturing work.[35] Yet caution is advised: Much of the work required in contemporary manufacturing cells requires tacit, nonroutine knowledge (problem solving, interacting, negotiating).

EXHIBIT 6.12 **Titles and High-Level Definitions of the Great Eight Competencies™**

Factor	Competency Domain Title	Competency Domain Definition	Hypothesized Big Five, Motivation, and Ability Relationships[a]
1	Leading and deciding	Takes control and exercises leadership. Initiates action, gives direction, and takes responsibility.	Need for power and control, extroversion
2	Supporting and cooperating	Supports others and shows respect and positive regard for them in social situations. Puts people first, working effectively with individuals and teams, clients, and staff. Behaves consistently with clear personal values that complement those of the organization.	Agreeableness
3	Interacting and presenting	Communicates and networks effectively. Successfully persuades and influences these. Relates to others in a confident, relaxed manner.	Extroversion, general mental ability
4	Analyzing and interpreting	Shows evidence of clear analytical thinking. Gets to the heart of complex problems and issues. Applies own expertise effectively. Quickly takes on new technology. Communicates well in writing.	General mental ability, openness to new experience
5	Creating and conceptualizing	Works well in situations requiring openness to new ideas and experiences. Seeks out learning opportunities. Handles situations and problems with innovation and creativity. Thinks broadly and strategically. Supports and drives organizational change.	Openness to new experience, general mental ability
6	Organizing and executing	Plans ahead and works in a systematic and organized way. Follows directions and procedures. Focuses on customer satisfaction and delivers a quality service or product to the agreed standards.	Conscientiousness, general mental ability
7	Adapting and coping	Adapts and responds well to change. Manages pressure effectively and copes well with setbacks.	Emotional stability
8	Enterprising and performing	Focuses on results and achieving personal work objectives. Works best when work is related closely to results and the impact of personal efforts is obvious. Shows an understanding of business, commerce, and finance. Seeks opportunities for self-development and career advancement.	Need for achievement, negative agreeableness

[a] Where more than one predictor is shown, the second is expected to be of lesser importance than the first. The competency titles and definitions are taken from the SHL Universal Competency Framework™ Profiler and Designer Cards (copyright © 2004 by SHL Group plc, reproduced with permission of the copyright holder). These titles may be freely used for research purposes subject to due acknowledgment of the copyright holder.

Dave Bartram, SHL Group, "The Great Eight Competencies: A Criterion-Centric Approach to Validation," *Journal of Applied Psychology* 90, no. 6, 2005, 1185–1203.

Note: More detailed definitions of each of the Great Eight are provided by the competency component level of the SHL Universal Competency Framework™.

ADMINISTERING AND EVALUATING THE PLAN

Whatever plan is designed, whether job-based or person-based, a crucial issue is the fairness of its administration. Just as with job evaluation, sufficient information should be available to apply the plan, such as definitions of compensable factors, degrees, or details of skill blocks, competencies, and certification methods. Increasingly, online tools are available for managers to learn about these plans and apply them.[36] We have already mentioned the issue of employee understanding and acceptance. Communication and employee involvement are crucial for acceptance of the resulting pay structures. See **Chapter 18** for more discussion of pay communication.

There is vast research literature on job evaluation compared to person-based structures. Most of it focuses on the procedures used rather than the resulting structure's usefulness in motivating employee behaviors or achieving organization objectives. In virtually all the studies, job-based evaluation is treated as a measurement device; the research assesses its reliability, validity, costs, and its compliance with laws and regulations. Any value added by job evaluation (e.g., reducing pay dissatisfaction, improving employees' understanding of how their pay is determined) has been largely ignored.[37] In contrast, research on person-based structures tends to focus on their effects on behaviors and organization objectives and ignores questions of reliability and validity.

Reliability of Job Evaluation Techniques

A reliable evaluation would be one where different evaluators produce the same results. Most studies report high agreement when different people rank-order jobs—correlations between .85 and .96.[38] This is important because in practice, several different people usually evaluate jobs. The results should not depend on which person did the evaluation. However, even with what are normally considered to be "high" reliabilities (e.g., .90 or greater), practically important differences in assigned salaries can result when different people or groups assign job evaluation points. Consider the example in **Exhibit 6.13**. Two different sets of raters evaluated 9 jobs (Jobs A through I). In **Chapter 8**, we will see how job evaluation points can be translated into predicted salary rates using a pay policy line. In the present example, the pay policy line is Predicted Salary = $4,800 + $360 * Job Evaluation Points. Do we get the same predicted salaries regardless of whether we use Group 1 versus Group 2 as the job evaluation raters? The answer is a clear NO. For example, in the case of Job G, the predicted salary is $28,800 higher based on Group 1's job evaluation scores. That is despite the fact that the correlation between the Group 1 and Group 2 columns of job evaluation ratings (the inter-rater reliability) is high (r = .94). Some of the difference in predicted salaries is due to Group 1 giving out lower levels of job evaluation points on average. However, even when we eliminate that difference between the groups, as in the right side of **Exhibit 6.13**, there remain predicted salary differences of an uncomfortably large size. And, remember that each job has multiple employees. Thus, many employees will be affected. Now, an important caveat is that, as we saw in **Chapter 5** and as we will discuss in **Chapter 8**, most organizations are now using market pricing, where many jobs are matched directly to jobs in pay surveys to determine salaries. In such cases, job evaluation results often have less influence on salaries. Nevertheless, it is important to remember that when job evaluation points do play a significant role in salary setting (e.g., for nonbenchmark jobs, those jobs that cannot be directly matched to pay survey jobs), even seemingly high reliability between different raters may still leave room for very different resulting salaries.

Reliability can be improved by using evaluators who are familiar with the work and trained in the job evaluation process. Some organizations use group consensus to increase reliability. Each evaluator makes a preliminary independent evaluation. Then, they discuss their results until consensus emerges. Consensus certainly appears to make the results more acceptable. However, some studies report that results obtained through consensus were not significantly different from those obtained either by independent evaluators or by averaging

EXHIBIT 6.13 Differences in Salaries despite "High" (.94) Interater Reliability

	Original Data						Equate Mean Job Evaluation Points across Group 1 and Group 2[a]				
Job	Job Evaluation Points		Predicted Salary		Salary	Job	Job Evaluation Points		Predicted Salary		Salary
	Group 1	Group 2	Group 1	Group 2	Difference		Group 1	Group 2	Group 1	Group 2	Difference
A	70	85	$ 30,000	$35,400	–$ 5,400	A	70	120	$ 30,000	$ 48,000	–$18,000
B	85	65	$ 35,400	$28,200	$ 7,200	B	85	100	$ 35,400	$ 40,800	–$ 5,400
C	200	180	$ 76,800	$69,600	$ 7,200	C	200	215	$ 76,800	$ 82,200	–$ 5,400
D	130	85	$ 51,600	$35,400	$ 16,200	D	130	120	$ 51,600	$ 48,000	$ 3,600
E	65	50	$28,200	$22,800	$ 5,400	E	65	85	$ 28,200	$ 35,400	–$ 7,200
F	135	105	$ 53,400	$42,600	$ 10,800	F	135	140	$ 53,400	$ 55,200	–$ 1,800
G	215	135	$ 82,200	$53,400	$ 28,800	G	215	170	$ 82,200	$ 66,000	$16,200
H	300	240	$112,800	$91,200	$ 21,600	H	300	275	$ 112,800	$103,800	$ 9,000
I	130	70	$ 51,600	$30,000	$ 21,600	I	130	105	$ 51,600	$ 42,600	$ 9,000
Mean	148	113	$58,000	$45,400		Mean	148	148	$ 58,000	$ 58,000	
Sum[b]					$124,200	Sum[b]					$75,600

Predicted salary = $4,800 + $360 * Job evaluation points

[a]Added 35 points to the Group 2 job evaluation score for each job.

[b]Sum of absolute values of differences.

individual evaluators' results. Others report that a forceful or experienced person on the committee can sway the results. So can knowledge about the job's present salary level. These reliabilities for job evaluation scores are higher than those we saw in **Chapter 4** for job analysis ratings. One possible reason is that those conducting job evaluation may already know the pay for the jobs, which may result in greater consistency across raters. Another factor is that job evaluation research has often had raters rely on job descriptions to assign job evaluation ratings. That (working from the same job description rather than starting "from scratch" with each evaluator observing jobs) may again result in greater consistency. In any case, as we have seen, even high reliabilities in job evaluation can still produce different pay rates for jobs that vary as a function of the rater/ raters.

As part of efforts to reduce costs, job evaluation committees are disappearing. Instead, managers do the evaluations online as part of the organization's "HR Toolkit" or "shared services." The reliability and validity of the results obtained this way have not been studied.

Validity

Validity refers to the degree to which the evaluation assesses what it is supposed to–the relative worth of jobs to the organization. Validity of job evaluation has been measured in two ways: (1) the degree of agreement between rankings that resulted from the job evaluation with an agreed-upon *ranking of benchmarks* used as the criterion, and (2) by **"hit rates"**–the degree to which the job evaluation plan matches (hits) an agreed-upon *pay structure for benchmark jobs*.[39] In both cases, the predetermined, agreed-upon ranking or pay structure is for benchmark jobs. It can be established by organization leadership or be based on external market data, negotiations with unions, or the market rates for benchmarks held predominantly by men (to try to eliminate any gender discrimination reflected in the market), or some combination of these.

Many studies report that when different job evaluation plans are compared to each other, they generate *very similar rankings* of jobs but *very low hit rates*–they disagree on how much to pay the jobs.[40] One study that looked at three different job evaluation plans applied to the same set of jobs reported similar rank order among evaluators using each plan but substantial differences in the resulting pay.[41] Some studies have found pay differences of up to $427 per month ($750/per month in today's dollars, or $9,000 a year) depending on the method used.

So it is clear that the definition of validity needs to be broadened to include impact on pay decisions. How the results are judged depends on the standards used. For managing compensation the correct standard is the pay structure–what jobholders get paid–rather than simply the jobs' rank order.

Studies of the degree to which different job evaluation plans produce the same results start with the assumption that if different approaches produce the same results, then those results must be "correct," that is, valid. But in one study, three plans all gave the same result (they were reliable) but all three ranked a police officer higher than a detective. They were not valid.[42] TV fans know that in U.S. police departments, the detectives outrank the uniforms. What accounts for the reliability of invalid plans? Either the compensable factors did not pick up something deemed important in the detectives' jobs or the detectives have more power to negotiate higher wages. So while these three plans gave the same results, they would have little acceptance among detectives.

You may wonder why any manager or employee cares about such details? Is this an example of compensation specialists inventing work for themselves? Not if your organization is facing challenges by dissatisfied employees or their lawyers. To miss this point is to place your organization at risk.[43]

Acceptability

Several methods are used to assess and improve employee acceptability. An obvious one is to include a *formal appeals process.* Employees who believe their jobs are evaluated incorrectly should be able to request reanalysis and/or skills reevaluation. Most firms respond to such requests from managers, but few extend the process to all employees unless it is part of a union-negotiated grievance process.[44] *Employee attitude surveys* can assess perceptions of how useful evaluation is as a management tool. Ask employees whether their pay is related to their job and how well they understand what is expected in their job.[45]

BIAS IN INTERNAL STRUCTURES

The continuing differences in jobs held by men, women, and people of color, and the accompanying pay differences, have focused attention on internal structures as a possible source of discrimination. Much of this attention has been directed at job evaluation as both a potential source of bias against women and a mechanism to reduce bias.[46] It has been widely speculated that job evaluation is susceptible to gender bias–jobs held predominantly by women are undervalued simply because of the jobholder's gender. But evidence does not support this proposition.[47] Additionally, there is no evidence that the job *evaluator's* gender affects the results.

In contrast to the gender of the jobholder or the evaluator, the evidence on compensable factors and bias is less clear. One study found that compensable factors related to job content (such as contact with others and judgment) did reflect bias against work done predominantly by women, but factors pertaining to employee requirements (such as education and experience) did not.[48]

Wages Criteria Bias

The second potential source of bias affects job evaluation indirectly, through the current wages paid for jobs. If job evaluation is based on the current wages paid and the jobs held predominantly by women are underpaid, then the results simply mirror bias in the current pay rates.[49] Since many job evaluation plans are purposely structured to mirror the existing pay structure, it is not surprising that current wages influence the results of job evaluation. One study of 400 compensation specialists revealed that market data had a substantially larger effect on pay decisions than did job evaluations or current pay data.[50] This study is a unique look at several factors that may affect pay structures.

Several recommendations seek to ensure that job evaluation plans are bias-free, including the following:

1. Define the compensable factors and scales to include the content of jobs held predominantly by women. For example, working conditions may include the noise and stress of office machines and the repetitive movements associated with the use of computers.
2. Ensure that factor weights are not consistently biased against jobs held predominantly by women. Are factors usually associated with these jobs always given less weight?
3. Apply the plan in as bias-free a manner as feasible. Ensure that the job descriptions are bias-free, exclude incumbent names from the job evaluation process, and train diverse evaluators.

At the risk of pointing out the obvious, all issues concerning job evaluation also apply to skill-based and competency-based plans. For example, the acceptability of the results of skill-based plans can be studied from the perspective of measurement (reliability and validity) and administration (costs, simplicity). The various points in skill certification at which errors and biases may enter into judgment (e.g., different views of skill-block definitions, potential favoritism toward team members, defining and assessing skill obsolescence) and whether skill-block points and evaluators make a difference all need to be studied. In light of the detailed bureaucracy that has grown up around job evaluation, we confidently predict a growth of bureaucratic procedures around person-based plans, too. In addition to bureaucracy to manage costs, the whole approach to certification may be fraught with potential legal vulnerabilities if employees who fail to be certified challenge the process. Unfortunately, no studies of gender effects in skill-based or competency-based plans exist. Little attention has been paid to assessor training or validating the certification process. Just as employment tests used for hiring and promotion decisions must be demonstrably free of illegal bias, it seems logical that certification procedures used to determine pay structures would face the same requirement.

THE PERFECT STRUCTURE

Exhibit 6.14 contrasts job-, skill-, and competency-based approaches. Pay increases are gained via promotions to more responsible jobs under job-based structures or via the acquisition of more-valued skills/competencies under the person-based structures. Logically, employees will focus on how to get promoted (experience, performance) or on how to acquire the required skills or competencies (training, learning).

Managers whose employers use job-based plans focus on placing the right people in the right job. A switch to skill-/competency-based plans reverses this procedure. Now, managers must assign the right work to the right people, that is, those with the right skills and competencies. A job-based approach controls costs by paying only as much as the work performed is worth, regardless of any greater skills the employee may possess. So, as **Exhibit 6.14** suggests, costs are controlled via job rates or work assignments and budgets.

In contrast, skill-/competency-based plans pay employees for the highest level of skill/competency they have achieved *regardless of the work they perform.* This maximizes flexibility. But it also encourages all employees to become certified at top rates. Unless an employer can either control the rate at which employees can certify skill/competency mastery or employ fewer people, the organization may experience higher labor costs than do competitors using job-based approaches. The key is to offset the higher rates with greater productivity. One consulting firm claims that an average company switching to a skill-based system experiences a 15 to 20 percent increase in wage rates, a 20 to 25 percent increase in training and development costs, and initial *increases* in head count to allow people to cross-train and move around.[51] Another study found costs were no higher.[52]

In addition to having potentially higher rates and higher training costs, skill/competency plans may become as complex and burdensome as job-based plans. Additionally, questions still remain about a skill/competency system's compliance with the U.S. Equal Pay Act.

So where does all this come out? What is the best approach to pay structures, and how will we know it when we see it? The answer is, it depends. The best approach may be to provide sufficient ambiguity (loosely linked internal alignment) to afford flexibility to adapt to changing conditions. Too generic an approach may not provide sufficient detail to make a clear link between pay, work, and results; too detailed an approach may become rigid. Bases for pay that are too vaguely defined will have no credibility with employees, will fail to signal what is really important for success, and may lead to suspicions of favoritism and bias.

This chapter concludes our section on internal alignment. Before we move on to external considerations, let's once again address the issue of, So what? Why bother with a pay structure? The answer should be, because it supports improved organization performance. An internally aligned pay structure, whether strategically loosely linked or tightly fitting, can be designed to (1) help determine pay for the wide variety of work in the organization and (2) ensure that pay influences peoples' attitudes and work behaviors and directs them toward organization objectives.

EXHIBIT 6.14 Contrasting Approaches

	Job Based	Skill Based	Competency Based
What is valued	Compensable factors	Skill blocks	Competencies
Quantify the value	Factor degree weights	Skill levels	Competency levels
Mechanisms to translate into pay	Assign points that reflect criterion pay structure	Certification and price skills in external market	Certification and price competencies in external market
Pay structure	Based on job performed/market	Based on skills certified/market	Based on competency developed/market
Pay increases	Promotion	Skill acquisition	Competency development
Managers' focus	Link employees to work content Promotion and placement Control costs via pay for job and budget increase	Utilize skills efficiently Provide training Control costs via training, certification, and work assignments	Be sure competencies add value Provide competency-developing opportunities Control costs via certification and assignments
Employee focus	Seek promotions to earn more pay	Acquire skills	Acquire competencies
Procedures	Job analysis Job evaluation	Skill analysis Skill certification	Competency analysis Competency certification
Advantages	Clear expectations Sense of progress Pay based on value of work performed	Continuous learning Flexibility Reduced work force	Continuous learning Flexibility Lateral movement
Limitations	Potential bureaucracy	Potential bureaucracy requires cost controls	Potential bureaucracy

Your Turn — Climb the Legal Ladder

Dewey & LeBoeuf, which just a few years previously had 2,500 employees (including 1,400 attorneys) in 26 offices around the world, filed for bankruptcy in 2012. The firm was formed in a merger of two blue-chip firm with very well-paid partners (and thus very high billing rates) just before the Financial Crisis of 2008. It also engaged in aggressive "poaching" of attorneys from other firms by offering large, multiyear, guaranteed pay packages. Very unfortunate timing to accumulate so much expensive high-level talent and then have business crater. When business declined, they were stuck with large fixed compensation costs and also, some would argue, a weakened culture, making it difficult to rally the troops. Indeed, most partners, once they felt things were going downhill, defected to other firms. In a firm like Dewey & LeBoeuf, top partners might earn 9 times what some other partners earn.

In contrast, in the more traditional law firm approach to compensation, the highest paid partners make 4 or 5 times as much as some other partners. In a lockstep model, partners are paid to an important degree based on seniority. Talent is largely groomed from within, as opposed to significant poaching of attorneys from other firms. Most large firms use pay structures with six to eight levels from associate to partner. The associate's level is typically based on experience plus performance (see **Exhibit 6.15**). In the world of associate attorneys, performance is measured as billable hours. So the associates who meet or exceed the expected billable hours advance to the next level each year. Similar to the tenure process in academic settings, after six to eight years associates are expected to become partners or "find opportunities elsewhere." The likelihood of making partner differs among firms, but the norm seems to be that fewer than one-third of the associates make it. Associates are expected to bill around 2,200 hours per year. For example, partners at Sullivan & Cromwell reportedly earn an average of over $3 million a year.

EXHIBIT 6.15 Pay Structure for Associates at Cravath Law Firm, by Year

Year	Base Salary	Year-End Bonus	Special Bonus
1st	$190,000	$15,000 (pro-rated)	$7,500 (pro-rated)
2nd	200,000	25,000	7,500
3rd	220,000	50,000	10,000
4th	255,000	65,000	20,000
5th	280,000	65,000	27,500
6th	305,000	80,000	32,500
7th	325,000	90,000	37,000
8th	340,000	100,000	40,000

Various estimates indicate clients are billed about $600/hour for each partner and about $300/hour for each associate by these large elite firms. So if associates hit or exceed their targets, they generate $660,000 annually ($300 times 2,200 hours). However, the most elite firms can charge even more for top partners and associates. For example, it is reported that at Kirkland & Ellis, partners are billing $1,000 to $1,800 per hour and associates are billing $600 to $1,100 per hour. Clearly, the revenue implications of these higher billing rates are substantial.

Many firms also use performance bonuses for associates. **Exhibit 6.15** above shows the 2021 pay structure at Cravath, typically the first large New York City firm each year to announce its associate base salary and bonus plan, which other such firms such as Sullivan & Cromwell typically follow (or nearly so). Like other firms, bonuses provide labor cost flexibility for law firms. When the economy is booming, especially when that translates into lucrative legal work on mergers and acquisitions, stock and bond offerings, and intellectual property matters, bonuses are higher to recognize contributions and to retain essential talent (and billable hours). (Note: A pandemic can create other types of business, such as bankruptcy.) **Exhibit 6.15** shows Cravath is including not only a Year-End Bonus, which is typical, but also a Special Bonus, this year.

1. Think about the research evidence discussed in this book. Would you expect associates to feel their pay structure (**Exhibit 6.15**) is fair? What comparisons would they likely make? What work behaviors would you expect this pay structure to motivate? Explain.
2. Partners make around 10 times the highest-paid associates. A *Wall Street Journal* writer laments that law firms form "giant pyramids . . . (in which) associates at the bottom funnel money to partners at the top." What is missing from the writer's analysis? Hint: Speculate about the likely differences in content and value of the work performed by partners compared to associates. Any parallels to Merrill Lynch's FAs and SVPIs?
3. A few years ago, Sullivan & Cromwell announced that year-end bonuses would be cut in half and in the following two years, bonuses were cut further. However, the trend was then reversed with bonuses subsequently being increased. Why do bonuses vary in this manner over time? How does this bonus variability over time compare to variability in salaries over time at these types of elite law firms? What explains the difference in the way salaries and bonuses are managed over time?
4. How does the more traditional approach to associate and partner compensation differ from that of Dewey & LeBoeuf? What are the advantages and disadvantages of each approach?
5. Why do think Cravath is offering not only the usual Year-End Bonus, but also a Special Bonus this year?

Sources: Kathryn Rubino. Cravath Bonuses Are Here! Good news! Cravath has spoken on 2020 bonuses. abovethelaw.com, November 23, 2020. Samantha Stokes. Law Firms Are Raking in Millions From Pandemic-Era Retail Bankruptcies: Several Am Law 100 firms are reaping the rewards from some of this spring's most active bankruptcies, including J. Crew, Neiman Marcus and J.C. Penney—some to the tune of more than $10 million. law.com, July 6, 2020; Kathryn Rubino. The Bigger The Biglaw Firm, The Bigger The Billing Rate: Putting the big in Biglaw. abovethelaw.com, July 14, 2020; Samantha Stokes. Will Billing Rates for Elite Firms Rise More in 2020? law.com, July 30, 2020.

Summary

This section of the book examines pay structures within an organization. The premise underlying internal alignment is that internal pay structures need to be aligned with the organization's business strategy and objectives, the design of the work flow, a concern for the fair treatment of employees, and the intent of motivating employees. The work relationships within a single organization are an important part of internal alignment.

The structures are part of the web of incentives within organizations. They affect satisfaction with pay, the willingness to seek and accept promotions to more responsible jobs, the effort to keep learning and undertake additional training, and the propensity to remain with the employer. They also reduce the incidence of pay-related grievances.

The techniques for establishing internally aligned structures include job analysis, job evaluation, and person-based approaches for skill-/competency-based plans. But in practice, aspects of both jobs and people are used. Although viewed by some as bureaucratic burdens, these techniques can aid in achieving the objectives of the pay system when they are properly designed and managed. Without them, our pay objectives of improving competitiveness and fairness are more difficult to achieve.

We have now finished the first part of the book. We discussed the techniques used to establish internal alignment as well as its effects on compensation objectives. The next part of the book focuses on the next strategic issue in our pay model: external competitiveness.

Review Questions

1. What are the pros and cons of having employees involved in compensation decisions? What forms can employee involvement take?
2. Why does the process used in the design of the internal pay structure matter? Distinguish between the processes used to design and administer a person-based and a job-based approach.
3. If you were managing employee compensation, how would you recommend that your company evaluate the usefulness of its job evaluation or person-based plans?
4. Based on the research on job evaluation, what are the sources of possible gender bias in skill-/competency-based plans?
5. How can a manager ensure that job evaluation or skill-/competency-based plans support a customer-centered strategy?

Endnotes

1. Robert Kanigel, *The One Best Way* (New York: Viking, 1997). See also Vanessa Hill and Harry Van Buren III, “Taylor Won: The Triumph of Scientific Management and Its Meaning for Business and Society,” in *Corporate Social Responsibility* (Bingley, UK: Emerald, 2018), pp. 265–294.
2. M. Marchington, D. Grimshaw, J. Rubery, and H. Willmott, eds., *Fragmenting Work: Blurring Organizational Boundaries and Disordering Hierarchies* (New York: Oxford University Press, 2004).
3. J. D. Shaw, N. Gupta, A. Mitra, and G. E. Ledford Jr., “Success and Survival of Skill-Based Pay Plans,” *Journal of Management* 31, no. 1 (2005): 28–49.
4. The Wisconsin Center for Education Research, University of Wisconsin-Madison (https://www.wcer.wisc.edu/) includes research on teacher pay, including skill-based pay. See, for example, Steven M. Kimball, Herbert G. Heneman III, Robin Worth, Jessica Arrigoni, and Daniel Marlin, “Teacher Compensation: Standard Practices and Changes in Wisconsin,” WCER Working Paper No. 2016-5, August 2016.
5. D. Southall and J. Newman, *Skill-Based Pay Development* (Buffalo, NY: HR Foundations, 2000).
6. G. Douglas Jenkins Jr., Gerald E. Ledford Jr., Nina Gupta, and D. Harold Doty, *Skill-Based Pay* (Scottsdale, AZ: American Compensation Association, 1992).
7. B. Murray and B. Gerhart, “An Empirical Analysis of a Skill-Based Pay Program and Plant Performance Outcomes,” *Academy of Management Journal* 41 (1998), pp. 68–78.
8. Gerald Ledford, “Factors Affecting the Long-Term Success of Skill-Based Pay,” *WorldatWork Journal,* First Quarter, 2008, pp. 6–18; Judy Canavan, “Overcoming the Challenge of Aligning Skill-Based Pay Levels to the External Market,” *WorldatWork Journal,* First Quarter (2008), pp. 18–24.
9. R. Batt, “Who Benefits from Teams? Comparing Workers, Supervisors, and Managers,” *Industrial Relations* 43 (2004), pp. 183–212; Greg L. Stewart, Stacy L. Astrove, Cody J. Reeves, Eean R. Crawford, and Samantha L. Solimeo, “Those with the Most Find It Hardest to Share: Exploring Leader

Resistance to the Implementation of Team-Based Empowerment," *Academy of Management Journal* 60, no. 6 (2017): pp. 2266–2293.

10. Gerald E. Ledford Jr., "Three Case Studies of Skill-Based Pay: An Overview," *Compensation and Benefits Review,* March/April 1991, pp. 11–23; Gerald Ledford, "Factors Affecting the Long-Term Success of Skill-Based Pay," *WorldatWork Journal,* First Quarter (2008), pp. 6–18.
11. Erich C. Dierdorff and Eric A. Surface, "If You Pay for Skills, Will They Learn? Skill Change and Maintenance Under a Skill-Based Pay System," *Journal of Management* 34 (2008), pp. 721–743; B. Murray and B. Gerhart, "An Empirical Analysis of a Skill-Based Pay Program and Plant Performance Outcomes," *Academy of Management Journal* 41 (1998), pp. 68–78.
12. Cynthia Lee, Kenneth S. Law, and Philip Bobko, "The Importance of Justice Perceptions on Pay Effectiveness: A Two-Year Study of a Skill-Based Pay Plan," *Journal of Management* 25(6), 1999, pp. 851–873.
13. K. Parrent and C. Weber, "Case Study: Does Paying for Knowledge Pay Off?" *Compensation and Benefits Review,* September–October 1994, pp. 44–50; B. Murray and B. Gerhart, "An Empirical Analysis of a Skill-Based Pay Program and Plant Performance Outcomes," *Academy of Management Journal* 41 (1998), pp. 68–78; A. Mitra, N. Gupta, and J. D. Shaw, "A Comparative Examination of Traditional and Skill-based Pay Plans," *Journal of Managerial Psychology* 26 (2010), pp. 278–296.
14. Kenneth Mericle and Dong-One Kim, "From Job-Based Pay to Skill-Based Pay in Unionized Establishments: A Three-Plant Comparative Analysis," *Relations Industrielles/Industrial Relations* 54, no. 3 (1999), pp. 549–580; Steve Farkas, Jean Johnson, Ann Duffett, et al., *Stand by Me: What Teachers Really Think about Unions, Merit Pay, and Other Professional Matters* (New York: Public Agenda, 2003), *www.publicagenda.org.*
15. Jason D. Shaw, Nina Gupta, Atul Mitra, and Gerald E. Ledford Jr., "Success and Survival of Skill-Based Pay Plans," *Journal of Management,* February 2005, pp. 28–49.
16. Gerald Ledford, "Factors Affecting the Long-Term Success of Skill-Based Pay," *WorldatWork Journal,* First Quarter (2008), pp. 6–18.
17. N. Fredric Crandall and Marc J. Wallace Jr., "Paying Employees to Develop New Skills," in *Aligning Pay and Results,* ed. Howard Risher (New York: American Management Association, 1999).
18. Patricia Zingheim, Gerald E. Ledford Jr., and Jay R. Schuster, "Competencies and Competency Models: Does One Size Fit All?" *ACA Journal,* Spring 1996, pp. 56–65.
19. TRW Corporate Competency Model.
20. Lyle M. Spencer Jr. and Signe M. Spencer, *Competence at Work* (New York: Wiley, 1993).
21. William M. Mercer, *Competencies, Performance and Pay* (New York: William M. Mercer, 1995).
22. TRW Corporate Competency Model.
23. James T. Kochanski and Howard Risher, "Paying for Competencies: Rewarding Knowledge, Skills, and Behaviors," in *Aligning Pay and Results,* ed. Howard Risher (New York: American Management Association, 1999).
24. C. A. Bartlett and Sumantra Ghoshal, "The Myth of the Generic Manager: New Personal Competencies for New Management Roles," *California Management Review* 40(1), 1997, pp. 92–105.
25. For a comprehensive discussion of best practices in competency modeling in compensation and other areas of human resources, see M. A. Campion, A. A. Fink, B. J. Ruggeberg, L. Carr, G. M. Phillips, and R. B. Odman, "Doing Competencies Well: Best Practices in Competency Modeling," *Personnel Psychology* 64 (2011), pp. 225–262; John P. Campbell and Brenton M. Wiernik, "The modeling and assessment of Work Performance," *Annual Review of Organizational Psychology and Organizational Behavior* 2, no. 1 (2015), pp. 47–74.

26. Edward E. Lawler III, "From Job-Based to Competency-Based Organizations," *Journal of Organizational Behavior* 15 (1994), pp. 3–15.

27. Patricia K. Zingheim and Jay R. Schuster, "Reassessing the Value of Skill-Based Pay: Getting the Runaway Train Back on Track," *WorldatWork Journal* 11(3), Third Quarter 2002.

28. Margaret E. Allredge and Kevin J. Nilan, "3M's Leadership Competency Model: An Internally Developed Solution," *Human Resource Management* 39 (Summer/Fall 2000), pp. 133–145.

29. Patricia Zingheim, Gerald E. Ledford Jr., and Jay R. Schuster, "Competencies and Competency Models," in American Compensation Association, *Raising the Bar: Using Competencies to Enhance Employee Performance* (Scottsdale, AZ: American Compensation Association, 1996).

30. T. H. Stone, B. D. Webster, and S. Schoonover, "What Do We Know About Competency Modeling?" *International Journal of Selection and Assessment*, 21(3), 2013, pp. 334–338.

31. Paul R. Sparrow and Heba Makram, "What Is the Value of Talent Management? Building Value-Driven Processes within a Talent Management Architecture," *Human Resource Management Review* 25, no. 3 (2015), pp. 249–263.

32. Peter Cappelli and J. R. Keller, "Talent Management: Conceptual Approaches and Practical Challenges," *Annual Review of Organizational Psychology and Organizational Behavior* 1, no. 1 (2014), pp. 305–331.

33. A. R. Levenson, W. A. Van der Stede, and S. G. Cohen, "Measuring the Relationship between Managerial Competencies and Performance," *Journal of Management* 32(3), 2006, pp. 360–380.

34. Wayne F. Cascio and John W. Boudreau, "The Search for Global Competence: From International HR to Talent Management," *Journal of World Business* 51, no. 1 (2016), pp. 103–114; Allen D. Engle Sr. and Mark E. Mendenhall, "Spinning the Global Competency Cube: Toward a Timely Transnational Human Resource Decision Support System," working paper, Eastern Kentucky University, Richmond, KY, 2000.

35. Jason D. Shaw, Nina Gupta, Atul Mitra, and Gerald E. Ledford Jr., "Success and Survival of Skill-Based Pay Plans," *Journal of Management,* February 2005, pp. 28–49.

36. For example, see https://au.hudson.com/talent-management/competency-scan-online.

37. An exception is the study cited in A. R. Levenson, W. A. Van der Stede, and S. G. Cohen, "Measuring the Relationship Between Managerial Competencies and Performance," *Journal of Management* 32(3), 2006, pp. 360–380.

38. Erich C. Dierdorff and Mark A. Wilson, "A Meta-Analysis of Job Analysis Reliability," *Journal of Applied Psychology,* August 2003, pp. 635–646; Vandra Huber and S. Crandall, "Job Measurement: A Social-Cognitive Decision Perspective," in *Research in Personnel and Human Resources Management,* vol. 12, Gerald R. Ferris, ed. (Greenwich, CT: JAI Press, 1994), pp. 223–269; Sheila M. Rutt and Dennis Doverspike, "Salary and Organizational Level Effects on Job Evaluation Ratings," *Journal of Business and Psychology,* Spring 1999, pp. 379–385.

39. Tjarda van Sliedregt, Olga F. Voskuijl, and Henk Thierry, "Job Evaluation Systems and Pay Grade Structures: Do They Match?" *International Journal of Human Resource Management* 12(8), December 2001, pp. 1313–1324.

40. R. M. Madigan and D. J. Hoover, "Effects of Alternative Job Evaluation Methods on Decisions Involving Pay Equity," *Academy of Management Journal,* March 1986, pp. 84–100.

41. D. Doverspike and G. Barrett, "An Internal Bias Analysis of a Job Evaluation Instrument," *Journal of Applied Psychology* 69 (1984), pp. 648–662; Kermit Davis Jr. and William Sauser Jr., "Effects of Alternative Weighting Methods in a Policy-Capturing Approach to Job Evaluation: A Review and Empirical Investigation," *Personnel Psychology* 44 (1991), pp. 85–127.

42. Judith Collins and Paul M. Muchinsky, "An Assessment of the Construct Validity of Three Job Evaluation Methods: A Field Experiment," *Academy of Management Journal* 36(4), 1993, pp. 895–904; Todd J. Maurer and Stuart A. Tross, "SME Committee vs. Field Job Analysis Ratings: Convergence, Cautions, and a Call," *Journal of Business and Psychology* 14(3), Spring 2000, pp. 489–499.

43. For example, see Kathryn May, "Government and Union Reach $45M Pay-Equity Deal," *Ottawa Citizen,* May 19, 2016, https://ottawacitizen.com/news/national/government-and-union-reach-45m-pay-equity-deal.

44. D. Lipsky and R. Seeber, "In Search of Control: The Corporate Embrace of Alternative Dispute Resolution," *Journal of Labor and Employment Law* 1(1), Spring 1998, pp. 133–157.

45. Hudson Employment Index, *www.hudson-index.com/node.asp?SID56755.*

46. D. J. Treiman and H. I. Hartmann, eds., *Women, Work and Wages: Equal Pay for Jobs of Equal Value* (Washington, DC: National Academy of Sciences, 1981); H. Remick, *Comparable Worth and Wage Discrimination* (Philadelphia: Temple University Press, 1984); Morley Gunderson, "The Evolution and Mechanics of Pay Equity in Ontario," *Canadian Public Policy* 28(1), 2002, pp. S117–S126; Deborah M. Figart, "Equal Pay for Equal Work: The Role of Job Evaluation in an Evolving Social Norm," *Journal of Economic Issues,* March 2000, pp. 1–19.

47. D. Schwab and R. Grams, "Sex-Related Errors in Job Evaluation: A 'Real-World' Test," *Journal of Applied Psychology* 70(3), 1985, pp. 533–559; Richard D. Arvey, Emily M. Passino, and John W. Lounsbury, "Job Analysis Results as Influenced by Sex of Incumbent and Sex of Analyst," *Journal of Applied Psychology* 62(4), 1977, pp. 411–416.

48. Michael K. Mount and Rebecca A. Ellis, "Investigation of Bias in Job Evaluation Ratings of Comparable Worth Study Participants," *Personnel Psychology,* Spring 1987, pp. 85–96.

49. D. Schwab and R. Grams, "Sex-Related Errors in Job Evaluation: A 'Real-World' Test," *Journal of Applied Psychology* 70(3), 1985, pp. 533–559.

50. S. Rynes, C. Weber, and G. Milkovich, "The Effects of Market Survey Rates, Job Evaluation, and Job Gender on Job Pay," *Journal of Applied Psychology* 74 (1989), pp. 114–123.

51. N. Fredric Crandall and Marc J. Wallace Jr., "Paying Employees to Develop New Skills," in *Aligning Pay and Results,* Howard Risher, ed. (New York: American Management Association, 1999); B. Murray and B. Gerhart, "An Empirical Analysis of a Skill-Based Pay Program and Plant Performance Outcomes," *Academy of Management Journal* 41 (1998), pp. 68–78.

52. Howard Risher, ed., *Aligning Pay and Results* (New York: American Management Association, 1999).

Part III
External Competitiveness: Determining the Pay Level

In **Part** II, our focus was on the internal structure or relative value organizations and markets assigned to different jobs. In Part III, we continue with that focus, but also examine how organizations choose their overall pay level and how and why different organizations choose different levels. For example, Organization A and Organization B may have the same relative pay (i.e., the same internal structure) for the jobs of engineer and senior engineer (e.g., a 20 percent difference in value), but Organization A might choose one pay level for the two jobs (e.g., $60,000 and $72,000, respectively), while Organization B might choose a higher pay level for the two jobs (e.g., $70,000 and $84,000, respectively). To identify organization pay-level differences, we can begin with a single job. Let's look at the job of software engineer. According to Glassdoor.com, as your textbook goes to press, the average national salary for this job is $104,749. But companies differ. Google's average salary for a software engineer is $140,000, whereas the average at IBM is $101,361, $97,655 at Lockheed Martin, and $82,656 at General Motors. Now, some part of that salary differential is likely related to geography/cost of living, because Glassdoor data also indicate that the average software engineer in San Jose, CA ("Silicon Valley") earns $135,851 versus $99,839 in Austin, TX, and $88,628 in Madison, WI. However, it is not all based on geography/cost of living (or tech versus others), because even when we look only at tech companies (consider why tech companies would pay more) and only salaries of software engineers in Silicon Valley, company pay levels still differ: Google ($132,269), Apple ($138,127), Qualcomm ($118,741). Some part of the remaining difference could be due to some organizations having more experienced and knowledgeable software engineers. In a similar vein, some organizations may have more challenging and more autonomous software engineer jobs, for which they feel higher pay levels are necessary to attract and retain more experienced and knowledgeable software engineers. (Important point: The same job title in different organizations does not mean the job is the same or has the same value.) Or perhaps some organizations have lower base salaries because they are higher on other forms of compensation (e.g., bonuses, stock awards/options, benefits)—in other words, they differ in "how" they pay, the topic of future chapters in **Part** IV. These are strategic pay decisions that organizations must consider and that we now focus on.

In **Part** IV, we will look at how much individuals within specific jobs and organizations earn. We can provide a quick preview. Examples of earnings are shown in **Exhibit III.1**. There are "real" people on this list. It's interesting to think about why these people get paid what they do. Why don't they get paid more? Why not less? What would they do if they were paid more or paid less? How well would their employers (where the person is not self-employed) do if they raised or lowered pay for these people and others in their jobs or other jobs? These are the kinds of questions we will address in Part III.

EXHIBIT III.1 Who Makes How Much?

Name	Age	Place	Job	Earnings
Allyn Bailey	26	Oxford, MS	Nurse Practitioner	$110,000
Christa Rogers	47	Charlotte, NC	Forester	$92,000
Cindy Firestein	40	Boston, MA	Director, Undergraduate Advising	$83,000
Ed O'Brien	61	Santa Ana, CA	Stagehand	$55,000
Danielle Wurth	46	Phoenix, AZ	Professional (Home) Organizer (with book on the topic)	$175,000
Fernando R. Salas	33	Tuscaloosa, AL	Hydrologist	$108,316
Eleno J. Banquil Jr.	39	Scottsdale, AZ	Restaurant Owner and Franchisor	$250,000
James Bauer	28	Aurora, CO	Emergency Medicine Physician Assistant	$105,000
Mollie Currid	23	Las Vegas, NV	Project Engineer	$63,000
Surya Patel	27	Manhattan, NY	Graphic Designer	$55,000
Sylvie Brouder	56	West Lafayette, IN	Professor of Agronomy (& president of agronomy society)	$213,757
Yaara Schwartz	27	Chicago, IL	Bridal Stylist and Group Fitness Instructor	$20,000

Source: "What People Earn 2020." *Parade*, April 3, 2020. Parade.com.

Let's shift from "everyday people" to celebrities. In the past year, both Russell Wilson and "The Rock" (Dwayne Johnson) earned $89 million. Ellen DeGeneres earned $81 million. Rihanna earned $62 million. Bradley Cooper earned $57 million. Ariana Grande earned $48 million.[1] (Not too long ago, Daniel Radcliffe earned $17 million—Blimey, Harry!) Not quite as glamorous perhaps, but not too shabby either, Equilar reported that the 50 highest-paid HR executives had an average annual compensation package of $4.3 million, up from $3.6 million the year before. The highest-paid HR executive was Deirde O'Brien of Apple at more than $19 million. [2] (We have not been able to verify whether she used our compensation book when she was in college and during her career, or if she feels what she learned from our book was the key to her success. However, we suspect this must have been the case.)

External competitiveness is the term we use to describe the "how *much* to pay" and "*how* to pay" questions. It is the next strategic decision in the total pay model, as shown in **Exhibit III.2**. Two aspects of pay translate external competitiveness into practice: (1) how much to pay relative to competitors—whether to pay more than competitors, to match what they pay, or to pay less—and (2) what mix of base, bonus, stock options, and benefits to pay relative to the pay mix of competitors. In a sense, "what forms" to pay (base, bonus, benefits) are the pieces of the pie. "How much" is the size of the pie. External competitiveness includes both questions.

EXHIBIT III.2 The Pay Model

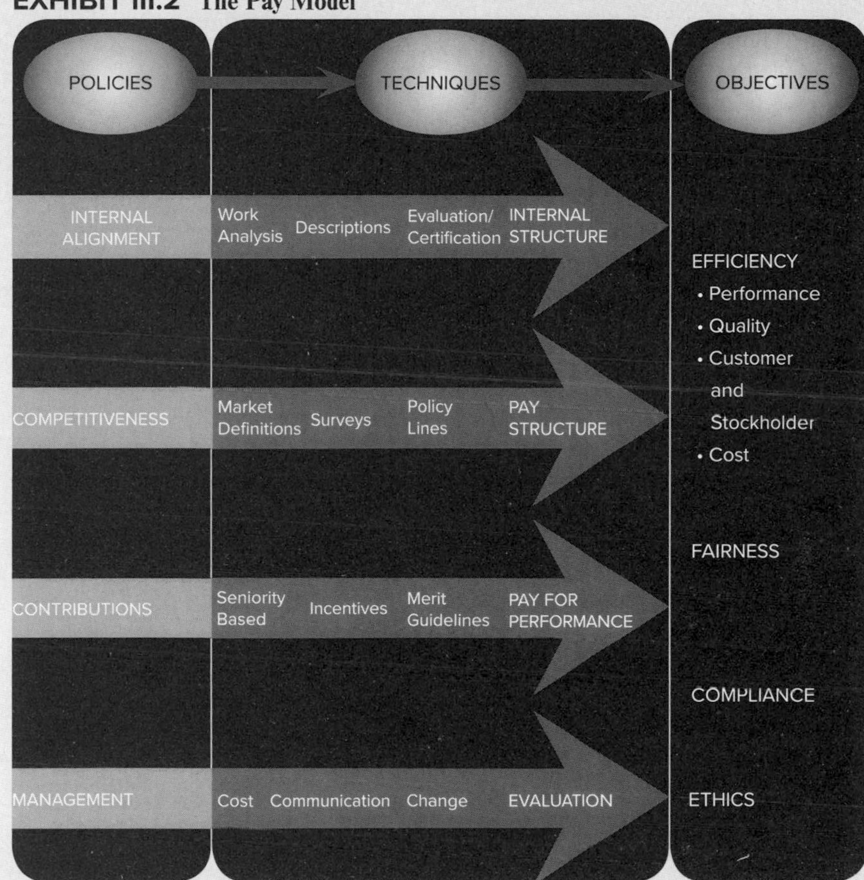

As we shall see in the next two chapters, a variety of answers exist. **Chapter 7** discusses choosing the external competitiveness policy, the impact of that choice, and related theories and research. **Chapter 8** has two parts: First, it discusses how to translate competitiveness policy into pay level and forms. Second, it discusses how to integrate information on pay levels and forms with the internal structure from **Part One**.

Chapter **SEVEN**
Defining Competitiveness

Chapter Outline

January is always a good month for travel agents in Ithaca, New York. In addition to the permanent population eager to flee Ithaca's leaden skies, graduating students from Ithaca's two colleges are traveling to job interviews with employers across the country–at company expense, full fare, no Saturday-night stayovers required. When they return from these trips, students compare notes and find that even for people receiving the same degree in the same field from the same college, the offers vary from company to company. What explains the differences? Location has an effect: Firms in San Francisco and New York City make higher offers. The kind of work also has an effect: In HR, for example, jobs in employment pay a little less than jobs in compensation. (Now aren't you glad you didn't drop this course?) And the industry to which the different firms belong has an effect: Pharmaceuticals, brokerage houses, and petroleum firms tend to offer more than consumer products, insurance, and heavy-manufacturing firms.[3]

Students would like to attribute these differences to themselves: differences in grades, courses taken, interviewing skills, and so on. But the same company makes the identical offer to most of its candidates at the school. So it is hard to make the case that an individual's qualifications totally explain the offers. Why would companies extend identical offers to most candidates? And why would different companies extend different offers? This chapter discusses these choices and what difference they make for the organization.

Pay levels at firms are not completely static. They also can adjust over time to changing market conditions and/or business strategies. The unemployment rate has dropped significantly in recent years, making for increased competition among retailers to hire and retain hourly workers. As a result, Amazon, Gap, Walmart, and Target all raised their lowest wage rate recently.[4]

Health insurance company Aetna, Inc. also announced a plan to increase pay at its lowest levels, by as much as one-third for some of those workers. A Deutsche Bank economist explained this increase as being due to the tightening of the labor market: "We are getting to the stage where companies can no longer find the right workers." However, Aetna's chief executive officer also cited a strategic rationale: "We're preparing our company for a future where we're going to have a much more consumer-oriented business" and for that reason Aetna wants to have "a better and more informed work force."[5]

The sheer number of economic theories related to compensation can make this chapter heavy going. Another difficulty is that the reality of pay decisions doesn't necessarily match the theories. The key to this chapter is to always ask: So what? How will this information help me?

COMPENSATION STRATEGY: EXTERNAL COMPETITIVENESS

In **Part II**, Internal Alignment, we looked at comparisons *inside* the organization. In **external competitiveness,** our second pay policy, we look at comparisons *outside* the organization–comparisons with other employers that hire people with the same skills. A major strategic decision is whether to mirror what competitors are paying or to design a pay package that may differ from those of competitors but better fits the business strategy.

External competitiveness is expressed in practice by (1) setting a **pay level** that is above, below, or equal to that of competitors; and (2) determining the **pay mix** relative to those of competitors.

External competitiveness refers to the pay relationships among organizations—the organization's pay relative to its competitors.

Pay level refers to the *average* of the array of rates paid by an employer:

(base + bonuses + benefits + value of stock holdings)/number of employees

Pay mix refers to the various types of payments, or pay forms, that make up total compensation.

Both pay-level and pay-mix decisions focus on two objectives: (1) control costs and increase revenues and (2) attract and retain employees.

Control Costs and Increase Revenues

Pay-level decisions have a significant impact on expenses. Other things being equal, the higher the pay level, the higher the labor costs:

Labor costs = (pay level) times (number of employees)

Furthermore, the higher the pay level relative to what competitors pay, the greater the relative costs to provide similar products or services. So you might think that all organizations would pay the same job the same rate. However, as we saw in the opening to **Part III**, they do not. Why would Google pay more than IBM for software engineers? What would any company pay above whatever minimum amount is required to hire engineers or other employees?

Paying employees above market can be an effective or ineffective strategy. It all depends on what the organization gets in return and whether that return translates into revenues that exceed the cost of the strategy. Let's look at a few examples. **Exhibit 7.1** compares labor costs at the U.S. Big Three automakers with those at two Japanese automakers (Toyota, Honda) in the United States. It also compares what the companies get in return. As of 2007, U.S. automakers had higher labor costs, but lower reliability and lower road-test performance ratings, on average. GM and Chrysler (subsequently becoming part of Fiat Chrysler and now, part of Stellantis after merging with Peugot) subsequently went through bankruptcy. One might infer that the Big Three's pay-level strategy has not worked for it. (In **Chapter 1**, we also noted the huge drop in employment among U.S. producers like GM.) As part of the bankruptcy process and also as a result of government involvement, agreements were reached with the United Auto Workers to reduce labor costs to make them competitive with other producers. Indeed, there was no increase in hourly wage between 2007 and 2015. The Big Three have long preferred profit sharing and other forms of variable pay (e.g., bonuses/lump sum payments) to increasing their fixed labor costs. As **Exhibit 7.1** indicates, as of 2019, labor costs for Ford, GM, and Chrysler were significantly lower than previously. It was not only the modest increase in fixed costs (wages), but also the continued use of two-tier wages (which can also include lower benefits), under which it takes Tier 2 new hires 8 years to reach the (higher) Tier 1 wage. (See also the end of chapter **Your Turn: Two-Tier Wages**.) Additionally, the use of temporary workers (also with lower wages and benefits) is another strategy to keep labor costs lower. In the most recent contract, which runs through 2023, labor costs are expected to once again increase significantly, widening the labor cost disadvantage relative to other producers, such as Toyota and Honda. One reason is the increase in the Tier 1 wage. Another reason is the

EXHIBIT 7.1 Comparing Compensation Costs and Outcomes Across Automakers Over Time in the United States

	2007		through 2019 (negotiated 2015)		through 2023 (negotiated 2019)	
	Ford GM Chrysler	Toyota Honda	Ford GM Chrysler	Toyota Honda	Ford GM Chrysler	Toyota Honda
Labor Cost						
Average Hourly Total Compensation[a]	$73	$48	$56–$60	$50–$52	$66–$71	$54
Hourly Wages	$29	$15–$26		$23–$25		b
Hourly Wages (Tier 1)			$29.71		$32.32	
Hourly Wages (Tier 2)			$17–$28		$17–$32.32	
Labor cost per vehicle			$2,600–$2,700	$1,042	$3,100–$3,500	<$1,300[c]
Quality and Reliability/Dependability[d]						
Consumer Reports						
Road-Test Performance (higher is better)	59	77	74, 74, 85	67, 78	74, 75, 74	74, 74
Reliability (higher is better)[e]	43	77	3, 2, 3	5, 3	1, 3, 3	4, 3
J.D. Power Dependability (lower is better)[f]	143	114	152, 144, 211	127, 140	118, 119, 144	90, 127
Productivity						
Total Labor Hours per Vehicle[g]	32.2	31.2	*	*	*	*

Note: Chrysler merged with Fiat to become Fiat Chrysler and then merged with Group PSA (Peugot S.A.) to become Stellantis.

[a] Average hourly total compensation includes wages and benefits. For 2007, it also includes legacy costs for Ford, GM, and Chrysler: retiree health care and pension payments.

[b] Nonunion. Thus, no contractual wage for future years.

[c] This is an estimate.

[d] Ford uses (unweighted) average of Ford and Lincoln brands; GM uses (unweighted) average of Cadillac, Chevrolet, and GMC brands; Chrysler uses average of Chrysler, Dodge, and Jeep Brands; Toyota uses average of Lexus and Toyota brands; Honda uses average of Acura and Honda brands; All averages are unweighted by production volume.

[e] In 2018, switched to 1-to-5 rating (5 = best).

[f] J.D. Power Vehicle Dependability Study, problems per 100 vehicles (lower is better)

[g] Total labor hours per vehicle is hours for assembly, stamping, engine, and transmission. These data are no longer publicly available. Two-tier wages came into effect in 2007.

Sources: Michael Martinez. Detroit 3 labor costs to 'rise steadily' over next 4 years under new UAW contract. Automotive News, January 15, 2020. www.autonews.com. Charlsy Panzino. GM, Ford, Fiat Chrysler to see increased hourly labor costs through 2023. S&P Global Market Intelligence. www.spglobal.com. Original data from Center for Automotive Research. Hentry Payne. Honda Marysville: A non-union auto plant prospers. Detroit News, September 30, 2019. www.detroitnews.com. J.D. Power Vehicle Dependability Study 2018, 2021, www.jdpower.com; Oliver Wyman, The Harbour Report™, North America 2008, www.oliverwyman.com; Consumer Reports, April 2008, April 2018, April 2021; David Leonhardt, "$73 an Hour: Adding It Up," New York Times, December 10, 2008; Chris Woodyard, "VW Exec Knows of No Talks to Unionize Tennessee Plant," USA Today, August 1, 2011; Bernie Woodall, "For UAW Members, Two-Tier Wage Issue Is Personal," Reuters.com, June 2, 2015; Michael Martinez, "Ford: Labor Costs Up about 1.5% Yearly after UAW Deal," Detroit News, November 30, 2015; Brent Snavely, "Chrysler Has Lowest Per-Worker Labor Costs," Detroit Free Press, March 24, 2015; "GM Contract May Yield Flat Per-Vehicle Labor Costs even with Hourly Raises, Study Says," Automotive News, November 20, 2015; Phoebe Wall Howard, "Why Investors Like Detroit Automaker-UAW Profit-Sharing," Detroit Free Press, February 9, 2018.

fact that under the new contract, current (but not future) Tier 2 workers can advance to the higher Tier 1 wage in 4 years (rather than the previous 8 years). It would be easy to criticize the Big Three for agreeing on new contracts having much higher labor costs. However, it must be kept in mind that the United Auto Workers (UAW) union had something to say about this. The UAW went on strike at GM in 2019 during contract negotiation. The strike lasted 29 days, involved 46,000 workers, and resulted in 1.33 million lost work days. It was the longest strike in the auto industry in 50 years by the UAW. One estimate is that the strike cost GM as much as $4 billion in lost profit (earnings before interest and taxes).[6] What about Ford and Chrysler, where no strike took place? Why are their labor costs increasing at essentially the same rate as at GM? The UAW chooses a strike target (GM in this case) it deems has the highest ability to pay. Once a contract is reached there, it is used as a "pattern" (called pattern bargaining) at the other two unionized producers. If Ford or Chrysler decline to agree on the same contract negotiated with GM, they can expect a (costly) strike.

Labor cost can be evaluated in combination with product quality (here, road test performance and reliability of the cars). According to **Exhibit 7.1**, the Big Three have made major strides on product quality. However, even if the Big Three match Toyota and Honda here, they seem destined to remain at a disadvantage due to their higher labor costs. Ordinarily, higher labor costs are sustainable only when the product is better or else when the product better matches consumer preferences. However, for the time being, the American consumer's love for trucks and SUVs, which have larger profit margins than cars for the Big Three, has been a key to recent strong profits.

Driving a hard bargain in contract negotiation is not the only way to control labor costs. Having control over where production is located is critical. In a global competitive market, automakers have a choice as to where to locate production to best achieve cost, productivity, and quality goals. Since 2005, automobile production in the United States has declined by 9 percent. It has increased by 138 percent in Mexico.[7] Labor costs are substantially lower in Mexico than in the United States (Volkswagen estimates they are 50 percent lower than in Tennessee, which are already lower than in the northern states and lower than in Germany, where Volkswagen is headquartered). Mexico also has free-trade agreements that give it duty-free access to markets that represent about 60 percent of the world's economic output. (One thing General Motors did achieve in its most recent contract with the UAW was the right to close some plants in the United States.) Automakers seem to feel they are able to also achieve vehicle production efficiency and quality goals there as well.[8] As the decline in U.S. production noted above would suggest, few new plants have opened in the United States and all of those have been in southern states, where labor costs are lower and union strength is likewise lower. Indeed, no foreign-owned automobile plants (BMW, Honda, Hyundai-Kia, Mercedes, Nissan, Subaru, Toyota, Volkswagen, Volvo) are unionized. Since 2005, a new plant was announced in 2008 (opened in 2011) by Volkswagen in Chattanooga, Tennessee. Chinese-owned Volvo opened its plant in 2018 in South Carolina, the state with the lowest unionization rate. Most recently, Mazda and Toyota, in a joint-venture, are opening a new plant in Alabama.

Oops, sorry, but there is actually one more plant, and one of some note, that opened since 2005. More specifically, an existing (nonunion) plant outside of the South (in Fremont, California) changed ownership in 2010. One can perhaps be forgiven for overlooking it for a while. It produced less than 3,000 vehicles per year initially, not very impressive compared to several U.S. plants producing over 300,000 vehicles per year at the time. Now, it is harder to ignore as its Fremont plant production is now around 500,000 per year and, at $800 billion, it is also now one of the 10 most valuable companies in the world and its value dwarfs that of any other automobile company. Its name is Tesla. And, it appears that its success is causing the rest of the industry to move toward making electric cars. The implications for employment and compensation in the industry are likely substantial.

Let us now turn from automobiles to the airline industry, an industry that, together with its employees, has faced tremendous challenges during the pandemic. We will trace some developments over the longer term. As part of this, we will use 2019 rather than the more recent 2020 data, given the (hoped) uniqueness of 2020 (when revenues were down 60% from 2019 for Southwest, for example). **Exhibit 7.2** traces the history of two "legacy" airlines, USAir and American, and relative newcomer, Southwest. As in the automobile industry, we can look at what employees cost and what the airlines receive in return that would help drive revenues. American was the last major airline to go through bankruptcy (and Southwest never did), entering in 2011 and exiting in late 2013, which included a proposed merger (subsequently executed) with USAir. Note that by 2014 the new combined company actually had lower labor costs and lower operating costs per available seat mile (ASM) than Southwest. However, with consolidation and a healthier profit outlook for the airline industry overall, American (and others) has faced increasing pressures from employees to increase wages and salaries and thus labor costs. In 2000, USAir and American trailed Southwest in terms of efficiency, with overall operating costs of 14 cents per ASM, almost double that of Southwest at 7.7 cents per ASM. Likewise, USAir had labor costs per ASM roughly double (5.5 cents versus 2.8 cents) that of Southwest Airlines. American, while not having labor costs

EXHIBIT 7.2 **Revenues, Capacity, Operating Costs, and Labor Costs of USAir, American, and Southwest Airlines**

	2000 American	2000 USAir	2000 Southwest	2014 American (including former USAir)	2014 Southwest	2019 American (including former USAir)	2019 Southwest
Revenues (in millions)	$19,703	$9,269	$5,650	$ 30,802	$18,605	$45,768	$22,428
Operating Costs (in millions)	$18,322	$9,322	$4,628	$ 31,885	$16,380	$42,703	$19,471
Labor Costs (in millions)	$ 6,783	$3,637	$ 1,683	$ 8,508	$ 5,434	$12,609	$8,293
Employees	93,951	43,467	29,274	94,400	46,278	133,700	60,767
Available Seat Miles (ASM) (in millions)	167,286	59,910	59,910	237,522	131,004	285,088	157,254
Labor Costs/ Revenues	34.4%	39.2%	29.8%	27.6%	29.2%	27.5%	37.0%
Labor Costs/ Employees	$ 0.072	$0.084	$0.058	$ 0.090	$ 0.117	$0.094	$0.136
Operating Costs/ASM	$ 0.110	$ 0.156	$0.077	$ 0.134	$ 0.166	$0.150	$0.124
Labor Costs/ASM	$ 0.041	$0.061	$0.028	$ 0.036	$ 0.055	$0.044	$0.053
Retiree Pension and Health Care Liabilities				Not reduced		Not reduced	

	2000 American	2000 USAir	2000 Southwest	2014 American (including former USAir)	2014 Southwest	2019 American (including former USAir)	2019 Southwest
Operating Income (in millions)	$ 1,381	($53)	$ 1,021	($1,083)	$2,225	$3,065	$2,957
Customer Complaints (per 100,000)	3.5	2.6	0.5	2.1	0.5	1.6	0.3
American Customer Satisfaction Index®	63	62	70	66	78	73	79

Sources: Financial data come from company 10-K reports, available at www.sec.gov. Annual data on customer complaints are from the U.S. Department of Transportation and appear each year in the February issue of *American Travel Consumer Reports*, available at http://www.dot.gov/airconsumer/air-travel-consumer-reports. American Customer Satisfaction Index® is available at http://www.theacsi.org/.

Notes: For 2014, only mainline data were used for American because labor cost was not reported for combined regional and mainline operations. For 2000, the number of employees at American came from U.S. Bureau of Transportation Statistics. In 10-K reports, labor cost data may appear as salaries, wages, and benefits. USAir filed for bankruptcy in 2002. American filed for bankruptcy in 2011. The two airlines officially announced their merger in December 2013. USAir, during its bankruptcy, was able to reduce retiree-related costs. American was less able to do so, apparently because courts have judged the airline is able to compete without reducing such costs. For 2014 (and 2019), American financial data are post-merger, thus including data on both the former American Airlines and the former USAir.

as high as those of USAir, still had a significantly higher cost structure than Southwest. USAir and other so-called legacy airlines realized that they needed to move their costs lower to compete with Southwest. (Question: What would labor costs and operating income be at American and USAir in 2000 if their labor cost/ASM had been the same as Southwest's?) By 2008 (not shown), both USAir and American had made considerable progress, at least with respect to labor costs, basically drawing even with Southwest on labor cost per ASM. By 2014, the new merged company had lower labor costs than Southwest (though only Southwest had positive operating income). Part of USAir's success in reducing labor costs was due to its having gone through bankruptcy in 2002 (the first major airline to do so, subsequently followed by all others) and using that as an opportunity to reduce pay and benefits costs. However, American (including the former USAir) remains at a disadvantage with respect to the passenger experience. In all years, at least until recently (e.g., see 2017), Southwest has had many fewer customer complaints and higher customer satisfaction. If anything, Southwest's advantage in customer satisfaction seemed to have increased between 2000 and 2014 as USAir and American cut costs. By 2019, however, Southwest's advantage on the customer experience had narrowed considerably. Even though Southwest continued to improve, American improved much more. As such, although Southwest may continue to be a somewhat better bet going forward due to its continued advantage in terms of the customer experience, that advantage of late has eroded. It will be interesting to see if American can continue to improve on this metric. In any case, the history of Southwest suggests that it is not necessarily how much it pays that is the key. Rather, it can be argued that it is its ability to pay competitively and get a great deal in return from its employees. Southwest has been widely studied for its total compensation strategy, which includes employee profit sharing and stock, but also having fun at work and strong employee relations. Southwest is unique in the airline industry both for its 40+ consecutive years (until the pandemic) of profitability (compare, for example, USAir's consecutive years of losses, from 1989 to 1999) and Southwest was the lone major airline not to go through bankruptcy. However, there is growing concern that Southwest's labor costs are or may become a problem. It will be interesting to see what the future brings in the airline industry for companies using different compensation and human resource approaches. Although both were profitable in 2019, the market has been more positive on Southwest, which had stock price appreciation of about 9 percent over the 3-year period ending year-end 2019, versus a 38 percent decline in stock price over the same period at American.

Attract and Retain the Right Employees

One company may pay more because it believes its higher-paid engineers are more productive than those at other companies. Their engineers may be better trained; maybe they are more innovative in dreaming up new applications. Maybe they are less likely to quit, thus saving the company recruiting and training costs. Another company may pay less because it is differentiating itself on nonfinancial returns–more challenging and interesting projects, possibility of international assignments, superior training, more rapid promotions, or even greater job security. Different employers set different pay levels; that is, they deliberately choose to pay above or below what others are paying for the same work. That is why there is no single "going rate" in the labor market for a specific job.[9]

Not only do the rates paid for similar jobs vary among employers, but a single company may set a different pay level for different job families.[10] The company in **Exhibit 7.3** illustrates the point. The *top chart* shows that this particular company pays about 2 percent above the market for its entry-level engineer. (Market is set at zero in the exhibit.) However, it pays 13 percent above the market for most of its marketing jobs and over 25 percent above the market for marketing managers. Office personnel and technicians are paid below the market. So this company uses very different pay levels for different job families.

These data are based on comparisons of **base wage.** When we look at **total compensation** in the bottom of the exhibit, a different pattern emerges. The company still has a different pay level for different job families. But when bonuses, stock options, and benefits are included, only marketing managers remain above the market. Every other job family is now substantially below the market. Engineering managers take the deepest plunge, from only 2 percent below the market to over 30 percent below.[11]

The exhibit, based on actual company data, makes two points. First, companies often set different pay-level policies for different job families. Second, how a company compares to the market depends on what competitors it compares to and what pay forms are included. It is not clear whether the company in the exhibit deliberately chose to emphasize marketing managers and de-emphasize engineering in its pay plan or if it is paying the price for not hiring one of you readers to design its plan.[12] Either way, the point is, people love to talk about "the market rate" as if a single rate exists for any job, with the implication that organizations are constrained to pay that same rate to their own employees in that job. Nevertheless, **Exhibit 7.4** instead shows that organizations can and do vary in how closely they match the "going rate." There is no single "going mix" of pay forms, either. **Exhibit 7.4** compares the pay mix for the same job (software marketing manager) at two companies in the same geographic area. Both companies offer about the same total compensation. Yet the percentages allocated to base, bonuses, benefits, and options are very different.

WHAT SHAPES EXTERNAL COMPETITIVENESS?

Exhibit 7.5 shows the factors that affect decisions on pay level and pay mix. The factors include (1) competition in the *labor market* for people with various skills; (2) competition in the *product and service markets,* which affects the financial condition of the organization; and (3) characteristics unique to each organization and its employees, such as its business strategy, technology, and the productivity and experience of its workforce. These factors act in concert to influence pay-level and pay-mix decisions.

EXHIBIT 7.3 A Single Company's Market Position May Differ Depending on Whether Comparing Base Pay or Total Compensation

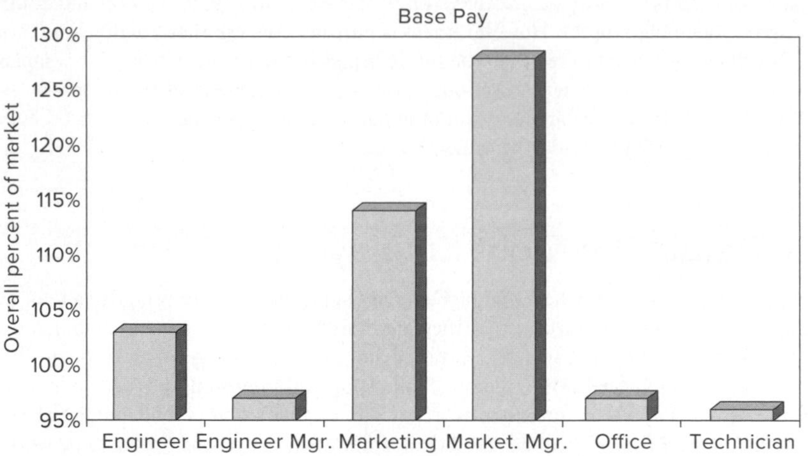

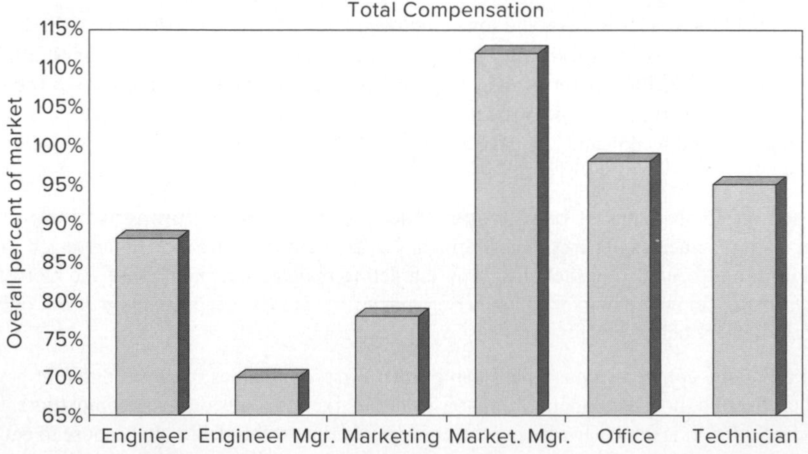

EXHIBIT 7.4 **Two Companies: Same Total Compensation, Different Mixes**

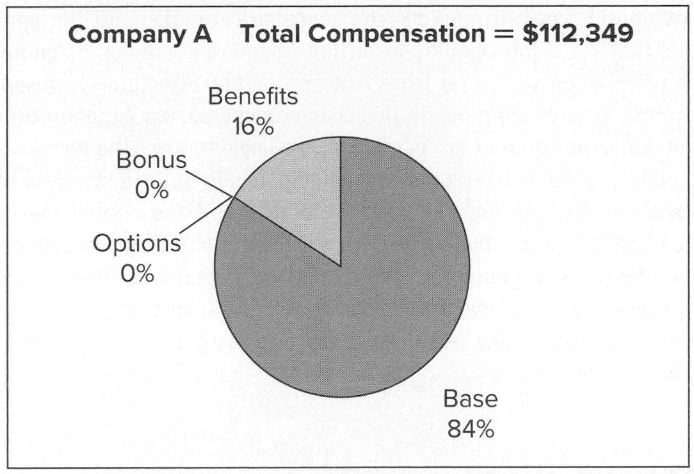

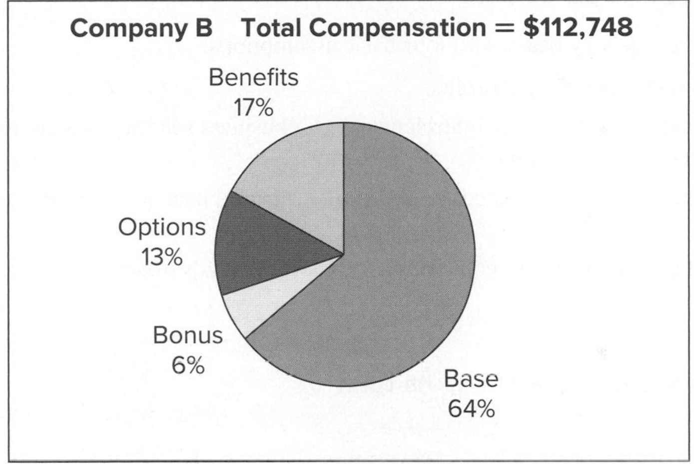

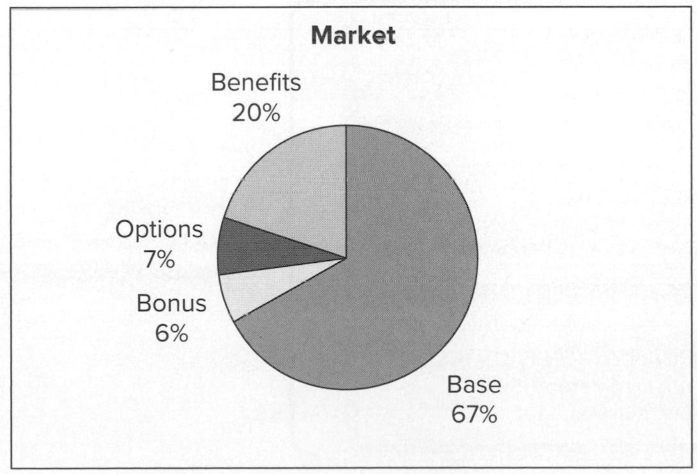

LABOR MARKET FACTORS

Economists describe two basic types of markets: the **quoted-price market** and the **bourse.** Stores that label each item's price or ads that list a job opening's starting wage are examples of quoted-price markets. You cannot name your own price when you order from Amazon, but at Priceline supposedly you can. However, Priceline does not guarantee that your price will be accepted, whereas an Amazon order arrives in a matter of days. In contrast with Amazon's quoted price, eBay allows haggling over the terms and conditions until an agreement is reached; eBay is a *bourse.* Graduating students usually find themselves in a quoted-labor market, though some negotiation does occur.[13] In both the bourse and the quoted market, employers are the buyers and the potential employees are the sellers. If the inducements (total compensation) offered by the employer and the skills offered by the employee are mutually acceptable, a deal is struck. It may be formal contracts negotiated by unions, professional athletes, and executives, or it may be a brief letter or maybe only the implied understanding of a handshake. All this activity makes up the labor market; the result is that people and jobs match up at specified pay rates.

How Labor Markets Work

Theories of labor markets usually begin with four basic assumptions:

1. Employers always seek to maximize profits.
2. People are all the same and therefore interchangeable; a business school graduate is a business school graduate is a business school graduate.
3. The pay rates reflect all costs associated with employment (e.g., base wage, bonuses, holidays, benefits, even training).
4. The markets faced by employers are competitive, so there is no advantage for a single employer to pay above or below the market rate.

EXHIBIT 7.5 **What Shapes External Competitiveness?**

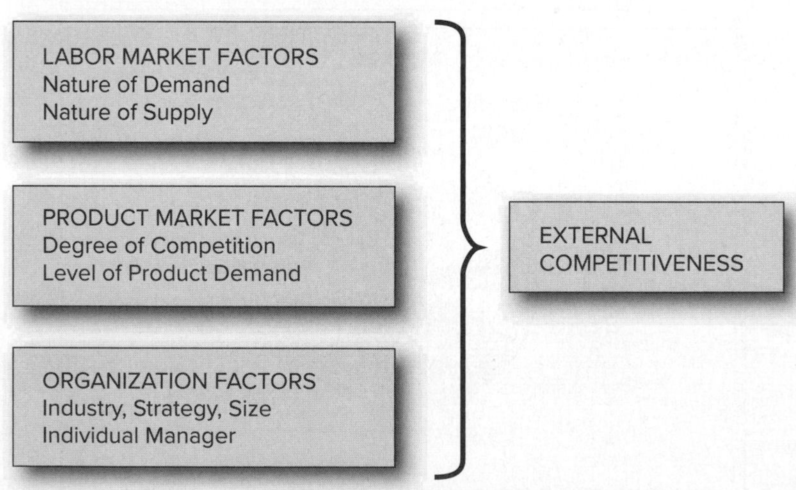

Although these assumptions oversimplify reality, they provide a framework for understanding labor markets.

Organizations often claim to be "market-driven"; that is, they pay competitively with the market or even are market leaders. Understanding how markets work requires analysis of the demand and supply of labor. The demand side focuses on the actions of the employers: how many new hires they seek and what they are willing and able to pay new employees. The supply side looks at potential employees: their qualifications and the pay they are willing to accept in exchange for their services.

Exhibit 7.6 shows a simple illustration of demand and supply for business school graduates. The vertical axis represents pay rates from $40,000 to $80,000 a year. The horizontal axis depicts the number of business school graduates in the market. The line labeled "Demand" is the sum of *all* employers' hiring preferences for business graduates at various pay levels. At $80,000, only a small number of business graduates will be hired, because only a few firms are able to afford them. At $40,000, companies can afford to hire a large number of business graduates. However, as we look at the line labeled "Supply," we see that there aren't enough business graduates willing to be hired at $40,000. In fact, only a small number are willing to work for $40,000. As pay rates rise, more graduates become interested in working, so the labor supply line slopes upward. *The market rate is where the lines for labor demand and labor supply cross.* In this illustration, the interaction among all employers and all business graduates determines the $60,000 market rate. Because any single employer can hire all the business graduates it wants at $60,000 and all business graduates are of equal quality (i.e., assumption 2 above), there is no reason to pay any wage other than $60,000.

Labor Demand

If $60,000 is the market-determined rate for business graduates, how many business graduates will a specific employer hire? The answer requires an analysis of **labor demand.** In the short term, an employer cannot change any other factor of production (i.e., technology, capital, or natural resources). Thus, its level of production can change only if it changes the level of human resources. Under such conditions, a single employer's demand for labor coincides with the **marginal product of labor.**

EXHIBIT 7.6 **Supply and Demand for Business School Graduates in the Short Run**

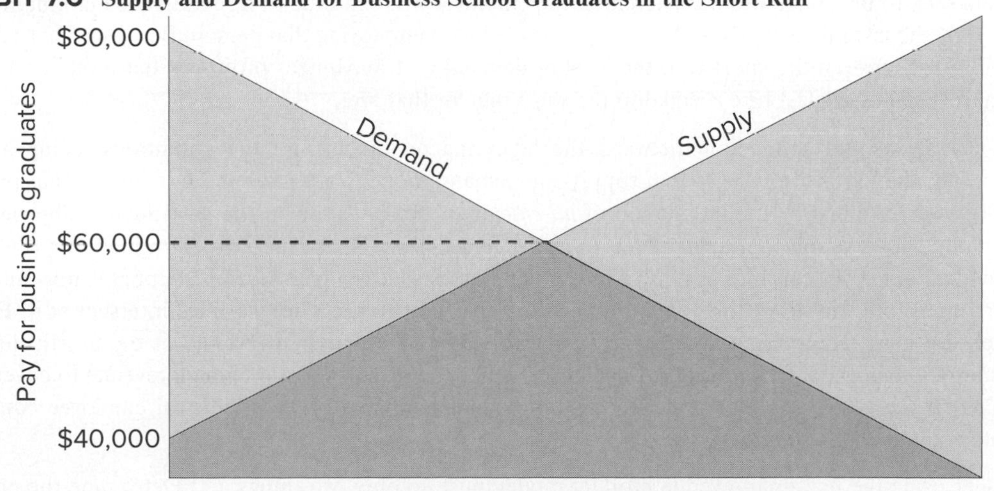

The **marginal product of labor** is the additional output associated with the employment of one additional person, with other production factors held constant.

The **marginal revenue of labor** is the additional revenue generated when the firm employs one additional person, with other production factors held constant.

Marginal Product

Assume that two business graduates form a consulting firm that provides services to 10 clients. The firm hires a third person, who brings in four more clients. The marginal product (the change in output associated with the additional unit of labor) of the third person is four clients. But adding a fourth employee generates only two new clients. This diminishing marginal productivity results from the fact that each additional employee has a progressively smaller share of the other factors of production with which to work. In the short term, these other factors of production (e.g., office space, number of computers, telephone lines, hours of clerical support) are fixed. Until these other factors are changed, each new hire produces less than the previous hire. The amount each hire produces is the marginal product.

Marginal Revenue

Now let's look at marginal revenue. Marginal revenue is the money generated by the sale of the marginal product, the additional output from the employment of one additional person. In the case of the consulting firm, it's the revenues generated by each additional hire. If each new client generates $20,000 in revenue, then if the third employee has four clients, that will generate $80,000 in additional revenue. But perhaps the fourth employee will only be able to bring three clients, or $60,000, in additional revenue. This $60,000 is exactly the wage that must be paid that fourth employee. So the consulting firm will break even on the fourth person but will lose money if it hires beyond that. Recall that our first labor market theory assumption is that employers seek to maximize profits. Therefore, the employer will continue to hire until the marginal revenue generated by the last hire is equal to the costs associated with employing that person. Because other potential costs will not change in the short run, the level of demand that maximizes profits is that level at which the marginal revenue of the last hire is equal to the wage rate for that hire.

Exhibit 7.7 shows the connection between the labor market model and the conditions facing a single employer. On the left is the *market level* supply-and-demand model from **Exhibit 7.6**, showing that pay level ($60,000) is determined by the interaction of *all employers'* demands for business graduates. The right side of the exhibit shows supply and demand for an *individual employer.* At the market-determined rate ($60,000), the individual employer can hire as many business graduates as it wants. Therefore, supply is now an unlimited horizontal line. However, the demand line still slopes downward. The two lines intersect at 4. For this employer, the market-determined wage rate ($60,000) equals the marginal revenue of the fourth hire. The marginal revenue of the fifth graduate is less than $60,000 and so will not add enough revenue to cover costs. The point on the graph at which the incremental income generated by an additional employee equals the wage rate is the *marginal revenue product*.

A manager using the marginal revenue product model must do only two things: (1) Determine the pay level set by market forces, and (2) determine the marginal revenue generated by each new hire. This will tell the manager how many people to hire. Simple? Of course not.

The model provides a valuable analytical framework, but it oversimplifies the real world. In most organizations, it is almost impossible to quantify the goods or services produced by an individual employee, since most production is through joint efforts of employees with a variety of skills. Even in settings that use piece rates (i.e., 50 cents for each soccer ball sewn), it is hard to separate the contributions of labor from those of other resources (efficient machines, sturdy materials, good lighting, and ventilation).

So neither the marginal product nor the marginal revenue is directly measurable. However, managers do need some measure that reflects value. In **Chapter 5** and **Chapter 6**, we discussed compensable factors, skill blocks, and competencies. If compensable factors define what organizations value, then job evaluation reflects the job's contribution and may be viewed as a proxy for marginal revenue product. However, compensable factors are usually defined as input (skills required, problem solving required, responsibilities) rather than value of output. This same logic applies to skills and competencies.

Labor Supply

Now let us look more closely at the assumptions about the behavior of potential employees. This model assumes that many people are seeking jobs, that they possess accurate information about all job openings, and that no barriers to mobility (discrimination, licensing provisions, or union membership requirements) exist.[14]

Just as with the analysis of labor demand, these assumptions greatly simplify the real world. As the assumptions change, so does the supply. For example, the upward-sloping supply assumes that as pay increases, more people are willing to take a job. But if unemployment rates are low, offers of higher pay may not increase supply—everyone who wants to work is already working. If competitors quickly match a higher offer, the employer may face a higher pay level but no increase in supply. For example, when Giant Foods raised its hourly pay $1 above the minimum wage in the Chicago area, Wendy's and Burger King quickly followed suit. The result was that the supermarket was paying more for the employees it already had but was still shorthanded. Although some firms find lowering the job requirements and hiring less-skilled workers a better choice than raising wages, this choice incurs increased training costs (which are included in assumption 3).

MODIFICATIONS TO THE DEMAND SIDE

The story is told of the economics professor and the student who were strolling through campus together. "Look," the student cried, "there's a $100 bill on the path!"

EXHIBIT 7.7 Supply and Demand at the Market and Individual Employer Level

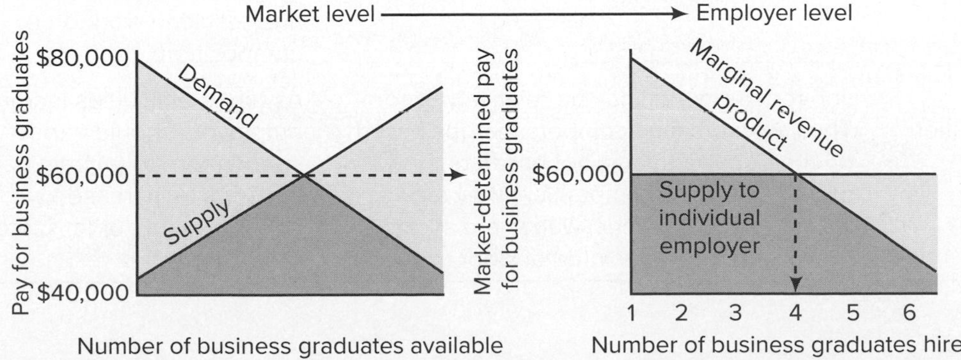

"No, that cannot be," the wiser head replied. "If there were a $100 bill, someone would have picked it up."

The point of the story is that economic theories must frequently be revised to account for reality. When we change our focus from *all* the employers in an economy to a *particular* employer, models must be modified to help us understand what actually occurs. A particularly troublesome issue for economists is why an employer would pay more than what theory states is the market-determined rate. **Exhibit 7.8** looks at three modifications to the model that address this phenomenon: compensating differentials, efficiency wage, and signaling.

Compensating Differentials

More than 200 years ago, Adam Smith argued that individuals consider the "whole of the advantages and disadvantages of different employments" and make decisions based on the alternative with the greatest "net advantage."[15] If a job has negative characteristics–for example, if the necessary training is very expensive (medical school), job security is tenuous (stockbrokers, CEOs), working conditions are disagreeable (highway construction), or chances of success are low (professional sports)–then employers must offer higher wages to compensate for these negative features.

EXHIBIT 7.8 Labor Demand Theories and Implications

Theory	Prediction	So What?
Compensating Differentials	Work with negative characteristics requires higher pay to attract/retain workers.	Job evaluation and compensable factors must capture these negative characteristics.
Efficiency Wage	Above-market wage/pay level may improve efficiency by attracting higher-ability workers (sorting effect, **Chapter 1**) and by discouraging shirking (incentive effect, **Chapter 1**) because of risk of losing high-wage job. A high-wage policy may substitute for intense monitoring (e.g., use of many supervisors).	The payoff to a higher wage depends on the employee selection system's ability to validly identify the best workers. See **Appendix 7-A** on utility. An efficiency wage policy may require the use of fewer supervisors.
Sorting & Signaling	Pay policies signal to applicants the attributes that fit the organization. Applicants may signal their attributes (e.g., ability) by the investments they have made in themselves.	How much, but also how (e.g., pay mix and emphasis on performance) will influence attraction-selection-attrition and resulting workforce composition.
Job Competition	Job requirements may be relatively fixed. Thus, workers may compete for jobs based on their qualifications, not based on how low of a wage (wage competition) they are willing to accept. Thus, wages are sticky downward. See also internal labor markets.	As hiring difficulties increase, employers should expect to spend more to (a) train new hires, (b) to increase compensation, or (c) search/recruit more.

Such **compensating differentials** explain the presence of various pay rates in the market. Although the notion is appealing, it is hard to document, due to the difficulties in measuring and controlling all the factors that go into a net-advantage calculation.

Efficiency Wage

According to **efficiency wage theory,** high wages may increase efficiency and actually lower labor costs if they:

1. Attract higher-quality applicants.
2. Lower turnover.
3. Increase worker effort.
4. Reduce **shirking behavior** (the term economists use to mean "screwing around"). The higher the wage, the less likely it is that an employee would be able to find another job that pays as well. Also, the risk of losing one's high-paying job depends on how likely it is that the employee can be replaced. One indicator is the unemployment rate. (Karl Marx referred to the unemployed as a "reserve army" that employers can use to replace current workers.) Thus, efficiency wage predicts that high effort will be most likely, and shirking less likely, to the degree that the wage premium is high and the unemployment rate is high.
5. Reduce the need to supervise employees (academics say "monitoring").

So, basically, efficiency increases by hiring better employees or motivating present employees to work smarter or harder. The underlying assumption is that pay level determines effort–again, an appealing notion that is difficult to document. In **Appendix 7-A**, we show how **utility theory** can help compare the costs and benefits of different pay-level policies. We will also discuss how business strategy plays a role in pay-level choice.

There is some research on efficiency wage theory, however.[16] One study looked at shirking behavior by examining employee discipline and wages in several auto plants. Higher wages were associated with lower shirking, measured as the number of disciplinary layoffs. However, the authors of the study were unable to say whether shirking was reduced enough to offset (cover) the costs of the higher wage.[17]

Research shows that higher wages actually do attract more qualified applicants.[18] But higher wages also attract more unqualified applicants. Few companies evaluate their recruiting programs well enough to show whether they do in fact choose only superior applicants from the larger pool. So an above-market wage does not guarantee a more productive workforce.

Does an above-market wage allow an organization to operate with fewer supervisors? Some research evidence says yes. A study of hospitals found that those that paid high wages to staff nurses employed fewer nurse supervisors.[19] The researchers did not speculate on whether the higher wages attracted better nurses or caused average nurses to work harder. They also did not say whether the hospital was able to reduce its overall nursing costs.

An organization's **ability to pay** is related to the efficiency wage model. Firms with higher profits than competitors are able to share this success with employees. This could be done via "leading" competitors' pay levels and/or via bonuses that vary with profitability. Academics see this as "rent sharing." **Rent** is a return (profits) received from activities that are in excess of the minimum (pay level) needed to attract people to those activities.[20] Pay levels at more profitable firms were about 15 percent greater than at firms with lower profits, according to one study.[21]

Notice that the discussion so far has dealt with pay level only. What forms to pay–the mix question–is virtually ignored in these theories. The simplifying assumption is that the pay level includes the value of different forms. Abstracted away is the distinct possibility that some people find more performance-based bonus pay or better health insurance more attractive. Signaling theory is more useful in understanding pay mix.

Sorting and Signaling

Sorting, introduced in **Chapter 1**, is the effect that pay strategy has on the composition of the workforce–who is attracted and who is retained. There, we saw in a study by Lazear that introduction of an incentive plan to replace a flat hourly pay plan resulted in a 44 percent increase in productivity. Half of that was what we call an incentive effect: workers who were at the company under the flat hourly pay plan were 22 percent more productive under the incentive plan. However, the other one-half of the 44 percent increase resulted from a 22 percent increase in productivity due to less productive workers leaving (because they would not benefit or even lose money) with the introduction of the incentive and being replaced by productive workers (who would have higher earnings).

Signaling is a closely related process that underlies the sorting effect. Signaling theory holds that employers deliberately design pay levels and pay mix as part of a strategy that signals to both prospective and current employees the kinds of behaviors that are sought.[22] Viewed through a marketing lens, how much to pay and what forms of pay are offered establishes a "brand" that sends a message to prospective employees, just like brands of competing products and services.[23]

A policy of paying below the market for **base pay** yet offering generous bonuses or training opportunities sends a different signal, and presumably attracts different people, than does a policy of matching the market wage and offering no performance-based pay. An employer that combines lower base pay with high bonuses may be signaling that it wants employees who are risk takers. Its pay policy helps communicate expectations.

Check out **Exhibit 7.4** again. It shows a breakdown of forms of pay for two competitors, as well as their relationship to the market. The pay mix at company A emphasizes base pay (84%) more than does the mix at company B (64%) or the market average (67%). Company A pays no bonuses, no stock options, and somewhat lighter benefits. Company B's mix is closer to the market average. What is the message that A's pay mix is communicating? Which message appeals to you, A's or B's? The astute reader will note that at A, you can earn the $112,349 with very little apparent link to performance. Maybe just showing up is enough. At B, earning the $112,748 requires performance bonuses and stock options as well. Riskier? Why would anyone work at B without extra returns for the riskier pay? Without a premium, how will B attract and retain employees? Perhaps with more interesting projects, flexible schedules, or more opportunity for promotions–all part of B's "total pay brand."

A study of college students approaching graduation found that both pay level and pay mix affected their job decisions.[24] Students wanted jobs that offered high pay, but they also showed a preference for individual-based (rather than team-based) pay, fixed (rather than variable) pay, job-based (rather than skill-based) pay, and flexible benefits. Job seekers were rated on various personal dimensions–materialism, confidence in their abilities, and risk aversion–that were related to pay preferences. Pay level was most important to materialists and less important to those who were risk-averse. So applicants appear to select among job opportunities based on the perceived match between their personal dispositions and the nature of the organization, as signaled by the pay system. Both pay level and pay mix send a signal, which results in sorting effects (i.e., who joins and who stays with the organization).

Signaling works on the supply side of the model, too, as suppliers of labor signal to potential employers. People who are better trained, have higher grades in relevant courses, and/or have related work experience signal to prospective employers that they are likely to be better performers. (Presumably they signal with the same degree of accuracy as employers.) So both characteristics of the applicants (degrees, grades, experience) and organization decisions about pay level (lead, match, lag) and mix (higher bonuses, benefit choices) act as signals that help communicate.

MODIFICATIONS TO THE SUPPLY SIDE (ONLY TWO MORE THEORIES TO GO)

Two theories shown in **Exhibit 7.9**–**reservation wage** and **human capital**–focus on understanding employee behavior: the supply side of the model.

Reservation Wage

At times, it seems that economists must have quite a sense of humor. How else do we explain why they would choose to describe pay using the term "noncompensatory"? What they mean is that job seekers have a reservation wage level below which they will not accept a job offer, no matter how attractive the other job attributes. If pay level does not meet their minimum standard, no other job attributes can make up (i.e., compensate) for this inadequacy. Other theorists go a step further and say that some job seekers–satisfiers–take the first job offer they get where the pay meets their reservation wage. A reservation wage may be above or below the market wage. The theory seeks to explain differences in workers' responses to offers. Reservation levels likely exist for pay forms, too, particularly for health insurance. A young high school graduate recently told us, "If I can't find a job that includes health insurance, I will probably go to college."

Human Capital

The theory of human capital, perhaps the most influential economic theory for explaining pay-level differences, is based on the premise that higher earnings flow to those who improve their potential productivity by investing in themselves (through additional education, training, and experience).[25] The theory assumes that people are in fact paid at the value of their marginal product. (Importantly, pay does not have to equal marginal product at a single point in time. Rather, pay and marginal product are expected to be equal over the course of a career. One can be "underpaid" and "overpaid" at different points in one's career.) Improving

EXHIBIT 7.9 **Labor Supply Theories and Implications**

Theory	Prediction	So What?
Reservation Wage	Job seekers won't accept jobs if pay is below a certain wage, no matter how attractive other job aspects.	Pay level will affect ability to recruit. Pay must meet some minimum level.
Human Capital	General and specific skills require an investment in human capital. Firms will invest in firm-specific skills, but not general skills. Workers must pay for investment in general skills.	Skill/ability requires investment by workers and firms. There must be a sufficient return (e.g., pay level) on investment for the investment to take place. Workers, for example, must see a payoff to training.

productive abilities by investing in training or even in one's physical health will increase one's marginal product. In general, the value of an individual's skills and abilities is a function of the time, expense, and effort to acquire them. Consequently, jobs that require long and expensive training (engineering, physicians) should receive higher pay than jobs that require less investment (clerical work, elementary school teaching).[26] As pay level increases, the number of people willing to make that investment increases, thereby creating an upward-sloping supply. In fact, different types of education do get different levels of pay. In the United Kingdom, new graduates with a degree in math, law, or economics will earn around 25 percent more than job seekers their age who do not have a college degree. An extra year of education adds about $4,200 per year.

A number of additional factors affect the supply of labor.[27] Geographic barriers to mobility among jobs, union requirements, lack of information about job openings, the degree of risk involved, and the degree of unemployment also influence labor markets. Also, nonmonetary aspects of jobs (e.g., time flexibility) may be important aspects of the return on investment.

PRODUCT MARKET FACTORS AND ABILITY TO PAY

The supply and demand for labor are major determinants of an employer's pay level. However, any organization must, over time, generate enough revenue to cover expenses, including compensation. It follows that an employer's pay level is constrained by its ability to compete in the product/service market. So product market conditions to a large extent determine what the organization can afford to pay.

Product demand and the degree of competition are the two key product market factors. Both affect the ability of the organization to change what it charges for its products and services. If prices cannot be changed without decreasing sales, then the ability of the employer to set a higher pay level is constrained.

Product Demand

Although labor market conditions (and legal requirements) put a floor on the pay level required to attract sufficient employees, the product market puts a lid on the maximum pay level that an employer can set. If the employer pays above the maximum, it must either pass on to consumers the higher pay level through price increases or hold prices fixed and allocate a greater share of total revenues to cover labor costs.

Degree of Competition

Employers in highly competitive markets, such as manufacturers of automobiles or generic drugs, are less able to raise prices without loss of revenues. At the other extreme, single sellers of a Lamborghini or a breakthrough cancer treatment are able to set whatever price they choose. However, too high a price often invites the eye of government regulators.

Other factors besides product market conditions affect pay level. Some of these have already been discussed. The productivity of labor, the technology employed, the level of production relative to plant capacity available–all affect compensation decisions. These factors vary more across than within industries. The technologies employed and consumer preferences may vary among auto manufacturers, but the differences are relatively small compared to the differences between the technology and product demand of auto manufacturers versus those of the oil or financial industry.

A Different View: What Managers Say

Discussions with managers provide insight into how all of these economic factors translate into actual pay decisions. In one study, a number of scenarios were presented in which unemployment, profitability, and labor market conditions varied.[28] Managers were asked to make wage adjustment recommendations for several positions. Level of unemployment made almost no difference. One manager was incredulous at the suggestion that high unemployment should lead to cutting salaries: "You mean take advantage of the fact that there are a lot of people out of work?" The company's profitability was considered a factor for higher management in setting the overall pay budget but not something managers consider for individual pay adjustments. What it boiled down to was "whatever the chief financial officer says we can afford!" They thought it shortsighted to pay less, even though market conditions would have permitted lower pay. In direct contradiction to efficiency-wage theory, managers believed that problems attracting and keeping people were the result of poor management rather than inadequate compensation. They offered the opinion that "supervisors try to solve with money their difficulties with managing people."[29]

Of course, what managers say that they would do in a hypothetical situation is not necessarily what they would do when they actually experience a situation. Nor are their views or decisions necessarily the same as those of managers in other companies that do things differently. In this same vein, what managers think is not always what their employees think. In 2009–2011 when the unemployment rate was higher than it had been in two decades, companies did indeed make pay cuts, either outright or by requiring employees to take days off (often called furloughs) without pay. Another common cut was reducing contributions to 401k retirement plans. Other companies imposed pay freezes.[30] Such cuts also took place during the pandemic in 2020, but in many cases were more short-lived because business rebounded more quickly than in 2009–2011. Such cuts were hard to find leading up to early 2020 when the unemployment rate was at its lowest level in decades, making attraction and retention priority one. Starting in 2021, the economy seemed on its way back to that attraction and retention mode as the unemployment rate began to decline again, while business continued to tick upwards. With respect to differences in manager/employer and employee views, consider employee retention. A national survey found that pay was the most often cited reason (51%) among high-performing employees for leaving, whereas relationship with supervisor was cited only 1 percent of the time by such employees. Employers, however, somewhat underestimated the role of pay (with 45% citing its role versus 51% of employees) and they very much overestimated the role of relationship with supervisor (with 31% citing its role versus 1% of employees).[31]

Segmented Supplies of Labor and (Different) Going Rates

However, faced with significant competition, a number of employers have cut pay. As we saw earlier, the U.S. airline industry is a notable example. Significant differences in wages paid around the world and the ease of offshoring work have also led many companies to consider this action.[32] Other options to reduce labor costs include segmenting the source of labor.

People Flow to the Work

Consider how a hospital staffs and pays its nursing positions and what each method costs. The number of nurses the hospital needs on each shift depends on the number of patients. To deal with fluctuating patient numbers, the hospital uses four different sources of nurses, as shown in **Exhibit 7.10**.

The segmented supply results in nurses working the same jobs side by side on the same shift, but earning significantly different pay and/or benefits and having different relationships with the hospital and the other nurses and health care professionals. This is a case of people flowing to the work. The hospital cannot send its nursing work to other cities or other nations.

Work Flows to the People—On-Site, Off-Site, Offshore

DELMIA Apriso (part of Dassault Systemes) in California designs and installs computer-assisted manufacturing software that is used in factories around the world. When Apriso competes for a project, the bid is structured in part on the compensation paid to people in different locations. Apriso can staff the project with employees who are on-site (in California), off-site (contract employees from throughout the United States), or offshore. Design engineers in California earn about twice as much as those in Krakow, Poland. Apriso can "mix and match" its people from different sources. Which source Apriso includes in its bid depends on many factors: customer preferences, time schedules, the nature of the project. To put together its bids, Apriso managers need to know pay levels and the mix of forms of pay, not only in the market in California but also in other locations, including Krakow, Shanghai, Vancouver, and Bangalore. (We return to this topic later in this chapter.)

There are three points ("so whats?") to take with you from this discussion:

1. Reality is complex and theories are abstract. It is not that our theories are useless. They simply abstract away the detail, clarifying the underlying factors that help us understand how reality works. Theories of market dynamics, the interaction of supply and demand, form a useful foundation.
2. The segmented sources of labor means that determining pay levels and pay mix increasingly requires understanding market conditions in different, even worldwide, locations.
3. Managers also need to know the jobs required to do the work, the tasks to be performed, and the knowledge and behaviors required to perform them (sound like job analysis?) so that they can bundle the various tasks to send to different locations.

EXHIBIT 7.10 Different Sources of Labor, Nurse Types

Nurse Type	Description	Relative Hourly Wage	Benefits?	Fee Paid by Hospital to Agency?
Regular	Full-time employees	100%	Yes	No
Pool	On call, part-time employees	132%	No	No
Registry	Agency employees who can work for multiple area hospitals. Benefits paid by agency.	150%	Yes	Yes
Travelers	Agency employees from outside the area who are sent on extended assignments (e.g., six months) to hospitals around the country. Benefits paid by agency.	150%	Yes	Yes

ORGANIZATION FACTORS

Although product and labor market conditions create a range of possibilities within which managers create a policy on external competitiveness, organizational factors influence pay-level and pay-mix decisions, too.[33]

Industry and Technology

The industry in which an organization competes influences the technologies used. Labor-intensive industries such as education and health care tend to pay lower than technology-intensive industries such as petroleum or pharmaceuticals, whereas professional services such as consulting firms pay high. In addition to differences in technology across industries affecting compensation, the introduction of new technology *within an industry* influences pay levels. The next time you are waiting in line at the supermarket, think about the pay the checkout person gets. The use of universal product codes, scanners, scales built into the counter, even do-it-yourself checkout lanes have reduced the skills required of checkers. As a result, their average pay has declined over time.[34]

Qualifications and experience tailored to particular technologies is important in the analysis of labor markets. Machinists and millwrights who build General Electric diesel locomotives in Erie, Pennsylvania, have very different qualifications from machinists and millwrights who build Boeing airplanes in St. Louis.[35]

Employer Size

There is consistent evidence that large organizations tend to pay more than small ones. A study of manufacturing firms found that firms with 100 to 500 workers paid 6 percent higher wages than did smaller firms; firms of more than 500 workers paid 12 percent more than did the smallest firms.[36] This relationship between organization size, ability to pay, and pay level is consistent with economic theory that says that talented individuals have a higher marginal value in a larger organization because they can influence more people and decisions, thereby leading to more profits. Compare the advertising revenue that former Late Night host Stephen Colbert was able to bring to CBS versus the potential revenue to station WBNS if his Late Night show was only seen on WBNS in Athens, Ohio (or even on Comedy Central). No matter how cool he was in Athens, WBNS (and/or Comedy Central) could not generate enough revenue to be able to afford to pay Mr. Colbert his multimillion dollar salary; CBS could. However, theories are less useful in explaining why practically everyone at bigger companies such as CBS, including janitors and compensation managers, is paid more. It seems unlikely that everyone has Colbert impact on revenues.

People's Preferences

What pay forms (health insurance, eye care, bonuses, pensions) do employees really value? Better understanding of employee preferences is increasingly important in determining external competitiveness. Markets, after all, involve both employers' and employees' choices.[37] However, there are substantial difficulties in reliably measuring preferences. In response to the survey question "What do you value most in your work?" who among us would be so crass as to (publicly) rank money over cordial co-workers or challenging assignments? Researchers find that people place more importance on pay than they are willing to admit.[38]

Organization Strategy

A variety of pay-level and pay-mix strategies exist. Some employers adopt a low-wage, no-services strategy; they compete by producing goods and services with the lowest total compensation possible. Nike and Reebok reportedly do this. Both rely heavily on outsourcing to manufacture their products. Nike, for example, outsources 99 percent of its footwear production to independent contract suppliers in China, Vietnam, Indonesia, and Thailand, all of which have much lower labor costs than found in the United States. Others select a low-wage, high-services strategy. Marriott offers its low-wage room cleaners a hotline to social workers who assist with child care and transportation crises. English and citizenship courses are available for recent immigrants. Seminars cover how to manage one's paycheck and one's life. Still other employers use a high-wage, high-services approach. Medtronic's "fully present at work" approach, discussed in **Chapter 2**, is an example of high wage, high services. Obviously, these are extremes on a continuum of possibilities. One study found that like the company in **Exhibit 7.3**, a variety of pay-level strategies exist within some organizations. Pay levels that lead competition are used in jobs that most directly impact the organization's success (research and development and marketing in pharmacy companies). In jobs with less impact (human resource management and manufacturing), pay levels reflect a "meet competition" policy.

As noted earlier, efficiency wage argues that some firms, for a variety of reasons (e.g., their technology depends more heavily on having higher-quality workers or it is more difficult to monitor employee performance) do indeed have efficiency reasons to pay higher wages. Higher pay levels, either for the organization as a whole or for critical jobs, may be well suited to particular strategies, such as higher value-added customer segments.[39] (Recall our example of Costco from **Chapter 1**.) Similarly, evidence suggests that organizations making greater use of so-called high-performance work practices (teams, quality circles, total quality management, job rotation) and computer-based technology and having higher-skilled workers also pay higher wages.[40] This is consistent with our discussion in **Chapter 2** about the need for human resources practices designed to encourage ability, motivation, and opportunity to contribute (AMO theory) to reinforce each other. The observable benefits of higher wages may include: higher **pay satisfaction,** improved attraction and retention of employees, and higher quality, effort, and/or performance.[41]

Returning to the Costco example, other retailers following a higher wage strategy include QuikTrip (the convenience store where the CEO's phone number is in the bathroom in case it needs cleaning), Trader Joe's, and Mercadona (Spain's largest supermarket chain). These companies, in addition to paying higher wages than many of their competitors, are known for providing employees with more predictable work schedules, strong growth opportunities (promotion from within), and more involvement in improving operations and the customer experience. In return, the company often has lower turnover, higher productivity, and higher customer loyalty.[42]

Ultimately, higher wages must bring something in return (e.g., higher productivity, quality, and/or innovation). Otherwise, a firm's ability to compete and survive is in question. (See our discussion of General Motors and the U.S. automobile industry in **Chapter 1** and elsewhere in this chapter.) Evidence shows that in manufacturing, productivity (defined as sales value of production divided by employee hours worked) is positively correlated ($r = .45$) with hourly wage level.[43] Thus, the relationship, while far from perfect, is meaningful in manufacturing.

RELEVANT MARKETS

Economists take "the market" for granted–as in "The market determines wages." But managers at St. Luke's and Apriso realize that defining the **relevant markets** is a big part of figuring out how and how much to pay.

Although the notion of a single homogeneous labor market may be a useful analytical device, each organization operates in many labor markets, each with unique demand and supply. Some, as in the case of hospitals, face segmented supplies for the same skills in the same market. Others, such as Apriso, think more broadly about which markets to use as sources of talent. They seek to answer the question, What is the right pay to get the right people to do the right things?

Consequently, managers must define the markets that are relevant for pay purposes and establish the appropriate competitive positions in these markets. The three factors usually used to determine the relevant labor markets are the occupation (skill/knowledge required), geography (willingness to relocate, commute, or become virtual employees), and competitors (other employers in the same product/service and labor markets).

Defining the Relevant Market

How do employers choose their relevant markets? Surprisingly little research has been done on this issue. But if the markets are incorrectly defined, the estimates of competitors' pay rates will be incorrect and the pay level and pay mix inappropriately established.

e-Compensation

Select several companies that you believe might be labor market competitors (e.g., Microsoft, Oracle, IBM; or Johnson & Johnson, Merck, Pfizer). Compare their job postings on their websites. Do any of the companies list salaries for their jobs? Do they quote a single salary? Do they allow room for haggling?

Two studies do shed some light on this issue.[44] They conclude that managers look at both *competitors*–their products, location, and size–and the *jobs*–the skills and knowledge required and their importance to the organization's success (e.g., lawyers in law firms, software engineers at Microsoft). So depending on its location and size, a company may be deemed a relevant comparison even if it is not a product market competitor. We will see an example in **Chapter 8** when we look at how Google and Microsoft define their relevant markets for paying executives.

The data from product market competitors (as opposed to labor market competitors) are likely to receive greater weight when:

1. Employee skills are specific to the product market (recall the differences in Boeing millwrights versus GE locomotive millwrights).
2. Labor costs are a large share of total costs.
3. Product demand is responsive to price changes. That is, people won't pay $4 for a bottle of Leinenkugel; instead, they'll go to Trader Joe's for a bottle of Charles Shaw wine, a.k.a. "two-buck Chuck" (the best $2 wine we have ever tasted).[45]
4. The supply of labor is not responsive to changes in pay (recall the earlier low-wage, low-skill example).

Globalization of Relevant Labor Markets: Offshoring and Outsourcing

We will discuss globalization and international issues more fully in **Chapter 16**. For now, we note that work flowing to lower wage locations is not new. Historically, clothing (needle trades) and furniture jobs flowed from New England to southern states. Nor is work flowing across national borders new. First, it was low-skill and low-wage jobs (clothing and Mardi Gras beads) from the U.S. to China and Central America; then higher-paid blue collar jobs (electronics, appliances); now it is service and professional jobs (accounting, legal, engineering, radiology). Vastly improved communication and software connectivity have accelerated these trends. For example, programming code and radiographic images can now be transported in an instant across the world.

In **Chapter 4**, we discussed characteristics of jobs (e.g., easily routinized, inputs/outputs easily transmitted electronically, little need for interaction with other workers, little need for local knowledge such as unique social and cultural factors) that are thought to increase susceptibility to offshoring (i.e., moving jobs to other countries). Here, we discuss why firms use offshoring, as well as challenges in doing so.

Several years ago, IBM found that a computer programmer (one of the occupations reported in **Chapter 4** to be most susceptible to offshoring) in the United States with three to five years of experience cost $56 per hour in total compensation. In China, a similarly qualified programmer cost $12.50 per hour.[46] Based on these data, IBM estimated that it could save $168 million per year by shifting some of these programmer jobs to countries like China, India, and Brazil. That sort of savings is difficult to ignore, especially when competing firms are either based in lower labor cost countries (e.g., Infosys in India) or are offshoring or expanding operations there.

As noted, offshoring is also happening to lawyers and financial services jobs. In Mumbai, India, Pangea3 LLC employs Indian lawyers to do legal work for Wall Street banks. Whereas starting associates in the United States might bill more than $200 per hour, similar lawyers in India might bill something closer to $75 to $100 per hour.[47] In financial services, Copal Partners of India has seen large increases in its business as Wall Street firms not only outsource or offshore "back office" work (e.g., processing of transactions), but increasingly also production of research reports, trading recommendations, and so forth. Citigroup now employs over 20,000 people in India and Deutsche Bank has about 6,000. According to one observer, "There's a huge amount of grunt work that has been done by $250,000-a-year Wharton M.B.A.s" but "some of that stuff, it's natural to outsource it."[48] It is possible that more sophisticated jobs will increasingly follow.

While large differences in labor costs cannot simply be ignored, there are other factors to consider in deciding where jobs will be.[49] First, as we saw in **Chapter 1** and as we will see in more detail in **Chapter 16**, countries with lower average labor costs also tend to have lower average productivity. So, a company must assure itself that labor costs savings, such as those available in China (relative to the United States), will not be neutralized by the offshore country's lower productivity. One determinant of productivity is the skill level of the workforce. According to the Global Competitiveness Report, China ranks 41st of 141 countries in terms of "ease of finding skilled employees," whereas the United States ranks 1st. There may also be other risks. Again, in the case of China, intellectual property protection continues to be a concern. The Global Competitiveness Report ranks China 58th on intellectual property protection, compared to a rank of 12th for the United States. (Finland is ranked 1st.) China ranks 140 (out of 141) on freedom of the press (compared to the United States at 42) and 72nd on corporate governance (compared to 31st in the United States).[50] Second, agency theory, which we discuss later, tells us that companies must devote resources to systems that monitor worker effort or output. This, as well as coordination of efforts, can be more difficult and more costly when geographic or cultural distance is great (and time zones different), even with advances in technology.[51] Third, customers' reactions must be considered. For example, Delta Air Lines Inc. decided to stop using call centers in India to handle sales and reservations, despite the fact that call-center workers in India earn roughly $500 a month (about one-sixth of U.S.-based call-center workers). Delta said that customers had trouble communicating with India-based representatives. Delta's CEO explained that "customer acceptance of call centers in foreign countries is low," adding, "Our customers are not shy about letting us have that feedback."[52] Fourth, if labor costs are the driving force behind placing jobs, one must ask how long the labor cost advantage at a significantly lower wage will hold up, and whether sufficiently qualified employees will continue to be available as other companies also tap into this pool of labor. However, nothing is forever, and labor cost savings from offshoring and/or outsourcing can, of course, have a substantial effect on profits for many years before the cost advantage becomes small enough to be offset by other factors. We return to this issue in **Chapter 16**.

A compelling example is Apple's manufacturing strategy for its iPad and iPhone. The labor cost savings that Apple realizes by outsourcing assembly of these products to (and likewise populating its supply chain with) low cost countries are big, very (very) big. This is interesting and important enough to devote a couple of different analyses/exhibits to it. **Exhibit 7.11** shows that under Scenario 1, assembly of the iPhone and iPad in the United States would decrease operating income by $8.0 billion (24%). Under Scenario 2, operating income would be decreased by $14.8 billion (44%). Thus, if these products were assembled in the States, Apple would need to either (a) tell shareholders that profits (and thus shareholder return) will be reduced by billions of dollars, or (b) pass along the increased cost to the consumer, which, unless demand is inelastic (unlikely) would result in lower sales and thus, once again, lower profits and shareholder return. Option (c) would be to invest in technology/automation to replace the more expensive labor in a country like the United States. However, that would again increase costs (at least in the short run) that would need to be covered somehow. By the way, it is important to note that iPhones and other such small and light products can be transported across oceans by planes rather than ships to product markets, thus helping create flexibility in where production takes place.

The results in **Exhibit 7.11** are a bit dated and more current data of this specific type does not seem to be available. Thus, we come at the estimation of Apple costs in two other ways using more recent data. Panel A seeks to estimate cost only of assembly of only the iPhone in China, compared to in the United States. Our estimate is that it would cost almost $12 billion per year more to assemble the iPhone in the United States. Based on Panel C, that would reduce Apple's most recent annual operating income from about $66 billion to $52 billion. Panel B includes much more. Apple's annual report, states that "Substantially all of the Company's hardware products are manufactured by outsourcing partners that are located primarily in Asia," Further, Apple's Supplier Responsibility 2020 Progress Report states there are "millions of people who work in our supply chain." (These are not Apple employees. These workers are employees of companies in its supply chain.) "Millions of people" means, at a minimum, two million workers. We use this 2,000,000 (lower bound perhaps?) estimate of workers in Part B. We estimate that if a supply chain containing 2,000,000 workers was located in the United States rather than in Asia, the labor cost would be higher by over $62 billion per year. Based on Part C, that would nearly wipe out Apple's annual operating income. Again, Apple could counteract these higher costs in a number of ways (see above), including by raising prices on the iPhone and other products. However, if its competitors continue to have their assembly and supply chains in low cost countries in Asia, that would not likely work out well for Apple. Thus, competitive pressures play a huge factor in Apple's strategy (assembly and supply chain outsourced to companies operating in low cost countries) of how to produce a product like the iPhone.

COMPETITIVE PAY POLICY ALTERNATIVES

Compensation theories offer some help in understanding the variations in pay levels we observe among employers. They are less helpful in understanding differences in the mix of pay forms. Relevant markets are

EXHIBIT 7.11 Effect of Annual Labor Costs (China versus U.S.) on Apple Annual Operating Income

Operating Income	$33,790,000,000					
iPhone Units Sold, 2011	Labor Cost Difference per Unit United States–China		Total Labor Cost Difference United States–China			
72,293,000	Estimate 1[a]	$65.00	$4,699,045,000			
72,293,000	Estimate 2[b]	$158.57	$11,463,501,010			
iPad Units Sold	Labor Cost Difference per Unit United States–China		Total Labor Cost Difference United States–China			
33,394,000	Estimate[c]	$100.00	$3,339,400,000			
			Added Labor Cost, if iPhone and iPad Assembled in United States	% of Operating Income	New Operating Income	New Operating Income (% change)
Scenario 1 (Using iPhone labor cost Estimate 1)			$8,038,445,000	24%	$25,751,555,000	−24%
Scenario 2 (Using iPhone labor cost Estimate 2)			$14,802,901,010	44%	$18,987,098,990	−44%

Note: Exhibit shows annual data from 2011.

[a] Charles Duhigg and Keith Bradsher, "How the U.S. Lost Out on iPhone Work," *The New York Times*, January 21, 2012.

[b] Julie Froud, Sukhdev Johal, Adam Leaver, and Karel Williams, "Apple Business Model: Financialization across the Pacific," University of Manchester, Centre for Research in Socio-Cultural Change, Working Paper No. 111, April 2012.

[c] Source: Tim Winstall. "If Apple Onshored iPad Production It Would Create 67,000 American Manufacturing Jobs!," Forbes, December 18, 2011, http://www.forbes.com/sites/timworstall/2011/12/18/if-apple-onshored-ipad-production-it-would-create-67000-american-manufacturing-jobs.

EXHIBIT 7.12 Labor Costs for Apple iPhone and Other Products, China or Asia versus United States

A. Apple iPhones ONLY, Annual Cost to Produce, China versus United States

	China	United States	Difference
iPhones produced	200,000,000	200,000,000	
Workers	383,562	383,562	
Earnings	10,560	41,760	
Labor Cost (Workers x Earnings)	4,050,414,720	16,017,549,120	11,967,134,400
Note: (Excludes cost of benefits)			

B. Apple Supply Chain Workers Cost in Asia versus U.S. Workers Cost, Annual Basis

	Asia	United States	Difference
Workers	2,000,000	2,000,000	
Earnings	10,560	41,760	
Labor Cost (Workers x Earnings)	21,120,000,000	83,520,000,000	62,400,000,000
Note: (Excludes cost of benefits)			

C. Apple Operating Income			66,288,000,000

Notes to Part A: In 2016, the New York Times reported that at peak iphone production, the Zhengzhou Foxconn factory could have 350,000 workers producing 500,000 iPhones per day. At that rate, it would produce 182,500,000 iPhones per year. Forbes reported that in 2021, iPhone worldwide annual sales totaled 200,000,000. Based on the above information, that output would require 383,562 workers. (These workers would be distributed across multiple plants. These do not operate at peak year-round. There are two Taiwanese companies producing iPhones in China: Foxconn and Pegatron. A third Taiwanese company, Wistron, also produces iPhones, but recently sold its operation in China to a Chinese company.) In 2019, the New York Times reported that starting hourly pay at the plant was $3.15. With 2080 hours in a year, that would imply annual earnings of $6,552. However, an article in the South China Morning Post reported that workers at the plant could earn $880 per week, which would imply annual earnings of $10,560. (At least part of the discrepancy is that workers work much more than 40 hours per week during peak production.) We use the higher estimate of $10,560. According to the U.S. Bureau of Labor Statistics, mean annual earnings for production workers in the United States is $41,760. (That does not include benefits, which would add roughly another 40%.)

Notes to Part B: In its annual report (form 10-K, dated October 31, 2020), Apple notes that although some Mac computers are manufactured in the U.S. and Ireland, "Substantially all of the Company's hardware products are manufactured by outsourcing partners that are located primarily in Asia." It further notes that it "had approximately 147,000 full-time equivalent employees." In its Supplier Responsibility 2020 Progress Report, by contrast, it says there are "millions of people who work in our supply chain." Thus, the vast majority of workers producing Apple products are not Apple employees, instead being employed by Apple's outsourcing partners in Asia (e.g., Foxconn). Use of the word "millions" implies at least two million workers in Asia in Apples' supply chain. We use the same earnings estimates as in Part A.

General notes: Not all workers in either example are production workers. Managerial and professional workers would have higher earnings. However, UBS data indicate that although the percentage differential between production workers and managers/professionals is almost the same in China as in the United States, the dollar differential is much greater in the United States. Thus, the labor cost differences using only production worker wages underestimates the actual labor cost difference. Apple also produces iPhones and other products outside of China in Asia. However, almost all of these countries (e.g., India) have lower labor costs than China.

Sources: Dwight Silverman. Apple Back on Top. Forbes.com, February 22, 2021; Cissy Zhou and Zhou Xin. "iPhone 12 Production at China Factory Ramps up to 24 Hours a Day ahead of New Model Launch." South China Morning Post, September 29, 2020. www.scmp.com; Jack Nicas. "A Tiny Screw Shows Why iPhones Won't Be Assembled in U.S.A." New York Times, January 18, 2019, www.nytimes.com; David Barboza. "An iPhone's Journey, from the Factory Floor to the Retail Store." New York Times, December 12, 2016. www.nytimes.com. Supplier Responsibility 2020 Report. Apple. https://www.apple.com/supplier-responsibility/; Annual Report (Form 10-K, dated October 31, 2020). www.sec.gov.

shaped by pressures from the labor and product markets and the organization. But so what? How, in fact, do managers set pay-level and pay-mix policy, and what difference does it make? In the remainder of this chapter, we will discuss those two issues.

Recall that pay level is the average of the array of rates inside an organization. There are three conventional pay-level policies: to lead, to meet, or to follow competition. Newer policies emphasize flexibility: among policies for different employee groups, among pay forms for individual employees, and among elements of the employee relationship that the company wishes to emphasize in its external competitiveness policy.

What Difference Does the Pay-Level Policy Make?

The basic premise is that the competitiveness of pay will affect the organization's ability to achieve its compensation objectives, and this in turn will affect its performance.[53] The probable effects of alternative policies are shown in **Exhibit 7.13** and discussed in more detail below. The problem with much pay-level research is that it focuses on base pay and ignores bonuses, incentives, options, employment security, benefits, or other forms of pay. Yet the exhibits and discussion in this chapter should have convinced you that base pay represents only a portion of compensation. Comparisons on base alone can mislead. In fact, many managers believe they get more bang for the buck by allocating dollars away from base pay and into variable forms that more effectively shape employee behavior.[54]

General Mills, for example, seeks to pay at the 50th percentile of base salary (among consumer packaged goods companies) but at the 75th percentile for total cash (base salary variable pay) for managers if they have superior performance.[55] As **Exhibit 7.14** shows, this seems to be a common strategy.

Pay with Competition (Match)

Given the choice to match, lead, or lag, the most common policy is to match rates paid by competitors.[56] Managers historically justify this policy by saying that failure to match competitors' rates would cause murmuring among present employees and limit the organization's ability to recruit. Many nonunionized companies tend to match or even lead competition in order to discourage unions. A **pay-with-competition policy** tries to ensure that an organization's wage costs are approximately equal to those of its product competitors and that its ability to attract applicants will be approximately equal to its labor market competitors.

EXHIBIT 7.13 **Probable Relationships between External Pay Policies and Objectives**

	Compensation Objectives				
Policy	Ability to Attract	Ability to Retain	Contain Labor Costs	Reduce Pay Dissatisfaction	Increase Productivity
Pay above market (lead)	+	+	?	+	?
Pay with market (match)	=	=	=	=	?
Pay below market (lag)	–	?	+	–	?
Hybrid policy	?	?	+	?	+
Employer of choice	+	+	+	–	?

EXHIBIT 7.14 Competitive Pay Policy Objectives, Base Salary, and Total Cash

Base Salary Target
What Is Your Organization's *Base Salary* Target (or Goal) Compared to the Relevant Labor Market?

	<25th Percentile	25th–40th Percentile	40th–60th Percentile	60th–75th Percentile	>75th Percentile	Varies/ No Target
Senior Management (*n* = 1,034)	0%	1%	73%	14%	3%	9%
Middle Management (*n* = 1,045)	0%	1%	85%	7%	2%	5%
Professional (*n* = 1,042)	1%	1%	86%	6%	2%	4%
Sales (*n* = 1,037)	1%	1%	85%	6%	1%	7%
Administrative (*n* = 1,037)	1%	2%	86%	6%	1%	5%
Production (*n* = 835)	0%	3%	84%	6%	1%	6%

Total Cash Target
What Is Your Organization's *Total Cash* Target (or Goal) Compared to the Relevant Labor Market?

	<25th Percentile	25th–40th Percentile	40th–60th Percentile	60th–75th Percentile	>75th Percentile	Varies/ No Target
Senior Management (*n* = 1,037)	0%	1%	50%	24%	5%	20%
Middle Management (*n* = 1,041)	0%	1%	61%	18%	3%	18%
Professional (*n* = 1,035)	0%	1%	64%	14%	2%	18%
Sales (*n* = 1,896)	0%	1%	63%	15%	3%	18%
Administrative (*n* = 1,033)	0%	2%	65%	13%	2%	18%
Production (*n* = 837)	0%	3%	63%	12%	2%	20%

Source: Reprinted from "Job Evaluation and Market-Pricing Practices," Contents ©WorldatWork. Reprinted with permission from WorldatWork. Content is licensed for use by purchaser only. No part of this article may be reproduced, excerpted or redistributed in any form without express written permission from WorldatWork.

Classical economic models predict that employers meet competitive wages. While this avoids placing an employer at a disadvantage in pricing products, it may not provide a competitive advantage in its labor markets.

Lead Pay-Level Policy

A **lead pay-level policy** maximizes the ability to attract and retain quality employees and minimizes employee dissatisfaction with pay. It may also offset less attractive features of the work, à la Adam Smith's "net advantage." Combat pay premiums paid to military personnel offset some of the risk of being fired upon.[57] The higher pay offered by brokerage firms offsets the risk of being fired when the market tanks.

As noted earlier, sometimes an entire industry can pass high pay rates on to consumers if pay is a relatively low proportion of total operating expenses or if the industry is highly regulated. But what about specific firms within a high-pay industry? For example, Merrill Lynch adheres to a pay leadership position for financial analysts *in its industry.* Do any advantages actually accrue to Merrill Lynch? If all firms in the industry have similar operating expenses, then the lead policy must provide some competitive advantage to Merrill Lynch that offsets the higher costs.

A number of researchers have linked high wages to ease of attraction, reduced vacancy rates and training time, and better-quality employees.[58] Research also suggests that higher pay levels reduce turnover and absenteeism.[59] **Exhibit 7.15** summarizes several studies on the degree to which higher pay is associated with lower quits (turnover). These studies suggest that pay level can have a substantial influence on quit rates. Consistent with this, there is also consistent evidence that quits, especially if voluntary, result in higher pay, as shown in **Exhibit 7.16**. Internal moves (promotion) also result in pay gains. However, there is a constraint on promotions because the number of jobs as one moves up the hierarchy/structure diminishes, meaning that not everyone has the opportunity to be promoted, at least not at the same rate. That means a substantial number of people will choose to leave to advance their careers and increase their pay or to find a job that better matches their abilities and preferences. Of course, it also depends on how much growth there is at one's present organization, relative to growth at other organizations. Low (high) employment growth at one's current organization, combined with high (low) employment growth at other organizations, will translate into more room for advancement elsewhere (at one's current organization). An economy where employees are able to move to organizations with more growth for better career opportunities is generally viewed as essential to the efficient operation of the economy and, of course, for those growing organizations.[60]

However, an employer wishing to control turnover will need to carefully choose the pay level that is most optimal in the sense of achieving the desired turnover target, especially for high performing/high value employees at an acceptable cost. (The choice and design of benefits and non-compensation attributes of the employment deal are also important.) In addition, an employee who receives an outside offer (many of which are unsolicited and the result of cold calls rather than active search) will often give their current employer a chance to make a *counteroffer*. As one example, several years ago, the University of Wisconsin-Madison reported on its efforts during that academic year to retain 232 of its faculty, including 144 who received outside offers (and another 88 where preemptive retention efforts were made).[61] Of the 144, 29 (20%) left, 111 (77%) stayed, and 4 cases (3%) were not yet resolved. In cases where details of the outside offer were known, the salary was a median 30 percent higher than the faculty member's current Wisconsin salary. The reports states that "Salary was the most common issue reported as a consideration in outside offers and responsive actions." To retain the 88 + 111 = 199 faculty, the University spent $23.56 million, some in the form of salary, most in the form of funds to support their research (which might also be taken in the form of salary in some cases). That works out to $118,400 per faculty member. This is only part of the cost to the University or any other organization in responding to outside job offers. Internal equity, which is fundamental to most compensation strategies means that if one faculty member receives a 20 percent increase in salary and/or support in the form of a counteroffer to stay, other faculty will, to varying degrees, seek their own salary adjustments to restore what they see as equity based on their own performance/contributions and how it is recognized with pay. Typically, that pursuit will begin internally. If that does not result in satisfactory action, they can turn to outside opportunities, especially after seeing faculty colleagues' success in obtaining a salary increase, either by moving or by virtue of a counteroffer to stay.

As noted above, pay satisfaction helps explain the influence of pay level on quits. **Exhibit 7.17** shows the relationship of pay satisfaction with turnover (quits) and also determinants of pay satisfaction. In addition to pay level, we see, consistent with equity theory, that fairness/justice perceptions, both distributive (based on how much they receive) and procedural (what process was used to decide how much), matter.[62] Nevertheless, there is no simple relationship between pay level and financial performance. Several studies have found that the use of variable pay (bonuses and long-term incentives) is related to an organization's improved financial

EXHIBIT 7.15 **Effect of Pay Levels on Quits, Organization Level Studies**

Study	Sample	Results	Elasticity
Riddell, *Industrial Relations* (2011)	390 firms in Greater Toronto, 6 occupational groups	A 10% increase in ratio of firm pay to market pay associated with quit rate going from .106 to .095, a 10% reduction	−1.01
Falch, *American Economic Review* (May 2011)	161 primary and secondary schools in Norway	Schools having teacher "shortage" and located in far north eligible to pay teachers wage premium of 10%. Introduction (also studied its removal) of 10% wage premium associated with quit rate going from .18 to .12, a 35% reduction	−3.50
Siebert & Zubanov, *Academy of Management Journal* (2009)	325 retail clothing stores in the United Kingdom	A 10% increase in ratio of store wage/county wage associated with separation rate going from .0500 to .0364, a 28% reduction	−2.78
Shaw, Delery, Jenkins, & Gupta, *Academy of Management Journal* (1998)	227 trucking companies in the United States	Regression coefficient (beta) = −.31 for quits on pay level. A 10% increase in average annual pay level ($34,912 to $38,403) associated with quit rate going from .256 to .200, a 22% reduction	−2.20
Raff & Summers, *Journal of Labor Economics* (1987)	Ford Motor Company in 1914	Increasing daily wage *100%*, from $2.50 to $5.00, associated with turnover reduction from 370% to 54%, an 85% reduction	−0.85

Elasticity = % change in y/% change in x

performance but that pay level is not.[63] We have conjectured that pay level is so important that paying "too low" or "too high" for any extended period has such significant potential drawbacks that organizations do not differentiate much on pay level (alone). It may be that high pay levels have beneficial effects on performance only when the pay level itself depends on performance (i.e., there is a high pay level AND strong pay for performance).[64]

A lead policy can also have negative effects. It may force the employer to increase wages of current employees too, to avoid internal misalignment and murmuring. Additionally, a lead policy may mask negative job

EXHIBIT 7.16 What Happens to Pay when People (Voluntarily) Quit to Change Employers in United States?

Study	Sample	Results
Groysberg, Healy, & Lin, ILR Review (2020)	Global executive search firm	13% increase (in salary plus bonus) after employer change
Bidwell, Organization Science (2015)	MBA alumni from a leading U.S. business school	35% increase in earnings from voluntary employer change within same job function. 4% increase from involuntary employer change. Internal moves (promotion) experienced 34% earnings increase. (Mean of 5.4 years post-MBA work experience. During that time, 87% changed employer at least once; 2.6 moves per person, with 65% being internal, 26% voluntary external, and 9% involuntary external.)
Dreher & Cox Academy of Management Journal (2000)	Recent MBA graduates	Pay was 20% higher among those who had changed employer at least once
Keith & McWilliams, ILR Review (1999)	National sample of young adults	Pay was 8% to 11% higher for those who voluntarily quit their job relative to stayers. Pay was 14% to 18% higher if searched prior to voluntarily quitting.
Gomez-Mejia & Balkin, Academy of Management Journal (1992)	College and university faculty	Each employer change associated with 25.4% higher 9-month salary
Topel & Ward, Quarterly Journal of Economics (1992)	National sample of young adults	10% increase in wage from employer change (first 10 years in labor market: 84% moved and 40% of wage growth due to employer changes)

attributes that contribute to high turnover later on (e.g., boring assignments or hostile colleagues). Remember the managers' view mentioned earlier that high turnover was more likely to be a managerial problem than a compensation problem.[65]

Lag Pay-Level Policy

A policy of paying below-market rates may hinder a firm's ability to attract potential employees. But if a **lag pay-level policy** is coupled with the promise of higher future returns (e.g., stock ownership in a high-tech start-up firm), this combination may increase employee commitment and foster teamwork, which may increase productivity. How long this promise works, in the face of flat or declining stock markets, is unknown. Unmet expectations probably have negative effects. Additionally, it is possible to lag competition on pay level but to lead on other returns from work (e.g., hot assignments, desirable location, outstanding colleagues, cool tools, work/life balance).

Different Policies for Different Employee Groups

In practice, many employers go beyond a single choice among the three policy options. They may vary the policy for different occupational families, as did the company in **Exhibit 7.3**. They may vary the policy for different forms of pay, as did the companies in **Exhibit 7.4**. They may also adopt different policies for different business units that face very different competitive conditions.

EXHIBIT 7.17 **Pay Satisfaction Correlations with Determinants and Consequences**

Meta-Analysis	Dependent Variable	Independent Variable	*K* (# studies)	*N* (# employees)	Correlation
Judge et al., *Journal of Vocational Behavior* (2010)	Pay Satisfaction	Pay Level	48	15,576	.23
Williams et al., *Journal of Applied Psychology* (2006)	Pay Satisfaction	Pay Level	64	29,574	.29
	Pay Satisfaction	Perceived Pay Discrepancy	64	29,754	−.54
	Pay Satisfaction	Distributive Justice	10	6,595	.79
	Pay Satisfaction	Procedural Justice	8	2,291	.42
	Turnover/ Quits	Pay Satisfaction	9	1,362	−.17
	Turnover Intention	Pay Satisfaction	37	15,893	−.31

Notes: Correlation is ρ, the correlation corrected for artifacts (e.g., unreliability in the independent and/or dependent variable). Perceived pay discrepancy = Perceived amount should be paid minus the perceived amount actually paid. Both studies (Judge et al., 2010 and Williams et al., 2006) are meta-analyses that use primary studies conducted at the individual/employee level of analysis.

Not by Pay Level Alone: Pay-Mix Strategies

Thus far, we have devoted limited attention to pay-mix policies. Some obvious alternatives include *performance driven, market match, work/life balance,* and *security.* **Exhibit 7.18** illustrates these four alternatives. Compared to the other three, incentives and stock ownership make up a greater percent of total compensation in *performance-driven* policies. The *market match* simply mimics the pay mix competitors are paying. How managers actually make these mix decisions is a ripe issue for more research.

How managers position their organization's pay against competitors is changing. Some alternatives that are emerging focus on total returns from work (beyond financial returns) and offering people choices among these returns. Rather than "flexible," perhaps a better term would be "fuzzy" policies.

Such pay-mix policy alternatives exist among enterprises in other countries, too. Apache Footware, located in Quingyuan, China, offers base plus bonus, which matches local practice. It also offers benefits that include a new medical clinic, housing for married couples, a school, sports facilities, and a shopping mall. Steve Chen, Apache's chief executive, states, "It's not just about pay, it's about lifestyle. We're building a community so people will stay." (Reminiscent of SAS, whose strategy was discussed in **Chapter 2**.) In contrast, Top Form Undergarment Wear, located in the same region, phased out its employee housing. It opted to pay employees over 20 percent higher base pay than local practice. Top Form executive Charles Lee says, "Workers need to have a life of their own. They are not children. We pay them more and let each worker decide what is best for them."[66]

EXHIBIT 7.18 **Pay-Mix Policy Alternatives**

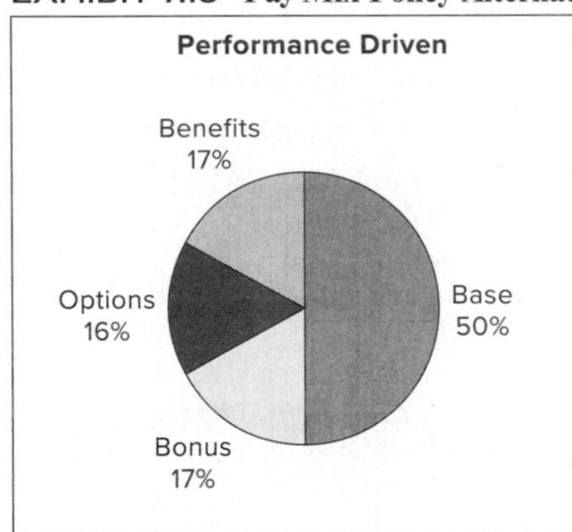

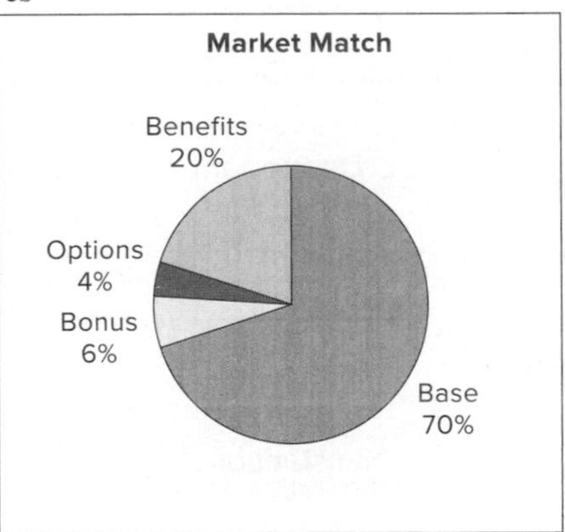

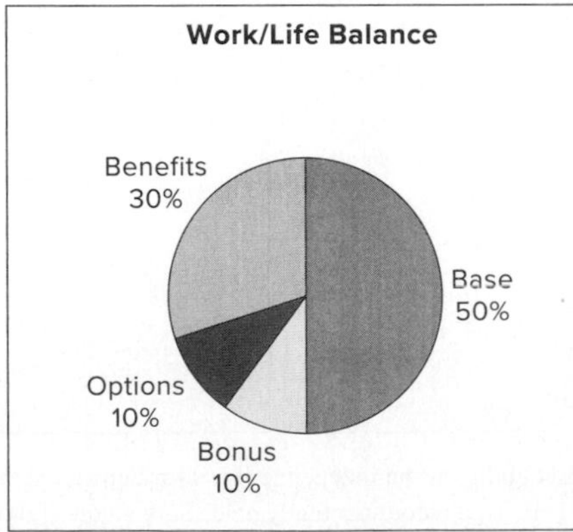

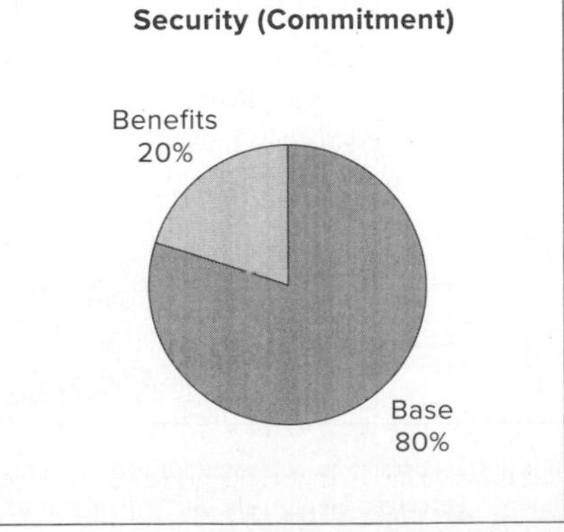

Employer of Choice/Shared Choice

Some companies compete based on their overall reputation as a place to work, beyond pay level and pay mix. For example, IBM compares within the information technology marketplace and positions its pay "among the best" in this group. Further, it claims to "strongly differentiate based on business and individual results." It leads the market with its strong emphasis on performance. IBM also offers extensive training opportunities, challenging work assignments, and the like. In a sense, **employer of choice** corresponds to the brand or image the company projects as an employer.

Shared choice begins with the traditional alternatives of lead, meet, or lag. But it then adds a second part, which is to *offer employees choices* (within limits) in the pay mix. This "employee as customer" perspective is not all that revolutionary, at least in the United States. Many employers offer choices on health insurance (individual versus dependent coverage), retirement investments (growth or value), and so on. (See flexible benefits in **Chapter 13**. See also **Chapter 2** for how Whole Foods uses an employee vote every three years in choosing its benefits package.) More advanced software is making the employee-as-customer approach more feasible. Mass customization–being able to select among a variety of features–is routine when purchasing a new laptop or auto. It is now possible with total compensation, too. Does offering people choices matter? One risk is that employees will make "wrong" choices that will jeopardize their financial well-being (e.g., inadequate health insurance). Another is the "24 jars of jam" dilemma. Supermarket studies report that offering consumers a taste of just a few different jams increases sales. But offering a taste of 24 different jams decreases sales. Consumers feel overwhelmed by too many choices and simply walk away. Perhaps offering employees too many choices of different kinds of pay will lead to confusion, mistakes, and dissatisfaction.[67]

An example of a company that does give employees a choice in pay mix is Netflix. Each November, employees have their performance evaluations. In December, each employee chooses how much compensation to receive in cash and how much to receive in stock options. Roughly two-thirds of Netflix employees choose 100 percent cash. Of the remaining one-third, the average share of compensation taken in the form of stock options is 7 to 8 percent. (The share allocated to options was initially restricted, but no longer is. So, these results may change.) The apparent preference among most employees for cash rather than (more risky) options at Netflix is consistent with agency theory, which is covered in **Chapter 9**.[68]

Pitfalls of Pies

The pie charts in **Exhibit 7.18** contrast various pay-mix policies. However, thinking about the mix of pay forms as pieces in a pie chart has limitations. These are particularly clear when the value of stock is volatile. The pie charts in **Exhibit 7.19** show how a well-known software company's mix changed after a major stock market decline (stock prices plummeted 50% within a month). Base pay went from 47 to 55 percent of total compensation, whereas the value of stock options fell from 28 to 16 percent. (The reverse has happened in this company, too.) The mix changed even though the company made no overt decision to change its pay strategy. But wait, it can get worse. One technology company was forced to disclose that three-quarters of all its stock options were "under water," that is, exercisable at prices higher than the market price. Due to stock market volatility, the options had become worthless to employees. So what is the message to employees? To competitors? The company's intended strategy has not changed, but in reality the mix has changed. So the possible volatility in the value of different pay forms needs to be anticipated.

Some companies prefer to report the mix of pay forms using a "dashboard," as depicted in **Exhibit 7.20**. The dashboard changes the focus from emphasizing the relative importance of each form within a single company to comparing each form by itself to the market (many companies). In the example, the value of stock options is 79 percent of competitors' median, base pay is at 95 percent of competitors' median, and overall total compensation is 102 percent of (or 2 percent above) the market median. Pies, dashboards–different terms, but both recognize the importance of the mix of pay forms.

Keep in mind that the mix employees receive differs at different levels in the internal job structure. **Exhibit 7.21** shows the different mix of base, cash incentives, and stock programs Merrill Lynch pays at different organization levels. Executive leadership positions receive less than 10 percent in base, about 20 percent in stock, and the rest in annual incentives. This compares to 50 percent in base, 40 percent in annual incentives, and 10 percent in stock for mid-level manager/professional positions, and 80 percent base, 20 percent incentives, and no stock for entry- and lower-level jobs. While the percentages vary among organizations, greater emphasis on performance (through incentives and stock) at higher levels is common practice. This is based on the belief that jobs at higher levels in the organization have greater opportunity to influence organization performance.

CONSEQUENCES OF PAY-LEVEL AND PAY-MIX DECISIONS: GUIDANCE FROM THE RESEARCH

Earlier we noted that external competitiveness has two major consequences: It affects (1) operating expenses and (2) employee attitudes and work behaviors. **Exhibit 7.22** summarizes these consequences, which have been discussed throughout this chapter.

Efficiency

A variety of theories make assumptions about the effects of relative pay levels on an organization's efficiency. Some recommend lead policies to diminish shirking and permit hiring better-qualified applicants. Others–such as marginal productivity theory–recommend matching. One study, using utility theory, concluded that a lag pay-level policy was the best choice for bank tellers.[69] However, as we will see in **Appendix 7-A**, utility theory tells us that for higher impact jobs, the conclusion could differ. No research suggests under what circumstances managers should choose which pay-mix alternative.

EXHIBIT 7.19 **Volatility of Stock Value Changes Total Pay Mix**

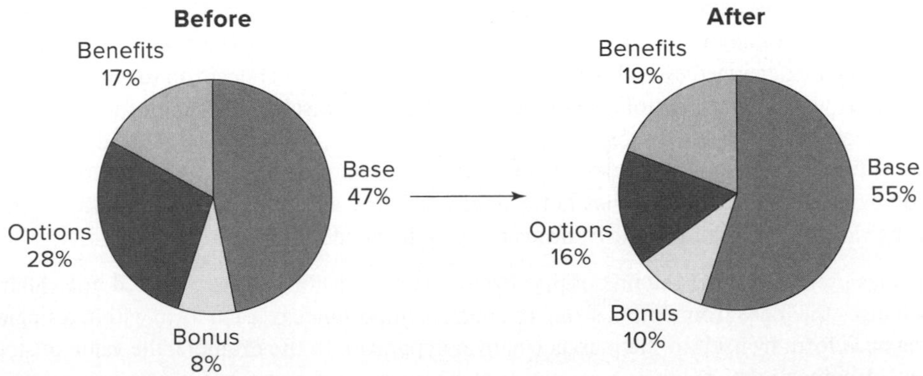

Which Policy Achieves Competitive Advantage?

Research on the effect of pay-level policies is difficult because companies' stated policies often do not correspond to reality. For example, HR managers at 124 companies were asked to define their firm's target pay level. All 124 of them reported that their companies paid above the median![70]

Beyond opinions, there is little evidence of the consequences of different policy alternatives. We do know that pay level affects costs; we do not know whether any effects it might have on productivity or attracting and retaining employees are sufficient to offset costs. Nor is it known how much of a pay-level variation makes a difference to employees; will 5 percent, 10 percent, or 15 percent be a noticeable difference? Although lagging competitive pay could have a noticeable reduction in short-term labor costs, it is not known whether this savings is accompanied by a reduction in the quality and performance of the workforce. It may be that an employer's pay level will not gain any competitive *advantage;* however, the wrong pay level may put the organization at a serious *disadvantage.* Similarly, we simply do not know the effects of the different pay-mix alternatives or the financial results of shifting the responsibility for choosing the mix to employees. Perhaps it is the message communicated by pay mix and levels that is the key to achieving competitive advantage.

EXHIBIT 7.20 Dashboard: Total Pay Mix Breakdown vs. Competitors*

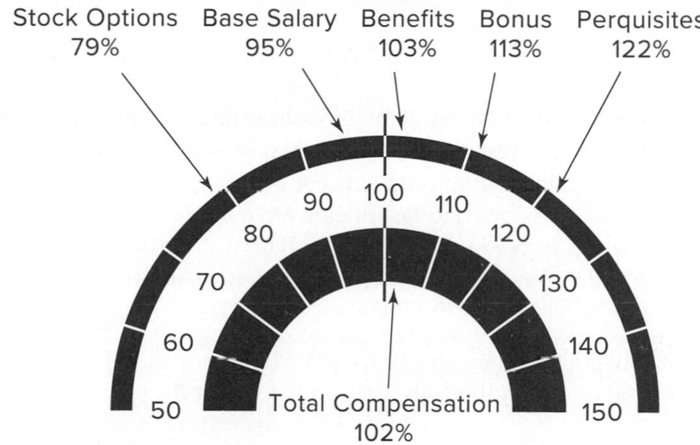

*100 = Chosen market position, e.g., market median

EXHIBIT 7.21 Merrill Lynch's Pay Mix Varies within the Structure

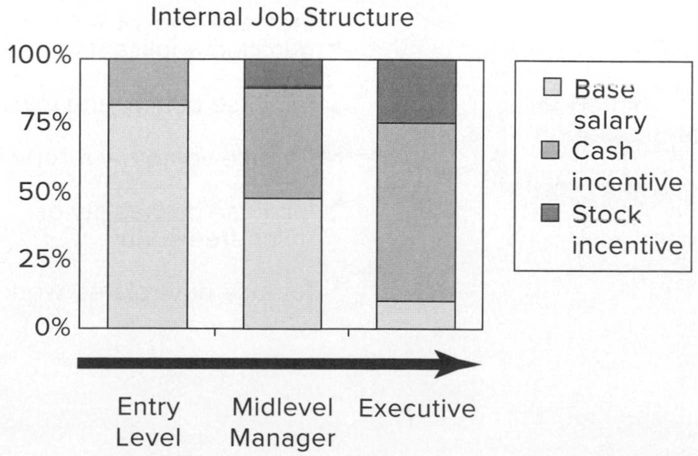

So where does this leave the manager? In the absence of convincing evidence, the least-risk approach may be to set both pay level and pay mix to match competition. An organization may adopt a lead policy for skills that are critical to its success, a match policy for less-critical skills, and a lag policy for jobs that are easily filled in the local labor market. An obvious concern with flexible policies is to achieve some degree of business alignment and fair treatment for employees among the choices. (The appendix to this chapter shows how utility analysis can help evaluate pay-level strategies.)

Fairness

Satisfaction with pay is directly related to the pay level: More is better.[71] But employees' sense of fairness is also related to how others are paid. A friend at Stanford claims that if all but one of the faculty in their business school got $1,000,000 and one person received $1,000,001, the others would all be lined up at the dean's office demanding an explanation. Employers have many choices about how and where to invest their resources. Even if the decision is made to invest in improving people's feelings about fairness of their pay, there is little research to tell us this will improve employees' overall feeling about fair treatment in the workplace.[72]

Compliance

It's not enough to say that an employer must pay at or above the legal minimum wage. Provisions of prevailing wage laws and equal rights legislation must also be met. In fact, we will return to the subject of market wages again when we discuss pay discrimination and the concept of "living wage." In addition to pay level, various pay forms are also regulated. Pensions and health care are considered part of every citizen's economic security and are regulated to some degree in most countries. This is discussed again when we look at international practices and benefits. Employers must also exercise caution when sharing salary information to avoid antitrust violations.[73]

No matter the competitive pay policy, it needs to be translated into practice. The starting point is measuring the market through use of a salary survey. For this, we turn to **Chapter 8**.

EXHIBIT 7.22 **Some Consequences of Pay Levels**

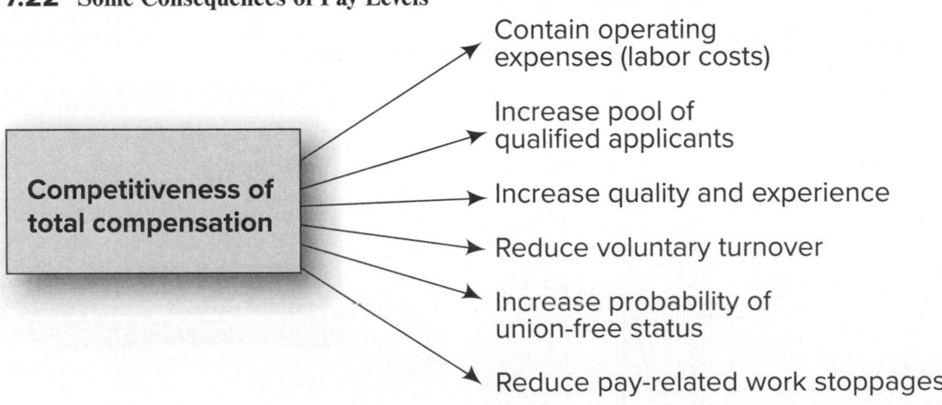

Your Turn

Two-Tier Wages

In this chapter we talked about the implications of different pay-level strategies for costs and revenues. We saw examples both of employers seeking to control/reduce pay levels and of employers increasing pay levels. Here, we continue our earlier discussion on how U.S. automakers have used two-tier wage structures to control labor costs and consider what might happen going forward. Also important is their use of profit sharing as a way to keep fixed labor costs under control and to make labor costs move more in line with profitability, so that labor costs decline when profits decline and labor costs increase when profits increase. That reduces the problem of having high, fixed labor costs when the company is under financial duress.

As we noted earlier, automobile production in the United States has declined over time. Employment has too. At the beginning of this century (January 2000), the motor vehicle and parts manufacturing industry (including both domestic and overseas owned U.S. producers) employed about 1,300,000 in the United States. That number bottomed out at 660,000 in 2009 during the recession and bankruptcies of that era. As of January 2020, it was back up to 976,000, or about 25% less than in January 2000. (We use January 2020 here to avoid the temporary effect on employment of the pandemic in 2020. For example, employment was down as low as 627,000 in April 2020.) Looking only at motor vehicle manufacturing (without parts), employment in January 2000 was 292,000, hitting its low of 123,000 in 2009, and growing to 235,000 by January 2020.[74] Consider that, according to Bloomberg, in the late 1970s, GM alone had U.S. employment of over 600,000, including over 500,000 hourly employees. As of January 2020, GM's U.S. employment was 96,000, including 48,000 hourly employees.[75] As we noted earlier, Mexico, by contrast, with its much lower labor costs, proximity to the large U.S. market, and access to export markets elsewhere, has, by contrast, grown its production and employment significantly over time.

As we saw earlier in this chapter, a two-tier wage structure allows a company to pay new hires at a lower wage. That is a major tool in reducing labor costs. At the Big Three (GM, Ford, Fiat Chrysler), as a result of their most recent contract agreements with the United Automobile Workers (UAW), the hourly wage for Tier 1 workers is $32.32 (up from $28 previously). In contrast, the wage for Tier 2 workers is up to $17 to $29.94, up from the previous $17 to $28. New hires start at $17 and progress through higher wage rates over time. For already employed Tier 2 employees at GM, under the previous contract, it took 8 years for a Tier 2 employee to progress to the top $28 rate. Under the new contract at GM (https://uaw.org/wp-content/uploads/2019/10/56100-UAW_hourly-1.pdf) that runs through 2023, in contrast, it will take already employed GM Tier 2 employees only 4 years to progress to the top rate, now $32.32. However, it appears that new Tier 2 employee hires going forward will still take 8 years to progress to the $32.32 top rate.[76] It is estimated that 20% and 45% of Big Three hourly employees, depending on the company, are on the Tier 2 wage scale. Thus, the savings are substantial.

In the GM UAW contract, there are also separate wage rates for "GMCH" (GM Components Holdings) employees and for "CCA" (GM's Customer Care and Aftersales) employees. The GMCH rate starts at $16.25 and tops out (after 8 years on the job) at $22.50. The CCA wage rate starts at $17.00 and tops out (again, it appears after 8 years) at $31.57. There are also "supplemental" (temporary) employees at the GM (and the Big Three). These employees also have lower wages ($16.67) and have the least job security, offering the company a way to easily reduce headcount when demand declines. In addition, there are flex temps and part-time temps.[77] Finally, it appears that, except for Tier 1 employees, the retirement plan is switched from a defined benefit to defined contribution plan (a 401k—discussed in Chapter 13) and there is no retiree health care benefit.[78]

Here are some questions to consider:

1. Besides Tier 1 employees, what are the other categories of hourly workers at GM? How many categories are there? How does the wage rate of each compare to that of Tier 1 employees?

2. How much more would it cost today if all Tier 2 employees at GM were paid the same as Tier 1 employees are paid today? How much more will it cost in each of the four years of the recent contract to implement the contract agreement to move current Tier 2 employees to Tier 1 wage levels over time? Hint: Use the information on the percentage of employees who are Tier 1 and Tier 2. Compute the average wage in each year and multiple it times the number of employees in each Tier and multiply by 2,080 hours per year.
3. Refer back to our earlier exhibit (**EXHIBIT 7.1**) and use the difference in average hourly compensation (which includes benefits costs) between GM and Toyota/Honda to compute the labor cost difference between them.
4. Look at the GM annual report (10-K) dated February 5, 2020 (again, to look at financials pre-pandemic). What is its operating cost and what is its operating income? Compare the labor costs you computed above to these financials? How big of an effect on costs and operating income do two-tier wages have?
5. To what extent is the renewed job growth in the automobile industry in the United States due to the use of two-tier wages and the associated lower labor costs? What if labor costs had been higher or go higher in the future. What is the risk for employees? (Hint: Recall that automobile production has increased substantially in Mexico.)
6. To what degree is two tier-wage system sustainable? Consider, for example, that a previous Fiat Chrysler CEO stated, in the "long term, (the system) is not a viable structure. It creates two classes of workers within the plant. It doesn't work in the same direction we are working . . . to get this organization to work in unison."[79] It seems the concern is with cooperation and unity of vision/goals among everyone. Explain why that might be under a two-tier system. How serious of a concern do you think this is? When would we expect any such drawbacks to materialize?
7. Will the two-tier wage structure go away in the near future? Summarize the pressures to eliminate it as well as the pressures to keep it. Be sure to consider labor costs and productivity of workers and plants at other companies and in other parts of the world.

Your Turn — Combining Pay Survey and Job Evaluation Data

Return to the job evaluation scores and job structure you created for Whole Foods in the Your Turn at the end of **Chapter 5**. To prepare for **Chapter 8**, where the internal job structure is combined with external market (pay survey) data to develop actual rates of pay for jobs (a pay structure), it will be helpful for you to now begin to become familiar with pay survey data. The U.S. Bureau of Labor Statistics provides Occupational Employment Statistics. For this exercise, we will use "National Industry-Specific Occupational Employment and Wage Estimates for the Food and Beverage Stores Industry" (NAICS 4450A1). Use the following link.[80]

https://www.bls.gov/oes/current/naics4_4450A1.htm#11-0000

Look for occupations that appear to match the occupations from Whole Foods.[81] As examples, consider:

11-9051 Food Service Managers

41-2011 Cashiers

43-5081 Stock Clerks (and order filers)

For each occupation, click on its name to show 10th, 25th, 50th (median), 75th, and 90th percentile wage levels for the occupation.

QUESTIONS:

1. What pay level (e.g., 50th or other) would you recommend be used for the Whole Foods jobs? Would you use the same pay level for all jobs? Explain.
2. How strongly do relative job evaluation points and relative survey pay correspond? For example, what is the ratio of job evaluation points you assigned to Job B (Cashier) and Job F (Team Member, Stock and Display) in the **Chapter 5** Your Turn? What is the ratio of survey pay from Occupational Employment Statistics for 41-2011 Cashiers and 43-5081 Stock Clerks? Are the two ratios the same? (In **Chapter 8**, we will discuss why these ratios, one based on internal worth and the other based on external worth, may differ.) If these two ratios or other ratios you compute using other Whole Foods/pay survey jobs differ, which ratio (internal, based on job evaluation, or external, based on the pay survey) would you recommend be emphasized or receive priority in setting actual pay?
3. What are the limitations of the Occupational Employment Statistics data?

Summary

One reviewer of this book told us, "There are three important contributions of this chapter: (1) that there is no 'going rate' and so managers make conscious pay-level and pay-mix decisions influenced by several factors; (2) that there are both product market and labor market competitors that impact the pay-level and pay-mix decisions; and (3) that alternative pay-level and pay-mix decisions have different consequences." That is a great summary of the key points.

The pay model used throughout this book emphasizes strategic policy issues: objectives, alignment, competitiveness, contributions, and management. Policies need to be designed to achieve specific pay objectives. This part of the book is concerned with external competitiveness, or pay comparisons among organizations. Does Apple Computer pay its accountants the same wage that Florida Power pays its accountants? Probably not. Different companies pay different rates; the average of the overall array of rates in an organization constitutes the pay level. Different companies also use different forms of pay. To achieve the objectives stipulated for the pay system, both the pay level and the pay mix must be properly positioned relative to competitors. Each integrated job structure or career path within the organization may have its own competitive position in the market. **Chapter 8** considers the decisions involved and the variety of techniques available to implement those decisions.

Before we proceed, let us reemphasize that the major reason we are interested in the external competitiveness policy–pay level and mix of pay forms–is that it has profound consequences on the organization's objectives. Theories and practical experience support this belief. But as we have also noted, more research is needed to guide us in making decisions. We have clearly established that differences among organizations' competitive policies and their pay levels and forms exist. We have examined the factors that determine these differences. What remains to be better understood is the potential effects of various policies.

Review Questions

1. Distinguish policies on external competitiveness from policies on internal alignment. Why is external competitiveness so important?
2. What factors shape an organization's external competitiveness?
3. What does marginal revenue product have to do with pay?

4. What pay level does the efficiency wage predict? Does the theory accurately predict organization behavior? Why or why not?
5. What is a relevant market? What difference does it make when determining people's pay?
6. Can you think of any companies that follow a lag and/or lead policy? Why do they believe it pays to pay differently? Can you think of any companies that follow performance-driven and/or work/life balance policies?

APPENDIX 7-A

Utility Analysis

One way to quantify and think about the effects of a compensation program is to use utility analysis. We define *utility* as the dollar value created by increasing revenues and/or decreasing costs by changing one or more human resource practices.[82] Utility analysis has most typically been used to analyze the payoff for making better hiring decisions. Compensation plays a major role here because a higher pay level may increase an organization's ability to hire and keep the best talent. In addition, as our discussion of sorting effects in **Chapter 1** suggested, differences in pay mix may also have major effects. For example, a pay mix that emphasizes performance-based pay may also have an impact by being especially attractive to high performers. In the broader picture, compensation decisions can be analyzed by modeling the cost and value created by different pay-level and pay-mix strategies. What does each strategy cost and what does it do for revenues via attraction, selection, and retention of a workforce that has a particular level of ability and motivation? Here, we will use a very basic form of utility analysis, which focuses only on the quality of the workforce initially hired.

To estimate utility in this basic approach, we model it as a function of several parameters:

$$u = r \times SDy \times Z - C/SR$$

where:

u = utility (revenue − cost) per hire per year.

r = validity coefficient, the correlation between criterion, y, and one or more pre-employment assessments used to make hiring decisions. It is the accuracy of our predictions regarding which applicants will perform well as employees.

SDy = standard deviation of the dollar value of different employee performance levels. In essence, this parameter measures the value of high performance versus average or low performance in a job. (This parameter would be higher for jobs like CEO, actors, athletes, attorneys, real estate brokers, and consultants where star performers can generate much more profit than weaker performers and lower for most lower-skill or highly structured jobs, where performance differences are less consequential.) Although the accuracy of utility estimates depends on accurate estimations of SDy, we will use a very rough rule of thumb here to keep things more manageable: SDy equals 40 percent of salary.

Z = mean standard score (z distribution, mean = 0, SD = 1) of those hired on the predictor used to select/hire employees.

C = cost per applicant. Note that in the utility formula, C is divided by the selection ratio. Thus, C/SR becomes large (and drives the utility estimate lower) as either cost per applicant increases or our selectivity increases (i.e., SR decreases). For example, a cost per applicant of \$200 and a selection ratio of .5 yields \$200/.5 = \$400, but a cost per applicant of \$200 and a selection ratio of .05 yields \$200/.05 = \$4,000. Thus, there is a trade-off between the gains from increasing average hire quality (Z) and the cost of being more selective in hiring to achieve this higher quality.

SR = selection ratio, which is hires/applicants.

It is important to note how Z changes as we become more selective (lower SR) in our hiring. Based on the standard normal distribution function:

SR	Z
5%	2.06
10%	1.75
20%	1.40
50%	0.80
80%	0.35
100%	0.00

In other words, if we hire all (100 percent of) applicants, our average z (Z) score would be .00, indicating that the average quality of our hires would be the same as the average quality of the applicant pool. However, if we are more selective and hire 50 percent of our applicants, then our average quality (Z) will be higher, .80. At a still higher selectivity of 5 percent, Z will be 2.06, indicating that our hires would be 2.06 standard deviations above the mean in the applicant pool.

Let us assume we are filling a position that will cost us a salary of \$100,000 under our new selective hiring approach (versus \$90,000 under the old system). If we are able to increase the quality of our hires to Z = 2.06 (from Z = .80) through selective hiring, what would the impact be on utility? Assume that the average cost per applicant is \$200. (Some applicants can be screened out quickly and cheaply, while other applicants will require higher costs to do more intensive screening.)

Old Selection Strategy

$SR = .50\ (Z = .80),\ r = .40,\ SD = \$40{,}000,\ cost = \$200$

$u = .40 \times \$40{,}000 \times .80 - \$200/.50 = \$12{,}400/\text{hire}$

New Selection Strategy

$SR = .05\ (Z = 2.06),\ r = .40,\ SD = \$40{,}000,\ cost = \$200$

$u = .40 \times \$40{,}000 \times 2.06 - \$200/.05 = \$28{,}960/\text{hire}$

In other words, our new, more selective hiring approach yields a utility gain of \$28,960 − \$12,400 = \$16,560 per hire.

But hold on. We are paying a $10,000 higher salary to enable us to be more selective in our hiring in the new approach. Thus, the utility gain is instead $16,560 − $10,000 = $6,560. Further, benefits, on average, add about another 40 cents on top of every dollar of direct pay. So, perhaps we should use 1.4 × $10,000 = $14,000 as the incremental compensation cost of the new selection strategy. The incremental utility would then be $16,560 − $14,000 = $2,560 per hire.[83]

Of course, our conclusion depends entirely on the estimates and assumptions we put into the model. Paying more will, of course, not always generate higher utility. It really depends on the situation and the organization's strategy. More-accurate estimates of utility of compensation can be obtained by following more complex models that have been developed.[84] Estimates obtained with these models would very likely change and be more accurate because they more fully recognize sorting effects (including retention patterns of high and low performers) and gains and losses to compensation decisions that accumulate over time. We have tried to keep things simpler here in the interest of introducing some basic ideas and logic.

Endnotes

1. "What People Earn 2020." Parade, April 3, 2020. Parade.com.
2. HRE Editorial Staff. "Introducing HR's Elite, the industry's highest-paid execs." Human Resource Executive, September 15, 2020. hrexecutive.com.
3. Erica Groshen, "Five Reasons Why Wages Vary Among Employers," *Industrial Relations* 30 (1991), pp. 350–381; B. Gerhart and S. Rynes, *Compensation: Theory, Evidence and Strategic Implications* (Thousand Oaks, CA: Sage, 2003); B. Gerhart and G. Milkovich, "Organization Differences in Managerial Compensation and Financial Performance," *Academy of Management Journal* 33 (1990), pp. 663–691.
4. Karen Weise, "Amazon to Raise Minimum Wage to $15 for All U.S. Workers," *New York Times,* Oct. 2, 2018; Steven Greenhouse, "Gap to Raise Minimum Hourly Pay," *New York Times*, February 19, 2014; Hiroko Tabuchimarch, "Target Plans to Raise Pay to at Least $9 an Hour," *New York Times*, March 19, 2015, p. B5.
5. Anna Wilde Mathews and Theo Francis, "Aetna Sets Wage Floor: $16 an Hour," *Wall Street Journal*, January 13, 2015, p. B1.
6. Michael Wayland. "UAW strike cost GM up to $4 billion for 2019, substantially higher than estimated." CNBC.com, October 29, 2019.
7. Production Statistics from: International Organization of Motor Vehicle Manufacturers, http://www.oica.net/.
8. William Boston, "In Germany, Mexican Workers Learn Audi's Ways," *Wall Street Journal*, March 18, 2015, p. A11; Dudley Althaus and William Boston, "Trade Pacts Given Mexico an Edge," *Wall Street Journal*, March 18, 2015, p. A1.
9. The National Association of Colleges and Employers, Bethlehem, PA, publishes a quarterly survey of starting-salary offers to college graduates; data are reported by curriculum, by functional area, and by degree at *www.naceweb.org*. It is one of several sources employers may use to establish the offers they extend to new graduates.
10. Adapted from our analysis of CHiPS data set, by arrangement with Clark Consulting, Boston, MA.
11. C. Trevor and M. Graham, "Deriving the Market Wage: Three Decision Areas in the Compensation Survey Process," *WorldatWork* 9(4), 2000, pp. 69–77.

12. Barry Gerhart and George Milkovich, "Employee Compensation: Research and Practice," in *Handbook of Industrial and Organizational Psychology,* 2nd ed., M. D. Dunnette and L. M. Hought, eds. (Palo Alto, CA: Consulting Psychologists Press, 1992).
13. Barry Gerhart and Sara Rynes, "Determinants and Consequences of Salary Negotiations by Male and Female MBA Graduates," *Journal of Applied Psychology* 76(2), 1991, pp. 256–262.
14. Morris M. Kleiner, *Licensing Occupations: Ensuring Quality or Restricting Competition?* (Kalamazoo, MI: Upjohn Institute, 2006).
15. Thomas A. Mahoney, *Compensation and Reward Perspective* (Burr Ridge, IL: Irwin, 1979), p. 123.
16. David Levine, Dale Belman, Gary Charness, et al., *Changes in Careers and Wage Structures at Large American Employers* (Kalamazoo, MI: Upjohn Institute, 2001); David I. Levine, D. Belman, Gary Charness, et al., *The New Employment Contract: Evidence About How Little Wage Structures Have Changed* (Kalamazoo, MI: Upjohn Institute, 2001); Edward P. Lazear, *Personnel Economics* (New York: Wiley, 1998); Carl M. Campbell III, "Do Firms Pay Efficiency Wages? Evidence With Data at the Firm Level," *Journal of Labor Economics* 11(3), 1993, pp. 442–469.
17. Peter Cappelli and Keith Chauvin, "An Interplant Test of the Efficiency Wage Hypothesis," *Quarterly Journal of Economics,* August 1991, pp. 769–787.
18. L. Rynes and J. W. Boudreau, "College Recruiting in Large Organizations: Practice, Evaluation, and Research Implications," *Personnel Psychology* 39 (1986), pp. 729–757.
19. E. Groshen and A. B. Krueger, "The Structure of Supervision and Pay in Hospitals," *Industrial and Labor Relations Review,* February 1990, pp. 134S–146S.
20. P. Milgrom and J. Roberts, *Economics, Organizations, and Management* (Englewood Cliffs, NJ: Prentice-Hall, 1992).
21. A. K. G. Hildreth and A. Oswald, "Rentsharing and Wages: Evidence From Company and Establishment Panels," *Journal of Labor Economics* 15 (1997), pp. 318–337.
22. C. O. L. H. Porter, D. E. Conlon, and Allison Barber, "The Dynamics of Salary Negotiations: Effects on Applicants' Justice Perceptions and Recruitment Decisions," *The International Journal of Conflict Management* 15(3), 2005, pp. 273–303; A. VanVinnen, "Person-Organization Fit: The Match Between Newcomers' and Recruiters' Preferences for Organization Cultures," *Personnel Psychology* 53 (2000), pp. 115–125.
23. Christopher J. Collins and Jian Han, "Exploring Applicant Pool Quantity and Quality: The Effects of Early Recruitment Practice Strategies, Corporate Advertising, and Firm Reputation," *Personnel Psychology,* Autumn 2004, pp. 685–717.
24. Daniel M. Cable and Timothy A. Judge, "Pay Preferences and Job Search Decisions: A Person-Organization Fit Perspective," *Personnel Psychology,* Summer 1994, pp. 317–348.
25. Gary S. Becker, *Human Capital* (Chicago: University of Chicago Press, 1975); Barry Gerhart, "Gender Differences in Current and Starting Salaries: The Role of Performance, College Major, and Job Title," *Industrial and Labor Relations Review* 43 (1990), pp. 418–433; Robert Bretz, C. Quinn Trank, and S. L. Rynes, "Attracting Applicants in the War for Talent: Differences in Work Preferences Among High Achievers," *Journal of Business and Psychology* 16 (2002), pp. 331–345.
26. Occupational earnings information for the United States is available at www.bls.govloes/curent/os_nat.htm. Earnings by education level is available at www.bls.gov/cps/earings.htm#demographic.
27. George F. Dreher and Taylor Cox Jr., "Labor Market Mobility and Cash Compensation: The Moderating Effects of Race and Gender," *Academy of Management Journal* 43(5), 2000, pp. 890–900.
28. Peter Drucker, "They're Not Employees, They're People," *Harvard Business Review,* February 2002, pp. 70–77; David I. Levine, "Fairness, Markets, and Ability to Pay: Evidence From Compensation

Executives," *American Economic Review,* December 1993, pp. 1241–1259; B. Klaas, "Containing Compensation Costs: Why Firms Differ in Their Willingness to Reduce Pay," *Journal of Management* 25(6), 1999, pp. 829–850.

29. David I. Levine, "Fairness, Markets, and Ability to Pay: Evidence From Compensation Executives," *American Economic Review,* December 1993, p. 1250.
30. Dana Mattioli, "Salary Cuts: Ugly, But It Could Be Worse," *The Wall Street Journal,* April 9, 2009; Matthew Quinn, "Survey: One in Four Companies Has Frozen Salaries," *Workforce Management,* February 9, 2009.
31. Watson Wyatt, "Aligning Rewards With the Changing Employment Deal," *WorldatWork,* 2007, www.watsonwyatt.com.
32. "National Wages Council Recommends the Restructuring of Wage System for Competitiveness–Ministers and Top Civil Servants to Lead with Wage Cuts," *Singapore Straits,* May 22, 2003; Marek Szwejczewski and Sri Srikanthan, "The Risks of Outsourcing: Unexpected Consequences," *Financial Times,* April 14, 2006, p. 8; Thomas Friedman, *The World Is Flat* (New York: Farrar, Straus and Giroux, 2006); "CEO's Marital Duties Outsourced to Mexican Groundskeeper," *The Onion* 39(48), December 10, 2003, p. 1.
33. Erica L. Groshen and David Levine, *The Rise and Decline (?) of Employer Wage Structures* (New York: Federal Reserve Bank, 2000).
34. John W. Budd and Brian P. McCall, "The Grocery Stores Wage Distribution: A Semi-Parametric Analysis of the Role of Retailing and Labor Market Institutions," *Industrial and Labor Relations Review* 54(2A), 2001, pp. 484–501.
35. D. M. Raff, "The Puzzling Profusion of Compensation Systems in the Interwar Automobile Industry," Working Paper, NBER, 1998. Raff attributes the fantastic diversity of compensation programs for blue-collar employees (firm-based, piece rate, companywide, team-based) to differences in technology employed among competitors.
36. Walter Oi and Todd L. Idson, "Firm Size and Wages," in *Handbook of Labor Economics, ed.* O. Ashenfelter and D. Card (Amsterdam: North Holland, 1999), pp. 2165–2214.
37. H. Heneman and T. Judge, "Pay and Employee Satisfaction," in *Compensation in Organizations: Current Research and Practice,* S. L. Rynes and B. Gerhart, eds. (San Francisco, CA: Jossey-Bass, 2000); T. R. Mitchell and A. E. Mickel, "The Meaning of Money: An Individual Differences Perspective," *Academy of Management Review* 24 (1999), pp. 568–578; Watson Wyatt, *Playing to Win: Strategic Rewards in the War for Talent* (New York: Watson Wyatt, 2001); Hudson Employment Index, *Transforming Pay Plans: 2006 Compensation and Benefits Report,* www.hudson-index.com/node.asp?SID = 6755.
38. Sara L. Rynes, Amy E. Colbert, and Kenneth G. Brown, "HR Professionals' Beliefs about Effective Human Resource Practices: Correspondence between Research and Practice," *Human Resource Management* 41(2), Summer 2002, pp. 149–174; Sara L. Rynes, Amy E. Colbert, and Kenneth G. Brown, "Seven Common Misconceptions about Human Resource Practices: Research Findings Versus Practitioner Beliefs," *Academy of Management Executive* 16(3), 2002, pp. 92–102.
39. Larry W. Hunter, "What Determines Job Quality in Nursing Homes?" *Industrial 8 Labor Relations Review* 53, (2000) pp. 463–481; Rosemary Batt, "Explaining Intra-Occupational Wage Inequality in Telecommunications Services: Customer Segmentation, Human Resource Practices, and Union Decline," *Industrial and Labor Relations Review* 54 (2A), 2001, pp. 425–449.
40. P. Osterman, "The Wage Effects of High Performance Work Organization in Manufacturing," *Industrial and Labor Relations Review* 59 (2006), pp. 187–204.

41. A. E. Barber and R. D. Bretz Jr., "Compensation, Attraction and Retention," in *Compensation in Organizations,* S. L. Rynes and B. Gerhart, eds. (San Francisco, CA: Jossey-Bass, 2000), pp. 32–60; S. C. Currall, A. J. Towler, T. A. Judge, and L. Kohn, "Pay Satisfaction and Organizational Outcomes," *Personnel Psychology* 58 (2005), pp. 613–640; H. G. Heneman III and T. A. Judge, "Compensation Attitudes," in *Compensation in Organizations,* S. L. Rynes and B. Gerhart, eds. (San Francisco, CA: Jossey-Bass, 2000); M. L. Williams, M. A. McDaniel, and N. T. Nguyen, "A Meta-Analysis of the Antecedents and Consequences of Pay Level Satisfaction," *Journal of Applied Psychology* 91 (2006), pp. 392–413; B. Gerhart and S. L. Rynes, *Compensation: Theory, Evidence, and Strategic Implications* (Thousand Oaks, CA: Sage, 2003); B. S. Klaas and J. A. McCledon, "To Lead, Lag, or Match: Estimating the Financial Impact of Pay Level Policies," *Personnel Psychology* 49 (1996), pp. 121–141.
42. Hazhir Rahmandad and Zeynep Ton. If Higher Pay Is Profitable, Why Is It So Rare? Modeling Competing Strategies in Mass Market Services. Organization Science, 2020, 1053-1071.
43. Mark C. Long, Kristin M. Dziczek, Daniel D. Luria, and Edith A. Wiarda, "Wage and Productivity Stability in U. S. Manufacturing Plants," *Monthly Labor Review* 131(5), 2008, pp. 24–36.
44. Charlie Trevor and M. E. Graham, "Deriving the Market Wage: Three Decision Areas in the Compensation Survey Process," *WorldatWork Journal* 9(4), 2000, pp. 69–77.
45. Trader's Joe's, *http://www.traderjoes.com/product_categories.html#Booze,* August 31, 2009.
46. William M. Bulkeley, "IBM Documents Give Rare Look at Sensitive Plans on 'Offshoring,'" *The Wall Street Journal,* January 19, 2004.
47. Nira Sheth and Nathan Koppel, "With Times Tight, Even Lawyers Get Outsourced," *The Wall Street Journal,* November 26, 2008.
48. Heather Timmons, "Cost-Cutting in New York, But a Boom in India," *The New York Times,* August 12, 2008.
49. P. J. Dowling, M. Festing, and A. D. Engle, Sr., *International Human Resource Management,* 7th ed. (Boston: Cengage, 2017).
50. Klaus Schwab, *The Global Competitiveness Report 2019,* World Economic Forum. www.weforum.org. Note: The 2020 report was not used because it appeared, due to the pandemic, that the ranking data normally reported, was not.
51. Kendall Roth and Sharon O'Donnell, "Foreign Subsidiary Compensation Strategy: An Agency Theory Perspective," *Academy of Management Journal* 39 (1996), pp. 678–703.
52. Paulo Prada and Niraj Shethapril, "Delta Air Ends Use of India Call Centers," *The Wall Street Journal,* April 18, 2009.
53. Margaret Williams, Michael McDaniels, and Njung Nguyen, "A Meta-Analysis of the Antecedents and Consequences of Pay Level Satisfaction," *Journal of Applied Psychology,* March 2006, pp. 392–413; David I. Levine, "Fairness, Markets, and Ability to Pay: Evidence from Compensation Executives," *American Economic Review,* December 1993, pp. 1241–1259.
54. See, for example, any of the surveys conducted by leading consulting firms: Hewitt, *www.hewitt.com;* Wyatt Watson, *www.watsonwyatt.com;* Hay, *www.haygroup.com;* Mercer, *www.mercer.com;* Towers Perrin, *www.towersperrin.com;* Executive Alliance, *www.executivealliance.com.*
55. Laura Johnson and Darrell Cira, "Taking the Best Path to Implementing a Global Pay Structure: The General Mill's Experience," paper at WorldatWork Conference, Seattle, WA, June 1, 2009.
56. Brian S. Klaas and John A. McClendon, "To Lead, Lag, or Match: Estimating the Financial Impact of Pay Level Policies," *Personnel Psychology* 49 (1996), pp. 121–140.
57. Robert Kaplan, *Imperial Grunts* (New York: Random House, 2005).

58. B. Gerhart and S. Rynes, *Compensation: Theory, Evidence and Strategic Implications* (Thousand Oaks, CA: Sage, 2003).

59. Robert Bretz, J. W. Boudreau, W. R. Boswell, and T. A. Judge, "Personality and Cognitive Ability as Predictors of Job Search Among Employed Managers," *Personnel Psychology* 54 (2001), pp. 25–50; Charlie Trevor, Barry Gerhart, and John Boudreau, "Voluntary Turnover and Job Performance: Curvilinearity and the Moderating Influences of Salary Growth and Promotions," *Journal of Applied Psychology* 82 (1997), pp. 44–61; A. L. Heavey, J. A. Holwerda, and J. P. Hausknecht, "Causes and Consequences of Collective Turnover: A Meta-analytic Review," *Journal of Applied Psychology*, 98(3), 2013, p. 412.

60. Gerhart, B., & Feng, J. (2021). The Resource-Based View of the Firm, Human Resources, and Human Capital: Progress and Prospects. *Journal of Management.* Engbom, N. 2020. Labor Market Fluidity and Human Capital Accumulation. Working Paper. Organisation for Economic Co-operation and Development (OECD). 2019. Barriers to exit–Background note. OECD. Lazear, E. P., & Spletzer, J. R. 2012. Hiring, churn, and the business cycle. *American Economic Review*, 102: 575-79. Jovanovic, B., & Moffitt, R. 1990. An estimate of a sectoral model of labor mobility. *Journal of Political Economy*, 98: 827-852.

61. UW-Madison. "Summary of Outside Offers and Retention Efforts, 2015-16." https://apir.wisc.edu/faculty-staff/recruitment-and-retention/.

62. R. Folger and M. A. Konovsky, "Effects of Procedural and Distributive Justice on Reactions to Pay Raise Decisions," *Academy of Management Journal* 32 (1989), pp. 115–30; J. Greenberg, "Determinants of Perceived Fairness of Performance Evaluations," *Journal of Applied Psychology* 71 (1986), pp. 340–342.

63. B. Gerhart and G. Milkovich, "Organizational Differences in Managerial Compensation and Financial Performance," *Academy of Management Journal* 33 (1990), pp. 663–691; M. Bloom and J. Michel, "The Relationships among Organization Context, Pay, and Managerial Turnover," *Academy of Management Journal* 45 (2002), pp. 33–42; M. Bloom and G. Milkovich, "Relationships among Risk, Incentive Pay, and Organization Performance," *Academy of Management Journal* 41(3), 1998, pp. 283–297; B. Hall and J. Liebman, "Are CEOs Really Paid Like Bureaucrats?" *Quarterly Journal of Economics,* August 1998, pp. 653–691. Variable pay is discussed in Chapters 9 through 11. "Variable" indicates that the pay increase (bonus) is not added to base pay; hence, it is not part of fixed costs but is variable, since the amount may vary next year.

64. B. Gerhart and G. Milkovich, "Organizational Differences in Managerial Compensation and Financial Performance," *Academy of Management Journal* 33 (1990), pp. 663–691.

65. David I. Levine, "Fairness, Markets, and Ability to Pay: Evidence from Compensation Executives," *American Economic Review,* December 1993, pp. 1241–1259.

66. Mei Fong, "A Chinese Puzzle," *The Wall Street Journal,* August 16, 2005, p. B1.

67. L. Gaughan and J. Kasparek, "Employees as Customers: Using Market Research to Manage Compensation and Benefits," *Workspan* (9), 2000, pp. 31–38; M. Sturman, G. Milkovich, and J. Hannon, "Expert Systems' Effect on Employee Decisions and Satisfaction," *Personnel Psychology* (1997), pp. 21–34; J. Shaw and S. Schaubrock, "The Role of Spending Behavior Patterns in Monetary Rewards," Working Paper, University of Kentucky, 2001; S. Dubner, "Calculating the Irrational in Economics," *The New York Times,* June 28, 2003.

68. Reed Hastings, "How to Set Your Employees Free," *Bloomberg Businessweek*, April 12, 2012; Jeffrey Goldfarb and Reynolds Holding, "Incentives Play Role in Success of Netflix," *The New York Times,* May 8, 2011; National Center for Employee Ownership Report, "Equity Compensation Case Study: Netflix,"

November–December 2007; David F. Larcker, Allan McCall, and Brian Tayan, "Equity on Demand: The Netflix Approach to Compensation," Stanford Graduate School of Business, Case CG-19, January 15, 2010.

69. Brian Klaas and John A. McClendon, "To Lead, Lag, or Match: Estimating the Financial Impact of Pay Level Policies," *Personnel Psychology* 49 (1996), pp. 121–140; M. C. Sturman, C. O. Trevor, J. W. Boudreau, and B. Gerhart, "Is It Worth It to Win the Talent War? Evaluating the Utility of Performance-Based Pay," *Personnel Psychology* 56 (2003), pp. 997–1035.
70. Barry Gerhart and George Milkovich, "Employee Compensation: Research and Practice," in *Handbook of Industrial and Organizational Psychology,* 2nd ed., M. D. Dunnette and L. M. Hough, eds. (Palo Alto, CA: Consulting Psychologists Press, 1992).
71. Jason D. Shaw, "Pay Levels and Pay Changes," in *Handbook of Industrial, Work, and Organizational Psychology,* ed. H. Heneman and T. Judge (Thousand Oaks, CA: Sage, 2015); Shaw, "Pay and Employee Satisfaction," in *Compensation in Organizations: Current Research and Practice,* ed. S. Rynes and B. Gerhart (San Francisco: Jossey-Bass, 2000).
72. B. Gerhart and S. Rynes, *Compensation Theory, Evidence and Strategic Implications* (Thousand Oaks, CA: Sage, 2003).
73. Kris Maher, "Nurses Win Settlement over Wages," *Wall Street Journal,* March 9, 2009, p. A6.
74. U.S. Bureau of Labor Statistics. Automotive Industry: Employment, Earnings, and Hours. Not seasonally adjusted data. https://www.bls.gov/iag/tgs/iagauto.htm#emp_national
75. One part of the drop in GM employment is that it spun off Delphi, its in-house parts production unit, into an independent company in 1999. However, that was 43,150 employees and so cannot account for much of the decline from over 500,000 U.S. hourly employees to 48,000. Also, Bloomberg reports that GM now has one-quarter of the production plants it had in the late 1970s. David Welch. "GM Is Now Detroit's Smallest Auto-Making Employer." bloomberg.com, August 29, 2019.
76. Chris Brooks. "GM workers shocked to learn new hires will still take eight years to reach top pay." labornotes.org, November 15, 2019.
77. However, like with Tier 2 employees, GM and the other companies agreed to change their status over time, in this case to more permanent regular employee status. That took place for a substantial number of temporary employees at GM and Ford in 2021. Kalea Hall. "GM, Ford convert hundreds of temps to permanent employees." The Detroit News, January 4, 2021. www.detroitnews.com.
78. Chris Brooks. "GM workers shocked to learn new hires will still take eight years to reach top pay." labornotes.org, November 15, 2019.
79. Jerry Hirsch, "Automakers Plan to Hire Thousands of Workers this Year," *Los Angeles Times*, January 12, 2012.
80. As we will see later, matching is more complex than we will treat it here and must be done well (i.e., with careful attention to the comparability and relative value of jobs in the survey versus jobs in our organization) to avoid significant mistakes in setting rates of pay for jobs. Here, we will temporarily put that important issue aside in the interest of simply becoming familiar with one example of survey data.
81. Contracts are available at UAW Auto Bargaining Resources, https://uaw.org/uaw-auto-bargaining/.
82. Wayne F. Cascio and John W. Boudreau, "Investing in People: Financial Impact of Human Resource Initiatives" (Upper Saddle River, NJ: Financial Times Press, 2008); H. E. Brogden, "When Testing Pays Off," *Personnel Psychology* 2 (1949), pp. 171–185; J. W. Boudreau and C. J. Berger, "Decision-Theoretic Utility Analysis Applied to Employee Separations and Acquisitions," *Journal of Applied Psychology* [monograph] 73 (1985), pp. 467–481; J. W. Boudreau, "Utility Analysis for Decisions in Human Resource Management, in *Handbook of Industrial and Organizational Psychology,* 2nd ed., M. D.

Dunnette and L. M. Hough, eds. (Palo Alto, CA: Consulting Psychologists Press, 1991); I. S. Fulmer and R. E. Ployhart, "'Our Most Important Asset': A Multidisciplinary/Multilevel Review of Human Capital Valuation for Research and Practice," *Journal of Management*, doi: 0149206313511271. November 2013.

83. The accuracy of utility estimates depends on whether higher-quality applicants actually accept job offers. To the degree they do not, the *Z* parameter estimate will be biased upward, biasing utility estimates upward as well. Kevin R. Murphy, "When Your Top Choice Turns You Down: Effect of Rejected Offers on the Utility of Selection Tests," *Psychological Bulletin* 99 (1986), pp. 133–138. Compensation level is one way to increase the probability of job offer acceptance.

84. B. S. Klaas and J. A. McCledon, "To Lead, Lag, or Match: Estimating the Financial Impact of Pay Level Policies," *Personnel Psychology* 49 (1996), pp. 121–141; M. C. Sturman, C. O. Trevor, J. W. Boudreau, and B. Gerhart, "Is It Worth It to Win the Talent War? Evaluating the Utility of Performance-Based Pay," *Personnel Psychology* 56 (2003), pp. 997–1035.

Chapter **Eight**
Designing Pay Levels, Mix, and Pay Structures

Chapter Outline

In **Chapter 7**, we discussed market and organization factors that influence these policies. Now we examine in more details the tools and strategies managers use to determine pay levels, mix of forms, and structures.

MAJOR DECISIONS

The major decisions in setting externally competitive pay and designing the corresponding pay structures are shown in **Exhibit 8.1**. They include (1) specify the employer's competitive pay policy, (2) define the purpose of the survey, (3) select relevant market competitors, (4) design the survey, (5) interpret survey results and construct the market line, (6) construct a pay policy line that reflects external pay policy, and (7) balance competitiveness with internal alignment through the use of **ranges,** flat rates, and/or bands. This is a lengthy list. Think of **Exhibit 8.1** as a road map through this chapter. The guideposts are the major decisions you face in designing a pay structure. Don't forget to end with, So what? "So what" means ensuring that pay structures both support business success and treat employees fairly.

SPECIFY COMPETITIVE PAY POLICY

The first decision–determining the external competitive pay policy–was covered in **Chapter 7**. Translating any external pay policy into practice requires information on the external market. Surveys provide the data for translating that policy into pay levels, pay mix, and structures.

> A **survey** is the systematic process of collecting and making judgments about the compensation paid by other employers.

THE PURPOSE OF A SURVEY

An employer conducts or participates in a survey for a number of reasons: (1) to adjust the pay level in response to changing rates paid by competitors, (2) to set the mix of pay forms relative to that paid by

EXHIBIT 8.1 Determining Externally Competitive Pay Levels and Structures

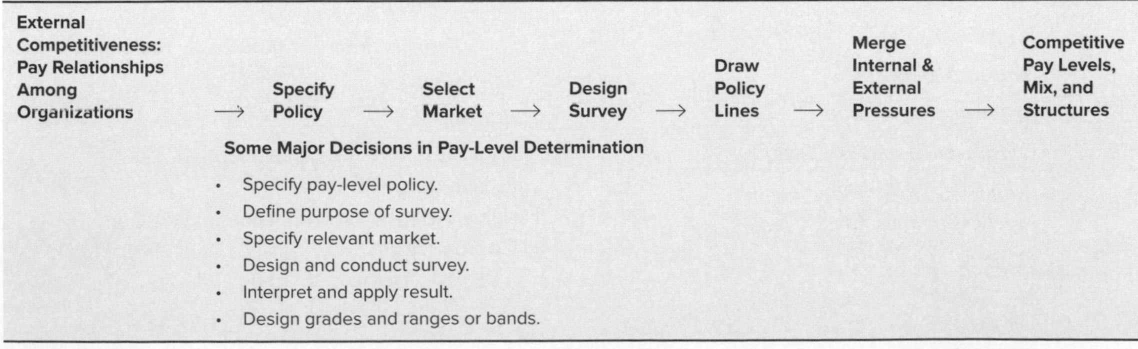

competitors, (3) to establish or price a pay structure, (4) to analyze pay-related problems, or (5) to estimate the labor costs of product/service market competitors.

Adjust Pay Level—How Much to Pay?

Most organizations make adjustments to employees' pay on a regular basis. Such adjustments can be based on the overall movement of pay rates caused by the competition for people in the market. Adjustments may also be based on performance, ability to pay, or terms specified in a contract.

Adjust Pay Mix—What Forms?

Adjustments to the different forms of pay competitors use (base, bonus, stock, benefits) and the relative importance they place on each form occur less frequently than adjustments to overall pay level. It is not clear (without good research) why changes to the pay mix occur less frequently than changes in the pay level. Perhaps the high costs of redesigning a different mix create a barrier. Perhaps inertia prevails. More likely, insufficient attention has been devoted to mix decisions. That is, the mix organizations use may have been based on external pressures such as health care costs, stock values, government regulations, union demands, and what others did. Yet some pay forms may affect employee behavior more than others. So good information on total compensation, the mix of pay competitors use, and costs of various pay forms is increasingly important.

Adjust Pay Structure?

Many employers use market surveys to validate their own job evaluation results. For example, job evaluation may place purchasing assistant jobs at the same level in the job structure as some secretarial jobs. But if the market shows vastly different pay rates for the two types of work, most employers will recheck their evaluation process to see whether the jobs have been properly evaluated. Some may even establish a separate structure for different types of work. Recall from **Chapter 5 (Exhibit 5.16)** that most organizations have multiple pay structures with the mode being 5 or more separate pay structures. IBM, for example, has set pay according to market conditions for each separate occupation (finance, engineering, law). Thus, the job structure that results from internal job evaluation may not match competitors' pay structures in the external market. Reconciling these two pay structures is a major issue.

Rather than integrating an internal and external structure, some employers go straight to market surveys to establish their internal structures. Such "market pricing" mimics competitors' pay structures. Accurate market data are increasingly important as organizations move to more generic work descriptions (associate, leader) that focus on the person's skill as well as the job. Former relationships between job evaluation points and dollars may no longer hold. Accurate information and informed judgment are vital for making all these decisions.

Study Special Situations

Information from specialized surveys can shed light on specific pay-related problems. A special study may focus on a targeted group such as patent attorneys, retail sales managers, secretaries, or software engineers. Unusual increases in an employer's turnover in specific jobs may require focused market surveys to find out if market changes are occurring.[1]

Estimate Competitors' Labor Costs

Survey data are used as part of employers' broader efforts to gather **competitive intelligence.**[2] To better understand how competitors achieve their market share and price their products/services, companies seek to examine (i.e., benchmark) practices, costs, and so forth against competitors, including in the area of compensation. One source of publicly available labor cost data is the Employment Cost Index (ECI), one of four types of salary surveys published regularly by the Department of Labor on its website at *www.bls.gov/ncs/*.[3] The ECI measures quarterly changes in employer costs for compensation. The index allows a firm to compare changes in its average costs to an all-industry or specific-industry average. However, this comparison may have limited value because industry averages may not reflect relevant competitors.[4]

SELECT RELEVANT MARKET COMPETITORS

We are up to the third of our major decisions shown in **Exhibit 8.1**: Specify relevant markets. To make decisions about pay level, mix, and structures, a relevant labor market must be defined that includes employers who compete in one or more of the following areas:

1. The same occupations or skills
2. Employees within the same geographic area
3. The same products and services[5]

Exhibit 8.2 shows how Microsoft and Google select relevant market competitors in establishing executive compensation. Both explicitly include product market ("technology") and labor market competitors. The geographic level is national or international.

Exhibit 8.3 shows how qualifications interact with geography to define the scope of relevant labor markets. As the importance and the complexity of the qualifications increase, the geographic limits also increase.[6] Competition tends to be national or international for managerial and professional skills (as in **Exhibit 8.2**) but local or regional for clerical and production skills.

However, these generalizations do not always hold true. In areas with high concentrations of scientists, engineers, and managers (e.g., Boston or San Jose/Silicon Valley), the primary market comparison may be regional, with national data used only secondarily. As **Exhibit 8.4** shows, pay varies among localities (i.e., there are geographic differentials).[7] A job (computer programmer in this example) that averages $95,640 nationally can pay from $70,890 in Jackson, Mississippi to $113,500 in Silicon Valley (San Jose, California). However, some larger firms ignore local market conditions.[8] Instead, they emphasize internal alignment across geographic areas to facilitate the use of virtual teams. But it turns out that team members in different locations compare their pay. What a surprise.

Some writers argue that if the skills are tied to a particular industry–as underwriters, actuaries, and claims representatives are to insurance, for example–it makes sense to define the market on an industry basis, and some research agrees.[9] If accounting, sales, or clerical skills are not limited to onc particular industry, then industry considerations are less important. From the perspective of cost control and ability to pay, including competitors in the product/service market is crucial.[10] However, this becomes a problem when the major competitors are based in countries with far lower pay rates, such as China or Mexico. But a segmented labor supply (see **Chapter 7**) requires multiple country comparisons.[11] Legal regulations, tax policies, and customs vary among countries. Because of tax laws, managers in Korea and Spain receive company credit cards to use for personal expenses (groceries, clothing). In the United States, these purchases count as taxable income, but they do not in Korea and Spain.

EXHIBIT 8.2 External Competitiveness Compensation Strategy for Top Executives, Microsoft and Google

MICROSOFT
Peer Group

Primary Peer Group-Technology. Primary Peer Group of bellwether technology companies, which reflect Microsoft's more direct competitors for executive talent.

Secondary Peer Group-General Industry. Secondary Peer Group of "large cap" general industry companies, which reflect the complexities of operating large, global, innovative businesses and Microsoft's broader competition for executive talent.

We give greater weight to the pay levels and practices of our technology peers because they more closely represent the labor market in which we compete for key talent.

Primary Peer Group-Technology		Secondary Peer Group-General Industry	
Adobe	IBM	Accenture	Pfizer
Alphabet	Intel	AT&T	Proctor & Gamble
Amazon	Oracle	Comcast	Tesla
Apple	Qualcomm	Honeywell	Verizon
Cisco Systems	Salesforce	Johnson & Johnson	Walt Disney
Facebook		Merck	

Market Position Target

Cash compensation target	"below median" (2008 proxy. No clear statement since. The 2017 proxy says base salary "at or below market median." Note that in 2017 proxy, base salary is expected to be only 10% or less of total compensation.)
Equity award target	"above median" (2008 proxy. No clear statement in more recent proxies.)
Overall	"While . . . market analysis and supplemental data inform the decisions of the independent Board members and the Compensation Committee . . . we do not tie executive officer compensation to specific market percentiles" (2017 proxy).

ALPHABET (formerly GOOGLE)
Peer Group

- High-technology or media company
- Key talent competitor
- High-growth, with a minimum of 50 percent of Alphabet's revenue growth and/or headcount growth over the previous two-year period
- $25 billion or more in annual revenues
- $200 billion or more in market capitalization

Considering these criteria, the Leadership Development and Compensation Committee selected the following peer companies:

Amazon.com, Inc.	IBM
Apple Inc.	Microsoft
Cisco Systems	Netflix
Comcast	Oracle
Facebook	Salesforce
Intel	Walt Disney

An earlier year's proxy also included: While peer group analysis provides a benchmark for our named executive officers' current roles, we also consider job opportunities our named executive officers could take if they were to leave Google. While we have not lost any named executive officer to other companies thus far, we intend to remain competitive with their potential opportunities. Therefore, we also benchmark compensation levels for our named executive officers against the following:

- CEO roles at other S&P 100 companies
- Founder and CEO roles at start-ups

We regularly review our compensation levels against our peer group. We also assess executives based on their individual performance and overall company performance. Management uses this information to develop compensation recommendations for our named executive officers. The Leadership Development and Compensation Committee then reviews these recommendations and makes the final decision on compensation for named executive officers.

Market Position Target

Element of Compensation	Percentile (2008)	Percentile (2011, 2014)	Percentile (2017, 2020)
Base Salary	50th to 70th	90th	No clear statement
Target Total Cash	75th	90th to 95th (90th in 2014)	No clear statement
Target Equity	90th	90th to 95th	No clear statement

Source: Microsoft 2008, 2011, 2015, 2017, and 2020 Proxy Statements; Google 2008, 2011, and 2014 Proxy and Alphabet 2018, 2020 Proxy. Statements. Available at www.sec.gov.

While the quantity of data available for international comparisons is improving, using the data to adjust pay still requires a lot of judgment. Labor markets have emerged relatively recently in some regions (China, Russia). Historically, state planning agencies set nationwide wage rates, so there was no need for surveys.[12] Japanese companies historically shared information among themselves but not with outsiders, making surveys unavailable.[13]

EXHIBIT 8.3 Relevant Labor Markets by Geographic and Employee Groups

Geographic Scope	Production	Office and Clerical	Technicians	Scientists and Engineers	Managerial Professional	Executive
Local: Within relatively small areas such as cities or Metropolitan Statistical Areas (e.g., Dallas metropolitan area)	Most likely	Most likely	Most likely			
Regional: Within a particular area of the state or several states (e.g., oil-producing region of southwestern United States)	Only if in short supply or critical	Only if in short supply or critical	Most likely	Likely	Most Likely	
National: Across the country				Most likely	Most likely	Most likely
International: Across several countries				Only for critical skills or those in very short supply	Only for critical skills or those in very short supply	Sometimes

EXHIBIT 8.4 Pay Differences by Location: Annual Mean Wage by Metro Area, Computer Programmer

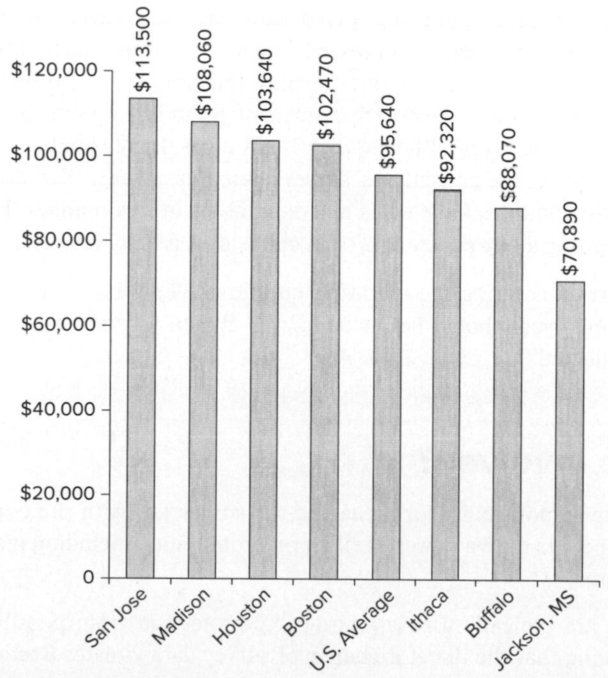

Source: U.S. Bureau of Labor Statistics. www.bls.gov/oes.

But even with good international survey data, judgment is still required. For example, salaries at international companies in developing economies are low by U.S., Western European, and Japanese standards, but they are often very high compared to salaries at domestic companies in those countries. Pay practices of foreign companies can disrupt emerging local markets in developing economies.[14] IBM software engineers in India told us that while they are paid very well by Indian standards, they feel underpaid compared to IBM engineers in the United States who work on the same projects.[15]

Fuzzy Markets

Walk through a bay of cubicles (plastered with *Dilbert* cartoons) at Yahoo! and you are likely to find former kindergarten teachers, software engineers, and sales representatives all collaborating on a single team. Yahoo! combines technology, media, and commerce into one company. What is the relevant labor market? Which firms should be included in Yahoo!'s surveys?

Even within traditional companies, unique talent is required for unique jobs. West Publishing, a provider of legal information to law firms, designed the position of Senior Director of Future Vision Services. The holder of this mouthful title is responsible for ensuring that West's customers (litigious lawyers) increase their purchases over the Web plus increase their satisfaction with West's services. The job was filled by a software engineer with e-commerce, marketing, and theater experience. Try finding that job in the market. These new organizations and jobs fuse together diverse knowledge and experience, so "relevant" markets appear more like "fuzzy" markets.[16] Organizations with unique jobs and structures face the double bind of finding it hard to get comparable market data at the same time they are placing more emphasis on external market data.

DESIGN THE SURVEY

Consulting firms offer a wide choice of ongoing surveys covering almost every job family and industry group imaginable. Their surveys are getting better and better.[17] While we would like to attribute this to the fact that our textbook has improved the sophistication of compensation education (the first edition of our book was published in 1985, and at least some of those early readers ought to be in power positions by now), it is more likely that the improvement is the result of technological advances. Increasingly, consultants offer clients the option of electronically accessing the consultants' survey databases. Clients then do whatever special analysis they need. General Electric conducts most of its market analysis in this manner. **Exhibit 8.5** provides some factors to consider in designing a pay survey and/or in choosing a pay survey vendor/consultant.[18]

Designing a survey requires answering the following questions: (1) Who should be involved in the survey design? (2) How many employers should be included? (3) Which jobs should be included? and (4) What information should be collected?

Who Should be Involved?

In most organizations, the responsibility for managing the survey lies with the compensation manager. But because compensation expenses have a powerful effect on profitability, including managers and employees on the task forces makes sense.

Outside consulting firms are typically used as third-party protection from possible "price-fixing" lawsuits. Suits have been filed alleging that the direct exchange of survey data violates Section 1 of the Sherman Act, which outlaws conspiracies in restraint of trade. Survey participants may be guilty of price fixing if the overall effect of the information exchange is to *interfere with competitive prices* and *artificially hold down wages.* Identifying participants' data by company name is considered price fixing.[19]

How Many Employers?

There are no firm rules on how many employers to include in a survey. Large firms with a lead policy may exchange data with only a few (6 to 10) top-paying competitors.[20] Merrill Lynch aims for the 75th percentile among 11 peer financial firms. A small organization in an area dominated by two or three employers may decide to survey only smaller competitors. National surveys conducted by consulting firms often include

EXHIBIT 8.5 Getting the Most Out of Pay Surveys

Look for communication from survey vendor	The vendor should communicate regularly, not just when it is time to collect data and later provide the survey results. Also, a sure way to tell if survey data are credible is if the vendor follows up with questions about pay data you submitted. There should be stringent quality assurance mechanisms in place.
Focus on your specific business needs	Ideally, the survey should provide data on at least 75 percent of the positions you want to price. Be sure that the survey includes organizations that are your specific labor market competitors—those specific organizations from which you hire employees and to which you most often lose employees. (Of course, product market competitors should also be included.)
Look for easy access to data	The data should come in the format (hard copy, PDF, Excel) that works best for you. Increasingly, data can be accessed at any time. The ability to tailor analyses by running custom reports that capture specific peer groups is important as is the recency of the data and/or the ability to accurately age the data.
Avoid time-consuming data input	Participation in a survey can take anywhere from one hour to several weeks, depending on the complexity and efficiency of data collection. Work with your human resource information system group to estimate the time and cost of responding to a survey. Make sure you are not required to submit data that will not appear in the survey results.
Stretch your salary budget	Participate in free surveys. Check job boards for salary information. Talk to recruiters to get real-time information on the latest market movements. Also, of course, participation (i.e., providing data) in a survey typically reduces the cost of purchasing the survey results.
Antitrust issues—use caution	Make sure that the survey is managed by a third party, pay information provided to participants is at least three months old, at least five participants report data for each survey question, data are weighted so that no single company accounts for more than 25 percent of any single data point. Always consult legal counsel with questions.
Look for added value	Events like job matching meetings and presentations of survey results provide participants the opportunity to meet peers, network, and learn from one another.

Source: Adapted from Rebecca Toman and Kristine Oliver, "Ways to Get the Most out of Salary Surveys," *Workspan,* February 2011, 17–21.

more than 100 employers. Clients of these consultants often stipulate special analyses that report pay rates by selected industry groups, geographic region, and/or pay levels (e.g., top 10 percent).

Publicly Available Data

In the United States, the **Bureau of Labor Statistics (BLS)** is the major source of publicly available compensation (cash, bonus, and benefits but not stock ownership) data. The BLS publishes extensive information on various occupations.

While some private firms may track the rate of change in BLS data as a cross-check on other surveys, the data are often not specific enough to be used alone. Tailoring analysis to specific industry segments, select companies, and specific job content is not feasible.

"Word of Mouse"

Once upon a time individual employees had a hard time comparing their salaries to others'. Information was gathered haphazardly, via word of mouth. Today, a click of the mouse (or trackpad) makes a wealth of data available to everyone. Employees are comparing their compensation to data from the BLS or Salary.com or occupation-specific websites.[21] This ease of access means that managers must be able to explain (defend?) the salaries paid to employees compared to those a mouse click away. Whole Foods confronted this issue via an "open book" list of last year's pay of all employees.[22] Unfortunately, the quality of some salary data on the Web is unclear. Few of the sites (except the BLS, of course) offer any information on how the data were collected, what pay forms are included, and so on. Most are based on information volunteered by site users. Some popular websites even misuse the cost-of-living index when making geographic salary comparisons.[23] On the other hand, Salary.com includes a compensation glossary, identifies where the site's information comes from, and explains what the statistics mean. (Glassdoor.com is another website that can provide this sort of detailed salary-by-job description data.) However, much of what used to be free on Salary.com appear now to require payment. **Exhibit 8.6** shows previous Salary.com pay data for three levels of the programmer job, both at the national level and in Boston. We can see that moving up two levels from I to III in Boston would bring a salary increase from $70,683 to $113,295, an increase of 60 percent. Importantly, there are data on not only salary, but also bonus pay. By comparison, all programmer positions are included in a single category in the BLS survey, making it all but impossible to get a good match and there is no breakout of compensation components.

Many Surveys (But Few That Are Validated)

Opinions about the value of consultant surveys are rampant; research is not. Do Korn Ferry Hay, Mercer, Willis Towers Watson, and Aon surveys yield significantly different results? The fact that companies typically use three or more surveys (for all job types) suggests that different surveys do, in fact, imply different pay levels.[24] Many firms select one survey as their primary source and use others to cross-check or "validate" the results. Some employers routinely combine the results of several surveys and weight each survey in this composite according to somebody's judgment of the quality of the data reported.[25] No systematic study of the effects of differences in market definition, participating firms, types of data collected, quality of data, analysis performed, and/or results is available. Issues of sample design and statistical inference are seldom considered. For staffing decisions, employment test designers report the test's performance against a set of standards (reliability, validity, etc.). Job evaluation's reliability and validity (or lack of) has been much studied and debated. Yet for market surveys and analysis, similar standards do not exist.[26] Without reliability and validity metrics, survey data are open to challenge.

EXHIBIT 8.6 **Salary Survey Data on the Web for Computer Programmer from U.S. Bureau of Labor Statistics and Salary.com**

	Percentile		
	25th	**50th**	**75th**
Bureau of Labor Statistics			
National			
Computer programmer	$ 67,370	$ 89.190	$116.220
Boston			
Computer programmer		$102,470[a]	
Salary.com Salary			
National			
Programmer I	$ 54,322	$ 62,112	$ 70,532
Programmer III	$ 88,111	$ 99,950	$110,310
Programmer V	$109,726	$122,625	$137,344
Boston			
Programmer I	$ 61,830	$ 70,683	$ 80,266
Programmer III	$100,270	$113,295	$125,533
Programmer V	$124,868	$139,548	$156,297
Salary.com Salary + Bonus			
National			
Programmer I	$ 55,031	$ 63,027	$ 71,593
Programmer III	$ 90,432	$102,964	$115,995
Programmer V	$115,626	$132,836	$150,919
Boston			
Programmer I	$ 62,626	$ 71,725	$ 81,833
Programmer III	$ 102,912	$ 117,173	$132,003
Programmer V	$ 131,582	$ 151,168	$171,745

U.S. Department of Labor, Bureau of Labor Statistics, Occupational Employment Statistics. https://www.bls.gov/oes/tables.htm. Accessed April 12, 2021; Salary.com. Accessed March 27, 2018. Use of Salary.com data like that in the exhibit are no longer available for free.

[a]Mean.

Note: The 50th percentile is the median. Median salaries differ from mean salaries for computer programmers reported earlier in the chapter.

e-Compensation

For a demonstration of online surveys, go to ***www.haypaynet.com*** or ***www.salary.com*** or ***www.bls.gov/bls/blswage.htm***. How do the sites compare? Do they give information on which employers are included and which ones are not? Where do their data come from? Do the sites tell you? Which would you use to design a pay system? Explain.

Which Jobs to Include?

There are several approaches to selecting jobs for inclusion.

Benchmark-Job Approach

In **Chapter 5** we noted that benchmark jobs have stable job content, are common across different employers, and include sizable numbers of employees. If the purpose of the survey is to price the entire structure, then benchmark jobs can be selected to include the entire job structure–all key functions and all levels, just as in job evaluation. In **Exhibit 8.7**, the more heavily shaded jobs in the structures are benchmark jobs. Benchmark jobs are chosen from as many levels in each of these structures as can be matched with the descriptions of the benchmark jobs that are included in the survey. **Exhibit 8.8** indicates that about one in three organizations are able to match over 80 percent of jobs to salary survey jobs, with the remaining organizations report less success in matching.

The degree of match between the survey's benchmark jobs and each company's benchmark jobs is assessed by various means. One approach, benchmark conversion/survey leveling is discussed below. As another example, the Korn Ferry Hay Group has installed the same job evaluation plan in many companies that participate in its surveys. Consequently, jobs in different organizations can be compared on their job evaluation points and the distribution of points among the compensable factors. Other surveys simply ask participants to check

EXHIBIT 8.7 Benchmarks

Managerial Group	Technical Group	Manufacturing Group	Administrative Group
		Assembler I Inspector I	
Vice Presidents	Head/Chief Scientist	Packer	Administrative Assistant
Division General Managers	Senior Associate Scientist	Material Handler Inspector II	Principal Administrative Secretary
Managers	Associate Scientist	Assembler II	Administrative Secretary
Project Leaders	Scientist	Drill Press Operator Rough Grinder	Word Processor
Supervisors	Technician	Machinist I Coremaker	Clerk/Messenger

the degree of match (e.g., my company's job is of moderately less value, slightly less value, equal value, etc.). A good survey will include this information in its results. A consultant friend insists that when the compensation manager of a company changes, the job matches change too.

Low-High Approach

If an organization is using skill-competency-based structures or generic job descriptions, it may not have benchmark jobs to match with jobs at competitors who use a traditional job-based approach. Market data must be converted to fit the skill or competency structure. The simplest way to do this is to identify the lowest- and highest-paid benchmark jobs for the relevant skills in the relevant market and to use the wages for these jobs as anchors for the skill-based structures. Work at various levels within the structure can then be slotted between the anchors. For example, if the entry market rate for operator A is $12 per hour and the rate for a team leader is $42 per hour, then the rate for operator B can be somewhere between $12 and $42 per hour.[27]

The usefulness of this approach depends on how well the extreme benchmark jobs match the organization's work and whether they really do tap the entire range of skills. Hanging a pay system on two pieces of market data raises the stakes on the accuracy of those data.

Benchmark Conversion/Survey Leveling

In cases where the content (e.g., job description) of an organization's jobs does not sufficiently match that of jobs in the salary survey, an effort can be made to quantify the difference via **benchmark conversion.** If an organization uses job evaluation, then its job evaluation system can be applied to the survey jobs. The magnitude of difference between job evaluation points for internal jobs and survey jobs provides an estimate of their relative value and thus guidance for adjusting the market data. (Again, a judgment.)

EXHIBIT 8.8 Percentage of Jobs in Organizations That Match to External Pay Survey Jobs

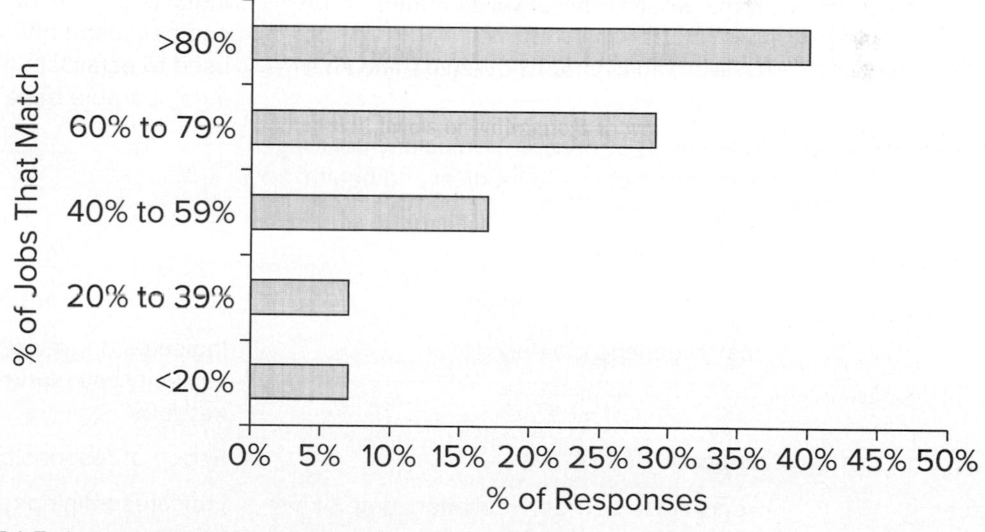

Source: "Job Evaluation and Market-Pricing Practices Survey," WorldatWork, February 2020.

What Information to Collect?

Three basic types of data typically are requested: (1) information about the organization, (2) information about the total compensation system, and (3) specific pay data on each incumbent in the jobs under study. **Exhibit 8.9** lists the basic data elements and the logic for including them. No survey includes all the data that will be discussed. Rather, the data collected depend on the purpose of the survey and the jobs and skills included.

EXHIBIT 8.9 Possible Survey Data Elements and Rationale

Basic Elements	Examples	Rationale
Nature of Organization		
Identification	Company, name, address, contact person	Further contacts
Financial performance	Assets, sales, profits, cash flow	Indicates nature of product/service markets, ability to pay, size, and financials
Size	Profit centers, product lines	Importance of specific job groups
	Total number of employees	Impact on labor market
Structure	Organizational charts Percent of employees at each level	Indicates how business is organized Indicates staffing pattern
Nature of Total Compensation System		
Cash forms used	Base pay, pay-increase schedules, long- and short-term incentives, bonuses, cost-of-living adjustments, overtime and shift differentials	Indicate the mix of compensation offered; used to establish a comparable base
Noncash forms used	Benefits and services, particularly coverage and contributions to medical and health insurance and pensions	
Incumbent and Job		
Date	Date survey data in effect	Update to current date
Job	Match generic job description	Indicates degree of similarity with survey's key jobs
	Reporting levels	Scope of responsibilities
Individual	Years since degree, education, date of hire	Indicates training tenure
Pay	Actual rates paid to each individual, total earnings, last increase, bonuses, incentives	

Basic Elements	Examples	Rationale
HR Outcomes		
Productivity	Revenues/employee Revenues/labor costs	Reflect organization performance and efficiency
Total labor costs	Number of employees × (average wages + benefits)	Major expense
Attraction	Yield ratio: Number accepting offers/ Number of job offers	Reveals recruiting success, a compensation objective
Retention	Turnover rate: Number of high or low performers who leave/Number of employees	Reveals outflow of people, which is related to a compensation objective
Employee views	Total pay satisfaction	Reveals what employees think about their pay

Organization Data

This information reflects the similarities and differences among organizations in the survey. Surveys of executive and upper-level positions include financial and reporting relationships data, since compensation for these jobs is more directly related to the organization's financial performance. Typically, financial data are simply used to group firms by size, expressed in terms of sales or revenues, rather than to analyze competitors' performance. These data are used descriptively to report pay levels and mix by company size. The competitors' data have not been used to compare competitors' productivity (revenues to compensation) or labor costs.

But this is changing. The increased gathering of "competitive intelligence" is changing the type of organization data collected and the way it gets used. Metrics of organization performance such as turnover and revenues are being collected. Other outcomes that may or may not be included are earnings per share, market share, customer satisfaction, employee pay satisfaction, and recruiting yield ratios are not included. Financial data are gathered from other, often publicly available sources (e.g., Finance-Google, Yahoo Finance). Examples include metrics on organization success (revenues, net income, customer satisfaction), turnover (voluntary quit rates), and recruiting (yield ratios).[28]

Total Compensation Data

Information on all types of pay forms is required to assess the total pay package and competitors' practices.[29] The list shown in **Exhibit 8.9** reveals the range of forms that could be included in each company's definition of total compensation. As a practical matter, it can be hard to include *all* the pay forms. Too much detail on benefits, such as medical coverage deductibles and flexible work schedules, can make a survey too cumbersome. Alternatives range from a brief description of a benchmark benefit package to including only the most expensive and variable benefits to an estimate of total benefit expenses as a percentage of total labor costs. Three alternatives–base pay, total cash (base, profit sharing, bonuses), and total compensation (total cash plus benefits and **perquisites**)–are the most commonly used measures of compensation. **Exhibit 8.10** draws the distinction between these three alternatives and highlights the usefulness and limitations of each. **Exhibit 8.11** shows some results of conducting a pay survey that includes these three measures on a sample of engineers.

A: *Base pay.* This is the amount of *cash* the competitors decided *each job and incumbent* is worth. A company might use this information for its initial observations of how "good" the data appear to fit a range of jobs. The market line A is based on base pay.

B: *Total cash.* This is base plus bonus–line B in the exhibit. Total cash measures reveal competitors' use of performance-based cash payments.

EXHIBIT 8.10 Advantages and Disadvantages of Measures of Compensation

Base pay	Tells how competitors are valuing the work in similar jobs	Fails to include performance incentives and other forms, so will not give true picture if competitors offer low base but high incentives.
Total cash (base + bonus)	Tells how competitors are valuing work; also tells the cash pay for performance opportunity in the job	All employees may not receive incentives, so it may overstate the competitors' pay; plus, it does not include long-term incentives.
Total compensation (base + bonus + stock options + stock awards + benefits)	Tells the total value competitors place on this work	All employees may not receive all the forms. Be careful: Don't set base equal to competitors' total compensation. Risks high fixed costs.

EXHIBIT 8.11 Pay Survey Results for Different Measures of Compensation

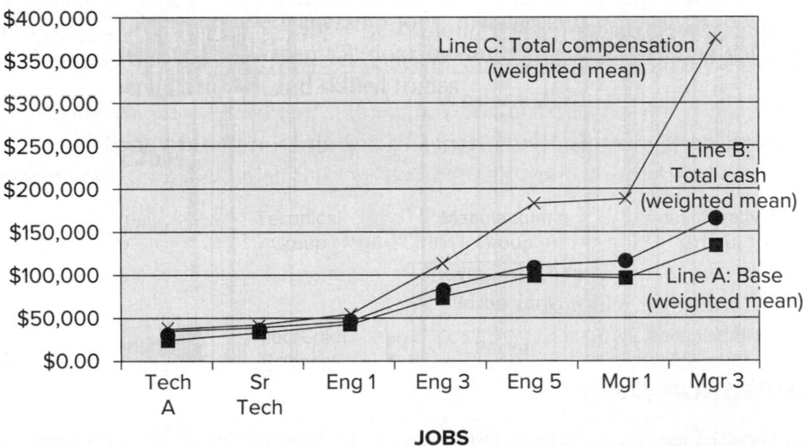

Survey Job	A: Base, Wtd Mean	B: Cash, Wtd Mean	C: Total Comp, Wtd Mean
Tech A	$22,989	$24,554	$30,831
Sr Tech	$37,748	$42,510	$51,482
Eng 1	$46,085	$48,289	$56,917
Eng 3	$73,134	$81,285	$112,805
Eng 5	$102,415	$112,587	$179,449
Mgr 1	$95,260	$115,304	$188,509
Mgr 3	$134,173	$171,030	$378,276

C: *Total compensation.* This includes total cash plus stock options and benefits. Total compensation reflects the total overall value of the employee (performance, experience, skills, etc.) plus the value of the work itself.

It is no surprise that for all seven jobs, total compensation is higher than base pay alone or base plus bonus. However, the variability and magnitude of the difference may be a surprise: from $7,842 (34 percent) for the job of technician A to $244,103.38 (182 percent) for the job of manager 3. Base pay is, on average, only 35 percent of total compensation for the manager 3s in this survey. So the measure of compensation is an important decision. Misinterpreting competitors' pay practices can lead to costly mispricing of pay levels and structures.

INTERPRET SURVEY RESULTS AND CONSTRUCT A MARKET LINE

Survey data today are typically exchanged online. Technology has made processing data and spitting out reports easy. The greatest challenge of total compensation surveys is to understand how to evaluate the information. In the best total compensation projects, each firm sees the survey as a customizable database project where they can specify the characteristics of the employers and jobs to analyze.

After the survey data are all collected, the next step is to analyze the results and use statistics to construct a **market pay line.** More than 20 years ago, Belcher interviewed compensation professionals to discover how survey data are actually analyzed. He reported:

> Every organization uses its own methods of distilling information from the survey; uses different surveys for different purposes; and uses different methods for company surveys. I could find no commonality in these methods of analysis by industry, by firm size, or by union presence. For example, some did nothing except read the entire survey, some emphasized industry data, others geographic competitors (commuting distances), some made comparisons with less than five competitors, some emphasized only large firms, others threw out the data from large firms.[30]

His conclusion still holds today. We hope this diversity reflects flexibility in dealing with a variety of circumstances and the use of improved compensation software. We worry that it reflects expediency and a lack of business- and work-related logic.

Verify Data

A common first step is to check the *accuracy* of the job matches, and then check for anomalies (i.e., an employer whose data are substantially out of line from data of others), age of data, and the nature of the organizations (e.g., industry, size—State Farm Insurance versus Google). **Exhibit 8.12** is a survey that was conducted at the behest of FastCat, a small start-up familiar to many readers. While there were a number of jobs included in the survey, we use information for just one job—engineer 1—to illustrate. As you can see, surveys do not make light reading. However, they contain a wealth of information. To extract that information, step through the portal . . . to being the FastCat analyst.[31]

EXHIBIT 8.12 External Pay Survey Data

A. Job Description: Engineer 1

Participates in develcpment, testing, and documentation of software programs. Performs design and analysis tasks as a project team member. Typical minimum requirements are a bachelor's degree in a scientific or technical field or the equivalent and up to two years of experience.

B. Individual Salary Data (partial data; for illustration only)

Job	Base	Bonus	Total Cash	Stock Option	Benefits	Total Comp
Engineer 1					JE Points:	50
					Number of Incumbents:	585
Company 1						
Engineer 1	$158,000	$1,000	$79,500	$0	$16,502	$175,502
Engineer 1	131,000	5,000	136,000	0	16,502	152,502
Engineer 1	130,000	0	130,000	0	16,502	146,502
Engineer 1	116,000	8,000	124,000	0	16,502	140,502
Engineer 1	115,860	6,000	121,860	0	16,502	138,362
Engineer 1	114,400	4,000	118,400	0	16,502	134,902
Engineer 1	112,000	2,200	114,200	0	16,502	130,702
Engineer 1	108,000	0	108,000	0	16,502	124,502
Engineer 1	105,000	0	105,000	0	16,502	121,502
Engineer 1	103,000	3,000	106,000	0	16,502	122,502
Engineer 1	98,000	6,600	104,600	0	16,502	121,102
Engineer 1	97,000	0	97,000	0	16,502	113,502
Engineer 1	73,000	0	73,000	0	16,502	89,502
Company 2						
Engineer 1	115,196	0	115,196	57,778	$17,036	190,010
Engineer 1	114,00	0	114,000	63,680	$17,036	194,666
Engineer 1	110,000	0	110,000	40,220	$17,036	167,256
(and so on...)						

C. Company Data (partial data; for illustration only)

	# Incumbents		Base	Short Term	Total Cash	LTI	Benefits	Total Comp
Company 1								
	13	**Avg.**	$112,404	$2,752	$115,156	0	16,502	$131,656
		Min.	73,000	0	73,000	0	16,500	89,500
		Max.	158,000	8,000	166,000	0	16,500	175,500
Company 2								
	13	**Avg.**	105,528	2,946	108,474	42,136	17,036	167,644
		Min.	94,752	0	94,752	9,756	17,034	130,832
		Max.	115,196	7,432	122,628	63,628	17,034	194,664
Company 8								
	14	**Avg.**	108,492	8,494	116,896	0	14,408	131,394
		Min.	90,000	1,720	91,720	0	14,408	110,796
		Max.	124,000	16,788	140,788	0	14,408	150,808
Company 12								
	35	**Avg.**	100,918	2,246	103,164	3,250	15,386	122,070
		Min.	84,000	0	84,000	0	15,386	105,212
		Max.	128,530	3,340	131,870	18,152	15,386	147,258

+ more data in the same format from 9 other companies (Company 4, Company 13, Company 14, Company 15, Company 15, Company 51, Company 57, Company 58, Company 59). Statistics below based on 13 companies.

D. Summary Data for Engineer 1 (13 companies, 585 Engineer 1 incimbents)

Base Salary		Total Cash		Total Compensation		Bonuses	Stock Options
Wtd Mean:	$92,170	*Wtd Mean:*	$96,578	*Wtd Mean:*	$113,834	Mean: $4,740	Mean: $32,580
Mean:	$98,184	*Mean:*	$101,880	*Mean:*	$131,048	As a % of Base:	As a % of Base:
50th:	$90,000	*50th:*	$92,844	*50th:*	$106,542	5.2%	34.0%
25th:	$85,200	*25th:*	$87,538	*25th:*	$101,186	% Who Receive:	% Who Receive
75th:	$97,000	*75th:*	$103,708	*75th:*	$121,500	93.0%	8.4%

Accuracy of Match (and Improving the Match)

Part A of the survey contains the description of the survey job. For jobs that match perfectly, things are easy. However, in most cases, the match is either poor or not perfect. In the latter case, one does not need to make a yes/no (all or nothing) decision. Rather, if the company job is sufficiently close to the survey job, especially on the most fundamental aspects, the benchmark conversion/survey leveling approach discussed earlier in this chapter can be used; that is, multiply the survey data by some factor that the analyst judges to be the difference between the company job and the survey job.[32] One way to execute this process is to conduct a job evaluation of the organization's benchmark job and the corresponding survey job and then determine their relative values.

Anomalies

Part B of the survey shows actual engineer 1 salaries. Perusal of salary data gives the analyst a sense of the quality of the data and helps identify any areas for additional consideration. For example, Part B of **Exhibit 8.12** shows that no engineer 1 at company 1 receives stock options, and all but five receive bonuses. The bonuses range from $1,000 to $8,000. (Because there are 585 engineer 1s in this survey, we have not included all their salary information.) Individual-level data provide a wealth of information about specific practices. Understanding minimums, maximums, and what percent actually receive bonuses and/or options is essential. Unfortunately, many surveys provide only summary information such as company averages.

Part C of **Exhibit 8.12** provides company data. Again, the first step is to look for anomalies:

1. *Does any one company dominate?* If so (i.e., company 13), a separate analysis of the largest company's data will isolate that employer's pay practices and clarify the nature of its influence.
2. *Do all employers show similar patterns?* Probably not. In our survey, base pay at company 1 ranges from $73,000 to $158,000 for a single job. This raises the possibility that this company might use broad bands (discussed later in this chapter). While the bonus to base ratio overall is 5.2 percent, company 8 pays an average bonus of $9,001 for a bonus-to-base ratio of 8.4 percent.
3. ***Outliers***? Company 2 gives one of its engineers options valued at $63,628 on top of base pay. An analyst may consider dropping a company with such an atypical pay practice. The question is, What difference will it make if certain companies are dropped? What difference will it make if they are included?

The best way to answer questions on anomalies is to do an analysis of them alone. They may have deliberately differentiated themselves with pay as part of their strategy. Learning more about competitors that differentiate can offer valuable insights. Combining outliers' pay data with their financials may reveal that the most successful competitors also use larger bonuses for their engineers.

Part D at the bottom of **Exhibit 8.12** contains summary data: five different measures of base pay, cash, and total compensation, as well as the percent of engineers who receive bonuses and options. The data suggest that most of FastCat's competitors use bonuses but are less likely to use options for this particular job. Summary data help abstract the survey information into a smaller number of measures for further statistical analysis. Statistics help FastCat get from pages of raw data (**Exhibit 8.12**) to graphs of actual salaries (**Exhibit 8.13**) and from there to a market line that reflects its competitive pay policy.

Statistical Analysis

While the statistics necessary to analyze survey data, including **regression,** are covered in basic statistics classes, a number of websites are probably more fun. Our favorite lets us click anywhere we want on a graph to see how adding that new data point (the mouse click) changes a regression line.[33] A useful first step in our analysis is to look at a frequency distribution of the pay rates.

Frequency Distribution

Exhibit 8.13 shows the frequency distribution of base wages for the 585 engineers based on the data in the **Exhibit 8.12** survey. Frequency distributions help visualize information and may highlight anomalies. For example, the base wage above $158,000 may be considered an outlier. Is this a unique person? Or an error in reporting the data? A phone call (or e-mail) to the survey provider may answer the question.

Shapes of frequency distributions can vary. Unusual shapes may reflect problems with job matches, widely dispersed pay rates, or employers with widely divergent pay policies. If the data look reasonable at this point, one wag has suggested that it is probably the result of two large errors that offset one another.

Central Tendency

A measure of **central tendency** reduces a large amount of data into a single number. **Exhibit 8.14** defines commonly used measures. The distinction between "mean" and "weighted mean" is important. If only company averages are reported in the survey, a *mean* may be calculated by adding each company's base wage and dividing by the number of companies. While use of the mean is common, it may not accurately reflect actual labor market conditions, since the base wage of the largest employer is given the same weight as that of the smallest employer. The *Weighted mean* ($92,170) is calculated by adding the base wages for all 585 engineers in the survey and then dividing by 585. A weighted mean gives equal weight to *each individual employee's* wage.

Variation

The distribution of rates around a measure of central tendency is called *variation.* The frequency distribution in **Exhibit 8.13** provides an example of variation. Variation tells us how the rates are spread out in the market.

EXHIBIT 8.13 **Frequency Distribution**

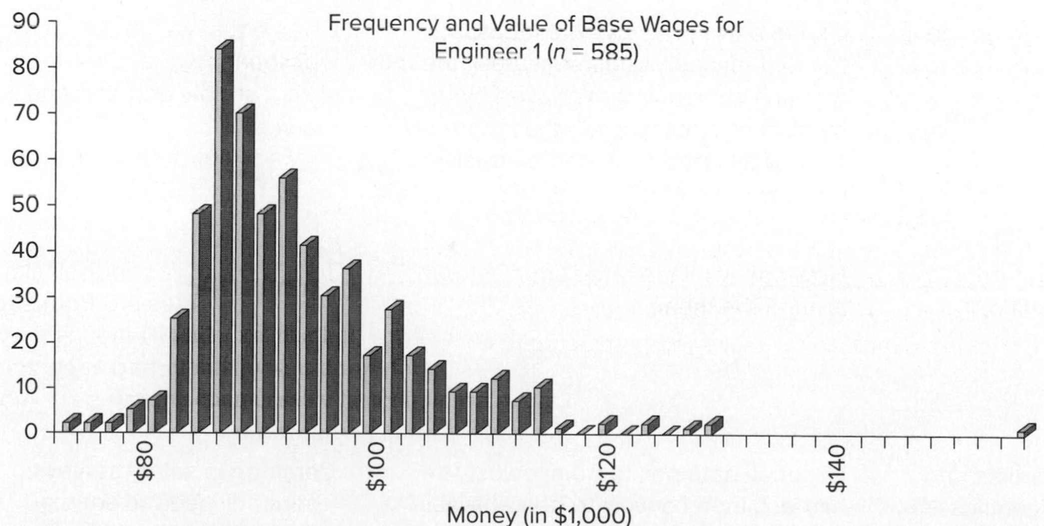

Standard deviation is probably the most common statistical measure of variation, although its use in pay surveys is rare. One reason is the pay distributions do not necessarily follow a distribution.

Thus, *quartiles* and *percentiles* are more common measures in pay survey analysis. Recall from the chapter introduction that someone's policy was "to be in the 75th percentile nationally." This means that 75 percent of all pay rates are *at or below* that point and 25 percent are *above*. Quartiles (25th and 75th percentiles) are often used to set pay ranges. More on pay ranges later in this chapter.

Update the Survey Data

Because they reflect decisions of employers, employees, unions, and government agencies, wages paid by competitors are constantly changing. Additionally, competitors adjust their wages at different times. Universities typically adjust to match the academic year. Unionized employers adjust on dates negotiated in labor

EXHIBIT 8.14 **Statistical Measures to Analyze Survey Data**

Measure	What Does It Tell Us?	Advantage/Disadvantage
Central Tendency		
Mode	Most commonly occurring rate.	Must draw frequency distribution to calculate it.
Mean	Sum all rates and divide by number of rates. If have only company (rather than individual) data, wage of largest employer given same weight as smallest employer.	Commonly understood (also called the "average"). However, if have only company data, will not accurately reflect actual labor market conditions.
Median	Order all data points from highest to lowest; the one in the middle is the median.	Minimizes distortion caused by outliers.
Weighted mean	If have only companywide measures (rather than individual measures), the rate for each company is multiplied by the number of employees in that company. Total of all rates is divided by total number of employees.	Gives equal weight to each individual's wage. Captures size of supply and demand in market.
Variation		
Standard deviation	How tightly all the rates are clustered around the mean.	Tells how similar or dissimilar the market rates are from each other. A small SD means they are tightly bunched at center; a large SD means rates are more spread out.
Quartiles and percentiles	Order all data points from lowest to highest, then convert to percentages.	Common in salary surveys; frequently used to set pay ranges or zones.

agreements. Some employers operating in competitive locations (e.g., Minsk, Shanghai) update every quarter or even every month. Many employers adjust each employee's pay on the anniversary of the employee's date of hire. Even though these changes do not occur smoothly and uniformly throughout the year, as a practical matter we assume that they do. Therefore, a survey that requires three months to collect and analyze is probably outdated before it is available. The pay data are usually updated (a process often called *aging* or *trending*) to forecast the competitive rates for the future date when the pay decisions will be implemented.

The amount to update is based on several factors, including historical trends in the labor market, prospects for the economy in which the employer operates, and the manager's judgment, among others. Some recommend using the **Consumer Price Index (CPI).** We do not. The CPI measures the rate of change in prices for goods and services in the product market, not wage changes in labor markets. **Chapter 18** has more information on this distinction.

Exhibit 8.15 illustrates updating. In the example, the base pay rate of $90,000 collected in the survey was in effect at January 1 of the current year–already in the past. The compensation manager will use this information for pay decisions that go into effect on January 1 of the plan year. So if base pay has been increasing by approximately 5 percent annually, and we assume that the future will be like the past, the rate is multiplied by 105 percent to account for the change expected by the end of the current year (to $94,500) and then by an additional percentage to estimate pay rates for the plan year.

Construct a Market Pay Line

Look again at **Exhibit 8.11**. It shows the results of the FastCat analyst's decisions on which salary survey jobs to include that are judged to closely match internal benchmark jobs (the seven jobs on the x [horizontal] axis), which companies to include and which measures of pay to use. For each of the compensation metrics, a line has been drawn connecting the pay for the seven jobs. Jobs are ordered on the horizontal axis according

EXHIBIT 8.15 **Choices for Updating Survey Data Reflect Pay Policy**

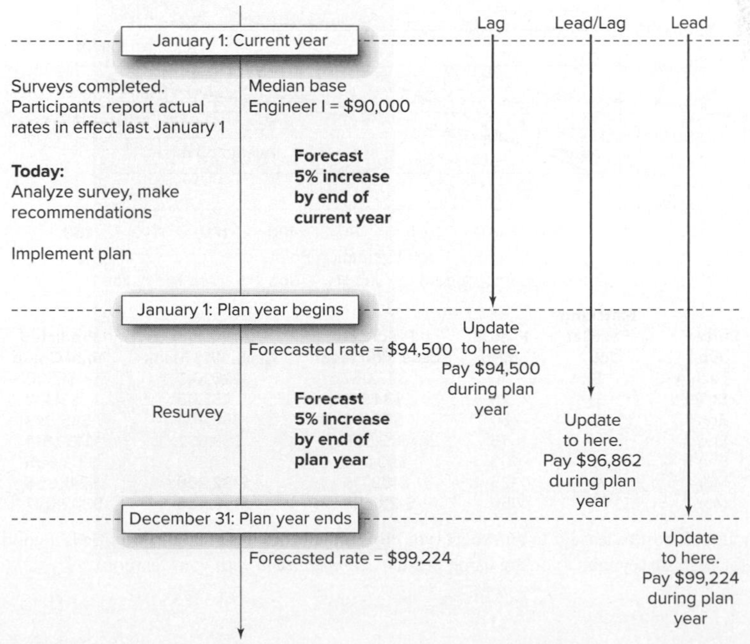

to their position (i.e., number of job evaluation points) in the internal structure. Thus, the line trends upward to create a market line.

A **market line** links a company's benchmark job evaluation points on the horizontal axis (internal structure) with market rates paid by competitors (market survey) on the vertical axis. It summarizes the distribution of going rates paid by competitors in the market.

A market line may be drawn freehand by connecting the data points, as was done in **Exhibit 8.11**, or statistical techniques such as regression analysis may be used. Regression generates a straight line that best fits the data by minimizing the variance around the line. **Exhibit 8.16** shows the regression lines that use the pay survey data in **Exhibit 8.11** as the dependent variable(s) and the job evaluation points of matched FastCat jobs as the independent variable. Compare the data tables in **Exhibit 8.11** and **Exhibit 8.16**. **Exhibit 8.11** shows the market rates for survey jobs. **Exhibit 8.16** shows the job evaluation points for the FastCat jobs that match these survey jobs plus the regression's statistical "prediction" of each pay measure for each job. The actual base pay for the survey job Tech A is $22,989 (**Exhibit 8.11**); the "predicted" base pay for the job is $23,058 (**Exhibit 8.16**).

In **Exhibit 8.17**, we focus in on the regression results that use base pay from the survey as the dependent variable. The diamonds are the actual results of the survey and the solid line is the regression result. Regression smooths large amounts of data while minimizing variations. As the number of jobs in the survey increases, the advantage of the straight line that regression provides becomes clear.

EXHIBIT 8.16 From Regression Results to a Market Line

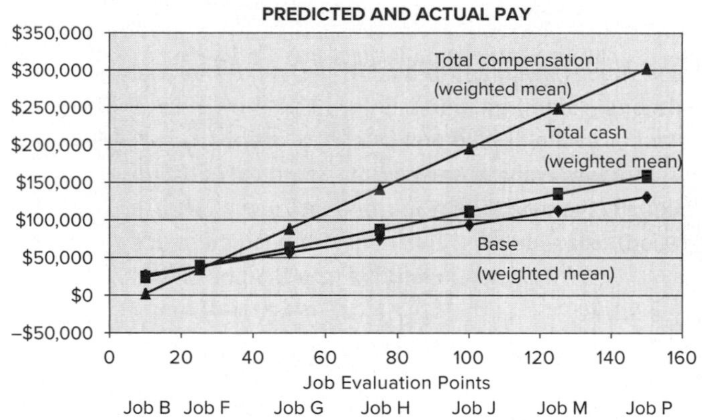

Survey Job	Matching FastCat Job*	FastCat JEPts	Predicted Base, Wtd Mean	Predicted Cash, Wtd Mean	Predicted Total Comp
Tech A	B	10	$23,057	$20,543	–$1,330
Sr Tech	F	25	$34,361	$35,116	$31,172
Eng 1	G	50	$53,199	$59,404	$85,343
Eng 3	H	75	$72,038	$83,692	$139,514
Eng 5	J	100	$90,876	$107,980	$193,685
Mgr 1	M	125	$109,715	$132,268	$247,856
Mgr 3	P	150	$128,553	$156,556	$302,027*

*We thought it best to leave it to an expert (you) to decide which FastCat job/job title is a good match for each survey job, if you are using *Cases in Compensation* with your textbook.

Setting Pay for Benchmark and Non-Benchmark Jobs

Setting pay for benchmark jobs is straightforward to the degree that good matches with survey jobs are found. Once it is known what other organizations pay for each job, a pay level can be chosen that is a function of what other organizations pay and what role the job plays in executing the strategy of one's own organization. For non-benchmark jobs (i.e., those jobs for which there is no good match among jobs included in the pay survey), the market pay lines in **Exhibit 8.16** are especially useful. For example, take a job, Job Z, that has no match, but for which we have assigned a job evaluation points score of 110. How might we estimate its base pay? From **Exhibit 8.16**, we know that FastCat Job J has 100 job evaluation points and matches a survey job, Eng 5, that has a base pay of $90,876. So, one approach is to pay Job Z 110/100 × $90,876 = $99,964. Or, we can use the market survey line regression equation shown in **Exhibit 8.17**. The predicted base pay = $15,522.56 + $753.54 (110 job evaluation points) = $98,412. The results are close, but not identical. (Remember, the regression line smooths the relationship, resulting in a small difference in predicted base pay.) So, our market line is very valuable. Even though only benchmark jobs in our company can be directly matched to the survey, the market line allows us to estimate the market pay for non-benchmark jobs. (See also our discussion of survey leveling earlier in this chapter.)

Before we leave survey data analysis, we must emphasize that not all survey results look like our examples and that not all companies use these statistical and analytical techniques. There is no one "right way" to analyze survey data. It has been our intent to provide some insight into the kinds of calculations that are useful and the assumptions that underlie salary surveys.

Calculating a Pay Market Line Using Regression Analysis

Regression analysis uses the mathematical formula for a straight line:

$y = a + bx$, where

y = dollars

x = job evaluation points

a = the y value (in dollars) at which $x = 0$ (i.e., where the straight line crosses/intercepts the y axis)

b = the slope of the regression line

Using the dollars from the market survey data and the job evaluation points from the internal structure, replicate our Exhibits 8.16 and 8.17 results.

The market line can be written as

Pay for job A = a + (b × job evaluation points for job A)

Pay for job B = a + (b × job evaluation points for job B)

and so on.

Regression estimates the values of a and b in an efficient manner, so errors of prediction are minimized.

(We are now beyond the halfway point of this long chapter. For those of you who are still going strong, great! But, for those of you who need at least a brief diversion from so much compensation material, perhaps a brief detour to the wizarding world would be welcome. Perhaps you would like to consider resorting to the Puking Pastilles, one of the Weasleys' Wizarding Wheezes described in the fifth Harry Potter book? The Puking Pastilles make you just ill enough to convince your professor to give you an extension on an assignment before you magically recover to enjoy your illicit time off.)[34]

Combine Internal Structure and External Market Rates

At this point, two parts of the total pay model have merged. Their relationship to each other can be seen in **Exhibit 8.18.**[35]

- The *internally aligned structure* (developed in **Chapters 3-6**) is shown on the horizontal (x) axis. For this illustration, our structure consists of jobs A through P. Jobs B, F, G, H, J, M, and P are the seven benchmark jobs that have been matched in the survey. Jobs A, C, D, E, I, K, L, N, and O have no direct matching jobs in the salary survey.
- The salaries paid by relevant competitors for those benchmark jobs, as measured by the survey–*the external competitive data*, are shown on the vertical (y) axis.

These two components–internal alignment and external competitiveness–come together in the pay structure. The pay structure has two aspects: the *pay-policy line* and *pay ranges.*

FROM POLICY TO PRACTICE: THE PAY-POLICY LINE

There are several ways to translate external competitive policy into practice. You have already made some of the choices that help you do this.

EXHIBIT 8.17 Understanding Regression

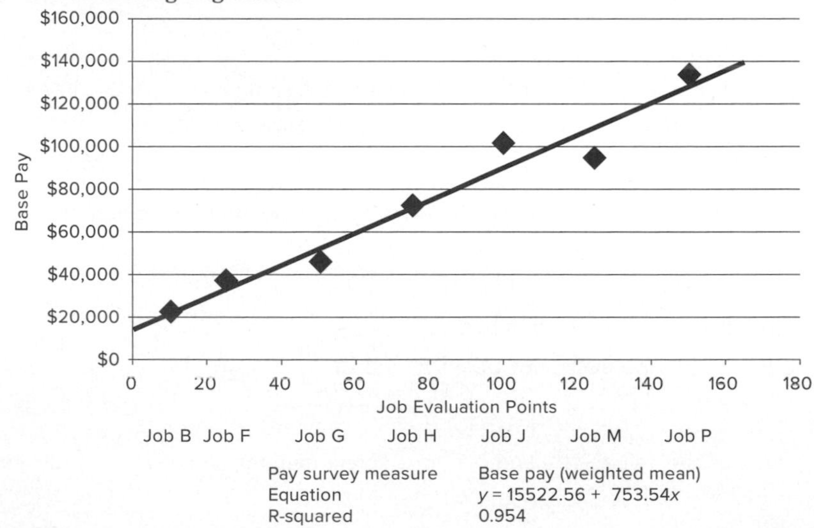

Choice of Measure

Lincoln Electric is a company that has set a target of the 45th percentile for base pay and the 65th percentile for total cash compensation as compensation measures in its regression.

Updating

Look again at **Exhibit 8.15**. The arrows on the right side of the exhibit show how updating survey data reflects policy. If the company chooses a "match" policy but then updates survey data to the end of the current year/start of the plan year and keeps this rate in effect throughout the plan year, the company will actually be lagging the market. It will match its desired market pay level only at the beginning of the plan year. The market rates continue to rise throughout the year; the company's rates do not.

Aging the market data to a point halfway through the plan year (middle arrow in **Exhibit 8.15**) is called *lead/lag.* The original survey rates are updated to the end of the current year plus half the projected amount for the plan year ($96,862). An employer who wants to lead the market may age data to the *end* of the plan year ($99,224) and pay at this rate throughout the plan year.

Policy Line as Percent of Market Line

Another way to translate pay-level policy into practice is to simply *specify a percent* above or below the regression line (market line) that an employer intends to match and then draw a new line at this higher (or lower) level. This **pay-policy line** would carry out a policy statement, "We lead the market by 10 percent." Other possibilities exist. An employer might lead by including only a few top-paying competitors in the analysis and then

EXHIBIT 8.18 Develop Pay Grades

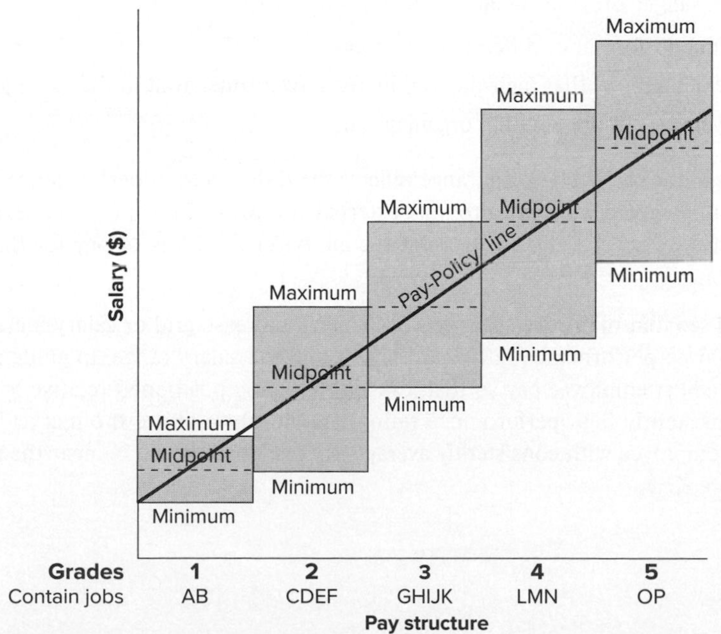

matching them ("pay among the leaders") or lead for some job families and lag for others. The point is that there are alternatives among competitive pay policies, and there are alternative ways to translate policy into practice. If the practice does not match the policy (e.g., we say one thing but do another), then employees receive the wrong message.

FROM POLICY TO PRACTICE: GRADES AND RANGES

The next step is to design **pay grades** and **pay ranges.** These analyses are usually done with base pay data, since base pay reflects the basic value of the work rather than performance levels of employees (see **Exhibit 8.10** for a comparison of metrics).

Why Bother with Grades and Ranges?

Grades and ranges offer flexibility to deal with pressures from external markets and differences among organizations. These include:

1. *Differences in quality (skills, abilities, experience) among individuals applying for work* (e.g., Microsoft may have stricter hiring requirements for engineers than does FastCat, even though job descriptions appear identical).
2. *Differences in the productivity or value of these quality variations* (e.g., the value of the results from a software engineer at Microsoft probably differs from that of the results of a software engineer at Best Buy).
3. *Differences in the mix of pay forms competitors use* (e.g., Oracle uses more stock options and lower base compared to IBM).

In addition to offering flexibility to deal with these external differences, an organization may use differences in rates paid to employees on the same job. *A pay range exists whenever two or more rates are paid to employees in the same job.* Hence, ranges provide managers the opportunity to:

1. Recognize individual performance differences with pay.
2. Meet employees' expectations that their pay will increase over time, even in the same job.
3. Encourage employees to remain with the organization.

From an internal alignment perspective, the range reflects the differences in performance or experience that an employer wishes to recognize with pay. From an external competitiveness perspective, the range is a control device. A range maximum sets the lid on what the employer is willing to pay for that work; the range minimum sets the floor.

In **Chapter 11**, we will see that many organizations use a merit increase grid or salary increase matrix, which uses two factors, employee performance rating and position in the salary range, to guide pay increases. The goal is to continually adjust employee pay so that it is appropriately positioned relative to the market. Thus, an employee with consistently high performance ratings should move above the market median and **range midpoint,** whereas an employee with consistently average performance should be near the range midpoint.

Develop Grades

The first step in building flexibility into the pay structure is to group different jobs that are considered substantially equal for pay purposes into a grade. Grades enhance an organization's ability to move people among jobs with no change in pay. In **Exhibit 8.18**, the jobs are grouped into five grades on the horizontal axis.

The question of which jobs are substantially equal and therefore slotted into one grade requires the analyst to reconsider the original job evaluation results. Each grade will have its own pay range, and *all the jobs within a single grade will have the same pay range.* Jobs in different grades (e.g., jobs C, D, E, and F in grade 2) should be dissimilar from those in other grades (grade 1 jobs A and B) and will have a different pay range.

Although grades permit flexibility, they are challenging to design. The objective is for all jobs that are similar for pay purposes to be placed within the same grade. If jobs with relatively close job evaluation point totals fall on either side of grade boundaries, the magnitude of difference in the salary treatment may be out of proportion to the magnitude of difference in the value of the job content. Resolving such dilemmas requires an understanding of the specific jobs, career paths, and work flow in the organization, as well as considerable judgment.

Establish Range Midpoints, Minimums, and Maximums

Grades group job evaluation data on the horizontal axis; ranges group salary data on the vertical axis. Ranges set upper and lower pay limits for all jobs in each grade. A range has three salient features: a midpoint, a minimum, and a maximum. **Exhibit 8.19** is an enlargement of grade 2 in **Exhibit 8.18**, which contains the engineer 1 job. The midpoint is \$54,896. This is the point where the pay-policy line crosses the center of the grade. The range for this grade has been set at 20 percent above and 20 percent below the midpoint. Thus, all FastCat engineer 1s are supposed to receive a salary higher than \$43,917 but lower than \$65,875.[36]

What Size Should the Range Be (Range Spread)?

Range spread is defined as maximum pay/minimum pay − 1. **Exhibit 8.20** shows typical range spreads by type of pay structure and by job level, with market-based structures being most common. We see that broadbands have the largest range spreads. Further, range spreads are larger at higher job levels, reflecting the greater opportunity for individual discretion and performance variations in the work.

EXHIBIT 8.19 Range Midpoint, Minimum, and Maximum

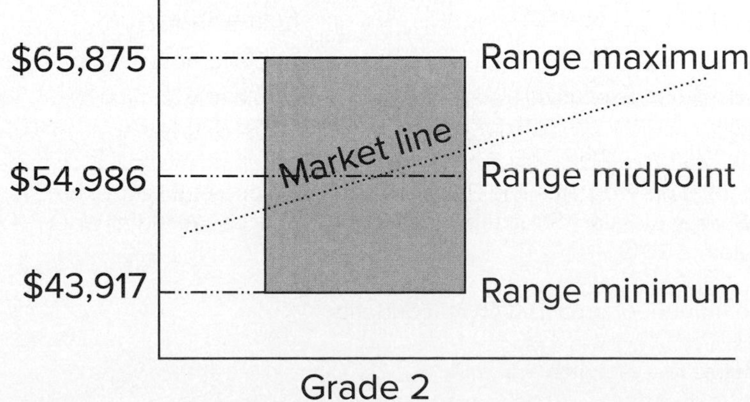

Some compensation managers use the actual survey rates, particularly the 75th and 25th percentiles, as maximums and minimums. Others ensure that the proposed range includes at least 75 percent of the rates in the survey data. Still others establish the minimum and maximum separately, with the amount between the minimum and the midpoint a function of how long it takes a new employee to become fully competent. Short training time may translate to minimums much closer to the midpoints. The maximum becomes the amount above the midpoint that the company is willing to pay for sustained performance on the job. In the end, the size of the range is based on judgment that weighs all these factors.

Overlap (and Midpoint Progression)

Exhibit 8.21 shows two extremes in overlap between adjacent grades. The high degree of overlap and low midpoint differentials in **Exhibit 8.21**(a) indicate small differences in the value of jobs in the adjoining grades. Being promoted from one grade to another may include a title change but not much change in pay. The smaller ranges in **Exhibit 8.21**(b) create less overlap, which permits the manager to reinforce a promotion into a new grade with a larger pay increase. The downside is that there may be fewer opportunities for promotion.

Promotion Increases Matter

The size of differentials between grades should support career movement through the structure. A managerial job would typically be at least one grade higher than the jobs it supervises. Although a 15 percent pay differential between manager and employee has been offered as a rule of thumb, large overlap and possible overtime in some jobs but not in managerial jobs can make it difficult to maintain manager–employee differentials. We are cautious about such rules of thumb. They are often ways to avoid thinking about what makes sense.

What is the optimal relationship between grades? The midpoint progression (differential between midpoints of adjacent grades) ought to be large enough to induce employees to seek promotion into a higher grade (and

EXHIBIT 8.20 **Range Spread Practices, by Pay Structure Type and Job Level**

Pay Structure Type	Range Spread
Market-based (N = 167)	55%
Traditional (N = 73)	30%
Broadbands (N = 15)	>80%
Job Level (N = 561 to 645)	**Range Spread**
Hourly	40% to 50%
Salaried, except Executive	50% to 60%
Executive	70% to 80%

"Compensation Programs and Practices Survey." World at Work, 2019; "2019 Survey of Salary Structure Policies and Practices." World at Work and Deloitte, 2019.

N is the number of organization respondents.

Range spread = max/min – 1.

the grade/range overlap should not be too large, again to induce interest in promotion to a higher grade/range). However, there is virtually no research to indicate how much of a differential or midpoint progression is necessary to influence employees to do so. Tracing how an employee might move through a career path in the structure (e.g., from engineer 1 to engineer 2 . . . to manager 3) and what size pay increases will accompany that movement will help answer that question. **Exhibit 8.22** provides benchmarking data. We see in **Exhibit 8.22** that midpoint progression percentages used by organizations as a function of the type of pay structure they use. Most organizations use market-based structures with midpoint progressions that average around 15 percent. Broadbands, as we saw just above, have larger pay spreads and with that, **Exhibit 8.22** shows broadbands also have larger midpoint progression. **Exhibit 8.22** also shows how to compute the needed number of salary grades/ranges that would be needed using different midpoint progressions. We apply this to an example case where midpoints go from 40,000 to 200,000. One would need 13 grades/ranges in this case.

Not all employers use grades and ranges. Skill-based plans establish single *flat rates* for each skill level regardless of performance or seniority. And many collective bargaining contracts establish single flat rates for each job (i.e., all senior machinists II receive $17.50 per hour regardless of performance or seniority). This flat rate often corresponds to some midpoint on a survey of that job. And increasingly, *broad bands* (think "really fat ranges") are being adopted for even greater flexibility.

FROM POLICY TO PRACTICE: BROAD BANDING

Exhibit 8.23 collapses salary grades into only a few broad bands, each with a sizable range. This technique, known as **broad banding,** consolidates as many as four or five traditional grades into a single band with one minimum and one maximum. Because the band encompasses so many jobs of differing values, a range midpoint is usually not used.[37]

Contrasts between ranges and broad bands are highlighted in **Exhibit 8.24**. Supporters of broad bands list several advantages over traditional approaches. First, broad bands provide flexibility to define job responsibilities more broadly. They support redesigned, downsized, or boundary-less organizations that have eliminated layers of managerial jobs. They foster cross-functional growth and development in these new organizations. Employees can move laterally across functions within a band in order to gain depth of experience. Companies with global operations such as 3M and Medtronic used bands to move managers among worldwide assignments. The emphasis on lateral movement with no pay adjustments helps manage the reality of fewer promotion opportunities in flattened organization structures. The flexibility of banding eases mergers and acquisitions since there are not a lot of levels to argue over.[38]

EXHIBIT 8.21 **Range Overlap**

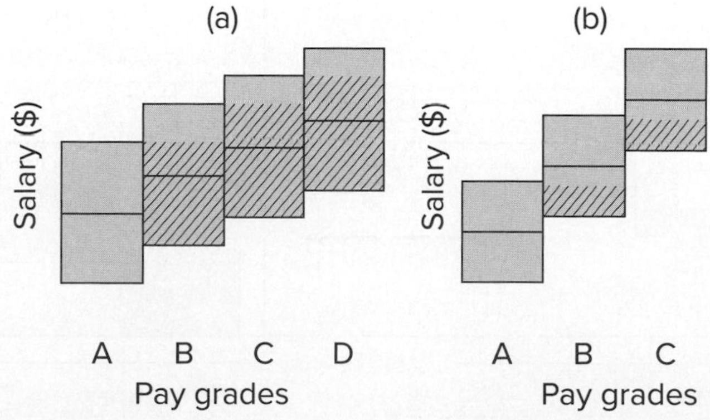

Broad bands are often combined with more traditional salary administration practices by using midpoints, **zones,** or other control points within bands.[39] Perhaps the most important difference between the grades-and-ranges and broad-banding approaches is the location of the controls. The grade-and-range approach has guidelines and controls designed right into the pay system. Range minimums, maximums, and midpoints ensure consistency across managers. Managers using bands have only a total salary budget limiting them. But as experience with bands has advanced, guidelines and structure are increasingly designed into them (e.g., reference market rates or shadow ranges).

Bands may add flexibility: Less time will be spent judging fine distinctions among jobs. But perhaps the time avoided judging jobs will now be spent judging individuals, a prospect managers already try to avoid. How will an organization avoid the appearance of salary treatment based on personality and politics rather than objective criteria? Ideally, with a well-thought-out performance management system.

EXHIBIT 8.22 Midpoint Progression Practices and Number of Grades Needed

Example:

Lowest Grade Salary Midpoint =	40,000
Highest Grade Salary Midpoint =	200,000

Pay Structure Type	Midpoint Progression	Grades Needed
Market-based (N = 167)	15%	13
Traditional (N = 73)	12%	15
Broadband (N = 15)	24%	8

Source: Midpoint progression percentages based on "Salary Structure Policies and Practices," World at Work and Deloitte, 2019. N is the number of organization respondents.

Midpoint Progression = percentage differential between adjacent grade midpoints.

Grades Needed = [natural log (Highest Salary Midpoint/Lowest Salary Midpoint)] ÷ [natural log (1 + Midpoint Progession)] + 1

[Hint: In Excel, use the in function for natural log.]

EXHIBIT 8.23 From Grades to Bands

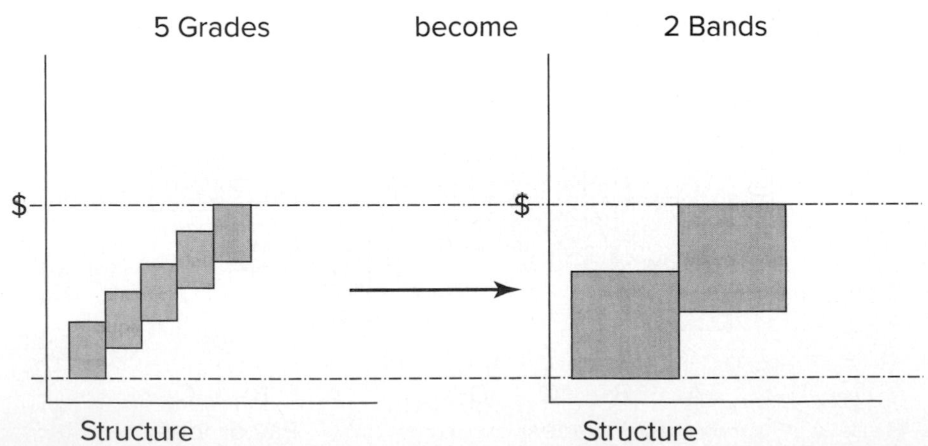

Banding takes two steps:

1. *Set the number of bands.* Merck used six bands for its entire pay structure. Band titles range from "contributor" to "executive." A unit of General Electric replaced 24 levels of work with 5 bands. Usually bands are established at the major "breaks," or differences, in work or skill/competency requirements. Titles used to label each band reflect these major breaks, such as "associate" (entry-level individual contributor), "professional" (experienced, knowledgeable team member), "leader" (project or group supervisor), "director," "coach," or even "visionary." The challenge is how much to pay people who are in the same band but in different functions performing different work.
2. *Price the bands: reference market rates.* The four bands in **Exhibit 8.25** (associates, professionals, lead professionals, senior professionals) include multiple job families within each band, for example, finance, purchasing, engineering, marketing, and so on. It is unlikely that General Electric pays associates and professionals with business degrees the same as associates and professionals with engineering degrees. Usually external market differences exist, so the different functions or groups within bands are priced differently. As the pop-out in **Exhibit 8.25** depicts, the three job families (purchasing, finance, and engineering) in the professional band have different *reference rates,* drawn from survey data.

You might say that this is beginning to look a lot like grades and ranges within each band. You would be correct. The difference is that ranges traditionally serve as controls, whereas reference rates act as guides. Today's guides grow to tomorrow's bureaucracy and perhaps lack of cost control. Not surprisingly perhaps then survey data show that grades/ranges are used almost 10 times more often than bands by organizations (86% versus 9%).[40]

Flexibility Control

Broad banding encourages employees to seek growth and development by moving cross-functionally (e.g., from purchasing to finance). The assumption is that this cross-fertilization of ideas will benefit the organization. Hence, career moves within bands are more common than between bands. According to supporters, the principal payoff of broad banding is this flexibility. But flexibility is one side of the coin; chaos and favoritism is the other. Banding presumes that managers will manage employee pay to accomplish the organization's objectives (and not their own) and treat employees fairly. Historically, this is not the first time managers have sought greater flexibility. Indeed, the rationale for using grades and ranges was to reduce inconsistencies and

EXHIBIT 8.24 Contrasts between Ranges and Bands

Ranges Support:	Bands Support:
Some flexibility within controls	Emphasis on flexibility within guidelines
Relatively stable organization design	Global organizations
Recognition via titles or career progression	Cross-functional experience and lateral progression
Midpoint controls, comparatives	Reference market rates, shadow ranges
Controls designed into system	Controls in budget, few in system
Give managers "freedom with guidelines"	Give managers "freedom to manage" pay
To 150 percent range-spread	100–400% spread

favoritism in previous generations. The challenge today is to take advantage of flexibility without increasing labor costs or leaving the organization vulnerable to charges of inconsistent or illegal practices.

BALANCING INTERNAL AND EXTERNAL PRESSURES: ADJUSTING THE PAY STRUCTURE

Up until now, we have made a distinction between the job structure and the pay structure. A **job structure** orders jobs on the basis of internal factors (reflected in job evaluation or skill certification). The **pay structure,** on the other hand, is anchored by the organization's external competitive position and reflected in its pay-policy line.

Reconciling Differences

The problem with using two standards (internal and external) to create a structure is that they are likely to result in two different structures. The order in which jobs are ranked on internal versus external factors may not agree. Differences between market structures and rates and job evaluation rankings warrant a review of the basic decisions in evaluating and pricing a particular job. This may entail a review of the job analysis, the evaluation of the job, or the market data for the job in question. Often this reanalysis solves the problem. Sometimes, however, discrepancies persist. Survey data may be discarded, or benchmark-job matches may be changed.

EXHIBIT 8.25 **Reference Rates within Bands**

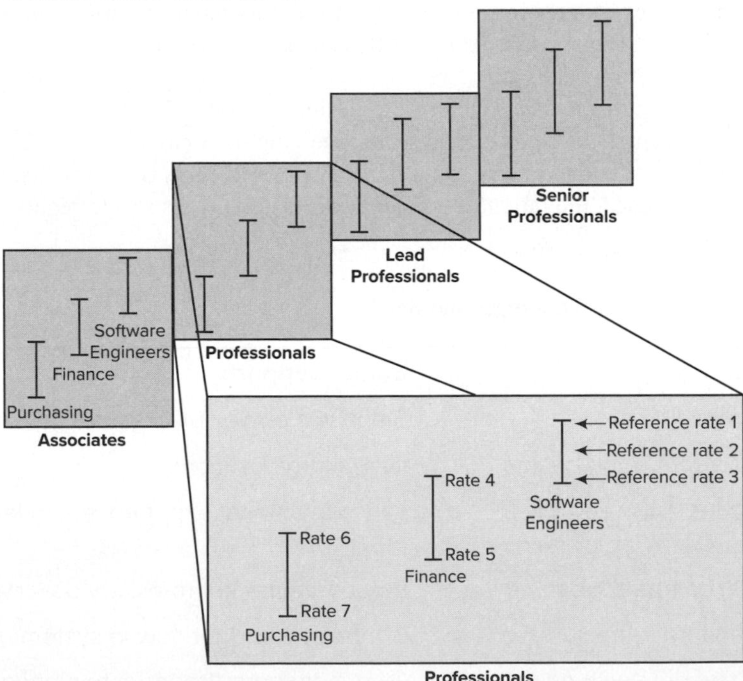

One study of how differences are actually reconciled found that managers weigh external market data more heavily than internal job evaluation data. In light of all the judgments that go into internal evaluation, market data are often considered to be more objective.[41] Yet this chapter and research show that market data are also based on judgment.

Sometimes differences arise because a shortage of a particular skill has driven up the market rate. But reclassifying such a job into a higher salary grade, where it will remain long after the supply/demand imbalance has been corrected, creates additional problems. Creating a special range that is clearly designated as *market responsive* may be a better approach. Decisions made on the basis of expediency may undermine the integrity of the pay decisions.

MARKET PRICING

Some organizations adopt pay strategies that emphasize external competitiveness and deemphasize internal alignment. In fact, we saw in **Chapter 5** that this approach is now quite common. Indeed, it has been said that "the core change" in compensation from the past "is the diminished concern with internal salary relationships."[42] Called *market pricing,* this approach sets pay structures almost exclusively on external market rates.[43] Market pricers match a large percentage of their jobs with market data and collect as much market data as possible. The competitive rates for jobs for which external market data are available are calculated; then the remaining (non-benchmark) jobs are blended into the pay hierarchy created by the external rates ("rank to market"). Pfizer, for example, begins with job analysis and job descriptions. This is immediately followed by market analysis and pricing for as many jobs as possible. After that, the few remaining (non-benchmark) jobs are blended in and the internal job relationships are reviewed to be sure they are *"reasonable in light of organization work flow and other uniqueness."* The final step is pricing the non-benchmark jobs. This is done by comparing the value of these jobs to the Pfizer jobs already priced in the market.

Market pricing goes beyond using benchmark jobs and slotting non-benchmarks. The objective of market pricing is to base most, if not all, of the internal pay structure on external rates, breaking down the boundaries between the internal organization and the external market forces. Some companies even match all forms of pay for each job to its competitors in the market. For example, if the average rate for a controller job is $150,000, then the company pays $150,000. If 60 percent of the $150,000 is base pay, 20 percent is annual bonus, 5 percent is stock options, and 15 percent is benefits, the company matches not only the amount but also this mix of pay forms. Another $150,000 job, say, director of marketing, may have a different pattern among market competitors, which is also matched.

Business Strategy (More than "Follow the Leader")

Pure market pricing carried to this extreme ignores internal alignment completely. Gone is any attempt to align internal pay structures with the business strategy and the work performed. Rather, the internal pay structure is aligned with competitors' decisions as reflected in the market. In a very real sense, the decisions of its competitors determine an organization's pay.

Why should competitors' pay decisions be the sole or even primary determinant of another company's pay structure? If they are, then *how much or what mix of forms* a company pays is no longer a potential source of competitive advantage. It is not unique, nor is it difficult to imitate. The implied assumption is that little value is added through internal alignment.

Any unique or difficult-to-imitate aspects of the organization's pay structure, which may have been based on unique technology or the way work is organized, are deemphasized by market pricers. Fairness is presumed to be reflected by market rates; employee behavior is presumed to be reinforced by totally market-priced structures, which are the very same as those of competitors.

In contrast, an organization may choose to differentiate its pay strategy from that of its competitors to better execute its own strategy.[44] We saw earlier that organizations may choose different overall pay levels, depending on their business strategy. We also saw earlier that an organization may choose to pay some of its jobs above market, but other jobs at or below market.[45] For example, according to resource dependence theory, employees who are more central to strategy execution in terms of their criticality in obtaining resources from the environment would be expected to be paid better relative to the market than would other employees. For example, in a study of universities, it was found that private universities, which rely more on private fundraising to operate, paid their chief development (fundraising) officers more than did public universities, which rely more on state funds. On the other hand, public universities, which typically rely more heavily on athletic programs to build alumni relations, paid their athletic directors more than did private universities.[46] Other evidence shows that in capital intensive and highly diversified firms, where finance expertise is especially important, compensation for managers in finance jobs was higher relative to market than for other jobs on average. Likewise, managers in marketing were paid more in firms with large expenditures on marketing and advertising, and managers in research in development were paid more relative to market than other managers in firms focusing on product innovation.[47]

In sum, the process of balancing internal and external pressures is a matter of judgment made with an eye on the pay system objectives. De-emphasizing internal alignment may lead to unfair treatment among employees and inconsistency with the strategy and fundamental culture of the organization. Neglecting external competitive pay practices, however, will affect both the ability to attract applicants and the ability to retain valued employees. External pay relationships also directly impact labor costs and hence the ability to compete in the product/service market. Thus, while differentiating pay strategy from competitors can lead to competitive advantage, the reasons for being different must be clearly reasoned and articulated. Otherwise, being different may only lead to lack of competitiveness in the product market or labor market, hindering organization success and strategy execution.

REVIEW

The end of **Part Two** of the textbook is a logical spot for a midterm exam. **Exhibit 8.26** has been designed to help you review.

EXHIBIT 8.26 **Open-Book Midterm Exam**

Answer true or false to the following questions:

You know you are spending too much time working on compensation when you:

- Use "pay mix" and "external competitiveness" when you e-mail home for money.
- Think that paying for lunch requires a strategic approach.
- Ask your date to specify his or her competencies.
- Can explain the difference between traditional pay grades and ranges and new broad bands with shadow ranges.
- Believe your answer to the above.

- Would cross the street to listen to economists and psychologists discuss the "likely effects of alternative external competitiveness policies."
- Consider your Phase II assignment a wonderful opportunity to increase your human capital.
- Think adding points to your project grade creates a "balanced scorecard."
- Are willing to pay your instructor to teach any other course.
- Are surprised to learn that some people think a COLA is a soft drink.
- Turn your head to listen rather than roll your eyes when someone talks about being "incentivized" with pay.
- Believe that instead of your mom, "the market" knows best.

How did you do? Good. Let's keep going!

Your Turn

Google's (now Alphabet's) Evolving Pay Strategy

In **Chapter 2**, we talked about how Microsoft had changed its pay strategy to rely less on stock options, more on stock grants, and then to rely less on stock grants and more on cash as its product cycle phase changed from growth to maintenance and its stock price growth slowed (at least back then it had). Google went public in 1994 and its stock price, already at around $100/share at that point, then rose rapidly (a great big understatement), peaking at around $370[48] in November 2007. However, as of May 2012, Google's stock price was right around $300 (with a 52-week high of about $335). As a result, Google was subjected to comments such as "Google isn't the hot place to work" and has "become the safe place to work" (per someone recruiting engineers for then start-ups such as Facebook).[49] Perhaps following in the footsteps of Microsoft, Google announced that it was giving a 10 percent across the board increase in salary. Not stock options. Not stock grants (but, see below). Salary.[50] The cost of the salary increase was estimated by Barclay's to be $400 million.[51]

"Analysts say Google is facing what all Silicon Valley companies struggle with when they graduate from start-up status and into the realm of Big Tech."[52] With or without the 10 percent increase, one report says that Google was "paying computer science majors just out of college as much as $20,000 more than it was paying a few months ago" and that salary "is so far above the industry average that start-ups cannot match Google's salaries."[53] (Actually, one might ask how many non-start-ups are likely to match such salaries.)

It is also noteworthy that Google repriced 7.64 million stock options in 2009. Of 20,200 total employees, 15,642 took advantage of the opportunity to replace their existing options, which had an average exercise price of $522, with new options having an exercise price of $308.57.[54] By one estimate, Google was on a path to spend $2 billion on stock-related compensation in 2011.[55] Subsequently, Google moved from stock options to restricted stock units for employees. The latter are actual grants of stock and are restricted in the sense that employees need to remain with Google for a minimum amount of time.

As of early 2015, Google's stock price was around $560 and during mid-2021 (now as Alphabet), the stock price was much higher still—over $2,200! Thus, employee stock-related wealth has soared. That goes along with their high salaries (see above) and their well-known extensive benefits. (Recall from **Chapter 2** that they have regularly topped Fortune's list and Forbes' list of top employers. We will talk more about employee stock plans and benefits in **Part Three** of your text. In retrospect, it looks like it may have been premature to conclude that Google had transitioned from a growth company to a maintenance/mature company. (Much as what happed with Microsoft.)

QUESTIONS:

1. What is Google's pay level? How do you define and measure its pay level? How well is it captured by salary alone?
2. Does your answer to the above question depend on what point in time it is answered? For example, what was Google's pay level the day before it repriced employee stock options? What was Google's pay level the day after it repriced employee stock options? And now?
3. Why did Google reprice its stock options and also give a 10 percent salary increase (in an era when 2 to 3 percent annual salary increase budgets are the norm)? Is it because its business strategy and/or product life cycle changed? Is it because it was concerned that employees' perceived value of compensation did not match what Google was spending?
4. Do you think Google has made the right choices in changing its compensation strategy? How much do these changes cost? How do these costs compare to Google's total costs and operating income? Are these increased compensation costs likely to be a good investment? In other words, will they pay for themselves (and more)? Explain.
5. Do you get the sense that companies act on the best information they have at the time, but that in retrospect, they are not so good at predicting the future?
6. Will Google's pay strategy work "forever"? What changes might be needed going forward?

Still Your Turn

Word-of-Mouse: Dot-Com Comparisons

More compensation information is available than ever before. Click on the website ***www.salary.com*** or on ***www.glassdoor.com***. These websites, which we have used in the opening to **Part Three** and in the present chapter, provide pay data on hundreds of jobs in cities all over the United States in many different industries. Identify several jobs of interest to you, such as accountant, financial analyst, product manager, or stockbroker. Select specific cities or use the U.S. national average. Obtain the median, the 25th and 75th percentile base wage, and total cash compensation rates for each job. Then consider the following questions:

1. Which jobs are paid more or less? Is this what you would have expected? Why or why not? What factors could explain the differences in the salaries?
2. Do the jobs have different bonuses as a percentage of their base salaries? What could explain these differences?
3. Do the data include the value of stock options? What are the implications of this?
4. Read the job descriptions. Are they accurate descriptions for jobs that you would be applying for? Why or why not? Are there jobs for which you cannot find an appropriate match? Why do you think this is the case?
5. If you are majoring in computer science, you may find that some surveys include data on software developers, but not software engineers (and vice versa). How similar are these jobs and can you use data on one of these job titles to estimate pay rates for the other title? Also, where does the job of computer programmer fit in?
6. Check out pay levels for these types of jobs in your school's career office. How does the pay for jobs advertised in your career office differ from the pay levels on salary.com? Why do you think these differences exist?

7. How could you use this information while negotiating your salary in your job after graduation? What data would you provide to support your "asking price"? What factors will influence whether or not you get what you ask for?
8. What is the relevant labor market for these jobs? How big are the differences between salaries in different locations?
9. For each job, compare the median salary to the low and high averages. How much variation exists? What factors might explain this variation in pay rates for the same job?
10. Look for a description of how these salary data are developed. Do you think it provides enough information? Why or why not? Discuss some of the factors that might impair the accuracy of these data. What are the implications of using inaccurate salary data for individuals or companies?
11. With this information available for free, why would you bother with consultants' surveys?
12. If you were a manager, how would you justify paying one of your employees either higher or lower than the results shown on this website?

Summary

This chapter has detailed the decisions and techniques that go into setting pay levels and mix and designing pay structures. Most organizations survey other employers' pay practices to determine the rates competitors pay. An employer using the survey results considers how it wishes to position its total compensation in the market: to lead, to match, or to follow competition. This policy decision may be different for different business units and even for different job groups within a single organization. The policy on competitive position is translated into practice by setting pay-policy lines; these serve as reference points around which pay grades and ranges or bands are designed.

The use of grades and ranges or bands recognizes both external and internal pressures on pay decisions. No single "going rate" for a job exists in the market; instead, an array of rates exists. This array results from conditions of demand and supply, variations in the quality of employees, and differences in employer policies and practices. It also reflects the fact that employers differ in the values they attach to the jobs and people. And, very importantly, it reflects differences in the mix of pay forms among companies.

Internally, the use of ranges is consistent with variations in the discretion in jobs. Some employees will perform better than others; some employees are more experienced than others. Pay ranges permit employers to recognize these differences with pay.

Managers are increasingly interested in broad banding, which offers even greater flexibility than grades and ranges to deal with the continuously changing work assignments required in many successful organizations. Broad banding offers freedom to adapt to changes without requiring approvals. However, it risks self-serving and potentially inequitable decisions on the part of the manager. Recently, the trend has been toward approaches with greater flexibility to adapt to changing conditions. Such flexibility also makes mergers and acquisitions easier and global alignment possible.

Let us step back for a moment to review what has been discussed and preview what is coming. We have examined two strategic components of the total pay model. A concern for internal alignment means that analysis and perhaps descriptions and evaluation are important for achieving a competitive advantage and fair treatment. A concern for external competitiveness requires competitive positioning, survey design and analysis, setting the pay-policy line (how much and what forms), and designing grades and ranges or broad bands. The next part of the book is concerned with employee contributions–paying the people who perform the work.

This is perhaps the most important part of the book. All that has gone before is a prelude, setting up the pay levels, mix, and structures by which people are to be paid. It is now time to pay the people.

Review Questions

1. Which competitive pay policy would you recommend to an employer? Why? Does it depend on circumstances faced by the employer? Which ones?
2. How would you design a survey for setting pay for welders? How would you design a survey for setting pay for financial managers? Do the issues differ? Will the techniques used and the data collected differ? Why or why not?
3. What factors determine the relevant market for a survey? Why is the definition of the relevant market so important?
4. What do surveys have to do with pay discrimination?
5. Contrast pay ranges and grades with bands. Why would you use either? Does their use assist or hinder the achievement of internal alignment? External competitiveness?

Endnotes

1. Consulting firms list their specialized surveys on their websites. See, for example, the Mercer/Gartner information technology pay survey at https://www.imercer.com/ecommerce/products/information-technology-survey. See also Aon: https://humancapital.aon.com/solutions/rewards/compensation-surveys; Willis Towers Watson: https://www.towerswatson.com/en/Services/our-solutions/global-data-services; Korn Ferry: http://engage.kornferry.com/pay.
2. Christopher Murphy, *Competitive Intelligence: Gathering, Analysing and Putting It to Work* (Routledge, 2016); Benjamin Gilad and Leonard Fuld, "Only Half of Companies Actually Use the Competitive Intelligence They Collect," *Harvard Business Review* (Jan. 26, 2016).
3. "Employer Costs for Employee Compensation, June 2018," https://www.bls.gov/news.release/ecec.nr0.htm; *National Compensation Survey: Guide for Evaluating Your Firm's Jobs and Pay,* www.bls.gov/ncs/ocs/sp/ncbr0004.pdf, revised, 2013.
4. Sara L. Rynes and G. T. Milkovich, "Wage Surveys: Dispelling Some Myths About the 'Market Wage,'" *Personnel Psychology*, Spring 1986, pp. 71–90; B. Gerhart and S. Rynes, *Compensation: Theory, Evidence, and Strategic Implications* (Thousand Oaks, CA: Sage, 2003).
5. Charlie Trevor and Mary E. Graham, "Deriving the Market Wage Derivatives: Three Decision Areas in the Compensation Survey Process," *WorldatWork Journal* 9(4), 2000, pp. 69–77; Brian Klaas and John A. McClendon, "To Lead, Lag, or Match: Estimating the Financial Impact of Pay Level Policies," *Personnel Psychology* 49 (1996), pp. 121–140.
6. F. Theodore Malm, "Recruiting Patterns and the Functioning of the Labor Markets," *Industrial and Labor Relations Review* 7 (1954), pp. 507–525; "Job Evaluation and Market Pricing Practices," *WorldatWork,* February 2009.
7. M. C. Sturman, A. D. Ukhov, & S. Park, "The Effect of Cost of Living on Employee Wages in the Hospitality Industry," *Cornell Hospitality Quarterly,* 58(2) (2017), pp. 179–189.
8. Andrew Klein, David G. Blanchflower, and Lisa M. Ruggiero, "Pay Differentials Hit Employees Where They Live," *Workspan,* June 2002, pp. 36–40; Stephen Ohlemacher, "Highest Wages in East, Lowest in South," U.S. Census Bureau, *www.census.gov/hhes/www/saipe/index.html,* 2005.

9. Charlie Trevor and Mary E. Graham, "Deriving the Market Wage Derivatives: Three Decision Areas in the Compensation Survey Process," *WorldatWork Journal* 9(4), 2000, pp. 69–77.
10. Barry Gerhart and George Milkovich, "Employee Compensation," in *Handbook of Industrial and Organizational Psychology,* 2d ed., M. D. Dunnette and L. M. Hough, eds. (Palo Alto, CA: Consulting Psychologists Press, 1992); B. Gerhart and S. Rynes, *Compensation: Theory, Evidence, and Strategic Implications* (Thousand Oaks, CA: Sage, 2003).
11. Pay survey data for many countries is available. See, for example, https://www.imercer.com/ecommerce/products/global-pay-summary.
12. M. Bloom, G. Milkovich, and A. Mitra, "International Compensation: Learning from How Managers Respond to Variations in Local-Host Conditions," *International Journal of Human Resource Management,* December 2003, pp. 1350–1367.
13. Yoshio Yanadori, "Minimizing Competition? Entry-Level Compensation in Japanese Firms," *Asia Pacific Journal of Management* 21 (2004), pp. 445–467.
14. Daniel Vaughn-Whitehead, *Paying the Price: The Wage Crisis in Central and Eastern Europe* (Handmill Hampshire, UK: McMillin Press Ltd., 1998).
15. M. Bloom, G. Milkovich, and A. Mitra, "International Compensation: Learning from How Managers Respond to Variations in Local-Host Conditions," *International Journal of Human Resource Management,* December 2003, pp. 1350–1367.
16. Michael Wanderer, "Dot-Comp: A 'Traditional' Pay Plan with a Cutting Edge," *WorldatWork Journal,* Fourth Quarter 2000, pp. 15–24.
17. Earlier footnotes in this chapter provide survey examples. See, for example, https://humancapital.aon.com/solutions/rewards/compensation-surveys.
18. See also R. J. Greene, "Compensation Surveys: The Rosetta Stones of Market Pricing," *WorldatWork Journal*, First Quarter 2014, pp. 23–31.
19. In response to a lawsuit, the Boston Survey Group agreed to publish only aggregated (rather than individual employee) information and to not categorize information by industry. Eight hospitals in Utah made the mistake of exchanging information on their *intentions* to increase starting pay offers. They were charged with keeping entry-level wages for registered nurses in the Salt Lake City area artificially low. As part of the legal settlement, no health care facility in Utah can design, develop, or conduct a wage survey. They can respond in writing (only) to a written request for information for wage survey purposes from a third party, but only after the third party provides written assurance that the survey will be conducted with particular safeguards. *District of Utah U.S. District Court v. Utah Society for Healthcare Human Resources Administration, et al.,* 59 Fed. Reg. 14,203 (March 25, 1994). The resulting guidelines may buy legal protection, but they also give up control over the decisions that determine the quality and usefulness of the data. Prohibiting exchange of industry data eliminates the ability to make industry or product market comparisons. This might not be important in nursing or clerical jobs, but industry groups are important in comparisons among competitors. See Chapter 17 of this book (e.g., the table summarizing federal pay-related laws) for more recent examples of employers running afoul of antitrust laws prohibiting anti-competitive practices in the labor market (e.g., the HighTech and Animation Workers cases).
20. Chockalingam Viswesvaran and Murray Barrick, "Decision-Making Effects on Compensation Surveys: Implications for Market Wages," *Journal of Applied Psychology* 77(5), 1992, pp. 588–597.
21. John A. Menefee, "The Value of Pay Data on the Web," *Workspan,* September 2000, pp. 25–28.
22. Charles Fishman, "The Anarchist's Cookbook," *Fast Company,* July 2004, Issue 84.

23. Some websites treat the federal government's Consumer Price Index as a measure of the cost of living in an area. It is not. The Consumer Price Index measures the rate of *change* in the cost of living in an area. So it can be used to compare how quickly prices are rising in one area versus another, but it cannot be used to compare living costs between two different areas.
24. "Job Evaluation and Market-Pricing Practices," *WorldatWork* report, November 2015.
25. Sara L. Rynes and G. T. Milkovich, "Wage Surveys: Dispelling Some Myths about the 'Market Wage,'" *Personnel Psychology,* Spring 1986, pp. 71–90; Frederic Cook, "Compensation Surveys Are Biased," *Compensation and Benefits Review,* September–October 1994, pp. 19–22.
26. George F. Dreher, "Wage and Salary Surveys," *Wiley Encyclopedia of Management* (2015): 1-1; Sara L. Rynes and G. T. Milkovich, "Wage Surveys: Dispelling Some Myths about the 'Market Wage,'" *Personnel Psychology,* Spring 1986, pp. 71–90.
27. Years-since-degree (YSD), or maturity curves, commonly used for scientists, are discussed in Chapter 14.
28. See, for example, Saratoga Benchmarking, https://www.pwc.com/us/en/services/hr-management/people-analytics/benchmarking.html; and the Society of HR Management, *www.shrm.org.*
29. Joseph R. Rich and Carol Caretta Phalen, "A Framework for the Design of Total Compensation Surveys," *ACA Journal,* Winter 1992–1993, pp. 18–29.
30. Letter from D. W. Belcher to G. T. Milkovich, in reference to D. W. Belcher, N. Bruce Ferris, and John O'Neill, "How Wage Surveys Are Being Used," *Compensation and Benefits Review,* September–October 1985, pp. 34–51.
31. Users of Milkovich and Gerhart's *Cases in Compensation,* edition 11.1e, will recognize the software company FastCat. The casebook offers the opportunity for hands-on experience. For more information, contact the authors at casesincompensation@gmail.com.
32. Margaret A. Coil, "Salary Surveys in a Blended-Role World," in *2003–2004 Survey Handbook and Directory* (Scottsdale, AZ: WorldatWork, 2002), pp. 57–64.
33. For an online tutorial in statistics, go to *www.robertniles.com;* for reading on the bus, try Larry Gonick and Woollcott Smith, *Cartoon Guide to Statistics* (New York: Harper Perennial, 1993); for the fun stuff, see e-Compensation 2 in this chapter.
34. J. K. Rowling, *Harry Potter and the Order of the Phoenix* (New York: Scholastic, 2003).
35. Brian Hinchcliffe, "Juggling Act: Internal Equity and Market Pricing," *Workspan,* February 2003, pp. 42–45.
36. See Cases in Compensation (described in the Preface of this book) for more tools for choosing number of grades and the size of pay ranges.
37. Charles Fay, Eric Schulz, Steven Gross, and David VanDeVoort, "Broadbanding, Pay Ranges and Labor Costs," *WorldatWork Journal,* Second Quarter 2004, pp. 8–24; Gene Baker and Joe Duggan, "Global Banding Program and a Consultant's Critique," *WorldatWork Journal,* Second Quarter 2004, pp. 24–35; Kenan S. Abosch and Beverly Hmurovic, "A Traveler's Guide to Global Broadbanding," *ACA Journal,* Summer 1998, pp. 38–47.
38. "Life with Broadbands," ACA Research Project, 1998; "Broad Banding Case Study: General Electric," *WorldatWork Journal,* Third Quarter 2000, p. 43.
39. Kenan S. Abosch and Janice S. Hand, *Broadbanding Models* (Scottsdale, AZ: American Compensation Association, 1994); Charles Fay, Eric Schulz, Steven Gross, and David VanDeVoort, "Broadbanding, Pay Ranges and Labor Costs," *WorldatWork Journal,* Second Quarter 2004, pp. 8–24; Gene Baker and Joe Duggan, "Global Banding Program and a Consultant's Critique," *WorldatWork Journal,* Second Quarter 2004, pp. 24–35.

40. WorldatWork. 2019 Survey of Salary Structure Policies and Practices. Scottsdale, AZ. www.worldatwork.org.
41. S. Rynes, C. Weber, and G. Milkovich, "Effects of Market Survey Rates on Job Evaluation, and Job Gender on Job Pay," *Journal of Applied Psychology* 74 (1989), pp. 114–123.
42. Howard Risher, "Second Generation Banded Salary Systems," *WorldatWork Journal* 16(1), 2007, p. 20.
43. WorldatWork, "Job Evaluation and Market Pricing Practices, 2015," https://www.worldatwork.org/docs/research-and-surveys/survey-brief-job-evaluation-and-market-pricing-2015.pdf.
44. B. Gerhart and S. L. Rynes, *Compensation: Theory, Evidence, and Strategic Implications* (Thousand Oaks, CA: Sage, 2003); B. Gerhart, C. Trevor, and M. Graham, "New Directions in Employee Compensation Research," in G. R. Ferris, ed., *Research in Personnel and Human Resources Management* (Greenwich, CT: JAI Press, 1996), pp. 143–203.
45. Y. Yanadori and S. C. Kang, "Intra-firm Differentiation of Compensation Systems: Evidence from U.S. High-Technology Firms," *Human Resource Management Journal* 21 (2011), pp. 236–257.
46. Jeffrey Pfeffer and Alison Davis-Blake, "Understanding Organizational Wage Structures: A Resource Dependence Approach," *Academy of Management Journal* 30 (1987), pp. 437–455.
47. Mason Carpenter and James Wade, "Micro-Level Opportunity Structures as Determinants of Non-CEO Executive Pay," *Academy of Management Journal* 45 (2002), pp. 1085–1103.
48. Google's stock split in 2014. Thus, the pre-2014 stock price values mentioned here have been adjusted by multiplying them by .50.
49. Amir Efrati and Pui-Wing Tam, "Google Battles to Keep Talent," *The Wall Street Journal,* November 10, 2010.
50. Amir Efrati and Pui-Wing Tam, "Google Battles to Keep Talent," *The Wall Street Journal,* November 10, 2010.
51. Rolfe Winkler, "The High Cost of Googling Growth," *The Wall Street Journal,* October 15, 2011, B16.
52. David Goldman, "Google's Fight to Keep Its Top Minds," *CNNMoney.com*, November 10, 2010.
53. Claire Cain Miller and Jenna Wortham, "Silicon Valley Hiring Perks: Meals, iPads and a Cubicle for Spot," *New York Times,* March 26, 2011.
54. Andrew Ross Sorkin, "Google Reprices 7.6 Million Employee Stock Options," *The New York Times,* March 11, 2009; Martin Peers, "Searching Google for Pay," *The Wall Street Journal,* November 11, 2010.
55. Rolfe Winkler, "The High Cost of Googling Growth," *The Wall Street Journal,* October 15, 2011, B16.

Part **IV**
Employee Contributions: Determining Individual Pay

The first two sections of the pay model outlined in **Exhibit IV.1** essentially deal with fairness. Alignment, covered in **Part I**I, is all about internal fairness: describing jobs and determining their worth relative to each other based on content of the jobs and impact on the organization's objectives. **Part I**II extended our discussion of fairness to the external market. It's not enough that jobs within a company are treated fairly in comparison to each other; we also need to look at external competitiveness with similar jobs in other companies. This raises questions of conducting salary surveys, setting pay policies, and arriving at competitive pay levels and equitable pay structures. This fourth part of the book finally brings people into the pay and fairness equation. How do we design a pay system so that individual contributors are rewarded according to their value to the organization? Let's hope the following example, from a photo caption, isn't a role model for today's practices:

> Another 4th dynasty tomb, beautifully carved and painted with vibrantly colored scenes, belonging to a priest of the royal cult and senior scribe named Kay. A fascinating glimpse into an ancient economic exchange is offered by the inscription at the entrance to this tomb, which reads: It is the tomb makers, the draftsmen, the craftsmen, and the sculptors who made my tomb. I paid them in bread and beer and made them take an oath that they were satisfied.
>
> —Zahi Hawass, *Mountains of the Pharaohs: The Untold Story of the Pyramid Builders* (Cairo: American University in Cairo Press, 2006, p. 136)

EXHIBIT IV.1 **The Pay Model**

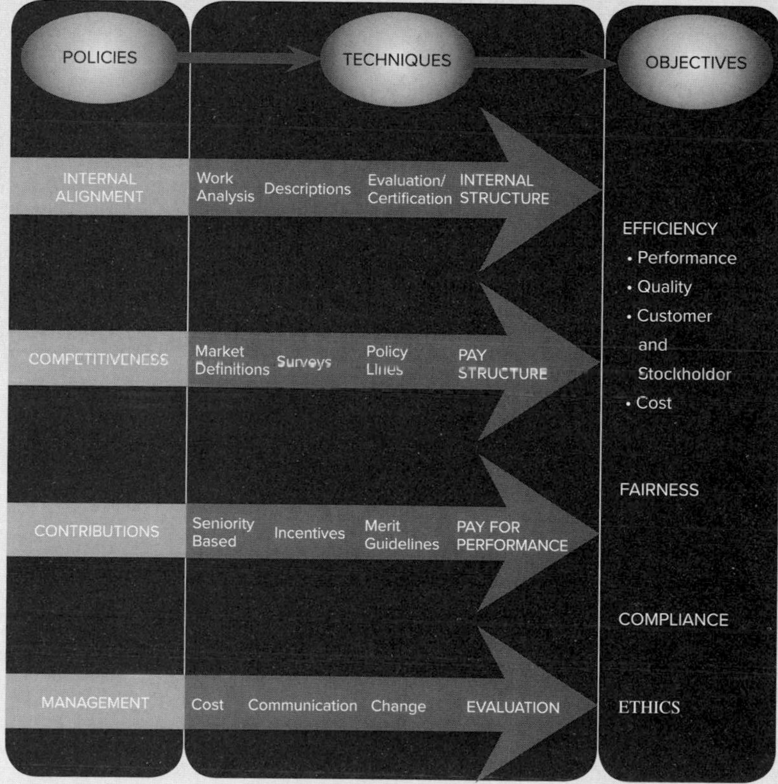

How much should one employee be paid relative to another when they both hold the same jobs in the same organization? If this question is not answered satisfactorily, all prior efforts to evaluate and price jobs may have been in vain.

For example, suppose that the compensation manager determines that all customer service representatives (CSRs) should be paid between $28,000 and $43,000.

But where in that range should each individual be paid? Should a good CSR be paid more than a poor one? If the answer is yes, how should performance be measured and what should be the differential reward? Similarly, should the CSR with more years of experience (i.e., higher seniority) be paid more than a CSR with less time on the job? Again, if the answer is yes, what is the trade-off between seniority and performance in assigning pay raises? Should Wesley, the compensation manager's son-in-law, be paid more just because he's family? What are the legitimate factors to consider in the reward equation? As **Exhibit IV.1** suggests, all of these questions involve the concept of employee contribution (and fairness/equity). For the next three chapters, we will be discussing different facets of employee contribution.

Chapter 9 asks whether companies should invest in pay-for-performance plans. In other words, does paying for performance result in higher performance? The answer may seem obvious, but there are many ways to complicate this elegant notion.

Chapter 10 looks at actual pay-for-performance plans. The compensation arena is full of programs that promise to link pay and performance. We identify these plans and discuss their relative advantages and disadvantages.

Chapter 11 acknowledges that performance can't always be measured objectively. What do we do to ensure that subjective appraisal procedures are as free from error as possible? Much progress has been made here, and we provide a tour of the different strategies for measuring performance.

Chapter Nine
Pay-for-Performance: Theory and Evidence

Chapter Outline

The primary focus of **Part 3** was on determining the worth of jobs, independent of who performed those jobs. **Job analysis, job evaluation,** and **job pricing** all have a common theme. They are techniques to identify the value a firm places on its jobs. Now we introduce people into the equation. Now we declare that different people performing the same job may add different value to the organization. Wesley is a better programmer than Kelly. Erinn knows more programming languages than Ian. Who should get what?

If you stop and think about it, employment is about a contract. When you accept a job, you agree to perform work–to complete tasks–in exchange for rewards. Sometimes this contract is simple. You agree to cut your neighbor's grass for $25. When you're done, she pays you the money. As we grow up, the contracts become more complex. Your first job after college will involve a contract, although the terms of that contract won't be spelled out fully. You will sign an agreement to perform tasks to the satisfaction of your employer. Rarely are the "satisfaction" terms clearly defined upfront. You hope you'll get feedback along the way that helps make the performance standards more apparent. In exchange, the contract reads, you will receive a certain amount of pay. Let's hope it's a big number! But you might be a bit disappointed in the rest of the contract, because it's rare that there will be any mention of other rewards (e.g., how interesting your work is and how collaborative your co-workers are) besides money (and perhaps related benefits). You take it on faith that the employer will do right by you beyond just the monetary component of the job.

At the extreme of employment contracts are those between an employer and a union representing workers (**Chapter 15**). Unionized employees aren't willing to take it on faith that the employer will provide fair compensation for work performed. Some union contracts are hundreds of pages long and specify in the tiniest detail what a worker will get as rewards under different work conditions.

Whether the employment contract is simple or complex, though, we still struggle with both sides of the agreement. How do we decide if a worker is performing the job satisfactorily and how much should we pay for that performance?

Entering people into the compensation equation greatly complicates the compensation process. People don't behave like robots. Believe us, the auto industry has tried replacing people with robots. On some jobs, like welding car parts together, robots work just fine. Robots can tighten a bolt and oil a joint. But for many jobs (though not as many as in the past) it's easier and cheaper to do things the old-fashioned way–with people. The challenge is to design a performance and reward system so that employees support what the company is trying to accomplish. Indeed, there is growing evidence that the way we design HR practices, like performance management, strongly affects the way employees perceive the company. Well-known organizations, like The Container Store and Costco, both pay more and have more sophisticated performance-tracking methods that lead to happier employees.[1] And this directly affects corporate performance.[2] The simple (or not so simple, as we will discuss) process of implementing a performance appraisal system that employees find acceptable goes a long way toward increasing trust for top management.[3] And that new performance appraisal and reward system has an impact on other parts of HR. The pool of people we recruit and select from changes as our HR system changes. In **Chapter 2**, we talked about sorting effects. Not everyone "appreciates" an incentive system or even a merit-based pay system. People who prefer pay systems that are less performance-based will "sort themselves" out of organizations that have these pay practices and philosophies. Those people either won't respond to recruitment ads, or, if already employed, may seek employment elsewhere.[4] So as we discuss pay and performance in this chapter and in **Chapters 10** and **11**, remember that there are other important outcomes that also depend on building good performance measurement tools.

In **Chapter 1** we talked about compensation objectives complementing overall human resource objectives and both of these helping an organization achieve its overall strategic objectives. But how does an organization achieve its overall strategic objectives? In this part of the book, we argue that organizational success ultimately depends on human behavior. Why did the St. Louis Cardinals in 1967, the Cleveland Cavaliers in 2016, and the Los Angeles Lakers in 2020 win a championship? Answer: It was a team effort, but it sure helped to have had on those teams, respectively, Bob Gibson ("Bullet"), LeBron James ("Greatest player on the planet"), and, again...LeBron James. Bob Gibson went 3-0 as a pitcher (in a best-of-seven series!) and gave up a total of three earned runs in those three (complete) games he pitched. It is said that Major League Baseball lowered the height of the pitching mound because of how dominant Bob Gibson was. LeBron has won titles with three different teams. (Reaching way back in baseball, Babe Ruth hit more home runs in a season than any other entire team in the league hit–twice.) In American football, the New England Patriots won in 2019 for a change. Did the Patriots, Coach Bill Belichik, and Tom Brady win again in 2021? What's that you say? Coach Belichik did not win, but Tom Brady did? With some team in Florida? Interesting. Or how did Dumbledore's Army and the Order of the Phoenix win the Battle of Hogwarts? Surely, it was because of superior wizarding talent (and not being evil)! OK, just one more. If the Night King and an army of wights is coming for you, it does not hurt to have some very specialized high level talent on your side, such as Daenerys Stormborn of House Targaryen, the First of Her Name, Queen of the Andals and the First Men, Protector of the Seven Kingdoms, the Mother of Dragons, the Khaleesi of the Great Grass Sea, the Unburnt, the Breaker of Chains.[5] (Someone who can handle herself up close and personal with the Night King, specifically Arya, is also pretty important it turns out.) These are all examples of valuable human capital and behaviors essential in executing strategies successfully. (Admittedly, there are more down to earth examples like highly talented programmers/coders.) Our compensation decisions and practices should be designed to increase the likelihood that employees will engage in behaviors that help the organization achieve its strategic objectives (incentive effect) and to attract and retain such employees to the organization (sorting effect). This chapter is organized around employee behaviors. First, we identify the four kinds of behaviors organizations are interested in. Then we note what theories say about our ability to motivate these behaviors. And, finally, we talk about our success, and sometimes lack thereof, in designing compensation systems to elicit these behaviors.

WHAT BEHAVIORS DO EMPLOYERS CARE ABOUT? LINKING ORGANIZATION STRATEGY TO COMPENSATION AND PERFORMANCE MANAGEMENT

The simple answer is that employers want employees to perform in ways that lead to better organizational performance. **Exhibit 9.1** shows how organizational strategy is the guiding force that determines what kinds of employee behaviors are needed.

As an illustration, Nordstrom's department stores are known for extremely good quality merchandise and high levels of customer satisfaction–this is the organization strategy they use to differentiate themselves from competitors. Nordstrom's success isn't a fluke. You can bet that some of their corporate goals, strategic business unit goals (SBU goals, where a strategic business unit might be a store), department-level goals, and, indeed, individual employee goals are linked to pleasing customers and selling high-quality products. The job of Human Resources is to devise policies and practices (and compensation falls in this mix) that lead employees (the last box in **Exhibit 9.1**) to behave in ways that ultimately support corporate goals. When you walk into a Nordstrom's, you see employees politely greeting you, helping without suffocating, and generally making the shopping experience a pleasant one. These are behaviors that support Nordstrom's strategic plan. Every organization, whether they realize it or not, has human resource practices that can either work together or conflict with each other in trying to generate positive employee behaviors. One way of looking at this process is evident from **Exhibit 9.2**, which says that behavior is a function of the ability, motivation, and opportunity to perform. We first saw this idea in **Chapter 2**.

EXHIBIT 9.1 The Cascading Link Between Organization Strategy and Employee Behavior

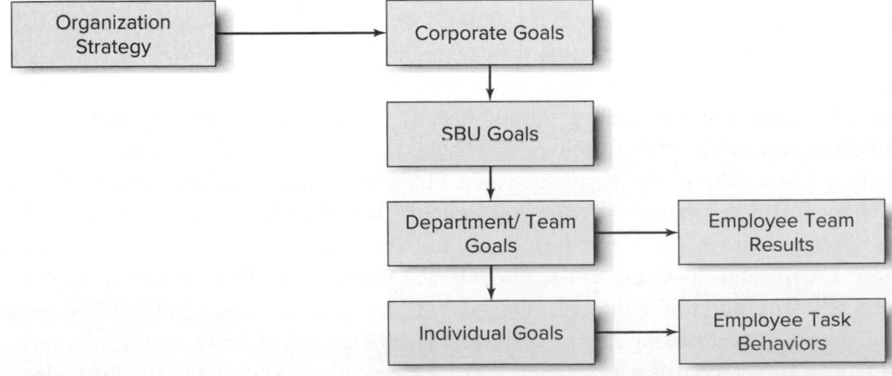

Let's use an example from the classroom. You have to make a presentation tomorrow. Twenty percent of your grade (the reward) depends on it. Do you have the ability? Can you speak clearly, be interesting, and send a good message? Are you motivated? (Or is this class unimportant to you? Would you prefer to watch the finale of "Walking Dead" on TV?) And is the opportunity to do well (e.g., without environmental obstacles) present? (One of your authors was making a presentation a few years ago in Indonesia when an earthquake hit. Ruined the speech!)

Wanting to succeed isn't enough. Having the ability but not the motivation also isn't enough. Many a player with lots of talent doesn't have the motivation to endure thousands of hours of repetitive drills, or to endure weight training and general physical conditioning. Even with both ability and motivation, a player's work environment (both physical and political) must be free of obstacles. A home run hitter drafted by a team with an enormous ball park (home run fences set back much farther from home plate) might never have the opportunity to reach his full potential.

The same thing is true in more traditional jobs. Success depends on finding people with ability–that's the primary job of recruitment, selection, and training. Once good people are hired, they need to be motivated to behave in ways that help the organization. (Note, part of selection is also to hire motivated people, so the triangles interact with each other, as denoted by the three-pronged arrow in the center of **Exhibit 9.2**.) This is where compensation enters the picture. Pay and other rewards should reinforce desired behaviors. But so, too, should performance management, by making sure that what is expected of employees, and what is measured in regular performance reviews, is consistent with what the compensation practices are doing. And perhaps most important of all, the culture of the organization (the informal rules and expectations that are evident in any company) should point in the same direction. Finally, HR needs to establish policies and practices that minimize the chances that outside "distractors" hinder performance.

In the 1980s, Nabisco was slow to recognize customer demand for "soft batch" cookies. Why? They had a centralized organization structure in which it took a long time for sales information to reach the top decision makers. No matter how much ability or motivation the sales staff has, it's hard to sell cookies the public doesn't want. What did Nabisco do? They decentralized the company (organization design), creating divisions responsible for different product lines. Now when sales people say consumer preferences are changing, response is much more rapid. Similarly, if we don't recognize changing **skill requirements** (human resource

EXHIBIT 9.2 **The Big Picture, or Compensation Can't Do It Alone!**

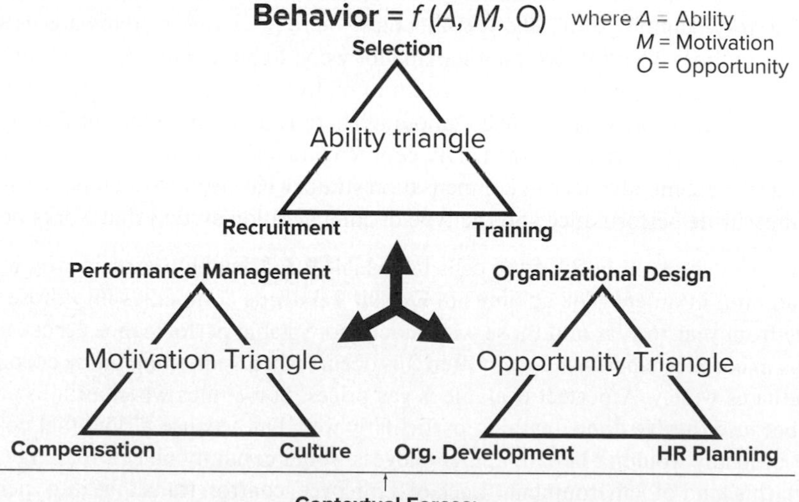

planning), it's hard to set up revised training programs or develop compensation packages to reward these new skills instantly. Knowing in advance about needed changes makes timely completion easier. As a further illustration, if we have inefficient processes (such as too many steps in getting approval for change), organization development (the process for changing the way a company operates) can free up motivated workers to use their skills.

The key lesson from **Exhibit 9.2** is important: Compensation can't do it all alone. Try changing behavior by developing a compensation system to reward/motivate that behavior. If you haven't selected the right people (and/or provided the necessary training/development) or if you haven't designed the work and the culture to provide the opportunity to leverage employees' motivation and ability, you're destined for failure. Not taking into account the importance of differences in how people respond to different pay systems is another potential pitfall.[6] When you're out working in HR, and your boss asks you to "fix" something (such as pay or performance appraisal), make sure the change fits with what other HR programs in the organization are trying to do. Otherwise trouble lurks.

So, what behaviors does compensation need to reinforce? First, compensation should be sufficiently attractive to make it possible to recruit and hire good potential employees (attraction).[7] Second, we need to make sure the good employees stay with the company (retention). The recession of 2008–2010 severely tested companies' (no) layoff strategies. Losing money? Lay off workers! But sometimes laying off workers means cutting future stars. Some wiser companies kept costs down by reducing labor costs without layoffs–by, for example, temporarily reducing salaries, bonuses, 401(k) retirement contributions, and/or work hours. Caterpillar, FedEx, Black and Decker, Honeywell, the *New York Times,* and the State of Pennsylvania are examples of organizations that reduced labor costs without layoffs.[8] As we noted earlier (Chapter 2), Nucor has weathered huge declines in revenues without layoffs. So too has Lincoln Electric. Honeywell too.[9] Not all companies can always avoid layoffs, but there is evidence that some companies probably still resort too readily to layoffs.[10] If we can succeed at these first two things, we can then concentrate on building further knowledge and skills (develop skills). And, finally, we need to find ways to motivate employees to perform well in their jobs–to take their knowledge and abilities and apply them in ways that contribute to organizational performance.

For example, whether we've developed a sound compensation package can only be determined by the impact on performance. We can't tell if our compensation system helps recruit and select good employees if we don't know how to measure what constitutes *good.* We can't tell if employees are building the kinds of knowledge base they need if we can't measure knowledge accumulation. We can't reward performance if we can't measure it! As a simple example, think about companies where piece-rate systems are used to pay people. Recently, one of the authors went to a sawmill, looking for wood to build a dining room table. Talks with the manager revealed they used a simple piece-rate system to motivate workers. For every board foot of lumber cut using giant saws, workers were paid a fixed amount. There is little ambiguity in this measure of performance, and this makes it easy to create a strong link between units of performance and amount of compensation. One of the biggest recent advances in compensation strategy has been to document and extend this link between ease of measuring performance and the type of compensation system that works best.

Let's take a minute to talk about each of the cells in **Exhibit 9.3**. They help explain why incentives work in some situations and not in others. The columns in **Exhibit 9.3** divide companies into those with widely variable performance from year to year and those with much more stable performance across time. What might cause wide swings in corporate performance? Often this occurs when something in the corporation's external environment fluctuates widely. A perfect example is gas prices. Sometimes when airlines are reporting high profits, it is not because they've done anything particularly well, but because airline fuel costs have dropped significantly.[11] It probably wouldn't be fair, and employees would certainly object, if a large part of pay were incentive-based in this kind of environment. Lack of employee control translates into perceptions of lack of opportunity to perform well and unfair treatment if pay is tied to these uncontrollable things. Situations B and D both suggest that a low-incentive component is appropriate in organizations with highly variable annual performance. Conversely, as situations A and C indicate, larger-incentive components are appropriate in companies with stable annual performance.

The rows in **Exhibit 9.3** note that individual employee performance also can vary. Some jobs are fairly stable, with expectations fairly consistent across time. What I do today is basically the same thing I did yesterday. And tomorrow looks like a repeat too! In other jobs, though, there might be high fluctuation in the kinds of things expected of employees, and for these jobs there is high demand for employees who are willing to be flexible and adjust to changing demand. Here, using incentive pay exclusively might not work. Incentive systems are notorious for getting people to do exactly what is being incentivized. Pay me big money to sell suits, and that's just what I'm going to do. You want me to handle customer returns, too? No way, not unless the compensation system rewards a broader array of duties. Evidence suggests that companies are best able to get employees to adjust, be flexible, and show commitment when a broader array of rewards, rather than just money, is part of the compensation package.[12] For example, why does Lincoln Electric (a major producer of welding machines) outproduce other companies in the same industry year after year? Normally we think it's because the company has a well-designed incentive system that links to level of production. Certainly this is a big factor! But when you talk to people at Lincoln Electric, they suggest that part of the success comes from other forms of reward, including the strong commitment to job security–downsizing simply isn't part of the vocabulary there–which reinforces a willingness to try new technologies and new work processes (a culture that supports innovation). Situation A, with low variability in corporate performance but unclear performance measures for employees, describes the kind of reward package that fits these job and organizational performance characteristics.

When we distill all of this, what can we conclude? We think the answer depends on how we respond to the following four questions:

1. How do we attract good employment prospects to *join* our company?
2. How do we *retain* these good employees once they join?

EXHIBIT 9.3 Performance Measurement Relationship to Compensation Strategy

		Variability in Corporate Performance	
		Low Variability	**High Variability**
Variability and ability to measure individual performance	**Unstable and unclear performance measures**	**Situation A** Provide a wide array of awards beyond just money. Include significant incentive component.	**Situation B** Provide a wide array of awards beyond just money. Emphasize base pay with low-incentive portion.
	Stable and clear performance measures	**Situation C** Emphasize monetary rewards with large-incentive component.	**Situation D** Emphasize monetary rewards: large base pay with low-incentive portion.

This table extrapolates the findings from two studies: Matthew C. Bloom and George T. Milkovich, "The Relationship among Risk, Incentive Pay, and Organizational Performance," *Academy of Management Journal* 14(3), 1998, pp. 283–297; Anne Tsui, Jone L. Pearce, Lyman W. Porter, and Angela M. Tripoli, "Alternative Approaches to the Employee-Organization Relationship: Does Investment in Employees Pay Off?" *Academy of Management Journal* 40(5), 1997, pp. 1089–1121.

3. How do we get employees to *develop skills* for current and future jobs?
4. How do we get employees to *perform well* while they are here?

First, how do we get good people to join our company? How did Nike get LeBron James to serve as a corporate spokesperson? Part of the answer is cold hard cash–$90 million guaranteed before LeBron had even played his first NBA game.[13] But it isn't always just about the money. LeBron asked for and got artistic input on the products designed by Nike. Even when the decision doesn't involve millions of dollars, the long-run success of any company depends on getting good people to accept employment. One particularly good study of this very question found that job characteristics (including rewards and tasks/abilities required) and recruiter behaviors were key elements in the decision to join a company.[14]

Second, the obvious complement to the decision to join is the decision to stay. How do we retain employees? It doesn't do much good to attract exceptional employees to our company only to lose them a short time later. Once our compensation practices get a good employee in the door, we need to figure out ways to ensure it's not a revolving door. Max Scherzer left the Detroit Tigers, a perennial pick for a division title, to play with the Washington Nationals. Was it the $210 million contract, including a $50 million signing bonus and an annual average salary of $30 million? Or was it because the Washington Nationals were favored to win the World Series? What does it take to retain key people? Money?[15] Or are other rewards important? And does their absence lead us to use money as the great neutralizer?

Third, we also must recognize that what we need employees to do today may change–literally overnight! A fast-changing world requires employees who can adjust more quickly. How do we get employees, who traditionally are resistant to change, to willingly develop skills that might not be vital on the current job but are forecast to be critical in the future? Another compensation challenge!

Finally, we want employees to do well on their current jobs. This means performing–and performing well–tasks that support our strategic objectives. What motivates employees to succeed? The compensation challenge is to design rewards that enhance job performance.

WHAT DOES IT TAKE TO GET THESE BEHAVIORS? WHAT THEORY SAYS

Another way of phrasing these same questions is to ask, "What motivates employees?" For example, we know that people differ in the importance they attribute to money. That is partly because people differ in the value they place on money and partly because the same person may place a different value on money depending on their circumstances (e.g., their age, wealth, aspirations).[16] We all know someone who just isn't motivated by the almighty dollar. But even for these people, it's possible to design a pay system that is appreciated–one in which the link between effort and pay is evident. Although money is not everyone's prime motivator, money is, on average, the most important reward in surveys of employees. Also, whatever money's importance, given most people's strong preference to be treated fairly, almost nobody likes to be underpaid or reacts well to it. Is it any wonder, then, that figuring out the motivation equation is a major pastime for compensation experts?[17] In the simplest sense, *motivation* involves three elements: (1) what's important to a person, and (2) offering it in exchange for some (3) desired behavior. As to the first element, what's important to employees, data suggest most employees prefer pay systems that are influenced primarily by individual performance and the market rate, with seniority also important to some.[18] To narrow down specific employee preferences, though, there has been some work on what's called **flexible compensation.** Flexible compensation is based on the idea that only the individual employee knows what package of rewards would best suit personal needs. Employees who hate risk could opt for more base pay and less incentive pay. Trade-offs between pay and benefits could also be selected. The key ingredient in this new concept is careful cost analysis to make sure the dollar cost of the package an employee selects meets employer budgetary limits.[19] Absent widespread adoption of flexible compensation systems, we need to answer these three questions the old-fashioned way—by going back to theories of motivation to see what "makes people tick."

In **Exhibit 9.4** we briefly summarize some of the important motivation theories.[20] These theories try to answer the three questions we posed above: What's important? How do we offer it? How does it help deliver desired behaviors? Pay particular attention to the "So What?" column, in which we talk about the theories' views on how employee behavior is delivered.

EXHIBIT 9.4 Motivation Theories

Theory	Essential Features	So What? Implications for Pay and Pay for Performance (PFP)
Maslow's need hierarchy	People are motivated by needs. Needs form a hierarchy from most lower/basic (food and shelter) to higher-order (e.g., self-esteem, love, self-actualization). Unmet needs motivate. Met needs do not. Unmet higher-order needs become motivating after lower-order needs have been met.	Base pay must be set high enough to provide individuals with the economic means to meet their basic living needs. PFP works best when focused on unmet needs. In cases when basic needs are met, PFP is motivating to the extent that performance is instrumental in gaining achievement, recognition, and/or approval in addition to higher pay.
Herzberg's two-factor theory	Hygiene/maintenance factors (e.g., pay) prevent dissatisfaction, but do not motivate or cause satisfaction. Hygiene factors, which include pay, help with basic living needs, security, and fair treatment. Satisfiers/motivators, such as recognition, promotion, and achievement, motivate performance.	Base pay must be set high enough to provide individuals with the economic means to meet hygiene needs, but it alone cannot motivate performance. As with need hierarchy theory, performance-based pay is motivating to the extent it is connected with meeting employees' needs for recognition, attainment, achievement, and the like. Low pay will cause dissatisfaction. High pay, by itself, does not motivate. It only motivates if it is instrumental in achieving higher-level needs.

Theory	Essential Features	So What? Implications for Pay and Pay for Performance (PFP)
Expectancy	Motivation is the product of the following three perceptions:	Job tasks and responsibilities should be clearly defined.
	Expectancy is employees' assessment of their ability to perform required job tasks.	Line of sight is critical—employees must believe they can influence performance targets. Selection and training, as well as job design, matter here.
	Instrumentality is employees' beliefs that higher job performance will be rewarded by the organization.	Pay must be clearly linked to performance and this link must be perceived as strong. Rewards for high performance must be perceived as significant.
	Valence is the value employees attach to the organization rewards received for job performance.	People choose to put forth effort toward the behavior (e.g., low, average, high performance) with the highest motivational force. Selection, training, job design, and compensation decisions influence this choice.
	Motivational force to choose high performance is higher to the degree expectancy, instrumentality, and valence are high for that choice.	
Equity	Employees experience equity and will be motivated to perform when the ratio of their perceived outputs (e.g., pay) to perceived inputs (e.g., effort, performance) is equal to the perceived outputs/inputs of a comparison person.	The pay/performance link is critical; increases in performance must be matched by commensurate increases in pay to achieve equity/fairness, particularly among high performers. Employees evaluate the adequacy of their pay via comparisons with other employees. That means that relative pay (and relative contribution) matters.
	If the two ratios above are not equal, perceived inequity results and the person is motivated to take action to restore equity.	Perceived inequity can lead to lower effort, theft, lawsuits, and/or turnover. Perceptions of pay and contribution may or may not be accurate. Organizations must focus on communicating accurate information on

Theory	Essential Features	So What? Implications for Pay and Pay for Performance (PFP)
	Some actions employees take (e.g., lower effort) to restore perceived equity are not helpful to organizations.	pay and contribution. Otherwise, inaccurate information and perceptions play a larger role and can influence motivation and behaviors.
Reinforcement	Rewards reinforce (motivate and sustain) performance. Rewards are most effective when they follow directly after behaviors to be reinforced. Behaviors that are not rewarded will be discontinued (extinction).	Performance-based payments work best when they closely follow performance. Rewards tightly coupled to desired performance objectives generate higher effort. Withholding payouts discourages unwanted behaviors.
Goal setting	Challenging and specific performance goals generate the most employee effort. Goals serve as feedback standards to which employees can evaluate their performance. Employees must be motivated to choose and persevere in (be committed to) pursuing performance goals.	Performance-based pay that is contingent upon continued achievement of challenging, specific performance goals increases performance. Regular and specific feedback on performance/goal attainment is important.
Agency	Pay directs and motivates employee performance. Employees are risk-averse. They prefer certain/fixed income flows (wage, salary) to variable income flows (e.g., performance-based pay).	Performance-based pay can be used to direct and induce employee performance. Depending on risk and monitoring challenges, a choice of efficient "contract" is made: either behavior-based or outcome-based.[21] Employees are risk-averse, meaning that a compensating differential (wage premium) is necessary when using an

Theory	Essential Features	So What? Implications for Pay and Pay for Performance (PFP)
	If performance can be accurately monitored without undue cost or if risk due to variability in outcomes (e.g., profits) is large (increasing risk-bearing concerns among employees), payments should be based upon behaviors (satisfactory completion of work duties). If monitoring of behaviors is difficult or costly and if risk due to variability in outcomes is not large, pay should be based on outcomes (e.g., profits).	outcome-based contract. However, stronger incentives are typically possible under outcome-based contracts. In each situation, the question is whether the positive of strong incentives outweighs the negative of a compensating differential paid for risk-bearing by employees.

Some of the theories in **Exhibit 9.4** focus on content–identifying what is important to people. Maslow's and Herzberg's theories, for example, both fall in this category. People have certain needs–such as physiological, security, and self-esteem needs–that influence behavior. Although neither theory is clear on how these needs are offered and how they help deliver behavior, presumably if we offer rewards that satisfy one or more needs, employees will behave in desired ways. These theories often drive compensation decisions about the breadth and depth of compensation offerings. Flexible compensation, with employees choosing from a menu of pay and benefit choices, clearly is driven by the issue of needs. Who best knows what satisfies an employee's needs? The employee! So let employees choose, within limits, what they want in their reward package.

Theories of a second sort, best exemplified by expectancy theory, equity theory, and agency theory, focus less on need states and what rewards best satisfy those needs and focus more on motivational processes, including how perceptions of needs and other factors (equity/fairness, risk, linkages between effort, performance, and pay) are processed cognitively to determine motivation and behavior.[22] Many of our compensation practices recognize the importance of a fair exchange. We evaluate jobs using a common set of compensable factors (**Chapter 5**) in part to let employees know that an explicit set of rules governs the evaluation process. We collect salary survey data (**Chapter 8**) because we want the exchange to be fair compared to external standards. We design incentive systems (**Chapter 10**) to align employee behavior with the needs (desired behaviors) of the organization. All of these pay decisions, and more, owe much to understanding how the employment exchange affects employee motivation.

Expectancy theory argues that people behave as if they cognitively evaluate what behaviors are possible (e.g., the probability that they can complete the task) in relation to the value of rewards offered in exchange. According to this theory, we choose behaviors that yield the most satisfactory exchange. Equity theory also focuses on what goes on inside an employee's head. Not surprisingly, equity theory argues that people are highly concerned about equity, or fairness of the exchange process. Employees look at the exchange as a ratio between what is expected and what is received. Some theorists say we judge transactions as fair when others around us don't have a more (or less) favorable balance between the give and get of an exchange.[23] Even greater focus on the exchange process occurs in the last of this second set of theories, agency theory.[24] Here, employees are depicted as agents who enter an exchange with principals–the owners or their designated managers. It is assumed that both sides to the exchange seek the most favorable exchange possible and will act opportunistically if given a chance (e.g., try to "get by" with doing as little as possible to satisfy the contract). Compensation is a major element in this theory, because it is used to keep employees in line: Employers identify important behaviors and important outcomes and pay specifically for achieving desired levels of each. Such incentive systems penalize employees who try to shirk their duties by giving proportionately lower rewards.

At least one of the theories summarized in **Exhibit 9.4** focuses on the third element of motivation: desired behavior. Identifying desired behaviors–and goals expected to flow from these behaviors–is the emphasis of a large body of goal-setting research. Most of this research says that how we set goals (the process of goal setting, the level and difficulty of goals, etc.) can influence the performance levels of employees.[25] For example, workers assigned "hard" goals consistently do better than workers told to "do your best."[26]

A final theory we will mention (not shown in **Exhibit 9.4**) purports to integrate motivation theories under a broad umbrella. Called self-determination theory (SDT), this approach believes that employees are motivated not only by monetary rewards (referred to as extrinsic motivation), but also by intrinsic motivation, which is enjoyment or satisfaction that comes from performing the work itself and produces a sense of autonomy. According to SDT, intrinsic motivation produces the highest-quality motivation.[27]

WHAT DOES IT TAKE TO GET THESE BEHAVIORS? WHAT PRACTITIONERS SAY

In the past, compensation people didn't ask this question very often. Employees learned what behaviors were important as part of the socialization process or as part of the performance management process.[28] If it was part of the culture to work long hours, you quickly learned this. One of our daughters worked as a business consultant for Accenture, a very large consulting company. She learned quickly that 70- to 80-hour work weeks were fairly common. Sure, she had very good wages for someone with a bachelor's degree in biology and no prior business experience, but it didn't take long to burn out when weeks of long hours turned into months. If your performance appraisal at the end of the year stressed certain types of behaviors, or if your boss said certain things were important to her, then the signals were pretty clear: Do these things! Compensation might have rewarded people for meeting these expectations, but usually the compensation package wasn't designed to be one of the signals about expected performance. That has not been true for many years![29] Now compensation people talk about pay in terms of a neon arrow flashing "Do these things." Progressive companies ask, "What do we want our compensation package to do? How, for example, do we get our product engineers to take more risks?" Compensation is then designed to support this risk-taking behavior. Compensation people will also tell you, though, that money isn't everything. But they will also tell you that money (and the sense of achievement and recognition that go with it) is very important. Indeed, there is no better way to ensure that you will hear from an employee than if that employee feels his/her pay is not equitable/fair, given what that employees sees as his/her contributions.

e-Compensation

The International Society for Performance Improvement has web information on performance journals, strategies for improving performance, and conferences covering the latest research on performance improvement techniques. Go to the society's website, ***www.ispi.org***.

Here, however, we do want to identify the many other rewards in addition to compensation that influence employee behavior. Sometimes this important point is missed by compensation experts. Going back at least to Henry Ford, we tend to look at money as the great equalizer. Job boring? No room for advancement? Throw money at the problem! More money is a solution sometimes (e.g., as a compensating wage differential to offset undesirable job attributes). In other cases, however, workers may value improvement in another reward area. To find out, you can ask them (e.g., in a survey). Surveys of workers in general (not as useful as a survey of your own workforce, but still of some use) report that workers generally also highly value other job rewards such as empowerment, recognition, and opportunities for advancement.[30] Entire books, for example, illustrate hundreds of ways to give meaningful recognition to employees.[31] And there is growing sentiment for letting workers choose their own "blend" of rewards from the 13 we note in **Exhibit 9.5**. We may be overpaying in cash *and* missing the opportunity to let employees construct both a more satisfying and less-expensive reward package. Known as flexible compensation, this idea introduced earlier is based on the notion of different rewards having different dollar costs associated with them. Armed with a fixed sum of money, employees move down the line, buying more or less of the 13 rewards as their needs dictate.[32] While widespread use of this type of system may be a long time in the future, the cafeteria approach still underscores the need for integration of rewards in compensation design.

If we don't think about the presence or absence of rewards other than money in an organization, we may find the compensation process producing unintended consequences. Consider the following three examples, which show how compensation decisions have to be integrated with total reward system decisions:

Example 1: A few years ago McDonald's completed a worldwide "employment branding" exercise. Their goal was to find out what people liked about jobs at McDonald's and to feature these rewards in the recruitment strategy for new employees. Three things emerged as strengths at McDonald's: (1) an emphasis on family and friends in a social work environment; (2) flexibility in work assignments and work schedules; and (3) development of skills that helped launch future careers.[33]

Example 2: This example comes from airline industry leader Southwest Airlines.[34] Southwest Airlines promotes a business culture of fun and encourages employees to find ways to make their jobs more interesting and relevant to them personally. All this is accomplished (at least on the surface) without using incentives as a major source of competitive advantage. Indeed, pay at Southwest isn't any higher than for competitor airlines, yet it's much easier to recruit top people there. Fun, a good social environment, is a reward! A somewhat different view is that fun and a good social environment are indeed crucial to Southwest's culture and competitive advantage. However, it may be that incentives are too. Southwest "pays by the trip," meaning that employees earn more, the more flights they work. (Planes only make money for Southwest when they are in the air.) Southwest employees also have significant ownership in the company through a discount stock purchase program, and they receive profit-sharing checks when the airline is profitable, which it has been for 45 years in a row![35] For example, in the most recent year, Southwest paid out $543 million in profit sharing to its 56,110 employees, which works out to an average of $9,677 per employee.[36] Of course, earning more money for working more flights and from ownership and profit sharing only happens when Southwest does well.

That is an example of alignment between the interests of Southwest Airlines and its employees. Add fun and a good social environment, and apparently you can be profitable 45 years in a row, even in an industry marked by regular bankruptcies.

Example 3: Consider the relationship between the different forms of compensation and another of the general rewards listed in **Exhibit 9.5**: security. Normally we think of security in terms of job security. Drastic reductions in middle-management layers during the downsizing decade of the 1980s increased employee concerns about job security and probably elevated the importance of this reward to employees today. Maybe that's why new millennial workers are concerned not only about employment risk but also about compensation risk. There is evidence that compensation at risk (variable pay, which is a payment based on performance objective achievement that does not become part of base pay in future years) may leave employees less satisfied both with their pay level and with the process used to determine pay.[37] Security as an issue, it appears, is creeping into the domain of compensation. It used to be fairly well established that employees would make more this year than they did last year, and employees counted on such *security* to plan their purchases and other economic decisions. The trend today is toward less stable and less secure compensation packages. The very design of compensation systems today contributes to instability and insecurity. And that in turn leads some potential employees to reject a firm or some current employees to decide it's time to leave. Of course, it may be the case that when such plans offer enough upside earnings potential for high performance that high performers may actually prefer to work under such plans (see incentive and sorting effects discussed in **Chapter 1**, later in this chapter, and in **Chapter 10**).

Exhibit 9.6 outlines the different types of compensation components, roughly in order from least risky to most risky for employees. We define risk as variance (lack of stability) of income and/or the inability to

EXHIBIT 9.5 Components of a Total Reward System

1.	Compensation	Wages, commissions, and bonuses
2.	Benefits	Vacations, health insurance
3.	Social interaction	Friendly workplace
4.	Security	Stable, consistent position and rewards
5.	Status/recognition	Respect, prominence due to work
6.	Work variety	Opportunity to experience different things
7.	Workload	Right amount of work (not too much, not too little)
8.	Work importance	Work is valued by society
9.	Authority/control/ autonomy	Ability to influence others; control own destiny
10.	Advancement	Chance to get ahead
11.	Feedback	Receive information helping to improve performance
12.	Work conditions	Hazard free
13.	Development opportunity	Formal and informal training to learn new knowledge skills/ abilities

predict income level from year to year. Base pay is, at least as far as there are any guarantees, the guaranteed portion of income, as long as employees remain employed. Since the Depression there have been very few years when base wages did not rise or at least stay the same.[38] Across-the-board increases, cost-of-living increases, and merit increases all help the base pay component increase on a regular basis. Of course, there always has to be an exception to the rule–and the Great Recession of 2008–2010 spawned many cuts in corporate base wages. The next seven components are distinguished by increasing levels of risk/uncertainty for employees. In fact, risk-sharing plans actually include a provision for cuts in base pay that are only recaptured in years when the organization meets performance objectives. For example, under a plan at E.I. du Pont de Nemours & Company, all employees put 6 percent of their salaries at risk and were paid a sliding percent of this based on how close the firm comes to its annual goals. If the company achieved less than 80 percent of goal, there was no pay increase. In the 80 to 100 range the increase was 3 to 6 percent. At 101 to 150 percent, increases were very lucrative to "pay for" employees taking a risk in the first place–in the 7 to 19 percent range.[39]

EXHIBIT 9.6 **Wage Components**

Wage Component	Definition	Level of Risk to Employee
Base pay	The guaranteed portion of an employee's wage package.	As long as employment continues, this is the secure portion of wages.
Across-the-board increase	Permanent base wage/salary increase granted to all employees, regardless of performance. Size related to some subjective assessment of employer ability to pay.	Some risk to employee, because at discretion of employer. But not tied to performance differences, so risk lower in that respect.
Cost-of-living increase	Same as across-the-board increase, except magnitude based on change in cost of living (e.g., as measured by the Consumer Price Index [CPI]).	Same as across-the-board increases.
Merit pay	Permanent wage/salary increase granted to employee as function of some (typically primarily subjective) assessment of individual employee performance.	Two types of risk faced by employees. Size of total merit pool at discretion of employer and individual portion of pool depends on performance, which also is not totally predictable.
Merit bonus	Nonpermanent (variable) payment (bonus or lump sum) form of variable pay granted to employee as function of some (typically primarily subjective) assessment of individual employee performance.	Three types of risks faced here. Both types mentioned under merit pay, plus not added into base—requires annually "re-earning" the added pay.
Individual incentive	Variable pay tied directly to objective measure of individual performance such	Most risky compensation component if sole element of

Wage Component	Definition	Level of Risk to Employee
	as sales, production volume, or production quality.	pay, but often combined with a base pay. No or low fixed-base pay means each year employee is dependent upon meeting performance target to determine pay.
Success-sharing plans	A generic term for variable pay plans that tie pay to measures of group/organization performance. Distinguished from risk-sharing plans because employees share in any success—any performance above standard—but are not penalized for performance below standard.	All success-sharing plans have risks noted in above pay components plus the risk associated with group performance measures. Now individual worker is also dependent upon the performance of others included in the group.
Profit sharing	Variable pay plan where payout depends on company profitability. (Can also be used at lower levels such as the division. Size of payouts to individuals can be modified based on other measures such as individual performance.)	Profit measures are influenced by factors beyond employee control (e.g., economic climate, accounting write-offs). Less control means more risk.
Gainsharing	Variable pay plan where payout depends not on company level performance such as profitability, but rather on performance at some sub-unit such as a plant/facility. Also, performance is often defined more broadly than just financial terms. Performance examples include labor cost/revenue, safety, cost of scrap, cost of utilities, customer (including patient) satisfaction.	Less risk to individual than profit sharing because performance measure is more controllable in a sub-unit than for an entire organization and because the performance measures themselves may be more controllable for employees than profits.
Risk sharing plans	A generic term for variable pay plans that tie pay to measures of group/organization performance. Distinguished from success-sharing plans in that failure to achieve baseline performance results in lower (total) direct pay. However, upside reward opportunity may be higher than in success-sharing plans in good years.	Greater risk than success-sharing plans. Typically, employees absorb a "temporary" cut in base pay. If performance targets are met, this cut is neutralized by one component of variable pay. Risk to employee is increased though because even base pay is no longer totally predictable.

All of this discussion of risk is only an exercise in intellectual gymnastics unless we add one further observation: Over the last several decades, companies have been moving more toward greater use of variable pay programs, which are higher on the risk continuum. We will say more on the degree to which organizations use pay for performance, including variable pay, in **Chapter 10**.

This greater compensation risk that employees are now asked to bear reflects the result of an evolution over time in forms of pay that are less entitlement-oriented and more variable and linked to individual, group, and corporate performance.[40] Employees increasingly are expected to bear a share of the risks that businesses have solely born in the past. It's not entirely clear what impact this shifting of risk will have in the long run. Some are concerned that efforts to build employee loyalty and commitment may be a casualty of this greater use of variable pay and risk in pay systems.[41] Indeed, some surveys suggest a downward trend in engagement levels for employees, although it may be that such trends, whether upward or downward, depend as much or more on the cyclical nature of the economy.[42] Consistent with the idea of a compensating pay differential for risk, some surveys suggest that employees may need a risk premium (higher pay) to stay and perform in a company with pay at risk.[43] Even a premium might not work for employees who are particularly risk-averse. Security-driven employees actually might accept lower wages if they come in a package that is more stable.[44] On the other hand, some employees may be willing to accept higher risk in return for a greater chance to earn large payouts when performance is high. Also, some employees are not interested in a traditional employment model of lifetime employment with one organization and steady but modest merit increases over the course of their careers. As always, there are pros and cons to each approach, and employees will to some degree self-select/sort themselves into organizations that fit their preferences and out of organizations that do not.

In any case, for the remainder of this chapter, we will return to the more general question of what impact these different forms of pay have on motivating the four general behaviors we noted earlier.

DOES COMPENSATION MOTIVATE BEHAVIOR?

Now let's look at the role of compensation in motivating the four types of behavior outlined earlier: the decision to join, to stay, to develop skills, and to perform well.

Do People Join a Firm Because of Pay?

Level of pay and pay system characteristics influence a job candidate's decision to join a firm, but this shouldn't be too surprising.[45] Pay is one of the more visible rewards in the whole recruitment process. We know, for example, that high-ability applicants do select companies because they provide pay for good performance.[46] This so-called sorting effect has been shown both for good employees choosing a company and for bad employees leaving a company—all because they do (or do not) like the pay system being used.[47] Job offers spell out the level of compensation and may even include discussions about the kind of pay, such as bonuses and profit-sharing participation. Less common are statements such as "You'll get plenty of work variety," or "Don't worry about empowerment," or "The workload isn't too heavy."[48] These other rewards are subjective and tend to require actual time on the job before we can decide if they are positive or negative features of the job. Not so for pay. Being perceived as more objective, it's more easily communicated in the employment offer.

Recent research suggests job candidates look for organizations with reward systems that fit their personalities.[49] Below we outline some of the ways that "fit" is important.

Person Characteristics	Preferred Reward Characteristics
Materialistic	Relatively more concerned about pay level[50]
Low self-esteem	Want large, decentralized organization with little pay for performance[51]
Risk takers	Want more pay based on performance[52]
Risk-averse	Want less performance-based pay[53]
Individualists ("I control my destiny")	Want pay plans based on individual performance, not group performance[54]

None of these relationships is particularly surprising. People are attracted to organizations that fit their personalities. Evidence suggests that talented employees are attracted to companies that have strong links between pay and performance.[55] One way to get this linkage is to give employees some control over the rewards they received. Thirty years ago no company ceded this control to employees. Now almost all major companies allow employees to have some reward choice. And the impact of reward choice is positive: up to 40 percent improvement in performance but only if the choices available are attractive to employees.[56]

It's not a big jump, then, to suggest that organizations should design their reward systems to attract people with the desired personalities and values. For example, if we need risk takers, maybe we should design reward systems that have elements of risk built into them.

Do People Stay in a Firm (or Leave) Because of Pay?

Employee decisions to leave are influenced by their performance and the degree to which pay is performance-based.[57] How does pay affect this relationship? Much of the equity theory research in the 1970s documented that workers who feel unfairly treated in pay react by leaving the firm for greener pastures.[58] This is particularly true under incentive conditions. Turnover is much higher for poor performers when pay is based on individual performance (a good outcome!). Conversely, group incentive plans may lead to more turnover of better performers–clearly an undesirable sorting effect.[59] When AT&T shifted from individual to team-based incentives a number of years ago, star performers either reduced their output or quit. Out of 208 above-average performers, only one continued to report performance increases under the group incentive plan. The rest felt cheated because the incentives for higher individual performance were now spread across all group members.[60]

Clearly, as we saw in **Chapter 7**, pay can be a major factor in decisions to stay or leave. Data suggest that dissatisfaction with pay can be a key factor in turnover.[61] Too little pay triggers feelings of being treated unfairly. The result? Turnover. Supporting this, pay that employees find reasonable can help reduce turnover.[62] Even the way we pay has an impact on turnover. Evidence suggests that some employees are uncomfortable with pay systems that put any substantial future earnings at risk or pay systems that link less to personal effort and more to group effort.[63] Another recent study found that superior-performing employees were less likely to leave if they received bonuses. No such positive result was found with pay increases (thus changing base pay) in that study.[64] We need to make sure, as one critic has noted, that we don't let our design of new reward systems rupture our relationships with existing employees.[65] However, as we have argued, negative sorting effects (high performers leaving) are more likely if base-pay growth does not keep up with performance over time.[66] Recent efforts to use different types of compensation as a tool for retaining workers have focused on what is called *scarce talent.* For example, information technology employees have been scarce for much of the past decade, if not longer. One way to retain these workers is to develop a variable-pay component for each project. For example, reports of variable pay linked to individual length of stay on a project, to peer ratings, and to project results suggest that this pay-for-performance combination may appeal to scarce talent.[67]

The next time you go into an Applebee's restaurant, think about how the company has historically used compensation to reduce turnover. In an industry where manager turnover hovers around 50 percent, Applebee's has been known to allow general managers to earn as much as $30,000 above base salary for hitting targets for sales, profitability, and customer satisfaction. To discourage turnover, this extra compensation is deferred for two years.[68]

Besides money, other rewards also influence the decision to stay in a firm (retention). According to one recent study, the rewards that are effective in helping to retain employees in tough economic times are as follows:[69]

Rewards That Lead People to Stay	Description
Job satisfaction	Work enjoyment
Pay and benefits	Self-explanatory
Social	Coworkers are fun
Organizational commitment	Not a job jumper; loyal
Organizational prestige	Respect afforded company in industry, region

Source: John P. Hausknecht, Julianne Rodda, and Michael J. Howard, "Targeted Employee Retention: Performance-Based and Job-Related Differences in Reported Reasons for Staying," *Human Resource Management* 48, no. 2 (2009), pp. 269–288.

Reminder: Not All Turnover is Bad (and at least some is necessary)

Although many organizations would benefit from reducing turnover, we would be remiss if we did not remind you the reader that not all turnover is bad. In fact, unless hiring decisions are perfect and people and their jobs never change, some amount of turnover is actually essential for a continued good match/fit between the job/organization and the person. At some point, a better match may be best achieved by turnover.[70] That turnover can be voluntary to varying degrees, but even organizations known for having strong employee relations (e.g., the SAS Institute) have healthy levels of involuntary turnover. Sorting effects, which we have seen are fundamental to how compensation influences performance, require turnover.

Do Employees More Readily Agree to Develop Job Skills Because of Pay?

We don't know the answer to this question. Skill-based pay (**Chapter 6**) is intended, at least partially, to pay employees for learning new skills—skills that hopefully will help employees perform better on current jobs and adjust more rapidly to demands on future jobs. For example, the U.S. Army pays ROTC cadets in college to learn new languages. Hot spots like the Mideast command monthly premiums of $100 to $250 per month.[71] Anyone know Farsi (spoken in Iran)?

We do know that one complaint about skill-based pay centers on cost implications. More employees request training, spurred by the promise of skill-based increments. Poorly administered plans, allowing more people to acquire certification in a skill than are actually required, creates cost inefficiencies. This leads to plan abandonment. So is the net result positive? Whether the promise of skill-based pay is fulfilled is unclear. Evidence suggests that while pay for skill may sometimes but not always increase productivity, it does focus people on believing in the importance of quality and in turning out significantly higher quality products.[72]

Do Employees Perform Better on Their Jobs Because of Pay for Performance? The Short Answer is "Yes" (especially compared to the alternative)

No matter what stand you take on this question, someone is going to disagree with you.[73] However, a well-designed plan linking pay to behaviors of employees generally results in better individual and organizational performance.[74] One study looked at the HR practices of over 3,000 companies.[75] One set of questions asked: (1) Did the company have a formal appraisal process, (2) Was the appraisal tied to the size of pay increases, and (3) Did performance influence who would be promoted? Organizations significantly above the mean (by one standard deviation) on these and other "high-performance work practices" had annual sales that averaged $27,000 more per employee. WorldatWork surveyed 1,001 organizations (most, but not all, in the private sector) and 92 percent reported they used individual performance to determine salary increases. Further, 84 percent also used variable pay that was tied to performance.[76]

In his review, Heneman reports that 40 of 42 studies looking at merit pay show higher performance when pay is tied to performance.[77] Strong evidence suggests that linking pay to performance does increase motivation of workers and lead to improved performance.[78] Locke and colleagues analyzed studies where individual incentives (which, strictly defined, are much less common than merit pay, but elements of which are present in especially higher level jobs) were introduced into actual work settings. Productivity increased on average 30 percent.[79] In a study discussed in more detail just below, Kim, Gerhart, and Fang found that performance was higher by 24 percent with individual incentive pay than under a flat hourly pay rate. Further, performance in the incentive group and was still 19.5 percent higher after adjusting for the fact that the incentive group earnings were higher (thus costing more).[80] Other meta-analyses draw similar conclusions–money does motivate performance.[81]

Looking at this from the opposite direction, consulting firm data indicate that high performers received not only significantly higher merit increases than average performers (4.5% versus 2.6%) but also higher bonuses (140% of target versus 99% of target).[82] One study of 841 union and nonunion companies found gainsharing and profit-sharing plans (both designed to link pay to performance) increased unit performance 18 to 20 percent.[83] How, though, does this translate into corporate performance? A review of 26 studies gives high marks to profit-sharing plans: Organizations with such plans had 3.5 to 5 percent higher annual performance.[84] Gerhart and Milkovich took the performance-based pay question one step further. Across 200 companies they found an 8 to 20 percent increase in return on assets for a 10 percentage point (from 10% to 20%) increase in the size of a bonus (as a percentage of base salary).[85] Further, they found that the variable portion of pay (which also included the percent of employees eligible for long-term incentives) had a stronger impact on individual and corporate performance than did the level of base pay.

If all this research isn't enough to convince you, consider Google's position on the matter. In recent speeches the top HR person at Google, Laszlo Bock, says the people you hire and the way you treat them (the rewards) make for happier and more productive workers. With evangelical zeal he advocates transparency in communications, obtainable goal setting, and less hierarchical organizations (fewer levels so employees can empower themselves to grow and learn).[86] Bock also advocates "Pay unfairly (it's more fair!)." Bock explains that a small percentage of employees create a large percentage of the value and that their pay must recognize their disproportionate contributions. A final consideration is: what is the alternative to paying for performance? Not paying for performance? Paying everyone the same, regardless of contribution? Best of luck in making that work in a world of competitors paying for performance and realizing positive incentive and sorting effects? (Try to think of where you have seen a total disconnect between pay and performance and think also of how well that worked.)

Pay for Performance: Harmful Effects on Intrinsic Motivation (Claims and Evidence)

There are legitimate concerns and challenges with making pay for performance work (and avoiding unintended, unwanted outcomes). We will get a bit of a start on that discussion here with some well-known concerns. Critics such as Alfie Kohn, argue that incentives are both morally and practically wrong.[87] The moral argument suggests that incentives are flawed because they involve one person controlling another. The counterargument to this notes that employment is a reciprocal arrangement. Also, how much control does an employee have when no matter how much they contribute, their pay stays the same? In periods of low unemployment especially, workers can choose whether they want to work under compensation systems with strong pay-for-performance linkages (as in the case of incentive systems). We do know that applicants aren't totally risk-averse. Some, especially high performers, tend to prefer performance-based pay rather than a totally fixed salary. Generally, if pay depends on individual performance, applicants find the company more attractive. Team-based incentives, in contrast, are less attractive, although it depends on the person.

Kohn also suggests that incentive systems can actually harm productivity, a decidedly negative practical outcome. His rationale is based on citations mostly to laboratory studies where subjects work in isolation on a task for either pay or no pay. His conclusion, based heavily on the work of Deci and colleagues, is that rewarding a person for performing a task reduces interest in that task–**extrinsic rewards** (money) reduce intrinsic rewards (enjoyment of the task for its own sake).[88] Critics of this interpretation point out at least two important flaws in Kohn's conclusions.[89] First, the pragmatics of business demand that some jobs be performed–indeed, many jobs–that aren't the most intrinsically interesting. Although Target may be a great store for shopping, spending day after day stocking shelves with towels and other nonbreakables falls far down the intrinsic-interest scale.[90] If incentives are required for real-world jobs to be completed and thus to create value for an organization and its consumers, so be it. This may simply be one of the costs of doing business. However, the idea that pay-for-performance would only be used to compensate people for doing uninteresting jobs flies in the face of reality. As we have seen, pay-for-performance is much more likely to be used for higher-level jobs and the payouts are also much higher in higher level jobs. That is likely because high level jobs have more impact on organization performance. Higher level jobs are also interesting, challenging (yes, intrinsically motivating), but people in intrinsically interesting jobs still want to be recognized for their achievements, earn a good living for themselves and their families, and be paid equitably (in line with other high achievers).[91]

Second, studies cited by Kohn frequently looked at people in isolation. In the real-world people interact with each other, know who is performing and who isn't, and react to this when rewards are allocated. Without any link to performance, the less-motivated employees will eventually recognize that harder work isn't necessary. These issues raise the basic question, "Should we tie pay to performance?" One view says, "Not always." Employers are less likely to offer performance-based pay when the job involves multitasking, important quality control issues, or team work. In all three cases performance is harder to measure, and employers shy away from linking pay as a consequence.[92] Alternatively, we could break the issue down to a series of questions.

The first question perhaps should focus on an obvious but often overlooked issue: Do employees think any link at all should be made between pay and performance? Substantial evidence indicates that management and workers alike believe pay should be tied to performance. Dyer and colleagues asked 180 managers from 72 different companies to rate nine possible factors in terms of the importance they should receive in determining the size of salary increases.[93] This group believed the most important factor for salary increases should be job performance. Following close behind is a factor that presumably would be picked up in job evaluation (nature of job) and a motivational variable (amount of effort expended). Other research supports these findings.[94]

Another way to make the pay-for-performance argument is to look at the ways HR professionals try to cut costs. At the top of the list: Create greater distinction between high and low performers![95] In other words, really pay for performance! Once we move away from the managerial ranks, though, other groups express a different view of the pay-performance link. The role that performance levels should assume in determining pay increases is less clear-cut for blue-collar workers.[96] As an illustration, consider the frequent opposition to compensation plans that are based on performance ratings (merit pay). Unionized workers prefer seniority rather than performance as a basis for pay increases.[97] Part of this preference may stem from a distrust of subjective performance measurement systems. Unions ask, "Can management be counted on to be fair?" In contrast, seniority is an objective index for calculating increases. Some evidence also suggests that women might prefer allocation methods not based on performance.[98] It's probably a good thing that, in general, workers believe pay should be tied to performance, because the research we've reported suggests this link makes a difference.[99]

Sorting and Incentive Effects

We suggest that pay for performance generally has a positive effect. How does this performance improvement occur? To start, differentiation between individuals in the pay they receive is necessary, even though some degree of collaboration and cooperation is necessary in most jobs. (**See the section, Differentiation and Dispersion in Teams, in Chapter 3.**) As we have emphasized (see **Chapter 1**), the two specific mechanisms through which differentiation occurs and pay for performance affects behavior are the *incentive effect* and the *sorting effect*.[100] The incentive effect means pay can motivate current employees to perform better. For example, **Exhibit 9.7** summarizes a meta-analytic review by Kim, Gerhart, and Fang of 82 studies that included 7,978 subjects. Kim et al. found that in 74 of the 82 studies, performance was higher in the incentive group than in the non-incentive group. Overall, performance was higher by 24 percent in the incentive group and was still 19.5 percent higher after adjusting for the fact that the incentive group earnings were higher (thus costing more). **Exhibit 9.7** reports performance differences in terms of the effect size d, which is the performance in the incentive group minus the performance in the non-incentive group, divided by the (pooled) standard deviation (SD) of performance in the two groups. Overall, we see that performance in the incentive group was .52 SD higher. The higher performance in the incentive group was robust across performance type, setting, and how interesting or noninteresting the task/work was.

The sorting effect means people sort themselves into and out of jobs based on what is important to them. So if Company X pays for performance, and you don't want to play by those rules (i.e., work harder or smarter to perform better) you sort yourself out, most easily by leaving Company X and finding another company with different rules for getting rewards.

In the studies summarized earlier by Kim et al.'s meta-analysis in **Exhibit 9.7**, the typical design was to randomly assign subjects to either the individual incentive or non-incentive (flat/fixed pay) group and then compare performance. In such a design, each subject is observed under one pay condition and subjects cannot choose their pay condition. Thus, sorting effects cannot be estimated.

In contrast, the study by Cadsby et al., summarized in **Exhibit 9.8**, has 8 rounds where performance is measured, each subject works in both an individual incentive and non-incentive condition, and each subject can choose in some rounds whether to work under and incentive or not. Thus, sorting effects can be estimated. One key finding in **Exhibit 9.8** is that performance is always higher under the individual incentive condition. A second even more striking finding is that the performance difference widens after subjects have an opportunity to experience each pay condition and their performance under each. Specifically, note that in Rounds 1-6, the performance advantage in the individual incentive condition is around 10 percent. However, by the last two rounds, when permitted to choose (sort) themselves into pay condition, subjects in the individual incentive condition outperform those in the fixed salary condition by 38 percent, a performance difference 3 to 4 times higher than in earlier rounds. Thus, the sorting effect accounts for roughly (38-10)/38 = 74 percent of the individual incentive effect. High performers/those motivated by the individual incentive sort themselves into that condition. (The extent of sorting is indicated by the fact that 35 of 115 subjects switched their choice of pay condition between Rounds 1 and 2 and Rounds 7 and 8.)

The Lazear study we discussed in **Chapter 1** provides another example of the importance of the sorting effect, this time in a company setting. Employee productivity (windshields installed per employee) at Safelite Glass increased 44 percent when pay practices switched from salaries (which were unlinked to windshields installed) to individual incentives (where pay depended on number of windshields installed). The interesting hook in this study was a separate analysis of employees who were present before and after the change in pay system (stayers) versus those who left and were replaced. Only one-half of the 44 percent increase (i.e., a 22 percent increase) came from increased productivity of the "stayers" (i.e., the incentive effect). The other half (i.e., the other 22 percent increase) was due to the sorting effect: Less productive workers (who did worse under the new incentive system) left and were replaced by more productive workers who would earn more money under the new incentive system.[101]

EXHIBIT 9.7 Effect Size (Performance in Incentive Group versus in Non-Incentive Group in Standard Deviation Units), Overall, and by Performance Type, Study Setting and Task Type

	N	*K*	$\bar{d}$
Overall performance	7978	82	.52
Performance measure			
Quantity	4909	40	.51
Quality	892	15	.28
Composite	2177	27	.63
Setting			
Laboratory	3993	57	.51
Field	3297	14	.43
Simulation	688	11	1.02
Task type			
Interesting tasks			
Overall	2140	38	.55
Quantity	706	16	.71
Quality	522	10	.30
Composite	912	12	.63
Noninteresting tasks			
Overall	5838	44	.51
Quantity	4203	24	.48
Quality	370	5	.27
Composite	1265	15	.68

N = number of subjects; K = number of effect sizes; Effect size (d) = (Incentive Group Performance minus Non-Incentive Group Performance)/pooled standard deviation (SD) of performance. In the subset of studies reporting sufficient information, there was 24 percent higher performance in the incentive group versus the non-incentive group. After adjusting for the higher average pay in the incentive group, performance was 19.5 percent higher in the incentive group. In addition, 74 of the 82 primary study effect sizes (which represented N = 7,422 6 of the total N of 7,978) are positive, indicating higher performance in the incentive group. Composite is a combination of performance quantity and performance quality.

Source: Kim, J.H., Gerhart, B., & Fang, M. (2021). Do Financial Incentives Help or Harm Performance in Interesting Tasks? *Journal of Applied Psychology*, forthcoming.

Thus, people sort themselves into or out of organizations (and, of course, organizations do their own sorting of prospective employees as well) based on a preference for being paid based on personal performance or something else.[102] The most obvious sorting factor is ability. Higher-ability individuals are attracted to companies that will pay for performance, thus recognizing their greater contribution.[103] (Just a reminder: Ability translates into performance when motivation and opportunity to contribute are also sufficiently high–see **Exhibit 9.2**.) High performers will also leave firms that don't reward their performance (pay for something like seniority rather than performance) and go to those that do. Coming at this from a different angle, data also suggest that some people make job choices based on effort aversion. "Find me a job where I don't have to work hard!" Obviously, jobs where high performance is expected are less likely to be attractive to these prospective employees.[104]

Any management practice, including an incentive plan or other pay for performance plan that has major consequences for important employee outcomes such as pay or retaining one's job can cause stress, anxiety and/or other negative reactions.[105] Thus, an organization implementing a plan like that in the Lazear study above, must be prepared for such reactions and think about whether it is prepared to rely on sorting to address what happens when employees who used to fit the job now fit less well and experience difficulty.

Finally, as noted in **Chapter 1**, sorting effects are more important to the degree that high performers create a disproportionately high amount of value for organizations, as in the case where performance is better characterized as having a power distribution rather than the usual normal distribution.[106] See also our discussion of "stars" from **Chapter 1**.

When we look at pay and group performance (instead of individual performance), the evidence is more mixed. In general, though, we think that group pay (whether the group is a team or an entire organization) leads to small increases (relative to individual pay for performance) in productivity. One study suggests that, to be effective, group incentives are most effective when paired with complementary HR practices. Specifically, group incentives work if you have implemented a team-based structure where members monitor team performance and personally sanction "free riders."[107]

EXHIBIT 9.8 **Difference in Performance (Solving Anagrams), Individual Incentive versus Fixed Pay**

Rounds of Experiment	Assigned versus Choice (of Fixed Pay or Individual Incentive)	Performance in Solving Anagrams		
		Individual Incentive	Fixed Pay	Difference
Rounds 1 & 2	Subjects Choose Fixed Pay or Individual Incentive	86.0	75.5	10.5 (14%)
Rounds 3, 4, 5, & 6	Everyone Assigned to Fixed Pay (Rounds 3 and 5) and Assigned to Individual Incentive (Rounds 4 and 6)	88.0	78.0	10.0 (13%)
Rounds 7 & 8	Subjects Choose Fixed Pay or Individual Incentive	96.0	69.5	26.5 (38%)

*Performance is expressed as a percentage of the pretest score for that anagram (used to control for difficulty of the anagram) obtained using a different sample.

Note: 52 percent chose incentive in Rounds 1 & 2 and 50 percent chose incentive in Rounds 7 & 8. However, the correlation between these choices was .39, indicating substantial switching (35 of 115 subjects) of incentive/Fixed condition choices.

Source: Cadsby, C. B., Song, F., & Tapon, F. (2007). Sorting and incentive effects of pay for performance: An experimental investigation. *Academy of Management Journal*, 50(2), 387–405.

Risk (Unintended Consequences)

Before we rush to add a variable-pay component (one form of pay for performance) to the compensation package, though, we should recognize that such plans can, and do, fail. Sometimes, ironically, the failure arises because the incentive works too well, leading employees to exhibit rewarded behaviors to the exclusion of other desired behaviors. (See **Chapter 10** for further discussion of the risks of such plans.) **Exhibit 9.9** documents one such embarrassing incident that haunted Sears for several years.[108]

Apparently the Sears example is no fluke. Other companies have found that poorly implemented incentive pay plans can hurt rather than help. Green Giant, for example, used to pay a bonus based on insect parts screened in its pea-packing process. The goal, of course, was to cut the number of insect parts making their way into the final product (anyone planning on vegetables for dinner tonight?). Employees found a way to make this incentive system work for them. By bringing insect parts from home, inserting, and inspecting, their incentive dollars rose. Clearly, the program didn't work as intended. Experts contend this is evidence that the process wasn't managed well. The second author of your book also recollects the first author was working with an oil drilling company. They attached a sizable incentive to compensation for geologists if they could reduce the time to explore for a well site and set up the drilling operation. They couldn't figure out why so many more wells were being reported as dry (no oil) than had been the case historically![109] (Could it be that well sites were suddenly being chosen more on the basis of their ease of setting up a drilling operation–perhaps those in less remote locations–and chosen less on the basis of how much oil is in the ground there?) What does this mean in terms of design? We return to the risks (as well as the potential returns) possible from the use of incentive pay in **Chapter 10**.

DESIGNING A PAY-FOR-PERFORMANCE PLAN

Our pay model suggests effectiveness is dependent on three things: efficiency, equity, and compliance in designing a pay system.

Efficiency

Efficiency involves three general areas of concern.

EXHIBIT 9.9 Sears Makes a Mistake

Strategic Goal	Supporting Compensation Component as Translated for Tire and Auto Centers	Unintended Consequence
Cut costs by $600 million, provide facelift to stores, cut prices, make every employee focus on profits.	Set high quotas for generating dollars from repairs and back up with commissions.	The California Consumer Affairs Division went undercover posing as customers. On 34 of 38 undercover runs, Sears charged an average of $235 for unnecessary repairs.

Strategy

Does the pay-for-performance plan support corporate objectives? For example, is the plan cost-effective, or are we making payouts that bear no relation to improved performance on the bottom line? Similarly, does the plan help us improve quality of service? Some pay-for-performance plans are so focused on quantity of performance as a measure that we forget about quality. Defect rates rise. Customers must search for someone to handle a merchandise return. A number of things happen that aren't consistent with the emphasis on quality that top organizations insist upon.

The plan also should link well with HR strategy and objectives. If other elements of our total HR plan are geared to select, reinforce, and nurture risk-taking behavior, we don't want a compensation component that rewards the status quo. Be careful, though. The Federal National Mortgage Association, also known as Fannie Mae, which buys mortgages from banks and re-sells them to investors, changed its performance metrics from return on assets and cost management to total earnings and earnings per share. No problem, you say? One view is that it was a problem because the CEO of Fannie Mae was part of the "team" that wrote legislation and he took this as an opportunity to influence the laws to fit his company's strategy. In this telling, he got rich but also helped start the 2008 financial crisis.[110]

Finally, we address the most difficult question of all—how much of an increase makes a difference? What does it take to motivate an employee? Is 3 percent, the recent average of pay increases, really enough to motivate higher performance? One review of the evidence suggests that an increase must be at least 6 to 7 percent "to be seen as meaningful" and goes on to say: "Obviously, people prefer *any* raise to no raise at all. But small raises, when presented as rewards for merit, can be dysfunctional. Organizations with small pay raise pools may wish to think seriously about their allocation of merit raises."[111]

Structure

Is the structure of the organization sufficiently decentralized to allow different operating units to create flexible variations on a general pay-for-performance plan? For example, IBM adapted performance reviews to the different needs of different units, and the managers in them, resulting in a very flexible system. In this system, midpoints for pay grades don't exist. Managers get a budget, some training on how to conduct reviews, and a philosophical mandate: Differentiate pay for stars relative to average performers, or risk losing stars. Managers are given a number of performance dimensions. Determining which dimensions to use for which employees is totally a personal decision. Indeed, managers who don't like reviews at all can input merit increases directly, anchored only by a brief explanation for the reason.[112] Different operating units may have different competencies and different competitive advantages. We don't want a rigid pay-for-performance system that detracts from these advantages, all in the name of consistency across divisions.

Standards (Performance objectives/criteria)

Operationally, the key to designing a pay-for-performance system rests on standards. Specifically, we need to be concerned about the following:

Objectives: Are they specific yet flexible? Can employees see that their behavior influences their ability to achieve objectives (called the "line-of-sight" issue in industry)?

Measures: Do employees know what measures (individual appraisals, peer reviews of team performance, corporate financial measures, etc.) will be used to assess whether performance is sufficiently good to merit a payout?

Eligibility: How far down the organization will the plan run? Companies like PepsiCo and Starbucks believe all employees should be included. Others think only top management can see how their decisions affect the bottom line.

Funding: Will you fund the program out of extra revenue generated above and beyond some preset standard? If so, what happens in a bad year? Many employees become disillusioned when they feel they have worked harder but economic conditions or poor management decisions conspire to cut or eliminate bonuses.

It is important to recognize that performance standards are rarely static. Instead, organizations are in an ongoing state of what might be called experimentation and testing of performance standards. The ongoing challenge is to make the plan simple, clear and objective enough to create motivation and line of sight, while at the same time trying not to exclude important standards, including those that ensure that results/objective standards are achieved in a way consistent with ethical principles and values. As **Exhibit 9.10** shows, even looking at only an interval of one year, 38 percent of organizations modified at least one of their short-term incentive plans. The two most common modifications are adding or deleting performance standards/measures. Under reasons, we see that most modifications are made as part of a regular review of short-term incentive plans, followed by change in business strategy as a driver of change.

Equity/Fairness

Our second design objective is to ensure that the system is fair to employees. Two types of fairness are concerns for employees. The first type is fairness in the *amount* that is distributed to employees. Not surprisingly, this type of fairness is labeled *distributive justice*.[113] Does an employee view the amount of compensation received as fair? As we discussed earlier in the section on equity theory, perceptions of fairness here depend on the amount of compensation actually received relative to input (e.g., productivity) compared against some relevant standard. Notice that several of the components of this equity equation are frustratingly removed from the control of the typical supervisor or manager working with employees. A manager has little influence over the size of an employee's paycheck. It is influenced more by external market conditions, pay-policy decisions of the organization, and the occupational choice made by the employee. Indeed, recent research suggests that employees may look at the relative distribution of pay. For example, some major league baseball teams have met with mixed success in trying to buy stars via the free-agent market. Some speculate that this creates feelings of inequity among other players. Some evidence suggests that narrower ranges for pay differences may actually have positive impacts on overall organizational performance.[114]

EXHIBIT 9.10 Short-Term Incentive Plans, Most Common Modifications (and Reasons)

Modified a short-term incentive plan for current performance year	38%
Modifications (most common)[a]	
Added one or more new performance measures	65%
Eliminated one or more performance measures	47%
Increased performance goals	22%
Increased the use of discretion in determining payouts	15%
Reasons for modification (most common)[a]	
Regular annual review and update of plan	68%
Change in business strategy	40%

Source: WorldatWork and Deloitte Consulting LLP, Incentive Pay Practices Survey: Publicly Traded Companies, 2018.

[a]The percentages are of those organizations making modifications. Multiple responses were permitted.

Managers have somewhat more control over the second type of equity. Employees are also concerned about the fairness of the *procedures* used to determine the amount of rewards they receive. Employees expect *procedural justice*.[115] Evidence suggests that organizations using fair procedures and having supervisors who are viewed as fair in the means they use to allocate rewards are perceived as more trustworthy and command higher levels of commitment.[116] Some research even suggests that employee satisfaction with pay may depend more on the procedures used to determine pay than on the actual level distributed.[117]

A key element in fairness is communications. Employees want to know in advance what is expected of them. They want the opportunity to provide input into the standards or expectations. And if performance is judged lacking relative to these standards, they want an appeals mechanism. The importance of open communication also extends to upper management. In firms that practice greater transparency of pay practices, executives perform better when told what the linkage is between pay and performance.[118] In a union environment, this is the grievance procedure. Something similar needs to be set up in a nonunion environment.[119] As evidence, only 15 percent of employees who feel well informed indicate they are considering leaving their company. This jumps to 41 percent who think about leaving if they feel poorly informed about the way the pay system operates.[120]

Compliance

Finally, our pay-for-performance system should comply with existing laws. We want a reward system that maintains and enhances the reputation of our firm. Think about the companies that visit a college campus. The interview schedules fill up quickly for some of these companies because students gravitate to them. Why? The companies' reputations.[121] We tend to undervalue the reward value of a good reputation. To guard this reputation, we need to make sure we comply with compensation laws.

Your Turn

Burger Boy

This is a true case. Jerry Newman (second author of this book) spent 14 months working in seven fast-food restaurants. He wrote about his experiences in the book *My Secret Life on the McJob* (McGraw-Hill, 2007). This is a description of events in one store—which we'll call "Burger Boy."

Person	Job Title	Base Salary	Other Wage Information	Avg Hrs/ Wk
Otis	Assistant Store Manager	34k	Exempt (no overtime pay)	55
Leon	Shift Supervisor	23k	Nonexempt	55
Marge	Crew Member (fries)	$6.25/hr	Nonexempt	30
Me	Cook	$6.50/hr	Nonexempt	20
Chuck	Drive-Through Window	$7.00/hr	Nonexempt	30
Lucy	Sandwich Assembler	$7.00/hr	Nonexempt	35

It's a hot Friday in Florida, and lunch rush is just beginning. Chuck is working the pay window and is beginning to grouse about the low staffing for what is traditionally the busiest day of the week. "Where the heck is LaVerne?" he yells to no one. Chuck has only worked here for six weeks but has prior experience at another Burger Boy. Marge, typically working the fries station (the easiest job at this Burger Boy), has been pressed into service on the front drive-through window because two of 10 scheduled workers have called in sick. She can handle the job when business is slow, but she clearly is getting flustered as more cars enter the drive-through line. I'm cooking, my third day on job, but my first one alone. I've worked the grill for 10 years as a volunteer at Aunt Rosie's Women's Fast-Pitch Softball Tournament, but nothing prepared me for the volume of business we will do today. By 11:30 I've got the grill full of burgers. Lucy is going full-speed trying to keep up with sandwich assembly and wrapping. She's the best assembler the place has and would be a supervisor if she could just keep from self-destructing. Yesterday she lit a can of vegetable spray with a lighter and danced around the floor, an arc of flame shooting out from the can. She thinks this is funny. Everyone else thinks she's nuts. But she's rumored to be a friend of the manager, Nancy, so everyone keeps quiet.

"Marge, you've got to get moving girl. The line's getting longer. Move girl, move," shouts Otis, unfazed by the fact that Marge really isn't good enough to work the window and clearly is showing signs of heavy stress. "I'll help her," chimes in Chuck. "I can work the pay window, then run up front to help Marge when she gets way behind." Otis says nothing and goes back to the office where he begins to count the morning receipts for the breakfast rush.

My job as cook also includes cooking baked potatoes in the oven and cooking chicken in the pressure cooker, so I have little time to do anything besides stay on top of my job. Finally, at noon, in comes Leon. He will replace Otis at three, but for now he is a sorely needed pair of hands on the second sandwich assembly board. Leon looks over at me and shouts above the din, "Good job, Jerry. Keeping up with Friday rush on your third cooking day. Good job." That's the first compliment I've received in the two weeks I've worked here, so I smile at the unexpected recognition. By 12:30 we're clearly all frazzled. Even with Chuck's help, Marge falls farther behind. She is now making mistakes on orders in her effort to get food out the drive-through window quickly. Otis comes barreling up front from the office and shouts for everyone to hear: "We're averaging 3:05 (minutes) on drive time. Someone's in trouble if we don't get a move on." He says this while staring directly at Marge. Everyone knows that drive times (the amount of time from an order being placed until the customer receives it) should be about 2:30 (two minutes, thirty seconds). In my head I do some mental math. The normal staffing for a Friday is 13 people (including management). Because of absenteeism we're working with eight, including Otis and Leon. By noon Marge is crying, but she stays at it. And finally things begin to slow at 1 p.m. We know rush is officially over when Lucy tells Leon she's "going to the can." This starts a string of requests for rest breaks that are interrupted by Otis, "All right, for God's sake. Here's the order of breaks." He points to people in turn, with me being next to last, and Marge going last. After Lucy, Chuck is second, and the others fill in the gap ahead of me. When my turn finally comes I resolve to break quickly, taking only 6 minutes instead of the allotted 10. When I return Otis sneers at me and chides, "What was that, about a half hour?" I snap, I'm angry, and let him know it. "If I could tell time, would I be working fast food?" Now I realize I've done the unforgivable, sassing my boss. But I'm upset, and I don't care. My only care is I've just claimed fast food is work for dummies, and I absolutely don't believe this. But as I said, I was mad. Otis looks me over, staring at my face, and finally decides to let out a huge bellow, "You're okay, Newman. Good line!"

It's now 2:10 and Marge has told Otis twice that she has to leave. Her agreement with the store manager at the time of hire was that she would leave no later than 2:30 every day. Her daughter gets off the school bus at 2:45, and she must meet her at that time. Otis ignores her first request, and is nowhere to be seen when, at 2:25, Marge looks around frantically and pleads to no one in particular, "What should I do? I have to leave." I look at her and declare, "Go. I'll tell Otis when he comes out again." Marge leaves. Ten minutes later we have a mini-surge of customers. Leon yells, "Where the hell is Marge? That's it; she's out of here tomorrow. No more chances for her." When he's done ranting, I explain the details of Marge's plight. Angrily Leon stomps back to the manager's office and confronts Otis. The yelling quickly reaches audible levels. Everyone in the store, customers included, hear what is quickly broadening into confrontations about other unresolved issues:

Leon: "I'm sick of coming in here and finding nothing stocked. Otis, it's your job to make sure the lunch shift [roughly 10 a.m.–2 p.m.] stocks items in their spare time. It never happens and I'm sick of it. Now you tell me you're leaving and sticking me with a huge stocking job."

Otis: "I'm sick of your whining, Leon. I work 50–60 hours a week. I'm sick of working 10–12 hours a day for crappy wages. You want things stocked . . . you do it. I'm going home and try to forget this place."

With that Otis drops what he has in his hands, a printout of today's receipts so far, and walks out the door. Leon swears, picks up the spreadsheet, and storms back to the office. I finish my shift and happily go home. No more Burger Boy for this burger boy.

1. What appear to be the problems at this Burger Boy?
2. How many of these problems could be explained by compensation issues?
3. How many other problems could be lessened with diligent use of rewards other than pay?
4. Are hours of work a reward? What might explain why I was happy to be working 20 hours per week, but Chuck was unhappy with 30 hours per week? How might schedules be used as a reward?

Summary

Why not admit it? We don't know what makes people tick! Reading this chapter should prove that we have more unanswered questions than supposed truths. We know that employee performance depends upon some blend of skill, knowledge, and motivation. If any of these three ingredients is missing, performance is likely to be suboptimal. This chapter concentrates on the motivation component of this performance triangle. Rewards must help organizations attract and retain employees; they must make high performance an attractive option for employees; they must encourage employees to build new skills and gradually foster commitment to the organization. A tall order, you say! The problem is especially big because we are just starting to realize all the different things that can serve as rewards (or punishments) for employees. This chapter outlines 13 rewards and makes a strong case that fair administration of these rewards can lead a company to higher performance levels.

Review Questions

1. A father decides to put his two sons to work landscaping. The business involves going to a customer's home and providing landscaping services (cut grass, edge sidewalk, pull weeds in flower beds, prune bushes and trees, rake leaves). Instead of paying a flat wage, the father decides to pay an incentive according to the following schedule (average across all lawns).

Task	Piece Rate Incentive per Person	Physical Effort	Time to Complete per Person	Charge to Customer
Cut grass	$4	Easy	.4 hr	$30
Edge sidewalk	$1	Easy	.1 hr	$ 5

Task	Piece Rate Incentive per Person	Physical Effort	Time to Complete per Person	Charge to Customer
Pull weeds	$6	Very Hard	.5 hr	$40
Prune bushes, etc.	$5	Hard	.5 hr	$30
Rake leaves	$5	Hard	.5	$25

At the end of the second week under this arrangement the boys are quarreling with each other and not happy with their dad. All of the disagreements revolve around the incentive system. What might be the problems?

2. Father Michael's Wraps (pitas, wraps, flat breads) is experiencing turnover in the range of 100 percent. Most of this occurs in the first 18 months of employment. How would you determine if this turnover rate is high? How would you justify to your boss that lower turnover is strategically important? What would you look at in both pay and other forms of rewards to identify ways of reducing turnover? Justify your choices based on your reading of this chapter.
3. Eric Dempsey Associates (EDA) is a relatively small public relations/advertising firm in western New York. It recently shifted its strategic plan to focus almost exclusively on clients who generate $200,000 or more in revenue for the firm. There are six employees in the firm who focus exclusively on business development, identifying new client prospects and making "pitches" to these prospects about ways that EDA can help them. While the payout for landing these prospects is high, averaging four times the revenue of the typical EDA client in the past, the likelihood of getting these new clients is considerably lower. In the past the development associates (as they are called) were paid heavily on incentive pay (4 percent of revenue generated by clients landed by the associate) along with a base pay that was 95 percent of the market rate for comparable jobs in western New York. What changes do you think should be made in compensation to reflect changes in the strategic plan of EDA?
4. Companies focus heavily on cost-saving strategies to be competitive today. Identify both monetary and nonmonetary ways of cost saving that would be relevant to a compensation person's job.
5. You supervise in a company that is a low payer relative to competitors. What things do you have control over to increase the likelihood that workers will feel fairly treated?

Endnotes

1. Sarah Gray, "Costco Is Set to Raises Wages for 130,000 Employees: Here's How Much," *Fortune,* June 1, 2018, http://fortune.com/2018/06/01/costco-is-set-to-raises-wages-for-130000-employees-heres-how-much/; Rachael Feintzeig, "Container store bets on $50,000 retail worker," *Wall Street Journal,* October 15, 2014, p. B6.
2. I. S. Fulmer, B. Gerhart, and K. Scott, "Are the 100 Best Better? An Empirical Investigation of the Relationship between Being a Great Place to Work and Firm Performance," *Personnel Psychology* 56 (2003), pp. 965–993; A. Carvalho and A. Nelson, "'Great Places to Work': Resilience in Times of Crisis," *Human Resource Management* 55, no. 3 (2016), pp. 479–498. Part of the performance advantage may be due to an advantage in employee recruiting and retention. See Brian R. Dineen and David G. Allen, "Third Party Employment Branding: Human Capital Inflows and Outflows Following 'Best Places to Work' Certifications," *Academy of Management Journal* 59, no. 1 (2016), pp. 90–112.

3. Elaine Farndale and Clare Kelliher, "Implementing Performance Appraisal: Exploring the Employee Experience," *Human Resource Management* 52, no. 6 (2013), pp. 879–897; Bonnie G. Mani, "Performance Appraisal Systems, Productivity, and Motivation: A Case Study," *Public Personnel Management* 31(2), 2000, pp. 141–159; R. Mayer and J. Davis, "The Effect of the Performance Appraisal System on Trust for Management," *Journal of Applied Psychology* 84(1) (1999), pp. 123–136.
4. Barry Gerhart, Sara L. Rynes, and Ingrid Smithey Fulmer, "Pay and Performance: Individuals, Groups and Executives," in eds. A. P. Brief and J. P. Walsh, *Academy of Management Annals,* vol. 3 (Mahwah, NJ: Lawrence Erlbaum, 2009).
5. Fandom. Daenerys Targaryen https://gameofthrones.fandom.com/wiki/Daenerys_Targaryen. Accessed April 13, 2021.
6. I. Smithey Fulmer and J. D. Shaw, "Person-Based Differences in Pay Reactions: A Compensation-Activation Theory and Integrative Conceptual Review," *Journal of Applied Psychology* 103, no. 9 (2018), p. 939.
7. M. Bidwell and J. R. Keller, "Within or Without? How Firms Combine Internal and External Labor Markets to Fill Jobs," *Academy of Management Journal* 57(4), 2014, pp. 1035–1055; Sara L. Rynes, Kenneth G. Brown, and Amy E. Colbert, "Seven Common Misconceptions about Human Resource Practices: Research Findings Versus Practitioner Beliefs," *Academy of Management Executive* 16(3), 2002, pp. 92–102; B. Becker and B. Gerhart, "The Impact of Human Resource Management on Organizational Performance: Progress and Prospects," *Academy of Management Journal* 39(4), 1996, pp. 779–801.
8. S. J. Sucher and S. Gupta, "Layoffs That Don't Break Your Company," *Harvard Business Review*, May–June 2018; S. Kirchoff and D. Jones, "Caterpillar Joins Other Companies Cutting Pay," Reuters, December 23, 2008, p. B1; J. McGregor, "Cutting Salaries Instead of Jobs," *BusinessWeek*, June 8, 2009, pp. O46–O48.
9. David Cote. "Honeywell's CEO on How He Avoided Layoffs," *Harvard Business Review*, June 2013. www.hbr.org.
10. Cascio, W. F., Chatrath, A., & Christie-David, R. A. (2021). Antecedents and Consequences of Employment and Asset Restructuring. *Academy of Management Journal* 64, 587–613
11. Andrew Ross Sorkin, "Mergers Pare Competition at 30,000 Feet," *The New York Times*, March 24, 2015, p. B1.
12. Anne Tsui, Jone L. Pearce, Lyman W. Porter, and Angela M. Tripoli, "Alternative Approaches to the Employee-Organization Relationship: Does Investment in Employees Pay Off?" *Academy of Management Journal* 40(5), 1997, pp. 1089–1121.
13. Hunter Atkins, "LeBron James Signs Largest Deal in Nike History," *Forbes,* December 7, 2015, https://www.forbes.com/sites/hunteratkins/2015/12/07/lebron-james-signs-largest-endorsement-deal-in-nike-history/#7d9fc61e328d.
14. Krista L. Uggerslev, Neil E. Fassina, and David Kraichy, "Recruiting through the Stages: A Meta-Analytic Test of Predictors of Applicant Attraction at Different Stages of the Recruitment Process," *Personnel Psychology*, Autumn 65(3), 2012, pp. 597–660.
15. http://www.spotrac.com/mlb/washinton-nationals/max-scherzer/, accessed March 31, 2015.
16. S. L. Rynes, B. Gerhart, and K. A. Minette, "The Importance of Pay in Employee Motivation: Discrepancies between What People Say and What They Do," *Human Resource Management* 43, no. 4 (2004), pp. 381–394; E. L. Lawler, *Pay and Organization Effectiveness: A Psychological View* (New York: McGraw Hill, 1971).

17. M. A. Maltarich, A. J. Nyberg, G. Reilly, D. D. Abdulsalam, and M. Martin, "Pay-for-Performance, Sometimes: An Interdisciplinary Approach to Integrating Economic Rationality with Psychological Emotion to Predict Individual Performance," *Academy of Management Journal* 60 (2017), pp. 2155–2174; Sanford E. Devoe, Jeffrey Pfeffer, and Byron Y. Lee, "When Does Money Make Money More Important? Survey and Experimental Evidence," *Industrial and Labor Relations Review* 66(5), 2013, pp. 1078–1097.

18. Dow Scott, Michelle Brown, John Shields, Richard J. Long, Conny H. Antoni, Ewa J. Beck-Krala, Ana Maria Lucia-Casademunt, and Stephen J. Perkins, "A global study of pay preferences and employee characteristics," *Compensation & Benefits Review* 47, no. 2 (2015): 60–70; Barry Gerhart and Meiyu Fang, "Pay, Intrinsic Motivation, Extrinsic Motivation, Performance, and Creativity in the Workplace: Revisiting Long-Held Beliefs," *Annual Review of Organizational Psychology and Organizational Behavior,* 2, no. 1 (2015): 489–521; Lee Dyer, Donald P. Schwab, and Roland D. Theriault, "Managerial perceptions regarding salary increase criteria," *Personnel Psychology* 29, no. 2 (1976): 233–242; A. Mamman, M. Sulaiman, and A. Fadel, "Attitude to Pay Systems: An Exploratory Study Within and Across Cultures," *International Journal of Human Resource Management* 7(1), 1996, pp. 101–121.

19. Xavier Baeten and Bart Verwaeren, "Flexible Rewards from a Strategic Rewards Perspective," *Compensation & Benefits Review* 44, no. 1 (2012), pp. 40–49; IOMA, "Are You Ready to Serve Cafeteria Style Comp?" *Pay for Performance Report,* June 2000, pp. 1, 13.

20. For a discussion of developments in motivation theory (albeit with no attention to the role of compensation in motivation), see the special topic forum, including the following articles in the 2004 issue of *Academy of Management Review* 29(2): R. Steers, R. Mowday, and D. Shapiro, "The Future of Work Motivation," pp. 379–387; E. Locke and G. Latham, "What Should We Do about Motivation Theory? Six Recommendations for the Twenty-First Century," pp. 388–403; Y. Fried and L. H. Slowik, "Enriching Goal-Setting Theory with Time: An Integrated Approach," pp. 404–422; and M. Seo, L. Barrett, and J. Bartunek, "The Role of Affective Experience in Work Motivation," pp. 423–438.

21. Martin, G. P., Wiseman, R. M., & Gomez-Mejia, L. R. (2019). The interactive effect of monitoring and incentive alignment on agency costs. *Journal of Management*, 45(2), 701–727; Eisenhardt, K. M. (1989). Agency theory: An assessment and review. *Academy of management review*, 14(1), 57–74.

22. Barry Gerhart, Sara L. Rynes, and Ingrid Smithey Fulmer, "Pay and Performance: Individuals, Groups and Executives," in *Academy of Management Annals,* vol. 3, ed. A. P. Brief and J. P. Walsh (Mahwah, NJ: Lawrence Erlbaum, 2009); J. P. Campbell and R. D. Pritchard, "Motivation Theory in Industrial and Organizational Psychology," in *Handbook of Industrial and Organizational Psychology,* ed. M. D. Dunnette, pp. 63–130 (Chicago: Rand McNally, 1976).

23. J. S. Adams, "Toward an Understanding of Inequity," *Journal of Abnormal and Social Psychology* 67 (1963), pp. 422–436; J. S. Adams, "Injustice in Social Exchange," in *Advances in Experimental Social Psychology,* vol. 2, L. Berkowitz, ed. (New York: Academic Press, 1965); R. Cosier and D. Dalton, "Equity Theory and Time: A Reformulation," *Academy of Management Review* 8 (1983), pp. 311–319; Pinder, Craig C. *Work motivation in organizational behavior*. Psychology Press, 2014.

24. Eugene F. Fama and Michael C. Jensen, "Separation of Ownership and Control," *Journal of Law and Economics* 26, no. 2 (1983), pp. 301–325; Douglas A. Bosse and Robert A. Phillips, "Agency Theory and Bounded Self-Interest," *Academy of Management Review* 41, no. 2 (2016), pp. 276–297; B. Oviatt, "Agency and Transaction Cost Perspectives on the Manager-Shareholder Relationship: Incentives for Congruent Interests," *Academy of Management Review* 13 (1988), pp. 214–225.

25. D. Knight, C. Durham, and E. A. Locke, "The Relationship of Team Goals, Incentives, and Efficacy to Strategic Risk, Tactical Implementation, and Performance," *Academy of Management Journal* 44(2), 2001, pp. 326–338.

26. E. A. Locke, K. N. Shaw, L. M. Saari, and G. P. Latham, "Goal Setting and Task Performance: 1969–1980," *Psychological Bulletin* 90 (1981), pp. 125–152.

27. Edward L. Deci, Anja H. Olafsen, and Richard M. Ryan, "Self-Determination Theory in Work Organizations: The State of a Science," *Annual Review of Organizational Psychology and Organizational Behavior* 4 (2017), pp. 19–43; Richard M. Ryan and Edward L. Deci, "Self-Regulation and the Problem of Human Autonomy: Does Psychology Need Choice, Self-Determination, and Will?" *Journal of Personality* 74, no. 6 (December 2006), pp. 1557–1586. For a different view, see Barry Gerhart and Meiyu Fang, "Pay, Intrinsic Motivation, Extrinsic Motivation, Performance, and Creativity in the Workplace: Revisiting Long-Held Beliefs," *Annual Review of Organizational Psychology and Organizational Behavior* 2, no. 1 (2015), pp. 489–521.

28. M. R. Louis, B. Z. Posner, and G. N. Powell, "The Availability and Helpfulness of Socialization Practices," *Personnel Psychology* 36 (1983), pp. 857–866; E. H. Schein, "Organizational Socialization and the Profession of Management," *Industrial Management Review* 9 (1968), pp. 1–16.

29. P. Zingheim and J. Schuster, "Creating a High-Performance Culture by Really Paying for Performance," in IOMA, *Complete Guide to Best Practices in Pay for Performance,* 2005, pp. 117–122.

30. Byron Wine, Shawn Gilroy, and Donald Hantula, "Temporal (In) Stability of Employee Preferences for Rewards," *Journal of Organizational Behavior Management* 32(1), 2012, pp. 58–64.

31. Bob Nelson, *1501 Ways to Reward Employees* (New York: Workman, 2012).

32. J. Tropman, *The Compensation Solution: How to Develop an Employee-Driven Rewards System* (San Francisco, CA: Jossey-Bass, 2001).

33. Jerry M. Newman, Richard Floersch, and Mike Balaka, "Employment Branding at McDonalds: Leveraging Rewards for Positive Outcomes," Workspan, March 2012, pp. 20–24.

34. N. Stein, "America's Most Admired Companies," *Fortune,* March 3, 2003, pp. 81–87; J. Pfeffer, "Six Dangerous Myths about Pay," *Harvard Business Review,* May–June 1998, pp. 109–119.

35. https://www.southwest.com/html/about-southwest/careers/workperks.html.

36. News Release, Southwest Media, January 25, 2018, https://www.swamedia.com/releases/release-6383d3d445691e933fc53daff613311e-southwest-airlines-reports-record-fourth-quarter-and-annual-profit-45th-consecutive-year-of-profitability?query=profit+sharing.

37. K. Brown and V. Huber, "Lowering Floors and Raising Ceilings: A Longitudinal Assessment of the Effects of an Earnings-at-Risk Plan on Pay Satisfaction," *Personnel Psychology* 45 (1992), pp. 279–311; Elena Belogolovsky and Peter A Bamberger, "Signaling in Secret: Pay for Performance Incentive and Sorting Effects of Pay Secrecy," *Academy of Management Journal,* 57(6), 2014, pp. 1706–1733; B. Gerhart, S. L. Rynes, and I. S. Fulmer, "Pay and Performance: Individuals, Groups, and Executives," *Academy of Management Annals*, 3 (2009), pp. 251–315.

38. Please note, though, that most of the declines in base pay have occurred since 1980.

39. http://www.payscale.com/research/US/Employer=E.I._Du_Pont_De_Nemours_%26_Co_(DuPont)/Salary, accessed November 11, 2018.

40. B. Gerhart, "Incentives and Pay for Performance in the Workplace," *Advances in Motivation Science* 4 (2017), pp. 91–140; IOMA, *Complete Guide to Best Practices in Pay for Performance* (Newark, NJ: BNA Subsidiaries, 2005), pp. 1.8–1.10; J. R. Schuster and P. K. Zingheim, *The New Pay: Linking Employee and Organizational Performance* (New York: Lexington Books, 1992).

41. Mercer, "What's Working Survey," http://inside-employees-mind.mercer.com/global.

42. Aon Hewitt, "Trends in Global Employee Engagement," www.aon.com/attachments/thoughtleadership/Trends_Global_Employee_Engagement_Final.pdf; Aon, "Employee Engagement Rebounds to Match All-Time High," http://www.aon.com/2018-global-employee-engagement-trends/index.html.

43. Aon Hewitt, "Trends in Global Employee Engagement," www.aon.com/attachments/thoughtleadership/Trends_Global_Employee_Engagement_Final.pdf.

44. D. M. Cable and T. A. Judge, "Pay Preferences and Job Search Decisions: A Person-Organization Fit Perspective," *Personnel Psychology* 47 (1994), pp. 317–348.

45. Julie Wayne and Wendy Casper, "Why Does Firm Reputation in Human Resource Policies Influence College Students? The Mechanisms Underlying Job Pursuit Intentions," *Human Resource Management* 51(1), 2012, pp. 121–142; Sara Rynes, Barry Gerhart, and Kathleen Minette, "The Importance of Pay in Employee Motivation: Discrepancies between What People Say and What They Do," *Human Resource Management* 43(4), Winter 2004, pp. 381–394; S. L. Rynes, K. G. Brown, and A. E. Colbert, "Seven Common Misconceptions about Human Resource Practices: Research Findings Versus Practitioner Beliefs," *Academy of Management Executive* 16(2), 2002, pp. 92–103; E. E. Lawler, *Pay and Organizational Effectiveness: A Psychological View* (New York: McGraw-Hill, 1971); E. E. Lawler and G. D. Jenkins, "Strategic Reward Systems" in *Handbook of Industrial and Organizational Psychology,* M. D. Dunnette and L. M. Hough, eds. (Palo Alto, CA: Consulting Psychologist Press, 1992), pp. 1009–1055; W. Mobley, *Employee Turnover: Causes, Consequences and Control* (Reading, MA: Addison-Wesley, 1982).

46. E. Lazear, "Performance Pay and Productivity," *American Economic Review* 90 (2000), pp. 1346–1361.

47. Barry Gerhart and Meiyu Fang, "Pay for (Individual) Performance: Issues, Claims, Evidence and the Role of Sorting Effects," *Human Resource Management Review* 24(1), March 2014, pp. 41–52.

48. David A. Comerford and Peter A. Ubel, "Effort Aversion: Job Choice and Compensation Decisions Overweight Effort," *Journal of Economic Behavior & Organization* 92, August 2013, pp. 152–162.

49. D. M. Cable and T. A. Judge, "Pay Preferences and Job Search Decisions: A Person-Organization Fit Perspective," *Personnel Psychology* 47 (1994), pp. 317–348.

50. D. M. Cable and T. A. Judge, "Pay Preferences and Job Search Decisions: A Person-Organization Fit Perspective," *Personnel Psychology* 47 (1994), pp. 317–348.

51. D. B. Turban and T. L. Keon, "Organizational Attractiveness: An Interactionist Perspective," *Journal of Applied Psychology* 78 (1993), pp. 184–193.

52. D. M. Cable and T. A. Judge, "Pay Preferences and Job Search Decisions: A Person-Organization Fit Perspective," *Personnel Psychology* 47 (1994), pp. 317–348; A. Kohn, *Punished by Rewards: The Trouble With Gold Stars, Incentive Plans, A's, Praise and Other Bribes* (Boston, MA: Houghton-Mifflin, 1993).

53. D. M. Cable and T. A. Judge, "Pay Preferences and Job Search Decisions: A Person-Organization Fit Perspective," *Personnel Psychology* 47 (1994), pp. 317–348; A. Kohn, *Punished by Rewards: The Trouble With Gold Stars, Incentive Plans, A's, Praise and Other Bribes* (Boston, MA: Houghton-Mifflin, 1993).

54. D. M. Cable and T. A. Judge, "Pay Preferences and Job Search Decisions: A Person-Organization Fit Perspective," *Personnel Psychology* 47 (1994), pp. 317–348; A. Kohn, *Punished by Rewards: The Trouble With Gold Stars, Incentive Plans, A's, Praise and Other Bribes* (Boston, MA: Houghton-Mifflin, 1993).

55. T. R. Zenger, "Why Do Employers Only Reward Extreme Performance? Examining the Relationships among Performance Pay and Turnover," *Administrative Science Quarterly* 37 (1992), pp. 198–219.

56. B. Gerhart, S. L. Rynes, and I. S. Fulmer, "Pay and Performance: Individuals, Groups, and Executives," *Academy of Management Annals* 3 (2009), pp. 251–315.

57. Barry Gerhart and Meiyu Fang, "Pay for (Individual) Performance: Issues, Claims, Evidence and the Role of Sorting Effects," *Human Resource Management Review Volume* 24(1), March 2014, pp. 41–52; C. O. Trevor, B. Gerhart, and J. W. Boudreau, "Voluntary Turnover and Job Performance: Curvilinearity and the Moderating Influences of Salary Growth and Promotions," *Journal of Applied Psychology* 82, no. 1 (1997), p. 44; David A. Harrison, Meghna Virick, and Sonja William, "Working

Without a Net: Time, Performance, and Turnover Under Maximally Contingent Rewards," *Journal of Applied Psychology* 81(4), 1996, pp. 331–345; A. Nyberg, "Retaining Your High Performers: Moderators of the Performance–Job Satisfaction–Voluntary Turnover Relationship," *Journal of Applied Psychology* 95, no. 3 (2010), p. 440.

58. Arran Caza, Matthew W. McCarter, and Gregory Northcraft, "Performance Benefits of Reward Choice: A Procedural Justice Perspective," *Human Resource Management Journal*, forthcoming; M. R. Carrell and J. E. Dettrich, "Employee Perceptions of Fair Treatment," *Personnel Journal* 55 (1976), pp. 523–524.
59. Barry Gerhart and Meiyu Fang, "Pay for (Individual) Performance: Issues, Claims, Evidence and the Role of Sorting Effects," *Human Resource Management Review Volume* 24(1), March 2014, pp. 41–52.
60. A. Weiss, "Incentives and Worker Behavior: Some Evidence," in *Incentives, Cooperation and Risk Sharing,* ed. H. R. Nalbantian (Totowa, NJ: Rowan and Littlefield, 1987), pp. 137–150.
61. Margaret L. Williams, Michael A. McDaniel, and Nhung T. Nguyen, "A Meta-Analysis of the Antecedents and Consequences of Pay Level Satisfaction," *Journal of Applied Psychology* 91, no. 2 (2006), p. 392; R. Heneman and T. Judge, "Compensation Attitudes: A Review and Recommendations for Future Research," in *Compensation in Organizations: Progress and Prospects,* ed. S. L. Rynes and B. Gerhart (San Francisco: New Lexington Press, 1999).
62. P. W. Hom and R. W. Griffeth, *Employee Turnover* (Cincinnati, OH: Southwestern, 1995); M. Kim, "Where the Grass Is Greener: Voluntary Turnover and Wage Premiums," *Industrial Relations* 38 (October 1999), p. 584.
63. Barry Gerhart and Meiyu Fang, "Pay for (Individual) Performance: Issues, Claims, Evidence and the Role of Sorting Effects," *Human Resource Management Review Volume* 24(1), March 2014, pp. 41–52; D. M. Cable and T. A. Judge, "Pay Preferences and Job Search Decisions: A Person-Organization Fit Perspective," *Personnel Psychology* 47 (1994), pp. 317–348.
64. S. Salamin and P. Hom, "In Search of the Elusive U-Shaped Performance-Turnover Relationship: Are High Performing Swiss Bankers More Liable to Quit?" *Journal of Applied Psychology* 90(6), 2005, pp. 1–9.
65. A. Kohn, *Punished by Rewards: The Trouble with Gold Stars, Incentive Plans, A's, Praise and Other Bribes* (Boston: Houghton-Mifflin, 1993).
66. C. O. Trevor, B. Gerhart, and J. W. Boudreau, "Voluntary Turnover and Job Performance: Curvilinearity and the Moderating Influences of Salary Growth and Promotions," *Journal of Applied Psychology* 82, no. 1 (1997), p. 44.
67. P. Zingheim and J. R. Shuster, *Pay People Right* (San Francisco, CA: Jossey-Bass, 2000); J. Boudreau, M. Sturman, C. Trevor, and B. Gerhart, "Is It Worth It to Win the Talent War? Using Turnover Research to Evaluate the Utility of Performance-Based Pay," Working Paper 99–06, Center for Advanced Human Resource Studies, Cornell University, 2000.
68. Allison Perlik, "Payback Time," *Restaurants and Institutions,* Chicago, January 15, 2003, pp. 22–29.
69. John P. Hausknecht, Julianne Rodda, and Michael J. Howard, "Targeted Employee Retention: Performance-Based and Job-Related Differences in Reported Reasons for Staying," *Human Resource Management* 48, no. 2 (2009), 269–288.
70. Gerhart, B., & Feng, J. (2021). The Resource-Based View of the Firm, Human Resources, and Human Capital: Progress and Prospects. *Journal of Management;* Maltarich, M. A., Reilly, G., & DeRose, C. (2020). A theoretical assessment of dismissal rates and unit performance, with empirical evidence. *Journal of Applied Psychology,* 105(5), 527. Weller, I., Hymer, C. B., Nyberg, A. J., & Ebert, J. (2019).

How matching creates value: Cogs and wheels for human capital resources research. *Academy of Management Annals*, 13(1), 188–214.

71. Aamer Madhani, "ROTC Recruits Paid to Command New Languages," *USA Today,* December 23, 2008, p. B1.
72. Atul Mitra, Nina Gupta, and Jason D. Shaw, "A Comparative Examination of Traditional and Skill-Based Pay Plans," *Journal of Managerial Psychology* 26, no. 4 (2011), pp. 278–296; E. C. Dierdorff and E. A. Surface, "If You Pay for Skills, Will They Learn? Skill Change and Maintenance under a Skill-Based Pay System," *Journal of Management* 34, no. 4 (2008), pp. 721–743; Jason D. Shaw, Nina Gupta, Atul Mitra, and Gerald E. Ledford Jr., "Success and Survival of Skill-Based Pay Plans," *Journal of Management* 31, no. 1 (2005), pp. 28–49; Brian Murray and Barry Gerhart, "An Empirical Analysis of a Skill-Based Pay Program and Plant Performance Outcomes," *Academy of Management Journal* 41, no. 1 (1998), pp. 68–78; Kevin J. Parent and Caroline L. Weber, "Does Paying for Knowledge Pay Off?" *Compensation and Benefits Review,* September 1994, pp. 44–50.
73. J. Pfeffer, *The Human Equation: Building Profits by Putting People First* (Boston: Harvard Business School Press, 1998).
74. Barry Gerhart, Sara L. Rynes, and Ingrid Smithey Fulmer, "Pay and Performance: Individuals, Groups, and Executives," *Academy of Management Annals* 3, no. 1 (2009), pp. 251–315; Barry Gerhart and Sara Rynes, *Compensation: Theory, Evidence, and Strategic Implications* (Thousand Oaks, CA: SAGE, 2003); R. L. Heneman, *Strategic Reward Management: Design, Implementation, and Evaluation* (Greenwich, CT: Information Age, 2002); W. N. Cooke, "Employee Participation Programs, Group Based Incentives, and Company Performance," *Industrial and Labor Relations Review* 47 (1994), pp. 594–610; G. W. Florkowski, "The Organizational Impact of Profit Sharing," *Academy of Management Review* 12 (1987), pp. 622–636.
75. Mark A. Huselid, "The Impact of Human Resource Management Practices on Turnover, Productivity, and Corporate Financial Performance," *Academy of Management Journal* 38(3), 1995, pp. 635–672.
76. Barry Gerhart and Meiyu Fang, "Pay for (Individual) Performance: Issues, Claims, Evidence and the Role of Sorting Effects," *Human Resource Management Review* 24(1), March 2014, pp. 41–52.
77. *Merit Pay: Linking Pay Increases to Performance Ratings* (Reading, MA: Addison-Wesley, 1992).
78. Shaw, Jason D., and Atul Mitra, "The Science of Pay-for-Performance Systems: Six Facts That All Managers Should Know," (2017); Jason D. Shaw, Atul Mitra, and Nina Gupta, "Let the evidence speak again! Financial incentives are more effective than we thought," *Human Resource Management Journal* 25, no. 3 (2015): 281–293; Gerhart, B. (2017). "Incentives and Pay for Performance in the Workplace," *Advances in Motivation Science,* 4, 91; Gerhart, B., & Fang, M. (2014). "Pay for (individual) performance: Issues, claims, evidence and the role of sorting effects," *Human Resource Management Review,* 24(1), 41–52.
79. E. A. Locke, D. B. Feren, V. M. McCaleb, K. N. Shaw, and A. T. Denny, "The Relative Effectiveness of Four Methods of Motivating Employee Performance" in *Changes in Working Life,* K. D. Duncan, M. M. Gruenberg, and D. Wallis, eds. (New York: Wiley, 1980), pp. 363–388.
80. Kim, J. H., Gerhart, B., & Fang, M. (2021). Do Financial Incentives Help or Harm Performance in Interesting Tasks? Journal of Applied Psychology, forthcoming.
81. Yvonne Garbers and Udo Konradt, "The Effect of Financial Incentives on Performance: A Quantitative Review of Individual and Team-Based Financial Incentives," *Journal of Occupational and Organizational Psychology* 87, no. 1 (2014), pp. 102–137; D. G. Jenkins Jr., A. Mitra, N. Gupta, and J. D. Shaw, "Are Financial Incentives Related to Performance? A Meta-Analytic Review of Empirical Research," *Journal of Applied Psychology* 83 (1998), pp. 777–787.

82. Original data from Mercer LLC, *2016/2017 United States Compensation Planning Survey and 2017/2018 United States Compensation Planning Survey*, www.mercer.com.

83. W. N. Cooke, "Employee Participation Programs, Group Based Incentives and Company Performance: A Union–Non Union Comparison," *Industrial and Labor Relations Review* 47(4), 1994, pp. 594–610.

84. D. L. Kruse, *Profit Sharing: Does It Make a Difference?* (Kalamazoo, MI: Upjohn Institute, 1993).

85. B. Gerhart and G. Milkovich, "Organizational Differences in Managerial Compensation and Financial Performance," *Academy of Management Journal* 33 (1990), pp. 663–690.

86. Christopher Mims, "At Google, the Science of Working," *The Wall Street Journal*, March 30, 2015, p. b1; Laszlo Bock, *Work Rules!: Insights from Inside Google That Will Transform How You Live and Lead Hardcover* (New York: Twelve Publishing, 2015).

87. A. Kohn, *Punished by Rewards. The Trouble with Gold Stars, Incentive Plans, A's, Praise and Other Bribes* (Boston: Houghton-Mifflin, 1993).

88. E. Deci, R. Ryan, and R. Koestner, "A Meta-Analytic Review of Experiments Examining the Effects of Extrinsic Rewards on Intrinsic Motivation," *Psychological Bulletin,* 125(6), 1999, pp. 627–668.

89. R. McKensie and D. Lee, *Managing Through Incentives* (New York: Oxford University Press, 1998); R. Eisenberger and J. Cameron, "Detrimental Effects of Rewards," *American Psychologist,* November 1996, pp. 1153–1156.

90. One of your book's authors knows this all too well, based on what was at one time the daily venting of his daughter, a short-term Target employee.

91. B. Gerhart and M. Fang, "Pay, Intrinsic Motivation, Extrinsic Motivation, Performance, and Creativity in the Workplace: Revisiting Long-Held Beliefs," *Annual Review of Organizational Psychology and Organizational Behavior* 2, no. 1 (2015), pp. 489–521; B. Gerhart, "Incentives and Pay for Performance in the Workplace," *Advances in Motivation Science* 4 (2017), pp. 91–140; Barry Gerhart and Meiyu Fang, "Competence and Pay for Performance," in *Handbook of Competence and Motivation: Theory and Application*, ed. Andrew J. Eliot, Carol S. Dweck, and David S. Yeager, pp. 232–250 (New York: Guilford Press, 2017).

92. Vera Brencic and John B. Norris, "On-the-Job Tasks and Performance Pay: A Vacancy-Level Analysis," *Industrial and Labor Relations Review* 63(3), 2010, pp. 511–544.

93. L. Dyer, D. P. Schwab, and R. D. Theriault, "Managerial Perceptions Regarding Salary Increase Criteria," *Personnel Psychology* 29 (1976), pp. 233–242.

94. J. Fossum and M. Fitch, "The Effects of Individual and Contextual Attributes on the Sizes of Recommended Salary Increases," *Personnel Psychology* 38 (1985), pp. 587–603. For a review of multiple studies, including in different countries, see: B. Gerhart. "Compensation and National Culture." Global Compensation: Foundations and perspectives (2008): 142–57.

95. Ken Abosch, "3 Ways to Make the Most of Your Merit Budget," *Compensation Focus,* October 2015, www.wordlatwork.com; Laszlo Bock, *Work Rules! Insights from Inside Google That Will Transform How You Live and Lead* (Ashland, OR: Hachette, 2015); IOMA, *Complete Guide to Best Practices in Pay for Performance* (Newark, NJ: BNA Subsidiaries, 2005), pp. 1–5.

96. L. V. Jones and T. E. Jeffrey, "A Quantitative Analysis of Expressed Preferences for Compensation Plans," *Journal of Applied Psychology* 48 (1963), pp. 201–210; Opinion Research Corporation, *Wage Incentives* (Princeton, NJ: Opinion Research Corporation, 1946); Opinion Research Corporation, *Productivity from the Worker's Standpoint* (Princeton, NJ: Opinion Research Corporation, 1949).

97. D. Koys, T. Keaveny, and R. Allen, "Employment Demographics and Attitudes That Predict Preferences for Alternative Pay Increase Policies," *Journal of Business and Psychology* 4 (1989), pp. 27–47.

98. Emily Grijalva, Daniel A. Newman, Louis Tay, M. Brent Donnellan, P. D. Harms, Richard W. Robins, and Taiyi Yan, "Gender Differences in Narcissism: A Meta-Analytic Review," *Psychological Bulletin,* 2015, 141(2), pp. 261–310; B. Major, "Gender, Justice and the Psychology of Entitlement," *Review of Personality and Social Psychology* 7 (1988), pp. 124–148.

99. Barry Gerhart, Sara L. Rynes, and Ingrid Smithey Fulmer, "Pay and Performance: Individuals, Groups, and Executives," *Academy of Management Annals* 3, no. 1 (2009), pp. 251–315; Barry Gerhart, and Sara Rynes, *Compensation: Theory, Evidence, and Strategic Implications* (Thousand Oaks, CA: SAGE, 2003); G. Green, "Instrumentality Theory of Work Motivation," *Journal of Applied Psychology* 53 (1965), pp. 1-25; R. D. Pritchard, D. W. Leonard, C. W. Von Bergen, Jr., and R. J. Kirk, "The Effects of Varying Schedules of Reinforcement on Human Task Performance," *Organizational Behavior and Human Performance* 16 (1976), pp. 205–230; D. P. Schwab and L. Dyer, "The Motivational Impact of a Compensation System on Employee Performance," *Organizational Behavior and Human Performance* 9 (1973), pp. 215-225; D. Schwab, "Impact of Alternative Compensation Systems on Pay Valence and Instrumentality Perceptions," *Journal of Applied Psychology* 58 (1973), pp. 308–312.

100. Barry Gerhart, Sara L. Rynes, and Ingrid Smithey Fullmer, "Pay and Performance: Individuals, Groups and Executives," *Academy of Management Annals* 3, ed. A. P. Brief and J. P. Walsh (Newark, NJ: Erlbaum, 2009).

101. E. Lazear, "Performance Pay and Productivity," *American Economic Review* 90(6), 2000, pp. 1346–1361.

102. B. Gerhart and G. T. Milkovich, "Employee Compensation: Research and Practice," in *Handbook of Industrial & Organizational Psychology,* 2nd ed., M. D. Dunnette and L. M. Hough, eds. (Palo Alto, CA: Consulting Psychologists Press, 1992).

103. C. Q. Trank, S. L. Rynes, and R. D. Bretz, Jr., "Attracting Applicants in the War for Talent: Differences in Work Preferences Among High Achievers," *Journal of Business and Psychology* 16 (2001), pp. 331–345.

104. David A. Comerford and Peter A. Ubel, "Effort Aversion: Job Choice and Amount of Effort Required in Work," *Journal of Economic Behavior and Organizations* 92(8), August 2013, 152–162.

105. Dahl, M. S., & Pierce, L. (2020). Pay-for-performance and employee mental health: Large sample evidence using employee prescription drug usage. Academy of Management Discoveries, 6(1), 12–38; Ho, H., & Kuvaas, B. (2020). Human resource management systems, employee well-being, and firm performance from the mutual gains and critical perspectives: The well-being paradox. *Human Resource Management*, 59(3), 235–253; Parker, S. L., Bell, K., Gagné, M., Carey, K., & Hilpert, T. (2019). Collateral damage associated with performance-based pay: the role of stress appraisals. *European Journal of Work and Organizational Psychology*, 28(5), 691–707.

106. E. H. O'Boyle and H. Aguinis, "The Best and the Rest: Revisiting the Norm of Normality of Individual Performance," *Personnel Psychology* 65 (2012), pp. 79–119; H. Aguinis and E. O'Boyle, "Star Performers in Twenty-First Century Organizations," *Personnel Psychology* 67, no. 2 (2014), pp. 313–350; H. Aguinis, E. O'Boyle, E. Gonzalez-Mulé, and H. Joo, "Cumulative Advantage: Conductors and Insulators of Heavy-Tailed Productivity Distributions and Productivity Stars," *Personnel Psychology*, 2014; K. F. Hallock, *Pay: Why People Earn What They Earn and What You Can Do Now to Make More* (Cambridge: Cambridge University Press, 2012). A key part of the argument is that performance is not normally distributed. For an alternative view of the evidence questioning whether the performance distribution is nonnormal, see J. W. Beck, A. S. Beatty, and P. R. Sackett, "On the Distribution of Job Performance: The Role of Measurement Characteristics in Observed Departures from Normality," *Personnel Psychology* 67 (2014) pp. 531–566.

107. Derek Jones, Panu Kalmi, and Antii Kauhanen, "Teams, Incentive Pay, and Productive Efficiency: Evidence from a Food-Processing Plant," *Industrial and Labor Relations Review* 63(4), 2010, pp. 606-626.

108. K. Kelly and E. Schine, "How Did Sears Blow This Gasket?" *BusinessWeek,* June 29, 1992, p. 38.

109. Jerry Newman, personal correspondence, April 5, 2015.

110. G. Morenson and J. Rosner, *Reckless Endangerment: How Outsized Ambition, Greed, and Corruption Led to Economic Armageddon,* Time Magazine books, 2011.

111. Atul G. Mitra, G. Douglas Jenkins Jr., Nina Gupta, and Jason D. Shaw, "The Utility of Pay Raises/Cuts: A Simulation Experimental Study," *Journal of Economic Psychology* 49 (2015), pp. 150-166.

112. A. Richter, "Paying the People in Black at Big Blue," *Compensation and Benefits Review,* May/June 1998, pp. 51-59.

113. John Thibaut and Laurens Walker, *Procedural Justice: A Psychological View* (Hillsdale, NJ: Wiley, 1975).

114. M. Bloom, "The Performance Effects of Pay Dispersion on Individuals and Organizations," *Academy of Management Journal* 4(1), 1999, pp. 25-40.

115. Joel Brockner, "Making Sense of Procedural Fairness: How High Procedural Fairness Can Reduce or Heighten the Influence of Outcome Favorability," *Academy of Management Review* 27(1), 2002, pp. 58-76.

116. Robert Folger and Mary Konovsky, "Effects of Procedural and Distributive Justice on Reactions to Pay Raise Decisions," *Academy of Management Journal* 32(1), March 1989, pp. 155-130.

117. S. Alexander and M. Ruderman, "The Role of Procedural and Distributive Justice in Organizational Behavior," *Social Justice Research* 1 (1987), pp. 177-198.

118. Gus Defranco, "The Effect of Disclosure on the Pay-Performance Relation," *Journal of Accounting and Public Policy*, 32, 2013, 117-136.

119. G. S. Leventhal, J. Karuza, and W. R. Fry, "Beyond Fairness: A Theory of Allocation Preferences," in *Justice and Social Interaction,* G. Mikula, ed. (New York: Springer Verlag, 1980), pp. 167-218.

120. IOMA, *Complete Guide to Best Practices in Pay for Performance* (Newark: NJ: Institute of Management and Administration, 2005).

121. K. B. Stone, B. A. Backhaus, and K. Heiner, "Exploring the Relationship between Corporate Social Performance and Employer Attractiveness," *Business and Society,* September 2002, pp. 28-41.

Chapter **Ten**
Pay-for-Performance: Types of Plans

Chapter Outline

WHAT IS A PAY-FOR-PERFORMANCE PLAN?

Good question! Many different compensation practices are lumped under the name **pay for performance.** When your Mom told you last summer she would give you 20 dollars to cut the grass, that's a pay-for-performance plan! When you didn't do a very good job because you were rushing to make a pickup game on the local court, and she paid you anyway, that's still a pay-for-performance plan, just not a very good one. Indeed, it sounds like your Mom learned about pay for performance from many of the managers we've met, whose plan seems to be "Don't distinguish between good and bad performance and pay everyone about the same."

Listen long enough and you will hear about **incentive, variable pay plans, compensation at risk, earnings at risk, success sharing, risk sharing,** and others. (Recall our discussion of these in **Chapter 9**.) Sometimes these names are used interchangeably. They shouldn't be. The major thing all these plans have in common is a shift in thinking about compensation. We used to think of pay as primarily an entitlement. If you went to work and did well enough to avoid being fired, you were entitled to the same size check as everyone else doing the same job as you. Pay-for-performance plans signal a movement–sometimes a very *slow* movement–away from entitlement and toward pay that varies with some measure of individual or organizational performance. Of the pay components we discussed in **Chapter 9**, only base pay and across-the-board increases don't fit the pay-for-performance category. Curiously, though, many of the surveys on pay for performance tend to omit the grandfather of all these plans, **merit pay**, which, as we will see, is very widely used.

Exhibit 10.1 provides another way to classify pay-for-performance plans–in this case, short-term incentive/variable pay plans–and shows the breadth of these types of plans in use.

How Widely Used Is Pay for Performance (PFP)?

Exhibit 10.1 also provides data on the use of the short-term incentive plans (where the performance period is 12 months or less) in organizations. We see that 99 percent of organizations surveyed use some form of short-term incentive plan for at least some of their employees, and also that most have multiple short-term incentive plans. What in the past was primarily a compensation tool for top management (and is still significantly more likely to be used for them) is now often used for lower-level employees too. The use of variable pay in general has increased. For example, in 1990 the average budget for base salary increases was 5.5 percent. More recently, it was down to 3.0 percent. One reason is a decline in wage and price inflation. However, that does not explain the simultaneous increase in merit bonus/variable pay budgets from 4.2 percent in 1990 to roughly 13 percent today.[1]

The greater interest in variable pay probably can be traced to two trends. First, the increasing competition from foreign producers forces American firms to cut costs and/or increase productivity. Well-designed variable pay plans have a proven track record in motivating better performance and helping cut costs. Plus, variable pay is, by definition, a variable cost. No profits, or poor profits, means no extra pay beyond base pay–when times are bad, compensation is lower.[2] Second, today's fast-paced business environment means that workers must be willing to adjust what they do and how they do it. There are new technologies, new work processes, and new work relationships. All these require workers to adapt in new ways and with a speed that is unparalleled. Failure to move quickly means market share goes to competitors. If this happens, workers face possible layoffs and terminations. To avoid this scenario, compensation experts are focusing on ways to design reward systems so that workers will be able–and willing–to move quickly into new jobs and new ways of performing old jobs. The ability and incentive to do this come partially from reward systems that more closely link worker interests with the objectives of the company.[3]

Other evidence points to the very strong overall reliance on pay for performance (PFP), including variable pay, especially in private sector organizations. World-at-Work surveys its members (compensation professionals) about practices in organizations. Its survey results indicate that pay for performance (PFP) is very widely used. Specifically, 94 percent of organizations have merit pay programs, 99 percent (as we have seen) have short-term incentive plans (payment based on attainment of financial, operational, and individual goals during a period of 12 months or less), and 91 percent have long-term incentive plans (payment based on attainment of goals over a period of longer than 12 months usually related to performance in terms of company stock price/return). However, these percentages underestimate the use of PFP in the private sector, given that 22 percent of responding organizations were in the nonprofit, not-for-profit, or public sectors, where we know that the use of PFP (as well as its intensity when it is used) is considerably lower than in the private sector. Also, the typical long-term incentive plan, which, as noted, is based on company stock performance, is not possible in organizations where there is no stock/ownership. Thus, the typical U.S. private sector company relies especially heavily on PFP, and the percentage of private sector organizations using two or more of the above PFP plans is probably close to 100 percent.

EXHIBIT 10.1 **Use of Short-Term Incentive/Variable Pay Plans**

Type of Short-Term Incentive (Variable Pay) Plan	Percentage of Organizations Using the Plan for at Least Some Employee Groups	Short-Term Incentive Plan Description
Any short-term incentive plan	99%	Incentive plan based on attainment of goals during a period of 12 months or less.
Have multiple short-term incentive plans	76%	Organization has two or more short-term incentive plans.
Specific Programs:		
Annual incentive plan	98%	Payout solely or primarily based on a predefined formula that can include a variety of performance metrics.
Spot cash awards	57%	To recognize a special contribution accomplished over a short period.
Retention bonus	44%	Payout designed to keep employee until completion of a crucial business event (e.g., a merger or an acquisition).
Annual discretionary bonus plan	35%	Management determines whether there is a bonus and its size after the fact at the end of the period.
Project bonus	23%	Paid to an employee or a department for achieving a specific project.
Profit-sharing plans	22%	Payout solely or primarily based on a predefined formula linked to profits.
Team/small-group incentives	20%	Programs where payout is based on performance of a small group.
Gain-sharing plans	7%	Programs designed to share productivity and other performance improvements that take place in subunits of the organization.

Source: WorldatWork and Deloitte Consulting LLP, *Incentive Pay Practices Survey: Publicly Traded Companies*, 2018.

One important caveat is that the roughly 13 percent merit bonus/variable pay percentage applies only to organizations that use such plans and only to the employee groups in such companies covered by such plans. (By contrast, merit pay plans cover almost all employees and, as we will see shortly, nearly all organizations.) **Exhibit 10.2** reports short-term incentive/variable payouts and the performance basis used for them as a percentage of base pay, by employee group, in organizations using such plans and in all organizations (on average), adjusted for the fact that not all organizations use such plans and that organizations using such plans do not use them for all employee groups. Again, we see that short-term incentive payouts as a percentage of salary are larger than merit increases. Moreover, for some employee groups (those at higher job/pay levels), short-term incentive/variable payouts are much larger than merit increases. We also see that the most common performance basis for short-term incentive/variable payouts is a combination of corporate, unit, and individual objectives.

The details on performance objectives beyond the split across corporate, business unit, and individual reported in **Exhibit 10.2** gets a bit confusing, which reflects the great variety in design specifics of plans in different organizations and for different employee groups. But here goes: In almost all (97% of) short-term incentive plans, payouts are based to some degree on financial (i.e., organization-level) performance–most commonly revenue (43%), followed closely by various (organization-level) profit measures. In addition, "overall individual performance (e.g., performance evaluation or rating)" was used by 48 percent of organizations. (These plans would be closer to the definition of a merit bonus plan, specifically.) Operational measures of performance were often used also, with the most common being customer satisfaction (28%).

EXHIBIT 10.2 **Estimated Short-Term Incentive/Variable (Bonus) Pay as a Percentage of Salary and Performance Basis, by Employee Group**

Employee Group	Percentage of Organizations Where Eligible	Bonus/Variable Pay as a Percentage of Salary (Target)		Performance Basis for Bonus Payout		
	(A)	In Organizations Using Such Plans (B)	All Organizations (A x B)	Corporate	Division/Business Unit	Individual
Officers/executives	99%	49%	49%	62%	19%	19%
Exempt, salaried	99	15	15	48	28	26
Nonexempt, salaried	48	6	3	44	29	26
Nonexempt, hourly nonunion	54	5	3	40	32	27

Source: Data are from: WorldatWork and Deloitte Consulting LLP, "Incentive Pay Practices Survey: Publicly Traded Companies," 2018. The logic for developing the A X B estimate is covered in: Barry Gerhart and Meiyu Fang, "Pay for (Individual) Performance: Issues, Claims, Evidence and the Role of Sorting Effects," *Human Resource Management Review* 24 (2014), pp. 41–52; Barry Gerhart, "Incentives and Pay for Performance in the Workplace," *Advances in Motivation Science* 4 (2017), pp. 91–140;

Note: The "All Organizations" column estimates reflect an adjustment for the fact that not all organizations use such plans and for the fact that organizations that do use such plans do not use them for all employee groups. The term "nonexempt" refers to employees covered by the Fair Labor Standards Act and the term "exempt" refers to employees not covered by the Act. See **Chapter 17**.

Note: Although "merit bonus" (for a significant role for subjective performance) and "short-term incentive" (primarily for objective performance) are defined differently, the terms tend not to be as distinct in surveys.

Long-term incentive plans (where the performance period is more than 12 months) are also more likely to be used for officers/executives and other higher job levels. Indeed, **Exhibit 10.3** shows that, on average, the lowest job levels, where most employees are, receive only a very small percentage of the value of long-term incentives granted by organizations. Long-term incentive plans (especially for top executives) will be covered further in **Chapter 14**. Here, we note that they include stock grants, stock option grants, performance share grants, performance units, and other programs where the payout depends on shareholder return and/or other corporate financial performance measures.

The Important Role of Promotion (internal or external) in Pay for Performance

As noted above, merit pay is widely used by organizations and for all types of employees. As we will see in our discussion below, the average merit pay increase is about 3 percent per year. At that rate, it would take an employee about 23 years to double his/her salary from say $70,000 to $140,000 or from $100,000 to $200,000. Yet, we know that many of you will go on to earn much more than $140,000 or even $200,000 per year. Although it is true that if you are a higher performer, you will get larger merit pay increases and that your salary will increase faster, it will still take a while. So, how will some of you end up making much higher salaries than described here? The answer is that you will get promoted to higher job levels (i.e., salary ranges/grades) and that salary increases due to promotion are much larger than 3 percent. For instance, if you return to **Chapter 3** and examine the pay structure for engineers at Lockheed Martin, you will see that a promotion brings a salary increase of roughly 21 to 23 percent. At that rate, one's salary doubles after three

EXHIBIT 10.3 **Allocation and Use of Long-Term Incentive Plans**

Employee Group	Median Percentage of Long-Term Incentive Grants Allocated
CEO	13%
Officers/executives (excluding CEO)	50%
Exempt, salaried	25%
Nonexempt, salaried	0%
Nonexempt, hourly nonunion	0%
	Practices/Use
Percentage of organizations using long-term incentive	91%
Number of long-term incentive plans used	
One plan	18%
More than one plan	82%

Source: Barry Gerhart. "Incentives and Pay for Performance in the Workplace," in *Advances in Motivation Science* 4 (2017), 91–140; updated using: WorldatWork and Deloitte Consulting LLP, "Incentive Pay Practices Survey: Publicly Traded Companies," 2018.

Note: The term "nonexempt" refers to employees covered by the Fair Labor Standards Act and the term "exempt" refers to employees not covered by the Act. See **Chapter 17**.

or four promotions. Except at higher job levels, promotion increases are probably more in the range of 15 percent (based on looking at typical midpoint progressions–the percentage difference in salary midpoints of adjacent salary ranges).[4] Using 15 percent, an employee's salary would double after five promotions.

Because promotion is based importantly on performance, any discussion of how strongly pay and performance are related must recognize that it is about much more than merit pay increases, which are within-grade increases. For many employees, their performance will be rewarded with higher pay more strongly through their high performance leading to promotions to higher levels, either within their current organization or in a different organization following turnover/mobility.[5]

PAY-FOR-PERFORMANCE: MERIT PAY PLANS

A **merit pay** system links increases in base pay (called *merit pay increases*) to how highly employees are rated on a performance evaluation. (**Chapter 11** covers performance evaluation.) However, most organizations use a merit increase grid, which determines merit pay increases not only on the basis of performance rating, but also on the basis of an employee's position in the salary range/grade (i.e., how close to the minimum versus maximum). Position in range is nicely captured by the compa-ratio, defined as employee salary divided by salary range midpoint. Thus, in a salary range that goes from a minimum of $50,000 to a maximum of $70,000 with a midpoint of $60,000, an employee with a current salary of $53,000 would have a compa-ratio of $53,000/$60,000 = .88, whereas an employee in that same salary range with a salary of $67,000 would have a compa-ratio of $67,000/$60,000 = 1.12. If both employees have the highest performance rating, the employee with the compa-ratio of .88 would get a larger merit increase than the employee with a compa-ratio of 1.12 because the lower-paid employee (with the compa-ratio of .88) is farther away from where his/her salary should be in the salary range if his/her performance were to stay at that high level over time. For example, in the following merit increase grid, the first employee (with the compa-ratio of .88) would receive a 7 percent merit increase (resulting in a new salary of $56,710), whereas the second employee (with the compa-ratio of 1.12) would receive a merit increase of 3 percent (resulting in a new salary of $69,010). One can imagine what would happen without the compa-ratio element of the merit increase grid. If a high-performing employee received a 7 percent salary increase each year, his/her salary would double every 10 years! That would be fine if the value generated for the organization of that same level of high performance also doubled every 10 years. However, that may not be likely in most jobs. Typically, to double one's contribution to the organization, one must get promoted to higher-level jobs that allows more impact on organization performance.

Exhibit 10.4 provides an example of a merit increase grid. We can also look at the degree to which companies award different merit increases to employees with different performance ratings. **Exhibit 10.5** shows that, on average, in companies using a 5-point rating scale, employees with the highest rating of 5 receive a 4.5 percent merit increase on average, compared to, for example, a 2.6 percent merit increase for an employee in the middle performance category. **Exhibit 10.5** also shows that about 7 percent of employees receive the highest rating and about 56 percent of employees receive the middle category performance rating. Of course, this distribution of employees across performance rating categories will have major cost implications. In some companies, as we discuss further in **Chapter 11**, most employees fall into the top two performance categories, which would translate into more higher merit pay increases and more cost. Finally, **Exhibit 10.5** shows that higher performance ratings translate not only into higher merit pay increases, but also into higher short-term incentive payouts.

At the end of a performance year, the employee is evaluated, usually by the direct supervisor. A key feature of a merit pay increase is that, unlike variable pay programs (short-term incentives and long-term incentives), the increase is added into base pay. This point is important. In effect, what an employees does this year in terms of performance is rewarded *every year* for as long as the employee remains with the employer. Once awarded, that merit pay increase is there forever. With compounding, this can amount to tens of thousands of dollars over an employee's work career.[6]

Year after year, there are concerns about merit pay. One concern is that it increases fixed compensation costs over time. One response has been to use merit bonuses and/or other forms of variable pay plans. Another concern is that merit pay becomes costly if too many high-performance ratings are awarded. A response is to control the number of high ratings and/or improve the accuracy and credibility of performance ratings. (See **Chapter 11**.) Another concern is that merit pay differentials based on performance are too small to motivate performance. That is a challenge. However, larger differentials can be used. Additionally, as discussed above, the strength of merit pay differentials will be greatly underestimated if the role of performance in promotions and resulting salary growth over time is not included. Another potential problem, true of any pay-for-performance program, is that individual performance is a deficient measure in organizations where work is interdependent and requires cooperation to achieve team/organization objectives. A possible solution is to broaden performance criteria to include cooperation and other factors that contribute to team/organization success. Our view is that it has been difficult to study and document the effects of merit pay plans on performance. However, the evidence that does exist is positive.[7] Further, when one considers the theory and evidence on pay-for-performance plans broadly, it appears to us that organizations use such plans with good reason: in their absence, an environment is created that does not reward excellence and employees who aspire to excellence will decide to look elsewhere.[8]

In this vein, it is important to again keep in mind the idea of *incentive* and *sorting* effects, first introduced in **Chapter 1**. Most discussion of merit pay focuses on incentive effects: how does merit pay influence performance of current employees. However, merit pay may have a significant sorting effect in that people who don't want to have their pay tied to performance don't accept jobs at such companies or leave when pay for performance is implemented. By contrast, people who do prefer to be paid for their performance (likely higher performers on average) are more likely to join and stay with companies that more strongly link pay to performance via merit pay and other pay-for-performance programs.[9]

Meanwhile, at the state and municipal levels, public schools in Minnesota, Ohio, Denver, and Philadelphia led the way to merit pay for teachers.[10] In Cincinnati, for example, teachers began to be held accountable for things they control: good professional practices. Teachers argue they should be held to standards similar to those for doctors: not a promise of a long healthy life but a promise that the highest professional standards will be followed. To assess teacher professional practices in Cincinnati, six evaluations were conducted over the school year, four by a trained teacher evaluator (essentially a trained teacher) and two by a building administrator. The size of pay increases was directly linked to performance during these observational

EXHIBIT 10.4 Merit Increase Grid Example

Recommended Salary Increases by Performance Rating and Compa-Ratio			
	Compa-Ratio[a]		
	80–90%	91–110%	111–120%
Performance rating			
Exceeds expectations	7%	5%	3%
Meets expectations	4%	3%	2%
Below expectations	2%	0%	0%

[a]Employee salary divided by midpoint of their salary range.

reviews. However, in this case the plan did not survive.[11] Perhaps because of these pioneering attempts, in 2006 Congress appropriated $99 million per year to school districts, charter schools, and states on a competitive basis to fund development and implementation of performance-related pay programs for principals and teachers.[12] In another vein, the public sector is also experimenting with bonuses for better student test scores. Teachers who show improved student scores can receive up to $8,000 in annual bonuses in Chicago and up to $15,000 in Nashville.[13] Be careful what you wish for, though! New York State teachers and principals recently were caught cheating on the grading process for regents' exams. The lure of bonuses totaling as much as $3,500 for teachers, and increased funding for principals' schools if pass rates improved, was too tempting.[14]

Of course, we could always design a system like that used in South Korea, a country whose students consistently outperform ours. Teachers in private schools often are paid on incentive. The dollar amount can be staggering if you're judged to be a good teacher. Kim Hi-Koon is an after-school tutor who makes 4 million per year because of his performance. He teaches three hours of lectures then spends 50 or so hours tutoring students online, developing lesson plans, and writing texts.[15]

If we want merit pay to live up to its potential, it needs to be managed better.[16] This requires a complete overhaul of the way we allocate raises: improving the accuracy of performance ratings, allocating enough merit money to truly reward performance, and making sure the size of the merit increase differentiates across performance levels. To illustrate the latter point, consider the employee who works hard all year, earns a 5 percent increase as our guidelines above indicate, and compares herself with the average performer who coasts to a 3 percent increase. First, we take out taxes on that extra 2 percent. Then, we spread the raise out over 52 paychecks. It's only a slight exaggeration to suggest that the extra money won't pay for a good cup of coffee. Unless we make the reward difference larger for every increment in performance, many employees are going to say, "Why bother?"

EXHIBIT 10.5 Distribution of Performance Rating and Average Merit Increase and Short-Term Incentive Payout by Performance Rating

Performance Rating	Percent of Employees	Merit Increase	Short-Term Incentive Payout (as % of Target)
Highest rating	7%	4.8%	140%
Next highest rating	30%	3.8%	119%
Middle rating	57%	2.9%	99%
Low rating	5%	1.1%	51%
Lowest rating	1%	.2%	8%

Source: Mercer *2019/2020 United States Compensation Planning Survey* and *2016/2017 United States Compensation Planning Survey*.

Note: Incentive payouts from 2016/2017 survey. Merit increases from 2019/2020 survey. Merit increases nearly identical (4.7%, 3.6%, 2.6%, 1.0%, 0.1%) in 2016/2017 survey.

PAY-FOR-PERFORMANCE: SHORT TERM INCENTIVE PLANS (INDIVIDUAL-BASED)

Merit Bonuses aka Lump-Sum Bonuses

Merit bonuses differ from merit pay increases in that employees receive an end-of-year bonus that does not build into base pay. Because employees must earn this increase every year, it is viewed less as an entitlement than as merit pay.[17] It also provides employers a way to make pay vary more in line with variations in company performance by reducing fixed salary costs that can grow rapidly through merit pay increases. As **Exhibit 10.6** indicates, merit bonuses can be considerably less expensive than merit pay over the long run.

Notice how quickly base pay rises under a merit pay plan. After just five years, base pay is almost $14,000 higher than it is under a merit bonus plan. It should be no surprise that cost-conscious firms report switching to merit bonuses. It also should be no surprise that employees aren't particularly fond of merit bonuses. After all, the intent of merit is to cause shock waves in an entitlement culture. By giving merit for several years, a company is essentially freezing base pay. Gradually this results in a repositioning relative to competitors. The message becomes loud and clear: "Don't expect to receive increases in base pay year after year–new rewards must be earned each year." Consider the bonus system developed by Prometric Thomson Learning call centers, which register candidates for computerized tests. The centers have very clear targets that yield specific employee bonuses, as shown in **Exhibit 10.7**. At Prometric, each day is a new day when it comes to earning bonuses.

Individual Spot Awards

Spot awards are seen by many organizations as being effective.[18] Usually these payouts are awarded for exceptional performance, often on special projects or for performance that so exceeds expectations as to be deserving of an add-on bonus. The mechanics are simple: After the fact, someone in the organization alerts

EXHIBIT 10.6 Relative Cost Comparisons

	Merit Pay	Merit Bonus
Base pay	$50,000	$50,000
Year 1 payout 5%	2,500	2,500
New base pay	52,500	50,000
Extra cost total	2,500	2,500
Year 2 payout 5%	($2,625 = .05 × 52,500)	(2,500 = .05 × 50,000)
New base pay	55,125 (52,500 + 2,625)	50,000
Extra cost total	5,125	5,000
After 5 years:		
Year 5 payout	3,039	2,500
New base pay	63,814	50,000

top management to the exceptional performance. If the company is large, there may be a formal mechanism for this recognition, and perhaps some guidelines on the size of the spot award (so named because it is supposed to be awarded "on the spot"). Smaller companies may be more casual about recognition and more subjective about deciding the size of the award. The Pharmacy School at the University of California at San Francisco has a pretty typical spot award program. Awards are given for such behaviors as "effectively resolved a complaint situation," or "went beyond the expected by staying late to get a grant out on time."[19]

Individual Incentive Plans

These plans differ from the merit and lump-sum payments because they offer a promise of pay for some objective, preestablished level of performance. All incentive plans have one common feature: an established standard against which worker performance is compared to determine the magnitude of the incentive pay. For individual incentive systems, this standard is compared against individual worker performance. Because it's often difficult to find good, objective individual measures, individual incentive plans don't work for every job. How, for example, would you come up with an incentive plan for construction laborers? Maybe this wouldn't be difficult if they did the same thing all day: Your goal is to dig 5 feet of trench, 2 feet wide by 18 inches deep, every hour. But construction laborers aren't limited to shovel jobs. They also help pour concrete, assist carpenters and masons framing buildings, etc. The job is too complex for an individual incentive plan. Even a repetitive job like working on an assembly line isn't well suited to individual incentives. Jerry Newman, a founding author of your textbook, used to work on a Ford assembly line building Lincolns. Even if workers wanted to build faster to make more money, the line went by with a new car frame every 55 seconds. There is no room here for individual differences, we would argue.

Despite this constraint, a number of different individual incentive plans exist. Their differences can be reduced to variation along two dimensions and can be classified into one of four cells, as illustrated in **Exhibit 10.8**.

The first dimension on which incentive systems vary is in the *method of rate determination*. Plans set up a rate based either on units of production per time period or on time period per unit of production. On the surface, this distinction may appear trivial, but, in fact, the deviations arise because tasks have different cycles of operation.[20] Short-cycle tasks, those that are completed in a relatively short period of time, typically have as a standard a designated number of units to be produced in a given time period. For example, a book distributor we worked with had an incentive plan for packers. Number of books packed is a short-cycle task, with only seconds taken to get a book from a supply stack and place in a shipping box. For long-cycle tasks, this would not be appropriate. It is entirely possible that only one task or some portion of it may be completed in a day. Consequently, for longer-cycle tasks, the standard is typically set in terms of time required to complete

EXHIBIT 10.7 Customer Service Bonus Scheme at Prometric Thomson Learning Call Centers

Performance Measure	Minimum Performance	Bonus	Target Performance	Bonus	Superior Performance	Bonus
Average call wait	<32 min/day	.5%	<28 min/day	1%	<20 min/day	1.75%
Average talk time	3 min 50 sec	.5	<3 min 20 sec	1	3 min	1.75
Attendance	2 occurrences	.5	1 occurrence	1	0 occurrence	1.75
Quality	As monitored	.5	As monitored	1	As monitored	.75
Total Bonus		2%		4%		7%

one unit of production. Individual incentives are based on whether or not workers complete the task in the designated time period. Auto mechanics work off a blue book that tells how long, for example, a fuel injection system should take to replace. Finish faster than the allotted time and the full pay is awarded.

The second dimension on which individual incentive systems vary is the *specified relationship between production level and wages.* The first alternative is to tie wages to output on a one-to-one basis, so that wages are some constant function of production. In contrast, some plans vary wages as a function of production level. For example, one common alternative is to provide higher dollar rates for production above the standard than for production below the standard.

Each of the plans discussed in this section has as a foundation of a standard level of performance determined by some form of time study or job analysis completed by an industrial engineer or trained personnel administrator. The variations in these plans occur in either the way the standard is set or the way wages are tied to output. As in **Exhibit 10.8**, there are four general categories of plans:

1. *Cell 1:* The most frequently implemented incentive system is a **straight piecework system.** Rate determination is based on units of production per time period, and wages vary directly as a function of production level. The major advantages of this type of system are that it is easily understood by workers and, perhaps consequently, is more readily accepted than some of the other incentive systems.
2. *Cell 2:* Two relatively common plans set standards based on time per unit and tie incentives directly to level of output: (1) **standard hour plans** and (2) **Bedeaux plans.** A standard hour plan is a generic term for plans setting the incentive rate based on completion of a task in some expected time period. A common example we introduced earlier can be found in any neighborhood gasoline station or automobile repair shop. Let us assume that you need a new transmission. The estimate you receive for labor costs is based on the mechanic's hourly rate of pay, multiplied by a time estimate for job completion derived from a book listing average time estimates for a wide variety of jobs. If the mechanic receives $40 per hour and a transmission is listed as requiring four hours to be removed and replaced, the labor cost would be $160. All this is determined in advance of any actual work. Of course, if the mechanic is highly experienced and fast, the job may be completed in considerably less time than indicated in the book. However, the job is still charged as if it took the quoted time to complete. The "surplus" money is split between the employee and the service station. Standard hour plans are more practical than straight piecework plans for long-cycle operations and jobs that are nonrepetitive and require numerous skills for completion.[21]

EXHIBIT 10.8 **Individual Incentive Plans**

		Method of Rate Determination	
		Units of production per time period	*Time period per unit of production*
Relationship between Production Level and Pay	*Pay constant function of production level*	(1) Straight piecework plan	(2) Standard hour and Bedeaux plans
	Pay varies as function of production level	(3) Taylor differential piece-rate system Merrick multiple piece-rate system	(4) Halsey 50-50 method Rowan plan Gantt plan

3. A *Bedeaux* plan provides a variation on straight piecework and standard hour plans. Instead of timing an entire task, a Bedeaux plan requires division of a task into simple actions and determination of the time required by an average skilled worker to complete each action. After the more detailed time analysis of tasks, the Bedeaux system functions similarly to a standard hour plan.

4. *Cell 3:* The two plans included in cell 3 provide for variable incentives as a function of units of production per time period. Both the **Taylor plan** and the **Merrick plan** provide different piece rates, depending on the level of production relative to the standard. The Taylor plan establishes two piecework rates. One rate goes into effect when a worker exceeds the published standard for a given time period. This rate is set higher than the regular wage incentive level. A second rate is established for production below standard, and this rate is lower than the regular wage.
   The Merrick system operates in the same way, except that three piecework rates are set: (1) high for production exceeding 100 percent of standard, (2) medium for production between 83 and 100 percent of standard, and (3) low for production less than 83 percent of standard. **Exhibit 10.9** compares these two plans.

5. *Cell 4:* The three plans included in cell 4 provide for variable incentives linked to a standard expressed as a time period per unit of production. The three plans include the Halsey 50–50 method, the Rowan plan, and the Gantt plan.

The **Halsey 50–50 method** derives its name from the shared split between worker and employer of any savings in direct cost. An allowed time for a task is determined via time study. The savings from completion of a task in less than the standard time are allocated 50–50 (most frequent division) between the worker and the company.

The **Rowan plan** is similar to the Halsey plan in that an employer and employee both share in savings resulting from work completed in less than standard time. The major distinction in this plan, however, is that a worker's bonus increases as the time required to complete the task decreases. For example, if the standard time to complete a task is 10 hours and it is completed in 7 hours, the worker receives a 30 percent bonus. Completion of the same task in 6 hours would result in a 40 percent bonus above the hourly wage for each of the 6 hours.

EXHIBIT 10.9 The Taylor and Merrick Plans

- Piece-rate standard: 10 units/hour
- Standard wage: $5/hour
- Piecework rate:

	Taylor		Merrick	
Output (Units/hour)	**Rate per Unit**	**Wage**	**Rate per Unit**	**Wage**
7	$.50	$3.50	$.50	$3.50
8	$.50	$4.00	$.50	$4.00
9	$.50	$4.50	$.60	$5.40
10	$.50	$5.00	$.60	$6.00
11	$.70	$7.70	$.70	$7.70
12 +	Calculations at same rate as for 11 units.			

The **Gantt plan** differs from both the Halsey and the Rowan plans in that the standard time for a task is purposely set at a level requiring high effort to complete. Any worker who fails to complete the task in the standard time is guaranteed a preestablished wage. However, for any task completed in standard time or less, earnings are pegged at 120 percent of the time saved. Consequently, workers' earnings increase faster than production whenever standard time is met or exceeded.

Individual Incentive Plans: Returns (But Also Risks)

Although individual incentive plans receive much attention (probably because they carry risks–see below), it turns out that they are not widely used, at least in the pure form(s) described above. One estimate is that fewer than 7 percent of U.S. employees are covered by individual incentive plans and almost half of those are in sales occupations. Thus, outside of sales occupations, fewer than 4 percent of employees work under such plans.[22] (If one defines "individual incentive" more broadly, there are clearly many more employees who could be included, whether it be managers/executives being paid based on financial performance or physicians being paid based, at least in part, on revenue.)[23] There is strong evidence that individual incentives, on average, have substantial positive effects on performance.[24] (Review **Chapter 9**, **"Do Employees Perform Better on Their Jobs Because of Pay?"**) However, besides not fitting many jobs in the new economy, another reason for their limited use is that with such plans, things can go wrong–sometimes spectacularly wrong.[25] For example, as we have noted, incentive plans can lead to unexpected, and undesired, behaviors. Certainly Sears, one of our examples in **Chapter 9**, did not want the public relations nightmare of having mechanics sell unnecessary repairs, but the incentive program encouraged that type of behavior. Please don't think Sears is an isolated example. Workers in a subsidiary of Caterpillar were placed on an incentive system to find problems with rail cars that could be repaired and charged back to their respective owners. Under pressure employees–just like at Sears–manufactured problems (smashing brakes with hammers, ruining wheels with chisels) and then making the "repairs."[26] This is a common problem with incentive plans: Employees and managers end up in conflict because the incentive system often focuses only on one small part of what it takes for the company to be successful.[27] Employees, being rational, do more of what the incentive system pays for. Sales staff provide a perfect example. Try developing a unit-based sales system that doesn't prioritize products by offering different levels of incentives. In this case the smart salesperson sells the easiest product to unload (e.g., discounted and bargain prices products).[28] As a sad example, New York teachers and administrators were put on an incentive system to get student pass rates and graduation numbers up. Both these rates increased, not because of better performance, but because standards were lowered so the incentive would be paid out. In another example, evidence suggests that hospitals using some types of pay for performance are more likely to "upcode" medical conditions into more complex categories, which brings higher reimbursements from Medicare.[29] The cause of the Great Financial Crisis is typically attributed in significant part to the fact that incentives were improperly designed such that they drove mortgage loan originators to sell/approve more mortgage loans to make more money for themselves and the company, but without an adequate incentive to be careful not to sell/approve mortgages for people unlikely to be able to afford them. Wells Fargo has paid substantial fines for creating incentives for its customer-facing employees to open more customer accounts to drive more revenue, even opening accounts for customers without their knowledge! **Exhibit 10.10** outlines some of the general potential problems, as well as potential advantages, with individual incentive plans.

These might be said to be examples of incentives working "too well." Individual incentives may do such a good job of motivating employees that they do whatever they get paid for and nothing else (e.g., ethical behavior, helping/mentoring others).[30] Anything not included explicitly in the incentive plan risks being ignored. This is referred to as the *equal compensation principle* by Milgrom and Roberts:

> *If an employee's allocation of time or attention between two different activities cannot be monitored by the employer, then either the marginal rates of return to the employee must be equal, or the activity with the lower marginal rate of return receives no time or attention.*[31]

Although subjectivity (judgment) in assessing performance is sometimes assumed to be a problem (and it is if its reliability and/or credibility is insufficient), a subjective assessment (rating) it is often necessary to make sure that objective performance (e.g., mortgages sold/revenue generated) that drives incentive payouts, say in a formula-based plan, is achieved using behaviors that are acceptable.[32] Related to this, if a formula-based plan is not working as anticipated (e.g., due to factors beyond the control of employees), a judgment may be needed about possibly modifying the plan.[33]

Individual Incentive Plans: Examples

Even though pure individual incentive systems are not as widely used as sometimes thought, there are notable successes. Of course, most sales positions have some part of pay based on commissions, a form of individual incentive. One of today's biggest success stories is the merger of individual incentives with efforts to reduce health care costs. For example, Jet Blue deposits $400 into employee health reimbursement accounts for participating in various activities such as smoking cessation programs or running in Ironman contests. In general, health incentives are on the rise: 57 percent of companies used them in 2009, while over 80 percent are expected to use them going forward.[34] Perhaps the longest-running success with individual incentives, going

EXHIBIT 10.10 Advantages and Disadvantages of Individualized Incentive Plans

Advantages

1. Substantial impact that raises productivity, lowers production costs, and increases earnings of workers.
2. Less direct supervision is required to maintain reasonable levels of output than under payment by time.
3. In most cases, systems of payment by results, if accompanied by improved organizational and work measurement, enable labor costs to be estimated more accurately than under payment by time. This helps costing and budgetary control.

Disadvantages

1. Greater conflict may emerge between employees seeking to maximize output and managers concerned about deteriorating quality levels.
2. Attempts to introduce new technology may be resisted by employees concerned about the impact on production standards.
3. Reduced willingness of employees to suggest new production methods for fear of subsequent increases in production standards.
4. Increased complaints that equipment is poorly maintained, hindering employee efforts to earn larger incentives.
5. Increased turnover among new employees discouraged by the unwillingness of experienced workers to cooperate in on-the-job training.
6. Elevated levels of mistrust between workers and management.

Sources: Michael Coates, *Psychology and Organizations, Heineman Themes in Psychology*, Boston: Heineman, 2001; T. Wilson, "Is It Time to Eliminate the Piece Rate Incentive System?," *Compensation and Benefits Review* 24, no. 2 (1992), 43–49; Pinhas Schwinger, *Wage Incentive Systems* (New York: Halsted, 1975).

back to before World War I, belongs to a company called Lincoln Electric. In **Exhibit 10.11**, the compensation package for factory jobs at Lincoln Electric is described. Notice how the different pieces fit together. This isn't a case of an incentive plan operating in a vacuum. All the pieces of the compensation and reward package fit together. Both culture and the performance review system support the different pay components. Lincoln Electric's success is so striking that it's the subject of many case analyses.[35]

EXHIBIT 10.11 Lincoln Electric's Compensation System

Description of culture	Reservoir of trust. Long history of employment stability even during severe economic downturns. Employees with 3+ years' seniority are guaranteed (on one year renewable basis) at least 75 percent full-time work for that year. In exchange, employees agree to flexible assignment across jobs.
Base wages	Set to be below market. However, total cash compensation (base + incentives) target is well above market and actual level is also in years when company financial performance is strong.
Individual incentive (short-term)	Time study department sets piece rate so that average worker can earn market rate. Piece rate paid only for quality production.
Bonus (short-term)	Board of directors sets year-end bonus pool as function of company performance. Employee's share in pool is function of semiannual performance review (see below).
Incentive (long-term)	Employees share in long-term company successes/failures in form of employee stock ownership plan (ESOP). Employees historically own roughly one-quarter of outstanding stock shares.
Performance review	Employees rated on four factors: (1) dependability, (2) quality, (3) output, and (4) ideas and cooperation in comparison to others in department. To ensure against rating inflation, the average score in department cannot exceed 100.
Hours worked	After two years of employment, guaranteed 30 hours per week. Hours go much higher (48 or above) when business is strong.
Benefits	Below market
Layoffs	None since founded in 1895. Labor costs automatically drop when revenues drop by reducing hours from 48 or more to 30, by not making bonus payments, and by having low fixed benefit costs.
Span of control (employees per supervisor)	Most recent estimates are 100 at Lincoln versus 9 at large companies overall. (In agency terms, Lincoln does not need to monitor employee behaviors as closely because it uses a results-based contract.)

PAY-FOR-PERFORMANCE: SHORT-TERM INCENTIVE PLANS ("GROUP"-BASED)

When we move away from individual incentive systems and start focusing on people working together, we shift to **group incentive plans.** We define the term "group" (and often similarly the term "team") in a very broad fashion to include team/group, department, unit, division, or the entire company. Or it might even be a pirate ship! Around 1750 Captain Henry Morgan, infamous pirate, recruited and motivated his men using a simple group incentive plan: an even split of all "booty" captured (of course, after distribution of shares to Captain Morgan and his top men). "No prey, no pay" was an early tagline, and it worked: A good day for a pirate was 1,000 pound sterling, far more than the 13 to 33 pounds sterling earned by merchant seamen in more legitimate vessels.[36] The basic concept is still the same, though. A standard is established against which worker performance (in this case, team performance) is compared to determine the magnitude of the incentive pay. With the focus on groups, now we are concerned about group performance in comparison against some standard, or level, of expected performance. The standard might be an expected level of operating income for a division. Or the measure might be more unusual, as at Litton Industries (now a part of Northrop Grumman Corp). One division has a team variable-pay measure that is based on whether customers would be willing to act as a reference when Litton solicits other business. The more customers willing to do this, the larger the team's variable pay.[37] In a second study, four food processing plants moved to team-based structures and implemented team incentive plans. The team incentive component resulted in productivity increases of 9–20 percent.[38] Some group incentive plans have even higher success goals–like winning a war. Napoleon took over an army that was underfed and demoralized. He developed one of the earliest profit-sharing plans by promising soldiers a share of any bounty achieved. When Napoleon defeated Italians in what is now the Piedmont region, he demanded gold and silver from the defeated foe. Morale soared when Napoleon then shared this with his troops.

Despite an explosion of interest in teams and team compensation, many of the reports from the front lines are not encouraging.[39] Companies report that they generally are not satisfied with the way their team compensation systems work. Failures of team incentive schemes can be attributed to at least five causes.[40] First, one of the problems with team compensation is that teams come in many varieties. There are full-time teams (work group organized as a team). There are part-time teams that cut across functional departments (experts from different departments pulled together to improve customer relations). There are even full-time teams that are temporary (e.g., cross-functional teams pulled together to help ease the transition into a partnership or joint venture).

With so many varieties of teams, it's hard to argue for one consistent type of compensation plan. Unfortunately, we still seem to be at the stage of trying to find the one best way. Maybe the answer is to look at different compensation approaches for different types of teams. Perhaps the best illustration of this differential approach for different teams comes from Xerox.

Xerox has used a **gainsharing plan** that pays off for units defined at a broader level than a typical team, usually at the level of a plant/facility or strategic business unit. For smaller teams, primarily intact work teams (e.g., all people in a department or function), there are group rewards based on supervisory judgments of performance. Units that opt to have their performance judged as teams (it is also possible to declare that a unit wouldn't be fairly judged if team measures were used) have managers who judge the amount to be allocated to each team based on the team's specific performance results. For new teams, the manager might also decide how much of the total will go to each individual on the team. More mature teams do individual allocations on their own. In Xerox's experience, these teams start out allocating equal shares, but as they evolve the teams allocate based on each worker's performance. Out of about 2,000 work teams worldwide at Xerox, perhaps 100 have evolved to this level of sophistication. For problem-solving teams and other temporary teams, Xerox has a reward component called the Xerox Achievement Award. Teams must be nominated for exceptional performance. A committee decides which teams meet a set of predetermined absolute standards. Even contributors outside the core team can share in the award. If nominated by team members, extended members who provide crucial added value are given cash bonuses equal to those of team members.

A second problem with rewarding teams is called the "level problem" or "line-of-sight" problem. (See Expectancy Theory in **Chapter 9**.) If we define teams at the very broad level–the whole organization being an extreme example–much of the motivational impact of incentives can be lost. As a member of a 1,000-person team, I'm unlikely to be at all convinced that my extra effort will significantly affect our team's overall performance. Why, then, should I try hard? Conversely, if we let teams get too small, other problems arise. TRW found that small work teams competing for a fixed piece of incentive awards tend to gravitate to behaviors that are clearly unhealthy for overall corporate success. Teams hoard star performers, refusing to allow transfers even for the greater good of the company. Teams are reluctant to take on new employees for fear that time lost to training will hurt the team–even when the added employees are essential to long-run success. Finally, bickering arises when awards are given. Because teams have different performance objectives, it is difficult to equalize for difficulty when assigning rewards. Inevitably, complaints arise.[41]

The last three major problems with team compensation involve the three Cs: *complexity, control,* and *communications.* Some plans are simply too complex. Xerox's Houston facility had a gain-sharing plan for teams that required understanding a three-dimensional performance matrix. Employees (and these authors!) threw their hands up in dismay when they tried to understand the "easy-to-follow directions." In contrast, Xerox's San Diego unit has had great success with a simple program called "bet the boss." Employees come to the boss with a performance-saving idea and bet their hard effort against the boss's incentive that they can deliver. Such plans have a simplicity that encourages employee buy-in. With a good line of sight as it's called, employees can see a clear link between their effort and the rewards they receive.

The second C is control. Praxair, a worldwide provider of gases (including oxygen) extracted from the atmosphere, works hard to make sure all its team pay comes from performance measures under the control of the team. If mother nature ravages a construction site, causing delays and skyrocketing costs, workers aren't penalized with reduced team payouts. Such uncontrollable elements are factored into the process of setting performance standards. Indeed, experts assert that this ability to foretell sources of problems and adjust for them is a key element in building a team pay plan.[42] Key to the control issue is the whole question of fairness. Are the rewards fair given our ability to produce results? Recent research suggests that this perception of fairness is crucial.[43] With it, employees feel that it is appropriate to monitor all members of the group–slackers beware! Without fairness, employees seem to have less sense of responsibility for the team's outcomes.[44]

The final C is a familiar factor in compensation successes and failures: communication. Team-based pay plans simply are not well communicated. Employees asked to explain their plans often flounder because more effort has been devoted to designing the plan than to deciding how to explain it. Conversely, the more transparent the plan, the more employees trust management and respond positively to the incentive effects of the plan.

Although there is much pessimism about team-based compensation, many companies still seek ways to reward groups of employees for their interdependent work efforts. Companies that do use team incentives typically set team performance standards based on productivity improvements (38% of plans), customer satisfaction measures (37%), financial performance (34%), or quality of goods and services (28%).[45] For example, Kraft Foods uses a combination of financial measures (e.g., income from operations and cash flow) combined with measures designed to gauge success in developing managers, building diversity, and adding to market share.[46] **Exhibit 10.12** summarizes some of these measures.

As **Exhibit 10.12** suggests, the range of performance measures used in organizations is extensive.[47] **Exhibit 10.13** describes the types of performance measures used in short-term incentive plans. Financial are the most common. **Exhibit 10.13** also indicates the strong reliance on a formula to determine payouts in such plans, with just under half of organizations relying on the formula alone, while the remainder introduce some subjectivity/judgment (discretion) to use in conjunction with the formula. Briefly, using a formula alone (Merrill Lynch is close to this approach) should provide maximum clarity and motivation. However, it also increases the risk that the payout will be obtained in a way not consistent with the organization's values and ethical principles. A discretionary component, to the degree it is done in a systematic and credible way, can help on this front.

Historically, financial measures have been the most widely used performance indicator for large group incentive plans. Increasingly, though, top executives express concern that these measures do a better job of communicating performance to stock analysts than to managers trying to figure out how to improve operating effectiveness.[48]

Whatever our thinking is about appropriate performance measures, the central point is still that we are now concerned about group performance. This presents both problems and opportunities. As **Exhibit 10.14** illustrates, we need to decide which type of group incentive plan best fits our objectives. Indeed, we should even

EXHIBIT 10.12 **A Sampling of Performance Measures**

Customer-Focused Measures	Financially Focused Measures
Time-to-Market Measures	**Value Creation**
• On-time delivery	• Revenue growth
• Cycle time	• Resource yields
• New product introductions	• Profit margins
	• Economic value added
Customer Satisfaction Measures	**Shareholder Return**
• Market share	• Return on invested capital
• Customer satisfaction	• Return on sales/earnings
• Customer growth and retention	• Earnings per share
• Account penetration	• Growth in profitability
Capability-Focused Measures	**Internal Process-Focused Measures**
Human Resource Capabilities	**Resource Utilization**
• Employee satisfaction	• Budget-to-actual expenses
• Turnover rates	• Cost-allocation ratios
• Total recruitment costs	• Reliability/rework
• Rate of progress on developmental plans	• Accuracy/error rates
• Promotability index	• Safety rates
• Staffing mix/head-count ratio	
Other Asset Capabilities	**Change Effectiveness**
• Patents/copyrights/regulations	• Program implementation
• Distribution systems	• Teamwork effectiveness
• Technological capabilities	• Service/quality index

ask if an incentive plan is appropriate. Recent evidence, for example, suggests that firms high on business risk and those with uncertain outcomes are better off not having incentive plans at all–corporate performance is higher.[49]

Comparing Group and Individual Incentive Plans

In this era of heightened concern about productivity, we frequently are asked if setting up incentive plans really boosts performance. As we noted in **Chapter 9**, the answer is yes. And individual–rather than group–incentives win the productivity "medal." We also are asked, though, which is better in a specific situation–group or individual incentive plans. Often this is a misleading question. Individual incentives yield higher productivity gains, but group incentives often are right in situations where team coordination is the issue. One study found that changing from individual incentives to gain sharing resulted in a decrease in grievances and a fairly dramatic increase in product quality (defects per 1,000 products shipped declined from 20.93 to 2.31).[50]

As we noted in **Exhibit 10.14**, things like the type of task, the organizational commitment to teams, and the type of work environment may preclude one or the other type of incentive plan. **Exhibit 10.15** provides a guide for when to choose group or individual plans. When forced to choose the type of plan with greater productivity "pep," experts agree that individual incentive plans have better potential for–and probably better track records in–delivering higher productivity. Group plans suffer from what is called the *free-rider problem.* See if this sounds familiar: You are a team member on a school project and at least one person doesn't carry his or her share of the load. Yet, when it comes time to divide the rewards, they are typically shared equally. Problems like this caused AT&T to phase out many of its team reward packages. Top-performing employees quickly grew disenchanted with having to carry free riders. End result–turnover of the very group that is most costly to lose.

Research on free riders suggests that the problem can be lessened through use of good performance measurement techniques. Specifically, free riders have a harder time loafing when there are clear performance standards. Rather than being given instructions to "do your best," poorer performers who were asked to deliver specific levels of performance at a specific time actually showed the most performance improvement.[51]

EXHIBIT 10.13 Short-Term Incentive (Bonus) Performance Measures and Formula versus Discretion in Determining Payouts

	Percent of Companies Using
Performance Measure	
Financial (e.g., revenue, income)	93%
Individual (performance, goal achievement)	57%
Operational (e.g., customer satisfaction, safety, efficiency)	24%
Formula versus Discretion in Determining Payouts	
Combination of formula and discretion	54%
Formula (only)	42%

Source: WorldatWork and Deloitte Consulting LLP, *Incentive Pay Practices Survey: Publicly Traded Companies*, 2018.

EXHIBIT 10.14 **Types of Group Variable Pay Plans: Advantages and Disadvantages**

Plan Type	What Is It?	Advantages	Disadvantages	Why?
Cash profit sharing	• Award based on organizational profitability • Shares a percentage of profits (typically above a target level of profitability) • Usually an annual payout • Can be cash or deferred 401(k)	• Simple, easily understood • Low administrative costs	• Profit influenced by many factors beyond employee control • May be viewed as an entitlement • Limited motivational impact	• To educate employees about business operations • To foster teamwork or "one-for-all" environment
Stock ownership or options	• Award of stock shares or options	• Option awards have minimal impact on the financial statements of the company at the time they are granted • If properly communicated, can have powerful impact on employee behavior • Tax deferral to employee	• Indirect pay/performance link • Employees may be required to put up money to exercise grants	• To recruit top-quality employees when organization has highly uncertain future (i.e., start-ups, high-tech, or biotech industries) • To address employee retention concerns
Balanced scorecard	• Awards that combine financial and operating measures for organization, business unit, and/or individual performance • Award pool based on achieving performance targets • Multiple performance measures may include:	• Communicates organizational priorities	• Performance criteria may be met, but if financial targets are not met, there may be a reduced payout or no payout at all • Can be complex	• To focus employees on need to increase shareholder value • To focus employees on organization, division, and/or individual goals • To link payouts to a specific financial and/or operational target

Plan Type	What Is It?	Advantages	Disadvantages	Why?
	1. Nonfinancial/operating: quality improvements, productivity gains, customer service improvements 2. Financial: EPS, ROE, ROA, revenues			
Gainsharing	• Awards that share economic benefits of improved productivity, quality, or other measurable results • Focus on department unit, plant, or division results • Designed to capitalize on untapped knowledge of employees	• Clear performance–reward links • Productivity and quality improvements • Employee's knowledge of business increases • Fosters teamwork, cooperation	• Can be administratively complicated • Unintended effects, like drop-off in quality • Management must "open the books" • Payouts can occur even if company's financial performance is poor	• To support a major productivity/quality initiative (such as TQM or reengineering) • To foster teamwork environment • To reward employees for improvements in activities that they control
Team/group incentives	• Awards determined based on team/group performance goals or objectives • Payout can be more frequent than annual and can also extend beyond the life of the team • Payout may be uniform for team/group members	• Reinforces teamwork and team identity/results • Effective in stimulating ideas and problem-solving • Minimizes distinctions between team members • May better reflect how work is performed	• May be difficult to isolate impact of team • Not all employees can be placed on a team • Can be administratively complex • May create team competition • Difficult to set equitable targets for all teams	• To demonstrate an organizational commitment to teams • To reinforce the need for employees to work together to achieve results

Source: Adapted from Kenan S. Abosch, "Variable Pay: Do We Have the Basics in Place?," *Compensation and Benefits Review* 30, no. 4 (1+998), pp. 12–22.

Large Group Incentive Plans

When we get beyond a small work team and try to incentivize large groups, there are generally two types of plans. Gain-sharing plans use operating measures to gauge performance. Profit-sharing plans use financial measures.

Gain-sharing Plans

Our discussion of team-based compensation often mentioned gain-sharing plans as a common component. As the name suggests, employees share in the gains in these types of group incentive plans. With profit-sharing plans (surprise), the sharing involves some form of profits. Realistically, though, most employees feel as if little they can do will affect profits; that's something top-management decisions influence more. So gain sharing looks at cost components of the income ledger and identifies savings over which employees have more impact (e.g., reduced scrap, lower labor costs, reduced utility costs). It was just this type of thinking that led the United States Post Office to an annual cost avoidance of $497 million under its gain-sharing plan.[52] Other studies of gain-sharing report similar positive results. Indeed, the empirical evidence on gain sharing appears to be quite favorable.[53] One study of 1,600 employees in an auto parts company showed gain sharing over five years reduced labor, material, tool purchase, scrap, rework, and supply costs. The total savings were $15 million over the five-year period. There were also decreases in absenteeism (by 20%) and grievances (by 50%).[54]

In a particularly good study of a major retailer, stores with gain-sharing incentives had 4.9 percent higher sales, 3.4 percent higher customer satisfaction, and 4.4 percent higher profit than stores without the incentive plan. In our experience, these effects are pretty typical of gain-sharing plans—improvements in the 4 to 5

EXHIBIT 10.15 The Choice between Individual and Group Plans

Characteristic	Choose an Individual Plan when . . .	Choose a Group Plan when . . .
Performance measurement	Good measures of individual performance exist. Task accomplishment not dependent on performance of others.	Output is group collaborative effort. Individual contributions to output cannot be assessed.
Organizational adaptability	Individual performance standards are stable. Production methods and labor mix relatively constant.	Performance standards for individuals change to meet environmental pressures on relatively constant organizational objectives. Production methods and labor mix must adapt to meet changing pressures.
Organizational commitment	Commitment strongest to individual's profession or superior. Supervisor viewed as unbiased and performance standards readily apparent.	High commitment to organization built upon sound communication of organizational objectives and performance standards.
Union status	Nonunion; unions promote equal treatment. Competition between individuals inhibits "fraternal" spirit.	Union or nonunion; unions less opposed to plans that foster cohesiveness of bargaining unit and which distribute rewards evenly across group.

Source: WorldatWork and Vivien Consulting, "Private Company Incentive Pay Practices," January 2012.

percent range. Keep in mind, though, gain-sharing plans can lead to the sorting effect we talked about in **Chapter 9**. Good employees want to be rewarded for their individual effort and performance. Changes to group plans, like gain-sharing, can lead to turnover. Just ask AT&T. They found that very-high- and very-low-performing individuals had much higher turnover rates under gain-sharing than other employees.[55] The following issues are key elements in designing a gain-sharing plan:[56]

1. *Strength of reinforcement (and what performance metrics are and are not included in the plan):* What role should base pay assume relative to incentive pay? Incentive pay tends to encourage only those behaviors that are rewarded. For example, try returning an unwanted birthday present to a store that pays its sales force solely for new sales. Tasks carrying no rewards are only reluctantly performed (if at all).
2. *Productivity standards:* What standard will be used to calculate whether employees will receive an incentive payout? Almost all group incentive plans use a historical standard. A historical standard involves choice of a prior year's performance to use for comparison with current performance. But which baseline year should be used? If too good (or too bad) a comparison year is used, the standard will be too hard (or easy) to achieve, with obvious motivational and cost effects. One possible compromise is to use a moving average of several years (e.g., the average for the past five years, with the five-year block changing by one year on an annual basis).
   One of the major problems with historical standards is that changing environmental conditions can render a standard ineffective. For example, consider the ice cream company that based profit sharing on a financial measure that had been easily achieved the prior year. What they didn't expect was a dramatic increase in milk costs. It was clear by the third month of the fiscal year that the goal wasn't going to be met, and grumblings among employees were mounting. The targets were adjusted and ice cream makers rejoiced.[57] Such problems are particularly insidious during economic swings and for organizations facing volatile economic climates. Care must be taken to ensure that the link between performance and rewards is sustained. This means that environmental influences on performance, which are not controllable by plan participants, should be factored out when identifying incentive levels.
3. *Sharing the gains split between management and workers:* Part of the plan must address the relative cuts between management and workers of any profit or savings generated. This also includes discussion of whether an emergency reserve (gains withheld from distribution in case of future emergencies) will be established in advance of any sharing of profits.
4. *Scope of the formula:* Formulas can vary in the scope of inclusions for both the labor inputs in the numerator and the productivity outcomes in the denominator.[58] Recent innovations in gain-sharing plans largely address broadening the types of productivity standards considered appropriate. Given that organizations are complex and require more complex measures, performance measures have expanded beyond traditional financial measures. For example, with the push for greater quality management, we could measure retention of customers or some other measure of customer satisfaction. Similarly, other measures include delivery performance, safety, absenteeism, turnaround time, and number of suggestions submitted. Four specific examples are:[59]

Performance Measure	Goal	Monthly Incentive Bonus
Error/Damage rate	20 per 10,000 units	To be Determined
Customer Dissatisfaction	1 per 100,000 lbs	TBD
Productivity Measure	10,000 lb/month	TBD
Cost	.1 lb below quota	TBD

5. Great care must be exercised with such alternative measures, though, to ensure that the behaviors reinforced actually affect the desired bottom-line goal. Getting workers to expend more effort, for example, might not always be the desired behavior. Increased effort may bring unacceptable levels of accidents. It may be preferable to encourage cooperative planning behaviors that result in more efficient work.
6. *Perceived fairness of the formula:* One way to ensure the plan is perceived as fair is to let employees vote on whether implementation should go forward. This and union participation in program design are two elements in plan success.[60]
7. *Ease of administration:* Sophisticated plans with involved calculations of profits or costs can become too complex for existing company information systems. Increased complexities also require more effective communications and higher levels of trust among participants.
8. *Production variability:* One of the major sources of problems in group incentive plans is failure to set targets properly. At times, the problem can be traced to volatility in sales. Large swings in sales and profits, not due to any actions by workers, can cause both elation (in good times) and anger (in bad times). As stated above, a good plan ensures that environmental influences on performance, which are not controllable by plan participants, should be factored out when identifying incentive levels. The second author once worked with an ice cream producer that experienced huge unexpected increases in milk costs. End result? The original profit goal was unattainable. To their credit, the company adjusted the profit target to reflect the uncontrollable cost change. One alternative would be to set standards that are relative to industry performance. To the extent data are available, a company could trigger gain-sharing when performance exceeds some industry norm. The obvious advantage of this strategy is that economic and other external factors hit all firms in the industry equally hard. If our company performs better, relatively, it means we are doing something as employees to help achieve success.
9. *(Lack of) Line of Sight:* One study of a gain-sharing plan, when shared with management, caused them to be reluctant to implement the plan at other locations. Concerns were that because the size of the bonus pool was not under the control of workers (see *Production Variability*, just discussed), their motivation was reduced. Also reducing their motivation was the lack of any individual performance determinant of bonus payout (unlike say at Lincoln Electric) and the small size of the bonuses. There was a belief that the participation aspect of the gainsharing plan was useful. But, the incentive part, in its current form, was not seen as actually incentivizing better productivity or quality.[61]

Exhibit 10.16 illustrates three different formulas that can be used as the basis for gain-sharing plans. The numerator, or input factor, is always some labor cost variable, expressed in either dollars or actual hours worked; the denominator is some output measure such as net sales or value added. Each of the plans determines employees' incentives based on the difference between the current value of the ratio and the ratio in some agreed-upon base year. The more favorable the current ratio relative to the historical standard, the larger the incentive award.[62] The three primary types of gain-sharing plans, differentiated by their focus on either cost savings (the numerator of the equation) or some measure of revenue (the denominator of the equation), are noted below.

EXHIBIT 10.16 **Three Gain-Sharing Formulas**

	Scanlon Plan (Single Ratio Volume)	Rucker Plan	Improshare
Numerator of ratio (input factor)	Payroll costs	Labor cost	Actual hours worked
Denominator of ratio (output factor)	Net sales (plus or minus inventories)	Value added	Total standard value hours

Scanlon Plan

Scanlon plans are designed to lower labor costs without lowering the level of a firm's activity. Incentives are derived as a function of the ratio between labor costs and **sales value of production (SVOP).**[63] The SVOP includes sales revenue and the value of goods in inventory. To understand how these two figures are used to derive incentives under a Scanlon plan, see **Exhibit 10.17**.

In practice, the $50,000 bonus in **Exhibit 10.17** is not all distributed to the workforce. Rather, 25 percent is distributed to the company, 75 percent of the remainder is distributed as bonuses, and the other 25 percent is withheld and placed in an emergency fund to reimburse the company for any future months when a "negative bonus" is earned (i.e., when the actual wage bill is greater than the allowable wage bill). The excess remaining in the emergency pool is distributed to workers at the end of the year.

To look at the impact of Scanlon plans, consider the retail chain that adopted a Scanlon plan in six of its stores and compared results against six control stores chosen for their similarity.[64] Presence of a Scanlon plan led to stores having higher customer satisfaction, higher sales, and lower turnover.

e-Compensation

HR Guide provides information about gain-sharing plans, including critiques of plans and statistical studies. The website is at *http://www.hr-guide.com/data/G443.htm*

Rucker Plan

The **Rucker plan** involves a somewhat more complex formula than a Scanlon plan for determining worker incentive bonuses. Essentially, a ratio is calculated that expresses the value of production required for each dollar of total wage bill. Consider the following illustration:[65]

1. Assume accounting records show that the company expended $.60 worth of electricity, materials, supplies, and so on, to produce $1.00 worth of product. The value added is $.40 for each $1.00 of sales value. Assume also that 45 percent of the value added was attributable to labor; a productivity ratio (PR) can be allocated from the formula in item 2.

EXHIBIT 10.17 **Examples of a Scanlon Plan**

2010 Data (base year) for Alton, Ltd.		
Sales value of production (SVOP)	=	$10,000,000
Total wage bill	=	$ 4,000,000
Total wage bill/SVOP	=	$ 4,000,000/10,000,00-0 = .40 = 40%
Operating Month, March 2012		
SVOP	=	$950,000
Allowable wage bill	=	.40 ($950,000) = $380,000
Actual wage bill (August)	=	$330,000
Savings	=	$ 50,000
50,000 available for distribution as a bonus.		

2. *PR* (labor) × .40 × .45 = 1.00. Solving yields *PR* = 5.56.
3. If the wage bill equals $100,000, the *expected* production value is the wage bill ($100,000) × *PR* (5.56) = $555,556.
4. If *actual* production value equals $650,000, then the savings (actual production value minus expected production value) is $94,444.
5. Since the labor contribution to value added is 45 percent, the bonus to the workforce should be .45 × $94,444 = $42,500.
6. The savings are distributed as an incentive bonus according to a formula similar to the Scanlon formula–75 percent of the bonus is distributed to workers immediately and 25 percent is kept as an emergency fund to cover poor months. Any excess in the emergency fund at the end of the year is then distributed to workers.

Implementation of the Scanlon/Rucker Plans

Two major components are vital to the implementation and success of a Rucker or Scanlon plan: (1) a productivity norm and (2) effective worker committees. Development of a productivity norm requires both effective measurement of base-year data and acceptance by workers and management of this standard for calculating bonus incentives. Effective measurement requires that an organization keep extensive records of historical cost relationships and make them available to workers or union representatives to verify cost accounting figures. Acceptance of these figures, assuming they are accurate, requires that the organization choose a base-year that is neither a "boom" nor a "bust" year. The logic is apparent. A boom year would reduce opportunities for workers to collect bonus incentives. A bust-year would lead to excessive bonus costs for the firm. The base-year chosen also should be fairly recent, allaying worker fears that changes in technology or other factors would make the base-year unrepresentative of a given operational year.

The second ingredient of Scanlon/Rucker plans is a series of worker committees (also known as productivity committees or bonus committees). The primary function of these committees is to evaluate employee and management suggestions for ways to improve productivity and/or cut costs. Operating on a plantwide basis in smaller firms, or a departmental basis in larger firms, these committees have been highly successful in eliciting suggestions from employees. It is not uncommon for the suggestion rate to be above that found in companies with standard suggestion incentive plans.[66]

Scanlon/Rucker plans foster this type of climate, and that is perhaps the most vital element of their success. Numerous authorities have pointed out that these plans have the best chance for success in companies with competent supervision, cooperative union-management attitudes, strong top-management interest and participation in the development of the program, and management open to criticism and willing to discuss different operating strategies.[67] It is beyond the scope of this discussion to outline specific strategies adopted by companies to achieve this climate, but the key element is a belief that workers should play a vital role in the decision-making process.

Similarities and Contrasts Between Scanlon and Rucker Plans

Scanlon and Rucker plans differ from individual incentive plans in their primary focus. Individual incentive plans focus primarily on using wage incentives to motivate higher performance through increased effort. While this is certainly a goal of the Scanlon/Rucker plans, it is not the major focus of attention. Rather, given that increased output is a function of group effort, more attention is focused on organizational behavior variables. The key is to promote faster, more intelligent, and more acceptable decisions through participation.

This participation is won by developing a group unity in achieving cost savings–a goal that is not stressed, and is often stymied, in individual incentive plans.

Even though Scanlon and Rucker plans share this common attention to groups and committees through participation as a linking pin, there are two important differences between the two plans. First, Rucker plans tie incentives to a wide variety of savings, not just the labor savings focused on in Scanlon plans.[68] Second, this greater flexibility may help explain why Rucker plans are more amenable to linkages with individual incentive plans.

Improshare

Improshare (Improved Productivity through Sharing) is a gain-sharing plan that has proved easy to administer and to communicate.[69] First, a standard is developed that identifies the expected hours required to produce an acceptable level of output. This standard comes either from time-and-motion studies conducted by industrial engineers or from a base-period measurement of the performance factor. Any savings arising from production of the agreed-upon output in fewer than the expected hours is shared by the firm and by the workers.[70] For example, if 100 workers can produce 50,000 units over 50 weeks, this translates into 200,000 hours (40 hours × 50 weeks) for 50,000 units, or 4 hours per unit. If we implement an Improshare plan, any gains resulting in less than 4 hours per unit are shared 50–50 between employees and management (wages times number of hours saved).[71]

One survey of 104 companies with an Improshare plan found a mean increase in productivity during the first year of 12.5 percent.[72] By the third year the productivity gain rose to 22 percent. A significant portion of this productivity gain was traced to reduced defect rates and downtime (e.g., repair time).

Profit-Sharing Plans

Profit sharing is also positively related to productivity and productivity growth. One study of 6 million employees across 275 firms found 3.5–5.0 percent higher profits in companies that used profit sharing than in those that didn't.[73] Productivity was much higher in plans where payouts were that year than in plans where payment was deferred (as in profit sharing used for a pension program). Also, these plans worked much better in smaller (less than 775 employees) companies. As always, careful design and implementation are keys to success.[74]

Even in companies that don't have profit-sharing plans, many variable pay plans still require a designated profit target to be met before any payouts occur. Our experience with chief executive officers is that they have a hard time giving employees extra compensation if the company isn't also profiting. Thus, many variable pay plans have some form of profit "trigger" linked to revenue growth or profit margins or some measure of shareholder return such as earnings per share or return on capital. Despite modestly positive results, profit sharing continues to be popular because the focus is on the measure that matters most to the most people: a predetermined index of profitability. When payoffs are linked to such measures, employees spend more time learning about financial measures and the business factors that influence them.

On the downside, most employees don't feel their jobs have a direct impact on profits. A small cog in a big wheel is difficult to motivate very well. For example, before the big crunch in the auto industry Ford Motor and GM gave profit-sharing checks of about $7,500, compared to $2,250 at Fiat-Chrysler.[75] You can bet the Chrysler employees wondered if their counterparts at Ford and GM were working more than three times as hard. If you guessed that they blamed the difference on bad management decisions, you're right on target.

The trend in recent variable-pay design is to combine the best of gainsharing and profit-sharing plans.[76] The company will specify a funding formula for any variable payout that is linked to some profit measure. As experts say, the plan must be self-funding. Dollars going to workers are generated by additional profits gained from operational efficiency. Along with having the financial incentive, employees feel they have a measure of control. For example, an airline might give an incentive for reductions in lost baggage, with the size of the payout dependent on hitting profit targets. Such a program combines the need for fiscal responsibility with the chance for workers to affect something they can control.

Earnings-at-Risk Plans

We probably shouldn't separate **earnings-at-risk plans** as a distinct category. In fact, any incentive plan could be an at-risk plan. Think of incentive plans as falling into one of two categories: success sharing or risk sharing. In success-sharing plans, employee base wages are constant and variable pay adds on during *successful years.* If the company does well, you receive a predetermined amount of variable pay. If the company does poorly, you simply forgo any variable pay–there is no reduction in your base pay, though. In a risk-sharing plan, base pay is reduced by some amount relative to the level that would be offered in a success-sharing plan. AmeriSteel's at-risk plan is typical of risk-sharing plans. Base pay was reduced 15 percent across the board in year 1. That 15 percent was replaced with a .5 percent increase in base pay for every 1 percent increase in productivity beyond 70 percent of the prior year's productivity. This figure would leave workers whole (no decline in base pay) if they only matched the prior year's productivity. Each additional percent improvement in productivity yielded a 1.5 percent increase in base wages. Everyone in AmeriSteel, from the CEO on down, is in this type of plan and the result has been an 8 percent improvement in productivity.[77]

Clearly, at-risk plans shift part of the risk of doing business from the company to the employee. The company hedges against the devastating effects of a bad year by mortgaging part of the profits that would have accrued during a good year. Not surprisingly, a key element of incentive design is to identify possible risks and incorporate design features that minimize them.[78] At-risk plans appear to be met with decreases in satisfaction with both pay in general and the process used to set pay.[79] In turn, this can result in higher turnover.

Group Incentive Plans: Advantages and Disadvantages

Clearly, group pay-for-performance plans are gaining popularity in today's team-based environment. Other factors play a role, though. One factor with intriguing implications suggests that group-based plans, particularly gain-sharing plans, cause organizations to evolve into learning organizations.[80] Apparently the suggestions employees are encouraged to make (how to do things better in the company) gradually evolve from first-order learning experiences of a more routine variety (maintenance of existing ways of doing things) into suggestions that exhibit second-order learning characteristics–suggestions that help the organization break out of existing patterns of behavior and explore different ways of thinking and behaving.[81]

Exhibit 10.18 outlines some of the general positive and negative features of group pay-for-performance plans.[82]

Group Incentive Plans: Examples

All incentive plans, as we noted earlier, can be described by common features:(1) the size of the group that participates in the plan, (2) the standard against which performance is compared, and (3) the payout schedule. **Exhibit 10.19** illustrates some of the more interesting components of plans for leading companies.

PAY-FOR-PERFORMANCE: LONG-TERM INCENTIVE PLANS

All of the individual and group plans we have discussed thus far focus on short time horizons for performance and payouts. Usually the time horizon is a year or less. Now we shift to variable pay plans where the time horizon is longer than a year. Such programs force executives to think long term and develop strategic plans that don't sacrifice tomorrow's riches for today's small gains.

EXHIBIT 10.18 **Group Incentive Plans: Advantages and Disadvantages**

Advantages

1. Positive impact on organization and individual performance of about 5 to 10 percent per year.
2. Easier to develop performance measures than it is for individual plans.
3. Signals that cooperation, both within and across groups, is a desired behavior.
4. Teamwork meets with enthusiastic support from most employees.
5. May increase participation of employees in decision-making process.

Disadvantages

1. Line-of-sight may be lessened, that is employees may find it more difficult to see how their individual performance affects their incentive payouts.
2. May lead to increased turnover among top individual performers who are discouraged because they must share with lesser contributors.
3. Increases compensation risk to employees because of lower income stability. May influence some applicants to apply for jobs in firms where base pay is a larger compensation component.

EXHIBIT 10.19 **Corporate Examples of Group Incentive Plans**

GE Information systems	A team-based incentive that also links to individual payouts. Team and individual performance goals are set. If the team hits its goals, the team members earn their incentive only if they also hit their individual goals. The team incentive is 12 to 15 percent of monthly base pay.
Corning Glass	A gain-sharing program (goal sharing) where 75 percent of the payout is based on unit objectives such as quality measures, customer satisfaction measures, and production targets. The remainder is based on Corning's return on equity.
3M	Operates with an earnings-at-risk plan. Base pay is fixed at 80 percent of market. Employees have a set of objectives to meet for pay to move to 100 percent of market. Additionally, there is a modest profit-sharing component.
DuPont Fibers	Earnings-at-risk plan where employees receive reduced pay increases over 5 years resulting in 6 percent lower base pay. If department meets annual profit goal, employees collect all 6 percent. Variable payout ranges from 0 (reach less than 80% of goal) to 19 percent (150% of goal).

Exhibit 10.20 shows different types of **long-term incentives** and their definitions. These plans are also grouped by the level of risk faced by employees having these incentives, as well as the expected rewards that might come from them.

Long-term incentives (LTIs) focus on performance beyond the one-year time line used as the cutoff for short-term incentive plans. Recent explosive growth in long-term plans appears to be spurred in part by a desire to motivate longer-term value creation.[83] The empirical evidence that stock ownership by management leads to better corporate performance varies by study.[84] There is some evidence, though, that stock ownership is likely to increase internal growth, rather than more rapid external diversification.[85]

All this talk about stock options neglects the biggest change in recent memory. As of June 2005 companies were required to report stock options as an expense.[86] Prior to this date, generally accepted accounting rules didn't require options to be reported as an overhead cost. They were (wrongly) viewed as a free good under old accounting rules.[87] Think about the executive issued 500,000 shares with a vesting period of five years (the shares can be bought in five years). After five years, the CEO can purchase the stock at the initial-offer price (if the market price is now lower than that, the stock option is said to be "underwater" and is not exercised).[88] If the executive bought the shares, they were typically issued from a pool of unissued shares. The

EXHIBIT 10.20 Long-Term Incentives and Their Risk/Reward Tradeoffs

Level One: Low Risk/Reward

1. *Time-based restricted stock:* An award of shares that actually are received only after the completion of a predefined service period. Employees who terminate employment before the restriction lapses must return their shares to the company.
2. *Performance-accelerated restricted stock:* Restricted stock granted only after attainment of specified performance objectives.
3. *Stock purchase plan:* Opportunity to buy shares of company stock either at prices below market price or with favorable financing.

Level Two: Medium Risk/Reward

4. *Time-vested stock option:* This is what most stock options are—the right to purchase stock at a specified price for a fixed time period.
5. *Performance-vested restricted stock:* This is a grant of stock to employees upon attainment of defined performance objective(s).
6. *Performance-accelerated stock option:* An option with a vesting schedule that can be shortened if specific performance criteria are met.

Level Three: High Risk/Reward

7. *Premium-priced stock option:* A stock option that has an exercise price about market value at the time of grant. This creates an incentive for employees to create value for the company, see the stock price rise, and thus be eligible to purchase the stock.
8. *Indexed stock option:* An option whose exercise price depends on what peer companies' experiences are with stock prices. If industry stock prices are generally rising, it would be difficult to attribute any similar rise in specific improvements beyond general industry improvement.
9. *Performance-vested stock option:* One that vests only upon the attainment of a predetermined performance objective.

money paid by the CEO was treated like money paid by any investor . . . found money? Not really. Options diluted the per-share earnings because they increase the denominator applied to net profits used to figure per-share earnings. (OK, OK we promise, no more accounting terms!) Cases like Enron, which did not expense options, gave an unrealistic picture of profits and helped to elevate stock prices. The publicity from this case increased pressure to change accounting rules and led to the changes that began affecting most companies in 2006.[89] Microsoft asserts that it will still continue to offer stock options to rank and file employees, but insiders admit that the modest movement in their stock prices have lessened the appeal of this vehicle for retaining top talent. No more instant multi-millionaires like the roaring 90s.[90] As a direct result of the changing rules, some companies, like Coca Cola, Dell Inc., Aetna Inc., Pfizer Inc., McDonald's Corp., Time Warner Inc., ExxonMobil Corp., and Microsoft Corp either stopped granting options or only grant them to executives.[91]

Employee Stock Ownership Plans (ESOPs)

Employee Stock Ownership Plans (ESOPs) are the most common form of employee ownership, with the number of employees in such plans increasing from 4 million in 1980 to about 14 million more recently in the United States. These 14 million are employed in over 6,000 companies and these ESOPs have assets of over $1.3 trillion in stock?[92] Including (see below) non-ESOP stock option, stock purchase, and stock-based retirement plans, it is estimated that about 28 million U.S. employees own some portion of the companies for which they work, controlling about 8 percent of U.S. corporate equity.

ESOPs specifically raise a number of unique issues. On the negative side, they can carry significant risk for employees. An ESOP must, by law, invest at least 51 percent of assets in its company's stock, resulting in less diversification of investment risk (in some cases, no diversification). Consequently, when employees buy out companies in poor financial condition to save their jobs, or when the ESOP is used to fund pensions, employees risk serious financial difficulties if the company does poorly.[93] This is not just a concern for employees, because, as agency theory suggests, employees may require higher pay to offset increased risks of this sort.

ESOPs can be attractive to organizations because they have tax and financing advantages and can serve as a takeover defense (under the assumption that employee owners will be "friendly" to management). ESOPs give employees the right to vote their securities (if registered on a national exchange).[94] As such, some degree of participation in a select number of decisions is mandatory, but overall participation in decision making appears to vary significantly across organizations with ESOPs. Overall, early research did not find much of an impact of ESOP use on productivity or profit on average.[95] A broad and more recent review using meta-analysis finds a small, positive relationship of employee ownership with firm performance.[96] Some studies suggest that the positive effects of ownership are larger in cases where employees have greater participation,[97] perhaps because the "employee–owner comes to psychologically experience his/her ownership in the organization and/or feel a norm of social exchange/reciprocity to contribute more."[98] More broadly, it has been argued that if more firms would combine ESOPs with high goal setting, improved employee communication with management, and greater participation in decision making by employees, ESOPs would have more positive results.[99] Another potential alignment issue concerns vertical pay dispersion. Some research indicates that higher vertical pay dispersion reduces the positive effect of employee ownership on productivity that was observed. The authors speculated that using stock ownership to encourage a feeling of all being owners and a feeling of everyone working together may be undermined if large top to bottom pay differentials seem to indicate otherwise.[100] Finally, we note that in Japan, most companies listed on Japanese stock markets have an ESOP, and these companies appear to have higher average productivity than non-ESOP companies.[101]

Performance Plans (Performance Share and Performance Unit)

Performance plans typically feature corporate performance objectives for a time three years in the future. They are driven by financial earnings or return measures, and they pay out for meeting or exceeding specific goals.

Broad-Based Stock Plans (BBSPs)

BBSPs are awards in the form of stock grants or stock option grants available to employees broadly, not just select groups (e.g., top executives). The company gives employees shares of stock (or allows them to purchase stock at a discount) or options over a designated time period. The potential strength of BBSPs is to better align the interests of people at all levels in the organization toward the same objectives.[102] Depending on the way they are distributed to employees, they can either reinforce a strong emphasis on performance (performance culture) or inspire greater commitment and retention (ownership culture) of employees. There is evidence that the incentive effect of BBSPs is relatively small and declines as the number of employees included grows. The smaller size of the effect in larger plans is explained by the free rider effect–"I can coast and get the same size benefit as others, and not get caught!"[103] The hope, of course, in agency theory terms, is to align interests of managers and employees so they think like owners. Examples of companies with BBSPs include Cisco Systems, Salesforce, Intuit, Cheesecake Factory, Adobe Systems, Publix, and Accenture. All of these companies (except Cheesecake Factory) also have employee stock purchase plans. Other companies with the latter type of plan include CarMax, Capital One, Edward Jones, Box, AbbVie, and Delta Airlines.[104] These plans typically allow employees to purchase the stock at a discount, encouraging them to take on ownership and hopefully then think more like owners.

The form of BBSP used at Starbucks ("Bean Stock") is a grant of restricted stock units (RSUs).[105] The "restricted" part means that you must remain employed at Starbucks to actually take ownership ("vesting" occurs) of the stock units. After one year of continuous employment with Starbucks, one-half of the grant vests. The other half vests after two years of continuous employment. Starbucks gives an example of an employee ("partner") receiving RSUs worth $500 (in a year). If the closing Starbucks stock price on the grant date is $52, then the employee would have $500 divided by $52 = 9.6 RSUs. If the Starbucks stock price subsequently goes up to $62, then the value of the RSUs would go to $62 × 9.6 = $595. Over the last 5 years, the Starbucks stock price has roughly doubled. If (and, of course, nobody really knows) that were to happen going forward, then, the value of the RSUs (granted in that one year) would go to $104 × 9.6 = $998. This program exists to send the clear signal that all employees, especially the two-thirds who are part-timers, are business partners. This effort to create a culture of ownership is viewed as the primary reason Starbucks has turnover that is only a fraction of the usually high turnover in the retail industry.

Combination Plans: Mixing Individual and Group

It's not uncommon for companies to use both individual and group incentives. The goal is to both motivate individual behavior and to insure that employees work together, where needed, to promote team and corporate goals. These combination programs start with standard individual (e.g., performance appraisal, quantity of output) and group measures (e.g., profit, operating income). Variable pay level depends on how well individuals perform and how well the company (or division/strategic business unit) does on its macro (e.g., profit) measures. A typical plan might call for a 75–25 split. Seventy-five percent of the payout is based on how well the individual worker does, the other portion is dependent on corporate performance. An alternative might be a completely **self-funding plan,** often favored by CEOs who don't like to make payouts when the company loses money. These plans specify that payouts only occur after the company reaches a certain profit target. Then variable payouts for individual, team, and company performance are triggered.

DOES VARIABLE PAY (SHORT-TERM AND LONG-TERM INCENTIVES) IMPROVE PERFORMANCE RESULTS? THE GENERAL EVIDENCE

As the evidence pointed out in **Chapter 9**, variable pay-for-performance plans (short-term incentives and long-term incentives) seem to have a positive impact on performance if designed well. Notice that we have qualified our statement that variable-pay plans can be effective *if they are designed well.* Too often though the plans have too small a payout for the work expected, unattainable (or too easy) goals, outdated or inaccurate metrics, or even too many metrics making it hard to determine what is important. A quite different problem is that the payouts are quite large for high performance, but the behaviors taken to achieve those particular aspects of performance cause major problems. As such, incentive pay plans are sometimes described as high return, but high-risk plans. When they go wrong, they go wrong in a big way. In the preceding sections, we have further addressed issues in design and the impacts they can have.

Your Turn — Pay at Delta and American Airlines

Exhibit 10.21, Panel A indicates that pilot pay is similar at Delta and American Airlines. Panel B, however, indicates that profit sharing (here, for all employees, including pilots) is another story. Profit-sharing payouts for employees at Delta are about 12x those at American on average. One reason for the difference is different profits. However, the formulas are also very different. American's plan pays out 5 percent of pre-tax earnings. In contrast, Delta's plan pays out 10 percent of pre-tax earnings 20 percent of pre-tax earnings above $2.5 billion. Just focusing on pilots, given the plan descriptions above, pilots at Delta would regularly receive anywhere from 2 to 4 times larger of a profit-sharing payout than pilots at American having the same salary, even if the two airlines were equally profitable.

Not surprisingly, American pilots and other employees have noticed the difference. American is now proposing a profit sharing plan identical to that of Delta.

1. Take a look at the American Customer Satisfaction Index for the airline industry for 2019 and 2020 at: https://www.theacsi.org/index.php?option=com_content&view=article&id=147&catid=&Itemid=212&i=Airlines. Is there any correlation between customer satisfaction and profit sharing? (You should answer "yes" because Delta and Southwest are highest, United and American lowest.) Why do you think that might be the case? For your consideration, note that Joseph Blasi, Director of Rutgers University's Institute for the Study of Employee Ownership and Profit Sharing states that profit sharing "helps companies keep employees invested in making a profit," Blasi said. "When they are getting some of the profits, employees are more motivated to work toward efficiencies and solving customer service problems." What do you think? Also, does agency theory apply here?

2. Any idea why American has a less lucrative profit-sharing plan? Is it possible that the pilots at American were traditionally more focused on negotiating higher base salaries, which do not fluctuate (unlike profit sharing)? Above, American was said to be "proposing a profit sharing plan identical to that of Delta." What will American want in return? Again, how would agency theory apply here?

3. Delta's profit sharing payout in 2020 was zero. Why? Is this the way a "variable pay" plan like profit sharing is supposed to work?

EXHIBIT 10.21 **Pay in the Airline Industry**

Part A. Pilot Hourly Pay by Plane Type and by Pilot Years of Experience

	Plane Type	
	Boeing 737	Airbus 320
American		
12 years experience	$278	$278
2 years experience	$257	$257
Delta		
12 years experience	$284	$266
2 years experience	$263	$274

Part B. Profit-Sharing Payments by Airlines (per employee)

Delta	$20,091
Southwest	$11,190
United	$ 6,191
American	$ 1,638

Source: Airline Pilot Central. https://www.airlinepilotcentral.com/airlines/legacy/delta_air_lines and https://www.airlinepilotcentral.com/airlines/legacy/american_airlines. Jeanne Sahadi, "Delta Gave Its Employees 2 Months of Extra Pay. Here's Why That's Good Business," January 21, 2020; Kyle Arnold, "American Airlines is Transforming the Way It Shares Profits with Employees: The Fort Worth-based Airline's New Proposal to Mechanics Could Match Profit Sharing at Rival Delta," *Dallas Morning News*, February 7, 2020; Kelly Yamanouchi, "Delta Pays Bonuses to Managers; No Profit Sharing Payouts for Workers: The Company Says Upper-Level Managers Had Bigger Cuts in Total Compensation, Since a Greater Share of Their Pay is At Risk and Dependent on the Company's Performance," *The Atlanta Journal- The Atlanta Journal-Constitution*, March 1, 2021.

Summary

Pay-for-performance plans can work. But as this chapter demonstrates, the design and effective administration of these plans is key to their success. Having a good idea is not enough. The good idea must be followed up by sound practices that recognize rewards can, if used properly, shape employee behavior.

Review Questions

1. As VP of HR at Pilsner Roofing, the eleventh largest roofing company in the world, you are experiencing turnover problems with the employees who actually install roofs (roofers). General Manager Roy Cranston has asked you to fix the problem. While your primary emphasis might be on having a competitive base pay, you need to decide if there is anything you can do in the incentive department. Before you can make this decision, what information would you like about (a) pay (base + incentive) at major competitors, (b) the nature of the turnover, and (c) next year's labor budget?

2. How is an earnings-at-risk plan different from an ordinary gain-sharing or profit-sharing plan? How might earnings-at-risk plans affect attraction and retention of employees? How does whether the economy is growing or contracting affect the viability of earnings-at-risk plans?
3. You own Falzer's Tool Coating Company, a high-tech firm specializing in the coating of cutting tools (e.g., drill bits, cutting blades) to provide longer life before resharpening is needed. You are concerned that the competition continues to develop new coating methods and new applications of coating in different industries. You want to create a work environment where employees offer more new product ideas and suggest new industries where these ideas might be applied. What type of compensation plan will you recommend? What are some of the problems you need to be aware of?
4. Why do the new accounting standards make stock options less popular?
5. You are the teacher in a class where team projects account for 25 percent of course grades. Each student is assigned to a team and that team is responsible for all team assignments. Students come to you and complain bitterly about one of their members who does absolutely nothing. You know this will affect your teaching ratings if you don't do something about it. What should you do?

Endnotes

1. B. Gerhart, "Incentives and Pay for Performance in the Workplace," *Advances in Motivation Science* 4 (2017), pp. 91–140; original data from K. Abosch, "The Quiet Revolution of Variable Pay," *Compensation Focus* (June 2015).
2. Kenan S. Abosch, "Rationalizing Variable Pay Plans," in *The Compensation Handbook,* ed. Lance A. Berger and Dorothy Berger (New York: McGraw-Hill, 2008), pp. 227–238.
3. Jeffrey Arthur and Lynda Aiman-Smith, "Gainsharing and Organizational Learning: An Analysis of Employee Suggestions Over Time," *Academy of Management Journal* 44(4), 2001, pp. 737–754.
4. WorldatWork (in cooperation with AonHewitt). Compensation Programs and Practices Survey. August 2016.
5. Gerhart, B. (2017). "Incentives and Pay for Performance in the Workplace." In *Advances in Motivation Science* (Vol. 4, pp. 91–140), Elsevier; Gerhart, B., & Milkovich, G. T. (1989). "Salaries, salary growth, and promotions of men and women in a large, private firm." In R. Michael, H. Hartmann, & B. O'Farrell (Eds.), *Pay equity: Empirical inquiries* (pp. 23–43), Washington, DC: National Academy Press; Trevor, C. O., Gerhart, B., & Boudreau, J. W. (1997). "Voluntary turnover and job performance: Curvilinearity and the moderating influences of salary growth and promotions." *Journal of Applied Psychology* 82, 44e61.WorldatWork. WorldatWork. (2016). Promotion guidelines." Scottsdale, AZ.
6. Jerry M. Newman and Daniel J. Fisher, "Strategic Impact Merit Pay," *Compensation and Benefits Review* (July/August 1992), pp. 38–45.
7. High performance ratings are almost always statistically related to high merit increases, and the reverse holds too. Removal of merit pay appears to result in lower subsequent performance, as well as lower satisfaction among top performers. Departments and strategic business units with better merit pay programs have higher subsequent performance. See Robert Heneman, *Merit Pay: Linking Pay Increases to Performance Ratings* (Reading, MA: Addison-Wesley, 1992); and R. E. Kopelman and L. Reinharth, "Research Results: The Effect of Merit-Pay Practices on White Collar Performance," *Compensation Review* 14(4), 1982, pp. 30–40.
8. B. Gerhart, "Incentives and Pay for Performance in the Workplace," *Advances in Motivation Science* 4 (2017), pp. 91–14; B. Gerhart, S. L. Rynes, and I. S. Fulmer, "Pay and Performance: Individuals, Groups, and Executives," *Academy of Management Annals* 3(1) (2009), pp. 251–315.

9. B. Gerhart and M. Fang, "Pay for (Individual) Performance: Issues, Claims, Evidence and the Role of Sorting Effects," *Human Resource Management Review* 24(1), 41–52; S. L. Rynes, B. Gerhart, and L. Parks, "Personnel Psychology: Performance Evaluation and Pay for Performance," *Annual Review of Psychology* 56 (2005), 571–600.

10. Hanover Research Institute, "Best Practices in Teacher Pay for Performance Models." December 2012, Hanover Research institute; S. Dillon, "Long Reviled, Merit Pay Gains Among Teachers," *The New York Times,* June 18, 2007, www.NYTimes.com, accessed June 29, 2009.

11. B. Keller, "Cincinnati Teachers Rebuff Performance Pay," *Education Week*, May 29, 2002.

12. M. Podgursky and M. Springer, "Teacher Performance Pay: A Review," *The National Center for Performance Incentives*, November 2006.

13. G. Toppo, "Teachers Take Test Scores to Bank," *USA Today,* October 22, 2008, p. A1.

14. www.huffingtonpost.com/2011/07/18/merit-based-teacher-bonus_n_901679.html visited May 2, 2012.

15. A. Ripley, "The $4 Million Teacher," *Wall Street Journal*, August 3, 2013, p. C1.

16. M. Hellerman and J. Kochanski, "Merit Pay," in *The Compensation Handbook,* 5th ed., Lance A. Berger and Dorothy Berger, eds. (New York: McGraw-Hill, 2008), pp. 85–93; D. Eskew and R. L. Heneman, "A Survey of Merit Pay Plan Effectiveness: End of the Line for Merit Pay or Hope for Improvement," in *Strategic Reward Management,* R. L. Heneman, ed. (Greenwich, CT: Information Age Publishing, 2002).

17. A. J. Nyberg, J. R. Pieper, and C. O. Trevor, "Pay-for-Performance's Effect on Future Employee Performance: Integrating Psychological and Economic Principles toward a Contingency Perspective," *Journal of Management* 42, no. 7 (2016), pp. 1753–1783; D. P. Schwab and C. A. Olson, "Merit Pay Practices: Implications for Pay-Performance Relationships," *Industrial and Labor Relations Review* 43(3), 1990, p. 237.

18. IOMA, *2002 Incentive Pay Programs and Results* (Newark NJ: Institute of Management and Administration, May 2002), p. 13.

19. UCSF School of Pharmacy, Office of the Associate Dean for Administration Personnel Unit, "Spot Awards," http://pharmacy.ucsf.edu/personnel/spot.html, July 6, 2009.

20. E. A. Locke, D. B. Feren, V. M. McCaleb, et al., "The Relative Effectiveness of Four Methods of Motivating Employee Performance," in *Changes in Working Life,* K. D. Duncan, M. M. Gruenberg, and D. Wallis, eds. (New York: Wiley, 1980), pp. 363–388; R. A. Guzzo, R. D. Jette, and R. A. Katzell, "The Effects of Psychologically Based Intervention Programs on Worker Productivity: A Meta-Analysis," *Personnel Psychology* 38 (1985), pp. 275–291.

21. Thomas Patten, *Pay, Employee Compensation, and Incentive Plans* (New York: Macmillan, 1977).

22. A. J. Barkume and T. G. Moehrle, "The Role of Incentive Pay in the Volatility of the Employment Cost Index: Compensation and Working Conditions," Summer 2001, pp. 13–18; B. Gerhart, "Incentives and Pay for Performance in the Workplace," *Advances in Motivation Science* 4 (2017), pp. 91–140.

23. For example, a study of thousands of physicians found that the higher the fee (and these change over time) for a health care service (e.g., a type of surgery), the more often that service was performed/delivered. According to the author (p. 908): "The results suggest that professionals do pay attention to opportunities for financial gain and that self-interest is an important motivator of professional work. While this finding may seem somewhat obvious, it contradicts existing theories of professions which tend to downplay the role of self-interest in shaping professionals' behaviors." Jillian Crown. Financial Incentives and Professionals' Work Tasks: The Moderating Effects of Jurisdictional Dominance and Prominence. *Organization Science*, 2020, 31, 897–908.

24. Kim, J. H., Gerhart, B., & Fang, M. (2021). Do Financial Incentives Help or Harm Performance in Interesting Tasks? *Journal of Applied Psychology*, forthcoming. D. G. Jenkins Jr., A. Mitra, N. Gupta, and J. D. Shaw, "Are Financial Incentives Related to Performance? A Meta-Analytic Review of Empirical Research," *Journal of Applied Psychology* 83 (1998), pp. 777–787; E. A. Locke, D. B. Feren, V. M. McCaleb, K. N. Shaw, and A. T. Denny, "The Relative Effectiveness of Four Methods of Motivating Employee Performance," In *Changes in Working Life,* ed. K. D. Duncan, M. M. Gruenberg, and D. Wallis, pp. 363-388 (New York: Wiley, 1980); R. A. Guzzo, R. D. Jette, and R. A. Katzell, "The Effects of Psychologically Based Intervention Programs on Worker Productivity: A Meta-Analysis," *Personnel Psychology* 38 (1985), pp. 275–291. For a review, see B. Gerhart, "Incentives and Pay for Performance in the Workplace," *Advances in Motivation Science* 4 (2017), pp. 91–140.

25. B. Gerhart, "Incentives and Pay for Performance in the Workplace," *Advances in Motivation Science* 4 (2017), pp. 91–140; B. Gerhart, C. O. Trevor, and M. E. Graham, "New Directions in Compensation Research: Synergies, Risk and Survival," in *Research in Personnel and Human Resource Management,* ed. G. R. Ferris (Bingley: Emerald, 1996); Uri Gneezy, Stephan Meier, and Pedro Rey-Biel, "When and Why Incentives (Don't) Work to Modify Behavior," *Journal of Economic Perspectives* 25, no. 4 (2011), pp. 191–210; Uri Gneezy and Aldo Rustichini, "Pay Enough or Don't Pay At All," *Quarterly Journal of Economics* 115, no. 3 (2000), pp. 791–810.

26. James R. Hagerty and Bob Tita, "Workers Say Train Repairs Were Often Bogus," *Wall Street Journal*, July 21, 2014, p. B1.

27. Thomas Wilson, "Is It Time to Eliminate the Piece Rate Incentive System?" *Compensation and Benefits Review,* March–April 1992, pp. 43–49.

28. Christopher W. Cabrera, *Game the Plan* (Austin, TX: River Grove Books, 2014).

29. www.huffingtonpost.com/2011/07/18/merit-based-teacher-bonus_n_901679.html; Hamsa Bastani, Joel Goh, and Mohsen Bayati, "Evidence of Upcoding in Pay-for-Performance Programs," *Management Science* (2018).

30. Wright, P. M., George, J. M., Farnsworth, S. R., & McMahan, G. C. (1993). Productivity and extra-role behavior: The effects of goals and incentives on spontaneous helping. *Journal of Applied psychology*, 78(3), 374.

31. P. Milgrom and J. Roberts. (1988). *Economics, organization & management*. Englewood Cliffs, NJ: Prentice Hall. p. 228.

32. He, W., Li, S. L., Feng, J., Zhang, G., & Sturman, M. C. (2021). When does pay for performance motivate employee helping behavior? The contextual influence of performance subjectivity. *Academy of Management Journal*, 64(1), 293–326.

33. A study, for example, found that in using a monthly incentive/commission with health care providers, performance was better if an occasional exception was made to prevent providers' income from dropping as much as the formula would determine in months when their sales were low. M. Maltarich, A. J. Nyberg, G. Reilly, D. Abdulsalam, and M. Martin, "Pay-for-Performance, Sometimes: An Interdisciplinary Approach to Integrating Economic Rationality with Psychological Emotion to Predict Individual Performance," *Academy of Management Journal*, 60 (2017), pp. 2155–2174; See also: Takahashi, S., Owan, H., Tsuru, T., & Uehara, K. (2021). Multitasking Incentives and the Informative Value of Subjective Performance Evaluations. *ILR Review*, 74(2), 511–543.

34. Thomas Beaton. "86% of Employers Use Financial Incentives in Wellness Programs," Health Payer Intelligence, May 7, 2018; Lauren Weber, "A health check for wellness programs." *Wall Street Journal,* October 8, 2014, B1.

35. Christopher W. Cabrera, *Game the Plan* (Austin, TX: River Grove Books, 2014). Daniel Eisenberg, "Where People Are Never Let Go," *Time,* June 18, 2001, p. 40; Kenneth Chilton, "Lincoln Electric's Incentive System: A Reservoir of Trust," *Compensation and Benefits Review,* November–December 1994, pp. 29–34.
36. Christopher W. Cabrera, *Game the Plan* (Austin, TX: River Grove Books, 2014).
37. J. Katzenbach and D. Smith, *The Wisdom of Teams* (New York: HarperCollins, 1993).
38. C. W. Cabrera, *Game the Plan* (Austin, TX: River Grove Books, 2014); D. C. Jones, P. Kalmi, and A. Kauhanen, "Teams, Incentive Pay, and Productive Efficiency: Evidence from a Food-Processing Plant," *Industrial & Labor Relations Review* 4, vol. 63 (2010), pp. 606–626.
39. B. Gerhart, S. L. Rynes, and I. S. Fulmer, "Pay and Performance: Individuals, Groups and Executives," *Academy of Management Annals*, 2009, 3(1), 251–315. K. D. Scott, J. Floyd, P. G. Benson, and J. W. Bishop, "The Impact of the Scanlon Plan on Retail Store Performance," *WorldatWork* 11(3), 2002, pp. 18–27.
40. Barry Gerhart, Sara L. Rynes, and Ingrid Smithey Fulmer. (2009). "Pay and Performance: Individuals, Groups and Executives." *Academy of Management Annals,* 3, 251–315.
41. Conversation with Thomas Ruddy, manager of research, Xerox Corporation, 1997.
42. J. G. Belcher, *Results Oriented Variable Pay System* (New York: AMACOM, 1996); S. E. Gross, *Compensation for Teams* (New York: AMACOM, 1995).
43. T. M. Welbourne, D. B. Balkin, and L. R. Gomez-Mejia, "Gainsharing and Mutual Monitoring: A Combined Agency-Organizational Justice Interpretation," *Academy of Management Journal* 38(3), 1995, pp. 881–899.
44. D. Terpstra and A. Honoree, "The Relative Importance of External, Internal, Individual, and Procedural Equity to Pay Satisfaction," *Compensation and Benefits Review,* November–December 2003, pp. 67–78.
45. R. E. Silverman, "Are You Happy in Your Job? Bosses Push Weekly Surveys," *Wall Street Journal*, December 3, 2014, p. B1; American Management Association, "Team-Based Pay: Approaches Vary, But Produce No Magic Formulas," *Compflash,* April 1994, p. 4.
46. E. Belogolovsky and P. A. Bamberger, "Signaling in Secret: Pay for Performance and the Incentive and Sorting Effects of Pay Secrecy," *Academy of Management Journal* 57(6), 2014, pp. 1706–1733; Conversation with Sharon Knight, director of compensation, and Martha Kimber, manager of compensation, both at Kraft Foods, 1997.
47. John G. Belcher, *Results Oriented Variable Pay System* (New York: AMACOM, 1996).
48. Personal communication to Jerry Newman from an anonymous client, 2013. F. McKenzie and M. Shilling, "Ensuring Effective Incentive Design and Implementation," *Compensation and Benefits Review,* May–June 1998, pp. 57–65.
49. M. Bloom and G. Milkovich, "Relationships among Risk, Incentive Pay, and Organizational Performance," *Academy of Management Journal* 11(3), 1998, pp. 283–297.
50. L. Hatcher and T. L. Ross, "From Individual Incentives to an Organization-Wide Gain-Sharing Plan: Effects on Teamwork and Product Quality," *Journal of Organizational Behavior* 12 (1991), pp. 169–183.
51. American Management Association, "Team-Based Pay: Approaches Vary, but Produce No Magic Formulas," *Compflash,* April 1994, p. 4.
52. G. K. Shives and K. D. Scott, "Gainsharing and EVA: The U.S. Postal Experience," *WorldatWork Journal,* First Quarter 2003, pp. 1–30.

53. B. Gerhart and G. Milkovich, "Employee Compensation: Research and Practice," in *Handbook of Industrial & Organizational Psychology,* 2nd edition, M. D. Dunnette and L. M. Hough, eds. (Palo Alto, CA: Consulting Psychologists Press, Inc., 1992); T. M. Welbourne and L. Gomez-Mejia, "Gain sharing: A critical review and a future research agenda," *Journal of Management* 21 (1995), pp. 559–609.
54. J. B. Arthur and G. S. Jelf, "The Effects of Gain Sharing on Grievance Rates and Absenteeism Over Time," *Journal of Labor Research* 20 (1999), pp. 133–145.
55. A. Weiss, "Incentives and Worker Behavior: Some Evidence," in *Incentives, Cooperation and Risk Taking,* ed. H. R. Nalbantian (Lanham, MD: Rowman and Littlefield, 1987).
56. Some of these issues are addressed at *www.hr-guide.com/data/G443.htm,* retrieved July 17, 2006.
57. R. Masternak, "How to Make Gainsharing Successful: The Collective Experience of 17 Facilities," *Compensation and Benefits Review,* September–October 1997, pp. 43–52.
58. John G. Belcher, "Gainsharing and Variable Pay: The State of the Art," *Compensation and Benefits Review,* May/June 1994, pp. 50–60.
59. John Belcher, "Design Options for Gain Sharing," unpublished paper, American Productivity Center, 1987.
60. D. Kim, "Determinants of the Survival of Gainsharing Programs," *Industrial and Labor Relations Review* 53(1), 1999, pp. 21–42.
61. A.M. Benson and S. S. Sajjadiani, "Are Bonus Pools Driven by Their Incentive Effects? Evidence from Fluctuations in Gainsharing Incentives," *Industrial and Labor Relations Review*, 71 (2018), pp. 567–99.
62. A. J. Geare, "Productivity from Scanlon Type Plans," *Academy of Management Review* 1(3), 1976, pp. 99–108.
63. A. J. Geare, "Productivity from Scanlon Type Plans," *Academy of Management Review* 1(3), 1976, pp. 99–108.
64. K. D. Scott, J. Floyd, and P. Benson, "The Impact of the Scanlon Plan on Retail Store Performance," *WorldatWork Journal* 11(3), 2002, pp. 4–13.
65. T. H. Patten, *Pay: Employee Compensation and Incentive Plans* (New York: Free Press, 1977); P. Schwinger, *Wage Incentive Systems* (New York: Halsted, 1975).
66. Matthew H. Roy and Sanjiv S. Dugal, "Using Employee Gainsharing Plans to Improve Organizational Effectiveness," *International Journal* 3, vol. 12, (2005), pp. 250–259.
67. B. Graham-Moore and T. Ross, *Productivity Gainsharing* (Englewood Cliffs, NJ: Prentice-Hall, 1983).
68. J. Newman, "Selecting Incentive Plans to Complement Organizational Strategy," in *Current Trends in Compensation Research and Practice,* eds. L. Gomez-Mejia and D. Balkin, eds. (Englewood Cliffs, NJ: Prentice-Hall, 1987).
69. Marshall Fein, "Improshare: A Technique for Sharing Productivity Gains with Employees," in *The Compensation Handbook,* M. L. Rock and L. A. Berger, eds. (New York: McGraw-Hill, 1993), pp. 158–175.
70. R. Kaufman, "The Effects of Improshare on Productivity," *Industrial and Labor Relations Review* 45(2), 1992, pp. 311–322.
71. Darlene O'Neill, "Blending the Best of Profit Sharing and Gainsharing," *HR Magazine,* March 1994, pp. 66–69.
72. John D. Stoll, "UAW's Rands Press to Close Pay Gap," *Wall Street Journal*, March 23, 2015, p. B2. D. L. Kruse, *Profit Sharing: Does It Make a Difference?* (Kalamazoo, MI: Upjohn Institute for Employment Research, 1993).
73. Douglas L. Kruse, *Profit Sharing: Does It Make a Difference?* (Upjohn Press, 1993).

74. Hambly, K., Kumar, R. V., Harcourt, M., Lam, H., & Wood, G. (2019). Profit-sharing as an incentive. *The International Journal of Human Resource Management*, 30(20), 2855-2875.

75. http://www.detroitnews.com/story/business/autos/2015/06/14/profit-sharing/71222980/.

76. Daniel P. Moynihan, "Designing Compensation Plans to Manage Today's Risk Environment," *Compensation & Benefits Review* 1, vol. 43 (January 1, 2011), pp. 17–22.

77. K. Brown and V. Huber, "Lowering Floors and Raising Ceilings: A Longitudinal Assessment of the Effects of an Earnings-at-Risk Plan on Pay Satisfaction," *Personnel Psychology* 45 (1992), pp. 279–311.

78. S. E. Gross and D. Duncan, "Gainsharing Plan Spurs Record Productivity and Payouts at AmeriSteel," *Compensation and Benefits Review,* November–December 1998, pp. 46–50.

79. R. Renn and W. K. Barksdale, "Earnings-at-Risk Incentive Plans: A Performance, Satisfaction, and Turnover Dilemma," *Compensation and Benefits Review,* July–August 2001, pp. 68–73.

80. P. M. Senge, *The Fifth Discipline: The Art and Practice of the Learning Organization* (New York: Doubleday, 1990).

81. Jeffrey Arthur and Lynda Aiman-Smith, "Gainsharing and Organizational Learning: An Analysis of Employee Suggestions Over Time," *Academy of Management Journal* 44(4), 2001, pp. 737–754.

82. T. H. Hammer and R. N. Stern, "Employee Ownership: Implications for the Organizational Distribution of Power," *Academy of Management Journal* 23 (1980), pp. 78–100.

83. B. J. Hall, "What You Need to Know about Stock Options," *Harvard Business Review,* March–April 2000, pp. 121–129.

84. Studies suggesting a positive relationship with corporate performance include: Anthony J. Nyberg, Ingrid Smithey Fulmer, Barry Gerhart, and Mason A. Carpenter, "Agency Theory Revisited: CEO Return and Shareholder Interest Alignment," *Academy of Management Journal* 53, no. 5 (2010), pp. 1029–1049; Brian J. Hall and Jeffrey B. Liebman, "Are CEOs Really Paid Like Bureaucrats?" *Quarterly Journal of Economics* 113, no. 3 (1998), pp. 653–691. For a study questioning such a positive relationship, see D. R. Dalton, S. T. Certo, and R. Roengpitya, "Meta-Analyses of Financial Performance and Equity: Fusion or Confusion?" *Academy of Management Journal* 46(1), 2003, pp. 13–26.

85. Barry Gerhart, "Pay Strategy and Firm Performance," in *Compensation in Organizations: Progress and Prospects,* S. Rynes and B. Gerhart, eds. (San Francisco: New Lexington Press, 1999).

86. Wikipedia, "Employee Stock Option," en.wikipedia.org/wiki/Employee_stock_option; retrieved July 24, 2006.

87. W. Zellner, "An Insider's Tale of Enron's Toxic Culture," *BusinessWeek,* March 31, 2003, p. 16.

88. T. Buyniski and B. Harsen, "The Cancel and Regrant: A Roadmap for Addressing Underwater Options," *Compensation and Benefits Review,* January–February 2002, pp. 28–32.

89. T. McCoy, "Emerging Option to Stock Options," *Pay for Performance Report* (Newark, NJ: Institute of Management & Administration, June 2001), p. 2.

90. N. Wingfield, "Microsoft to Boost Cash Pay for Employees," *The Wall Street Journal,* April 2, 2012, B5.

91. Mike Esterl and Joanne Lublin, "Coke Scales Back Stock Options," *Wall Street Journal,* October 2, 2014, p. B1. "Expensing Stock Options: The Rule Is Final' Or Is it?," *http://accounting.smartpros.com/x49842.xml;* accessed July 24, 2006.

92. "ESOPs by the Numbers," National Center for Employee Ownership, March 2018, https://www.nceo.org.

93. M. A. Conte and J. Svejnar, "The Performance Effects of Employee Ownership Plans," in Paying for Productivity, ed. A. S. Blinder (Washington, DC: Brookings Institution, 1990), pp. 245–294.

94. Conte and Svejnar, "Performance Effects of Employee Ownership Plans."

95. J. Blasi, M. Conte, and D. Kruse, "Employee Stock Ownership and Corporate Performance Among Public Companies," *Industrial and Labor Relations Review* 50 (1996), pp. 60–66.

96. E. H. O'Boyle, P. C. Patel, and E. Gonzalez-Mulé, "Employee Ownership and Firm Performance: A Meta-Analysis," *Human Resource Management Journal* 26(4) (2016), pp. 425–448.

97. Conte and Svejnar, "Performance Effects of Employee Ownership Plans."; T. H. Hammer, "New Developments in Profit Sharing, Gainsharing, and Employee Ownership," in *Productivity in Organizations*, ed. J. P. Campbell, R. J. Campbell and Associates (San Francisco: Jossey-Bass, 1988); K. J. Klein, "Employee Stock Ownership and Employee Attitudes: A Test of Three Models," *Journal of Applied Psychology* 72 (1987), pp. 319–32.

98. A. Kim and K. Han, "All for One and One for All: A Mechanism Through which Broad-Based Employee Stock Ownership and Employee-Perceived Involvement Practice Create a Productive Workforce," *Human Resource Management* 58(6), 2019, pp. 571–584; P. Cappelli, M. Conyon, and D. Almeda "Social Exchange and the Effects of Employee Stock Options," *ILR Review*, 73(1), 2020, pp. 124–152; J. L. Pierce, S. Rubenfeld, and S. Morgan, "Employee Ownership: A Conceptual Model of Process and Effects," *Academy of Management Review* 16 (1991), pp. 121–44.

99. J. Blasi, D. Kruse, J. Sesil, and M. Kroumova, "An Assessment of Employee Ownership in the United States with Implications for the EU," *International Journal of Human Resource Management* 14 (2003), pp. 893–919.

100. S. Sukanya and Y. Yoon, "Moderating Effect of Pay Dispersion on the Relationship between Employee Share Ownership and Labor Productivity," *Human Resource Management* 57, no. 5 (2018), pp. 1083–1096.

101. D. Jones and T. Kato, "The Productivity Effects of Employee Stock Ownership Plans and Bonuses: Evidence from Japanese Panel Data," *American Economic Review* 185 (1995), pp. 391–414. At the time of the study, 91% of Japanese companies had an ESOP.

102. S. Natarajan, I. P. Mahmood, and W. Mitchell, "Middle Management Involvement in Resource Allocation: The Evolution of Automated Teller Machines and Bank Branches in India," *Strategic Management Journal*, 40 (7), 2019, 1070–1096.

103. Kim E. Han and Paige Quimet, "Broad-Based Employee Stock Ownership: Motives and Outcomes," *Journal of Finance*, 69(3), 2014, pp. 1273–1319.

104. Corey Rosen, "Broad-Based Stock Plans Remain Prevalent in Fortune Best 100 Companies to Work For," www.nceo.org, February 21, 2020.

105. Bean Stock. https://starbucksbeanstock.com/en-us/welcome-en-us/. Accessed April 13, 2021.

Chapter **Eleven**
Performance Appraisals

Chapter Outline

Here's What Performance Appraisals Are Really Like:

Attention: Human Resources—submission of performance review for Joe Smith

Joe Smith, my assistant programmer, can always be found hard at work in his cubicle. Joe works independently, without wasting company time talking to colleagues. Joe never

thinks twice about assisting fellow employees, and he always
finishes given assignments on time. Often Joe takes extended
measures to complete his work, sometimes skipping
coffee breaks. Joe is an individual who has absolutely no
vanity in spite of his high accomplishments and profound
knowledge in his field. I firmly believe that Joe can be
classed as a high-caliber employee, the type which cannot be
dispensed with.

Regards,

Project Leader

e-mail to Attention: Human Resources

Joe Smith was reading over my shoulder while I wrote the report sent to you earlier today. Kindly read only the odd numbered lines [1, 3, 5, etc.] for my true assessment of his ability.

Regards,
Project Leader

In **Chapter 2**, **Exhibit 2.2**, Strategic Choices, we saw that the choice of corporate performance objectives led, in turn, to choices of business unit strategies, HR strategies, and compensation strategies, and ultimately, employee attitudes and behaviors and the degree to which corporate objectives are achieved. Likewise, at each of these levels, performance objectives must be chosen, which, again, ultimately, come to individual level performance objectives, their measurement, and evaluation.[1] If Nucor Steel and Lincoln Electric compete on cost, what role is played in achieving that objective at each level of the organization and at the level of the individual employee. If the SAS Institute competes by religious adherence to satisfying customer needs, how does that translate to each level and to each employee? And, how do we measure how each employee performed on his/her objectives. This measurement of individual performance is imperfect but is necessary in making compensation (and other HR decisions) and is the focus of this chapter.

Chapters 9 and **10** covered pay-for-performance plans. A key element of these plans is the choice of one or more measures of performance. Often, especially in merit pay decisions, subjective measures (ratings) play a key role and care must be taken to control errors and biases, lest we end up with less than useful ratings (as in the example above!). Organizations also use objective measures of performance. Blue Cross–Blue Shield of New Jersey, for example, uses data from insurance claims (number of tests ordered, treatments administered, drugs prescribed) to compare doctors with their peers. (The Centers for Medicare and Medicaid Services reports prices of procedures and treatments, by hospital.)[2] As we have seen, group incentive plans often rely primarily on objective performance measures. As we move down to the level of the individual and the team, these "hard" measures are not as readily available (thus explaining the rarity of pure individual incentive programs). We should be careful to note that "objective" measures are not necessarily better than subjective measures. Objective simply means that the score does not depend on judgment. However, objective measures are susceptible to problems, including "criterion deficiency"—excluding key aspects of performance. A secretary who is measured solely on words per minute in word processing would complain, legitimately, that he or she does other things that are far more vital to job performance. Paying a mortgage loan originator solely on the volume of loans (not their quality/risk) can, as we know, lead to major problems. This chapter focuses primarily on the challenges of measuring performance, particularly when we use subjective procedures.

THE ROLE OF PERFORMANCE APPRAISALS IN COMPENSATION DECISIONS

The first use of merit ratings apparently took place in a Scottish cotton mill around 1800. Wooden cubes, indicating different levels of performance, were hung above worker stations as a visible signal of who was doing well.[3] Some 200 years later, the Iraqi national soccer team reported that during the Saddam Hussein regime, players were frequently tortured for bad performance. Even though performance reviews don't usually lead to such outcomes, they are used for a wide variety of decisions in organizations–only one of which is to guide the allocation of merit increases. Unfortunately, as we will discover, the link between performance ratings and these outcomes is not always as strong as we would like. In fact, it's common to make a distinction between performance judgments and performance ratings.[4] Performance ratings–the things we enter into an employee's permanent record–are influenced by a host of factors besides the employee behaviors observed by raters. Such things as organization values (e.g., valuing technical skills or interpersonal skills more highly), competition among departments, differences in status between departments, and economic conditions (labor shortages which make for less willingness to terminate employees for poor performance)–all influence the way raters rate employees. There is even some evidence that much of job performance ratings can be attributed to a general performance factor (after accounting for error) that is present across a wide variety of jobs and situations.[5] Is it any wonder then that employees often voice frustration about the appraisal process?[6] A survey of 2,600 employees nationwide yielded the following rather disheartening conclusions:

39 percent felt their performance goals weren't clearly defined.

39 percent felt they didn't know how their performance was evaluated.

45 percent didn't believe their last performance review guided them on how to improve.

45 percent didn't think the reviews could differentiate among good, average, and poor performers.

48 percent didn't think doing a good job was recognized.[7]

This dissatisfaction makes a difference. Employees unhappy with the appraisal process were less satisfied with their firms, less satisfied with their pay, less committed, and more likely to turn over.[8] One trending approach by companies to deal with this is to conduct "Pulse" surveys as often as three times per week. Employers want to catch problems before they fester.[9] Perhaps the biggest complaint of all from employees (and managers too) is that appraisals are too subjective. And lurking behind subjectivity, always, is the possibility of unfair treatment by a supervisor. A good leader is key to making an employee believe that pay is linked to individual performance.[10] Is it any surprise that the subject of **performance metrics** is one of the hottest areas of study in both academic and business organizations? Critics of subjective measures want performance measures (metrics) that are fair to employees and reflect value for the organization.

Performance Metrics

Major advances in the development of metrics have been made over the past few decades. The first observation is that pay-for-performance programs evolve along multiple dimensions. First, is the measure (metric) result-oriented (e.g., financial measures, physical output, or sales being good examples) or behaviorally oriented (e.g., customer or supervisory ratings)? Second, does the measure focus on individual employees or aggregation up to team or even total organization?[11] Weaving these two issues together in an example, at the individual level (in this case, for an employee), it is very difficult to find good result-oriented measures. Just because something is quantifiable, though, doesn't mean it is an objective measure of performance. And this problem extends to even higher levels of analysis (e.g., firm level). As any accounting student knows, financial measures are arrived at through a process that involves some subjective decision making. Which year we choose to take write-offs for plant closings, for example, affects the bottom line reported to the public. Such potential for subjectivity has led some experts to warn that so-called objective data can be deficient **(criterion deficiency)** and may not tell the whole story.[12] Even with external audits, supposedly solid financial performance indicators can be misrepresented for extended periods. Just ask the folks at HealthSouth, who overstated earnings for almost 15 years without being caught by their auditor, Ernst and Young.[13] Despite these concerns, most HR professionals probably would prefer to work with quantitative data. Sometimes, especially at the individual level, performance isn't easily quantified. Either job output is not readily quantifiable or the components that are quantifiable do not reflect important job dimensions. As we noted earlier, a secretarial job could be reduced to words per minute and errors per page of keyboarding. But many secretaries, and their supervisors, would argue this captures only a small portion of the job. Courtesy in greeting clients and in answering phones, initiative in solving problems without running to the boss, dependability under deadlines–all of these intangible qualities can make the difference between a good secretary and a poor one. Such subjective goals are less easily measured. The end result, all too often, is a performance appraisal process that is plagued by errors.

One of the biggest challenges to individual performance measurement in general, and subjective appraisals in particular, comes from top names in the total-quality-management area. Edward Deming, the grandfather of the quality movement here and in Japan, launched an attack on appraisals because, he contended, the work situation (not the individual) is the major determinant of performance.[14] Variation in performance often arises because employees don't have the necessary information, technology, or control to adequately perform their jobs.[15] Further, Deming argued, individual work standards and performance ratings rob employees of pride and self-esteem.

Some experts argue that rather than throw out the entire performance appraisal process, we should apply total-quality-management principles to improving it.[16] A first way to improve performance appraisals, then, would be to recognize that part of performance is influenced more by the work environment and system than by employee behaviors. For example, sometimes when a student says "The dog ate my paper" (latest version: "The computer ate my flash drive"), they're reporting what really happened. When we tell teachers, or other raters, that the system sometimes does affect performance, raters are more sympathetic and rate higher.[17]

A second way to improve performance appraisal, which most of the remainder of this chapter discusses, concerns identifying strategies for understanding and measuring job performance better. This may help us reduce the number and types of rating errors illustrated later.

STRATEGIES FOR BETTER UNDERSTANDING AND MEASURING JOB PERFORMANCE

Efforts to improve the performance rating process take several forms.[18] First, researchers and compensation people alike devote considerable energy to defining job performance: What exactly should be measured when we evaluate employees? The answer depends on such factors as job level, type of occupation, the way work is organized, and the strategic goals of the organization.[19] Interestingly, managers can be grouped into three categories, based on the types of employee behaviors they focus on. One group looks strictly at task performance, how the employees perform the responsibilities of their jobs. A second group looks primarily at counterproductive performance, the negative behaviors employees show. The final group looks at both these types of behavior.[20] Studies that examine more specific factors focus on such performance dimensions as planning and organizing, training, coaching, developing subordinates, and technical proficiency.[21] As we noted earlier, one particularly good mega study found that much of performance can be accounted for by one general performance factor. Perhaps breaking performance ratings down into component performance dimensions may not be fruitful.[22] Countering this argument is the large amount of research and heavy adoption by industry of balanced scorecards.

The Balanced Scorecard Approach

A **balanced scorecard approach** is a way to look at what contributes value in an organization. Too often we just look at the bottom line, as measured by financial goals. The balanced scorecard acknowledges that bottom line success doesn't just happen. It depends on satisfied customers buying products and services from effective and satisfied employees who both serve the customers *and* produce goods (or deliver services) in the most operationally efficient way possible. If this is true, then we need to measure all four of the following dimensions and be prepared to say that success depends on high scores for each: customer satisfaction, employee internal growth and commitment, operational efficiency in internal processes, and financial measures. Besides the widespread enthusiasm in industry for this approach, data suggest that implementation of a balanced scorecard can have positive impacts on the bottom line and on rating accuracy.[23]

Exhibit 11.1 shows how the choice of performance measures can be guided by a desire to balance shareholder, customer, and employee objectives, as well as strategic imperatives (which related to operational efficiency in internal processes). Financial results can be seen as a lagging indicator that tells the company how it has done in the past, whereas customer and employee ("colleague") metrics like those in **Exhibit 11.1**, used by

EXHIBIT 11.1 Balanced Scorecard for Executives, Annual Incentive Awards, American Express

OBJECTIVES	WEIGHTING
Shareholder	55%
Revenue growth	
Earnings per share (EPS)	
Return on equity (ROE)	
Customer	15%
Net promoter score (customer satisfaction)	
Billings growth	
New accounts acquired	
Active locations in force	
Colleague	15%
Quantitative talent retention (retaining high potentials and high performers)	
Diversity (increase minority and women representation at managerial levels)	
Strategic Imperatives	15%
Leading in the premium consumer space (e.g., 16 products refreshed globally)	
Building on strength in commercial payments (e.g., #1 small business issuer)	
Strengthening our network (e.g., 99% of credit card accepting merchants accept AMEX card)	
Becoming digitally essential (e.g., 72% of new card members acquired via digital channels)	

Source: 2020 Proxy Statement, American Express. https://www.sec.gov/Archives/edgar/data/4962/000119312520083487/d804770ddef14a.htm.

American Express are leading indicators that tell the company how its financial results will be in the future. Focusing only financials does not provide a way to fix problems harming financials before it is too late. Effective leading indicators allow one to identify and fix problems that, left unaddressed, would cause lower (subsequent) financial performance. Importantly, empirical research should be conducted in each company to validate these or other hypothesized leading indicators of financial performance.[24] Another example of a balanced scorecard (for the Department of Energy) can be found in **Appendix 11-A.**

A second direction for performance research notes that the definition of performance and its components is expanding. Just consider the hugely successful company General Electric. In 1951, they began serious efforts to measure key performance indicators. More than a half century later they are still trying to achieve this goal.[25] Jobs are becoming more dynamic, and the need for employees to adapt and grow is increasingly stressed. This focus on individual characteristics, or personal competencies, is consistent with the whole trend toward measuring job competency.[26] Pizza Hut, for example, has five competencies that store managers must master: (1) sets high standards, (2) communicates well, (3) executes processes and routines, (4) holds self and others accountable, and (5) celebrates successes. Each of these competencies involves specific behaviors a Pizza Hut general manager must show at three different levels of mastery.[27]

A third direction for improving the quality of performance ratings centers on identifying the best appraisal format. If only the ideal format could be found, so the argument goes, raters would use it to measure job performance better–that is, make more accurate ratings. As you might expect, there is little evidence that an ideal format exists.

Recently attention has focused less on the rating format and more on the raters themselves. This fourth direction identifies possible groups of raters (supervisor, peers, subordinates, customers, self) and examines whether a given group provides more or less accurate ratings. The fifth direction attempts to identify how raters process information about job performance and translate it into performance ratings. Such information, including an understanding of the role played by irrelevant information in the evaluation of employees, may yield strategies for reducing the flaws in the total process. Finally, data also suggest that raters can be trained to increase the accuracy of their ratings. The following sections focus on these last four approaches to better understanding and measuring performance: improving the format, selecting the right raters, understanding how raters process information, and training raters to improve their rating skills.

Strategy 1: Improve Appraisal Formats

Types of Formats

Evaluation formats can be divided into two general categories: *ranking* and *rating.*[28] **Ranking formats** require that the rater compare employees against each other to determine the relative ordering of the group on some performance measure (usually some measure of overall performance). **Exhibit 11.2** illustrates three methods of ranking employees:

- The **straight ranking** procedure is just that employees are ranked relative to each other.
- The **alternation ranking** recognizes that raters are better at ranking people at extreme ends of the distribution. Raters are asked to indicate the best employee and then the worst employee. Working at the two extremes permits a rater to get more practice prior to making the harder distinctions in the vast middle ground of employees.

- The **paired comparison ranking** method simplifies the ranking process by forcing raters to make ranking judgments about discrete pairs of people. Each individual is compared separately with all others in the work group. The person who "wins" the most paired comparisons is ranked top in the group, and so on. Unfortunately, when the size of the work group goes above 10 to 15 employees, the number of paired comparisons becomes unmanageable.

The second category of appraisal formats–ratings–is generally more popular than ranking systems. This popularity, though, is not accompanied by any evidence that rating formats are particularly valid.[29] Such formats, especially those employing nonbehavioral anchors (see **Exhibit 11.3**, for example), provide more convenience than credibility.

The various **rating formats** have two elements in common. First, in contrast to ranking formats, rating formats require raters to evaluate employees on some absolute standard rather than relative to other employees.

EXHIBIT 11.2 Three Ranking Formats

Straight Ranking Method

Rank	Employee's Name
Best	1. ________
Next best	2. ________
Next best	3. ________
etc.	

Alternation Ranking

Rank	Employee's Name
Best performer	1. ________
Next best	2. ________
Next best	3. ________
Etc.	4. ________
Next worst	3. ________
Next worst	2. ________
Worst performer	1. ________

Paired Comparison Ranking Method

	John	Pete	Sam	Tom	Ranked Higher
Bill	x	x	x	x	4
John		x	x	x	3
Pete			x	x	2
Sam				x	1

Second, each performance standard is measured on a scale whereby appraisers can check the point that best represents the employee's performance. In this way, performance variation is described along a continuum from good to bad. It is the types of descriptors used in anchoring this continuum that provide the major difference in rating scales.

These descriptors may be adjectives, behaviors, or outcomes. When adjectives are used as anchors, the format is called a **standard rating scale. Exhibit 11.3** shows a typical rating scale with adjectives as anchors ("well above average" to "well below average"). Switching to behaviors as anchors, **behaviorally anchored rating scales (BARS)** seem to be the most common format using behaviors as descriptors. By anchoring scales with concrete behaviors, firms adopting a BARS format hope to make evaluations less subjective. When raters try to decide on a rating, they have a common definition (in the form of a behavioral example) for each of the performance levels. Consider, as an example, the following behaviors as recorded on a fictitious officer fitness report for the British Royal Navy. They are easily identifiable and, hopefully, humorous:

> "This Officer reminds me very much of a gyroscope–always spinning around at a frantic pace, but not really going anywhere."
>
> "He would be out of his depth in a car park puddle."
>
> "Works well when under constant supervision and cornered like a rat in a trap."
>
> "This man is depriving a village somewhere of an idiot."
>
> "Only occasionally wets himself under pressure."[30]

A more serious behavioral scale for a similar occupation was developed by the Royal Canadian Mounted Police.[31] On the leadership dimension, the top and bottom ratings a Mountie could get have behavioral descriptors that look like this:

Bottom rating–Ignores advice and views of other members: does not accept responsibility for own views and actions, blames others for own failures, provides others with incorrect information on policies and procedures.

Top rating–Takes charge of situations; consulted by other members for advice on operational and/or administrative policies and procedures.

This rating format directly addresses a major criticism of standard adjective rating scales: Different raters carry with them into the rating situation different definitions of the scale levels (e.g., different raters have different ideas about what "average work" is). **Exhibit 11.4** illustrates a complete behaviorally anchored rating scale for teamwork.

EXHIBIT 11.3 Rating Scale Using Absolute Standards

Standard Rating Scale with Adjective Anchors					
Communications Skills	Written and oral ability to clearly and convincingly express thoughts, ideas, or facts in individual or group situations				
Circle the number that best describes the level of employee performance	1 Well above average	2 Above average	3 Average	4 Below average	5 Well below average

EXHIBIT 11.4 **Standard Rating Scale with Behavioral Scale Anchors**

Teamwork:		Ability to contribute to group performance, to draw out the best from others, to foster activities building group morale, even under high-pressure situations.
Exceeds Standards	1	Seeks out or is regularly requested for group assignments. Groups this person works with inevitably have high performance and high morale. Employee makes strong personal contribution and is able to identify strengths of many different types of group members and foster their participation. Wards off personality conflicts by positive attitude and ability to mediate unhealthy conflicts, sometimes even before they arise. Will make special effort to ensure credit for group performance is shared by all.
	2	Seen as a positive contributor in group assignments. Works well with all types of people and personalities, occasionally elevating group performance of others. Good ability to resolve unhealthy group conflicts that flare up. Will make special effort to ensure strong performers receive credit due to them.
Meets Standards	3	Seen as a positive personal contributor in group assignments. Works well with most types of people and personalities. Is never a source of unhealthy group conflict and will encourage the same behavior in others.
	4	When group mission requires skill this person is strong in, employee seen as strong contributor. On other occasions will not hinder performance of others. Works well with most types of people and personalities and will not be the initiator of unhealthy group conflict. Will not participate in such conflict unless provoked on multiple occasions.
	5	Depending on the match of personal skill and group mission, this person will be seen as a positive contributor. Will not be a hindrance to performance of others and avoids unhealthy conflict unless provoked.
Does Not Meet Standards	6	Unlikely to be chosen for assignments requiring teamwork except on occasions where personal expertise is vital to group mission. Not responsive to group goals, but can be enticed to help when personal appeals are made. May not get along with other members and either withdraw or generate unhealthy conflict. Seeks personal recognition for team performance and/or may downplay efforts of others.
	7	Has reputation for noncontribution and for creating conflicts in groups. Cares little about group goals and is very hard to motivate toward goal completion unless personal rewards are guaranteed. May undermine group performance to further personal aims. Known to seek personal recognition and/or downplay efforts of others.
Rating:		Documentation of rating (optional except for 6 and 7).

In both the standard rating scale and the BARS, overall performance is calculated as some weighted average (weighted by the importance the organization attaches to each dimension) of the ratings on all dimensions. One way to derive an overall evaluation from the dimensional ratings appears in **Exhibit 11.5**. The employee evaluated in **Exhibit 11.5** is rated slightly above average. An alternative method for obtaining the overall rating would be to allow the rater discretion not only in rating performance on the individual dimensions but also in assigning the overall evaluation. The weights (shown in the far-right column of **Exhibit 11.5**) would not be used, and the overall evaluation would be based on a subjective and internal assessment by the rater.

Appendix 11-B gives an example of the rating scale and appraisal form used by Pfizer Pharmaceutical to assess leadership, one of the competencies tracked by Pfizer. Pay attention to how long and involved Pfizer's form is–and this covers only one of four competencies. Considerable money went into its development.

In addition to adjectives and behaviors, outcomes also are used as a standard. The most common form is **management by objectives (MBO).**[32] Management by objectives is both a planning tool and an appraisal tool, and has many variations across firms.[33] As a first step, organization objectives are identified from the strategic plan of the company. Each successively lower level in the organizational hierarchy is charged with identifying work objectives that will support attainment of organizational goals.[34]

Exhibit 11.6 illustrates a common MBO objective. Notice that the emphasis is on outcomes achieved by employees. At the beginning of a performance review period, the employee and supervisor discuss performance objectives (column 1).[35] Months later, at the end of the review period, the two again meet to record results formally (of course, multiple informal discussions should have occurred before this time). Results are then compared against objectives, and a performance rating is determined based on how well the objectives were met.

EXHIBIT 11.5 An Example of Employee Appraisal

Employee: Kelsey T. Mahoney
Job Title: Supervisor, Shipping and Receiving

Performance Dimension	Dimension Rating					Dimension Weight
	Well Below Average *1*	*Below* Average *2*	*Average* *3*	*Above* Average *4*	*Well Above* Average *5*	
Leadership				×		0.2 (×4) = 0.8
Ability						
Job knowledge					×	0.1 (×5) = 0.5
Work output				×		0.3 (×4) = 1.2
Attendance			×			0.2 (×3) = 0.6
Initiative			×			0.2 (×3) = 0.6

Sum of Rating × Weight = 3.7
Overall Rating = 3.7

Merck, the pharmaceutical giant, combines an MBO approach focusing on outcomes with a set of measures designed to assess how those outcomes were achieved—Merck calls this its multidimensional view of performance. The MBO portion of a performance review is regularly updated to ensure that individual objectives are aligned with corporate and department goals. At the end of the year, employees are reviewed both on goal performance and on five other measures: quality of work, resource utilization, timeliness of completing objectives, innovation, and leadership. Ratings on these latter measures must be accompanied by examples of behaviors shown by employees that justify particular ratings.

A review of firms using MBO indicates generally positive improvements in performance both for individuals and for the organization. This performance increase is accompanied by managerial attitudes toward MBO that become more positive over time, particularly when the system is revised periodically to reflect feedback of participants. Managers are especially pleased with the way MBO provides direction to work units, improves the planning process, and increases superior/subordinate communication. On the negative side, MBO appears to require more paperwork and to increase both performance pressure and stress.[36]

Exhibit 11.7 shows some of the common components of an MBO format and the percentage of experts who judge this component vital to a successful evaluation effort.

A final type of appraisal format does not easily fall into any of the categories yet discussed. In an **essay format,** supervisors answer open-ended questions, in essay form, describing employee performance. Because the descriptors used could range from comparisons with other employees to the use of adjectives describing performance, types of behaviors, and goal accomplishments, the essay format can take on characteristics of all the formats discussed previously. **Exhibit 11.8** illustrates the relative popularity of these formats in industry.

Evaluating Performance Appraisal Formats

What makes for a good appraisal format? Good ones score well on five dimensions: (1) employee development potential (amount of feedback about performance that the format offers), (2) administrative ease, (3) personnel research potential, (4) cost, and (5) validity. Admittedly, different organizations will attach different weights to these dimensions. For example, a small organization in its formative years is likely to be very cost-conscious. A large organization with pressing affirmative action commitments might place relatively high weight on validity and nondiscrimination and show less concern about cost issues. A progressive firm concerned with employee development might demand a format allowing substantial employee feedback. For example, some years ago Dow Chemical Company did away with performance ratings but kept performance reviews; stress was placed on using reviews to help develop employee skills. The five main criteria are explained below:[37]

EXHIBIT 11.6 **Example of MBO Objective for Communications Skill**

1. Performance Objective	2. Results
By July 1 of this year, Bill will complete a report summarizing employee reactions to the new performance appraisal system. An oral presentation will be prepared and delivered to all nonexempt employees in groups of 15–20. All oral presentations will be completed by August 31, and reactions of employees to this presentation will average at least 3.0 on a 5-point scale.	Written report completed by July 1. All but one oral presentation completed by August 31. Last report not completed until September 15 because of unavoidable conflicts in vacation schedules. Average rating of employees (reaction to oral presentation) was 3.4, exceeding minimum expectations.

1. *Employee development criterion:* Does the method communicate the goals and objectives of the organization? Is feedback to employees a natural outgrowth of the evaluation format, so that employee developmental needs are identified and can be attended to readily? We know that feedback has a positive impact on job performance.[38] There is also evidence that different kinds of feedback have different effects. Critical feedback that attacks the individual rather than focusing on the task has negative effects.[39] Employees respond better to feedback that tells them what went wrong on the task and how to improve.[40] Keep in mind, though, that the desire for feedback doesn't extend across all cultures. Lucent Technologies found that certain cultures are very reluctant to give feedback, either positive or negative. In most Asian cultures, feedback is viewed with great suspicion, and only the most reckless executive would jeopardize his reputation by giving feedback, particularly in public.
2. *Administrative criterion:* How easily can evaluation results be used for administrative decisions concerning wage increases, promotions, demotions, terminations, and transfers? Comparisons among individuals for personnel action require some common denominator. Typically this is a numerical rating of performance. Evaluation forms that do not produce numerical ratings cause administrative headaches. So, for example, an essay format (solely a written explanation of what the employee did well and not so well), with no numerical evaluation, is difficult to evaluate relative to other essays. Who did better is an important question when giving out merit increases.

EXHIBIT 11.7 Components of a Successful MBO Program

	Total No. of Responses*	Percent of Authorities in Agreement
1. Goals and objectives should be specific.	37	97
2. Goals and objectives should be defined in terms of measurable results.	37	97
3. Individual goals should be linked to overall organization goals.	37	97
4. Objectives should be reviewed "periodically."	31	82
5. The time period for goal accomplishment should be specified.	27	71
6. Wherever possible, the indicator of the results should be quantifiable; otherwise, it should be at least verifiable.	26	68
7. Objectives should be flexible; changed as conditions warrant.	26	68
8. Objectives should include a plan of action for accomplishing the results.	21	55
9. Objectives should be assigned priorities of weights.	19	50

*In this table, the total number of responses actually represents the total number of authorities responding; thus, percentages also represent the percentage of authorities in agreement with the statements made.

Source: From Mark L. McConkie. "A Clarification of the Goal Setting and Appraisal Process in MBO," *Academy of Management Review,* 1979, pp. 29–40.

EXHIBIT 11.8 An Evaluation of Performance Appraisal Formats

	Employee Development Criterion	Administration Criterion	Personnel Research Criterion	Economic Criterion	Validity Criterion
Ranking	Poor—ranks typically based on overall performance, with little thought given to feedback on specific performance dimensions.	Poor—comparisons of ranks across work units to determine merit raises are meaningless. Other administrative actions similarly hindered.	Average—validation studies can be completed with rankings of performance.	Good—inexpensive source of performance data. Easy to develop and use in small organizations and in small units.	Average—good reliability but poor on rating errors, especially halo.
Standard rating scales	Average—general problem areas identified. Some information on extent of developmental need is available, but no feedback on necessary behaviors/outcomes.	Average—ratings valuable for merit increase decisions and others. Not easily defended if contested.	Average—validation studies can be completed, but level of measurement contamination unknown.	Good—inexpensive to develop and easy to use.	Average—content validity is suspect. Rating errors and reliability are average.
Behaviorally anchored rating scales	Good—extent of problem and behavioral needs are identified.	Good—BARS good for making administrative decisions. Useful for legal defense because job-relevant.	Good—validation studies can be completed and measurement problems on BARS less than many other criterion measures.	Average—expensive to develop but easy to use.	Good—high content validity. Some evidence of inter-rater reliability and reduced rating errors.
Management by objectives	Excellent—extent of problem and outcome deficiencies are identified.	Poor—MBO not suited to merit income decisions. Level of completion and difficulty of objectives hard to compare across employees.	Poor—nonstandard objectives across employees and no overall measures of performance make validity studies difficult.	Poor—expensive to develop and time-consuming to use.	Excellent—high content validity. Low rating errors.
Essay	Unknown—depends on guidelines or inclusions in essay as developed by organization or supervisors.	Poor—essays not comparable across different employees considered for merit or other administrative actions.	Poor—no quantitative indices to compare performance against employee test scores in validation studies.	Average—easy to develop but time-consuming to use.	Unknown—unstructured format makes studies of essay method difficult.

3. *Personnel research criterion:* Does the instrument lend itself well to validating employment tests? Can applicants predicted to perform well be monitored through performance evaluation? Similarly, can the success of various employees and organizational development programs be traced to impacts on employee performance? As with the administrative criterion, evaluations typically need to be quantitative to permit the statistical tests so common in personnel research.
4. *Cost criterion:* Does the evaluation form initially require a long time to be developed? Is it time-consuming for supervisors to use the form in rating their employees? Is it expensive to use? All of these factors increase the format cost.
5. *Validity criterion:* By far the most research on formats in recent years has focused on reducing error and improving accuracy. Success in this pursuit would mean that decisions based on performance ratings (e.g., promotions, merit increases) could be made with increased confidence. In general, the search for the perfect format to eliminate rating errors and improve accuracy has been unsuccessful. The high acclaim, for example, accompanying the introduction of BARS has not been supported by research.[41]

Exhibit 11.8 provides a report card on the five most common rating formats relative to the criteria just discussed.

Which of these appraisal formats is the best? Unfortunately, the answer is a murky "It depends." Keeley suggests that the choice of an appraisal format is dependent on the type of tasks being performed.[42] He argues that tasks can be ordered along a continuum from those that are very routine to those for which the appropriate behavior for goal accomplishment is very uncertain. In Keeley's view, different appraisal formats require assumptions about the extent to which correct behavior for task accomplishment can be specified. The choice of an appraisal format requires a matching of formats with tasks that meet the assumptions for that format. At one extreme of the continuum are behavior-based evaluation procedures that define specific performance expectations against which employee performance is evaluated. Keeley argues that behaviorally anchored rating scales fall into this category. The behavioral anchors specify performance expectations representing the different levels of performance possible by an employee. Only for highly routine, mechanistic tasks is it appropriate to specify behavioral expectations. For these routine tasks, it is possible to identify the single sequence of appropriate behaviors for accomplishing a goal. Consequently, it is possible to identify behavioral anchors for a performance scale that illustrate varying levels of attainment of the proper sequence of activities.

However, when tasks are less routine, it is more difficult to specify a single sequence of procedures that must be followed to accomplish a goal. Instead, multiple strategies are both feasible and appropriate to reach a final goal. Under these circumstances, the appraisal format should focus on evaluating the extent to which the final goal can be specified.[43] Thus, for less certain tasks, an MBO strategy would be appropriate. As long as the final goal can be specified, performance can be evaluated in relation to that goal without specifying or evaluating the behavior used to reach that goal. The focus is exclusively on the degree of goal accomplishment.

At the other extreme of the continuum are tasks that are highly uncertain in nature. There is not much consensus on the characteristics of successful performance. Moreover, the nature of the task is so uncertain that it may be difficult to specify expected goals. For this type of task, Keeley argues that judgment-based evaluation procedures–as exemplified by standard rating scales–may be the most appropriate. Raters make subjective estimates about the levels of employee performance on tasks for which neither the appropriate behavior nor the final goal is well specified. The extent of this uncertainty makes this type of appraisal very subjective and may well explain why trait rating scales are openly criticized for the number of errors that occur in performance evaluations.

Strategy 2: Select the Right Raters

A second way that firms have tried to improve the accuracy of performance ratings is by focusing on who might conduct the ratings and which of these sources is more likely to be accurate.[44] For example, recent evidence indicates raters who are not particularly conscientious and raters who are too agreeable tend to give artificially high evaluations of employees.[45] To lessen the impact of a single reviewer, and to increase participation in the process, a method known as **360-degree feedback** (or multisource feedback) has grown more popular in recent years–and evidence suggests that it has value.[46] Generally, this system is used in conjunction with supervisory reviews. The method assesses employee performance from five points of view: supervisor, peer, self, customer, and subordinate. The flexibility of the process makes it appealing to employees at all levels within an organization; most companies using the system report that their employees are satisfied with its results. They feel that the 360-degree system has outperformed their old systems in improving employee understanding and self-awareness, promoting communication between supervisors and staff, and promoting better performance and results.[47] Hershey Foods, for example, uses a 360-degree feedback process that identifies areas for leadership training, and employees have voiced support for continuation of the program.[48]

Regardless of the positive responses from those who have implemented the 360-degree feedback system, today most companies still use it only for evaluation of their top-level personnel and for employee development, rather than for appraisal or pay decisions.[49] Some companies report frustration with the number of evaluation surveys each rater has to complete and the time necessary to complete the entire process.[50] More seriously, some research indicates that the different types of raters are very similar in their evaluations–so, given the extra costs, why ask for multiple views?[51] In response, recent research shows a distinct impact of rating source–raters do provide differing views.[52] As future HR professionals, you will face conflicting information daily. Part of your job will be to evaluate choices. Let's take a closer look at the role and benefit of each of the raters.

Supervisors as Raters

Who rates employees? Some estimates indicate that more than 80 percent of the input for performance ratings comes from supervisors.[53] There are good reasons supervisors play such a dominant role. Supervisors assign (or jointly determine) what work employees are to perform. This makes a supervisor knowledgeable about the job and the dimensions to be rated. Also, many supervisors have considerable prior experience in rating employees, thus giving them some pretty firm ideas about what level of performance is required for any given level of performance rating.[54] Although some credible sources question the validity of supervisory ratings,[55] the dominant view is that supervisors tend to provide accurate appraisals of their subordinates.[56] Supervisor ratings also tend to be more reliable than those from other sources.[57] On the negative side, though, supervisors are particularly prone to halo and leniency errors.[58]

Peers as Raters

One of the major strengths of using peers as raters is that they work more closely with the ratee and probably have an undistorted perspective of typical performance, particularly in group assignments (as opposed to what a supervisor might observe in a casual stroll around the work area). Balanced against this positive aspect are at least two powerful negatives. First, peers may have little or no experience in conducting appraisals, leading to rather mixed evidence about the reliability of this rating source. Second, in a situation where teamwork is promoted, giving co-workers the burden of rating peers can create group tensions (in the case of low evaluations) or yield ratings second only to self-ratings in level of leniency.[59] One exception to this leniency effect comes from top performers–who, it seems, give the most objective evaluations of peers.[60] However, Motorola, one of the leaders in the use of teams and in peer ratings, reports that peer ratings help team members exert pressure on co-workers to perform better.[61]

Self as Rater

Some organizations have experimented with self-ratings. Obviously self-ratings are done by someone who has the most complete knowledge about the ratee's performance. Unfortunately, though, self-ratings are generally more lenient and possibly more unreliable than ratings from other sources.[62] One compromise in the use of self-ratings is to use them for developmental rather than administrative purposes. In addition, increasingly firms are asking employees to rate themselves as the first step in the appraisal process.[63] Forcing employees to think about their performance before they go into the formal appraisal with their boss may lead to more realistic self-assessments, ones that are also more in tune with a supervisor's own perceptions.

Customer as Rater

This is the era of the customer. The drive for quality means that more companies are recognizing the importance of customers. One logical outcome of this increased interest is ratings from customers. For example, McDonald's surveys its customers, sets up 800 numbers to get feedback, and hires mystery customers to order food and report back on the service and treatment they receive. In a more personal example, co-author Newman used to be a mystery shopper for the car wash company discussed several times in this book. He would go for a car wash, write down the names of employees who did things out of the ordinary (either good or bad), and send headquarters a written report. For example, one time he asked for a new type of wax finish advertised on billboards–the employee had no idea about this wash and "bluffed" that no such option was available. Bad boy! In exchange for regular reports on performance, Newman got car washes and oil changes for free. Yes, he's incredibly cheap!

Increasingly we can expect the boundaries between organizations and the outside world to fade. Although much of the customer rating movement is directed at the performance of business units, we can expect some of this to distill down to individual workers. As another example, Home Depot prints its Web address on receipts and encourages feedback about specific employees. Great feedback can result in a $2,000 bonus.[64]

Subordinate as Rater

Historically, upward feedback has been viewed as countercultural, but the culture within organizations has undergone a revolution in the past 10 years and views are everchanging.[65] The notion of subordinates as raters is appealing because most superiors want to be successful with the people who report to them. Hearing how they are viewed by their subordinates gives them the chance to both see their strengths and their weaknesses as a leader and to modify their behavior.[66] The difficulty with this type of rating is in attaining candid reviews and also in counseling the ratee on how to deal with the feedback. Research shows, not surprisingly, that subordinates prefer to give their feedback to managers anonymously. If their identity is known, subordinates give artificially inflated ratings of their supervisors.[67]

Inter-Rater Reliability (and Multiple Raters)

As we saw in **Chapter 6**, an important criterion for any measure is that variance in scores due to error be minimized and variance in scores due to true differences, whether in job attributes there or in job performance here, be maximized. Reliability is defined as: true variance/(true variance + error variance). One clear path to maximizing reliability when ratings are used, inter-rater reliability, is to use multiple raters (as long as they are as well positioned and qualified). That is accomplished by including more than one rater per source (e.g., peers) and/or using multiple types of sources (see above). With more raters, the idiosyncrasy (error) present in each individual rater's ratings becomes less important and the shared part of their ratings, which is more likely to represent true variance, becomes more dominant. In fact, there is a formula, known as the Spearman-Brown prophecy formula,[68] that tells us how inter-rater reliability will change as we add more raters (**Exhibit 11.9**).

The inter-rater correlations, $\bar{r}_{ij}$, are .54 between Rater 1 and Rater 2, .48 between Rater 1 and Rater 3, and 0.32 between Rater 2 and Rater 3. The mean of these three correlations is 0.45. Thus, in this case, inter-rater reliability, if we used only $k = 1$ rater, as estimated by the Spearman-Brown formula would be $1(.45)/(1 + (1 - 1) \times 0.45 = 0.45$. If, however, we were to use the average of all three ratings for each employee (i.e., $k = 3$), then inter-rater reliability would instead be $3(0.45)/(1 + (3 - 1)\ 0.45) = 0.71$. Because each rater rates the same five employees, we can determine here that the three raters differ in their leniency/severity by the fact that their column means of 3.6, 4.4, and 4.6 are different. It is crucial to adjust for these mean differences to the degree possible in the case where not all raters rate all employees. Otherwise, employees rated by "easier" raters would get larger pay increases, more promotions, etc.

EXHIBIT 11.9 Inter-Rater Reliability Using Spearman-Brown Prophecy Formula

$$r_{kk} = \frac{k\bar{r}_{ij}}{1 + (k - 1)\bar{r}_{ij}}$$

where r_{kk} is the expected inter-rater reliability, k is the number of raters to be used, and $\bar{r}_{ij}$ is the mean correlation between raters, which is also the inter-rater reliability in the case of one rater. As an example, in the following data set, three raters each rate the same five employees.

Employee	Performance Rating Assigned by:			Mean
	Rater 1	Rater 2	Rater 3	
A	3	4	5	4.0
B	4	5	4	4.3
C	2	3	4	3.0
D	4	6	5	5.0
E	5	4	5	4.7
Mean	3.6	4.4	4.6	4.2
SD	1.0	1.0	.5	.7

To see the consequences of different inter-rater reliability, we can compute confidence intervals. As a first step, we compute the so-called true score, which equals mean score + (observed score − mean score) × inter-rater reliability. The true score adjusts observed scores to be closer to the mean score to the degree to which they are extreme and obtained under a condition of low reliability to be closer to the mean (i.e., less likely to be as extreme if repeated ratings were conducted). We will choose an observed score of 3. With a mean score of 4.2 and a reliability of 0.45, the true score = 4.2 + (3 − 4.2) × 0.45 = 3.7. The standard error of measurement (SEM) is given by SD × $(1 - \text{reliability})^{1/2}$ where SD is the standard deviation of the mean score of each employee. Here, SEM is equal to 0.70 × (1 − 0.45) = 0.39. To form a 95% confidence interval, we use the formula true score ± $z_{0.95}$(SEM), which here yields 3.7 ± 1.96(0.39), or a 95% confidence interval that ranges from a performance rating score of 2.9 to 4.5. Obviously, that is an awfully wide interval (1.6 ratings wide) to be using to make important decisions such as how large a merit pay increase to give an employee. What if we used the average of three ratings instead? From above, we know that this produces an inter-rater reliability of .71 using Spearman–Brown. That, in turn, yields a true score of 4.2 + (3 − 4.2) × 0.71 = 3.3, and a SEM of 0.70 × (1 − 0.71) = 0.21. The resulting confidence interval is 3.3 ± 1.96(0.21), or 2.9 to 3.7, still not as precise as we might like, but the interval is now only half as wide as the confidence interval produced above using a single rater and the related lower reliability. To summarize, as this example shows, using more raters, all else being equal, improves inter-rater reliability, which directly translates into more precise estimates of performance. (As noted, if different raters rate different employees, it is crucial to adjust for any rater differences in leniency/severity.)

e-Compensation

The American Compensation Association has an extensive website, including a bookstore. Go to ***https://www.worldatwork.org/resources/specialty-publications*** to find information about other books on performance measurement, including the advantages and disadvantages of using multiple raters.

Strategy 3: Understand How Raters Process Information

A third way to improve job performance ratings is to understand how raters think.[69] When we observe and evaluate performance, what else influences ratings besides an employee's performance?[70] We know, for example, that feelings, attitudes, and moods influence raters. If your supervisor likes you, then regardless of how well you perform, you are likely to get better ratings.[71] Your boss's general mood also influences performance ratings. Hope for a rater who is generally cheerful rather than grumpy; it could influence how you are evaluated![72]

Researchers continue to explore how raters process information about the performance of the people they rate. In general, we think the following kinds of processes occur:

1. The rater observes the behavior of a ratee.
2. The rater encodes this behavior as part of a total picture of the ratee (i.e., the rater forms stereotypes).
3. The rater stores this information in memory, which is subject to both short- and long-term decay. Simply put, raters forget things.
4. When it comes time to evaluate a ratee, the rater reviews the performance dimensions and retrieves stored observations/impressions to determine their relevance to the performance dimensions.
5. The information is reconsidered and integrated with other available information as the rater decides on the final ratings.[73]

Quite unintentionally, this process can produce errors, and they can occur at any stage.

Errors in the Rating Process

Ideally raters should notice only performance-related factors when they observe employee behavior. In fact, all of the processing stages should be guided by performance relevancy. Unless a behavior (or personality trait) affects performance, it should not influence performance ratings. Fortunately, studies show that performance actually does play an important role, perhaps the major role, in determining how a supervisor rates a subordinate.[74] Employees who are technically proficient and do not create problems on the job tend to receive higher ratings than these who are weaker on these dimensions.[75] Indeed, political skill (among other things, your ability to ingratiate yourself–get in good–with your boss) pays off in a number of ways in performance ratings.[76] On the negative side, though, performance-irrelevant factors appear to influence ratings, and they can cause errors in the evaluation process.[77]

Common Errors in Appraising Performance: Criterion Contamination

Suppose you supervise 1,000 employees. How many would you expect to rate at the highest level? How many would be average or below? If you're tempted to argue that the distribution should look something like a normal curve, you might get an A in statistics but fail Reality 101. One of the authors had a consulting project with a county department of social services. Part of the project required collecting performance ratings for the prior 10 years. With more than 10,000 performance reviews, guess how many times people were rated "average" or "below average"? Three times! Do you think that's just an aberration? **Criterion contamination,** or allowing nonperformance factors to affect performance scores, occurs in every company and every job, and probably affects each of us at sometime during our careers. Sound a bit over the top? Consider the following: One survey of 1,816 organizations reported that only 4.6 percent of the managers were rated below average. See **Exhibit 11.10**; it looks like we all live in Lake Wobegone.

Now, we might argue that people who get to the managerial level do so because they are better-than-average performers.[78] So, of course, most of them rate average or better in their jobs. But the truth is that as raters we tend to make mistakes. Our ratings differ from those that would occur if we could somehow, in a moment of clarity, divine (and report!) the truth. We make errors in ratings. Recognizing and understanding the errors, such as those noted in **Exhibit 11.11**, are the first steps to communicating and building a more effective appraisal process.

Not surprisingly, the potential for errors causes employees to lose faith in the performance appraisal process. Employees, quite naturally, will be reluctant to have pay systems tied to such error-ridden performance ratings. At the very least, charges that the evaluation process is political will abound.[79] There are several factors that lead raters to give inaccurate appraisals: (1) guilt, (2) embarrassment about giving praise, (3) taking things for granted, (4) not noticing good or poor performance, (5) the halo effect (seeing one good attribute

EXHIBIT 11.10 Ratings of Managers

Rating	Percent of Managers Receiving Rating
Above average	46
Average	49
Below average	5

and leaping to positive ratings of remaining attributes), (6) dislike of confrontation, and (7) spending too little time on preparation of the appraisal. To counter such problems, companies and researchers alike have expended considerable time and money to identify ways job performance can be measured better.

Errors in Observation (Attention)

Generally researchers have varied three types of input information to see what raters pay attention to when they are collecting information for performance appraisals. First, it appears that raters are influenced by general appearance characteristics of the ratees. Males are rated higher than females (other things being equal). A female ratee is observed not as a ratee but as a female ratee. A rater may form impressions based on stereotypic beliefs about women rather than the reality of the work situation and quite apart from any performance information. Females are rated less accurately when the rater has a traditional view of women's "proper" role; raters without traditional stereotypes of women are not prone to such errors.[80] Race also matters in performance ratings. Both in layoff decisions and in performance ratings, blacks are more likely to do worse than whites.[81]

Researchers also look at change in performance over time to see if this influences performance ratings. Both the pattern of performance (performance gets better versus worse over time) and the variability of performance (consistent versus erratic) influence performance ratings, even when the overall level (average) of

EXHIBIT 11.11 Common Errors in the Appraisal Process

Halo error	An appraiser giving favorable ratings to all job duties based on impressive performance in just one job function. For example, a rater who hates tardiness rates a prompt subordinate high across all performance dimensions exclusively because of this one characteristic.
Horn error	The opposite of a halo error. Downgrading an employee across all performance dimensions exclusively because of poor performance on one dimension.
First-impression error	Developing a negative or positive opinion of an employee early in the review period and allowing that to negatively or positively influence all later perceptions of performance.
Recency error	The opposite of first-impression error. Allowing performance, either good or bad, at the end of the review period to play too large a role in determining an employee's rating for the entire period.
Leniency error	Consistently rating someone higher than they deserve.
Severity error	The opposite of leniency error. Rating individuals consistently lower than they deserve.
Central tendency error	Avoiding extremes in ratings across employees.
Clone error	Giving better ratings to individuals who are like the rater in behavior and/or personality.
Spillover error	Continuing to downgrade an employee for performance errors in prior rating periods.

performance is controlled.[82] Workers who start out high in performance and then get worse are rated lower than workers who remain consistently low.[83] Not surprisingly, workers whose performance improves over time are seen as more motivated, while those who are more variable in their performance are tagged as lower in motivation. All of us have seen examples of workers and students who intuitively recognize this type of error and use it to their advantage. The big surge of work at the end of an appraisal period is often designed to "color" a rater's perceptions.

Errors in Storage and Recall

Research suggests that raters store information in the form of traits.[84] More importantly, they tend to recall information in the form of trait categories. For example, a rater observes a specific behavior such as an employee resting during work hours. The rater stores this information not as the specific behavior but rather in the form of a trait, such as "That worker is lazy." Specific instructions to recall information about the ratee, as for a performance review, elicit the trait–lazy. Further, in the process of recalling information, a rater may remember events that didn't actually occur, simply because they are consistent with the trait category.[85] The entire rating process, then, may be heavily influenced by the trait categories that the rater adopts, regardless of their accuracy.

Errors in storage and recall also appear to arise from memory decay. At least one study indicates that rating accuracy is a function of the delay between performance and subsequent rating. The longer the delay, the less accurate the ratings.[86] Some research suggests that memory decay can be avoided if raters keep a diary and record information about employee performance as it occurs.[87] And should you ever have to go to court to defend your performance rating of an employee (e.g., discrimination charges sometimes come down to this), the judiciary likes witnesses who keep diaries documenting employee performance.

Errors in the Actual Evaluation

The context of the actual evaluation process also can influence evaluations.[88] Several researchers indicate that the purpose of an evaluation affects the rating process.[89] For example, performance appraisals sometimes serve a political end.[90] Supervisors have been known to deflate performance to send a signal to an employee–"You're not wanted here."[91] Supervisors also tend to weigh negative attributes more heavily than positive attributes: You are more likely to receive a much lower score if you do one task badly than you are to receive a proportionally higher score if you perform one task particularly well.[92]

If the purpose of evaluation is to divide up a fixed pot of merit increases, ratings also tend to be less accurate. Supervisors who know ratings will be used to determine merit increases are less likely to differentiate among subordinates than they are when the ratings will be used for other purposes.[93]

Rank and Yank: Good Idea or Bad?

Jack Welch, a hugely popular and successful former CEO of General Electric when it was most successful, popularized what came to be called **"rank and yank."** Over the years a substantial number companies in the Fortune 500 have used this approach, sometimes with "gentler" names, such as "talent assessment."[94] Rank and yank requires managers to force-rank employees according to some preset distribution. McDonald's, GE, and Sun Microsystems, for example, use something like a 20–70–10 distribution (top 20 percent,[95] vital 70 percent, bottom 10 percent). Employees in the bottom 10 percent are given a chance to improve. Failure to move into the middle 70 percent usually results in termination. Some consultants and academics view forced ranking as the cure for inflated ratings and poor appraisal processes. As a result, these supporters claim, company performance improves.[96] Some managers wonder, though, if there is a limit to this yank strategy—after ridding yourself of the deadwood, don't you start cutting good employees? One simulation study, asking just this question, suggested as much as 16 percent average improvement over the first four years of rank and yank, but that benefits fall off dramatically after that.[97] This suggests the method has strong short-term benefits, but that it is perhaps best used with a sunset provision so that the method is used for a specified period of time. A recent survey indicates that 30 percent of companies use some form of ranking (i.e., 70% do not).[98]

Also, being required to provide feedback to subordinates about their ratings yields less accuracy than a secrecy policy.[99] Presumably, anticipation of an unpleasant confrontation with the angry ratee persuades the rater to avoid confrontation by giving a rating higher than is justified. However, when raters must justify their scoring of subordinates in writing, the rating is more accurate.[100]

Strategy 4: Training Raters to Rate More Accurately

Although there is some evidence that training is not effective[101] or is less important in reducing errors than are other factors,[102] most research indicates that rater training is an effective method for reducing appraisal errors.[103] Rater training programs can be divided into three distinct categories:[104] (1) **rater error training,** in which the goal is to reduce psychometric errors (e.g., leniency, severity, central tendency, halo) by familiarizing raters with their existence; (2) **performance-dimension training,** which exposes supervisors to the performance dimensions to be used in rating (e.g., quality of work, job knowledge), thus making sure everyone is on the same page when thinking about a specific performance dimension; and (3) **performance-standard training,** which provides raters with a standard of comparison or frame of reference for making appraisals (what constitutes good, average, and bad). Several generalizations about ways to improve rater training can be summarized from this research:

1. Straightforward lecturing to ratees (the kind we professors are notorious for) about ways to improve the quality of their ratings generally is ineffective.
2. Individualized or small-group discussion sections are more effective in conveying proper rating procedures.
3. When these sessions are combined with extensive practice and feedback sessions, rating accuracy significantly improves.
4. Longer training programs (more than two hours) generally are more successful than shorter programs.
5. Performance-dimension training and performance-standard training generally work better than rater-error training, particularly when they are combined.
6. The greatest success has come from efforts to reduce halo errors and improve accuracy.

Leniency errors are the most difficult form of error to eliminate. This shouldn't be surprising. Think about the consequences to a supervisor of giving inflated ratings versus those of giving accurate or even deflated ratings. The latter two courses are certain to result in more complaints and possibly reduced employee morale. The easy way out is to artificially inflate ratings.[105] Unfortunately, this positive outcome for supervisors may come back to haunt them: With everyone receiving relatively high ratings, there is less distinction between truly good and poor performers. Obviously, it is also harder to pay for real performance differences.

Strategy 5: Improving Rater Motivation and Opportunity to Rate More Accurately

If we return to our basic model first introduced in **Chapter 2**–that any performance behavior is a function of ability, motivation, and opportunity to perform–it is probably reasonable to describe the four strategies above as focusing primarily on rater ability and rater opportunity to perform (i.e., to produce valid/accurate performance ratings). However, we do not want to end this discussion without recognizing that there are often rater motivation-related factors as well. For example, what can happen when a supervisor does not give a high performance rating and/or generally positive performance feedback to a subordinate? Sometimes the subordinate will be grateful for the opportunity to improve and sometimes will improve. Other times, the subordinate will perceive the evaluation as unfair and unjustified, and it will make the working relationship more tense. We will say more about this issue shortly. But the challenge is to develop a culture (including rewards) in which employees, both as raters and ratees, value constructive performance feedback as a necessary tool to improve their performance and that of the organization so that both can benefit from its success. To be clear, that is easier said than done.[106]

A basic tool that some organizations use is sometimes called a calibration session, which involves higher-level managers and same-level managers who meet to review draft performance ratings and modify them as necessary to improve consistency (inter-rater reliability) and accuracy/validity. According to WorldatWork, about one-half of organizations it surveyed use such sessions.[107] Use of such sessions may also help supervisors deliver less positive feedback to low performers, but it may also serve to make high performers more visible. Following are the basic steps in a calibration session:[108]

- Managers prepare preliminary performance appraisals, including proposed appraisal ratings.
- Managers who supervise similar groups of employees meet and post names and ratings for all to review.
- Participants review and discuss their proposed appraisal ratings for every employee.
- Participants adjust ratings to assure accuracy and consistency.
- Final performance appraisals are prepared.

PUTTING IT ALL TOGETHER: THE PERFORMANCE EVALUATION PROCESS

A good performance evaluation doesn't begin on the day of the performance interview.[109] We outline here some of the key elements in the total process that from day one make for a good appraisal outcome.[110] First, figure out what your culture and strategy are. This should help you figure out what the key factors are that should be measured. Second, make sure your job descriptions are up to date and employees know what is expected of them. Third, periodically have informal discussions with employees about progress and any barriers that the supervisor needs to remove. Fourth, when evaluating performance, focus on behavior, not the person, in providing feedback. If employees don't know what you expect of them, how can they possibly please you?[111]

Second, we need to involve employees in every stage of developing performance dimensions and building scales to measure how well they perform on these dimensions. One extreme case of involvement is illustrated by Emmitt Smith, Hall of Fame football player. At age 21, Emmitt walked into the office of Jerry Jones (Dallas Cowboys owner) and handed him a slip of paper indicating how he wanted to be evaluated over his career. On that paper were five goals, including winning the Super Bowl more than once and becoming the NFL all-time leading rusher.[112] In such cases where employees themselves have clear performance goals, they respond more positively to ratings, regardless of how well they do. They are happier with the system's fairness and the appraisal accuracy. They give better evaluations of managers and indicate intentions to stay with their organization. Managers also respond well to this type of "due process" system. They feel they have a greater ability to resolve work problems. They have higher job satisfaction and less reason to distort appraisal results to further their own interests.[113] Employees also provide a unique perspective on what will or won't work. Consider the performance appraisal system developed by Alcatel-Lucent Technologies for its overseas operations. A performance dimension that worked well in Alcatel-Lucent U.S. operations was translated in local cultures as "obsession with serving our customers." It turns out that the word *obsession* in Saudi Arabia, Thailand, the Caribbean, and Latin America has very, very erotic and negative connotations. The problem was discovered only when managers reported employees speaking with one voice: "I don't care how important the customer is–I'm not doing this!"[114]

Third, we need to make sure raters are trained in use of the appraisal system and that all employees understand how the system operates and what it will be used for. A Harvard Business Review book discusses the importance of supervisors wearing both performance review and coaching hats.[115] Coaching addresses current performance and opportunities for growth through development of new skills. By fostering a creative environment and allowing employees to achieve goals using their unique individual skills, the performance review hat is easier to wear.

Fourth, as we have noted, we need to make sure raters are motivated to rate accurately. One way to achieve this is to ensure that managers are rated on how well they utilize and develop human resources. A big part of this would be evaluation and feedback to employees. Less than one-half of managers report that they provide feedback, and of those who do give feedback, most admit they are unsure if their feedback is worthwhile.[116] Almost one-half of employees agreed with this assessment, feeling performance reviews did little to guide performance.[117] Regardless of the quality of feedback one receives, don't assume that every review will improve performance![118] More generally, as we noted, it is necessary to develop a mindset that constructive performance feedback will lead to improvement that will benefit everyone.

Fifth, raters should maintain a diary of employee performance, both as documentation and to jog the memory.[119] This will help ensure that supervisors are knowledgeable about subordinates' performance and will serve as an objective exhibit in any court-based allegation of discrimination.[120] Sixth, raters should attempt a performance diagnosis to determine in advance if performance problems arise because of motivation, skill deficiency, or external environmental constraints;[121] this process in turn tells the supervisor whether the problem requires motivation building, training, or efforts to remove external constraints.

And finally, feedback to employees should be timely. Recent research indicates that "millennials" like to have feedback frequently. At the company Facebook, for example, feedback is encouraged after any meeting, presentation, or project completion.[122] More companies are also trying to make the feedback developmental. A recent trend is to minimize negative feedback that can crush self-confidence. Such well-regarded firms as Boston Consulting Group have taken up the "accentuate the positive" movement.[123]

"New" Performance Appraisal

Despite being so central to compensation human resource management, there is not as much solid evidence as we might like on what works.[124] Further, what works may depend. Different firms and firms at different stages may find different approaches to be effective. Not surprisingly, we see that firms often revisit their approaches. For example, a number of companies now focus on more timely (and frequent) performance feedback, sometimes as often as every two weeks (instead of one annual performance review). Or, as the *Wall Street Journal* put it: "Welcome to the era of the never-ending performance review."[125] The accounting firm PricewaterhouseCoopers LLP overhauled its performance reviews and now relies on a tool called "snapshots," a review that is meant to take only a few minutes to conduct and that an employee can request from his/her supervisor at any time. In the finance industry at firms like Goldman Sachs and J. P. Morgan, employees can use software to request "mini-reviews" from supervisors and colleagues at any time, which might be especially useful during or after work on a project or deal. Managers and employees differ, of course, in their reaction to such systems. One reaction is that "it is tough learning to give–and receive–constant critiques" and that when on the receiving end, "You really have to put your ego aside."[126]

One view is that the role of the manager in performance management is developmental: "to build commitment to and engagement with the organization and its broad goals and to assist and support employees who are having difficult carrying out their particular roles..." This view also argues it is "ineffective" for the manger to play the role of "a judge to evaluate deviations from plans and strategies that are imposed [from] above and forcing employees to get back on track."[127] Everyone seems to agree that development is important in performance appraisal. On the other hand, there is concern with the role of evaluation and its consequences, leading, for example, to the idea of "ratingless reviews."

Gerry Ledford and colleagues describe these new approaches as being defined primarily by three attributes: "ratingless reviews, ongoing feedback and crowdsourced feedback."[128] In the systems above, the emphasis is often on providing ongoing, regular, constructive, detailed feedback "in words," not as a number or rating. Crowd-sourced feedback refers to the use of "social media platforms to permit peer feedback in a free-form manner compared to 360 reviews." In their study of (only) companies that use such practices, they found that 97 percent use ongoing feedback, 51 percent use ratingless reviews, and 27 percent use crowd-sourced feedback. They conclude that use of these "new" practices appears to have a positive impact, at least according to the companies that use them. (Of course, such a measure of effectiveness may have some limitations.)

The "ratingless" aspect has received much attention. However, to be clear, the term does not mean that performance reviews have gone away.[129] To the contrary, there is more performance review, but with a focus on getting performance feedback to individuals in time and in a form that can be used immediately (rather than waiting for the end-of-year review). Also, "ratingless" does not mean an end to differentiation in pay and promotion (pay for performance) based on performance differences. Such decisions will still be made–and performance ratings, whether transmitted to employees or not, and whether formally recorded or not, will exist somewhere, if only in the mind of decision makers who choose which employees receive promotions and which receive larger pay adjustments.

A Checklist of Recommended Behaviors for Managers and Employees

If you would like to have a checklist of performance objectives to evaluate your performance in performing performance management (it's ok to smile), here are two helpful lists.[130]

For Managers

1. Set clear expectations, priorities, success criteria, and standards.
2. Revise expectations in real time, so employees know what to do.
3. Provide informal feedback daily to praise, coach, and course-correct employee performance. [Comment: Different employees may have different preferences regarding frequency and amount of feedback.]
4. Check in regularly with employees to stay in touch and provide guidance.
5. Coach employees and help them solve problems to enable success.

For Employees

1. Clarify their performance expectations to ensure they understand priorities and standards; revisit expectations when necessary.
2. Set expectations with peers about who is doing what, and by when.
3. Ask for and accept feedback openly and nondefensively.
4. Use feedback to course-correct and continuously improve own performance.

EQUAL EMPLOYMENT OPPORTUNITY AND PERFORMANCE EVALUATION

Equal employment opportunity (EEO) and **affirmative action** have influenced HR decision making for more than 40 years. While there are certainly critics of these programs, at least one important trend can be traced to the civil rights vigil in the workplace. Specifically, EEO has forced organizations to document decisions and to ensure they are firmly tied to performance or expected performance. For example, in a recent court case several female employees at Northern States Power Company in Minneapolis filed a lawsuit alleging that male workers in their job classification were paid more. While the case was dismissed, the problem of inequality remains.[131] This may well be the legacy of EEO. While it doesn't directly reduce segregation in the workforce, research shows that EEO affects HR practices and legal practices of companies that have been found guilty, and this in turn yields gradual positive changes in practices.[132] Nowhere is this more apparent than in the performance appraisal area. Just ask folks at the Social Security Administration, who settled an $8 million class action suit brought by black employees who successfully argued there was bias in the performance appraisal process.[133] Performance appraisals are subject to the same scrutiny as employment tests. Consider the use of performance ratings in making decisions about promotions. In this context, a performance appraisal takes on all the characteristics of a test used to make an initial employment decision. If employees pass the test–are rated highly in the performance evaluation process–they are predicted to do well at higher-level jobs. This interpretation of performance evaluation as a test, subject to validation requirements, was made in ***Brito v. Zia Company.***[134] In this case, Zia Company used performance evaluations based on a rating format to layoff employees. The layoffs resulted in a disproportionate number of minorities being discharged. The court held that:

> Zia, a government contractor, had failed to comply with the testing guidelines issued by the Secretary of Labor, and that Zia had not developed job-related criteria for evaluating employees' work performance to be used in determining employment promotion and discharges which is required to protect minority group applicants and employees from the discriminatory effects of such failure.[135]

Since the *Brito* case there has been growing evidence that the courts have very specific standards and requirements for performance appraisal.[136] The courts stress six issues in setting up a performance appraisal system.[137]

1. Courts are favorably disposed to appraisal systems that give specific written instructions on how to complete the appraisal. Presumably, more extensive training in other facets of evaluation would also be viewed favorably by the courts.
2. Organizations tend to be able to support their cases better when the appraisal system incorporates clear criteria for evaluating performance. Performance dimensions and scale levels that are written, objective,

and clear tend to be viewed positively by courts in discrimination suits.[138] In part, this probably arises because behaviorally oriented appraisals have more potential to provide workers feedback about developmental needs.

3. As pointed out by every basic personnel book ever printed–and reinforced by this text–the presence of adequately developed job descriptions provides a rational foundation for personnel decisions. The courts reinforce this by ruling more consistently for defendants (companies) when their appraisal systems are based on sound job descriptions.
4. Courts also approve of appraisal systems that require supervisors to provide feedback about appraisal results to the employees affected. Absence of secrecy permits employees to identify weaknesses and to challenge undeserved appraisals.
5. The courts seem to like evaluation systems that incorporate a review of any performance rating by a higher-level supervisor.
6. Perhaps most importantly, the courts consistently suggest that the key to fair appraisals depends on consistent treatment across raters, regardless of race, color, religion, sex, or national origin.

The focal question then becomes: Are similarly situated individuals treated similarly? This standard is particularly evident in a court case involving performance appraisal and merit pay.[139] A black male filed suit against General Motors, claiming race discrimination in both the timing and the amount of a merit increase. The court found this case without merit. General Motors was able to show that the same set of rules was applied equally to all individuals. There also has been a recent jump in lawsuits challenging as discriminatory the practice of "rank and yank." Employees are arguing they've been "ranked and yanked" not because of performance, but because of age.[140] As a result, there has been a noticeable drop in the number of companies using this method.

A final word of caution about the role of equal employment and performance appraisal: Experts note that firms approaching performance appraisal primarily as a way to defend against discrimination claims may actually create more claims. Documentation of performance to discourage such claims only causes poor employee relations, and it can lead to solid employees feeling like plaintiffs themselves.[141] A better strategy is to follow the guidelines we developed earlier. They permit both effective performance reviews and a strong foundation in case legal issues arise.

TYING PAY TO SUBJECTIVELY APPRAISED PERFORMANCE (MERIT PAY)

Think, for a moment, about what it really means to give employees merit increases. Bill Peterson makes $40,000 per year. He gets a merit increase of 3 percent, the approximate average increase over the past several decades. Bill's take-home increase (adjusted for taxes) is a measly $16 per week more than he used to make. Before we console Bill, though, consider Jane Krefting, who is a better performer than Bill and receives a 6 percent merit increase. Should she be thrilled by this pay-for-performance differential and be motivated to continue as a high achiever? One the one hand, probably not. After taxes, her paycheck (assuming a base salary similar to Bill's) is only $15 dollars per week more than Bill's check. BUT, as we saw in **Chapter 10**, merit pay often DOES MATTER if we look at the bigger picture. As discussed there, first, higher performance ratings and what seem like only modestly higher pay increases, through the magic of compound interest, do add up over time. Second, higher performance ratings lead to more promotions to higher job levels, which is THE most important determinant of how much you are paid over your career. Third, of course, an organization can always choose to make merit increases for high performers higher and those for lower performers lower. Likewise, they can make promotions even more dependent on performance.

The central issue involving merit pay is, "How do we get employees to view raises as a reward for performance?" The short answer is organizations must try to communicate the reality described above that merit pay is often much more consequential than it may first appear. **Chapter 9** illustrated this difficulty in theoretical terms. Now it is addressed from a pragmatic perspective. Very simply, organizations frequently grant increases that are not designed or communicated to be related to performance. Perhaps the central reason for this is the way merit pay is managed. Many companies view raises not as motivational tools to shape behavior but as budgetary line items to control costs.[142] Frequently this results in **pay increase guidelines** with little motivational impact. Three pay increase guidelines that particularly fit the low-motivation scenario will be discussed briefly below before we outline standards that attempt to link pay to performance.

Two types of pay increase guidelines with low-motivation potential provide equal increases to all employees regardless of performance. The first type, a general increase, typically is found in unionized firms. A contract is negotiated that specifies an across-the-board, equal increase for each year of the contract. Similarly, in the second type, across-the-board increases often are linked to cost-of-living changes. When the Consumer Price Index (CPI) rises, some companies adjust base pay for all employees to reflect the rising costs. (This is discussed in more detail in **Chapter 18**.) The third form of guideline comes somewhat closer to tying pay to performance. **Seniority increases** tie pay increases to a preset progression pattern based on seniority. For example, a pay grade might be divided into 10 equal steps, with employees moving to higher steps based on seniority. To the extent that performance improves with time on the job, this method has the rudiments of paying for performance.

In practice, tying pay to performance requires three things. First, we need some definition of performance. One set of subjective measures, as we discussed in **Chapter 6**, involves the competencies that people possess or acquire. Increasingly companies assert that corporate performance depends on having employees who possess key competencies. Xerox identifies 17 core competencies. As a company with strong strategic objectives linked to customer satisfaction and quality, it's not surprising to find that Xerox values such competencies as quality orientation, customer care, dependability, and teamwork. Recent trends in compensation center on finding ways to build competencies in employees. Merit increases may be linked to employee ability and willingness to demonstrate key competencies. For example, showing more of the following behaviors might be tied to higher merit increases:

Competency: Customer Care

1. Follows through on commitments to customers in a timely manner
2. Defines and communicates customer requirements
3. Resolves customer issues in a timely manner
4. Demonstrates empathy for customer feelings
5. Presents a positive image to the customer
6. Displays a professional image at all times
7. Communicates a positive image of the company and individuals to customers

Whether we measure performance by behaviors, competencies, or traits, there must be agreement that higher levels of performance will have positive impacts on corporate strategic objectives. Second, we need some continuum that describes different levels from low to high on the performance measure. Third, we need to decide how much of a merit increase will be given for different levels of performance. Decisions about these three questions lead to some form of merit pay guide.

As noted previously in **Chapter 10**, a merit increase grid ties pay not only to performance but also to position in the pay range (or equivalently the compa-ratio, the ratio of employee pay to the midpoint of his/her pay range/grade). **Exhibit 11.12** illustrates such a system for a food market firm. The percentages in the cells of **Exhibit 11.12** are changed yearly to reflect changing economic conditions. Two patterns are evident in this merit guideline. First, as would be expected in a pay-for-performance system, lower performance is tied to lower pay increases. In fact, in many organizations the poorest performers receive no merit increases. The second relationship is that pay increases at a decreasing rate as employees move through a pay range. For the same level of performance, employees low in the range receive higher percentage increases than employees who have progressed further through the range. In part this is designed to forestall the time when employees reach the salary maximum and have their salaries frozen. In part, though, it is also a cost-control mechanism tied to budgeting procedures, as discussed in **Chapters 10** and **18**.

Performance- and Position-Based Guidelines

Given a salary (or merit) increase matrix (or grid), merit increases are relatively easy to determine. As **Exhibit 11.12** indicates, an employee at the top of his or her pay grade who receives a "competent" rating would receive a 2 percent increase in base salary. A new trainee starting out below the minimum of a pay grade would receive an 8 percent increase for a "superior" performance rating. **Exhibit 11.13** shows that organizations vary in the degree to which a merit increase matrix allows a manager discretion in assigning a base pay increase based on an employee's place in the matrix, with the most common approach being that the matrix is used as a guide.

Designing Merit Guidelines

Designing merit guidelines involves answering four questions. First, what should the poorest performer be paid as an increase? Notice that this figure is seldom negative. Base wages are, unfortunately, considered an entitlement. Wage cuts tied to poor performance are very rare. Most organizations, though, are willing to give no increases to very poor performers, perhaps as a prelude to termination if no improvements are shown.

EXHIBIT 11.12 **Merit Increase Grid (or Matrix)**

	Performance Rating				
Position in Range	**Not Satisfactory**	**Needs Improvement**	**Competent**	**Commendable**	**Superior**
Fourth quartile	0%	0%	2%	3%	4%
Third quartile	0	0	3	4	5
Second quartile	0	0	4	5	6
First quartile	0	1	5	6	7
Below minimum of range	0	2	6	7	8

The second question involves average performers: How much should they be paid as an increase? Most organizations try to ensure that average performers are kept whole (wages will still have the same purchasing power) relative to cost of living. This dictates that the midpoint of the merit guidelines equal the percentage change in the local or national consumer price index. Following this guideline, the 4 percent increase for an average performer in the second quartile of **Exhibit 11.12** would reflect the change in CPI for that area. In a year with lower inflation, all the percentages in the matrix probably would be lower.

Third, how much should the top performers be paid? In part, budgetary considerations (**Chapter 18**) answer this question. But there is also growing evidence that employees do not agree on the size of increases that they consider meaningful (**Chapter 8**). Continuation of this research may help determine the approximate size of increases that is needed to make a difference in employee performance.[143]

Finally, matrixes can differ in the size of the differential between different levels of performance. **Exhibit 11.12** basically rewards successive levels of performance with 1 percent increases (at least in the portion of the matrix in which any increase is granted). A larger jump between levels would signal a stronger commitment to recognizing performance with higher pay increases. Most companies balance this, though, against cost considerations. Larger differentials cost more. When money is tight, this option is less attractive. **Exhibit 11.14** shows how a merit grid is constructed when cost constraints (merit budget) are known. Finally, **Exhibit 11.15** shows how Room & Board, a well-known and respected furniture and accessories firm, designs its pay-performance linkage.

EXHIBIT 11.13 How Organizations Use a Merit Increase Matrix

"If your organization allocates annual increases based on performance, indicate the method for determining the actual increase:"	
A merit matrix is published that managers use as a GUIDE, but they have discretion to deviate if deemed appropriate	44%
A merit matrix is published that managers MUST follow in which a specific RANGE of increases is published for each box of the matrix	11%
A merit matrix (position in range and performance rating) is published that managers MUST follow in which a specific percentage increase is published for each box of the matrix	10%
A specific guide providing one increase percentage or a range of increase percentages for each level of performance (position in salary range is not considered) is published as a GUIDE only	9%
A specific guide providing one increase percentage or a range of increase percentages for each level of performance (position in salary range is not considered) is published that MUST be followed	5%
Other type of guidance is provided	8%
No guidance is provided other than the overall budget figure	13%

Source: WorldatWork and Aon Hewitt, *Compensation Programs and Practices Survey*, August 2016.

EXHIBIT 11.14 Merit Increase Grids

Merit grids combine three variables: level of performance, distribution of employees within their job's pay range, and merit increase percentages.

Example

1. Assume a performance rating scale of A through D: 30 percent of employees get A, 35 percent get B, 20 percent get C, and 15 percent get D. Change the percents to decimals.

A	B	C	D
.30	.35	.20	.15

2. Assume a range distribution as follows: 10 percent of all employees are in the top (fourth) quartile of the pay range for their job, 35 percent in the third quartile, 30 percent in second quartile, and 25 percent in the lowest quartile. Change the percents to decimals.

1	.10
2	.35
3	.30
4	.25

3. Multiply the performance distribution by the range distribution to obtain the percent of employees in each cell. Cell entries = performance 3 range.

	A	B	C	D
1	.30 × .10 = .03	.35 × .10 = .035	.20 × .10 = .02	.15 × .10 = .015
2	.30 × .35 = .105	.35 × .35 = .1225	.20 × .35 = .07	.15 × .35 = .0525
3	.30 × .30 = .09	.35 × .30 = .105	.20 × .30 = .06	.15 × .30 = .045
4	.30 × .25 = .075	.35 × .25 = .0875	.20 × .25 = .05	.15 × .25 = .0375

Cell entries tell us that 3 percent of employees are in the top quartile of pay range and received an A performance rating, 10.5 percent of employees are in the second quartile of pay range and received an A performance rating, etc.

4. Distribute increase percentage among cells, varying the percentages according to performance and range distribution, for example, 6 percent to those employees in cell A1, 5 percent to those employees in B1.

5. Multiply increase percentages by the employee distribution for each cell. The sum of all cells should equal the total merit increase percentage.

   Example: 6% × cell A1 = .06 × .03 = .0018
   5% × cell B1 = .05 × .035 = .00175
   Etc. ________
   Targeted merit increase percentage = Sum

6. Adjust increase percentages among cells if needed in order to stay within budgeted increase.

EXHIBIT 11.15 Room & Board

As we begin our current business planning process, we are targeting a 3 percent payroll increase. This is a guideline and is not meant as a template for you to apply to your team across the board. This range should be kept in mind as you work through your team to help ensure that we do not exceed our plan for payroll.

To determine salary increases for your team members this year, you should take into account individuals' Priorities & Measures, your team assessment, scorecard data, as well as your market and location performance as a support to your individual decision making. Salaries should match one's contribution. We want to consider our long-term strategy of rewarding top performers and ensuring they get competitive increases each year. However, we do not want to be so aggressive in any given year that we do not leave ourselves room for competitive increases in future years.

Strong Contributor/Top Performer

Strong increases should be given to those individuals who have shown exemplary performance and have challenged themselves to grow and evolve with our business and gone above and beyond your expectations. (As a guide post, it is our assumption that only a small number of your team may fit this definition.) Your criteria for performance should encompass both subjective and objective measures as well as the manner in which the individuals performed. Staff members who have challenged themselves, improved their productivity, and at the same time conducted themselves in a manner consistent with our culture should receive strong increases.

Strong Increase Example

Hourly Staff Member = $.75–$1.00

(For a staff member earning $18.00/hour, this equates to an increase of 4.2%–5.6%.)

Salaried individuals earning $40,000–$55,000 = $2,000 or $2,500

(At a $45,000 annual salary, this represents an increase of 4.4%–5.5%.)

Staff members earning in excess of $55,000 a year should receive approximately 4%.

Solid, Core Contributor

Individuals who made a good contribution to the business yet are paid fairly for what they bring to our organization should see a moderate increase. Again, our assumption is that they are core, stable performers, immersed and learning every day, and they are paid fairly. The vast majority of your team members should fit these criteria. This approach helps individuals keep pace with the market while reserving more dollars for you to reward your key contributors. If you have core performers whom you feel are not paid fairly for their role, talk this through with your HR Partner to discuss this need for a stronger increase.

Moderate Increase Example:

Hourly Staff Member = $.50–$.75

(For a staff member earning $18.00/hour, this equates to an increase of 2.8%–4.2%.)

Salaried individuals earning $40,000–$55,000 = $1,000–$1,500

(At a $45,000 annual salary, this represents an increase of 2.2%–3.3%.)

Staff members earning in excess of $55,000 a year should receive approximately 3%.

Noncontributors

As in any year, those that have not contributed at a significant level and/or struggled in terms of their contribution and/or behavior should not be considered for an increase. Our expectation is that you have engaged these individuals in conversation throughout the year and your decision not to reward them with an annual increase will not come as a surprise.

It is also our expectation that those individuals not receiving an increase continue to be aggressively managed and will therefore either attain an acceptable level of contribution within a reasonable time period or be coached out of our organization.

Source: Based on documents provided by Nancy McGough, Human Resource Director at Room & Board, April 7, 2011.

Your Turn

Performance Appraisal at American Energy Development

Background

American Energy Development (AED) drills for oil using both vertical and horizontal ("fracking") drilling procedures. Financing for these operations in Pennsylvania and Texas comes largely through limited partnerships. The company identifies investors who become limited partners sharing in any successful drilling operations for the wells they have partially funded.

The founder of AED, Ron Robertson, recently passed away. His son John Robertson took over as CEO in 2014 and is steering a much more aggressive land acquisition strategy (for drilling wells) than was advocated by his father. Two hundred million dollars was raised last year to purchase land in Texas. Indeed, much of the operation is shifting to Texas and away from Pennsylvania because Texas has more lenient environmental laws governing fracking. Sixteen months ago, six new employees were hired to help kick-start the Texas operation. Additionally, seven employees were voluntarily relocated to Dallas–Fort Worth (DFW) from the Buffalo, NY, headquarters. John Robertson also relocated to DFW as a sign of his commitment to this new facility. Don Welch, chief operating officer and president, remains behind in Buffalo to run that operation.

Present

John Robertson is a transplant from the aggressive, fast-moving trenches of Wall Street, where as a broker he was weaned on tough performance appraisals and an incentive system that richly rewarded success stories and quickly discarded poor performers. He wants to instill a culture exactly like that in the DFW office. When he hired the six new key employees sixteen months ago, his early discussions with them included the fact that failure would not be accepted. No one was entitled to a job, and it must be earned each day. Of the six new employees, two stand out for different reasons.

Billy Ray Jenson

Billy Ray is a petroleum engineer with 30 years' experience after graduating from the University of Texas petroleum engineering program. He was hired in as senior engineer at a base wage of $216,000, a figure that matched the market rate. Market rate is a difficult figure to determine in Texas these days. More than 100,000 employees have been terminated in one of the worst downturns in the gas and oil economy in recent decades. Billy Ray is very grateful to get a job with a very competitive salary. He also is eligible for a 3 percent bonus on any wells that "hit" if he is the engineer of record for that field. As per agreement with John Robertson, Billy Ray will get his first full performance review in two weeks.

Elizabeth Andrews

Elizabeth also is a petroleum engineer. She has 14 years' experience and is paid $165,000 with the same bonus arrangement as other petroleum engineers. Elizabeth is very bright and brimming over with initiative. She has made several suggestions for drilling procedures using a holographic technology that has reduced the number of dry wells by 11 percent.

The Performance Appraisal System

John Robertson told the new employees when they were hired that they would be evaluated by him based on his perceptions of their performance. About one year ago he provided a performance appraisal form that had four performance dimensions rated on a 5-point scale. He also communicated base pay increases that would be associated with each rating. The factors and merit increases are as follows:

Performance Dimension	Performance Scale				
	Very Good	Good	Average	Not Good	Bad
	1	2	3	4	5
Merit increase (%)	8	5	3	1	0
Teamwork					
Productivity					
Quality					
Hard Working					

Teamwork: Someone who works well with fellow team players and values their efforts and contributions as much as his/her own.

Productivity: Amount of assigned work completed in an agreed upon time frame

Quality: Elimination of errors and absence of complaints

Hard Working: Shows up on time and works more hours than expected.

John Robertson's Concerns

John Robertson clearly has his dad's DNA. He purposely chose general performance dimensions because he believes the oil business is fast-changing and demands people who are willing to work with a great deal of ambiguity. He doesn't want to be tied down to specific performance dimensions that employees can then use to "lawyer up" on him if they believe they didn't get a fair shake. He gave average or good ratings to most of his employees. Two employees, though, are causing him some problems. He likes to link ratings to performance. He's inclined to give Billy Ray Jenson a very good rating, and this would be associated with an 8 percent increase. John is reluctant to give Billy Ray this large an increase because he feels he overpaid the Petroleum Engineer to begin with. After all, there are hundreds of people who could fill his job in Texas, and all of them he believes would work for less. He can't rate Billy Ray Very Good and only give him a 3 percent increase. The merit pay guide is known to all employees. John has decided, therefore, to rate Billy Ray only Average. Billy Ray was great on the teamwork and hardworking dimensions. No question. So John has decided he'll downgrade Billy Ray on productivity and quality. Billy Ray has some promising wells that look like they might deliver, and he is right on target with the number of wells sunk in a one-year time frame. But none of the wells have produced yet. So John figures he can rate Billy Ray lower on that. John also has decided to rate Billy Ray lower on quality. There aren't any hard and fast measures of quality, so John can justify whatever he wants to get an overall rating of average.

John has a different issue with Elizabeth Andrews. She is hard-driving and aggressive. She shows great initiative, but he has had many complaints from other engineers that she isn't a team player. They ask her for help using her holographic technology, claiming it will help them decide whether a well is worth pursuing. For the most part she turns these requests down, claiming that she is too busy exploring her own wells. She suggests that the others take the same online class at UT Dallas to learn to use holographic technology. On other dimensions Elizabeth is quite good. She works as hard as Billy Ray, has two wells that are producing already, far better than the industry standard for one year, and there have been no quality problems that he knows of. John is inclined to give Elizabeth an average rating because of complaints from other workers. The guys just don't think she is a team player.

John's Action

John gives both workers an average rating. In the performance review Billy Ray takes the news and feedback stoically. However, six days later he tenders his letter of resignation, effective in one week. Two days after that, though, in a very bizarre move, he asks to have the resignation revoked and return to his job. John accepts his change of heart and continues Billy Ray as an employee.

Elizabeth is far more confrontational. She maintains that she was indeed a good team player, and that others were taking advantage of her so much that she didn't have time to do her own job. She asserts that she took an online course on her own time and at her own initiative, and that others could do that too. Plus, she says, in response to his rating of her on the quantity dimension, she has two producing wells in only one year's time. That is a phenomenal record, she maintains, and certainly better than any of the other petro engineers John hired for the new office. This statement is accurate. Elizabeth says nothing else during the meeting but leaves the office unhappy, perhaps unhappy enough to do something about it.

QUESTIONS FOR YOU

1. What problems do you see in the performance appraisal system and accompanying merit pay system? Did any of these problems contribute to the people problems John had with his two employees in the performance review process?
2. What might John have done differently in the early communications process to improve later performance review sessions?
3. Should Billy Ray have quit? Why? Should John have accepted his return? What other action might Billy Ray have taken that could have been hurtful to the company?
4. Was Elizabeth treated fairly? Should initiative be a performance dimension? What other action might she take? Could she make a case that she was discriminated against? What defense, if any, might the company have?

Summary

The process of appraising employee performance can be both time-consuming and stressful. These difficulties are compounded if the appraisal system is poorly developed or if a supervisor lacks the appropriate training to collect and evaluate performance data. Development of sound appraisal systems requires an understanding of organizational objectives balanced against the relative merits of each type of appraisal system. For example, despite its inherent weaknesses, an appraisal system based on ranking of employee performance may be appropriate in small organizations that, for a variety of reasons, choose not to tie pay to performance; a sophisticated MBO appraisal system may not be appropriate for such a company.

Training supervisors effectively to appraise performance requires an understanding of organizational objectives. We know relatively little about the ways raters process information and evaluate employee performance. However, a thorough understanding of organizational objectives combined with a knowledge of common errors in evaluation can make a significant difference in the quality of appraisals.

Review Questions

1. We talked in depth about four ways to improve performance ratings. Pick one that you think shows the most promise and defend your position.
2. You own a nonunion company with 93 nonexempt employees. All of these employees pack books into boxes for shipment to customers throughout the United States. Because of wide differences in performance, you have decided to try performance appraisal, something never done before. Until now, you have given every worker the same size increase. Now you want to measure performance and reward

the best performers with bigger increases. Without any further information, which of the five types of appraisal formats do you think would be most appropriate? Justify your answer. Do you anticipate any complaints, or other comments, from employees after you implement your new system?

3. Think about the last group project you worked on. Describe that project and identify three performance criteria you think would be appropriate for evaluating the team members. Should every team member be able to rate one another on all these dimensions? Should the team-member ratings be used for feedback only or for feedback and part of the overall grade (with teacher approval, of course)? Should the teacher rate each team member on performance (all three criteria) in the group assignment? How are these questions relevant to setting up a 360° performance review?
4. Angela Lacy, an African American employee in your accounts receivable department, has filed a charge of discrimination, alleging she was unfairly passed over for promotion and regularly receives smaller pay increases than do employees who perform less well (she alleges). You have to go to your boss, the VP of HR, and explain what elements of your HR system can be used in your legal defense. What things do you hope you did in setting up and administering your systems to counter this discrimination charge?

APPENDIX 11-A

Balanced Scorecard Example: Department of Energy (Federal Personal Property Management Program)

THE BSC PERSPECTIVE

Customer Perspective

The Customer Perspective enables organizations to align the core measure (customer satisfaction) to targeted customers. For this perspective, the primary objectives are to provide effective service to and establish effective partnerships with external and internal customers. Effective service and partnerships are key ingredients in assessing the health of any federal personal property management program.

Internal Business Processes Perspective

The objectives in the Internal Business Processes Perspective collectively assure that an effective federal personal property management program is established to (1) support customer needs; (2) provide efficient life cycle management (accountability, utilization and disposition) of direct operations personal property; and (3) maintain oversight of entities that have federal personal property management program responsibilities. Key processes in the federal personal property management program must be monitored to ensure that the outcomes satisfy program objectives. This perspective is important because it not only addresses the internal business processes that must be developed and maintained to meet customer and stakeholder requirements and expectations, but also the process results that lead to financial success and satisfied customers. Within any personal property management organization, there are a number of internal business processes that require focused management attention to ensure requirements and expectations are met as effectively as possible, while accommodating cost efficiency issues addressed in the Financial Perspective.

Learning and Growth

The two objectives under the Learning and Growth Perspective promote organizational and individual growth that will provide long-term benefits to the federal personal property management program. These objectives must be achieved if program performance is going to improve over time. While the objectives in the other perspectives identify where the program must excel to achieve breakthrough performance, the Learning and Growth objectives provide the infrastructure needed to enable the objectives in the other perspectives to be achieved. The Learning and Growth objectives are the drivers for achieving excellence in the other perspectives.

This perspective is important because it promotes individual and organizational growth–factors that are crucial to future success. Support for this perspective equates to recognition of the link between top-level strategic objectives and activities needed to re-skill and motivate employees; supply information; and align individuals, teams, and organizational units with the Department's strategy and long-term objectives. An analysis of the cause-and-effect relationships of the measures in this perspective clearly shows that employee satisfaction, employee alignment, and information availability are vital contributors to meeting the objectives stated in the other perspectives.

Financial Perspective

The objective of the Financial Perspective is to strive for optimum efficiency in the federal personal property management program. To achieve that, processes need to be analyzed to determine (1) cost and performance trends over time and (2) process changes that can be implemented to produce optimum efficiencies. Success for entities charged with federal personal property management program responsibilities should be measured by how effectively and efficiently these entities meet the needs of their constituencies. This perspective is important because optimizing the cost efficiency of the federal personal property management program ensures that the maximum amount of funds are available for accomplishing the primary missions of the Department and its field organizations. Managers must ensure that federal personal property management program operating costs are optimized in order to meet the challenge of creating business programs that work better and cost less.

OBJECTIVES, MEASURES, AND TARGETS

General

Each federal personal property BSC should contain both national and local performance objectives, measures, and targets. The national elements of the BSC are developed by the Department in support of the Departmental mission, vision, and strategy. The local elements of the BSC are developed locally, based on site-specific missions and needs.

National (Core) Measures

The core measures contained in the federal personal property BSC are measures that the Department expects all entities charged with federal personal property management program responsibilities to implement where applicable. The formulae and measuring methods should be maintained as standard as practicable from self assessment to self assessment. Some core measures may contain core and optional elements. Core elements are aspects of the federal personal property management program that the Department expects all entities to take into consideration, where applicable, when measuring. Optional elements are aspects of the federal personal property management program that the Department suggests, but does not require, for measurement where applicable.

Local Measures

The federal personal property BSC should also include local measures to track performance in areas of importance to the local site. The following measures are provided as examples of local measures that are currently in use throughout the DOE complex:

1. ***Customer Perspective***

- Percent accuracy of key property data elements (e.g., property control number, nomenclature, part/model number, and serial number), where customers maintain or update databases.

2. ***Internal Business Processes Perspective***

- Number of property system processes re-engineered during period.
- Percent and/or value (acquisition cost) of personal property items lost, damaged, destroyed, and/or stolen during the period.
- Value (acquisition cost) of personal property items found during the period.
- Percent of scheduled property management reviews conducted during period.
- Percent of scheduled management walk-throughs completed during period.
- Percent of excess or surplus property shipped within XX days of receipt of requisitions or transfer orders.
- Percent of usable property with sale value sold within XX days after completion of required screening.
- Extent to which reliable property, administrative, and financial systems are in place and integrated.
- Percent of government equipment issues resolved in a timely (defined locally) fashion.

3. ***Learning and Growth***

- Number of classes/training sessions, supporting BSC objectives, provided to personal property custodians/representatives during the period.
- Percent of personal property custodians/representatives who attended the classes that were provided during the period in support of BSC objectives.
- Percent of personal property custodians/representatives who have been trained regarding their property management responsibilities.
- Percent of professional personal property employees who have attended a basic property administration course.
- Percent of professional personal property employees who have attended property management related training (e.g., demilitarization, high risk, NPMA).
- Number of employee suggestions, supporting BSC objectives, that were adopted during the period.
- Percent of personal property professional staff with professional certifications related to BSC objectives.

4. *Financial Perspective*

- Net proceeds from the sale of surplus assets as a percent of asset acquisition cost. Dollar value of site-generated excess property reutilized internally at the site.
- Dollar value of externally generated excess property (i.e., by other DOE sites and other federal agencies) utilized by the site.
- Reutilization screening transactions (number and dollar value) completed during period.

APPENDIX 11-B

Sample Appraisal Form for Leadership Dimension: Pfizer Pharmaceutical

PERFORMING FOR RESULTS

Reaching for the Future

District Manager/Regional Manager Capabilities

District Manager Baseline Capability Assessment

Employee Name:	**Self-Assessment:**	[ ]	**(Select one)**
Title:	**Manager Assessment:**	[ ]	
District:	**Manager's Name:**		

I. Strategic Capability Assessment	Unacceptable/ Needs Improvement	Stage I	Stage II	Stage III	Stage IV	Comments
1. Leadership						
2. Recruiting and Selection						
3. People Development						
4. Strategic Perspective						

Capabilities Cross-Reference Table

II. Core Behaviors Assessment	U	NI	S	RO	A	Comments
1. Planning & Organizing						
2. Impact						
3. Job Knowledge						
4. Problem Analysis						
5. Communication Ability						
6. Facilitation Skills						
7. Judgment						
8. Flexibility						
9. Political Savvy/Protocol						
10. Sensitivity						
11. Teamwork						

III. Employee Comments

Employee Signature:	Date:
Supervisor Signature:	Date:

	Key
U	"Unacceptable"
NI	"Needs Improvement"
S	"Sometimes"
RO	"Routinely"
A	"Always"

District Manager Strategic Capabilities

Levels of Development

Stage I Stage II Stage III Stage IV

Outlined below are four strategic capabilities for the District Manager (DM) role.

1. Leadership

	Stage I	Stage II	Stage III	Stage IV
Descriptor	*Is learning to manage the district, and is becoming involved in the TACU process.*	*Coordinates district activities for the division and participates in the TACU process (e.g., completes the business plan).*	*Successfully leads and manages own representatives while actively contributing to the TACU process.*	*Emerges as a leader within the region, division, and TACU. Is willing to take on reasonable risk to push representatives/TACU/district/region toward more forward thinking.*
Leads implementation of sales strategy and tactics	• Provides direction to representatives regarding what work activities are important (e.g., communicates district standards to representatives).	• Ensures representatives are following through on work activities that need to be executed in the territory (e.g., physician calls, sample drops, computer data entry, etc.). • Implements the tactical aspects of targeted account selling.	• Ensures that representatives understand how their activities affect district, regional, state, and U.S. Pharmaceuticals' objectives (e.g., regularly reviews territory, district, and regional results to reinforce line-of-sight). • Designs and manages a full targeted account selling process, including copromotes, government relations, CECs, Specialty, LMMs, and MSLs.	• Takes a lead role in implementing and inspiring a vision of success for the district, region, and TACU (e.g., works with TACU members to clearly define outcomes based on what is best for the customer and Pfizer and develops innovative approaches that are adopted across U.S. Pharmaceuticals lines). • Understands the politics at work in district, region, and U.S. Pharmaceuticals (e.g., among local community leaders, employer groups, corporate affiliations, MCOs, medical groups, and deans of schools) and applies this understanding to developing targeted account selling strategies.
Leverages internal/external relationships to deliver value	• Attends TACU meetings. • Focuses primarily on issues related to own products or division at TACU meetings.	• Suggests agenda items for TACU discussions.	• Advocates the TACU as a strategic advantage in the selling process.	• Optimizes the value of the TACU and LAT processes as critical elements in meeting U.S. Pharmaceuticals' strategic objectives.

	• Pays attention to other DMs' successes to learn management and leadership techniques and approaches. • Discourages or confronts the exchange of negative disrespectful comments.	• Actively networks with DMs from other districts to learn from their successes.	• Works seamlessly with copromote partners. Regularly engages in activities to strengthen copromote relationships to maximize their benefits (e.g., openly shares resources, knowledge, and experience to facilitate representative/DM mastery of market issues).	• Encourages and facilitates collaborating with CECs, MSLs, MSMs, Headquarters, and other field force members (e.g., identifies opportunities where a pooling of resources will increase the likelihood of success, matches up field force members who would benefit from collaboration).
	• Often focuses on individual contributors but is beginning to encourage a team approach (e.g., encourages representatives to coordinate business plan, goals, speakers, and call cycles).	• Recognizes and encourages a team approach to achieving results (e.g., acknowledges a representative's support of a priority copromote selling effort).	• Focuses on growing Pfizer's market share and profitability [e.g., adopts a customer-focused (versus division-focused) selling approach].	
Raises performance in the field and develops high-performing teams	• Holds self to the same standards as representatives (e.g., is always punctual, files reports on time, willingly performs details, etc.). • Closely manages representative activities.	• Leads by example—personally demonstrates the core behaviors, skills, knowledge, and traits that representatives need to be successful. • Understands the principles of situational leadership and how it can	• Raises performance of representatives by setting high performance standards that are perceived by representatives as being challenging but achievable. • Applies the principles of situational leadership (e.g., uses multiple leadership styles and	• Raises performance of the field beyond division, TACU, district, and regional lines. • Sought out by peers for advice on developing high-performing teams. • Recognized by representatives, peers, RM, and Sales VP as a situational leadership role model as measured by

		improve performance (e.g., acknowledges individual differences but tends to rely on one preferred leadership style/approach). • Imparts a sense of responsibility among team members (e.g., requires representatives to assess their contributions and impact on district results, does not micro-manage or under manage representatives, etc.).	adapts approach to individual needs/circumstances).	IMDI, EQ, 360 Degrees, and Situational Leadership surveys.
Manages conflicts and makes tough decisions to position the district for success	• Learning to surface and manage conflicts when dealing with individual representatives and at the TACU level (e.g., points out when representatives are making excuses).	• Does not wait until problems arise before addressing performance issues (e.g., addresses significant work activity performance shortfalls early).	• Recognizes opportunities to improve policies and/or practices and takes action to do so. • Makes tough decisions within an appropriate time frame and with the appropriate documentation (e.g., places a representative on final probation after several performance discussions and demonstrates to the representative how to correct his/her behaviors).	• Sought out by peers, Headquarters, and sales leadership for advice, counsel, and assistance regarding business, customer, market, and people issues (e.g., is recommended by RM or Sales VP for various advisory panels).
Capitalizes on the benefits of diversity (field force and customers)	• Understands that representatives and customers have individual needs and	• Helps representatives respect and understand individual differences.	• Adapts management style to respond to individual and customer needs/styles.	• Recognizes and draws on individual backgrounds, experiences, and strengths to optimize district performance.

	styles and respects these differences.	• Hires diverse candidates to complement the current field force (e.g., works with minority recruiters to select top talent).		• Is considered to be a role model by representatives, peers, and RM for his/her commitment to using diversity to increase effectiveness (e.g., helps others develop relationships with minority recruiting centers).
			• Utilizes a diverse set of skills and perspectives to enhance the overall effectiveness of the team.	• Assesses individuals' backgrounds and strengths and matches them to specific initiatives to optimize district performance.

Note: DMs will be expected to maintain demonstration/mastery of behaviors from prior stages.

Endnotes

1. E. D. Pulakos, R. Mueller-Hanson, & S. Arad "The Evolution of Performance Management: Searching for Value." *Annual Review of Organizational Psychology and Organizational Behavior* 6 (2019), pp. 249–271.
2. Centers for Medicare and Medicaid Services, The Inpatient Utilization and Payment Public Use File, www.cms.gov, accessed November 19, 2018; L. Landro, "Pay for Performance Reaches Out to Specialists," *The Wall Street Journal,* December 15, 2004, p. D3.
3. R. Heilbroner, *The Worldly Philosophers* (New York: Simon & Schuster, 1953).
4. K. Murphy and J. Cleveland, *Understanding Performance Appraisal* (Thousand Oaks, CA: Sage, 1995).
5. C. Viswesvaran, F. L. Schmidt, and D. Ones, "Is There a General Factor in Ratings of Job Performance? A Meta-Analytic Frame Disentangling Substantive and Error Influences," *Journal of Applied Psychology* 90(1), 2005, pp. 108–131; John P. Campbell and M. Wiernik Brenton, "The Modeling and Assessment of Work Performance," *Annual Review of Organizational Psychology and Organizational Behavior* 2, no. 1 (2015), pp. 47–74.
6. Joo Hun Han, Kathryn M. Bartol, and Kim Seongsu, "Tightening Up the Performance-Pay Linkage: Roles of Contingent Reward Leadership and Profit-Sharing in the Cross-Level Influence of Individual Pay-For-Performance," *Journal of Applied Psychology* 100, no. 2 (2015), pp. 417–430.
7. Mercer homepage, *www.mercerhr.com,* April 24, 2003.
8. M. J. Ducharme, P. Singh, and M. Podolsky, "Exploring the Links between Performance Appraisals and Pay Satisfaction," *Compensation and Benefits Review,* September–October 2005, pp. 46–52; K. Murphy and J. Cleveland, *Understanding Performance Appraisal* (Thousand Oaks, CA: Sage, 1995).
9. Rachel Emma Silverman, "Are You Happy in Your Job? Bosses Push Weekly Surveys," *Wall Street Journal*, December 3, 2014, p. B1; Theresa M. Welbourne, "The Potential of Pulse Surveys: Transforming Surveys into Leadership Tools," *Employment Relations Today* 43, no. 1 (2016), pp. 33–39.
10. Joo Hun Han, Kathryn M. Bartol, and Kim Seongsu, "Tightening Up the Performance-Pay Linkage: Roles of Contingent Reward Leadership and Profit-Sharing in the Cross-Level Influence of Individual Pay-For-Performance," *Journal of Applied Psychology* 100, no. 2 (2015), pp. 417–430.
11. B. Gerhart and S. L. Rynes, *Compensation: Theory, Evidence, and Strategic Implications* (Thousand Oaks, CA: Sage, 2003).
12. Robert L. Cardy and Gregory H. Dobbins, *Performance Appraisal: Alternative Perspectives* (Cincinnati: South-Western, 1994).
13. J. Weil, "HealthSouth Becomes Subject of a Congressional Probe," *The Wall Street Journal,* April 23, 2003, p. C1.
14. W. E. Deming, *Out of the Crisis* (Cambridge, MA: MIT Press, 1986).
15. David Waldman, "The Contributions of Total Quality Management to a Theory of Work Performance," *Academy of Management Review* 19 (1994), pp. 510–536.
16. David Antonioni, "Improve the Performance Management Process Before Discontinuing Performance Appraisals," *Compensation and Benefits Review,* May–June 1994, pp. 29–37.
17. R. L. Cardy, C. L. Sutton, K. P. Carson, and G. H. Dobbins, "*Degree of Responsibility: An Empirical Examination of Person and System Effects on Performance Ratings*," paper presented at the National Meeting of the Academy of Management, San Francisco, 1990.
18. R. Arvey and K. Murphy, "Performance Evaluation in Work Settings," *Annual Review of Psychology* 49 (1998), pp. 141–168.

19. B. Gerhart, "Compensation Strategy and Organizational Performance," in eds. S. L. Rynes and B. Gerhart, *Compensation in Organizations* (San Francisco: Jossey-Bass, 2000).

20. P. Gwynne, "How Consistent Are Performance Review Criteria," *MIT Sloan Management Review* (Summer 2002), pp. 15-22.

21. W. Borman and D. Brush, "More Progress Towards a Taxonomy of Managerial Performance Requirements," *Human Performance* 6(1), 1993, pp. 1-21.

22. C. Viswesvaran, F. L. Schmidt, and D. Ones, "Is There a General Factor in Ratings of Job Performance? A Meta-Analytic Frame Disentangling Substantive and Error Influences," *Journal of Applied Psychology* 90(1), 2005, pp. 108-131.

23. Shujun Ding and Philip Beaulieu, "The Role of Financial Incentives in Balanced Scorecard-Based Performance Evaluations: Correcting Mood Congruency Biases," *Journal of Accounting Research* 49(5) 2011, pp. 1223-1247; Rachael Griffith and Andrew Neely, "Performance Pay and Managerial Experience in Multitask Teams: Evidence from within a Firm," *Journal of Labor Economics* 27(1), 2009, pp. 49-82.

24. Christopher D. Ittner and David F. Larcker. "Coming up short on nonfinancial performance measurement." *Harvard Business Review* 81, no. 11 (2003), pp. 88-95.

25. Robert D. Austin, *Measuring and Managing Performance in Organizations* (New York: Dorsett Press, 1996).

26. D. Coleman, *Working with Emotional Intelligence* (New York: Bantam Books, 1998).

27. Based on a personal visit to Pizza Hut headquarters, March 2009.

28. Daniel Ilgen and Jack Feldman, "Performance Appraisal: A Process Focus," *Research in Organizational Behavior* 5 (1983), pp. 141-197.

29. Barry Gerhart, Sara L. Rynes, and Ingrid Smithey Fulmer, "Pay and Performance: Individuals, Groups and Executives," in *Academy of Management Annals,* vol. 3, ed. A. P. Brief and J. P. Walsh (Newark, NJ: Lawrence Erlbaum, 2009).

30. Royal Navy and Marines fitness reports, *Technical Report S206,* Royal Navy Publications, 2004.

31. Victor M. Catano, Wendy Darr, and Catherine A. Campbell, "Performance Appraisal of Behavior Based Competencies," *Personnel Psychology* 60 (2007), pp. 201-230.

32. H. Levinson, "Management by Whose Objectives," *Harvard Business Review,* January 2003, pp. 1007-1016.

33. Mark L. McConkie, "A Clarification of the Goal Setting and Appraisal Processes in MBO," *Academy of Management Review* 4(1), 1979, pp. 29-40.

34. Chiara Mio, Andrea Venturelli, and Rossella Leopizzi, "Management by Objectives and Corporate Social Responsibility Disclosure," *Accounting, Auditing and Accountability Journal*, 28(3), 2015, pp. 325-364.

35. Mark L. McConkie, "A Clarification of the Goal Setting and Appraisal Processes in MBO," *Academy of Management Review* 4(1), 1979, pp. 29-40.

36. J. S. Hodgson, "Management by Objectives: The Experiences of a Federal Government Department," *Canadian Public Administration* 16(4), 1973, pp. 422-431.

37. Bruce McAfee and Blake Green, "Selecting a Performance Appraisal Method," *Personnel Administrator* 22(5), 1977, pp. 61-65.

38. Abraham N. Kluger and Angelo DeNisi, "The Effects of Feedback Interventions on Performance: A Historical Review, A Meta-Analysis and A Preliminary Feedback Intervention Theory," *Psychological Bulletin* 119(2) (1996), pp. 254-284.

39. Rachel Feintzeig, "You're Awesome! Firms Scrap Negative Feedback," *Wall Street Journal*, February 11, 2015, p. B1.

40. A. N. Kluger and A. DeNisi, "The Effects of Feedback Interventions on Performance: A Historical Review, a Meta-Analysis and a Preliminary Feedback Intervention Theory," *Psychological Bulletin* 119(2) (1996), pp. 254–284.

41. H. John Bernardin, "Behavioral Expectation Scales v. Summated Ratings: A Fairer Comparison," *Journal of Applied Psychology* 62 (1977), pp. 422–427; H. John Bernardin, Kim Alvares, and C. J. Cranny, "A Recomparison of Behavioral Expectation Scales to Summated Scales," *Journal of Applied Psychology* 61 (1976), pp. 284–291; C. A. Schriesheim and U. E. Gattiker, "A Study of the Abstract Desirability of Behavior-Based v. Trait-Oriented Performance Rating," *Proceedings of the Academy of Management* 43 (1982), pp. 307–311; F. S. Landy and J. L. Farr, "Performance Rating," *Psychological Bulletin* 87 (1980), pp. 72–107.

42. Michael Keeley, "A Contingency Framework for Performance Evaluation," *Academy of Management Review* 3 (1978), pp. 428–438.

43. H. Risher, "Refocusing Performance Management for High Performance," *Compensation and Benefits Review* (September–October 2003), pp. 20–30.

44. Harvard Business Review, *HBR Guide to Coaching Employees* (Boston: Harvard Business Review Press, 2015).

45. H. J. Bernardin, K. Cooke, and P. Villanova, "Conscientiousness and Agreeableness as Predictors of Rating Leniency," *Journal of Applied Psychology* 85(2) (2000), pp. 232–234.

46. K. Y. Kim, L. Atwater, P. C. Patel, and J. W. Smither, "Multisource Feedback, Human Capital, and the Financial Performance of Organizations," *Journal of Applied Psychology* 101, no. 11 (2016), p. 1569; S. L. Rynes, B. Gerhart, and L. Parks, "Personnel Psychology: Performance Evaluation and Pay for Performance," *Annual Review of Psychology* 56 (2005), pp. 571–600.

47. Mark R. Edwards and Ann J. Ewen, *360 Degree Feedback: The Powerful New Model for Employee Assessment and Performance Improvement* (Toronto: American Management Association, 1996).

48. IOMA, "Perils and Payoffs of Multi-Rater Feedback Programs," *Pay for Performance Report,* May 2003, p. 2.

49. Mark R. Edwards and Ann J. Ewen, *360 Degree Feedback: The Powerful New Model for Employee Assessment and Performance Improvement* (Toronto: American Management Association, 1996).

50. IOMA, "Perils and Payoffs of Multi-Rater Feedback Programs" (Newark, NJ: BNA Subsidiaries, 2007); D. Waldman, L. Atwater, and D. Antonioni, "Has 360 Degree Feedback Gone Amok?" *Academy of Management Executive* 12(2) (1998), pp. 86–94.

51. C. Viswesvaran, F. L. Schmidt, and D. S. Ones, "The Moderating Influence of Job Performance Dimension on Convergence of Supervisory and Peer Ratings of Job Performance: Unconfounding Construct-Level Convergence and Rating Difficulty," *Journal of Applied Psychology* 87 (2002), pp. 245–354.

52. Brian Hoffman, Charles E. Lance, Bethany Bynum, and William A. Gentry, "Rater Source Effects Are Alive and Well After All," *Personnel Psychology* 63 (2010), pp. 119–151.

53. Susan E. Jackson, Randall S. Schuller, and J. Carlos Rivero, "Organizational Characteristics as Predictors of Personnel Practices," *Personnel Psychology* 42 (1989), pp. 727–786.

54. E. Pulakos and W. Borman, *Developing the Basic Criterion Scores for Army-Wide and MOS-Specific Ratings* (Alexandria, VA: U.S. Army Research Institute, 1983).

55. K. R. Murphy, "Explaining the Weak Relationship between Job Performance and Ratings of Job Performance," *Industrial and Organizational Psychology: Perspectives on Science and Practice* 1, (2008), pp. 148–160.

56. Deniz S. Ones, Chockalingam Viswesvaran, and Frank L. Schmidt, "No New Terrain: Reliability and Construct Validity of Job Performance Ratings," *Industrial and Organizational Psychology* 1 (2008), pp. 174–179.

57. Deniz S. Ones, Frank L. Schmidt, and Chockalingam Viswesvaran, "Comparative Analysis of the Reliability of Job Performance Ratings," *Journal of Applied Psychology* 81(5), 1996, pp. 557–574.

58. F. S. Landy and J. L. Farr, "Performance Rating," *Psychological Bulletin* 87 (1980), pp. 72–107.

59. M. M. Harris and J. Schaubroeck, "A Meta Analysis of Self-Supervisor, Self-Peer, and Peer-Supervisor Ratings," *Personnel Psychology* 4 (1988), pp. 43–62.

60. R. Saavedra and S. Kwun, "Peer Evaluation in Self Managing Work Groups," *Journal of Applied Psychology* 78(3), 1993, pp. 450–462.

61. Conference on Performance Management, Center for Effective Organizations, April 23, 2003.

62. M. M. Harris and J. Schaubroeck, "A Meta Analysis of Self-Supervisor, Self-Peer, and Peer-Supervisor Ratings," *Personnel Psychology* 41(1), 1988, pp. 43–62.

63. C. Longenecker and L. Fink, "On Employee Self-Appraisals: Benefits and Opportunities," *Journal of Compensation and Benefits* 22(3), 2006, pp. 12–16.

64. Patti Bond, "Home Depot Uses Customer Ratings for Employee Incentives," Cox News Service, Wednesday, June 21, 2006; visited July 7, 2009 *http://www.statesman.com/news/content/shared/money/stories/coxnews/HOME_DEPOT_0621_COX.html.*

65. Mark R. Edwards and Ann J. Ewen, *360 Degree Feedback: The Powerful New Model for Employee Assessment and Performance Improvement* (Toronto: American Management Association, 1996).

66. William L. Bearly and John E. Jones, *360 Degree Feedback: Strategies, Tactics, and Techniques for Developing Leaders* (Amherst, MA: HRD Press, 1996).

67. D. Antonioni, "The Effects of Feedback Accountability on Upward Appraisal Ratings," *Personnel Psychology* 47 (1994), pp. 349–356.

68. J. Nunnally, *Psychometric Theory*, 2nd ed. (New York: McGraw-Hill, 1978).

69. E. Belogolovsky and P. A. Bamberger, "Signaling in Secret: Pay for Performance and the Incentive and Sorting Effects of Pay Secrecy," *Academy of Management Journal*, 57(6), 2014, pp. 1706–1733.

70. J. Schaubroeck and S. Lam, "How Similarity to Peers and Supervisor Influences Organizational Advancement in Different Cultures," *Academy of Management Journal,* 45(6) 2002, pp. 1125–1136; K. Murphy and J. Cleveland, *Understanding Performance Appraisal* (Thousand Oaks, CA: Sage, 1995).

71. J. Lefkowitz, "The Role of Interpersonal Affective Regard in Supervisory Performance Ratings: A Literature Review and Proposed Causal Model," *Journal of Occupational and Organizational Psychology* 73(1), 2000, pp. 61–85; R. L. Cardy and G. H. Dobbins, "Affect and Appraisal Accuracy: Liking as an Integral Dimension in Evaluating Performance," *Journal of Applied Psychology* 71 (1986), pp. 672–678; Robert C. Liden and Sandy J. Wayne, "Effect of Impression Management on Performance Ratings: A Longitudinal Study," *Academy of Management Journal* 38(1), 1995, pp. 232–260; Angelo S. DeNisi, Lawrence H. Peters, and Arup Varma, "Interpersonal Affect and Performance Appraisal: A Field Study," *Personnel Psychology* 49 (1996), pp. 341–360.

72. G. Alliger and K. J. Williams, "Affective Congruence and the Employment Interview," in *Advances in Information Processing in Organizations,* vol. 4, eds. J. R. Meindl, R. L. Cardy, and S. M. Puffer (Greenwich, CT: JAI Press, 1986).

73. F. S. Landy and J. L. Farr, "Performance Rating," *Psychological Bulletin* 87 (1980), pp. 72–107; A. S. DeNisi, T. P. Cafferty, and B. M. Meglino, "A Cognitive View of the Performance Appraisal Process: A Model and Research Propositions," *Organizational Behavior and Human Performance* 33 (1984), pp. 360–396; Jack M. Feldman, "Beyond Attribution Theory: Cognitive Processes in Performance Appraisal," *Journal of Applied Psychology* 66(2), 1981, pp. 127–148; W. H. Cooper, "Ubiquitous Halo," *Psychological Bulletin* 90 (1981), pp. 218–244.

74. A. DeNisi and G. Stevens, "Profiles of Performance, Performance Evaluations, and Personnel Decisions," *Academy of Management* 24(3), 1981, pp. 592–602; W. Cascio and E. Valtenzi, "Relations Among Criteria of Police Performance," *Journal of Applied Psychology* 63(1), 1978, pp. 22–28; W. Bigoness, "Effects of Applicant's Sex, Race, and Performance on Employer Performance Ratings: Some Additional Findings," *Journal of Applied Psychology* 61(1), 1976, pp. 80–84; D. P. Moore, "Evaluating In-Role and Out-of-Role Performers," *Academy of Management Journal* 27(3), 1984, pp. 603–618; W. Borman, L. White, E. Pulakos, and S. Oppler, "Models of Supervisory Job Performance Ratings," *Journal of Applied Psychology* 76(6), 1991, pp. 863–872.

75. W. Borman, L. White, E. Pulakos, and S. Oppler, "Models of Supervisory Job Performance Ratings," *Journal of Applied Psychology* 76(6) (1991), pp. 863–872.

76. D. C. Treadway, G. R. Ferris, A. B. Duke, et al., "The Moderating Role of Subordinate Political Skill on Supervisors' Impressions of Subordinate Ingratiation and Ratings of Subordinate Interpersonal Facilitation," *Journal of Applied Psychology* 92(3) 2007, pp. 848–855.

77. H. J. Bernardin and Richard Beatty, *Performance Appraisal: Assessing Human Behavior at Work* (Boston: Kent, 1984).

78. American Management Association, "Top Performers? Most Managers Rated Average or Better," *Compflash,* September 1992, p. 3.

79. C. Longnecker, H. Sims, and D. Gioia, "Behind the Mask: The Politics of Employee Appraisal," *Academy of Management Executive* 1(3) (1987), pp. 183–193.

80. G. Dobbins, R. Cardy, and D. Truxillo, "The Effects of Purpose of Appraisal and Individual Differences in Stereotypes of Women on Sex Differences in Performance Ratings: A Laboratory and Field Study," *Journal of Applied Psychology* 73(3) (1988), pp. 551–558.

81. M. Elvira and C. Zatzick, "Who's Displaced First? The Role of Race in Layoff Decisions," *Industrial Relations* 49(2) (2002), pp. 329–361.

82. A. S. DeNisi and G. E. Stevens, "Profiles of Performance, Performance Evaluations, and Personnel Decisions," *Academy of Management Journal* 24(3), September 1981, pp. 592–602; William Scott and Clay Hamner, "The Influence of Variations in Performance Profiles on the Performance Evaluation Process: An Examination of the Validity of the Criterion," *Organizational Behavior and Human Performance* 14 (1975), pp. 360–370; Edward Jones, Leslie Rock, Kelly Shaver, George Goethals, and Laurence Ward, "Pattern of Performance and Ability Attributions: An Unexpected Primacy Effect," *Journal of Personality and Social Psychology* 10(4), 1968, pp. 317–340.

83. B. Gaugler and A. Rudolph, "The Influence of Assessee Performance Variation on Assessor's Judgments," *Personnel Psychology* 45 (1992), pp. 77–98.

84. F. J. Landy and J. L. Farr, "Performance Rating," *Psychological Bulletin* 87 (1980), pp. 72–107; H. J. Bernardin and R. W. Beatty, *Performance Appraisal: Assessing Human Behavior at Work* (Dallas: Scott, Foresman, 1984).

85. N. Cantor and W. Mischel, "Traits v. Prototypes: The Effects on Recognition and Memory," *Journal of Personality and Social Psychology* 35 (1977), pp. 38–48; R. J. Spiro, "Remembering Information From Text: The 'State of Schema' Approach," in R. C. Anderson, R. J. Spiro, and W. E. Montatague, eds.,

Schooling and the Acquisition of Knowledge (Hillsdale, CA: Erlbaum, 1977); T. K. Srull and R. S. Wyer, "Category Accessibility and Social Perception: Some Implications for the Study of Person Memory and Interpersonal Judgments," *Journal of Personality and Social Psychology* 38 (1980), pp. 841–856.

86. Robert Heneman and Kenneth Wexley, "The Effects of Time Delay in Rating and Amount of Information Observed on Performance Rating Accuracy," *Academy of Management Journal* 26(4), 1983, pp. 677–686.
87. B. P. Maroney and R. M. Buckley, "Does Research in Performance Appraisal Influence the Practice of Performance Appraisal? Regretfully Not," *Public Personnel Management* 21 (1992), pp. 185–196.
88. Robert Liden and Terence Mitchell, "The Effects of Group Interdependence on Supervisor Performance Evaluations," *Personnel Psychology* 36(2), 1983, pp. 289–299.
89. Dick Grote, *Forced Ranking: Making Performance Management Work* (Boston, MA: Harvard Business School Press, 2005); G. H. Dobbins, R. L. Cardy, and D. M. Truxillo, "The Effects of Purpose of Appraisal and Individual Differences in Stereotypes of Women on Sex Differences in Performance Ratings: A Laboratory and Field Study," *Journal of Applied Psychology* 73(33), 1986, pp. 551–558.
90. Samuel Y. Todd, Kenneth J. Harris, Ranida B. Harris, and Anthony R. Wheeler, "Career Success Implications of Political Skill," *Journal of Social Psychology* 149(3), June 2009, pp. 179–204.
91. G. R. Ferris and T. A. Judge, "Personnel/Human Resource Management: A Political Influence Perspective," *Journal of Management* 17 (1991), pp. 1–42.
92. Yoav Ganzach, "Negativity (and Positivity) in Performance Evaluation: Three Field Studies," *Journal of Applied Psychology* 80(4) (1995), pp. 491–499.
93. D. Winstanley, "How Accurate Are Performance Appraisals?" *Personnel Administrator* 25(8), 1980, pp. 55–58; F. S. Landy and J. L. Farr, "Performance Rating," *Psychological Bulletin* 87 (1980), pp. 72–107; R. L. Heneman and K. N. Wexley, "The Effects of Time Delay in Rating and Amount of Information Observed on Performance Rating Accuracy," *Academy of Management Journal* 26 (1983), pp. 677–686.
94. Leslie Kwoh, "'Rank and Yank' Retains Vocal Fans," *The Wall Street Journal,* (January 31, 2012), p. B6.
95. Conversation between Jerry Newman and Lisa Emerson, VP Global Total Compensation, McDonalds, Fall 2008.
96. D. Grote, *Forced Ranking: Making Performance Management Work* (Boston, MA: Harvard Business School Press, 2005).
97. S. Scullen, P. Bergey, and L. Aiman-Smith, "Forced Distribution Rating Systems and the Improvement of Workforce Potential: A Baseline Simulation," *Personnel Psychology* 58(1), 2005, pp. 1–33; S. H. Moon, S. E. Scullen, and G. P. Latham, "Precarious Curve Ahead: The Effects of Forced Distribution Rating Systems on Job Performance," *Human Resource Management Review* 26, no. 2 (2016), pp. 166–179.
98. WorldatWork. Compensation Programs & Practices Survey (2019). Worldatwork.org.
99. L. Cummings and D. Schwab, *Performance in Organization* (Glenview, IL: Scott Foresman, 1973).
100. Neal P. Mero and Stephan J. Motowidlo, "Effects of Rater Accountability on the Accuracy and the Favorability of Performance Ratings," *Journal of Applied Psychology* 80(4), 1995, pp. 517–524.
101. H. J. Bernardin and E. C. Pence, "Effects of Rater Training: Creating New Response Sets and Decreasing Accuracy," *Journal of Applied Psychology* 6 (1980), pp. 60–66.
102. Sheldon Zedeck and Wayne Cascio, "Performance Appraisal Decision as a Function of Rater Training and Purpose of the Appraisal," *Journal of Applied Psychology* 67(6), 1982, pp. 752–758.

103. Erich C. Dierdorff, Eric A. Surface, and Kenneth G. Brown, "Frame-of-Reference Training Effectiveness: Effects of Goal Orientation and Self-Efficacy on Affective, Cognitive, Skill-Based, and Transfer Outcomes," *Journal of Applied Psychology* 6, vol. 95 (2010), pp. 1181–1191; E. Rogers, C. Rogers, and W. Metlay, "Improving the Payoff From 360-Degree Feedback," *Human Resource Planning,* 25(3), 2002, pp. 44–54; H. J. Bernardin and M. R. Buckley, "Strategies in Rater Training," *Academy of Management Review* 6(2), 1981, pp. 205–212; D. Smith, "Training Programs for Performance Appraisal: A Review," *Academy of Management Review* 11(1), 1986, pp. 22–40; B. Davis and M. Mount, "Effectiveness of Performance Appraisal Training Using Computer Assisted Instruction and Behavioral Modeling," *Personnel Psychology* 3 (1984), pp. 439–452; H. J. Bernardin, "Effects of Rater Training on Leniency and Halo Errors in Student Ratings of Instructors," *Journal of Applied Psychology* 63(3), 1978, pp. 301–308; J. M. Ivancevich, "Longitudinal Study of the Effects of Rater Training on Psychometric Error in Ratings," *Journal of Applied Psychology* 64(5), 1979, pp. 502–508.

104. H. J. Bernardin and M. R. Buckley, "Strategies in Rater Training," *Academy of Management Review* 6 (1981), pp. 205–221.

105. C. O. Longnecker, H. P. Sims Jr., and D. A. Gioia, "Behind the Mask: The Politics of Employee Appraisal," *Academy of Management Executive* 1(3), August 1987, pp. 183–193.

106. S. Adler, M. Campion, A. Colquitt, A. Grubb, K. Murphy, R. Ollander-Krane, and E. D. Pulakos, "Getting Rid of Performance Ratings: Genius or Folly? A Debate," *Industrial and Organizational Psychology* 9(2) (2016), pp. 219–252.

107. WorldatWork, "Research Report: Performance Management and Rewards 2017," https://www.worldatwork.org/docs/research-and-surveys/surveys/worldatwork-research-report-performance-management-and-rewards/performance-mngmnt-rewards-2017.pdf.

108. Stephen Miller, "Improving Performance Evaluations Using Calibration: Get Managers Onboard and Keep the Process on Track," May 23, 2014, https://www.shrm.org/resourcesandtools/hr-topics/compensation/pages/calibration-sessions.aspx.

109. S. Waugh, "Solid Performance Reviews," *Supervision* 67(5), 2006, pp. 16–17.

110. Doug Blizzard, "Effective Performance Management," *Journal of Accountancy*, 218(1), 2014, pp. 18–19.

111. Ann Podolske, "Creating a Review System that Works," *Pay for Performance Report* (March 1996), pp. 2–4.

112. Greg Bustin, *Accountability: The Key to Driving a High-Performance Culture* (New York: McGraw-Hill, 2014).

113. Stephen J. Carroll, J. Kline Harrison, Monika K. Renard, et al., "Due Process in Performance Appraisal: A Quasi-Experiment in Procedural Justice," *Administrative Science Quarterly* 40 (1995), pp. 495–523.

114. IOMA, *Pay for Performance Report* (Newark, NJ: BNA Subsidiaries, January 2002, p. 13).

115. Harvard Business Review, *HBR Guide to Coaching Employees* (Cambridge, MA: Harvard Business Review Press, 2014).

116. Ann Podolske, "Creating a Review System That Works," *Pay for Performance Report,* March 1996, pp. 2–4.

117. Mercer homepage, *www.mercerhr.com,* April 24, 2003.

118. Avraham N. Kluger and Angelo DeNisi, "The Effects of Feedback Interventions on Performance: A Historical Review, a Meta-Analysis, and a Preliminary Feedback Intervention Theory," *Psychological Bulletin* 119(2), 1996, pp. 254–284.

119. A. DeNisi, T. Robbins, and T. Cafferty, "Organization of Information Used for Performance Appraisals: Role of Diary-Keeping," *Journal of Applied Psychology* 74(1), 1989, pp. 124–129.

120. Angelo S. DeNisi, Lawrence H. Peters, and Arup Varma, "Interpersonal Affect and Performance Appraisal: A Field Study," *Personnel Psychology* 49 (1996), pp. 341–360; F. J. Landy, J. L. Barnes, and K. R. Murphy, "Correlates of Perceived Fairness and Accuracy of Performance Evaluations," *Journal of Applied Psychology* 63 (1978), pp. 751–754.

121. S. Snell and K. Wexley, "Performance Diagnosis: Identifying the Causes of Poor Performance," *Personnel Administrator,* April 1985, pp. 117–127.

122. Rachel Emma Silverman, "Yearly Reviews? Try Weekly," *The Wall Street Journal,* September 6, 2011, p. B6.

123. Rachel Feintzeig, "You're Awesome! Firms Scrap Negative Feedback," *Wall Street Journal*, February 11, 2015, p. B1.

124. E. D. Pulakos, R. Mueller-Hanson, and S. Arad, "The Evolution of Performance Management: Searching for Value," *Annual Review of Organizational Psychology and Organizational Behavior* 6(2019), 249–271; T. C. Brown, P. O'Kane, B. Mazumdar, and M. McCracken, "Performance Management: A Scoping Review of the Literature and an Agenda for Future Research," *Human Resource Development Review* 18(1), 2019, 47–82; S. L. Rynes, B. Gerhart, and L. Parks, "Personnel Psychology: Performance Evaluation and Pay for Performance," *Annual Review of Psychology* 56 (2005), pp. 571–600; R. D. Bretz, Jr., G. T. Milkovich, and W. Read, "The Current State of Performance Appraisal Research and Practice: Concerns, Directions, and Implications," *Journal of management* 18(2) (1992) 321–352.

125. Rachel Feintzeig, "Your Manager Wants to See You. Again," *Wall Street Journal*, May 10, 2017, p. B7.

126. Rachel Feintzeig, "Your Manager Wants to See You. Again," *Wall Street Journal*, May 10, 2017, p. B7.

127. K. R. Murphy, "Performance Evaluation Will Not Die, But It Should," *Human Resource Management Journal* 30(1) (2020), pp. 13–31.

128. G. Ledford, G. Benson, and E. Lawler, "A Study of Cutting Edge Performance Management Practices: Ongoing Feedback, Ratingless Reviews, and Crowd-Sourced Feedback," *WorldatWork Journal* 25(2), 2016.

129. Adler, S., Campion, M., Colquitt, A., Grubb, A., Murphy, K., Ollander-Krane, R., & Pulakos, E. D. (2016). Getting rid of performance ratings: Genius or folly? A debate. *Industrial and Organizational Psychology* 9(2), 219–252.

130. Pulakos, E. D., Mueller-Hanson, R., & Arad, S. (2019). The evolution of performance management: Searching for value. *Annual Review of Organizational Psychology and Organizational Behavior* 6, 249-271.

131. HR Specialist, "Be Ready to Explain Male/Female Pay Differences," Minnesota Employment Law, 4(4), 2011, pp. 1–2.

132. Elizabeth C. Hirsh, "The Strength of Weak Enforcement: The Impact of Discrimination Charges, Legal Environments, and Organizational Conditions on Workplace Segregation," *American Sociological Review* 74(2), 2009, pp. 245–271.

133. LRP Publications, "Black SSA Employees Get 7.75 Million Settlement," *Federal Human Resources Week* 8(39), 2002, pp. 1, 3.

134. *Brito v. Zia Company,* 478 F.2d 1200 (1973).

135. *Brito v. Zia Company,* 478 F.2d 1200 (1973).

136. G. L. Lubben, D. E. Thompson, and C. R. Klasson, "Performance Appraisal: The Legal Implications of Title VII," *Personnel* 57(3), 1980, pp. 11–21; H. Feild and W. Halley, "The Relationship of Performance Appraisal System Characteristics to Verdicts in Selected Employment Discrimination Cases," *Academy of Management Journal* 25(2), 1982, pp. 392–406; *Albermarle Paper Company v. Moody,* U.S. Supreme Court, no. 74–389 and 74–428, 10 FEP Cases 1181 (1975); *Moody v. Albermarle Paper Company,* 474 F.3d. 134.

137. H. S. Feild and W. H. Holley, "The Relationship of Performance Appraisal System Characteristics to Verdicts in Selected Employment Discrimination Cases," *Academy of Management Journal* 25(2), 1982, pp. 392–406; Gerald Barrett and Mary Kernan, "Performance Appraisal and Terminations: A Review of Court Decisions Since *Brito v. Zia* with Implications for Personnel Practices," *Personnel Psychology* 40 (1987), pp. 489–503.

138. D. Martin and K. Bartol, "The Legal Ramifications of Performance Appraisal: An Update," *Employee Relations* 17(2), 1991, pp. 286–293.

139. *Payne v. General Motors,* 53 FEP Cases 471 (D. C. Kan. 1990).

140. J. McGregor, "The Struggle to Measure Performance," *BusinessWeek,* January 9, 2006, p. 26.

141. C. Wood, "Measuring Progress, Avoiding Liability in Evaluating Employees," *Employment Law Weekly,* December 1999, pp. 1–9.

142. George Milkovich and Carolyn Milkovich, "Strengthening the Pay-Performance Relationship: The Research," *Compensation and Benefits Review,* November–December 1992, pp. 22–31.

143. A. Mitra, A. Tenhia¨la¨, and J. D. Shaw, "Smallest Meaningful Pay Increases: Field Test, Constructive Replication, and Extension," *Human Resource Management* 55(1) 2016, pp. 69–81.

Part V
Employee Benefits

Dig two holes in the ground. In the first, bury $10.74. In the second, put $20.39. Now every hour, Monday through Friday, 8 a.m. until 4 p.m., dig up those holes and add the corresponding amount.[1] Leave the money in these holes as very expensive fertilizer for your geraniums. Why these amounts, you ask? Why bury them in the backyard, you ask? Well, those dollar amounts are the cost of a full-time employee's benefits each hour of every workweek in, respectively, a private sector firm and a state or local government job. (See Chapter 13.) Burying the money in the backyard is our way of saying it's not clear the money is any worse off in the ground than invested in employee benefits. A bit harsh? Especially since more than 75 percent of employees claim benefits are either extremely important (33%) or very important (45%) in the decision to accept or reject a job.[2] But stop and think about what we know is fact—not faith—in the benefits area. Which of the issues covered in the pay model (see **Exhibit V.1**), for example, can we answer with respect to benefits? Does effective employee benefit management facilitate organization performance? The answer is unclear. We do know that benefit costs can be cut, and this affects the bottom line (admittedly an important measure of organization performance). But what about other alignment and management efforts? Do benefits complement organization strategy and performance? We don't know. Or do employee benefits impact an organization's ability to attract, retain, and motivate employees? Conventional wisdom says employee benefits can affect retention, but there is no definitive research to support this conclusion. A similar lack of research surrounds each of the other potential payoffs to a sound benefits program.

EXHIBIT V.1 The Pay Model

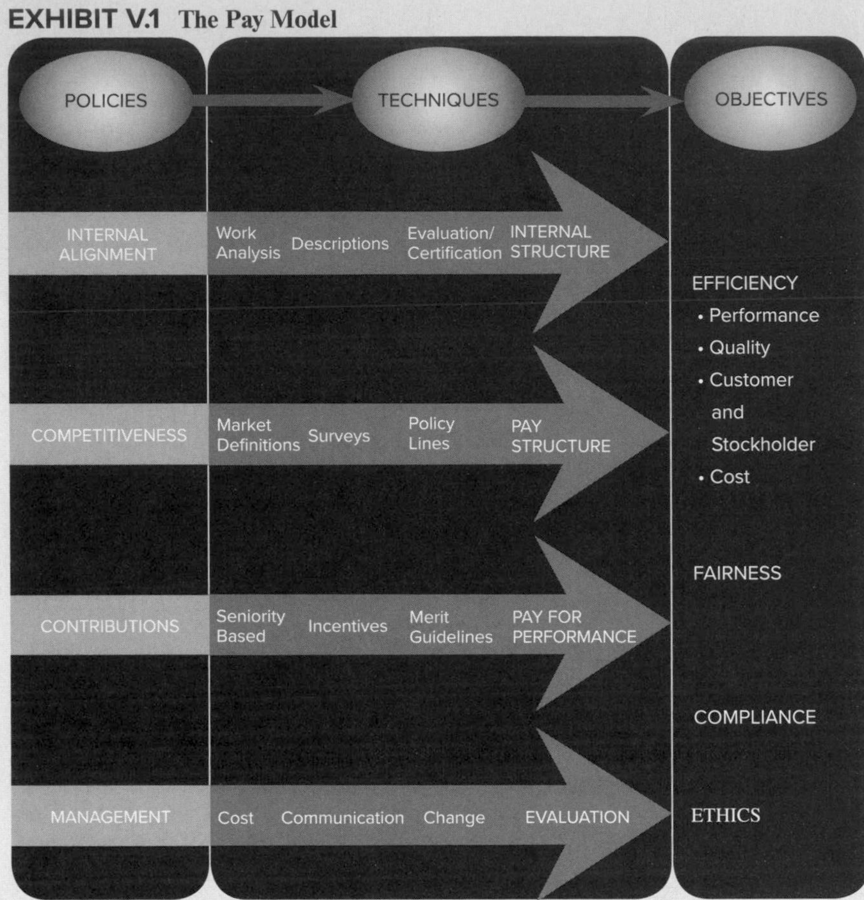

The only absolute reality is this: Employee benefits cost trillions of dollars per year. Obviously then, it is important to examine whether all of this money is being well spent and how to get the best return possible. Not surprisingly, firms are increasingly paying attention to this compensation component. It represents a huge labor cost, but with no solid evidence on returns in most organizations.

Compounding this concern is the ever-present entitlement problem. Employees perceive benefits as a right, independent of how well they or the company perform. Efforts to reduce benefit levels or eliminate parts of the package altogether would meet with employee resistance and dissatisfaction. Just ask workers and retirees at GM, Ford, or Fiat Chrysler (now part of Stellantis).[3] In an effort to stop the competitive bleeding, the auto industry is cutting benefits for both current and retired employees.

Assuming that organizations must find ways to control the costs of benefits wherever possible, this section of the book focuses on identifying ways to maximize the returns from benefit expenditures. As a first step in this direction, **Chapter 12** identifies issues organizations should face in developing and maintaining a benefit program. A model of the benefit determination process is also presented, to provide a structure for thinking about employee benefits. **Chapter 13** provides a summary of the state of employee benefits today. Hopefully, this will provide the groundwork for the innovative and effective benefit packages of tomorrow.

Chapter **Twelve**
The Benefit Determination Process

Chapter Outline

What can you do with a few trillion dollars?[4] Help balance the budget? Buy a few new copies of this book? Well, the answer is, you can cover the cost of all employee benefits in the United States today. It's hard to believe that employee benefits cost this much. This is particularly hard to believe when we take a look at what used to pass as benefits in the not-too-distant past:

- "In 1875, American Express introduced a formal pension plan permitting workers to retire at half-pay at age 60 with 20 or more years of service. Up to this point in time, pension benefits, if any, were given on an informal basis by companies to those who were no longer able to work."[5] Eventually it was common for companies to settle on a retirement age of 65. At the time, life expectancy at age 35 was age 66. Today, life expectancy at age 35 is age 78. "As life expectancy continued to improve, financing this benefit would become an increasing concern."[6]
- In 1880, a carriage shop published a set of rules for employees that stated, in part: "Working hours shall be from 7 a.m. to 9 p.m. every day except the Sabbath.... After an employee has been with this firm for five years he shall receive an added payment of five cents per day, provided the firm has prospered in a

manner to make it possible.... It is the bounden duty of each employee to put away at least 10 percent of his monthly wages for his declining years so he will not become a burden upon his betters."

- In 1915, employees in the iron and steel industry worked a standard 60 to 64 hours per week. By 1930 that schedule had been reduced to 54 hours.
- It was not until 1929 that the Blue Cross concept of prepaid medical costs was introduced.
- Prior to 1935, only one state (Wisconsin) had a program of unemployment compensation benefits for workers who lost their jobs through no fault of their own.
- Before World War II, very few companies paid hourly employees for holidays. In most companies, employees were told not to report for work on holidays and to enjoy the time off, but their paychecks were smaller the following week.[7]

In comparison to these "benefits" from the past, today's reality seems staggering. Consider the kinds of things that are common in companies that made the *Fortune* magazine list of "100 Best Companies to Work For in America."[8] These companies recognize the importance of taking care of employees' needs as a key factor in attracting and retaining the best employees. A first-class benefit plan includes some mix of the following benefits: education reimbursement; on-site child care services, car cleaning, financial counseling, concierge services, and retirement benefits.[9] Just consider some of the extra benefits beyond the norm at Google (AKA, Alphabet), a company typically at the top of best employers lists: The parental leave program has been upgraded. New parents, regardless of gender, now get up to twelve weeks of fully paid baby-bonding time. This also included $500 "Baby Bonding Bucks." Along with this are liberal policies for volunteering, on-site fitness centers and medical care, lavish paid lunches daily, and reimbursement for college tuition.[10]

Clearly Google would argue that these extra services are important benefits of employment that perhaps make it easier to attract, retain, and motivate. But the truth is, we don't know if even ordinary benefits have positive payoffs. We do know that employees consistently rate benefits a key factor in job satisfaction even though fewer than 50 percent of employees are actually satisfied with their benefits.[11] Additionally, there is a mismatch between cost to employer and perceived value to employee: the cost is much higher than employees estimate.[12]

OVERVIEW

Controlling labor costs is not possible without controlling benefits costs. Employers continue to be focused on cost control, which has included shifting health care costs and responsibility for retirement (retiree income, but also retiree health care coverage and costs) increasingly to employees. Employers also seek to make benefits costs, like compensation costs generally, move more in the same direction of revenues and profits (rather than being solely fixed costs). Adjusting the amount they contribute to employee 401(k) retirement plans depending on business conditions is an example.

On the behavioral side, benefits seem to influence whether potential employees come to work for a company, whether they stay, when they retire–perhaps even how they perform.[13] However, as with compensation generally (see our discussion of Sorting Effects in **Chapter 1** and elsewhere), different employees look for different types of benefits. For example, at consulting, financial services and tech firms, where long working hours had long been the norm, some firms decided to move toward shorter work weeks and/or (aim to) be more supportive to paid leave (including for fathers) to have better success with that the part of the applicant pool interested in more work-life balance.[14] The SAS Institute, which we discussed in **Chapter 2**, has long had a 35-hour work week, which had historically been unusual in the tech industry. Benefits can also be more directly tailored to different employee preferences via flexible benefits plans (discussed later) and as part of broader individualized employment agreements between a manager and employee referred to as an "i-deal."[15]

Thus, as we will see, benefits can be used to differentiate an employer from competitors, allowing it to tap in to what in some cases may be a valuable, but underutilized, part of the pool of human capital.[16] In addition, it may be that employers can sometimes offer benefits that not only are better at matching applicant/ employee preferences, but may be able to do it cheaper, giving it an edge on rivals. One example is Disney, which gives its employees free access to its parks and large discounts at its hotels, restaurants, and on its merchandise. Although rival employers could try to imitate Disney by offering its own products/services (think for a moment what these might be) for free or at a discount, it seems unlikely that this would successfully create a comparable level of value to their employees at the same cost, given Disney's uniqueness.[17]

Although it makes sense to think of benefits as part of total compensation, benefits are also unique in some important aspects. As noted above, different employees will have different preferences for specific benefits. Another way benefits are unique is their complexity. It is relatively easy to understand the value of a dollar as part of a salary but not as part of a benefits package. The advantages and disadvantages of different types of medical coverage, pension provisions, disability insurance, and investment options for retirement funds are often difficult to grasp, and their value (beyond a general sense that they are good to have) is rarely as clear as the value of one's salary. Most fundamentally, employees may not even be aware of the benefits available to them; and if they are aware, they may not understand how to use them. When employers spend large sums of money on benefits but employees do not understand the benefits or attach much value to them, the return on employers' benefits investment will be fairly dismal. One reason for giving more responsibility to employees for retirement planning and other benefits is to increase their understanding of the value of such benefits.

Finally, the pandemic has helped us see that benefits and benefits flexibility are critical in dealing with a crisis.[18] Fidelity Investments began a pilot program that allows employees to reduce their hours to 30, to allow them more time for other needs. Their salary will be reduced, but not their benefits. Fidelity will hire additional employees to cover the work so that colleagues are not overwhelmed. Elephant Ventures, a software and data engineering company is not reducing hours, but rather going to a 4 day, 10 hour week, with Fridays off, with "pencils down, no e-mails or Slack" on Fridays. The company says it made this move after it had started to notice some employees, especially working parents, were struggling. Software firm Red Hat has started shutting down operations on quarterly recharge days. One software engineer at Red Hat, a father of three young children, reported that some of his co-workers cried when they received the e-mail announcing the recharge days: "People do need time and space to heal themselves." Some of this response may last beyond the pandemic, not only in work-life balance flexibility, but also in areas like more telework, greater attention to employee well-being (including mental and financial), and telehealth (including mental health services).[19]

WHY THE GROWTH IN EMPLOYEE BENEFITS?

As **Exhibit 12.1** illustrates, **employee benefits** can no longer realistically be called "fringe benefits." Among private sector employers in the United States, the average cost of benefits is $10.72/hour, which accounts for 30 percent of total compensation (wages and salaries + benefits) and adds 42 cents on top of every dollar of wages and salaries. **Exhibit 12.1** also shows that the cost of total compensation, including both wages and salaries and benefits, is substantially higher in larger than in smaller firms.[20]

As an example of how the costs of benefits operate in a specific firm, visualize cars rolling down the assembly lines at the Big Three (Ford, General Motors, Fiat Chrysler/Stellantis). Historically, the cost of health insurance coverage for workers building their cars has been more than the cost of steel for the cars, and these health care costs remain high.[21] To make matters more challenging still, the Big Three are competing with foreign automakers, whose workers in their U.S. factories are younger and healthier and thus have much lower health insurance costs. (Also, few, if any, have retired, making their retirement benefits costs lower also.) That makes it challenging for the Big Three to compete by offering a car of similar quality at a similar price.

As **Exhibit 12.2** shows, the cost of employer benefits has risen over time. Over one 20-year period (1955–1975), employee benefit costs rose at a rate almost four times greater than employee wages or the consumer price index.[22] (Note: benefits costs are higher in **Exhibit 12.2** than **Exhibit 12.1** because the former includes public sector workers.) Not so long ago, the Big Three automobile manufacturers spent about $1,200 per $20,000 car on worker health insurance. Since then, they have managed to reduce costs. Still, even as of a few years ago, Ford's health insurance costs hit $800 million per year for its U.S. hourly bargaining-unit workers. With U.S. vehicle production that year of 2,492,168, that worked out to a cost of about $320/vehicle just to cover health insurance costs.[23]

Pension costs also are a major challenge for companies. Just ask General Electric, which has the country's most underfunded pension plan in dollar terms at $31 billion. (Intel and Delta Airlines are the most underfunded in percentage terms, with both funding just under 50 percent of their pension liabilities.) More generally, a recent edition of the *Milliman Corporate Pension Funding Study* reports that underfunding is widespread. Even after a run of strong investment returns, the 100 largest U.S. company pensions remain significantly underfunded. On average, 86 percent of pension liabilities are funded and the total amount of underfunding is $252 billion.[24] Underfunding is worse in the public sector. Milliman's analysis of the 100 largest public sector pension plans finds an average funding ratio of 71 percent.[25] The highest funded plan (98.2 percent) is the Wisconsin Retirement System. The worst-funded plans are in Connecticut, Illinois, Kentucky, and New Jersey. For example, the plans in Illinois are funded at 30.6 to 39.6 percent of liabilities, depending on the plan. With looming retirements of baby boomers, this likely spells trouble for already burdened state budgets. (Your increasingly elderly textbook authors, only one of whom lives in Wisconsin, thank you in advance for helping to finance these obligations.)

EXHIBIT 12.1 Total Hourly Compensation and Benefits Costs, U.S. Private Industry Workers, by Establishment Size

	Establishment Size		
	All	1–99 Employees	500 Or More Employees
Total Compensation	$36.23	$29.99	$53.83
Wages and Salaries	$25.48	$22.21	$34.94
Benefits	$10.74	$7.78	$18.88
Benefits/Total Compensation	30%	26%	35%
Benefits/Wages and Salaries	42%	35%	54%

Source: Bureau of Labor Statistics, U.S. Department of Labor. *Employer Costs for Employee Compensation–December 2020.* USDL-20-0437. March 18, 2021. www.bls.gov.

Employee benefits are that part of the total compensation package, other than pay for time worked, provided to employees in whole or in part by employer payments (e.g., life insurance, pension, workers' compensation, vacation).

Exhibit 12.2 shows that benefits costs have grown over time and now represent 31.7 percent of total compensation. There are several factors that have contributed to the growth in benefits costs.

Wage and Price Controls

During both World War II and the Korean War, the federal government instituted strict **wage and price controls.** The compliance agency charged with enforcing these controls was relatively lenient in permitting reasonable increases in benefits. With strict limitations on the size of wage increases, both unions and employers sought new and improved benefits to satisfy worker demands. This was the catalyst for growth in pensions, health care coverage, time off, and a broad spectrum of benefits virtually unthinkable before 1950.

Unions

The climate fostered by wage and price controls created a perfect opportunity for unions to flex the muscles they had acquired under the Wagner Act of 1935. Several National Labor Relations Board rulings during the 1940s freed unions to negotiate over employee benefits. With little freedom to raise wages during the war, unions fought for the introduction of new benefits and the improvement of existing benefits. Success on this front during the war years led to further postwar demands. Largely through the efforts of unions, most

EXHIBIT 12.2

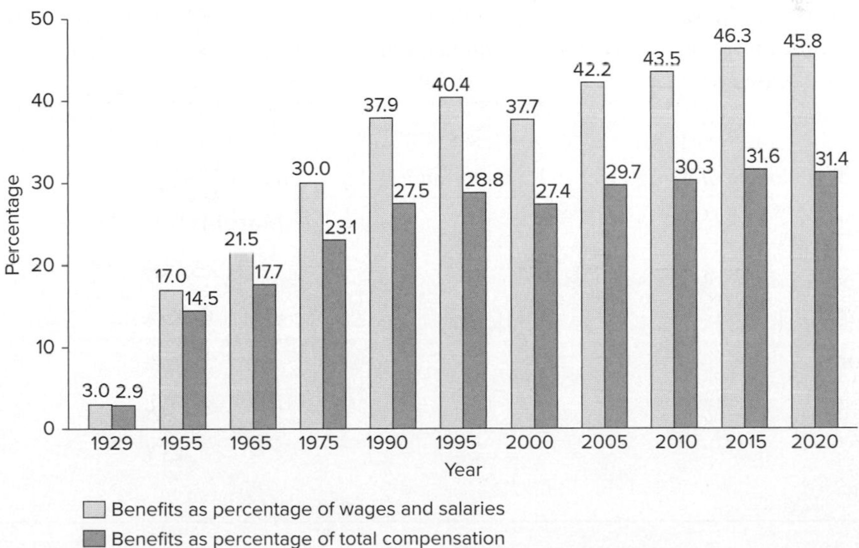

Source: Data through 1990, U.S. Chamber of Commerce Research Center, Employee Benefits 1990, Employee Benefits 1997, Employee Benefits 2000, Washington, DC: U.S. Chamber of Commerce, 1991, 1997, and 2000. Data from 1995 onward: Bureau of Labor Statistics, U.S. Department of Labor. "Employer Costs for Employee Compensation."

notably the autoworkers and steelworkers, several benefits common today were given their initial impetus: pattern pension plans, supplementary unemployment compensation, extended vacation plans, and guaranteed annual wage plans.[26]

Employer Impetus

Many of the benefits in existence today were provided at employer initiative. Much of this initiative can be traced to pragmatic concerns about employee satisfaction and productivity. Rest breaks often were implemented in the belief that fatigue increased accidents and lowered productivity. Savings and profit-sharing plans were implemented (e.g., Procter & Gamble's profit-sharing plan was initiated in 1885) to improve performance and provide increased security for worker retirement years. Indeed, many employer-initiated benefits were designed to create a climate in which employees perceived that management was genuinely concerned for their welfare. Notice, though, these supposed benefits were taken on faith. But their costs were quite real: Without hard data about payoffs, employee benefits slowly became a costly entitlement of the American workforce.

Cost (Including Tax) Effectiveness of Benefits

Another important and sound impetus for the growth of employee benefits is their cost effectiveness in two situations. The first cost advantage is that most employee benefits are not taxable. Provision of a benefit rather than an equivalent increase in wages avoids payment of federal and state personal income tax. Although cash has the advantage of being fungible (i.e., it can be used by each person in the way that fits his/her preferences), an extra dollar paid in cash is not an extra dollar received in the paycheck, as **Exhibit 12.3** demonstrates. In this example, the government collects about 40 cents of the extra dollar when paid in the form of cash, leaving 60 cents to the employee in his/her paycheck. Thus, it can be more efficient to put some of those extra dollars in earnings in the form of benefits.

A second cost-effectiveness component of benefits arises because many group-based benefits (e.g., life, health, and legal insurance) can be obtained at a lower rate than could be obtained by employees acting on their own. Group insurance also has relatively easy qualification standards, giving security to a set of employees who might not otherwise qualify.

EXHIBIT 12.3 Example of Marginal Tax Rates for an Employee Salary of $80,000

	(Marginal) Tax Rate
Federal	25.00%
State (New York)	6.09%
City (New York)	3.82%
Social Security	6.20%
Medicare	1.45%
Total tax rate	43%

Note: Local taxes (state, city, and property taxes) up of to $10,000 total are deductible on the federal return, if itemizing deductions. In this case, the effective marginal tax rate would be 40% (rather than 43%).

Government Impetus

Obviously the government has played an important role in the growth of employee benefits. Three employee benefits are mandated by either the state or federal government: **workers' compensation** (state), **unemployment insurance** (federal), and **social security** (federal). These legally required benefits came about as part of the New Deal in the 1930s in response to the Great Depression, when the national unemployment rate went above 20 percent and no unemployment insurance yet existed. (Question: What has the highest U.S. unemployment rate been in your lifetime?) In addition, most other employee benefits are affected by such laws as the **Employee Retirement Income Security Act (ERISA),** which affects pension administration, and various sections of the Internal Revenue Code.

THE VALUE OF EMPLOYEE BENEFITS

Exhibit 12.4 shows the relative importance that employees attached to different types of benefits across five studies.

In general, the five studies reported in **Exhibit 12.4** show remarkably consistent results over the past two decades. For example, medical benefits continue to be ranked tops in importance for most employee groups. These rankings have added significance when we note that today an employer pays an average of $6,277 for health coverage of a single employee and $15,574 for family coverage. (Employees additionally pay an average of $1,243 for single coverage and $5,588 for family coverage.)[27]

Let's take a firm that pays the above health insurance premiums for 10,000 employees, 60 percent of whom have family coverage and the rest single coverage. That comes to (.60 × 10,000 × $15,574) + (.40 × 10,000 × $6,277), which equals roughly $119 million. One recurring question will be whether that large expenditure is a good investment. A major concern is evidence that employees frequently undervalue the benefits provided

EXHIBIT 12.4 Ranking of Employee Benefits

	Study				
	1	**2**	**3**	**4**	**5**
Medical	1	1	3	1	1
Pension	2	3	8	3	2
Paid vacations and holidays	3	2	nr	2	3
Sickness	4	nr	5	8	nr
Dental	5	nr	6	6	nr
Long-term disability	7	nr	7	9	6
Life insurance	8	nr	4	nr	5

Note: nr = indicates a benefit that was not rated in this study.

Compiled from five sources. Some of the reward components rated in some of the studies were not traditional employee benefits and have been deleted from the rankings here. The five sources were: Employee Benefits Research Institute and Matthew Greenwald and Associates, "Worker Ranking of Employee Benefits," www.ebri.org/pdf/publications/facts/fastfacts/fastfact062905.pdf, June 26, 2006; "Employees Value Basic Benefits Most" (A on survey), *Best's Review* 103(4) (2002), pp. 1527–1591; "The Future Look of Employee Benefits" (Hewitt Associates survey), *The Wall Street Journal*, September 8, 1988, p. 23; Kermit Davis, William Giles, and Hubert Feild, *How Young Professionals Rank Employee Benefits:* Two Studies (Brookfield, WI: International Foundation of Employee Benefit Plans, 1988); Kenneth Shapiro and Jesse Sherman, "Employee Attitude Benefit Plan Designs," *Personnel Journal*, July 1987, pp. 49–58.

by their organization (or in some cases may even be unaware of them). For example, in one study employees were asked to recall the benefits they received. The typical employee could recall less than 15 percent of them.[28] In another study, employees underestimated by 62 percent what it cost employers to provide health benefits.[29] Using our example of an employer spending $100 million on health insurance coverage, that implies employees might estimate the employer's spending as being only (1 − .62) × $100 million = $38 million! All the same, employees regularly report benefits as a top factor in their job satisfaction and retention decisons.[30]

One possible avenue to improve employer return on investment in benefits is to provide employees with greater choice in the benefits they receive.[31] In fact, up to 70 percent of employees in one study indicated they would be willing to pay more out of pocket for benefits if they were granted greater choice in designing their own benefit package. We do know, in support of this, that the perceived value of benefits rises when employers introduce choice through a flexible benefit package.[32] We also saw earlier (in **Chapter 2**), for example, that employees at Whole Foods are given the opportunity to vote on what benefits will be offered. Maybe better planning, design, and administration of benefits would offer an opportunity to improve benefit effectiveness. Indeed, preliminary evidence indicates that employers are making serious efforts to educate employees about benefits, with an outcome of increased employee awareness.[33] For example, the simple act of stating in an employment ad that benefits are generous leads to applicants' focusing on this characteristic and relying more heavily on it in job choice. Some experts speculate that a key element in reward attractiveness (and benefits, in this example) may be their visibility. Not only do we have to plan and design effective benefit programs; we also need to communicate their value to employees.

KEY ISSUES IN BENEFIT PLANNING, DESIGN, AND ADMINISTRATION

Benefits Planning and Design Issues

What do you want–or expect–the role of benefits to be in your overall compensation package?[34] For example, if a major compensation objective is to attract good employees, we need to ask, "What is the best way to achieve this?" The answer is not always, or even frequently, "Let's add another benefit."

Put yourself in the following situation as the benefits manager. A casino opens up in the Niagara Falls area. The Seneca Indians own this casino, and they needed to fill thousands of entry-level jobs. The wages for a blackjack dealer were $4.60 per hour plus tips. The combination of the two exceeds minimum wage, but not by much. How do we attract more dealers, and other applicants, given these low wages? One temptation might be to set up a day care center to attract more mothers of preschool children. Certainly this is a popular response today, judging from all the press that business-sponsored day care centers are receiving. A more prudent compensation policy would ask the question: "Is day care the most effective way to achieve my compensation objective?" Sure, day care may be popular with working mothers, but can the necessary workers be attracted to the casino using some other compensation tool that better meets needs? If we went to compensation experts in the gaming industry, they might say (and we would be impressed if you said this along with them): "We target recruitment of young females for our entry-level jobs. Surveys of this group indicate day care is an extremely important factor in the decision to accept a job."

If you used this kind of logic in your arguments as benefits manager, we think you're well on the way to a successful career. As a second example, how do we deal with undesirable turnover? Rich Floersch, senior vice president of HR at McDonald's, faced this very question. After looking at other alternatives to reduce turnover, Rich decided that the best strategy was to design a benefit package that improved progressively with seniority, thus providing a reward for continuing service. Keep in mind, though, Rich only made this decision after evaluating the effectiveness of other compensation tools (e.g., increasing wages, introducing incentive compensation).

In addition to integrating benefits with other compensation components, the planning process also should include strategies for ensuring external competitiveness and adequacy of benefits.[35] Competitiveness requires an understanding of what other firms in your product and labor markets offer as benefits. Firms conduct benefit surveys much as they conduct salary surveys. Either our firm must have a package comparable to that of survey participants or there should be a sound justification of why deviation makes sense for the firm.

In contrast, ensuring that benefits are adequate is a somewhat more difficult task. Most organizations evaluating adequacy consider the financial liability of employees with and without a particular benefit (e.g., employee medical expenses with and without medical expense benefits). There is no magic formula for defining benefit adequacy.[36] In part, the answer may lie in the relationship between benefit adequacy and the third plan objective: cost of effectiveness. More organizations need to consider whether employee benefits are cost justified. All sorts of ethical questions arise when we start asking this question. How far should we go with elder care? Can we justify paying for a $250,000 surgical procedure that will likely buy only a few more months of life? Companies face these impossible questions when designing a benefit system. And more frequently than ever before, companies are saying no to absorbing the cost increases of benefits. Additionally, we know that employers have increasingly shifted increased benefit costs to employees by implementing higher deductibles and copays and such.[37]

e-Compensation

Benefitslink, at ***www.benefitslink.com/index.shtml***, provides a wealth of information about types of benefits, a message board for interacting in discussions with others interested in benefits, and an "Ask the Expert" question-and-answer column.

Benefit Administration Issues

Four major administration issues arise in setting up a benefit package: (1) Who should be protected or benefited? (2) How much choice should employees have from an array of benefits? (3) How should benefits be financed?[38] and (4) Are the chosen benefits legally defensible?[39]

The first issue–who should be covered–ought to be easy to answer. The answer is *employees*, of course. But every organization has a variety of employees with different employment statuses. Should these individuals be treated equally with respect to benefits coverage? Historically companies have provided far fewer benefits for part-time workers.

As a second example, should retired automobile executives be permitted to continue purchasing cars at a discount price, a benefit that could be reserved solely for current employees or–given the state of the auto industry–perhaps eliminated entirely? In fact, a whole series of questions need to be answered:[40]

1. What probationary periods (for eligibility of benefits) should be used for various types of benefits? Does the employer want to cover employees and their dependents immediately upon employment or provide such coverage only for employees who have established more or less permanent employment with the employer? Is there a rationale for different probationary periods with different benefits?
2. Which dependents of active employees should be covered?
3. Should retirees (as well as their spouses and perhaps other dependents) be covered, and for which benefits?
4. Should survivors of deceased employees (and/or retirees) be covered? If so, for which benefits? Are benefits for surviving spouses appropriate?
5. What coverage, if any, should be extended to employees who are suffering from disabilities?
6. What coverage, if any, should be extended to employees during layoffs, leaves of absence, strikes, and so forth?
7. Should coverage be limited to full-time employees?[41]

The answers to these questions depend on the policy decisions regarding adequacy, competition, and cost effectiveness discussed in the previous section.

The second administrative issue concerns choice (flexibility) in plan coverage. In the standard benefit package, employees typically have not been offered a choice among employee benefits. Rather, a package is designed with the average employee in mind, and any deviations in needs simply go unsatisfied. The other extreme (discussed in greater detail later) is represented by "cafeteria-style," or flexible, benefit plans. Under this concept employees are permitted great flexibility in choosing the benefit options of greatest value to them. Picture an individual allotted x dollars walking down a cafeteria line and choosing menu items (benefits) according to their attractiveness and cost. The flexibility in this type of plan is apparent. **Exhibit 12.5** illustrates a typical choice among packages offered to employees under a flexible benefit system. Imagine an employee whose spouse works and already has family coverage for health, dental, and vision. The temptation might be to select package A. An employee with retirement in mind might select option B with its contributions to a **401(k)** pension plan. **Exhibit 12.6** summarizes some of the major advantages and disadvantages of flexible benefits.

EXHIBIT 12.5 Possible Options in a Flexible Benefit Package

	Package			
	A	B	C	D
Health	No	No	Yes	Yes
Dental	No	No	No	Yes
Vision	No	Yes	Yes	Yes
Life insurance	1 × AE*	2 × AE	2 × AE	3 × AE
Dependent care	Yes	No	No	No
401(k) savings	No	Yes	No	No
Cash back	Yes	No	No	No

* AE = average earnings.

Even companies that are not considering a flexible benefit program are offering greater flexibility and choice. Such plans might provide, for example, (1) optional levels of group term life insurance; (2) the availability of death or disability benefits under pension or profit-sharing plans; (3) choices of covering dependents under group medical expense coverage; and (4) a variety of participation, cash distribution, and investment options under profit-sharing, thrift, and capital accumulation plans.[42]

The level at which an organization finally chooses to operate on this choice/flexibility dimension really depends on its evaluation of the relative advantages and disadvantages of flexible plans, noted in **Exhibit 12.6.**[43] Many companies cite the cost savings from flexible benefits as a primary motivation. Companies also offer flexible plans in response to cost pressures related to the increasing diversity of the workforce. Flexible benefit plans, it is argued, increase employee awareness of the true costs of benefits and, therefore, increase employee recognition of benefit value.[44]

Another way to increase employee awareness, and probably the biggest trend today in health care, is to offer **market-based,** or **customer-driven,** health care. Although there are many variants on **consumer-driven health care benefits,** here are the basic issues.[45]

- In a consumer-driven or high-deductible plan, an employee pays all health care costs up to some predetermined rate. That rate can be as high as $3,000 to $6,000. After that amount the employee pays a rate of 10 to 35 percent of any additional medical services (called coinsurance). Each employer sets some out-of-pocket maximum, typically in the range of $6,000 to $12,000 (single vs. family). After that the employer pays.[46]
- The obvious inducement to an employee is to shop around for the lowest rate. Need an MRI? The cost can vary between $415 and $4,530.[47] Before these high-deductible plans were implemented, the employee had no motivation to choose a low-cost provider. For the employer this yields a huge cost saving. Monthly premiums can dip to as low as $100. Of course, this can cause a health care crisis for an employee who foregoes a procedure because of cost.

The third administrative issue involves the question of how to finance benefit plans. Alternatives include:

EXHIBIT 12.6 Advantages and Disadvantages of Flexible Benefit Programs

Advantages

1. Employees choose packages that best satisfy their unique needs.
2. Flexible benefits help firms meet the changing needs of a changing workforce.
3. Increased involvement of employees and families improves understanding of benefits.
4. Flexible plans make introduction of new benefits less costly. Any new option is added merely as one among a wide variety of elements from which to choose.
5. Cost containment: Organization sets dollar maximum; employee chooses within that constraint.

Disadvantages

1. Employees make bad choices and find themselves not covered for predictable emergencies.
2. Administrative burdens and expenses increase.
3. Adverse selection: Employees pick only benefits they will use; the subsequent high-benefit utilization increases its cost.
4. Flexible benefit plans are subject to nondiscrimination requirements in Section 125 of the Internal Revenue Code.

1. Noncontributory (employer pays total costs).
2. Contributory (costs are shared between employer and employee).
3. Employee financed (employee pays total costs for some benefits–by law the organization must bear the cost for certain benefits).

In general, organizations prefer to make benefit options contributory, reasoning that a "free good," no matter how valuable, is less valuable to an employee. Furthermore, employees have no personal interest in controlling the cost of a free good. And with the cost of benefits rising considerably more than other goods and services, employers are increasingly turning to ways for cutting their costs.

Finally, benefits have to comply with hundreds of arcane sections of the tax code and other "devils" designed to turn any benefit administrator's hair gray. Because there are so many rules and regulations, benefit administrators should develop a compliance checklist and regularly conduct audits to ensure that they are complying with the avalanche of new and existing requirements.[48]

COMPONENTS OF A BENEFIT PLAN

Exhibit 12.7 outlines a model of the factors influencing benefit choice, from both the employer's and the employee's perspective. The remainder of this chapter briefly examines each of these factors.

Employer Factors

As **Exhibit 12.7** indicates, a number of factors affect employer preference in determining desirable components of a benefit package.

EXHIBIT 12.7 Factors Influencing Choice of Benefit Package

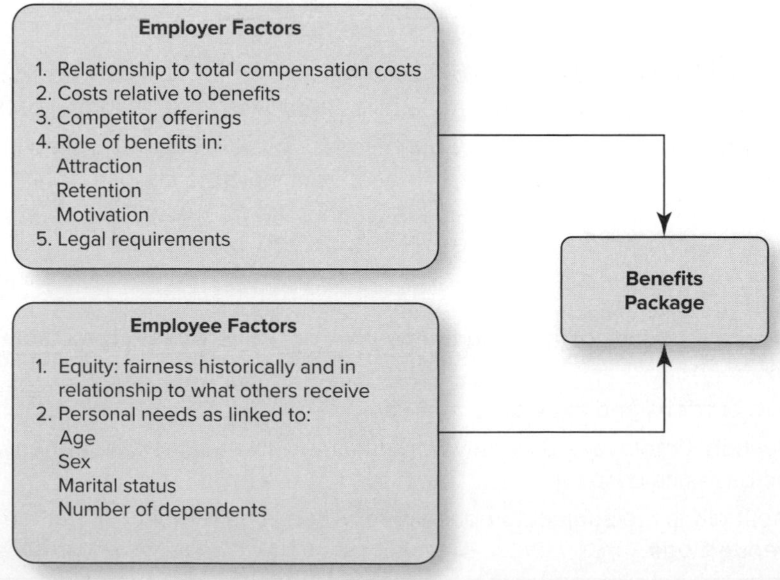

Relationship to Total Compensation Costs

A good compensation manager considers employee benefit costs as part of a total package of compensation costs. Frequently employees think that just because an employee benefit is attractive, the company should provide it. A good compensation manager thinks somewhat differently: "Is there a better use for this money? Could we put the money into some other compensation component and achieve better results?" Benefit costs are only one part of a total compensation package. Decisions about outlays have to be considered from this perspective. Let's take a perfect example provided by former Governor of Tennessee Phillip Bredesen.[49] He argued that Tennessee could keep its employees whole with respect to health care and save the state $146 million. How, you ask? Under the Patient Protection and Affordable Care Act employees could purchase health insurance in part subsidized by the government. The governor calculated how much it would cost to keep state employees whole if they accepted this government support. By eliminating health coverage for state employees and providing an incentive keeping each worker whole, and paying the government-imposed fine of $2,000, the state saved $146 million.

Costs Relative to Benefits

A major reason for the proliferating cost of benefit programs is that too frequently the costs/advantages of a particular benefit inclusion are viewed in isolation, without reference to total package costs or forecasts of rising costs in future years. To control spiraling benefit costs, it is useful to adopt a broader, cost-centered approach. As a first step, this approach would require policy decisions on the level of benefit expenditures acceptable both in the short and the long runs. Historically, benefit managers negotiated or provided benefits on a package basis rather than a cost basis. The current cost of a benefit would be identified, and if the cost seemed reasonable, the benefit would be provided for or negotiated with employees. This failed to recognize that rising costs of this benefit were expected to be borne by the employer. The classic example of this phenomenon is health-care coverage. An employer considering a community-based medical plan like Blue Cross during the early 1960s no doubt agreed to pay all or most of the costs of one of the Blue Cross options. As costs of this plan skyrocketed throughout the rest of the century, the employer was expected to continue coverage at the historical level. In effect, the employer became locked into a level of coverage rather than negotiating a level of cost. In subsequent years, then, the spiraling costs were essentially out of the control of the benefit manager.

A cost-centered approach requires that benefit administrators, in cooperation with insurance carriers and armed with published forecasts of anticipated costs for particular benefits, determine the cost commitments for the existing benefit package. Budget dollars not already earmarked may then be allocated to new benefits that best satisfy organizational goals. Factors affecting this decision include an evaluation of benefits offered by other firms and the competitiveness of the existing package. Also important is compliance with various legal requirements as they change over time (**Chapter 13**). Finally, the actual benefit of a new option must be explored in relation to employee preferences. The benefits that top the list of employee preferences should be evaluated in relation to current and future costs. Because future cost estimates may be difficult to project, it is imperative that benefit administrators reduce uncertainty.

If a benefit forecast suggests future cost containment may be difficult, the benefit should be offered to employees only on a cost-sharing basis. Management determines what percentage of cost it can afford to bear within budget projections, and the option is offered to employees on a cost-sharing basis, with projected increases in both employer and employee costs communicated openly. In the negotiation process, then, employees or union representatives can evaluate their preference for the option against the forecasted cost burden. In effect, this approach defines in advance the contribution an employer is willing to make. And it avoids the constraints of a defined-benefit strategy that burdens the employer with continued provision of that defined-benefit level despite rapidly spiraling costs.

Competitor Offerings

Benefits must be externally equitable, too. This begs the question, what is the absolute level of benefit payments relative to important product and labor market competitors? A policy decision must be made about the position (market lead, market lag, or competitive) the organization wants to maintain in its absolute level of benefits relative to the competition. One of the best strategies for determining external equity is to conduct a benefit survey. Alternatively, many consulting organizations, professional associations, and interest groups collect benefit data that can be purchased. A widely used source of data is the annual benefit survey conducted by the U.S. Bureau of Labor Statistics, parts of which we saw earlier in **Exhibits 12.1** and **12.2**.[50] The Employee Benefits Research Institute is also a first-rate source for benefits information.[51]

Role of Benefits in Attraction, Retention, and Motivation

Given the rapid growth in benefits and the staggering cost implications, it seems only logical that employers would expect to derive a fair return on this investment. In fact, there is at best only anecdotal evidence that employee benefits are cost-justified.[52]

This evidence falls into three categories.[53] First, employee benefits are widely claimed to help in the retention of workers. Benefit schedules are specifically designed to favor longer-term employees. For example, retirement benefits increase with years of service, and most plans do not provide for full employee eligibility until a specified number of years of service have been reached. Equally, the amount of vacation time increases with years of service, and employees' savings plans, profit-sharing plans, and stock purchase plans frequently provide for increased participation or benefits as seniority increases. By tying these benefits to seniority, it is assumed that workers are more reluctant to change jobs.

There is also some research to support this common assumption that benefits increase retention. Two studies found that higher benefits reduced mobility.[54] More detailed follow-up studies, though, found that only two specific benefits curtailed employee turnover: pensions and medical coverage.[55] Virtually no other employee benefit was observed to have a significant impact on turnover.

We've been assuming here that turnover is bad and stability is good. In fact, there are times when turnover may be good–something we may not want to discourage. For example, at one time or another 3 Americans in 10 have stayed in a job they wanted to leave simply because they could not give up their health-care coverage.[56] This "job lock" probably is not a desirable outcome for employers. Indeed, over time, U.S. companies have moved away from the use of defined benefit retirement plans (pensions), which provide a disincentive to mobility, to greater use of defined contribution plans, which do not inhibit mobility. (We define and discuss these plans in **Chapter 13**.)

Employee benefits also might be valued if we could prove they increase employee satisfaction. As noted, surveys show that employees rank benefits (and pay) as quite important to both their job satisfaction and to their decisions about whether to stay with or leave an employer. However, there was a substantial difference between the percentage of employees reporting that benefits are very important to them (60 percent) and the percentage saying they were very satisfied with their benefits (27 percent).[57] Benefits also would be valuable if we could show a link to increased productivity or other direct measures of performance. Unfortunately, no strong data exist linking benefits level and employee productivity. Perhaps as a result, some companies are cutting benefits, especially medical insurance, as a cost reduction strategy. If we want to argue that benefits matter, first we need to show that benefits are well-designed–in part this means they must meet employee needs. Critics argue that companies haven't responded to long-term changes in the workforce. Ever-increasing numbers of women in the labor force, coupled with increasing numbers of dual-career families and higher educational attainments, suggest changing values of employees.[58] Changing values, in turn, necessitate a reevaluation of benefit packages.

One response to these workforce changes is increased interest in work/life balance benefits. Things like day care, elder care, time off to volunteer, remote working, and paid maternity/paternity leave can help with this balance and, along with other benefits (such as on-site fitness centers and weight-loss programs), may additionally foster a perception that the company cares about its employees. One well-constructed research study found that this caring attitude led to greater worker involvement in suggesting ways to improve productivity and in helping others with their work.[59] Maybe benefits can pay off; we just need to document this better.

Legal Requirements

Employers obviously want a benefit package that complies with all aspects of the law. **Exhibit 12.8** shows part of the increasingly complex web of legislation in the benefit area. Greater details on the three legally mandated benefits (workers' compensation, social security, and unemployment insurance) are provided in **Chapter 13**. A broader discussion of the legal environment for compensation is provided in **Chapter 17**.

Absolute and Relative Compensation Costs

Any evaluation of employee benefits must be placed in the context of total compensation costs. Cost competitiveness means the total package–not just specific segments–must be competitive. Consequently, decisions on whether to adopt certain options must be considered in light of the impact on total costs and in relationship to expenditures of competitors (as determined in benefit surveys–again, see, for example, **Exhibits 12.1** and **12.2** from earlier in this chapter).

Employee Factors

Employee preferences for various benefit options are determined by individual needs. The benefits perceived to best satisfy individual needs are the most highly desired. In part, these needs arise out of feelings of perceived equity or inequity.

Equity

To illustrate the impact of equity, consider the example of government employees working in the same neighborhood as autoworkers. Imagine the dissatisfaction with government holidays that arises when government employees leave for work every morning, knowing that the autoworkers are home in bed for the whole week between Christmas and New Year's Day. The perceived unfairness of this difference need not be rational, especially considering the large number of layoffs in the auto industry in contrast to the relative job security in the public sector. But it is, nevertheless, a factor that must be considered in determining employee needs. Occasionally this comparison process leads to a "bandwagon" effect, in which new benefits offered by a competitor are adopted without careful consideration, simply because the employer wants to avoid hard feelings. This phenomenon is particularly apparent for employers with strong commitments to maintaining a totally or partially nonunion work force. Benefits obtained by a unionized competitor or a unionized segment of the firm's workforce are frequently passed along to nonunion employees. While the effectiveness of this strategy in thwarting unionization efforts has not been demonstrated, many nonunion firms would prefer to provide the benefit as a safety measure.

Personal Needs of Employees

One way to gauge employee preferences is to look at demographic differences. The demographic approach assumes that demographic groups (e.g., young versus old, married versus unmarried) can be identified for which benefit preferences are fairly consistent across members of the group. Furthermore, it assumes that meaningful differences exist between groups in terms of benefit preferences.

There is some evidence that these assumptions are only partially correct. In an extensive review of employee preference literature, Glueck traced patterns of group preferences for particular benefits.[60] As one might expect, older workers showed stronger preferences than younger workers for pension plans.[61] Also, families with dependents had stronger preferences for health/medical coverage than families with no dependents.[62] The big surprise in all these studies, though, is that many of the other demographic group

EXHIBIT 12.8 **Impact of Legislation on Selected Benefits**

Legislation	Impact on Employee Benefits
Fair Labor Standards Act 1938	Created time-and-a-half overtime pay. Benefits linked to pay (e.g., social security) increase correspondingly with those overtime hours.
Employee Retirement Income Security Act 1974	If an employer decides to provide a pension (it is not mandated), specific rules must be followed. Plan must vest (employee has right to both personal and company contributions into pension) after five years' employment. Pension Benefit Guaranty Corporation, as set up by this law, provides worker some financial coverage when a company and its pension plan go bankrupt.
Tax reforms—1982, 1986	Permit individual retirement accounts (IRAs) for eligible employees. Established 401(k) programs, a matched-contribution saving plan (employer matches part or all of employee contribution) that frequently serves as part of a retirement package.
Maintenance Act 1973	Required employers to offer alternative health coverage (e.g., health maintenance organizations) options to employees.
Discrimination legislation (Age Discrimination in Employment Act, Civil Rights Act, Pregnancy Disability Act, various state laws)	Benefits must be administered in a manner that does not discriminate against protected groups (on basis of race, color, religion, sex, national origin, age, pregnancy).
Consolidated Omnibus Budget Reconciliation Act (COBRA) 1984	Employees who resign or are laid off through no fault of their own are eligible to continue receiving health coverage under employer's plan at a cost borne by the employee.
Family Medical Leave Act (1993)	Mandates 12 weeks of leave for all workers at companies that employ 50 or more people.
The Patient Protection and Affordable Care Act (2010)	Creates employer mandate (for those with 50 or more full-time) employees to provide qualifying health insurance coverage or face financial penalties.

breakdowns fail to result in differential benefit preferences. Traditionally, it has been assumed that benefit preferences ought to differ among males versus females, blue collar versus white collar, and married versus single. Few of these expectations have been born out by these studies. Rather, the studies have tended to be more valuable in showing preference trends that are characteristic of all employees. Among the benefits available, health/medical and stock plans are highly preferred benefits, while such options as early retirement, profit sharing, shorter hours, and counseling services rank among the least-preferred options. (Note: by our definition several of these options don't really fall under the category of employee benefits.) Beyond these conclusions, most preference studies have shown wide variation in individuals with respect to benefits desired.

The weakness of this demographic approach has led some organizations to undertake a second and more expensive empirical method of determining employee preference: surveying individuals about needs. One way of accomplishing this requires development of a questionnaire on which employees evaluate various benefits. For example, **Exhibit 12.9** illustrates a questionnaire format.

A third empirical method of identifying individual employee preferences is commonly known as a **flexible benefit plan** (also called a section 125 plan after the section of the Tax Code or a *cafeteria-style plan*). As previously noted, employees are allotted a fixed amount of money and permitted to spend that amount in the purchase of benefit options. From a theoretical perspective, this approach to benefit packaging is ideal. Employees directly identify the benefits of greatest value to them, and by constraining the dollars employees have to spend, benefit managers are able to control benefit costs.

ADMINISTERING THE BENEFIT PROGRAM

The job description for an employee benefit manager at Sony Brothers, shown in **Exhibit 12.10**, includes many areas of responsibility. Here, we note three in particular: (1) benefits strategy, which includes deciding on what benefits will be provided (discussed in this and the next chapter), (2) communicating about the benefits program, and (3) cost containment.[63] In other words, it is about forming a benefits strategy, and then getting the maximum return on investment from that strategy by both controlling costs and maximizing actual value and perceived value to employees.

Employee Benefit Communication

Benefits communications revolves around four issues: What is communicated, to whom, how it's communicated, and how frequently. Much of the effort to achieve benefit goals today focuses on identifying methods (how) of communication. One method still used by firms is the employee benefit handbook.[64] A typical handbook contains a description of all benefits, including levels of coverage and eligibility requirements. To be most effective, the benefit handbook should be accompanied by ease of access and repetition of the message in multiple media (e.g., newsletters, e-mail, web/intranet, and social media).[65]

An effective communications package should match the message with the appropriate medium. Technological advances have made tremendous improvements in employee benefit communication and self-service such that employees can now often use web-based applications to access benefit information, complete annual benefit enrollment, change personal data, update retirement contributions (e.g., in a 401[k]), and complete other benefits-related actions on their own. **Exhibit 12.11** shows some benefits communication methods and the percentage of HR professionals rating each method as very effective.

Benefits communication, however conducted, remains very important because failure to understand benefit components and their value is still one of the root causes of employee dissatisfaction with a benefit package and/or a low return on investment for employers. Employers report that less than one-fifth of their employees have a high understanding of their benefits package.[66] This can be remedied, though. One study of 500 employees in seven Canadian organizations found that perceived fairness of a plan was significantly higher when there was extensive communications and employee participation in plan design.[67] An organization must spell out its benefit objectives and it must ensure that any communications achieve these objectives. **Exhibit 12.12** provides some advice on how to better communicate the value of benefits to employees.

EXHIBIT 12.9 Questionnaire Format for Benefit Surveys

Employee Benefit Questionnaire

1. In the space provided in front of the benefits listed below indicate how important each benefit is to you and your family. Indicate this by placing a "1" for the most important, and "2" for the next most important, etc. Therefore, if life insurance is the most important benefit to you and your family, place a "1" in front of it.

Importance		Improvement
________	Dental insurance	________
________	Disability (pay while sick)	________
________	Educational assistance	________
________	Holidays	________
________	Life insurance	________
________	Medical insurance	________
________	Retirement annuity plan	________
________	Savings plan	________
________	Vacations	________
________	________	________
________	________	________

Now, go back and in the space provided after each benefit, indicate the priority for improvement. For example, if the savings plan is the benefit you would most like to see improved, give it a "1," the next a priority "2," etc. Use the blank lines to add any benefits not listed.

2. Would you be willing to contribute a portion of your earnings for new or improved benefits beyond the level already provided by the Company?

- ☐ Yes
- ☐ No

If yes, please indicate below in which area(s):

- ☐ Dental insurance
- ☐ Disability benefits
- ☐ Life insurance
- ☐ Medical insurance
- ☐ Retirement annuity plan
- ☐ Savings plan

EXHIBIT 12.10 **Director, Benefits, Sony Corporation of America. Duties/Responsibilities:**

- Setting short and long-term retirement, health and welfare and wellbeing strategy and plan design
- Providing thought leadership and engagement with other key leaders across the organization
- Aligning benefit strategies with overall Total Rewards, HR, and business strategy and objectives
- Collaborating with finance, company leadership, and external consultants to set, assess and report on financial performance of benefit programs
- Advising, supporting, and serving as Secretary to the benefits committee in the development of short-term and long-range benefits planning
- Supporting M&A activity, including benefits due diligence, integration and change management
- Collaborating with affiliates and subsidiaries as needed on benefits matters
- committee.
- Engaging in regular benchmarking activities, assessing the marketplace against current and future employee needs as well as best practices, to maintain competitive programs and services
- Preparing annual department budget and monitoring on monthly basis
- Providing detailed analysis of budget to Finance team to prepare the annual Fringe Budget
- Overseeing administration of all benefits programs
- Managing all employee benefits communications
- Executing on benefit plan modifications
- Establishing and maintaining collaborative relationships with key benefit stakeholders across the organization (e.g., payroll, finance, legal, HRBPs) to support benefits administration
- Manage compliance of benefit programs, including timely completion of regulatory reporting and filings (such as Forms 5500, 1095/1094, etc.).
- Leading request for proposal (RFP) processes as needed for vendor review and selection
- Ongoing vendor management

EXHIBIT 12.11 **Effectiveness of Benefits Communication Methods (Percentage Rated Very Effective by HR)**

Benefits Communication Method	% Very Effective
Face-to-Face: Fosters open communication. Requires coordination and planning.	
One-on-one	51%
Orientation/on-boarding	40%
Group communications	37%
Benefits fairs	26%
Lunch-and-learn	21%
Virtual: Provides on-demand access and wide reach. Requires technology and training.	
Bulletins to screensavers	20%
Webinars	15%

Benefits Communication Method	% Very Effective
Social media	15%
Virtual education	14%
<u>Information Portal</u>: One-stop-shop for benefits. Requires ongoing maintenance and intuitive user interface.	
Online benefits portal	32%
Intranet	21%
<u>Materials</u>: Allows for personalized communication methods. Requires current contact information.	
Enrollment materials	35%
E-mails	31%
Text messages	25%
Direct mail to home/residence	16%
Handouts/pamphlets	15%
Newsletters	13%

Source: Society for Human Resource Management. *Strategic Benefits Survey*, December 29, 2017.

EXHIBIT 12.12 Steps to Better Communicating the Value of Benefits to Employees

Learn more about what benefits your employees value or would like to have

Help employee understand benefits as a connected set of resources and offer a range of options they can personalize (and change as their priorities evolve)

Personalize communications to different employee groups

Engage employees as if they were customers

Communicate benefits more effectively. Employees' most preferred channels are:

- Company's benefits website
- Provider's website
- In-person group presentations
- Benefits handbooks
- One-on-one guidance

Communicate the value of benefits throughout the year.

Sources: Navigating Together: Supporting Employee Well-being in Uncertain Times. MetLife's 18th Annual U.S. Employee Benefits Trends Study 2020. Metlife.com; Thriving in the New Work-Life World. MetLife's 17th Annual U.S. Employee Benefits Trends Study 2019. Metlife.com.

Cost Containment

Increasingly, employers are auditing their benefit options for **cost containment** opportunities. The most prevalent practices include:

1. **Probationary periods**–excluding new employees from benefit coverage until some term of employment (e.g., three months) is completed.
2. **Benefit limitations**–it is not uncommon to limit disability income payments to some maximum percentage of income and to limit medical/dental coverage for specific procedures to a certain fixed amount.
3. **Copay**–requiring that employees pay a fixed or percentage amount for coverage.
4. Deductible–Employee must pay for expenses up to some dollar amount per year, after which the employer plan pays.
5. Administrative cost containment–controlling costs through policies such as seeking competitive bids for program delivery.
6. Deny service or charge more for preexisting conditions. (Health plans covered by the Affordable Care Act are not permitted to do this. An exception is if enrollment in a plan began prior to March 23, 2010. Note also that smokers can be charged a 50% higher premium, unless prohibited by state law.)
7. Claims processing (see below).
8. Negotiate lower fees with providers.
9. Develop programs that encourage wellness (e.g., smoking cessation).
10. Outsource benefits and administration.
11. Self-insure.
12. Provide accommodations for employees to return to work after illness or disability.

Probably the biggest cost-containment strategy in recent years is the movement to **outsourcing.** As with payroll, companies may find that their benefits can be administered best by a company that specializes in benefits administration. Such an outsourcing company might be able to administer the company's benefits not only less expensively but also better, given that outsourcing company does the same work for many companies and it is their area of expertise.

Claims Processing

Claims processing is included above (#7) under **Cost Containment** and may require additional explanation. It arises when an employee asserts that a specific event (e.g., disability, hospitalization, unemployment) has occurred and demands that the employer (or its agent with outsourcing) fulfill a promise of payment. As such, a claims processor must first determine whether the act has, in fact, occurred. For example, consider a claim from a man asserting he had an on-the-job back injury. The injury allegedly was so severe that the employee's physical activities were drastically limited. The case was quickly dismissed when an insurance investigator caught the individual on video lifting car engine blocks without a winch.

If the event did occur, the second step involves determining if the employee is eligible for the benefit. If payment is approved at this stage, the claims processor calculates the payment level. It is particularly important at this stage to ensure coordination of benefits. This may occur, for example, if multiple insurance companies are liable for payment (e.g., working spouses covered by different insurers).

Your Turn

World Measurement

World Measurement is the global leader in product testing for safety. The recent problem with Chinese-made toy products (for example, Mattel recalled 19 million toys with evidence of lead paint) combined with the global recession has caused a 7 percent decline in sales and a 12 percent decline in net profits. The president of the company, Lewis Jacobs, is convinced that he must get concessions from the workers if World Measurement is to compete effectively with increasing foreign competition. In particular, Jacobs is displeased with the cost of employee benefits. He doesn't mind conceding a competitive wage increase (maximum 3 percent), but he wants the total compensation package to cost 3 percent less. The current costs are shown in **Exhibit 12.13**.

EXHIBIT 12.13 Current Compensation Costs

Average yearly wage	$34,800	
Average hourly wage	$17.06	
Dollar value of yearly benefits, per employee	$11,600	
Total compensation (wages plus benefits)	$46,400	
Daily average number of hours paid	8.0	
Benefits (by Category)		**Cost/Employee**
1. **Legally required payments (employer's share only)**		**$2,783**
a. Old-age, survivors, disability, and health insurance (FICA) taxes	$1,962	
b. Unemployment compensation	$380	
c. Workers' compensation (including estimated cost of self-insured)	$404	
d. Railroad retirement tax, railroad unemployment and cash sickness insurance, state sickness benefits insurance, etc.	$12	

2. **Pension, insurance, and other agreed-upon payments (employer's share only)**		**$4,061**
a. Pension plan premiums and pension payments not covered by insurance-type plan (net)	$1,898	
b. Life insurance premiums; death benefits; hospital, surgical, medical, and major medical insurance premiums; etc. (net)	$1,855	
c. Short-term disability	$108	
d. Salary continuation or long-term disability	$74	
e. Dental insurance premiums	$66	
f. Discounts on goods and services purchased from company by employees	$35	
g. Employee meals furnished by company	$0	
h. Miscellaneous payments (compensation payments in excess of legal requirements, separation or termination pay allowances, moving expenses, etc.)	$31	
3. **Paid rest periods, lunch periods, wash-up time, travel time, clothes-change time, get-ready time, etc. (60 minutes)**		**$945**
4. **Payments for time not worked**		**$3,600**
a. Paid vacations and payments in lieu of vacation (16 days average)	$2,025	
b. Payments for holidays not worked (9 days)	$1,265	

c. Paid sick leave (10 days maximum)	$224	
d. Payments for state or national guard duty; jury, witness, and voting pay allowances; payments for time lost due to death in family or other personal reasons, etc.	$92	
5. **Other items**		**$204**
a. Profit-sharing payments	$0	
b. Contributions to employee thrift plans	$92	
c. Christmas or other special bonuses, service awards, suggestion awards, etc.	$0	
d. Employee education expenditures (tuition refunds, etc.)	$52	
e. Special wage payments ordered by courts, payments to union stewards, etc.	$60	
Total		**$11,389**

Your assistant has surveyed other companies that are obtaining concessions from employees. You also have data from a consulting firm that indicates employee preferences for different forms of benefits (**Exhibit 12.14**). Based on all this information, you have two possible concession packages that you can propose, labeled "Option 1" and "Option 2" (**Exhibit 12.15**).

EXHIBIT 12.14 **Benefit Preferences**

Benefit Type or Method of Administering	Importance to Workers
Pensions	87
Hospitalization	86
Life insurance	79
Paid vacation	82

Benefit Type or Method of Administering	Importance to Workers
Holidays	82
Long-term disability	72
Short-term disability	69
Paid sick leave	70
Paid rest periods, lunch periods, etc.	55
Dental insurance	51
Christmas bonus	31
Profit sharing	21
Education expenditures	15
Contributions to thrift plans	15
Discount on goods	5
Fair treatment in administration	100

Note: 0 = unimportant; 100 = extremely important.

EXHIBIT 12.15 Two Possible Packages for Cutting Benefit Costs

Option 1

Implement Copay for Benefit	Amount of Copay
Pension	$400.00
Hospital, surgical, medical, and major medical premiums	460.00
Dental insurance premiums	95.00

Reduction of Benefit

Eliminate 10-minute paid break (workers leave work 10 minutes earlier)

Eliminate one paid holiday per year

Coordination with **legally required benefit;** social security coordinated with Lightning Industries pension plan

Option 2

Improved claims processing:

- Unemployment compensation
- Workers' compensation
- Long-term disability

Require probationary period (one year) before eligible for:

Discounts on goods

Employee meal paid by company

Contributions to employee thrift plans

Deductible ($100 per incident):

Life insurance, death benefits, hospital, etc.

Dental insurance

Copay	**Amount of Copay**
Hospital, surgical, medical and major medical premiums	$460.00

1. Cost out these packages, given the data in **Exhibit 12.13** and the information obtained from various insurance carriers and other information sources (**Exhibit 12.16**).
2. Which package should you recommend to Jacobs? Why?
3. Which of the strategies do you think will require less input from employees in terms of their reactions?

EXHIBIT 12.16 **Analysis of Cost Implications for Different Cost-Cutting Strategies: Lightning Industries**

Cost-Saving Strategy	Savings as Percent of Benefit-Type Cost
Copay	**Dollar-for-dollar savings equal to amount of copay**
Deductible ($100 per incident):	
Life insurance premiums, death benefits, hospital, etc.	10%
Dental insurance	15
Require probationary period before eligible (one year):	
Discount on goods and services	10
Employee meals furnished by company	15
Contributions to employee thrift plans	10
Improved claims processing:	
Unemployment compensation	8
Workers' compensation	3
Long-term disability	1

Cost-Saving Strategy	Savings as Percent of Benefit-Type Cost
Coordination with legally required benefits:	
Coordinate social security with Lightning pension plan	15

Summary

Given the rapid escalation in the cost of employee benefits over the past 15 years, organizations would do well to evaluate the effectiveness of their benefit adoption, retention, and termination procedures. Specifically, how do organizations go about selecting appropriate employee benefits? Are the decisions based on sound evaluation of employee preferences balanced against organizational goals of legal compliance and competitiveness? Do the benefits chosen serve to attract, retain, and/or motivate employees? Or are organizations paying billions of dollars of **indirect compensation** without any tangible benefit? This chapter has outlined a benefit determination process that identifies major issues in selecting and evaluating particular benefit choices. **Chapter 13** catalogs the various benefits available and discusses some of the decisions confronting a benefit administrator.

Review Questions

1. Early in this chapter, we identified reasons for the historical growth in the size of benefits packages. Which of these reasons still affect the growth of employee benefits today? Which actually might be current reasons for declines in the size of benefit packages?
2. Erinn Kelly, VP of Human Resources at Lawson Chemical, just purchased a local salary survey that has employee benefits data. She was shocked to see that Lawson has a larger benefits bill (38 percent of payroll) than the average in the community (31 percent). In a memo to you, she demands an explanation for why our package is significantly bigger. What sound reasons might save you from getting fired?
3. You are the benefits manager in a firm metaphorically described as part of the rust belt, in Syracuse, NY. The average age of your 600-person workforce is 43. Eighty-eight percent of your workforce is male, and there is hardly any turnover. Not much is happening on the job front. How do these facts influence your decisions about designing an employee benefit program?
4. As HR director at Crangle Fixtures, your bonus this year is based on your ability to cut employee benefit costs. Your boss has said that it's okay to shift some of the costs over to employees (right now they pay nothing for their benefits) but that he doesn't want you to overdo it. In other words, at least one-half of your suggestions should not hurt the employee's pocket book. What alternatives do you want to explore, and why?
5. Google is famous for paying wages significantly above the market and also providing employee benefits that one might call lavish. The European Union fined Google for its monopolistic behavior, claiming that the company's internet search function systematically favors its own comparison shopping product in its search results pages (their products turn up earlier in the search effort). Speculate on what (if anything) Google might change about its benefits package as a consequence of this ruling.

Endnotes

1. Bureau of Labor Statistics, www.data.bls.gov/cgi-bin/surveymost, June 21, 2006.
2. The *McKinsey Quarterly* Chart Focus Newsletter, June 2006, Member Edition.
3. I. Watson, "GM Puts Salaried Staff in Firing Line," *Knight Ridder Tribune Business News,* March 26, 2006, p. 1.
4. U.S. Department of Labor, Bureau of Labor Statistics, "Employer Costs for Employee Compensation-USDL-18-1499," September 18, 2018, www.bls.gov.
5. Bruce R. Ellig, "American History's Impact on Employee Pay and Benefits," self-published, 2015, see p. 33.
6. James W. Glover, Department of Commerce, Bureau of the Census, *United States Life Tables, 1921* (Washington, DC: U.S. Government Printing Office, 1921), pp. 26–27, https://www.cdc.gov/nchs/data/lifetables/life1890-1910.pdf.
7. Society for Human Resource Management, "2010 Employee Benefits," February 2010, http://www.shrm.org/Research/SurveyFindings/Articles/Documents/10-0280%20Employee%20Benefits%20Survey%20Report-FNL.pdf.
8. Pault Fronstin, "2013 Health and Voluntary Workplace Benefits Survey," Employee Benefits Research Institute, 2013, fronstin@ebri.org.
9. S. Bates, "Benefit Packages Nearing 40 Percent of Payroll," *HR Magazine*, March 2003, pp. 36–38, http://fortune.com/best-companies/google-1/.
10. http://fortune.com/best-companies/google-1/.
11. Pault Fronstin, "2013 Health and Voluntary Workplace Benefits Survey," Employee Benefits Research Institute, 2013, fronstin@ebri.org.
12. Stephen Miller, "Survey: Employees Undervalue Benefits," *HR Magazine* 52(8), 2008, p. 7.
13. Steve Werner and David B. Balkin, "Strategic Benefits: How Employee Benefits Can Create a Sustainable Competitive Edge," *The Journal of Total Rewards*, Q1, 2021, pp. 8–22; Brian Murray and James H. Dulebohn, "Strategic Benefits Management: What We Think, What We Know and What We Need to Know," *The Journal of Total Rewards*, Q1, 2021, pp. 23–35.
14. C. Rexrod, "Citigroup to Millennial Bankers: Take a Year Off," Wall Street Journal, March 16, 2016; C. C. Miller, "Silicon Valley's Struggle Adapting to Families," *New York Times*, April 8, 2015, p. A3; L. Gellman and Justin Baer, "Goldman Sachs Sweetens Deal for Young Bankers," Wall Street Journal, November 5, 2015; D. Huang and L. Gellman, "Millennial Employees Confound Big Banks," *Wall Street Journal*, April 8, 2016.
15. Ingrid Smithey Fulmer, Yan Chen, and Junting Li. "Strategic Idiosyncratic Deals (I-Deals) Policy: Individually Negotiated Arrangements as an Alternative Approach for Delivering Customized Benefits," *The Journal of Total Rewards*, Q1, 2021, pp. 45–54.
16. Daniel Alfonso, Monica Franco-Santos, Luis R. Gomez-Mejia, "Revisiting Benefits Design Approaches: The Strategic Value of Identity-Based Benefits," *The Journal of Total Rewards*, Q1, 2021, pp. 71–80.
17. D. Kryscynski, R. Coff, and B. Campbell, "Charting a Path Between Firm-Specific Incentives and Human Capital-Based Competitive Advantage," *Strategic Management Journal* 42(2), 2021, pp. 386–412.
18. Joanne Lipman, "Stressed Out Over the Covid-19 Pandemic? Some Companies Invent a Holiday," *WSJ*, Nov. 12, 2020; Chip Cutter, "Companies Offer Creative Solutions to Worker Burnout During the Pandemic From Surprise Days off to 30-Hour Workweeks," managers are devising ways to help

employees. *WSJ*, November 8, 2020; Kathryn Vasel, "To Fight Pandemic Burnout, This Company Is Trying Four-Day Workweeks," *CNN.com*, August 4, 2020.

19. Atul Mitra and Jason D. Shaw, "Strategic Benefits to Help Survive and Thrive in Times of COVID-19," *The Journal of Total Rewards*, Q1, 2021: Cara Murez, "Health Care After COVID: The Rise of Telemedicine," Usnews.com. January 5, 2021; Kathryn Dill and Julia Carpenter, "Employers Craft Health Benefits to Cushion Covid-19 Shock," *WSJ.com*, November 12, 2020.
20. In this and Chapter 13, we draw freely from Raymond A. Noe, John R. Hollenbeck, Barry Gerhart, and Patrick M. Wright, *Human Resource Management: Gaining a Competitive Advantage,* 11th ed. New York: McGraw-Hill, 2019.
21. Steve Finlay, "GM Is Getting Sick of High Health-Care Costs," WardsAuto, March 1, 2004; Melissa Burden and Michael Martinez, "Health Care Costs Key Issue in UAW Talks," *Detroit News,* July 13, 2015; Michael Wayland, "Toyota's Per-Car Profits Lap Detroit's Big 3 Automakers," *Detroit News,* February 22, 2015.
22. John Hanna, "Can the Challenge of Escalating Benefits Costs Be Met?" *Personnel Administration* 27(9), 1977, pp. 50–57.
23. David Barkholz, "UAW's Rich Health Care Wears a Bull's-Eye: Cuts Could Help Union Achieve Other Goals," *Automotive News,* May 30, 2015; International Organization of Motor Vehicle Manufacturers, production statistics, http://www.oica.net/category/production-statistics/2015-statistics/.
24. Katherine Chiglinsky, Brandon Kochkodin, and Rick Clough, "GE's $31 Billion Problem," Bloomberg.com, February 7, 2018; *Milliman Corporate Pension Funding Study,* http://us.milliman.com/PFS/, accessed April 28, 2018; Brandon Kochkodin and Laurie Meisler, "S&P 500's Biggest Pension Plans Face $382 Billion Funding Gap," Bloomberg.com, July 20, 2017.
25. *Milliman Corporate Pension Funding Study,* http://us.milliman.com/PFS/, accessed April 28, 2018.
26. Bashker D. Biswas, *A Guide to Employee Benefits Design and Planning* (Upper Saddle River, NJ: Pearson Education, 2014).
27. Henry J. Kaiser Family Foundation, *2020 Employer Health Benefits Survey (Report), www.kff.org.*
28. M. L. Williams and E. Newman, "Employees' Definitions of and Knowledge of Employer-Provided Benefits," paper presented at Academy of Management meetings, Atlanta, GA, 1993; Richard Huseman, John Hatfield, and Richard Robinson, "The MBA and Fringe Benefits," *Personnel Administration* 23(7), 1978, pp. 57–60.
29. Marie Wilson, Gregory B. Northcraft, and Margaret A. Neale, "The Perceived Value of Fringe Benefits," *Personnel Psychology* 38, no. 2 (1985), pp. 309–320.
30. Society for Human Resource Management, "Employee Job Satisfaction and Engagement: Revitalizing a Changing Workforce," 2016, https://www.shrm.org/hr-today/trends-and-forecasting/research-and-surveys/Documents/2016-Employee-Job-Satisfaction-and-Engagement-Report.pdf.
31. Bashker D. Biswas, *A Guide to Employee Benefits Design and Planning* (Upper Saddle River, NJ: Pearson Education, 2014).
32. D. M. Cable and T. A. Judge, "Pay Preferences and Job Search Decisions: A Person-Organization Fit Perspective," *Personnel Psychology* 47 (1994), pp. 317–348.
33. Carol Danehower and John Lust, "How Aware Are Employees of Their Benefits?" *Benefits Quarterly* 12(4), 1996, pp. 57–61.
34. Burton Beam Jr. and John J. McFadden, *Employee Benefits* (Chicago: Dearborn Financial, 1996).
35. Bashker D. Biswas, *A Guide to Employee Benefits Design and Planning* (Upper Saddle River, NJ: Pearson Education, 2014).

36. Ibid.
37. Laura Ungar and Jayne O'Donnell, "Dilemma over Deductibles," *USA Today,* January 2, 2015, p. A1. Rebecca Mazin, The Employee Benefits Answer Book (San Francisco: Pfeiffer, 2011).
38. Bashker D. Biswas, *A Guide to Employee Benefits Design and Planning* (Upper Saddle River, NJ: Pearson Education, 2014); E. Parmenter, "Employee Benefit Compliance Checklist," *Compensation and Benefits Review,* May/June 2002, pp. 29–39.
39. Bashker D. Biswas, *A Guide to Employee Benefits Design and Planning* (Upper Saddle River, NJ: Pearson Education, 2014).
40. E. Parmenter, "Employee Benefit Compliance Checklist," *Compensation and Benefits Review*, May/June 2002, pp. 29–39.
41. Rebecca Mazin, *The Employee Benefits Answer Book* (San Francisco: Pfeiffer, 2011).
42. Melissa W. Barringer and George T. Milkovich, "A Theoretical Exploration of the Adoption and Design of Flexible Benefit Plans: A Case of Human Resource Innovation," *Academy of Management Review* 23 (1998), pp. 306–308; Commerce Clearing House, "Flexible Benefits" (Chicago: Commerce Clearing House, 1983); American Can Company, "Do It Your Way" (Greenwich, CT: American Can Co., 1978); L. M. Baytos, "The Employee Benefit Smorgasbord: Its Potential and Limitations," *Compensation Review,* First Quarter 1970, pp. 86–90; "Flexible Benefit Plans Become More Popular," *The Wall Street Journal*, December 16, 1986, p. 1; Richard Johnson, *Flexible Benefits: A How-to Guide* (Brookfield, WI: International Foundation of Employee Benefit Plans, 1986).
43. EBRI, *Employee Benefits Research Institute Databook on Employee Benefits* (Washington, DC: Employee Benefits Research Institute, 1995).
44. Ibid.
45. Tara Siegel Bernard, "High Deductible Plans Projected to Grow," *Wall Street Journal*, September 2014, p. B1.
46. Kaiser Family Foundation, "2014 Employer Health Benefits," 2014 Annual Survey, KFF.org, accessed January 3, 2015.
47. Tara Siegel Bernard, "High Deductible Plans Projected to Grow," *Wall Street Journal*, September 2014, p. B1.
48. E. Parmenter, "Employee Benefit Compliance Checklist," *Compensation and Benefits Review* 34(3), 2002, pp. 29–39.
49. Philip Bredesen, "ObamaCare's Incentive to Drop Insurance," *The Wall Street Journal* online, visited March 21, 2012, http://online.wsj.com/article/SB10001424052702304510704575562643804015252.html.
50. Bureau of Labor Statistics. U.S. Department of Labor. Employer Costs for Employee Compensation. www.bls.gov.
51. Paul Fronstin, "Offering Benefits Still Gives Employers a Competitive Advantage," fronstin@ebri.org, 2013.
52. Donald P. Crane, *The Management of Human Resources*, 2nd ed. (Belmont, CA: Wadsworth, 1979); J. Foegen, "Are Escalating Employee Benefits Self-Defeating?" *Pension World* 14(9), September 1978, pp. 83–84, 86.
53. Olivia Mitchell, "Fringe Benefits and Labor Mobility," *Journal of Human Resources* 17(2), 1982, pp. 286–298; Bradley Schiller and Randal Weiss, "The Impact of Private Pensions on Firm Attachment," *Review of Economics and Statistics* 61(3), 1979, pp. 369–380.

54. W. Even and D. Macpherson, "Employer Size and Labor Turnover: The Role of Pensions," *Industrial and Labor Relations Review* 49(4) (1996), pp. 707–729; Olivia Mitchell, "Fringe Benefits and the Cost of Changing Jobs," *Industrial and Labor Relations Review* 37(1), 1983, pp. 70–78.

55. Ibid.

56. *The New York Times* and CBS poll, as reported in *Human Resource Management News* (Chicago: Remy, 1991).

57. Society for Human Resource Management, "Employee Job Satisfaction and Engagement: Revitalizing a Changing Workforce," 2016, https://www.shrm.org/hr-today/trends-and-forecasting/research-and-surveys/Documents/2016-Employee-Job-Satisfaction-and-Engagement-Report.pdf. See also Paul Fronstin, "Offering Benefits Still Gives Employers a Competitive Advantage," fronstin@ebri.org, 2013.

58. S. Lambert, "Added Benefits: The Link between Work-Life Benefits and Organizational Citizenship Behavior," *Academy of Management Journal* 43(5) (2000), pp. 801–815.

59. William F. Glueck, *Personnel: A Diagnostic Approach* (Plano, TX: Business Publications, 1978).

60. William F. Glueck, *Personnel: A Diagnostic Approach* (Plano, TX: Business Publications, 1978).

61. Ludwig Wagner and Theodore Bakerman, "Wage Earners' Opinions of Insurance Fringe Benefits," *Journal of Insurance*, June 1960, pp. 17–28; Brad Chapman and Robert Otterman, "Employee Preference for Various Compensation and Benefits Options," *Personnel Administrator* 25 (November 1975), pp. 31–36.

62. Stanley Nealy, "Pay and Benefit Preferences," *Industrial Relations*, October 1963, pp. 17–28.

63. Robert M. McCaffery, *Managing the Employee Benefits Program*, rev. ed. (New York: American Management Association, 1983).

64. See "Towers Perrin Survey Finds Dramatic Increase in Companies Utilizing the Web for HR Transactions: Two- to Threefold Increase Compared to 1999 Survey," www.towers./Users/f-com/towers/news, October 20, 2000; Towers, Perrin, Forster, and Crosby, "Corporate Benefit Communication . . . Today and Tomorrow" (New York: Towers, Perrin, Forster, and Crosby, 1988).

65. Ellen Anreder, "Communicating the Value of Your Benefits," *Benefits Magazine*, 52(5), 2015, pp. 28–33.

66. International Foundation of Employee Benefits Plans, Benefits Communication Survey Results, February 2016, https://www.ifebp.org/pdf/benefits-communication-survey-results.pdf.

67. Ibid.

Chapter **Thirteen**
Benefit Options

Chapter Outline

A Historical Perspective

The idea of employee benefits in the United States dates back to colonial days. Plymouth Colony settlers established a retirement program in 1636 for the military. American Express began the first private pension plan in 1875. Montgomery Ward, a now defunct competitor of JC Penneys, started the first group health and life insurance programs in 1910. In 1915, employees in the iron and steel industry worked a standard 60 to 64 hours per week. By 1930 that schedule had been reduced to 54 hours. It was not until 1929 that the Blue Cross concept of prepaid medical costs was introduced. Before that health care was the responsibility of the worker's family. Prior to 1935 only one state (Wisconsin) had a program of unemployment compensation benefits for workers who lost their jobs through no fault of their own. Before World War II, very few companies paid hourly employees for holidays. In most companies, employees were told not to report for work on holidays and to enjoy the time off, but their paychecks were smaller the following week.[1]

The biggest early push for benefits, though, came from Uncle Sam. In 1935 the federal government mandated retirement income protection under Social Security. Coverage for the disabled and elderly followed in the 1950s and 1960s. Fast forward several decades and companies are in an ongoing struggle to control benefits costs, especially health care costs. And some of the measures to cut these costs are attracting public attention. For example, the Affordable Care Act allows insurance companies to charge up to 50 percent higher premiums to smokers. (It is up to each state to decide.) Likewise, depending on the state, an employer may choose not to hire someone who smokes. The argument runs, if you're going to continue habits that raise our health insurance costs, we're going to charge you or even not hire you (law in the state permitting). A key fact that explains the focus on smokers and health generally is that a relatively small number of people account for a majority of health care costs. By one estimate, 20 percent of the population accounts for 85 percent of health care costs and 1 percent of the population accounts for 30 percent of costs.[2] Consider also that with the explosion of research on the human genome, a company could test applicants not only for expensive health conditions, but also for a disposition to have such conditions *years in the future.* All of this makes the study of employee benefits that much more interesting. Eager to control the cost of employee health insurance and other benefits, companies are experimenting with a variety of approaches to encourage, incentivize (and/or penalize) employees to become more health. They are also using analytics to identify where the costs are (see the 20%/85% cost distribution above) and how to take action on those (e.g., coming up with ways to avoid premature births, reducing emergency care visits, and so forth). Happy reading!

For years we've asked our students and HR professionals to rate different kinds of rewards in terms of importance. Usually, at least in the past, employee benefits lagged behind such rewards as pay, advancement opportunity, job security, and recognition. Recently, though, we've noticed a shift in this admittedly unscientific poll. As benefits costs, especially health care, have increased, so too interest in them.

With this increased popularity comes a need for HR professionals to understand what benefits are important to employees. As we noted in **Chapter 12**, several years ago McDonald's unveiled a new benefits program for crew members. When we asked then chief HR officer, Rich Floersch, why McDonald's was modifying its health care package as part of a total benefits upgrade, he cited the rising value of benefits to workers and the strategic importance of its hundreds of thousands of employees (and around two million, including its franchises). Likewise, a survey by the Society for Human Resource Management (SHRM) found that employers believe the two most import benefits for employees are health care and investment/retirement and that health care was the main area where employers had increased benefits of late.[3] Of course, things can change quickly, at least for the short term. During the pandemic, leave and remote work arrangements quickly became critical benefits.

Our goal in this chapter is to give you a clearer appreciation of the role of employee benefits in compensation, including their scope and their cost. **Exhibit 13.1** reports employer costs of wages and salaries, benefits, and specific benefits categories. In private industry, total compensation equals $36.23, of which $25.48 (70%) is wages and salaries and $10.74 (30%) is benefits. Insurance and legally required benefits are the most costly benefit categories. Overall, benefits add almost 42 cents on top of every dollar of wages and salaries (and account for 30% of total compensation). Employer costs are higher in state and local government, where benefits are a higher share, 38 percent of total compensation (and add 61 cents on top of every dollar of wages/salaries!). It seems to pay to work for the government! Before getting too animated, however, there are important caveats. First, government employees earn more partly because they have higher average education.[4] Second, government workers having a graduate degree actually earn less total compensation (wages/salaries plus benefits) than private industry workers with a graduate degree. Third, stock option/grant payouts, received only by private sector employees, are not included in these figures. (Note that the very top executive in government in the United States, the President, has a salary of $400,000. We saw in **Chapter 1** and will see more in **Chapter 14** that the total compensation for private industry top executives is "somewhat" higher than that. On the other hand, it does seem like the POTUS does have some perquisites that even top executives in private industry cannot match.)

EXHIBIT 13.1 **Employer Cost of Benefit per Hour Worked: Private Industry and State/Local Government**

	Private Industry Average ($)	State and Local Government Average ($)
Total Compensation	**36.23 (100%)**	**53.47 (100%)**
Wages and salaries	**25.48 (70%)**	**33.08 (62%)**
Benefits	**10.74 (30%)**	**20.39 (38%)**
Paid leave	**2.69**	**4.04**
Holiday	.80	1.14
Vacation	1.38	1.52
Sick leave	.37	1.03
Personal leave	.14	.35
Supplemental pay[a]	**1.25**	**.54**
Insurance	**2.81**	**6.23**
Life insurance	.04	.07
Health insurance	2.65	6.07
Short-term disability	.07	.03
Long-term disability	.04	.05
Retirement	**1.25**	**6.65**
Defined benefit	.42	6.18
Defined contribution	.82	.47

	Private Industry Average ($)	State and Local Government Average ($)
Legally required	**2.75**	**2.94**
Social security & Medicare	2.14	2.29
Federal and state unemployment insurance	.17	.06
Workers' compensation	.45	.58

Source: Bureau of Labor Statistics, U.S. Department of Labor. *Employer Costs for Employee Compensation–December 2020.* USDL-21-0437. March 18, 2021. Table 1.

[a]Includes overtime and other premiums, shift differentials, and nonproduction bonuses.

Exhibit 13.2 shows employee access to selected benefit programs, by establishment size. We can see that larger establishments are much more likely than smaller establishments to offer many types of benefits.

Many students tell us they are struck by how low the retirement and health insurance figures are. The follow-up question we get is, "Doesn't everyone get a retirement package?" The answer is no! Many Americans work in jobs with no paid retirement. Many also receive no health coverage.

To organize the rest of this chapter, we will use a somewhat more detailed categorization of employee benefits (**Exhibit 13.3**). We will use these seven categories to illustrate important principles affecting strategic and administrative concerns for each benefit type.

EXHIBIT 13.2 **Percentage of Full-Time Workers in U.S. Private Industry with Access to Selected Benefits Programs, by Establishment Size**

	Establishment Size		
	All	**1–99 Employees**	**500 or More Employees**
Medical care	70%	56%	91%
Short-term disability insurance	42	30	63
Long-term disability insurance	34	24	58
All retirement	67	53	88
Defined benefit pension	15	7	39
Defined contribution plan	64	51	82
Life insurance	56	40	82
Paid leave			
Sick	75	67	88
Vacation	79	71	90
Holidays	80	73	91
Family	20	15	31

Source: U.S. Bureau of Labor Statistics, National Compensation Survey. *Employee Benefits in the United States–March 2020.* Bulletin 2793. www.bls.gov/ncs/ebs.

EXHIBIT 13.3 Categorization of Employee Benefits

Type of Benefit

1. Legally required payments (employers' share only)
   a. Workers' compensation (including estimated cost of self-insured)
   b. Social Security (old-age, survivors, disability, and health insurance [employer FICA taxes] and railroad retirement tax)
   c. Unemployment compensation
   d. Family leave and health insurance (FMLA, COBRA, HIPAA)
2. Retirement and savings plan payments (employers' share only)
   a. Defined benefit pension plan contributions (401(k) type)
   b. Defined contribution plan payments
   c. Profit sharing
   d. Stock bonus and employee stock ownership plans (ESOPs)
   e. Pension plan premiums (net) under insurance and annuity contracts (insured and trusted)
   f. Administrative and other costs
3. Life insurance and death benefits (employers' share only)
4. Medical and medical-related benefit payments (employers' share only)
   a. Hospital, surgical, medical, and major medical insurance premiums (net)
   b. Retiree hospital, surgical, medical, and major medical insurance premiums (net)
   c. Short-term disability, sickness, or accident insurance (company plan or insured plan)
   d. Long-term disability or wage continuation (insured, self-administered, or trust)
   e. Dental insurance premiums
   f. Other (vision care, physical and mental fitness benefits for former employees)
5. Paid rest periods, coffee breaks, lunch periods, wash-up time, travel time, clothes-change time, get-ready time, etc.
6. Payments for time not worked
   a. Payments for or in lieu of vacations
   b. Payments for or in lieu of holidays
   c. Sick leave pay
   d. Parental leave (maternity and paternity leave payments)
   e. Other
7. Miscellaneous benefit payments
   a. Discounts on goods and services purchased from company by employees
   b. Employee meals furnished by company
   c. Employee education expenditures
   d. Child care
   e. Other

Source: U.S. Chamber of Commerce, *Employee Benefits Study*, 2008. Reprinted with permission.

LEGALLY REQUIRED BENEFITS

Virtually every employee benefit is somehow affected by statutory or common law (many of the limitations are imposed by tax laws). In this section, the primary focus is on benefits that are required by statutory law: workers' compensation, social security, and unemployment compensation.

Workers' Compensation

What costs employers about $99 billion a year and is a major cost of doing business? Answer: workers' compensation. Of this total cost, $33 billion is to pay for premiums, deductibles, and other costs of the program. The other $66 billion is in the form of worker benefits, with roughly half of that to pay for medical benefit and the remaining one-half in the form of cash benefits for lost/covered wages.[5]

Prior to the first states passing workers' compensation laws early in the 20th century, "the many workers who were injured on the job, often badly, rarely received any compensation." Suing employers was costly and difficult. However, the situation was also difficult for employers in that they "faced potentially heavy liability, because it was very difficult to predict how much employees would be awarded when they did win such suits."[6] Such laws now provide benefits (see below) in the form of no-fault insurance (employees are eligible even if their actions caused the accident) covering injuries and diseases that arise out of, and while in the course of, employment. Workers who are covered cannot sue the employer or recover pain and suffering or other costs beyond wages and medical care. Benefits are given for:[7]

1. Medical care needed to treat the job injury or illness.
2. Temporary disability benefits to the employee to help replace lost wages.
3. Permanent disability payments to the employee to compensate for permanent effects of the injury.
4. Survivor death benefits.
5. Rehabilitation and training in most states, for those unable to return to their prior career.

Workers compensation costs have not been fairly stable and, when adjusted for growth in employment and wages, have declined.[8] Experts believe this relates to employer safety programs, with far fewer fatal accidents occurring and somewhat higher incidents of minor, less costly accidents.

States vary in the size of the payout for claims.[9] New York State, for example, has a payout formula for totally or partially disabled that is based on his/her average weekly wage for the previous year. The following formula is used in New York State to calculate cash benefits for permanently disable workers:[10]

2/3 × pre-injury weekly wage × percent of disability = weekly benefit

Therefore, a claimant who was earning $800 per week and is totally (100%) disabled would receive $533 per week. A partially disabled claimant (50%) would receive $267 per week. The maximum weekly cash benefit at the time of this writing was $966.78/week.

Some states provide "second-injury funds." These funds relieve an employer's liability when a pre-employment injury combines with a work-related injury to produce a disability greater than that caused by the latter alone. For example, if a person with a known heart condition is hired and then breaks an arm in a fall triggered by a heart attack, medical treatments for the heart condition would not be paid from workers' compensation insurance; treatment for the broken arm would be compensated.

Workers' compensation is covered by state, not federal, laws. For details on each state's laws, go to the e-Compensation website below:

e-Compensation

Each state differs in its workers' compensation law. If you're a glutton for punishment, visit https://www.workerscompensation.com/.

As **Exhibit 13.4** shows, in general the states are similar in some ways. However, both the level of worker cash benefits and employer cost vary significantly by state. For example, the cash benefit paid to workers per $100 of covered wages is $0.63 in New York State. (That is lower than the 2/3 or $0.67 in the formula above because there is a maximum weekly benefit, as noted above, of $966.78. Thus, high wage workers do not receive the full 2/3.) In contrast, it is $0.11 in Texas and $0.14 in Arkansas. Employer cost is $1.41 per $100 of covered wages in New York. In contrast, Texas is $0.55 and Arkansas is $0.70, or one-half or less of New York.[11]

e-Compensation

This website from the Department of Labor provides extensive information about legally required benefits and specific requirements for compliance: ***http://www.dol.gov/dol/topic/***.

Social Security: Old Age, Survivors, Disability & Health (OASDI) + Medicare

When Social Security was introduced in 1937 (under the Social Security Act of 1935), only about 60 percent of all workers were eligible.[12] Today, nearly all American workers (96%) are covered.[13] Whether a worker

EXHIBIT 13.4 **Commonalities in State Workers' Compensation Laws**

Issue	Most Common State Provision
Type of law	Compulsory (in 47 states)
	Elective (in 3 states)
Self-insurance coverage	Self-insurance permitted (in 48 states)
	All industrial employment
	Farm labor, domestic servants, and casual employees usually exempted
	Compulsory for all or most public sector employees (in 47 states)
Occupational diseases	Coverage for all diseases arising out of and in the course of employment No compensation for "ordinary diseases of life"

Source: *NCCI.com.*

retires, becomes disabled, or dies, Social Security benefits are paid to replace part of the lost family earnings. Ever since its passage, the Social Security Act has been designed and amended to provide a foundation of basic security for American workers and their families. **Exhibit 13.5** outlines the initial provisions of the law and its subsequent broadening over the years.[14] In combination, this law and its updates provide coverage in the form of: retirement insurance; survivors insurance; disability insurance; hospital and medical insurance for the aged, the disabled, and those with end-stage renal disease; prescription drug benefit Extra Help with Medicare Prescription Drug Costs supplemental security income; and special veterans benefits.[15]

The money to pay these benefits comes from the Social Security contributions made by employees, their employers, and self-employed people during working years. As contributions are paid in each year, they are immediately used to pay for the benefits to current beneficiaries. Herein lies a major problem with Social

EXHIBIT 13.5 Changes in Social Security over the Years

1939	Survivor's insurance was added to provide monthly life insurance payments to the widow and dependent children of deceased workers.
1950–1954	Old-age and survivor's insurance was broadened.
1956	Disability insurance benefits were provided to workers and dependents of such employees.
1965	Medical insurance protection was provided for the aged, and later (1973) for the disabled under age 65 (Medicare).
1972	Cost-of-living escalator was tied to the consumer price index—guaranteed higher future benefits for all beneficiaries.
1974	Existing state programs of financial assistance to the aged, blind, and disabled were replaced by SSI (supplemental security income) administered by the Social Security Administration.
1983	Effective 1984, all new civilian federal employees were covered. All federal employees covered for purpose of Medicare.
1985	Social Security Administration (SSA) became an independent agency administered by a commissioner and a bipartisan advisory board.
1994	Amendments were enacted imposing severe restrictions on benefits paid to drug abusers and alcoholics (together with treatment requirements and a 36-month cap on the payment of benefits).
1996	Contract with America Advancement Act of 1996 (CWAAA) was enacted, eliminating substance abuse as a disabling impairment. Substance abuse may no longer be the basis for a finding of disability.
2000	Depression-era limits on amount of money that workers age 65 to 69 may earn without having their Social Security benefits reduced were eliminated—retroactive to January 1, 2000. The rules governing individuals who take early retirement at age 62 and the status of workers age 70 and over were not changed by the new law.
2003	The Medicare Prescription Drug, Improvement and Modernization Act of 2003 (P.L.108-173) archive. Seniors must choose from among a variety of plans written in bureaucratic hieroglyphics.

Source: Social Security Administration, *Social Security Handbook*.

Security. While the number of retired workers continues to rise (because of earlier retirement and longer life spans), no corresponding increase in the number of contributors to Social Security has offset the costs. Combine the increase in beneficiaries with other cost stimulants (e.g., liberal cost-of-living adjustments) and the outcome is not surprising. To maintain solvency, there has been a major increase over time in both the maximum earnings base and the rate at which that base is taxed. **Exhibit 13.6** illustrates the trends in tax rate, maximum earnings base, and maximum tax for Social Security.

As of 2021, the total Social Security Tax on earnings is 7.65 percent (6.2% OASDHI + 1.45% Medicare), which is *paid by both employees and employers* (for a total of 15.3%). Although not shown in **Exhibit 13.6**, the federal government did not forget about the self-employed, who, in the absence of a separate employer, pay a tax rate of 15.3 percent (12.4% OASDHI tax plus a 2.9% Medicare tax). Also not shown is a tax added as of 2013 by the Affordable Care Act, referred to by the Social Security Administration as the High Income Tax and by the Internal Revenue Service as the Additional Medicare Tax, which is 0.9 percent on adjusted gross income above $200,000 for single filers and $250,000 for married filers. (This latter tax is paid only by individuals. Employers do not pay this tax.) So, when tennis star Naomi Osaka makes $37 million, she will pay 6.2 percent ($8,854) on the first $142,800 and 1.45% ($536,500) on the entire $37 million. She will then also pay 0.9 percent ($331,200) on the portion above $200,000. That is $481,854. (And, income taxes are still to be paid on top of that.) For the super rich (even with royalties, textbook authors need not apply), this may leave a mark.

Despite the above, funding of the Social Security and Medicare system continues to be a concern. In 1940, the ratio of social security covered workers (those paying into the fund) to beneficiaries was 159.4 to 1 and 5.1 to 1 in 1960. In 1990, the ratio was 3.4 to 1, and it is now under 3.0 to 1.[16] Consequently, the Trustees have stated "The Old-Age and Survivors Insurance (OASI) Trust Fund, which pays retirement and survivors benefits, will be able to pay scheduled benefits on a timely basis until 2034, the same as reported last year. At that time, the fund's reserves will become depleted and continuing tax income will be sufficient to pay 76

EXHIBIT 13.6 **Social Security Taxes, by Year**

	Old Age, Survivors, Disability, and Health Insurance (OASDHI)		Medicare	
Year	Maximum Taxable Earnings	Tax Rate	Maximum Taxable Earnings	Tax Rate
1980	$25,900	5.08%	$25,900	1.05%
1990	51,300	6.20	51,300	1.45
1995	61,200	6.20	No maximum	1.45
2000	76,200	6.20	No maximum	1.45
2005	90,000	6.20	No maximum	1.45
2010	106,800	6.20	No maximum	1.45
2015	118,500	6.20	No maximum	1.45
2020	137,700	6.20	No maximum	1.45
2021	142,800	6.20	No maximum	1.45

Source: U.S. Social Security Administration Office of Retirement and Disability Policy, *www.ssa.gov/policy/docs/quickfacts/prog_highlights/index.html,* April 6, 2015; U.S. Social Security Administration, Contribution and Benefit Base, Social Security, https://www.ssa.gov/oact/COLA/cbb.html, accessed April 29, 2018.

Note: In 2011 the OASDHI tax was reduced for one year from 6.2% to 4.2%.

percent of scheduled benefits."[17] They also provide a similar analysis of Medicare and the other related programs. The Social Security Administration, based on the Trustees report, provides a set of options to address the funding challenge.[18]

Benefits under Social Security

The majority of benefits under Social Security fall into four categories: (1) old-age (retirement) or disability benefits, (2) benefits for dependents of retired or disabled workers, (3) benefits for surviving family members of a deceased worker, and (4) lump-sum death payments. To qualify for the retirement benefit, worker must work in covered employment and earn a specified amount of money ($1,470 this year) for each quarter-year of coverage for 40 quarters.[19] The amount received under the four benefit categories noted above varies, but in general it is tied to the amount contributed during eligibility quarters.

For those born in 1940, Social Security retirement (old-age insurance) benefits for fully insured workers begin at age 65 years and 6 months (full benefits) or age 62 (at a permanent reduction of 22.5% in benefits). The "full retirement age" now rises with birth year, reaching age 67 for those born in 1960 or later. Although the amount of the benefit depends on one's earnings history, benefits do not go up after reaching a certain earnings level. Thus high earners help subsidize benefit payments to low earners. In 2021, the maximum benefit (for someone with a high earning history) at full retirement age was $3,148/month ($37,776/year). However, the highest maximum benefit ($3,895/month, $46,470/year) is, in fact, obtained by waiting beyond the "full retirement age" until age 70 to retire. Cost-of-living increases are provided each year that the consumer price index increases. There is also a spousal benefit of up to 50 percent of the primary recipient's (full retirement age) benefit (if larger than the spouse's own benefit).

An important attribute of the Social Security retirement benefit is that for those at full retirement age, it is free from state tax in about half of the states and free from federal tax if no other income is received or if that other income falls below a certain level (recently, $25,000 for single tax return filers, $34,000 for married/joint filers). At high income levels, a maximum of 85% of benefits are subject to federal tax. Additionally, the federal tax code has an earnings test for those who are still earning wages (and not yet at full retirement age). In 2021, beneficiaries (who must be 62 or older) below the full retirement age were allowed to make $18,960; in the year an individual reaches full retirement age, the earnings test is $50,250. If these amounts are exceeded, the Social Security benefit is reduced $1 for every $2 in excess earnings for those under the full retirement age and $1 for every $3 in the year a worker reaches the full retirement age. These provisions are important because of their effects on the work decisions of those between age 62 and full retirement age. The earnings test increases a person's incentive to retire (otherwise, full Social Security benefits are not received), and if she continues to work, the incentive to work part time rather than full time increases. A major change made in January 2000 is that there is no earnings test once full retirement age is reached. Therefore, these workers no longer incur any earnings penalty (and thus have no tax-related work disincentive).

Unemployment Insurance

The earliest union efforts to cushion the effects of unemployment for their members (ca. 1830s) were part of benevolent programs of self-help. Working members made contributions to their unemployed brethren. Wisconsin, in 1932, was the first state to introduce unemployment insurance. With passage of the unemployment insurance law (as part of the Social Security Act of 1935), this floor of security for unemployed workers became less dependent upon the philanthropy of co-workers. The Great Depression started in 1929, and as we have noted, the unemployment rate eventually went as high as 25 percent. Think of that and the fact that no unemployment insurance existed until several years into the Great Depression.

The unemployment insurance program has four major objectives: (1) to offset lost income during involuntary unemployment, (2) to help unemployed workers find new jobs, (3) to provide an incentive for employers to stabilize employment, and (4) to preserve investments in worker skills by providing income during short-term layoffs (which allows workers to return to their employer rather than start over with another employer). Unemployment insurance laws vary by state. The following discussion will cover some of the major characteristics of different state programs.

Financing

In the majority of states, unemployment compensation paid out to eligible workers is financed exclusively by employers that pay federal and state unemployment insurance tax. The federal tax amounts to 0.6 percent of the first $7,000 earned by each worker.[20] In addition, states impose a tax above the $7,000 figure. The extra amount a company pays depends on its **experience rating**–lower percentages are charged to employers who have terminated fewer employees. The tax rate may fall to almost 0 percent in some states for employers that have had no recent experience (hence the term "experience rating") with downsizing and may rise to 10 percent for organizations with large numbers of layoffs.

Coverage

All workers except a few agricultural and domestic workers are currently covered by unemployment insurance (UI) laws. These covered workers though, must still meet eligibility requirements to receive benefits:

1. You must meet the state requirements for wages earned or time worked during an established (one year) period of time referred to as a "base period." [In most states, this is usually the first four out of the last five completed calendar quarters prior to the time that your claim is filed.]
2. You must be determined to be unemployed through no fault of your own [determined under state law], and meet other eligibility requirements of state law.[21]

Duration

Until 1958, the maximum number of weeks any claimant could collect UI was 26 weeks. However, the recessions of 1958 and 1960–1961 yielded large numbers of claimants who exhausted their benefits, leading many states temporarily to revise upward the maximum benefit duration. In 2008 Congress enacted the Emergency Unemployment Compensation program (EUC08). The program provided additional weeks of benefits to long term unemployed, extending benefits to as long as 53 weeks.[22] This program expired in 2013 and maximum benefits duration returned to 26 weeks.

(During the pandemic, unemployment compensation was expanded in key ways, including in terms of duration, benefit amount, and including independent contractors for the first time. However, these changes were temporary.)

Weekly Benefit Amount

In general, benefits are based on a percentage of an individual's earnings over a recent 52-week period–up to the state maximum amount.[23] For example, in many states, the compensation will be half your earnings, up to a maximum amount (e.g., $505/week in New York State).[24]

Controlling Unemployment Taxes

Every unemployed worker's **unemployment benefits** are "charged" against the firm or firms most recently employing that currently unemployed worker. The more money paid out on behalf of a firm, the higher is the unemployment insurance tax rate for that firm (i.e., the tax is based on the experience rating defined above). Efforts to control these costs quite logically should begin with a well-designed **human resource planning system.** Realistic estimates of human resource needs will reduce the pattern of hasty hiring followed by morale-breaking terminations. Additionally, a benefit administrator should attempt to audit pre-layoff behavior (e.g., lateness, gross misconduct, absenteeism, illness, leaves of absence) and compliance with UI requirements after termination (e.g., refusing a job can disqualify an unemployed worker). The government can also play an important part in reducing unemployment expenses by decreasing the number of weeks that people are unemployed. Research shows that unemployment duration decreases by three weeks simply by stepping up enforcement of sanctions against fraudulent claims.[25]

Family and Medical Leave Act (FMLA)

The 1993 **Family and Medical Leave Act** applies to all employers having 50 or more employees within a 75-mile radius and entitles all eligible employees to receive unpaid leave up to 12 weeks per year for specified family or medical reasons.[26] Common reasons for leave under FMLA include caring for a newborn or seriously ill spouse, child, or parent.[27] Employees are guaranteed the same or a comparable job on their return to work. Employees with less than one year of service or who work less than 25 hours per week or who are among the 10% highest paid are not covered. More state legislatures are now moving toward some form of paid family and medical leave for workers.

Consolidated Omnibus Budget Reconciliation Act (COBRA)

In 1985 Congress enacted this law to provide current and former employees and their spouses and dependents with a temporary extension of group health insurance when coverage is lost due to qualifying events (e.g., layoffs). All employers with 20 or more employees must comply with COBRA. An employer may charge individuals up to 102 percent of the premium for coverage (100% premium plus 2% administration fee), which can extend up to 36 months (standard 18 months), depending on the category of the qualifying event.[28] The biggest concern for individuals getting health insurance under COBRA is the relatively brief qualifying period. After 18 months you're not eligible. With passage of the Affordable Care Act COBRA participants can opt into the Health Insurance Marketplace.[29]

Health Insurance Portability and Accountability Act (HIPAA)

The 1996 HIPAA is designed to (1) lessen an employer's ability to deny coverage for a preexisting condition and (2) prohibit discrimination on the basis of health-related status.[30] Perhaps the most significant element of HIPAA began in 2002, when stringent new privacy provisions added considerable compliance problems for both the HR people charged with enforcement and the information technology people delegated the task of building secure health information systems. Just watch next time you visit a new doctor. You will have to sign a HIPAA document that, should you choose to read it, will make your eyes glaze over.

RETIREMENT AND SAVINGS PLAN PAYMENTS

Pensions have been around for a long, long time. The first plan was established in 1759 to protect widows and children of Presbyterian ministers. After decades of steady growth in private pension plan coverage, today, as we saw earlier, only 67 percent of workers have access to a retirement plan (53% in smaller companies). Also not all workers with access to a plan actually participate.

Blame competitive pressures from globalization, the recession, and paltry growth in productivity, but the reality is, as we saw above, that fewer people are paying into Social Security and more are drawing benefits. Employer-provided retirement plans are thus more important than ever if people are going to be able to retire and hopefully do so with confidence. In this vein, employees with employer-provided retirement plans are more likely to have sufficient savings for a comfortable retirement than those who do not have these plans.[31] Two generic types of retirement plans are discussed below: **defined benefit plans** (the term "pension plan" most often refers to these) and **defined contribution plans. Exhibit 13.7** provides a comparison of the two types of plans. As you read their descriptions, keep in mind that defined benefit plans have become less common and those that remain are often not open to new enrollees. Prominent companies such as IBM and Verizon have frozen their traditional defined benefit pension payouts. Workers still get their pensions, but there isn't any growth in the amount as a function of additional time on the job. Rather, many companies are shifting to 401(k) plans (a popular type of defined contribution plan) where the dollar contribution is known and controllable. As we saw earlier, only 15 percent of private sector employers are covered by defined benefit plans, whereas 64 percent are covered by defined contribution plans, such as a 401(k). A few decades ago, these percentages would have been reversed. To understand why this major change occurred, we next explain the different cost and impacts of the two types of plans.

Defined Benefit Plans

In a defined benefit (DB) plan an employer agrees (promises) to provide a specific level of retirement pension ("defined benefit"), which is expressed as either a fixed dollar amount or a percentage-of-earnings amount, which typically varies (increases) with years of seniority in the company. The firm finances this obligation by following an actuarially determined benefit formula and making current payments that will yield the future pension benefit for a retiring employee.[32]

EXHIBIT 13.7 Retirement Plans, Defined Benefit versus Defined Contribution

Defined Benefit	Defined Contribution
Pension	e.g., 401k, profit sharing
Retirement Benefit is Defined/Promised	Employer Contribution is Defined/Promised
Investment Risk Borne by Employer	Investment Risk Borne by Employee
Cost Does Not Vary With Ability to Pay	Cost Varies with Ability to Pay
Employee Has No Active Role or Responsibility	Employee Must Manage Investments
Encourages Retention	Facilitates Mobility
	Bad Investment Decisions Mean Lower Retirement Income

The majority of defined benefit plans calculate average earnings over the last 3 to 5 years of service for a prospective retiree and offer a pension that is about one-half this amount (varying from 30% to 80%) adjusted for years of seniority, at least for employees who have been with the firm for a sufficiently long period of time.

So what is it about defined benefit plans that make them prime targets for cost cutting? The major complaints by chief financial officers (CFOs) center on funding: If I've got to pay Jim $40,000 a year at retirement, I have to start investing now to have that cash available. How much should I invest, though? Given how volatile the stock market is, it's hard to predict how much is needed. CFOs report that this is a drag on corporate financial health and a distraction from running the core business. As an example, General Motors (GM) recently eliminated its defined benefit plan for salaried employees. New hires already were covered by a defined contribution (DC) plan. Now all salaried employees are enrolled in DC plans. Why? GM had a $12 billion shortfall in funding its pension. As one step to eliminate their pension burden, GM paid Prudential $2.5 billon to take over 25 percent of GM's pension burden.[33] What companies do is purchase annuities with insurance companies. GM had a total of $25 billion in annuities with Prudential. Verizon had a $7.5 billion annuity, also with Prudential. Motorola and Bristol Meyers Squibb paid a combined $4.5 billion to Prudential to take over all pension payments. These companies buy the annuity at a premium (often 10%). When interest rates fluctuate in the future, now these companies won't have to worry about significantly higher pension costs. The annuity stabilized the cost of their pension obligation.[34]

Defined Contribution Plans

In a defined contribution (DC) plan the employer makes provisions for contributions to an account set up for each participating employee. Years later when employees retire, the pension is based on their contributions, employer contributions, and any gains (or losses) in stock investments. There are three popular forms of defined contribution plans. A **401(k) plan,** so named for the section of the Internal Revenue Code describing the requirements, is a savings plan in which employees are allowed to defer pretax income. Employers typically match employee savings at a rate of 50 cents on the dollar.[35] The growing use of defined contribution plans (and drop in use of defined benefit plans) has some advantages for younger employees (like many of you). Historically these plans are faster to vest (the company's matched share of the contribution permanently shifts over to employee ownership) and they are also more portable–job hopping employees can take their retirement fund accruals along to the next job. On the negative side, whereas employers bear the investment risk under a defined benefit plan, investment risk is borne by employees under defined contribution plans, a point unfortunately driven home to many during the recession of 2008–2010, when many employees saw their 401(k) portfolios decimated. Another problem with such plans is that many employees do not invest enough (i.e., contribution rates are low). About 40 percent of all employees don't contribute enough to get the full employer match.[36] To sum up, under a defined contribution plan, whether an employee will be able to afford to retire depends on decisions made by the employee. As such, employers must consider how to help employees learn the basics of investing (including the importance of diversification).

Several factors affect the amount of income that will be available to an employee upon retirement. First, the earlier the age at which investments are made, the longer returns can accumulate. As **Exhibit 13.8** shows, an annual investment of $3,000 made between ages 21 and 29 will be worth much more at age 65 than a similar investment made between ages 31 and 39. Second, different investments have different historical rates of return. Between 1928 and 2020 the average annual return was 10.3% for stocks, 6.1% for bonds, and 3.3% for cash (e.g., short-term Treasury bills or bank savings accounts). As **Exhibit 13.8** shows, *if* historical rates of return were to continue, an investment in a mix of 70% stock and 30% bonds between the ages of 21 and 29 would be worth about <u>10</u> times as much at age 65 as would the same amount kept in the form of cash. A third consideration is the need to counteract investment risk by diversification because stock and bond prices can be volatile in the short run. Although stocks have the greatest historical rate of return, that is no guarantee of future performance, particularly over shorter time periods. (This fact becomes painfully obvious during the dramatic drops in stock market values that are experienced every so often, most recently a drop of 38% in the S&P 500 in 2008 and a drop of 20% in the 1st quarter of 2020 before recovering to gain 4% for the year.) Thus, investment advisers often recommend a mix of stock, bonds, and cash, as shown in **Exhibit 13.8**, to reduce investment risk. Younger investors may wish to have more stock, while those closer to retirement age typically have less stock in their portfolios.

It's also important–indeed, extraordinarily important–not to invest too heavily in any single stock. Some Enron employees had 100 percent of their 401(k) assets in Enron stock. When the price dropped from $90 to less than $1 and Enron entered bankruptcy, their retirement money was gone. (More on Enron just below.) Employees at Bear Stearns, a storied Wall Street firm, also learned the hard way what can happen when you put all your eggs in one basket–company stock. When the stock price fell from its peak of $160 to $2 and Bear was purchased by JP Morgan Chase, the value of employee-owned shares fell from $6.3 billion to $79 million, a loss of 99 percent. Risk is compounded further by risk of job loss when one's employer struggles financially. So, repeat several times: Always diversify, and don't put all your retirement eggs in one basket.

The second type of DC plan is an **employee stock ownership plan (ESOP).** In a basic ESOP, a company makes a tax-deductible contribution of stock shares or cash to a trust. The trust then allocates company stock (or stock bought with cash contributions) to participating employee accounts. The amount allocated is based on employee earnings. When an ESOP is used as a pension vehicle (as opposed to an incentive program), the

EXHIBIT 13.8 **The Relationship of Retirement Savings to Age When Savings Begins and Type of Investment Portfolio**

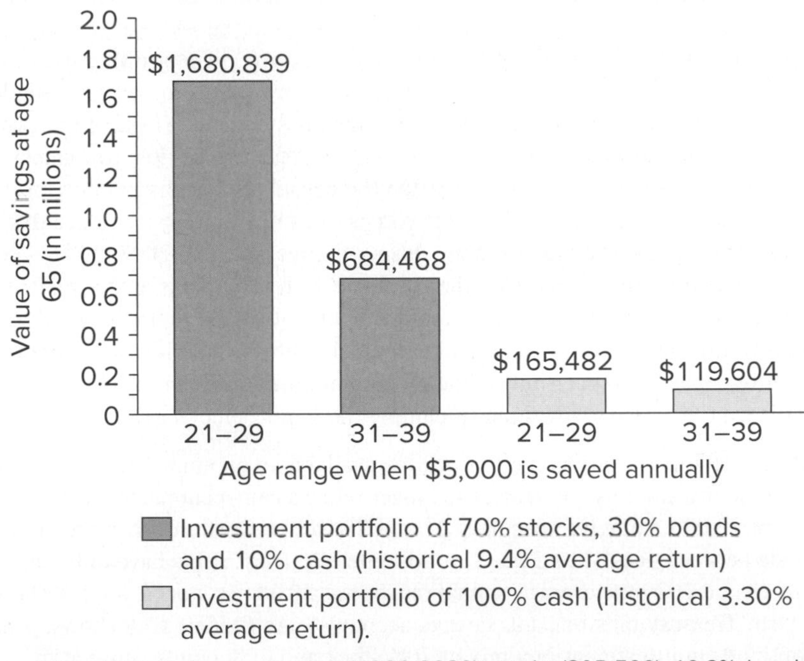

Note: Historical rates of return (1926-2020): stocks (S&P 500), 10.3%; bonds (long-term investment grade), 6.1%; cash (3-month Treasury Bill), 3.3%.

Source: Vanguard. "Vanguard Portfolio Allocation Models." https://investor.vanguard.com/investing/how-to-invest/model-portfolio-allocation.

employees receive cash at retirement based upon the stock value at that time. ESOPs have one major disadvantage, which limits their utility for pension accumulations. Many employees are reluctant to "bet" most of their future retirement income on just one investment source. If the company's stock takes a downturn, the result can be catastrophic for employees approaching retirement age. The classic example described above is Enron . . . yes, the same Enron linked to all the ethics problems. Under Enron's 401(k), employees could elect to defer a portion of their salaries. The employees were given 19 different investment choices, one of which was Enron common stock. Enron matched contributions, up to 6 percent of an employee's compensation. Enron's contributions were made in Enron stock and had to be held until the employee was at least age 50. This feature resulted in 60 percent of the total plan value being in Enron stock in 2001. Guess what? When Enron's shares went through the floor in 2001–2002, thousands of employees saw their retirement nest eggs destroyed. Recently 401(k) contributions have shifted away from company stock. The majority (53%) of companies allow less than 10 percent of assets in company stock.[37] Corey Rosen, founder of the National Center for Employee Ownership, advises, "Employees need to think very carefully about investing their own money beyond 10% in company stock." That implies that 47 percent of companies still have too much of retirement assets in company stock.[38]

Consider what has happened at General Electric (GE). The drop in its stock price in late 2017 and early 2018 resulted in an estimated $140 billion in wealth disappearing, more than was lost at Enron (and at Lehman and Bear Stearns). Compared to its 2000 peak, GE's market value dropped more than $460 billion. That, of course, had consequences for GE employees and retirees who for years took advantage of GE's stock purchase plan, under which GE would match up to 50 percent of worker stock purchases. When Gary Zabroski retired in 2016 from being a punch press operator at GE, he did so with an annual pension of $85,000 and GE stock valued at $280,000. A few years later, however, the value of his GE stock had fallen to $110,000. He decided he needed to find a job even though he hadn't planned on "having to go back to work." His monthly mortgage payment and the cost of supporting his partially disabled wife made his financial situation "kind of scary" after the drop in the value of his GE stock.[39]

Finally, a **profit-sharing plan** can be considered a defined contribution plan if the distribution of profits is delayed until retirement. **Chapter 10** explains the basics of profit sharing.

Not surprisingly, both DB and DC compensation plans are subject to stringent tax laws. For **deferred compensation** to be exempt from current taxation (i.e., to be a qualified deferred compensation plan), specific requirements must be met. To qualify, an employer cannot freely choose who will participate in the plan. Instead, they must meet nondiscrimination tests that are intended to encourage companies to spread benefits coverage to all employees. This requirement eliminated the common practice of building tax-friendly, extravagant pension packages (only) for executives and other highly compensated employees (a term precisely defined by the Internal Revenue Service in performing equally precise nondiscrimination tests).[40] The major advantage of a qualified plan is that the employer receives an income tax deduction for contributions made to the plan even though employees may not yet have received any benefits. The disadvantage arises in recruitment of high-talent executives. A plan will not qualify for tax exemptions if an employer pays high levels of deferred compensation to entice executives to the firm unless proportionate contributions also are made to lower-level employees.

A hybrid of defined benefit and defined contribution plans has emerged in recent years. **Cash balance plans** are defined benefit plans that look like a defined contribution plan. Employees have a hypothetical account (like a 401[k]) into which is deposited what is typically a percentage of annual compensation. The dollar amount grows both from contributions by the employer and from some predetermined interest rate (e.g., often set equal to the rate given on 30-year treasury certificates).

In 2009, 401(k) contributions were suspended by many companies in the wake of the Great Financial Crisis in the United States. General Motors, FedEx, Sears Holdings, and Eastman Kodak are among companies who suspended contributions. (During the 2020–2021 pandemic, 401(k) contributions were again reduced or suspended by a number of companies.) Such flexibility (in terms of what if any contributions are made when times are hard) can be viewed as another advantage (from the employer's point of view) of a defined contribution plan.

Individual Retirement Accounts (IRAs)

An **individual retirement account (IRA)** is a tax-favored retirement savings plan that individuals can establish themselves. That's right, unlike the other pension options, IRAs don't require an employer to set them up. Even people not in the workforce can establish an IRA. Currently, IRAs are used mostly to store wealth accumulated in other retirement vehicles, rather than as a way to build new wealth.[41]

Employee Retirement Income Security Act (ERISA)

The early 1970s were a public relations and economic disaster for private pension plans. Many people who thought they were covered were the victims of complicated rules, insufficient funding, irresponsible financial management, and employer bankruptcies. Some pension funds, including both employer-managed and union-managed funds, were mismanaged; other pension plans required long vesting periods. The result was a pension system that left far too many lifelong workers poverty stricken. Enter the Employee Retirement Income Security Act (ERISA) in 1974 as a response to these problems.

ERISA does not require that employers offer a pension plan. But if a company decides to have one, it is rigidly controlled by ERISA provisions.[42] These provisions were designed to achieve two goals: (1) to protect the interest of approximately 100 million active participants,[43] and (2) to stimulate the growth of such plans. The actual success of ERISA in achieving these goals has been mixed at best. In the first two full years of operation (1975 and 1976) more than 13,000 pension plans were terminated. A major factor in these terminations, along with the recession, was ERISA. Employers complained about the excessive costs and paperwork of living under ERISA. Some disgruntled employers even claimed ERISA was an acronym for "Every Ridiculous Idea Since Adam." To examine the merits of these claims, let us take a closer look at the major requirements of ERISA.

General Requirements

ERISA requires that employees be eligible for pension plans beginning at age 21. Employers may require 12 months of service as a precondition for participation. The service requirement may be extended to three years if the pension plan offers full and immediate vesting.

Vesting and Portability

These two concepts are sometimes confused but have very different meanings in practice. **Vesting** refers to the length of time an employee must work for an employer before he or she is entitled to employer payments made into the pension plan. The vesting concept has two components. First, any contributions made by the employee to a pension fund are immediately and irrevocably vested. The vesting right becomes questionable only with respect to the employer's contributions. The Economic Growth and Tax Relief Reconciliation Act of 2001 states that the employer's contribution must vest at least as quickly as one of the following two formulas: (1) full vesting after three years (down from five years previously) or (2) 20 percent after two years (down from three years) and 20 percent each year thereafter, resulting in full vesting after six years (down from seven years).

The vesting schedule an employer uses is often a function of the demographic makeup of the workforce. An employer who experiences high turnover may wish to use the three-year service schedule. By so doing, any employee with less than three years' service at time of termination receives no vested benefits. Or the employer may use the second schedule in the hopes that earlier benefit accrual will reduce undesired turnover. The strategy adopted is, therefore, dependent on organizational goals and workforce characteristics.

Portability of pension benefits becomes an issue for employees moving to new organizations. Should pension assets accompany the transferring employee in some fashion?[44] ERISA does not require mandatory portability of private pensions. On a voluntary basis, though, the employer may agree to let an employee's pension benefits transfer to the new employer. For an employer to permit portability, of course, the pension rights must be vested.

Pension Benefit Guaranty Corporation

Despite the wealth of constraints imposed by ERISA, the potential still exists for an organization to go bankrupt or in some way fail to meet its vested pension obligations. In the event of severe financial difficulties that force the company to terminate or reduce employee pension benefits, the **Pension Benefit Guaranty Corporation (PBGC)** provides some protection of benefits. Established by the Employee Retirement Income Security Act (ERISA) of 1974, the PBGC guarantees a basic benefit, not necessarily complete pension benefit replacement, for employees who were eligible for pensions at the time of termination. The maximum annual benefit for terminated single-employer plans is limited to the lesser of an employee's annual gross income during a PBGC-defined period or (in 2021) $32,584 at age 55, $47,066 at age 60, $72,413 at age 65, $120,199 at age 70, and $220,124 at age 75.[45] We guarantee you, there are many Eastman Kodak employees who lose sleep over this issue! The PBGC is funded by employer premiums paid annually and these premiums are larger for underfunded plans. (Note that the PBGC does not guarantee retiree health care benefits.)

Pension Protection Act of 2006 (PPA)

Remember Enron? Maybe you didn't know that many Enron employees lost more than their jobs. As we noted earlier, many employees had their retirement funds allocated to Enron stock. When the stock went through the floor, so did many retirement dreams. The PPA was passed by Congress in the wake of Enron and WorldCom. Its purpose was to protect employees' retirement income as well as transfer some responsibility for retirement savings from the employer to the employee. A key provision of the law allows employees in publicly traded companies the freedom to sell off any employer stock purchased through deferrals or after-tax contributions. We expect this provision will motivate employees toward investing in defined contribution plans and reduce some of the burden on employers. The law also aims at employers who fail to set aside enough reserves to cover current and future pension obligations by defining plans less than 70 percent funded as 'at risk' plans. There are at least two other important provisions of the PPA. One is that defined contribution plans holding publicly traded securities must provide employees with at least three investment options other than employer securities. The other provision is to allow employers to enroll workers in their 401(k) plan automatically and to increase a worker's 401(k) contribution automatically to coincide with a raise or a work anniversary. Workers can decline, but the onus is on them to do so.

How Much Retirement Income to Provide?

The level of pension a company chooses to offer depends on the answers to five questions. First, what level of retirement compensation would a company like to set as a target, expressed in relation to pre-retirement earnings? Second, should Social Security payments be factored in when considering the level of income an employee should have during retirement? One integration approach reduces normal benefits by a percentage (usually 50%) of Social Security benefits.[46] Another feature employs a more liberal benefit formula on earnings that exceed the maximum income taxed by Social Security. Regardless of the formula used, about one-half of U.S. companies do not employ the cost-cutting strategy. Once a company has targeted the level of income it wants to provide employees in retirement, it makes sense to design a system that integrates private pension and social security to achieve that goal. Any other strategy is not cost-effective.

Third, should other post-retirement income sources (e.g., savings plans that are partially funded by employer contributions) be integrated with the pension payment? Fourth, a company must decide how to factor seniority into the payout formula. The larger the role played by seniority, the more important pensions will be in retaining employees. Most companies believe that the maximum pension payout for a particular level of earnings should be achieved only by employees who have spent an entire career with the company (e.g., 30 to 35 years). As **Exhibit 13.9** vividly illustrates, job hoppers are hurt financially by this type of strategy *if* they are covered by a defined benefit plan. In our example–a very plausible scenario–job hopping cuts final defined benefit amounts in half. (Question: Would someone changing jobs perhaps prefer to be covered by a defined contribution plan such as a 401k instead?)

Finally, companies must decide what they can afford. As noted earlier, defined benefit plans at both companies and governments are often chronically underfunded. Of course, the decline in the use of defined benefit programs (especially in private industry) and a concurrent shift toward greater use of defined contribution plans can be explained in large part by a desire to get away from these funding challenges/financial obligations in the future, instead shifting them to employees.

EXHIBIT 13.9 The High Cost of Job Hopping (under a defined benefit plan)*

Career History	Years in Company	Percent of Salary for Pension		Salary at Company (Final)	Annual Pension
Sam					
Job 1	10	10%	×	$ 35,817	= $ 3,582
Job 2	10	10%	×	$ 64,143	= 6,414
Job 3	10	10%	×	$ 114,870	= 11,487
Job 4	10	10%	×	$205,714	= 20,571
Total pension					$42,054
Ann					
Job 1	40		×	$205,714	= $82,286
Total pension					$82,286

Source: Federal Reserve Bank of Boston.

*Assumptions: (1) Starting salary of $20,000 with 6 percent annual inflation rate. (2) Both employees receive annual increases equal to inflation rate. (3) Pensions based on 1 percentage point (of salary) for each year of service multiplied by final salary at time of exit from company.

LIFE INSURANCE

As we saw earlier, 56 percent of private sector employees have access to paid life insurance.[47] Typical coverage would be a group term insurance policy with a face value of one to two times the employee's annual salary.[48] Most plan premiums are paid completely by the employer.[49] The cost is about ten cents per hour per employee.[50] Slightly over 30 percent include retiree coverage. To discourage turnover, almost all companies make this benefit forfeitable at the time of departure from the company.

Life insurance is one of the benefits heavily affected by movement to a flexible benefit program. Flexibility is introduced by providing a core of basic life coverage (e.g., $25,000). The option then exists to choose greater coverage (usually in increments of $10,000 to $25,000) as part of the optional package.

MEDICAL AND MEDICALLY RELATED PAYMENTS

General Health Care

Health care costs continue to increase. As touched on earlier, annual premiums to provide family coverage now average $21,342, up 4 percent from the previous year, with (74%) paid by the employer and $5,588 (26%) paid by the employee. By comparison, in 2000, the average annual premium for family coverage was $6,438. Single coverage was $7,470, up 5 percent from the previous year, with employers paying $6,227 (83%) and employees paying $1,243 (17%).[51] **Exhibit 13.10** shows the percentage increase in annual premium costs over time, which have substantially outstripped increases in inflation and worker earnings. More costly technology, the explosion of lawsuits, the increased number of elderly people, and a system that does not encourage cost savings have all contributed to the rapidly rising costs of medical insurance. Not surprisingly, employers continue to seek ways to cut health care costs, including by passing more of them on to employees, or eliminate them completely from their benefits package. For example, not included in premium costs are payments made by employees in the form of co-insurance (paying a percentage of the cost of a medical service received, co-payments (paying a flat fee that covers part of the cost of a medical service received), and deductibles (paying the first x dollars of cost for medical services received during a year before insurance coverage, funded by premiums, kicks in to cover the cost). These three costs average an additional $800 annually for employees of large firms. The largest increase over time has been in deductibles.[52] After a discussion of the types of health care systems, we return to these (employer) cost-cutting strategies.

Before 1930, health care coverage essentially didn't exist. Health issues were the responsibility of the family. After the Great Depression, though, Blue Cross (BC) and Blue Shield (BS) appeared as the first institutional health care. Envious of the profits made by BC/BS, insurance companies began to offer plans for hospitalization along with doctor and surgical coverage. Then, of course, the government got involved. In the 1960s national health insurance emerged to cover the elderly (Medicare) and the poor (Medicaid).

The Affordable Care Act was signed into law in 2010 and its provisions as they affect employers came into full effect in 2018. The Act isn't intended to change the way health care is delivered, but rather is aimed at expanding health care coverage through both an individual mandate to purchase health insurance and an employer mandate (for those with 50 or more employees) to provide qualifying health insurance coverage or face financial penalties. "Under the law, the number of uninsured nonelderly Americans decreased from 44 million in 2013 (the year before the major coverage provisions went into effect) to less than 28 million as of the end of 2016."[53] Although the individual mandate was eliminated in 2018, the employer mandate remains in place. **Exhibit 13.11** summarizes provisions of the Act that pertain to employers.

As noted, the Affordable Care Act hasn't changed the basic underlying structure of health care delivery. The first method is through commercial insurance companies like Prudential, Aetna and Humana. Plans through these companies are called indemnity plans or so-called pay-for-service plans. Under these plans an employee can choose any health care provider. The second method of delivery is through a Health Maintenance Organization (HMO). An HMO pulls together a group of providers (e.g., hospitals and doctors) willing to provide services at an agreed upon rate in exchange for the employer limiting employees to these providers for health services. Employees make prepayments in exchange for guaranteed health care services on demand. Third, to provide employees with more options in selecting doctors and hospitals, Preferred Provider Organizations (PPOs) arose. Employers select certain providers who agree to provide price discounts and submit to strict utilization controls (e.g., strict standards on number of diagnostic tests that can be ordered). In turn, the employer influences employees to use these providers by charging higher fees if employees make selections outside the provider network. Finally, a **point-of-service plan (POS)** is a hybrid plan combining HMO and PPO benefits. The POS plan permits an individual to choose which plan to seek treatment from at the time that services are needed. POS plans, therefore, provide the economic benefits of the HMO with the freedom of the PPO. The HMO component of the POS plan requires office visits to an assigned primary care physician, with the alternative of receiving treatment through the PPO component. The PPO component does not require the individual to first contact the primary care physician but does require that in-network physicians be used. When POS plan participants receive all of their care from physicians in the network, they are fully covered, as they would be under a traditional HMO. Point-of-service plans also allow individuals to see a doctor outside the network, for which payment of an annual deductible ranging between $100 and $5,000 is required.[54]

EXHIBIT 13.10

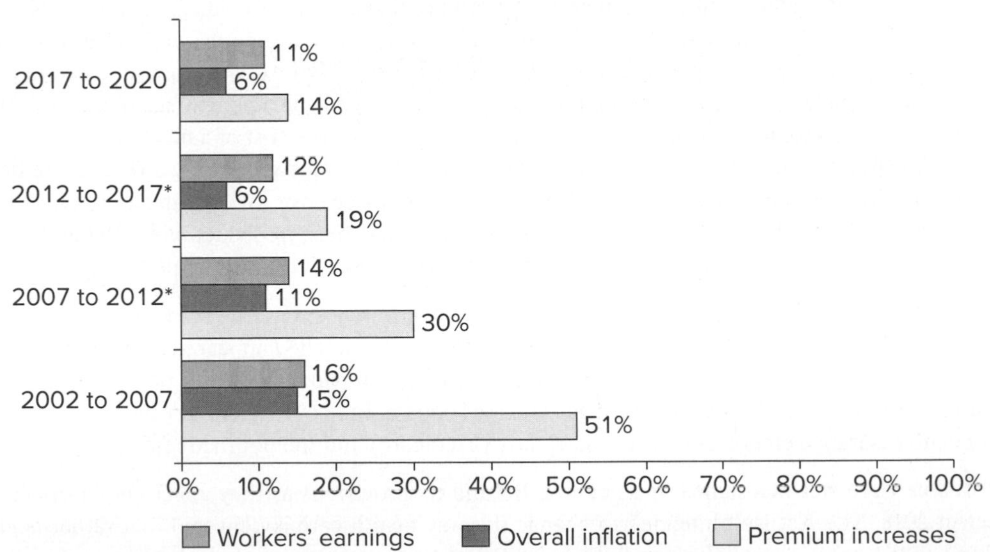

Note: the 2017 to 2020 growth period is shorter (3 years) than the other (5 year) growth periods, which makes the growth percentages smaller, all else equal.

Sources: Henry J. Kaiser Family Foundation. Health Costs, *Employer Health Benefits Survey*, September 19, 2017. Henry J. Kaiser Family Foundation, 2020 Employer Health Benefits Survey (Report), www.kff.org. https://www.bls.gov/data/inflation_calculator.htm; U.S. Bureau of Labor Statistics. Usual Weekly Earnings of Wage and Salary Workers. https://www.bls.gov/news.release/wkyeng.toc.htm.

EXHIBIT 13.11 The Affordable Care Act: Impact on Employers

Penalties for not Providing Health Benefits (The "Employer Mandate")

The health reform law does not require employers to provide health benefits. However, it does impose penalties in some cases on larger employers (those with 50 or more full-time workers or 50 or more full-time equivalents [FTE]) that do not provide affordable and minimum value health insurance to 95% of their full-time employees and children through age 26. Affordable is if employee contributions do not exceed 9.83% of an employee's household income in 2021. Minimum value is if it pays at least 60% of the cost of covered services (deductibles, copays, and coinsurance). Full-time is 30 hours or more.

Covered employers that do not provide health coverage are assessed a penalty if any one of their workers receives a tax credit when buying insurance on their own in a health insurance exchange. Workers with income up to 400% of the poverty level are eligible for tax credits. The employer penalty is equal to as much as $4,060 multiplied by the number of workers in the business in excess of 30 workers

Businesses with fewer than 25 FTEs and average annual wages of less than $54,000 that pay at least half of the cost of health insurance for their employees are eligible for a tax credit.

Taxes

The law increases the Medicare Hospital Insurance (Part A) payroll tax on earnings for higher-income taxpayers (more than $200,000/individual and $250,000/couple) by 0.9 percentage points, from 1.45% to 2.35%. Employers will be responsible for withholding these taxes.

(The law created a new tax on so-called "Cadillac" insurance plans provided by employers on plans valued at $10,200 or more for individual coverage or $27,500 or more for family policies. Such plans were to be subject to an excise tax of 40% on the value of the plan that exceeds these thresholds. This tax never went into effect. It was initially delayed and then repealed in 2019.)

Coverage of Dependents

The ACA requires plans and issuers that offer dependent coverage to make the coverage available until a child reaches the age of 26. Both married and unmarried children qualify for this coverage. This rule applies to all plans in the individual market and to new employer plans. It also applies to existing employer plans unless the adult child has another offer of employer-based coverage (such as through his or her job). Children up to age 26 can stay on their parent's employer's plan even if they have another offer of coverage through their own employer.

Wellness Programs

Employers can provide rewards to employees of up to 30% of the total plan premium as part of a wellness program incentive, up from the previous limit of 20%. Under the law, the Secretary of Health and Human Services may increase this limit to 50% if deemed appropriate. (This was done for programs targeting tobacco use.) Wellness programs must be "reasonably designed to promote health or prevent disease." The law also created a five-year grant program to encourage small employers that did not currently have wellness programs to establish them, which ran through 2015. Importantly, there is currently some legal uncertainty about whether employers can still use incentives at the above levels. This uncertainty has to do with rule-making by the Equal Employment Opportunity (EEOC, part of the U.S. Department of Labor), as part of its enforcement of the Americans with Disabilities Act (ADA). The ADA requires employee participation in a wellness programs that includes medical questions to be voluntary. The question is whether using strong incentives, in effect, compels participation. Before proceeding, it would be prudent to check for updated rules from the EEOC.

Sources: Internal Revenue Service, "Questions and Answers on Employer Shared Responsibility Provisions under the Affordable Care Act," www.irs.gov, accessed March 12, 2021; Internal Revenue Service. "Affordable Care Act Tax Provisions." www.irs.gov, Accessed March 12, 2021; Cigna. Employer Mandate. www.cigna.com. Accessed March 12, 2021. Chris Arey. ACA Employer Mandate Penalties Increasing in 2021. acatimes.com, November 19, 2020; Kaiser Family Foundation. Employer Responsibility Under the Affordable Care Act. July 2, 2019. www.kff.org; Conner, Strong, & Buckelew. New Wellness Rules Expected from EEOC. June 30, 2020. www.conner-strong.com.

Health Care: Cost Control Strategies

We noted above that employers use a variety of approaches (e.g., deductibles) to control costs by passing them on to employees. There are three general strategies available to benefit managers for controlling the rapidly escalating costs of health care.[55] First, organizations can motivate employees to change their demand for health care, through changes in either the design or the administration of health insurance policies. Included in this category of control strategies are (1) deductibles, or the first x dollars of health care cost are paid by the employee (at the extreme the state of Georgia recently told employees that certain name brand drugs will require a $100 copay, clearly signaling that enough is enough);[56] (2) coinsurance rates (premium payments are shared by the company and employee); (3) maximum benefits (defining a maximum payout schedule for specific health problems); (4) coordination of benefits (ensure no double payment when coverage exists under the employee's plan and a spouse's plan); (5) auditing of hospital charges for accuracy; (6) requiring preauthorization for selected visits to health care facilities; (7) mandatory second opinion whenever surgery is recommended; (8) using intranet technology to allow employees access to online benefit information, saving some of the cost of benefit specialists;[57] and (9) providing incentives to employees for using providers who meet certain high performance criteria.[58] The more questions answered online, the fewer specialists needed.

The second general cost control strategy involves changing the structure of health care delivery systems and participating in business coalitions (for data collection and dissemination). At the extreme are companies that simply decline to provide any health care coverage whatsoever.

Less extreme are choices like HMOs, PPOs, POSs, and consumer-directed health care plans. Also called Consumer Driven Health Plans and High Deductible Plans, this increasingly popular option for companies cuts costs by shifting much of the burden of purchasing health care over to employees. Employees choose from any of the traditional providers (HMO, PPO, Indemnity Plans), but the employer sets its contribution equal to the lower cost of these three (usually HMO). If the employee wants a more expensive option, the extra cost is out-of-pocket. These plans usually are accompanied by high deductibles, sometimes reaching several thousand dollars.[59] Typically an employer helps lessen the cost of the deductible by setting up Health Savings (HSA) or Health Reimbursement (HRA) accounts. Funds in these accounts are either contributed by employees with pretax dollars (HSA) or by the employer up to some fixed dollar amount (HRA). All of this complexity is introduced simply to force employees to make choices in the most economical way while hopefully not neglecting important health issues.

A final category of cost control strategies links incentives to healthy behaviors. We know that preventable illnesses account for 70 percent of all health care costs.[60] Obesity, for example, is preventable. Dieting, however, is not a favorite pastime. How, then, do we get people to lose weight? The answer may be health incentives. For example, Caesar's Casinos give a $40 award to employees who get screened to measure cholesterol level and then make efforts (e.g., by losing weight) to lower their levels. More than two-thirds of medium and large employers with wellness programs have incentives to get employees involved in wellness.[61] JetBlue provides a maximum of $400 in Health Reimbursement Accounts to be used by employees in roughly 45 activities (e.g., smoking cessation). On the negative incentive side, CVS drugstores charge employees $600 more in health premiums for not completing wellness assessment activities like annual checkups. In general, incentives are becoming much more popular. In 2009, only 57 percent of companies had any of these incentives. Now 75 percent use these motivational tools.[62]

e-Compensation

The Health Insurance Association of America provides research about a wide variety of specific health-related issues at its website, **www.ahip.org/**.

Short- and Long-Term Disability

A number of benefit options provide some form of protection for disability. For example, workers' compensation covers disabilities that are work related. Even Social Security has provisions for disability income to those who qualify. Beyond these two legally required sources, there are two private sources of disability income: employee **salary continuation plans** and **long-term disability plans.**[63]

Many companies have some form of salary continuation plan we include here vacation days that might be used for sick leave as a last resort that pays out varying levels of income depending on duration of illness.

At one extreme is short-term illness covered by sick leave policy and typically reimbursed at a level equal to 100 percent of salary.[64] The most prevalent practice these days is to give paid time off (PTO) rather than sick days. This reduces the need for companies to "police" whether employees are indeed sick, and allows employees more flexibility in life planning. After such benefits run out, disability benefits become operative. **Short-term disability (STD)** pays a percentage of your salary (about 60% on average) for temporary disability because of sickness or injury (on-the-job injuries are covered by workers' compensation). **Long-term disability plans (LTD),** if available, typically kick in after the short-term plan expires. Long-term disability is usually underwritten by insurance firms and provides 60 to 70 percent of pre-disability pay for a period varying between two years and life.[65]

Dental Insurance

A rarity decades ago, dental insurance is now much more prevalent, with most larger employers offering coverage. In many respects dental care coverage follows the model originated in health care plans. The dental equivalent of HMOs and PPOs is the standard delivery system. For example, a dental HMO enlists a group of dentists who agree to treat company employees in return for a fixed monthly fee per employee.

At the start of the century, the typical cost for employee dental coverage was $219.[66] Since then, of course, cost increases have been an issue and employers now typically require employee contributions.[67] The relatively modest increase in dental care costs can be traced to stringent cost control strategies (e.g., plan maximum payouts are typically $1,000 or less per year) and an excess supply of dentists.

Vision Care

Vision care dates back only to the 1976 contract between the United States Auto Workers and the Big Three automakers. Since then, this benefit has spread to other auto-related industries and parts of the public sector. Most large employers offer a vision plan. Most plans are noncontributory and usually cover partial costs of eye examination, lenses, and frames.

MORE BENEFITS

Paid Time off during Working Hours

Paid rest periods, lunch periods, wash-up time, travel time, clothes change time, and get-ready time benefits are self-explanatory.

Payment for Time Not Worked

Included within this category are several self-explanatory benefits:

1. Paid vacations and payments in lieu of vacation
2. Payments for holidays not worked
3. Paid sick leave
4. Other (payments for National Guard, Army, or other reserve duty; jury duty and voting pay allowances; payments for time lost due to death in the family or other personal reasons).

Twenty years ago, it was relatively rare to grant time off for anything but vacations, holidays, and sick leave. Now many organizations have a policy of ensuring payments for civic responsibilities and other obligations. Any outside pay for such civic duties (e.g., jury duty) is usually nominal, so companies often supplement this pay, frequently to the level of 100 percent of wages lost. There is also increasing coverage for parental leaves. Maternity and, to a lesser extent, paternity leaves are much more common than they were 25 years ago. Indeed, passage of the Family and Medical Leave Act in 1993 provides up to 12 weeks of unpaid leave (with guaranteed job protection) for the birth or adoption of a child or for the care of a family member with a serious illness. The following sick policy, taken from Motley Fool's employee manual, shows just how far such policies have come:

> Unlike other companies, The Motley Fool doesn't make you wait for six months before accruing vacation or sick time. Heck, if you're infected with some disgusting virus–stay home! We like you, but don't really want to share in your personal anguish. In other words, if you're bleeding out your eyes and coughing up a lung–don't be a hero! Stay home. Out of simple Foolish courtesy, we expect you to call your supervisor and let him or her know you won't be in. And yes, you will get paid. So, pop quiz: You're feeling like you're going to snap any moment if you don't take some personal time off, you've made a small deposit on an M-16 rifle and are scoping out local clock towers, BUT you've only been a paid Fool for a short time ... what do you do, what do you do?[68]

Many companies are switching from **traditional time-off plans (TTO),** as described above, to **paid-time-off (PTO) plans.** These lump all time off together into one total allotment and deduct any day missed from this bank. Not only is this administratively easier for companies to track, but it also eliminates the need for employees to lie and say they're sick when the reality is, for example, a scheduled dentist appointment.[69]

Family-Friendly Policies (including child care, family leave, and flexible work)

To ease employees' conflicts between work and nonwork (and to help in recruiting and retention), organizations may use *family-friendly policies* (also known as policies that help balance work and family) such as child care, family leave policies, and flexible work arrangements.[70]

Relatively few companies directly provide child care. However, it's becoming quite common for employers to offer flexible spending accounts with child care expenditures as a legitimate expense. The employee, employer, or both pay into an account with pretax monies, and individuals can then use these funds to pay local child care providers. Here again, the tax-advantaged nature of benefits is important to consider.

A flexible spending account permits pretax contributions of up to $2,750 to an employee account that can be drawn on to pay for uncovered health care expenses (like deductibles or co-payments). A separate account of up to $5,000 per year is permitted for pretax contributions to cover dependent care expenses. The federal tax code requires that funds in the health care and dependent care accounts be earmarked in advance and spent during the plan year. Remaining funds revert to the employer. Therefore, the accounts work best to the extent that employees have predictable expenses. The major advantage of such plans is the increase in take-home pay that results from pretax payment of health and dependent care expenses. Consider again the hypothetical employee with an effective total marginal tax rate of 43 percent we discussed earlier. Now, examine **Exhibit 13.12**, which shows that the take-home pay from an additional $10,000 in salary with and without a flexible dependent care account is: $3,990–$2,700, or an extra $1,290 per year with it. Even more money can be saved using a dependent care account, which allows a maximum contribution of $5,000 for joint filers. (Note: During the pandemic the limit was temporarily increased from $5,000 to $10,500.)

As noted earlier in this chapter, the ***Family and Medical Leave Act*** requires organizations with 50 or more employees within a 75-mile radius to provide as much as 12 weeks of unpaid leave after childbirth or adoption; to care for a seriously ill child, spouse, or parent; or for an employee's own serious illness. In the United States, as we saw in **Exhibit 13.2** earlier, paid family leave is not the norm. It is the norm in some other parts of the world (e.g., Europe and Japan) where it is mandated by law. Back to the United States, the main avenue to paid leave has been the Pregnancy Discrimination Act of 1978, which requires employers that offer disability plans to treat pregnancy as they would any other disability.

EXHIBIT 13.12 **Saving Money by Using a Flexible Spending Care Account**

	No Flexible Spending Care Account	Flexible Spending Care Account
Salary portion	$10,000	$10,000
Pretax contribution	0	−3,000
Taxable salary	10,000	7,000
Tax (43%)	−4,300	−3,010
After-tax cost of dependent care	−3,000	0
Take-home pay	$2,700	$3,990

A number of U.S. employers, especially larger ones, however, have chosen to offer paid family leave. Reasons include believing it is the right thing to do and striving to better attract and retain employees rather than forcing some to have to choose between employment and family obligations. Although such programs seem targeted to particular group of employees, it has been argued that symbolize a general corporate concern for employees, human resources, thus promoting loyalty and commitment among employees broadly, which can benefit organizational performance.[71] Further, one estimate is that less than 10 percent of American families fit the image of a husband working outside the home and a wife who stays home to take care of the children (not to mention others needing care). Thus, these programs may not be relevant to more employees than initially thought.

Sweden-based IKEA is an example of a company that recently began to provide paid family leave in the United States, even for low-paid employees, of 12–16 weeks, depending on how long employees have been with the company. The policy applies to mothers and fathers and to births, adoptions, and foster children. Employees with at least one year of tenure will receive 12 weeks, with 100% of their salary paid for the first 6 weeks and 50% of their salary paid for the remaining 6 weeks. Employees with at least three years of tenure will receive 16 weeks, with 8 weeks of 100% pay and the remaining 8 weeks at 50% of pay. IKEA's plan is to use interim assignments to do the work and to encourage managers, one-half of whom are women, to use the program themselves as part of its strategy to make hourly workers comfortable using it.[72]

Perhaps not coincidentally, given the low unemployment rates at the time, IKEA also raised its minimum wage at about the same time it implemented its paid family leave program. When Google expanded its paid leave policy from 12 to 18 weeks years ago, it reports the retention of post-maternity women increased by 50 percent. Best Buy reports that it decreased turnover by 14 percentage points (from 46% to 32%) over four years through introduction of what it calls a paid leave program (despite a drop in unemployment rates during that same period).[73]

As we discussed at the beginning of **Chapter 12**, flexible work arrangements go a big boost during the pandemic. There, we discussed initiatives undertaken by Fidelity, Elephant Ventures, and Red Hat. For example, Fidelity Investments began a pilot program that allows employees to reduce their hours to 30, to allow them more time for other needs. Their salary will be reduced, but not their benefits. Fidelity will hire additional employees to cover the work so that colleagues are not overwhelmed.[74] We also discussed there (and in **Chapter 2**), the SAS Institute, which has long had a 35-hour work week, historically unusual in the tech industry, although that has evolved also. Finally, the pandemic, as also discussed also increased (and some contend the change will be somewhat lasting) the ability to work remotely.[75]

Elder Care

With longer life expectancy than ever before and the aging of the baby-boom generation, one benefit that will become increasingly important is elder care assistance. The majority of companies report that they provide employees paid or unpaid time off to provide elder care.[76]

Domestic Partner Benefits

Domestic partner benefits are benefits that are voluntarily offered by employers to an employee's unmarried partner, whether of the same or opposite sex. The major reasons motivating U.S. corporations to provide domestic partner benefits include fairness to all employees regardless of their sexual orientation or marital status.

Legal Insurance

Prior to the 1970s, prepaid legal insurance was practically nonexistent. Even though such coverage was offered only by approximately 7 percent of all employers in 1997, that percentage has more than tripled in the past decade (to 24%).[77] A majority of plans provide routine legal services (e.g., divorce, real estate matters, wills, traffic violations) but exclude provisions covering felony crimes, largely because of the expense and potential for bad publicity. Keep in mind, though, that most legal insurance premiums are paid by the employee, not the employer. Technically, then, this doesn't qualify as a traditional employee benefit.

Addressing Financial Precarity (and Financial Wellness)

In the United States, it has been reported that "money-related concerns are a more prevalent source of distress than those related to health, work, or family" and that "most people ... do not have $400 in savings to cover an emergency," and there is some evidence that such "financial precarity" can adversely affect employee performance at the workplace.[78] In addition to higher wages, of course, employers can also take steps to encourage/incentivize employees to save enough money for an emergency (e.g., by cooperating with banks), through programs that help with balancing work and family, and by programs that encourage wellness.[79]

More broadly, financial precarity and financial wellness have short-term (as above), but also longer-term dimensions. (In a Bank of America survey, 78% of employers reported feeling "very/extremely responsible for helping employees with sustaining assets through retirement, up from 33% in 2012.) There is much work to be done, however, as only 49% of employees rate their financial wellness as good or excellent. Although part of that in 2020 was due to the pandemic, as the rating was higher (55%) in 2019 and 2018 (61%), even in the best year, 39% of employees reported lower than desired financial wellness. Similarly, 38% of employees agreed with the statement "I don't have any spare money after my monthly expenses." Ascend Performance Materials of Houston, Texas, recently won an award for its financial planning program from the Plan Sponsor Council of America (PSCA). The program provides an individual meeting opportunity with a consultant from Transamerica. The program is tailored to employees based on age and financial situation. Three educational challenges are addressed for each employee: Money Management Basics, Financial Planning 101, and Get Ready to Retire. Points were awarded to employees based on their progress through these "courses." The Hy-Vee supermarket chain also won a PSCA award. They also provided one-on-one meetings with a consultant. In addition, it also included webinars and monetary credits for completing steps in the program.

BENEFITS (OR LACK THEREOF): CONTINGENT AND ALTERNATIVE WORK ARRANGEMENTS WORKERS

Contingent workers, defined as workers who do not expect their jobs to last or who report their jobs are temporary, according to the U.S. Bureau of Labor Statistics (BLS), represent between 1.3 and 3.8 percent of the workforce.[80] Additionally, alternative work arrangements, which include independent contractors (6.9%), on-call workers (1.7%), temporary help agency workers (0.9%), and workers provided by contract firms (0.6%) represent another 10.1 percent of the workforce. BLS also specifically counted contingent workers who "obtained short jobs or tasks through websites or mobile apps that both connected them with customers and facilitated payment for the tasks" (i.e., Gig workers like those at Uber and Lyft). This group had 1.6 million workers, or about 1 percent of all workers in the U.S. economy.[81] Because it reduces direct workforce costs (because there are no legally required benefits for nonemployees and other benefits may not be offered), and permits easier expansion and contraction of the workforce (because there is typically no explicit implicit promise of job security) in response to expansion and contraction of production/services (sales), use of contingent workers and/or alternative work arrangements offers a way to meet rapidly changing economic conditions.[82] We say more about this subject in **Chapter 14** and more about legal issues in **Chapter 17.**

Your Turn

Evolving Benefits: Paid Leave

Organizations have implemented and expanded paid family leave practices in an effort to help employees better balance work and family and also to help them be more successful in attracting and retaining employees who place a priority on such balance. A number of organizations report that improvements in paid leave have helped improve employee retention (and recruiting success).

Earlier, we saw examples of companies that believed they documented tangible benefits, including Google and Best Buy. As another example, In Austin, Texas, a study of the implementation of a citywide paid sick days ordinance reported that city businesses saved $4.5 million annually due primarily to lower turnover and the community was estimated to save $3.8 million annually due to fewer emergency room visits, less flu contagion, and other public health improvements. (In the time of Covid-19, one presumes these health benefits would have been still larger.) Anecdotal evidence is less systematic and large scale but can provide further insight. For example, one recruiter reports that having paid leave policy "often sealed the deal, especially for women and younger candidates" and that such groups often raised the paid leave question "right off the bat" in talking about the position.

1. Earlier, we saw in (**EXHIBIT 13.2**) that paid family leave is offered by few organizations. Why do you think that is? What does paid family leave cost? Would a paid family leave benefit be important to all employees? What about you? Why or why not?

2. What role might paid family leave play in helping employees stay in the work force? What is the business case broadly for (or against) offering family leave?

Sources: Joan Michelson. How Small Companies Can Offer Great Paid-Leave Programs Harvard Business Review, January 7, 2021. HBR.org. National Partnership for Women & Families. Paid Sick Days Are Good for Business. Fact Sheet. October 2020; T. L. Rhodes, "Paid Family Leave Is Increasing Employee Retention Rates," Risk & Insurance, July 18, 2018, https://riskandinsurance.com; A. Van Abbema, "How Best Buy Cut Its Staff Turnover More Than 30 Percent in Four Years," Minneapolis/St. Paul Business Journal, December 6, 2018;

(Still) Your Turn

Evolving Benefits: Telehealth

Telehealth is providing health care from a distance and telemedicine refers more specifically to the technology used to help provide that care. Whether for domestic or expatriate employees, telehealth (typically for nonemergency care) is growing as a way to provide increased and faster access to general medical advice. It offers the opportunity to avoid waiting potentially weeks for an in-person appointment and/or having to take the time to travel to and from and potentially wait at the appointment. In the case of an expatriate employee, which by one estimate number over 60 million, it offers the additional advantage (see above) of eliminating any language barrier, as well as the need to deal with the idiosyncrasies of the foreign health care system. It may also save the employer a significant amount of money.

In some cases, a 10 or 15 minute teleconsultation may help avoid a costly and drawn-out visit to an emergency room or doctor's office. There are, of course, challenges and risks in using telemedicine. For example, a virtual exam has limitations compared to an in-person exam. For example, it may be possible to diagnose the concern raised by the patient, but other concerns that might be noticed by a doctor in an in-person exam may go unnoticed. Another challenge in the case of expatriates is that some countries may ban doctors from providing health care unless they hold a license in that country. And/or they may not permit the doctor to write prescriptions in that country. In such cases, some sort of partnership with a local doctor would be necessary.

Of course, telemedicine exploded during the pandemic. In a survey of large employers, 80 percent said that telehealth will play a key role in health care delivery going forward, up from 64 percent the previous year, and up from 52 percent two years ago. Almost all of these employers offer telehealth for minor, acute services and 91 percent offer telemental health and emotional well-being care. Virtual musculoskeletal care will be offered by 29 percent in the coming year. As one example of supporting telehealth, game developer Zynga Inc. waived copays for virtual appointments and accelerated implementation of a global mental-health support program. From the perspective of a physician, telehealth helped in bringing health care to patients. For example, one family physician noticed a patient missed an appointment. It was discovered the patient had no transportation. The telehealth option allowed the physician to "see" the patient and check on the patient's diabetes and mental health, which might not have happened otherwise. At UCLA Health in Los Angeles, there had been a push pre-pandemic to increase the use of telehealth, without much success (about 100 such appointments per day). During the first few months of the pandemic, virtual appointments jumped to 3,000 to 4,000 per day. More recently, telehealth appointments seem to have stabilized at around 2,700 per day.

DISCUSSION QUESTIONS

1. Have you ever had a health problem while overseas and needed care? Describe your experience. Was telehealth available? If not, would it have been helpful?
2. How do you feel about using telehealth versus in-person care? Explain.
3. To what degree can telehealth help employers control health care costs while also achieving health care quality goals for their employees?

Sources: Cara Murez. Health Care After COVID: The Rise of Telemedicine. Usnews.com. January 5, 2021; Kathryn Dill and Julia Carpenter. Employers Craft Health Benefits to Cushion Covid-19 Shock. WSJ.com, November 12, 2020; No Author. How Telehealth Can Improve Medical Care for Expats. Goexpat.com, March 30, 2020; Large U.S. Employers Accelerating Adoption of Virtual Care, Mental Health Services for 2021, Business Group on Health Survey Finds. Businessgrouphealth.org. August 18, 2020; T. Starner, "Improving Access to Healthcare for Expat Workers," Human Resource Executive, October 30, 2018, hrexecutive.com; T. Anderson, "The Magic of Telemedicine," International Travel and Health Insurance Journal, October 28, 2018, www.itij.com.

Summary

Since the 1940s, employee benefits have been the most volatile area in the compensation field. From 1940 to 1980, dramatic changes came in the form of more and better types of employee benefits. The result should not have been unexpected. Employee benefits are now a major, and many believe prohibitive, component of doing business. Look for this century to be dominated by cost-saving efforts to improve the competitive position of American industry. A part of these cost savings will come from tighter administrative controls on existing benefit packages. But another part, as already seen in the auto industry, may come from a reduction in existing benefit packages. If this does evolve as a trend, benefit administrators will need to develop a mechanism for identifying employee preferences (in this case "least preferences") and use them as a guideline to meet agreed upon savings targets.

Review Questions

1. James A. Klingon has a mandate from his boss to cut employee benefit costs. In a company expanding by 10 percent in employees every year, Jim decides to control costs through his selection strategy. Is he crazy? Or crazy like a fox? Explain.
2. Explain the concept of experience rating using examples from unemployment insurance. Would the same concept apply to workers' compensation? Using the Internet, find out if experience rating plays a role in insurance coverage.
3. The CEO of Krinkle Forms Inc. says there is a serious problem with turnover, with data for her observation provided below.

Seniority	Turnover Rate
0–2 yrs	61%
2–5 yrs	21%
5+ yrs	9%

   The CEO wants to use employee benefits to lessen this problem. Before agreeing to look at this as the solution, what should run through your mind as a trained professional? What might you do, specifically, in the areas of pension vesting, vacation and holiday allocation, and life insurance coverage in the effort to reduce turnover?
4. Why are defined contribution pension plans gaining in popularity in the United States and defined benefit plans losing popularity?
5. Some experts argue that consumer-directed health care is, amongst other things, a great communications tool for employee benefits. Defend this position.

Endnotes

1. R. McCaffery, *Managing the Employee Benefits Program* (New York: American Management Association, 1972), pp. 1–2.
2. Deloitte. "The 80/20 Rule" Is it still true? And what can it tell us about Population Health in 2018 and beyond? www.deloitte.com.
3. SHRM Employee Benefits 2019. www.shrm.org.
4. Congressional Budget Office, "Comparing the Compensation of Federal and Private-Sector Employees," January 2012, http://www.cbo.gov/sites/default/files/cbofiles/attachments/01-30-FedPay.pdf.
5. National Academy of Social Insurance, *Worker's Compensation: Benefits, Coverage, and Costs (2018 Data)* (Washington, DC: National Academy of Social Insurance), November 2020. The total cost to employers is described in the report as "equal to the sum of: premiums and deductibles paid to private insurers and state funds; plus benefits and administrative costs paid by self-insured employers; plus assessments paid to special funds (e.g., guaranty funds, second-injury funds)."
6. National Academy of Social Insurance, *Worker's Compensation: Benefits, Coverage, and Costs (2018 Data)* (Washington, DC: National Academy of Social Insurance, November 2020.
7. http://www.wcb.ny.gov/content/main/Employers/getInsurance.jsp.

8. National Academy of Social Insurance, *Worker's Compensation: Benefits, Coverage, and Costs (2018 Data)* (Washington, DC: National Academy of Social Insurance), November 2020. See Figure 1.
9. National Academy of Social Insurance, *Worker's Compensation: Benefits, Coverage, and Costs (2018 Data)* (Washington, DC: National Academy of Social Insurance), November 2020. See Appendix D.
10. http://www.wcb.ny.gov/content/main/Workers/LostWageBenefits.jsp.
11. National Academy of Social Insurance, *Worker's Compensation: Benefits, Coverage, and Costs (2018 Data)* (Washington, DC: National Academy of Social Insurance, November 2020. See Table 11 for worker cash benefits and see Table 14 for employer costs.
12. Employee Benefit Research Institute, *Fundamentals of Employee Benefit Programs* (Washington, DC: EBRI, 2011).
13. www.ebri.org, visited April 22, 2015.
14. William J. Cohen, "The Evolution and Growth of Social Security," in *Federal Policies and Worker Status Since the Thirties,* J. P. Goldberg, E. Ahern, W. Haber, and R. A. Oswald, eds. (Madison, WI: Industrial Relations Research Association, 1976), p. 62.
15. http://www.ssa.gov/OP_Home/handbook/handbook.01/handbook-0100.html, visited April 22, 2015.
16. "Social Security History: Frequently Asked Questions, Ratio of Covered Workers to Beneficiaries," https://www.ssa.gov/history/ratios.html, accessed April 14 2021; Social Security Online Actuarial Publications Table IV.B2. Covered Workers and Beneficiaries, Calendar Years 1945-2086. https://www.ssa.gov/oact/TR/2011/lr4b2.html.
17. Social Security and Medicare Boards of Trustees. Status of the Social Security and Medicare Programs. A Summary of the 2020 Annual Reports. https://www.ssa.gov/OACT/TRSUM/index.html.
18. Office of the Chief Actuary. Social Security Administration. Summary of Provisions that Would Change the Social Security Program. July 1, 2020. https://www.ssa.gov/OACT/solvency/provisions/summary.pdf.
19. Social Security Administration, "Fact Sheet, Social Security: 2018 Social Security Changes," https://www.ssa.gov/news/press/factsheets/colafacts2018.pdf.
20. http://www.workforcesecurity.doleta.gov/unemploy/uitaxtopic.asp, visited April 24, 2015.
21. http://www.workforcesecurity.doleta.gov/unemploy/uitaxtopic.asp, visited April 24, 2015.
22. Center on Budget and Policy Priorities, "Introduction to Unemployment Insurance," www.cbpp.org/cms/index.cfm?fa=view&id=1466.
23. U.S. Department of Labor, www.workforcesecurity.doleta.gov/uitaxtopic.asp, visited May 15, 2003.
24. Department of Labor, New York. Unemployment Insurance: A Bridge to Your Next Career. https://dol.ny.gov/system/files/documents/2021/03/ui-handbook-mar-08_2021.pdf. Accessed April 14, 2021.
25. http://www.dol.gov/whd/fmla/, visited April 24, 2015.
26. Employee Benefit Research Institute, *Fundamentals of Employee Benefit Programs* (Washington, DC: EBRI, 2009).
27. http://www.dol.gov/whd/fmla/, visited April 24, 2015.
28. "Continuation of Health Coverage' COBRA," http://www.dol.gov/dol/topic/health-plans/cobra.htm.
29. U.S. Department of Labor, Employee Benefits Security Administration, www.dol.gov/ebsa, August 18, 2009.
30. U.S. Department of Health and Human Services, http://www.hhs.gov/ocr/privacy/index.html, February 5, 2009.

31. Institute of Management & Administration (IOMA), *Managing 401(k) Plans* (Newark, NJ: BNA Subsidiaries, August 2000).

32. Employee Benefit Research Institute, *Fundamentals of Employee Benefit Programs* (Washington, DC: EBRI, 1997), pp. 69–73.

33. http://www.gurufocus.com/news/330501/thoughts-on-gms-2014, visited April 27, 2015.

34. Vipal Monga, "Pension Dropouts Cause Pinch," *Wall Street Journal,* October 7, 2014, p. B7.

35. "Employee Benefits News," *Benefits Marketplace* 22(16), 2009, pp. 19–22.

36. www.401k.org/, visited April 11, 2012.

37. www.ebri.org/publications/benfaq/index.cfm?fa=retfaq14, visited April 11, 2012.

38. Jason Zweig, "A Singular Focus Can Crack Your Nest Egg," *Wall Street Journal*, July 15–16, 2017, p. B1.

39. Thomas Gryta, "Retired from GE, Now Pinching Pennies," *Wall Street Journal*, April 23, 2018, p. A1.

40. A Guide to Common Qualified Plan Requirements. www.irs.gov.

41. Employee Benefit Research Institute, "EBRI Research Highlights: Retirement Benefit," Special Report SR-42 (Washington, DC: EBRI, June 2003).

42. In 2001, the Economic Growth and Tax Relief Reconciliation Act of 2001 was passed. This act replaced some of the aspects of the original ERISA and came into effect for plans starting after December 31, 2001.

43. Employee Benefit Research Institute, *Fundamentals of Employee Benefit Programs* (Washington, DC: EBRI, 2009).

44. Stuart Dorsey, "Pension Portability and Labor Market Efficiency: A Survey of the Literature," *Industrial and Labor Relations Review,* January 1, 1995, pp. 43–58.

45. https://www.pbgc.gov/.

46. Burton T. Beam and John J. McFadden, *Employee Benefit 5* (Chicago, IL: Dearborn Financial, 1992).

47. U.S. Department of Labor, Bureau of Labor Statistics, "Employee Benefits Survey," https://www.bls.gov/ncs/ebs/#bulletin_coverage.

48. Ibid.

49. Employee Benefit Research Institute, *Fundamentals of Employee Benefit Programs* (Washington, DC: EBRI, 2009).

50. Bureau of Labor Statistics, "Employer Costs for Employee Compensation," December 2014, Bureau of Labor Statistics USDL-15-1386.

51. Kaiser Family Foundation. 2020 Employer Health Benefits Survey. October 08, 2020. https://www.kff.org/health-costs/report/2020-employer-health-benefits-survey/.

52. G. Claxton, L. Levitt, M. Rae, and B. Sawyer, "Increases in Cost-Sharing Payments Continue to Outpace Wage Growth," *Peterson-Kaiser Health System Tracker*, June 15, 2018, www.healthsystemtracker.org; Murphy, "Survey: Companies Keep Passing Health Costs to Workers"; P. Hubel, "Bait and Switch: The Sneaky Way Your Employer Just Passed Healthcare Costs onto You," *Forbes*, February 28, 2018, www.forbes.com.

53. Henry J. Kaiser Family Foundation. Key Facts about the Uninsured Population. November 29, 2017. https://www.kff.org/uninsured/fact-sheet/key-facts-about-the-uninsured-population/.

54. Bashker D. Biswas, *A Guide to Employee Benefits Design and Planning* (Upper Saddle River, NJ: Pearson Education, 2014).

55. S. Smith, "New Trends in Health Care Cost Control," *Compensation and Benefits Review,* January 2002, pp. 38–44; Regina Herzlinger and Jeffrey Schwartz, "How Companies Tackle Health Care Costs: Part I," *Harvard Business Review,* July–August 1985, pp. 69–81.
56. Tracey Walker, "Benefit Designs Continue to Evolve," *Managed Healthcare Executive* 15(9), 2005, p. 9.
57. "GE Workers Plan Strike over Benefit Cost-Shifting," *Business Insurance,* January 6, 2003, pp. 23–26.
58. Bashker D. Biswas, *A Guide to Employee Benefits Design and Planning* (Upper Saddle River, NJ: Pearson Education, 2014).
59. EBRI, "Characteristics of the Population with Consumer-Driven and High-Deductible Health Plans, 2005–2012," and "Retirement Plan Participation and Asset Allocation, 2010." Employee Benefits Research Institute, April 2013, Vol. 34, No. 4.
60. Barry Hall, "Health Incentives: The Science and Art of Motivating Healthy Behaviors," *Benefits Quarterly,* 2008 (second quarter), pp. 12–22.
61. Stephanie Armour, "CEO's Say Federal Limits Are Ailing Wellness Programs," *Wall Street Journal,* September, 4, 2014, p. B3.
62. Lauren Weber, "A Health Check for Wellness Programs," *Wall Street Journal,* October 8, 2014, p. B1.
63. The Health Insurance Association of America provides research about a wide variety of specific health-related issues at its website, *www.hiaa.org/pubs/.*
64. Employee Benefit Research Institute, *Fundamentals of Employee Benefit Programs* (Washington, DC: EBRI, 2009).
65. U.S. Department of Labor, "Disability Insurance," https://www.dol.gov.
66. U.S. Chamber of Commerce, "1999 Employee Benefits Survey," 2000, p. 10.
67. Bruce Jaspen, "Deductibles Hit $2,000 As Employers Intensify Cost Shift." Forbes, October 4, 2018. www.forbes.com
68. The Motley Fool, "The Fool Rules! A Global Guide to Foolish Behavior," *Motley Fool Employees Manual* (Alexandria, VA: The Motley Fool, 1997), p. 14.
69. *www.cbsnews.com/stories/2009/05/28/eveningnews.*
70. Y. Chen and I. Smithey Fulmer, "Fine-Tuning What We Know about Employees' Experience with Flexible Work Arrangements and Their Job Attitudes," *Human Resource Management* 57, no. 1 (2018), pp. 381–395
71. N. Bloom, T. Kretschmer, and J. Van Reenen, "Are Family-Friendly Workplace Practices a Valuable Firm Resource?" *Strategic Management Journal* 32 (2011), pp. 343–367; S. L. Grover and K. J. Crooker, "Who Appreciates Family Responsive Human Resource Policies: The Impact of Family-Friendly Policies on the Organizational Attachment of Parents and Non-parents," *Personnel Psychology* 48 (1995), pp. 271–288; T. J. Rothausen, J. A. Gonzalez, N. E. Clarke, and L. L. O'Dell, "Family-Friendly Backlash: Fact or Fiction? The Case of Organizations' On-Site Child Care Centers," *Personnel Psychology* 51 (1998), p. 685; M. A. Arthur, "Share Price Reactions to Work-Family Initiatives: An Institutional Perspective," *Academy of Management Journal* 46 (2003), p. 497; J. E. Perry-Smith and T. Blum, "Work-Family Human Resource Bundles and Perceived Organizational Performance," *Academy of Management Journal* 43 (2000), pp. 1107–1117.
72. B. Lam, "IKEA's Leave Policy Actually Includes Most of Its Workers," *The Atlantic*, December 6, 2016; A. D'Innocenzio, "As Workforce Tightens, IKEA Expands Parental Leave," *Milwaukee Journal Sentinel*, December 6, 2016.
73. Joan Michelson. How Small Companies Can Offer Great Paid-Leave Programs Harvard Business Review, January 7, 2021. HBR.org. National Partnership for Women & Families. Paid Sick Days Are

Good for Business. Fact Sheet. October 2020; A. Van Abbema, "How Best Buy Cut Its Staff Turnover More Than 30 Percent in Four Years," *Minneapolis/St. Paul Business Journal*, December 6, 2018.

74. Chip Cutter. Companies Offer Creative Solutions to Worker Burnout During the Pandemic From surprise days off to 30-hour workweeks, managers are devising ways to help employees. WSJ, Nov. 8, 2020.
75. Atul Mitra and Jason D. Shaw, "Strategic Benefits to Help Survive and Thrive in Times of COVID-19," *The Journal of Total Rewards*, Q1, 2021.
76. Kenneth Matos, Ellen Galinsky, and James T. Bond, "National Study of Employers," Society for Human Resource Management, 2017, www.shrm.org.
77. David Schlaifer, "Legal Benefit Plans Help Attract and Retain Employees," *HR Focus,* December 1999, pp. S7–S8.
78. Jirs Meuris and Carrie Leana, "The Price of Financial Precarity: Organizational Costs of Employees' Financial Concerns," *Organization Science,* 2018, 29, 398–417.
79. Jirs Meuris and Carrie R. Leana, "The High Cost of Low Wages: Economic Scarcity Effects in Organizations," *Research in Organizational Behavior* 35 (2015), pp. 143–158; Anne Tergensen, "Workers Schooled in Money: More Firms Pay Workers to Shore Up Their Finances through Education, Cutting Debt," *Wall Street Journal,* February 21, 2018.
80. Bureau of Labor Statistics. U.S. Department of Labor. Contingent and Alternative Employment Arrangements–May 2017. June 7, 2018. www.bls.gov.
81. U.S. Bureau of Labor Statistics. U.S. Department of Labor. Contingent and Alternative Employment Arrangements–May 2017. June 7, 2018. www.bls.gov.
82. Lauren Weber, "For Videogame Makers, Hiring Is a Last Resort: Staffers Do the Most Critical Jobs while Outside Labor Comes and Goes," *Wall Street Journal*, April 11, 2017, p. A1; Lauren Weber, "Outsourcing Grabs More of the Workforce," *Wall Street Journal*, December 12, 2017.

Part **VI**
Extending the System

You've now read about three strategic policies in the pay model. The first, which focused on determining the structure of pay, dealt with internal alignment. The second examined determining pay level based on external competitiveness, and the third dealt with determining the pay for employees according to their performance. Strategic decisions regarding alignment, competitiveness, and performance are directed at achieving the objectives of the pay system. Specific objectives vary among organizations; helping achieve competitive advantage and treating employees fairly are basic ones.

We now extend the basic pay model to the strategic issue of execution. A number of employee groups require, because of their importance to strategic success, special consideration in the way we design their compensation packages. In fact, **Chapter 14** is titled just that: "**Compensation of Special Groups**." Here we talk about employee groups that don't quite fit our basic model. Their special employment status, for reasons we will discuss in a moment, dictates the design of compensation administration programs that sometimes differ from the more traditional designs covered in **Parts 2** through **5**.

In **Chapter 15**, we look at compensation in unionized firms. Although less than 15 percent of the workforce in the United States is unionized, the role of unions in wage determination extends far beyond the size of this small group. Firms looking to remain nonunion often pay considerable attention to the way rewards are distributed to union employees. As we shall see, the role of a compensation person in a unionized organization is, indeed, different.

Our final extension of the system focuses on international employees. Different cultures, different laws, and different economies all can lead to different strategic and administrative decisions for international employees. If we are truly to embrace the globalization of business, the globalization of compensation must be a key ingredient.

EXHIBIT VI.1 The Pay Model

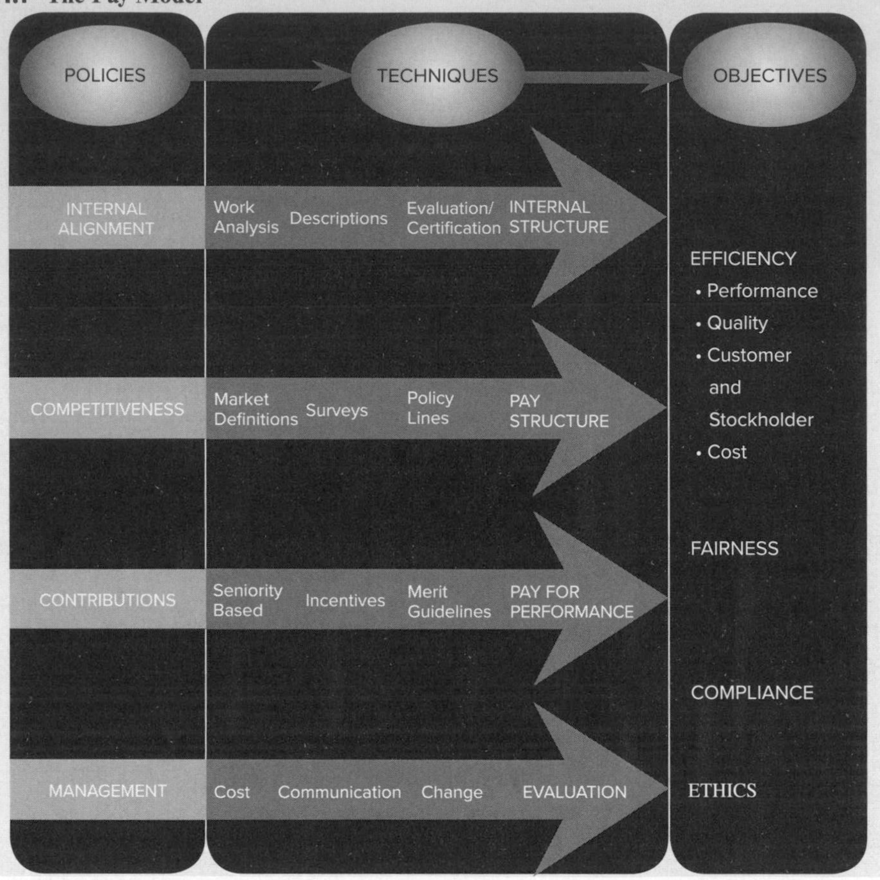

Chapter **Fourteen**
Compensation of Special Groups: Executives and Others

Chapter Outline

Chief executive officers (CEOs) in the 500 largest U.S. public companies earn, on average, more than $12 million per year. Assuming a 55-hour workweek, this translates into an hourly pay of about $4,200. So, in the time it might take you to read this chapter, $4,200 would be earned. Some of you would be fine (ok, ecstatic) with such an hourly rate. Perhaps some of you would be fine (OK, maybe ecstatic) to make that much money in a week. No wonder so many news articles and blogs discuss (well, usually question) executive pay. Well, what about earning that $4,200 hourly pay yourself? Considering that there are about 150 million people employed in the United States, it is simply a question of beating out some other people (149,999,500 of them) for one of those 500 CEO jobs. Not so easy, but someone, possibly you, will accomplish that and the payoff is pretty good. (See tournament theory in **Chapter 3.**) Executives below the CEO level get paid well too and there are a lot more greater companies than the 500 largest (not to mention other types of firms). And some of the largest companies today will give way to what were once smaller companies (see the FANG companies, Tesla, and many others). Yes, indeed, to paraphrase one of Shakespeare's characters, the world is your oyster.

This chapter takes a look at groups that, for reasons we will discuss, receive compensation that is anything but common. Some jobs simply don't fit the basic pay model. Some aspect of the job doesn't fit. Maybe the content of the job (from job evaluation) doesn't seem to match the pay that the job commands in the market. If you looked at the job description of a CEO, it might not be obvious to you that the pay would be over $12 million and, as we will see, can go a lot higher. Or take sales staff–their pay is also hard to explain. Often sales employees are paid incentives that can amount to well over one-half their salaries. Our standard pay model up until now doesn't account as well for such jobs. This chapter looks more closely at the compensation of these special groups.

SPECIAL GROUPS: OVERVIEW

There is a pattern to the compensation of groups that we discuss in this chapter, a pattern that doesn't follow the pay model. Special treatment, either in the form of add-on packages not received by other employees or in the form of compensation components entirely unique in the organization, tends to focus on a few specific groups. This chapter argues that special groups share two characteristics. First, special groups tend to be strategically important to the company. If they don't succeed at their jobs, success for the whole organization is in jeopardy. Second, their positions tend to have built-in conflict, conflict that arises because different factions place incompatible demands on members of the group.

As the first characteristic explains, the work these employees perform is central to the strategic success of the company. As an example, consider the contrast in compensation treatment for engineers in two different organizations. One is a high-tech firm with a strong research and development component. The other organization employs a few engineers, but their role is not central to the mission of the organization. A survey of this type of difference in employee composition and organizational strategy found that research and development organizations with heavy concentrations of engineers had evolved unique compensation systems that were responsive to the special needs of the engineering contingent. Organizations with a different focus and with fewer engineers merged this group's compensation with the standard package offered to other employees.

Exhibit 14.1 describes the nature of the conflicts faced by such special groups as supervisors, top management, boards of directors, scientists and engineers, sales personnel, and contingent workers. When both of the characteristics we've been discussing are present, we tend to find distinctive compensation practices adopted to meet the needs of these special groups.

Supervisors

Remember, supervisors are caught between the demands of upper management to meet production goals and the needs of employees to receive rewards, reinforcements, and general counseling.[1] Conflict arises when management wants more output from workers and workers balk because their rewards don't increase. The major challenge in compensating supervisors centers on equity. Some incentive must be provided to entice nonexempt employees to accept the challenges of being a supervisor. Supervisor jobs often are classified as exempt, meaning they are exempt from overtime pay. If the job requires more than forty hours of work per week (which is very common), every extra hour is either just part of the job with no extra pay or paid at straight time rather than time and a half. Picture a "recently promoted" supervisor working alongside a team member who collects overtime–and the financial incentive to be a supervisor quickly disappears. Jerry Newman once worked undercover at fast-food restaurants as part of research for a book (*My Secret Life on the McJob*). On one of his jobs, the assistant manager earned $32,000 per year. As an exempt employee the assistant manager received nothing for the extra 15 or so hours he worked every week. The shift supervisor who reported to him was classified nonexempt. He received overtime pay and made more money than the assistant manager when the overtime was factored in. One day this inequity came to a head, ending in a profane screaming match over ... tomatoes. The assistant manager was tired of doing all the condiment stocking tasks for no extra money. He accused the shift supervisor of being a slacker who milked the job and never filled the tomato tray ... until he was on overtime! More recently, organizations have devised several strategies to attract workers into supervisory jobs. The most popular method is to key the base salary of supervisors to some amount (typically 5–30 percent) above the pay of the top-paid subordinate in the unit.

Another method for maintaining equitable differentials is simply to pay supervisors for scheduled overtime. Companies that do pay overtime are about evenly split between paying straight time and paying time-and-a-half for overtime hours.

The biggest trend in supervisory compensation centers on increased use of variable pay. Slightly more than half of all companies now have a variable pay component for supervisors, up from 16 percent in prior years.[2]

Corporate Directors

A board of directors comprises individuals from both inside and outside a firm who provide strategic advice on decision making. Because directors usually play a major role in setting executive compensation, they are

EXHIBIT 14.1 Conflicts Faced by Special Groups

Special Group	Type of Conflict Faced
Supervisors	Caught between upper management and employees. Must balance need to achieve organization's objectives with importance of helping employees satisfy personal needs. If unsuccessful, either corporate profit or employee morale suffers.
Corporate directors	Face possibility that disgruntled stockholders may sue over corporate strategies that don't "pan out."
Executives	Stockholders want healthy return on investment. Government wants compliance with laws. Executives must decide between strategies that maximize short-run gains at expense of long-run versus directions that focus on long-run gains.
Professional employees	May be torn between goals, objectives, and ethical standards of their profession (e.g., should an engineer leak information about a product flaw, even though that information may hurt corporate profits) and demands of an employer concerned more with profits.
Sales staff	Often spend extended periods in the field with little supervision. Challenge is to stay motivated and continue making sales calls even in the face of limited contact or scrutiny from manager. Conflict is inevitable between customers who want product now and production facilities that can't deliver that quickly.
Contingent workers	Play an important "safety valve" role for companies. When demand is high, more are hired; when demand drops, they are the first workers let go. Employment status is highly insecure, and challenge is to find low-cost ways to motivate.

also a lightning rod for complaints about CEO pay. Most boards have 8 to 11 directors. Increasingly, these directors are expected to put in more hours on board activities such as cybersecurity (remember the breach on Target!) and risk oversight.[3]

Probably because of the increased attention to CEO pay and concerns about impartiality, companies are trying to populate their boards with outside directors who aren't beholden to the CEO who appointed them. Outside directors are harder to bring up to speed about a company's values and environment, but they are perceived to be less prone to bias than internal directors. CEOs influence the selection of directors, and often will favor people who have served on other boards with CEOs who are like-minded.[4] What used to be a "rubber stamp" process by internal board members beholden to the CEO is now a highly charged analysis of, among other things, CEO compensation. There is considerable risk in these jobs. Stockholders are prone to sue directors when CEOs receive large pay increases despite poor company performance on key financial measures.[5] In fact, if companies offer liability insurance to protect against these lawsuits, director compensation is lower. Maybe it pays to be uninsured?[6]

In exchange for assuming this risk, directors are well rewarded. A typical director works 30–40 hours per month.[7] In exchange, the median annual compensation is $290,000.[8] And as a reflection of greater concern about performance, the mix of compensation is shifting away from base pay toward incentives. Last year, for example, average base pay (primarily in the form of a "retainer") was $107,500 while stock-based compensation averaged $182,500.[9]

Executives

Median annual pay for a CEO in the S&P 500 is over $12 million.[10] As **Exhibit 14.2** shows, pay can go much higher than that. In the case of Tesla, its market value has increased from under $2 billion in 2010 to $600 billion in 2021. Thus, the $595 million annual compensation paid to Elon Musk represents 0.10 percent of wealth (i.e., $1 of every $1,000 in wealth) created over that time period. (Adding his compensation up over all years would make this share higher.) As a Tesla shareholder, would you be concerned about how much Elon Musk is paid?

CEO pay is higher in large companies. For example, the $12 million in the S&P 500 is over twice (2.3×) as large as the CEO pay in the Russell 3000, the largest 3,000 companies.[11] Of course, the Russell 3000 includes the S&P 500, so we may wish to compare the S&P 500 with the S&P SmallCap 600. Here, CEO pay differs by a factor of 3.7.

How do Americans feel about these CEO pay levels and how much CEOs make relative to other employees (the CEO pay ratio)? In a broad survey conducted across demographic groups, 74 percent of respondents said they thought that chief executive officers (CEOs) were overpaid. Interestingly, that opinion was based on inaccurate perceptions of what CEOs are paid, with the median estimate from respondents being $1 million in the 500 largest U.S. companies, which is a bit short of their actual pay of about $12 million.[12] One can

EXHIBIT 14.2 Highest Paid Executives

Executive	Company	Total Compensation
Elon Musk	Tesla, Inc.	$595 million
Tim Cook	Apple, Inc.	$134 million
Tom Rutledge	Charter Communications, Inc.	$117 million

Source: Anders Melin and Cedric Sam. "Wall Street Gets the Flak, But Tech CEOs Get Paid All the Money." Bloomberg.com, July 10, 2020.

only imagine how much higher than 74 percent the disapproval rate would be if respondents learned that CEOs actually make 12 times more than they'd estimated. Also of interest, when given a scenario where the average worker in a company made $50,000, the median respondent said that the CEO should make no more than $300,000, or 6 times more. As we saw above, will see shortly, rather than CEOs making 6 times more than the average worker, they make 275 times more in the largest 500 companies. Finally, when asked how much a CEO should be given if the value of a company increased by $100 million, the median answer was $500,000, or 0.5 percent. In a separate survey conducted by the same group, this time of public company directors (of which 41 percent were CEOs), only 18 percent disapproved of CEO compensation and 76 percent approved (6 percent were unsure).[13] Further, 91 percent of corporate directors stated they believed that "CEO compensation is aligned with company performance." In response to the question, "In your best estimate, what percentage of a company's overall performance is directly attributable to the efforts of the CEO?" the median answer was 30 percent, and when asked about the senior management team (including the CEO), the median answer was 60 percent. When asked if stock options encourage CEOs to engage in excessive risk taking, 83 percent said no and 15 percent said yes (2 percent were unsure). Finally, directors were asked how much a CEO should be given if the value of a company increased by $100 million. The median answer was $1.5 million, or 1.5 percent, or about 3 times as high as respondents in the broad survey.

These results nicely capture the divergence of opinions on CEO pay in the United States. Our own perspective is that there is no right or wrong answer to how much CEOs should be paid or how much they should be paid relative to the average worker. It comes down to how much of a company's value is created by the CEO versus other employees, what shareholders are willing to approve, and two other important factors: how the industry/product market the company is in is doing overall, and an often overlooked factor: luck. On the other hand, we see little reason to disagree on the need to align CEO pay with company performance.

How Aligned are Executive Pay and Performance?

Our research (Gerhart and colleagues Nyberg, Fulmer, and Carpenter) suggests that although there are certainly egregious cases of CEO pay gone bad, on the whole CEO pay and company performance are strongly aligned. Without going into detail, our review of previous studies found that the pay/performance relationship for CEOs was often not studied in an optimal manner. For example, in some cases the time period during which company performance and CEO pay were measured was not appropriate. In other cases, major components of CEO compensation were excluded. After correcting for these and other issues, we found a strong positive relationship between CEO return (i.e., change in CEO's employment-based wealth) and the total shareholder return (i.e., the change in shareholder wealth). Specifically, the addition of shareholder return to the model, after controlling for other determinants of CEO return, resulted in an increase in the (adjusted) R^2 from 22 percent to 67 percent. Further, we found that over the course of multiple years a CEO at a firm with shareholder return in the 75th percentile had a mean CEO return of $21.6 million, compared to a mean CEO return of $9.5 million in a firm with shareholder return at the median (50th percentile) and a mean CEO return (loss) of −$709,841 for a firm with shareholder return at the 25th percentile.[14] We also observed that at median shareholder return, CEOs received 6 percent of that return and at the 75th percentile of shareholder return, CEOs received 4 percent of that return. **Exhibit 14.3** summarizes some of these results.

To be sure, there are overpaid executives who earn a lot and produce little in return for shareholders (or other stakeholders such as employees). And there have been examples of egregious CEO behavior such as manipulating accounting data to inflate share prices (as a means to increase their compensation), hiding information on losses or product problems, and so forth.

There is a legitimate concern with how the structure of CEO compensation can sometimes contribute to CEOs engaging in behaviors that can have very negative consequences. For example, heavy use of bonuses and stock-based compensation may result in executives "swinging for the fences" (i.e., engaging in excessively risky behavior, especially with "other people's money").[15] In fact, some believe that part of the global economy meltdown in 2008–2009 (the Great Financial Crisis) can be traced directly to executive compensation. CEOs such as Dick Fuld at Lehman Brothers and Jimmy Cayne at Bear Stearns let their firms take huge risks and then the firms paid the price when the value of their shareholdings evaporated. Who else paid the price? Yes, the shareholders took huge losses, but so also did the government, and ultimately the taxpayers. The public is understandably looking for someone to blame, and executive compensation is one legitimate target. One consequence of the The Great Financial Crisis was the passage of the Dodd-Frank Wall Street Reform and Consumer Protection Act, which states as its purpose: "To promote the financial stability of the United States by improving accountability and transparency in the financial system, to end 'too big to fail,' to protect the American taxpayer by ending bailouts, to protect consumers from abusive financial services practices, and for other purposes." Note that the Act includes provisions such as the following as part of that purpose: "The Corporation, as receiver of a covered financial company, may recover from any current or former senior executive or director substantially responsible for the failed condition of the covered financial company any compensation received during the two-year period preceding the date on which the Corporation was appointed as the receiver of the covered financial company, except that, in the case of fraud, no time limit shall apply." (This sometimes called a "clawback" provision.)

Let's return to the argument that CEO compensation is not aligned with or related to company performance. In some cases, what looks like a lack of an alignment probably is not. Consider the example of Richard Fairbank, the CEO of Capital One, as reported one year in the *Wall Street Journal*.[16] The Journal reported that Capital One shareholders earned a one-year return of 2.7 percent, and over five years had earned a return of 5.8 percent. The survey reported that Fairbank received $249.3 million in total direct compensation from Capital One in the most recent year. That $249.3 million was widely interpreted as being way out of line with the modest shareholder return. However, most of the $249.3 million received by Fairbank arose from his exercise of stock options granted to him 10 years earlier that were about to expire and be lost if he did not exercise them. Over that longer 10-year period, shareholder wealth at Capital One increased by $23 billion, for a cumulative shareholder return of 802 percent.[17] In other words, the CEO of Capital One received $249.3 million/$23 billion = 1.08 percent of the shareholder wealth generated during that 10-year time period when he was CEO. As we asked in the case of Tesla, if you were a shareholder of Capital One, would the level of compensation paid to CEO Richard Fairbank concern you?

Say on Pay (Shareholder Votes)

Wait a minute! Has anyone ever actually asked shareholders (not that some of you aren't shareholders too, but...) whether they approve of how much executives running their companies get paid? Well, you may be surprised to learn that the answer is yes! The Dodd-Frank Act introduced a requirement that (at least every three years) shareholders vote to approve or disapprove the company's proposed compensation plan for its five highest-paid executives. This vote is nonbinding. In other words, a company may choose to execute its

EXHIBIT 14.3 Chief Executive Officer (CEO) Return and Shareholder Return

Shareholder Return	Shareholder Return in $ (change in wealth)	CEO Return in $ (change in wealth)
25th percentile	−198 million	−0.7 million
Median	+163 million	+9.5 million
75th percentile	+553 million	+21.6 million

Source: Nyberg, A., Fulmer, I. S., Gerhart, B., and Carpenter, M. A. "Agency Theory Revisited: CEO Returns and Shareholder Interest Alignment," *Academy of Management Journal*, vol. 53, 2010, 1029–1049.

proposed executive compensation plan, despite a majority of shareholders voting against the plan. Before telling you the typical outcome of such votes, what would your guess be? Recall that in a survey of a broad cross-section of the general public, 74 percent disapproved of executive pay versus 76 percent approval in a separate survey of public company directors. But, again, what about shareholders? **Exhibit 14.4** reports the results of shareholder votes from 2011 through 2020. It shows that in the vast majority (97 to 99 percent) of company votes during that time period, shareholders have approved executive pay. Further, the average percentage of shareholders in each company voting to approve has been 90 to 92 percent. In summary, unlike the general public, shareholders generally support how executives are paid.

Even though the say-on-pay vote required by Dodd-Frank is nonbinding, most companies view a no-vote as a public relations disaster.[18] Of the 2 percent or less of companies that don't pass the "say on pay" vote, most try to overhaul their systems to obtain stockholder approval. For example, Abercrombie & Fitch split their chairman and CEO jobs and restructured short- and long-term incentives to gain a positive vote.[19] The exceptions are sometimes companies still run by their founders, a group not likely to be voted out of office easily. For example, Oracle, where its founder, Larry Ellison, is chairman of the board of directors, lost (received support from less than 50 percent of voting shareholders) say-on-pay votes for six years in a row.[20] A possible reason is that recently, "even with consistent negative feedback from investors, Oracle awarded its three most senior executives over $100 million in aggregate compensation." When a company does not respond to negative say-on-pay votes, shareholders sometimes use a strategy of attempting to remove members of the board of directors, especially those on the board's compensation committee. That is what happened at Oracle, and perhaps that is what contributed to recent changes in executive compensation, which included an announcement that it was "cutting its executive long-term equity grants in half for fiscal year 2018 and it didn't expect any new grants until 2022. Moreover, the new grants will vest only if the company meets share price, market capitalization, and operational goals."[21]

One other item of interest is that say-on-pay vote results are significantly influenced by the recommendations of two proxy advisor organizations, Glass Lewis and Institutional Shareholder Services (ISS). We focus on ISS. ISS recommends approval roughly 90 percent of the time. When ISS recommends approval, say-on-pay vote approval occurs roughly 94 percent of the time. By contrast, when ISS recommends against approval, shareholder say-on-pay vote approval occurs only about 64 percent of the time. How does ISS

EXHIBIT 14.4 Say-on-Pay Vote Results, By Year

Year	Percent of Companies Where Shareholders Voted to Approve Executive Pay Plan	Average Percent of Shareholders Voting to Approve Executive Pay Plan
2020	98%	91%
2019	97%	91%
2018	98%	91%
2017	99%	92%
2016	98%	91%
2015	97%	91%
2014	98%	91%
2013	98%	91%
2012	97%	90%
2011	99%	91%

Source: Semler Brossy, "2020 Say on Pay and Proxy Results," *Russell 3000*, February 4, 2021.

evaluate company executive compensation plans? It uses three dimensions: pay for performance, problematic pay practices, and compensation committee communication and responsiveness.[22] To evaluate pay for performance, it uses both qualitative and quantitative measures. With respect to the latter, ISS states that it examines "how well a company's CEO pay has been aligned with shareholder returns and fundamental financial performance" and that it "identifies companies that demonstrate a significant level of misalignment between the CEO's pay and company performance, either on an absolute basis or relative to a group of peers similar in size and industry." Much greater detail is available from ISS if you are interested.[23] **Exhibit 14.5** shows some of the most serious examples on the second dimension ISS uses, problematic pay practices. Examples include repricing or replacing of underwater stock options (where the current company stock price is below the exercise/strike price, reducing the value of the option) and "excessive change in control [CIC] agreements," which describe what executives get paid when the company is acquired by/merged with another company. These CIC provisions are sometimes referred to as "golden parachutes."[24]

The third and final dimension used by CIC to evaluate executive pay refers to how the compensation committee (part of the company's board of directors) responds (i.e., by modifying the executive pay plan) to say-on-pay votes where there is less than 70 percent support.

It is also important to note that large shareholders can influence executive pay, as well as other governance practices. This could be an individual, but it is often a so-called institutional investor such as the California Public Employees' Retirement System (CALPERS), the world's largest public-pension fund (assets of $444 billion as of this writing). Even highly regarded companies run by legends can expect such investors to share their views on how best to run the company to obtain the best financial returns for the shareholders they represent. For example, Berkshire Hathaway, headed up by Warren Buffet (aka "The Oracle of Omaha") heard

EXHIBIT 14.5 Institutional Shareholder Services (ISS), List of the Most Problematic Executive Compensation Practices

Practices that "will likely result in adverse vote recommendations":

- Repricing or replacing of underwater stock options/stock appreciation rights without prior shareholder approval (including cash buyouts and voluntary surrender of underwater options);
- Extraordinary perquisites or tax gross-ups, potentially including gross-ups related to a secular trust or restricted stock vesting, and home loss buyouts, or any lifetime perquisites;
- New or extended executive agreements that provide for:
  - Excessive change in control (CIC) payments (exceeding three times base salary and average/target/most recent bonus);
  - CIC severance payments without involuntary job loss or substantial diminution of duties ("single" or "modified single" triggers);
  - CIC severance payments triggered by questionable "good reason" definitions (e.g., bankruptcy, de-listing)
  - CIC payments with excise tax gross-ups (including "modified" gross-ups);
  - Multiyear guaranteed awards that are not at risk due to rigorous performance conditions; or
  - Liberal CIC definition combined with any single-trigger CIC benefits.
- Any other provision or practice included in the ISS fuller list of problematic practices deemed to be egregious and present a significant risk to investors.

Source: Institutional Share Services, "U.S. Compensation Policies Frequently Asked Questions," Updated December 21, 2020.

from CALPERS (and from proxy advisors, ISS and Glass Lewis) that it needed to "refresh" the board of directors and that new directors should be more responsive to shareholder concerns about climate-risk and executive pay. CALPERS is withholding votes to re-elect certain current board members.[25]

Components of an Executive Compensation Package

There are five basic elements of most executive compensation packages: (1) **base salary,** (2) short-term (annual) incentives or bonuses, (3) long-term incentives (e.g., stock options and stock grants), (4) benefits, and (5) perquisites.[26] **Exhibit 14.6** shows total CEO compensation, which includes all five components, over time. Most recently, it was $12.7 million. **Exhibit 14.6** reports the first three components of CEO compensation separately. It is important to note that the great majority of CEO pay is not in the form of base salary, which accounted for just 8.7 percent ($1.1 million/$12.7 million). Instead, long-term incentives (stock) and short-term incentives (bonuses) account for the bulk of CEO pay. (As **Exhibit 14.6** notes, although the median stock option grant is $0, the mean is $2.0 million.) These facts suggest that CEO compensation must be significantly linked to short-term and long-term company performance, which are usually defined, respectively, in terms of profitability and total shareholder return (TSR). In the absence of strong profitability and TSR, the main components of CEO pay become smaller. Some indication of the degree of linkage between CEO total pay and company performance can be seen in **Exhibit 14.6**. As the value of the S&P 500 increases or decreases (an indicator of changes in TSR), total CEO pay also increases and decreases, primarily due to increases and decreases in stock options and stock grants. For example, after peaking at $17.1 million in 2007, total CEO pay fell by 40 percent to $8.5 million by 2010 (including a drop in stock-related compensation from $13.1 million to $5.5 million), as TSR dropped (as reflected in repeated declines in the value of the S&P 500). We also saw earlier (in **Exhibit 14.3**) evidence of substantial linkage between executive pay and performance.

Exhibit 14.6 also shows average weekly earnings of production and nonsupervisory workers "Worker Pay" in all companies (not just the 500 largest) and the ratio of CEO pay (in the largest 500 companies only) to worker pay. As such, the most recent year's ratio of 297 in **Exhibit 14.6** is a bit of an "apples and oranges" comparison, as it compares CEO pay where it is highest (in the 500 largest companies) with worker pay in all companies, not the same large companies where worker pay would also be higher. However, these data are useful for documenting that since 1990, CEO pay in large companies has grown faster than worker pay, and thus the CEO pay/worker pay ratio has also increased over that time period. There is some belief that a larger ratio will negatively influence firm performance because of more negative employee relations due to their perception of pay inequity. Direct tests of that (where employee perceptions are actually measured) are hard to find. However, one study found, consistent with other pay dispersion research (see **Chapter 3**) that larger dispersion between CEO and employee pay is most likely to negatively influence future firm performance when high CEO pay is not explained by high past firm performance.[27]

Base Salary

Although formalized job evaluation still plays an occasional role in determining executive **base pay,** other sources are much more important. Particularly important is the analysis of a compensation committee, composed usually of the company's board of directors or a subset of the board.[28] Frequently the compensation committee will take over some of the data analysis tasks previously performed by the chief personnel officer, even going so far as to analyze salary survey data and performance records for executives of comparably sized firms.[29] One empirical study suggests the most common approach (60% of the cases) of executive compensation committees is to identify major competitors and set the CEO's compensation at a level between the best and worst of these comparison groups.[30] Where pay fell in this range depended on a number of factors. CEOs who are particularly likely to be raided, or who have greater power over the wage setting process or

EXHIBIT 14.6 CEO Pay, S&P 500 Market Value, Worker Pay, and CEO Pay/Worker Pay, by Year

Year	Salary	Bonus	Salary Plus Bonus	Stock Options	Stock Grants	CEO Pay (total)	Annual Change in CEO Pay	Annual Change in S&P 500 Market Value	Worker Pay*	CEO Pay/ Worker Pay
2020	$1.1 million	$1.8 million	$2.9 million	$0.0***	$7.1 million	$12.7 million	3%	16%	****	—
2019	$1.2 million	$2.0 million	$3.2 million	$0.0***	$6.5 million	$12.3 million	3%	29%	$41,442	297
2018	1.2 million	2.1 million	3.3 million	0.0***	6.4 million	12.0 million	1%	−6%	40,463	297
2017	1.1 million	2.0 million	3.1 million	1.1 million	5.6 million	11.9 million	3%	19%	39,212	303
2016	1.1 million	2.0 million	3.1 million	1.1 million	5.5 million	11.5 million	11%	12%	38,089	302
2015	1.1 million	2.0 million	3.1 million	1.1 million	5.1 million	10.4 million	1%	1%	37,186	280
2014	1.1 million	2.1 million	3.2 million	1.2 million	4.7 million	10.3 million	1%	14%	36,455	283
2013	1.1 million	2.0 million	3.1 million	1.4 million	4.2 million	10.2 million	11%	32%	35,555	287
2012	1.0 million	1.9 million	2.9 million	1.3 million	3.8 million	9.2 million	4%	16%	34,519	269
2011	1.0 million	2.0 million	3.0 million	1.7 million	3.3 million	8.9 million	**	2%	33,800	263
2010			3.0 million	3.0 million	2.5 million	8.5 million	−29%	15%	33,119	258
2009			3.0 million	3.3 million	5.8 million	12.1 million	−14%	26%	32,093	377
2008			3.6 million	3.6 million	6.9 million	14.1 million	−18%	−37%	31,617	446
2007			4.0 million	4.9 million	8.2 million	17.1 million	34%	5%	30,682	558
2006			3.8 million	2.4 million	6.5 million	12.7 million	3%	16%	29,529	431
2005			3.7 million	2.1 million	6.6 million	12.4 million	—	—	28,305	438
2000			2.9 million	4.5 million	7.0 million	14.3 million	—	—	25,013	573
1995			2.0 million	0.7 million	0.7 million	3.3 million	—	—	20,804	160
1990			1.6 million	0.3 million	0.7 million	2.6 million	—	—	18,187	144

*Worker pay (annual) is based on establishment survey data on earnings of production and nonsupervisory workers on private nonfarm payrolls, U.S. Bureau of Labor Statistics, Employment & Earnings Online, Establishment Data from the Current Employment Statistics Survey (CES), National, Table B-8a, https://www.bls.gov/opub/ee. The December average weekly earnings number is multiplied by 52 to obtain worker pay (annual).

**Not computed due to change in definition of total compensation from a mean to a median.

*** This indicates that the median was $0.0. However, the mean is not $0.0. For example, in 2020, the mean was $1.7 million.

**** Not yet available

Note: Through 2010, the three pay-category averages of salary plus bonus, stock awards, and stock options add up to equal average total pay. Beginning in 2011, the pay categories do not add up to total pay because some compensation categories (non-equity incentive plan compensation, change in pension value and nonqualified deferred compensation earnings, all other compensation) reported in the Summary Compensation Table of company proxy statements are excluded and because medians are used. For 2016, only CEOs in that role for at least two years were included.

Sources: Through 2010, CEO pay data are averages from *Forbes* magazine. Through 1999 (1995 here), *Forbes* data pertain to the 800 largest companies. Beginning with year 2000 through 2010, *Forbes* data pertain to the 500 largest U.S. companies (S&P 500). Beginning in 2011, CEO pay data pertain to the 500 largest U.S. companies (S&P 500) and are medians (versus averages) from Equilar, CEO Pay Trends (multiple years). www.equilar.com.

successfully made strategic changes, were more likely to have higher compensation than peers.[31] Larger companies also tended to hit the high end of the compensation range by selecting "peer companies" to benchmark against that were tilted toward the high-paying end.[32]

Annual Incentive Plan/Bonuses

Annual (short-term) incentive plan bonuses, as we have seen, play a major role in executive compensation and are primarily designed to motivate better short-term (defined as measured over a period of one year or less) performance. The first annual executive cash bonus may have been introduced by pharmaceutical giant Pfizer in 1901. The CEO got a five year contract with an annual bonus of 25 percent of company profits. In 1918 GM got a bit more complicated with a bonus of 10 percent less a deduction of 7 percent for capital employed.[33] Only 20 years ago, just 36 percent of companies gave annual bonuses. Today, as we saw in **Chapter 10**, essentially 100 percent of executives in private sector companies are covered by bonus plans. As we also saw in **Chapter 10**, for all executives (not just CEOs), the basis for short-term incentive payouts is 69 percent corporate performance, 19 percent business unit performance, and 19 percent individual performance. In the case of a CEO, the business unit performance component would not be relevant and so the corporate performance component would be substantially larger than 69 percent.

FW Cook conducts a survey of annual incentive plan practices for CEO among the 250 largest companies in the S&P 500.[34] They report that 83 percent of the Top 250 use non-discretionary plans, all of which use one or more financial measures (one to three is most common). The most commonly used financial measures in such plans are profit (92%), revenue (46%), and cash flow (25%). Nonfinancial measures are also common, being used in 52 percent of these plans. The most common nonfinancial measures in this group of companies (52% × 83% = 43% of the Top 250) are strategic (42%; e.g., safety, customer service, quality, and employee engagement), individual (38%; typically with goals/objectives defined for each individual), and discretionary (12%; allows for subjective decision to increase or decrease the incentive payout). In determining the size of annual incentive/bonus payouts, financial measures on average carry a weight of 82%, compared to 18% for nonfinancial measures. An additional 17% of the Top 250 use a discretionary annual incentive plan. FW Cook notes that "although payouts are not formulaically tied to specific goals or targets, many of these plans consider company financial performance when determining payouts, so as to avoid disconnects between pay and performance that could draw outside criticism from proxy advisory firms [see ISS], shareholders, and others."[35]

As we saw in **Exhibit 14.6**, if we look back far enough (say, to 1990), we can see that bonuses have become a smaller portion of executive compensation. One potential explanation may pertain to a shift in the time horizon that companies want executives to focus on. Bonuses are a short-term incentive and thus reward good short-term results. The concern was that this caused CEOs to approve decisions with great short-term payouts but not necessarily desirable long-term consequences for the firm. That (agency) problem would be exacerbated to the degree executive tenure with a firm was short. (The CEO would be gone by the time the negative long-term consequences came to pass.)

Following the same logic as used with balanced scorecards, although companies have in common many of the same performance measures in their annual incentive plans, they typically tailor these to their own objectives and strategies.[36] As an example, a growth company might be interested in the level of innovation or progress in branding its products.[37] In contrast, an automobile company like Ford chooses a different emphasis. **Exhibit 14.7**, drawing on publicly available information in the proxy Ford filed with the SEC, shows that Ford's (non-discretionary) annual incentive bonus plan for its top five executives determines payouts using the following performance measures (and weights): revenue (20%), operating margin (30%), operating cash flow (20%), Ford Credit profit before tax (10%), and quality (20%). Ford notes that "The amount earned under the Incentive Bonus Plan was determined pursuant to a pre-established sliding scale, based on various levels of achievement for each metric."[38] The target payout for the top five executives is 200% of salary for the CEO and 125% of salary for the other four. In this case, actual resulting performance ranged from 55% of target (operating margin) to 146% of target (Ford Credit profit before tax). The resulting overall performance to target was 100%. That resulted in 2018 of a bonus payments of $3.6 million for the president and CEO, $1.1 million for the executive vice president and president for global operations, $1.0 million for the executive vice president and president for global markets, and $0.9 million for the executive vice president and chief financial officer. Ford's proxy statement also notes, "If minimum performance levels had not been met for all metrics, the payout would have been zero." This statement later proved to be true. According to Ford's 2021 Proxy Statement, the overall performance to target declined to 23 percent (during the pandemic) and as a consequence, the bonus payment for the president and CEO was $449,100, down from $3.6 million in 2018. More broadly, total compensation (from the Summary Compensation Table) of the president and CEO in the 2021 Proxy Statement was $11.8 million, down from $16.7 million in the 2018 Proxy Statement.

Exhibit 14.8 provides more detail on the quality part of Ford's annual incentive, showing that it is a composite of three equally weighted measures: Industry-provided data on "things that go wrong" and customer satisfaction at Ford, as well as Ford's own warranty spend. All three quality measures are taken "at three months in service."

A **balanced scorecard** (e.g., see **Chapter 11**) traditionally includes financial performance, as well as measures of performance in customer, employee, and internal process/strategies, which are chosen (preferably based on empirical evidence) because they are leading indicators of financial performance. Increasingly, these scorecards include diversity and inclusion objectives under Employee ("Colleague" in this example) objectives, as American Express does in the balanced scorecard example we saw in **Chapter 11**.

Long-Term Incentives

Long-term incentive plans assess performance over a period of longer than one year. **Exhibit 14.9**, courtesy of Bruce R. Ellig, provides a detailed classification of long-term incentive plans. We can also use the FW Cook three-part classification of stock options/stock appreciation rights (SAR; we will include phantom stock here), restricted stock, and performance awards (which include performance shares and performance units).

Using this classification, we see in **Exhibit 14.10** that performance awards are the most used long-term incentive program for executives, followed by restricted stock and stock option/SAR. FW Cook also reports that

EXHIBIT 14.7 Annual Incentive Plan for Top Five Executives, Ford Motor Company

	INCENTIVE BONUS PLAN PERFORMANCE RESULTS			
	Performance (Based on 100% Target)	Target (Bils)	Weighting	Total Weighted Performance (Weighting × Performance)
Revenue	133%	$142.9	20%	**26%**
Operating Margin	55%	6.00%	30%	**16%**
Operating Cash Flow	106%	$3.582	20%	**21%**
Ford Credit Profit before Tax	146%	$1.519	10%	**15%**
Quality	107%	Various	20%	**22%**
				Overall Performance = 100%

Source: Ford's 2018 Proxy Statement. The plan is similar in later years, except that Ford Credit Profit before Tax is eliminated and weightings change (e.g., cash flow is weighted 50% in the 2021 Proxy Statement).

performance awards likewise comprise most (59%) of the value of long-term incentives in the Top 250 companies, followed by restricted stock at 22 percent, and stock options/SAR at 18 percent.[39]

We note that FW Cook data from 2008 showed that 79 percent of companies used stock options/SAR at that time. The drop of 20 percentage points since then (see **Exhibit 14.10**) in the view of FW Cook is due to "accounting regulators who imposed an explicit expense on stock options and proxy advisory firms taking

EXHIBIT 14.8 Annual Incentive Plan for Top Five Executives, Ford Motor Company, Quality Measures

	Incentive Bonus Plan Results – Quality Performance		
	Performance (Based on 100% Target)	Target – Year-over-Year Global Target Improvement/(Deterioration)	Weighting
Things gone wrong	91%	10%	33%
Customer satisfaction	92%	2%	33%
Warranty spend	137%	(16)%	33%
Total quality performance	**107%**		

Source: Ford's 2018 proxy statement. These same metrics are used in Ford's 2021 Proxy Statement.

EXHIBIT 14.9 Description of Long-Term Incentives for Executives

Type	Description	Comments
Incentive stock options	Purchase of stock at a stipulated price, conforming with Internal Revenue Code (Section 422A).	No taxes at grant. Company may not deduct as expense.
Nonqualified stock options	Purchase of stock at a stipulated price, not conforming with Internal Revenue Code.	Excess over fair market value taxed as ordinary income. Company may deduct.
Phantom stock plans	Cash or stock award determined by increase in stock price at a fixed future date.	Taxed as ordinary income. Does not require executive financing.
Stock appreciation rights	Cash or stock award determined by increase in stock price during any time chosen (by the executive) in the option period.	Taxed as ordinary income. Does not require executive financing.
Restricted stock plans	Grant of stock at a reduced price with the condition that it may not be sold before a specified date.	Excess over fair market value taxed as ordinary income.
Performance share/unit plans	Cash or stock award earned through achieving specific goals.	Taxed as ordinary income. Does not require executive financing.

Source: Ellig, B., *The Complete Guide to Executive Compensation* (New York: McGraw-Hill Education, 2014).

the stance that service-vesting stock options are not performance-based equity." The second issue refers once again to a body like ISS, which, as we have seen, produces evaluations and voting recommendations pertaining to executive pay packages.

Let us return to the first issue, the change in accounting treatment of stock options from "intrinsic value" (APB 25) to "fair value" (FAS 123 recommended in 1995 and FAS 123(R) required it in 2004). Under the former intrinsic value standard, compensation expense was zero at the time of the stock option grant as long as the stock price and the option/exercise/strike price was equal at the time of the grant. This accounting treatment allowed companies to issue stock options at no expense unless and until the stock price rose and executives (and/or a broader group of employees in some companies) exercised their option to purchase the stock. This strategy was especially attractive as a means to attract, motivate, and retain employees in small firms that had limited cash and preferred to use it to invest in the company rather than pay it out in salary and benefits (if it had an alternative like stock options). However, with the change to fair value, stock options must be taken as an expense at the time they are granted. The expense can be estimated using pricing models such as Black-Scholes.

How does a stock option work? Consider an employee at a company with a current stock price of $50/share. This year the employee receives a grant of 100 stock options having an option price of $50 (the same as the current stock price). That means that until the stock options expire, the employee can purchase the stock at $50/share, regardless of the actual stock price when the shares are purchased. One year later, the stock price has risen to $60/share. The employee can then choose to exercise her stock options to purchase the stock at $50 and earn a $10 profit ($60 − $50 = $10) on each share. If she exercises all 100 options, she would make 100 × $10 = $1,000. Of course, if the stock price had gone up more or if she had received more options, she would have made much more money. Now consider the case where the stock price falls to $40/share, a situation where the options are said to be "under water." If the employee cannot sell the stock options (and they typically cannot), the options are now worthless, at least in the short run. However, if a market can be made (as was done at Google), the options are not worthless. Even in the absence of such a market, the options are not worthless as long as there is a non-zero probability of the stock price rebounding above the option price in the future. (But that may be cold comfort to those holding underwater options in a company with seemingly poor prospects.)

This discussion brings up the question of how one computes the value of a stock option. The most rigorous approach is to use an options pricing model such as Black-Scholes. One can now easily go to the Internet and find spreadsheets to use for this purpose. Here, we provide a demonstration of some basic properties of the Black-Scholes options pricing model. **Exhibit 14.11** shows the impact of two parameters on option value, expressed here as percentage of the stock price. First, and perhaps somewhat surprising to many, is that the higher the volatility (i.e., how much the stock price fluctuates/varies over time), the better (i.e., the option is worth more). The reason is that with more variation, there is a greater chance that the stock price will exceed the option price and exceed it by a greater amount before the stock option expires (usually after 10 years, according to FW Cook). Second, the lower the dividend rate, the greater the Black-Scholes value of an

EXHIBIT 14.10 Percentage of Companies Using Long-Term Incentive Programs for Executives, Top 250

Long-Term Incentive Program	Percentage of Companies
Performance Awards	93%
Restricted Stock	65%
Stock Options/Stock Appreciation Rights	50%

Source: FW Cook, *2020 Top 250 Report*, October 2020. www.fwcook.com.

option, because returns to shareholders for their investment take the form of either dividends or price appreciation (an increase in stock price). To apply **Exhibit 14.11**, let's again take the example where an employee (perhaps you) receives 100 stock options with an option price = stock price = $50/share. In the absence of any dividend (0%) and a volatility of 50%, each stock option would be worth .69 × $50 = $34.50, and with 100 options, the value of the total option grant would be $34.50 × 100 = $3,450. Of course, if the stock options are held, there is no guarantee that will be the realized value. That would depend on what the stock price actually does.

One concern with stock options (and potentially any long-term incentive, depending on whether it is designed to make payouts based on absolute or relative stock price performance) is that stock options sometimes do not link as closely as desired to performance of the executive.[40] Consider a rising stock market. If everyone's stock is going up, as often happens in a bull market, should CEOs be rewarded because their company's stock price also rises? It can happen easily in boom markets if performance is not relative (e.g., stock price increase relative to a comparison group). In a stock market that is rising on all fronts, executives can exercise options at much higher prices than the initial grant price–and the payouts are more appropriately attributed to general market increases than to any specific action by the executive. In a falling market, stock options are under water–the market price is below the exercise price. If I can exercise options at $23 per share, but they're valued at $18, I would be a fool to exercise. One potential response by the corporate compensation committee is to issue new stock options with a lower exercise price, a practice that is perceived by many as inappropriate and that, we have seen, ISS frowns upon.[41] A final reason for the concern about stock options as an incentive tool is the ability to "game the system." For example, when a CEO's actions drive up the stock price and thus the value of his/her own options, is it because of improved performance in fundamentals of the business such as higher sales? Not necessarily. For example, there can be manipulation of accounting numbers. A legal path to higher stock prices is a large stock buyback. That reduces the number of shares of stock outstanding. Shares just happen to be the denominator in an equation with profits as the numerator in computing earnings per share. Reducing the denominator makes earnings per share higher, which is often an important metric for deciding executive bonuses under annual incentive plans. In the spirit of the long-ago children's show, Mister Rogers' Neighborhood, "Can you say 'manipulation'?"[42] (Of course, the alternative view is that sometimes a stock buyback may be the best way to return cash to shareholders and may especially make sense if there is not currently a way for the company to invest that money in new products and/or services that would produce as large of a return.)

Whatever the challenges in paying them, executive decisions have an important impact on corporate success. Linking executive compensation to stock price is a very effective way to make sure executives are motivated to seek corporate successes (or in the language of agency theory, that executive goals/interests are aligned with those of shareholders). In comparison, **base wages** seem like an entitlement. As long as the executive doesn't get fired, wages are guaranteed. Annual/short-term incentives/bonuses also are not adequate alone. They pay off for good short-term performance. What's good in the short run isn't necessarily good for the company in

EXHIBIT 14.11 Effect of Volatility and Dividend Rate on Option Value (as % of stock price)

Dividend Rate	Volatility			
	10%	30%	50%	70%
0%	.45	.56	.69	.81
4%	.15	.29	.41	.51
8%	.02	.14	.24	.32

Source: Hall, B. J., "What You Need to Know about Stock Options," *Harvard Business Review* 78, no. 2 (2000), pp. 121–129.

the long run. Thus, it is not surprising that essentially all private sector companies, as we saw in **Chapter 10**, use long-term incentives and rely on them most heavily to pay executives. As we saw earlier in **Exhibit 14.3**, in U.S. companies, when shareholders do better, executives do better.

We saw earlier that performance awards are now the most important long-term incentive program in terms of use and as a determinant of executive long-term incentive payouts. Returning to the survey of corporate directors of public companies, when asked to choose the single best metric to measure company performance, 40 percent chose total shareholder return (TSR), followed by return on capital (18 percent), operating income (16 percent), free cash flow (15 percent), other (primarily earnings per share, 9 percent), and sales (0 percent).[43] FW Cook (see **Exhibit 14.12**) also provides data on the most frequently used performance metrics under performance share plans. We see that TSR is the most common performance measure and note also that it is typically used in a relative manner (i.e., the executive is evaluated on whether the firm's TSR is better than that of competitors). The next most often used performance measures are profit, capital efficiency, and revenue. Nonfinancial ("other" in **Exhibit 14.12**) measures are used much less often.

We saw earlier that performance awards are now the most important long-term incentive program in terms of use and as a determinant of executive long-term incentive payouts. Returning to the survey of corporate.

Vesting. Importantly, long-term incentive plan grants are not immediately owned by the recipient (e.g., an executive). Rather, they are owned when fully vested and this vesting takes place over time. The typical (92% of companies) vesting schedule for performance awards is 3 years. For stock options and restricted stock, 3 years is also typical (61% of companies), but 4 years is also common (33% of companies).[44]

Executive Benefits

Because many benefits are tied to income level (e.g., life insurance, disability insurance, pension plans), executives typically receive higher benefits than most other exempt employees. Beyond the typical benefits outlined in **Chapter 13**, however, many executives also receive additional life insurance, exclusions from deductibles for health-related costs, and supplementary pension income exceeding the maximum limits permissible under ERISA guidelines for qualified (eligible for tax deductions) pension plans.

Of course, various sections of ERISA and the tax code restrict employers' ability to provide benefits for executives that are too far above those of other workers. The assorted clauses require that a particular benefit plan (1) cover a broad cross-section of employees (generally 80 percent), (2) provide definitely determinable benefits, and (3) meet specific vesting (see **Chapter 13**) and nondiscrimination requirements. The nondiscrimination requirement specifies that the average value of benefits for low-paid employees must be at least 75 percent of the average value of those for highly paid employees.[45]

Executive Perquisites

Perquisites, or "perks," probably have the same genesis as the expression "rank has its privileges." Indeed, life at the top has its rewards, designed to satisfy unique needs and preferences. Since 1978, various tax and regulatory agency rulings have slowly been requiring companies to place a value on perks.[46] Despite this obstacle perks rose in value seven percent last year. Examples of interesting perks are the following:[47]

1. The most interesting perk pays for an executive's death. If the CEO of the Shaw group, James Bernhard, should die, the company will pay his family $18 million for him (the deceased) to not compete in Shaw's industry for two years. Is executive compensation insane, or what?
2. Seven percent of Fortune 500 firms give cash allowances, averaging $32,000. Explain why executives making millions of dollars need an allowance? Ken Chenault, CEO of American Express, gets $21 million in salary but still needs a $35,000 allowance for incidentals? Or Paul Murray, CEO of Calvin Klein needs a $20,000 clothing allowance?[48]

3. SL Green Realty spent $51,882 on a personal car for chairman Stephen Green–plus another $119,050 for a chauffeur. These are footnoted figures that work out to $468 a day, or enough to drive 233 miles a day for a year in a New York City cab.[49]
4. Our personal favorite, and now a classic of abuse: When Dennis Kozlowski's second wife hit the magic age of 40 in 2001, shortly after they wed, the then Tyco chief threw the party of parties. Guests were treated to a weeklong Roman-themed party on the island of Sardinia. Total cost? Over $2 million (nearly $3 million in today's dollars), half paid by Tyco.[50]

Exhibit 14.13 shows common perks today in the S&P 500.

EXHIBIT 14.12 Performance Metrics Used in Performance Share Long-Term Incentive Plans for Executives, Top 250 Companies

Performance Measure Categories						
		Percent of Companies with Performance Awards		Performance Measurement Approach*		
Category	**Performance Measures**	**2015**	**2020**	**Absolute**	**Relative**	**Both**
Total Shareholder Return (TSR)	Stock Price Appreciation Plus Dividends	54%	**67%**	3%	92%	5%
Profit	EPS, Net Income EBIT, EBITDA Operating/Pretax Profit	51%	**55%**	90%	8%	2%
Capital Efficiency	Return on Equity, Return on Assets, Return on Capital,	41%	**38%**	76%	12%	12%
Revenue	Revenue, Organic Revenue	20%	**23%**	85%	15%	0%
Cash Flow	Cash Flow, Operating Cash Flow, Free Cash Flow	11%	**15%**	94%	6%	0%
Other	Safety, Quality Assurance, New Business, Individual Performance	14%	**14%**	N/A	N/A	N/A

Source: FW Cook, *2015 Top 250 Report, 2017 Top 250 Report, and 2020 Top 250 Report. www.fwcook.com.*

*Based on 2017 Report.

Why is Everyone So Interested in Executive Compensation? And ... Some Different Perspectives

Well, let's face it. Most of us don't earn $12 million per year like CEOs (of the largest companies) do. Perhaps it makes us wonder whether anyone could ever be worth that much, let alone the much higher amounts received by the top-earning CEOs last year. One issue has to do with income inequality in the United States (See **Chapter 1**) and in other countries. Should anyone get paid so much if others in society are earning so little that they cannot get by? Another perspective is that executive pay in almost every other country, particularly in more developed economies, is lower than in the United States. (One issue here is that executive pay is positively related to company size. The United States has a disproportionate share of large companies in the world). Another part of the argument, which relates to income equality, notes that the difference in pay between a CEO and the average worker has exploded. As **Exhibit 14.6** shows, in 1990 an executive made 144 times as much as the typical worker (in the largest 500 U.S. companies). Today that executive earns 275 times as much. No shock that the average worker, like the average citizen (as we saw in the survey results of the U.S. public earlier) isn't a supporter of executives' high pay.

Comparisons across countries indicate that U.S. CEOs are paid more than counterparts in Europe and Japan.[51] That means CEO pay/worker pay ratios are also higher in the United States. However, as briefly noted earlier in talking about income inequality generally, such comparisons must take care to avoid "apples to oranges" comparisons that can result if "large" are compared and "large" companies in the United States are larger on average. Still, after factoring that in, CEO pay and the CEO/worker pay ratio is still likely larger in the United States.

Think about the job of the compensation directors sitting on an executive pay committee. Why do they recommend that executives be paid as much and how they are? The most basic reason presumably is that the

EXHIBIT 14.13 Popular Perks Offered to Executives

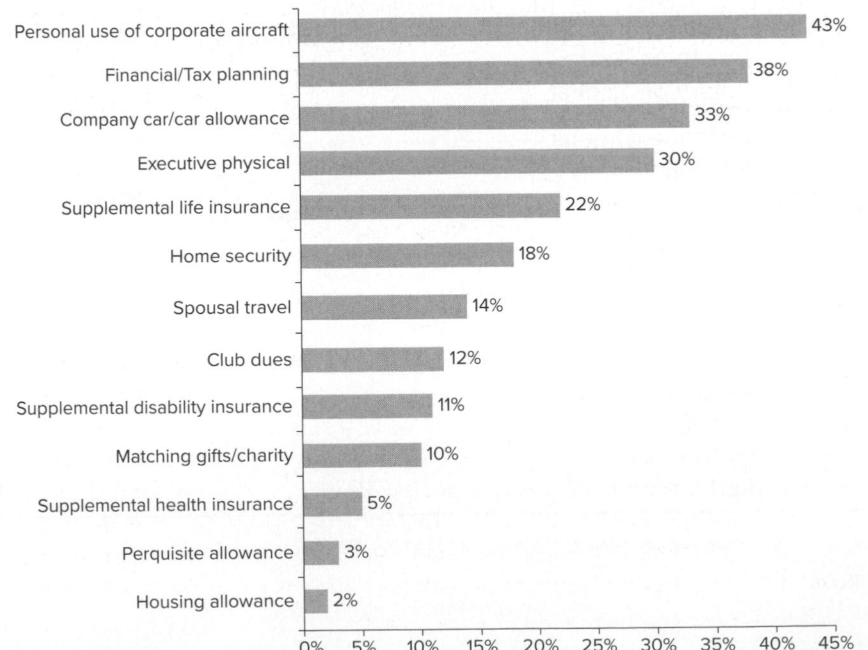

Source: Ahmed, Minha, "Executive Compensation Bulletin: An Update on Executive Perquisite Trends in the S&P 500," Willis Towers Watson, February 17, 2016.

committee and the Board are responsible for representing shareholder interests. Although CEO pay is a major cost to shareholders, it may pale in comparison to the difference in shareholder return that could come from having a high-performing versus low-performing CEO. Related to this, an argument could be that executive compensation is simply a reflection of changes in the market. Yes, executive compensation has risen dramatically since 1900, but so has the pay of other groups. For example, the top 25 hedge fund managers earned more in 2005 than all 500 CEOs in the S&P 500.[52] In 2017 it was a little closer, with the top 25 hedge fund managers earning a total of $16.8 billion (about $672 million per manager), which is more than the average CEO total compensation of about $12 million times 500 companies, or about $600 million.[53] (Actually, the $12 million is a median. Perhaps you would like to point out the problem with this computation?) By 2020, the top 25 highest-paid hedge fund managers combined made $32 billion, or an average of 1.28 billion each.[54] Not even Tesla CEO Elon Musk made that much. And the median CEO's pay is really starting to look kind of small by comparison. Top professional ballplayers (football, baseball, and basketball) making more than $5 million in 1994 increased their wages by a factor of 10 over the next 10 years. During the same period, the salaries of top lawyers increased by a factor of 2.5. Compare this, say the supporters of executive pay, to the increase in CEO pay during the same period–a multiplier of 4 or 5.[55] As another comparison, the average National Basketball Association player salary increased by a factor of 7× from 1990 to present.[56] Based on **Exhibit 14.6**, CEO pay increased by a factor of 4.7 over the same period. Even if you don't buy these arguments–and many critics don't[57]–there is still strong evidence that there is a strong pay-for-performance link in the pay of executives. If the company performance exceeds industry standards, big short-term and long-term incentive payouts should happen. Poor financial performance means much smaller pay packages. How did executive pay get to where it is today? **Exhibit 14.14** gives a brief history.

e-Compensation

For a union view of CEO wages, visit ***www.aflcio.org/paywatch/***. This site is maintained by the AFL-CIO and is designed to monitor executive compensation. The union view is that CEOs are overpaid and that monitoring is the first step to curbing excess.

One explanation for the high pay of executives involves *social comparisons*.[58] In this view, executive salaries bear a consistent relative relationship to compensation of lower-level employees. When salaries of lower-level employees rise in response to market forces, top executive salaries also rise to maintain the same relative relationship. In general, managers who are in the second level of a company earn about two-thirds of a CEO's salary, while the next level down earns slightly more than half of a CEO's salary.[59] Much of the criticism of this theory–and an important source of criticism about executive compensation in general–is the gradual increase in the spread between executives' compensation and the average salaries of the people they employ. Comparisons over time can be tricky because it is important to use the same size companies. In our earlier **Exhibit 14.6**, data from 2000 and later pertain to the largest 500 U.S. companies. We see that the CEO Pay/Worker pay ratio was actually larger (573) in 2000 than recently (275). Going back farther in time, however, paints a dramatically different picture. An analysis of the 350 largest U.S. companies reports that the CEO Pay/Worker pay ratio in 2020 was 278 versus 20 in 1965.[60] If one were to try to explain this, it would probably rely in part on the fact that CEOs used to be paid a salary, but then thinking shifted to the idea that they should be paid differently to better align their interests with those of owners (see Agency Theory). That meant making them owners.

A second approach to understanding executive compensation focuses less on the difference in wages between executive and other jobs and more on explaining the level of executive wages.[61] The premise in this economic approach is that the worth of CEOs, or their subordinates, should correspond closely to some measure of company success, such as profitability or sales or firm size. Intuitively, this explanation makes sense. There is also empirical support. Numerous studies over the past 30 years have demonstrated that executive pay bears some relationship to company success, including the ability to make strategic changes and negotiate

EXHIBIT 14.14 Brief History of Executive Compensation: Key Events

1974	Michael Bergerac cracks the $1 million mark when recruited to Revlon.
1979	Chrysler's Lee Iacocca takes $1 million plus 400,000 option shares.
1983	William Bendix of Bendix becomes the first executive to collect a huge golden parachute (contract clause for payment in a takeover leading to termination) of $3.9 million over five years.
1984	Congress tries to limit excessive golden parachutes but gives rise to unintended consequences—the rules actually lead to larger amounts.
1986	New law gives favorable tax treatment to stock option awards. Sizes increase.
1987	Lee Iacocca receives first mega-grant of stock options: 820,000 option shares worth 15.3 times his salary and bonus that year.
1987	Junk bond expert Michael Milkin explodes through the $5 million mark in salary and bonus.
1987	Leon Hirsch of U.S. Surgical gets even larger megastock option award, worth 126 times his salary and bonus.
1992	Securities and Exchange Commission rules CEO salaries must be disclosed more often in proxy statements. Easier availability of peer compensation data serves to drive up the standard.
1992	Michael Eisner of Walt Disney exercises low-cost stock options for pretax profit of $126 million.
1993	New tax law sets upper limit on tax-deductible executive compensation at $1 million but has unintended effect of raising bar to that level.
2000	Charles Wang, Computer Associates Intl. executive, cracks two-thirds of billion-dollar mark.
2006	Steve Jobs lost the top-paid CEO position to Oracle's Lawrence J. Ellison, who was compensated $192.92 million in 2007.
2010	Dodd-Frank Act gives power to shareholders by giving them a nonbinding (but image important) vote on appropriateness of an executive's compensation.
2014	The top five paid executives average about $75 million/year, less than before the Great Financial Crisis.
2017	Total Compensation of CEOs in the S&P 500 is about $12 million, still well below the peak of $17 million reached in 2007.
2020	Total Compensation of CEOs in the S&P 500 remains at about $12 million.

Source: *BusinessWeek,* April 17, 2000, p. 100, April 23, 2003; *The Wall Street Journal,* April 10, 2006, pp. R1–R4; "Executive Pay," *BusinessWeek,* April 17, 2009, pp. 23–31, Forbes.com, visited May 5, 2015. "Equilar 100: Highest-Paid CEOs at the Largest Companies by Revenue." April 11, 2018. www.equilar.com.

mergers/acquisitions successfully.[62] A recent article analyzing the results from over 100 executive pay studies concluded that firm size (sales or number of employees) is the best predictor of CEO compensation. (Consider why. Would you recommend the same pay for someone to lead a $500 thousand firm as for someone to lead a $5 billion firm?)[63] A different economic perspective looks at labor markets. CEO salaries are strongly influenced by labor markets–competitor pay levels matter. CEOs who are in demand (their companies are performing well relative to competitors) are more likely to receive higher wages, or have pay tied less to annual performance (good long-term track records mean less reliance on yearly performance).[64]

Some research suggests taking into account environmental performance and social responsibility when measuring company value.[65] One interesting study found that environmental performance (e.g., pollution prevention) is an important determinant of CEO pay in polluting industries. This suggests that CEOs are rewarded for setting and working toward environmental goals. Remember it's still difficult to determine if these green goals have tangible benefits; they are not measured in typical bottom-line accounting.[66] Two other studies combined both social comparison and economic explanations to try to better understand CEO salaries.[67] Both of these explanations turned out to be significant. Size and profitability affected level of compensation, but so did social comparisons. In one study, the social comparison was between wages of CEOs and those of the board of directors. It seems that CEO salaries rose, on average, 51 percent for every $100,000 more that was earned by directors on the board.[68] Recognizing this, CEOs sometimes lobby to get a board loaded with directors who are highly paid in their primary jobs.

A third view of CEO salaries, called **agency theory,** incorporates the political motivations that are an inevitable part of the corporate world.[69] Sometimes, this argument runs, CEOs make decisions that aren't in the economic best interest of the firm and its shareholders. One variant on this view suggests that the normal behavior of a CEO is self-protective. CEOs will make decisions to solidify their positions and to maximize the rewards they personally receive.[70] When given stock options, they will engage in more risk-taking. But CEOs are also motivated to protect their current wealth, depending on the incentives, and taking risks could result in personal losses. A new variant on agency theory, called behavioral agency theory, suggests CEOs are conflicted about stock options, tempted to both be risky to accumulate future wealth but also tempted to be conservative to protect current wealth.[71] Actually, riskiness and time horizon (short term, long term) may depend on how much stock-related wealth is accumulated and how much opportunity is provided to accumulate additional wealth through actions that would maximize the payout of recent stock option grants.[72] Other research suggests that as CEO tenure with a company increases, it may be that less pay at risk is preferred because of accumulated firm-specific wealth and the desire to avoid taking actions that would put that wealth at risk. In contrast, a new CEO might prefer greater risk and upside earnings potential.[73]

As further evidence of this self-motivated behavior, consider the following description (based on one person's view) of how executives ensure themselves high compensation.[74] The description comes from the experience of a well-known executive compensation consultant, now turned critic, who specialized for years in the design of executive compensation packages:

1. *If the CEO is truly underpaid:* A compensation consultant is hired to survey actual competitors of the company. The consultant reports to the board of directors that the CEO is truly underpaid. Salary is increased to a competitive or higher level.
2. *If the CEO is not underpaid and the company is doing well:* A compensation consultant is hired. Specific companies are recommended to the consultant as appropriate for surveying. The companies tend to be selected because they are on the top end in terms of executive compensation. The consultant reports back to the board that its CEO appears to be underpaid. Salary is increased.
3. *If the CEO is not underpaid and the company is doing poorly:* A compensation consultant is hired. The CEO laments with the consultant that wages are so low for top management that there is a fear that good people will start leaving the company and going to competitors. Of course, no one ever asks why

the company is underperforming if it has such a good management team. Anyway, the result is that the consultant recommends a wage increase to avoid future turnover.

In each of these scenarios CEO pay manages to increase.

Despite this jaundiced view of the compensation determination process, agency theory argues that executive compensation should be designed to ensure that executives have the best interests of stockholders in mind when they make decisions.[75] Consistent with this logic, as we have seen, almost all companies now design executive compensation plans such that the vast majority of pay is tied closely to performance through short-term and long-term incentive plans and almost all companies receive the strong support of shareholders (through say-on-pay votes) to design executive pay plans in this way. As we have also seen, there is compelling evidence that the resulting alignment between shareholder return and executive pay is very strong.[76]

Scientists and Engineers in High-Tech Industries

Scientists and engineers are classified as **professionals.** According to the Fair Labor Standards Act, this category includes any person who has received special training of a scientific or intellectual nature and whose job does not entail more than a 20 percent time allocation for lower-level duties. If you take a look at firms hiring scientists and engineers, they struggle to figure out what pay should be. For example, one of the authors recently worked with a company that recently purchased land in Texas and Oklahoma for oil and gas exploration. This was the first venture south of the Mason-Dixon line. Should they pay those petroleum engineers the same as they pay their engineers in the Marcellus shale in Pennsylvania? Should they pay the market rate in Texas or Oklahoma? But given the layoff of over 100,000 employees in the Texas/Oklahoma oil industry because of falling gas prices, wouldn't wages reported on recent salary surveys be hugely overstated? You can begin to see the complexity. Some experts argue that salaries are beginning to lag compared to common comparisons like pharmacists, and this is causing drops in demand for engineering training.[77] To restore our lead in the generation of scientific knowledge, more attention needs to be paid to knowledge workers who should be paid for their special scientific or intellectual training. Here, though, lies one of the special compensation problems that scientists and engineers face. Consider the freshly minted electrical engineer who graduates with all the latest knowledge in the field. For the first few years after graduation this knowledge is a valuable resource on engineering projects where new applications of the latest theories are a primary objective. Gradually, though, this engineer's knowledge starts to become obsolete, and team leaders begin to look to newer graduates for fresh ideas. If you track the salaries of engineers and scientists, you will see a close parallel between pay increases and knowledge obsolescence (**Exhibit 14.15**). Early years bring larger-than-average increases (relative to employees in other occupations). After 10 years, increases drop below average, and they become downright puny in 15 to 20 years.

Partly because salary plateaus arise, many scientists and engineers make career changes such as moving into management or temporarily leaving business to update their technical knowledge. In recent years some firms have tried to deal with the plateau effect and also accommodate the different career motivations of mature scientists and engineers. The answer is something called **a dual-career ladder. Exhibit 14.16** shows a typical dual career ladder.

Notice that dual ladders provide exactly that: two different ways of progressing in an organization, each reflecting different types of contributions to the organization's mission. The managerial ladder offers a promotion path with increasing responsibility for management of people. The professional track rises with increasing technical responsibility. At some point in a scientist's career, the choice to opt for one or the other track arises. The idea is that talented technical people shouldn't feel that they have to take management jobs in order to advance in their careers, that they can advance through the excellence of their technical work. The titles are different in each ladder, but pay and perquisites are supposed to be comparable across the rungs.[78]

A second problem in designing the compensation package of scientists and engineers centers on the question of equity. The very nature of technical knowledge and its dissemination requires the relatively close association of these employees across organizations. They mingle at trade association meetings. They keep in touch and cross-fertilize knowledge by discussing recent developments in the field. Scientists and engineers tend to compare themselves for equity purposes with graduates who entered the labor market when they did. Partially because of this and partially because of the volatile nature of both jobs and salaries in these occupations, organizations rely very heavily on external market data in pricing scientists' and engineers' base pay.[79] The result is the use of something called **maturity curves** (**Exhibit 14.15** again).

Maturity curves reflect the relationship between scientist/engineer compensation and years of experience in the labor market. Generally, surveying organizations ask for information about salaries as a function of years since the incumbent(s) last received a degree. This is intended to measure the half-life of technical obsolescence. In fact, a plot of this data, with appropriate smoothing to eliminate aberrations, typically shows curves that are steep for the first 5 to 7 years and then rise more gradually as technical obsolescence erodes the value of jobs. **Exhibit 14.15** illustrates such a graph with somewhat greater sophistication built into it, in that different graphs are constructed for different levels of performance. To construct such graphs, the surveying

EXHIBIT 14.15 **Maturity Curve: Relative Salary by Years Since Degree and Performance**

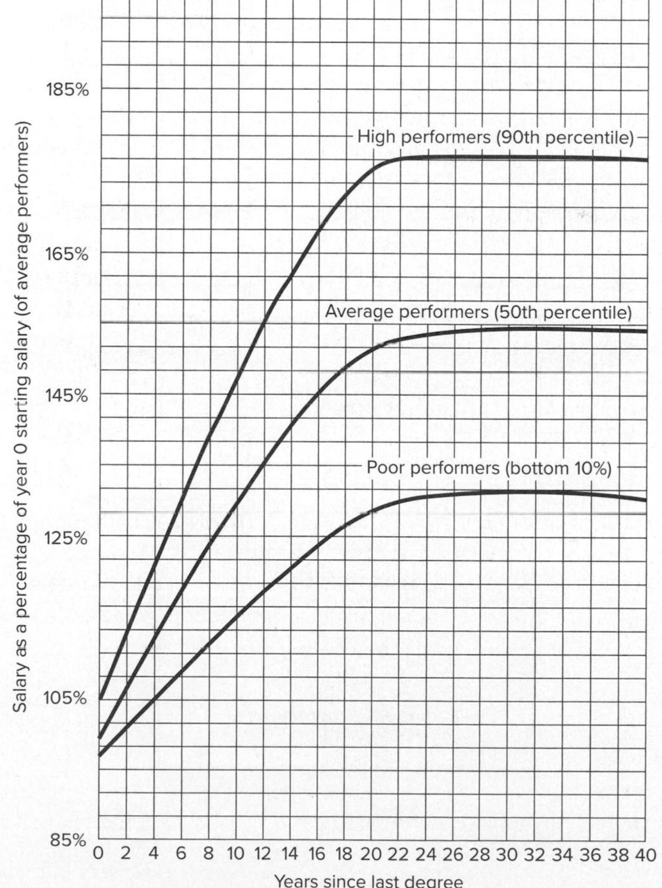

organization must also ask for data broken down by broad performance levels. Notice in the illustration that the high performers begin with somewhat higher salaries and the differential continues to broaden over the first few years.

Scientists and engineers also receive compensation beyond base pay. More than half get a bonus either linked to company profits or personal performance. The incentives, though, tend to be small, averaging less than 5 percent of pay. Other incentives link payment of specific cash amounts to completion of specific projects on or before agreed-upon deadlines. Post-hiring bonuses are also paid for such achievements as patents, publications, elections to professional societies, and attainment of professional licenses.[80]

Finally, organizations have devoted considerable creative energy to development of perks that satisfy the unique needs of scientists and engineers. These perks include flexible work schedules, large offices, campus-like environments, and lavish athletic facilities. The strategic importance of these groups dictates that both mind and body be kept active.

EXHIBIT 14.16 IBM Dual Ladders

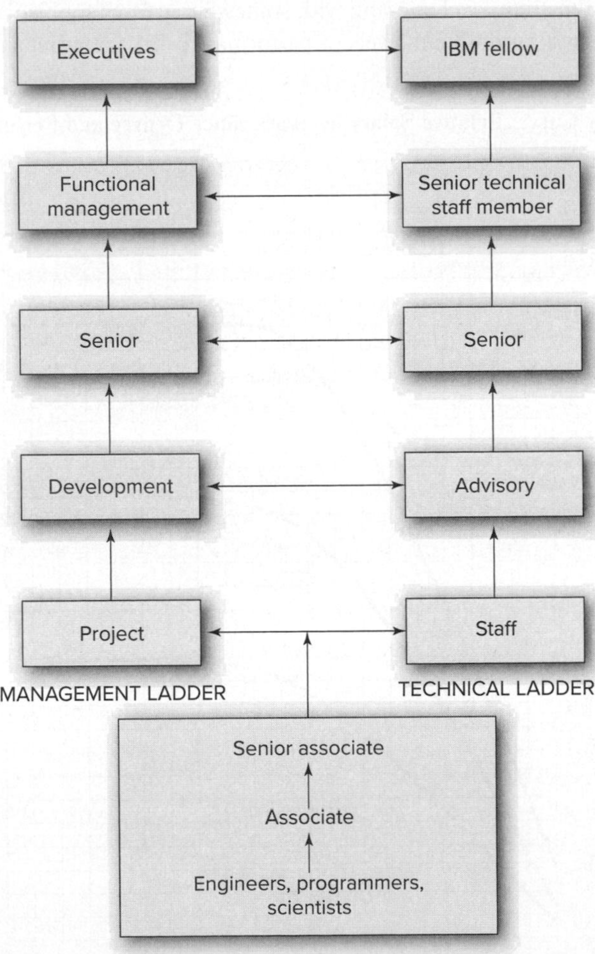

Sales Forces

The sales staff spans the all-important boundary between the organization and consumers of the organization's goods or services. To meet this need in an increasingly complex environment, the sales job has morphed into a variety of forms. For example, the job can be outsourced and called either indirect sales force or manufacturing reps or even simply independent reps. If the sales job remains in-house it can still be broken down by inside or outside sales reps. Inside reps perform sales calls (the dreaded cold calls included in this) or sales support functions. Outside reps generally travel and visit potential customers.[81] The role of interacting in the field with customers requires individuals with high initiative who can work under low supervision for extended periods of time. The standard compensation system is not designed for this type of job. As you might expect, there is much more reliance on incentive payments tied to individual performance. Thus, even when salespeople are in the field–and relatively unsupervised–there is always a motivation to perform. If the product is in high demand, and "sales ability" isn't a difference maker, the compensation mix is mostly base salary with a small incentive component. However, as the sales person's ability becomes more important, the size of the incentive component rises significantly. Think about the last door-to-door salesperson you saw (if ever). That is a tough sale, no matter what the product. Here the incentive component is likely to be large. The typical sales job has a base/incentive ratio of somewhere between 55/45 and 60/40.[82]

Designing a Sales Compensation Plan

Six major factors influence the design of sales compensation packages: (1) the nature of people who enter the sales profession, (2) organizational strategy, (3) market maturity, (4) competitor practices, (5) economic environment, and (6) product to be sold.

The Nature of the People Popular stereotypes of salespeople characterize them as being heavily motivated by financial compensation.[83] One study supports this perception, with salespeople ranking pay significantly higher than five other forms of reward. In the study, 78 percent of the salespeople ranked money as the number-one motivator, with recognition and appreciation being ranked as the number-two motivator.[84] Promotional opportunities, sense of accomplishment, personal growth, and job security were all less highly regarded. These values almost dictate that the primary focus of sales compensation should be on direct financial rewards (base pay plus incentives).

Organizational Strategy A sales compensation plan should link desired behaviors of salespeople to organizational strategy.[85] This is particularly true in the Internet age. As more sales dollars are tied to computer-based transactions, the role of sales personnel will change.[86] Salespeople must know when to stress customer service and when to stress volume sales. And when volume sales are the goal, which products should be pushed hardest? Strategic plans signal which behaviors are important. For example, emphasis on customer service to build market share or movement into geographic areas with low potential may limit sales volume (see cell labeled New Concept Selling). Ordinarily, sales representatives under an incentive system will view customer service as an imposition, taking away from moneymaking sales opportunities. And woe be to the sales supervisor who assigns a commission-based salesperson to a market with low sales potential. Salespeople who are asked to forgo incentive income for low-sales tasks should be covered under a compensation system with a high base pay and small incentive component. **Exhibit 14.17** outlines the strategy as a function of type of buyers.

Alternatively, an organization may want to motivate aggressive sales behavior. A straight commission-based incentive plan will focus sales efforts in this direction, to the possible exclusion of supportive tasks such as processing customer returns. Such incentive plans include both a statement about the size of the incentive and a discussion of the performance objective necessary to achieve the incentive.[87] Typical performance measures include overall territory volume, market share, number of product placements in retail stores, number of new accounts, gross profit, percentage of list-price attainment (relative to other salespeople in the organization), consistency of sales results, expense control, productivity per square foot (especially popular in retail stores), and bad debt generated by sales.[88] Each measure, of course, corresponds to a different business goal. For example, an organization might use a volume measure such as number of units, orders, invoices, or cash received if the business goal is to increase sales growth. Alternatively, if the goal is profit improvement, the appropriate measurement would be gross margin on sales or price per unit. Percentage account erosion would be stressed if improved account retention became a major focus of attention, while customer satisfaction indices are increasingly popular because of greater emphasis on quality. A good sales plan also factors in the KISS principle: Keep It Simple Stupid. Few plans have more than four sales objectives. The most common plan has three components (30%). Twenty-five percent of sales plans have two sales components.[89]

Generally, there are two types of sales compensation plans: (1) unit rate plans and (2) add-on plans.[90] Unit rate plans differ by the amount they pay for each unit of sales. Flat commissions have the same rate for each unit sold (e.g., $8 for each sale). Ramped commissions have one rate up to a target level, then a higher rate tied to more difficult "above-target" sales (e.g., 4 percent of the first $100,000 in sales, 6 percent thereafter). Declining commissions offer one rate up to a target level, then lesser rates thereafter. One of our authors bought a whole life insurance plan in 1972 (yes, he's very old). The agent got 100 percent of the first year residual and then declining amounts in following years. These declining amounts reflect the reduction in work the sales person must do in later years of the plan. Finally, with pooled commissions, a plan recognizes that a sales person works as part of a team. Your stockbrokers get a large chunk of the commission you pay to have them make investment decisions, but they also share with various assistants and market analysts who provide vital information on stock trends. Or, an organization can even have sales teams, individuals working together to sell services or products. There is evidence that sales teams shouldn't be any larger than two people, and they sell better when the team incentive component isn't too large relative to the individual component or base salary.[91] The second type of sales compensation plan tries to get sales staff to focus on specific types of sales. We've just introduced a new line of suits at a high-end men's clothing store. The sales staff gets an extra incentive for each sale of that line. Usually this stress on one product is short-lived, and then the focus turns to yet another sales item.[92]

Market Maturity As the market of a product matures, the sales pattern for that product will change, and companies need to adapt the compensation for their sales force accordingly.[93] A recent study showed that with maturing markets, companies move toward a more conservative sales pattern, focusing even more on customer satisfaction and retention. This leads companies to employ more conservative, rather than aggressive, salespeople, who can comply with the companies' customer retention plans. In maturing markets,

EXHIBIT 14.17 **Sales Strategy Matrix**

		Sales Strategy Mix	
Buyers	Prospects	*Conversion Selling* **(grow base)**	*New Concept Selling* **(develop markets)**
	Customers	*Retention Selling* (protect base)	*Penetration Selling* (penetrate accounts)
		Existing	**New/Additional In-Line**
		Prospects	

Source: Colletti, Jerome A., and Fiss, Mary S., "Sales Compensation," in Lance A. Berger and Dorothy R. Berger, eds., *The Compensation Handbook* (New York: McGraw-Hill, 2008), pp. 239–257.

companies focus both on performance-based pay tied to customer satisfaction and on greater base salaries to retain conservative salespeople.[94]

Competitor Practices In selecting an appropriate pay level, organizations should recognize that external competitiveness is essential. The very nature of sales positions means that competitors will cross paths, at least in their quest for potential customers. This provides the opportunity to chat about relative compensation packages, an opportunity which salespeople will frequently take.

Economic Environment The economic environment also affects the way a compensation package is structured. In good economic climates with roaring sales, companies can afford to hire mid- and low-level sales personnel to capture the extra sales. In a recession environment, however, companies need to react to the decreasing level of sales by focusing more on the top-level performers and rewarding those that achieve high levels of sales despite the economic downturn.

Product to Be Sold The nature of the product or service to be sold may influence the design of a compensation system. For a product that, by its very technical nature, is difficult to understand, it will take time to fully develop an effective sales presentation. Such products are said to have high barriers to entry, meaning considerable training is needed to become effective in the field. Compensation in this situation usually includes a large base-pay component, thus minimizing the risk a sales representative will face, and an encouraging entry into the necessary training program. At the opposite extreme are products with lower barriers to entry, where the knowledge needed to make an effective sales presentation is relatively easy to acquire. These product lines are sold more often using a higher incentive component, thus paying more for actual sales than for taking the time to learn the necessary skills.

Products or services that sell themselves, where sales ability isn't as crucial, inspire different compensation packages than do opportunities where the salesperson is more prominent. Base compensation tends to be more important with easily sold products. Not surprisingly, incentives become more important when willingness to work hard may make the difference between success and failure. Clearly, figuring out what that sales target should be is a major challenge. Too easy a target and the sales staff receive undeserved compensation. An impossible target, in contrast, can be demotivating. One survey puts correct goal setting as the number one challenge in program design (57 percent of respondents). The second biggest challenge is making the forecast of expected sales as accurate as possible (35 percent). The linkage between these two issues is clear. Bad forecasts lead to inaccurate goals. A local oil and gas company found this out the hard way. Salespeople received incentives for finding customers to become limited partners in oil and gas exploration. Sales quotas based on gas priced at $4 per gallon made sales easy. When gas dropped below $3, the quotas became impossible to meet.[95]

Most jobs do not fit the ideal specifications for either of the two extremes represented by straight salary or straight commission plans. A combination plan is intended to capture the best of both these plans. A guaranteed straight salary can be linked to performance of nonsales functions such as customer service, while a commission for sales volume yields the incentive to sell. A plan combining these two features signals the intent of the organization to ensure that both types of activities occur in the organization.

A final caveat, though, in incentive system design. Salespeople are famous for finding loopholes in sales incentive plans and "milking" them for personal profit. For example, if you design a sales plan based on unit sales, and don't prioritize sales, the staff will sell the easiest items at the expense of more profitable items that are harder to sell. Or beware the incentive plan that works too well: During Hurricane Sandy in 2012, Uber (car service) saw an opportunity to help stranded New Yorkers. They incentivized drivers to brave the horrible road conditions by doubling tolls. The plan worked–drivers went out. But the plan was also a PR nightmare. Customers blitzed social media with complaints about price gouging. Uber responded by dropping rates but bumping up base compensation to get drivers on the road. Beware of your incentive plan! It may not do what you want it to.

Contingent Workers and Workers under Alternative Work Arrangements (Including Independent Contractors, Gig Workers)

Explaining work classifications in the new economy is a challenge.[96] At the end of **Chapter 13**, we provided some basic statistics on the prevalence of contingent and alternative work arrangements. Wages vary. For example, working through a temporary-help agency usually means low pay in administrative or day labor positions. In contrast, the wages for an independent contractor might be higher than those for a more permanently employed counterpart. Indeed, independent contractors are sometimes people who have been downsized and then reemployed by the company. When DuPont cut its workforce by 47,000, about 14,000 of these workers were subsequently hired as vendors or contractors.[97] Alternatively, some companies regularly rely on nonemployees. For example, Bloomberg Business reports that about one-half of Google workers are "contractors," not employees.[98] Because the employment status of contingent workers is temporary and employee benefits are less or nonexistent, wages at times tend to compensate by being somewhat higher.

Be careful, though, in the way you define the status of your contingent workers. It simply isn't enough to declare them temporary or consultant status and, ipso facto, it's true. In **Chapter 17**, we talk about legal pitfalls using Microsoft and FedEx as examples.

Why the move to contingent workers? One answer may signal a permanent change in the way we do business. As we came out of the "Great Recession," companies were not hiring at the level we would expect. Rather, they were taking on contractor and/or temporary workers as a way to insulate themselves in a volatile economy. Temp workers afford a level of flexibility that allows expansion and contraction of the workforce in response to market changes. Employers tend to be cautious in such circumstances. Their first move is to hire temps to satisfy greater customer demand. Of course, these temporary workers would rather be hired permanently. And this clearly could affect long-term loyalty and morale.[99] One summary of almost 100 studies of contingent workers showed lower levels of job satisfaction for part-timers and temps but levels comparable to full-time workers for contract employees.[100] But the arguments for hiring temps are persuasive. Usually the wages and benefits are lower and often the productivity is higher.[101] And terminating a non-employee does not necessarily have as negative of an impact on employee relations as terminating an employee.

A major compensation challenge for contingent workers, as with all our special-group employees, is identifying ways to deal with equity problems. Contingent workers may work alongside permanent workers yet often receive lower wages and benefits for the same work. Employers deal with this potential source of inequity on two fronts, one traditional and one that challenges the very way we think about employment and careers. One company response is to view contingent workers as a pool of candidates for more permanent hiring status. High performers may be moved off contingent status and afforded more employment stability. Cummins Engine, for example, is famous for its hiring of top-performing contingent workers. The traditional reward of a possible "promotion," then, becomes a motivation to perform. Another part of the equity challenge is to actually classify a worker correctly.

A second way to look at contingent workers is to champion the idea of boundaryless careers.[102] At least for high-skilled contingent workers, it is increasingly popular to view careers as a series of opportunities to acquire valuable increments in knowledge and skills. In this framework, contingent status isn't a penalty or cause of dissatisfaction. Rather, employees who accept the idea of boundaryless careers may view contingent status as part of a fast-track developmental sequence. Lower wages are offset by opportunities for rapid development of skills—opportunities that might not be so readily available in more traditional employment arrangements. Companies like General Electric that promote this reward—enhanced employability status through acquisition of highly demanded skills—may actually have tapped an underutilized reward dimension.

However, there are also high-paid "gig" workers.[103] According to the U.S. Bureau of Labor Statistics, "a gig describes a single project or task for which a worker is hired, often through a digital marketplace, to work on demand." A gig can be a short-term job as an employee, and some gigs can be self-employment. Consider the case of James Knight, who recently left his full-time job as a programmer at Google to do freelance programming. That meant leaving behind Google's famously extensive benefits package and a secure job and income. He was willing to do that because he believes he can earn twice as much money writing code for dating and other apps while having the flexibility to "travel to Spain and hopscotch across Europe." The Bureau of Labor Statistics notes that gigs are not new, but that "companies connecting workers with these jobs through websites or mobile applications (more commonly known as apps) is a more recent development." Uber, Lyft, Airbnb, Amazon Flex, and Freelancer are some of the better-known examples, mostly of gig work that does not pay as well.

Another example of a highly paid gig worker is Martin Langhoff, 39, formerly a chief technology officer for an organization. He grew tired of the "bureaucracy and endless meetings" that some people view as part of the deal for employees of big companies, and wanted to have more flexibility and be able to focus more on writing code. Now, his services are available through 10X, and he can sometimes be found writing code aboard the 41-foot sailboat that, in line with the sharing economy, he shares with other owners. He recently helped develop a security product for a large U.S. company. Langhoff says he earns 50 percent more than when he had a traditional job.

McKinsey estimates that roughly 70 percent of gig workers ("free agents" and "casual earners") prefer that arrangement, whereas the remaining 30 percent ("reluctants" and "financially strapped") would choose traditional full-time jobs if they were available. A study of Uber drivers also indicates that many are attracted to the flexibility. Specifically, for many, driving is not their primary job, but rather is something they can scale up or down, depending on their income from their primary job and/or depending on their income goals.[104] In the case of the freelance programmers we discussed here, the gig route again seems to be their preference. That is an important fact for organizations to recognize as they think about how to sustain their access to human capital in the long run and what its cost will be, especially where it is valuable and/or scarce. For other types of employees with less valuable and/or scarce human capital (and thus with less leverage to choose whether to be a gig worker or not), organizations will need to consider whether the potential cost savings and flexibility of such a model outweigh what may be lost in terms of employee commitment and the development of uniquely valuable organization-specific skills. Organizations will also need to consider how evolving regulation of the gig economy and workers may affect their choices going forward. (More on this in **Chapter 17.**)

Your Turn

A Sports Sales Plan

The Buffalo Bisons are a Triple A affiliate of the Toronto Blue Jays. Players on this team are one level below the Major Leagues where salaries can be huge. In the early days of the team's most recent incarnation, sell outs were very common. Filling almost 20,000 seats was fairly easy in the early 90's when the stadium was still new and the team was a perennial contender. In recent years, the selling effort has become more difficult. Typical attendance is about 8,000 per game. (The following information is a fictional, but realistic, account of the sales plan used by the Bisons.)

The VP of Operations, Michael Salamone, wants to design a sales incentive plan that will reinvigorate the fan base for the Bisons. He recognizes several realities:

1. Three staff members serve as full-time sales agents. They have two major jobs:
   a. Sell tickets to games. Because the Bisons had a weak team last year, projections are that it will be difficult to exceed an average of 14,000 seats no matter what the plan design is. Further, architecture of the stadium makes sales above 12,000 more challenging because the seats are not as desirable. If last year is any indication, fans will buy less expensive seats, then switch to premium seats that are unoccupied after the game begins. For PR reasons, staff look the other way when this occurs, unless late-arriving fans find their seats occupied. The goal for Mike Salamone is to focus on sale of premium seats, thus reducing the "seat shifting" by fans buying standard and bleacher seats. Statistics for last year are as follows:

Type of Seat	Cost to Fan	Number of These Seats	Average Paid Occupancy
Premium	$12	6,000	1,500
Standard	$9	13,000	6,000
Bleacher	$7	1,900	500

   b. Sell advertising—Advertising dollars come from placement of product information throughout the stadium, including on billboards, outfield fences, scoreboards, even dugout roofs. The dollar amount sold last year was $908,013.
2. Increases in advertising sales are dependent on team performance. Team performance drives ticket sales. In turn, advertising depends on number of seats sold.
3. The three staff members are heavily dependent on the total administrative team (seven other individuals) for ancillary activities in the selling event (e.g., they send out brochures, answer phone queries, provide follow-up information after the initial sales contact, etc.). Mike Salamone wants to have a simple plan for advertising sales that rewards the total group yet still motivates the three sales staff.

QUESTIONS:

1. Of the above information, what is most important in your design of a sales incentive plan for the three sales staff? How does this information affect your plan design?
2. Your book talks about unit rate plans. Which of these types of plan would you use for sales of tickets? Which plan might be appropriate for sales of advertising? Why?
3. What factors influence the dollar amount you can pay for increases in ticket sales?

Summary

Special groups are portrayed here as sharing two common characteristics: They all have jobs with high potential for conflict, and resolution of this conflict is central to the goals of the organization. Probably because of these characteristics, special groups receive compensation treatment that differs from the approach for other employees. Unfortunately, most of this compensation differentiation is prescriptive in nature (i.e., all we have is opinion to guide us, not hard data), and little is known about the specific roles assumed by special groups and the functions compensation should assume in motivating appropriate performance. Future practice and research should focus on answering these questions.

Review Questions

1. We read an article the other day that said it's getting harder to find good people willing to serve on a corporate board of directors. Given what you learned in this chapter, speculate on why it's hard to attract good people to this job.
2. What makes professional/scientist jobs different, such that they qualify for special group status in many companies? Why is the compensation of knowledge workers so frequently linked to the amount of time these workers have been out of school?
3. The differential between the salary of top executives and the lowest paid workers in the same country is quite small in Japan, at least in comparison to the United States. The same is true in unions (president of union versus union workers). Explain why the differential might be small in Japan and in U.S. unions but much larger in private U.S. corporations.
4. Romance Novels, Inc., located in Cheektowaga, NY, has gradually increased the number of contingent workers (full-time, temporary) from 10 percent of the workforce to about 28 percent today. Why might they do this? Also, what equity problems can arise from hiring contingent workers, especially when they work alongside regular employees?
5. Why is it easier to explain a $2 million payout to Jordan Spieth for working four days to win a Masters Championship than it is to explain why William Clay Ford made $30 million as CEO of Ford Motor Company?

Endnotes

1. P. Frost, "Handling the Pain of Others: The Hidden Role of Supervisors," *Canadian HR Reporter,* April 7, 2003, pp. 7–8.
2. IOMA, *Pay for Performance Report,* May 2000, p. 6.
3. Jesse Rhodes, "Historic Norms Return to Board Pay," 2013–14 Director Compensation Report. NACD Directorship March/April, 2014.
4. David Zhu and James Westpahl, "How Directors' Prior Experience with Other Demographically Similar CEOs Affects Their Appointments onto Corporate Boards and the Consequences for CEO Compensation," *Academy of Management Journal* 57(3), 2014, pp. 791–813.
5. G. Strauss, "$228,000 for a Part-Time Job? Apparently, That's Not Enough," *USA Today,* March 4, 2011, p. A1.
6. Iness Aguir, Natasha Burns, Sattar Mansi, and John Waki, "Liability Protection, Director Compensation, and Incentives," *Journal of Financial Intermediation* 23(4), October 2014, pp. 570–589.
7. Gary Strauss, "Part-Time Job Pays $240,000," http://www.usatoday.com/story/money/business/2014/09/23/big-company-director-pay-now-up-to-nearly-240000-a-year/16113497/, visited May 4, 2015; Emily Glazer and Joann Lublin, "Funds Get Active Over Director Pay," *Wall Street Journal,* May 21, 2013, p. B1.
8. Willis Towers Watson, "S&P 500 Director Compensation Trends in 2020." December 15, 2020. www.willistowerswatson.com.
9. Ibid.
10. See CEO Pay exhibit that follow below shortly. See also: EY Center for Board Matters, "Corporate Governance by the Numbers." The general location for such reports is www.ey.com/boardmatters. The specific location for this report is https://assets.ey.com/content/dam/ey-sites/ey-com/en_us/topics/board-matters/ey-cgbtn-december-2020.pdf.

11. Ibid.
12. "Americans and CEO Pay: 2016 Public Perception Survey on CEO Compensation," Rock Center for Corporate Governance, Stanford University, www.gsb.stanford.edu/cgri.
13. "CEOs and Directors on Pay: 2016 Survey on CEO Compensation," Rock Center for Corporate Governance, Stanford University, www.gsb.stanford.edu/cgri.
14. A. J. Nyberg, I. Fulmer, B. Gerhart, and M. A. Carpenter, "Agency Theory Revisited: CEO Returns and Shareholder Interest Alignment," *Academy of Management Journal* 53 (2010), pp. 1029–1049.
15. Yuval Deutsch, Thomas Keil, and Tom Laamanen, "A Dual Agency View of Board Compensation: The Joint Effects of Outside Director and CEO Stock Options on Firm Risk," *Strategic Management Journal* 32(2), 2011, pp. 212–227. W. G. Sanders and D. C. Hambrick, "Swinging for the Fences: The Effects of CEO Stock Options on Company Risk Taking and Performance," *Academy of Management Journal*, 50(5) 2007, pp. 1055–1078.
16. *Wall Street Journal*/Mercer CEO Compensation Survey (April 13, 2006).
17. Ingrid Smithey Fulmer, "The Elephant in the Room: Labor Market Influences on CEO Compensation," *Personnel Psychology* 62 (2009), pp. 659–695.
18. Emily Chasan, "Companies Say 'No Way' to 'Say on Pay'," *Wall Street Journal,* August 26, 2014, p. B1.
19. Ibid.
20. Robin Ferracone, "Oracle's Road to Moving the Needle on 'Say on Pay' Votes," Forbes.com, February 26, 2018.
21. Robin Ferracone, "Oracle's Road to Moving the Needle on 'Say on Pay' Votes," Forbes.com, February 26, 2018.
22. Institutional Share Services, "U.S. Compensation Policies Frequently Asked Questions," December 14, 2017, issgovernance.com.
23. Ibid.
24. A. P. Cowen, A. W. King, and J. J. Marcel, "CEO Severance Agreements: A Theoretical Examination and Research Agenda," *Academy of Management Review* 41(1) (2016), pp. 151–169.
25. Justin Baer. Impatient Investors Pressure Buffett as Returns Decline. *Wall Street Journal*, May 1-2, 2021, A1.
26. Joann S. Lublin, "Boards Tie CEO Pay More Tightly to Performance," *The Wall Street Journal,* February 11, 2006, p. A1.
27. Rouen, E. (2020). Rethinking measurement of pay disparity and its relation to firm performance. *The Accounting Review* 95(1), 343–378.
28. Dan Lin and Lu Lin, "The Interplay Between Director Compensation and Ceo Compensation," *International Journal of Business & Finance Research* 8(3), 2014, pp. 11–26.
29. Gary Strauss and Barbar Hansen, "Median Pay for CEOs of 100 Largest Companies Rose 25%," *USA Today,* April 10, 2006, p. B1.
30. Ingrid Smithey Fulmer, "The Elephant in the Room: Labor Market Influences on CEO Compensation," *Personnel Psychology* 62 (2009), pp. 659–695.
31. Seemantini Pathak, Robert E. Hoskisson, and Richard A. Johnson, "Settling Up in CEO Compensation: The Impact of Divestiture Intensity and Contextual Factors in Refocusing Firms," *Strategic Management Journal* 35(8), August 2014, pp. 1124–1143; Marc Van Essen, Jordan Otten, and Edward J. Carberry, "Assessing Managerial Power Theory: A Meta-Analytic Approach to Understanding the Determinants of CEO Compensation," *Journal of Management* 41(1), 2015,

pp. 164–202; J. Bizjak, M. Lemmon, and T. Nguyen, "Are All Ceos Above Average? An Empirical Analysis of Compensation Peer Groups and Pay Design," *Journal of Financial Economics* 100(3) (2011), pp. 538–555.

32. Ibid.
33. Bruce R. Ellig, *The Complete Guide to Executive Compensation* (New York: McGraw-Hill, 2014).
34. FW Cook, "2016 Annual Incentive Plan Report," January 2017, https://www.fwcook.com/content/documents/publications/1-16-17_FWC_2016_Incentive_Plan_Report.pdf. As of April 2021, this was the most recent annual incentive report.
35. FW Cook, "2016 Annual Incentive Plan Report," January 2017, https://www.fwcook.com/content/documents/publications/1-16-17_FWC_2016_Incentive_Plan_Report.pdf, p. 13.
36. Bruce R. Ellig, *The Complete Guide to Executive Compensation* (New York: McGraw-Hill, 2014).
37. Bruce R. Ellig, *The Complete Guide to Executive Compensation* (New York: McGraw-Hill, 2014).
38. William Clay Ford Jr., Chairman of the Board, "Notice of 2018 Virtual Annual Meeting of Shareholders and Proxy Statement," March 29, 2018, p. 51, http://s22.q4cdn.com/857684434/files/doc_financials/proxy/Ford-Motor-Company.pdf.
39. FW Cook, 2020 Top 250 Report, October 2020. www.fwcook.com.
40. Ryan Krause, Kimberly A. Whitler, and Matthew Semadeni, "Power to the Principals! An Experimental Look at Shareholder Say-on-Pay Voting," *Academy of Management Journal* 57(1), 2014, pp. 94–115.
41. Floyd Norris, "G. E. Is Latest to Reconfigure Stock Options," *New York Times,* August 1, 2002, *http://www.nytimes.com/2002/08/01/business/01PLAC.html,* October 7, 2009.
42. Scott Thurm and Serena Ng, "Stock Buybacks Propel Executive Bonuses," *Wall Street Journal,* May 6, 2013, p. B1.
43. CEOs and Directors on Pay. 2016 Survey on CEO Compensation. Rock Center for Corporate Governance, Stanford University. www.gsb.stanford.edu/cgri.
44. FW Cook, 2020 Top 250 Report. www.fwcook.com.
45. A. Henderson and J. Fredrickson, "Top Management Team Coordination Needs and the CEO Pay Gap: A Competitive Test of Economic and Behavioral Views," *Academy of Management Journal* 44(1), 2001, pp. 96–107; A. Simon, *Administrative Behavior,* 2nd ed. (New York: Macmillan, 1957); Conference Board, *Top Executive Compensation* (New York: Conference Board, 1996).
46. *United for a Fair Economy,* "Executive Excess 2007," 14th Annual Compensation Survey, www.faireconomy.org/files/pdf/ExecutiveExcess2007.pdf, August 29, 2007.
47. "Hard Times Haven't Cut What Some Execs Get," *USA Today,* April 12, 2011, pp. 1–2B.
48. Gary Strauss, "Some CEOs Get Cash Allowances," *Wall Street Journal*, May 28, 2014, p. B2.
49. *Forbes Magazine*, http://www.forbes.com/pictures/fhkd45jid/driving-in-style/, visited May 4, 2015.
50. Kathy Kristof, "8 Outrageous Executive Perks," 2011, http://us.lrd.yahoo.com/SIG=10ule8q1e/** http://www.kiplinger.com/.
51. CEO pay landscape in Japan, the U.S. and Europe – 2020 analysis. www.willistowerswatson.com, December 9, 2020.
52. S. Kaplan and J. Rauh, "Wall Street and Main Street: What Contributes to The Rise in The Highest Incomes?" working paper, University of Chicago, 2008.
53. Nathan Vardi. The 25 Highest-Earning Hedge Fund Managers And Traders. forbes.com. April 27, 2018.
54. Robert Frank. 25 highest-paid hedge fund managers made $32 billion in 2020, a record. cnbc.com, February 22, 2021.

55. Steven N. Kaplan, "Are U.S. CEOs Overpaid?" *Academy of Management Perspectives* 22(2), 2008, pp. 5–19.
56. Dimitrije Curcic. The Ultimate Analysis of NBA Salaries [1991-2019]. RunRepeat. runrepeat.com, March 2, 2021.
57. Ibid.
58. Charles O'Reilly, Brian Main, and Graef Crystal, "CEO Compensation as Tournament and Social Comparison: A Tale of Two Theories," *Administrative Science Quarterly* 33, 1988, pp. 257–274.
59. Ibid.
60. Lawrence Mishel and Julia Wolfe. CEO compensation has grown 940% since 1978 Typical worker compensation has risen only 12% during that time. Economic Policy Institute, August 14, 2019. Figure C. www.epi.org.
61. Marc J. Wallace, "Type of Control, Industrial Concentration, and Executive Pay," *Academy of Management Proceedings* (1977), pp. 284–288; W. Lewellan and B. Huntsman, "Managerial Pay and Corporate Performance," *American Economic Review* 60, 1977, pp. 710–720.
62. Seemantini Pathak, Robert E. Hoskisson, and Richard A. Johnson, "Settling Up in CEO Compensation: The Impact of Divestiture Intensity and Contextual Factors in Refocusing Firms," *Strategic Management Journal* 35(8), 2014, pp. 1124–1143; Eliezer M. Fich, Laura T. Starks, and Adam S. Yore, "CEO Deal-Making Activities and Compensation," *Journal of Financial Economics* 114(3), 2014, pp. 471–492; H. L. Tosi, S. Werner, J. Katz, and L. Gomez-Mejia, "A Meta Analysis of CEO Pay Studies," *Journal of Management* 26(2), 2000, pp. 301–339.
63. Peter Kostiuk, "Firm size and Executive compensation," *Journal of Human Resources* 25(1), 2010, pp. 90–105.
64. Ingrid Smithey Fulmer, "The Elephant in the Room: Labor Market Influences on CEO Compensation," *Personnel Psychology* 62, 2009, pp. 659–695.
65. Michele Fabrizi, Christine Mallin, and Giovanna Michelon, "The Role of CEO's Personal Incentives in Driving Corporate Social Responsibility," *Journal of Business Ethics,* 124, 2014, pp. 311–326.
66. Pascual Berone and Luis R. Gomez-Mejia, "Environmental Performance and Executive Compensation: An Integrated Agency-Institutional Perspective," *Academy of Management Journal* 52(9), 2009, pp. 103–126.
67. A. Henderson and J. Fredrickson, "Top Management Team Coordination Needs and the CEO Pay Gap: A Competitive Test of Economic and Behavioral Views," *Academy of Management Journal* 44(1) (2001), pp. 96–107; Charles O'Reilly, Brian Main, and Graef Crystal, "CEO Compensation as Tournament and Social Comparison: A Tale of Two Theories," *Administrative Science Quarterly* 33 (1988), pp. 257–274.
68. C. Daly, J. Johnson, A. Ellstrand, and D. Dalton, "Compensation Committee Composition as a Determinant of CEO Compensation," *Academy of Management Journal* 41(2), 1998, pp. 209–220.
69. B. Ellig, *The Complete Guide to Executive Compensation* (New York: McGraw-Hill, 2002).
70. Daniel J. Miller, "CEO Salary Increases May Be Rational After All: Referents and Contracts in CEO Pay," *Academy of Management Journal* 38(5), 1995, pp. 1361–1385. Kalin Kolev, Robert M. Wiseman, and Luis R. Gomez-Mejia. Do CEOs Ever Lose? Fairness Perspective on the Allocation of Residuals between CEOs and Shareholders. *Journal of Management*, 2017, 43, 610–637.
71. R. M. Wiseman and L. R. Gomez-Mejia, "A Behavioral Agency Model of Managerial Risk-Taking," *Academy of Management Review,* 23, 1998, pp. 133–153.
72. Geoffrey P. Martin, Robert M. Wiseman, and Luis R. Gomez-Mejia, "Going Short-Term or Long-Term?

CEO Stock Options and Temporal Orientation in the Presence of Slack," *Strategic Management Journal* 37 (2016), pp. 2463–2480.

73. Wanrong Hou, Richard L. Priem, and Maria Goranova, "Does One Size Fit All? Investigating Pay-Future Performance Relationships over the 'Seasons' of CEO Tenure," *Journal of Management* 43 (2017), pp. 864–891.
74. Graef S. Crystal, *In Search of Excess: The Overcompensation of American Executives* (Hopewell, NJ: Ecco Press, 1991); L. Bebchuk and J. Fried, "Pay Without Performance," *Academy of Management Perspective,* February 2006, pp. 5–24. A more recent study of how benchmarking interacts with CEO power to influence CEO compensation is: T. Shin, "Fair Pay or Power Play? Pay Equity, Managerial Power, and Compensation Adjustments for CEOs," *Journal of Management* 42(2) (2016), pp. 419–448.
75. B. Ellig, *The Complete Guide to Executive Compensation* (New York: McGraw–Hill, 2002).
76. A. Nyberg, I. S. Fulmer, B. Gerhart, and M. A. Carpenter, "Agency Theory Revisited: CEO Returns and Shareholder Interest Alignment," *Academy of Management Journal* 53 (2010), pp. 1029–1049; B. J. Hall and J. B. Liebman, "Are CEOs Really Paid Like Bureaucrats?" *Quarterly Journal of Economics* 113(3) (1998), pp. 653–691.
77. Leland Teschler, "How to Get More Engineers? Pay Them!" *Machine Design* 78(20), 2006, pp. 10–13.
78. Richard Demers, "Dual Career Ladders," *www.cincomsmalltalk.com/userblogs/rademers/blog-View?showComments=true˜entry=3253517059,* June 16, 2006.
79. http://www.worldatwork.org/waw/community/discussions/discuss.jsp?did=19791, visited October 26, 2012.
80. Jo C. Kail, "Compensating Scientists and Engineers," in *New Perspectives on Compensation,* eds., David B. Balkin and Luis R. Gomez-Mejia (Englewood Cliffs, NJ: Prentice–Hall, 1987), pp. 247–281.
81. Pankaj M. Madhani, "Managing Sales Compensation Across the Economic Cycle: Direct Sales Force Versus Independent Reps," *Compensation & Benefits Review* 46, 2014, pp. 16–24.
82. Ibid.
83. B. Davenport, "Now Is the Time to Redesign Your Sales Comp Plan," *Report on Salary Surveys 2006 Year book* (New York: IOMA, 2006), p. 10–12.
84. Charles Warner, "Recognition and Appreciation Is Vital for Salespeople," www.charleswarner.us/recogsls.htm, April 10, 2003.
85. David J. Cichelli, *Compensating the Sales Force* (New York: McGraw-Hill), 2010.
86. Ibid.
87. V. Kumar, Sarang Sunder, and Robert P. Leone, "Measuring and Managing a Salesperson's Future Value to the Firm," *Journal of Marketing Research* 51(5), 2014, pp. 591–608.
88. David J. Chchelli (ed.) 2011 Sales Compensation Trends Survey© Results, Alexander Group, 2011.
89. Ibid.
90. Ibid.
91. Noah Lim and Hua Chen, "When Do Group Incentives for Salespeople Work?" *Journal of Marketing Research* 51, June 2014, pp. 320–334.
92. David J. Chchelli (ed.), 2011 Sales Compensation Trends Survey© Results, Alexander Group, 2011.
93. Pankaj M. Madhani, "Managing Sales Compensation Across the Economic Cycle: Direct Sales Force Versus Independent Reps," *Compensation & Benefits Review* 46, 2014, pp. 16–24.
94. Bill O'Connell, "Dead Solid Perfect: Achieving Sales Compensation Alignment," *Compensation and Benefits Review* March/April 1996, pp. 41–48.

95. Personal consulting assignment for Jerry Newman.

96. P. Cappelli and J. R. Keller, "Classifying Work in the New Economy," *Academy of Management Review* 38(4), 2013, pp. 575–596.

97. Kim Clark, "Manufacturing's Hidden Asset: Temp Workers," *Fortune,* November 10, 1997, pp. 28–29.

98. Mark Bergen and Josh Eidelson. "Inside Google's Shadow Workforce." Bloomberg Business. July 25, 2018. www.bloomberg.com.

99. Elizabeth G. Olson, "The Rise of the Permanently Temporary Worker," *Fortune,* May 5, 2011, http://management.fortune.cnn.com/2011/05/05/the-rise-of-the-permanently-temporary-worker/, visited online March 25, 2012.

100. Christa L. Wilkin, "I Can't Get No Job Satisfaction: Meta-analysis Comparing Permanent and Contingent Workers," *Journal of Organizational Behavior* 34(1), 2013, pp. 47–64.

101. Andrea Garnero, Stephan Kampelmann, and Francois Rycx, "Part-Time Work, Wages and Productivity: Evidence from Belgian Match Panel Data," *Industrial and Labor Relations Review* 67(3), 2014, pp. 926–955.

102. Jan Aylsworth, "Boundaryless and Protean Careers," Examiner.com, visited October 26, 2012.

103. This section draws on multiple sources: Raymond A. Noe, John R. Hollenbeck, Barry Gerhart, and Patrick M. Wright, *Human Resource Management: Gaining a Competitive Advantage* (Boston: McGraw-Hill/Irwin, 2019); E. Torpey and A. Hogan, "Working in a Gig Economy," U.S. Bureau of Labor Statistics, *Career Outlook*, May 2016, https://www.bls.gov/careeroutlook/2016/article/what-is-the-gig-economy.htm; S. Wang, "Why an Ex-Google Coder Makes Twice as Much Freelancing," *Bloomberg*, January 19, 2016; J. Manyika, S. Lund, J. Bughin, K. Robinson, J. Mischke, and D. Mahajan, "Independent Work: Choice, Necessity, and the Gig Economy," *McKinsey Global Institute*, October 2016.

104. J. V. Hall and A. B. Krueger, "An Analysis of the Labor Market for Uber's Driver-Partners in the United States," *ILR Review* 71(3) 2018, 705–732.

Chapter Fifteen
Union Role in Wage and Salary Administration

Chapter Outline

Although labor unions still influence the workplace and compensation in the United States, especially in certain industries (e.g., government, utilities, transportation, warehousing) and occupations (e.g., education, training, and library; protective services), their presence, specifically in the private sector, is greatly reduced. Union membership has consistently declined since the 1950s, when it peaked at 35 percent of employment, and now, according to the U.S. Bureau of Labor Statistics (BLS), it stands at 10.8 percent overall. However, that overall trend masks an important fact: although 34.8 percent of public sector workers are union members, only 6.3 percent of private sector workers are union members. Just since 1983, in the private sector, the number of workers in unions has dropped from 11.9 million to 7.1 million and the membership rate dropped from 16.8 percent to 6.3 percent.[1]

Four popular explanations are usually offered for this decline: (1) the structure of American industry is changing, and declining industries are the most heavily unionized, whereas growing industries are less so; (2) unionization is declining because workers don't view unions as a solution to their problems; (3) union organizing efforts have declined (this is frequently cited as a reason several large and powerful unions, including the Teamsters, broke off from the AFL-CIO in 2005); and (4) management is taking an increasingly hard stance against unions in general and against union demands in particular.[2] A classic example is management's increasing use of temps to combat unionization. Beyond their use during strikes, temps are now also used to prevent unions from forming and to weaken existing unions.[3] A large portion of this management opposition to unions is spurred by increasing pressure from both domestic and international competitors. Management more frequently resists wage increases that would give nonunion competitors, both domestic and foreign, a competitive price advantage. The end result of these competitive pressures is a decline in the difference between union and nonunion wages. In fact, one study shows that a 10 percent rise in import share (a popular measure of international competition) has the effect of lowering the union wage differential (the difference between union and nonunion wages) by approximately 2 percent.[4]

Such competitive pressures, which started in the 1980s and continue today, have triggered lower-than-normal wage increases in unionized firms and even some wage concessions. As a cost-cutting strategy, in the early part of this century, unions agreed to have two tiers of wages. New workers would be paid less than existing workers, often as little as half as much. We saw an example of a two-tier wage system in the automobile industry in **Chapter 7**. There too, we saw that consistent with the overall trend in private sector union membership, the number of autoworkers represented by the United Automobile Workers (UAW) union has dropped dramatically over time. In general, though, recent improvements in the economy have enabled labor unions to steady things a bit and even make some gains. For example, in 2015, workers at the Big Three automobile companies represented by the UAW, received their first wage increases (3% in 2016 and 3% in 2017) in eight years.[5] Over that preceding eight years, instead of raises, it was variable pay they received such as profit-sharing payments, which, as we know, companies find useful for controlling increases in fixed labor costs. The UAW also was able to negotiate a path for Tier 2 workers in the two-tiered wage structures to achieve Tier 1 worker level wages over time. However, automakers were able to continue to hire new workers at the lower Tier 2 wage of $17/hour (versus a Tier 1 wage level of $28 and up). For example, new hires at Ford will start at $17/hour and progress to $28 after 84 months.[6] In the most recent UAW contracts with the Big Three, negotiated in 2019 and running to 2023, there are pay raises of 3 percent in years 2 and 4 of the contract, which will bring the hourly wage to $32.32. However, in years 1 and 3, there are lump sums (bonuses) of 4 percent instead. There was also a substantial ratification bonus of $11,000 and elimination of the cap of $12,000 on profit-sharing bonuses. Recall that the bonuses to not become part of base pay and thus do not accumulate in higher base pay over time, unlike the (base) pay raises in years 2 and 4. The most recent contracts continue with two-tiered wage structures. Now, current two-tier workers will advance to the Tier 1 wage of $32.32 by year 4 of the contract. Nevertheless, Tier 2 workers hired during the new four-year contract will continue to start at the lower Tier 2 wage and will still take eight years to progress to the Tier 1 wage.[7] However, in years 1 and 3, there are lump sums (bonuses) of 4 percent instead. There was also a substantial ratification bonus of $11,000 and elimination of the cap of $12,000 on profit-sharing bonuses. Recall that the bonuses to not become part of base pay and thus do not accumulate in higher base pay over time, unlike the (base) pay raises in years 2 and 4. The most recent contracts continue with two-tiered wage structures. Now, current two-tier workers will advance to the Tier 1 wage of $32.32 by year 4 of the contract. However, Tier 2 workers hired during the new four-year contract will continue to start at the lower Tier 2 wage and will still take eight years to progress to the Tier 1 wage. As we saw in **Chapter 7**, complete elimination of the two-tier wage system would drive up labor costs for the Big Three U.S. automakers and make it difficult for them to compete with Toyota, Honda, Hyundai, and others. If they cannot compete, they will sell fewer cars and need fewer workers. Thus, the UAW has to balance its goal of wage gains and the traditional core union value of equal pay for equal work against the need to help its members' employers be competitive and provide jobs to its members.

Let us return to the general decline in unionism in the private sector noted above. Despite this decline, roughly one-half (48%) of nonunion workers would support being represented by a union, up from roughly one-third in earlier. The same study also reports that a strong majority (83%) of current union members would vote to support a union again. Some of the issues where nonunion workers would like more voice are in areas like respect for employees, protection from harassment and discrimination, and the ability to provide more input in how to do and improve their jobs, including the impact of technology. However, workers ranked as even more important "bread-and-butter" issues: having increased voice regarding benefits, compensation, opportunities for promotion, and job security. The authors of this study interpret these results to mean "the decline in the number of workers joining unions cannot be attributed to a lack of interest" and suggest instead that "the effectiveness of employer resistance to organizing efforts" (which is commonly viewed as having increased over time) is an important explanation.

You want to invite a unionization effort? Show little respect for employees or concern for their welfare and be unwilling to give them a role in decisions that influence their workplace. And these are not just blue-collar and/or manufacturing, transportation, and construction workers. Just ask the nurses, teachers, physicians, nuclear engineers, psychologists, and judges who have decided to unionize. Unions may be down, but they are not out just yet. Again, you can learn this the hard way by seeing what happens if you do not manage people effectively and/or do not pay wages and benefits that are seen as fair. There does not have to be a union in your workplace for unions to have an influence there. You will find that a union drive to organize your workers will also give you plenty of opportunity to deal with a union and the workers you helped encourage to support it. Just ask Amazon. Although Amazon ended up winning a decisive victory in 2021 against an attempt by the Retail, Wholesale and Department Store Union (RWDSU) to organize its facility in Bessemer, Alabama, it devoted a substantial amount of time, attention, and resources to achieve that outcome. Otherwise, it would have been left to deal with the possibility that once the RWDSU got a foot in the door, it would go after the remaining 800 Amazon U.S. facilities.

THE IMPACT OF UNIONS IN WAGE DETERMINATION

Despite strong management efforts to lessen the impact of unions, they still have an important effect on wages. Even in a nonunion firm, compensation managers will adjust rewards (usually upward) when there is a hint of nearby union activity. This section outlines four specific areas of union impact: (1) impact on general wage and benefit levels, (2) impact on the structure of wages, (3) impact on nonunion firms (also known as **spillover effect**), and (4) impact on wage and salary policies and practices in unionized firms. This chapter's concluding section focuses on union response to the changing economic environment of the 1980s and the alternative compensation systems that have evolved in response to these changes.

e-Compensation

This site gives detailed information about dozens of unions, including specifics of union contracts: **https://irle.berkeley.edu/digital-collection/bargaining/**.

Union Impact on Compensation

Do unions raise wages? Are unionized employees better off than they would be if they were nonunion? Unfortunately, comparing "what is" to "what might have been" is no easy chore, for a variety of reasons–including the fact that union status may be confounded with other (unmeasured) factors (such as individual worker human capital/productivity) that influence wages, benefits, and total compensation. However, we can begin by looking at basic differences in wages, benefits, and total compensation between union and nonunion workers. **Exhibit 15.1** reports the results of two surveys that collect compensation data, one a survey of employees and one a survey of employers/establishments that provide data on their employees. In general, the two surveys indicate that across all types of employees, wages are 19 percent higher for union members than for nonunion employees. The union advantage on benefits is much larger, resulting in a total compensation union advantage of 43 percent. According to the employee survey, the largest union wage advantage is for employees in service or production occupations. In comparison, there is no union wage advantage for management and professional employees. (That, however, does not rule out union-nonunion differences on non-compensation issues, such as voice in how the work is done, staffing level, etc.)

As noted, to infer that the differences between union and nonunion wages are caused by union status would require us to be confident that union and nonunion workers would have received the same pay in the absence of a union. If not, there are alternative explanations. For example, the causality could be that a union organizes an employer and negotiates a higher wage. The employer accordingly responds by raising hiring standards, which results in hiring more productive workers. The less productive workers who would have been employed prior to unionization might eventually disappear. Thus, the union did raise wages at the employer, but did not necessarily raise wages for individual workers over time, which is the goal of the union. Of course,

EXHIBIT 15.1 Compensation, Union versus Nonunion Employees, United States, Worker Survey and Employer Survey

	Worker Survey			
	% in Union	Median Weekly Earnings, Full-Time Workers		
		Union Members	Nonunion	Union/ Nonunion
All	11	$ 1,144	$ 958	1.19
Men	11	1,216	1,051	1.16
Women	11	1,067	862	1.24
Industry				
Public sector	35	1,186	1,022	1.16
Private sector	6	1,089	948	1.15
Occupation				
Management & professional	11	1,313	1,366	.96
Service	11	931	599	1.55
Production, transportation, & material moving	13	954	720	1.33
		Employer Survey (Hourly Rate)		
Total compensation		$49.74	$34.72	1.43
Wages and salaries		29.62	24.84	1.19
Benefits		20.12	9.88	2.04

Sources: Median weekly earnings and percentages in union data based on the Current Population Surveys: U.S. Bureau of Labor Statistics, Union Members–2020, News Release, USDL-21-0081, January 22, 2021; wages/salaries, benefits, and total compensation data, based on a survey of employers, are from U.S. Bureau of Labor Statistics, National Compensation Survey (NCS), Employer Costs for Employee Compensation–September 2020, News Release USDL-20-2266, December 17, 2020; the worker survey includes civilian (private-sector and public-sector) employees. The employer survey includes private-sector employees only.

it is also possible to underestimate the effect of unions on wages. For example, as part of a strategy to remain nonunion, a company may choose to pay higher wages so that wages are not an issue that a union could use in an effort to organize the company's workers. (This is referred to as the union spillover or threat effect on wages.)

One source of continuing data on unionized and nonunionized firms is the Bureau of Labor Statistics. From 1969 to 1985, the union wage premium more than doubled, from 17.6 to 35.6 percent.[8] In 2000, the union wage premium was back down to 26 percent overall, and it was 24 percent in the private sector. In 2017, the union wage premium (based on the worker survey) was 26 percent overall and 21 percent in the private sector. By 2020, as **Exhibit 15.1** shows, the union wage premium was down to 19 percent overall and 16 percent in the private sector. Thus, since 2000, the union wage premium was fairly stable until 2017, but declined as of 2020. We will have to see whether the 2020 decline is temporary, reflecting the influence of the pandemic, or part of a longer-term decline.

Returning to the question of how much of the unadjusted union effect that we see in **Exhibit 15.1** remains after controlling for worker characteristics and other possible covariates, a summary of 114 different studies, albeit mostly older studies during a different labor relations environment, reached the following two conclusions:[9]

1. *Unions do make a difference in wages, across all studies and all time periods.* Union workers earn between 8.9 and 12.4 percent more than their nonunion counterparts, after adjusting for other factors related to union status and wages. So, depending on the time period (see above), one might say that roughly one-third to one-half of the unadjusted union wage premiums shown in **Exhibit 15.1** remain after adjusting for other factors.
2. *The size of the gap varies from year to year.* During periods of higher unemployment, the impact of unions is larger. During strong economies the union–nonunion gap is smaller. Part of the explanation for this time-based phenomenon is related to union resistance to wage cuts during recessions and the relatively slow response of unions to wage increases during inflationary periods (because it's hard to respond quickly when a union is tied to a multiyear labor contract).

More recent evidence likewise concludes the union wage premium remains after attempts to equate union and nonunion worker attributes to the degree possible. This estimate put the adjusted union wage premium at around 15 percent.[10] Whether that too would be somewhat smaller in line with smaller (unadjusted) wage premiums we have seen in 2020 (**Exhibit 15.1**) is not known. Finally, recall that the union premium for total compensation is much larger than the wage premium alone.

e-Compensation

These sites provide union employment and wage information: ***www.unionstats.com*** and ***http://stats.bls.gov/news.release/union2.nr0.htm***

The Structure of Wage Packages

The second compensation issue involves the structuring of wage packages. In particular, results from the employer survey in **Exhibit 15.1** show that the union effect on benefits (a 2.04 union/nonunion ratio) far exceeds the union effect on wages/salaries (a union/nonunion ratio of 1.19). As such, the effect of unions on total compensation (1.43 times higher for union members) also exceeds the union effect on wages/salaries. So not only is the total compensation pie bigger in unionized companies, the share devoted to benefits is bigger too. Typically the higher benefits costs show up in the form of higher pension expenditures or higher insurance benefits. One particularly well-controlled study found unionization associated with a 213 percent higher level of pension expenditures and 136 percent higher health insurance expenditures.[11]

A second dimension of the wage structure issue, as we noted earlier in this chapter (and in **Chapter 7**), is the evolution of **two-tier pay plans.** Basically a phenomenon of the union sector, two-tier wage structures differentiate pay based upon hiring date. A contract is negotiated which specifies that employees hired after a given target date will receive lower wages than their higher-seniority peers working on the same or similar jobs. From management's perspective, wage tiers are a viable alternative compensation strategy. Tiers can be used as a cost control strategy to allow expansion or investment or as a cost-cutting device to allow economic survival.[12] Two-tier pay plans initially spread because unions viewed them as less painful than wage freezes and staff cuts among existing employees. The trade-off, however, was a bargaining away of equivalent wage treatment for future employees. Recognize, this is a radical departure from the most basic precepts of unionization. Unions evolved and continue to endure, in part based on the belief that all members are equal.[13] Two-tier plans are obviously at odds with this principle. The contract may specify that the wage differential may be permanent, or, as we saw with the most recent contract between the UAW and Big Three, the lower tier may be scheduled ultimately to catch up with the upper tier. Eventually the inequity from receiving different pay for the same job usually causes employee dissatisfaction. This is not new. Consider the Roman emperor Carcalla, who implemented a two-tier system for his army in AD 217.[14] He was assassinated by his disgruntled troops shortly thereafter. Although such extreme expressions of dissatisfaction are unlikely today, unions are reluctant to accept a two-tier structure, but may view it as a strategy of last resort to save jobs.

Union Impact: The Spillover (or Threat) Effect

Although union wage settlements have declined in recent years, the impact of unions in general would be understated if we did not account for what is termed the *spillover effect.* Specifically, employers seek to avoid unionization by offering workers the wages, benefits, and working conditions won in rival unionized firms. The nonunion management continues to enjoy the freedom from union "interference" in decision making, and the workers receive the spillover of rewards already obtained by their unionized counterparts. Several studies document the existence of this phenomenon, although smaller as union power diminishes, providing further evidence of the continuing role played by unions in wage determination.[15]

Role of Unions in Wage and Salary Policies and Practices

Perhaps of greatest interest to current and future compensation administrators is the role unions play in administering wages. The role of unions in administering compensation is outlined primarily in the contract. The following illustrations of this role are taken from major collective bargaining agreements.

Basis of Pay

The vast majority of contracts specify that one or more jobs are to be compensated on an hourly basis and that overtime pay will be paid beyond a certain number of hours. Notice the specificity of the language in the following contract clause:

> A. Overtime pay is to be paid at the rate of one and one-half (1 1/2) times the basic hourly straight-time rate.
>
> B. Overtime shall be paid to employees for work performed only after eight (8) hours on duty in any one service day or forty (40) hours in any one service week. Nothing in this section shall be construed by the parties or any reviewing authority to deny the payment of overtime to employees for time worked outside of their regularly scheduled work week at the request of the Employer.
>
> C. Penalty overtime pay is to be paid at the rate of two (2) times the basic hourly straight-time rate. Penalty overtime pay will not be paid for any hours worked in the month of December.
>
> D. Excluding December, part-time flexible employees will receive penalty overtime pay for all work in excess of ten (10) hours in a service day or fifty-six (56) hours in a service week.[16]

Further, many contracts specify a premium be paid above the worker's base wage for working nonstandard shifts:

> Double time will be paid as follows, except as provided in paragraph 4: (a) for time worked on the calendar Sunday; (b) for time worked on the calendar holidays designated in subparagraph (273).[17]

Alternatively, agreements may specify a fixed daily, weekly, biweekly, or monthly rate. In addition, agreements often indicate a specific day of the week as payday and sometimes require payment on or before a certain hour.

Much less frequently, contracts specify some form of incentive system as the basis for pay. The vast majority of clauses specifying incentive pay occur in manufacturing (as opposed to nonmanufacturing) industries:

> *Section 7. Establishment of Labor Standards.* The Company and the Union, being firmly committed to the principle that high wages can result only from high productivity, agree that the Company will establish Labor Standards that:
>
> a. Are fair and equitable to both the Company and the workers; and
>
> b. Are based on the working capacity of a normally qualified worker properly motivated and working at an incentive pace; and
>
> c. Give due consideration to the quality of workmanship and product required; and
>
> d. Provide proper allowances for fatigue, personal time, and normal delays, and
>
> e. Provide for payment of incentive workers based on the earned hours produced on standard (except when such Employees are working on a Preliminary Estimate, etc.), and for each one per cent (1%) increase in acceptable production over standard, such workers shall receive a one per cent (1%) increase in pay over the applicable incentive rate.
>
> The Company will, at its discretion as to the time and as to jobs to be placed on or removed from incentive, continue the earned-hour incentive system now in effect, and extend it to jobs in such other job classifications which, in the opinion of the Company, can properly be placed on incentive, with the objective

of increasing productivity and providing an opportunity for workers to enjoy higher earnings thus made possible. The plan shall be maintained in accordance with the following principles [not shown here].[18]

Occupation-Wage Differentials

Most contracts recognize that different occupations should receive different wage rates. Within occupations, though, a single wage rate prevails:

Occupational Code	Classification	Rate/hr
C5	Sheet and metal fabricator	$19.78
D1	Machinist grind, lap, and hone	20.45
D2	Machinist turn, drill, bore, and mill	20.45
F16	Spot welder	19.78
M26	Miscellaneous processor	18.63

Source: Agreement between John Deere and Company and International Union United Automobile Aerospace and Agricultural Implement Workers of America, October 2015.

Although rare, there are some contracts that do not recognize occupational/skill differentials. These contracts specify a single standard rate for all jobs covered by the agreements. Usually such contracts cover a narrow range of skilled groups.

Experience/Merit Differentials

Single rates are usually specified for workers within a particular job classification. Single-rate agreements do not differentiate wages on the basis of either seniority or merit. Workers with varying years of experience and output receive the same single rate. Alternatively, agreements may specify wage ranges. The following example is fairly typical:

	Years of Experience							
Job Title	**None**	**1**	**2**	**3**	**4**	**6**	**10**	**14**
Computer operators	$14.20	$14.60	$14.88	$15.44	$15.72	$16.02	$17.32	$19.54
Lab assistants	$12.20	$12.50	$12.76	$13.01	$13.32	$13.88	$14.99	$19.13

Source: Negotiated agreement between District School Board of St. Johns County and St. Johns School Support Association.

The vast majority of contracts, as in the example above, specify seniority as the basis for movement through the range. *Automatic progression* is an appropriate name for this type of movement through the wage range, with the contract frequently specifying the time interval between movements. This type of progression is most appropriate when the necessary job skills are within the grasp of most employees. Denial of a raise is rare and frequently is accompanied by the right of the union to grieve the decision.

A second, and far less common, strategy for moving employees through wage ranges is based exclusively on merit. Employees who are evaluated more highly receive larger or more rapid increments than average or poor performers. Within these contracts, it is common to specify that disputed merit appraisals may be submitted to grievance. If the right to grieve is not explicitly excluded, the union also has the implicit right to grieve.

The third method for movement through a range combines automatic and merit progression in some manner. A frequent strategy is to grant automatic increases up to the midpoint of the range and permit subsequent increases only when merited on the basis of performance appraisal.

Of course, it should be kept in mind that even though merit/performance (including the merit increase grids we saw in **Chapters 9** and **10**) may be rarely used in a union setting to determine base pay increases, performance will typically play a significant role in determining which workers are promoted to higher paying jobs, especially jobs not covered by the collective bargaining contract.

Other Differentials

There are a number of remaining contractual provisions that deal with differentials for reasons not yet covered. A first example deals with different pay to unionized employees who are employed by a firm in different geographic areas. Very few contracts provide for different wages under these circumstances, despite the problems that can arise in paying uniform wages across regions with markedly different costs of living.

A second category where differentials are mentioned in contracts deals with part-time and temporary employees. Few contracts specify special rates for these employees. Those that do, however, are about equally split between giving part-time and temporary employees wages above full-time workers (because they have been excluded from the employee benefit program) or below full-time workers.

Vacations and Holidays

Vacation and holiday entitlements are among the clauses frequently found in labor contracts. They, too, use very specific language, as the following example illustrates:

> *26.01 Observance*
>
> The following holidays will be observed:
>
> New Year's Day–First Day in January;
>
> Martin Luther King, Jr.'s Birthday–Third Monday in January;
>
> President's Day–Third Monday in February;
>
> Memorial Day–Last Monday in May;
>
> Juneteenth-19th day of June;
>
> Independence Day–Fourth day of July;
>
> Labor Day–First Monday in September;
>
> Columbus Day–Second Monday in October;
>
> Veterans' Day–Eleventh day of November;
>
> Thanksgiving Day–Fourth Thursday in November;
>
> Christmas Day–Twenty-fifth day of December;
>
> Any other day proclaimed by the Governor of the State of Ohio or the President of the United States.

When a holiday falls on a Sunday, the holiday is observed on the following Monday. When a holiday falls on a Saturday, the holiday is observed on the preceding Friday. For employees whose work assignment is to a seven (7) day operation, the holiday shall be celebrated on the day it actually falls. A holiday shall start at 12:01 A.M. or with the work shift that includes 12:01 A.M.

26.02 Work on Holidays

Employees required to work on a holiday will be compensated at their discretion either at the rate of one and one-half (1 1/2) times their regular rate of pay, or granted compensatory time at the rate of one and one-half (1 1/2) times, plus straight-time pay for the holiday. The choice of compensatory time or wages will be made by the employee. Holiday work beyond regularly scheduled work shall be distributed among employees by the provisions covered in Article 13. No employees' posted regular schedule or days off shall be changed to avoid holiday premium pay. Once posted, the employee's schedule shall not be changed, except that an employee who is scheduled to work on the holiday may be directed not to report to work on the holiday. The Agency reserves the right to determine the number of employees needed to work the holiday.[19]

Wage Adjustment Provisions

Frequently in multiyear contracts some provision is made for wage adjustment during the term of the contract. There are three major ways these adjustments might be specified: (1) deferred wage increases, (2) **reopener clauses,** and (3) **cost-of-living adjustments (COLAs)** or escalator clauses. A *deferred wage increase* is negotiated at the time of initial contract negotiations with the timing and amount specified in the contract. A *reopener clause* specifies that wages, and sometimes such nonwage items as pension and benefits, will be renegotiated at a specified time or under certain conditions. Finally, a *COLA clause,* as noted earlier, involves periodic adjustments based typically on changes in the consumer price index:

Section 4. Cost of Living Adjustment

A. Definitions

1. "Consumer Price Index" refers to the "National Consumer Price Index for Urban Wage Earners and Clerical Workers," published by the Bureau of Labor (1967 = 100) and referred to herein as the "Index."
2. "Consumer Price Index Base" refers to the Consumer Price Index for the month of October 2001 and is referred to herein as the "Base Index."

B. Effective Dates of Adjustment

Each employee covered by this Agreement shall receive cost-of-living adjustments, upward, in accordance with the formula in Section 4.C, below, effective on the following dates:

–the second full pay period after the release of the January 2002 Index

–the second full pay period after the release of the July 2002 Index

–the second full pay period after the release of the January 2003 Index

–the second full pay period after the release of the July 2003 Index

C. The basic salary schedules provided for in this Agreement shall be increased 1 cent per hour for each full 0.4 of a point increase in the applicable Index above the Base Index. For example, if the increase in the Index from October 2011 to January 2012 is 1.2 points, all pay scales for employees covered by this Agreement will be increased by 3 cents per hour. In no event will a decline in the Index below the Base Index result in a decrease in the pay scales provided for in this Agreement.[20]

Role of Unions in Discipline, Job Security, and Assignments

One of the most important purposes of a labor union is to protect its members from arbitrary and capricious treatment by management in the form of unfair discipline, including discharge. Of course, from the perspective of management, it may at times seem that the union seeks to protect all of its members, regardless of their conduct and performance on the job. Our point here is to be sure to make the point that, in contrast to nonunion workers, who with some important exceptions, can be fired at will (but, we strongly recommend you check with a very competent lawyer before contemplating any such action), most union workers cannot be. From management's perspective, that sometimes means that employees whose performance is not what the company feels it needs to compete not only may remain on the job, but will continue to receive wages and all benefits that go with the job. Given that, as we have seen (**Exhibit 15.1**), the total compensation of union members, primarily due to higher benefits, is about twice what nonunion members receive, it is clear that the enhanced job security of union members can translate into a major labor cost (and productivity) problem.

What is the basis for the greater protection of union members from discipline? In the great majority of union contracts, there is a formal grievance procedure that must be followed to discipline an employee (or for such discipline to be upheld). Although similar grievance procedures sometimes exist in nonunion settings also, what is unique and central to the standard union grievance procedure is that if agreement on discipline between union and management cannot be reached in the successive steps of the process, the final decision is made by an independent outside arbitrator and his/her decision is final and binding on the parties. For example, the Agreement between the University of Vermont Medical Center and Vermont Federation of Nurses and Health Professionals (VFNHP), AFT Vermont, AFL-CIO, Local 5221 states under its Article 39, Discipline & Discharge, that "No bargaining unit employee, except for bargaining unit employees in a probationary period, shall be disciplined or discharged except for just cause." If VFNHP feels discipline/discharge was not for just cause, it can file a grievance. The grievance process has four steps. The process ends at whichever step leads to resolution of the grievance. Step 1 is to present the grievance to the employees immediate supervisor. Step 2 is to present the grievance to the next level supervisor. Step 3 is to present the grievance to the Chief Nursing Officer. Step 4 is final and binding arbitration with an arbitrator acceptable to both union and management and the arbitration is conducted in accordance with American Arbitration Procedures.[21]

What types of issues most commonly reach arbitration? Data from the FMCS on a total of 2,473 grievances show that discharge and disciplinary issues topped the list with 913 cases. Other frequent issues include the use of seniority in promotion, layoffs, transfers, work assignments, and scheduling (309 cases); wages (178); and benefits (127).[22] As such, these data indicate that management discretion is not limited by a collective bargaining contract just in the area of discipline/discharge. It may also be limited when it comes to other personnel actions/assignments, including promotions, layoffs, transfers, work assignments, and scheduling. The combined effect may not only be a workforce that is not what management would choose, but also utilization of that workforce in a way that management did not choose. Clearly, these limits on management discretion can have consequences for labor costs, productivity, and other objectives.

UNIONS AND ALTERNATIVE REWARD SYSTEMS (AND VARIABLE PAY)

International competition causes a fundamental problem for unions. If a unionized company settles a contract and raises prices to cover increased wage costs, there is always the threat that an overseas competitor with lower labor costs will capture market share. Eventually, enough market share erosion means the unionized company is out of business. To keep this from happening, unions have become much more receptive in recent years to alternative reward systems that link pay to performance. After all, if worker productivity rises, product prices can remain relatively stable even with wage increases.

Willingness to try such plans is higher when the firm faces extreme competitive pressure and where bargaining is more decentralized (versus national).[23] In the unionized firms that do experiment with these alternative reward systems, though, the union usually insists on safeguards that protect both the union and its workers. The union insists on group-based performance measures with equal payouts to members. This equality principle cuts down strife and internal quarrels among the members and reinforces the principles of equity that are at the very foundation of union beliefs. To minimize bias by the company, performance measures more often tend to be objective in unionized companies. Most frequently the measures rely on past performance as a gauge of realistic targets rather than on some time study or other engineering standard that might appear more susceptible to tampering.[24] Below we offer specific feedback about union attitudes toward alternative reward concepts.

Lump-Sum Awards/Bonuses

As discussed in **Chapter 10**, **lump-sum awards** are one-time cash payments (bonuses) to employees that are not added to an employee's base wages. As such, they are variable pay. These awards are typically given in lieu of merit increases, which are more costly to the employer. This higher cost results both because merit increases are added on to base wages and because several employee benefits (e.g., life insurance and vacation pay) are figured as a percentage of base wages. Lump-sum payments are a reality of union contracts. In recent years, a stable one-third of all major collective bargaining agreements in the private sector have contained a provision for lump-sum payouts. The elements related to compensation, including fixed (base pay increases) and variable (lump sum and other bonuses, profit sharing, and so forth), included in the most recent contract agreed upon by Ford and the UAW (for Tier 1 workers) are shown in **Exhibit 15.2**. We see that there will be base wage increase of 3 percent, but only during two of the four years of the contract. Most of the compensation "action" will be in the form of variable pay: lump sums of 4 percent (again in only two of the four years), modest-sized competitiveness bonuses, inflation protection payments, and profit sharing payments. Again, these are all one-time lump sums/bonuses, representing a firm commitment to keeping fixed labor costs from growing much over time.

Employee Stock Ownership Plans (ESOPs)

An alternative strategy for organizations hurt by intense competition is to control base wages (and perhaps get employees to think more like owners) in exchange for giving employees part ownership in the company.[25] For example, Southwest Airlines has an employee stock ownership plan that, together with its profit-sharing plan, is aimed at aligning employee interests with those of the company. (As we have previously noted, it is important that employee ownership programs not result in too little diversification in employee investment portfolios.)

Pay-for-Knowledge Plans

Pay-for-knowledge plans do just that: pay employees more for learning a variety of different jobs or skills. For example, the UAW negotiates provisions giving hourly-wage increases for learning new skills on different parts of the assembly process. By coupling this new wage system with drastic cuts in the number of job classifications, organizations have greater flexibility in moving employees quickly into high-demand areas. Unions also may favor pay-for-knowledge plans because they make each individual worker more valuable, and less expendable, to the firm. In turn, this also lessens the probability that work can be subcontracted out to nonunion organizations.

Gainsharing Plans

Gainsharing plans are designed to align workers and management in efforts to streamline operations and cut costs. Any cost savings resulting from employees' working more efficiently are split, according to some formula, between the organization and the workers. Some reports indicate gainsharing is more common in unionized than nonunionized firms.[26] In our experience, success is dependent on a willingness to include union members in designing the plan. Openness in sharing financial and production data, key elements of putting a gainsharing plan in place, are important in building trust between the two parties.

While unions aren't always enthusiastic about gainsharing, they rarely directly oppose it, at least initially. Rather, the most common union strategy is to delay taking a stand until real costs and benefits are more apparent.[27] Politically, this may be the wisest choice for a union leader. As **Exhibit 15.3** illustrates, there are numerous possible costs and benefits to union members for agreeing to a gainsharing plan. Until the plan is actually implemented, though, it is unclear what the impact will be in any particular firm.

EXHIBIT 15.2 Fixed and Variable Pay Components of the UAW–General Motors Contract, Tier 1 Workers, by Year

	2015	2016	2017	2018	2019	2020	2021	2022	2023
Ratification bonus	$8,000				$11,000				
Wage increase	3%		3%			3%		3%	
Lump sum bonus		4%		4%	4%		4%		
Profit sharing	TBD	TBD	TBD	TBD	TBD	TBD			
Lump sum performance bonus		$1,000	$1,000	$1,000	$1,000	$1,000	$1,000	$1,000	$1,000
Quality performance payment		TBD	TBD	TBD	TBD	TBD	TBD	TBD	

Source: United Auto Workers, UAW-General Motors Contract Summary: Hourly Workers, November 2015–October 2019.

TBD = To be determined (by formula). Exhibit 15.4 for what actual payouts were up to $500 if quality goals met.

The only fixed pay component is "Wage Increase." All other pay components are variable.

Profit-Sharing Plans

Unions have debated the advantages of profit-sharing plans for at least 80 years.[28] Walter Reuther, president of the CIO in 1948 (which became the AFL-CIO in 1955) championed the cause of profit sharing in the auto industry. In years past, the primary goal of unions was to secure sound, stable income levels for members. Coming out of the great recession, saving and creating jobs is rapidly becoming the top priority. Consider the auto industry. As we saw in **Chapter 7**, the Big Three U.S. automakers have been in constant struggle to contain their labor costs, especially fixed labor costs, which typically far exceed those of foreign producers with U.S. plants. The U.S. producers have been able to get the UAW to agree to greater profit sharing in lieu of wage increases to allow labor costs to vary more with their ability to pay/profitability rather than carry large fixed labor costs even when times are bad.[29]

As **Exhibit 15.4** shows, these profit-sharing payouts have been substantial in recent years as the Big Three have rebounded from some lean years. Note, however, the substantial variance across companies and years, which coincides, as desired, with ability to pay/profitability. For example, profit-sharing payments at General Motors have ranged from as little as $4,800 to as much as $12,000. Another way to look at it is that General Motors can shed roughly $7,200 ($12,000 − $4,800) in labor cost per worker when it goes from strong profitability to significantly weaker profitability. As of 2020, General Motors had 46,000 union-represented hourly U.S. employees. As such, a savings of $7,200 per worker would translate into a total savings of $331.2 million.

EXHIBIT 15.3 Union Perceptions of Gainsharing

The Top Nine Reasons for Unions Favoring Gain Sharing:	The Top Nine Reasons for Unions Opposing Gain Sharing:
1. Increased recognition	1. Management may try to substitute it for wages
2. Better job security	2. Management cannot be trusted
3. Increased involvement with job activities	3. Peer pressure to perform may increase
4. More money	4. Bonus calculations are not understood or trusted
5. Increased feeling of achievement or contributing to the organization	5. Union influence is undermined
6. Increased influence of union	6. Increased productivity may reduce need for jobs
7. Greater contributions to the nation's productivity	7. Grievances may go unprocessed
8. Compatibility with union goals	8. Gain sharing is incompatible with union goals
9. Fewer grievances	9. Employees really do not want more involvement

Source: http://www.bovino-consulting.com.

EXHIBIT 15.4 Profit-Sharing Payouts to UAW Hourly Workers at the Big Three, by Year

Year	Fiat Chrysler	Ford	General Motors
2010	$0	$5,000	$4,800
2011	$1,500	$6,200	$7,000
2012	$2,250	$8,343	$6,750
2013	$2,500	$8,781	$7,500
2014	$2,750	$6,898	$7,000
2015	$4,000	$9,345	$11,000
2016	$5,000	$9,000	$12,000
2017	$5,500	$7,500	$11,500
2018	$6,000	$7,600	$10,750
2019	$7,280	$6,590	$8,000
2020	$8,010	$3,625	$9,000

Profit Sharing Payouts ($)

Year

Source: Howard, Phoebe Wall, "Why Investors Like Detroit Automaker-UAW Profit-Sharing Checks," *Detroit Free Press*, February 9, 2018; Breana Noble. "Stellantis workers to get larger profit share thanks to improved formula." *Detroit News*, March 3, 2021, www.detroitnews.com.

Note: Fiat Chrysler is now part of Stellantis.

Your Turn

Collective Bargaining and Compensation in Health Care

We have focused on wages and compensation of production workers in the automobile industry. However, the largest U.S. unions by membership, the National Education Association (NEA) and Service Employees International Union (SEIU) now primarily represent workers in other occupations, including teachers and health care workers. As of 2020, there were more union members (1.1 million) in the occupation, healthcare practitioners and technical occupations, than in production occupations (870,000). Here, we would like you to take some time to familiarize yourself with a contract in the health care area.

One excellent resource is found at: https://www.seiuhealthcaremn.org/worksites/. (Should the link not work, search for: SEIU HEALTHCARE MINNESOTA. Then look for "contracts" and/or "worksites.") It provides access to many collective bargaining contracts in healthcare in Minnesota for workers represented by the SEIU. You can check the different worksites and you will see that some have links to contracts. One example at the time your book goes to press can be found under: HealthPartners Stillwater Medical Group. In this particular contract, wage rates appear on pp. 14–15 and in Appendix A. Whatever contract(s) you examine, check for information on wage rates, wage progression, and other aspects of compensation.

1. As you may recall, in **Chapter 10**, you read a section called "The Important Role of Promotion in Pay for Performance." Toward the end of **Chapter 11**, you read a section on merit increase grids. In those sections, the emphasis was on the importance of performance (typically assessed with a performance rating assigned by the immediate supervisor and sometimes others also) in determining pay growth/increases over time, both in (a) promotions (to higher grade/pay levels) and (b) pay (merit) increases within grade levels. When you look at Article 18 and Appendix A, what role does performance rating play in promotions and pay increases within grades?

2. Your answer to the above question should be: "Performance does not play a role." OK, so what does play a role (or more accurately perhaps, "the role") in this contract in determining pay growth over time?

3. Take a moment to comment on the different wage scales for different occupations. Also, briefly comment on the degree to which rates of progression are similar or different (in percentage terms).

4. If you were a manager in this healthcare setting, how would the presence of the contract and its provisions on how pay is determined influence your ability to achieve effectiveness goals?

5. If you would like to delve in deeper to the contract, have a look at the other provisions (e.g., shift differentials) that affect pay.

Summary

Other countries continue to make inroads in product areas traditionally the sole domain of American companies. The impact of this increased competition has been most pronounced in the compensation area. Labor costs are often under pressure to be cut to improve ability to compete. Alternative compensation systems (often including a variable pay element) to achieve this end are regularly being devised. Unions face a difficult situation. How should they respond to these attacks to traditional compensation systems? Many unions believe that the crisis demands changing attitudes from both management and unions. Labor and management identify compensation packages that both parties can abide. Sometimes these packages include cuts in traditional forms of wages in exchange for compensation tied more closely to the success of the firm. We expect the beginning of the 21st century to be dominated by more innovation in compensation design and increased exploration between unions and management for ways to improve the competitive stance of American business.

Review Questions

1. What is spillover? How does it lead to underestimation of the impact unions have on wages?
2. Why don't many public sector unions have the right to strike, a weapon almost universally guaranteed in the private sector? Make your explanation based on compensation.
3. If merit pay is supposed to increase individual equity and unions are very concerned about equity, why do unions frequently oppose merit pay for their membership?
4. It is probably true that, if given a choice, unions would prefer to implement a skill-based pay system rather than some form of gainsharing plan. Why?

Endnotes

1. Bureau of Labor Statistics, United States Department of Labor, "Union Members–2020," www.bls.gov. January 22, 2021.

2. www.bls.gov/opub/ted/2008/feb/wk2/art01.htm; accessed September 9, 2008.

3. Erin Hatton, "Temporary Weapons: Employers' Use of Temps against Organized Labor," *Industrial and Labor Relations Review* 67(1) 2014, pp. 86–111.

4. David A. Macpherson and James B. Steward, "The Effect of International Competition on Union and Non-Union Wages," *Industrial and Labor Relations Review* 43(4), 1990, pp. 434–446.

5. UAW-Ford Contract Summary: Hourly Workers, November 2015, https://uaw.org/app/uploads/2015/11/reducedFINAL-FORD-HOURLY-11-9-15-1229p-FINAL-with-numbers-p24-headings-page-6-charts-p25.pdf; Lydia DePillis, "General Motors Workers Return to Raises with New Contract: It Doesn't Get Them Back to Pre-Recessionary Highs, But it Does Allow Them to Stay in the Middle Class and Preserve U.S. Jobs in the Future," *Washington Post*, October 29, 2015. www.washingtonpost.com.

6. See page 5 of UAW-Ford Contract Summary: Hourly Workers, November 2015, https://uaw.org/app/uploads/2015/11/reducedFINAL-FORD-HOURLY-11-9-15-1229p-FINAL-with-numbers-p24-headings-page-6-charts-p25.pdf.

7. *Contract Summary: Hourly Workers*. UAW General Motors. October 2019. UAW.org.

8. David A. Macpherson and James B. Steward, "The Effect of International Competition on Union and Non-Union Wages," *Industrial and Labor Relations Review* 43(4), 1990, pp. 434–446.

9. Stephen B. Jarrell and T. D. Stanley, "A Meta-Analysis of the Union–Non-Union Wage Gap," *Industrial and Labor Relations Review* 44(1), 1990, pp. 54–67.

10. A. Kulkarni, B. T. Hirsch. "Revisiting Union Wage and Job Loss Effects Using the Displaced Worker Surveys," *ILR Review*, April 2020.

11. Loren Solnick, "Unionism and Fringe Benefits Expenditures," *Industrial Relations* 17(1), 1978, pp. 102–107.

12. James E. Martin and Thomas D. Heetderks, *Two Tier Compensation Structures: Their Impact on Unions, Employers and Employees* (Kalamazoo, MI: Upjohn Institute for Employment Research, 1990).

13. James Martin and Melanie Peterson, "Two-Tier Wage Structures: Implications for Equity Theory," *Academy of Management Journal* 30(2), 1987, pp. 297–315.

14. Ann C. Foster, "Union-Nonunion Wage Differences, 1997," *Compensation and Working Conditions,* 2006, p. 46.

15. Craig A. Olson, "Union Threat Effects and the Decline in Employer-Provided Health Insurance," *ILR Review* 72, 2019, 417–445; Richard B. Freeman and Joel Rogers, *What Workers Want* (Ithaca, NY: ILR Press, 1999); David Neumark and Michael L. Wachter, "Union Effects on Nonunion Wages: Evidence from Panel Data on Industries and Cities," *Industrial and Labor Relations Review* 31(1), 1978, pp. 205–216.

16. Past bargaining agreement between the American Postal Workers Union, AFL-CIO and U.S. Postal Service. For recent contract language on overtime pay at the U.S. Postal Service, see https://about.usps.com/manuals/elm/html/elmc4_015.htm.

17. DaimlerChrysler Corporation and International Union, United Automobile Aerospace and Agricultural Implement Workers of America (UAW) Local 12 (Jeep Unit). For a recent example of a complete contract for the Jeep Unit, Local 12 (in Toledo), see https://digitalcommons.ilr.cornell.edu/cgi/viewcontent.cgi?referer=&httpsredir=1&article=1238&context=blscontracts.

18. Past contract between Maytag, Maytag and Admiral Products, and UAW.

19. State of Ohio and Ohio Civil Service Employees Association (OCSEA) collective bargaining agreement, May 12, 2018–February 28, 2021.

20. Past bargaining agreement between American Postal Workers Union, AFL-CIO, and U.S. Postal Service. For recent contract language on overtime pay at the U.S. Postal Service, see https://about.usps.com/manuals/elm/html/elmc4_015.htm.

21. Agreement between the University of Vermont Medical Center and Vermont Federation of Nurses and Health Professionals (VFNHP), AFT Vermont, AFL-CIO, Local 5221, July 9, 2015 to July 9, 2018, www.vfnhp.org. http://unitednurses.info/sites/default/files/Executed%20Final%20Nurses%20Contract.pdf.

22. U.S. Federal Mediation and Conciliation Service, *Fiftieth Annual Report, Fiscal Year 2006* (Washington, DC: U.S. Government Printing Office, 2006), www.fmcs.gov.

23. Bechter, B., Braakmann, N., & Brandl, B. (2021). Variable Pay Systems and/or Collective Wage Bargaining? Complements or Substitutes?. ILR Review, 74, 443-469; L. B. Cardinal and I. B. Helbrun, "Union Versus Nonunion Attitudes Toward Share Agreements," in *Proceedings of the 39th Annual Meeting of the Industrial Relations Research Association* (Madison, WI: IRRA, 1987), pp. 167–173.

24. R. L. Heneman, C. von Hippel, D. E. Eskew, and D. B. Greenberger, "Alternative Rewards in Union Environments," *American Counseling Association Journal*, Summer 1997, pp. 42–55.

25. E. H. O'Boyle, P. C. Patel, and E. Gonzalez-Mulé, "Employee Ownership and Firm Performance: A Meta-Analysis," *Human Resource Management Journal* 26(4) (2016), pp. 425–448; D. L. Kruse, J. R. Blasi, and R. Park, *Shared Capitalism in the US Economy* (Chicago, IL: University of Chicago Press, 2010).

26. R. L. Heneman and C. von Hippel, "Alternative Rewards in Unionized Environments," *ACA Journal* 6 (1995), pp. 42–55.

27. T. Ross and R. Ross, "Gainsharing and Unions: Current Trends," in *Gainsharing: Plans for Improving Performance,* eds. B. Graham-Moore and T. Ross (Washington, DC: Bureau of National Affairs), pp. 200–213.

28. J. Zalusky, "Labor's Collective Bargaining Experience with Gainsharing and Profit Sharing," paper presented at the 39th Annual Meeting of the Industrial Relations Research Association, December 1986, pp. 175–182; William Shaw, "Can Labor Be Capitalized?" *American Federationist* 17 (June 1910), p. 517.

29. Matthew Dolan, "UAW Wants Union Jobs," *The Wall Street Journal,* July 25, 2011, pp. B1, 11.

Chapter **Sixteen** International Pay Systems

Chapter Outline

All around the world, competitive forces have changed the way people work and how they get paid.[1] Toyota and other Japanese companies have moved from a seniority-based pay system to a merit-based system.[2] Toshiba offers stock awards, which until some years ago were not even legal in Japan.[3] Deutsche Bank, Nokia, Seimens, and other European companies shifted to variable pay and performance-based (rather than personality-based) appraisal in their search for ways to improve productivity and control labor costs.[4] Toyota and Hitachi, two of Japan's largest companies have moved China's employment system has experienced a "fundamental transformation from stable and permanent employment with good benefits (often called the iron rice bowl) to a system characterized by highly precarious employment with no benefits for about 40 percent of the population."[5] In 1990, multinational companies employed 28 million people in their foreign affiliates.

By 2010, it was 61 million, and by 2019, it was estimated at 82 million.[6] In 2000, General Motors produced 4.2 million vehicles in the United States and 3.9 million vehicles in other countries (including 30,000 vehicles in China and 443,000 vehicles in Mexico). In 2017, by contrast, GM produced 2.1 million vehicles in the United States and 4.8 million vehicles in other countries (including 2.0 million in China and 806,000 in Mexico).[7] In addition, the supply chain for a company often includes many overseas workers who are employees of other (supplier) companies. For example, as we saw in **Chapter 7**, Apple reports it presently has "millions of people who work in our supply chain" and that "Substantially all of the Company's hardware products are manufactured by outsourcing partners that are located primarily in Asia, with some Mac computers manufactured in the United States and Ireland."[8]

Global acquisitions of former competitors change pay systems. As part of its takeover and restructuring of Tungsram Electric in Poland, General Electric changed from a rigid seniority-based pay system to broad bands, market-based wage rates, and performance bonuses. India's leading software companies, such as Tata Consultancy Services, Wipro, and Infosystems, all use performance-based bonus plans for their software engineers. Prior to Daimler's acquisition of Chrysler in 1998, the pay for Chrysler's CEO was equal to the combined total pay of the top 10 Daimler executives. As little as 25 percent of Chrysler managers' total compensation was in the form of base pay, whereas Daimler managers' base pay accounted for up to 60 percent of their total compensation. The merged DaimlerChrysler adopted a Chrysler-like approach to executive compensation. Some have even claimed that the attractive pay was the reason Daimler executives were eager to acquire Chrysler![9]

This merger, described by some as a "marriage made in hell," ended unhappily after 10 years (but presumably Daimler executives got to keep the "engagement ring" of higher pay).[10] One might also say that Daimler in particular had "hell to pay" to get out of the marriage. Daimler paid $36 billion for Chrysler in 1998, but received only $7.4 billion in 2006 when it sold 80.1 percent of Chrysler to Cerberus Capital Management.[11] As part of Chrysler's bankruptcy, Daimler appears to have received nothing for its remaining stake. Rather, it had to write off $1.5 billion in loans it made to Chrysler in 2008 and also had to make a payment of $600 million to Chrysler's pension plan.[12] Daimler will not be having bouts of nostalgia looking back at its marriage with Chrysler.

Perhaps Daimler and Chrysler underestimated the challenges posed by the differences in contextual factors of the sort we highlight in this chapter. Any merger or acquisition, even between companies in the same country, has challenges. Adding an international component adds another layer of challenges.[13] Nevertheless, another suitor burst onto the scene. The Italian car maker, Fiat, initially acquired 20 to 35 percent ownership in Chrysler and later increased it to 58.5 percent and then to 100 percent. Although Fiat is more similar (its product portfolio includes basic vehicles) than Daimler (high-end vehicles) to Chrysler in some ways, it is more similar to Daimler in its experience on a number of the other factors we will discuss in this chapter (ownership structure, regulation, trade union experience, social contract).[14] Thus, it was not clear whether things would work out better the second time around for a Chrysler merger with a European company that is used to operating in a different context.[15] Nevertheless, opinion seems to be that the Fiat-Chrysler merger is working.[16] And, of course, Chrysler went on to be part of yet another cross-country merger in 2021 when FiatChrysler merged with Groupe PSA (which includes Peugot) to form Stellantis, which will be headquartered in Amsterdam.

Sometimes changes in pay are directly tied to cataclysmic sociopolitical change, as in China, Russia, and Eastern Europe, where government authorities had long dictated pay rates.[17] Now companies in these countries face the challenge of devising pay systems responsive to business and market pressures while maintaining a sense of social justice among the people. In China, the only hope for profitability in many state-owned enterprises is to reduce the massively bloated head count. Yet an army of unemployed people without social support is a threat to government survival.[18] Some state-owned enterprises, such as Baogang, the country's largest steelmaker, have moved to more "market- and performance-based" systems, even though labor markets are just emerging in many regions in China. Shanghai Shenyingwanguo Security Company and Shanghai Bank have implemented job-based structures to help them retain key employees and increase pay satisfaction. Most surprising of all is that some town-owned enterprises are using stock ownership as part of their employee compensation.[19] China may still be striving to become a worker's paradise, but the experimentation with compensation approaches might already qualify it as a pay pundit's paradise.

However, too much change and experimentation can have a dark side that threatens to create social unrest. Following the breakup of the USSR, workers in some of the formerly socialist countries reported going unpaid for months. At one point more than half the Russian workers said they were owed back wages; their average wait to be paid was 4.8 months.[20] A friend in Russia maintains that "the most effective pay delivery system is a brown bag under the table."

So it is a time of unprecedented global change. Or is it? Let's step back to gain some historical perspective:

> There [is] hardly a village or town anywhere on the globe whose wages are not influenced by distant foreign markets, whose infrastructure is not financed by foreign capital, whose engineering, manufacturing, and even business skills are not imported from abroad, or whose labor markets are not influenced by the absence of those who had emigrated or by the presence of strangers who had immigrated.[21]

This is not a description of the 21st century–it is from 100 years ago. In the late 1800s, trade barriers were being reduced, free trade was being promoted, and mass migrations of people were under way. Thanks to transoceanic telegraphic cables, the speed of communication had increased dramatically, and investment capital flowed among nations. Yet by 1917 these global links had been replaced with a global war. Citizens desired security rather than face the greater risks and uncertainty of globalization. Nations began to raise tariffs to protect domestic companies hurt by foreign competitors. Immigrants were accused of "robbing jobs." Historians conclude that "globalization is neither unique nor irreversible; it has and can again sow seeds of its own destruction."[22]

THE GLOBAL CONTEXT

Understanding international compensation begins with recognizing differences and similarities and figuring out how best to manage them. How people get paid around the world depends on variations shown in **Exhibit 16.1**–*economic, institutional, organizational,* and *employee characteristics*. These factors have been discussed throughout the book; now they can be applied globally. But once we shift from a domestic to an international perspective, the discussion must necessarily broaden.

Organizations must first determine the degree to which each of these contextual factors constrain their compensation decisions and practices. Some constraints are regulatory (i.e., laws), while others may be more normative (national culture, the social contract).[23] In some cases (e.g., laws/regulations), there may be little room to exercise strategy.[24] On the other hand, in the case of other contextual factors (e.g., national culture), the constraint may be less than often believed.[25] So, to be sure, there are differences, on average, between organizations, depending on the country.[26] However, there is also evidence that different management approaches are used within the same country.[27] To the degree that strategy can be exercised, an organization must decide the degree to which it will choose compensation practices similar to those used by other organizations and the degree to which it will be different. Being the same is perhaps less risky, but, by necessity, following the pack means there is little chance to stand out from the pack and thus little chance to achieve anything better than average performance.[28] Also, in the international context, it is not always simple to follow the pack. A multinational corporation (MNC) having the United States as its home country may see a typical way of doing things there, but may see a different typical way of doing things in another country where it operates. If they want to play follow the pack or follow the leader, which do they follow? (There seem to be a lot of metaphors available here! Bonus points for you if you can name the group that sang "Leader of the Pack." Double bonus points if you can name the best-known sound effect in the song's performance and in which country the song was banned from the airwaves.) Evidence indicates that MNCs are influenced by the institutional pressures both in their home country and in the local context.[29] To follow the (leader, pack, herd, lemmings, you choose), companies must balance pressures toward localization ("when in Rome . . .")–where compensation practice is tailored to each country–and standardization (where the objective is consistency, not with the local context, but instead with the organization's business strategy).[30] Finally, organizations may weight the home and local country context differently for different jobs. For example, in higher-level jobs, the local country context influence may be weaker.[31]

In the following discussion, we highlight five specific contextual factors we feel are especially relevant in international compensation. These are variations in (1) social contracts, including the legal framework and regulation; (2) cultures; (3) trade unions; (4) ownership and financial markets; and (5) managers' autonomy.

EXHIBIT 16.1 The International Context of Compensation

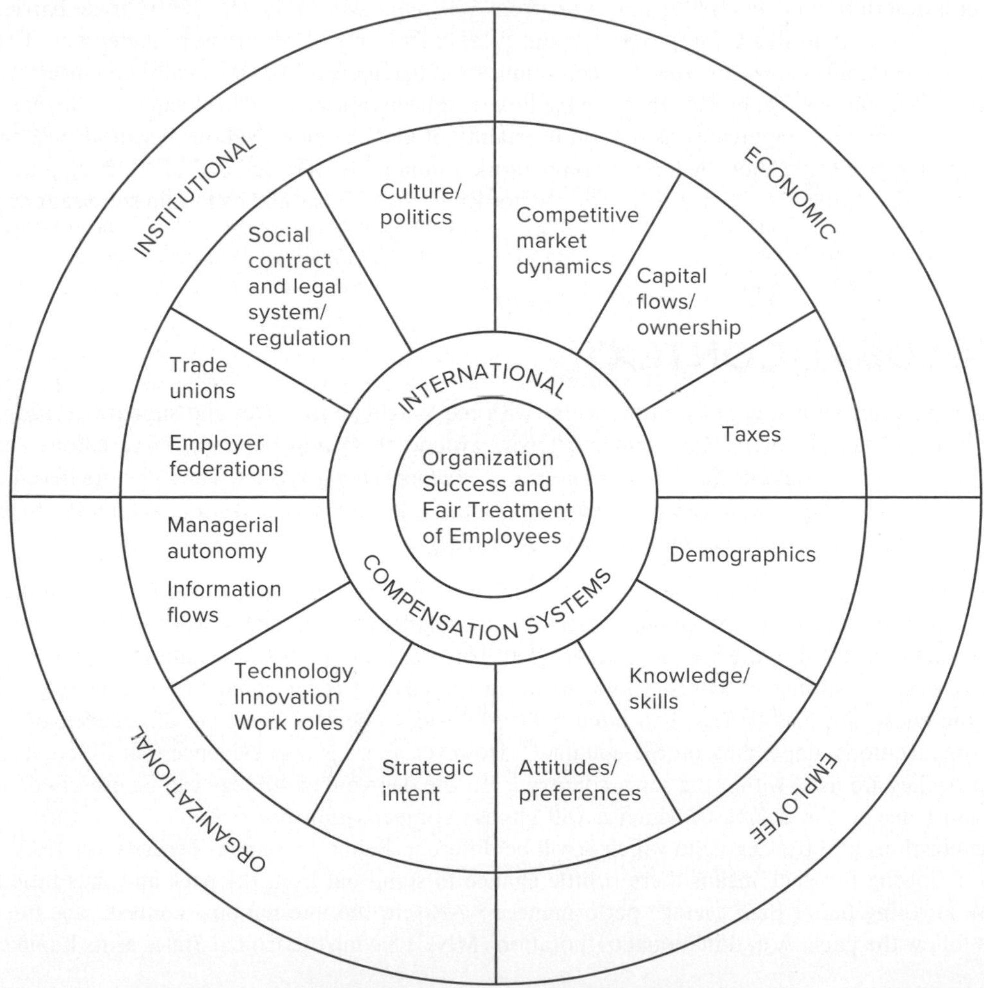

Although we separate the factors to clarify our discussion, they do not separate so easily in reality. Instead, they overlap and interact.

THE SOCIAL CONTRACT

Viewed as part of the social contract, the employment relationship is more than an exchange between an individual and an employer. It includes the government, all enterprise owners (sometimes acting individually and sometimes collectively through owner associations), and all employees (sometimes acting individually and sometimes in trade unions). The relationships and expectations of these parties form the social contract. As you think about how people get paid around the world, it will be clear that different people in different countries hold differing beliefs about the role of government, employees, unions, and employers. Understanding how to manage employee compensation in any country requires an understanding of the social contract in that country. Changing employee compensation systems–for example, to make them more responsive to customers, encourage innovative and quality service, or control costs–require changing the expectations of parties to the social contract.

The social contract evolves over time, sometimes very quickly. One need to look no further than the United States for recent examples. Compared to many countries (such as those in the European Union), government has traditionally played a relatively modest role in the employment relationship. However, that role changed in response to crises, at least in two key sectors of the U.S. economy: automobiles and financial services. Consider that Chrysler and General Motors (GM) have went through bankruptcy as a result of the 2008 Great Financial Crisis and upon their exit, major shareholders were the United Automobile Workers (UAW) union and the U.S. government (in return for the many billions in funds it has provided to stave off liquidation). In the financial services industry, the U.S. government also played a major role during the 2008 Great Financial Crisis in saving firms, either by providing funds (e.g., Citibank, Goldman Sachs, Capital One, and many others) under the Troubled Assets Relief Program (TARP) or by actively facilitating mergers and acquisitions (e.g., Bank of America's acquisition of Merrill Lynch). The TARP program in the United States provided $700 billion (in return for warrants enabling the U.S. government to buy stock in the companies), an amount roughly the same as the total economic output (gross domestic product) of Turkey, the seventeenth largest economy in the world. As one of the "strings attached" to the TARP funds, the U.S. Treasury Department issued special executive compensation regulations for firms while they have TARP funding (see **Chapter 17**). In 2020 and 2021, in response to the pandemic, the U.S. government stepped in to provide trillions in relief to individuals and businesses. In summary, the social contract in the United States, known for the small role of government and the lack of a tripartite relationship between government, employees (and their representatives), and employers, has done a rapid "about-face" in response to crises.

Centralized or Decentralized Pay-Setting

Perhaps the most striking example of the social contract's effects on pay systems is in **Exhibit 16.2**, which contrasts the degree of centralization of pay setting among countries.[32] Companies in the United States, United Kingdom, and some central European countries use highly decentralized approaches with little government involvement. In contrast, in western and northern European countries, wage bargaining is more likely to be centralized, taking place primarily at the industry or national level, with government involvement being typical in national-level bargaining countries.

Although understanding differences in wage bargaining levels is important, it should also be understood that things continue to evolve.[33] For example, not so long ago, countries like the Czech Republic and

Sweden would have been placed in the national level bargaining group in **Exhibit 16.2**. Japan, not included in **Exhibit 16.2**, has become more decentralized in its wage bargaining.[34] Also, even where bargaining is primarily centralized, there is also typically bargaining at other levels.[35] Likewise, there may be exceptions, under particular circumstances, that permit companies to deviate from the centralized agreement. Thus, differences across countries in the degree of pay-setting centralization translate, but not perfectly, into differences in wage flexibility. Such flexibility is generally desirable to employers who do not want to be "locked in" to a particular wage level when product market conditions (i.e., level and growth of sales and profits) are in flux. **Exhibit 16.3** shows judgments of wage flexibility gathered from an international sample of executives. We can see that countries with more centralized bargaining levels (e.g., Germany, Sweden) generally have less wage flexibility, while countries with more decentralized bargaining (e.g., the United Kingdom, Czech Republic, United States) generally have higher wage flexibility, as does Japan.

Regulation

The social compact also relates to the legal/regulatory environment for human resource decisions in each country. The country differences in wage flexibility relate not only to degree of bargaining centralization, but also to regulatory restrictions such as maximum hours of work. The European Union Working Time Directive limits the workweek to no more than 48 hours. Countries such as France have experimented with a 35-hour workweek, which was in effect from 1998 until 2008.[36] In contrast, in countries like Japan and the United States, there is no maximum workweek and, as we saw, wage flexibility is high.

Another indicator of employment regulation (i.e., restriction on flexibility) is the degree of legal restriction in hiring and firing workers. As shown in **Exhibit 16.4**, employers in the United States have more flexibility than employers in the European Union, South America, and Japan. Interestingly, Korea and China are not so different from the United States. As a final example of how the legal framework comes into play and affects employer flexibility, consider the role of works councils and co-determination in a European country like Germany.[37] A works council may be formed by employees in any business unit having five or more permanent employees. It operates separately from the trade union and collective bargaining process (although works council members are often union members) and may not, for example, call a strike. In general, the German works council deals with issues of a collective nature (i.e., that affect two or more employees). It has rights to information and consultation in these matters. In the area of compensation, consider that:

EXHIBIT 16.2 The Social Contracts and Primary Bargaining Level in Selected European Union Countries and the United States

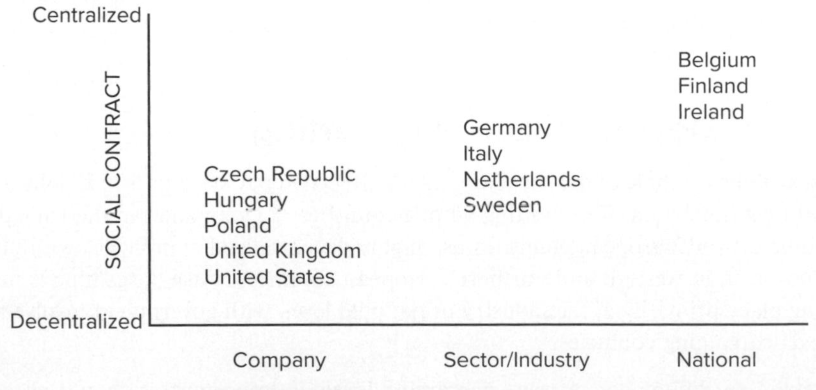

Source: European Industrial Relations Observatory Online, "Changes in National Collective Bargaining Systems Since 1990," 2005.

> the employer must obtain the consent of the Works Council on collective rules regarding criteria to be applied for determining wages and salaries of all employees, the implementation of systems that classify wages according to performance or time spent (e.g., bonus schemes), the mode of payment, and the method of determining criteria for pension rights.[38]

An employer must consult the Works Council and give it an opportunity to respond prior to taking actions in the area of compensation as well as in a wide range of other human resource and operational areas. The Works Council has "veto-rights and rights of consent," including "the right to block management decisions until an agreement is reached or a decision by the labor court is taken overruling the veto."[39]

In addition, the co-determination law in Germany requires that in companies with 500 to 2,000 employees, one-third of the supervisory board (akin to the board of directors in a United States company) must be employee representatives. In companies with over 2,000 employees, one-half of the board must be composed

EXHIBIT 16.3 Flexibility of Wage Determination

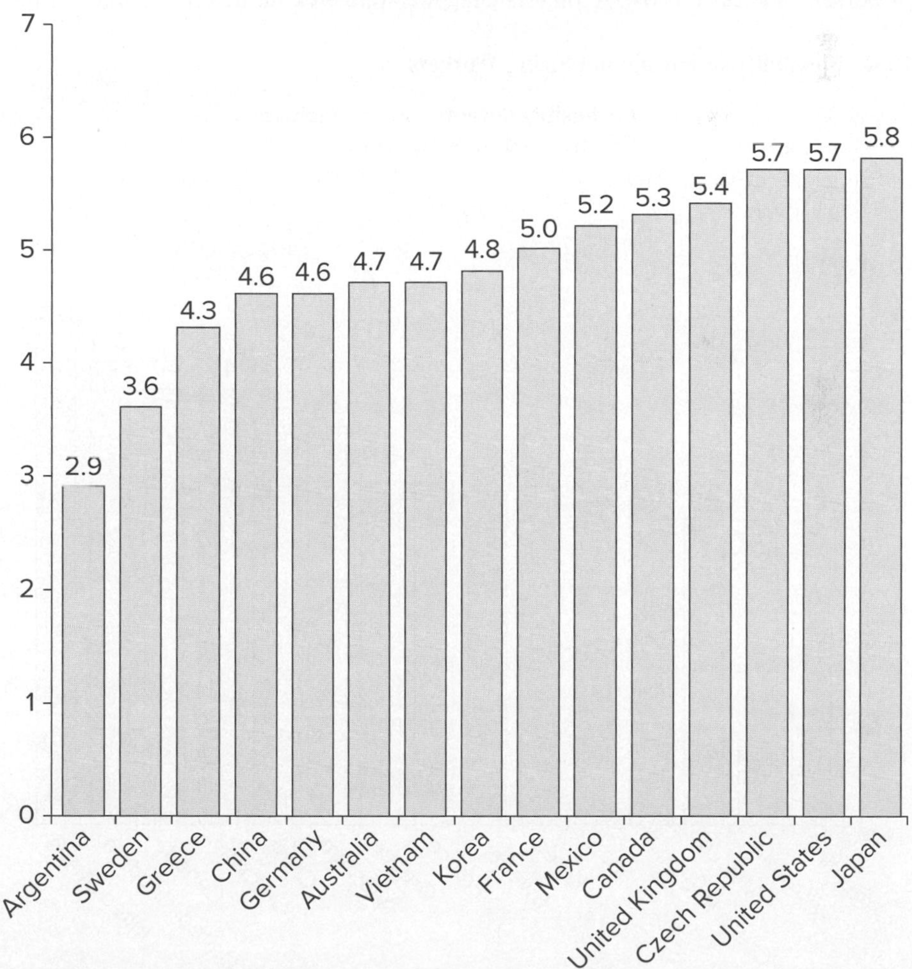

Source: World Economic Forum. *The Global Competitiveness Report 2019.*

of employee representatives. However, there is not true parity here because shareholders elect the chairperson, who has the power to cast a tie-breaking vote.[40] By way of contrast, neither works councils or co-determination are legally required in the United States and are quite rare. Clearly, an employer from the United States that becomes an employer in Germany will find that things work very differently.

In Europe, like in the United States, laws can also vary within countries. Further, there are also, as we have seen, directives that apply across countries such as that dealing with working time in the European Union (EU). Another EU directive gives employees the right to information and consultation on company decisions in companies having 1,000 or more employees, including 150 or more in at least two member countries through the establishment of a European works council. Thus, a company operating in multiple EU countries might have consultation obligations with a works council in each country as well as a European works council. The EU has a goal of providing common labor standards in all its member countries. The purpose of standards is to avoid "social dumping," or the relocation of a business in a country with lower standards and labor costs. At present, average hourly labor costs vary substantially among the EU countries, sometimes in countries right next door, such as Germany, which, as we saw in **Chapter 1**, has much higher labor costs than Czechia (Czech Republic).

Finally, the social compact in Europe, with its regulatory and institutional limits on employer flexibility and protection of workers, comes at a cost. A long-standing literature seeks to determine whether more generous

EXHIBIT 16.4 Flexibility in Hiring and Firing Workers

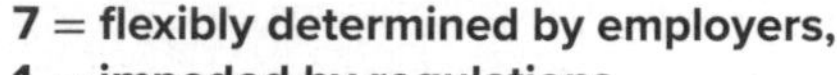

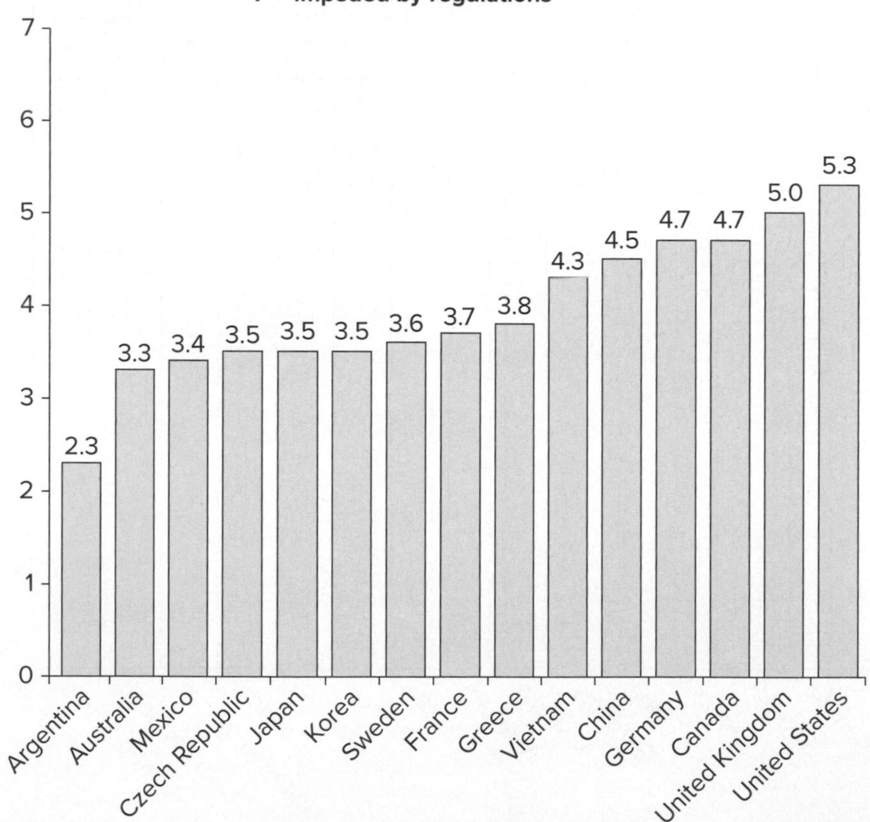

Source: World Economic Forum, *The Global Competitiveness Report 2019*.

worker protection (e.g., unemployment benefits) undermines incentives for workers to put forth effort on the job (as efficiency wage theory would suggest) or look for work (thus resulting in higher unemployment rates and higher public expenditures). Here, we will simply look at how expenditures vary across countries, as well as how taxes, which of course are needed to fund such expenditure, also vary. **Exhibit 16.5** shows that the tax burden in countries like Germany and France is roughly 60 percent higher than in the United States, Canada, Australia, and Japan. One purpose of these higher taxes is to help insulate workers from income losses due to unemployment.

As **Exhibit 16.6** indicates, some European countries (again, France and Germany) tend to spend more on unemployment than the United States (and other countries shown). To illustrate, consider that the annual gross domestic product (GDP) of the United States is roughly $21 trillion. As such, spending 0.14 percent (pre-pandemic during historically low unemployment) of that on unemployment benefits as is done in the United States costs just over $29 billion. However, if spending in the United States on unemployment benefits was 1.52 percent of GDP as in France, that would cost about $319 billion (i.e., $290 billion more).

(NATIONAL) CULTURE

Culture is defined as shared mental programming which is rooted in the values, beliefs, and assumptions held in common by a group of people and which influences how information is processed.[41] The assumption that pay systems must be designed to fit different *national cultures* is based on the belief that most of a country's inhabitants share a national character. The job of the global manager, according to this assumption, is to define the national characteristics that influence pay systems. Typical of this thinking is the widely used list of national cultural attributes proposed by Hofstede (power distance, individualism–collectivism, uncertainty avoidance, and masculinity–femininity).[42] (See **Exhibit 16.7**.) Advocates of this view believe that "it is crucial that companies adjust their compensation practices to the cultural specifics of a particular host country."[43]

EXHIBIT 16.5 Combined Employer-Employee Tax Rate on Wages

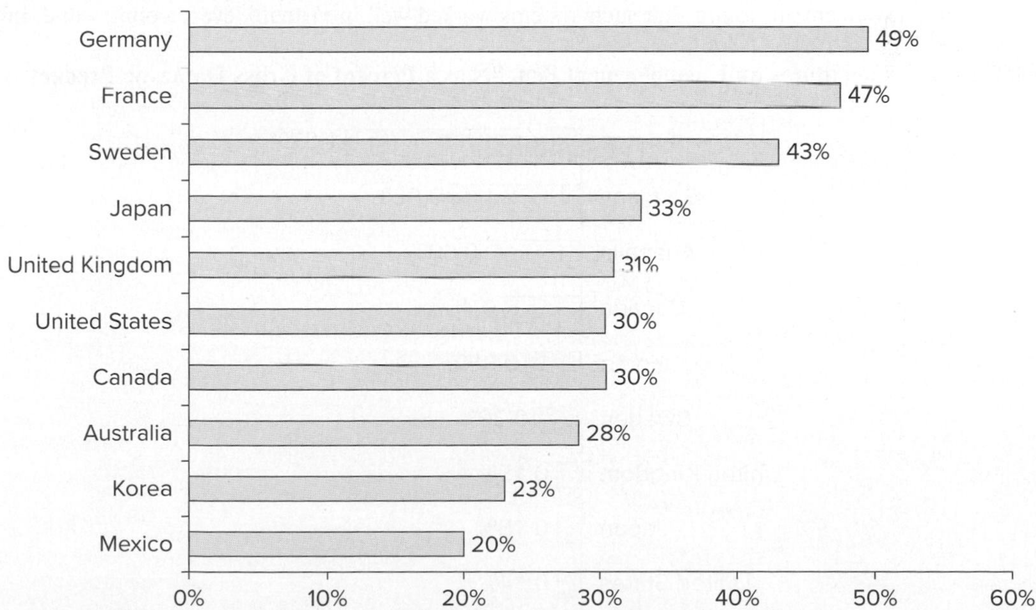

Source: Organization for Economic Cooperation and Development. *Tax Wedge*. 2019.

Accordingly, in Malaysia and Mexico, where the culture is alleged to emphasize respect for status and hierarchy (high power distance), hierarchical pay structures are appropriate. In low-power-distance nations such as Australia and the Netherlands, egalitarianism is said to be a better approach.[44]

Advice can get even more specific. Companies operating in nations with supposedly "collectivistic" cultures, such as Singapore, Japan, Israel, and Korea, should use egalitarian pay structures, equal pay increases, and group-based rather than individual-based performance incentives. Employers in the more "individualistic" national cultures, such as the United States, United Kingdom, and Hong Kong, should use individual-based pay and performance-based increases.[45]

But such thinking risks stereotyping.[46] The question is not, What are the cultural differences among nations? Rather, the question is, Which culture matters?[47] Any group of people may exhibit a shared set of beliefs. Look around your college or workplace; engineers, lawyers, accountants, and technicians may each share some beliefs and values. Employees of organizations may, too. Your school's culture probably differs from Microsoft's, Toshiba's, or the London Symphony Orchestra's. You may even have chosen your school because of its culture. However, you are likely part of many cultures. You are not only part of your university but also part of your family, your social/political/interest groups, your region of the state or country, and so on. Cultures may be similar or different among all these categories.

Is National Culture a Major Constraint on Compensation?

In our view, theory and evidence increasingly say no. At the very least, the importance of national culture in terms of how well employees accept pay for performance and in terms of how national culture influences the effectiveness of compensation and other human resource practices in different countries has been overstated. For example, research shows that respondents from what are seen as very different national cultures (e.g., China and the United States) have nearly identical beliefs in the importance of basing pay on performance (versus paying people equally or based on need).[48] Additionally, a meta-analysis (see **Exhibit 16.8**.) of the effectiveness of "high-performance work systems" (HPWSs), which typically include pay for performance, as well as worker involvement in decisions, use of teams, and ability/performance-based hiring and advancement, found that such systems worked well in virtually every country and, in fact,

EXHIBIT 16.6 Expenditures on Unemployment Benefits as a Percent of Gross Domestic Product

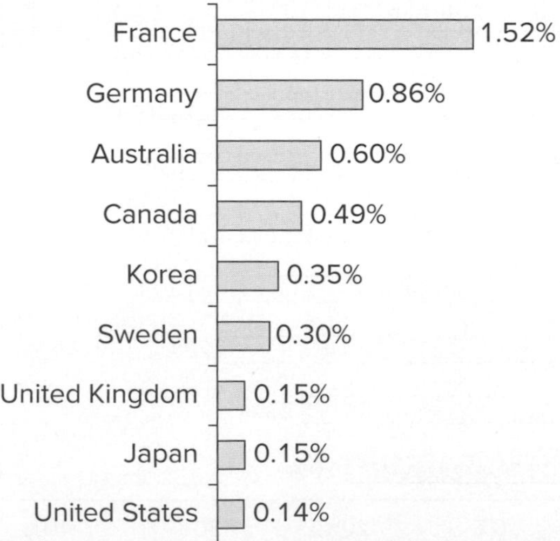

Source: Organisation for Economic Cooperation and Development, *Public Unemployment Spending*. Latest available data (2016–2019).

some evidence suggested they worked better (not worse) in countries where they did not (according to conventional wisdom) fit the national culture as well. (Often, such practices are argued to work only in the United States or countries with a similar "Anglo-Saxon" approach to management. Note, however, how different in **Exhibit 16.7** China and the United States are. Yet, HPWS appeared more, not less, effective in China than the United States, based on **Exhibit 16.8**.) One explanation is that being out in front of within-country competitors in successfully implementing more effective management systems can be a source of competitive advantage. Deviating from what everyone else does carries a risk, but so does deviating from a global management practice standard that may be different from the domestic standard, but is more effective. That is especially true if a company competes not just domestically, but also in the global economy. It is also possible that organizations adapted/executed HPWS principles in different ways in different national contexts to reduce the possibility of misfit.[49]

Culture classifiers consider the United States a country of risk takers who rank high on the individualistic (rather than collectivistic) scale. In contrast, the country of Slovenia has been classified as more collectivistic and security-conscious (as opposed to risk taking).[50] Slovenia was the first country to break off from the former Yugoslavia. (How is that for taking a risk?) It has a population of less than 3 million and by most

EXHIBIT 16.7 Hofstede's National Culture Dimensions and Scores for Four Countries

Hofstede Culture Dimensions	United States	Germany	China	Japan
Power Distance The extent to which the less powerful members of organizations and institutions accept and expect that power is distributed unequally.	Low (40)	Low (35)	High (80)	Medium (54)
Uncertainty Avoidance The extent to which a culture programs its members to feel either uncomfortable or comfortable in unstructured situations. Unstructured situations are unknown, surprising, different from usual and societies differ in the degree to which they try to control the uncontrollable.	Low (46)	Medium (65)	Medium (60)	High (92)
Individualism On the one side versus its opposite, collectivism, it is the degree to which individuals are supposed to look after themselves or remain integrated into groups, usually around the family.	High (91)	High (67)	Low (20)	Medium (47)
Masculinity versus Femininity This refers to the distribution of emotional roles between the genders; it opposes "tough" masculine to "tender" feminine societies. Masculine societies emphasize assertiveness, performance, and competition.	High (62)	High (66)	Medium (50)	High (95)
Long-term versus Short-term Orientation This refers to the extent to which a culture programs its members to accept delayed gratification of their material, social, and emotional needs.	Low (29)	Medium (31)	High (118)	High (80)

Sources: G. Hofstede. "Cultural Constraints in Management Theories," *Academy of Management Executive* 7 (1993), pp. 81–94; G. Hofstede. *Culture's Consequences: Comparing Values, Behaviors, Institutions, and Organizations Across Nations*, 2nd ed. (Thousand Oaks, CA: Sage, 2001), xix–xx.

standards would be considered very homogeneous. So you might expect Slovenian managers to be very different from U.S. managers. However, a study found that Slovenian managers tended, on average, to be more risk taking and individualistic than U.S. managers. The most striking finding, as shown in **Exhibit 16.9**, was that the degree of variation among managers on cultural dimensions was virtually the same in both the Slovenian and the U.S. data. Thus, one can find employees with different values or personality traits (e.g., risk-averse collectivists and risk-taking individualists) in both nations.[51]

Indeed, re-analysis of data from Hofstede's seminal work on national differences in culture finds that the variance between individuals within countries is far larger than the variance between countries.[52] In other

EXHIBIT 16.8 Correlation (r) between Degree of Use of High Performance Work Systems (HPWS) and Business Performance, by Country

Country or Region	K	N	Mean r	95% Confidence Interval for Mean r
United States	48	11,309	.23	.20 to .26
Non-United States	108	24,458	.22	.18 to .26
China	16	3,692	.35	.26 to .43
Korea	8	1,899	.26	.17 to .36
Spain	13	3,430	.20	.14 to .26
United Kingdom	13	2,758	.16	.06 to .26

K = Number of samples; N = Number of organizations across samples

Source: T. Rabl, M. Jayasinghe, B. Gerhart, and T. A. Kühlmann, "Meta-Analysis of Country Differences in the High Performance Work System-Business Performance Relationship: The Roles of National Culture and Managerial Discretion," *Journal of Applied Psychology* 99 (2014), pp. 1011–41.

EXHIBIT 16.9 Understanding the "Full House" of Variation Within a Culture

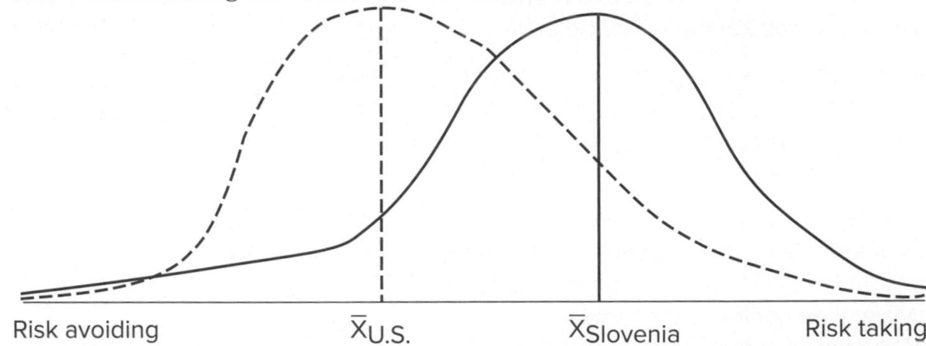

words, knowing what country someone is from tells us much less than the national culture literature seems to suggest. In fact, based on Hofstede's data, about 4 percent of the variance in individual level cultural values is explained by country. That means that 96 percent is not explained by country.[53] Of course, it is critical to keep the following "formula" in mind as well:

National Culture ≠ Country

This is meant to emphasize that if countries differ on some measure, it is necessary to determine which specific country characteristic causes the difference. National culture is a possibility. However, so too are all the other dimensions (see **Exhibit 16.1**) on which countries differ, including the legal system, economic system/role of markets, trade unions, demographics, and so forth. (For you statisticians, think in terms of multilevel modeling and variance decomposition.)[54]

So how useful is the notion of a *national* culture when managing international pay? In the absence of better data on variations such as those in **Exhibit 16.9**, it may offer a starting point. However, *it is only a starting point.*[55] National culture can be thought of as the "average" in **Exhibit 16.9**. It provides some information about what kinds of pay attitudes and beliefs you are likely to find in an area. But overreliance on the "average" can seriously mislead to the degree the variance around the average is large, which is certainly the case when it comes to cultural values within a country. This point is critical for managing international pay.

To claim that all organizations and people within Germany or within China share a certain mind-set ignores variations and differences within each nation, and reviews of empirical work bear out the fact that differences in worker preferences across countries (including China and the United States) for the use of performance-based pay, for example, tend to be small in practical terms.[56] Again, country is just too rough of a proxy to use in making compensation decisions. Considerable diversity among companies and people within any country exists. The Chinese computer company Lenovo, which purchased IBM's PC division, illustrates the point. Throughout its short history, Lenovo has relied heavily upon government support. Yet Lenovo's approach to compensating employees does not reflect widely held beliefs about Chinese national culture.[57] For example, the CEO uses 20 percent of the company's profits to award high-performing employees with "special merit" bonuses. Pay differentials among jobs, which in 1990 were 2 to 1, are now up to 30 to 1. Most amazing is a benefits plan in which individual employees select the specific benefits that best meet their personal preferences. All this diversity in a company in which the Chinese government still owns controlling interest!

So keep in mind our basic premise in this chapter: The interplay among economic, institutional, organizational, and individual conditions within each nation or region, taken as a whole, forms distinct contexts for determining compensation. Understanding these factors in the global guide is useful for managing employee compensation. However, do not assume uniformity (the average) within a country. Understanding the full range of individuals within nations is even more important.[58]

So how may understanding cultural diversity within a nation matter to global pay? Perhaps with an eye to attracting and motivating those risk-taking, entrepreneurial Slovenians, a multinational firm may use performance bonuses, stock awards, and hierarchical pay structures rather than simply matching the "average" Slovenian culture.

TRADE UNIONS AND EMPLOYEE INVOLVEMENT

Labor unions remain a major force in Europe. Even though union membership as a percentage of employment is not always so different (e.g., 17% in Germany and 8% in France, compared to 10% in the United States), the major difference is that the terms and conditions of employment are much more likely to be covered by a union contract in Europe, even for those not members of a union.[59] This union coverage rate is 56 percent in Germany and 99 percent in France, compared to 12 percent in the United States. In the European Union overall, the union coverage rate is 61 percent. Japan's union coverage rate is 17 percent and Mexico is 10 percent. In addition to having higher rates of union coverage, as we have seen, workers in countries like Germany have the right to establish works councils, which must be involved in any changes to a pay plan.[60] China, although it has a substantial union coverage rate (41%), has a different model. Labor unions are still closely linked to the Communist Party and thus not independent in the Western sense. They do sometimes assert themselves (especially at foreign companies with operations in China).[61]

OWNERSHIP AND FINANCIAL MARKETS

Ownership and financing of companies differ widely around the world. These differences are important to international pay. In the United States, corporate ownership and access to capital is far less concentrated than in most other countries. Fifty percent of American households own stock in companies either directly or indirectly through mutual funds and pension funds.[62] Direct stock ownership is only a few mouse clicks away. In Korea, six conglomerates control a significant portion of the Korean economy, and the six are closely linked with specific families. In Germany, the national Bundesbank and a small number of other influential banks have ownership interests in most major companies. These patterns of ownership make certain types of pay systems almost nonsensical because ownership in the companies is not readily available for individual investors. For example, linking performance bonuses to increased shareholder value or offering stock options to employees makes little sense in the large conglomerates in Germany, Korea, and Japan. However, ownership in small start-ups in the nations is outside the traditional channels, so these firms do offer stock options to attract new employees.[63] Recent tax law changes in many countries have made stock options more attractive, but limited ownership of many companies remains the rule.

The most vivid illustrations of the importance of ownership occur in China and in eastern Europe (Poland, Hungary, Slovenia, Czech Republic, and Slovakia), where a variety of forms are emerging. State-owned enterprises still play a major role in China, but now township enterprises, wholly privately owned enterprises, joint ventures with foreign companies, and wholly owned foreign enterprises (WOFEs) play a much larger role in China than in the past.[64] Indeed, according to the China Statistical Yearbook, National Bureau of Statistics China, the total wage bill of employed persons in urban units in state-owned units went from 77 percent of the national total in 1995 to 36 percent in 2019.[65] Chinese employees switching from government-owned enterprises to these newer organizations find that both the pay and the employer expectations (i.e., the social contract) are substantially different.[66] Individuals attracted to work in these various enterprises have different values and expectations. One study found that those working for local or town-owned enterprises prefer more performance-based pay than those working in federal-owned enterprises.[67] Many families find it makes sense to have one wage earner working at a safe but low-paying government enterprise and another wage earner working at a private enterprise where expectations and pay are high. So it is clear that ownership differences may influence what forms of pay make sense. It is very misleading to assume that every place is like home.

MANAGERIAL AUTONOMY

Managerial autonomy, an organizational factor in the global guide in **Exhibit 16.1**, refers to the degree of discretion managers have to make total compensation a strategic tool. It is inversely related to the degree of centralization and regulatory intensity discussed earlier. (See **Exhibits 16.2**, **16.3**, and **16.4**.) Thus, most U.S.- and UK-based organizations have relatively greater freedom to change employee pay practices or to hire and downsize than do most European companies. As already noted, the centralized pay setting found in

European Union countries limits organizations' autonomy to align pay to business strategies and changing market conditions.[68] Volkswagen AG, which is trying to reduce labor costs to better compete with Toyota and others, must negotiate changes with both IG Metall, a powerful trade union, and also with a federal labor agency.[69] Works councils also have information and consultation rights. In contrast, in Singapore the National Wage Council issues guidelines that are voluntary (e.g., "Wage freezes for most companies," "Emphasize variable and performance-based pay"). Most government organizations adhere to these guides, but private organizations do so to varying degrees.[70] Yet, even in countries with centralized bargaining, employers sometimes find ways to exercise autonomy. For example, subcontracting work seems to be one avenue for reducing the degree of constraint.[71] Also, even though Volkswagen must negotiate with IG Metall in Germany, it does not have to do so at its (nonunion) U.S. plant in Chattanooga, Tennessee.

e-Compensation

A good source of free information on labor laws throughout the world is the NATLEX database produced by the International Labor Organization (ILO): ***natlex.ilo.org***.

Governments and trade unions are not the only institutions to limit managerial autonomy. Corporate policies often do so as well. Compensation decisions made in the home-country corporate offices and exported to subunits around the world may align with the corporate strategy but discount local economic and social conditions. While IBM corporate in Armonk, New York, expects all its worldwide operations to "differentiate people on performance" with total compensation, some IBM units in Tokyo remain convinced that Japanese IBMers in Japan prefer more egalitarian practices.[72] Nevertheless, managers are expected to comply with Armonk.

In sum, as the global guide depicts, international compensation is influenced by economic, institutional, organizational, and individual conditions. Globalization really means that these conditions are changing–hence, international pay systems are changing as well.

COMPARING COSTS (AND PRODUCTIVITY)

In **Chapter 8,** we discussed the importance of obtaining accurate information on what competitors pay in domestic markets. Similar comparisons of total compensation among nations can be very misleading. Even if wage rates appear the same, expenses for health care, living costs, and other employer-provided allowances complicate the picture. Outside the United States, many nations offer some form of national health care. An organization may pay for it indirectly through payroll taxes, but since all people in a nation share similar coverage, its value as part of total compensation is diminished.

Comparisons between a specific U.S. firm and a specific foreign competitor may be even more misleading. Accurate data are usually difficult to obtain. While consulting firms are improving their global data collection, much of their data is still from U.S. companies' operations in global locations. Other foreign and local-national companies' data are often not available. Thus, international data may be biased toward U.S. companies' practices.[73]

Labor Costs and Productivity

Nevertheless, substantial differences in (average) labor costs (wages/salaries plus benefits and social insurance expenditures and/or labor-related taxes) do exist (see **Exhibit 16.10**). Companies may find that it makes sense to move or grow employment in lower-cost countries if productivity can be maintained at a workable level. (Of course, there are reasons other than labor cost to grow employment in a country, such as proximity to customers/markets.) As we saw in **Chapter 1**, **Exhibit 1.2**, it is important to compare not only labor costs, but productivity as well, across countries. There, we saw, for example, that although Mexico's salary level was 73 percent lower than that of the United States, its productivity was also lower (by 65%). Of course, productivity at the national level is of limited use in telling us what productivity will be at a well-designed, technologically up to date plant that is well-managed (including how workers are selected, trained, developed, and compensated and encouraged to contribute ideas to run the plant better) and well-integrated with its supply chain. It also depends on the product and type of work. As we have noted, Apple has millions of (non-Apple) workers in its supply chain, primarily in Asia and many of these are in countries like China where the average salary is 81 percent lower than in the United States, based on data we saw in **Exhibit 1.2**, **Chapter 1**.

Exhibit 16.11 shows further information on wage rates in Asia, reporting annual labor costs by country for two occupations in manufacturing: worker and manager. Note that China is a low-wage country compared to some Asian countries, but its pay is much higher than in some others (e.g., India, Vietnam, Sri Lanka).[74] Note also that market pay rates can change quickly in a number of these countries. That occurs because of wage growth in the local currency and/or due to changes in the exchange rate. (Given that labor costs in **Exhibit 16.11** are reported in U.S. dollars, weakening of the dollar against any of the local currencies will result in an increase in labor costs expressed in U.S. dollars.) Thus, our **Chapter 8** discussion of the importance of aging/updating salary survey data to be up to date and account for market movement (and in the international context, currency exchange rates also) remains highly (or even more) relevant.

Of course, most companies are not average and so each has to do its own analysis of the pros and cons of where to locate employment, as we discussed in **Chapter 7**. Also, while differences in labor costs are often the impetus to do the analysis, many other factors must be considered.

Consider the case of a small custom software company in the Midwest that provides high-end web applications to meet clients' core business needs (e.g., online registration or customer service). It sets up longstanding web development teams to provide client support on an ongoing basis. Here we have a case involving knowledge work where responsiveness to customers is key. The engineering work (software coding, architecture, testing, graphics production, database) is all done in a former Soviet Bloc country in Eastern Europe. Some employees work in teams that write HTML code (which tells web browsers how to present a page). Not many years ago, new college graduates were hired at a rate of about $6,000 per year, with more senior team leads earning up to $15,000 per year. (We suspect that many readers of this book expect to make considerably more than that upon graduating from college.) Other employees, software engineers, with two to four years of experience, and writing applications in more complex languages, earned $10,000 per year, with the more senior and most highly skilled engineers earning $22,000 to $30,000 per year. You may wish to compare these salaries to those we saw in **Chapter 7** for engineers (and programmers). There, we saw that an engineer fresh out of college could expect $60,000 to $70,000 per year, and more senior engineers could advance to earning well over $100,000 per year. Thus, the labor cost savings for this Midwest customer software company were too large to ignore.

Of course, it is not quite that simple. In a global market, some of the very best engineering talents from Eastern Europe migrate to where they can command higher pay and be at the epicenter of the most exciting work being done (e.g., Silicon Valley in California). Thus, the productivity of the company's engineers in Eastern Europe is not as high. That is not necessarily a problem if the work to be done is relatively routine and not oriented toward innovation.

What about setting up a team that is several time zones and a 16- to 20-hour round trip away? This company's experience has been that it can take six months to a year to get off the ground and fine-tune. Other differences are harder to quantify. Former Soviet Bloc countries do not have the same consumer- and marketing-oriented culture as in the United States–until recently, ordinary consumers in those countries did not have multiple options when it came to toothpaste, apartments, cars, and so forth. So most workers in those countries will not have the underlying shared experiences and knowledge that most U.S. engineers will have. Think of someone who has never had a credit card. How would a software engineer go about designing an online shopping experience without an inherent understanding of credit cards and comparison shopping?

Nevertheless, in some cases, especially in manufacturing, the focus can sometimes be entirely on labor cost. As we saw in **Chapter 7**, by outsourcing assembly of the iPhone and iPad to plants in China owned by

EXHIBIT 16.10 Average Hourly Labor Cost (Cash and Benefits) for Production Workers in Manufacturing, Annual Salary for All Employees, and Hourly Salary (estimated) for All Employees, by Country and Year, in U.S. Dollars

	Average Hourly Labor Cost (Production Workers in Manufacturing only)	Hourly Salary (estimated)	Annual Salary	Hourly Salary (estimated)	Annual Salary
	1990	2016	2016	2019	2019
Canada	$16.62	$30.08	51,563	$31.86	53,198
Mexico	1.94	3.91	16,981	8.23	17,594
United States	14.88	39.03	63,079	37.01	65,836
Czechia		10.71	25,819	16.38	29,281
Germany	18.05	43.18	51,623	38.70	53,638
China		5.37[a]	10,161	[c]	12,430[b]
Japan	12.52	26.46	37,896	23.49	38,617
Republic of Korea	3.79	22.98	38,617	21.50	42,285

Sources: Hourly labor cost (salary plus benefits) data for 1990 are from the U.S. Bureau of Labor Statistics and for 2016 are from the Conference Board. Neither provides such data for more recent years. Annual salary (not including benefits) and annual hours worked data (not shown) from the Organization for Economic Cooperation and Development (OECD.org), https://data.oecd.org/earnwage/average-wages.htm and https://data.oecd.org/emp/hours-worked.htm. Note that Annual Salary is in constant (2016) U.S. dollars and is adjusted for country differences in purchasing power. Hourly salary (estimated) = Annual Salary/ Annual Hours Worked. Note country differences in hourly salary may differ from those in annual salary because of differences in hours worked. For example, Germany's annual salary is 1.83 times that of the Czech Republic, but its hourly salary (estimated) is 2.36 times higher because annual hours worked is considerably less (1,386) in Germany than in the Czech Republic (1,788).

[a]Most recent Conference Board data for China were from 2014. The 2016 estimate for China was obtained by inflating the 2014 Conference Board estimate based on wage inflation data from the National Bureau of Statistics of China.

[b]Table 4-12, China Statistical Yearbook 2019, National Bureau of Statistics of China, http://www.stats.gov.cn/tjsj/ndsj/2019/indexeh.htm. Converted from yuan to USD using average exchange rate for 2019.

[c]Hourly salary (estimated) for China cannot be computed because the OECD does not provide annual hours worked for China.

Foxconn and others, Apple likely saves many billions of dollars per year in labor costs, which we saw likely has a major impact on its operating income. Thus, even though wages are growing in China, eroding its labor cost advantage and leading some companies to look for lower labor cost countries,[75] labor costs remain much lower in China than in more advanced economies, such as the United States, and that appears to mean that companies will continue to manufacture in China. However, as also discussed, companies like Apple are looking to diversify the locations of their supply chains so as not to be too dependent on any one country. **Exhibit 16.12**, based on a survey of global manufacturing executives, provides the average importance of factors that go into location decisions. We see that labor cost, but also the quality of the labor available, are the most important factors. Taxes and the legal/regulatory environment, other factors addressed in the current chapter, are also important.

Cost of Living and Purchasing Power

If comparing total compensation is difficult, comparing living costs and standards across borders is even more complex. (Recall our discussion of the limitations of the CPI for wage setting in **Chapter 8**.) However, companies need such data to adjust pay for employees who transfer among countries. The objective is to maintain the same level of *purchasing* power.[76] **Exhibit 16.13** provides several types of relevant data for this purpose. In

EXHIBIT 16.11 Annual Labor Costs in Select Asian Countries (U.S. Dollars)

	Annual Salary	
Country	**Manufacturing Worker**	**Manufacturing Manager**
Australia	$52,318	$90,153
Korea	37,812	59,467
Singapore	31,931	71,616
Hong Kong	30.646	61,110
Taiwan	20,648	46,101
China	10,613	26,371
Thailand	8,135	26.725
Malaysia	7,048	26,071
Indonesia	6,098	18,489
India	4,208	19,737
Vietnam	4,132	16,494
Cambodia	3,280	13,501
Laos	3,132	10,760
Sri Lanka	2,353	8,246
Bangladesh	1,848	11,220

Source: Japan External Trade Organization (JETRO), 2020 JETRO *Survey on Business Condition of Japanese Companies Operating Overseas (Asia and Oceania)*, December 23, 2020, Section 9, "Wages (4) Annual Salary." "Annual salary" includes salary, bonuses, and benefits.

the first two columns are Gross and Net (after taxes and deductions) Hourly Pay. The third column is Price Level (i.e., cost of goods and services). The fourth column is Purchasing Power (how much in goods and services can be bought, given Net Hourly Pay and Price Level). These four columns are all expressed as a percentage of the value for New York City. For example, a worker in Copenhagen, although having gross hourly pay slightly higher than a worker in New York City, has much lower purchasing power. Thus, to maintain the purchasing power of an expatriate from New York moving to Copenhagen, additional compensation beyond that paid in New York would be necessary. In contrast, a move to Kuala Lumpur at New York City pay levels would provide an economic windfall. On the other hand, paying a New York–based expatriate in Jakarta at the local level would result in a serious decline in living standard. The last column, working hours required to buy an iPhone X, provides another index of purchasing power. It takes 54 hours in New York City, versus 243 hours in Kuala Lumpur, 299 hours in Moscow, and 306 hours in Shanghai.

COMPARING SYSTEMS

We have made the points that pay systems differ around the globe and that the differences relate to variations in economic pressures, sociopolitical institutions, and the diversity of organizations and employees. In this section we compare several compensation systems. The caution about stereotyping raised earlier applies here as well. Even in nations described by some as homogeneous, pay systems differ from business to business. One does not even need to look overseas for examples. In **Chapters 1** and **2**, we highlighted the different compensation strategies used by companies just within the United States.

Sometimes, the assumption is made that most employers in a country adopt similar pay practices (and/or that constraints make this necessary). Hopefully, we have made it clear that such an assumption is usually at least partly and often largely wrong because of the large within-country variance in many practices. That said, there are some average differences between countries that are meaningful and useful to examine. Thus, we briefly describe some typical practices in traditional companies in Japan and Germany. However, use of

EXHIBIT 16.12 Drivers of Countries' Global Manufacturing Competitiveness

Rank	Component	Importance 10 = High, 1 = Low
1	Quality and availability of labor force	10.00
2	Cost competitiveness of materials	9.06
3	Cost competitiveness of labor	9.05
4	Health of economic and financial system	8.96
5	Quality and availability of scientists, researchers and engineers	8.85
6	Capacity for manufacturing innovation	8.82
7	Cost competitiveness of energy	8.23
8	Tax system	7.45
9	Quality of physical infrastructure	7.15
10	Legal and regulatory environment	7.13

Source: Deloitte and U.S. Council on Competitiveness. *2010 Global Manufacturing Competitiveness Index*. Deloitte, 2010, appendix table A1.

the word "traditional" is important because many companies do not follow the traditional model. For example, revisit our examples at the beginning of the chapter of Japanese companies such as Toyota, Hitachi, and Fujitsu that have moved toward greater use of performance versus seniority in compensation.

EXHIBIT 16.13 Cost of Living, Domestic Purchasing Power, and Minutes of Working Time Required to Buy a Bread, Rice, and iPhone

	Hourly Pay (NYC = 100)		Price Level	Purchasing Power	Working Time (Hours) Required to Buy:
	Gross	Net	(NYC = 100)	(NYC = 100)	iPhone X
Cairo	5	6	30	17	
Chicago	90	95	87	106	55
Copenhagen	101	92	94	77	70
Hong Kong	60	72	82	100	75
Kuala Lumpur	21	24	48	44	243
London	69	76	88	83	91
Moscow	18	23	57	34	299
Mumbai	6	7	42	25	
Munich	86	87	76	91	81
Nairobi	10	11	45	24	
New York City	100	100	100	100	54
Paris	69	69	88	66	102
Prague	27	26	55	39	275
Rio de Janeiro	25	30	53	46	316
Seoul	40	46	77	59	147
Shanghai	19	22	57	32	306
Sydney	80	91	84	97	68
Taipei	61	63	73	83	93
Tel Aviv	56	62	77	80	
Tokyo	79	85	90	85	71
Toronto	87	87	72	102	64
Zurich	120	154	104	129	38

Source: UBS, *Cost of Living in Cities Around the World: Prices and Earnings* 2018.

Notes: Price Level is based on prices for a basket of 128 goods and services (including rent). Net Hourly Pay is equal to Gross Hourly Pay minus deductions and taxes. Both are based on 15 professions. Purchasing Power is Net Hourly Pay divided by Price Level (excluding rent).

Japanese Traditional National System

Traditionally, Japan's employment relationships were supported by "three pillars":

1. Lifetime security within the company
2. Seniority-based pay and promotion systems
3. Enterprise unions (decentralized unions that represent workers within a single company)

Japanese pay systems tend to emphasize the person rather than the job; seniority and skills possessed rather than job or work performed; promotions based on a combination of supervisory evaluation of trainability, skill/ability levels, and performance rather than on performance alone; internal alignment over competitors' market rates; and employment security based on the performance of the organization and the individual (formerly lifetime security). Japanese pay systems can be described in terms of three basic components: base pay, bonuses, and allowances/benefits.[77]

Base Pay

Base pay is not based on job evaluation or market pricing (as predominates in North America), nor is it attached to specific job titles. Rather, it is based on a combination of employee characteristics: career category, years of service, and skill/performance level.

Career Five career categories prevail in Japan: (1) general administration, (2) engineer/scientific, (3) secretary/office, (4) technician/blue-collar job, and (5) contingent.

Years of Service Seniority remains a major factor in determining base pay. Management creates a matrix of pay and years of service for each career category. In general, salary increases with age until workers are 50 years old, when it is reduced. Employees can expect annual increases no matter what their performance level until age 50, although the amount of increase varies according to individual skills and performance.

Skills and Performance Each skill is defined by its class and rank within the class. Employees advance in rank as a result of their supervisor's evaluation of their:

- Effort (e.g., enthusiasm, participation, responsiveness)
- Skills required for the work (e.g., analytical, decision making, leadership, planning, process improvement, teamwork)
- Performance (typical MBO-style ratings)

To illustrate how the system works, say you are a graduate fresh from college who enters at class 1, rank 1. After one year, you and all those hired at the same time are evaluated by your supervisors on their effort, abilities, and performance. Early in your career (the first three years) effort is more important; in later years abilities and performance receive more emphasis. The number of ranks you move each year (and therefore your increase in base pay) depends on this supervisory rating (e.g., receiving an A on an appraisal form lets you move up three ranks within the class, a B moves you two ranks, and so on).

Theoretically, a person with an A rating could move up three ranks in class each year and shift to the next class in three years. However, most companies require both minimum and maximum years of service within each class. So even if you receive four A ratings, you would still remain in class 1 for the minimum of six years. Conversely, if you receive four straight D grades, you would still get promoted to the next skill class after spending the maximum number of years in class 1. Setting a minimum time in each class helps ensure that the employee knows the work and returns value to the company. However, the system slows the progress of high-potential performers. Additionally, even the weakest performers eventually get to the top of the pay structure, though they do not get the accompanying job titles or responsibility. The system reflects the traditional

Japanese saying, "A nail that is standing too high will be pounded down." An individual employee will not want to stand out. Employees work to advance the performance of the group or team rather than themselves.

Since the Japanese system is so seniority-based, labor costs increase as the average age of the workforce increases. In fact, a continuing problem facing Japanese employers is the increasing labor costs caused by the cumulative effects of annual increases and lifetime employment security. Early retirement incentives and "new jobs" with lower salaries are being used to contain these costs.[78]

Bonuses

Bonuses provide additional pay equivalent to one to five months of annual salary, depending on the level in the organization and often the financial results of the organization.[79] Generally, the higher up you are, the larger the percent of annual salary received as bonus. Typical Japanese companies pay bonuses twice a year (July and December). The bonuses are an *expectable* additional payment to be made twice a year, even in bad financial times. They are not necessarily related to performance.

The amount of bonuses is calculated by multiplying employees' monthly base pay by a multiplier. The size of the multiplier is determined by collective bargaining between employers and unions in each company. According to the Japan Institute of Labor, for most employees (other than managers) bonuses are variable pay that help control the employer's cash flow and labor costs. They do not necessarily act as a motivator. Japanese labor laws encourage the use of bonuses to achieve cost savings by omitting bonuses from calculations of many other benefit costs (i.e., pension plan, overtime pay, severance pay, and early retirement allowances).

The timing of the bonuses is very important. In Japan both the summer festival and the new year are traditional gift-giving times; in addition, consumers tend to make major purchases during these periods. Employees use their bonuses to cover these expenses. Thus, the tradition of the bonus system is deeply rooted in Japanese life and is today considered an indispensable form of pay.

Benefits and Allowances

The third characteristic of Japanese pay systems, the allowance, comes in a variety of forms: family allowances, commuting allowances, housing and geographic differential allowances, and so on. Company housing in the form of dormitories for single employees or rent or mortgage subsidies is a substantial amount. Life-passage payments are made when an employee marries or experiences a death in the immediate family. Commuting allowances are also important. Family allowances vary with number of dependents. Some employers even provide matchmaking allowances for those who tire of life in company dorms.

Legally Mandated Benefits Legally mandated benefits in Japan include social security, unemployment, and workers' compensation. Although these three are similar to the benefits in the United States, Japanese employers also pay premiums for mandated health insurance, preschool child support, and employment of the handicapped.

German Traditional National System

Traditional German pay systems are embedded in a social partnership between business, labor, and government that creates a generous *vater staat,* or "nanny state."[80] *Vergutung* is the most common German word for "compensation." Pay decisions are highly regulated; over 90 different laws apply. Different **tariff agreements** (pay rates and structures) are negotiated for each industrial sector (e.g., banking, chemicals, metals, manufacturing) by the major employers and unions. Thus, the pay rates at major companies in the same industry (e.g., automobiles) are similar. Methods for job evaluation and career progression are included in the tariff agreements. However, these agreements do not apply to managerial jobs. Even small organizations that are not legally bound by tariffs tend to use them as guidelines.

Base Pay

Base pay is based on job descriptions, job evaluations, and employee age. A tariff agreement creates *tariff groups* (akin to job families and grades). Generally, a rate will be negotiated for one of the levels, for example, and the other levels in that group will be calculated as a percentage of the negotiated rate.

e-Compensation

A number of web locations offer currency conversions to change euros into U.S. dollars, Canadian dollars, Hong Kong dollars, and any number of other currencies. Try ***www.xe.com*** or ***www.globaldevelopment.org*** over a period of several weeks to appreciate the complexity that currency conversion adds to managing compensation.

Bonuses

While there is a trend toward performance-based bonuses, they have not been part of a traditional German pay system for unionized workers. However, some percentage of the base wages may be set aside to be paid as an "efficiency allowance." Systems for measuring this efficiency are negotiated with the works councils for each location. In reality, the efficiency allowances become expected annual bonuses. Performance bonuses for managerial positions not included in tariffs are based on company earnings and other company objectives. Top executives increasingly receive stock options.

Allowances and Benefits

As discussed, Germany's social contract includes generous social benefits.[81] These nationally mandated benefits, paid by taxes levied on employers and employees, include liberal social security, unemployment protection, health care, nursing care, and other programs. Employer and employee contributions to the social security system can add up to more than one-third of wages. Additionally, companies commonly provide other benefits and services such as pension plans, savings plans, building loans, and life insurance. Company cars are always popular. The make and model of the car and whether or not the company provides a cell phone are viewed as signs of status in an organization. German workers also receive much more extensive vacation and holiday time than those of us in the United States. Indeed, the average German works about 400 fewer hours (eight to nine weeks) per year than the average U.S. worker![82]

Comparison of Traditional Systems in Japan, Germany, United States

As we have emphasized, speaking of *the* German, Japanese, or U.S. system is too simplistic, as there are important variations between firms within each country. Nevertheless, in looking at the average firm in each country, Japanese and German traditional systems still reflect different approaches compared to U.S. pay systems. **Exhibit 16.14** uses the basic choices outlined in the total pay model—objectives, internal alignment, competitiveness, and contributions—as a basis for comparisons. Both the Japanese and the German sociopolitical and culture systems constrain organizations' use of pay as a strategic tool. German companies face pay rates, job evaluation methods, and bonuses identical to those of their competitors, set by negotiated tariff agreements. The basic strategic premise, that competitive advantage is sustained by aligning with business strategy, is limited by laws and unions. Japanese companies do not face pay rates fixed industry-wide; rather, they voluntarily meet to exchange detailed pay information. However, the end result appears to be the same: similar pay structures across companies competing within an industry. In contrast, managers in U.S. companies possess considerable flexibility to align pay systems with business strategies. As a result, greater variability exists among companies within and across industries.

The pay objectives in traditional German systems include mutual long-term commitment, security, egalitarian pay structures, and cost control through tariff agreements, which apply to competitors' labor costs too. Japanese organizations set pay objectives that focus on the long term (age and security), support high commitment (seniority-based/ability-based), are also more egalitarian, signal the importance of company and individual performance, and encourage flexible workers (person-based pay). U.S. companies, in contrast, focus on the shorter term (less job security); are market-sensitive (competitive total pay); emphasize cost control (variable pay based on performance); reward performance improvement, meritocracy, and innovation (individual bonuses and stock, etc.); and encourage flexibility.

In Japan, person-based factors (seniority, ability, and performance) carry important weight in setting base pay. Market comparisons are monitored in Japan, but internal alignment based on seniority remains far more important. Job-based factors (job evaluation) and seniority are also used in Germany. Labor markets in Germany remain highly regulated, and tariff agreements set pay for union workers. So, like the Japanese system, the German system places much greater emphasis on internal alignment than on external markets.

Each approach has advantages and disadvantages. Clearly, the Japanese approach is consistent with low turnover/high commitment and high security, greater acceptance of change, and the need to be flexible. U.S. firms face higher turnover and greater skepticism about change. U.S. firms encourage innovation; they also recognize the contributions to be tapped from workforce diversity. German traditional systems tend to be more bureaucratic and rule-bound. Hence, they are more inflexible. However, they also offer more stability. Both the Japanese and the German national systems face challenges from the high costs associated with an aging workforce. Japan has taken very limited advantage of women's capabilities. The U.S. challenges include the impact of increased uncertainty that employees face, the system's short-term focus, and employees' skepticism about continuous change.

Evolution and Change in the Traditional Japanese and German Models

The slow economic growth that Japan has experienced combined with the emphasis in its traditional model on seniority-based pay creates a challenge in controlling labor costs. At the same time, cheaper labor in emerging Asian countries (e.g., China) puts further pressure on controlling labor costs and/or increasing productivity. Faced with these pressures, many companies are trying to maintain *long-time employment* (rather than **lifetime employment**) and are looking for other ways to reward less senior employees. These younger employees, who have been paid relatively poorly under the seniority-based pay system, are increasingly finding alternative job opportunities in non-Japanese firms operating in Japan, which have in the past rewarded individual ability and performance more strongly.[83]

EXHIBIT 16.14 Country Similarities and Differences in "Typical" Compensation Systems

	Japan	United States	Germany
Objectives	Long-term focus	Short/intermediate focus	Long-term focus
	High commitment	High commitment	High commitment
	Egalitarian—internal fairness	Performance—market—meritocratic	Egalitarian—fairness
	Flexible workforce	Flexible workforce	Highly trained
	Control cash flow with bonuses	Cost control; varies with performance	Cost control through tariff negotiations
Internal alignment	Person based: age, ability, performance determines base pay	Work based: jobs, skills, accountabilities	Work based: jobs and experience
	Many levels	Fewer levels	Many levels
	Small pay differences	Larger pay differences	Small pay differences
External competitiveness	Monitor age-pay charts	Market determined	Tariff based
	Consistent with competitors	Compete on variable and performance-based pay	Same as competitors
Employee contribution	Bonuses vary with performance only at higher levels in organization	Bonuses an increasing percentage of total pay	Tariff negotiated bonuses
	Performance appraisal influences promotions and small portion of pay increases	Increases based on individual, unit, and corporate performance	Smaller performance bonuses for managers
Advantages	Supports commitment and security	Supports performance—competitor focus	Supports commitment and security
	Greater predictability for companies and employees	Costs vary with performance	Greater predictability for companies and employees
	Flexibility—person based	Focus on short-term payoffs (speed to market)	Companies do not compete with pay
Disadvantages	High cost of aging workforce	Skeptical workers, less security	Inflexible; bureaucratic
	Discourages unique contributors	Fosters "What's in it for me?"	High social and benefit costs
	Discourages women and younger employees	No reward for investing in long-term projects	Not a strategic tool

To compete, as we have noted, companies such as Toyota, Hitachi, and Fujitsu are increasingly using performance-based pay. As a result, more variation in pay systems has emerged among traditional Japanese companies.[84] As **Exhibit 16.15** shows, 41 percent of Japanese companies, even as of the mid-1990s, reported placing a high emphasis on performance in compensation decisions.[85] Only 12 percent reported that performance received a low emphasis. In another survey, 58 percent of Japanese companies reported they had adopted merit pay as of 2018, up from 18 percent in 1999.[86]

Likewise, **Exhibit 16.16** shows that Japan has been similar for some years now to other countries such as the United States in its degree of performance-based differentiation in the merit increase process. Also, national data indicate a decline in the role of seniority in pay in Japan, as well as less lifetime employment (as noted above).[87] China too moved more toward pay for (individual) performance many years ago.[88] Apparently, the fact that China and Japan (as well as Singapore) are medium high or high on collectivism and uncertainty avoidance, national culture characteristics thought to be inconsistent with individual pay for performance and lack of job security, did not prevent these countries from making major changes in these areas when faced with sufficiently strong competitive forces that called into question the sustainability of their traditional employment practices. (We also know that there have been similar, perhaps even bigger changes in Korea, which had previously modeled its employment system on Japan.)[89]

Like many advanced economies, Germany, along with a number of other Western European countries, faces serious challenges. An aging population, low birth rates, earlier retirement ages, and high pension and unemployment benefits are pushing up the costs of the social support system. A relatively inflexible labor market means that employers are finding it easier to move to (or expand in) other EU countries (e.g., just across the border to countries like Poland or Czechia where labor costs are much lower) as well as to China and India. All these factors are causing a rethinking of the traditional German social contract and the resulting total compensation systems. Companies are asking for greater autonomy in negotiating tariff agreements to better reflect each company's economic conditions, the use of performance-based pay, and ways to link job security to company performance.

A number of studies report substantial changes in the traditional German model, including greater use of pay for performance, similar to the shifts seen in Japan. Again, foreign multinationals have played some part.[90] As **Exhibit 16.15** indicates, 47 percent of German companies, even by the late 2000s put a high emphasis

EXHIBIT 16.15 Use of Performance (versus Seniority) in Compensation Decisions

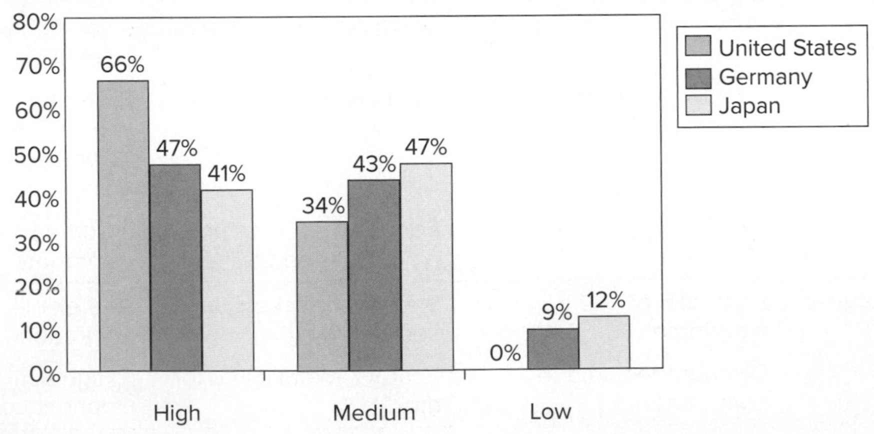

Source: Markus Pudelko, "The Seniority Principle in Japanese Companies: A Relic of the Past?" *Asia Pacific Journal of Human Resources* 44, no. 3 (December 2006), pp. 276–294.

on performance in compensation decisions and only 9 percent reported that it received little emphasis. **Exhibit 16.16** demonstrates further that the magnitude of merit pay increases for top versus average performers is similar in Germany, China, the United States, and the United Kingdom, with Japan being somewhat different. Finally, the use of stock options in Germany has gone from near zero in 1990 (prior to the lifting of legal restrictions in 1998) to being commonplace in large firms.[91]

STRATEGIC MARKET MIND-SET

A global study of pay systems used by companies with worldwide operations identifies three general compensation strategies: (1) localizer, (2) exporter, and (3) globalizer.[92] These approaches reflect the company's business strategy.[93]

Localizer: "Think Global, Act Local"

If a localizer operates in 150 countries, it may have 150 different systems. The company's business strategy is to seek competitive advantage by providing products and services tailored to local customers. Localizers operate independently of the corporate headquarters. One manager compared his company's pay system this way: "It's as if McDonald's used a different recipe for hamburgers in every country. So, too, for our pay system." Another says, "We seek to be a good citizen in each nation in which we operate. So should our pay system." The pay system is consistent with local conditions.

Exporter: "Headquarters Knows Best"

Exporters are virtual opposites of localizers. Exporters design a total pay system at headquarters and "export" it worldwide for implementation at all locations. Exporting a basic system (with some adjustments for

EXHIBIT 16.16 **Merit Pay Increase for Top Performer versus Average Performer, by Country**

Country	Number of Companies	Type of Employee	Top Performer	Average Performer	Top/Average Ratio
United Kingdom	266	All Employees	3.5%	2.8%	1.3
Germany	262	All Employees	3.4%	2.7%	1.3
China	227	All Employees	8.9%	6.1%	1.5
Japan	115	Professional/ Technical	6.4%[a]	4.3%[a]	1.5[a]
Singapore	201	All Employees	5.4%	3.6%	1.5
United States	835	Management	4.7%	3.0%	1.6

Source: Aon Global Salary Increase Survey 2019 and 2020 (Ken Abosch, Aon, personal communication). Data for Japan only from: Hewitt Associates, *Salary Increase Survey* 2008 and 2009 from Japan.

[a]Data for Japan only are from 2008/2009.

national laws and regulations) makes it easier to move managers and professionals among locations or countries without having to change how they are paid. It also communicates consistent corporatewide objectives. Managers say that "one plan from headquarters gives all managers around the world a common vocabulary and a clear message about what the leadership values." Common software used to support compensation decisions and deployed around the world makes uniform policies and practices feasible. However, not everyone likes the idea of simply implementing what others have designed. One manager complained that headquarters rarely consulted managers in the field: "There is no notion that ideas can go both ways. It's a one-way bridge."

Globalizer: "Think and Act Globally and Locally"

Similar to exporters, globalizers seek a common system that can be used as part of the "glue" to support consistency across all global locations. But headquarters and the operating units are heavily networked to share ideas and knowledge. Managers in these companies said:

> "No one has a corner on good ideas about how to pay people. We need to get them from all our locations."
>
> "'Home country' begins to lose its meaning; performance is measured where it makes sense for the business, and pay structures are designed to support the business."
>
> "Compensation policy depends more on tax policies and the dynamics of our business than it does on 'national' culture. The culture argument is something politicians hide behind."

Some believe the globalizer is the business model for the 21st century. IBM, for example, calls itself a "globally integrated enterprise." The aim is for all its operations, from production to marketing to R&D to be integrated around the world.[94] They continue to compete as multinationals. The point is that rather than emphasizing national pay systems as the key to international compensation, the three strategic **global approaches** focus first on the global business strategy and then adapt to local conditions.

When it comes to one dimension of compensation, variable pay, **Exhibit 16.17** seems to suggest that "Headquarters Knows Best" is the dominant strategy (53% in 2016 and 2019), at least among these particular firms, which are almost entirely headquartered in North America. Less than 5 percent of companies report that variable pay programs "are designed...at the local level to ensure they are meeting the unique needs of local employees." In this vein, the 2019 survey reported that in seven world regions (e.g., U.S./Canada, Asia-Pacific), use of individual incentives varied only from 47 percent of companies to 55 percent of companies. In other words, there was almost no difference by region. The 2019 survey also reported that 82 percent of companies said their compensation philosophy was the same across countries and 85 percent said their performance management system was "applied consistently" across countries. Likewise, use of bonuses varied only from 79 percent to 91 percent depending on world region.

EXPATRIATE PAY

Multinationals operate, by definition, in many nations. Employees temporarily working and living in a foreign country are called **expatriates** (or "expats"). One key decision for companies is the degree of reliance on expatriates relative to local employees.[95]

- Expatriates who are citizens of the employer's parent or home country and living and working in another country (e.g., a Japanese citizen working for Toshiba in Toronto) are called parent-country nationals (PCNs).
- Expatriates who are citizens of neither the employer's parent country nor the foreign country where they are living and working (e.g., a German citizen working for Toshiba in Toronto) are called third-country nationals (TCNs).
- **Local country nationals (LCNs)** are citizens of a foreign country where the parent employer operates (e.g., a Canadian citizen working for Toshiba in Toronto).

Hiring LCNs has advantages. LCNs know local conditions and have relationships with local customers, suppliers, and government regulators. The company saves relocation expenses and the other often substantial expenses associated with the use of expatriates. It also avoids concerns about employees adapting to the local culture. Employment of LCNs satisfies nationalistic demands for hiring locals. Only rarely do organizations decide that hiring LCNs is inappropriate.

However, expats or TCNs may be brought in for a number of reasons.[96] The foreign assignment may represent an opportunity for selected employees to develop an international perspective; the position may be sufficiently confidential that information is entrusted only to a proven domestic veteran; or the particular skills required for a position may not be readily available in the local labor pool. **Exhibit 16.18** catalogs a number of reasons for asking employees to take work assignments in another country.

Designing expatriate pay is a challenge. A company that sends a U.S. employee (base salary of $100,000) with a spouse and two children to London for three years can expect to spend $1,000,000 to $1,300,000. Obviously, the high cost of expatriate assignments must be offset by the value of the employee's contributions.

EXHIBIT 16.17 Degree of Variable Pay Program Standardization across Countries

	2016	2019
Variable pay programs are designed primarily at the corporate level, and all employees usually participate in the same programs, with flexibility for local countries [to make limited adaptations or implement unique programs of nominal cost].[a]	53%	53%
Variable pay programs are designed exclusively at the corporate level, and all employees worldwide participate in the same programs.	31%	32%
Variable pay programs are designed with significant input from local HR and/or line management. One or a few core variable pay programs exist companywide; however, different countries have significant latitude to implement additional local programs based on local practice and competitive factors.	15%	12%
Variable pay programs are designed and administered primarily at the local level to ensure they are meeting the unique needs of local employees.	1%	4%

Source: WorldatWork. Compensation Programs and Practices Survey, 2016 (N = 165 companies), 2019 (N = 112 companies). Respondents are almost entirely North American companies.

[a]The part in brackets was included in 2016, but not in 2019.

Elements of Expatriate Compensation

"(W)e are becalmed. There has been little real innovation in the expatriate compensation field in years," according to a leading consultant.[97] We would add, "So much money, going to so many people, with so little evidence of added value." **Exhibit 16.19** is a shopping list of items that can make up expatriate compensation. The list includes everything from household furnishing allowances to language and culture training, spousal employment assistance, and rest and relaxation leaves for longer-term assignments. Usually such lists are organized into four major components: salary, taxes, housing, and allowances and premiums.[98]

Salary

The base salary plus incentives (merit, eligibility for profit sharing, bonus plans, etc.) for expatriate jobs is usually determined via job evaluation or some system of "job leveling."[99] 3M applies a global job evaluation plan for its international assignments. Common factors describe different 3M jobs around the world. With this system, the work of a general manager in Brussels can be compared to the work of a manager in Austin, Texas, or in Singapore. General Mills has recently implemented a similar system.[100]

Beyond salaries and incentives, the intent of the other components is to help keep expatriate employees financially whole and minimize the disruptions of the move. This means maintaining a standard of living about equal to their peers in their home or base country. This is a broad standard that often results in very costly packages.

EXHIBIT 16.18 Why Expatriates Are Selected

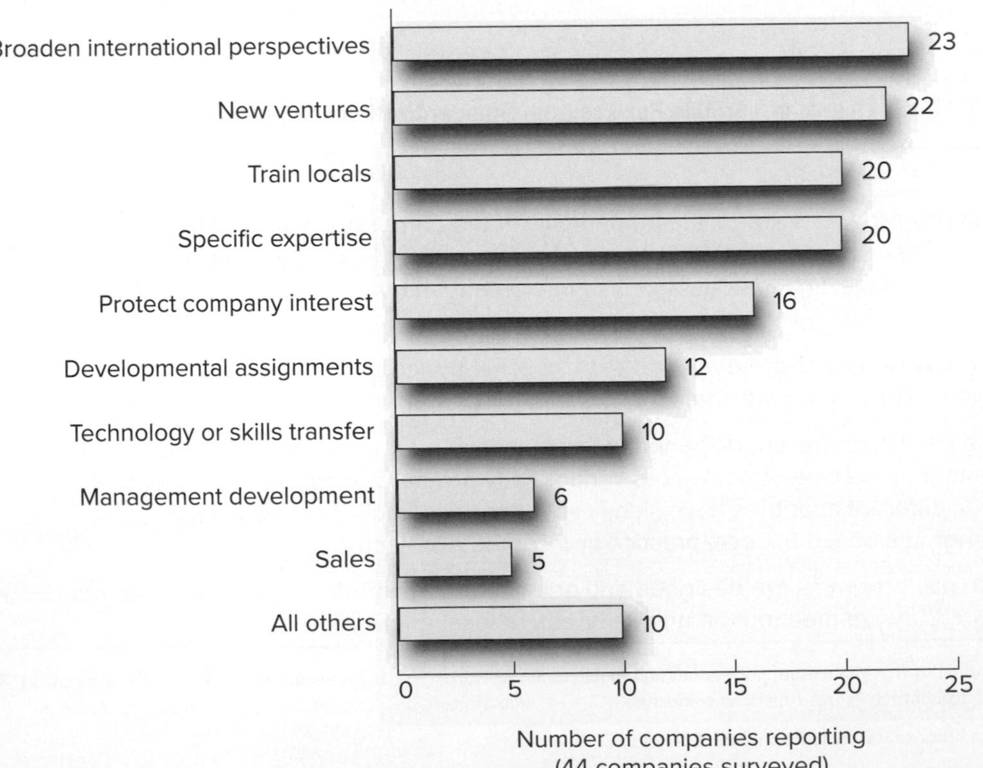

Taxes

Income earned in foreign countries has two potential sources of income tax liability.[101] With few exceptions (Saudi Arabia is one), foreign tax liabilities are incurred on income earned in foreign countries. For example, money earned in Japan is subject to Japanese income tax, whether earned by a Japanese or a Korean citizen. The other potential liability is the tax owed in the employee's home country. The United States has the dubious distinction of being the only developed country that taxes its citizens for income earned in another country, even though that income is taxed by the country in which it was earned. Most employers pay whatever income taxes are due to the host country and/or the home country via **tax equalization.**[102] Taxes are deducted from employees' earnings up to the same amount of taxes they would pay had they remained in their home country.

This allowance can be substantial. For example, the marginal income tax rate in Sweden is 57 percent and 56 percent in Denmark, which is higher than in the United States (roughly 40 percent with federal and where applicable, state and local taxes). However, most notable is that Denmark and Sweden apply this tax rate starting at income levels around $65,000.[103] Thus, if a Swedish expatriate is sent to a lower-tax country, say, Great Britain, the company keeps the difference. If a British expatriate goes to Sweden, the company makes up the difference in taxes. The logic here is that if the employee kept the windfall from being assigned to a low-tax country, then getting this person to accept assignments elsewhere would become difficult.

EXHIBIT 16.19 Common Allowances in Expatriate Pay Packages

Financial Allowances	**Social Adjustment Assistance**
Reimbursement for tax return preparation	Emergency leave
Tax equalization	Home leave
Housing differential	Company car/driver
Children's education allowance	Assistance with locating new home
Temporary living allowance	Access to Western health care
Goods and services differential	Club membership
Transportation differential	General personal services (e.g., translation)
Foreign service premium	Personal security (manager and family)
Household furnishing allowance	General culture-transition training (manager)
Currency protection	Social events
Hardship premium	Career development and repatriation planning
Completion bonus	Training for local-culture customs (manager)
Family Support	Orientation to community (manager and family)
Language training	Counseling services
Assistance locating schools for children	Rest and relaxation leave
Training for local culture's customs (family)	Domestic staff (excluding child care)
Child care providers	Use of company-owned vacation facilities
Assistance locating spousal employment	

Housing

Appropriate housing has a major impact on an expatriate's success. Most international companies pay housing allowances or provide company-owned housing. **Expatriate colonies** often grow up in sections of major cities where many different international companies group their expatriates.

Allowances and Premiums

A friend in Moscow cautions that when we take the famed Moscow subway, we should pay the fare at the beginning of the ride. Inflation is so high there that if we wait to pay until the end of the ride, we won't be able to afford to get off! Cost-of-living allowances, club memberships, transportation assistance, child care and education, spousal employment, local culture training, and personal security are some of the many service allowances and premiums expatriates receive. The logic supporting these allowances is that foreign assignments require that the expatriate (1) work with less direct supervision than a domestic counterpart, (2) often live and work in strange and sometimes uncongenial surroundings, and (3) represent the employer in the host country. The size of the premium is a function of both the expected hardship and hazards in the host country and the type of job. An assignment in London will probably yield fewer allowances than one in Tehran, where the "National Day of Campaign against Global Arrogance" is observed every year on the anniversary of the takeover of the American Embassy in 1979.

The Balance Sheet Approach

Most North American, European, and Japanese global firms combine these elements of pay in a **balance sheet approach.**[104] The name stems from accounting, where credits and debits must balance. It is based on the premise that employees on overseas assignments should have the same spending power as they would in their home country. Therefore, the home country is the standard for all payments. The objective is to:

1. Ensure mobility of people to global assignments as cost-effectively as feasible.
2. Ensure that expatriates neither gain nor lose financially.
3. Minimize adjustments required of expatriates and their dependents.

Notice that none of these objectives link (explicitly) to performance.

Exhibit 16.20 depicts the traditional balance sheet approach. Home-country salary is the first column. A person's salary (based on job evaluation, market surveys, merit, and incentives) must cover taxes, housing, and goods and services, plus other financial obligations (a "reserve").

The proportions set for each of the components in the exhibit are *norms* (i.e., assumed to be "normal" for the typical expatriate) set to reflect consumption patterns in the home country for a person at that salary level with that particular family pattern. They are not actual expenditures. These norms are based on surveys conducted by consulting firms. Using the norms is supposed to avoid negotiating with each individual, although substantial negotiation still occurs.

Let us assume that the norms suggest that a typical manager with a spouse and one child, earning $84,000 ($7,000 per month) in the United States, will spend $2,000 per month on housing, $2,000 on taxes, and $2,000 on goods and services and put away a reserve of $1,000 per month. The next building block is the equivalent costs in the host country where the assignment is located. For example, if similar housing costs $3,000 in the host country, the expatriate is expected to pay the same $2,000 paid in the United States and the company pays the employee the difference; in our example, an extra $1,000 per month. In the illustration, the taxes, housing, and goods and services components are all greater in the host country than in the home country. The expatriate bears the same level of costs (white area of right-hand column) as at home. The employer is responsible for the additional costs (shaded area). (Changing exchange rates among currencies complicates these allowance calculations.)

However, equalizing pay may not motivate an employee to move to another country, particularly if the new location has less personal appeal. Therefore, many employers also offer some form of financial incentive or bonus to encourage the move. The right-hand column in **Exhibit 16.20** includes a relocation bonus. Most U.S. multinational corporations pay relocation bonuses to induce people to take expatriate assignments.

If gaining international experience is really one of the future competencies required by organizations, then the need for such bonuses ought to be reduced, since the expatriate experience should increase the likelihood of future promotions. Either the experience expatriates obtain is unique to each situation and therefore not transferable or companies simply do not know how to value it. Whatever the reason, research reveals that **U.S. expatriates** feel their U.S. organizations still do not value their international expertise.[105] So the rhetoric of the value of global competencies has yet to match the reality–hence the need for relocation incentives. Another way to look at it is that the employee takes a risk going overseas. Near-term promotion opportunities may be lost. While international experience could have a handsome payoff in later promotions for some, this payoff is not certain and not true for all. Moreover, a nontrivial share of expatriate assignments are cut short, due either to performance problems or family-related problems (e.g., spouse and/or children having difficulties adapting).[106] Thus, consistent with our earlier discussion of agency theory, a compensating differential for risk may be required.

Alternatives to Balance Sheet Approach

Employers continue to explore alternatives to the balance sheet, due primarily to the cost. Although in **Exhibit 16.20** the expatriate premium was 46 percent ($10,200/$7,000 - 1), that premium can be much higher. For example, **Exhibit 16.21** shows survey data on the cost of a manager (married plus one child/dependent) with a U.S. salary of $116,000 posted to Singapore. The balance sheet approach cost ranged from

EXHIBIT 16.20 Balance Sheet Approach

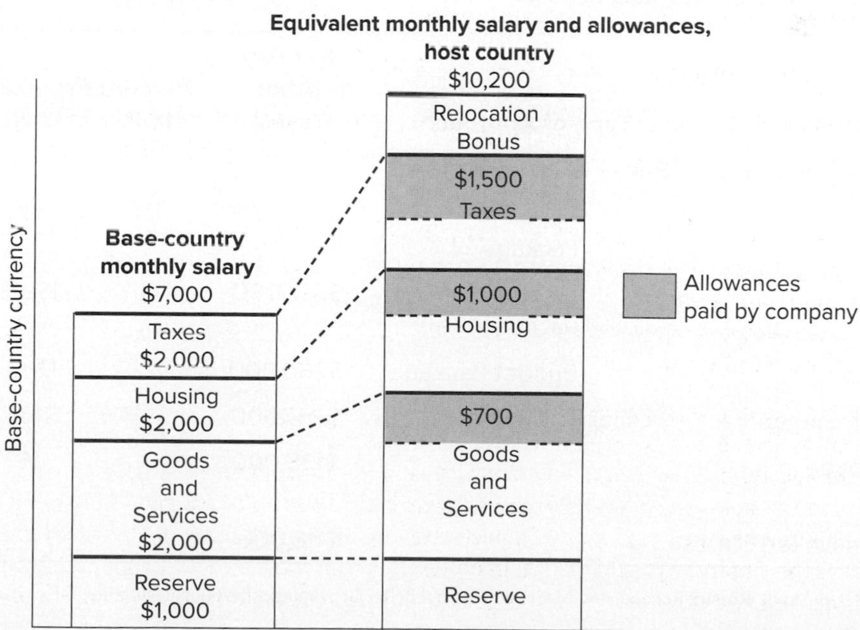

a "budget package" cost of $260,000 to a "premium package" cost of $393,000, or a 239 percent premium. The "standard package" was $312,000, a 169 percent premium and had the following components:

Home Net Base Salary	$115,500
Cost of Living Adjustment	$ 16,570
Mobility Premium	$ 16,570
Accommodation/Housing	$115,500
Car Benefit	$ 14,400
Education Benefit	$ 33,600
Total	$312,140

Negotiation simply means the employer and employee find a mutually agreeable package. The arrangements tend to be relatively costly (or generous, depending on your point of view), create comparability problems when other employees are asked to locate overseas ("but Mike and Sarah got . . ."), and need to be renegotiated with each transfer.

Another alternative, *localization,* or *local plus,* ties salary to the host country's salary scales and provides some cost-of-living allowances for taxes, housing, and dependents. The allowances tend to be similar to those under the balance sheet, but the salary can vary with the location. As **Exhibit 16.21** shows, in the case of Singapore, the localization approach would, on average, result in a cost of $247,000, a 113 percent premium, in contrast to the premium of as much as 239 percent for the balance sheet approach.

While the balance sheet approach ties salary to the home country, the *modified balance sheet* ties salary to a region (Asia-Pacific, Europe, North America, Central America, or South America). The logic is that if an employee of a global business who relocates from San Diego, California, to Portland, Maine, receives only a

EXHIBIT 16.21 Manager Working in Singapore or United States ("Married Plus One" Situation)

Type of Employee	Type of Approach	Net Pay (After Taxes)	Percent Premium Relative to Pay in United States
Expatriate in Singapore	Balance Sheet Approach		
	Premium Package	$393,000	239%
	Standard Package	$312,000	169%
	Budget Package	$260,000	124%
Expatriate in Singapore	Local Plus Package	$247,000	113%
Local Employee in Singapore		$135,000	16%
Employee in United States		$116,000	

Source: Carole Mestre, Anne Rossier-Renaud, and Madeline Berger, "Better Benchmarks for Global Mobility," *Workspan*, April 2009.

moving allowance, why should all the extras be paid for international moves of far less distance (e.g., from Germany to Spain)? In Europe, many companies no longer view European managers who work outside their home country as expats. Instead, they are Europeans running their European businesses. And the use of a common currency, the euro, makes this easier. In this vein, a study compared the over-base pay allowance provided by 17 multinational companies to an employee earning 100,000 euros being transferred from Frankfurt, Germany, to Paris, France.[107] The median premium was 23,000 euros, or 13 percent and the range was from as little as 5,000 euros, a 5 percent premium, to 45,000 euros, a 45 percent premium. Thus, in all 17 companies, the premium was modest relative to what we have seen.

Another common modification is to decrease allowances over time. The logic is that the longer the employee is in the host country, the closer the standard of living should come to that of a local employee. For example, if Americans eat a $10 pizza twice a week in the United States, should they eat a $30 pizza twice a week in Tokyo, at the employer's expense? More typically, after a couple of months, the expatriate will probably learn where the nationals find cheaper pizza or will switch to sushi. We had a friend posted to London by a U.S. company. The expatriate and spouse ate dinner out each night, leased a nice apartment in an upscale centrally located neighborhood, had a car, and the spouse went back to school. All this was paid for by the company, so the couple's entire paycheck went into the bank and investments. They were living in London with all expenses paid! When they had to eventually return to the United States, at the behest of the company, it was with great reluctance and after running out of extensions to the assignment.

The *lump-sum/cafeteria approach* offers expats more choices. This approach sets salaries according to the home-country system and simply offers employees lump sums of money to offset differences in standards of living. For example, a company will still calculate differences in cost of living, but instead of allocating them housing, transportation, goods and services, and so on, it simply gives the employee a total allowance. Perhaps one employee will trade less spacious housing for private schooling and tutors for the children; another employee will make different choices. We know of one expatriate who purchased a winery in Italy with his lump-sum allowance. He has been reassigned to Chicago but still owns and operates his winery.

Finally, a company can consider using fewer expatriates and more *local country nationals.* As we stated at the beginning of our discussion of expatriate pay, such a strategy has many advantages, including lower cost, and greater familiarity with the aspects of the business environment unique to that country. Another advantage is that such a strategy can be combined with a strategy of greater integration of talent into the career planning and development system. An increasing number of companies have foreign-born managers and executives in key posts. Some of these key people would not be where they are now making important contributions if they had not had the opportunity at some point to gain experience in key jobs in their home countries and then build on that to progress through the company's ranks.[108] Along these same lines, greater use of **third-country nationals (TCNs)** can also fit this strategy. In addition, TCNs can be less expensive if they come from countries having lower compensation levels. For example, whereas we saw in our earlier example that a U.S. expatriate earning $116,000 at home and posted to Singapore would cost $312,000, a comparable TCN from India posted to Singapore would cost $209,000.[109] In addition, given that the Indian TCN would earn $49,000 in India, the premium he or she would realize would be quite substantial and thus perhaps the assignment would have higher value than it would to a comparable expatriate from the United States.

Expatriate Systems → Objectives? *Quel dommage!*

Talk to experts in international compensation, and you soon get into complexities of taxes, exchange rates, housing differences, and the like. What you do not hear is how the expatriate pay system affects competitive advantage, customer satisfaction, quality, or other performance concerns. It does emphasize maintaining employee purchasing power and minimizing disruptions and inequities. But the lack of attention to aligning expatriate pay with organization objectives is glaring. Sadly, the major innovation in expat pay over the past decade seems to have been to relabel expats and TCNs as "international assignees."

Expatriate compensation systems are forever trying to be like Goldilocks' porridge: not too high, not too low, but just right. The expatriate pay must be sufficient to encourage the employee to take the assignment yet not be so attractive that local nationals will feel unfairly treated or that the expatriate will refuse any future reassignments. These systems also presume that expats will be repatriated to their home country. However, the relevant standard for judging fairness may not be home-country treatment. It may be the pay of other expats, that is, the expat community, or it may be local nationals. And how do local nationals feel about the allowances and pay levels of their expat co-workers? Very little research tells us how expats and those around them judge the fairness of expat pay.

Employee Preferences

Beyond work objectives, costs, and fairness, an additional consideration is employees' preferences for international assignments. For many Europeans, working in another country is just part of a career. Yet for many U.S. employees, leaving the United States means leaving the action. They may worry that expatriate experience sidetracks rather than enhances a career. Employees undoubtedly differ in their preferences for overseas jobs, and preferences can vary over time. Having children in high school or elderly parents to care for, divorce, working spouses, and other life factors exert a strong influence on whether an offer to work overseas is a positive or negative opportunity. Research does inform us of the following:

- 68 percent of expatriates do not know what their jobs will be when they return home.
- 54 percent return to lower-level jobs. Only 11 percent are promoted.
- Only 5 percent believe their company values overseas experience.
- 77 percent have less disposable income when they return home.
- Only 13 percent of U.S. expatriates are women. (Yet 49% of all U.S. managers and professionals are women.)
- More than half of returning expatriates leave their company within one year.[110] Unfortunately, while research does highlight the problem, it does not offer much guidance for designers of expat pay systems. Consequently, we are at the mercy of conjecture and beliefs.[111]

We should emphasize that, of course, some companies do a much better job of managing expatriates. Also, there is disagreement over what the evidence actually says on rates of success and failure of expatriates, especially those from the United States.[112]

BORDERLESS WORLD → BORDERLESS PAY? GLOBALISTS

Some corporations, particularly those attempting to become "globally integrated enterprises," are creating cadres of globalists: managers who operate anywhere in the world in a borderless manner. They expect that during their career, they will be located in and travel from country to country. According to a former CEO of General Electric, "The aim in a global business is to get the best ideas from everyone, everywhere." To support this global flow of ideas and people some companies are also designing borderless, or at least regionalized, pay systems. One testing ground for this approach is the European Union. As our global guide points out, one difficulty with borderless pay is that base pay levels and the other components depend too much on differences in each nation's laws and customs.

Focusing on expatriate compensation may blind companies to the issue of appropriate pay for employees who seek global career opportunities. Ignoring these employees causes them to focus only on the local operations, their home country pay, and devote less attention to integrating operations in global firms. It is naive to expect commitment to a long-term global strategy in which local managers have little input and receive limited benefits. Paradoxically, attempts to localize top management in subsidiaries may reinforce the differences in focus between local and global management.

Your Turn

Globalization of the Labor Market: The English Premier League

According to Forbes, depending on the year, three of the five (or ten) most valuable sports teams in the world are football teams. In 2020, they were: Real Madrid ($4.2 billion), Barcelona ($4.0 billion), and Manchester United ($3.3 billion). As you can see, we are not talking about American football teams. We are talking about what some of us call soccer. (The most valuable sports team in the world in 2020 was the the Dallas Cowboys at $5.5 billion).

The English Premier League, where Manchester United plays, is the top soccer league in the world, based on revenue generated. (La Liga in Spain, where Real Madrid and Barcelona play, as well as the Bundesliga in Germany, where, for example, Bayern Munich plays, are other top leagues.) There are 500 players in the British Premier League (20 teams x 25 players each). The average annual salary (before the pandemic) was about £3 million. At today's British pound/U.S. dollar exchange rate, that is about $4.1 million. In 1992–1993, the average player salary was about $210,000 (adjusted for inflation). Besides the salaries, one other thing that has changed is where the players come from. In 1992–1993, 69 percent of the players were English. Today, it is 31 percent. Thus, it is no longer the case that the majority of players in the English Premier League are English. Indeed, there is now a rule that of the 25 players on the roster, 8 must be "home grown." Of the top 20 goal scorers in the most recent year, 7 were from England.

Some economists have noted the benefits of this globalization of the English Premier League and open borders/free movement of players ("workers"). Arguably, the quality of play in the League has improved because it draws the best talent from around the world rather than being mostly limited to local talent. That, in turn, has led to globalization of the product market. Specifically, English Premier League football is watched around the world, not only because of the elite quality of play and players, but also likely because many countries have players in the League, which probably increases interest in those countries. That brings in large amounts of revenue from outside of England in the form of television rights, jersey sales, and advertising. To help see the global reach of the League, one can look at the players' jerseys. The jerseys for the club Tottenham, for example, carry the logo of AIA, an Asian-based insurance company that has no offices in England. The book *Soccernomics* refers to the League as "the most successful product in sporting history."

So, what's not to like? Greg Dyke, chairman of the Football Association, which governs English soccer, has asked how many English players in the English football academies dream of playing football but "cannot get a first-team game." He has proposed limits on the number of foreign players in the Premier League.

QUESTIONS:

1. Has the globalization of the English Premier League been a good thing? Who is better off as a result? Who is worse off? Think carefully about owners, fans/consumers, and players. Are there others who have been affected as well?

2. Consider the proposal by Mr. Dyke to limit the number of foreign players in the English Premier League. Take the perspective of owners, players, and fans/consumers. Who would benefit and who would lose under this proposal?
3. Do players from England play in elite leagues outside of England? Does that affect your evaluation of the proposal? If so, how?
4. One concern expressed by Mr. Dyke is that the English national team may be suffering because fewer English players can develop in the English Premier League. Jürgen Klinsmann, former coach of the U.S. National team, has criticized players who play in the Major League Soccer (MLS) league in the United States, rather than in one of the European elite leagues, because he feels MLS does not provide strong enough competition for the U.S. players to develop their full potential. Comment on the arguments by Mr. Dyke and Mr. Klinsmann. What would be best for the English national team?

Sources: Sean Ingle. "Average annual salary of Premier League players tops £3m for first time." The Guardian, December 23, 2019. www.theguardian.com; https://www.premierleague.com/stats/top/players/goals?se=-1. Based on the 2019/2020 season, accessed April 18, 2021; Kurt Badenhausen. "The World's Most Valuable Sports Teams 2020. Forbes, July 32, 2020. www.forbes.com; Binyamin Appelbuam, "Globalization under Attack, on the Soccer Field," *New York Times*, April 2, 2015, p. A3; https://www.premierleague.com/stats/top/players/goals?se=-1. Based on the 2019/2020 season, accessed April 18, 2021.

Summary

Studying employee compensation only in your neighborhood, city, or country is like being a horse with blinders. Removing the blinders by adopting an international perspective deepens your understanding of local issues. Anyone interested in compensation must adopt a worldwide perspective. The globalization of businesses, financial markets, trade agreements, and even labor markets is affecting every workplace and every employment relationship. And employee compensation, so central to the workplace, is embedded in the different political-socioeconomic arrangements found around the world. Examining employee compensation with the factors in the global pay model offers insights into managing total compensation internationally.

The basic premise of this book is that compensation systems have a profound impact on individual behavior, organization success, and social well-being. We believe this holds true within and across all national boundaries.

Review Questions

1. Rank the factors in the global guide according to your belief in their importance for understanding and managing compensation. How does your ranking differ from those of your peers? From those of international peers? Discuss how the rankings may change over time.
2. Distinguish between nationwide and industrywide pay determination. How do they compare to a business strategy–market approach?
3. Develop arguments for and against "typical" Japanese-style, "typical" German-style, and "typical" U.S.-style approaches to pay. Using the global guide, what factors are causing each approach to change?
4. Distinguish between global workers, expatriates, local nationals, and third-country nationals.
5. In the balance sheet approach to paying expats, most of total compensation is linked to costs of living. Some argue that expatriate pay resembles a traditional Japanese pay system. Evaluate this argument.

Endnotes

1. Holger M. Mueller, Paige P. Ouimet, and Elena Simintzi, "Wage Inequality and Firm Growth," *American Economic Review* 107, no. 5 (2017), pp. 379–383; Ariel Burstein and Jonathan Vogel, "International Trade, Technology, and the Skill Premium," *Journal of Political Economy* 125, no. 5 (2017), pp. 1356–1412; Ken Abosch, Jill Schermerhorn, and Lori Wisper, "Broad-Based Variable Pay Goes Global," *Workspan,* May 2008, pp. 57–62; Jie Shen, "HRM in Chinese Privately Owned Enterprises," *Thunderbird International Business Review* 50, no. 2 (2008), pp. 91–101; Fay, C. H., "The Global Convergence of Compensation Practices," in *Global Compensation: Foundations and Perspectives,* L. R. Gomez-Mejia and S. Werner, Eds. (Oxon, UK: Routledge, 2008), pp. 32–141.
2. Markus Pudelko, "The Seniority Principle in Japanese Companies: A Relic of the Past?" *Asia Pacific Journal of Human Resources* 44 (2006), pp. 276–294; Tetsushi Kajimoto and Izumi Nakagawa, "Japan's Efforts to Raise Wages Wane as Firms Embrace Merit-Based Pay," *The Japan Times,* February 12, 2020; Makiko Yamazaki and Noriyuki Hirata, "With Shift Toward Merit-Based Pay," Japan's Hitachi to drop old ways, www.reuters.com, July 16, 2020.
3. Interviews with Toshiba managers, included in M. Bloom, G. Milkovich, and A. Mitra, "Managing the Chaos of Global Pay Systems," *International Journal of Human Resource Management* 14 (2003), pp. 1350–1367.
4. Geraldine Fabrikant, "U.S.-Style Pay Packages Are All the Rage in Europe," *The New York Times,* June 16, 2006; "New Equity Incentive Programs Gain Favor with Employers Around the World," *Towers Perrin Monitor,* July 22, 2005; *European Total Rewards Survey 2005,* www.merhr.com/totalrewardseurope.
5. S. Kuruvilla, C. K. Lee, and M. E. Gallagher, eds., *From Iron Rice Bowl to Informalization: Markets, Workers, and the State in a Changing China* (Ithaca, NY: Cornell University Press, 2011). [Kuruvilla et al. estimated at the time that 40% of the population in China was in a precarious situation.] No author, "The Social Cracks in Breaking China's 'Iron Rice Bowl': State Firms Have Long Provided not only Jobs but Also a Range of Welfare Benefits," *South China Morning Post,* December 18, 2016.
6. United Nations, *World Investment Report 2011,* table I.5; *World Investment Report* 2014, table 2; *World Investment Report 2020,* Table I.7 (p. 22) and Table IV.1 (p. 124). unctad.org.
7. International Association of Automobile Manufacturers, http://oica.net/category/production-statistics/, accessed April 18, 2021.
8. Apple Inc. 2020 Form 10-K (Annual Report); Apple, Inc. Supplier Responsibility, 2020 Progress Report. https://www.apple.com/supplier-responsibility/. [Scroll down for pdf file containing each year's report.]
9. Geraldine Fabrikant, "U.S. Style Pay Packages Are All the Rage in Europe," *The New York Times,* June 16, 2006; Thomas Li Ping Tang, Toto Sutarso, Adebowale Akande, et al., "The Love of Money and Pay Level Satisfaction: Measurement and Functional Equivalence in 29 Geopolitical Entities Around the World," paper presented at the Annual Meeting of the Academy of Management, August 11–16, 2006, Atlanta, GA.
10. "Marriages Made in Hell," *The Economist,* May 20, 2009, *www.economist.com,* August 2009.
11. "Costs of Chrysler Sale Blamed in Daimler Loss," *The New York Times,* October 25, 2007, *www.nytimes.com,* August 2009.
12. Parmy Olson, "The Carmaker Finally Rids Itself of 19.9% Stake," *Forbes,* April 28, 2009, *www.forbes.com,* August 2009.
13. Torsten Kühlmann and Peter J. Dowling, "DaimlerChrysler: A Case Study of a Cross Border Merger," in *Mergers and Acquisitions: Managing Cultures and Human Resources,* ed. Günther Stahl and Mark E. Mendenhall (Stanford, CA: Stanford Business Books, 2005).

14. Carmelo Cennamo, "Shareholders' Value Maximization and Stakeholders' Interest," in *Global Compensation: Foundations and Perspectives,* Luis R. Gomez-Mejia and Steve Werner eds. (London: Routledge, 2008). See especially Table 8.1.

15. Mike Ramsey, "Chrysler Installs Fiat Production System before Plants Restart," *www.bloomberg.com,* June 29, 2009; "The Italian Solution: Fiat's Ambitions," *The Economist,* May 9, 2009, *www.economist.com,* August 2009; Serena Saitto, "Detroit Suburbs Beckon Fiat Executives with $1,595 Sandals," *www.bloomberg.com,* June 29, 2009.

16. Bill Vlasic, "A Merger Once Scoffed at Bears Fruit in Detroit," *The New York Times,* January 9, 2012; Jeremy Cato, "Chrysler and Fiat: The Odd Couple Triumphs," *The Globe and Mail,* May 3, 2012; Larry P. Vellequette, "How a Merger Made a Dart: First Test of Synergy Shows Chrysler, Fiat Can Listen, Communicate," *Automotive News,* May 14, 2012.

17. S. Basu, S. Estrin, and J. Svejnar, "Employment Determination in Enterprises under Communism and in Transition: Evidence from Central University," *Industrial and Labor Relations Review,* April 2005, pp. 353–369; J. Banister, "Manufacturing Compensation in China," *Monthly Labor Review,* November 2005, pp. 22–40; *Overview of the Chinese Economy,* Report by the Joint Economic Committee of United States Congress, July 2005; N. Zupan, "HRM in Slovenian Transitional Companies," presentation at CAHRS International Conference, Berlin, June 2002.

18. D. Dong, K. Goodall, and M. Warner, "The End of the Iron Rice Bowl," *International Journal of Human Resource Management,* April 2, 2000, pp. 217–236; Hesan A. Quazi, *Compensation and Benefits Practices in Selected Asian Countries* (Singapore: McGraw Hill, 2004).

19. Zhong-Ming Wang, presentation to Cornell University Global HRM Distance Learning seminar, Shanghai, China, March 2000; comments by Ningyu Tang, instructor in Shanghai for Global HRM Distance Learning seminar; Jing Zhou and J. J. Martocchio, "Chinese and American Managers' Compensation Award Decisions," *Personnel Psychology* 54 (Spring 2001), pp. 115–145; Mei Fong, "A Chinese Puzzle," *The Wall Street Journal,* August 16, 2005, p. B1; Zaohui Zhao, "Earnings Differentials between State and Non-State Enterprises in Urban China," *Pacific Economic Review* 7, no. 1 (2002), pp. 181–197.

20. *Doing Business in the Russian Federation,* PricewaterhouseCoopers, April 2004; John S. Earle and Klara Sabirianova Peter, "Complementarity and Custom in Wage Contract Violation," Upjohn Institute Staff Working Paper 06–129, July 2006.

21. Kevin O'Rourke and J. G. Williamson, *Globalization and History: The Evolution of a 19th Century Atlantic Economy* (Cambridge, MA: MIT Press, 1999), p. 2.

22. Kevin O'Rourke and J. G. Williamson, *Globalization and History: The Evolution of a 19th Century Atlantic Economy* (Cambridge, MA: MIT Press, 1999), chapter 14. Also see W. Keller, L. Pauly, and S. Reich, *The Myth of the Global Corporation* (Princeton, NJ: Princeton University Press, 1998); B. Kogut, "What Makes a Company Global?" *Harvard Business Review,* January–February 1999, pp. 165–170.

23. T. Kostova, "Transnational Transfer of Strategic Organizational Practices: A Contextual Perspective," *Academy of Management Review* 24 (1999), pp. 308–324; W. R. Scott, *Institutions and Organizations* (Thousand Oaks, CA: Sage Publications, 2000); T. Kostova and K. Roth, "Adoption of Organizational Practice by Subsidiaries of Multinational Corporations: Institutional and Relational Effects," *Academy of Management Journal* 45 (2002), pp. 215–233; R. Whitley, *Divergent Capitalisms: The Social Structuring and Change of Business Systems* (Oxford: Oxford University Press, 1999); Peter Hall and David Soskice, eds., *Varieties of Capitalism: The Institutional Foundations of Comparative Advantage* (New York: Oxford University Press, 2001); Tony Edwards and Sarosh Kuruvilla, "International HRM: National Business Systems, Organizational Politics and the International Division of Labour in MNCs," *International Journal of Human Resource Management* 16 (2005), pp. 1–21; Luis R. Gomez-Mejia and Steve Werner, eds., *Global Compensation: Foundations and Perspectives* (London:

Routledge, 2008); P. J. Dowling, M. Festing, and A. D. Engle, Sr., *International Human Resource Management,* 5th ed. (London: Thomson Learning, 2008); P. Evans, V. Pucik, and J. L. Barsoux, *The Global Challenge: International Human Resource Management* (New York: McGraw-Hill/Irwin, 2002); Gregory Jackson and Richard Deeg, "Comparing Capitalisms: Understanding Institutional Diversity and Its Implications for International Business," *Journal of International Business Studies* 39 (2008), pp. 540–561; Chris Brewster, "Different Paradigms in Strategic HRM: Questions Raised by Comparative Research," in *Research in Personnel and Human Resources Management,* Supplement 4, Patrick Wright, Lee Dyer, John Boudreau, and George T. Milkovich, eds. (Greenwich, CT: JAI Press, 1999).

24. C. Oliver, "Strategic Responses to Institutional Processes," *Academy of Management Review* 16 (1991), pp. 145–179.
25. K. Y. Au, "Intra-Cultural Variation: Evidence and Implications for International Business," *Journal of International Business Studies* 30 (1991), pp. 799–812; M. Bloom and G. T. Milkovich, "A SHRM Perspective on International Compensation and Rewards," in P. M. Wright, L. Dyer, J. W. Boudreau, and G. T. Milkovich, *Research in Personnel and Human Resources Management,* Supplement 4, (Stamford, CT: JAI Press, 1999), pp. 283–303; Barry Gerhart, "How Much Does National Culture Constrain Organization Culture?" *Management and Organization Review* 5 (2009), pp. 244–259; Barry Gerhart, "Cross-Cultural Management Research: Assumptions, Evidence, and Suggested Directions," *International Journal of Cross Cultural Management* 8 (2008), pp. 259–274; Barry Gerhart and Meiyu Fang, "National Culture and Human Resource Management: Assumptions and Evidence," *International Journal of Human Resource Management* 16 (2005), pp. 975–990; R. Nelson and S. Gopalan, "Do Organizational Cultures Replicate National Cultures? Isomorphism, Rejection, and Reciprocal Opposition in the Corporate Values of Three Countries," *Organization Studies* 24 (2003), pp. 1115–1151; B. Gerhart, "Compensation and National Culture," in *Global Compensation: Foundations and Perspectives,* S. Werner and L. R. Gomez-Mejia, eds. (London, U.K.: Routledge, 2008); Barry Gerhart, "Does National Culture Constrain Organization Culture and Human Resource Strategy? The Role of Individual Mechanisms and Implications for Employee Selection," *Research in Personnel and Human Resources Management* 28 (2009), pp. 1–48.
26. Russell D. Lansbury, Nick Wailes, Jim Kitay, and Anja Kirsch, eds., *Globalization and Employment Relations in the Auto Assembly Industry,* Bulletin of Comparative Labor Relations 64 (Alphen aan den Rijn, Netherlands: Wolters Kluwer, 2008).
27. H. C. Katz and O. Darbishire, *Converging Divergences: Worldwide Changes in Employment Systems* (Ithaca, NY: ILR Press/Cornell University Press, 2000); R. Batt and H. Nohara, "How Institutions and Business Strategies Affect Wages: A Cross-National Study of Call Centers," *Industrial and Labor Relations Review* 62 (2009), pp. 533–552.
28. J. B. Barney, "Organizational Culture: Can It Be a Source of Sustained Competitive Advantage?" *Academy of Management Review* 11 (1986), pp. 656–665; J. B. Barney, "Firm Resources and Sustained Competitive Advantage," *Journal of Management* 17 (1991), pp. 99–120; Barry Gerhart, "How Much Does National Culture Constrain Organization Culture?" *Management and Organization Review* 5 (2009), pp. 244–259. J. Du and J.N. Choi, "Pay for Performance in Emerging Markets: Insights from China," *Journal of International Business Studies* 41, pp. 671–689.
29. M. Pudelko and A. W. K. Harzing, "The Golden Triangle for MNCs: Standardization Towards Headquarters Practices, Standardization Towards Global Best Practices and Localization," *Organizational Dynamics* 37, no. 4 (2008), pp. 394–404; M. Pudelko and A. W. K. Harzing, "How European Is Management in Europe? An Analysis of Past, Present and Future Management Practices in Europe," *European Journal of International Management* 1, no. 3 (2007), pp. 206–224; M. Pudelko and A. W. K. Harzing, "Country-of-Origin, Localization or Dominance Effect? An Empirical

Investigation of HRM Practices in Foreign Subsidiaries," *Human Resource Management* 46 (2007), pp. 535–559; Anthony Ferner, "Country of Origin Effects and HRM in Multinational Companies," *Human Resource Management Journal* 7, no. 1 (1997), pp. 19–37; Anthony Ferner and Javier Quintanilla, "Multinationals, National Business Systems and HRM: The Enduring Influence of National Identity or a Process of 'Anglo-Saxonization,'" *International Journal of Human Resource Management* 9, no. 4 (1998), pp. 710–731; Ingmar Björkman, Carl F. Fey, and Hyeon Jeong Park, "Institutional Theory and MNC Subsidiary HRM Practices: Evidence from a Three-Country Study," *Journal of International Business Studies* 38 (2007), pp. 430–446.

30. Marion Festing, Judith Eidems, and Susanne Royer, "Strategic Issues and Local Constraints in Transnational Compensation Strategies: An Analysis of Cultural, Institutional and Political Processes," *European Management Journal* 25 (2007), pp. 118–131; Allen D. Engle, Sr., Peter J. Dowling, and Marion Festing, "State of Origin: Research in Global Performance Management: A Proposed Research Domain and Emerging Implications," *European Journal of International Management* 2 (2008), pp. 153–169; C.A. Bartlett and S. Ghoshal, *Managing Across Borders: The Transnational Solution* (Boston: Harvard Business School Press, 1989); Matt Bloom, George T. Milkovich, and Atul Mitra, "International Compensation: Learning From How Managers Respond to Variations in Local Host Contexts," *International Journal of Human Resource Management* 14 (2008), pp. 1350–1367.
31. Y. Yanadori, "Paying Both Globally and Locally: An Examination of the Compensation Management of a U.S. Multinational Finance Firm in the Asia Pacific Region," *International Journal of Human Resource Management* 18 (2011), pp. 3867–3887. T. Greckhamer, "Cross-Cultural Differences in Compensation Level and Inequality across Occupations: A Set-theoretic Analysis," *Organization Studies* 32, pp. 85–115.
32. Fran Blau and Lawrence Kahn, *At Home and Abroad: U.S. Labor Market Performance in International Perspective* (New York: Russell Sage Foundation, 2002).
33. Harry C. Katz, Wonduck Lee, and Joohee Lee, eds., "The New Structure of Labor Relations," *Tripartism and Decentralization* (Ithaca, NY: Cornell University Press, 2004).
34. *World of Work Report* (Geneva, Switzerland: International Labour Organization, 2008). See especially table 3.3.
35. Matthew M. C. Allen, Heinz-Joseph Tuselmann, Hamed El-Sa'id, and Paul Windrum, "Sectoral Collective Agreements: Remuneration Straitjackets for German Workplaces?" *Personnel Review* 36 (2006), pp. 963–967; European Industrial Relations Observatory Online (2005), "Changes in National Collective Bargaining Systems Since 1990," www.eurofound.europa.eu/eiro, retrieved 6/30/2009.
36. Bruce Crumley, "Goodbye to France's 35-Hour Week," *Time,* July 24, 2008.
37. Baker & McKenzie LLP, "Worldwide Guide to Trade Unions and Works Councils," www.gurn.info/en/, June 30, 2009.
38. Ibid., p. 105.
39. Ibid., p. 104.
40. John W. Budd, *Labor Relations: Striking a Balance,* 2nd ed. (New York: McGraw-Hill/Irwin, 2008).
41. G. Hofstede, *Culture's Consequences: International Differences in Work-Related Values* (Beverly Hills, CA: Sage, 1980); G. Hofstede, *Culture's Consequences: Comparing Values, Behaviors, Institutions, and Organizations Across Nations,* 2nd ed. (Thousand Oaks, CA: Sage, 2001); R. J. House, P. J. Hanges, M. Javidan, P. W. Dorfman, and V. Gupta, *Culture, Leadership, and Organizations: The Globe Study of 62 Societies* (Thousand Oaks, CA: Sage Publications, 2004); Trompenaars, *Riding the Waves of Culture: Understanding Diversity in Global Business* (Burr Ridge, IL: Irwin, 1995); H. C. Triandis, "Cross-Cultural Industrial and Organizational Psychology," in *Handbook of Industrial and*

Organizational Psychology, M. D. Dunnette and L. M. Hough, eds. (Palo Alto, CA: Consulting Psychologists Press, 1994), pp. 103–172.

42. G. Hofstede, "The Cultural Relativity of Organizational Practices and Theories," *Journal of International Business Studies* 14 (1983), pp. 75–89; G. Hofstede, "Cultural Constraints in Management Theories," *Academy of Management Executive,* 7 (1993), pp. 81–94; G. Hofstede, *Culture's Consequences: International Differences in Work-Related Values* (Beverly Hills, CA: Sage, 1980); G. Hofstede, *Culture's Consequences: Comparing Values, Behaviors, Institutions, and Organizations Across Nations,* 2nd ed. (Thousand Oaks, CA: Sage, 2001).
43. R. Schuler and N. Rogovsky, "Understanding Compensation Practice Variations Across Firms: The Impact of National Culture," *Journal of International Business Studies* 29 (1998), pp. 159–178.
44. L. R. Gomez-Mejia and T. Welbourne, "Compensation Strategies in a Global Context," *Human Resource Planning* 14 (1994), pp. 29–41; Sunny C. L. Fong and Margaret A. Shaffer, "The Dimensionality and Determinants of Pay Satisfaction: A Cross-Cultural Investigation of a Group Incentive Plan," *International Journal of Human Resource Management* 14, no. 4 (June 2003), pp. 559–580.
45. P. C. Early and M. Erez, *The Transplanted Executive: Why You Need to Understand How Workers in Other Countries See the World Differently* (New York: Oxford University Press, 1997).
46. G. Milkovich and M. Bloom, "Rethinking International Compensation: From Expatriates and National Cultures to Strategic Flexibility," *Compensation and Benefits Review,* April 1998; L. Markoczy, "Us and Them," *Across the Board,* February 1998, pp. 44–48; Brendan McSweeney, "Hofstede's Model of National Cultural Differences and Their Consequences: A Triumph of Faith, A Failure of Analysis," *Human Relations,* January 2002, pp. 89–118; Paul Gooderham and Odd Nordhaug, "Are Cultural Differences in Europe on the Decline?" geert-hofstede.international-business-center.com.
47. M. Bloom, G. Milkovich, and A. Mitra, "International Compensation: Learning from How Managers Respond to Variations in Local Host Contexts," *International Journal of Human Resource Management* special issue, 2003; Allen D. Engle, Sr., and Mark Mendenhall, "Transnational Roles and Transnational Rewards: Global Integration in Executive Compensation," presentation at international HR conference, Limerick, Ireland, June 2003; Paul Evans, Vlado Pucik, and Jean-Louis Barsoux, *The Global Challenge* (New York: McGraw-Hill, 2002); G. Hundley and J. Kim, "National Culture and the Factors Affecting Perceptions of Pay Fairness in Korea and the U.S.," *International Journal of Organization Analysis* 5, no. 4 (October 1997), pp. 325–341; David Landes, *Culture Matters: How Values Shape Human Progress* (New York: Basic Books, 2001).
48. B. Gerhart, "Compensation and National Culture," in *Global Compensation: Foundations and Perspectives*, S. Werner and L. R. Gomez-Mejia, eds. (London, U.K.: Routledge, 2008); Barry Gerhart, "Does National Culture Constrain Organization Culture and Human Resource Strategy? The Role of Individual Mechanisms and Implications for Employee Selection," *Research in Personnel and Human Resources Management* 28 (2009), pp. 1–48.
49. T. Rabl, M. Jayasinghe, B. Gerhart, and T. A. Kühlmann, "Meta-Analysis of Country Differences in the High Performance Work System-Business Performance Relationship: The Roles of National Culture and Managerial Discretion," *Journal of Applied Psychology* 99 (2014), pp. 1011–1041.
50. M. Bloom, G. Milkovich, and N. Zupan, "Contrasting Slovenian and U.S. Employment Relations: The Links between Social Contracts and Psychological Contracts," *CEMS Business Review,* no. 2 (1997), pp. S95–S109; Chun Hui, Cynthia Lee, and Denise Rousseau, "Psychological Contract and Organizational Citizenship Behavior in China: Investigating Generalizability and Instrumentality," *Journal of Applied Psychology* 89, no. 2 (2004), pp. 311–321.
51. M. Bloom and G. T. Milkovich, "A SHRM Perspective on International Compensation and Rewards" in P.M. Wright, L. Dyer, J.W. Boudreau, and G.T. Milkovich, *Research in Personnel and Human*

Resources Management, Supplement 4 (Stamford, CT: JAI Press, 1999), pp. 283–303; Barry Gerhart, "Does National Culture Constrain Organization Culture and Human Resource Strategy? The Role of Individual Mechanisms and Implications for Employee Selection," *Research in Personnel and Human Resources Management,* 2009; K. Y. Au, "Intra-Cultural Variation: Evidence and Implications for International Business," *Journal of International Business Studies* 30 (1999), pp. 799–812; D.V. Caprar, "Foreign Locals: A Cautionary Tale on the Culture of MNC Local Employees," *Journal of International Business* 42, pp. 608–628.

52. Barry Gerhart, "Cross-Cultural Management Research: Assumptions, Evidence, and Suggested Directions," *International Journal of Cross Cultural Management* 8 (2008), pp. 259–274; Barry Gerhart, and Meiyu Fang, "National Culture and Human Resource Management: Assumptions and Evidence," *International Journal of Human Resource Management* 16 (2005), pp. 975–990.
53. Barry Gerhart, and Meiyu Fang, "National Culture and Human Resource Management: Assumptions and Evidence," *International Journal of Human Resource Management* 16 (2005), pp. 975–990. An analysis of studies other than Hofstede's study generally yields similar conclusions. See Exhibit 4 of: Barry Gerhart, "Does National Culture Constrain Organization Culture and Human Resource Strategy? The Role of Individual Mechanisms and Implications for Employee Selection," *Research in Personnel and Human Resources Management,* 1999.
54. Weller, I., & Gerhart, B. (2018). Methodological challenges for quantitative research in comparative HRM. In *Handbook of Research on Comparative Human Resource Management*. Edward Elgar Publishing.
55. B. Gerhart, "Compensation and National Culture," in *Global Compensation: Foundations and Perspectives,* S. Werner & L.R. Gomez-Mejia, eds. (London, U.K.: Routledge, 2008); H. Yeganeh and Z. Su, "The Effects of Cultural Orientations on Preferred Compensation Policies," *International Journal of Human Resource Management* 22 (2011), pp. 2609–2628.
56. R. Fischer and P. Smith, "Reward Allocation and Culture: A Meta-Analysis," *Journal of Crosscultural Psychology* 34 (2003), pp. 251–268; B. Gerhart, "Compensation and National Culture," in *Global Compensation,* S. Werner and L. Gomez-Mejia, eds. (London, UK: Routledge, 2008).
57. Go to *geert-hofstede.international-business-center.com/* for Hofstede's description of Chinese national culture.
58. Zhijun Ling and Martha Avery, *The Lenovo Affair: The Growth of China's Computer Giant and Its Takeover of IBM-PC* (New York: John Wiley & Sons, 2006). See especially pp. 266–273. Also see D. Z. Ding, S. Akhtar, and G. L. Ge, "Organizational Differences in Managerial Compensation and Benefits in Chinese Firms," *International Journal of Human Resource Management* 17, no. 4 (April 2006), pp. 693–715; and Wan Lixin, "The Student Job Crunch," *China International Business,* June 2006, pp. 18–25.
59. International Labor Organization. https://ilostat.ilo.org/topics/union-membership/ and https://ilostat.ilo.org/topics/collective-bargaining/. February 10, 2021.
60. Baker & McKenzie LLP, "Worldwide Guide to Trade Unions and Works Councils," *www .gurn.info/en/,* 6/29/2009.
61. Elfstrom, M., and S. Kuruvilla, "The Changing Nature of Labor Unrest in China," *Industrial & Labor Relations Review* 67, no. 2 (2014), pp. 453–480.
62. The website of the National Center for Employee Ownership (NCEO) has information and referrals concerning employee stock ownership plans (ESOPs) and other forms of employee ownership: *www.esop.org.* Worker ownership around the world is discussed at *www.activistnet.org.*
63. Lowell Turner, ed., *Negotiating the New Germany: Can Social Partnership Survive?* (Ithaca, NY: Cornell University Press, 1998); Wolfgang Streeck, *Social Institutions and Economic Performance: Studies of Industrial Relations in Advanced Capitalist Economies* (London: Sage, 1992).

64. Ryan Rutkowski, "A Shrinking Leviathan: State Employment in China Looms Smaller than Expected," Peterson Institute for International Economics, January 24, 2013, https://piie.com/blogs/china-economic-watch/shrinking-leviathan-state-employment-china-looms-smaller-expected.

65. National Bureau of Statistics China. China Statistical Yearbook 2019. Table 4-10. http://www.stats.gov.cn/tjsj/ndsj/2019/indexeh.htm.

66. Wei He, Chao C. Chen, and Lihua Zhang, "Rewards Allocation Preferences in Chinese State-Owned Enterprises: A Revisit after a Decade's Radical Reform," in *The Management of Enterprises in the People's Republic of China,* Anne S. Tsui and Chung-Ming Lau, eds. (Boston: Kluwer Academic, 2002); Marshall Meyer, Yuan Lu, Hailin Lan, and Xiaohui Lu, "Decentralized Enterprise Reform: Notes on the Transformation of State-Owned Enterprises," in Anne S. Tsui and Shung-Ming Lau, eds., *The Management of Enterprises in the People's Republic of China* (Boston: Kluwer Academic, 2002); Chun Hui, Cynthia Lee, and Denise Rousseau, "Psychological Contract and Organizational Citizenship Behavior in China: Investigating Generalizability and Instrumentality," *Journal of Applied Psychology* 89, no. 2 (April 2004), pp. 311–321.

67. Jing Zhou and J. J. Martocchio, "Chinese and American Managers' Compensation Award Decisions," *Personnel Psychology* 54 (Spring 2001), pp. 115–145.

68. The European Trade Union Institute's website is at www.etuc.org/etui/default.cf.

69. Stephen Power and Guy Chazan, "Europe Auto Relations Get Testy," *The Wall Street Journal,* June 15, 2006, p. A8.

70. Hesan Ahmed Quazi, *Compensation and Benefits Practices in Selected Asian Countries* (Singapore: McGraw Hill, 2004).

71. R. Batt and H. Nohara, "How Institutions and Business Strategies Affect Wages: A Cross-National Study of Call Centers," *Industrial and Labor Relations Review* 62, pp. 533–552.

72. Samuel Palmisano, "Multinationals Have Been Superseded," *Financial Times,* June 11, 2006.

73. Mercer Human Resource Consulting, *2006 Worldwide Pay Survey* (London: October 3, 2005); Marie-Claire Guillard, "A Visual Essay: International Labor Market Comparisons," *Monthly Labor Review,* April 2006, pp. 33–37; Nic Paton, "Performance-Related Pay Becoming a Global Phenomenon," *www.management-issues.com,* accessed January 13, 2006; Chris Giles, "Moscow Is Now World's Costliest City for Expatriates," *Financial Times,* June 26, 2006, p. 2.

74. "Shanghai Raises Minimum Wage 13% as China Seeks to Boost Demand," *Bloomberg News,* February 27, 2012. www.bloomberg.com, accessed May 24, 2012.

75. John Gapper and Barney Jopson, "Coach to Cut Output in China," *Financial Times,* May 13, 2011; Ben Blanchard, "Foxconn to Raise Wages Again at China Plant," www.reuters.com, accessed October 19, 2010; Joe Manget and Pierre Mercier, "As Wages Rise, Time to Leave China?" *Bloomberg Businessweek*, December 1, 2010; and Shai Oster, "China's Rising Wages Propel U.S. Prices," *The Wall Street Journal,* May 9, 2011. Tim Worstall, "Apple's Foxconn to Double Wages Again," *Forbes,* May 28, 2012.

76. W. Lane and M. Schmidt, "Comparing U.S. and European COI and the HICP," *Monthly Labor Review* 129, no. 5 (May 2006), pp. 20–27; J. Abowd and M. Bognanno, "International Differences in Executive and Managerial Compensation," in *Differences and Changes in Wage Structures,* R. B. Freeman and L. Katz, eds. (Chicago: NBER, 1995), pp. 67–103; "Big Mac Index," *The Economist,* February 4, 2009, *www.economist.com.*

77. S. Jacoby, *The Embedded Corporation* (Princeton: Princeton University Press, 2005); J. Abegglen, *Twenty-First Century Japanese Management: New System, Lasting Values* (New York: Palgrave-Macmillan, 2006); Toyo Keizai, *Japan Company Handbook* (Tokyo: Japan Labour Bureau, Summer 2001).

78. T. Kato, "The End of Lifetime Employment in Japan? Evidence from National Surveys and Field Research," *Journal of the Japanese and International Economies* 15 (2002), pp. 489–514; T. Kato and M. Rockell, "Experiences, Credentials, and Compensation in the Japanese and U.S. Managerial Labor Markets: Evidence from New Micro Data," *Journal of the Japanese and International Economies* 6 (1992), pp. 30–51; P. Evans, V. Pucik, and J. Barsoux, *The Global Challenge: Frameworks for International Human Resource Management* (New York: McGraw-Hill/Irwin, 2002).

79. B. D. Singh, *Industrial Relations: Emerging Paradigms,* 2nd ed. (New Dehli: Excel Books. 2009), p. 448.

80. We thank Thomas Gresch and Elke Stadelmann, whose manuscript, *Traditional Pay System in Germany* (Ruesselsheim, Germany: Adam Opel AG, 2001), is the basis for this section of the chapter; Geoff Dyer, "A Tale of Two Corporate Cultures," *Financial Times,* May 23, 2006, p. 8; Paul DeGrauwe, "Germany's Pay Policy Points to a Eurozone Design Flaw," *Financial Times,* May 5, 2006, p. 13.

81. Bertrand Benoit, "Benefit Check: Why Germany Is Confronted with a Welfare State Fiasco," *Financial Times,* June 26, 2006.

82. Organization for Economic Cooperation and Development. Data for 2019. http://stats.oecd.org. Labour, Subsection, Labour Force Statistics, accessed February 20, 2021.

83. Hiroshi Ono, "Careers in Foreign-Owned Firms in Japan," *American Sociological Review* 72 (2007), pp. 267–290.

84. See S. Jacoby, *The Embedded Corporation* (Princeton: Princeton University Press, 2005), especially pp. 75–77; S. Strom, "In Japan, from Lifetime Job to No Job at All," *The New York Times* Online, February 3, 1999; M. Bloom, G. Milkovich, and A. Mitra, "International Compensation: Learning From How Managers Respond to Variations in Local Host Contexts," *International Journal of Human Resource Management,* special issue, 2003; T. Kato, "The End of Lifetime Employment in Japan? Evidence from National Surveys and Field Research," *Journal of Japanese and International Economies* 15 (2002), pp. 489–514; T. Kato and M. Rockell, "Experiences, Credentials, and Compensation in the Japanese and U.S. Managerial Labor Markets: Evidence from New Micro Data," *Journal of the Japanese and International Economies* 6 (1992), pp. 30–51; Hiromichi Shibata, "Wage and Performance Appraisal Systems in Flux: Japan-U.S. Comparison," *Industrial Relations* 41, no. 4 (2002), pp. 629–652; National Personnel Authority, *Current Status of Private Firms' Remuneration Systems* (Tokyo: Japan Labour Bureau, 2006); D. Raj Adhikari, *National Factors in Employment Relations in Japan* (Tokyo: Japan Institute of Labor Policy, 2005).

85. Markus Pudelko, "The Seniority Principle in Japanese Companies: A Relic of the Past?" *Asia Pacific Journal of Human Resources* 44 (2006), pp. 276–294.

86. Tetsushi Kajimoto and Izumi Nakagawa. Japan's efforts to raise wages wane as firms embrace merit-based pay. The Japan Times, February 12, 2020. The article refers to surveys conducted by the Japanese Productivity Center.

87. Hamaaki, J., Hori, M., Maeda, S., and Murata, K., "Changes in the Japanese Employment System in the Two Lost Decades," *Industrial & Labor Relations Review* 65, no. 4 (2012), pp. 810–846.

88. Meng, X., *Labour Market Reform in China* (Cambridge University Press, 2000). Xiu, L., and Gunderson, M., "Performance Pay in China: Gender Aspects," *British Journal of Industrial Relations* 51, no. 1 (2013), pp. 124–147.

89. Bae, J., and Lawler, J. J., "Organizational and HRM Strategies in Korea: Impact on Firm Performance in an Emerging Economy," *Academy of Management Journal* 43 (2000), pp. 502–517.

90. Antje Kurdelbusch, "Multinationals and the Rise of Variable Pay in Germany," *European Journal of Industrial Relations* 8 (2002), pp. 324–349; James Arrowsmith, Heidi Nicolaisen, Barbara Bechter, and Rosa Nonell, "The Management of Variable Pay in Banking: Forms and Rationale in Four

European Countries," in *Challenges of European Employment Relations and Employment Regulation,* Roger Blanplain and Linda Dickens, eds. (The Netherlands: Kluwer Law International, 2008); Matthias Schmitt and Dieter Sadowski, "A Cost-Minimization Approach to the International Transfer of HRM/IR Practices: Anglo-Saxon Multinationals in the Federal Republic of Germany," *International Journal of Human Resource Management* 14 (2003), pp. 409–430.

91. William Gerard Sanders and Anja Tuschke, "The Adoption of Institutionally Contested Organizational Practices: The Emergence of Stock Option Pay in Germany," *Academy of Management Journal* 50 (2007), pp. 33–56.

92. M. Bloom, G. Milkovich, and A. Mitra, "International Compensation: Learning From How Managers Respond to Variations in Local Host Contexts," *International Journal of Human Resource Management,* special issue, 2003. See also N. Napier and Van Tuan Vu, "International HRM in Developing and Transitional Economy Context," *Human Resource Management Review* 8, no. 1 (1998), pp. 39–71.

93. Thomas Friedman, *The World Is Flat: A Brief History of the Twenty-First Century* (New York: Farrar, Straus and Giroux, 2006); J. W. Walker, "Are We Global Yet?" *Human Resource Planning* (First Quarter 2000), pp. 7–8; R. Locke and K. Thelen, "Apples and Oranges Revisited: Contextualized Comparisons and Comparative Labor Policies," *Politics and Society* 23, no. 2 (1996), pp. 337–367; M. Mendenhall and Gary Oddou, *Readings and Cases in International Human Resource Management* (Cincinnati: Southwestern, 2000).

94. Samuel Palmisano, "The Globally Integrated Enterprise," *Foreign Affairs,* May/June 2006.

95. P. J. Dowling, M. Festing, and A. D. Engle, Sr., *International Human Resource Management,* 5th ed. (London: Thomson Learning, 2008).

96. G. Latta, "The Future of Expatriate Compensation," *WorldatWork* (Second Quarter 2006), pp. 42–49; Geoffrey Latta, "Expatriate Policy and Practice: A 10-Year Comparison of Trends," *Compensation and Benefits Review* 31, no. 4 (1999), pp. 35–39; C. Reynolds, "Global Compensation and Benefits in Transition," *Compensation and Benefits Review* 32, no. 1 (January/February 2000), pp. 27–37; J. Stewart Black and Hal B. Gregerson, "The Right Way to Manage Expats," *Harvard Business Review,* March–April 1999, pp. 52–62; Roger Heron, "The Cardinal Sins of Expatriate Policies," *Organization Resources Counselors: Innovations in International HR,* Fall 2001.

97. G. Latta, "The Future of Expatriate Compensation," *WorldatWork,* Second Quarter 2006, pp. 42–49; Cris Prystay and Tom Herman, "Tax Hike Hits Home for Americans Abroad," *The Wall Street Journal,* July 19, 2006, pp. D1, D5.

98. Runzheimer International, *www.runzheimer.com,* publishes monthly newsletters on the costs of relocation.

99. Bobby W. Watson, Jr., and Gangaram Singh, "Global Pay Systems: Compensation in Support of a Multinational Strategy," *Compensation and Benefits Review* 37, no. 1 (January/February 2005), pp. 33–36; Sherrie Webster Brown, "Spanning the Globe for Quality Pay Data," in *2003-2004 Survey Handbook and Directory* (Scottsdale, AZ: WorldatWork, 2002), pp. 95–100; Margaret A. Coil, "Salary Surveys in a Blended-Role World," in *2003-2004 Survey Handbook and Directory* (Scottsdale, AZ: WorldatWork, 2002), pp. 57–64.

100. Laura Johnson and Darrell Cira, "Taking the Best Path to Implementing a Global Pay Structure: The General Mill's Experience," World at Work Conference, Seattle, Washington, June 1, 2009.

101. W. Lane and M. Schmidt, "Comparing U.S. and European COI and the HICP," *Monthly Labor Review,* May 2006, pp. 20–27.

102. C. Reynolds, "Expatriate Compensation in Historical Perspective," *International Human Resource Journal,* Summer 1997, pp. 118–131.

103. Elke Asen. Insights into the Tax Systems of Scandinavian Countries . Tax Foundation, February 24, 2020. taxfoundation.org.

104. *Global Rewards: A Collection of Articles From WorldatWork* (Scottsdale, AZ: WorldatWork, 2005); Cal Reynolds, "International Compensation," in *Compensation Guide,* William A. Caldwell, ed. (Boston: Warren, Gorham and Lamont, 1998).

105. Chun Hui, Cynthia Lee, and Denise Rousseau, "Psychological Contract and Organizational Citizenship Behavior in China: Investigating Generalizability and Instrumentality," *Journal of Applied Psychology* 89, no. 2 (April 2004), pp. 311–321; Richard A. Guzzo, Katherine A. Noonan, and Efrat Elron, "Expatriate Managers and the Psychological Contract," *Journal of Applied Psychology* 7, no. 4 (1994), pp. 617–626; Steve Gross and Per Wingerup, "Global Pay? Maybe Not Yet!" *Compensation Benefits Review* 31 (1999), pp. 25–34.

106. P. J. Dowling, M. Festing, and A. D. Engle, Sr., *International Human Resource Management,* 5th ed. (London: Thomson Learning, 2008).

107. Carole Mestre, Anne Rossier-Renaud, and Madeline Berger, "Better Benchmarks for Global Mobility," *Workspan,* April 2009.

108. P. J. Dowling, M. Festing, and A. D. Engle, Sr., *International Human Resource Management,* 5th ed. (London: Thomson Learning, 2008).

109. Carole Mestre, Anne Rossier-Renaud, and Madeline Berger, "Better Benchmarks for Global Mobility," *Workspan,* April 2009.

110. Garry M. Wederspahn, "Costing Failures in Expatriate Human Resource Management," *Human Resource Planning* 15, no. 3, pp. 27–35; Soo Min Toh and Angelo S. DeNissi, "Host Country National Reactions to Expatriate Pay Policies: A Model and Implications," *Academy of Management Review,* 28, no. 4 (2003), pp. 606–621.

111. Paul Evans, Vlado Pucik, and Jean-Louis Barsoux, *The Global Challenge* (New York: McGraw-Hill, 2002); Allen D. Engle, Sr. and Peter Dowing, "Global Rewards: Strategic Patterns in Complexity," presentation at international HR conference, Ljubljana, Slovenia, June 2004.

112. For a very helpful review and analysis of this issue, see P. J. Dowling, M. Festing, and A. D. Engle, Sr., *International Human Resource Management,* 5th ed. (London: Thomson Learning, 2008). Also, see Claus Christensen and Anne-Wil Harzing, "Expatriate Failure: Time to Abandon the Concept?" *Career Development International* 9 (2004), pp. 616–626.

Part VII
Managing the System

The last part of our total pay model is management. This means ensuring that the right people get the right pay for achieving the right objectives in the right way. We have touched on aspects of management already—the use of budgets in merit increase programs; the "message" that employees receive from their variable pay bonuses, communication, and cost control in benefits; and the importance of employee involvement in designing the total compensation system.

Several important issues remain. The first, already noted in the global guide in **Chapter 16**, is the significant role that government plays in managing compensation. Laws and regulations are the most obvious government intervention. In the United States, minimum-wage legislation, the Equal Pay Act, and Title VII of the Civil Rights Act, among others, regulate pay decisions. Legal issues in compensation in the United States are covered in **Chapter 17**.

Government is more than a source of laws and regulations, however. As a major employer, as a consumer of goods and services, and through its fiscal and monetary policies, government affects the supply of and the demand for labor.

Chapter 18 covers several aspects of managing compensation: costs and added value, communication, and change. One of the key reasons for being systematic about pay decisions is to manage the costs associated with those decisions. As **Chapter 18** will show, a total compensation system is really a device for allocating money in a way that is consistent with the organization's objectives. Recent developments in how to evaluate the value gained from compensation programs are discussed.

Communication and change are linked. What is to be communicated to whom is an important, ongoing issue. Compensation itself communicates. A pay increase tells people how they are doing. Changes in the pay system also communicate; they may signal change in business direction or even reinforce restructuring of the organization. Any system will founder if it is ineffectively communicated and managed.

Chapter 18 also discusses enterprise software that holds out the promise of helping users make pay decisions faster and smarter. Perhaps most critical of all, we return to look at ethics and the increasing importance of personal standards when no professional standards exist.

EXHIBIT VII.1 The Pay Model

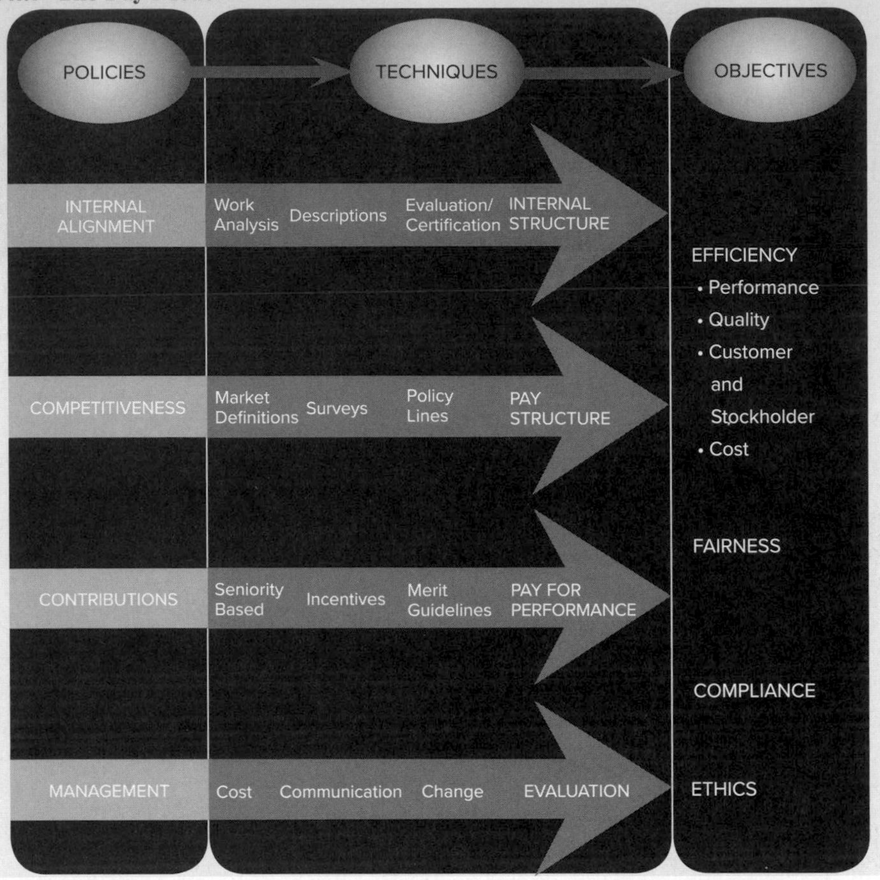

Chapter **Seventeen** Government and Legal Issues in Compensation

Chapter Outline

A 1939 pay policy handbook for a major U.S. corporation outlines the following justification for paying different wages to men and women working on the same jobs:[1]

> The . . . wage curve . . . is not the same for women as for men because of the more transient character of the former, the relative shortness of their activity in

> industry, the differences in environment required, the extra services that must be provided, overtime limitations, extra help needed for the occasional heavy work, and the general sociological factors not requiring discussion herein. Basically then we have another wage curve . . . for women below and not parallel with the men's curve.

The presumption that people should be paid different wages based on "general sociological factors" was still evident in the United States in the 1960s, in newspaper help-wanted ads that specified "perky gal Fridays" and in whites-only local unions. The 1960s civil rights movement and subsequent legislation were intended to end such practices.

Are you thinking you have stumbled into a history class by mistake? Not so. These historical practices and subsequent legislation still affect pay decisions. However, legislation does not always achieve what it intends nor intend what it achieves. Consequently, *compliance* and *fairness* are continuing compensation objectives.

In democratic societies, the legislative process begins when a problem is identified (not all citizens are receiving fair treatment in the workplace) and corrective legislation is proposed (the Civil Rights Act). If enough support develops, often as a result of compromises and trade-offs, the proposed legislation becomes law. Employers, along with other stakeholders, attempt to influence the form any legislation will take.

Once passed, laws are enforced by agencies through rulings, regulations, inspections, and investigations. Companies respond to legislation by auditing and perhaps altering their practices, perhaps defending their practices before courts and agencies, and perhaps lobbying for still further legislative change. The laws and regulations issued by governmental agencies created to enforce the laws are a significant influence on compensation decisions throughout the world.

In the United States, there are three branches of *federal* government and each plays a role in the legal and regulatory framework in which employers work toward compliance objectives. The *legislative* branch (Congress) passes laws (or statutes). The *executive* branch, headed by the President, enforces laws through agencies and its other bodies (e.g., the Department of Labor), and the *judicial* branch interprets laws and considers their constitutionality. Over time, the legislative branch may change existing laws or pass new ones. The way that the judicial branch interprets laws can also change. The great interest in Supreme Court justice appointments and the difficulty sometimes encountered in gaining their confirmation is based on the belief that who the justices are will matter. Finally, enforcement priorities and intensity can vary from one presidential administration to the next. Compliance efforts by employers must take that fact into account.

Of course, the regulatory environment is also a function of *state and local* laws, which often cover employers not covered by federal laws and/or include requirements that go beyond federal laws. For example, Title VII of the (federal) Civil Rights Act, which prohibits employment (including pay) discrimination on the basis of race, color, religion, sex, or national origin, covers employers with 15 or more employees. But, under the Wisconsin Fair Employment Act, all employers are covered and discrimination on the basis of some characteristics (e.g., sexual orientation) not included in Title VII is prohibited. As another example, in our discussion of minimum wage laws later in this chapter, we will see that some states have minimums greater than the federal minimum. (California often comes up in discussing state laws. One reason is that if California was a country, it would have the fifth largest economy in the world, just ahead of the United Kingdom.) We will also see that some cities have living wage laws. Finally, of course, as we saw in **Chapter 16**, laws differ by country.[2]

Our objective in this chapter is to help you become more familiar with the legal and regulatory framework of compensation. Importantly, however, you will not be an attorney after reading this chapter. Compliance will require legal advice.

To help motivate you to speak promptly to an attorney should you encounter legal compliance risks, consider **Exhibit 17.1**, which reports payments by employers to come into compliance with regulatory actions brought by two U.S. government agencies, the Department of Labor's Equal Employment Opportunity Commission (EEOC) and its Wage and Hour Division (WHD). Compliance issues fall into two corresponding areas: employment discrimination (especially Title VII of the Civil Rights Act) and wage and hour (especially the Fair Labor Standards Act, FLSA). Over the five-year period 2016–2020, the EEOC recovered more than $2 billion from employers to resolve employment discrimination issues (some, but not all, having to do with compensation issues), with most of that relating to Title VII. During that same period, the WHD recovered over $1.4 billion in back wages payments (i.e., wages for work employees previously performed, but for which they were not fully paid) from employers. Employees may also bring private plaintiff lawsuits (i.e., without involving government agencies) against employers. These are most costly when they are class action suits that include many similarly situated employees combining to bring a single joint lawsuit. In the area of employment discrimination, **Exhibit 17.1** shows that the 10 largest private plaintiff class-action lawsuit settlements alone cost employers almost $1.2 billion over the five-year period. On the wage and hour side, the 10 largest class action lawsuit settlements cost employers more than $2.2 billion over the five-year period. These, we think you will agree, are big numbers, and it would be great if you could help your future employer comply with the law so as not to be part of paying out these very large amounts of money either from court decisions or to settle lawsuits. (Beyond that, some people report that dealing with legal concerns can be challenging and require a substantial time commitment.)

GOVERNMENT AS PART OF THE EMPLOYMENT RELATIONSHIP

Overviews

People differ in their view of what role government should play in the contemporary workplace. Some call for organizations and the government to act in concert to carry out a public policy that protects the interests of employees.[3] Others believe that the best opportunities for employees are created by the constant change and reconfiguring that is inherent in market-based economies; the economy ought to be allowed to adapt and transform, undistorted by government actions.[4] All countries throughout the world must address these issues. However, as we saw in **Chapter 16**, different countries take different approaches.[5]

Governments' usual interests in compensation decisions are whether procedures for determining pay are fair (e.g., pay discrimination), providing safety nets for the unemployed and/or those unable to work (e.g., unemployment compensation, workers compensation), and worker protection (e.g., overtime pay, minimum wage, child labor restrictions).

In addition to being a party to all employment relationships, government units are also employers and purchasers. Consequently, government decisions also affect conditions in the labor market. The U.S. federal government employs 2.9 million people; state and local governments employ 18.6 million. Overall, government employment is 21.4 million, representing 15 percent of the total U.S. nonfarm employment of 143 million.[6] In addition to being a big employer, and thus competing with private sector organizations for employees, government also indirectly affects labor demand in the private sector through its spending and purchases (military aircraft, computer systems, paper clips) and tax policy. In addition to government fiscal policy (i.e., total spending and budget, tax policy, taxes), the federal government influences overall economic growth/demand and business activity through its monetary policy (level of interest rates and money supply). Increased business activity translates into increased demand for labor and upward pressure on wages. In addition to being an employer, government affects labor supply through legislation. Laws aimed at protecting specific groups also tend to restrict those groups' participation in the labor market. Compulsory schooling laws restrict the

EXHIBIT 17.1 Payments by Employers to Settle Employment Discrimination and Wage and Hour Claims, Government Agency (EEOC, WHD) Enforcement Actions and Private Class Action Lawsuits

Year	Employment Discrimination			Wage and Hour		
	EEOC Enforcement Activity (Settlements + Litigation)[a]		Private Plaintiff Class Action	WHD Enforcement Activity[b]		Private Plaintiff Class Action
	Monetary Recovery From:		Lawsuit Settlements	Back Wages Recovery from:		Lawsuit Settlements
	All Acts	Title VII (only)	10 Largest[3]	All Acts	FLSA (only)	10 Largest[c]
2020	$438 million	$307 million	$423 million	$258 million	$182 million	$295 million
2019	$386 million	$271 million	$139 million	$322 million	$225 million	$449 million
2018	$408 million	$256 million	$216 million	$305 million	$227 million	$254 million
2017	$398 million	$256 million	$294 million	$270 million	$189 million	$525 million
2016	$400 million	$262 million	$80 million	$267 million	$207 million	$696 million
5-Year Total	$2.03 billion	$1.35 billion	$1.15 billion	$1.42 billion	$1.03 billion	$2.22 billion

[a]U.S. Equal Employment Opportunity Commission. Enforcement and Litigation Statistics. Does not include charges filed with state or local Fair Employment Practices Agencies. https://www.eeoc.gov/statistics/enforcement-and-litigation-statistics. Each dollar amount is the sum of monetary benefits from (a) charges resolved and filed + (b) EEOC enforcements suits filed and resolved in federal district courts. For example, for 2020, these amounts for All Acts were $332.2 million + $106.1 million = $438.3 million.

[b]U.S. of Labor. Wage and Hour Division. Fiscal Year Data for WHD, Fair Labor Standards Act Back Wages, https://www.dol.gov/whd/data/datatables.htm#panel1 and https://www.dol.gov/whd/data/datatables.htm#panel2.

[c]17th Annual Workplace Class Action Litigation Report, 2021 edition. Published by Seyfarth Shaw LLP. https://www.workplaceclassaction.com.

Notes: Title VII monetary recovery amounts include all Title VII related charges, not just those related to pay.

WHD = Wage and Hour Division, Department of Labor.

EEOC = Equal Employment Opportunity Commission, Department of Labor.

FLSA = Fair Labor Standards Act.

supply of children available to sell hamburgers or to assemble soccer balls. Licensing requirements for certain occupations (plumbers, cosmetologists, attorneys, physicians, psychologists) restrict the number of people who can legally offer a service.[7] Immigration policy and how rigorously it is enforced is an increasingly important factor in labor supply.[8]

This chapter will examine the laws and regulations that most directly affect compensation in the United States. **Exhibit 17.2** provides an overview of the regulatory framework, especially as it applies to wages and salaries and other forms of direct pay. See **Chapters 12** and **13** for information on benefits-related regulations (e.g., the Employee Retirement Income Security Act, ERISA).

FAIR LABOR STANDARDS ACT OF 1938

The **Fair Labor Standards Act of 1938 (FLSA)** covers all employees (with some exceptions, discussed later) of companies engaged in interstate commerce or in the production of goods for interstate commerce. In spite of its age, this law remains a cornerstone of pay regulation in the United States. The FLSA's major provisions are:

1. Minimum wage
2. Hours of work (including overtime)
3. Child labor

An additional provision requires that records be kept of employees, their hours worked, and their pay. As noted earlier, in recent years, U.S. employers have paid out billions of dollars (see **Exhibit 17.1**) as a result of FLSA lawsuits and enforcement activity by the DOL Wage and Hour Division. **Exhibit 17.3** provides a breakdown of the claim types covered in such settlements. We see that overtime violations are the most common type of claim. The industries with the most FLSA claims are food/food services, retail, financial services/insurance, and transportation/shipping.

Minimum Wage

Minimum-wage legislation is intended to provide an income floor for workers in society's least productive jobs. When first enacted in 1938, the minimum wage was 25 cents an hour. It has been raised periodically; in 2009, it was raised to $7.25 and has remained there.

Exhibit 17.4 shows the purchasing power of the federal minimum wage over time, adjusted for inflation. We can see, for example, that in 2021, the minimum wage would need to be raised by almost $4/hour to $11.04 to have the same purchasing power it had in 1970. The decline in real purchasing power has been used to argue for indexing the minimum wage to changes in the consumer price index.

Estimates from the U.S. Bureau of Labor Statistics indicate that approximately 1.6 million U.S. workers (down from 3.83 million in 2011) are paid at or below the minimum wage. The majority (1.1 million) of those earning minimum wage or less are in service occupations, mostly food service, where tips supplement hourly wages for many workers. The proportion of hourly paid workers earning minimum wage or less has trended downward since 1979 when data first began to be collected systematically. In 1979, 13.4 percent of hourly paid workers (7.7% of men and 20.2% of women) earned at or below minimum. (Note that 58% of employees in the United States are paid an hourly rate.) More recently, the figures are 1.9 percent of hourly workers (1.3% of men and 2.6% of women). As a percentage of all civilian wage and salary workers, those earning at or below minimum wage has declined from 7.9 percent in 1979 to 1.1 percent more recently.[10] An important

EXHIBIT 17.2 U.S. Federal Pay Regulations

1931	**Davis-Bacon Act**	Requires that mechanics and laborers on public construction projects be paid the "prevailing wage" in an area.
1934	**Securities Exchange Act**	Created the Securities and Exchange Commission (SEC). Currently, the SEC requires companies that have more than $10 million in assets and whose securities are publicly traded and held by more than 500 owners to periodically report information, which is available to the public. This includes disclosure of compensation received by the CEO, CFO, and three other highest paid executives.
1936	**Walsh-Healey Public Contracts Act**	Extends prevailing-wage concept to manufacturers or suppliers of goods for government contracts.
1938	**Fair Labor Standards Act (FLSA)**	Sets minimum wage, hours of work, overtime premiums; prohibits child labor.
1963	**Equal Pay Act**	Equal pay required for men and women doing "substantially equal" work in terms of skill, effort, responsibility, and working conditions.
1964	**Title VII of Civil Rights Act of 1964**	Prohibits discrimination in all employment practices on basis of race, sex, color, religion, or national origin.
1965	**Executive Order 11246**	Prohibits discrimination by federal contractors and subcontractors in all employment practices on basis of race, sex, color, religion, or national origin.
1967	**Age Discrimination in Employment Act (ADEA)**	Protects employees age 40 and over against age discrimination.
1978	**Pregnancy Discrimination Act (PDA)**	Pregnancy must be covered to same extent that other medical conditions are covered.
1990	**Americans with Disabilities Act (ADA)**	Requires that "essential elements" of a job be called out. If a person with a disability can perform these essential elements, reasonable accommodation must be provided.
1990	**Immigration Act of 1990**	Created the H-1B classification for temporary employment of foreign workers in specialty occupations or as fashion models. Intent is to help employers who cannot otherwise obtain needed business abilities and skills from the U.S. workforce.
1991	**Civil Rights Act of 1991**	Increases burden of proof on employers to rebut some discrimination claims. Stronger remedies available in cases of international discrimination.
1993	**Family and Medical Leave Act (FMLA)**	Requires employers to provide up to 12 weeks' unpaid leave for family and medical emergencies.
1997	**Mental Health Act**	Mental illness must be covered to same extent that other medical conditions are covered.

2000	**Worker Economic Opportunity Act**	Income from most stock plans need not be included in calculating overtime pay.
2002	**Sarbanes-Oxley Act**	Executives cannot retain bonuses or profits from selling company stock if they mislead the public about the financial health of the company.
2004	**Financial Accounting Standards Board (FASB) Statement 123 R**	Value of all employee stock options must be expensed at estimates of fair value on financial statements (as/when they vest).
2006	**Securities and Exchange Commission (SEC) rule change on executive compensation disclosure**	Adopts enhanced executive compensation disclosure requirements. For example, the Compensation Discussion and Analysis in the proxy statement must address the objectives and implementation of executive compensation programs.
2009	**Lilly Ledbetter Fair Pay Act**	Employers can be liable for current pay differences that are a result of discrimination (as defined under existing laws such as Title VII of the Civil Rights Act) that occurred many years earlier.
2009	**Troubled Asset Relief Program (TARP), American Recovery and Reinvestment Act of 2009 (ARRA)**	Financial institutions receiving funds from TARP have restrictions on compensation. Prohibits use of several compensation programs, including, but not limited to bonuses, retention awards, and incentive pay, except where part of a preexisting employment contract, during the period TARP funds are received. Restricted stock is permitted if one-third or less of annual compensation. In firms receiving the largest TARP assistance, restrictions cover senior executives and next 20 highest paid employees.
2010	**The Patient Protection and Affordable Care Act**	Creates employer mandate (for those with 50 or more employees) to provide qualifying health insurance coverage or face financial penalties. (See **Chapter 12** for further details.)
2010	**Dodd-Frank Wall Street Reform and Consumer Protection Act[a]**	
	Nominating Directors	Gives SEC authority to grant shareholders proxy access to nominate directors.
	Independent Compensation Committees	Standards for listing a company on an exchange require that compensation committees include only independent directors and that the committee has authority to hire its own compensation consultants.
	Clawbacks	Requires public companies to set policies to allow executive compensation to be taken back if it was based on inaccurate financial statements that did not comply with accounting standards.

	Executive Compensation Disclosure	Requires reporting of the ratio of chief executive officer (CEO) pay to worker pay (CEO Pay Ratio) and the magnitude of the relationship between executive pay and corporate financial performance.
	Increased Oversight of Financial Industry	Directs regulators to develop rules specific to the financial industry.
	"Say on Pay"	Nonbinding vote by shareholders to approve or disapprove executive pay.
2014	**Executive Order 13665**	Prohibits federal contractors and subcontractors from having pay secrecy policies.
2014/ 2021	**Executive Order 13658**	The original order required federal contractors to pay a minimum wage of $10.10/hour, indexed to inflation (resulting in $10.95 in 2021). In 2021, the rule was revised to require $15/hour, which will continue to be indexed to inflation.
Ongoing	**SEC**	Executive compensation rules and enforcement.
	Internal Revenue Service (IRS)	Tax treatment of employee and executive compensation, including rules (e.g., nondiscrimination tests) for which compensation costs can be deducted. Also monitors employer decisions to classify workers as employees versus independent contractors, which has tax revenue implications.
	Financial Accounting Standards Board (FASB)	Engages in ongoing rule-making regarding accounting treatment of executive and employee compensation. FASB rules are given great deference by the SEC.
	Federal Trade Commission	Enforces antitrust laws, which includes prohibiting employers from collusion in fixing prices (i.e., pay) in compensation or collusion in the form of agreeing not to recruit each other's employees (see Hi-Tech Employee Antitrust Settlement and Animation Workers Antitrust Settlements websites).[9]
	Arbitration (deferral to)	Many employers now ask employees to sign agreements that require them to use arbitration systems to resolve individual employment disputes in lieu of filing a lawsuit or filing a complaint with a government agency. The employer must provide "consideration" (something of value) in return for employees giving up their right to sue in individual dispute cases.
	Noncompete Agreements	Many employers ask employees to agree not to work for a competitor within a certain time of leaving the employer. Consideration must be provided to the employee in return for waiving this right. Enforceability varies by state and typically as a function of the level of the employee and the degree to which the employee has access to valuable information or resources related to competitiveness.
	Department of Labor (DOL)	The DOL's Wage and Hour Division (WHD) monitors and enforces compliance with the FLSA, FMLA, Davis-Bacon,

	Walsh-Healey, H-1B (temporary foreign) worker classification part of The Immigration Act of 1990, and other Acts. The DOL's Equal Employment Opportunity Commission (EEOC) monitors and enforces compliance with equal employment opportunity laws, including Title VII of the Civil Rights Act, ADA, ADEA, PDA, and the Equal Pact Act. The DOL's Office of Federal Contract Compliance (OFCCP) monitors and enforces compliance with equal employment opportunity laws, primarily Executive Order 11246, which applies to companies that do business (federal contractors and subcontractors) with the federal government.
Benefits	For further information on benefits-related regulation, see **Chapters 12** and **13**.
State and Local Laws	Examples: Minimum wage, classification of workers as employees or independent contractors, prohibition against asking applicant salary history.

[a]The SEC is responsible for developing specific rules/policies for implementing the different provisions of Dodd-Frank. Rules for the provisions listed have been issued at various points in time since 2010.

reason for the decline in those directly affected is that the federal minimum wage stayed unchanged at $5.15 from 1997 to 2007 (and, more recently, has stayed unchanged since 2009 from $7.25).

Changes to the federal minimum wage have direct effects (on workers having a current wage between any state minimum wage and the federal minimum wage). There are also indirect, spillover effects because as legislation forces pay rates at the lowest end of the scale to move up, pay rates above the minimum often increase in order to maintain differentials. This shift in pay structure does not affect all industries equally. The lowest rates paid in the software, chemical, oil, and pharmaceutical industries are already well above minimum; any legislative change has little direct impact on them. In contrast, retailing and hospitality firms tend to pay at or near minimum wage to many clerks, sales persons, and cleaning people.[11]

EXHIBIT 17.3 FLSA Wage and Hour Settlements, by Type of Claim

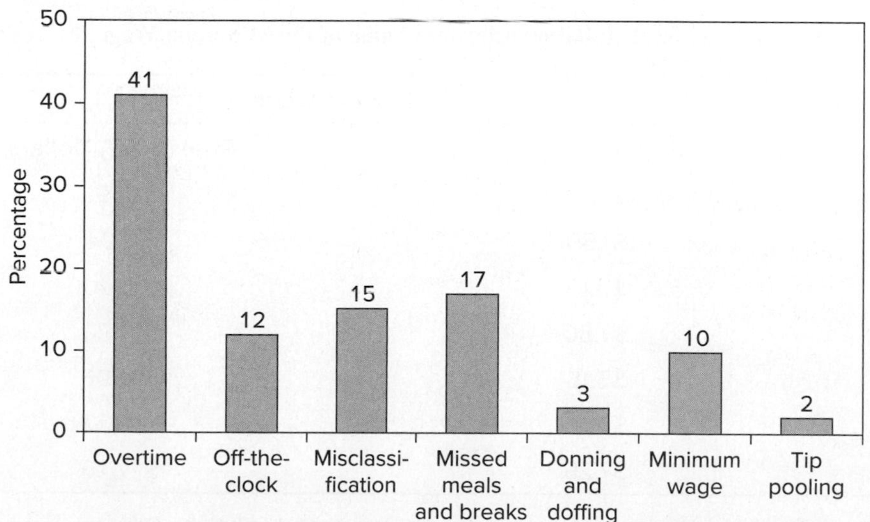

Source: Stephanie Plancich and Janeen McIntosh, *Trends in Wage and Hour Settlements: 2019 Update*, June 4, 2020, www.nera.com.

Forty-five states plus the District of Columbia have their own minimum wages to cover jobs omitted from federal legislation. If state and federal laws cover the same job, the higher rate prevails. Over half of the states have minimums higher than the federal rate, with some of the highest being Massachusetts ($13.50), Washington ($13.69), and California ($14.00, $13.00 if 25 employees or less). It is $15.00 in the District of Columbia.[12] A number of cities (and counties) also have minimum wage ordinances, including Chicago ($15.00 if 21 employees or more, $14.00 if 4 to 20 employees), San Francisco ($15.00), and Seattle ($15 to $15.75, depending on employer size).[13] Note also that a revised Executive Order issued (in preliminary form) in April 2021 requires federal contractors to pay a minimum wage of $15/hour.[14]

Why would anyone be opposed to a mandated minimum wage or making increases to it? The concern is that the resulting higher labor costs (as noted above, not only covered employees, but also other employees to the degree pay differentials are maintained) for affected firms may lead them to decrease their demand for workers and/or their hours worked. (See our discussion of supply and demand curves in **Chapter 7**.) In other words, a higher minimum wage, which is intended to help low wage workers, runs the risk of reducing employment opportunities for these very workers it is intended to help. So, whether a minimum wage "works" or not depends on whether the gains through higher wages are greater than the losses of jobs and/or hours.[15] For example, the Congressional Budget Office in 2021 projected the impact of a minimum wage rising gradually to $15 by 2025 as follows during the 2021 to 2031 period: an increase of $509 billion in pay for those employed, minus $175 billion lost to those (roughly 1% of U.S. employment) pushed into unemployment by the higher minimum wage. Thus, the net impact would be $333 billion higher pay, reduced poverty, but higher unemployment.[16] Another consideration in evaluating minimum wage law effectiveness is whether wage gains go primarily to workers from low-income families rather than going to workers from families with higher incomes.[17] Employers certainly have a stake in minimum wage public policy and thus may seek to influence it over time. In the shorter run, employers must be in compliance and will need to consider how changes to the minimum wage will affect their labor costs, to what degree they can pass the higher costs on to customers, and to what degree they will need to take some other action in the long run (e.g., using technology/automation, such as automated check-out in retail) to control or offset higher labor costs.

Exhibit 17.5 provides an example of how an employer can run afoul of minimum wage, hours worked, and overtime provisions of the FLSA, as well as the consequences.

EXHIBIT 17.4 Nominal and Real (Inflation-Adjusted) Value of the Minimum Wage, by Year

Year	Minimum Wage	
	Nominal Dollars	Real (2021) Dollars
1960	$1.00	$ 8.91
1970	$1.60	$11.04
1980	$3.10	$10.40
1990	$3.80	$ 7.80
2000	$5.15	$ 7.96
2010	$7.25	$ 8.72
2021	$7.25	$ 7.25

Real (2021) dollars computed using January data in each year from U.S. Bureau of Labor Statistics, Consumer Price Index for All Urban Consumers.

EXHIBIT 17.5 FLSA Wage and Hour Division Investigation Examples: LinkedIn and a Philadelphia Sports Bar and Restaurant Chain

LinkedIn Corp. has paid $3,346,195 in overtime back wages and $2,509,646 in liquidated damages to 359 former and current employees working at company branches in California, Illinois, Nebraska, and New York. An investigation by the U.S. Department of Labor's Wage and Hour Division found that LinkedIn was in violation of the overtime and record-keeping provisions of the FLSA. LinkedIn failed to record, account, and pay for all hours worked in a workweek, investigators found. The FLSA does not allow unpaid "off the clock" hours for employees covered by (nonexempt from) the FLSA. LinkedIn agreed to pay all the overtime back wages due and take proactive steps to prevent repeat violations.

Philadelphia sports bar and restaurant chain Chickie's & Pete's and its owner, Peter Ciarrocchi, Jr. have signed a consent judgment agreeing to pay 1,159 current and former employees at nine locations more than $6.8 million in back wages, plus damages (a $50,000 civil penalty) for improperly taking tips from servers and violating federal minimum wage, overtime, and record-keeping requirements. The proposed consent judgment has been filed in the U.S. District Court for the Eastern District of Pennsylvania and is subject to the review and approval by the court.

Under the Fair Labor Standards Act, tips are the property of the employee who receives them; however, restaurant operators can benefit by claiming a credit based on the tips toward their obligation to pay those employees the full minimum wage. If an employee's tips combined with the employer's direct wages do not equal the minimum wage, the employer must make up the difference during the pay period. An employer that claims a tip credit is required to pay a tipped employee only $2.13 an hour (unchanged since 1991) in direct wages provided that amount plus the tips received equals at least the federal minimum wage of $7.25 an hour.

Investigators from the Wage and Hour Division found that the company required servers to contribute a portion of their tips to an improper "tip pool," or tip-sharing arrangement, which was approximately between 2 and 4 percent of the server's daily table sales. The owner illegally retained approximately 60 percent of the tip pool. This amount had come to be known as "Pete's Tax" and was required to be paid to the manager in cash at the end of each shift.

Additionally, servers and bartenders were paid only a flat rate of $15 per shift at all locations except for Chickie's and Pete's airport establishment—an amount that was not sufficient in all cases to even cover the minimum cash wage of $2.13 per hour that must be paid to a tipped employee when an employer claims a tip credit under federal law. Additionally, the employer failed to pay the required overtime wages to these employees when they worked in excess of 40 hours in a week. Investigators also determined that employees were not paid for time spent in mandatory meetings and training, and were improperly required to pay for uniforms.

Under the provisions of the consent judgment the company will pay minimum wage and overtime back wages and is required to return the improperly retained tips to the servers, as well as pay liquidated damages. In addition, the company has agreed to enhanced compliance, including: External compliance monitoring for an 18-month period; Internal compliance monitoring for an additional 18-month period; Training for all employees on their rights under the FLSA; Providing a statement to any employee required to contribute to a tip pool detailing the amounts that were contributed by the employee, the job categories of workers included in the tip pool and the specific percentage each category receives; Peter Ciarrocchi, Jr., the owner, will write an article for a restaurant trade publication that addresses an employer's obligations under the FLSA; Chickie's & Pete's and Ciarrocchi are to be permanently enjoined and restrained from violating the provisions of the FLSA in the future.

Source: U.S. Department of Labor, WHD News Release, Number 14-0940-SANI and WHD News Release, Number 13-0044-PHI.

Overtime and Hours of Work

The overtime provision of the FLSA requires payment at one-and-a-half times the standard for working more than 40 hours per week. However, some of the largest wage and hour monetary settlements result from private class action suits brought by plaintiffs. Paying for all hours worked and/or for overtime are often central issues. For example, Bank of America paid $73 million to settle a nationwide class action lawsuit alleging that it had a company-wide policy that required nonexempt employees to perform off-the-clock work.[18] Walmart has settled or lost a number of lawsuits, including one for as much as $640 million (for allegedly not paying for all hours worked and for expecting workers to work through their breaks) and another for as much as $86 million (for not paying all wages due upon termination of employment). In another case, which it may appeal, a court ordered it to pay $188 million (for again expecting workers to skip or cut short rest and/or meal breaks).

One objective of the FLSA is to share available work by making the hiring of additional workers a less costly option than the scheduling of overtime for current employees. However, the conditions that inspired the legislation have changed since the law was passed. Contemporary employers face (1) an increasingly skilled workforce with higher training costs per employee and (2) higher benefits costs, the bulk of which are fixed per employee. These factors have lowered the break-even point at which it pays employers to schedule longer hours and pay the overtime premium, rather than hire, train, and pay benefits for more employees.

Again, state laws sometimes go beyond the FLSA. California, for example, requires time and a half pay for working more than 8 hours in a day and double time for working more than 12 hours in a day. It also requires premium pay for working a seventh day during a week.

Exemptions

The Wage and Hour Division of the Department of Labor, which is charged with enforcement of the FLSA, provides strict criteria that must be met in order for jobs to be **exempt** from minimum-wage and overtime provisions. These are summarized in **Exhibit 17.6**. (To check for possible updates on the salary test of $684/week, $35,568/year in **Exhibit 17.6**, go to the Wage and Hour Division website in the next e-compensation box.)

Some employers try to get around the overtime requirement by classifying employees as executives, even though the work of these "executives" differs only slightly from that of their co-workers. However, in the eyes of the Department of Labor, the job title is not relevant. Rather, it is the actual nature of the work that matters.

Merrill Lynch reached a $37 million settlement with financial analysts in California regarding overtime pay. A Merrill Lynch financial analyst argued that because his salary was entirely from commissions, he did not meet the "salary basis" test for the administrative exemption. The plaintiff also successfully argued that he did not exercise sufficient discretion and independent judgment. Instead, the financial analyst's work was considered "production," Merrill Lynch's practices were standard in the financial industry, and the impact of this ruling rippled through other financial service companies and brought changes to Merrill Lynch's pay system for analysts.[19]

Subsequently, Citigroup's Smith Barney brokerage unit settled an FLSA overtime lawsuit for $98 million, with UBS Financial Services and Morgan Stanley both also making substantial payments to settle similar suits. JPMorgan Chase & Co., reached a $42 million settlement with a class of 3,800 loan processors.[20] The U.S. Department of Labor ordered Walmart to pay $4.8 million in back wages and damages to 4,500 vision-center managers and asset-protection coordinators who worked at Walmart over a four-year period.[21] Insurance claims adjustors settled overtime lawsuits against Farmers Insurance for as much as $210 million

EXHIBIT 17.6 **Fact Sheet #17A: Exemption for Executive, Administrative, Professional, Computer & Outside Sales Employees under the Fair Labor Standards Act**

Executive Exemption

To qualify for the executive employee exemption, all of the following tests must be met:

- The employee must be compensated on a salary basis (as defined in the regulations) at a rate not less than $684 per week;
- The employee's primary duty must be managing the enterprise, or managing a customarily recognized department or subdivision of the enterprise;
- The employee must customarily and regularly direct the work of at least two or more other full-time employees or their equivalent; and
- The employee must have the authority to hire or fire other employees, or the employee's suggestions and recommendations as to the hiring, firing, advancement, promotion or any other change of status of other employees must be given particular weight.

Administrative Exemptions

To qualify for the administrative employee exemption, all of the following tests must be met:

- The employee must be compensated on a salary or fee basis (as defined in the regulations) at a rate not less than $684 per week;
- The employee's primary duty must be the performance of office or non-manual work directly related to the management or general business operations of the employer or the employer's customers; and
- The employee's primary duty includes the exercise of discretion and independent judgment with respect to matters of significance.

Professional Exemption

To qualify for the learned professional employee exemption, all of the following tests must be met:

- The employee must be compensated on a salary or fee basis (as defined in the regulations) at a rate not less than $684 per week;
- The employee's primary duty must be the performance of work requiring advanced knowledge, defined as work which is predominantly intellectual in character and which includes work requiring the consistent exercise of discretion and judgment;
- The advanced knowledge must be in a field of science or learning; and
- The advanced knowledge must be customarily acquired by a prolonged course of specialized intellectual instruction.

To qualify for the creative professional employee exemption, all of the following tests must be met:

- The employee must be compensated on a salary or fee basis (as defined in the regulations) at a rate not less than $684* per week;
- The employee's primary duty must be the performance of work requiring invention, imagination, originality or talent in a recognized field of artistic or creative endeavor.

Computer Employee Exemption

To qualify for the computer employee exemption, the following tests must be met:

- The employee must be compensated either on a salary or fee basis (as defined in the regulations) at a rate not less than $684 per week;
- The employee must be employed as a computer systems analyst, computer programmer, software engineer or other similarly skilled worker in the computer field performing the duties described below;
- The employee's primary duty must consist of:
    1. The application of systems analysis techniques and procedures, including consulting with users, to determine hardware, software or system functional specifications;
    2. The design, development, documentation, analysis, creation, testing or modification of computer systems or programs, including prototypes, based on and related to user or system design specifications;
    3. The design, documentation, testing, creation or modification of computer programs related to machine operating systems; or
    4. A combination of the aforementioned duties, the performance of which requires the same level of skills.

Outside Sales Exemption

To qualify for the outside sales employee exemption, all of the following tests must be met:

- The employee's primary duty must be making sales (as defined in the FLSA), or obtaining orders or contracts for services or for the use of facilities for which a consideration will be paid by the client or customer; and
- The employee must be customarily and regularly engaged away from the employer's place or places of business.

Highly Compensated Employees

Highly compensated employees performing office or nonmanual work and paid total annual compensation of $107,432 or more (which must include at least $684 per week paid on a salary or fee basis) are exempt from the FLSA if they customarily and regularly perform at least one of the duties of an exempt executive, administrative or professional employee identified in the standard tests for exemption.

NOT Exempt

Blue-collar workers. The exemptions do not apply to manual laborers or other "blue-collar" workers who perform work involving repetitive operations with their hands, physical skill and energy.

Police, fire fighters, paramedics, and other first responders.

These employee groups are not exempt, but rather are covered by the FLSA.

State Laws

When the state laws differ from the federal FLSA, an employer must comply with the standard most protective to employees.

Source: U.S. Department of Labor, Wage and Hour Division. "Fact Sheet #17A: Exemption for Executive, Administrative, Professional, Computer & Outside Sales Employees Under the Fair Labor Standards Act (FLSA)." Revised September 2019. https://www.dol.gov/sites/dolgov/files/WHD/legacy/files/fs17a_overview.pdf.

and against State Farm Insurance for $135 million. Both of these lawsuits were brought under California law, under which it was more difficult than under federal law (i.e., the FLSA) to meet the administrative employee exemption. Indeed, similar lawsuits brought under FLSA have not succeeded.

e-Compensation

Go the website of the Wage and Hour Division, **http://www.dol.gov/whd/overtime_pay.htm**, and check for updates on the FLSA exemption criteria shown in **Exhibit 17.6**.

Another challenge in compliance is that "in an evolving, always-on workplace where employees routinely put in extra hours and shoot off e-mails late at night from mobile devices, when the workday begins and ends has become an issue for employers."[22] For example, writers at *ABC News* asked that they be paid overtime for using their smartphones for work purposes after business hours. As a result, ABC News asked writers to sign an agreement waiving rights to overtime for such activity. Writers who declined to sign had their smartphones taken away.[23] One survey reports that just over half of large firms have restricted the use of communications devices outside of the office and one-third have restricted telecommuting.[24]

In response to these types of lawsuits, some companies have reclassified some employees. For example, IBM voluntarily reclassified 7,000 technical and support employees after settling a class-action overtime lawsuit for $65 million. The employees, who had been earning an average of $77,000 per year, had their base salaries cut by 15 percent to account for the potential overtime that the company would need to pay them going forward.[25]

The impact of FLSA and other laws depends importantly on the degree to which they are enforced. A Government Accountability Office (GAO) report found that the Labor Department's Wage and Hour Division "mishandled" 9 of 10 cases brought by GAO undercover agents posing as workers who had experienced FLSA violations.[26] As one example, an agent posing as a dishwasher called four times to complain that he had not been paid overtime for almost five months. His calls were not returned until 4 months later and he was then told it would take another 8 to 10 months to begin an investigation. GAO also investigated existing files. In another case, an undercover agent posing as an employer who had violated the law appeared to escape any penalty by simply saying that business was bad, so he could not afford to pay anything. The Department of Labor investigator was quoted as saying, "OK, so you're not in a position where you can pay?" and when the undercover agent said that was correct, the investigator seemed to give up and said that he would let the worker know that he could pursue the case on his own (i.e., need to hire an attorney). To increase enforcement of the FLSA, the Department of Labor since added wage-and hour investigators.[27]

In Japan, unpaid overtime is (also) a major issue. The Japanese Trade Union Confederation reports that two-thirds of men work more than 20 hours of unpaid overtime each month.[28] Only in 2008 did Toyota begin to pay factory workers for participating in quality control programs that were held outside of normal work hours. Some large companies have introduced "no overtime" days on which employees are to leave at 5:30 p.m. However, the concern is that many employees just take the work home, which is referred to as *furoshiki*, or "cloaked overtime."[29] "Death by overwork" (*karoshi*) has resulted in lawsuits against companies in Japan.

What Time Is Covered?

As we have seen, employers are sometimes guilty of not paying employees for hours worked (i.e., of having them "work off the clock"). In addition to the FLSA, other laws come into play. Occupational Safety and Health Administration legislation specifies the number of breaks that must be provided in an eight-hour workday. The Portal-to-Portal Act provides that time spent on activities before beginning the "principal activity" is generally not compensable. The original issue that inspired the act was the time that miners were forced to spend traveling to and from the actual underground site where the mining was occurring. The meat processing industry has been the source of several cases defining time spent at work. Time spent sharpening knives and cutting tools is compensable time, as is the time spent donning protective gear and walking in this "integral" gear to the production area.[30]

The law is also relevant to "on-call employees" who must be available to respond outside the usual workday. Firefighters and emergency personnel are traditional examples. Today, telecommunications and software services personnel who must respond quickly to problems outside their regularly scheduled workday are newer categories of employees eligible for "beeper pay." (See also our ABC News example earlier.) In general, if employees can use this "on-call" time for their own purposes, there is no legal requirement to pay employees for such time, even if they are required to carry a beeper or must let their employer know where they can be reached. However, if they are required to stay on the employer's premises while on call, then they must be compensated for that time. Sometimes a flat rate is paid for the added inconvenience of being on call. These payments must be included when computing overtime pay.[31]

A related area concerns the "donning and doffing" issue in **Exhibit 17.3**. Some recent examples involving Starbucks and Apple come from the California Supreme Court (and based on California state wage and hour law). In the case of Apple, the Court ruled that Apple must pay its store employees for the time they spend waiting for mandatory bag and iPhone searches at the end of their shifts. The Court stated that "The exit searches burden Apple employees by preventing them from the leaving the premises with their personal belongings until they undergo an exit search–a process that can take five to 20 minutes to complete..."[32]

What Income Is Covered?

FLSA specifies one and a half times pay for overtime, but one and a half of what? As more employees became eligible for bonuses, there was an argument over whether bonus, gain-sharing, and stock option payments needed to be included for calculating overtime pay. A 1999 advisory from the Wage and Hour Division said they did. But the extra bookkeeping and calculations provided enough of a burden that employers simply did not offer these forms of pay to **nonexempt employees**. The Worker Economic Opportunity Act, a 2000 amendment to FLSA, allows stock options and bonuses to be exempt from inclusion in overtime pay calculations. Gifts or special-occasion bonuses have never needed to be included, because they are at the employer's discretion rather than a pay form promised to employees if certain conditions are met.

Compensatory Time Off

The changing nature of the workplace and of pay systems has led to calls to reform FLSA to allow for more flexible scheduling and easier administration of variable pay plans.

Federal legislation has been proposed (but not yet passed) that would give employees and employers the option of trading overtime pay for time off. Rather than being paid overtime after 8 hours for a 10-hour workday, an employee would have the option of taking 2 or more hours off at another time. Or, a 50-hour workweek could be banked against a future 30-hour workweek.[33] The employee would get more scheduling flexibility to attend to personal matters, and the employer would save money. This kind of change has a lot of appeal for employees who are also raising children and/or caring for elderly parents. One poll reported that 81 percent of women would prefer compensatory time off in lieu of overtime wages.[34]

Child Labor

Generally, persons under 18 cannot work in hazardous jobs such as meat packing and logging; persons under 16 cannot be employed in jobs involving interstate commerce except for nonhazardous work for a parent or guardian. Additional exceptions and limitations also exist.[35]

The union movement in the United States has taken a leading role in publicizing the extent of the use of child labor outside the United States to produce goods destined for U.S. consumers. Government guidelines help importers monitor the employment practices of subcontractors producing goods for the U.S. market. A recent International Labour Organization report finds that globally, child labor is declining, particularly in Latin America. Brazil and Mexico, where half the children in Latin America live, have made the greatest strides, which the study attributed to increased political will, awareness, poverty reduction, and education. The steepest declines were among children 14 and younger, and among hazardous occupations. The highest rates of child labor are in sub-Saharan Africa, where high population growth, grinding poverty, and the HIV/AIDS epidemic have left a lot of families in need of the income that children can provide.[36]

LIVING WAGE

Although living wage provisions are not part of the FLSA, we cover the topic here because of its similarity to FLSA minimum wage provisions.

Rather than (solely) push for changes in the FLSA, an alternative approach in recent years has been to push for a "living wage" at local levels that provides a minimum wage tailored to living costs in an area.[37] These laws have narrower coverage than minimum wage laws, as they cover only city (or state) employees and/or employers that do business with the city (i.e., contractors and subcontractors). Sometimes they cover only base wages, but more frequently they require health insurance, vacations, sick pay, job security, and provide incentives to unionize.

Maryland was the first to adopt a statewide **living wage** ordinance, effective in 2009, covering "certain contractors and subcontractors working on State funded service contracts."[38] The minimum at the time ranged from $10.36 to $13.79, depending on location, compared to a then $9.25 state minimum wage. More than 100 ordinances have been put into effect in the United States by cities, counties, universities, and other public entities. Companies too can implement a living wage. Unilever, for example, has revised its Code of Business Principles. As of 2020, it reports all employees worldwide are paid a living wage. In addition, it has committed to have "everyone who directly provides goods and services to Unilever" (e.g., workers in other companies in Unilever's supply chain) to earn at least a living wage by 2030.[39]

Los Angeles's law covers "contractors/subcontractors who have agreements with the city." As of 2021, the law mandates $15.00/hour with health benefits of $1.25/hour or $16.25/hour if no health benefits are provided. The required wage rate is higher for airport workers ($16.50/hour with health benefits of $5.55/hour or $22.05/hour if no health benefits are provided).[40] An early study of the Los Angeles law's effects found that 7,735 of the covered employees got an average wage increase of 20 percent.[41] Another 149 noncovered employees got increases in order to maintain pay differentials. Employers adjusted to the law by making only very minor adjustments in employment–an estimated 112 jobs, or 1 percent of covered jobs, were lost. Benefits were cut for less than 5 percent of affected jobs, including cuts in health benefits, merit pay, bonuses, and employer-provided meals. Training for new hires stayed the same, but nonaffected firms were increasing their training. Firms benefited via reduced turnover and absenteeism. New hires tended to be better qualified, with higher levels of education and training than those hired before the law was passed. The new hires also included a higher proportion of males: 56 percent, compared to 45 percent of hires before the living wage. The study also found that 70 percent of the benefit of the law went to low-income families.

Living wage laws are increasingly popular. Coalitions of union members and church groups often support them. Because they are so narrowly tailored, there is some speculation that their real intention is to reduce any cost savings a municipality might receive from outsourcing. Reduced outsourcing means more government jobs, which generally translates into more union members.[42]

EMPLOYEE OR INDEPENDENT CONTRACTOR?

As we saw in **Chapter 12**, U.S. employers are legally obligated to pay Social Security, unemployment compensation, and workers compensation taxes on wages and salaries on behalf of their employees. As we saw in **Chapter 13**, the average total compensation per employee in private industry was $36.23 per hour, with $25.48 of that being in the form of wages and salaries and the remaining $10.74 being for benefits. Of the $10.25, $2.75 was for the legally required benefits just mentioned.[43] However, in the case of a worker who is an independent contractor rather than an employee, the employer is not obligated to pay the legally required benefits. In addition, independent contractors would also typically not receive other benefits. An independent contractor would also not be eligible for overtime (time and a half). Thus, whether a worker is classified as an employee or an independent contractor can have substantial cost implications for an employer, which of course increases with the number of workers involved. Less obvious perhaps is that law-abiding employers are put at a disadvantage because complying with the law results in higher costs than those borne by employers that misclassify (unless those not in compliance are discovered). Finally, of course, workers suffer if they are denied access to benefits and legal protections that they should receive.

As with the FLSA exceptions discussed a few pages earlier, the decision of whether to classify a worker as an employee or independent contractor requires careful attention to compliance issues. Both tax law–enforced by the Internal Revenue Service (IRS)–and the Employee Retirement Income Security Act (ERISA)–enforced by the Department of Labor–are relevant. To get an idea of the potential revenue losses to government of misclassification of workers, consider that Ohio's attorney general estimated that Ohio alone at one point had 92,500 misclassified workers, estimated to cost the state up to $35 million in lost unemployment insurance taxes, up to $103 million in lost workers' compensation taxes, and up to $223 million in income tax revenue. (Note: some estimates suggest that misclassified independent contractors do not report 30 percent of their income.)[44] The most widely used classification criteria are provided by the IRS and shown in **Exhibit 17.7**. Two general criteria have to do with behavioral and financial control. The more control a firm is able to exercise, the more likely it is that the IRS will see the worker as an employee rather than an independent contractor. The IRS also considers the type of relationship, including its permanence. The Supreme Court, in *Nationwide v. Darden*, has applied similar criteria in deciding whether a worker is an employee under ERISA.[45] Among the most often misclassified are truck drivers, construction workers, home health aides, and high-tech engineers.[46]

Microsoft hired workers as independent contractors. It had these workers sign agreements acknowledging their independent contractor status. However, after an audit by the IRS concluded that these workers were actually employees, Microsoft agreed to begin paying legally required taxes (see above). Microsoft had used the workers on projects, often working on teams with regular employees, doing similar work, working similar hours, and being supervised by the same managers. Microsoft also required them to work onsite and they were given office equipment and supplies.[47]

EXHIBIT 17.7 Employee or Independent Contractor: Internal Revenue Service Tests

Behavioral control. Facts that show whether the business has a right to direct and control how the worker does the task for which the worker is hired include the type and degree of:

Instructions that the business gives to the worker. An employee is generally subject to the business' instructions about when, where, and how to work. Even if no instructions are given, sufficient behavioral control may exist if the employer has the right to control how the work results are achieved. Examples of types of instructions include: when and where to do the work, what tools or equipment to use, what workers to hire or to assist with the work, where to purchase supplies and services, what work must be performed by a specified individual, what order or sequence to follow.

Training that the business gives to the worker. An employee may be trained to perform services in a particular manner. Independent contractors ordinarily use their own methods.

Financial control. Facts that show whether the business has a right to control the business aspects of the worker's job include:

The extent to which the worker has unreimbursed business expenses. Independent contractors are more likely to have unreimbursed expenses than are employees.

The extent of the worker's investment. An independent contractor often has a significant investment in the facilities he or she uses in performing services for someone else.

The extent to which the worker makes his or her services available to the relevant market. An independent contractor is generally free to seek out business opportunities. Independent contractors often advertise, maintain a visible business location, and are available to work in the relevant market.

How the business pays the worker. An employee is generally guaranteed a regular wage amount for an hourly, weekly, or other period of time. An independent contractor is usually paid by a flat fee for the job. However, it is common in some professions, such as law, to pay independent contractors hourly.

The extent to which the worker can realize a profit or loss. An independent contractor can make a profit or loss.

Type of relationship. Facts that show the parties' type of relationship include:

Written contracts describing the relationship the parties intended to create.

Whether or not the business provides the worker with employee-type benefits, such as insurance, a pension plan, vacation pay, or sick pay.

The permanency of the relationship. If you engage a worker with the expectation that the relationship will continue indefinitely, rather than for a specific project or period, this is generally considered evidence that your intent was to create an employer–employee relationship.

The extent to which services performed by the worker are a key aspect of the regular business of the company. If a worker provides services that are a key aspect of your regular business activity, it is more likely that you will have the right to direct and control his or her activities. For example, if a law firm hires an attorney, it is likely that it will present the attorney's work as its own and would have the right to control or direct that work. This would indicate an employer–employee relationship.

Source: Adapted from Internal Revenue Service, Department of U.S. Treasury, Publication 15-A, January 31, 2012.

Next, two separate suits (*Vizcaino v. Microsoft* and *Hughes v. Microsoft*) were filed against Microsoft to compel it to retroactively provide other benefits (e.g., a discounted stock purchase program) that it provided to its (other) employees. Some of the workers had been at Microsoft for several years with a few being there as long as 10 years. By classifying workers as consultants/independent contractors, Microsoft would also avoid paying those workers overtime wages when their hours exceeded 40 in a week. In *Vizcaino v. Microsoft*, the court declared these workers common-law employees. Before the case could go to the Supreme Court, Microsoft settled for $97 million, which, after attorneys' fees, was to be divided between 8,000 and 12,000 people employed at Microsoft for at least 9 months during a several year period.[48] Microsoft implemented new rules, including limiting independent contractor assignments to 12 months with at least 100 days between assignments.

FedEx has also had FLSA issues around how it classified workers. In one case, it classified workers as independent contractors to avoid paying them 2 hours of overtime for the mandated 10-hour days. However, these workers were ruled to be employees.[49]

The year 2016 was especially difficult (for almost $500 million reasons) for FedEx. It settled two lawsuits where it was alleged to have misclassified delivery drivers as of independent contractors to avoid paying them benefits and overtime. It settled the first lawsuit, in California, for $226 million and a second lawsuit, across 20 states, for $240 million.[50] In both cases, a major basis for the complaint was the significant amount of control (see **Exhibit 17.7** above), especially behavioral control, exercised by FedEx over drivers. In the multistate case, drivers will receive payments ranging from $250 to $116,000.[51]

We noted legal problems Microsoft had. However, Microsoft has also taken steps more recently to help workers. Specifically, Microsoft began to require that its suppliers provide their employees with at least 15 days of paid time off each year. More recently, Microsoft has implemented a new requirement that its suppliers, of which it says it has over 1,000, if they have at least 50 employees and "perform substantial work for Microsoft," must also provide a minimum of 12 weeks of paid parental leave and an additional 8 weeks for birth mothers. Microsoft went on to cite research it says shows that employers providing parental paid leave see "improved productivity, higher morale, and lower turnover rates."[52]

Of course, it is now difficult not to think of gig workers like Lyft and Uber drivers when discussing who is an employee and who is an independent contractor. This issue has been front and center in many countries around the world and in many U.S. states. Here again, we focus on California.[53] In California, the state recently passed a law (AB5) that a California court interpreted as meaning Uber and Lyft were required to reclassify their drivers as employees. Uber and Lyft made changes to how they treated drivers and argued that had come in compliance with the law. The state attorney general then sued the companies, arguing it was not in compliance and a court agreed. Uber and Lyft then threatened to stop service in California. A Court then ruled that Uber and Lyft did not have to reclassify workers immediately, forestalling at least temporarily any halt in service. Shortly thereafter, Proposition 22 appeared on a statewide ballot. A state voter guide described what a "yes" vote would mean: "A YES vote on this measure means: App-based rideshare and delivery companies could hire drivers as independent contractors. Drivers could decide when, where, and how much to work but would not get standard benefits and protections that businesses must provide employees." It also described an argument for a "No" vote: "Stop billion-dollar app companies like Uber, Lyft, and DoorDash from writing their own exemption to California law and profiting from it. 22 denies their drivers rights and safety protections they deserve: sick leave, healthcare and unemployment. Companies profit; exploited drivers lose rights and protections." Proposition 22 "yes" votes prevailed (59% to 41%). Thus, companies like Uber and Lyft now are permitted to classify drivers as self-employed/independent contractors. However, Proposition 22, with support from companies like Uber and Lyft does provide new benefits and protections to their workers. Specifically, the text of the law identifies these as including "a healthcare subsidy consistent with the average contributions required under the Affordable Care Act (ACA); a new minimum earnings guarantee tied to 120 percent of minimum wage with no maximum; compensation for vehicle expenses; occupational accident insurance to cover on-the-job injuries; and protection against discrimination and sexual harassment" (p. 30). Thus, these app companies, by agreeing to the new benefits and protections in the law, look to be able to maintain a key part of their desired business model: workers as independent contractors, not employees. The California Supreme Court threw out a challenge to the law after its passage.) It remains to be seen what will happen in other states or, with a change in presidential administration, whether federal regulation will follow. And, as noted, the issue will be addressed country by country as well.

PREVAILING WAGE LAWS

Prevailing wage laws set pay for work done to produce goods and services contracted by the federal government. A *government-defined prevailing wage* is the minimum wage that must be paid for work done on covered government projects or purchases. Consider, for example, "The Big Dig," Boston's $15 billion taxpayer-financed project to put its freeways underground.[54] A construction project of such magnitude attracts workers from a very wide area and distorts the labor market. Prevailing wage laws prevent contractors from using their size to drive down wages. The law was passed in response to conditions on projects such as the construction of the Hoover Dam during the Depression. Workers who collapsed from the July heat in Nevada or were killed in accidents were quickly replaced from a pool of unemployed men who were already camping near the job site.

To comply with the law, contractors must determine the "going rate" for construction labor in an area. As a practical matter, the "union rate" for labor becomes the going rate. That rate then becomes the mandated minimum wage on the government-financed project. One effect is to distort market wages and drive up the cost of government-financed projects. For example, some years back, the market wage for plumbers in Kentucky was $18.15 an hour, according to the Bureau of Labor Statistics. Yet a wage survey for Owsley County, Kentucky, required that plumbers on public projects receive $23.75 an hour, more than 30 percent above the government's own market wage.[55]

A number of laws contain prevailing-wage provisions. They vary on the government expenditures they target for coverage. The main prevailing wage laws include the Davis-Bacon Act, the Walsh–Healey Public Contracts Act, the Service Contract Act, and the National Foundation for the Arts and Humanities Act. A spate of new laws extends prevailing-wage coverage to new immigrants to the United States and to noncitizens who are working in the United States under special provisions. For example, the Nursing Relief for Disadvantaged Areas Act of 1999 allows qualified hospitals to employ temporary foreign workers as registered nurses for up to three years under a special visa program. The prevailing wage for registered nurses must be paid to these foreign workers. Similar acts target legal immigrants and farm workers.

Much of the legislation discussed so far was originally passed in the 1930s and 1940s in response to social issues of that time. While this legislation has continued to be extended up to the present, the Equal Rights movement in the 1960s pushed different social problems to the forefront. The Equal Pay Act and the Civil Rights Act were passed. Because of their substantial impact on human resource management and compensation, they are discussed at length below.

ANTITRUST ISSUES

In **Chapter 8**, we noted the need to avoid antitrust concerns in setting employee pay. A lawsuit (referred to as Hi-Tech) representing 64,000 former software engineers and programmers at Apple, Inc., Google, Inc., Intel Corp., and Adobe Systems alleged that these companies entered into an agreement between 2005 and

2009 that they would not poach or "cold call" (try to recruit away) each other's employees. It was also alleged that before making an offer to an employee of one of the other companies (who applied on their own for a job), it would notify the employee's current company. Finally, it was alleged that if an offer was made to such an employee, the other company would not make a counteroffer (with the intent of eliminating "bidding wars" for employees). Given that one of the main contributors to career earnings is advancement, either at one's present company or another company (typically with a higher salary), the companies' alleged action to avoid competing with each other and to avoid a bidding war for talent (through using anticompetitive actions) is argued to have resulted in lost pay for their employees. The lawsuit alleges that the main mastermind of the no poaching agreement was the late Steve Jobs, the former head of Apple, Inc. (Indeed, according to one claim in the papers filed, when in 2007 a Google recruiter contacted an Apple employee about a job, Mr. Jobs complained and the Google recruiter was fired, purportedly within an hour.) The two sides in the lawsuit eventually agreed to settle the case by having the companies (those above plus later Intuit, Inc., Lucasfilm, Ltd., and Pixar) pay $435 million in back pay (and legal fees). A similar case, Animation Workers, resulted in settlements totaling $168.95 million with several companies, including some (e.g., Lucasfilm, Ltd. and Pixar) who were part of the Hi-Tech settlement, as well as other well-known companies (e.g., Walt Disney Company, Sony Pictures Animation, Inc., and DreamWorks Animation SKG, Inc.).[56]

PAY DISCRIMINATION AND PAY EQUITY: WHAT ARE THEY?

Pay Discrimination

Before we look at specific federal pay discrimination laws, which are summarized in **Exhibit 17.8**, let us address the more general question of how to legally define discrimination. The law recognizes two types of discrimination: access discrimination and valuation discrimination. The charges of discrimination and reverse discrimination that most often make the news involve **access discrimination:** the denial of particular jobs, promotions, or training opportunities to qualified candidates on the basis of sex, race, and other protected classes. Over time, this can be seen in segregation by job, occupation, industry, and/or firm. The major case that established the application of Title VII in access discrimination was the U.S. Supreme Court decision in *Griggs v. Duke Power Co. (1971)*, which struck down the use of employment tests (requirement to have a high school degree, aptitude test scores) to select applicants for positions because use of these tests screened out a higher proportion of Blacks than whites, without adequate evidence that doing better on these tests was associated with significantly better performance on the job.

There are also limits on the nature of affirmative action steps organizations can take to proactively increase representation of underrepresented groups (which potentially raises the issue of reverse discrimination). The University of Michigan, for example, in an effort to increase minority group representation, was accused of (reverse) access discrimination for using differential standards among different racial groups to determine who is "qualified" for admission. Being a member of a minority group counted for 20 points, whereas the quality of the admission essay counted for 3 points. (Being an athlete also counted for 20 points.) In 2003, the Supreme Court ruled that while schools can take race into account for admission, this 20-point differential was illegal because it was applied in a mechanical way.[57] However, the admission process for Michigan's law school was upheld because it was narrowly tailored and more flexible. Minority candidates for the law school were interviewed and their entire record was examined, in contrast to the routine addition of 20 points that the undergraduate school used. (The court did not address the issue of the preferred treatment for athletes or children of alumni or big donors.)[58] Subsequently, however, the State of Michigan passed a constitutional amendment prohibiting race-conscious admission policies at the state's public universities.

EXHIBIT 17.8 Federal Pay Discrimination Law and Enforcement

	Equal Pay Act	Title VII, Civil Rights Act	Executive Order 11246
Year	1963	1964	1965
Discrimination Prohibited on Basis of:	Sex	Race, color, religion, sex, or national origin	Race, color, religion, sex, or national origin
Type of Pay Discrimination Prohibited	"for equal work on jobs the performance of which requires equal skill, effort, and responsibility, and which are performed under similar working conditions, except where such payment is made pursuant to (i) a seniority system; (ii) a merit system; (iii) a system which measures earnings by quantity or quality of production; or (iv) a differential based on any other factor other than sex" (Equal Pay Act)	"[in] compensation, terms, conditions, or privileges of employment" (Title VII, Civil Rights Act)	"statistically significant compensation disparities between similarly situated employees . . . after taking into account legitimate factors which influence compensation." ("Systemic Compensation Discrimination," Federal Register, June 16, 2006)
Coverage	Same as FLSA. Virtually all employers.	Employers having 15 or more employees. Those with 100 or more employees must also file annual EEO-1 reports, which report the number of employees by race, ethnicity and gender for each of nine job categories. Over 600,000 employers covered.*	Government contractors and subcontractors with $10,000 or more in government contracts. Contractors with 50 or more employees and $50,000 or more in contracts must also file annual EEO-1 reports, which report the number of employees by race, ethnicity and gender for each of nine job categories. Over 116,000 employers covered.**
Enforcement Agency	Equal Employment Opportunity Commission (EEOC)	Equal Employment Opportunity Commission (EEOC)	Office of Federal Contract Compliance Programs (OFCCP), Department of Labor
Primary Enforcement Action Trigger	Employee Complaint-Driven	Employee Complaint-Driven	Regular Audits

*U.S. Government Accountability Office, "Federal Agencies Should Better Monitor Their Performance in Enforcing Anti-Discrimination Laws," GAO Reports, Report Number GAO-08-799. Washington, D.C., August 2008.

**Department of Labor. Office of Federal Contracts Compliance. Government Contractors, Requirement to Report Summary Data on Employee Compensation. Federal Register / Vol. 79, No. 153 / Friday, August 8, 2014 / Proposed Rules.

A second legally recognized interpretation of discrimination is **valuation discrimination**, which looks at the pay women and minorities receive for the jobs they perform. This is the more salient definition for our purposes. The Equal Pay Act makes it clear that it is discriminatory to pay women less than males when they are performing equal work (i.e., working side by side, in the same plant, doing the same work, producing the same results). This definition of pay discrimination hinges on the standard of *equal pay for equal work.*

Pay Equity

Pay equity is a broad term, commonly used both as a goal (to eliminate pay discrimination) and to encompass an array of policies/practices intended to reduce/eliminate pay discrimination. The federal Equal Pay Act of 1963 discussed above provides a starting point. As shown in **Exhibit 17.8**, Title VII and Executive Order 11246 are other key federal laws in the area of pay equity. We will also see that state and local laws are important. As we will also see, these go beyond federal law in terms of broadening "equal pay for equal work" (e.g., equal pay for "substantially similar work"). Two other common ways they go beyond federal law are (a) banning asking candidates about their salary histories, and (b) requiring employers to be more transparent in their pay practices (e.g., submitting employee earnings data to the state and/or requirements to notify employees of promotion opportunities).[59]

As noted (and discussed further below), some states have gone beyond defining valuation discrimination as equal pay for equal work for equal pay for substantially similar work. A further step would be to examine valuation discrimination can also occur when men and women hold entirely different jobs. Such a situation may represent segregation that stems from a history of certain jobs being closed to certain groups, women in this case. For example, office and clerical jobs are typically staffed by women, and craft jobs (electricians, welders) are typically staffed by men. Further, if women had only a relatively small number of occupations open to them, the resulting "crowding" would give rise to excess supply (relative to demand) and depressed wages. This view argues it is illegal to pay employees in one job group less than employees in the other if the two job groups contain work that is not equal in content or results but is, in some sense, of **comparable worth** to the employer?[60] Existing federal laws in the United States do not support this standard. We return to this topic below.

THE EQUAL PAY ACT (AND RELATED STATE LAWS)

The Equal Pay Act (EPA) of 1963 (which is part of the FLSA) forbids wage discrimination on the basis of gender if employees perform equal work in the same establishment. Jobs are considered equal if they require equal skill, effort, and responsibility and are performed under similar working conditions.

Differences in pay between men and women doing equal work are legal if these differences are based on any one of four criteria, called an *affirmative defense:*

- Seniority
- Merit or quality of performance
- Quality or quantity of production
- Some factor other than sex

These terms for comparison and permitted defenses seem deceptively simple. Yet numerous court cases have been required to clarify the act's provisions, particularly its definition of "equal."

Definition of Equal

The Supreme Court first established guidelines to define equal work in the *Schultz v. Wheaton Glass* case back in 1970. Wheaton Glass Company maintained two **job classifications** for selector-packers in its production department: male and female. The female job class carried a pay rate 10 percent below that of the male job class. The company claimed that the male job class included additional tasks such as shoveling broken glass, opening warehouse doors, and doing heavy lifting that justified the pay differential. The plaintiff claimed that the extra tasks were infrequently performed and not all men did them. Further, these extra tasks performed by some of the men were regularly performed by employees in another classification ("snap-up boys"), and these employees were paid only 2 cents an hour more than the women. Did the additional tasks sometimes performed by some members of one job class render the jobs unequal?

The Court decided they did not. It ruled that the equal work standard required only that jobs be *substantially* equal, not identical. Additionally, in several cases where the duties employees actually performed were different from those in the job descriptions, the courts held that the *actual work performed* must be used to decide whether jobs are substantially equal.

Definitions of Skill, Effort, Responsibility, Working Conditions

The Department of Labor provides these definitions of the four factors.

1. *Skill:* Experience, training, education, and ability as measured by the performance requirements of a particular job.
2. *Effort:* Mental or physical—the degree of effort (not type of effort) actually expended in the performance of a job.
3. *Responsibility:* The degree of accountability required in the performance of a job.
4. *Working conditions:* The physical surroundings and hazards of a job, including dimensions such as inside versus outside work, heat, cold, and poor ventilation.

Guidelines to clarify these definitions have evolved through court decisions. For an employer to support a claim of *unequal* work, the following conditions must be met:

1. The effort/skill/responsibility must be substantially greater in one of the jobs compared.
2. The tasks involving the extra effort/skill/responsibility must consume a *significant amount* of time for *all* employees whose additional wages are in question.
3. The extra effort/skill/responsibility must have a *value commensurate* with the questioned pay differential (as determined by the employer's own evaluation).

Time of day (e.g., working a night shift) does not constitute dissimilar working conditions. However, if a differential for working at night is paid, it must be separated from the base wage for the job.

Factors Other than Sex

Of the four affirmative defenses for unequal pay for equal work, "a factor other than sex" has prompted the most court cases. Factors other than sex include shift differentials; temporary assignments; bona fide training programs; differences based on ability, training, or experience; and other reasons of "business necessity."

Factors other than sex have been interpreted as a broad exception that may include business reasons advanced by the employer. A practice will not automatically be prohibited simply because wage differences between men and women result. However, an employer is required to justify the business relatedness of the practice.[61] Usually a specific practice is not singled out; rather, the argument focuses on a "pattern of practices." That is what a group of female brokers at Merrill Lynch charged in their class action suit. They were concerned with how accounts from departing brokers, walk-ins, and referrals were being distributed. They felt that the top men brokers were given the most promising leads, while everyone else, including the 15 percent of brokers who were women, got the "crumbs." The women contended that Merrill Lynch discriminated against women in wages, promotions, account distributions, maternity leaves, and other areas. A negotiated settlement promised to establish a more open method for sharing leads and not to penalize brokers for time off in determining bonuses and production quotas.

Because such cases tend to be settled out of court, no legal clarification of a "factor other than sex" has ever been provided. It does seem that pay differences for equal work can be justified for demonstrably business-related reasons. But what is and is not demonstrably business-related has yet to be cataloged.

"Reverse" Discrimination

Many people dislike the term "reverse" discrimination, saying that it is still discrimination, even if the group penalized is white males. Several court cases deal with discrimination against men when pay for women is adjusted. The University of Nebraska created a model to calculate salaries based on estimated values for a faculty member's education, field of specialization, years of direct experience, years of related experience, and merit. Based on these qualifications, the university granted raises to 33 women whose salaries were less than the amount computed by the model. However, the university gave no such increases to 92 males whose salaries were also below the amount the model set for them based on their qualifications. The court found this system a violation of the Equal Pay Act. It held that, in effect, the university was using a new system to determine a salary schedule, based on specific criteria. To refuse to pay employees of one sex the minimum required by these criteria was illegal.

Viewed collectively, the courts have provided reasonably clear directions to interpret the Equal Pay Act. The design of pay systems must incorporate a policy of equal pay for substantially equal work. The determination of substantially equal work must be based on the actual work performed (the job content) and must reflect the skill, effort, responsibility, and working conditions involved. It is legal to pay men and women who perform substantially equal work differently if the pay system is designed to recognize differences in performance, seniority, quality, and quantity of results, or certain factors other than sex in a nondiscriminatory manner. Further, if a new pay system is designed, it must be equally applied to all employees.

But what does this tell us about discrimination on jobs that are *not substantially equal*–dissimilar jobs? Most working women are not in jobs substantially equal to jobs of men, so they are not covered by the Equal Pay Act. Title VII of the Civil Rights Act extends protection to them.

TITLE VII OF THE CIVIL RIGHTS ACT OF 1964 AND RELATED LAWS

The Civil Rights Act is a far-reaching law that grew out of the civil rights movement of the 1950s and 1960s. **Title VII** of the act prohibits discrimination on the basis of sex, race, color, religion, or national origin in any employment condition, including hiring, firing, promotion, transfer, compensation, and admission to training programs. Title VII was amended in 1972, 1978, and 1990. The EEOC is responsible for Title VII enforcement. As we saw earlier in **Exhibit 17.8**, the cost to employers of equal employment opportunity (EEO) issues broadly (including Title VII) was about $2 billion over a five-year period, taking into account both EEOC enforcement activity and private class action lawsuit settlements.

In addition to Title VII, other key EEO statutes, the 1967 **Age Discrimination in Employment Act (ADEA)** and the 1990 **Americans with Disabilities Act (ADA)** also prohibit discrimination based on age and disability, respectively. Compliance with the ADEA is typically a key concern when companies use workforce reduction programs. The ADEA pertains not only to age-related differences in pay and employment outcomes, but in addition, it was amended in 1990 to include the Older Workers Benefit Protection Act (OWBPA), which has detailed rules regarding how separation agreements (e.g., an early retirement incentive) involving older workers are used. As one example, at least 21 days must be given to consider the agreement.

Title VII cases of pay discrimination typically focus on differences in pay, promotions, pay raises, and performance reviews. Race-based differences in these areas were at the center of litigation against Merrill Lynch and gender-based differences were the issue at Bank of America. These companies settled with the plaintiffs for $160 million and $39 million, respectively.[62] Of course, these cases are very costly for the company not only in terms of legal expenses, but also in terms of unfavorable publicity, employee relations, and the allocation of time away from the core business. Organizations that can successfully be proactive in maintaining compliance increase their chances of avoiding such litigation.

These types of settlements are the result of class action lawsuits. A class action lawsuit is "any civil case in which parties indicated their intent to sue on behalf of themselves as well as others not specifically named in the suit at some point prior to the final resolution of the matter."[63] Employment-related class action lawsuits such as those that pertain to EEO/discrimination can be very costly to employers because they can include large numbers of potential plaintiffs (employees, former employees, potential employees). These potential plaintiffs can potentially be included as part of the class without contacting them in advance. Instead, they can be given the opportunity to opt out in the event the lead plaintiffs prevail in court or reach a settlement with the employer. (FLSA lawsuits differ.)[64] Such settlements typically include back pay (pay that would have received absent discrimination) for each member of the class. The bigger the class, the bigger the potential cost to the employer. Clearly, a key issue in class actions is the definition of the class. The easier it is to include large numbers of potential plaintiffs, the more potential liability the employer faces and the bigger the potential payoff for plaintiffs (and their attorneys). Rule 23 of the Federal Rules of Civil Procedure and 29 U.S.C. § 216(b) provide the requirements for forming a class and one requirement is a commonality of interests.[65] A 2011 U.S. Supreme Court decision in *Wal-Mart Stores, Inc., v. Dukes, et al.* made it more difficult for plaintiffs to certify a class of potential plaintiffs. The Supreme Court "reversed a class certification decision that joined the claims of 1.5 million female salaried and hourly employees who held any number of positions across Wal-Mart's 3,400 stores because the plaintiffs could not articulate a common question that was capable of common answers as to the entire class. The Supreme Court ruled that the plaintiffs were required to demonstrate that Wal-Mart operated under a 'general policy of discrimination,' which it concluded was 'entirely absent' [in the evidence presented in the case]."[66] Some experts believe the Wal-Mart ruling has already resulted in employers more aggressively challenging class action lawsuits and similarly in employers being less willing to settle such lawsuits to avoid litigation.[67] However, there is also evidence that plaintiffs and their attorneys are using new approaches to satisfy Rule 23 class action requirements and it is perhaps noteworthy that the Merrill Lynch settlement of a class action discrimination lawsuit for $160 million (see above) came after the Wal-Mart decision.[68] On the other hand, it has been observed since that the U.S. Supreme Court decision in Wal-Mart Stores "still lords over employment discrimination class actions."[69]

Another added impediment to bringing a class action lawsuit is a new strategy by employers to not only require employees to agree to resolve their individual employment discrimination complaints via arbitration (versus legal action), but to also require them to agree to give up their right to pursue their complaints as part of a class action lawsuit. (In return for waiving such a right, the employer must provide something in return referred to as "consideration.") Employers prefer arbitration because it is faster and cheaper, especially so if it can be used in lieu of costly class action litigation. At present, the law is not clear on whether such waivers are legal. The National Labor Relations Board had ruled that workers cannot be required to give up their (concerted action) right to be part of a class action lawsuit. However, another view is that a 2011 Supreme Court ruling (in a nonemployment context), *AT&T Mobility v. Concepcion,* can be applied to employment law to permit use of such waivers. Companies such as Sears, Nordstrom, Uber, and Haliburton are doing so, and more generally the use of such waivers is reported to have increased dramatically since the 2011 Supreme Court decision.[70] In 2018, The U.S. Supreme Court cleared up any confusion, ruling in its Epic Systems Corp. v Lewis decision that employers can require employees to submit all work-related disputes to individual arbitration, including waiving their ability to bring class or collective claims.[71]

Although class action lawsuits may provide more challenging to mount for plaintiffs, the passage in 2009 of the Lilly Ledbetter Fair Pay Act is expected to further increase the compliance challenge for employers. The statute of limitations for filing a claim of discrimination is within 180 days (300 days in states with their own equal employment opportunity agencies) of the date of the alleged discriminatory employment practice. Lilly Ledbetter's claim was made after she left her job as a supervisor in a tire plant and was based on the lasting effects of compensation decisions she alleged to be discriminatory that were made as much as 19 years earlier, far outside the 180-day period. In 2007 the Supreme Court ruled (*Ledbetter v. Goodyear Tire & Rubber Company*) that such decisions could not be litigated because they were outside the statute of limitations. However, the 2009 Act overturns this rule, instead stating that discrimination occurs–and starts the 180/300-day time period for filing a claim–"each time a discriminatory paycheck is issued, not just when the employer makes an adverse pay-setting decision."[72] According to the EEOC, "The Act restores the pre-Ledbetter position of the EEOC that each paycheck that delivers discriminatory compensation is a wrong which is actionable under the federal EEO statutes, regardless of when the discrimination began."[73] It has been argued that "employers will likely be called upon to defend against actions and decisions made by retired managers and supervisors that occurred years, and even decades, ago."[74]

Court cases have established two theories of discrimination behavior under Title VII: (1) **disparate treatment** and (2) **disparate impact**.

Disparate Treatment

Disparate or unequal treatment applies different standards to different employees: For example, asking women but not men if they plan to have children. In Japan, for example, women college students continue to report that recruiters ask them different questions than are asked of male college students. The mere fact of unequal treatment may be taken as evidence of the employer's intention to discriminate under U.S. law. In the pay context, an example would be requiring a woman to have higher performance than a man to be promoted to a higher-paying job.

Disparate Impact

Practices that have a differential effect on members of protected groups are illegal, unless the differences are work-related. As noted earlier. the major case that established this interpretation of Title VII is *Griggs v. Duke Power Co.,* which struck down employment tests (educational requirements and aptitude test scores) that screened out a higher proportion of Blacks than whites. Even though the practices were applied equally–both Blacks and whites had to pass the tests–they were prohibited because (1) they had the consequence of excluding a protected group disproportionately and (2) there was not sufficient evidence to document that the tests were not related to performance in the jobs in question. Under disparate impact, whether or not the employer intended to discriminate is irrelevant. A personnel decision can, on its face, seem neutral, but if its results are unequal, the employer must demonstrate that the decision is a business necessity (e.g., performance-related). The two standards of discrimination—disparate treatment versus disparate impact—remain difficult to apply to pay issues, since pay differences are legal for dissimilar work. It is still not clear what constitutes pay discrimination in dissimilar jobs in the United States.[75]

EXECUTIVE ORDER 11246

Enforced by the Office of Federal Contracts Compliance Programs (OFCCP), Department of Labor, Executive Order 11246 (E.O. 11246) prohibits discrimination on the basis of race, color, religion, sex, or national origin. It requires covered government contractors to file affirmative action plans, which have three parts. First, utilization analysis compares the contractor's workforce to the available external workforce. Underutilization exists if a group (e.g., women) represents a significantly smaller percentage of the employer's workforce than of the external workforce. Second, goals and timetables are developed for achieving affirmative action. Third, action steps are developed for achieving these goals and timetables. As discussed below, the OFCCP conducts audits and seeks remedies where it finds insufficient compliance. Importantly, covered employers also have an obligation to perform self-audits for pay discrimination

Here we focus specifically on the steps in the OFCCP's compliance review process as it applies to compensation.[76] It begins with a selection of contractors based, in part, on a mathematical model, called the Federal Contractor Selection System (FCSS), which is intended to predict the likelihood that a contractor is engaging in systemic (i.e., affecting a broad class of employees) discrimination. (Under a 1999 Memorandum of Understanding with the EEOC, individual complaints of compensation discrimination can be referred to the EEOC.) The OFCCP also selects contractors based on other factors (e.g., time since their previous review) and selects some contractors at random. In recent years, about 5 percent of all contractors have been selected for review.

If selected, the first step is a desk audit. The OFCCP will notify the employer that it is conducting an audit and will instruct the employer to provide complete information on its Affirmative Action Program and all supporting personnel activity (such as hiring, promotion decisions) and compensation data within 30 days. This is "analyzed for possible systemic discrimination indicators (i.e., a potential affected class of 10 or more applicants/workers)."[77] If such indicators are found, additional information for the desk audit will be requested. After the desk audit is completed, if the OFCCP decides the employer is in compliance, it ends the process by issuing a closure letter.

If the OFCCP believes systemic discrimination may be present, it conducts an onsite review, where it will delve deeper into statistical analyses of data (including using multiple regression analysis) and also conduct interviews with management and nonmanagement employees for "anecdotal evidence" to consider along with statistical evidence.[78] Based on its statistical analyses and anecdotal evidence, the OFCCP will decide whether there is evidence of systemic discrimination. If so, it will issue a Notice of Violation (NOV). However, that and other aspects of the investigative process have been revised (see below). If an NOV is issued, the OFCCP will seek to have the employer sign a conciliation agreement under which it agrees to stop and remedy practices identified as discriminatory. The employer may also be required to change its compensation levels for some employee groups to remedy disparities between similarly situated employees that the OFCCP judges to be the result of systemic discrimination. If the OFCCP cannot reach a settlement with the employer, it can refer the case to the Office of the Solicitor and disputes are addressed in a hearing in front of an administrative law judge. The OFCCP can also seek to disbar contractors from receiving future contracts from the government or to stop payments on current contracts.

In 2013, under President Obama, the OFCCP rescinded its previous (issued in 2006 under George W. Bush) standards for evaluating evidence of systemic pay discrimination, stating that these former standards "restrict[ed] OFCCP's ability to enforce the Executive Order's nondiscrimination mandate."[79] The OFCCP issued new standards (Directive 307)[80] giving it more "flexibility," which it argued was "critical because discrimination may be difficult to identify." Then, in 2018, under President Trump, the OFCCP stated that it had rescinded Directive 307 and replaced it with Directive 2018-05. In other words, this is another example of how the executive branch enforcement of laws changes with different presidential administrations (and their agency appointees). Directive 2018-05 is intended to provide greater clarity on how the OFCCP evaluates evidence and forms pay analysis groupings (PAGs) to identify possible discrimination. In this vein, it goes into some detail in describing how multiple regression is used. Both the directive and a Frequently Asked Questions document are available from the OFCCP. [81] Subsequently, two court decisions, OFCCP v. Analogic Corp. in 2019 and OFCCP v. Oracle America in 2020, cases brought during the Obama Administration, went against the OFCCP, essentially being consistent with the stricter standards for proving employer pay discrimination set out in Directive 2018-05. For example, in the Oracle America case, the administrative law judge noted the OFCCP's failure to identify an actual discriminatory personnel practice that caused the alleged underpayment to female, Asian, and Black employees. Similarly, the lack of anecdotal (i.e., nonstatistical evidence on practices) was noted as a limitation of the case. The judge also pointed to the OFCCP's disregard for how Oracle decided to pay different employees differently (e.g., by using market survey data, using a merit increase grid) and to the OFCCP's aggregation of dissimilar groups of employees (in terms of work content) in its comparisons. Although with the new Biden Administration coming in, some shift back toward the more aggressive enforcement of the Obama Administration is possible, these recent court decisions may temper that to a degree.[82]

In any case, the National Law Review advises employers that pay equity enforcement in the Biden administration will increase. To prepare, it advises: (a) "retaining legal counsel to conduct a privileged pay equity audit that will be protected from disclosure in the event of an OFCCP audit or employee lawsuit, (b) bolstering written compensation policies to identify all relevant factors the contractor may seek to rely upon in the event of an audit, and (c) reviewing the use of market compensation studies to ensure they are appropriately conducted and used in a way that does not perpetuate gender-based pay gaps."[83]

Although some forms of pay discrimination "can be easy to spot," such as paying men and women in the same job and with the same performance differently, as **Exhibit 17.9** shows, other forms may be more "complex." An example from **Exhibit 17.9** would be that "African-American sales workers are disproportionately assigned to territories with less potential," meaning "that no matter how well they perform, they can never have the same earnings opportunities as their white counterparts." The OFCCP goes on to state that "Title VII addresses all forms of compensation differences, including those that come from channeling a favored group into the better paying entry level jobs with better long-term opportunities, or where glass ceilings or other unfair promotion practices wrongly block advancement of talented workers on the basis of illegal criteria like race or gender. And even where base wages or salaries are fair, discrimination in access to overtime, or higher paying shifts, or bonuses, can add up to unequal take home pay in violation of federal civil rights law."

Most companies already have their hands full managing relationships with customers, investors, and suppliers. An onsite visit by an OFCCP compliance investigator can mean that at least some HR employees will be forced to put their work in managing employee relationships on hold and instead deal with the compliance review. Outside legal counsel may be necessary, which can be costly. If a NOV is issued, the company will face further challenges. So, what can a company do to avoid running afoul of E.O. 11246 and the OFCCP?

The simple answer is: Don't discriminate. The somewhat more complex answer is don't discriminate *and* collect and analyze data to document that you are not. In fact, regular self-audits by employers are actually required.[84]As with any analysis that can be seen as relevant to deciding whether an employer has engaged in or is engaging in discrimination, care must be taken to minimize legal risks. Obviously, as noted, obtaining prompt legal counsel is necessary. For the analyses to be privileged (and not open to discovery, for example, by a plaintiff's attorney in possible future litigation), they should be done under the direction of an attorney and strict communication protocols must be followed.[85]

PAY DISCRIMINATION AND DISSIMILAR JOBS

In 1981, the Supreme Court, in *Gunther v. County of Washington,* determined that pay differences for dissimilar jobs may reflect discrimination. In this case, four jail matrons in Washington County, Oregon, claimed that their work was comparable to that performed by male guards. The matrons also were assigned clerical duties, because guarding the smaller number of female prisoners did not occupy all of the work time.

Lower courts said the matrons had no grounds because the jobs did not meet the equal work requirement of the Equal Pay Act. But the Supreme Court stated that a Title VII pay case was not bound by the definitions in the Equal Pay Act. While the Supreme Court did not say that Washington County had discriminated, it did say that a claim of wage discrimination could also be brought under Title VII for situations where the jobs were not the same. Unfortunately, the Court did not say what might constitute evidence of pay discrimination in dissimilar jobs. The case was returned to a lower court for additional evidence of discrimination and was eventually settled out of court.

EXHIBIT 17.9 Examples of Employment Discrimination to Avoid, OFCCP

Type of Difference	Basis for Comparison of Employees	Examples of Differences
Differences in Salary or Hourly Rate	Similar job, different pay	Hispanic customer service agents are paid less than white employees in the same or similar positions due to highly subjective salary system.
Differences in Job Assignment or Placement	Similar qualifications, different job	Women hired into entry-level grocery store positions are disproportionately assigned to the bakery department. Men are assigned to the meat department where pay and promotion opportunities are better.
Differences in Training or Advancement Opportunities	Similar job, different opportunities to increase skills	Employees may participate in a management training program on a recommendation by a manager. Certain managers are referring only white males resulting in disproportionate participation. Resulting promotions to management positions are disproportionately awarded to white males.
Differences in Earnings Opportunities	Similar job, different earnings	African-American sales workers are disproportionately assigned to territories with less potential.
Differences in Access to Increases and Add-Ons	Similar job, different opportunities to increase pay	Female lawyers who get exactly the same base pay as male counterparts earn less on annual bonuses.

So if jobs are dissimilar and if no pattern of discrimination in hiring, promotion, or other personnel decisions exists, then what constitutes pay discrimination? Courts have ruled on the use of market data as well as the use of job evaluation. We will look at both of these possible standards in turn.

Evidence of Discrimination: Use of Market Data

In a landmark case regarding the use of market data, Denver nurse Mary Lemons claimed that her job, held predominantly by women, was illegally paid less than the city and county of Denver paid jobs held predominantly by men (tree trimmers, sign painters, tire servicemen, etc.). Lemons claimed that the nursing job required more education and skill. Therefore, to pay the male jobs more than the nurses' jobs simply because the male jobs commanded higher rates in the local labor market was discriminatory. She argued that the market reflected historical underpayment of "women's work." The court disagreed. The situation identified by *Lemons*–pay differences in dissimilar jobs–did not by itself constitute proof of intent to discriminate.

The courts continue to uphold use of market data to justify pay differences for different jobs. *Spaulding v. University of Washington* developed the argument in greatest detail. In this case, the predominantly female faculty members of the Department of Nursing claimed that they were illegally paid less than faculty in other departments. They presented a model of faculty pay comparisons in "comparable" departments that controlled for the effects of level of education, job tenure, and other factors. They asserted that any pay difference not accounted for in their model was discrimination.

But the courts have been dubious of this statistical approach. As the late Carl Sagan used to say, "Just because it's a light doesn't make it a spaceship." Far better to define discrimination directly, rather than concluding that it is "whatever is left." The judge in the *Spaulding* case criticized the statistical model presented, saying it "unrealistically assumed the equality of all master's degrees, ignored job experience prior to university employment, and ignored detailed analysis of day-to-day responsibilities." Without such data, "we have no meaningful way of determining just how much of the proposed wage differential was due to sex and how much was due to academic discipline." "Market prices," according to the judge, "are inherently job-related."

It is interesting to ask whether this judge's level of confidence in the objectivity of "the market" is justified. As you recall from **Chapter 8**, a lot of judgment goes into the wage survey process.[86] Which employers constitute the "relevant market"? Does the relevant market vary by occupation? Do different market definitions yield different wage patterns? Clearly, judgment is involved in answering these questions. Yet the courts have thus far largely neglected to examine those judgments for possible bias.

Evidence of Discrimination: Jobs of Comparable Worth

Comparable Worth: Overview

A second approach to determining pay discrimination on jobs of dissimilar content hinges on finding a standard by which to compare the value of jobs. The standard must do two things. First, it must permit jobs with dissimilar content to be declared equal or "in some sense comparable."[87] Second, it must permit pay differences for dissimilar jobs that are not comparable. Job evaluation has become that standard.[88] If an employer's own job evaluation study shows that jobs of dissimilar content are of equal value to the employer (equal total job evaluation points), then isn't failure to pay them equally proof of intent to discriminate? That was the issue considered in *AFSCME v. State of Washington,* where the state commissioned a study of the concept of comparable worth (discussed later in this chapter) and its projected effect on the state's pay system. The study concluded that by basing wages on the external market, the state was paying women approximately 20 percent less than it was paying men in jobs deemed of comparable value to the state. The state took no action on this finding, alleging it could not afford to adjust wages, so the American Federation of State, County, and Municipal Employees (AFSCME) sued the state. The union alleged that because the state was aware of the adverse effect of its present policy, failure to change the policy constituted discrimination.

But an appeals court ruled that the state was not obligated to correct the disparity. Even though the state had commissioned the study, it had not agreed to implement the study's results. Therefore, the employer had not, in the court's view, admitted that the jobs were equal or established a pay system that purported to pay on the basis of comparable worth rather than markets. Rather than appeal, the parties settled out of court. The state revamped its pay system and agreed to make more than $100 million in "pay equity" adjustments.

Since this case, many public employers have undertaken "pay equity studies" to assess the "gender neutrality" of pay systems. In states and cities which enacted comparable-worth legislation for public employees, the results of these studies are used to adjust pay for jobs held predominantly by women. In other places the results become part of the give and take of collective bargaining. We return to issues of pay equity and comparable worth later in this chapter where we discuss the mechanics of implementing these policies.

The state of Washington conducted a study that concluded that the job of a licensed practical nurse required skill, effort, and responsibility equal to that of a campus police officer. The campus police officer was paid, on average, one-and-a-half times what the state paid the licensed practical nurse.[89]

In Ontario, Canada, jobs that were deemed comparable based on numerical scores displayed a similar disparity in pay. A chief librarian made $35,050, while a dairy herd improvement manager made $38,766. A computer operations supervisor made $20,193, while a forestry project supervisor made $26,947. A typist made $10,531, while a sailor made $14,097. It is this type of wage difference between jobs judged in some sense to be comparable that is controversial. The notion of comparable worth says that if jobs require comparable skill, effort, and responsibility, the pay must be comparable, no matter how dissimilar the job content may be. (In Canada and the European Union, comparable worth is called *gender equity*.) Consider the experience of Bell Canada and its unions. After lawyers spent over a decade disputing the quality and results of a pay equity study, Bell Canada agreed to a $104 million ($91.5 million American) settlement. The point job evaluation plan used in the study to determine pay equity was then used in the contemporary workplace in Bell's operations.[90]

The Mechanics

Establishing a comparable-worth plan typically involves the following four basic steps:

1. *Adopt a single "gender neutral" point job evaluation plan for all jobs within a unit.* If employees are unionized, separate plans have been prepared for each bargaining unit and take precedence over previous agreements. The key to a comparable-worth system is a single job evaluation plan for jobs with dissimilar content. What a "gender neutral" point job evaluation plan is remains open to debate. Advocates of all persuasions offer often conflicting advice, and there is little research to provide guidance. Some advocates try to distinguish between "gender neutral" and "traditional" point job evaluation.[91] Close reading reveals that "traditional" refers to practices dating back 50 years that do not reflect contemporary point plan practices.
2. *All jobs with equal job evaluation results should be paid the same.* Although each factor in the job evaluation may not be equal, if the total points are equal, the wage rates must also be equal.
3. *Identify the percentages of male and female employees in each job group.* A job group is defined as a group of positions with similar duties and responsibilities that require similar qualifications, are filled by similar recruiting procedures, and are paid under the same pay schedule. Typically, a female-dominated job group is defined as having 60 percent or more female incumbents; a male-dominated job group has 70 percent or more male incumbents.

4. *The wage-to-job evaluation point ratio should be based on the wages paid for male-dominated jobs* since they are presumed to be the best estimate of nondiscriminatory wages.

These steps are based on the state of Minnesota's law that mandates comparable worth for all public-sector employees (e.g., the state, cities, school districts, libraries). Canadian federal and provincial labor departments have also published detailed guidance on procedures.[92]

To understand the mechanics more clearly, consider **Exhibit 17.10**. The solid dots represent jobs held predominantly by women (i.e., 60% or more employees are female). The circles represent jobs held predominantly by men (i.e., 70% or more employees are men). The policy line (solid) for the women's jobs is below the policy line (dotted) for men's jobs. A comparable-worth policy uses the results of the single job evaluation plan and prices all jobs as if they were male-dominated jobs (dotted line). Thus, all jobs with 100 job points receive $600; all those with 200 points receive $800, and so on.

Market rates for male-dominated jobs are used to convert the job evaluation points to salaries. The point-to-salaries ratio of male-dominated jobs is then applied to female-dominated jobs.

However, a mandated job evaluation, especially a single point plan that specifies a hierarchy of all jobs, seems counter to the direction in which most organizations are moving today. A partner of Hay Associates observed:

> We, ourselves, do not know of a single case where a large and diverse organization in the private sector concluded that a single job evaluation method, with the same compensable factors and weightings, was appropriate for its factory, office, professional, management, technical, and executive personnel in all profit center divisions and all staff departments.[93]

This point, plus the fact that job evaluation is typically used to capture and extend market rates, not replace them, raises serious limitations with the use of job evaluation for this purpose.

EXHIBIT 17.10 Job Evaluation Points and Salary

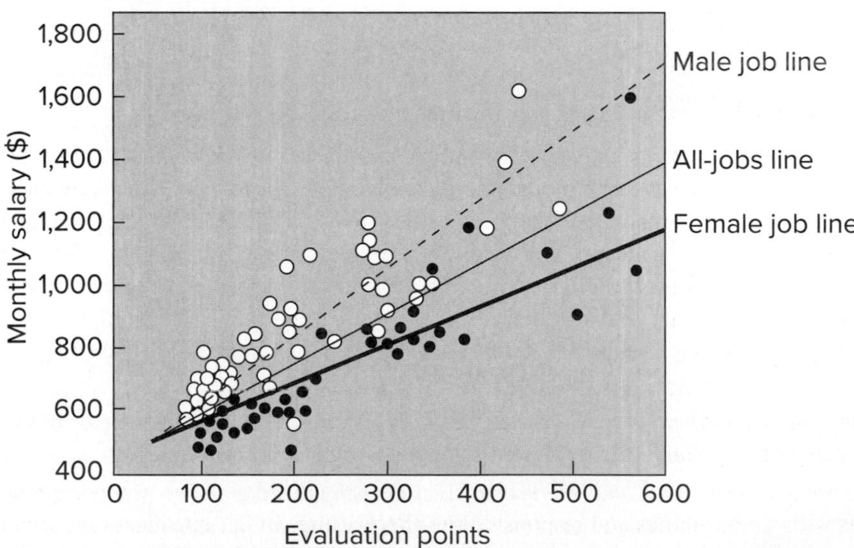

More Recent Developments

State Laws

As noted earlier, a number of states have laws that go beyond equal pay for equal work to instead require equal pay for employees performing "substantially similar work," including California, Illinois, and New Jersey. Other states require equal pay for employees performing "comparable work" (Massachusetts), "work of a comparable character" (Oregon and Maryland), or for those "similarly employed" (Washington).[94] The California statute, the California Fair Pay Act, which took effect in 2016, allows employees working at different establishments to be compared. It defines "substantially similar work" in terms of "when viewed as a composite of skill, effort, and responsibility, and performed under similar working conditions." The Act also bars employers from prohibiting employees from disclosing or discussing their own or others' wages.[95]

Canada

In 1988 the Canadian province of Ontario mandated comparable worth in both the private and public sectors. (See above discussion.) More recently, Canada passed the national Pay Equity Act, which is expected to come into force 2021. Employers will have three years to achieve pay equity. The Act defines pay equity the same as comparable worth. Specifically, the Canadian Human Rights Commission, which has enforcement responsibility for the Act states that "Pay equity is about equal pay for work of equal value" and that "Pay equity is not about equal pay for equal work." (Previous laws cover the latter.)

The United States (?)

As noted, the nature of federal pay equity efforts is likely to increase in the Biden administration. Of particular interest is the previously expressed view of the incoming OFCCP Director, Jenny Yang, that market compensation rates are not an appropriate justification for salary differentials.[96] This takes us back to the essential argument of comparable worth.

EARNINGS GAPS

Exhibit 17.11 shows that, across all races combined and limiting the analysis to full-time, year-round workers, women's median annual earnings compared to men's has changed from 60 percent to 82 percent from 1980 to 2019. The wage gap between men and women varies according to wage level, being relatively large at very high wages and even larger at very low wage levels. Since the 1990s, the gap at the top narrowed slightly, due mostly to education gains by women. The gap at the bottom narrowed more, mostly due to increases in overall years worked and years worked with current employer by women.[97]

Exhibit 17.12 shows that Asian men's earnings have risen over time to now be higher (by 25%) than those of white men. Black to white men's earning ratios have varied between about 68 to 79 percent, and the ratio of Hispanic to white men's earnings varied from about 55 to 72 percent. **Exhibit 17.13** compares earnings of Asian, Black, and Hispanic women to white women. We see a pattern similar to what we saw with men, with Asian women having the highest earnings. Perhaps this is in part because a larger percentage of Asian women have a bachelor's degree. The gap between Black and white women is less than the gap between Black and white men, again perhaps partly because of education differences, as Black women are more likely than Black men to have a college degree.[98]

EXHIBIT 17.11 **Women's Median Earnings as a Percentage of Men's Median Earnings, Full-Time, Year-Round Workers, 1980–2019**

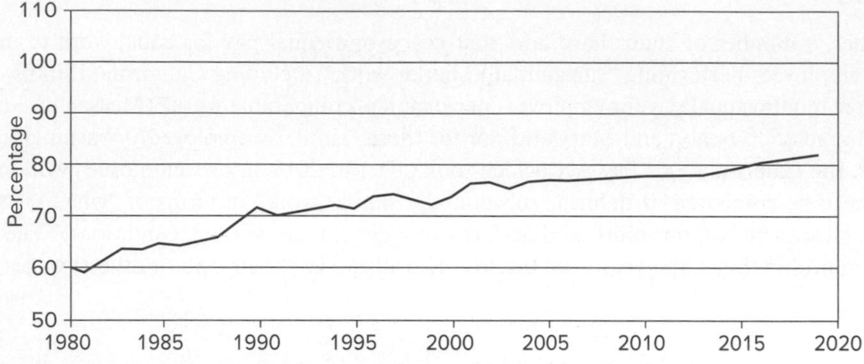

Source: U.S. Bureau of the Census, Historical Income Tables, Table P-40. census.gov.

EXHIBIT 17.12 **Asian, Black, and Hispanic Median Men's Earnings as a Percentage of White, Non-Hispanic Median Men's Earnings, Full-Time, Year-Round Workers, 1980–2019**

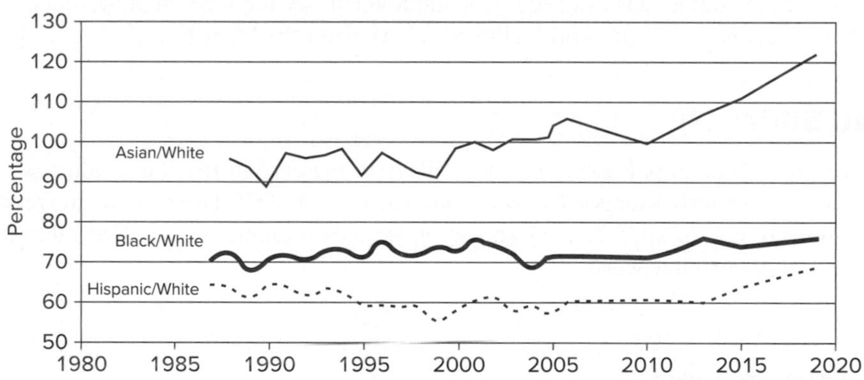

Source: U.S. Bureau of the Census, Historical Income Tables, Table P-38. census.gov.

EXHIBIT 17.13 **Asian, Black, and Hispanic Median Women's Earnings as a Percentage of White, Non-Hispanic Median Women's Earnings, Full-Time, Year-Round Workers, 1980–2019**

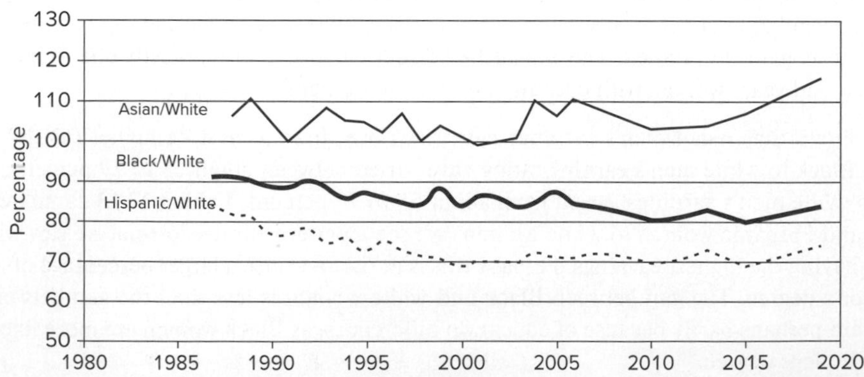

Source: U.S. Bureau of the Census, Historical Income Tables, Table P-38. census.gov.

What do we know about why these gaps exist? Some of the more important sources, shown in **Exhibit 17.14**, include the following:

- Work/occupation differences
- Work-related behavior
- Labor market conditions
- Firm/industry differences
- Union differences
- Discrimination

Let us first examine some data and then some conflicting beliefs.

Sources of the Earnings Gaps

Considerable research has examined the factors shown in **Exhibit 17.14**, which are the central sources of the wage differences between men and women and the racial/ethnic groups. The issue, especially any proposed remedies, continues to generate research and debate. Our reading of the recent research is that the primary sources contributing to the gender gap differ from the primary sources for the race/ethnic gaps. It appears that differences in the work/occupation (e.g., technician vs. clerical) and differences in work-related behaviors (e.g., work-life balance challenges) are central to understanding the remaining gender wage gaps.[99] In contrast, differences in qualifications, especially educational levels and work-related experience as well as differences in occupations, are important sources of the gaps for both Blacks and Hispanics compared to white men.[100]

EXHIBIT 17.14 Sources of Earnings Gaps

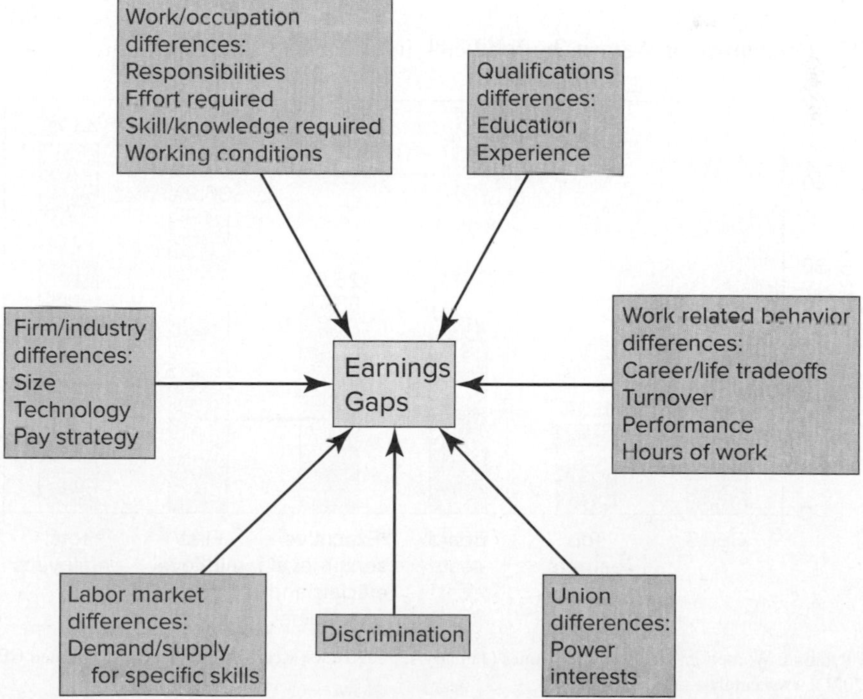

Differences in Occupations and Qualifications

There is evidence that women of all ethnic groups are more likely than men to seek part-time and flexible work arrangements and that they are more likely than men to interrupt their careers due to family responsibilities.[101] There is also evidence that gender differences in occupational choices and preferences continue to exist.[102] According to the Center for Education Statistics, for every 100 women who earn bachelor's degrees today, 74 men do.[103] However, men are much more likely to enroll, graduate, and continue working in engineering, computer science, and certain scientific specialties. Women's enrollment and graduation rates do exceed men's in the biological sciences. Women may be somewhat less likely to negotiate for higher pay than men (and/or receive less payoff when they do).[104] However, that difference seems to have diminished over time.[105] It may also vary by country (and perhaps national culture).[106] In addition, negotiation can take very different forms or strategies (asking, bending, and shaping is an example of one classification), which can go beyond salary issues, may involve multiple parties, and may vary to some extent between men and women.[107]

In the early 1970s, 53 percent of women workers were in administrative support (including clerical) and service occupations, compared to only 15 percent of men. At that time, less than one in five managers were women; professional women were frequently employed in traditionally female professions, such as nurse, teacher, dietitian, or librarian. Women were also underrepresented in blue-collar jobs, including higher-paying precision production and craft occupations. In 1960, almost half of the women who graduated from college became teachers, while today less than 10 percent do so. Today, the number of women in managerial jobs (economy-wide) is at parity with men. Despite progress, one notable concern (in addition to overall unexplained pay gaps) remains: lack of representation of women in executive and director level positions in organizations, sometimes referred to as the "Glass Ceiling" effect. **Exhibit 17.15** shows how the representation of women declines at higher levels of organizations (in this case the largest 500 U.S. companies). Note that some countries (not the United States) mandate a minimum number of women directors (on boards). For example, Norway and France both require 40 percent and the European Union may consider similar mandates.[108]

EXHIBIT 17.15 Percentage of Women, by Job Level, in S&P 500 Companies

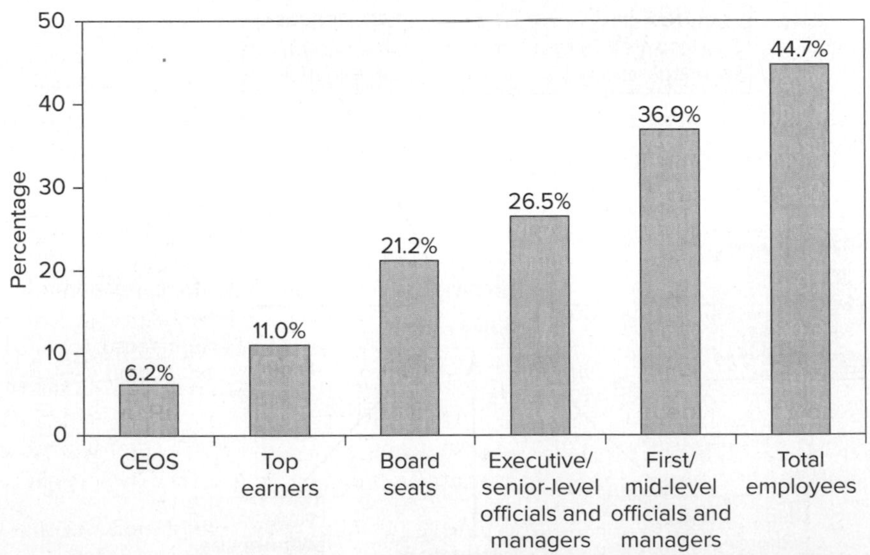

Source: Catalyst, Pyramid: Women in S&P 500 Companies (January 15, 2020). www.catalyst.org; Catalyst, Women CEOs of the S&P 500 (March 15, 2021). www.catalyst.org.

Evidence of increased levels of occupational attainment does not automatically mean that the wage gap will close. A study of women in science and engineering finds that even though they have already cleared the hurdles of the occasional misguided high school guidance counselor and/or lack of peer support or role models, women scientists and engineers are almost twice as likely to leave these occupations as are males.[109]

For a variety of reasons, a relatively small wage gap among younger cohorts (i.e., recent college graduates) tends to increase as the cohort ages. A key factor is that women continue to have more career interruptions/time out of the labor force than men, as noted above, which translates into lower work experience over time, an indicator of human capital. Interruptions also may result in depreciation in the value of human capital already obtained. Fran Blau and Lawrence Kahn estimate that gender differences in work experience explained 24 percent of the gender wage gap in 1980 and 16 percent using more recent data. They further estimate that about 18 to 31 percent of the narrowing of the gender wage gap over the past few decades is explained by the narrowing gap in work experience between women and men.[110]

One reason for career interruptions is family responsibility. Paid leave and other work-life balance programs are intended to make this less likely. Another potential reason women may be more likely to withdraw from the labor force is if they perceive opportunities declining at higher levels in the **job hierarchy,** referred to as the "Glass Ceiling." See **Exhibit 17.15**.

Wage differences among occupations were determined decades ago. While a variety of reasons account for these original wage differences, an important one is the belief about gender roles and "women's work" that prevailed at the time and the resulting segregation (and crowding) of women into a limited number of occupations, depressing their wages relative to men. There is also such segregation by industry (and firms, see below for more on both). Even though such segregation has been reduced somewhat over time, it remains substantial and Blau and Kahn estimate that occupation and industry together account for 50 percent of the gender wage gap.

Level of schooling and work-related experience appear to be primary (legitimate) sources of the pay gaps among both Black and Hispanic men and women. Almost half of Hispanic men have not completed high school and only 9 percent are college graduates.[111] This may be due to the considerable differences in continuing immigration among Hispanics. Generally, the longer Hispanic immigrants stay in the United States, the better they do educationally and financially. However, the continuing inflow of poorly educated new immigrants holds down the average wage for the whole category. Black men's high school dropout rates match those of Hispanic men. In contrast, more than half of Asian men are college graduates or hold higher degrees. All this research and discussion about sources of the earnings gaps does not mean there are not any discriminatory pay practices; it does mean that important sources of the pay gaps reside in other productivity-related factors such as level and quality of education, work-life/career tradeoffs, and occupational choices.

Differences in Industries and Firms

Other factors that affect earnings differences among men and women and among race/ethnic groups are the industries and the firms in which they are employed. A study of middle-aged lawyers revealed large differences between men and women lawyers in the types of firms that employed them. Men were much more likely than women to be in private practice and to be at large firms (over 50 lawyers). They were much *less* likely than women to be in the lower-paying nonprofit sector. Clearly, these differences are related to pay: the most highly paid legal positions are in private-practice law firms; the larger the law firm, the greater the average rate of pay.[112] There also may be different promotion opportunities among firms within the same industry.[113]

Some work has focused on pinpointing where women's pay falls behind that of men. One finding is that the pay gap is wider where bonus and incentive payments (not just base salary) are examined, especially to the degree subjective judgment is important. Other evidence indicates that women lose ground at the time they are hired and, in some cases, actually do better once they are employed for some time.[114] One interpretation is that when actual job performance (rather than the limited general qualification information available on applicants) is used in decisions (e.g., promotion), women may be less likely to encounter unequal treatment. If so, more attention needs to be devoted to ensuring fair treatment of applicants and new employees.[115] Also, two studies (one using multiple samples) report that women designated as high-potential earn more than men, regardless of whether they are designated as high potential. The authors suggest that high-potential women are especially valuable for helping organizations achieve performance and diversity goals.[116] Another study, in this case of university presidents, finds that the gender gap is smaller and then disappears as the focus becomes more limited to higher status universities.[117] Ultimately, what happens within firms is likely to differ by firm, as indicated, for example, by the fact that different studies find different results regarding gender-based differences in promotions and resulting pay increases.[118]

Differences in the firm's compensation policies within a specific industry is another factor that accounts for some of the earnings gap.[119] As noted in **Chapters 7** and **8**, some firms within an industry adopt pay strategies that place them among the leaders in their industry; other firms adopt policies that may offer more work-life balance benefits compared to cash compensation. The unknown here is whether *within an industry* some firms are more likely to attract women or minorities than other firms because of these pay-mix differences and whether this has any effect on earnings gaps.

Within a firm, differences in policies for different jobs may even exist. For example, many firms tie pay for secretaries to the pay for the manager to whom the secretary is assigned. The rationale is that the secretary and the manager function as a team. When the manager gets promoted, the secretary also takes on additional responsibilities and therefore also gets a raise. However, this traditional approach breaks down when layers of management are cut. When IBM went through a major restructuring a few years back, it cut pay by up to 36 percent for secretaries who had been assigned to managerial levels that no longer existed. IBM justified the cuts by saying the rates were way above the market.

We also know that the size of a firm is systematically related to differences in wages. Female employment is more heavily concentrated in small firms. Wages of men in large firms are 54 percent higher than wages of men in small firms. The gap was 37 percent for women in small versus large firms. Hispanic men are concentrated in construction and service firms. Other studies report that employees in some jobs can get a pay increase of about 20 percent simply by switching industries in the same geographic area while performing basically similar jobs.[120] Nevertheless, a recent study concludes that this pay premium associated with changing jobs is enjoyed primarily by white males. Women and minorities who were MBA graduates from five universities did not obtain the same (dollar) pay increases as their white male classmates when they switched jobs.[121]

However, a more recent study of executive moves, while finding that men earned (salary + performance bonus) 8.5 percent more than women before moving, after switching companies, the gap was reduced to 6.1 percent, a decline of 30 percent. Based on the results reported, one can compute that men received an average 10 percent increase, whereas women received an average 25 percent increase from switching companies. (No stock-related compensation was measured.)[122] (Note that the lower pre-switch compensation of women reinforces the relevance of salary history bans to avoid perpetuating (even further) women's lower pay when switching companies.)

To the extent that these differences in job setting are the result of an individual's preference or disposition, they are not evidence of discrimination. To the extent that these differences are the result of industry and firm practices that steer women and minorities into certain occupations and industries or lower-paying parts of a profession, they may reflect discrimination.

Challenges in Estimating Amount of Discrimination

We know that many factors affect pay and that discrimination can be one of them. Disagreement remains over what constitutes evidence of discrimination. Although the earnings gap is the most frequently cited example, closer inspection reveals the weaknesses in this statistic. Unfortunately, many studies of the earnings gap have little relevance to understanding discrimination in pay-setting practices within organizations. Some studies use aggregated data–for instance, treating all bachelor's degrees as the same, or defining an occupation too broadly (e.g., the U.S. Department of Labor categorizes LeBron James as well as the basketball game time-keeper in the same occupation–"sports professional"). Another problem is that mere possession of a qualification or skill does not mean it is work related. Examples of cab drivers, secretaries, and house painters with college degrees are numerous.

A standard statistical approach (and one that suffers from the problems just noted) for determining whether discrimination explains part of the gap is to try to relate pay differences to the factors discussed above (occupation, type of work, experience, education, and the like). The procedure typically regresses some measure of earnings on those factors thought to legitimately influence earnings. If the average wage of men with a given set of values for these factors is significantly different from the average wage of women with equal factors, then the residual portion of the gap is considered discrimination. Using this approach, Blau and Kahn estimate that 62 percent of the female-male wage gap can be explained, primarily, consistent with our discussion above, on the basis of differences between women and men in work experience, occupation, and industry.[123]

e-Compensation

You can track legal issues and read transcripts of Supreme Court decisions at ***www.law.cornell.edu***. Many states have their own web pages that include their compensation legislation. What information is available from your state? Compare the pay discrimination legislation in your state with another state's. What might explain these differences? Are there any unique characteristics of your state (e.g., unique industries, extent of unionization, etc.)?

Even if legitimate factors did fully explain gender, ethnic, and racial group pay differences (which they do not), discrimination still could have occurred because the factors shown in **Exhibit 17.14** themselves may be tainted by discrimination. For example, if women were historically discouraged from studying in certain fields/entering certain occupations or industries, then it is incomplete to simply say that occupation, and industry "explain" much of gender pay gap.

One challenge is that any worker who has a history of low wages/salaries will often find it is difficult to break out of that pattern because employers regularly ask applicants what they earned in current/previous jobs (their "salary history"). So, low earnings (including unjustifiably low earnings) tend to be perpetuated. Consequently, some jurisdictions (e.g., New York City, Delaware, Oregon, Massachusetts) have prohibited organizations from asking applicants to share their salary history, at least until after the applicant has been hired and/or been already offered a specific salary.[124]

Gaps Are Global

The gender wage gap is fairly universal. However, in a number of countries, the size of the gap is smaller than in the United States.[125] One analysis concludes that the difference can be found in narrower pay structures in European countries. In many countries, as the global guide in **Chapter 16** suggests, rates negotiated by federations of employers, unions, and government agencies rather than individual companies and employees mean a narrower range of pay rates for each job, as well as smaller differences between jobs.[126]

Earlier chapters have emphasized the wide range of pay rates in the U.S. market for any job. More centralized wage decision making permits a pay gap to be closed by political/institutional fiat. Multinational companies operating in different nations face wide differences in how wages are influenced by varying social policies and regulations.

COMPLIANCE: A PROACTIVE APPROACH

Compliance with laws and regulations can be a constraint and/or an opportunity for a compensation manager. The regulatory environment certainly constrains the decisions that can be made. Once laws are passed and regulations published, employers must comply. But a proactive compensation manager can influence the nature of regulations and their interpretation. Astute professionals must be aware of legislative and judicial currents to protect both employers' and employees' interests and to ensure that compensation practices conform to judicial interpretation.

How can a compensation manager best undertake these efforts? First, join professional associations to stay informed on emerging issues and to act in concert to inform and influence public and legislative opinion. Second, constantly review compensation practices and their results. Be sure to consult with legal counsel in doing so, as attorney-client privilege and protection of work product are important issues to understand prior to conducting analyses on an organization's compliance. The fair treatment of all employees is the goal of a good pay system, and that is the same goal of legislation. When interpretations of what is fair treatment differ, informed public discussion is required. Such discussion cannot occur without the input of informed managers.

Your Turn — From Barista to Manager

You work at an upscale coffee shop that is part of a nationwide chain of 200 such stores. You started as a barista, but then you moved up. Your title is now store manager. You are expected to work 55 hours per week. Your boss says you need to be in the store to get to know the customers and because, well, you are the manager. It is up to you to make sure everything runs smoothly and that there is a great customer experience, which translates into growth in store sales volume and store profit. By the way, however many hours you work, you get paid for 40 hours only (and no overtime pay) because . . . that's right, you are the manager.

However, as you think about how you spend your time at the store, you can't help but feel that a lot of your time seems to be spent on things that don't seem much like "management" to you—making coffee drinks, checking supplies, and sometimes cleaning bathrooms. So, this is the life of a manager. It seems a lot like being a barista, except that you work a lot more hours, have more responsibility, and you don't get paid all that much more. You do spend some time on training other employees and you interview job applicants. But, the district manager is around a lot and she seems to have her own ideas on who to hire most of the time and how to run the store. Plus, there are pretty clear corporate guidelines to be followed on how to run many aspects of the store.

The more you think about it, the more you think that it sure would be nice to get paid for working 55 hours. In fact, you have friends who work in other businesses and when they work over 40 hours in a week, they get time and a half for the hours beyond 40. That sounds awfully good. If you are going to spend all of your time at work, it would be nice to at least get paid what you deserve for it.

Now, "switch hats" and look at it from the company point of view. Is this company running afoul of the Fair Labor Standards Act (FLSA)? Refer back to our discussion earlier in this chapter. Would this company be able to document that the store managers are exempt from the FLSA (not to mention similar state laws)? Also, what would it cost to re-classify your store managers as nonexempt? If managers feel overworked and underpaid, what do you project that they will do when the economy picks back up? Is that a concern for the company? Is the company in compliance with the FLSA? What would it cost to have a lawsuit filed against the company? Have other companies in your industry (e.g., Starbucks, Caribou, Peet's, etc.) had any FLSA issues? If so, what can you learn from their experiences? Would you advise meeting with corporate counsel? What facts and observations would you recommend be presented at such a meeting?

Still Your Turn

The Case of Lady Gaga's (Former) Personal Assistant

According to the *New York Post,* pop superstar (and actor) Lady Gaga, whose real name is Stefani Germanotta, employed Jennifer O'Neill as a personal assistant for 13 months. Ms. O'Neill sued Gaga's touring company, Mermaid Touring, in the U.S. District Court for the Southern District of New York, alleging violations of the federal Fair Labor Standards Act (FLSA) and New York State Labor. [127]

Ms. O'Neill, 41, who was paid $75,000 ($90,000 in today's dollars) per year, reported that she had to cater to the 25-year-old Gaga's every whim, whether it was related to schedule, finances, or food, at any hour of the day or night. Ms. O'Neill worked for Gaga both in New York City (at her Upper West Side duplex) and also on the Monster Ball world tour, where she assisted Gaga in a variety of settings, including "stadiums, private jets, fine hotel suites, yachts, ferries, trains and tour buses."

According to Court papers, Ms. O'Neill alleged that there were no breaks for meals "or, at times, even sleep," and that she was required to be on hand for anything the Grammy Award-winning singer needed, at her "earliest waking hour" or for "spontaneous, random matters in the middle of the night." One of Ms. O'Neill's tasks was "ensuring the availability of chosen outfits," a task of presumably considerable magnitude, given Gaga's unique approach to style (e.g., wearing a meat dress to the MTV Video Music Awards).

Ms. O'Neill alleged that she worked 6,656 hours of unpaid overtime over a period of 56 weeks. She is asking to be paid $359,956.48 for unpaid overtime. Along with this request for back pay, Ms. O'Neill, a graduate of American University, also sought unspecified damages.

A spokeswoman for Gaga branded the lawsuit "completely without merit."

A judge declined to dismiss the lawsuit, ruling that it would go to a jury trial. However, the lawsuit was settled out of court prior to going to trial. The terms of the lawsuit were not disclosed.

QUESTIONS:

1. Is Ms. O'Neill exempt or nonexempt under the FLSA? Which exemption would be most relevant in this case?
2. Can you find any other examples in the news of similar lawsuits? If so, please again form an opinion on whether the plaintiff is exempt or not and which exemption is most relevant.

3. Does a settlement mean that Lady Gaga violated the FLSA or another wage and hour (e.g., state or local) law?
4. How common are settlements in lieu of going to trial?
5. Why would parties choose to settle instead of going to trial?

Summary

Governments around the world play varying roles in the workplace. Legislation in any society reflects people's expectations about the role of government. Beyond direct regulation, government affects compensation through policies and purchases that affect labor supply and demand.

In the United States, legislation reflects the changing nature of work and the workforce. In the 1930s, legislation was concerned with correcting the harsh conditions and arbitrary treatment facing employees, including children. In the 1960s, legislation turned to the issue of equal opportunity. Such legislation has had a profound impact on all of U.S. society. Nevertheless, more progress to eliminate discrimination in the workplace, including pay discrimination, is required. Contemporary issues include treatment of the recent waves of immigrants. Recent attention has shifted to increasing the transparency of compensation for executives and accounting for stock options.

Pay discrimination laws require special attention for several reasons. First, these laws regulate the design and administration of pay systems. Second, the definition of pay discrimination and thus the approaches used to defend pay practices are in a state of flux, especially as employers increase their international operations. Many of the provisions of these laws simply require sound pay practices that should have been employed in the first place. Sound practices are those with three basic features:

1. They are work related.
2. They are related to the mission of the enterprise.
3. They include an appeals process for employees who disagree with the results.

Achieving compliance with these laws rests in large measure on the shoulders of managers of compensation. It is their responsibility to ensure that the pay system is properly designed and managed.

The earnings gaps among various ethnic and racial groups for both women and men are attributable to many factors. The sources of the gender gap appear to center on differences in work/occupational attainment and work-life challenges. The sources for Blacks and Hispanics center on differences in educational levels, work-related experience, occupational attainment, and qualifications. Discrimination, whether access or valuation, is another factor. Others include market forces, industry and employer differences, and union bargaining priorities. Compensation managers need to constantly monitor pay practices to be sure that they are complying with regulations and are not discriminatory.

Is all this detail on interpretation of pay discrimination really necessary? Yes. Without understanding the interpretation of pay discrimination legislation, compensation managers risk violating the law, exposing their employers to considerable liability and expense, and losing the confidence and respect of all employees when a few are forced to turn to the courts to gain nondiscriminatory treatment.

Review Questions

1. What is the nature of government's role in compensation?
2. Explain why changes in minimum wage can affect higher-paid employees as well.

3. What is the difference between access discrimination and valuation discrimination?
4. Consider contemporary practices such as skill-competency-based plans, broad banding, market pricing, and pay-for-performance plans. Discuss how they may affect the pay discrimination debate.
5. What factors help account for the pay gap?
6. What kinds of proactive activities can an employer undertake to enhance the regulatory environment?

Endnotes

1. The job evaluation manual was introduced as evidence in *Electrical Workers (IUE) v. Westinghouse Electric Corp.,* 632 F.2d 1094, 23 FEP Cases 588 (3rd Cir. 1980), *cert. denied,* 452 U.S. 967, 25 FEP Cases 1835 (1981).
2. Philip M. Berkowitz, Anders Etgen Reitz, Thomas Müller-Bonanni, eds., *International Labor and Employment Law,* 2nd ed. (Chicago, IL: American Bar Association, 2008); Organisation for Economic Co-operation and Development, "The Price of Prejudice: Labour Market Discrimination on the Grounds of Gender and Ethnicity," *OECD Employment Outlook 2008* (Paris, France: OECD, 2008), includes a survey of equal employment opportunity regulation across OECD countries; Richard A. Posthuma, Mark V. Roehling, and Michael A. Campion, "Applying U.S. Employment Discrimination Laws to International Employers: Advice for Scientists and Practitioners," *Personnel Psychology* 59, no. 3 (2006), pp. 705–739; The U.S. Equal Employment Opportunity Commission, "The Equal Employment Opportunity Responsibilities of Multinational Employers," www.eeoc.gov/facts/multiemployers.html; The U.S. Equal Employment Opportunity Commission. Employee Rights When Working for Multinational Employers, www.eeoc.gov/facts/multiemployees.html.
3. Bruce Kaufman, ed., *Government Regulation of the Employment Relationship* (Ithaca, NY: Cornell University Press, 1998); Arthur Gutman, *EEO Law and Personnel Practices,* 2nd ed. (Thousand Oaks, CA: Sage, 2000).
4. Francine D. Blau and Lawrence M. Kahn, *At Home and Abroad: U.S. Labor Market Performance in International Perspective* (Thousand Oaks, CA: Sage, 2001).
5. C. E. Lindblom, *Politics and Markets: The World's Political Economic Systems* (New York: Basic Books, 1977), pp. 161–169; P. A. Hall and D. Soskice (eds.), *Varieties of Capitalism: The Institutional Foundations of Comparative Advantage* (Oxford: Oxford University Press, 2001).
6. U.S. Bureau of Labor Statistics, "The Employment Situation–February 2021." USDL-21-0365. Table B-1. Seasonally adjusted employment numbers. www.bls.gov.
7. Morris Kleiner, *Licensing Requirements: Ensuring Quality or Restricting Competition?* (Kalamazoo, MI: Upjohn, 2006).
8. OECD, "Migration Policy Debates. Is Migration Good for the Economy?" May 2014, www.oecd.org/migration.
9. http://www.hightechemployeelawsuit.com/ and http://www.animationlawsuit.com/.
10. Bureau of Labor Statistics, U.S. Department of Labor, "Characteristics of Minimum Wage Workers, 2016," April 2017; "Characteristics of Minimum Wage Workers, 2011," March 2, 2012; "The Employment Situation," May 2018.
11. Economic Policy Institute, "Issue Guide on Minimum Wage," www.epi.org.
12. U.S. Department of Labor, Wage and Hour Division (WHD). State Minimum Wage Laws. https://www.dol.gov/agencies/whd/minimum-wage/state, accessed March 26, 2021.
13. UC Berkeley Labor Center, http://laborcenter.berkeley.edu/minimum-wage-living-wage-resources/inventory-of-us-city-and-county-minimum-wage-ordinances/, accessed March 26, 2021.

14. Fact Sheet: Biden-Harris Administration Issues an Executive Order to Raise the Minimum Wage to $15 for Federal Contractors .https://www.whitehouse.gov/briefing-room/statements-releases/2021/04/27/fact-sheet-biden-harris-administration-issues-an-executive-order-to-raise-the-minimum-wage-to-15-for-federal-contractors/.
15. David Neumark and William L. Wascher, *Minimum Wages* (Cambridge, MA: MIT Press, 2008); Economic Policy Institute, "Issue Guide on Minimum Wage," 2008, www.epi.org; David Card and Alan Krueger, "Minimum Wages and Employment: A Case Study of the Fast-Food Industry in New Jersey and Pennsylvania," *American Economic Review,* September 1994, pp. 772–793; Lawrence F. Katz and Alan B. Krueger, "The Effect of the Minimum Wage on the Fast-Food Industry," *Industrial and Labor Relations Review* 46, no. 1 (October 1992), pp. 6–21; K. I. Simon and R. Kaestner, "Do Minimum Wages Affect Non-Wage Job Attributes? Evidence on Fringe Benefits," *Industrial and Labor Relations Review* 58, no. 1 (October 2004), pp. 52–70; Joseph Sabia, "Identifying Minimum Wage Effects: New Evidence from Monthly CPS Data," *Industrial Relations* 48 (2009), pp. 311–328; Hristos Doucouliagos and T. D. Stanley, "Publication Selection Bias in Minimum-Wage Research? A Meta-Regression Analysis," *British Journal of Industrial Relations* 47 (2009), pp. 406–428; "Hundreds of Economists Say: Raise the Minimum Wage," *Economic Policy Institute,* October 11, 2006.
16. Congressional Budget Office. The Budgetary Effects of the Raise the Wage Act of 2021. February 2021. www.cbo.gov.
17. Economic Policy Institute, Issue Guide on Minimum Wage. *www.epi.org,* 2008; David Neumark and William L. Wascher, *Minimum Wages* (Cambridge, MA: MIT Press, 2008); Richard V. Burkhauser and Joseph J. Sabia, "The Effectiveness of Minimum Wage Increases in Reducing Poverty: Past, Present and Future," *Contemporary Economic Policy* 25, no. 2 (April 2007), pp. 262–281.
18. Annual Workplace Class Action Litigation Report, 2014 edition and 2015 edition. Published by Seyfarth Shaw LLP. Miguel Bustillo, "Wal-Mart to Settle 63 Suits Over Wages," *The Wall Street Journal, December 24*, 2008; Wal-Mart must pay $188 million in workers' class action. Reuters. December 16, 2014. www.reuters.com. Extracted March 29, 2015.
19. Dale A. Hudson, "Plaintiff's Lawyers Bullish on Merrill Lynch: Brokerage Firm Agrees to Pay $37 Million to Settle Overtime Claims by Stockbroker," *Nixon Peabody Employment Law Alert,* August 26, 2005.
20. "Judge OKs $42 Million Settlement," *BNA Bulletin to Management,* October 18, 2011.
21. Ylan Q. Mui, "Walmart to Pay $4.8 million in Back Wages," *The Washington Post,* May 1, 2012.
22. Cindy Krischer Goodman, "Overtime under Fire: Workday Trends Blur Overtime Rules, Clogging Courts with Lawsuits," *Wisconsin State Journal,* August 17, 2008.
23. Ibid.
24. Paul Davidson, "More Americans Sue for Overtime Pay," *USA Today,* April 15, 2012.
25. Ibid.
26. Steven Greenhouse, "Labor Agency Is Failing Workers, Reports Says," *The New York Times,* March 25, 2009.
27. Paul Davidson, "More Americans Sue for Overtime Pay," *USA Today,* April 15, 2012.
28. Ian Rowley and Hiroko Tashiro, "Recession Puts More Pressure on Japan's Workers," *BusinessWeek,* January 5, 2009.
29. Ibid.
30. *IBP, Inc. v. Alvarez,* (03-1238) No. 03–1238, 339 F.3d 894, affirmed; No. 04–66, 360 F.3d 274, affirmed in part, reversed in part, and remanded.
31. Will Parsons, "On-Call Pay Premiums and Expenses," *Culpepper Pay Trends Survey e-Bulletin,* December 2005.

32. Joyce E. Cutler. Apple on Hook for Millions for Off-the-Clock Bag Searches. Daily Labor Report, February 13, 2020.

33. Peter Kuhn and Fernando Lozano, *The Expanding Workweek? Understanding Trends in Long Work Hours among U.S. Men, 1979–2004,* NBER Working Paper No. 11895, July 2006.

34. Kimberley Strassel, "Make My (Mother's) Day . . ." *The Wall Street Journal,* May 13, 2006, p. A11.

35. Douglas L. Kruse and Douglas Mahony, "Illegal Child Labor in the United States: Prevalence and Characteristics," *Industrial and Labor Relations Review* 54, no. 1 (October 2000), pp. 17–40; Faraaz Siddiqi and Harry Anthony Patrinos, "Child Labor: Issues, Causes, and Interventions," Human Capital Development and Operations Policy Working Paper 56, www.worldbank.org/html/extdr/hnp/hddflash/workp/wp_00056.html; Steven Greenhouse and Michael Barbaro, "An Ugly Side of Free Trade: Sweatshops in Jordan," *The New York Times,* May 3, 2006; B. Powell and D. Skarbek, "Sweatshops and Third World Living Standards: Are the Jobs Worth the Sweat?" *Journal of Labor Research* 27, no. 2 (Spring 2006), pp. 263–279.

36. *The End of Child Labour: Within Reach* (Geneva, Switzerland: International Labor Organization, 2006).

37. Jon Gertner, "What Is a Living Wage?" *The New York Times Magazine,* January 15, 2006.

38. Maryland's Living Wage Frequently Asked Questions (FAQs), Living Wage for State Service Contracts, http://www.dllr.state.md.us/labor/prev/livingwagefaqs.shtml#what, accessed June 2, 2018.

39. Unilever. "A Living Wage." https://www.unilever.com/planet-and-society/raise-living-standards/a-living-wage/, accessed March 26, 2021.

40. Living Wages Ordinance (LWO), http://bca.lacity.org/living-wages-ordinance-lwo, accessed March 26, 2021.

41. David Fairris, David Runsten, Carolina Briones, and Jessica Goodheart, *Examining the Evidence: The Impact of the Los Angeles Living Wage Ordinance on Workers and Businesses,* www.losangeleslivingwagestudy.org, accessed June 2, 2005.

42. David Neumark, "Living Wages: Protection for or Protection From Low-Wage Workers?" *Industrial and Labor Relations Review* 58, no. 1 (October 2004), pp. 27–51.

43. Bureau of Labor Statistics, U.S. Department of Labor, "Employer Costs for Employee Compensation–December 2014," March 11, 2015.

44. Steven Greenhouse, "U.S. Cracks Down on 'Contractors' as a Tax Dodge," *The New York Times,* February 18, 2010.

45. *Nationwide Mutual Ins. v. Darden* (90-1802), 503 U.S. 318 (1992).

46. Steven Greenhouse, "U.S. Cracks Down on 'Contractors' as a Tax Dodge," *The New York Times,* February 18, 2010.

47. Dennis D. Grant (2000), "Employee or Independent Contractor? The Implications of Microsoft III," *http://library.findlaw.com/2000/Feb/1/127759.html.*

48. Bill Virgin, "Microsoft Settles 'Permatemp' Suits: Two $97 Million Cases Reshape Employment for Temps Nationwide," *Seattle Post-Intelligencer,* December 13, 2000.

49. Steven Greenhouse, "Suits Point to Increasing Wage Theft by Employers," *Wall Street Journal,* September, 2014, p. A1.

50. Troutman Pepper. Self-Inflicted IC Misclassification Wounds: How Did FedEx Bludgeon Itself Into Pay Nearing $500 Million to Settle Claims That It Could Have Avoided? www.jdsupra.com, October 25, 2016; Troutman Pepper. $240 Million Settlement Closes Chapter on FedEx IC Misclassification Lawsuits. www.jdsupra.com, June 17, 2016.

51. Dave Stafford. Judge approves $227M in FedEx driver suit settlements. theindianalawyer.com, May 3, 2017.

52. L. Weber, "The End of Employees," *Wall Street Journal*, February 3, 2017. S. Salinas, "Microsoft Will Start Requiring Partners and Suppliers to Offer Paid Family Leave, and It Will Help Cover the Costs," www.cnbc.com, August 30, 2018; R. Lerman, "Microsoft Requires Contractors to Offer Paid Parental Leave," *The Seattle Times*, August 31, 2018, www.seattletimes.com.

53. Suhauna Hussain. California Supreme Court throws out challenge to Prop. 22 Los Angeles Times, February 3, 2021; Lauren Feiner and Lora Kolodny. Uber and Lyft eye other states after California ballot victory. CNBC.com, November 5, 2020. https://voterguide.sos.ca.gov/propositions/22/; Adam Clark. Firms Seek Gig-Work Union Pacts. The Wall Street Journal, December 31, 2020; Irina Ivanova. Legal ruling averts Uber and Lyft shutdown in California. Cbsnews.com, August 20, 2020; https://vig.cdn.sos.ca.gov/2020/general/pdf/topl-prop22.pdf.

54. Rebecca Knight, "Politicians Shifting Blame Put Boston's Big Dig Back in News," *Financial Times,* July 16, 2006, p. 4.

55. Aaron Morris, "Prevailing-Wage Law: Noble Goal, Costly Projects," *Bluegrass Institute,* March 7, 2006, *www.bipps.org/ARTICLE.ASP?ID=535.*

56. "Disney Settles Anti-Poaching Lawsuit," February 2, 2017, https://www.forbes.com/; David Streitfeld, "Engineers Allege Collusion in Silicon Valley," *New York Times*, March 1, 2014, p. A1; Jeff Elder, "Judge Rejects Settlement in Silicon Valley Wage Case," *Wall Street Journal*, August 8, 2014. See the settlement websites: "High-Tech Employee Antitrust Settlement," http://www.hightechemployee-lawsuit.com/; and "Animation Workers Antitrust Litigation," http://www.animationlawsuit.com/.

57. *Gratz v. Bollinger,* (02-516) 539 U.S. 244 (2003).

58. *Grutter v. Bollinger,* (02-241) 539 U.S. 306 (2003).

59. Seyfarth Shaw LLP. Developments in Equal Pay Litigation, 2021 Update. seyfarth-ebooks.com, March 2021.

60. Paula England, *Comparable Worth: Theories and Evidence* (Hawthorne, NY: Aldine deGruyter, 1992); Ben A. Barres, "Does Gender Matter?" *Nature* 442 (July 13, 2006); Morley Gunderson, "The Evolution and Mechanics of Pay Equity in Ontario," *Canadian Public Policy* 28, suppl. 1 (2002).

61. Michael E. Gold, "Towards a Unified Theory of the Law of Employment Discrimination," *Berkeley Journal of Employment and Labor Law,* February 2001.

62. Davan Maharaj, "Coca-Cola to Settle Racial Bias Lawsuit," *Los Angeles Times,* November 17, 2000.

63. *Annual Workplace Class Action Litigation Report*, 2015 edition (Seyfarth Shaw LLP, 2015).

64. FLSA-based lawsuits representing similarly situated employees are "collective actions" rather than class actions and employees are required to "opt in" (rather than opt out) under FLSA Section 216(b).

65. The Rule 23(a) requirements, specifically, identify four criteria. Numerosity. The number of putative (potential) plaintiffs is so large that to identify all of them individually by name would not be practical. Commonality. The lawsuit issues must be common to the proposed class. Typicality. The lawsuit issues and claims must be typical of those of the putative class members. Adequacy of Representation. The lead plaintiffs and their attorneys must be able to fairly and adequately protect the interests of the putative class. Annual Workplace Class Action Litigation Report, 2015 edition. Published by Seyfarth Shaw LLP. January 2015.

66. Gerald L. Maatman Jr., Ada Dolph, and Annette Tyman. *Wal-Mart Stores Inc. v. Dukes*: Has It Lived Up to the Hype? January 24, 2014. http://www.shrm.org/legalissues/employmentlawareas/pages/walmart-dukes-class-action-fallout.aspx. Extracted March 30, 2014.

67. Annual Workplace Class Action Litigation Report, 2015 edition. Published by Seyfarth Shaw LLP. January 2015. Gerald L. Maatman Jr., Ada Dolph and Annette Tyman. Wal-Mart Stores Inc. v. Dukes: Has It Lived Up to the Hype? January 24, 2014. http://www.shrm.org/legalissues/employmentlawareas/pages/wal-mart-dukes-class-actionfallout.aspx. Extracted March 30, 2014.
68. Gerald L. Maatman Jr., Ada Dolph and Annette Tyman. Wal-Mart Stores Inc. v. Dukes: Has It Lived Up to the Hype? January 24, 2014. http://www.shrm.org/legalissues/employmentlawareas/pages/walmart-dukes-class-action-fallout.aspx. Extracted March 30, 2014.
69. Seyfarth Shaw LLP. Class Certification Denied In Bus Company Discrimination Suit. www.lexology.com. November 10, 2020.
70. Lauren Weber. More Companies Block Employees From Filing Suits. The Wall Street Journal. March 31, 2015. www.wsj.com.
71. James N. Boudreau. Supreme Court Holds Employers Do Not Violate National Labor Relations Act by Requiring Employees to Agree to Arbitrate: The ruling comes in Epic Systems v. Lewis. americanbar.org, July 6, 2018; Lise Gelernter, "The Impact of Epic Systems in the Labor and Employment Context," *Journal of Dispute Resolution* 1 (2019), pp. 115–127.
72. U.S. Equal Employment Opportunity Commission, "Notice Concerning the Lilly Ledbetter Fair Pay Act of 2009," www.eeoc.gov/epa/ledbetter.html, June 22, 2009.
73. Ibid.
74. Brett A. Gorovsky, "Lilly Ledbetter Fair Pay Act of 2009: What's Next for Employers?" CCH Incorporated, http://www.cch.com/Press/news/CCHWhitePaper_LedbetterFairPayAct.pdf, June 22, 2009.
75. Michael E. Gold, "Towards a Unified Theory of the Law of Employment Discrimination," *Berkeley Journal of Employment and Labor Law,* February 2001.
76. U.S. Government Accountability Office, "Federal Agencies Should Better Monitor Their Performance in Enforcing Anti-Discrimination Laws," GAO Reports, Report Number GAO-08-799. Washington, D.C.; Debra Ann Millenson and David S. Fortney, "OFCCP Fundamentals," ABA Philadelphia Labor & Employment Conference, 2007, *www.abanet.org/labor/annualconference/2007/materials/data/papers/v1/009.pdf,* accessed June 12, 2009.
77. OFCCP Directive. Transmittal Number: 285, 09/17/2008, *www.dol.gov/esa/ofccp/regs/compliance/directives/dir285.htm,* June 21, 2009.
78. Office of Federal Contract Compliance Programs. Federal Contract Compliance Manual. Chapter 3—On-Site Review, *http://www.dol.gov/esa/ofccp/regs/compliance/fccm/ofcpch3.htm,* June 21, 2009.
79. The previous standards required the use of multiple regression analysis (for any similarly situated group (SSEG) that had 30 or more total employees and at least five employees in each group to be compared (the 30/5 rule). An SSEG was defined as "a grouping of employees who perform similar work, and occupy positions with similar responsibility levels and involving similar skills and qualifications." The OFCCP had stated that the multiple regression "must include [as control variables] factors that are important to how the contractor in practice makes pay decisions" and gave as examples: education, work experience with previous employers, seniority, time in salary grade, and performance ratings. SSEG group was also to be controlled in the regression. Finally, anecdotal evidence (e.g., reports of discrimination from employees) was also necessary. It noted that under these now rescinded standards, the OFCCP could "only establish a systemic compensation violation of the Executive Order by testing narrowly defined groupings of employees . . . [and] OFCCP [had been required to] use multiple regression analysis to test for pay disparities and [to] have anecdotal evidence to establish a systemic compensation violation, 'except in unusual cases' [despite the fact that] employment discrimination comes in many forms." OFCCP further argued that the anecdotal evidence requirement was "particularly burdensome for workers who frequently lack meaningful

access to information about pay." In summary, the OFCCP stated that "Fair and effective enforcement requires tailoring the compensation investigation and analytical procedures to the facts of the case based on Title VII principles." U.S. Department of Labor. Office of Federal Contract Compliance Programs (OFCCP). Advancing Equal Pay Enforcement. More Effective and Transparent Procedures for Investigating Pay Discrimination. http://www.dol.gov/ofccp/regs/compliance/CompGuidance/index.htm.

80. Under the new standards, the OFCCP (and employers performing self-evaluations) are to form "Pay Analysis Groups," defined as "A group of employees (potentially from multiple job titles, units, categories and/or job groups) who are comparable for purposes of the contractor's pay practices." In data analysis, "Regression analysis may be performed on different types of pay analysis groups. A pay analysis group may be limited to a single job or title, or may include multiple distinct units or categories of workers. A pay analysis group may combine employees in different jobs or groups, with statistical controls to ensure that workers are similarly situated." However, use of multiple regression is no longer mandated. In forming Pay Analysis Groups, "similarly situated" employees are used. "For purposes of evaluating compensation differences, employees are similarly situated where it is reasonable to expect they should be receiving equivalent compensation absent discrimination. Relevant factors in determining similarity may include tasks performed, skills, effort, level of responsibility, working conditions, job difficulty, minimum qualifications, and other objective factors. In some cases, employees are similarly situated where they are comparable on some of these factors, even if they are not similar on others." U.S. Department of Labor. Office of Federal Contract Compliance Programs (OFCCP). Directive. U.S. Department Of Labor Office of Federal Contract Compliance Programs. Number: 307 Date: February 28, 2013 ADM. Notice/Compensation.
81. Directive 2018-05 available at: https://www.dol.gov/ofccp/regs/compliance/directives/dir2018_05.html. Frequently asked questions available at: https://www.dol.gov/ofccp/regs/compliance/faqs/compguidance_faq.htm
82. After Record Settlements in 2020, Contractors Should Expect More Pay Equity Enforcement Under Biden. National Law Review, January 5, 2021. www.natlawreview.com.
83. Biden OFCCP Director Appointment Signals That More Pay Equity Enforcement is on the Horizon for Federal Contractors. www.natlawreview.com, January 22, 2021.
84. Ibid. The OFCCP until 2013 offered what it described as an "incentive" do so in that it "will coordinate its compliance monitoring activities with the contractor's self-evaluation approach." If the self-evaluation approach "reasonably meets the general standards outline in the Voluntary Guidelines, OFCCP will consider the contractor's compensation practices to be in compliance with Executive Order 11246." In other words, if the self-evaluation follows the standards and shows no disparities between similarly situated employee groups, the OFCCP would conclude the employer was in compliance. Again, as noted, this is no longer the case since 2013.
85. Murray S. Simpson, "Analyzing Pay Equity in an Uncertain Regulatory Environment," *Compensation & Benefits Review,* November/December, pp. 29–39.
86. Sara L. Rynes and George T. Milkovich, "Wage Surveys: Dispelling Some Myths about the 'Market Wage,'" *Personnel Psychology,* Spring 1986, pp. 71–90; Charlie Trevor and Mary E. Graham, "Deriving the Market Wage: Three Decision Areas in the Compensation Survey Process," *WorldatWork Journal,* Fourth Quarter 2000, pp. 69–76; Judith K. Hellerstein, David Neumark, and Kenneth R. Troske, "Market Forces and Sex Discrimination," *Journal of Human Resources* 37 no. 2 (Spring 2002), pp. 353–380.
87. H. Remick, ed., *Comparable Worth and Wage Discrimination* (Philadelphia: Temple University Press, 1984); B. F. Reskin and H. I. Hartmann, eds., *Women's Work, Men's Work: Segregation on the Job* (Washington, DC: National Academy Press, 1986); Morley Gunderson, *Women and the Labour*

Market: Transitions towards the Future (Toronto: ITP Nelson Publishing, 1998); Morley Gunderson and Nan Weiner, *Pay Equity: Issues, Options and Experiences* (Toronto: Butterworths, 1990).

88. *Job Evaluation: A Tool for Pay Equity* (Washington, DC: National Committee on Pay Equity, November 1987); Morley Gunderson, "The Evolution and Mechanics of Pay Equity in Ontario," *Canadian Public Policy* 28, suppl. 1 (2002).
89. Sharon Toffey-Shepela and Ann T. Viviano, "Some Psychological Factors Affecting Job Segregation and Wages," *Comparable Worth and Wage Discrimination,* in H. Remick, ed. (Philadelphia: Temple University Press, 1984); Helen Remick, "Beyond Equal Pay for Equal Work: Comparable Worth in the State of Washington," in Ronnie Steinber-Ratner, ed., *Equal Employment Policy for Women,* (Philadelphia: Temple University Press, 1980), pp. 405–448; "Supreme Court Decision a Victory for Pay Equity and Human Rights," press release from Public Service Alliance of Canada, June 26, 2003; Theresa Glomb, John Kammeyer-Mueller, and Maria Rotundo, "Emotional Labor Demands and Compensating Wage Differentials," *Journal of Applied Psychology* 89, no. 4 (2004), pp. 700–714.
90. "Bell Canada Operators Accept Pay Equity Deal," *Canadian Employment Law Today* June 20, 2006, *www.employmentlawtoday.com;* Judy Fudge, "The Paradoxes of Pay Equity: Reflections on the Law and the Market in Bell Canada and the Public Service Alliance of Canada," *Canadian Journal of Women and the Law* 12 (2000), pp. 312–344.
91. Ronnie Steinberg, "Emotional Labor in Job Evaluation: Redesigning Compensation Practices," *Annals of the American Academy of Political and Social Science* 561, no. 1 (1999), pp. 142–157.
92. Kenneth Kovach, "An Overview and Assessment of Comparable Worth Based on a Large Scale Implementation," *Public Personnel Management* 26, no. 1 (1997), pp. 109–122; Judith McDonald and Robert Thornton, "Private Sector Experience with Pay Equity in Ontario," *Canadian Public Policy* 24, no. 2 (1998), pp. 227–241; Nan Weiner and Morley Gunderson, *Pay Equity: Issues, Options, and Experiences* (Toronto: Butterworths, 1990); Lynda Ames, "Fixing Women's Wages: The Effectiveness of Comparable Worth Policies," *Industrial and Labour Relations Review* 48, no. 4 (1998), pp. 709–725.
93. Alvin O. Bellak, "Comparable Worth: A Practitioner's View," in *Comparable Worth: Issue for the 80s,* vol. 1 (Washington, DC: Equal Employment Advisory Council, 1980).
94. Christopher T. Patrick. Rethinking Pay Equity: Who is 'Comparable' for Pay Equity Purposes? www.jacksonlewis.com, March 21, 2019.
95. Seyfarth Shaw LLP. Developments in Equal Pay Litigation, 2021 Update. seyfarth-ebooks.com, March 2021.
96. Biden OFCCP Director Appointment Signals That More Pay Equity Enforcement is on the Horizon for Federal Contractors. www.natlawreview.com, January 22, 2021.
97. Sonja C. Kassenboehmer and Mathias G. Sinning, "Distributional Changes in the Gender Wage Gap," *Industrial and Labor Relations Review* 67 (2014), pp. 335–361.
98. U.S. Bureau of Census, "Educational Attainment in the United States: 2011—Detailed Tables," www.census.gov/hhes/socdemo/education/data/cps/2011/tables.html, accessed May 30, 2012.
99. U.S. Department of Labor, Bureau of Labor Statistics, "Highlights of Women's Earnings in 2007," Report 1008, October 2008; Francine D. Blau and Lawrence M. Kahn, "The Gender Pay Gap: Have Women Gone as Far as They Can?" *Academy of Management Perspectives;* D. A. Black, A. M. Haviland, S. G. Sanders, and L. J. Taylor, "Gender Wage Disparities among the Highly Educated," *Journal of Human Resources* 42 (2008), pp. 630–659. Cheri Ostroff and Leanne Atwater, "Does Whom You Work with Matter? Effects of Referent Group Gender and Age Composition on Managers' Compensation," *Journal of Applied Psychology,* August 2003, pp. 725–740; Paula England, "The Gender System: What's Changing? What's Not?" Alice Cook Memorial Lecture, Cornell University, Ithaca, NY, March 22, 2006; Nabanita Datta Gupta, Ronald L. Oaxaca, and Nina Smith, "Swimming Upstream, Floating Downstream: Comparing Women's Relative Wage Progress In the

United States and Denmark," *Industrial and Labor Relations Review,* January 2006, pp. 243-266; Warren Farrell, *Why Men Earn More: The Startling Truth behind the Pay Gap—and What Women Can Do About It* (New York: Amacom, 2005); Gerrit Mueller and Erik Plug, "Estimating the Effect of Personality on Male and Female Earnings," *Industrial and Labor Relations Review,* October 2006, pp. 3-22.

100. June O'Neill and Dave O'Neill, *What Do Wage Differentials Tell Us about Labor Market Discrimination?* NBER Working Paper W11240, April 2005.

101. Rachel Croson and Uri Gneezy, "Gender Differences in Preferences," *Journal of Economic Literature* 47 (2009), pp. 448-474; D. Anderson, M. Binder, and K. Krause, "The Motherhood Wage Penalty Revisited: Experience, Heterogeneity, Work Effort and Work-Schedule Flexibility," *Industrial and Labor Relations Review* 56, no. 2 (January 2003), pp. 273-295; Andrew M. Gill and Duane E. Leigh, "Community College Enrollment, College Major, and the Gender Wage Gap," *Industrial and Labor Relations Review* 54, no. 1 (October 2000), pp. 163-181; C. Brown and M. Corcoran, "Sex-Based Differences in School Content and the Male-Female Wage Gap," *Journal of Labor Economics* 15, no. 3 (1997), pp. 431-465; M. Montgomery and I. Powell, "Does an Advanced Degree Reduce the Gender Wage Gap? Evidence From MBAs," *Industrial Relations* 42, no. 3 (July 2003), pp. 396-418.

102. Laurie A. Morgan, "Major Matters: The Within-Major Gender Pay Gap for Early-Career College Graduates," *Industrial Relations* 47 (2008) pp. 625-650; Nicole M. Fortin, "The Gender Gap among Young Adults in the United States: The Importance of Money versus People," *Journal of Human Resources* 43 (2008), p. 884; C. A. Karlin, P. England, and Mary Richardson, "Why Do 'Women's Jobs' Have Low Pay for Their Educational Level?" *Gender Issues* 20, no. 4 (Fall 2002), pp. 3-22; Stephanie Boraas and William M. Rodgers III, "How Does Gender Play a Role in the Earnings Gap? An Update," *Monthly Labor Review,* March 2003, pp. 9-15. Francine Blau and Marianne Ferber, "Career Plans and Expectations of Young Women and Men," *Journal of Human Resources* 26, no. 4 (1998), pp. 581-607; Greg Hundley, "Male/Female Earnings Differences in Self-Employment: The Effects of Marriage, Children, and the Household Division of Labor," *Industrial and Labor Relations Review* 54, no. 1 (October 2000), pp. 95-114.

103. National Center for Educational Statistics. Digest of Education Statistics. Tables and Figures. Table 318.30. https://nces.ed.gov/. The gap at the graduate level (women getting more degrees) is larger still.

104. J. Säve-Söderbergh, "Gender Gaps in Salary Negotiations: Salary Requests and Starting Salaries in the Field," *Journal of Economic Behavior & Organization* 161 (2019), pp. 35-51.

105. K. Stevens and S. Whelan, "Negotiating the Gender Wage Gap," *Industrial Relations: A Journal of Economy and Society* 58, no. 2 (2019), pp. 141-188. [Stevens and Whelan provide a very helpful literature review]; K. G. Kugler, J. A. Reif, T. Kaschner, and F. C. Brodbeck, "Gender Differences in the Initiation of Negotiations: A Meta-Analysis," *Psychological Bulletin* 144, no. 2 (2018), pp. 198-222; B. Gerhart and S. Rynes, "Determinants and Consequences of Salary Negotiations by Graduating Male and Female MBAs," *Journal of Applied Psychology* 76 (1991), pp. 256-262. One study finds that to the degree there is a gender gap in negotiation propensity, it emerges "surprisingly early" in childhood, meaning that efforts to address this difference may need to likewise start early on. See S. H. Arnold and K. McAuliffe, "Children Show a Gender Gap in Negotiation," *Psychological Science* 32, no. 2 (2021), pp. 153-158.

106. W. Shan, J. Keller, and D. Joseph, "Are Men Better Negotiators Everywhere? A Meta-Analysis of How Gender Differences in Negotiation Performance Vary Across Cultures," *Journal of Organizational Behavior* 40, no. 6 (2019), pp. 651-675.

107. H. R. Bowles, B. Thomason, and J. B. Bear, "'Reconceptualizing What and How Women Negotiate for Career Advancement," *Academy of Management Journal* 62, no. 6 (2019), pp. 1645-1671.

108. Claire Zillman. The EU Is Taking a Drastic Step to Put More Women on Corporate Boards. Fortune.com. November 20, 2017. http://fortune.com/2017/11/20/women-on-boards-eu-gender-quota/.

109. Anne E. Preston, "Why Have All the Women Gone? A Study of Exit of Women from the Science and Engineering Professions," *American Economic Review,* December 1994, pp. 1446–1462; Joy A. Schneer and Frieda Reitman, "The Importance of Gender in Mid-Career: A Longitudinal Study of MBAs," *Journal of Organizational Behavior* 15 (1994), pp. 199–207.

110. Francine D. Blau and Lawrence M. Kahn, "The Gender Wage Gap: Extent, Trends, and Explanations," *Journal of Economic Literature* 55, pp. 789–865. Although the human capital-based explanation in the text is the traditional basis for why work experience matters, Blau and Kahn observe that other explanations (e.g., signaling) may also be important.

111. June O'Neill and Dave O'Neill, *What Do Wage Differentials Tell Us about Labor Market Discrimination?* NBER Working Paper W11240, April 2005; Finis Welch, "Catching Up: Wages of Black Men," American Economic Association Papers and Proceedings, May 2003, pp. 320–322; J. Heckman, "Detecting Discrimination," *Journal of Economic Perspectives* 12, no. 2 (1998), pp. 101–116.

112. Dan Black, Amelia Haviland, Seth Sanders, and Lowell Taylor, "Why Do Minority Men Earn Less? A Study of Wage Differentials among the Highly Educated," *Review of Economics and Statistics,* May 2006, pp. 300–313; Robert G. Wood, Mary E. Corcoran, and Paul N. Courant, "Pay Differences among the Highly Paid: The Male-Female Earnings Gap in Lawyers' Salaries," *Journal of Labor Economics* 11, no. 3 (1993), pp. 417–441.

113. Barry A. Gerhart and George T. Milkovich, "Salaries, Salary Growth, and Promotions of Men and Women in a Large, Private Firm," *Pay Equity: Empirical Inquiries* (Arlington, VA: National Science Foundation, 1989); Francine Blau and Jed DeVaro, *New Evidence on Gender Difference in Promotion Rates: An Empirical Analysis of a Sample of New Hires,* NBER Working Paper No. 12321, June 2006.

114. A. D. Sterling and R. M. Fernandez, "Once in the Door: Gender, Tryouts, and the Initial Salaries of Managers" *Management Science 64* (2018), pp. 5444–5460; B. Gerhart, "Gender Differences in Current and Starting Salaries: The Role of Performance, College Major, and Job Title," *ILR Review* 43, no. 4 (1990), pp. 418–433; B. Gerhart and G. T. Milkovich, "Salaries, Salary Growth, and Promotions of Men and Women in a Large, Private Firm," in Pay Equity: Empirical Inquiries, ed. R. Michael, H. Hartmann, and B. O'Farrell (Washington, DC: National Academy Press, 1989); K. W. Chauvin and R. A. Ash, "Gender Earnings Differentials in Total Pay, Base Pay, and Contingent Pay," *Industrial and Labor Relations Review* 47 (1994), pp. 634–49; M. M. Elvira and M. E. Graham, "Not Just a Formality: Pay System Formalization and Sex-Related Earnings Effects," *Organization Science* 13 (2002), pp. 601–617.

115. B. Gerhart, "Gender Differences in Current and Starting Salaries: The Role of Performance, College Major, and Job Title," *ILR Review* 43, no. 4 (1990), pp. 418–433.

116. G. T. Dreher, N. M. Carter, and T. Dworkin, "The Pay Premium for High-Potential Women: A Constructive Replication and Refinement," *Personnel Psychology* 72, no. 4, pp. 495–511; L. M. Leslie, C. F. Manchester, and P. C. Dahm, "Why and When Does the Gender Gap Reverse? Diversity Goals and the Pay Premium for High Potential Women," *Academy of Management Journal* 60 (2017), pp. 402–432.

117. D. P. Blevins, S. Sauerwald, J. M. Hoobler, and C. J. Robertson, "Gender Differences in Pay Levels: An Examination of the Compensation of University Presidents," *Organization Science* 30, no. 3 (2019), pp. 600–616.

118. See Footnote 1 of the following article for a summary of different study findings. M. Javdani and A. McGee, "Moving up or Falling Behind? Gender, Promotions, and Wages in Canada," *Industrial Relations* 58, no. 2 (2019), pp. 189–228. Another study finds that in some cases, the existence/size of a gap can depend on model specification (here, whether fixed effects are controlled); B. Artz and S. Taengnoi, "The Gender Gap in Raise Magnitudes of Hourly and Salary Workers," *Journal of Labor Research* 40, no. 1 (2019), pp. 84–105.

119. Mary E. Graham, Julie L. Hotchkiss, and Barry Gerhart, "Discrimination by Parts: A Fixed Effects Analysis of Starting Pay Differences across Gender," *Eastern Economic Journal* 26 (2000), pp. 9–27; Erica L. Groshen, "Sources of Intra-Industry Wage Dispersion: How Much Do Employers Matter?" *The Quarterly Journal of Economics* 106 (1991), pp. 869–884; Kimberly Bayard, Judith Hellerstein, David Neumark, and Kenneth Troske, "New Evidence on Sex Segregation and Sex Differences in Wages From Matched Employee-Employer Data," *Journal of Labor Economics* 21 (2003), pp. 887–922; George Johnson and Gary Solon, "Estimates of the Direct Effects of Comparable Worth Policy," *American Economic Review* 76 (1986), pp. 1117–1125; Barry Gerhart, "Gender Differences in Current and Starting Salaries: The Role of Performance, College Major, and Job Title," *Industrial and Labor Relations Review* 43 (1990), pp. 418–433.

120. George F. Dreher and Taylor H. Cox Jr., "Labor Market Mobility and Cash Compensation: The Moderating Effects of Race and Gender," *Academy of Management Journal* 43, no. 5 (2000), pp. 890–900; J. M. Brett and L. K. Stroh, "Jumping Ship: Who Benefits from an External Labor Market Career Strategy?" *Journal of Applied Psychology* 82 (1997), pp. 331–341; G. F. Dreher and T. H. Cox, Jr., "Race, Gender, and Opportunity: A Study of Compensation Attainment and the Establishment of Mentoring Relationships," *Journal of Applied Psychology* 81 (1996), pp. 297–308.

121. George F. Dreher and Taylor H. Cox, Jr., "Labor Market Mobility and Cash Compensation: The Moderating Effects of Race and Gender," *Academy of Management Journal* 43, no. 5 (2000), pp. 890–900.

122. B. Groysberg, P. Healy, and E. Lin, E, "Determinants of Gender Differences in Change in Pay among Job-Switching Executives," *ILR Review,* 2020

123. Francine D. Blau and Lawrence M. Kahn, "The Gender Wage Gap: Extent, Trends, and Explanations," *Journal of Economic Literature* 55 (2017), pp. 789–865. See their Table 4, Panel B.

124. Susan Milligan, "Are Salary Histories History?" *HR Magazine,* March 2018, pp. 54–59; Kelsey Gee, "Pay Queries in Job Interviews under Fire," *Wall Street Journal,* April 18, 2017.

125. Organisation for Economic Co-operation and Development, "The Price of Prejudice: Labour Market Discrimination on the Grounds of Gender and Ethnicity," *OECD Employment Outlook* 2008, chap. 3 (Paris: OECD, 2008).

126. Francine D. Blau and Lawrence M. Kahn, *The Sources of International Differences in Wage Inequality* (ILR Impact Brief #10), (Ithaca, NY: School of Industrial and Labor Relations, Cornell University, 2006); H. C. Jain, P. J. Sloane, and F. Horwitz, *Employment Equity and Affirmative Action: An International Comparison* (Armonk, NY: ME Sharpe, 2003); Janet C. Gornick, Marcia K. Meyers, and Katherine E. Ross, "Supporting the Employment of Mothers: Policy Variation across Fourteen Welfare States," *Journal of European Social Policy* 7, no. 1 (1997), pp. 45–70.

127. www.nypost.com/p/news/local/manhattan/was_gaga_slave_IyvXjE3n412CoMqKQnyS1L#ixzz1w-Tpq5Gaz, accessed May 31, 2012. www.employmentlawattorneyoh.com/2012/01/lady-gaga-subject-to-fair-labor-standards-act.shtml, accessed May 31, 2012.

Chapter **Eighteen** Management: Making It Work

Chapter Outline

This chapter is about making it work: ensuring that the right people get the right pay for achieving the right objectives in the right way. The greatest pay system design in the world is useless without competent management. So why bother with a formal system at all? If management is that important, why not simply let every manager pay whatever works best? Such total decentralization of decision making could create a chaotic array of rates. Managers could use pay to motivate behaviors that achieved their own immediate objectives, not necessarily those of the organization. Employees could be treated inconsistently and unfairly. Some employees would be overpaid (driving up costs), while others would be underpaid (driving up turnover and, in today's world, increasing the risk of a lawsuit).

This was the situation in the United States in the early 1900s. The "contract system" made highly skilled workers managers as well as workers. The employer agreed to provide the "contractor" with floor space, light, power, and the necessary raw or semifinished materials. The contractor hired *and* paid labor.[1] Pay inconsistencies for the same work were common. Some contractors demanded kickbacks from employees' paychecks; many hired their relatives and friends. Dissatisfaction and grievances were widespread, eventually resulting in legislation that outlawed the arrangement.

Corruption and financial malfeasance were also part of decentralized decision making in the early 1900s. Some see parallels today. To help avoid history repeating itself and to redeem HR (and compensation) vice presidents from the image of unindicted coconspirators, the compensation system should be managed to achieve the objectives in the pay model: efficiency, fairness, and compliance.

Any discussion of managing pay must again raise the basic questions: So what is the impact of the decision or technique? Does it help the organization achieve its objectives? How?

Although many pay management issues have been discussed throughout the book, a few remain to be called out explicitly. These include (1) managing labor costs, (2) managing revenues, (3) communication, and (4) designing the compensation department.

MANAGING LABOR COSTS AND REVENUES

Financial planning is integral to managing compensation. As we noted in **Chapter 1**, compensation decisions influence organization's performance by influencing costs and/or revenues. The cost implications of actions such as updating the pay structure, increasing merit pay, or instituting gain sharing are critical for making sound decisions. Budgets account for these costs. Creating a compensation budget requires trade-offs, such as how much of an increase should be allocated according to employee contributions versus across-the-board increases versus company performance. Trade-offs also occur over short- versus long-term incentives, over pay increases contingent on performance versus seniority, and over cash compensation compared to benefits.

Financial planning also requires understanding the revenues (or returns) gained from the allocation.[2] Total compensation makes up at least 50 percent of operating expenses in many organizations. Yet, most companies have not tried to analyze the returns from their compensation decisions.[3] As we noted in **Chapter 2**, compensation strategy influences effectiveness not only by its influence on (labor) costs, but also through its influence in helping increase revenues or returns as well. Returns might be the productivity increases expected from a new gain-sharing or profit-sharing plan, or the expected value added by boosting merit increases to the top performers.[4] In the past, financial planning in compensation was only about costs.[5] This is perhaps because costs are tangible and easy to measure, whereas the returns generated by compensation strategy may often be intangible and harder to quantify. It is important to keep in mind, however, that how easy or difficult it is to quantify something has little to do with how important it is. Fortunately, analysis of the expected returns compared to costs is becoming more common.[6] More on this later.

MANAGING LABOR COSTS

You already know many of the factors that affect labor costs. **Exhibit 18.1** shows a simple labor cost model. Using this model, there are three main factors to control in order to manage labor costs: employment (e.g., number of workers and the hours they work), average cash compensation (e.g., wages, bonuses), and average benefit costs. Cash compensation and benefits have been this book's focus. However, if our objective is to better manage labor costs, then all three factors require attention.

Number of Employees (a.k.a.: Staffing Levels or Headcount)

Using information about competitors' average pay helps improve understanding of labor costs. **Exhibit 18.2A** shows how one organization pays its engineers relative to its competitors at each of five job levels, E5-E1. The pay for each position is the cross-hatched bar. Market pay is the shaded bar, with the average falling in the middle of the unshaded part of the bar. So the organization meets competition by paying E5, E3, and E2 engineers at about the median. But the company leads competition at E4 and lags at the entry-level E1.

Exhibit 18.2B provides more insight into the organization's labor costs. This part of the exhibit compares the organization's distribution of engineers among the five job levels to its competitors' distributions. A larger percentage of the organization's engineers are at higher levels, E4 and E5, than its competitors. So even though the organization pays above market for only one of the five job levels, its labor costs may be higher than its competitors due to its staffing pattern. So what? Looking only at total headcount, as suggested in **Exhibit 18.1**, may mislead since the total employment level could be identical to competitors' but deployment among job levels may vary. Here, the organization differs from its competitors mostly at E4, where it employs a larger percentage of engineering talent and also pays them more. Something is going on at E4. More information is required to better understand what underlies these differences. Are the organization's engineers more experienced and thus promoted into E4? Does the company do more sophisticated work that requires more experienced engineers? Absent some sound business-related rationale, labor costs can be reduced by redeploying staffing levels and wages at E4.[7] Obviously, paying the same wages (e.g., meeting competition) to fewer employees is less expensive. The effects on all pay objectives–efficiency and fairness–also need to be considered before taking any action.

Reducing Headcount

The demand for labor is a derived demand, meaning that it depends on the demand for the company's product.[8] As is apparent from following the business news during any recession, organizations often reduce headcount to cut labor costs. Such cuts may take the form of layoffs (often with severance benefits that depend on length of service) or exit incentives that are designed to encourage employees to leave "by choice." A major advantage of a reduction in force (RIF) is that it also reduces benefits costs, something that a pay cut, furlough, or reduction in hours ordinarily does not achieve. (An exception would be Lincoln Electric, which has a very lean, low-cost benefits package.) To the degree that headcount reductions can be targeted based on performance, it can also be an opportunity for an organization to reshape its workforce in a way that creates positive sorting effects. Under such a scenario, stronger performers are unaffected (e.g., their pay is not cut), and the organization has an opportunity to maintain good employee relations with this important group.

EXHIBIT 18.1 Managing Labor Costs

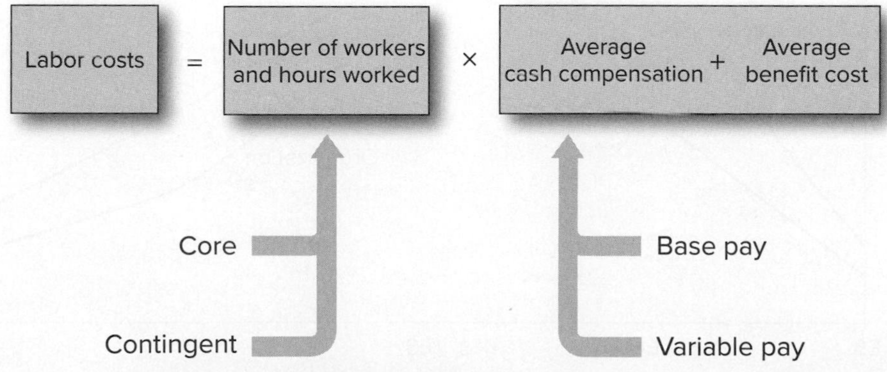

There are, however, several potential problems with headcount reductions. First, regulatory requirements make it difficult to make targeted cuts. The Age Discrimination in Employment Act (ADEA) often comes into play if organizations target reductions among higher paid employees (to maximize labor cost savings) because higher paid employees also tend to be older employees. In addition, the Older Worker Benefits Protection Act, part of the ADEA, requires that exit incentive programs be structured in very specific ways. For example, a program must give workers 40 years old and older 21 days to consider the offer and 7 days to change their mind if they accept the offer. These and other provisions tend to make it difficult to single out high-wage and/or poor-performing workers. If exit incentives cannot be effectively targeted and all employees are eligible, which employees do you think would be most likely to take the incentive and leave? Probably those most employable and most able to find another good job, right? That is indeed what a number of organizations have experienced. Thus, you may end up, in essence, paying your top performers to leave–a very undesirable sorting effect! Second, workforce reductions, especially if not handled well, can harm employee relations. Regulatory restrictions on headcount reductions can be quite stringent outside the United States. (See our discussion of works councils, for example, in **Chapter 16**.)[9] Third, organizations that make greater (involuntary) workforce reductions also experience greater voluntary turnover and may find that even "desirable" turnover can cause unanticipated problems.[10] Fourth, RIFs, while reducing costs over time, are very costly in tangible terms up front due to increases in unemployment insurance tax rates, disruption of work

EXHIBIT 18.2 Staffing Analysis Identifies Reasons for Pay Variances

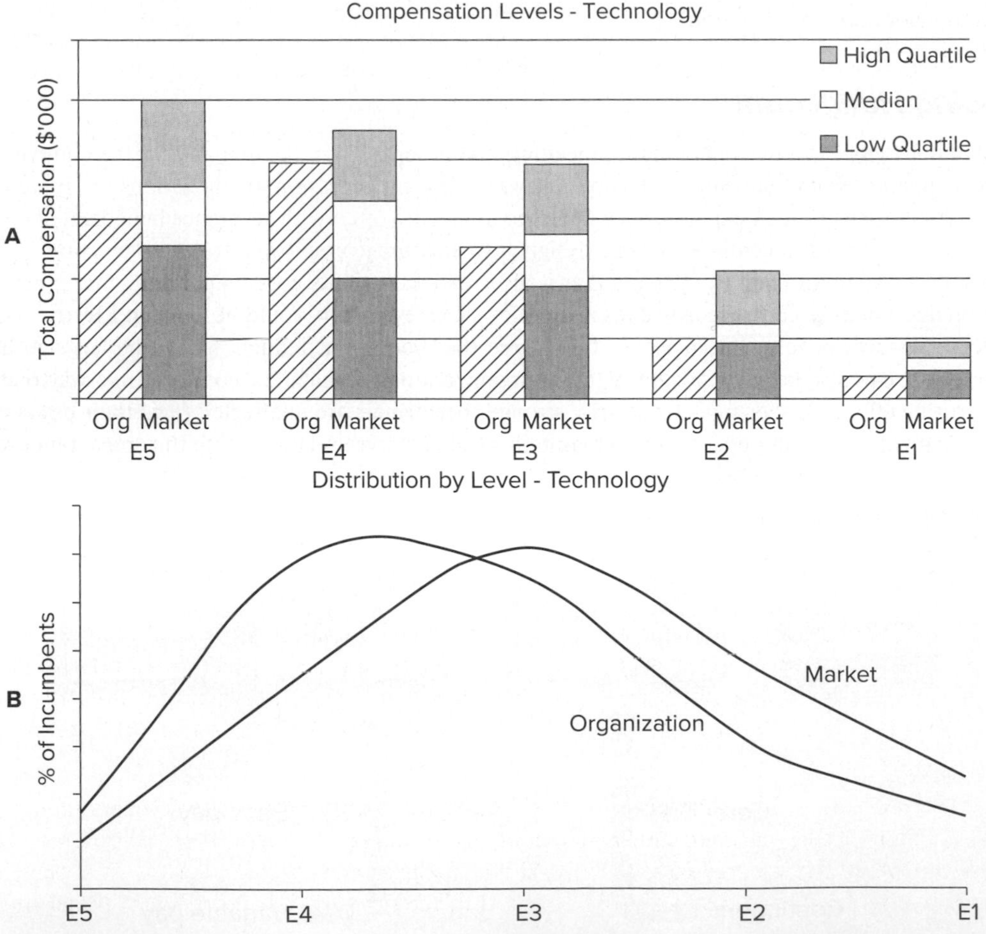

processes and serving customers, and administrative costs of handling exits. Exit incentives, if provided, further drive up costs. Fifth, some companies have learned to run so "lean" (i.e., very few employees on manufacturing lines) and have controlled hiring so successfully, that there may be little room to cut headcount.[11] Finally, where cuts can be made, if the cuts are too deep, an organization will be poorly positioned to generate revenue if business picks up again.[12] An organization may spend a lot of money reducing headcount and then spend a lot more a short time later to hire new employees to handle increased product demand. If other firms increase hiring at the same time, costs will be even greater. Announcements of layoffs and plant closings often have favorable short-run effects on stock prices as investors anticipate improved cash flow and lower costs. However, in the longer term, adverse effects such as loss of trained employees, unrealized productivity, and lowered morale often translate into lower financial gains than anticipated. Thus, it is somewhat reassuring that at least one study finds that "it appears that boards [of directors] do not allow CEOs to benefit from layoffs...unless firm performance benefits as well."[13] Some evidence indicates that close attention to process and employee relations during workforce reductions can help financial results.[14] In addition, reducing headcount without also divesting assets (part of the business) appears to have the least favorable financial consequences (perhaps because after some point, there is only so much of the original work that can be done well by a smaller number of employees).[15]

In addition, as we saw in **Chapter 17**, the regulatory environment differs from country to country. Many European countries have legislation as part of their social contracts that makes it very difficult to reduce headcount or wages. Managing labor costs is a greater struggle in such circumstances.

Many employers seek to buffer themselves from getting into a position where layoffs are necessary. A key is to avoid hiring/increasing headcount beyond a sustainable level. As discussed below, use of overtime is part of this strategy. In addition, organizations establish different relationships with different groups of workers. As **Exhibit 18.3** depicts, the two groups are commonly referred to as **core employees**, with whom a long-term relationship is desired, and *contingent workers*, whose employment agreements may cover only short, specific time periods. Contingent workers can be employees but can also be independent contractors/vendors or may be employed by staffing services firms/vendors. Rather than expand or contract the core workforce, many employers achieve flexibility and control labor costs by expanding or contracting the contingent workforce. Toyota, for example, while not cutting regular employees in either the United States or Japan during the recent recession, has cut its contract worker headcount.

The segmented supply of nurses at St. Luke's Hospital, discussed in **Chapter 7** and shown in **Exhibit 18.4**, illustrates the variable costs from use of different sources of nurses. Regular, pool, registry, and traveler nurses are paid differently. Some have benefits from St. Luke's, others have them from the contracting agencies, and still others must purchase their own benefits (pool nurses). The trade-offs in managing costs include balancing patient loads, nurse-to-patient ratios, costs of alternative sources, and quality of care.[16]

Hours

Rather than define employment as number of employees, hours of work is often used. For nonexempt employees in the United States, hours over 40 per week are more expensive (one-and-a-half times regular wage). Hence, another way to manage labor costs is to examine overtime hours versus hiring more employees. St. Luke's may guarantee its regular nurses a specific number of hours, but contract nurses (pool, registry, or travelers) are "on call."

The four factors in the labor cost model–number of employees, hours worked, cash compensation, and benefit costs–are not independent. Overtime hours require higher wages, but the incremental benefits cost is substantially lower than that incurred in hiring an additional regular nurse. The higher the fixed benefits costs, the more viable is the option to add overtime (even with the time and a half premium) rather than hiring another nurse. By not hiring, the organization avoids recruitment/selection costs. It also gains more flexibility to reduce labor costs if demand for its health care services declines in the future. In that case, rather than cutting headcount, it can reduce hours worked, which helps avoid employee relations problems as well as the monetary costs of reducing headcount.

During the most recent recession, a number of firms reduced hours and costs through the use of mandatory unpaid leave or furloughs to cut hours and thus labor costs. Allied Signal used furloughs and decided on that strategy rather than layoffs because it wanted to be prepared to scale its workforce back up to take advantage of growth/revenue/opportunities quickly when the recession ended and business picked up.[17] As another example, state employees in California were required to take two furlough days off per month, resulting in a 10 percent pay cut. Wendy Roberson, one such employee, partly as a joke, founded the "Fun Furlough Fridays

EXHIBIT 18.3 Core and Contingent Employees

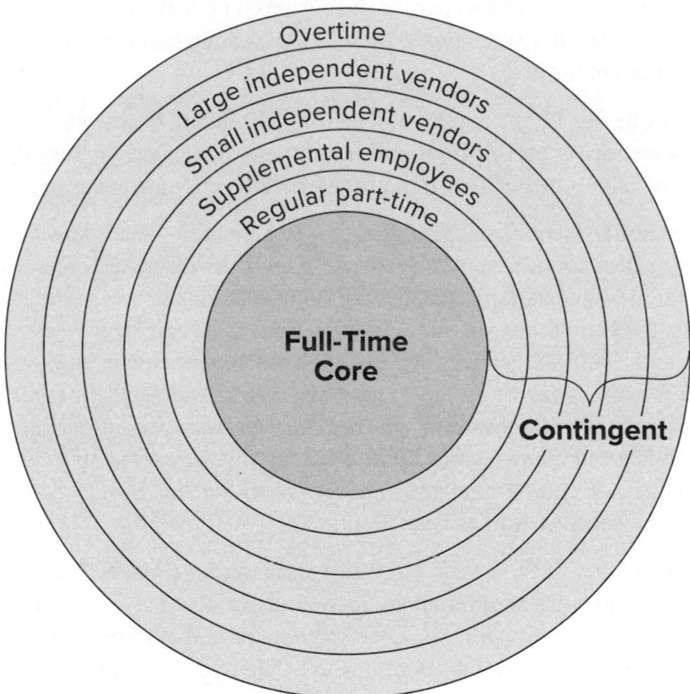

EXHIBIT 18.4 Segmented Supplies: St. Luke's Labor Cost Model

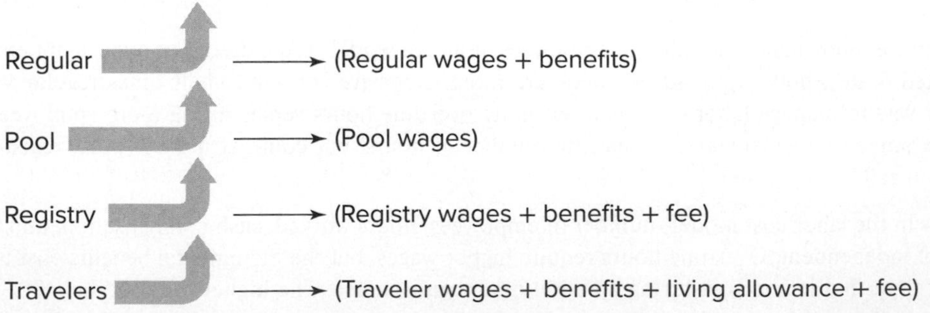

Source: ©George T. Milkovich.

Club." Nobody wants a pay cut, but if you are going to get some extra time off, you might as well make the best of it and enjoy it, right? Well, as it turns out, although the pay cut was real, the time off in many cases was not. The amount of work to be done did not decrease, so many "furloughed" employees found themselves at work, rather than having Fun Furlough Fridays.[18] Nevertheless, reducing hours and pay does mean that fewer headcount reductions are necessary and by avoiding these, there will be less disruption and private sector organizations should be better positioned to respond when business picks up again, at least so long as top performers don't find greener pastures in the meantime.[19]

Benefits

One of the most common approaches to reducing benefits costs recently has been for employers to suspend matching (made when employees contribute) to 401(k) retirement plans. Survey data from circa 2009 during the Great Recession showed about one in four companies either had already suspended their matching contributions or were considering doing so. Even the American Association for Retired Persons (AARP) decided it needed to suspend its 401(k) retirement plan match, a decision that was presumably not taken lightly![20] During the pandemic, especially early on in 2020, contributions to 401(k) plans were again paused and/or reduced at a significant number of companies. The average company match is 50 cents on the dollar up to 6 percent of pay. More companies may move to a model that makes matching contributions dependent on profits.[21] In any case, with improvements to the economy and corporate profits in more recent years, we have seen companies increase 401(k) contributions. In contrast to the depth of the Great Recession in 2009 when employers contributed 3.0 percent of salary, by 2016, after the economy bounced back and the labor market tightened, it was up to 4.7 percent.[22] Another action we have seen is organizations eliminating benefits such as defined benefit (pension) plans as part of seeking bankruptcy protection from creditors. Examples include several airlines (e.g., United, Delta, USAir, Northwest), automobile companies (General Motors, Chrysler), and automobile parts companies (e.g., Delphi). As noted in **Chapter 13**, the Pension Benefit Guaranty Corporation (PBGC) provides benefits to employees who were covered under such plans. However, as noted there, the maximum annual retirement benefit from the PBGC is $72,413 at age 65, meaning that more highly paid employees (e.g., airline pilots, executives) can experience a significant loss in pension benefits after bankruptcy. Other, more typical, ways of controlling or reducing benefits costs have to do with efforts by companies in the area of health care (as discussed in **Chapters 12** and **13**) and outsourcing, as Apple has done extensively (see **Chapter 7**).

Average Cash Compensation (Fixed and Variable Components)

Average cash compensation includes average salary (fixed payments) level plus variable compensation payments such as bonuses, gain sharing, stock plans, and/or profit sharing. The fixed component is typically paid regardless of business performance. In contrast, the variable component of compensation, in theory, will rise and fall in line with business performance. For example, a profit-sharing plan will ordinarily have lower than normal profit-sharing payouts in years when profits are lower than normal. If other firms are experiencing similar profit declines, then there may be less danger of losing employees through turnover when this happens and the full advantage of "automatic" labor cost flexibility can be experienced.

During the most recent recession (the "Great Recession" of 2007–2009) almost one-half of firms froze salaries, giving no annual increase,[23] resulting in an average salary increase budget across companies of just 1.9 percent in 2009. As **Exhibit 18.5** indicates, salary increase budgets have generally been in the neighborhood of 3 percent, except during difficult economic times (the late 2000s and the pandemic of 2020 and 2021). In addition, only 5 percent of firms froze salary increase budgets in 2011 (and less in subsequent years), down from 21 percent in 2010, and 48 percent in 2009.[24] However, in 2020 and 2021, the percentage of companies freezing salary budgets appeared to be more closer to 15 percent, with those not implementing such freezes giving pay increases of almost 3 percent (2.9%), resulting in an overall average of 2.5 to 2.6 percent in 2020 and 2021 (**Exhibit 18.5**). Another major tool used by organizations to control salary costs, in both good and bad times, is variable pay. (See **Chapters 8** and **10**.) As **Exhibit 18.6** shows, while the size of the merit increase budget has come down over time, the size of the variable pay (e.g., lump sum merit increases, profit sharing) budget has gone up very significantly. Unlike base salary increases, variable pay does not become a permanent part of base salary. Thus, the variable aspect allows companies to reduce labor costs when times are tough and to share success with (and reward) employees when times are good. As we saw earlier, the Big Three U.S. automobile companies have followed this strategy in recent years. (With respect to **Exhibit 18.6**, please keep in mind, as noted in **Chapter 10**, that while almost all companies use merit pay, variable pay plans of this sort are used in roughly one-half to two-thirds of companies and within those companies, higher level employees are more likely to be covered by such plans.)[25]

Adjustments to average cash compensation level (here, to simplify, we focus primarily on the salary component) can be made (1) *top down,* in which top management determines the amount of money to be spent on pay and allocates it "down" to each subunit for the plan year, and (2) *bottom up,* in which individual employees' pay for the plan year is forecasted and summed to create an organization-wide salary budget.

Budget Controls: Top Down

Top-down budgeting begins with an estimate from top management of the pay increase budget for the entire organization. Once the total budget is determined, it is then allocated to each manager, who plans how to distribute it among subordinates. There are many approaches to top-down budgeting. A typical one, **planned**

EXHIBIT 18.5 Base Salary Increases, as Percentage of Payroll, Salaried Exempt Employees, by Year

2008	2009	2010	2011	2012	2013	2014	2015	2016	2017	2018	2019	2020	2021
3.7%	1.9%	2.4%	2.7%	2.9%	2.9%	2.9%	3.0%	3.0%	3.0%	3.0%	3.1%	2.5%	2.6%*

Sources: Mercer. March 2021: U.S. Compensation Planning Pulse Survey Results. April 2021. www.imercer.com; The Conference Board. Salary Increase Budgets for 2021: Results of the 2020 Follow-up Survey. conference-board.org, March 2021. Accessed April 19, 2021; Ken Abosch, Aon, personal communication; * = projected.

EXHIBIT 18.6 Traditional Base Salary Increases and Variable Pay, as Percentage of Payroll, Salaried Exempt Employees, Changes over Time

	1991	2019
Base salary increase budget	5.0%	3.1%
Variable pay (merit bonus) budget	3.8%	11 %

Note: These budget numbers describe only organization that use these programs. In the case of base salary increase programs, that is nearly all organizations and nearly all employees are eligible. In contrast, the variable pay program is used in one-half to two-thirds of companies and primarily for employees at higher pay levels.

Source: Willis Towers Watson. "Most U.S. Employers Planning Raises, Bonuses for 2021." www.willistowerswatson.com. Mercer. March 2021: US Compensation Planning Pulse Survey Results. April 2021. www.imercer.com; The Conference Board. Salary Increase Budgets for 2021: Results of the 2020 Follow-up Survey. conference-board.org, March 2021. Accessed April 19, 2021; Ken Abosch, Aon, personal communication. Patricia Cohen. "Where Did Your Pay Raise Go? It May Have Become a Bonus," *New York Times*, February 10, 2018.

pay-level rise, is simply the percentage increase in average pay for the unit that is planned to occur. Several factors influence the decision on how much to increase the average pay level for the next period: how much the average level was increased this period, ability to pay, competitive market pressures, turnover effects, and cost of living.

Current Year's Rise

This is the percentage by which the average wage changed in the past year; mathematically:

$$\text{Percent pay-level rise} = 100 \times \frac{\text{average pay at year-end} - \text{average pay at year beginning}}{\text{average pay at year beginning}}$$

Ability to Pay

Any decision to increase the average pay level is in part a function of the organization's financial circumstances. Financially healthy employers may wish to maintain their competitive positions in the labor market or share financial success through bonuses and profit sharing. Conversely, financially troubled employers may not be able to maintain competitive market positions. As noted, the conventional response has been to reduce employment. As shown earlier, by analyzing pay and staffing at each level, potential cost savings can be discovered. Other options are to reduce the rate of increase in average pay by controlling adjustments in base pay and/or variable pay. Raising employees' copays and deductibles for benefits is another. Often as a last resort, firms decrease base wages (as well as variable pay). Airline pilots and mechanics have taken highly publicized pay cuts in recent years. Other alternatives also exist. Look again at the cost model for St. Luke's and its segmented labor supply. The hospital can reduce costs by reducing the different sources of contract nurses.

Competitive Market Pressures

In **Chapter 8**, we discussed how managers determine an organization's competitive position in relation to its competitors. Recall that a distribution of market rates for benchmark jobs was collected and analyzed into a single average wage for each benchmark. This "average market wage" becomes the "going market rate," and this market rate changes each year in response to a variety of factors in the external market.

Turnover Effects

Sometimes referred to as **"churn"** or "slippage," the **turnover effect** recognizes the fact that when people leave (through layoffs, quitting, retiring), they typically are replaced by employees who earn a lower wage. **Exhibit 18.2** illustrates where an organization is overstaffed compared to competitors. Reducing levels at E5 and E4 and replacing them with E1s and E2s will reduce labor costs. However, keep in mind the potential impact on revenues and customer satisfaction, as well as possible violation of the Age Discrimination in Employment Act.

The turnover effect can be calculated as annual turnover multiplied by the planned average increase. For example, assume that an organization whose labor costs equal $1 million a year has a turnover rate of 15 percent and a planned average increase of 6 percent. The turnover effect is .15 × .06 = .9%, or $9,000 (.009 × $1,000,000). So instead of budgeting an additional $60,000 to fund a 6 percent increase, only $51,000 is needed. The turnover effect will also reduce benefit costs linked to base pay, such as pensions.[26]

Cost of Living

Although there is little research to support **cost of living increases,** employees undoubtedly compare their pay increases to changes in their living costs. Unions consistently argue that increasing living costs justify increasing pay.

It is important to distinguish among three related concepts: the *cost of living, changes in prices in the product and service markets,* and *changes in wages in labor markets.* As **Exhibit 18.7** shows, changes in wages in labor markets are measured through pay surveys. These changes are incorporated into the system through market adjustments in the budget and updates of the policy line and range structure. Price changes for goods and services in the product and service markets are measured by several government indexes, one of which is the consumer price index (CPI). The third concept, the cost of living, refers to the expenditure patterns of individuals for goods and services. The cost of living is more difficult to measure because employees' expenditures depend on many things: marital status, number of dependents and ages, personal preferences, location, and so on. Different employees experience different costs of living, and the only accurate way to measure them is to examine the personal expenditures of each employee.

The three concepts are interrelated. Wages in the labor market are part of the cost of producing goods and services, and changes in wages create pressures on prices. Similarly, changes in the prices of goods and services create the need for increased wages in order to maintain the same lifestyle.

Many people refer to the CPI as a "cost-of-living" index, and many employers choose, as a matter of pay policy or in response to union pressures, to tie wages to it. However, the CPI does not necessarily reflect an individual employee's cost of living. Instead, it measures *changes in prices over time.* Changes in the CPI indicate whether prices have increased more or less rapidly in an area since the base period. For example, a CPI of 110 in Chicago and 140 in Atlanta does not necessarily mean that it costs more to live in Atlanta. It does mean that prices have risen faster in Atlanta since the base year than they have in Chicago, since both cities started with bases of 100.

EXHIBIT 18.7 Three Distinct but Related Concepts and Their Measures

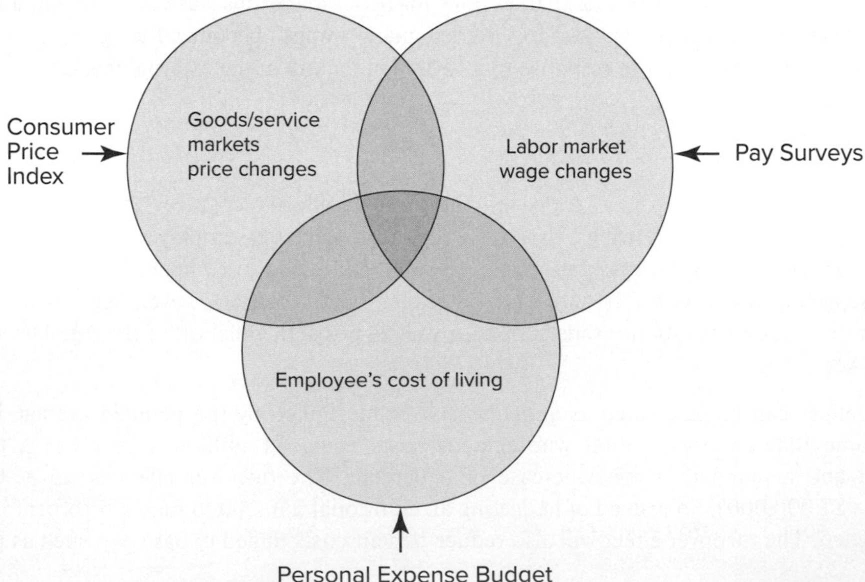

e-Compensation

A simple inflation calculator at ***www.westegg.com/inflation/*** uses the consumer price index to adjust any given amount of data from 1800 on. Most governments calculate some kind of consumer price index for their country. The Web page for the U.S. Bureau of Labor Statistics provides many of these indexes (***stats.bls.gov***). They vary on how realistically they capture actual changes in prices.

A word of caution: If you decide to use the CPI rather than labor market salary surveys to determine the merit budget, you basically are paying for inflation rather than performance or market changes.

e-Compensation

A quicker way to compare living costs is to use the "cost of living calculator" at ***https://www.salary.com/research/cost-of-living*** Enter your current city and potential new city to see what salary you need in the new city based on cost-of-living differences.

The CPI is of public interest because changes in it trigger changes in labor contracts, social security payments, federal and military pensions, and food stamp eligibility. Tying budgets or payments to the CPI is called *indexing.*

Rolling It All Together

Let us assume that the managers take into account all these factors–current year's rise, ability to pay, market adjustments, turnover effects, changes in the cost of living, and **geographic differentials**–and decide that the planned rise in average salary for the next period is 4 percent. This means that the organization has set a target of 4 percent as the increase in *average* salary that will occur in the next budget period. It does not mean that everyone's increase will be 4 percent. It means that at the end of the budget year, the average salary calculated to include all employees will be 4 percent higher than it is now.

The next question is, How do we distribute that 4 percent budget in a way that accomplishes management's objectives for the pay system and meets the organization's goals?

Distributing the Budget to Subunits

A variety of methods exist for determining what percentage of the salary budget each manager should receive. Some use a uniform percentage, in which each manager gets an equal percentage of the budget based on the salaries of each subunit's employees. Others vary the percentage allocated to each manager based on pay-related issues–such as turnover or performance–that have been identified in that subunit.

Once salary budgets are allocated to each subunit manager, they become a constraint: a limited fund of money that each manager has to allocate to subordinates. Typically, **merit increase guidelines** are used to help managers make these allocation decisions. Merit increase grids help ensure that different managers grant consistent increases to employees with similar performance ratings and in the same position in their ranges.

Additionally, grids help control costs. **Chapter 11** provides examples of merit increase grids. To limit the number of employees placed in high performance categories (and thus the number of employees receiving the largest merit increases), some companies used forced distribution approaches.

Budget Controls: Bottom Up

In contrast to top-down budgeting, where managers are told what their salary budget will be, bottom-up budgeting begins with managers' pay increase recommendations for the upcoming plan year. **Exhibit 18.8** shows the process involved.

1. *Instruct managers in compensation policies and techniques.* Train managers in the concepts of a sound pay-for-performance policy and in standard company compensation techniques such as the use of pay-increase guidelines and budgeting techniques. Communicate market data and the salary ranges.
2. *Distribute forecasting instructions and worksheets.* Furnish managers with the forms and instructions necessary to preplan increases. Most firms offer managers computer software to support these analyses and to enter information and perform what-if analyses.[27] Adjustments for each individual are fed into the summary merit budget, promotion budget, equity adjustment budget, and so on, on a summary screen. These recommendations are then submitted electronically.
   The type of information available to each supervisor to guide him or her in making recommendations might include performance rating history, past raises, training background, and stock allocations . Guidelines for increases based on merit, promotion, and equity adjustments are provided, and all the

EXHIBIT 18.8 Compensation Forecasting and Budgeting Cycle

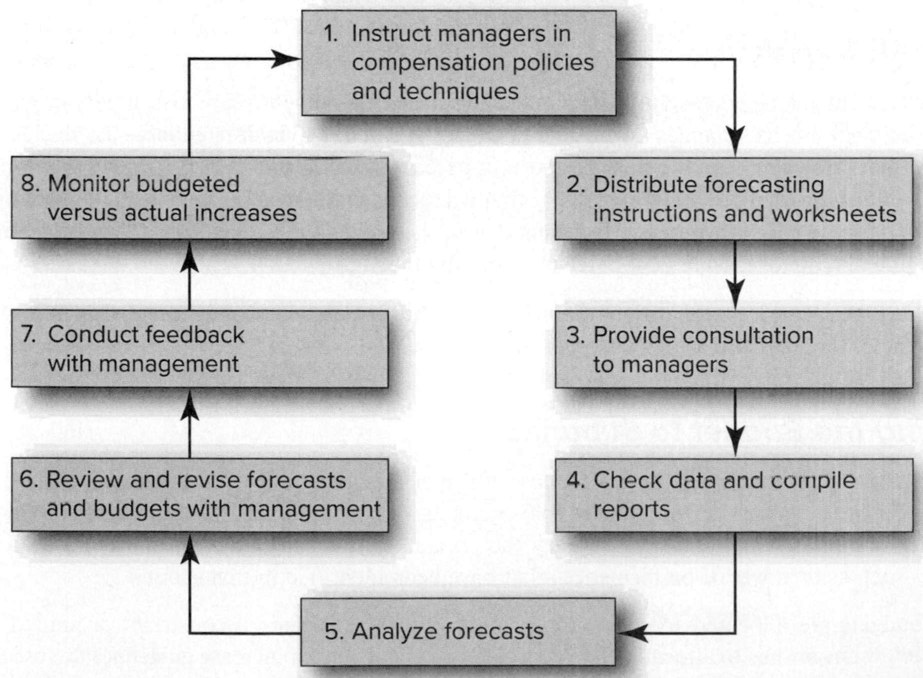

worksheets are linked so that the manager can model pay adjustments for employees and see the budgetary effects of those adjustments immediately.

Some argue that providing such detailed data and recommendations to operating managers makes the process biased. How would you like your instructor to look at your overall GPA before giving you a grade in this course? Pay histories, however, ensure that managers are at least aware of this information and that pay increases for any one period are part of a continuing message to individual employees, not some ad-hoc response to short-term changes.

3. *Provide consultation to managers.* Offer advice and salary information services to managers upon request. Dell's online approach makes it much easier to request and apply such guidance.
4. *Check data and compile reports.* Audit the increases forecasted to ensure that they do not exceed the pay guidelines and are consistent with appropriate ranges. Then use the data to feed back the outcomes of pay forecasts and budgets.
5. *Analyze forecasts.* Examine each manager's forecast, and recommend changes based on noted inequities among different managers.
6. *Review and revise forecasts and budgets with management.* Consult with managers regarding the analysis and any recommended changes. Obtain top-management approval of forecasts.
7. *Conduct feedback with management.* Present statistical summaries of the forecasting data by department, and establish unit goals.
8. *Monitor budgeted versus actual increases.* Control the forecasted increases versus the actual increases by tracking and reporting periodic status to management.

The result of the forecasting cycle is a budget for the upcoming plan year for each organization's unit as well as estimated pay treatment for each employee. The budget does not lock in the manager to the exact pay change recommended for each employee. Rather, it represents a plan, and deviations due to unforeseen changes such as performance improvements and unanticipated promotions are common. The approach places responsibility for pay management on the managers by requiring them to plan the pay treatment for each of their employees. The compensation manager takes on the role of advisor to operating management's use of the system.[28]

Embedded (Design) Controls

Controls on managers' pay decisions come from two different aspects of the compensation process: (1) controls that are inherent in the design of the techniques and (2) the formal **budgeting** process discussed above. Think back to the many techniques already discussed: job analysis and evaluation, skill- and competency-based plans, policy lines, **range minimums** and **maximums**, broad bands, performance evaluation, gain sharing, and salary-increase guidelines. In addition to their primary purposes, these techniques also regulate managers' pay decisions by guiding what managers can and cannot do. Controls are built into these techniques to direct them toward the pay system objectives. A few of these controls are examined below.

Range Maximums and Minimums

Ranges set the maximum and minimum dollars to be paid for specific work. The maximum is an important cost control. Ideally, it represents the highest value the organization places on the output of the work. With job-based structures, skills and knowledge possessed by employees may be more valuable in another job, but the range maximum represents the maximum worth to an organization of work performed in a particular job. When Walmart installed range maximums and minimums for its jobs, its critics accused the company of "capping wages" of its workers. Those readers who recall the discussion in **Chapter 8** on designing ranges recognize that specific jobs may have a maximum rate (a cap) but individuals may still be able to increase their pay through promotions, profit sharing, and so on.[29]

When employees are paid above the range maximum, these rates are called **red circle rates**. Most employers "freeze" red circle rates until the ranges are shifted upward by market update adjustments so that the rate is back within the range again. An organization also has the option to combine a salary freeze with the use of merit bonuses, which unlike merit increases, do not become part of base salary. If red circle rates become common throughout an organization, then the design of the ranges and the evaluation of the jobs should be reexamined. **Green circle rates** refer to instances where employees are paid below the minimum. As with red circle rates, organizations typically take steps to make sure these are temporary.

Range minimums are just that: the minimum value placed on the work. Often rates below the minimum are used for trainees. Pay below minimum may also occur if outstanding employees receive a number of rapid promotions and pay increases have not kept up.

Broad Bands

Broad bands are intended to offer managers greater flexibility compared to a grade-range design. Usually broad bands are accompanied by external market "reference rates" and "shadow ranges" that guide managers' decisions. Bands may be more about career management than pay decisions. Rather, the control is in the salary budgets given to managers. The manager has flexibility in pay decisions, as long as the total pay comes in under the budget.

Promotions and External versus Internal Hires

Promotion-based pay increases are often substantial, meaning that cost control efforts must monitor both rates of promotion and the salary increase that is given with promotions. Some organizations limit the number of promotions permitted within a time period and some also limit the number of grades/levels that an employee can advance as well as the size of the promotion salary increase.[30] Another, more strategic issue concerns the degree to which positions are filled from the inside via promotion versus the use of outside hires.[31] Outside hires often command a pay premium and, to the degree that their higher pay is known to other employees, internal equity pressures may, in some cases, result in higher pay for current employees as a means to preserve current norms regarding relative pay.

Compa-Ratios

Range midpoints reflect the pay policy line of the employer in relationship to external competition. To assess how managers actually pay employees in relation to the midpoint, an index called a **compa-ratio** is often calculated:

$$\text{Compa-ratio} = \frac{\text{average rate actual paid}}{\text{range midpoint}}$$

A compa-ratio of less than 1 means that, on average, employees in a range are paid below the midpoint. That is, managers are paying less than the intended policy. There may be several valid reasons for such a situation. The majority of employees may be new or recent hires; they may be poor performers; or promotion may be so rapid that few employees stay in the job long enough to get into the high end of the range.

A compa-ratio greater than 1 means that, on average, the rates exceed the intended policy. The reasons for this are the reverse of those mentioned above: a majority of workers with high seniority, high performance, low turnover, few new hires, or low promotion rates. Compa-ratios may be calculated for individual employees, for each range, for organization units, or for functions.

Other examples of controls designed into the pay techniques include the mutual sign-offs on job descriptions required of supervisors and subordinates. Another is slotting new jobs into the pay structure via job evaluation, which helps ensure that jobs are compared on the same factors. Similarly, an organization-wide performance management system is intended to ensure that all employees are evaluated on similar factors.

Variable Pay

The essence of variable pay is that it must be re-earned each period, in contrast to conventional merit pay increases or across-the-board increases that increase the base on which the following year's increase is calculated. We have distinguished between fixed and variable pay and noted multiple times that organizations have moved toward greater reliance on variable pay. It is important enough that it bears repeating again. As we saw in **Exhibit 18.6**, organizations have increased their use of variable pay relative to traditional base pay increases.

Increases added into base pay have compounding effects on costs, and these costs are significant. For example, a $15-a-week take-home pay added onto a $40,000 base compounds into a cash flow of $503,116 over 10 years. In addition, costs for some benefits also increase. By comparison, the organization could use that same $503,000 to keep base pay at $40,000 a year and pay a 26.8 percent bonus every single year. As the example shows, the greater the ratio of variable pay to base pay, the more flexible the organization's labor costs.

Apply this flexibility to the general labor cost model in **Exhibit 18.1**. The greater the ratios of contingent to core workers and variable to base pay, the greater the variable component of labor costs and the greater the options available to managers to control these costs. A caution: Although variability in pay and employment may be an advantage for managing labor costs, it may be less appealing from the standpoint of managing effective treatment of employees. The inherent financial insecurity built into variable plans may adversely affect employees' financial well-being, especially for lower-paid workers. Managing labor costs is only one objective for managing compensation.

Analyzing Costs

Costing out wage proposals is commonly done prior to recommending pay increases, especially for collective bargaining. For example, it is useful to bear in mind the dollar impact of a 1-cent-per-hour wage change or a 1 percent change in payroll as one goes into bargaining. Knowing these figures, negotiators can quickly compute the impact of a request for a 9 percent wage increase.

Commercial compensation software is available to analyze almost every aspect of compensation information. Software can easily compare past estimates to what actually occurred (e.g., the percentage of employees that actually did receive a merit increase and the amount). It can simulate alternate wage proposals and compare their potential effects. It can also help evaluate salary survey data and simulate the cost impact of incentive and gain-sharing options.

MANAGING REVENUES

Although the cost of compensation is most easily measured (and managed/controlled), we cannot forget that compensation, via its incentive and sorting effects on the workforce and its central role in supporting strategy execution, is also central to driving future revenues. According to one study, only about one-third of organizations actually calculate the cost and value added by their pay programs.[32] Not surprisingly, another survey reports that assessment of the impact of compensation on revenues falls especially short, with about 70 percent of the compensation specialists reporting their tools as "ineffective" to determine the value added. However, a handful of companies, supported by consultants and researchers, are beginning to analyze the value added (or return on investments) of pay decisions and how that influences revenues.[33] This analysis requires a shift in how compensation is viewed. Compensation becomes an investment as well as an expense. Decisions are based on analysis of the return on this investment. The hope is to answer questions such as, "So what" if returns are expected from spending more on the offensive team (as do the Seattle Seahawks), or from showering rewards on the top performers (as does General Electric), or from a new incentive plan based on a balanced scorecard (as does Citigroup)?[34]

Exhibit 18.9 illustrates the approach to assessing value gained in different ways, which directly or indirectly influence revenues. The company in this exhibit has already done an analysis that suggests that the top 10 percent of employees improve returns by about 2 to 5 percent of their average salary. Now the company is considering two actions:

1. Implement a bonus plan based on balanced scorecards for individual managers.
2. Increase the differentiation between top performers and average performers.

Exhibit 18.9 shows the analysis of potential value added by these two options. The returns are grouped into four types: recruiting and retaining top talent, reducing turnover of top performers, revenue enhancement, and productivity gains. The logic, assumptions, measures, and estimates of gains are described in the exhibit. The cautious reader will immediately see that the assumptions are critical and based on research evidence, best estimates, and judgments.

The practice of analyzing the returns from compensation decisions is in its early stages. The promise is that it will direct thinking beyond treating compensation as only an expense to considering the returns gained as well. Our discussion of utility analysis in the Appendix to **Chapter 7** is an example of one approach.[35] Advocates want to develop compensation managers' *analytical literacy*. Readers will recognize the similarity to topics in their finance and operations management classes. Nevertheless, managers still must use their heads as well as their models. Treating compensation as an investment and employees as human capital risks losing sight of them as people.[36] The fairness objective must not get lost in the search for ROI.

Using Compensation to Retain (and Recruit) Top Employees

Recall that one aspect of the sorting effect is that high performers will tend to move from organizations that do not adequately compensate them for the high value they create to organizations that do. Some in this group will be "pushed" to look for another job because of their perception that they are not equitably paid. However, a substantial share of employees, especially high performers, leave their jobs because of being "pulled" by opportunities elsewhere. They leave not as a result of being dissatisfied with their current job and/or as a result of looking for a new job, but rather because an unsolicited opportunity from a proactive organization came their way.[37] Indeed, Google's former top human resources executive takes the view that the best people are doing well where they are and that it is important to invest resources to learn who they are. They may not actively search or apply for jobs at Google, but Google wants to cultivate these "passive

EXHIBIT 18.9 Examples of How Compensation Can Influence Revenues (directly or indirectly)

			Value Added	
Description of Value	**Assumptions**	**Measure**	**Low Estimate**	**High Estimate**
		Recruiting/Retaining Top Talent		
Increase pool of top people applying; Increase percent accepting offers; Decrease time to fill position	Top performers improve returns by 2% to 5% of average salary ($68,000)	Increase top talent yield ratios and turnover rates	Increases revenues by $1,400/ top person	Improves revenues by $3,400/ top person
		Reduced Turnover/Replacement Costs		
Reduction of recruiting costs due to lower turnover of top performers	Reduction in turnover of one top performer results in a savings of $25,000 (based on an average salary of $68,000)	Savings of $25,000/ top performer Productivity savings reflected in "loss of revenue" section	$100,000 for a reduction of four "resigned" top employees	$500,000 for a reduction of 10 "resigned" top employees
		Revenue Enhancers		
Reduced loss of revenue due to faster time to fill key customer-facing (sales, technical support) and other key positions Greater revenue because of focus on revenue and customer goals as driven by the balanced scorecard Increased revenue because of stronger and longer-lasting customer relationships due to retention of key/top performers through market competitiveness and pay differentiation	Revenue will increase by some percentage (e.g., 5%) Headcount remains constant	Revenue increase Assume current revenue of $2 billion	2% or $40 million	5% or $100 million

Description of Value	Assumptions	Measure	Value Added: Low Estimate	Value Added: High Estimate
		Productivity Gains		
Increased productivity by retaining top performers through significant pay differentiation and market-competitive base pay	Retaining and engaging more of the top employees results in significant productivity gains and revenue generation because top employees are 25% to 50% more productive than the average employee	Increased revenue (reflected in revenue gains-above) Headcount reduction (need fewer employees or grow slower)	A reduction in 10 headcount results in a savings of $900,000 ($68,000 employee + benefit cost)	A reduction in 50 headcount results in a savings of $4.5-million
Increased productivity of all employees because of greater perception of "internal alignment" and "market competitiveness" resulting from paying competitive with the market and common programs	Increasing the productivity of all results in increased revenue, customer satisfaction, or fewer headcount		A reduction in 1 headcount results in a savings of $90,000	A reduction in 5 headcount results in a savings of $450,000
	Terminating low-productivity employees and replacing them with high-productivity employees result in significant productivity gains and revenue generation	Headcount reduction because *fewer* top performers achieve the same results as more *lower* performers		

job seekers," even if it takes years because Google sees successfully hiring such people as a path to higher revenues.[38] The implication is that their current employer would do well to keep compensation current and competitive (given their skills and value/revenues generated) because other (proactive) organizations will eventually find them. It also means that organizations can be proactive too not just in terms of keeping valuable employees they already have, but in looking for people employed elsewhere who can come and create value and higher revenues.

MANAGING PAY TO SUPPORT STRATEGY AND CHANGE

In **Chapter 2**, we noted the important role of pay in supporting the business strategy and the HR strategy. We saw that organizations with different business strategies often have correspondingly different compensation strategies. We also saw, using the ability-motivation-opportunity (AMO) framework that pay plays a crucial role. These alignment issues must be managed successfully to drive future revenues (and control costs). Compensation often plays a singular role when organizations restructure. Strategic changes in the business strategy mean the compensation strategy must be realigned as well. Looking back again to **Chapter 2**, pay's incentive effects can help redirect and reenergize employee efforts. Its sorting effects can help replace current employees who fit the old system, but not the new system, with new employees who do fit. The bigger the change, the bigger the sorting effects and the more likely that there will be a difficult period of adjustment as part of the change. The question is whether the short-term pain will be worth it to reposition the organization to better succeed going forward in terms of achieving the goals of stakeholders (owners, employees, customers, and so forth).

Pay is a powerful signal of change; changing people's pay captures their attention. At a broader level, pay changes can play two roles in any restructuring. Pay can be a *leading catalyst* for change or a *follower* of change. Shifts from conventional across-the-board annual increases to profit sharing or from narrow job descriptions and ranges to broad roles and bands signal major change to employees. Determining the role pay plays is an important part of a strategic perspective, as you will recall from the **Chapter 2** discussion of strategic mapping.

Microsoft's shift from its uniquely aggressive stock options to less risky stock awards illustrates the point. Microsoft used its change in the pay mix to communicate a shift from a "workaholic–get rich quick" to a "work hard–get paid well" approach. Whether this shift acts as a catalyst or a support is open to debate. As a catalyst, it communicates change more strongly and vividly than any rhetoric could. It helps drive recruiting and retention. Yet it may be that Microsoft had already changed as an organization. Faced with murmuring employees (their options were underwater) and external conditions (an accounting rule change that required options to be treated as an expense) the shift in pay mix merely confirmed reality–that Microsoft had changed.

Whether pay is a leading catalyst for change or a follower of change, compensation managers must learn how to implement and manage change. Not only must they know the strategic and technical aspects of compensation, they also must know how to bargain, resolve disputes, empower employees, and develop teams. Being able to grab bullets in midflight doesn't hurt, either.[39]

COMMUNICATION: MANAGING THE MESSAGE

Compensation communicates. It signals what is important and what is not. If you receive a pay increase for one more year of experience on your job, then one more year is important. If the pay increase is equal to any change in the CPI, then the CPI and its real meaning is important. If the increase is for moving to a bigger job or for outstanding performance, then a bigger job or outstanding performance is important. Changes in a pay system also send a powerful message. Microsoft's shift from stock options to grants tells everyone (current and future employees and stockholders) to expect lower risks and lower returns.

Pay Secrecy versus Transparency/Openness

Earlier in this book, we stressed that employees must understand the pay system. Their understanding is shaped indirectly through the paychecks they receive and directly via formal communication about their pay, their performance, and the markets in which the organization competes. An argument for employee involvement in the design of pay systems is that it increases understanding. Two surveys are revealing. A Watson Wyatt survey of 13,000 employees reported that about only 35 percent of them understood the link between their job performance and the pay they receive. (Watson Wyatt failed to point out that some workers may simply believe that in their organizations there is no real link!)[40] WorldatWork did a second survey of 6,000 employees. Only about one-third of them said they understood how pay ranges are determined or had a reasonable idea of what their increase would be if they were promoted. Fewer than half understood how their own pay increases are calculated.[41] **Exhibit 18.10** provides further insight into employee (lack of) pay knowledge. Of note is that only 8 and 4 percent, respectively, of compensation professionals strongly agree that employees know their own pay range (e.g., the maximum they can earn without getting promoted), the pay range above them (so, how much they could earn if they were promoted). By contrast, 15 and 20 percent, respectively, strongly disagree that employees have this information, which presumably is relevant to their work motivation. Finally, only a minority of respondents agree that pay-related information is "shared openly" in their organizations.

Two reasons are usually given for communicating pay information. The first is that considerable resources have been devoted to designing a fair and equitable system that is intended to attract and retain qualified people and motivate performance. For managers and employees to gain an accurate view of the pay system–one that perhaps influences their attitudes about it–they need to be informed. Of course, one might observe that increasing the accuracy of employee perceptions through pay openness is most useful in cases where the compensation system is well designed and will be perceived as fair and credible by employees. In that case, from a motivational point of view, it would certainly make sense to communicate and demonstrate to employees that those with consistently high performance receive higher compensation (including via more promotions) than others.[42] Thus, it is quite interesting (see **Exhibit 18.11**) that most (25% + 41% = 66%) U.S. private sector employees report working in organizations where pay secrecy is the policy and few (17%) report that pay information is made public. The lack of pay knowledge among employees discussed above now becomes easier to understand. As **Exhibit 18.11** also shows, there is much more pay openness in the public sector (both because of higher union coverage and because taxpayers wish to know how their tax dollars are spent).

Finally, it is important to keep in mind that a pay secrecy policy in private sector organizations may be illegal. Under the National Labor Relations Act, it is illegal if it interferes with "concerted action" by employees. In addition, Executive Order 13665, "Non-Retaliation for Disclosure of Compensation Information," prohibits federal contractors or subcontractors from "discharging or discriminating in any other way against employees or applicants who inquire about, discuss, or disclose their own compensation or the compensation of another employee or applicant."[43] It serves to modify existing Executive Order 11246 with the aim of making it more effective. A major rationale given is that to the degree discrimination explains why men and women are paid differently, "strictures against revealing compensation can conceal compensation disparities among

EXHIBIT 18.10 Pay Communication and Employee Knowledge of Pay

	Strongly Disagree	Disagree	Neither Agree nor Disagree	Agree	Strongly Agree
Employees know the pay ranges for their [*own*] pay grade or position	15%	26%	18%	33%	8%
Employees know what the pay ranges are for the grade or the positions *immediately above their own*	20%	40%	19%	17%	4%
Compensation program information is shared openly by the organization	12%	35%	17%	29%	7%

Source: Scott, Dow, Tom McMullen, Bill Bowbinl, and John Shields. "Alignment of Business Strategies, Organization Structures and Reward Programs: A Survey of Policies, Practices and Effectiveness," WorldatWork, May 2009.

employees. This makes it impossible for an employee to know he or she is being underpaid compared to his or her peers. If compensation remains hidden, employees who are being unfairly paid less because of their gender or race will remain unaware of the problem and will be unable to exercise their rights by filing a complaint pursuant to the Executive Order."

The second (and related) reason for communicating pay information is that, according to some research, employees seem to misunderstand the pay system. For example, they tend to overestimate the pay of those in lower-level jobs and to underestimate the pay of those in higher-level jobs. They assume that the pay structure is more compressed than it actually is. If differentials are underestimated, their motivational value is, as noted above, diminished, because they underestimate the payoff to high performance.

Further, there is some evidence to suggest that the goodwill engendered by the act of being open about pay may also affect perceptions of pay equity. Interestingly, the research also shows that employees in companies with open pay communication policies are as inaccurate in estimating pay differentials as those in companies in which pay secrecy prevails.[44] (Caution: Most of this research was done more than 20 years ago.) However, employers in companies with open pay policies tend to express higher satisfaction with their pay and with the pay system.[45]

But, it increasingly appears that employee reactions to pay transparency are not always positive.[46] For the most part, reactions are positive to *process* pay transparency, which concerns sharing information with employees about how pay is determined. On the other hand, reaction to outcome pay transparency, disclosure of actual pay levels, depends on one's pay. Those paid above the average react positively, whereas those below average react negatively (due to low perceived distributive justice) to this disclosure.[47] Other research agrees that employees who perceive themselves as being paid being well below average are not keen on outcome pay transparency, but also finds this reluctance among those who perceive themselves as paid well above average.[48] Further, research indicates that employee reactions to pay secrecy versus pay openness depend on equity sensitivity, with those more sensitive to whether pay is fair (given inputs like performance) being most likely to respond favorably (higher performance, stronger perceived performance–pay instrumentality) to pay openness.[49] Still other research, in a university setting, found that making pay information on other employees in the university systems more explicitly available resulted in more pay comparisons by employees (especially with peers in the same department) and lower satisfaction and greater search intentions among employees paid below the median (consistent with above) for their department and occupation. This finding led the study authors to conclude that "employers have a strong incentive to impose pay secrecy rules," but also noted that another result could be a change in the composition of the workforce.[50] Another way to put

EXHIBIT 18.11 Pay Secrecy Policies, Private and Public Sector

	Private Sector Workers	Public Sector Workers
The discussion of wages and salaries at work is ***formally prohibited,*** and/or employees caught discussing wage and salary information could be punished	25%	6%
The discussion of wages and salaries at work is ***discouraged by managers***	41%	9%
Wage and salary information ***can be discussed*** in the workplace	17%	15%
Wage and salary information is ***public***	17%	70%

Source: Institute for Women's Policy Research, Pay Secrecy and Wage Discrimination. Fact Sheet IWPR #C382, June 2011.

it is that being more open with pay information will decrease the satisfaction of some employees. One reason is that most employees believe their performance is above average (even though that is not possible).[51] So, an employer must be prepared to address that consequence. However, an employer will also want to consider who is dissatisfied and why. To the degree that pay is based on performance, being more open with pay could result in positive sorting effects over time to the extent that it is low performers who are dissatisfied and they leave and are replaced by higher performing employees. A laboratory study found some evidence that more open pay not only had positive incentive effects on performance (especially when performance was measured in relative terms), but also that there were positive sorting effects of the type just suggested.[52]

Pay Communication: General Principles

In the case of benefits too, communication plays a potentially important role. We know that employees greatly underestimate the value of their benefits, which is a major concern given that benefits add roughly 40 cents on top of every dollar spent on cash compensation.[53]

WorldatWork recommends a six-stage process of communication, similar to that shown in **Exhibit 18.12**.[54]

Step 1 is, not surprisingly, defining the objectives of the communication program. Is it to ensure that employees fully understand all the components of the compensation system? Is it to change performance expectations? Or is it to help employees make informed health care choices? While specifying objectives as a first step seems obvious, doing so is often overlooked in the rush to design an attractive brochure, website, or CD.

Step 2 is to collect information from executives, managers, and employees to assess their current perceptions, attitudes, and understanding of the subject. Information may be gathered through online opinion surveys and focus groups to identify problems in understanding the compensation system.

Step 3 is a communication program that will convey the information needed to accomplish the original objectives. There is no standard approach on what to communicate to individuals about their own pay or that of their colleagues. Some organizations adopt a *marketing approach.* That includes consumer attitude surveys about the product, snappy advertising about the pay policies, and elaborate websites expounding policies and rationale. The objective is to manage expectations and attitudes about pay. In contrast, the *communication approach* tends to focus on explaining practices, details, and the way pay is determined. The marketing

EXHIBIT 18.12 The Compensation Communication Cycle

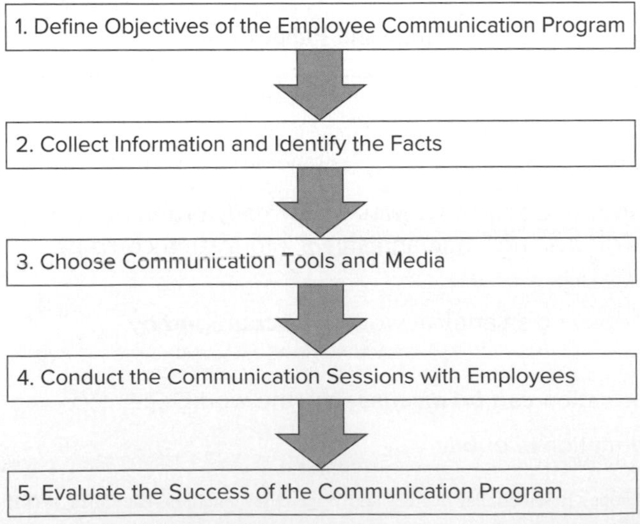

approach focuses on the strategy, values, and advantages of overall policies and may be silent on specifics such as range maximums, increase guides, and the like.

Steps 4 and 5 of the communication process are to determine the most effective media, in light of the message and the audience, and to conduct the campaign. The message can be fine-tuned, depending on the audience. Executives, for example, should be interested in how the compensation programs fit the business strategy. Managers need to know how to use the development and motivation aspects of the compensation program for the people they supervise. Employees may want to know the processes and policies as well as specifics about how their pay is determined. The danger is overload–information is so detailed that employees get snowed under sorting through it.

Step 6 of the communication process suggests that the program be evaluated. Did it accomplish its goals? Pay communication often has unintended consequences.[55] For example, improving employees' knowledge about pay may cause some initial short-term concerns. Over the years, employees may have rationalized a set of relationships between their pay and the perceived pay and efforts of others. Receiving accurate information may require that those perceptions be adjusted.

e-Compensation

One compensation manager reports having a great deal of difficulty with an employee who used the Moving.com ("Compare Cost of Living in Cities" section) website ***www.moving.com*** to determine that he should receive a 30 percent pay differential to accompany his transfer from one office to another. In contrast, the manager's information showed a differential of around 12 to 15 percent. How can you judge the accuracy of information obtained on the Web? How would you deal with the unhappy employee?

Say What? (Or, What to Say?)

As noted above, if the pay system is not based on work-related or business-related logic, then the wisest course is probably to avoid formal communication until the system is put in order. However, avoiding *formal* communication is not synonymous with avoiding communication. Employees are constantly getting intended and unintended messages through the pay treatment they receive.

Some employers communicate the range for an incumbent's present job and for all the jobs in a typical career path or progression to which employees can logically aspire. Some also communicate the typical pay increases that can be expected for poor, satisfactory, and top performance. The rationale given is that employees exchange data (not always factual) and/or guess at normal treatment and that the rumor mills are probably incorrect. However, as we saw just above, employee pay knowledge is often quite limited.

How people process information and make decisions, as shown in **Exhibit 18.13**, offers some new ideas when contemplating compensation communications.[56]

Opening the Books

There are some who advocate going beyond the sharing of pay information to the sharing of all financial information with employees.[57] Employees at engine rebuilder Springfield Remanufacturing receive weekly peeks at everything from revenues to labor costs. The employees, who own 31 percent of the company stock, believe that this "open-book" approach results in high commitment and an understanding of how to maintain competitiveness. Whole Foods' open-paybook approach was described in **Chapter 1**. Most employers don't share information with such gusto, but they are increasingly disclosing more to their employees. Some are even providing basic business and financial training to help employees better understand the information. Devotees of opening the books and providing financial training believe these methods will improve attitudes and performance, but there is no research to support this. With salary data available on the Internet (albeit often inaccurate and misleading), developing in-house compensation portals has appeal.

At the minimum, the most important information to be communicated is the work-related and business-related rationales on which pay systems are based. Some employees may not agree with these rationales or the results, but at least it will be clear that pay is determined by something other than the whims of their supervisors.

STRUCTURING THE COMPENSATION FUNCTION AND ITS ROLES

Compensation professionals seem to be constantly reevaluating where within the organization the responsibility for the design and administration of pay systems should be located. The organizational arrangements of the compensation function vary widely.[58] Other key issues include the use of enterprise information systems and ethics issues for compensation professionals.

Centralization–Decentralization (and/or Outsourcing)

An important issue related to structuring the function revolves around the degree of decentralization (or centralization) in the overall organization structure. *Decentralized* refers to a management strategy of giving separate business units the responsibility of designing and administering their own systems. This contrasts with

EXHIBIT 18.13 Guidance from the Research on Pay Communication

Behavior	What Is It?	So What?
Persistence of beliefs	Reluctance to accept evidence that contradicts existing beliefs.	Changing existing beliefs requires actively engaging employees in pay system design and communication.
Anchoring/framing	Initial data strongly affect decisions/beliefs.	First data matters, for example, market data swamps job-evaluation results. Previous bonus sets expectation for future bonus.
Herding	Following fashions in programs/techniques.	Benchmark selectively. Use pilot programs and test trials to guide.
Pattern recognition	People "discover" patterns in random events. They believe correlation means causation.	Higher pay may not mean higher performance; higher performance may not mean higher pay.

a *centralized* strategy, which locates the design and administration responsibility at corporate headquarters. A centralized compensation strategy and function is more likely to be found in smaller and/or single line of business organizations. This "one size fits all" approach is more likely to make sense when the entire company mostly competes in a single product market. Examples include Herman Miller (furniture) and McDonald's (quick service food).[59] However, in organizations (e.g., IBM) that are larger and/or compete in different product (or geographic) markets, human resource and compensation strategies are more likely to need to be tailored to fit those different contexts. In such cases, compensation professionals are increasingly likely to be embedded in each business unit. Typically, corporate will retain some number of compensation professionals, perhaps in what is known as a center for expertise. This group provides an internal consulting capability that human resource professionals in the business units, who are often human resource generalists, can be drawn on to assist in the design of compensation strategies. The mix of corporate and business unit compensation expertise is a balancing act. Too big of a corporate group risks becoming out of touch with specific business unit needs. Too many staff in the business units risks reinventing the wheel, duplication/redundancy of expertise, and higher costs. Over time, it is not unusual to see the pendulum swing within companies back and forth between more or less centralization.

Other, more decentralized organizations, such as Eaton and GE, have relatively small corporate compensation staffs. Sometimes, their primary responsibility is to manage the systems by which executives and the corporate staff are paid (although GE corporate compensation drives the salary planning process companywide). These professionals may operate in a purely advisory capacity to other organization subunits. The subunits, in turn, may employ their own compensation specialists. Or the subunits may choose to employ only personnel generalists rather than compensation specialists and may turn to outside compensation consultants to purchase the expertise required on specific compensation issues.

AES, an electric power company, has no compensation unit at all. They don't even have an HR department. Compensation functions are handled by teams of managers. Decentralizing certain aspects of pay design and administration has considerable appeal. Pushing these responsibilities (and expenses) close to the units, managers, and employees affected by them may help ensure that decisions are business-related. However, decentralization is not without dilemmas. For example, it may be difficult to transfer employees from one business unit to another. A pay system may support a subunit's objectives but run counter to the overall corporate objectives. Also, we have seen time and again that decentralization, which by definition includes less direct control of what managers do, can contribute to legal problems. As noted in **Chapter 17**, for example, Walmart is facing sex-discrimination claims in what would be the largest class action discrimination suit to date (1.6 million or more claimants). Interestingly, Walmart has argued that "establishing a national class is unwarranted because its store managers acted with discretion" in their decisions regarding promotion and pay of workers. So, in effect, Walmart's defense is that if its managers discriminated, it was because Walmart did not have centralized control over their decisions.[60]

Flexibility within Corporatewide Principles

The answers to these and related problems of decentralization can be found in developing a set of corporatewide principles or guidelines that all must meet. The principles may differ for each major pay technique. For example, GE's business units worldwide have the flexibility to design incentive plans tailored to each unique business unit's strategies and cultures. The only guidance is to ensure that the plans adhere to GE's basic beliefs, improve financial and business objectives, and maintain or enhance GE's reputation.

Keep in mind that the pay system is one of many management systems used in the organization. Consequently, it must be congruent with these other systems. For example, it may be appealing, on paper at least, to decentralize some of the compensation functions. However, if financial data and other management systems are not also decentralized, the pay system may be at odds with other systems.

Reengineering and Outsourcing

Value chain analysis and Six Sigma are processes used to improve quality and ensure that value is added by each technique and at each stage in a process. For the compensation system, the basic question to ask is, "Does each specific activity (technique) directly contribute to our objectives?" If some added value isn't apparent, then the question is, "How should it be redesigned? Or should it be dropped?" Of those activities that do add value, the next question is, "Who should do it?" "Should the activity be done in-house, or can others do it more effectively? That is, should it be outsourced?"

Outsourcing is a viable alternative as organizations struggle with activities that do not directly contribute to objectives. These are often referred to as transactional activities, which are not unique to the organization and might be done cheaper (and perhaps also better) by an outside provider. On the other hand, more transformational or strategic activities (e.g., what pay-for-performance strategy would best align with the business strategy) are less likely to be outsourced.[61]

Cost savings are the major potential advantage of outsourcing. All those compensation pros can be laid off and/or retrained and reassigned to other work. Sometimes, the quality of the service provided may increase also. A firm that does nothing but administer retirement benefits may be able to do a better job than a firm whose primary business is something else (e.g., making furniture or cars, selling quick service food). Major potential disadvantages include less responsiveness to unique employee–manager problems, less control over decisions that are often critical to all employees (i.e., their pay), and information leaks to rivals and competitors. In addition, as with any contract, while an agreement may be signed stating that an outsourcing firm will provide a certain set of services and at a certain level, either side may subsequently find that their vision of the agreement and their experience of what is actually delivered may end up being different.[62]

Balancing Flexibility and Control

One of the major attacks on traditional compensation plans is that they often degenerate into bureaucratic nightmares that hinder the organization's ability to respond to competitive pressures. Some recommend reducing the controls and guidelines inherent in any pay plan. Hence, banding eliminates or at least reduces the impact of range maximums and minimums. Replacing merit grids with bonuses eliminates the link between the pay increase and the employees' salary position in the range and performance rating. Replacing job evaluation with skill- or competency-based plans permits assigning employees to a variety of work, regardless of their pay.

Such approaches are consistent with the oft-heard plea that managers should be free to manage pay. Or, as some more bluntly claim, pay decisions are too important to be left to compensation professionals. Yet, permitting managers to be free to pay employees as they judge best rests on a basic premise: Managers will use pay to achieve the organization's objectives—efficiency, fairness, and compliance with regulations—rather than their own objectives. But the ongoing leadership scandals in some corporations and public agencies casts doubt on this premise.

Clearly, some balance between hidebound controls and chaos is required to ensure that pay decisions are directed at the organization's goals yet permit sufficient flexibility to respond to unique situations. Achieving the balance becomes the art of managing compensation.

A final issue related to pay design and administration is the skills and competencies required in compensation managers. The grandest strategy and structure may seem well designed, well thought out in the abstract, but could be a disaster if people qualified to carry it out are not part of the staff. In view of the importance of a well-trained staff, both WorldatWork and the Society of Human Resource Managers (SHRM) have professional development programs to entice readers into the compensation field.

Making Information Useful—Compensation Enterprise Systems

A friend of ours e-mailed from Shanghai that "six months after we have acquired this operation from the government, I still cannot get an accurate headcount. I do not know how many people we actually employ or who should get paychecks!" That manager clearly needs more information. But most managers find themselves overwhelmed with too much information. The challenge is to make the information useful.

Compensation software transforms data into useful information and guides decision making. Many software packages that serve a variety of purposes are available.[63] Some of them support *employee self-service,* by which employees can access their personal information, make choices about which health care coverage they prefer, allocate savings between growth or value investment funds, access vacation schedules, or check out a list of child or elder care service providers. *Manager self-service* helps managers pay their employees appropriately. *Communication portals,* designed for employees or managers, explain compensation policies and practices, answer frequently asked questions, and explain how these systems affect their pay.[64] Other software *processes transactions*. It standardizes forms, performs some analysis, and creates reports at the click of the mouse. The advantage is that all employees at all locations are on the same system.

While compensation software is proliferating, what remains a scarcer resource is the intellectual capital: the compensation knowledge and judgment required to understand which information, analyses, and reports are useful. Part of this intellectual capital includes analytical (read "statistical and math") skills. Another part is knowledge of the business. A shortage of this knowledge among compensation managers not only limits the usefulness of compensation software but also limits the contribution of compensation management.

Computers inevitably bring up the issue of confidentiality. If personal compensation data are accessible to employees and managers, privacy and security issues as well as ethical and legal issues emerge. Regulations vary around the world. The European Union has issued the Data Privacy Directive, which is significantly stronger than U.S. regulations.[65] Unauthorized users, both inside and outside the corporation, remain a threat.

Ethics: Managing or Manipulating?

Compensation ethics is not an oxymoron. But absent a professional code of behaviors and values, it is a challenge for compensation managers to ensure that their actions *are* ethical. The Web page for the compensation society WorldatWork includes the topic of ethics. Public discussion of ethics in compensation topics such as executive pay or backdating option grants benefits from the voices of informed compensation practitioners.

Managing compensation ethically is increasingly complicated for several reasons. First, pay really matters; it is important to all of us. Second is the fierce pressure to achieve results. The increased use of pay for performance, which is based on results achieved and exceeding targets, can contribute to these pressures. However, assessing results sometimes has a "smoke and mirrors" feel to it. At an organization's compensation strategy session that we attended, the chief financial officer observed that it was possible to "manage our reported earnings within several percentage points of the target. We can exceed analysts' and shareholder expectations by 1 to 10 percent." This was relatively easy for this particular company since about one-third of its earnings came from liquid investments in other companies. The remainder was revenue from its products and services. The implication of managing earnings for employees' profit-sharing payouts and executive stock valuations were not ignored. The point is that measures of financial performance do not provide an immutable gold standard. They can be "managed."[66]

Where Is the Compensation Professional?

Performance-based pay is not the only area that presents ethical dilemmas. Misusing and even failing to understand survey statistics, manipulating job evaluations, peer-company competitive data, masking overtime and pay discrimination violations, failure to understand that correlation does not mean causation, and recommending pay programs without addressing their expected costs and returns should force us to take a hard look at what we are doing.[67]

Stephen Landry, the former HR director at Sycamore Networks, reports that the company's chief financial officer pressured him to change the hiring dates of some employees to make their stock option grants worth more money. These actions were to be kept hidden from the company auditors. Instead, Landry told executives these actions were unethical and probably illegal. He was fired. Internal memos from the company reveal a "risk assessment" of the action becoming exposed. Changing the date on documents was judged a low risk since the original grant "has been deleted from the system in its entirety." Landry is suing and the SEC is investigating. If Mr. Landry's experience is not enough for the professional compensation community, over at Cablevision, they backdated stock grants to a dead executive.[68]

A starting point to judge the ethics of our behavior may be our compensation model, presented with the advice: "Strive to achieve both efficiency and fairness."

Your Turn — Communication by Copier

Deb Allen's life-altering discovery at work really "communicated" her company's pay practices. Swamped with work at an asset-management firm, she went into the office over the weekend and found a document abandoned on the copy machine. The document contained the base compensation, raises, performance ratings, and bonus information for 80 of her colleagues.

Ms. Allen was outraged that a noted screw-up was making $65,000 a year more than more competent colleagues, while some new hires were earning almost $200,000 more than their counterparts with more experience. The discovery led her to question why she was working weekends for less pay than others were getting. "I just couldn't stand the inequity of it," she says. Three months later she quit.

But Ms. Allen couldn't bring herself to share the information with her colleagues. "I would have been better off not knowing any of that," she explains. "I couldn't give it to people who were still working there because it would make them depressed, like it made me depressed."[69]

1. How would you have reacted if you were Ms. Allen? Explain why.
2. Put yourself in the place of the compensation director at Ms. Allen's company. Based on the pay model and what you now know about compensation, are there any possible business- and work-related explanations for what Ms. Allen observed (i.e., the screw-up getting $65,000 more; new hires earning $200,000 more than more-experienced employees; and Ms. Allen making less pay than others)?
3. As the compensation director, what would you do if Ms. Allen had brought you this document, and asked for your help in understanding what was going on. (Firing the person who left it on the copier is not an option. It may have been you.)

Still Your Turn

Managing Compensation Costs, Head-count, and Participation/Communication Issues

Cisco Systems, Hewlett-Packard, American Airlines, and General Motors are examples of companies that have cut employment or cut wages and/or benefits to reduce labor costs in hopes of becoming more competitive and more profitable. Indeed, American and GM went through bankruptcy in part to gain control over labor costs. In contrast, some companies—Southwest Airlines, Nucor, and Lincoln Electric—have a no-layoff practice and do not appear to have cut wages or benefits even in years when sales have declined significantly. (They have also not gone through bankruptcy.) What is the difference between these two sets of companies? Is it simply that one set of companies cares more about its employees than the other set of companies does? Or is it also the case that Southwest, Nucor, and Lincoln Electric have set up their compensation strategies in a way that makes them more able (than Cisco, HP, American, and GM) to cut labor costs when times are tough? (For more background, go to an online search engine and conduct a separate search for each company using its name and the term "layoff.") What about protecting investment in employees and employee relations?

What can an employer do to make labor costs flexible so that profits do not take as much of a beating during difficult economic times and so that fewer employees need to be laid off? If you were in charge of designing a compensation system for a company that is fairly new but is now reaching a stage and size where it needs a formal compensation system, how would you design the compensation system to have labor-cost flexibility? To what degree would you have others at the company participate in the design of the new compensation system? Who would participate? Would you follow a policy of pay openness in communicating your compensation system? Provide a rationale for your decisions.

Summary

We have now completed the discussion of the pay management process. Management includes control: control of the way managers decide individual employees' pay as well as control of overall costs of labor. As we noted, some controls are designed into the fabric of the pay system (embedded controls). The salary budgeting and forecasting processes impose additional controls. The formal budgeting process focuses on controlling labor costs and generating the financial plan for the pay system. The budget sets the limits within which the rest of the system operates.

We also noted that with the continuous change in organizations, compensation managers must understand how to manage change and be knowledgeable business partners. They are responsible for communicating information about pay in a way that treats employees fairly and honestly. The basic point is that pay systems are tools, and like any tools they need to be evaluated in terms of usefulness in achieving an organization's objectives.

Review Questions

1. How can employers control labor costs?
2. How does the management of the pay system affect pay objectives?

3. Why is the structure of the compensation function important?
4. Give some examples of how employers use inherent controls.
5. What activities in managing the pay system are likely candidates to be outsourced? Why?
6. Use **Exhibit 18.13** to explain how the research on individual decision making can be used in pay communication.

Endnotes

1. Sanford Jacoby, *The Embedded Corporation* (Princeton: Princeton University Press, 2005). For a broader historical perspective on compensation and benefits, see, Bruce R. Ellig, "*American History's Impact on Employee Pay and Benefits*" (2015, Self-published. Bruce R. Ellig LLC).
2. Wayne Cascio and John Boudreau, *Investing in People: Financial Impact of Human Resource Initiatives,* 2nd ed. (FT Press, 2015); Felix Barber and Rainer Strack, "The Surprising Economics of a 'People Business,'" *Harvard Business Review,* June 2005, pp. 81–90.
3. D. Scott, D. Morajda, T. McMullen, and R. Sperling, "Evaluating Pay Program Effectiveness," *WorldatWork Journal* 15, no. 2 (Second Quarter 2006), pp. 50–59.
4. Lindsay Scott, "Managing Labor Costs Using Pay-for-Performance," Lindsay Scott & Associates, Inc., *www.npktools.com.*
5. *Reward Transformation: Turning Rewards from Costs into an Investment* (New York: Deloitte, 2006), *www.deloitte.com.*
6. Personal communication from B. Dunn, president, McLagan Partners; D. Scott, D. Morajda, T. McMullen, and R. Sperling, "Evaluating Pay Program Effectiveness," *WorldatWork Journal* 15, no. 2 (Second Quarter 2006), pp. 50–59; John Boudreau and Peter Ramstad, "From 'Professional Business Partner' to 'Strategic Talent Leader:' What's Next for Human Resource Management," CAHRS Working Paper 02–10, Ithaca, NY.
7. B. Dunn, president, McLagan Partners; *The Lake Wobegon Salary Survey,* Lindsay Scott & Associates, Inc., www.npktools.com, 2006.
8. B. Gerhart and C. O. Trevor, "Employment Variability under Different Managerial Compensation Systems," *Academy of Management Journal* 39, no. 6 (1996), pp. 1692–1712.
9. Allen Smith, "Layoffs in Europe: Deal or No Deal?" *HR Magazine,* January 2009, pp. 71–73.
10. Charlie O. Trevor and Anthony J. Nyberg, "Keeping Your Headcount When All About You Are Losing Theirs: Downsizing, Voluntary Turnover Rates, and the Moderating Role of HR Practices," *Academy of Management Journal* 51 (2008), pp. 259–276; C. O. Trevor & R. Piyanontalee, "Discharges, Poor-Performer Quits, and Layoffs as Valued Exits: Is It Really Addition by Subtraction?" *Annual Review of Organizational Psychology and Organizational Behavior* 7 (2020), pp. 181–211.
11. Timothy Aeppel and Justin Lahart, "Lean Factories Find It Hard to Cut Jobs Even in Slump," *The Wall Street Journal,* March 9, 2009, p. A1.
12. Erin White, "Retaining Employees before an Upturn Hits," *The Wall Street Journal,* May 8, 2009, http://online.wsj.com/article/SB124178707883900633.html, September 14, 2009; Gray Yohe, "A Delicate Balance," *Human Resource Executive,* March 2, 2009, www.hreonline.com/HRE/story.jsp?storyId=1815633178query=morale, September 14, 2009.
13. F. S. Bentley, I. S. Fulmer, and R. R. Kehoe, "Payoffs for Layoffs? An Examination of CEO Relative Pay and Firm Performance Surrounding Layoff Announcements," *Personnel Psychology* 72, no. 1 (2019), pp. 81–106.
14. Clint Chadwick, Larry W. Hunter, and Stephen Walston, "Effects of Downsizing Practices on the Performance of Hospitals," *Strategic Management Journal* 25 (2004), pp. 405–427.

15. W. F. Cascio, A. Chatrath, and R. A. Christie-David, "Antecedents and Consequences of Employee and Asset Restructuring," *Academy of Management Journal* 64, no. 2 (2021), pp. 587–613.
16. Charles Duhigg, "Hospital Clients Nurture Firm's Scheduling Software," *Los Angeles Times,* June 21, 2006, p. C1.
17. David Cote, "Honeywell's CEO on How He Avoided Layoffs," *Harvard Business Review*, June 2013.
18. Susan Saulny and Robbie Brown, "On a Furlough, but Never Leaving the Cubicle," *The New York Times,* June 15, 2009; Jonathan Buck, "British Airways Urges Staff to Work without Pay," *The Wall Street Journal,* June 16, 2009; "The Quiet Americans: Employees Are Social in the Face of Pay Cuts and Compulsory Unpaid Leave," *The Economist,* June 25, 2009, www.economist.com/world/unitedstates/displaystory.cfm?story_id=13915822, September 14, 2009.
19. Riva Richmond, "How to Cut Payroll without Layoffs," *BusinessWeek*, April 3, 2009, www.businessweek.com/magazine/content/09_64/s0904048707309.htm, September 14, 2009; Matthew Boyle, "Cutting Work Hours without Cutting Staff," *BusinessWeek,* February 25, 2009, www.businessweek.com/magazine/content/09_10/b4122055789445.htm, September 14, 2009.
20. Ron Lieber, "Et Tu, AARP? Good Guys Cut 401(k)s, Too," *The New York Times,* June 27, 2009, p. B1.
21. Sandra Block, "Companies Rethink 401(k) Plan Contributions for Employees," *USA Today,* June 24, 2009,www.usatoday.com/money/perfi/retirement/2009-06-24-401kcontributions-economy_N.htm, September 14, 2009.
22. Sarah Krouse, "U.S. Companies Have a New 401(k) Fix: Spend More. Microsoft, Host Hotels, Others Raise Contributions to Retain Employees, Encourage Older Workers to Retire," *Wall Street Journal,* July 17, 2017. www.wsj.com; Vanguard. *How America Saves 2017.* https://pressroom.vanguard.com/nonindexed/How-America-Saves-2017.pdf.
23. Michael Sanserino, "Pay Raises Are the Smallest in Decades, Surveys Show," *The Wall Street Journal,* July 21, 2009; Aon Hewitt, *Annual Salary Increase Survey,* September 2011.
24. Aon Hewitt, *Annual Salary Increase Survey,* September 2011.
25. B. Gerhart and M. Fang "Pay for (Individual) Performance: Issues, Claims, Evidence and the Role of Sorting Effects," *Human Resource Management Review* 24, no. 1 (2014), pp. 41–52.
26. Carlos Tejada and Gary McWilliams, "New Recipe for Cost Savings: Replace Expensive Workers," *The Wall Street Journal,* June 11, 2003, pp. 1, A12.
27. John Watson, "Delivering Total Compensation Online at Dell," *ACA News* 42, no. 4 (April 1999), pp. 14–19.
28. Ronald T. Albright and Bridge R. Compton, *Internal Consulting Basics* (Scottsdale, AZ: American Compensation Association, 1996); John Watson, "Delivering Total Compensation Online at Dell," *ACA News* 42, no. 4 (April 1999), pp. 14–19.
29. Jennifer Hicks, an Oklahoma State University student, coined the term "yellow circle rates" while working as a compensation specialist for FastCat. Yellow circle rates result where, if you give an employee the percent raise indicated by the merit increase grid, that employee would become red circled. For Walmart information, see Steven Greenhouse and Michael Barbaro, "Wal-Mart to Add Caps and Part-Timers," *New York Times,* October 2, 2006, p. B1.
30. WorldatWork, Promotional Guidelines 2010, December 2010, www.worldatwork.org/waw/adimLink?id=45914, accessed June 22, 2012.
31. M. J. Bidwell and J. R. Keller, "Promote or Hire? Comparing Make or Buy and Competing Process Views in a Professional Service Firm," working paper, Wharton School, University of Pennsylvania. See the related article: Rachel Emma Silverman and Lauren Weber, "An Inside Job: More Firms Opt to Recruit From Within," *The Wall Street Journal*, May 29, 2012.

32. *Reward Transformation: Turning Rewards from Costs Into an Investment* (New York: Deloitte, 2006), *www.deloitte.com;* D. Scott, D. Morajda, T. McMullen, and R. Sperling, "Evaluating Pay Program Effectiveness," *WorldatWork Journal* 15, no. 2 (Second Quarter 2006), pp. 50–59.

33. Wayne Cascio, *Responsible Restructuring: Creative and Profitable Alternatives to Layoffs* (San Francisco: Berrett-Koehler, 2002); John Boudreau and Peter Ramstad, "Beyond Cost per Hire and Time to Fill: Supply-Chain Measurements for Staffing" (Los Angeles: Center for Effective Organizations, 2006); Jaap deJonge, *Watson Wyatt Human Capital Index* (New York: Watson Wyatt, 2003); S. Raza, *Optimizing Human Capital Investments for Superior Shareholder Returns* (New York: Hewitt Associates, 2006); M. Huselid and B. Becker, "Improving HR Analytical Literacy: Lessons from Moneyball," chapter 32 in M. Losey, S. Meisinger, and D. Ulrich, *The Future of Human Resource Management* (Hoboken, NJ: Wiley, 2005); J. Burton and S. Pollack, "ROI of Human Capital: The United States and Europe," *Workspan,* November 2006, pp. 28–27.

34. Ibid.

35. M. C. Sturman, C. O. Trevor, J. W. Boudreau, and B. Gerhart, "Is It Worth It to Win the Talent War? Evaluating the Utility of Performance-Based Pay," *Personnel Psychology* 56 (2003), pp. 997–1035; Wayne Cascio and John Boudreau, *Investing in People* (Saddle River, NJ: Pearson Education, 2008); Mark A. Huselid, Brian E. Becker, and Richard W. Beatty, *The Workforce Scorecard* (Boston: Harvard Business School Press, 2005).

36. Peter F. Drucker, "They're Not Employees, They're People," *Harvard Business Review,* February 2002, pp. 70–77.

37. Lee, T. H., B. Gerhart, I. Weller, and C. O. Trevor, "Understanding Voluntary Turnover: Path-Specific Job Satisfaction Effects and the Importance of Unsolicited Job Offers," *Academy of Management Journal*, 51 (2008), pp. 651–671.

38. Laszlo Bock, *Work Rules!* (New York: Twelve, 2015); Daniel Freedman, "Silicon Valley Star Search," *Wall Street Journal*, April 7, 2015, p. A11; M. L. Call, A. J. Nyberg and S. M. B. Thatcher, "Stargazing: An Integrative Conceptual Review, Theoretical Reconciliation, and Extension for Star Employee Research," *Journal of Applied Psychology* 100, no. 3 (2015), pp. 623–640.

39. Michael Beer and Mitin Nohria, "Cracking the Code of Change," *Harvard Business Review,* May–June 2000, pp. 133–141; Dave Ulrich, "A New Mandate for Human Resources," *Harvard Business Review,* January–February 1998, pp. 125–134.

40. "Growing Worker Confusion about Corporate Goals Complicates Recovery, Watson Wyatt WorkUSA Study Finds," Watson Wyatt news release, September 9, 2002.

41. Robert L. Heneman, Paul W. Mulvey, and Peter V. LeBlanc, "Improve Base Pay ROI by Increasing Employee Knowledge," *WorldatWork Journal* 11, no. 4 (Fourth Quarter 2002), pp. 22–27.

42. A. Bandura, *Social Learning Theory* (New York: General Learning Press, 1977); E. E. Lawler, *Pay and Organizational Effectiveness: A Psychological View* (New York: McGraw-Hill, 1977).

43. Federal Register/Vol. 79, No. 180/Wednesday, September 17, 2014/Proposed Rules. Department of Labor, Office of Federal Contract Compliance Programs, 41 CFR Part 60–1 RIN 1250–AA06. Government Contractors, Prohibitions Against Pay Secrecy Policies and Actions. Notice of proposed rulemaking.

44. Thomas A. Mahoney and William Weitzel, "Secrecy and Managerial Compensation," *Industrial Relations* 17, no. 2 (1978), pp. 245–251; Julio D. Burroughs, "Pay Secrecy and Performance: The Psychological Research," *Compensation Review,* Third Quarter 1982, pp. 44–54; George Milkovich and P. H. Anderson, "Management Compensation and Secrecy Policies," *Personnel Psychology* 25 (1972), pp. 293–302.

45. Adrienne Colella, Ramona Paetzold, Asghar Zardkoohi, and Michael Wesson, "Exposing Pay Secrecy," *Academy of Management Review* 32 (2007), pp. 55–71; Renae Broderick and Barry Gerhart, "Non-Wage

Compensation," in *The Human Resource Management Handbook,* Part 3; David Lewin, Daniel J. B. Mitchell, and Mahmood A. Zaidi, eds. (Greenwich, CT: JAI Press, 1997), pp. 95–135.

46. Smit, B. W., & Montag-Smit, T. (2018). The role of pay secrecy policies and employee secrecy preferences in shaping job attitudes. *Human Resource Management Journal* 28, no. 2, pp. 304–324.

47. I. SimanTov-Nachlieli and P. Bamberger, "Pay Communication, Justice, and Affect: The Asymmetric Effects of Process and Outcome Pay Transparency on Counterproductive Workplace Behavior," *Journal of Applied Psychology* 106 (2020), pp. 230–249.

48. B. W. Smit and T. Montag-Smit, "The Pay Transparency Dilemma: Development and Validation of the Pay Information Exchange Preferences Scale," *Journal of Applied Psychology* 104, no. 4, (2019), pp. 537–558.

49. P. Bamberger and E. Belogolovsky, "The Impact of Pay Secrecy on Individual Task Performance," *Personnel Psychology* 63 (2010), pp. 965–966.

50. David Card, et al., "Inequality at Work: The Effect of Peer Salaries on Job Satisfaction," *American Economic Review* 102, no. 6 (2012), pp. 2981–3003.

51. Todd Zenger, "The Case against Pay Transparency," *Harvard Business Review,* September 30, 2016; T. R. Zenger, "Explaining Organizational Diseconomies of Scale in R&D: Agency Problems and the Allocation of Engineering Talent, Ideas, and Effort by Firm Size," *Management Science* 40, no. 6 (1994), pp. 708–729.

52. Elena Belogolovsky and Peter A. Bamberger, "Signaling in Secret: Pay for Performance and the Incentive and Sorting Effects of Pay Secrecy," *Academy of Management Journal* 57, no. 6 (2014), pp. 1706–1733.

53. M. Wilson, G. B. Northcraft, and M. A. Neale, "The Perceived Value of Fringe Benefits," *Personnel Psychology* 38 (1985), pp. 309–320.

54. John A. Rubino, *Communicating Compensation Programs* (Scottsdale, AZ: American Compensation Association, 1997).

55. Jared Sandberg, "Why You May Regret Looking at Papers Left on the Office Copier," *The Wall Street Journal,* June 20, 2006, p. B1; John Case, "When Salaries Aren't Secret," case study, *Harvard Business Review,* May 2001.

56. A. Tversky and D. Kahneman, "The Framing of Decisions and the Psychology of Choice," *Science* 211 (1981), pp. 453–458; C. F. Camerer and U. Malmendier, "Behavioral Organizational Economics," July 8, 2006, working paper available from www.hss.caltech.edu/camerer/SS200/SS200.html; Sharla A. Stewart, "Can Behavioral Economics Save Us From Ourselves?" *University of Chicago Magazine* 97, no. 3 (February 2005), www.magazine.uchicago.edu/0502/features/economics.shtml.

57. Dori Meinert, "An Open Book: Involving Employees in Business Decisions Can Improve the Bottom Line. That's Why Fans of Open-Book Management Are So Dedicated to the Approach," *HR Magazine*, April 2013, pp. 43–46. "Rethinking Ways to Present Financial Information to Employees," *Employee Ownership Report,* March/April 2000, pp. 7, 10; Jack Stack and Bo Burlingham, *The Great Game of Business* (New York: Currency Doubleday, 1992); Jack Stack and Bo Burlingham, *A Stake in the Outcome* (New York: Currency Doubleday, 2002); John Case, "Opening the Books," *Harvard Business Review,* March–April, 1996, pp. 118–127.

58. *HR Services Delivery Research Report,* Towers Perrin, 2005, www.towersperrin.com; "The Psychology of Change Management," *McKinsey Quarterly,* July 2006.

59. Dave Ulrich, Jon Younger, and Wayne Brockbank, "The Next Evolution of the HR Organization," in *The Routledge Companion to Strategic Human Resource Management,* John Storey, Patrick M. Wright, and Dave Ulrich, eds. (London and New York: Routledge, 2009), pp. 182–203.

60. Alexandria Sage, "Wal-Mart Sex Discrimination Case Back in Court," *Reuters*, March 25, 2009, www.reuters.com/article/topNews/idUSTRE52O0P820090325.

61. Stephen Miller, "Companies Continue to Selectively Outsource HR Programs," *HRMagazine* (2009), p. 76; Dave Ulrich and Wayne Brockbank, *The HR Value Proposition* (Boston, MA: Harvard Business School Press, 2005); Brian S. Klaas, "Outsourcing and the HR Function: An Examination of Trends and Developments Within North American Firms," *International Journal of Human Resource Management* 19 (2008), pp. 1500–1514.
62. Michael Skapinker, "Much to Question on Outsourcing," *Financial Times,* June 30, 2003, p. 4.
63. A useful guide on selecting HR software is James G. Meade, *The Human Resources Software Handbook* (San Francisco: Jossey-Bass/Pfeiffer, 2003); Mark L. Lengnick-Hall and Steve Moritz, "The Impact of e-HR on the Human Resource Management Function," *Journal of Labor Research,* Summer 2003, pp. 365–379.
64. Diane Palframan, *HR Technology Strategies* (New York: Conference Board, 2003); James H. Dulebohn and Janet H. Marler, "e-Compensation: The Potential to Transform Practice?" in *Brave New World of e-HR: Human Resources in the Digital Age,* H. Gueutal and D. Stone, eds. (San Francisco: Jossey Bass, 2005), pp. 138–165.
65. Privacilla,www.privacilla.org/business/eudirective.html.
66. Flora Guidry, Andrew J. Leon, and Steve Rock, "Earnings-Based Bonus Plans and Earnings Management by Business-Unit Managers," *Journal of Accounting and Economics* 26 (1999), pp. 113–142.
67. Joseph P. O'Connor, Jr., Richard L. Priem, Joseph E. Coombs, and K. Matthew Gilley, "Do CEO Stock Options Prevent or Promote Fraudulent Financial Reporting?" *Academy of Management Journal,* June 2006, pp. 483–500; Frederic W. Cook, "Compensation Ethics: An Oxymoron or Valid Area for Debate?" Featured speech at ACA International Conference Workshop, 1999; Barrie Litzky, Kimberly Eddleston, and Deborah Kidder, "The Good, the Bad, and the Misguided: How Managers Inadvertently Encourage Deviant Behaviors," *Academy of Management Perspectives,* February 2006, pp. 91–102; Gretchen Morgenson, "Advice on Boss's Pay May Not Be So Independent," *The New York Times,* April 10, 2006, p. B1. The WorldatWork Ethics Initiative is described on their website, www.worldatwork.org. Also see their WorldatWork Standards of Professional Practice.
68. John Hechinger and James Bandler, "In Sycamore Suite, Memo Points to Backdating Claims," *The Wall Street Journal,* July 12, 2006, p. A3. Also see C. Forelle, J. Bandler, and Steve Stecklaw, "Brocade Ex-CEO, 2 Others Charged in Options Probe," *The Wall Street Journal,* July 21, 2006, p. A1, A8; Peter Grant, James Bandler, and Charles Forelle, "Cablevision Gave Backdated Grant to Dead Official," *The Wall Street Journal,* September 22, 2006, pp. A1, A8; Della Bradshaw, "MBA Students 'Cheat the Most,'" *Financial Times,* September 21, 2006, p. 8.
69. Source: Jared Sandberg. "Why You May Regret Looking at Papers Left On the Office Copier," *Wall Street Journal,* June 20, 2006.

Glossary

360-degree feedback A rating method that assesses employee performance from five points of view: supervisor, peer, self, customer, and subordinate.

401(k) plan A 401(k) plan, so named for the section of the Internal Revenue Code describing the requirements, is a savings plan in which employees are allowed to defer pretax income.

401(k) A 401(k) plan, so named for the section of the Internal Revenue Code describing the requirements, is a savings plan in which employees are allowed to defer pretax income.

ability to pay The ability of a firm to meet employee wage demands while remaining profitable; a frequent issue in contract negotiations with unions. A firm's ability to pay is constrained by its ability to compete in its product market.

ability An individual's capability to engage in a specific behavior.

access discrimination Discrimination that focuses on the staffing and allocation decisions made by employers. It denies particular jobs, promotions, or training opportunities to qualified women or minorities. This type of discrimination is illegal under Title VII of the Civil Rights Act of 1964.

affirmative action Firms with government contracts must take affirmative steps to hire women and minorities in proportion to their presence in the labor force.

Age Discrimination in Employment Act (ADEA) of 1967 (amended 1978, 1986, and 1990) Legislation that makes nonfederal employees aged 40 and over a protected class relative to their treatment in pay, benefits, and other personnel actions. The 1990 amendment is called the Older Workers Benefit Protection Act.

agency theory A theory of motivation that depicts exchange relationships in terms of two parties: agents and principals. According to this theory, both sides of the exchange will seek the most favorable exchange possible and will act opportunistically if given a chance. As applied to executive compensation, agency theory would place part of the executive's pay at risk to motivate the executive (agent) to act in the best interests of the shareholders (principals) rather than in the executive's own self-interests.

alternation ranking A job evaluation method that involves ordering the job description alternately at each extreme. All the jobs are considered. Agreement is reached on which is the most valuable and then the least valuable. Evaluators alternate between the next most valued and next least valued and so on until the jobs have been ordered.

Americans with Disabilities Act (ADA) Legislation passed in 1990 that requires that reasonable accommodations be provided to permit employees with disabilities to perform the essential elements of a job.

appeals processes Mechanisms are created to handle pay disagreements. They provide a forum for employees and managers to voice their complaints and receive a hearing.

balance sheet approach A method for compensating expatriates based upon the belief that the employee should not suffer financially for accepting a foreign-based assignment. The expatriate's pay is adjusted so that the amounts of the financial responsibilities the expatriate had prior to the assignment are kept at about the same level while on assignment—the company pays for the difference.

balanced scorecard A corporatewide, overall performance measure typically incorporating financial results, process improvements, customer service, and innovation.

base pay *See* base wage.

base salary *See* base wage.

base wage The basic cash compensation that an employer pays for the work performed. Tends to reflect the value of the work itself and ignore differences in individual contributions.

Bedeaux plan Individual incentive plan that provides a variation on straight piecework and standard hour plans. Instead of timing an entire task, a Bedeaux plan requires determination of the time required to complete each simple action of a task. Workers receive a wage incentive for completing a task in less than the standard time.

behaviorally anchored rating scales (BARS) Variants on standard rating scales in which the various scale levels are anchored with behavioral descriptions directly applicable to jobs being evaluated.

benchmark (key) job A prototypical job, or group of jobs, used as a reference point for making pay comparisons within or without the organization. Benchmark jobs have well-known and stable contents; their current pay rates are generally acceptable, and the pay differentials among them are relatively stable. A group of benchmark jobs, taken together, contains the entire range of compensable factors and is accepted in the external labor market for setting wages.

benchmark conversion Process of matching survey jobs by applying the employer's plan to the external jobs and then comparing the worth of the external job with its internal "match."

benefit limitation Limit of disability income payments to some maximum percentage of income and limit of medical/dental coverage for specific procedures to a certain fixed amount.

best-pay practices Compensation practices that allow employers to gain preferential access to superior human resource talent and competencies (i.e., valued assets), which in turn influence the strategies the organization adopts.

bourse market A market that allows haggling over terms and conditions until an agreement is reached.

Brito v. Zia Company Benchmark case that interpreted performance evaluation as a test, subject to validation requirements, and used these evaluations based on a rating format to lay off employees, resulting in a disproportionate number of minorities being discharged.

broad banding Collapsing a number of salary grades into a smaller number of broad grades with wide ranges.

budgeting A part of the organization's planning process; helps to ensure that future financial expenditures are coordinated and controlled. It involves forecasting the total expenditures required by the pay system during the next period as well as the amount of the pay increases. Bottom up and top down are the two typical approaches to the process.

Bureau of Labor Statistics (BLS) A major source of publicly available pay data. It also calculates the consumer price index.

career path A progression of jobs within an organization.

cash balance plan A defined benefit plan that looks like a defined contribution plan. Employees have a hypothetical account, such as a 401(k), into which is deposited what is typically a percentage of annual compensation. The dollar amount grows both from contributions by the employer and by some predetermined interest rate (e.g., often set equal to the rate given on 30-year treasury certificates).

central tendency A midpoint in a group of measures.

churn *See* turnover effect.

claims processing Procedure that begins when an employee asserts that a specific event (e.g., disablement, hospitalization, unemployment) has occurred and demands that the employer fulfill a promise for payment. As such, a claims processor must first determine whether the act has, in fact, occurred.

classification Job evaluation method that involves slotting job descriptions into a series of classes or grades that cover the range of jobs and that serve as a standard against which the job descriptions are compared.

commission Payment tied directly to achievement of performance standards. Commissions are directly tied to a profit index (sales, production level) and employee costs; thus, they rise and fall in line with revenues.

committee a priori judgment approach Compensable factor importance weights are assigned by a committee based on a priori judgment.

compa-ratio An index that helps assess how managers actually pay employees in relation to the midpoint of the pay range established for jobs. It estimates how well actual practices correspond to intended policy. Calculated as average rates actually paid divided by range midpoint.

comparable worth A policy that women performing jobs judged to be equal on some measure of inherent worth should be paid the same as men, excepting allowable differences, such as seniority, merit, production-based pay plans, and other non-sex-related factors. Objective is to eliminate use of the market in setting wages for jobs held by women.

compensable factor Job attributes that provide the basis for evaluating the relative worth of jobs inside an organization. A compensable factor must be work-related, business-related, and acceptable to the parties involved.

compensating differentials Economic theory that attributes the variety of pay rates in the external labor market to differences in attractive as well as negative characteristics in jobs. Pay differences must overcome negative characteristics to attract employees.

compensation at risk *See* risk sharing.

compensation All forms of financial returns and tangible services and benefits employees receive as part of an employment relationship.

competency-based pay system Compensation approach that links pay to the depth and scope of competencies that are relevant to doing the work. Typically used in managerial and professional work where what is accomplished may be difficult to identify.

competency-based structure Compensation approach that links pay to the depth and scope of competencies that are relevant to doing the work. Typically used in managerial and professional work where what is accomplished may be difficult to identify.

competency-based system Compensation approach that links pay to the depth and scope of competencies that are relevant to doing the work. Typically used in managerial and professional work where what is accomplished may be difficult to identify.

competency Basic knowledge and abilities employees must acquire or demonstrate in a competency-based plan in order to successfully perform the work, satisfy customers, and achieve business objectives.

competitive intelligence The collection and analysis of information about external conditions and competitors that will enable an organization to be more competitive.

competitive position The comparison of the compensation offered by one employer relative to that paid by its competitors.

compliance As a pay objective, conforming to federal and state compensation laws and regulations.

Consumer Price Index (CPI) A measure of the changes in prices in a fixed market basket of goods and services purchased by a hypothetical average family. Not an absolute measure of living costs; rather, a measure of how fast costs are changing. Published by the Bureau of Labor Statistics, U.S. Department of Labor.

consumer-driven health care benefits Costs link consumer choice of more or less expensive options to higher or lower individual costs. Also called consumer-directed health care plans.

content The work performed in a job and how it gets done (tasks, behaviors, knowledge required, etc.).

contingent workers People who have no expectation of continued employment and/or expect their employment to be temporary. (*See* U.S. Bureau of Labor Statistics.)

conventional job analysis Methods (e.g., functional job analysis) that typically involve an analyst using a questionnaire in conjunction with structured interviews of job incumbents and supervisors. The methods place considerable reliance on analysts' ability to understand the work performed and to accurately describe it.

copay Copay requires that employees pay a fixed or percentage amount for coverage.

core employees Workers with whom a long-term, full-time work relationship is anticipated.

correlation coefficient A common measure of association that indicates how changes in one variable are related to changes in another.

cost containment An attempt made by organizations to contain benefit costs, such as imposing deductibles and coinsurance on health benefits or replacing defined benefit pension plans with defined contribution plans.

cost cutter The cost cutter's efficiency-focused strategy stresses doing more with less by minimizing costs, encouraging productivity increases, and specifying in greater detail exactly how jobs should be performed.

cost-of-living adjustments (COLAs) Across-the-board wage and salary increases or supplemental payments based on changes in some index of prices, usually the consumer price index (CPI). If included in a union contract, COLAs are designed to increase wages automatically during the life of the contract as a function of changes in the CPI.

cost-of-living increase Same as across-the-board increase, except magnitude based on change in cost of living (e.g., as measured by the consumer price index [CPI]).

criterion contamination Allowing nonperformance factors to affect performance scores.

criterion deficiency A criterion is deficient if it fails to include all of the dimensions relevant to job performance (e.g., excluding keyboarding skills for a secretary's job performance).

criterion pay structure A pay structure to be duplicated with a point plan.

culture The informal rules, rituals, and value systems that influence how people behave.

customer-driven health care Medical care package where the employer finances the cost up to a dollar maximum and the employees search for options that best fit their specific needs.

customer-focused business strategy The customer-focused business strategy stresses delighting customers and bases employee pay on how well they achieve this.

customer-focused The customer-focused business strategy stresses delighting customers and bases employee pay on how well they achieve this.

deferred compensation Pay approach that provides income to an employee at some future time as compensation for work performed now. Types of deferred compensation programs include stock option plans and pension plans.

defined benefit plan A benefit option or package in which the employer agrees to give the specified benefit without regard to cost maximum. Opposite of defined contribution plan.

defined contribution plan A benefit option or package in which the employer negotiates a dollar maximum payout. Any change in benefit costs over time reduces the amount of coverage unless new dollar limits are negotiated.

delayering Eliminating some layers or job levels in the pay structure.

differentials Pay differences among levels within the organization, such as the difference in pay between adjacent levels in a career path, between supervisors and subordinates, between union and nonunion employees, and between executives and regular employees.

disparate impact Discrimination theory that outlaws the application of pay practices that may appear to be neutral but have a negative effect on females or minorities unless those practices can be shown to be business-related.

disparate treatment Discrimination theory that outlaws the application of different standards to different classes of employees unless the standards can be shown to be business-related.

distributive justice Fairness in the amount of reward distributed to employees.

dual-career ladders Presence of two different ways to progress in an organization, each reflecting different types of contribution to the organization's mission. The managerial ladder ascends through increasing responsibility for supervision or direction of people. The professional track ascends through increasing contributions of a professional nature that do not mainly entail the supervision of employees.

earnings-at-risk plans *See* risk sharing.

efficiency wage theory A theory that explains why firms are rational in offering higher-than-necessary wages.

employee benefits The parts of the total compensation package, other than pay for time worked, provided to employees in whole or in part by employer payments (e.g., life insurance, pension, workers' compensation, vacation).

employee contributions Comparisons among individuals doing the same job for the same organization.

Employee Retirement Income Security Act (ERISA) For employers who choose to have a retirement plan, this act sets some formidable rules that must be followed to be in compliance.

employee stock ownership plan (ESOP) A retirement plan in which the company contributes its stock as the retirement benefit.

employer of choice The view that a firm's external wage competitiveness is just one facet of its overall human resource policy and that competitiveness is more properly judged on overall policies. Challenging work, great colleagues, or an organization's prestige must be factored into an overall consideration of attractiveness.

entitlement Employee belief that returns and/or rewards are due regardless of individual or company performance.

entry jobs Jobs that are filled from the external labor market and whose pay tends to reflect external economic factors rather than an organization's culture and traditions.

equal employment opportunity A mandate that all firms make employment decisions that are "blind" to minority/gender status.

Equal Pay Act (EPA) of 1963 An amendment to the Fair Labor Standards Act of 1938 that prohibits pay differentials on jobs that are substantially equal in terms of skills, efforts, responsibility, and working conditions, except when they are the result of bona fide seniority, merit, production-based systems, or any other job-related factor other than sex.

essay format An open-ended performance appraisal format. The descriptors used can range from comparisons with other employees to adjectives, behaviors, and goal accomplishment.

essential elements The parts of a job that cannot be assigned to another employee. The Americans with Disabilities Act requires that if applicants with disabilities can perform the essential elements of a job, reasonable accommodations must then be made to enable the qualified individuals to perform the job.

exchange value The price of labor (the wage) determined in a competitive market; in other words, labor's worth (the price) is whatever the buyer and seller agree upon.

exempt Jobs not subject to provisions of the Fair Labor Standards Act with respect to minimum wage and overtime. Exempt employees include most executives, administrators, professionals, and outside sales representatives.

expatriate colony A section of a large city where expatriates tend to locate and form a community that takes on some of the cultural flavor of their home country.

expatriates Employees assigned outside their base country for any period of time in excess of one year.

experience rating Rating system in which insurance premiums vary directly with the number of claims filed. An experience rating is applied to unemployment insurance and workers' compensation and may be applied to commercial health insurance premiums. In a *community rating system,* insurance rates are based on the medical experience of the entire community.

external competitiveness The pay relationships among organizations; focuses attention on the competitive positions reflected in these relationships.

extrinsic rewards Rewards that a person receives from sources other than the job itself. They include compensation, supervision, promotions, vacations, friendships, and all other important outcomes apart from the job itself.

factor scales Measures that reflect different degrees within each compensable factor. Most commonly five to seven degrees are defined. Each degree may be anchored by typical skills, tasks and behaviors, or key job titles.

factor weights Measures that indicate the importance of each compensable factor in a job evaluation system. Weights can be derived through either a committee judgment or a statistical analysis.

Fair Labor Standards Act of 1938 (FLSA) A federal law governing minimum wage, overtime pay, equal pay for men and women in the same types of jobs, child labor, and recordkeeping requirements.

Family and Medical Leave Act Legislation passed in 1993 that entitles eligible employees to receive unpaid leave up to 12 weeks per year for specified family or medical reasons, such as caring for ill family members or adopting a child.

flat rate A single rate, rather than a range of rates, for all individuals performing a certain job. Ignores seniority and performance differences.

flexible benefit plan Benefit package in which employees are given a core of critical benefits (necessary for minimum security) and permitted to expend the remainder of their benefit allotment on options that they find most attractive.

flexible compensation The allocation of employee compensation in a variety of forms tailored to organization pay objectives and/or the needs of individual employees.

forms of compensation The various types of pay, which may be received directly in the form of cash (e.g., wages, bonuses, incentives) or indirectly through series and benefits (e.g., pensions, health insurance, vacations). This definition excludes other forms of rewards or returns that employees may receive, such as promotion, recognition for outstanding work behavior, and the like.

gain-sharing (group incentive) plans Incentive plans that are based on some measure of group performance rather than individual performance. Taking data on a past year as a base, group incentive plans may focus on cost savings (e.g., the Scanlon, Rucker, and Improshare plans) or on profit increases (profit-sharing plans) as the standard for distributing a portion of the accrued funds among relevant employees.

Gantt plan Individual incentive plan that provides for variable incentives as a function of a standard expressed as time period per unit of production. Under this plan, a standard time for a task is purposely set at a level requiring high effort to complete.

geographic differentials Local conditions that employees in a specific geographic area encounter, such as labor shortages and differences in housing costs.

global approach Substitution of a particular skill and experience level for job descriptions in determining external market rates. Includes rates for all individuals who possess that skill.

Green Circle Rate Pay rate that is below the minimum rate for a job or pay range for a grade

group incentive plans *See* gain-sharing (group incentive) plans.

Halsey 50–50 method Individual incentive method that provides for variable incentives as a function of a standard expressed as time period per unit of production. This plan derives its name from the shared split between worker and employer of any savings in direct costs.

hit rate The ability of a job evaluation plan to replicate a predetermined, agreed-upon job structure.

human capital An economic theory proposing that the investment one is willing to make to enter an occupation is related to the returns one expects to earn over time in the form of compensation.

human resource planning system Put in place by the benefit administrator to make realistic estimates of human resource needs and avoid a pattern of hasty hiring and morale-breaking terminations.

Improshare (IMproved PROductivity through SHARing) A gain-sharing plan in which a standard is developed to identify the expected hours required to produce an acceptable level of output. Any savings arising from production of agreed-upon output in fewer-than-expected hours are shared by the firm and the worker.

incentive effect The degree to which pay influences individual and aggregate motivation among employees at any point in time.

incentive Inducement offered in advance to influence future performance (e.g., sales commissions).

indirect compensation Noncash benefits provided to an employee.

individual retirement accounts (IRAs) Tax-favored retirement savings plans that individuals can establish themselves.

innovator The innovator stresses new products and short response time to market trends.

internal alignment The pay relationships among jobs or skill levels within a single organization; focuses attention on employee and management acceptance of those relationships. It involves establishing equal pay for jobs of equal worth and acceptable pay differentials for jobs of unequal worth.

interval scaling A particular numerical point difference has the same meaning on all parts of a scale.

job analysis The systematic process of collecting information related to the nature of a specific job. It provides the knowledge needed to define jobs and conduct job evaluation.

job classification (grade) A grouping of jobs that are considered substantially similar for pay purposes.

job content Information that describes a job. May include responsibility assumed and/or the tasks performed.

job description A summary of the most important features of a job. It identifies the job and describes the general nature of the work, specific task responsibilities, outcomes, and the employee characteristics required to perform the job.

job evaluation committee Group that may be charged with the responsibility of (1) selecting a job evaluation system, (2) carrying out or at least supervising the process of job evaluation, and (3) evaluating the success with which the job evaluation has been conducted. Its role may vary among organizations, but its members usually represent all important constituencies within the organization.

job evaluation A systematic procedure designed to aid in establishing pay differentials among jobs within a single company. It includes classification, comparison of the relative worth of jobs, blending internal and external market forces, measurement, negotiation, and judgment.

job family A group of jobs involving work of the same nature but requiring different skill and responsibility levels (e.g., computing and account recording are a job family; bookkeeper, accounting clerk, and teller are jobs within that family).

job hierarchy A grouping of jobs based on their job-related similarities and differences and on their value to the organization's objectives.

job pricing The process of assigning pay to jobs, based on thorough job analysis and job evaluation.

job specifications The job specifications that can be used as a basis for hiring are knowledge, skills, and abilities required to adequately perform the tasks.

job structure Relationship among jobs inside an organization, based on work content and each job's relative contribution to achieving the organization's objectives.

job-based structure Structure that relies on work content—tasks, behaviors, responsibilities.

job-based systems Systems that focus on jobs as the basic unit of analysis to determine the pay structure; hence, job analysis is required.

just wage doctrine A theory of job value that posits a "just" or equitable wage for any occupation based on that occupation's place in the larger social hierarchy. According to this doctrine, pay structures should be designed on the basis of societal norms, customs, and tradition, not on the basis of economic and market forces.

labor demand The employment level organizations require. An increase in wage rates will reduce the demand for labor, other factors constant. Thus, the labor demand curve (the relationship between employment levels and wage rates) is downward-sloping.

lag pay-level policy A wage structure that is set to match market rates at the beginning of the plan year only. The rest of the plan year, internal rates will lag behind market rates. Its objective is to offset labor costs, but it may hinder a firm's ability to attract and retain quality employees.

lead pay-level policy A wage structure that is set to lead the market throughout the plan year. Its aim is to maximize a firm's ability to attract and retain quality employees and to minimize employee dissatisfaction with pay.

lifetime employment Most prevalent in Japanese companies, the notion of employees' staying with the same company for their entire career, despite possible poor performance on the part of either an employee or the company.

line of sight An employee's ability to see how individual performance affects incentive payout. Employees on a straight piecework pay system have a clear line of sight—their pay is a direct function of the number of units they produce; employees covered by profit sharing have a fuzzier line of sight—their payouts are a function of many forces, only one of which is individual performance.

living wage Pay legislation in some U.S. cities that requires wages well above the federal minimum wage. Often applies only to city government employees.

local country nationals (LCNs) Citizens of a country in which a U.S. foreign subsidiary is located. LCNs' compensation is tied either to local wage rates or to the rates of U.S. expatriates performing the same job.

long-term disability (LTD) plan An insurance plan that provides payments to replace income lost through an inability to work that is not covered by other legally required disability income plans.

long-term incentives Inducements offered in advance to influence longer-rate (multiyear) results. Usually offered to top managers and professionals to get them to focus on long-term organization objectives.

lump-sum award Payment of entire increase (typically merit-based) at one time. Because amount is not factored into base pay, any benefits tied to base pay do not increase.

management by objectives (MBO) An employee planning, development, and appraisal procedure in which a supervisor and a subordinate, or group of subordinates, jointly identify and establish common performance goals. Employee performance on the absolute standards is evaluated at the end of the specified period.

marginal product of labor The additional output associated with the employment of one additional human resource unit, with other factors held constant.

marginal productivity In contrast to Marxist "surplus value" theory, a theory that focuses on labor demand rather than supply and argues that employers will pay a wage to a unit of labor that equals that unit's use (not exchange) value. That is, work is compensated in proportion to its contribution to the organization's production objectives.

marginal revenue of labor The additional revenue generated when the firm employs one additional unit of human resources, with other factors held constant.

market line A line on a graph that links a company's benchmark job evaluation points on the horizontal axis (internal structure) with market rates paid by competitors (market survey) on the vertical axis. It summarizes the distribution of going rates paid by competitors in the market.

market pay line Using key/benchmark jobs, a market pay policy line can be constructed that shows external market pay survey data as a function of internal job evaluation points. In many cases, the market pay policy line is obtained by using regression analysis, which yields an equation of the form "market pay = intercept + slope × job evaluation points." By plugging the job evaluation points for any job (both benchmark and non-benchmark jobs) into the equation, the predicted pay for each job can be obtained.

market pricing Setting pay structures almost exclusively through matching pay for a very large percentage of jobs with the rates paid in the external market.

market-based health care *See* customer-driven health care.

maturity curve A plot of the empirical relationship between current pay and years since a professional has last received a degree (YSLD), thus allowing organizations to determine a competitive wage level for specific professional employees with varying levels of experience.

merit bonus Payment of entire increase (typically merit-based) at one time. Because amount is not factored into base pay, any benefits tied to base pay do not increase. Also called lump-sum bonus or lump-sum award.

merit increase guidelines Specifications that tie pay increases to performance. They may take one of two forms: The simplest version specifies pay increases permissible for different levels of performance. More complex guidelines tie pay not only to performance but also to position in the pay range.

merit pay A reward that recognizes outstanding past performance. It can be given in the form of lump-sum payments or as increments to the base pay. Merit programs are commonly designed to pay different amounts (often at different times) depending on the level of performance.

Merrick plan Individual incentive plan that provides for variable incentives as a function of units of production per time period. It works like the Taylor plan, but three piecework rates are set: (1) high—for production exceeding 100 percent of standard; (2) medium—for production between 83 and 100 percent of standard; and (3) low—for production less than 83 percent of standard.

minimum wage A minimum-wage level for most Americans established by Congress as part of the Fair Labor Standards Act of 1938.

motivation An individual's willingness to engage in some behavior. Primarily concerned with (1) what energizes human behavior, (2) what directs or channels such behavior, and (3) how this behavior is maintained or sustained.

multiskill systems Systems that link pay to the number of different jobs (breadth) an employee is certified to do, regardless of the specific job he or she is doing.

National Electrical Manufacturers Association (NEMA) plan A point factor job evaluation system that evolved into the National Position Evaluation Plan sponsored by NMTA associates.

National Metal Trades Association (NMTA) plan A point factor job evaluation plan for production, maintenance, and service personnel.

nonexempt employees Employees who are subject to the provisions of the Fair Labor Standards Act.

nonexempt Employees who are subject to the provisions of the Fair Labor Standards Act.

offshoring Offshoring refers to the movement of jobs to locations beyond a country's borders.

outsourcing The practice of hiring outside vendors to perform functions that do not directly contribute to business objectives and in which the organization does not have a comparative advantage.

paid-time-off (PTO) plan Eliminates the distinction between sick days and other paid days off, thus eliminating the incentive to "fake" illness.

paired comparison ranking A ranking job evaluation method that involves comparing all possible pairs of jobs under study.

paired comparison A ranking job evaluation method that involves comparing all possible pairs of jobs under study.

pay discrimination Discrimination usually defined as including (1) access discrimination, which occurs when qualified women and minorities are denied access to particular jobs, promotions, or training opportunities; and (2) valuation discrimination, which takes place when minorities or women are paid less than white males for performing substantially equal work. Both types of discrimination are illegal under Title VII of the Civil Rights Act of 1964. Some argue that valuation discrimination can also occur when men and women hold entirely different jobs (in content or results) that are of comparable worth to the employer. Existing federal laws do not support the "equal pay for work of comparable worth" standard.

pay grade One of the classes, levels, or groups into which jobs of the same or similar values are grouped for compensation purposes. All jobs in a pay grade have the same pay range—maximum, minimum, and midpoint.

pay increase guidelines The mechanisms through which levels are translated into pay increases and, therefore, dictate the size and time of the pay reward for good performance.

pay level An average of the array of rates paid by an employer.

pay mix (or pay forms) Relative emphasis among compensation components such as base pay, merit, incentives, and benefits.

pay objectives What an organization seeks to achieve through its compensation strategy. Basic objectives are efficiency, fairness, ethics, and compliance with laws and regulations.

pay ranges The range of pay rates from minimum to maximum set for a pay grade or class. It puts limits on the rates an employer will pay for a particular job.

pay satisfaction A function of the discrepancy between employees' perceptions of how much pay they should receive and how much pay they do receive. If these perceptions are equal, an employee is said to experience pay satisfaction.

pay structures The array of pay rates for different jobs within a single organization; they focus attention on differential compensation paid for work of unequal worth.

pay techniques Mechanisms or technologies of compensation management, such as job analysis, job descriptions, market surveys, job evaluation, and the like, that tie the four basic pay policies to the pay objectives.

pay-for-knowledge plans A compensation practice whereby employees are paid for the number of different jobs they can adequately perform or the amount of knowledge they possess.

pay-for-performance plans Pay that varies with some measure of individual or organizational performance, such as merit pay, lump-sum bonus plans, skill-based pay, incentive plans, variable pay plans, risk sharing, and success sharing.

pay-policy line Representation of the organization's pay-level policy relative to what competitors pay for similar jobs.

pay-with-competition policy Policy that tries to ensure that a firm's labor costs are approximately equal to those of its competitors. It seeks to avoid placing an employer at a disadvantage in pricing products or in maintaining a qualified workforce.

pension benefit guaranty corporation (PBGC) Agency to which employers are required to pay insurance premiums to protect individuals from bankrupt companies (and pension plans!). In turn, the PBGC guarantees payment of vested benefits to employees formerly covered by terminated pension plans.

performance metrics Quantitative measures of job performance.

performance-dimension training Training that gives performance appraisers an understanding of the dimensions on which to evaluate employee performance.

performance-standard training Training that gives performance appraisers a frame of reference for making ratee appraisals.

perquisites (perks) The extras bestowed on top management, such as private dining rooms, company cars, and first-class airfare.

person-based structure A person-based structure shifts the focus to the employee: the skills, knowledge, or competencies the employee possesses, whether or not they are used in the employee's particular job.

planned pay-level rise The percentage increase in average pay that is planned to occur after considering such factors as anticipated rates of change in market data, changes in cost of living, the employer's ability to pay, and the efforts of turnover and promotions. This index may be used in top-down budgeting to control compensation costs.

point (factor) method A job evaluation method that employs (1) compensable factors, (2) factor degrees numerically scaled, and (3) weights reflecting the relative importance of each factor. Once scaled degrees and weights are established for each factor, each job is measured against each compensable factor and a total score is calculated for each job. The total points assigned to a job determine the job's relative value and hence its location in the pay structure.

point-of-service plan (POS) A point-of-service plan is a hybrid plan combining health maintenance organization (HMO) and preferred provider organization (PPO) benefits.

policy capturing Compensable factor importance weights are inferred using statistical methods such as regression analysis.

portability Transferability of pension benefits for employees moving to a new organization. ERISA does not require mandatory portability of private pensions. On a voluntary basis, the employer may agree to let an employee's pension benefit transfer to an individual retirement account (IRA) or, in a reciprocating arrangement, to the new employer.

Position Analysis Questionnaire (PAQ) A structured job analysis technique that classifies job information into seven basic factors: information input, mental processes, work output, relationships with other persons, job context, other job characteristics, and general dimensions. The PAQ analyzes jobs in terms of worker-oriented data.

prevailing-wage laws Legislation that provides for a government-defined prevailing wage as the minimum wage that must be paid for work done on covered government projects or purchases. In practice, these prevailing rates have been union rates paid in various geographic areas.

probationary period Period during which new employees are excluded from benefits coverage, usually until some term of employment (e.g., three months) is completed.

procedural justice/fairness Concept concerned with the process used to make and implement decisions about pay. It suggests that the way pay decisions are made and implemented may be as important to employees as the results of the decisions.

professional An employee who has specialized training of a scientific or intellectual nature and whose major duties do not entail the supervision of people.

profit-sharing plan A plan that focuses on profitability as the standard for group incentive. These plans typically involve one of three distributions: (1) Cash or current distribution plans provide full payment to participants soon after profits have been determined (quarterly or annually); (2) deferred plans have a portion of current profits credited to employee accounts, with cash payments made at time of retirement, disability, severance, or death; and (3) combination plans that incorporate aspects of both current and deferred options.

quantitative job analysis (QJA) Job analysis method that relies on scaled questionnaires and inventories that produce job-related data that are documentable, can be statistically analyzed, and may be more objective than other analyses.

quoted-price market Stores that label each item's price or ads that list a job's opening starting wage are examples of quoted-price markets.

range maximums The maximum values to be paid for a job grade, representing the top value the organization places on the output of the work.

range midpoint The salary midway between the minimum and maximum rates of a salary range. The midpoint rate for each range is usually set to correspond to the pay-policy line and represents the rate paid for satisfactory performance on the job.

range minimums The minimum values to be paid for a job grade, representing the minimum value the organization places on the work. Often, rates below the minimum are used for trainees.

ranges The range of pay rates from minimum to maximum set for a pay grade or class. It puts limits on the rates an employer will pay for a particular job.

rank and yank Requires managers to complete performance appraisals by ranking employees into a preset distribution of top, middle, and needs improvement categories. Often this latter category has employees who are "yanked" or terminated from the organization.

ranking format A type of performance appraisal format that requires that the rater compare employees against each other to determine the relative ordering of the group on some performance measure.

rater error training Training that enables performance appraisers to identify and suppress psychometric errors such as leniency, severity, central tendency, and halo errors when evaluating employee performance.

rating format A type of performance appraisal format that requires that raters evaluate employees on absolute measurement scales that indicate varying levels of performance.

red circle rates Pay rates that are above the maximum rate for a job or pay range/pay grade.

reengineering Making changes in the way work is designed to include external customer focus. Usually includes organizational delayering and job restructuring.

regression A statistical technique for relating present-pay differentials to some criterion, that is, pay rates in the external market, rates for jobs held predominantly by men, or factor weights that duplicate present rates for all jobs in the organization.

relational returns The nonquantifiable returns employees get from employment, such as social satisfaction, friendship, feeling of belonging, or accomplishment.

relative value of jobs The relative contribution of jobs to organizational goals, to their external market rates, or to some other agreed-upon rates.

relevant markets Those employers with which an organization competes for skills and products/services. Three factors commonly used to determine the relevant markets are the occupation or skills required, the geography (willingness to relocate and/or commute), and employers that compete in the product market.

reliability The consistency of the results obtained, that is, the extent to which any measuring procedure yields the same results on repeated trials. Reliable job information does not mean that it is accurate (valid), comprehensive, or free from bias.

rent Amount by which payment to a factor of production (capital or labor) exceeds the payment needed to keep it employed and/or its productivity. In the case of an employee (labor), economic rent would be compensation paid beyond what is necessary to retain the employee and/or beyond his/her marginal product.

reopener clause A provision in an employment contract that specifies that wages, and sometimes such nonwage items as pension/benefits, will be renegotiated under certain conditions (changes in cost of living, organization, profitability, and so on).

reservation wage A theoretical minimum standard below which a job seeker will not accept an offer, no matter how attractive the other job attributes.

risk sharing An incentive plan in which employees' base wages are set below a specified level (e.g., 80% of the market wage) and incentive earnings are used to raise wages above the base. In good years, an employee's incentive pay will more than make up for the 20 percent shortfall, giving the employee a pay premium. Because employees assume some of the risk, risk-sharing plans pay more generously than success-sharing plans in good years.

Rowan plan Individual incentive plan that provides for variable incentives as a function of a standard expressed as time period per unit of production. It is similar to the Halsey plan, but in this plan a worker's bonus increases as the time required to complete the task decreases.

Rucker plan A group cost-savings plan in which cost reductions due to employee efforts are shared with the employees. It involves a somewhat more complex formula than a Scanlon plan for determining employee incentive bonuses.

salary continuation plans Benefit options that provide some form of protection for disability. Some are legally required, such as workers' compensation provisions for work-related disability and social security disability income provisions for those who qualify.

salary Pay given to employees who are exempt from regulations of the Fair Labor Standards Act and hence do not receive overtime pay (e.g., managers and professionals).

Exempt pay is calculated at an annual or monthly rate rather than hourly.

sales value of production (SVOP) An incentive metric that calculates the dollar value of goods produced and in inventory.

scaling Determining the intervals on a measurement instrument.

Scanlon plan A group cost-savings plan designed to lower labor costs without lowering the level of a firm's activity. Incentives are derived as the ratio between labor costs and sales value of production (SVOP).

self-funding plans These plans specify that payouts only occur after the company reaches a certain profit target. Then variable payouts for individual, team, and company performance are triggered.

seniority increases Pay increases tied to a progression pattern based on seniority. To the extent performance improves with time on the job, this method has the rudiments of paying for performance.

shared choice An external competitiveness policy that offers employees substantial choice among their pay forms.

shirking behavior The propensity of employees to allow the marginal revenue product of their labor to be less than its marginal cost; to be lax.

short-term disability (STD) *See* workers' compensation.

skill analysis A systematic process to identify and collect information about the skills required to perform work in an organization.

skill blocks Basic units of knowledge employees must master to perform the work, satisfy customers, and achieve business objectives.

skill requirement Composite of experience, training, and ability as measured by the performance requirements of a particular job.

skill-based pay A pay structure in which workers are paid for the skills they are certified to have obtained.

skill-based structure Pay structure that links pay to the depth or breadth of the skills, abilities, and knowledge a person acquires that are relevant to the work.

social security Program based on federal law that provides retirement and disability benefits.

sorting effect The effect that pay can have on the composition of the workforce. Different types of pay strategies may cause different types of people to apply to and stay with an organization.

spillover effect The fact that improvements obtained in unionized firms "spill over" to nonunion firms seeking ways to lessen workers' incentives for organizing a union.

spot award One-time award for exceptional performance; also called a spot bonus.

standard hour plan Individual incentive plan in which rate determination is based on time period per unit of production and wages vary directly as a constant function of product level. In this context, the incentive rate in standard hour plans is set based on completion of a task in some expected time period.

standard rating scales Appraisal system characterized by (1) one or more performance standards being developed and defined for the appraiser and (2) each performance standard having a measurement scale indicating varying levels of performance on that dimension. Appraisers rate the appraisee by checking the point on the scale that best represents the appraisee's performance level. Rating scales vary in the extent to which anchors along the scale are defined.

straight piecework system Individual incentive plan in which rate determination is based on units of production per time period; wages vary directly as a constant function of production level.

straight ranking procedure A type of performance appraisal format in which the rater compares or ranks each employee relative to each other employee.

strategic perspective A focus on those compensation choices that help the organization gain and sustain competitive advantage.

strategy The fundamental direction of the organization. It guides the deployment of all resources, including compensation.

success sharing An incentive plan (e.g., profit sharing or gain sharing) in which an employee's base wage matches the market wage and variable pay adds on during successful years. Because base pay is not reduced in bad years, employees bear little risk.

surplus value The difference between labor's use and exchange values. According to Marx, under capitalism wages are based on labor's exchange value—which is lower than its use value—and thus provide only a subsistence wage.

survey The systematic process of collecting and making judgments about the compensation paid by other employers.

tacit work Complex work (as compared to transactional, or routine, work).

tariff agreements In some European countries, the wage rates negotiated by employer associations and trade union federations for all wage earners for all companies in an industry group.

task (work) data Information on the elemental units of work (tasks), with emphasis on the purpose of each task, collected for job analysis. Work data describe the job in terms of actual tasks performed and their output.

tax equalization A method whereby an expatriate pays neither more nor less tax than the assumed home-country tax on base remuneration.

Taylor plan Individual incentive plan that provides for variable incentives as a function of units of production per time period. It provides two piecework rates that are established for production above and below standard, and these rates are higher and lower than the regular wage incentive level.

team incentive Group incentive restricted to team members, with payout usually based on improvements in productivity, customer satisfaction, financial performance, or quality of goods and services directly attributable to the team.

third-country nationals (TCNs) Employees of a U.S. foreign subsidiary who maintain citizenship in a country other than the United States or the host country. TCNs' compensation is tied to comparative wages in the local country, the United States, or the country of citizenship.

Title VII A major piece of legislation prohibiting pay discrimination. It is much broader in intent than the Equal Pay Act, forbidding discrimination on the basis of race, color, religion, sex, pregnancy, or national origin.

topping out Situation in which employees in a skill-based compensation plan attain the top pay rate in a job category by accumulating and/or becoming certified for the top-paid skill block(s).

total cash Base wage plus cash bonus; does not include benefits or stock options.

total compensation The complete pay package for employees, including all forms of money, bonuses, benefits, services, and stock.

tournament theory The notion that larger differences in pay are more motivating than smaller differences. Like prize awards in a golf tournament, pay increases should get successively greater as one moves up the job hierarchy. Differences between the top job and the second-highest job should be the largest.

traditional time-off (TTO) plan Paid vacations, holidays (or pay if worked), sick leave, and personal leave, tracked separately.

transactional work Routine work.

turnover effect The downward pressure on average wage that results from the replacement of high-wage-earning employees with workers earning a lower wage.

two-tier pay plans Wage structures that differentiate pay for the same jobs based on hiring date. A contract is negotiated that specifies that employees hired after a stated day will receive lower wages than their higher-seniority peers working on the same or similar jobs.

U.S. expatriates (USEs) American citizens working for a U.S. subsidiary in a foreign country. Main compensation concerns are to "keep the expatriates whole" relative to their U.S.-based counterparts and to provide expatriates with an incentive wage for accepting the foreign assignment.

unemployment benefits *See* unemployment insurance.

unemployment insurance (UI) State-administered program that provides financial security for workers during periods of joblessness.

use value The value or price ascribed to the use or consumption of labor in the production of goods or services.

utility theory The analysis of utility, the dollar value created by increasing revenues and/or decreasing costs by changing one or more human resource practices. It has most typically been used to analyze the payoff to making more valid employee hiring/selection decisions.

validity The accuracy of the results obtained; that is, the extent to which any measuring device measures what it purports to measure.

valuation discrimination Discrimination that focuses on the pay women and minorities receive for the work they perform. Discrimination occurs when members of these groups are paid less than white males for performing substantially equal work. This definition of pay discrimination is based on the standard of "equal pay for equal work." Many believe that this definition is limited and that valuation discrimination can also occur when men and women hold entirely different jobs (in content or results) that are of comparable worth to the employer. Existing federal laws do not support the "equal pay for work of comparable worth" standard.

value The worth of the work; its relative contribution to organization objectives.

variable pay Pay tied to productivity or some measure that can vary with the firm's profitability.

vesting A benefit plan provision that guarantees that participants will, after meeting certain requirements, retain a right to the benefits they have accrued, or some portion of them, even if employment under their plan terminates before retirement.

wage and price controls Government regulations that aim at maintaining low inflation and low levels of unemployment. They frequently focus on "cost-push" inflation, limiting the size of pay raises and the rate of increases in prices charged for goods and services. Used for limited time periods only.

wage Pay given to employees who are covered by overtime and reporting provisions of the Fair Labor Standards Act. Pay for workers who are nonexempt usually is calculated at an hourly rate rather than a monthly or annual rate.

work flow analysis How work gets performed and where value is or is not added.

work flow The process by which goods and services are delivered to the customer.

workers' compensation Legally required programs in each state that provide payment of medical expenses and compensation for lost wages resulting from work-related injuries or disabilities.

zones Ranges of pay used as controls or guidelines within pay bands that can keep the system more structurally intact. Maximums, midpoints, and minimums provide guides to appropriate pay for certain levels of work. Without zones employees may float to the maximum pay, which for many jobs in the band is higher than market value.

Name Index

A

B

C

D

E

H

I

J

K

N

O

P

Q

R

S

T

U

V

W

X

Y

Z

Subject Index